The Correspondence and Unpublished Papers of Robert Persons, SJ

The rapid growth of early modern British Catholic studies, and its integration into the wider historiographical project, continues to focus attention on Robert Persons as one of the most significant public figures of the Reformation era in England. As the superior of the Jesuit English mission from 1580 until 1610, he was engaged in a controversial campaign for the reconversion of England that had wide political, ecclesiastical, pastoral, and polemical ramifications. Modern scholarship is engaged in lively debate over his role in international relations and conflicts within British Catholicism.

This volume of Robert Persons's correspondence is centred on his eight-year sojourn in Spain following the failure of the Spanish Armada of 1588. It was a period of incessant activity and constant travelling as he negotiated with the royal court and Spanish Jesuits, founded English seminaries in Valladolid and Seville, supervised the mission to England, and promoted the Catholic cause in printed works such as the *Philopater* and the *Conference about the Next Succession*. Increasing opposition amongst Catholic exiles in Flanders and Rome prompted him to return to Rome in 1597 to deal with disaffected students at the English College.

Studies and Texts 235

CATHOLIC AND RECUSANT TEXTS
OF THE LATE MEDIEVAL
& EARLY MODERN PERIODS 6

Edited by
FREDDY DOMINGUEZ, *University of Arkansas*
ANN M. HUTCHISON, *York University and PIMS*
MICHAEL QUESTIER, *University of Durham*
ALISON SHELL, *University College, London*

The Pontifical Institute of Mediaeval Studies acknowledges
the support of the late JOSEPH and CLAUDINE POPE,
who generously helped initiate the publication of Catholic and
Recusant Texts of the Late Medieval and Early Modern Periods.

The Correspondence and Unpublished Papers of Robert Persons, SJ

Volume 2: 1588–1597

Edited by

VICTOR HOULISTON

THOMAS M. McCOOG, SJ   ANA SÁEZ-HIDALGO

JAVIER BURRIEZA SÁNCHEZ   GINEVRA CROSIGNANI

Toronto
PIMS
PONTIFICAL INSTITUTE OF MEDIAEVAL STUDIES

Acknowledgments

The publication of this volume was made possible by funds generously provided by Ann M. Hutchison, James P. Carley, and the Janet E. Hutchison Foundation.

Library and Archives Canada Cataloguing in Publication

Title: The correspondence and unpublished papers of Robert Persons, SJ / edited by Victor Houliston, Ginevra Crosignani and Thomas M. McCoog, SJ.
Other titles: Correspondence
Names: Parsons, Robert, 1546–1610, author. | Houliston, Victor, 1954– editor. | Crosignani, Ginevra, editor. | McCoog, Thomas M., editor. | Sáez-Hidalgo, Ana, editor. | Burrieza Sánchez, Javier, editor. | Pontifical Institute of Mediaeval Studies, publisher.
Series: Studies and texts (Pontifical Institute of Mediaeval Studies) ; 235. | Catholic and recusant texts of the late medieval & early modern periods ; 6.
Description: Series statement: Studies and texts ; 235 | Catholic and recusant texts of the late Medieval & early modern periods ; 6 | Volume 2 edited by Victor Houliston, Thomas M. McCoog, SJ., Ana Sáez-Hidalgo, Javier Burrieza Sánchez, Ginevra Crosignani. | Includes bibliographical references and indexes. | Contents: Volume 2. 1588–1597 | Letters in Latin, Italian, Spanish and English, with English translations.
Identifiers: Canadiana (print) 20179058878 | Canadiana (ebook) 20240286170 | ISBN 9780888442352 (v. 2 ; hardcover) | ISBN 9781771104357 (v. 2 ; PDF)
Subjects: LCSH: Parsons, Robert, 1546–1610 – Correspondence. | LCSH: Jesuits – England – Correspondence. |LCSH: Catholic Church – England – History – Sources. | LCSH: Catholics – England – Correspondence. | LCSH: England – Church history – 16th century – Sources. | LCSH: England – Church history – 17th century – Sources. | LCSH: Catholic Church – History – Sources. | LCGFT: Personal correspondence.
Classification: LCC BX4705.P37683 A4 2017 | DDC 271/.5302–dc23

© Pontifical Institute of Mediaeval Studies 2024

Pontifical Institute of Mediaeval Studies
59 Queen's Park Crescent East
Toronto, Ontario M5S 2C4
Canada
pims.ca

PRINTED IN CANADA

Contents

Preface	vii
Abbreviations and Sigla	ix
Maps	xv
Using This Edition	xix
Introduction	1
The *Memorialistas*	1
The Seminaries: Valladolid, Seville, and St Omers	4
The Opposition in Flanders	9
The English College, Rome	12
The English Mission	16
The International Scene	20
Controversy and Publicity	23
The Correspondence Network	26
Archival Sources	29
Dramatis Personae	31
Valladolid, 1588–1592	38
Seville, November 1592–October 1594	222
After Allen, 1594–1596	411
Rome, 1597	640
Appendix A: Memorials and Memoranda, 1597	823
Appendix B: List of Rectors of the English Colleges	891
Appendix C: Cardinal Protectors of the English College, Rome	892
Appendix D: Provincial Superiors of the Society of Jesus	893
Index of Persons	895
Index of Places and Subjects	910

Preface

During the unforgivably long gap between the appearance of the first volume of his correspondence at the end of 2017 and the completion of the second, the place of Robert Persons in the historiography of early modern religion and politics has become even more secure. Peter Lake and Michael Questier have played a pivotal role in this, with their complementary command of cultural analysis and archival labyrinths. Lake's *Bad Queen Bess* (2016) raised awareness of the significance of Elizabethan Catholic publications such as *Leicester's Commonwealth* and the *Philopater*. Questier's *Dynastic Politics* (2019) continued the work of debunking the queen's mythical status, and their combined *All Hail to the Archpriest* (2019) featured Persons on the dustjacket as the central figure in a controversy they presented as much more than an internal squabble among the Catholic minority at the turn of the century. Questier's *Catholics and Treason* (2022) gave a longer view to Persons's engagement with the state.

Several other scholars have helped to enhance the context of the letters and documents we present here. Freddy Dominguez's *Radicals in Exile* (2020) and Deborah Forteza's *The English Reformation in the Spanish Imagination* (2022) bring a Spanish perspective to bear. The second and third volumes of Thomas M. McCoog's history of the Jesuits in Ireland, Scotland, and England will serve as companion to the second and third volumes of Persons's correspondence. Brill's journal *Jesuit Studies* and the attendant series, including Spencer J. Weinreich's comprehensive translation and study of Pedro de Ribadeneyra's history of the English Reformation (2017), have boosted scholarship on the early Jesuits. In Boston the Institute for Advanced Jesuit Studies has made a wide range of resources available. The Centre for Catholic Studies at Durham University has initiated early modern British and Irish Conferences.

As editors of the Persons correspondence, we have benefited greatly from the coming together of a growing number of excellent scholars contributing to our understanding of relevant religious politics, book history, biography, diplomacy, material culture, and education, many of whom are represented in Robert Scully's *Companion to Catholicism and Recusancy in Britain and Ireland* (2022). I would like to acknowledge the friendship and support of Maurice Whitehead at the Venerable English College in Rome, Janet Graffius at Stonyhurst, Peter Harris at Bishop's Stortford, Earle Havens and Elizabeth Patton at John Hopkins, Robert E. Scully, SJ and Christopher Warner at Le Moyne, Susannah Monta and Brad Gregory at Notre Dame, Alexandra Walsham at Cambridge, Katie McKeogh and Peter Davidson in Oxford, Gerard Kilroy in Bath and London,

Andrew Cichy in Australia, Hannah Thomas in York, James Kelly in Durham, and Clarinda Calma in London.

We have enjoyed whole-hearted support and encouragement from the general editors of the series Catholic and Recusant Texts of the Late Medieval & Early Modern Periods: originally Ann Hutchison, Thomas Freeman, and Alison Shell, and now, with the retirement of Tom Freeman, including Freddy Dominguez and Michael Questier. At the Pontifical Institute of Mediaeval Studies, James Carley, Megan Jones, and Fred Unwalla have been unfailingly helpful. I am also much indebted to Jonathan Brent for his careful copyediting of a long and complicated manuscript.

Persons's correspondence has taken us to several archives and libraries in Britain and Europe. I should like to acknowledge the generous help I have received at the Jesuit archives in London and Rome; the Archivio Apostolico Vaticano and the Biblioteca Apostolica Vaticana; the Archivio di Stato, Napoli; the Venerable English College, Rome; the Archivo General de Simancas; the Real Academia de la Historia, Madrid; the Real Biblioteca del Monasterio de San Lorenzo de El Escorial; the archive of the Royal College of St Alban's, Valladolid; the British Library; the Bodleian Library; the Cambridge University Library; and the Archives of the Archdiocese of Westminster. Special thanks go to Mauro Brunelli and Brian Mac Cuarta at the Archivum Romanum Societatis Iesu; Rebecca Somerset at the Archives of the British Province of the Society of Jesus; Maurice Whitehead at the Venerable English College, Rome; and Janet Graffius at Stonyhurst.

This edition would not have been possible without the financial and institutional support of the National Research Foundation of South Africa; the University of the Witwatersrand, Johannesburg; and the University of the Free State, Bloemfontein. I have continued to enjoy the hospitality of Campion Hall, Oxford, and the friendship of the master, Fr Nicholas Austin, SJ, and the community. I have been a frequent visitor at the Procura Generale of the Suore Missionarie Pallottine in Rome and the Royal College of St Alban's, Valladolid.

I would like to acknowledge the assistance of Marianne Dircksen with Latin translations, Lucia Ruggieri with Italian translations, Adam Worster and Sonia Fanucchi with transcriptions, and Andrea Campana, Carol Macdonald, Elani Boshoff, René Lombard, Ananke Meintjies, and Yonwaba Matshobotiyana with proofreading and checking. The index was compiled with the assistance of Lesego Maponyane. The maps were drawn by Karen van Niekerk.

To my co-editors, Ana Sáez-Hidalgo, Thomas M. McCoog, Ginevra Crosignani, and Javier Burrieza Sánchez, my heartfelt thanks are due, for your expert help and advice, and your patience.

Victor Houliston
Cambridge, Michaelmas, 2023

Abbreviations and Sigla

Frequently Used Sigla

A	Archivum Britannicum Societatis Iesu (ABSI)
B	Biblioteca Apostolica Vaticana (BAV)
G	Grene, Collectanea (at ABSI)
R	Archivum Romanum Societatis Iesu (ARSI)
S	Archivo General de Simancas (AGS)
V	Archivio Apostolico Vaticano (AAV)
Vd	Archivum Collegii Sancti Albani, Valladolid (ACSA)
W	Archives of the Archdiocese of Westminster (AAW)

The symbol Δ is used to denote "ducats" or "scudi."

Abbreviations

AAV	Archivio Apostolico Vaticano, Vatican City
AAW	Archives of the Archdiocese of Westminster, London
Acts of the Privy Council	Acts of the Privy Council of England, ed. John Roche Dasent et al., 46 vols. (London, 1890–1964).
ABSI	Archivum Britannicum Societatis Iesu, London
ACSA	Archivum Collegii Sancti Albani, Valladolid
AGS	Archivo General de Simancas
AHSI	*Archivum historicum Societatis Iesu*
Alford	Stephen Alford, *The Watchers: A Secret History of the Reign of Elizabeth I*, 2nd ed. (London, 2013).
Anstruther	Godfrey Anstruther, *The Seminary Priests*, vol. 1: *Elizabethan* (Ware and Durham, 1968).
ARCR	Antony Francis Allison and David McGregor Rogers, *The Contemporary Printed Literature of the English Counter-Reformation between 1558 and 1640*, 2 vols. (Aldershot, 1989–1994).

ARSI	Archivum Romanum Societatis Iesu, Rome
Astrain	Antonio Astrain, *Historia de la Compañía de Jesús en la asistencia de España*, 7 vols. (Madrid, 1902–1925).
Bartoli, *Inghilterra*	Daniello Bartoli, *Dell' istoria della Compagnia di Giesù l'Inghilterra, parte dell'Europa* (Rome, 1667).
BAV	Biblioteca Apostolica Vaticana, Vatican City
Blackfan Annals	John Blackfan, *The Blackfan Annals*, ed. Peter Harris (London, 2008).
Book of the Succession	See *Conference about the Next Succession*.
Caraman, *Henry Garnet*	Philip Caraman, *Henry Garnet 1555–1606, and the Gunpowder Plot* (London, 1964).
Conference about the Next Succession	R. Doleman (pseud.), *A Conference about the Next Succession to the Crowne of Ingland* (Antwerp, 1595), compiled by Robert Persons.
CP	Cecil Papers, Hatfield House, Hertfordshire
CRS	[Publications of the] Catholic Record Society
CSPD	*Calendar of State Papers, Domestic Series 1547–1625*, ed. Robert Lemon and Mary Anne Everett Green, 12 vols. (London, 1856–1872).
CSPS	*Calendar of Letters and State Papers Relating to English Affairs Preserved principally in the archives of Simancas*, ed. Martin A.S. Hume, 4 vols. (London, 1892–1899).
DBE	*Diccionario Biográfico Español* (Real Academia de la Historia), http://dbe.rah.es.
DBI	*Dizionario Biografico degli Italiani* (Istituto della Enciclopedia Italiana), www.treccani.it.
DHCJ	*Diccionario histórico de la Compañía de Jesús: Biográfico-temático*, ed. Charles E. O'Neill, and Joaquín M. Domínguez, 4 vols. (Rome and Madrid, 2001).
Dominguez, *Radicals in Exile*	Freddy Cristóbal Dominguez, *Radicals in Exile: English Catholic Books during the Reign of Philip II* (University Park, PA, 2020).
Edwards	Francis Edwards, *Robert Persons: The Biography of an Elizabethan Jesuit, 1546–1610* (St Louis, 1995).
Edwards, *More*	*The Elizabethan Jesuits*, ed. and trans. Francis Edwards (London, 1981).

Abbreviations and Sigla | xi

Foley	*Records of the English Province of the Society of Jesus*, ed. Henry Foley, 7 vols. in 8 (London, 1875–1883).
Gerard, *Autobiography*	*John Gerard: The Autobiography of an Elizabethan*, ed. Philip Caraman (London, 1956).
Hicks	Persons Transcripts (ABSI, 46/12/1–6)
Hicks, Garnet	Garnet Transcripts (ABSI, 46/12/1)
Hicks, *Seminaries*	Leo Hicks, "Father Persons, SJ, and the Seminaries in Spain," *The Month* 157 (1931): 193–204 (part 1), 410–417 (part 2), 497–506 (part 3); 158 (1931): 26–35 (part 4).
Kamen	Henry Kamen, *Philip of Spain* (New Haven, CT, 1997).
Kenny, "Inglorious Revolution"	Anthony Kenny, "The Inglorious Revolution 1594–97," *The Venerabile* 16 (1954): 240–258 (part 1); 17 (1955): 7–25 (part 2); 77–94 (part 3); 136–155 (part 4).
Knox, *Allen*	*Letters and Memorials of William, Cardinal Allen (1532–1594)*, ed. Thomas Francis Knox (London, 1882).
Knox, *Douay Diaries*	*The First and Second Diaries of the English College, Douay*, ed. Thomas Francis Knox (London, 1878).
Lake and Questier, *All Hail to the Archpriest*	Peter Lake and Michael Questier, *All Hail to the Archpriest: Confessional Conflict, Toleration, and the Politics of Publicity in Post-Reformation England* (Oxford, 2019).
Law, *Archpriest Controversy*	*The Archpriest Controversy: Documents Relating to the Dissensions of the Roman Catholic Clergy, 1597–1602*, ed. Thomas Graves Law, 2 vols. (London, 1896–1898).
Loomie, *Spanish Elizabethans*	Albert J. Loomie, *The Spanish Elizabethans: The English Exiles at the Court of Philip II* (London, 1965).
McCoog, *And Touching Our Society*	Thomas M. McCoog, *"And Touching Our Society": Fashioning Jesuit Identity in Elizabethan England* (Toronto, 2013).
McCoog, *Building the Faith of St Peter*	Thomas M. McCoog, *The Society of Jesus in Ireland, Scotland, and England, 1589–1597: Building the Faith of St Peter upon the King of Spain's Monarchy* (Farnham, Surrey, 2012).
McCoog, *English and Welsh Jesuits*	Thomas M. McCoog, *English and Welsh Jesuits, 1555–1650*, 2 vols., CRS 74–75 (London, 1994–1995).
McCoog, *Lest Our Lamp Be Entirely Extinguished*	Thomas M. McCoog, *The Society of Jesus in Ireland, Scotland, and England, 1598–1606: "Lest Our Lamp be Entirely Extinguished"* (Leiden, 2017).
McCoog, *Our Way of Proceeding*	Thomas M. McCoog, *The Society of Jesus in Ireland, Scotland, and England, 1541–1588: "Our Way of Proceeding?"* (Leiden, 1996).

MH	Milton House Archives, Georgetown University, Washington, DC
Milward	Peter Milward, *Religious Controversies of the Elizabethan Age* (London, 1978).
More	Henry More, *Historia missionis anglicanae Societatis Iesu* (Saint-Omer, 1660).
Morris	John Morris, *The Troubles of Our Catholic Forefathers*, 3 vols. (London, 1872–1877).
Murphy	Martin Murphy, *St Gregory's College, Seville, 1592–1767*, CRS 73 (London, 1992).
OED	*Oxford English Dictionary*, Oxford University Press (2014–), www.oed.com.
ODNB	*Oxford Dictionary of National Biography*, online ed., Oxford University Press (2004–), www.oxforddnb.com.
Parker	Geoffrey Parker, *Imprudent King: A New Life of Philip II* (New Haven, CT, 2014).
Petti	*The Letters and Despatches of Richard Verstegan (c. 1550–1640)*, ed. Anthony G. Petti, CRS 52 (London, 1959).
Philopater	Andreas Philopater (pseud.), *Elizabethae Angliae Reginae haeresim Calvinianum propugnantis, saevissimum in Catholicos sui regni edictum ... Cum responsione* (Antwerp, 1592), by Robert Persons.
Pollen, *Acts of English Martyrs*	*Acts of English Martyrs, Hitherto Unpublished*, ed. John Hungerford Pollen (London, 1891).
Pollen, "Colleges in Spain"	John Hungerford Pollen, MS History of the Jesuits in England, ABSI, MS 56/5A/1B, "Chapter 13: Colleges in Spain, 1589–1595" (folder 59/3/3).
Pollen, *Miscellanea II*	*Miscellanea II*, ed. John Hungerford Pollen, CRS 2 (London, 1906).
Pollen, *Unpublished Documents*	*Unpublished Documents Relating to the English Martyrs*, vol. 1: *1584–1603*, ed. John Hungerford Pollen, CRS 5 (London, 1908).
Pollen, *Miscellanea IX*	*Miscellanea IX*, ed. John Hungerford Pollen, CRS 14 (London, 1914).
Questier, *Catholics and Treason*	Michael C. Questier, *Catholics and Treason: Martyrology, Memory, and Politics in the Post-Reformation* (Oxford, 2022).

Renold, *Letters of Allen and Barret*	*Letters of William Allen and Richard Barret, 1572–1598*, ed. P. Renold, CRS 58 (London, 1967).
Renold, *Wisbech Stirs*	*The Wisbech Stirs (1595–1598)*, ed. P. Renold, CRS 51 (London, 1958).
Tierney	Mark Aloysius Tierney, *Dodd's Church History of England: From the Commencement of the Sixteenth Century to the Revolution in 1688*, 5 vols. (London: 1839–1843).
TNA	The National Archives, Kew
Valladolid Registers	*Registers of the English College at Valladolid, 1589–1862*, ed. Edwin Henson (London, 1930).
Weinreich	*Pedro de Ribadeneyra's "Ecclesiastical History of the Schism of the kingdom of England": A Spanish Jesuit's History of the English Reformation*, ed. Spencer J. Weinreich (Leiden, 2017).
Williams, *St Alban's College*	Michael E. Williams, *St Alban's College, Valladolid: Four Centuries of Catholic Presence in Spain* (London and New York, 1986).
Yellowlees	Michael Yellowlees, *"So Strange a Monster as a Jesuiste": The Society of Jesus in Sixteenth-Century Scotland* (Isle of Colonsay, 2003).

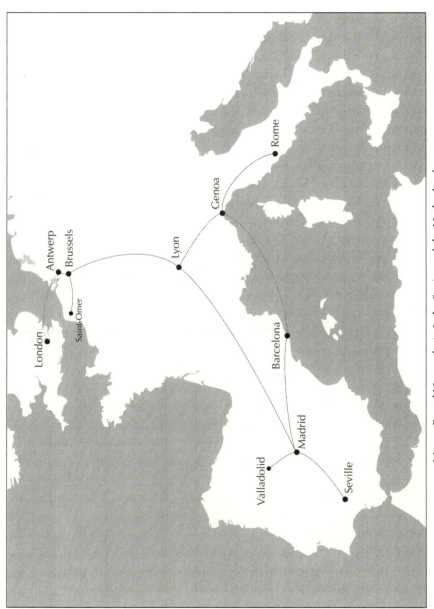

Map 1. Postal Networks in Italy, Spain, and the Netherlands

xvi | Maps

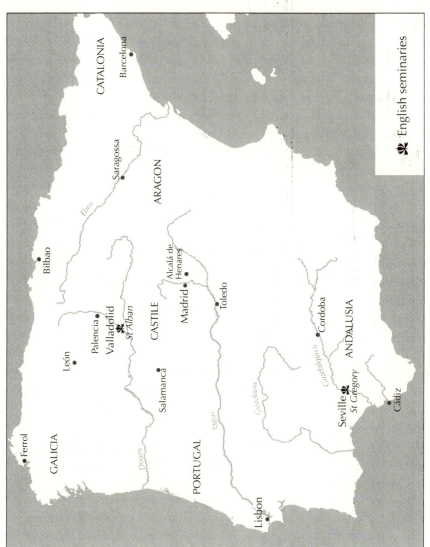

Map 2. Spain and Portugal

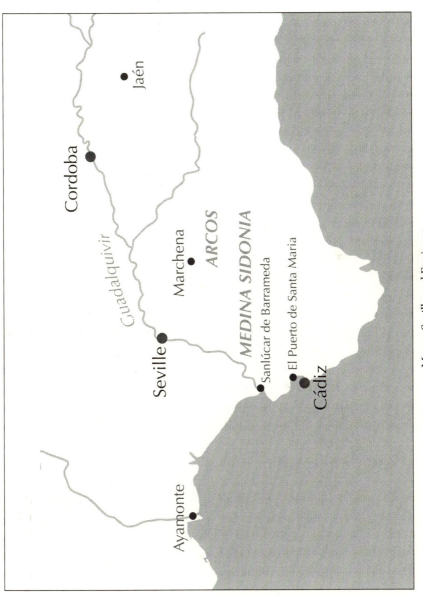

Map 3. Seville and Environs

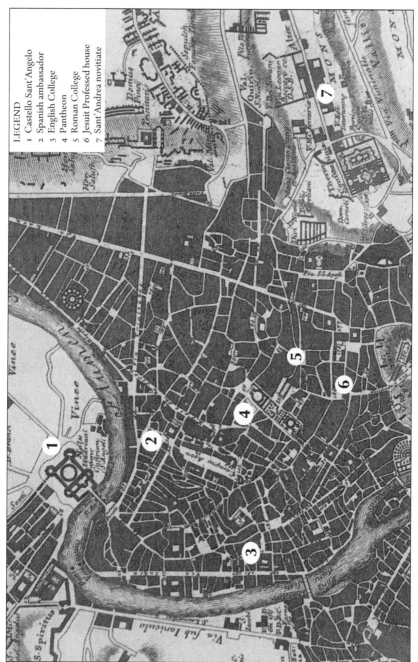

Map 4. Rome in the 1590s. Detail from a map by Leonardo Bufalino (1551), engraved by Jo. Bapt. Nolli (author's private collection)

Using This Edition

Inclusion of letters, translations, and token entries
For the sake of completeness, this edition includes letters both to and from Persons, as well as entries for letters for which we have references only but no text; this is why many of the early letters appear only as editorial summaries. Most of the letters are in languages other than English – Latin, Italian, and Spanish – for which translations have been provided. In these cases, textual notes appear as footnotes to the text in the original language, while explanatory notes appear as footnotes to the translation. Paratextual material such as endorsements, addresses, and other notes on the manuscripts have been transcribed wherever possible, but translated only where useful information would otherwise remain obscure.

Serial numbers
For ease of reference, the entry for each letter has been assigned a serial number, prefaced by A, B, or C, to indicate volumes 1, 2, and 3 of this edition. This applies also to entries where there is no extant text. In some cases, where there are significant alternative versions of the opening or conclusion of the letter, a separate subentry has been made, e.g., A121a.

Editorial material (introduction, headnotes, explanatory notes, and indices)
Given the complexity of Persons's career and his involvement in several countries, we have tried to arrange the editorial material as helpfully as possible. The headnotes to each letter summarize the contents briefly and explain the context in some detail, enabling the reader to follow the course of relevant events; explanatory footnotes then provide further detail. There are two indices: the Index of Persons is meant as a guide to the large number of personages referred to in the letters, and the Index of Places and Subjects as a guide to the main themes covered.

We have explained the significance of specialized Jesuit vocabulary: if necessary, the index should be consulted. Where the term "Ours" is capitalized, this is to indicate that it refers to members of the Society of Jesus.

Brief biographies and references are given at the end of the introduction for the personages mentioned most frequently in the letters and commentary.

There are four appendices. The first gathers the texts of several memorials Persons prepared in 1597 for the Roman curia and the Spanish court. The second, third, and fourth provide lists with dates of the rectors of the colleges in Rome, Valladolid, and

Seville; the cardinal protectors of the English College, Rome; and the provincial superiors of the relevant provinces of the Society of Jesus, with their dates.

Sigla
Frequently used sigla and abbreviations are listed on pages ix–xiii. See also the details of archives on pp. 29–30.

Editorial conventions
The objective of this edition is to provide as complete and reliable a record of Persons's correspondence as possible, with a critical apparatus that reflects the complexity of the composition, delivery, and reception of the letters. Each letter has been collated with all the extant witnesses, with significant variants recorded. It is notoriously difficult to draw a line between accidental and substantive variants in punctuation and spelling; as a general principle, this edition errs on the side of inclusiveness.

The text has been lightly regularized, substituting i for j, s for ſ, and u for v (and vice versa) according to standard conventions. For the Latin, we have used initial capitals for sentences, and v for u (and vice versa) for ease of reading. Contractions and abbreviations, such as V.P. (*Vestra Paternitas*) have been expanded for the same purpose. Punctuation is editorial but with minimal interference, except in the case of Persons's English letters, where the syntax is often hard to follow. Wherever there is ambiguity in the original, the intervention has been indicated and, where necessary, discussed.

In the Spanish and Italian texts, the original spelling has been retained but the punctuation and the diacritical accents are editorial, with minimal intervention. Where Latin text appears in letters written in English, Italian, or Spanish, the Latin text has been italicized both in the original and the translation, with Biblical and other references indicated in the notes to the translation. For ease of reading, underlining in the manuscript sources has been registered in the textual notes rather than appearing in the texts themselves. Ciphers have generally been retained in square brackets in the text, following the deciphered words.

In the footnotes, Biblical passages are rendered in the Rheims-Douai translation unless otherwise indicated.

Introduction

This second volume of Persons's correspondence is largely devoted to the period of Persons's sojourn in Spain, from 1589 to 1596, and ends where the first volume began: with trials at the English college in Rome. Only, where the earlier conflict, of 1578–1579, issued in a period when the college formed a relatively stable foundation for the English mission, the broils which compelled Persons to return to Rome in 1597 signalled an enduring rift in English Catholicism.

The death of William Cardinal Allen (1532–1594) in Rome in October 1594 was the catalyst for this change, which is reflected in the structure of this volume. The first two chapters cover the five years from 1589 to 1594 when Persons was carrying out a commission from the superior general of the Society of Jesus, Claudio Acquaviva (1543–1615, in office 1581–1615), to intervene in the *memorialista* controversy which was disturbing the Jesuits in Spain. During these years Persons was not only occupied as a Jesuit diplomat at the court of King Philip II (1527–1598, r. 1556–1598) as the crisis evolved and preparations were made for the Fifth General Congregation of the Society (November 1593 to March 1594), but also engaged in founding two English seminaries: St Alban's College, Valladolid (1589), and St Gregory's College, Seville (1592).

After Allen's death, Persons became increasingly concerned with the growth of opposition to his programme for the restoration of Catholicism in England, a programme led by the Jesuits and sponsored by Spain. Both in Rome and in Flanders, there was a vigorous campaign to have Owen Lewis (1532–1595), bishop of Cassano, appointed as cardinal, to shift the centre of gravity of the Catholic community in England and Wales and in exile. Chapters 3 and 4 deal, accordingly, with the repercussions of Allen's death on Persons's activities in Spain and with his return to Rome to deal with the situation at the English college there.[1]

The Memorialistas

At the time of the 1588 Armada, Pope Sixtus V (1520–1590, r. 1585–1590) intended that Allen and Persons should go to Flanders to support the exiles there and promote the

---

1. For biographical details, see Edwards, *Robert Persons* and Federico Eguiluz, *Robert Persons "El Architraidor"* (Madrid, 1990); see also McCoog, *Building the Faith of St Peter*.

English mission from close quarters. But with a crisis developing in the ranks of the Society in Spain, Acquaviva decided that Persons should go to Madrid instead, at least temporarily. For Persons, this also afforded an opportunity to approach Philip II in person, to restore his confidence in the English cause and ensure his continued support. He prepared himself for this double mission by going on pilgrimage to Loreto, where he acquired the services of Fr William Flack.[2]

The Society's problem had arisen from the competing interests of the Inquisition, the monarchy, and the Society's international character.[3] A growing number of influential Spanish Jesuits, who came to be known as the *memorialistas*, were critical of the Society's Institute or "way of proceeding," especially in its transnational character. They recalled that the Society was of Spanish origin and feared that Spanish predominance was being eroded by the non-Spanish superior generals Everard Mercurian (1514–1580, in office 1573–1580) and Acquaviva, even though more than half of the Society's provinces lay in Spanish territory. Memorials were drawn up and circulated, notably by Juan Bautista Carrillo, who was later expelled from the Society.[4] The *memorialistas* were determined to maintain and promote the Spanish character of the Society: they challenged the central authority of the Jesuit curia in Rome, called for a general congregation of the Society to deal with their concerns, and brought the power of the Inquisition and the monarchy to bear on provincial superiors of the Society who had a strong loyalty to the general. In 1586, Antonio Marcén, provincial of Toledo, was hauled before the Inquisition and jailed for failing to denounce persons to the Inquisition, implying thereby that Jesuit jurisdiction was sufficient.[5] Philip II was induced to place restrictions on Spanish Jesuits' movements outside of Spain, because of fears that they would be corrupted by contact with heretics. Things came to a head when the king threatened to appoint visitors to the Jesuit provinces from outside the Society, notably the inquisitor Jerónimo Manrique (c. 1538–1595), bishop of Cartagena.

In October 1588, Acquaviva instructed Persons and José de Acosta (1540–1600) to go to Madrid and persuade the king to stand back and allow standard Jesuit procedure to be followed.[6] The superior general's appointees might then carry out visitations which could reduce the influence of the *perturbatori* (disruptors of the peace) and go some way towards restoring unity. Acosta was chosen for this mission as a former provincial of Peru who had the ear of the king thanks to his reputation as an authority on the Spanish dominions. Acquaviva assumed Acosta would be suitably diffident about being appointed as a visitor himself,[7] but once Persons had spoken up for him to the king,

2. John E. Parish, *Robert Parsons and the English Counter-Reformation* (Houston, 1966), 39; Pollen, "Colleges in Spain," 1–4.

3. See Astrain, volume 3; for Persons's intervention, see Thomas M. McCoog, "Correcting the Damage: Robert Persons's Work for the Society of Jesus in Spain in the 1590s," forthcoming in William Sheils, ed., *Writing the Catholic Past: Essays in Memory of Michael Hodgetts* (London, 2024).

4. Astrain, 3: 505–510.

5. Astrain, 3: 376–380; Stefania Tutino, *Shadows of Doubt: Language and Truth in Post-Reformation Catholic Culture* (Oxford, 2014), 20.

6. Instructions for Fr Persons, 31 October 1588 (B1).

7. Acquaviva to Persons, 6 March 1589 (B6).

Acosta gravitated towards the *memorialistas*. After delivering the report on his visitation at the end of 1591, he retired to Valladolid and began agitating for a general congregation. In December 1592, he made an unauthorized visit to Rome and succeeded in persuading the new pope, Clement VIII (1535–1605, r. 1592–1605), to insist on a general congregation.[8]

The diplomatic mission had mixed success. Philip approved the Jesuit visitors early in 1589. Over the next seven years Persons had several audiences with him about the Society's organization and discipline, advising the king how to interpret the visitors' reports and reassuring him about the value of the Society in his dominions.[9] When Acquaviva was instructed by the pope to call a general congregation,[10] Persons had an important role to play, in concert with other trusted Jesuits. During carnival season in 1593, he had a meeting at Alcalá de Henares, involving Gil González Dávila (1532–1596), one of the visitors, and Alonso Sánchez (1547–1593), the celebrated missionary to the Philippines, whom Acquaviva had sent to Spain the previous year to strengthen his party. Here it was decided that Persons should discuss the prospects of the congregation with the king. The king listened politely, and so did his minister the count of Chinchón, Diego Fernández de Cabrera y Bobadilla (1536–1608), but more guardedly. This turned out to be the result of further lobbying by Acosta, so it was agreed that Sánchez should do what he could to warn the royal council against Acosta.[11] A few months later, González Dávila and the provincial of Andalusia, Bartolomé Pérez (1548–1614), informed Persons that they were more confident of the king's disposition, but hoped that he would be able to keep Philip in this frame of mind. In the run up to the general congregation, the provinces held their congregations to elect delegates (procurators) and to formulate concerns for the general congregations. As a senior professed father of the Society (that is, one who had pronounced the fourth vow), Persons was invited to some of the provincial congregations.[12] There he employed his skill to curtail the antics of the *memorialistas*.

While the delegates gathered in Rome for the general congregation, which took place from November 1593 to March 1594, Persons himself remained vigilant in Madrid. It was disappointing to learn that some of the king's ministers in Rome had interfered, and a delay in the post meant that Acquaviva failed in his attempt to detain Acosta in Rome

---

8. For accounts of Acosta's gradual estrangement from Acquaviva, see Claudio M. Burgaleta, *José de Acosta, S.J. (1540–1600): His Life and Thought* (Chicago, 1999), 60–63, and Thomas M. McCoog, "Correcting the Damage," citing John W. Padberg, in *For Matters of Greater Moment: The First Thirty Jesuit General Congregations*, ed. John W. Padberg, Martin D. O'Keefe, and John L. McCarthy (St Louis, 1994), 11.

9. Acquaviva to Persons, 17 April, 12 June, and 4 September 1589, 19 February 1590, 2 September 1591 (B10, B18, B31, B51, B119); Persons to Acquaviva, 22 March and 19 April 1593, 10 and 20 March 1594, 2 and 9 December 1595 (B173, B176, B219, B221, B303); to Creswell, 22 July 1589 (B24); to Ruiz de Velasco, 5 August 1589 (B27); to Barret, 7 November 1590 (B86); to Philip II, September/October 1595 (B293).

10. McCoog, *Building the Faith of St Peter*, 136, noting Acquaviva's suspicions that Acosta had engineered this via Philip II.

11. Persons to Acquaviva, 22 March and 19 April 1593 (B173, B176).

12. Persons to Acquaviva, 19 April 1593 (B176).

afterwards.¹³ The congregation made some concessions to Spanish interests and sensibilities, including a provision to exclude persons of Jewish descent from entering the Society. Acosta was the only delegate to vote against the relevant decree, which would have alienated Acquaviva even more. Persons now found himself in the position of having to support Acquaviva against his own better judgement: when news of the decrees reached him in May, he had to be nimble of foot because he had earlier tried to dissuade Philip's court from pursuing their discrimination against *conversos*. Even more agility was going to be required in response to the decree which prohibited Jesuits from taking any part in affairs of state. Persons asked Acquaviva how this would apply to the English mission, given that the Elizabethan state had politicized religion. Acquaviva's reply was guarded, leaving the matter to Persons's discretion so that no formal dispensation would be needed.¹⁴

The Seminaries: Valladolid, Seville, and St Omers

The question of Spanish nationalism had a bearing on the status of the English colleges Persons founded in Valladolid and Seville.¹⁵ There was something of an anomaly in the presence of Jesuit institutions exclusively for English students within the Spanish provinces. Nor was it merely a question of competition for funds, although this was a recurrent complaint. There were constitutional issues over academic collaboration with local Spanish colleges, St Ambrose in Valladolid and St Hermenegild in Seville. Although the rectors of the English colleges were Spanish, and the Spanish provincials were involved in their appointment, ultimately Persons had the management in his own hands, and he was answerable to no one but Acquaviva. The larger issue of the place of English Jesuits resident in Spanish provinces came to a head in the seventeenth century, prompting Acquaviva's successor, Muzio Vitelleschi (1563–1645, in office from 1615), to elevate the English mission from prefecture to vice province and province by 1623.¹⁶

13. Persons to Acquaviva, 18 April 1594 (B226).

14. Persons to Acquaviva, 12 May 1594 (B230); Acquaviva to Persons, 4 July 1594, addendum (B235). On the congregation, see John W. Padberg, Martin D. O'Keefe, and John L. McCarthy, *For Matters of Greater Moment: The First Thirty Jesuit General Congregations* (St Louis, 1994), 187–246. See also Robert Maryks, *The Jesuit Order as a Synagogue of Jews: Jesuits of Jewish Ancestry and Purity-of-Blood Laws in the Early Society of Jesus* (Leiden, 2010); Thomas M. McCoog, "'Rendering to Caesar': Religion, Politics, and the Society of Jesus in Elizabethan England," in McCoog, *And Touching our Society*, 349–369; and Harro Höpfl, *Jesuit Political Thought: The Society of Jesus and the State, c. 1540–1630* (Cambridge, 2004), 53–63.

15. For details of the foundations, see Hicks, *Seminaries*; Williams, *St Alban's College*; Murphy; see also the revised, Spanish version, Martin Murphy and José Miguel Santamaría, *Ingleses en Sevilla: el Colegio de san Gregorio, 1592–1767* (Seville, 2012). For a contemporary account of the foundation at Valladolid, see *Blackfan Annals*.

16. Thomas M. McCoog, *Pre-Suppression Jesuit Activity in the British Isles and Ireland* (Leiden, 2019), 32–46. On Persons's treatment of the relationship between the English identity of the

The progress of the two colleges, at Valladolid and Seville, followed a similar pattern. They began with a modest house of residence, negotiation with local Jesuits, and then the development of property with support from local notables. The king was forthcoming with financial and moral support, witness the amicable audiences he gave to Persons, who was able to inspire him with a vision of scholarship and missionary purpose. Both colleges were endorsed by the pope: Valladolid on 25 April 1592 and Seville in May 1594. Priests were prepared there for the English mission, travelling either from Seville to Cádiz or Sanlúcar de Barrameda, or from Valladolid through ports in Galicia.[17] Starting with Henry Walpole (1558–1595), it became customary for missionaries to pay their respects to the king in one of his palaces in or near Madrid.[18]

St Alban's College, Valladolid, originated in response to difficulties faced by Richard Barret (1544–1599), president at Rheims: the English college there was overcrowded, underfunded and under threat from the troops of Henry of Navarre (1553–1610), contesting the French crown after the assassination of Henry III (1551–1589). On arrival in Spain, Persons hoped to increase the level of royal funding for Rheims but conjectured that the king might be more enticed by a new foundation in Spain itself. Barret accordingly despatched three students, John Blackfan (1561–1641), Henry Floyd (1564–1641), and John Bosseville (or Bosvile, ca. 1567–ca. 1631), who reached Valladolid at the end of May 1589. They were arrested on arrival but then, released by the Inquisition, joined a handful of other English students in the city. Persons himself got to Valladolid in August, delayed by having first to obtain royal authorization. He found the students suffering in poor lodgings "beneath the tiles in the blazing summer heat."[19] Within three or four weeks, despite some local resistance from the abbot, Don Alfonso de Mendoza, and the brothers of the hospice of SS Cosmas and Damian (the accommodation appointed by the crown),[20] he astonished the townspeople by establishing a seminary of twelve students at a house rented in the Calle Don Sancho, only four minutes from the Jesuit college of St Ambrose in the Calle Alonso Pesquera, where the students were attending lectures.[21]

Persons recognized that Valladolid had the advantage, as a location for a seminary, that the Inquisition could endorse the English students, otherwise liable to suspicion of heresy, as already voiced by the abbot. For a similar reason, and because of the proximity of the ancient university of Valladolid, he declined Don Francisco de Fonseca's offer

---

colleges and the Spanish context, see Mark Netzloff, "The English Colleges and the English Nation: Allen, Persons, Verstegan, and Diasporic Nationalism," in *Catholic Culture in Early Modern England*, ed. Ronald Corthell et al. (Notre Dame, IN, 2008), 236–260.

17. Persons to Barret, 7 November 1590 (B86).
18. Persons to Idiáquez, Moura, and Ruiz de Velasco, July 1593 (B194).
19. *Blackfan Annals*, 12–13.
20. Persons to Ruiz de Velasco, 5 August 1589 (B27).
21. The college of St Ambrose, vacated after the suppression of the Society, became by grant of Carlos III the Scots college which later relocated to Salamanca. It is now the Centre for Spirituality of the archdiocese of Valladolid, attached to the National Shrine of the Great Promise.

of the rural castle of Coca. Instead, with support from a grandee from Palencia, Don Francisco de Reinosa Baeza (1534–1601, bishop of Cordoba from 1597 to 1601), and the reclusive Don Alfonso de Quiñones in Valladolid, he purchased the rented house, together with an adjoining house with a garden. Building operations commenced, and the church and sacristy were ready in 1591, but the half-completed hall had to be hurriedly furnished when the king paid an unscheduled visit in August 1592. Philip was on a state tour of Castile, and while the civic celebrations were taking place in Valladolid, the city of his birth, he decided not simply to commend the English college but to appear in person, together with the prince and the infanta. Persons made sure that the students put on a fine display of learning, devotion to their royal patron, and determination to sacrifice everything in the cause of the restoration of the faith in England.[22]

Despite these promising beginnings, the running of the college presented many challenges. The first rector, Bartolomé de Sicilia, who had accompanied Persons from Madrid, lasted only a month or two before being recalled to the court.[23] His successor, Pedro de Guzmán (ca. 1560–1590) died only a few months later, in June 1590. The next rector, Juan López de Manzano (d. 1602), fell seriously ill in the epidemic of 1591, to be replaced by the college confessor Rodrigo de Cabredo (ca. 1558–1618), a man whom Persons liked and trusted. Unfortunately, Cabredo was whisked off at the very end of 1594 to be assistant to the provincial.[24] The provincial then recommended Gonzalo del Río, whose main interest appears to have been in entertaining his friends sumptuously at the college's expense. Eventually, after trying his best by letter,[25] Persons had to tear himself away from Seville to deal with him, but it was not until September 1596, just as Persons was tying things up to be able to leave for Rome, that Alonso Rodríguez de Toro took charge.

Of the English Jesuits at the college, William Flack was minister, in effect the vice rector, from September 1589 until he left for Saint-Omer in 1593, to be succeeded by Charles Tancard. He also acted as Persons's amanuensis and *socius* (a Jesuit term for companion and advisor). Richard Gibbons (ca. 1547–1632), prefect of studies, was restless and fiery tempered. He had two short spells in Portugal but stayed on at Valladolid until 1594. His last months there were clouded by an acrimonious dispute with Tancard over a confidential letter he had found in Persons's study.[26] Thomas Wright (ca. 1561–

---

22. See Berta Cano Echevarría, Ana Sáez-Hidalgo, et al., "'Comfort without Offence'? The Performance and Transmission of Exile Literature at the English College of Valladolid, 1592–1600," *Renaissance and Reformation/Renaissance et Réforme* 31 (2008): 31–67, and Berta Cano Echevarría and Ana Sáez-Hidalgo, eds., *The Fruits of Exile: Emblems and Pamphlets from the English College at Valladolid* (Valladolid, 2009).

23. Bartolomé de Sicilia entered the Society as a lay brother in 1568 and was priested in 1589; his penchant for business and financial affairs often got him into trouble with his superiors but may also have commended him to Persons (*Valladolid Registers*, xvii–xviii n*, citing Astrain, 3: 612–617).

24. Acquaviva to Persons, 29 August 1594 (B242).

25. Correspondence with del Río, after 19 March, 1 and 12 May 1595 (B265, B271, B275).

26. Persons to Acquaviva, 16 June 1593, 12 July 1594 (B186, B237).

1623), a gifted theologian, was continually under threat of expulsion from the Society. As with Gibbons, Persons did his best to make allowances, but Wright returned to England in 1595 with an agenda opposed to Persons and the Spanish crown.[27]

The royal visit to St Alban's, Valladolid, in 1592 gave Persons the confidence to proceed with another foundation, St Gregory's College, at Seville. Persons had established a house of residence there in 1590 but, despite urging from the provincial of Andalusia, Bartolomé Pérez, he wisely delayed its conversion into a seminary. Now he went there with the backing of the king, who wrote supporting letters to the archbishop of Seville, Cardinal Rodrigo de Castro Osorio (1523–1600), and the duke of Medina Sidonia, Alonso Pérez de Guzmán y de Zúñiga-Sotomayor (1550–1615). Persons's *Philopater* (see below),[28] a lively rejoinder to the English royal proclamation of October 1591 against seminary priests and Jesuits, boosted public enthusiasm for the English and added impetus to the new project. At this time his burdens were eased slightly by the transfer of Joseph Creswell (1557–ca. 1623), rector of the English college. Creswell joined Persons in Valladolid in the summer of 1592 and travelled with him to Seville. Later, he settled in Madrid in the role of procurator for English affairs, managing the finances and court business of the colleges.[29]

Major celebrations took place on the feast days of St Catherine (25 November) and St Thomas (Becket) of Canterbury (29 December), attended by the archbishop, the duke of Medina Sidonia, and several other high-ranking aristocrats.[30] The occasion was marked by displays and speeches echoing those at Valladolid, enhanced by the contribution of Henry Walpole, recently arrived from Flanders. At first, the college was situated in the Plaza de la Magdalena, beyond the city wall to the east, which Persons described as a prime location. He fitted it out so as to be able to accommodate eighty, but he could do even better: in 1594 he purchased a splendid property in the Calle de las Armas (now the Calle Alfonso XII), next-door to the palace of the duke of Medina Sidonia and close to St Hermenegild, the Jesuit house of studies. Eighteen thousand ducats were spent on improving the building.[31] Persons continued to take an interest in the public profile of the college, as evidenced by the report of a tragicomedy, *Anglia lapsa resurgens*, performed in celebration of the feast of St Hyacinth on 17 August 1595, before Cardinal de Castro, the inquisitors, the regent, and the asistente. The play, which depicted the principal events in the reign of Queen Elizabeth, was written by a student, based on an outline by Persons.[32]

---

27. Persons to Acquaviva, 2 October 1594, 19 March 1595 (B245, B264); Garnet to Persons, 8 October 1597 (B418); Wright to Persons, 20 February 1595 (B260).

28. Persons to Acquaviva, 12 August 1592 (B153).

29. Loomie, *Spanish Elizabethans*, 191–193; Persons to Acquaviva, 15 July 1593 (B190); Acquaviva to Persons, 14 March 1594 (B220).

30. Persons to Acquaviva, 12 June 1595. See Ana Sáez-Hidalgo, "*E Duobus Elige*: The 'Devise' of Thomas Becket and Queen Elizabeth's Spanish Dilemma," forthcoming.

31. Persons to Acquaviva, 15 May 1595 (B276).

32. Murphy, 123.

The college at Seville benefited from having only one rector, Francisco de Peralta (ca. 1554–1622), from its inception until 1607. It also enjoyed a healthier climate than Valladolid, so that over the years several priests were transferred there.[33] Although students and priests were assigned to the two colleges on the basis of availability of places, they would normally go to Valladolid if they had already had some training at Rheims or Rome, whereas Seville catered to students who were beginning their courses of study and even to younger boys and laymen. Henry Piers (1567–1623) enrolled as a *convictor* (lay boarder) there in April 1598, admitted by the prefect of studies Richard Walpole (ca. 1562–1607), Henry's brother.[34] As in Valladolid, foreigners were subject to interrogation and approval by the Inquisition.

In 1593 Persons directed the foundation of a school for boys at Saint-Omer,[35] in the Spanish Netherlands near the French border, in response to threatened legislation that would have obliged Catholic parents in England – presumably those of the gentry – to hand their sons over to Protestant households for their reformation.[36] He sent his former *socius*, William Flack, to take charge as rector, obtaining generous funding from Philip II and enlisting the help of Acquaviva and Olivier Mannaerts (1523–1614), former provincial in Flanders, to reconcile the local Jesuits to the idea.[37] The city fathers of Saint-Omer were given assurances that this would not jeopardize the city's position on the French border. Later in 1593 Persons sent Henry Walpole, who was on his way to England, to help with the teething problems. Persons's success at Saint-Omer created some tension with the Scottish Jesuit William Crichton (ca. 1535–1617), who was concerned about the state of the Scots college at Douai. Persons tried to assist, without much success, as the college moved to Louvain.[38] He also lent a hand to Thomas White (1558–1622) and James Archer (ca. 1550–1620) with the Irish college established in Salamanca in 1592.[39]

The relation of the colleges in Spain to those in Douai and Rome was generally cooperative.[40] Douai was not a Jesuit college, but it was deeply imbued with the Jesuit ethos:

33. Williams, *St Alban's College*, 21.

34. *Henry Piers's Continental Travels, 1595–1598*, ed. Brian Mac Cuarta (Cambridge, 2018), 29, 34–35.

35. In this edition the school is referred to as St Omers, but the city as Saint-Omer.

36. Persons to Acquaviva, 22 March, 19 April, 16 June, 15 July, 11 August, and 4 December 1593 (B173, B176, B187, B190, B196, B210); Acquaviva to Persons, 12 April, 10 May, 30 August, and 27 September 1593 (B174, B180, B197, B202); Walpole to Persons, 13 and 19 November 1593 (B206, B207); despatches on behalf of Philip II, 24 February 1594 (B218). See also Leo Hicks, "The Foundation of the College of St Omers," *AHSI* 19 (1950): 146–180; Hubert Chadwick, *St Omers to Stonyhurst: A History of Two Centuries; St Omers, 1593, Bruges, 1762, Liège, 1773, Stonyhurst, 1794* (London, 1962); and Maurice Whitehead, *English Jesuit Education: Expulsion, Suppression, Survival, Restoration, 1762–1803* (Farnham, Surrey, 2013).

37. Acquaviva to Persons, 6 June 1594 (B231).

38. Persons to Acquaviva, 12 May 1594, 7 September 1594 (B230, B244); Persons to Crichton, 10 May 1596 (B323).

39. Acquaviva to Persons, 31 August 1592 (B155).

40. The college founded at Douai moved to Rheims in 1578 but returned to Douai progressively from 1592 to 1594. For ease of reading, it is referred to generically as Douai.

Douai students attended the Jesuit college in the city, and the college itself had a Jesuit spiritual director.[41] Richard Barret, Allen's assistant and then successor as president at Douai, intervened on behalf of the Jesuits in the English college in Rome, as we shall see. There was incompatibility, however, between him and his vice president, Thomas Worthington (1549–1627), whom Persons respected and even recommended for a bishopric in the event of a successful restoration in England.[42] Worthington wrote earnestly to Persons for advice about his vocation in January 1597, and succeeded Barret as president in 1599.[43] Douai and Rome provided the bulk of the teaching staff at St Alban's and St Gregory's. The curriculum conformed to the *Ratio studiorum*, which was finalized under Acquaviva's oversight in 1599.[44] Linguistic virtuosity, especially, was showcased at the public ceremonies in Valladolid and Seville in 1592, alongside glances at the Elizabethan regime. In the following years, there were public defences of theses and musical performances. Students were being prepared psychologically and spiritually for the mission, as well as honing their skills in theological debate. The place of St Thomas Aquinas (1225–1274) in the curriculum, although central, could also be a source of tension, when he was offered as the only authority on every question a student might have.[45] In the colleges, the chief officers were the rector, the minister (effectively the vice rector, dealing with logistics), the confessor, the prefect of studies, and the consultor, who advised the rector. According to Henry More (ca. 1587–1661), Seville was a popular destination for English students because of the quality of teaching they received nearby at St Hermenegild,[46] a centre of learning distinguished by widely known authors such as Melchor de Castro (1559–1609) and Juan de Pineda (1558–1637).

The Opposition in Flanders

It is as difficult to present an objective view of Persons's detractors in Flanders[47] as it is to give a name to the group (sometimes referred to as the "Scottish" or "French" party,

---

41. See Thomas M. McCoog, "'Replant the uprooted trunk of the tree of faith': The Society of Jesus and the Continental Colleges for Religious Exiles," in *Insular Christianity: Alternative Models of the Church in Britain and Ireland, c. 1500–c. 1700*, ed. Robert Armstrong and Tadhg Ó hAnnracháin (Manchester, 2013), 28–48.

42. Memorandum, 30 August 1596 (B340).

43. Worthington to Persons, 10 January 1597 (B353).

44. See Whitehead, *English Jesuit Education*, and "'Established and putt in good order': The Venerable English College, Rome, Under Jesuit Administration, 1579–1685," in *Jesuit Intellectual and Physical Exchange Between England and Mainland Europe, c.1580–1789: "The World is Our House"?*, ed. James E. Kelly and Hannah Thomas (Leiden, 2019), 315–336.

45. Persons to Acquaviva, 12 July 1594 (B236).

46. Henry More, *Historia missionis Anglicanae Societatis Jesu, 1580–1635* (Saint-Omer, 1660), 159–160.

47. In this edition, "Flanders" is the preferred term for the Spanish Netherlands, although "Belgium" is frequently used in Latin, especially for the Belgian province of the Society of Jesus.

opposed to the "Spanish" or "Jesuit" party),[48] partly because the bulk of the evidence comes from Persons and his associates: William Holt (1545–1599), William Allen, and Richard Barret. Persons's own account, presented in a long letter to Charles Paget in December 1597, traces their hostility back to 1582, when Guise invasion plans were mooted at a conference in Paris. Charles Paget (ca. 1546–1612) and Thomas Morgan (ca. 1542–1606), regarding themselves as agents of Mary Stuart (1542–1587, r. 1542–1567) in Paris, were initially excluded from these discussions and treated Persons warily ever after, despite various attempts on his part to bring about a reconciliation. Their Paris base was strengthened by the fact that Paget's brother Thomas Lord Paget (ca. 1540–1590) was a leading figure amongst the more aristocratic exiles,[49] and their interests coincided with those of Gilbert Gifford (1560–1590), renowned in history for his beer-barrel device for smuggling letters to Mary Stuart at Chartley, and his associate Edward Grately (1555–post 1588). These two had assisted in provoking opposition to Persons in Paris by writing against William Allen's defence of the surrender of Deventer.[50]

In 1588 Paget and Morgan removed to Flanders, but Morgan came under suspicion of spying for the English government: he was held in prison by Alessandro Farnese, duke of Parma (1545–1592, r. 1586–1592), and then expelled from the country. Paget remained in Brussels and built up his connections in the region. These included William Gifford (1557/8–1629), Gilbert's kinsman, who became dean of Lille in May 1595 and in due course was to play a major role in the English Benedictine revival, ending his career as archbishop of Rheims. Humphrey Ely (1539–1604), at Pont-à-Mousson, was a fellow traveller.[51] In the main the party, or faction as Persons preferred to call it, comprised clerics and lay people who resented the dominance of Persons and Allen, whom they saw as too much under Persons's influence, in English Catholic affairs. They were suspicious of Jesuit designs and nervous about relying overmuch on Spain. There was potential support from many whose Spanish royal pensions were delayed or, indeed, never paid. The predominance of Spanish and English interests in Persons's agenda also alienated some leading Jesuits, such as William Crichton, who was concerned about the sidelining of the Scots, and the Belgian provincial Olivier Mannaerts, formerly an ally. William Holt, the superior of the English Jesuits in Brussels, was thick with Hugh Owen (1538–1618), the organizer of an intelligence network devoted to foiling the devices of Walsingham and Cecil, and both seem to have had a knack for riling other exiles.[52] Innocenzo Malvasia (1552–1612), the papal agent in Brussels until late in 1595, was another who criticized them in the light of Spain's pretensions to be the Catholic power *par excellence*.

48. A partial view is given by Leo Hicks, *An Elizabethan Problem: Some Aspects of the Careers of Two Exile-Adventurers* (New York, 1964).
49. See Katy Gibbons, *English Catholic Exiles in Late Sixteenth-Century Paris* (Woodbridge, Suffolk, 2011).
50. See vol. 1: 684–686.
51. See, for instance, his account of the troubles in the English college in *Certaine briefe notes upon a briefe apologie set out under the name of the priestes united to the archpriest* (Paris, 1602).
52. Persons to Acquaviva, 12 May 1594 and 9 December 1595 (B230, B304).

The party was galvanized after the death of William Allen in October 1594. Although Allen and Persons acted as close allies in the 1580s, in France, the Netherlands, and Rome, there is some evidence of attempts to induce Allen to a more neutral stance once Persons had left for Spain. Allen had to warn Thomas Throckmorton against trusting Charles Paget, and opined that Owen Lewis had been compromised by entertaining support from "the faction." Throckmorton seems to have ignored his advice, so that Allen was reluctant to sanction Throckmorton's marriage to his niece, Mary Allen, fearing that it would send out a signal that Allen was changing his political and diplomatic stance.[53] The rector of the English college, Alfonso Agazzari, even attributed Allen's demise to his ambivalence: "When he began to leave this path [of support for the Jesuits], in a moment the thread of his plans and life were cut short together."[54] In Allen's last months, Thomas Morgan tried to enlist his support in a scheme to have Jane Dormer (1538–1612), duchess of Feria, come to Brussels, where she might provide a centre of attraction for the exiles.[55] Morgan appears to have been in Madrid when he heard of Allen's death, and he set to work, agitating for Owen Lewis to succeed as cardinal and leader of British Catholicism. Lewis, now bishop of Cassano but normally resident in Rome, was a close friend of Allen and popular both among the English community there and at the English college. Letters and memorials were soon being exchanged between Rome and Flanders, the two bases of his support. Mannaerts cautioned Persons against putting himself up as a rival candidate to Lewis,[56] and Malvasia composed a memorial for papal attention. Even after Lewis died in October 1595, the party remained focused on diminishing Persons's influence. William Gifford resumed a correspondence with Persons, professing admiration and willingness to cooperate, despite having previously spread vicious anti-Jesuit ideas.[57] Further canvassing was done by Robert Fisher, who left the college in Rome about July 1596 and made a tour of Flanders, gathering support for a memorial he forwarded to Rome.[58]

In response, Persons devised his own plans for a council for English affairs in Brussels and the appointment of two bishops, one based in England itself, the other in Brussels.[59] Once he got to Rome in March 1597, he intensified his efforts, lobbying both the Spanish ambassador and the papal curia.[60] For its part, the papacy was trying hard to

---

53. Allen to Throckmorton, 4 January 1591; Thomas Worthington to Thomas Allen (alias Hesketh), Douai, 18 Dec 1601 (Knox, *Allen*, 320–324, 396–397). Worthington cites a letter from William Allen shortly before his death, but his evidence, offered during the appellant controversy, should be treated with due caution. See McCoog, *Building the Faith of St Peter*, 202–203.

54. Pollen, "Colleges in Spain," 62–65.

55. Loomie, *Spanish Elizabethans*, 115–117.

56. Mannaerts to Persons, 24 November 1594 (B251); see also Persons to Mannaerts, 12 April 1597 (B364).

57. Gifford to Persons, 20 March 1597; see Kenny, "Inglorious Revolution," 86–87 (part 3).

58. Barret to Persons, 10 August 1597 (B392).

59. See the "Memorandum on the Establishment of a Special Council in Flanders to Advise the Governor on English Affairs" (probably to Martín de Idiáquez, 30 August 1596, B341) and the 1597 memorandum on the appointment of two bishops (appendix A, item BA 3).

60. Persons to Peña, 12 and 15 August 1597 (B393, B397); Persons to Pope Clement VIII, 13 August 1597 (B395).

bring Thomas Stapleton (1535–1598), the renowned theologian and controversialist, from Louvain, possibly to be made cardinal, certainly to occupy a position of dignity, and he and Persons exchanged friendly but guarded letters.[61]

The English College, Rome

The unrest at the English College, Rome,[62] was so closely related to the growth of the opposition party in Flanders that it could be treated as part of the same movement. Owen Lewis had been invited to assist in the remaking of the English hospice into a college in 1578–1579, and although his partiality to his fellow Welshmen contributed to the strife at that time and obliged him to retire to Milan, where he joined the household of Cardinal St Charles Borromeo (1538–1584), his friendship with Allen survived.[63] Within months of Allen's death, the students petitioned the pope to have Lewis elevated to cardinal. The old animosity between Welsh and English students played its part as the student body divided, with the majority party attached to Lewis. Edward Bennet (1569–1637) emerged as the leader, supported in the city by Thomas Throckmorton, who had come from Flanders to join Allen's entourage; he harboured strongly anti-Spanish views and was friendly with Thomas Morgan.[64]

The agitation led the minister at the college, Edmund Harewood (1554–1597) to try to quash it by setting up a new form of surveillance by informers called "guardian angels." This contrasted with the indulgent attitude of the rector, Girolamo Fioravanti (d. 1630), who liked feasting the students – as, indeed, did Lewis himself. The students strongly resented Harewood; their grievances even reached John Mush (ca. 1551–1612/13) in England, who wrote an earnest letter to Persons begging him to intervene in favour of a more understanding approach.[65] Harewood, too, wrote to Persons in desperation,[66] and was further distressed when he was heckled during an official visit from

---

61. Persons to Stapleton, 15 March 1597 (B358); Stapleton to Persons, 16 April and 6 July 1597 (B366, B385).

62. Much of what follows is indebted to Kenny, who supplies a comprehensive list of sources in "Inglorious Revolution," 240 n1 (part 1). Persons described the events in memoranda to Juan de Idiáquez, 1 and 22 May 1597, and in a letter to Garnet, 12/13 July 1598 (in Law, *Archpriest Controversy* 1: 21–38); "A Brief Account of the Stirs at the English College, Rome, 18–20 October 1597" may also be by Persons (appendix A, item BA 6).

63. Kenny, "Inglorious Revolution,"245 (part 1).

64. Thomas Throckmorton was the younger brother of Francis, executed in 1584 in relation to the Guise invasion attempts (the "Throckmorton plot"). He escaped with the aid of the countess of Arundel in October 1583 (*CSPD*, 2: 124), and Allen tried unsuccessfully to obtain a pension for him: Allen to Cardinal Como, papal secretary, 20 July 1584 (Knox, *Allen*, 234–235). According to A.L. Rowse, *Ralegh and the Throckmortons* (London, 1962), 114, he lived "impoverished in Paris on pittances from Philip and the Pope" (see also 9, 46, 102). He then arranged to be married to Allen's niece Mary, but arrived in Rome after Allen's death and the marriage fell through (Persons to Idiáquez, 22 May 1597, B378).

65. Mush to Persons, 24 March 1595 (B266).

66. Harewood to Persons, 25 October 1595 (B297).

Enrico Caetani (1550–1599), the cardinal protector with special oversight over the college. The pope then ordered a visitation by Monsignor Bernardino Morra (ca. 1549–1605), notary of the Congregation for Bishops and Religious, as a result of which Harewood was asked to retire to the novitiate of Sant'Andrea, and some students were sent away. Persons expressed his concern lest Harewood be seen to be removed at the students' behest.[67]

A more exhaustive visitation followed, conducted by Morra and Cardinal Filippo Sega (1537–1596), the vice-protector. Sega produced his report only in March 1596,[68] by which time it was certainly too late for the harsh disciplinary methods he recommended. Lewis had died in October 1595, but discontent with Jesuit rule intensified, despite the efforts of Richard Barret, president of the college at Douai, who came to Rome at this time to see if he could help.[69] When Sega died not long afterwards, he was succeeded as vice-protector by Cardinal Francisco de Toledo (1532–1596), a Spanish Jesuit, who had been instrumental in the rehabilitation of Henry of Navarre, now Henry IV of France.[70] Toledo was critical of Acquaviva and hostile to Philip II's policies, and with Caetani away in Poland from April 1596 to June 1597,[71] had a relatively free hand. His favourable stance to the students brought a measure of peace. He replaced Fioravanti with Persons's old ally Alfonso Agazzari (1549–1602), a previous rector, but this was not enough to reassure Acquaviva, who was still trying hard to let the college go when Toledo died in his turn, in September 1596.[72]

All the while, Persons had been in constant correspondence with Acquaviva, urging moderation and a continued Jesuit presence, and by this stage he was making plans to return. He received helpful reports from two young Jesuits at the college, Richard Cowling (1562–1618) and Henry Tichborne (1570–1606).[73] The balance of opinion among the English and Welsh community in Rome, outside the college, was shifting, thanks to the departure of Hugh Griffin (1555–1600), Lewis's nephew, for the position of archdeacon of Cambrai, where he joined forces with William Gifford.[74] Richard Barret took advantage of Griffin's departure and Thomas Throckmorton's death to woo Allen's nephew Thomas Hesketh (d. post 1602), the new leader of the English in Rome, over to the Jesuits' side.[75]

---

67. Persons to Acquaviva, 2 December 1595 (B303).

68. The report, BAV, Ott. Lat. 2473, can be found, "translated fairly accurately into English" (Kenny, "Inglorious Revolution," 240 n1 [part 1]) in Foley, 6: 1–66.

69. Barret to Persons, 10 April 1596 (B322).

70. Kenny, "Inglorious Revolution," 79–80 (part 3). Toledo had been given various diplomatic missions by Pope Gregory XIII, including one to the University of Louvain: see Josef Grisar, "Die Universität Löwen zur Zeit der Gesandschaft des P. Franciscus Toletus (1580)," *Miscellanea Historica in honorem Alberti de Meyer* (Leuven, 1946), 2: 941–968, and *DHCJ*, 4: 3807–3808.

71. Acquaviva to Persons, 8 April 1596 (B320).

72. Agazzari to Persons, 25 September 1596 (B343); Barret to Persons, 26/28 September 1596 (B344).

73. Cowling to Persons, 13 February and 8 April 1596 (B315, B321); Tichborne to Persons, 5 June 1596 (B327).

74. Agazzari to Persons, 25 September 1596 (B343).

75. Agazzari to Persons, 27 August and 25 September 1596 (B336, B343). Hesketh now adopted the surname Allen.

On arrival in Rome on 27 March 1597, Persons acted with his customary decisiveness. To begin with, he took up residence with Acquaviva at the Jesuit professed house. Before meeting with the pope and the cardinal nephews, he was briefed by Francisco de Peña (ca. 1540–1612), a high official in the Rota and advisor to the Spanish ambassador, on 2 April, presumably with a view to gauging the dynamic between the papal curia, the Spanish interest, and the Jesuits. Instead of dwelling on the question of the royal succession in England, as Peña had anticipated, Pope Clement VIII enquired about the troubles at the English College. Persons had already been approached by several students, including the leader of the discontented party, Edward Bennet, so the pope requested him to take up residence in the college itself. There he addressed all the students at the Easter vigil on 5 April, in a speech which to us looks like a bravura performance but is only obliquely mentioned in the correspondence and other contemporary documents. He continued to hold conferences with the students, winning their confidence partly because he had brought Edward Bennet's brother, John (ca. 1570–1623) with him from Valladolid. An agreement was reached, which was approved by the new protector, Cardinal Camillo Borghese, at a reconciliation ceremony on 15 May, the feast of the Ascension.[76]

Muzio Vitelleschi, future superior general of the Society, was brought back as rector for a few months, and the English Jesuit William Baldwin (1562–1632), sent by Garnet to Rome in the late summer or early autumn 1596, took Harewood's place as minister.[77] Persons kept Juan de Idiáquez (1540–1614), Philip II's secretary, apprised of developments and devised a new regimen for the students.[78] He took steps to ensure that dissident students who had been sent to join the mission in England were detained in Flanders and saw to the arrest and discipline of the students who were making a name for themselves in the taverns, impersonating German seminarians. Finally, in November, he took charge as rector.

An enthusiastic but clearly partisan endorsement of Persons's role at the English college is to be found in Henry Piers's *Discourse of His Travells*, composed in Ireland after a tour of the Continent. He arrived in Rome in September 1595, in the thick of the contestation, and joined the minority party who supported the Jesuits in their oversight of the college. A prominent member of the English clerical fraternity in Rome, Richard Haydock (ca. 1551–1605), whom Persons trusted as one who had played a constructive role during the earlier troubles,[79] helped Piers to navigate the Inquisition and to be admitted to the college as a lay student. Later, after a spell as a student in Seville, Piers

---

76. See Kenny, "Inglorious Revolution," 89–94 (part 3). There is conflicting evidence in the sources about the dating of Persons's meeting with Clement and his subsequent move to the college, which may have taken place after Easter.

77. Garnet to Persons/Baldwin, 25 November 1597 (B426); McCoog, *Building the Faith of St Peter*, 292–293.

78. Persons to Idiáquez, 1 May, 3 and 12 July 1597.

79. Persons to Idiáquez, 6 December 1595 (B302); Persons to Philip II, 26 March 1596 (B319); memorandum of 30 August 1596 (B340); see also vol. 1: 42, 51, 57.

summarized Persons's achievements in establishing colleges and residences: "Since the death of Cardinall Allen, Father Parsons hathe bene the cheefe man wch hathe wroght and travelled for the good of that Colledge, and for the Englishe natione on that side of the seas ... his deepe iudgmt, great zeale gravetie learninge, and rare witt is soe well knowen to the worlde, by his worckes and writtinges as I neede not make any further reporte of him."[80]

Whatever we make of Persons's motives and methods, his dealing with the students in Rome was a masterpiece of diplomacy. It was evidently hoped that the reconciliation celebrated on Ascension Day could help to bring about a rapprochement in Flanders as well, with Persons writing immediately to Holt on the one side, and Edward Bennet to Hugh Griffin in Cambrai, on the other.[81] Persons's success proved, however, to be localized and short lived. His attempts to keep the Catholic community to a common purpose of restoration by whatever means might be most effective – military, diplomatic, polemical, or pastoral – seem in retrospect to have been misjudged: his correspondence, personal action, and printed works generally treated the opposition in Flanders and Rome as unreasonable and obstructive, whereas we can detect the evolution of a more coherent alternative strategy, a qualified loyalism which was to furnish a rationale for the appellants in the Archpriest Controversy in the immediately succeeding years. The two most substantial figures in this respect were William Gifford and Thomas Wright, both of whom Persons would have liked to count as allies. They operated within different force fields from him: Gifford was caught up in the struggle for ascendancy in France,[82] while Wright, arriving in England from Valladolid in 1595, sought out Anthony Bacon and commended himself to Essex. By contrast, in the same year Persons dedicated the *Conference about the Next Succession* to the earl, either to embarrass him or to provoke him to show his hand. Wright was a theologian and controversialist to be reckoned with: in prison, but with a degree of latitude, he appears to have been instrumental in the conversion of Ben Jonson (1572–1637) and William Alabaster (1567–1640), and to have conspired with Alabaster to try to convert Essex.[83] His Latin treatise on the question of whether English Catholics should defend the realm against Spanish invasion represented

---

80. *Henry Piers's Continental Travels, 1595–1598*, ed. Mac Cuarta, 9, 17–21, 83.

81. Persons to Holt, 15 May 1597 (B375); Edward Bennet to Griffin, 16 May 1597, in Tierney, 3: lxxx–lxxxii, transcribed from a copy endorsed by Persons.

82. On Gifford, and his likely authorship of *De iusta reipublicae christiana in reges impios et hereticos authoritate* (Paris, 1590 and 1592), a tract that may have influenced the *Conference about the Next Succession*, see François Valérian, *Un prêtre anglais contre Henri IV, archéologie d'une haine religieuse* (Paris, 2011), 157–186, and Dominguez, *Radicals in Exile*, 165–169.

83. Thomas A. Stroud, "Father Thomas Wright: A Test Case for Toleration," *Biographical Studies* (now *British Catholic History*) 1 (1951): 189–219; Alexandra Gajda, *The Earl of Essex and Late Elizabethan Political Culture* (Oxford, 2012), 127–130. On Wright and Alabaster, see Dana F. Sutton's introduction to *Unpublished Works by William Alabaster (1568–1640)*, ed. Sutton (Salzburg, 1997), xv–xxx; on Wright and Jonson, see James P. Crowley, "'He took his religion by trust': The Matter of Ben Jonson's Conversion," *Renaissance and Reformation* 34 (1998): 53–70.

a middle way between Persons's presumed militancy and mere submission, and he made a cogent argument for church attendance.[84]

The English Mission

Throughout this period Persons continued to act as superior of the Jesuit mission to England. By migrating, first from Paris to Rome and then from Rome to Spain, he shifted the centre of operations and in effect established the king of Spain as patron: his original supporters, the Guises and the Catholic League, were now caught up in French domestic religious warfare. It was as promoter of the Guise plan for invasion of Scotland and England that Persons had met King Philip in 1582. At that time Philip preferred the Guises to give priority to the French dynastic struggle rather than English affairs,[85] but now he was receptive to Persons's missionary and seminary plans. The movement of Persons's library to Valladolid was symbolic,[86] even though he remained in contact with Ralph Emerson (1553–1604), the lay brother who acted as courier for books and holy objects, and Richard Verstegan (ca. 1550–1640), his source of news about England and the Spanish Netherlands.[87] His colleges in Spain became the hub of movement into England, although non-Jesuit missionaries from Rome often still went through Flanders. Persons was kept up to date not only with mission news but also with current affairs through Verstegan's regular despatches. He also maintained a regular correspondence with Henry Garnet (1553–1606).

Garnet arrived on English shores with Robert Southwell (ca. 1561–1595) in July 1586 and had to take over as Jesuit superior when William Weston (ca. 1550–1615) was arrested at the beginning of August. In 1588 Weston was transferred to Wisbech castle. The story of the mission in the years covered by this volume thus had three centres: Wisbech, the London prisons, and wherever Garnet happened to be based at any one time. At Wisbech, Weston created division by separating his followers from those he regarded as undisciplined. Some of those in the opposing camp, especially Christopher Bagshaw (1552–ca. 1625), liaised with the anti-Jesuit party in Flanders and originated the movement that was later to generate the appeal against the appointment of the archpriest.[88] Garnet tried to limit the damage, urging moderation.[89] He was distressed also by the

---

84. *An lictum sit Catholicis in Anglia arma sumere, & aliis modis Reginam, et regnum defendere contra Hispanos*, trans. John Stype, *Annals of the Reformation*, 4 vols. in 6 (Oxford, 1824), 3.2: 583–597; Ginevra Crosignani, *"De adeundis ecclesiis protestantium": Thomas Wright, Robert Parsons, S.J., e il dibattito sul conformismo occasionale nell'Inghilterra dell'età moderna* (Rome, 2004).

85. Stuart Carroll, *Martyrs and Murderers: The Guise Family and the Making of Europe* (Oxford, 2009), 247.

86. See the very patchy letter from Emerson to Persons, 25 April 1593 (B177).

87. See Petti.

88. For details, see Penelope Renold, ed., *The Wisbech Stirs (1595–1598)* (London, 1958).

89. Garnet to Persons, 6 September 1594 (B243).

arrest of Southwell in June 1592.[90] Southwell joined Philip Howard (1557–1595), earl of Arundel, in the Tower of London, and in 1594 Henry Walpole was added to their number, arrested almost immediately after landing in England. Initially imprisoned in York, he was brought to London so that Richard Topcliffe (1531–1604) could see what could be got out of him, and subsequently returned to York for execution. His story greatly affected not only Persons, who had seen him off not much more than a year previously, but also Joseph Creswell, whose printed account (see below) was to become bedtime reading for Luisa de Carvajal (1566–1614).[91] Howard died in prison, Southwell suffered at Tyburn in 1595, and in 1597 John Gerard (1564–1637), too, was incarcerated in the Tower, taking inspiration from being placed for a while in Walpole's cell. The following year he made his daring escape. Persons was kept informed of these developments, including frequent reports of Gerard's imminent execution.[92]

Garnet, meanwhile, was at large. From time to time, according to Jesuit custom, he gathered his fellow-Jesuits together, taking precautions not to have them all in one place at any one time.[93] There were Jesuits scattered through the kingdom, notably Richard Holtby (1552–1640) in the north and Robert Jones (ca. 1564–1615) in Wales, but it was a small cohort. All the same, the Jesuit network formed the only coherent group of priests on the mission. Given the alliance between Allen and Persons, there was, in effect, only one mission: the missionary priests were trained at Douai, the English college in Rome and the new seminaries in Spain, and they saw themselves as one body. Garnet and Verstegan reported the martyrdoms of Jesuits and seminary priests alike. Persons put many missionaries on the road to England, only a handful of whom were Jesuits. But the divisions in Wisbech, Flanders, and Rome, intensified by Allen's death, accelerated the process by which the two missions, Jesuit and secular, diverged.

The Continental opposition movement crossed into England when two priests, Richard Button (ca. 1575–post 1643) and Sylvester Norris (ca. 1572–1630), were sent from Rome in May 1596 with a view to establishing two clerical associations. Robert Fisher joined the campaign later in the year, and so did John Sacheverell (1568–1625), who came to be known as the Dominican Friar William.[94] Clearly this was intended to counter the strength of Jesuit influence among both clergy and laity, and Garnet was alarmed.[95] The anti-Jesuit party at Wisbech combined with other secular priests of a sim-

90. Persons to Acquaviva, 9 September 1592 (B156).

91. Glyn Redworth, *The She-Apostle: The Extraordinary Life and Death of Luisa de Carvajal* (Oxford, 2008), 75.

92. On these developments, see Caraman, *Henry Garnet*; Gerard, *Autobiography*; *William Weston: The Autobiography of an Elizabethan*, trans. Philip Caraman (London, 1955); Christopher Devlin, *The Life of Robert Southwell, Poet and Martyr* (New York, 1969); Augustus Jessop, *One Generation of a Norfolk House: A Contribution to Elizabethan History*, 2nd ed. (London, 1879); J.H. Pollen and William MacMahon, *The Ven. Philip Howard, Earl of Arundel, 1557–1595* (London, 1919).

93. Garnet to Persons/William Baldwin, 25 November 1597 (B426).

94. Relación of the Disturbances in the English College, Persons to Idiáquez, 22 May 1597 (B378).

95. Garnet to Persons, 23 February and 28 May 1597 (B355, B379).

ilar persuasion to launch the appellant campaign which was to dominate English Catholic discourse for several years, as we shall see in the next volume.[96] Allen's death underlined the question of jurisdiction in the English Catholic church, largely deprived of its hierarchy since the displacement of the bishops at the beginning of Elizabeth's reign. In 1598, as is well-known, controversy erupted over the decision to appoint an archpriest for England, rather than bishops, and this fuelled the opposition to Persons. In 1596 and 1597 we see him drawing up memorials for the establishment of bishoprics even in advance of a Spanish invasion. Later, he was to cite at least one of these memorials in his defence against the appellants. In his larger plan for restoration, spelled out in the *Memorial for the Reformation of England*, he envisaged a significant role for bishops, although he was cautious about their wealth and the size of their establishments. Even these proposals could give rise to suspicion, however.[97]

The wider Catholic community was being pulled in two directions: loyalism and opposition, recusancy and conformity, with many shades in between.[98] The polarity was exacerbated and complicated as the 1590s wore on by uncertainty over the succession, and rivalry between Robert Devereux, earl of Essex (1565–1601), and the Cecils, William Cecil Lord Burghley (1520–1598) and his son Robert Cecil (1563–1612). Apart from personal, regional, and local allegiances which cut across confessional lines, Catholics were unsure where in the court they might look for hope of toleration or relief. There was the Lord Chancellor Sir Christopher Hatton (1540–1591), who was sometimes thought to be soft on Catholicism.[99] There was Thomas Sackville (1536–1608), Lord Buckhurst, who had succoured Persons when he was expelled from Oxford in 1574. There was Essex, who cultivated the forward Protestant party but could be generous towards anyone he liked or admired. He was impressed by Gerard's courage in the Tower,[100] but took advantage of opportunities to increase his prestige by acts of anti-Catholic aggression, such as the prosecution of Roderigo López (ca. 1517–7 June 1594), the raid on Cádiz, and the war in Ireland. Notoriously, Persons put him on the spot by

---

96. See Lake and Questier, *All Hail to the Archpriest*.

97. Memorandum on considerations regarding the enterprise of England, probably to Martín Idiáquez, 30 August 1596 (B340), paragraphs 10–11; memorandum on the appointment of two bishops (Appendix A, item BA 3, citing *A Briefe Apologie or Defence of the Catholike Ecclesiastical Hierarchie*); *Memorial for the Reformation of England* 2.2.119–135. The *Memorial* exists in multiple manuscript copies – e.g., English version, ABSI, MS 19/3/36, with note by J.H. Pollen (owned by Ralph Slyfield or Sliford, who was at Seville in 1605); Latin version, ACSA, libro 30 – it was first published in a hostile but mainly accurate edition by Edward Gee, *The Jesuit's Memorial, for the Intended Reformation of England, under Their First Popish Prince: Published from the Copy That Was Presented to the Late King James II* (London, 1690). See Dominguez, *Radicals in Exile*, 181–204. Grateful thanks to the anonymous reviewer for this information and their comments.

98. For the most recent treatment, see Michael Questier, *Catholics and Treason: Martyrology, Memory, and Politics in the Post-Reformation* (Oxford, 2022), esp. (for this period) 179–258.

99. See Susan Doran, *Elizabeth I and her Circle* (Oxford, 2015), 153–154; Questier, *Catholics and Treason* 199, 214–220 and *passim*.

100. Garnet to Persons, 10/11 June 1597 (B381).

dedicating *A Conference about the Next Succession* to him, perhaps mischievously (see below).[101] It appears that Anthony Standen (ca. 1548–ca. 1615), Essex's agent, contacted Persons afterwards to sound him out further about the succession.[102] Burghley operated an espionage network to flush out Catholic plots,[103] but his anti-Catholic legislation was governed by considerations of state security rather than religious ideology, and he liked Catholics to imagine that conformity would bring a measure of toleration. He himself had been content to conform under Mary Tudor (1516–1558, r. 1553–1558), as his critics never tired of pointing out. Persons attacked him savagely in the *Philopater* (see below), but there was always the possibility that a Spanish alliance would suit the Cecils' purposes.

Another source of division was the question of occasional conformity,[104] a practical resort for many Catholics. The Jesuits continued to insist on heroic refusal to attend the state church, whatever the cost, and their position was strengthened by the example of Margaret Clitherow (1556–1586), who had been pressed to death in 1586. John Mush, her chaplain, spiritual adviser and biographer, made as much mileage as he could from this.[105] It is a measure of how things were changing that Mush, who, as we have seen, was friendly enough to Persons when he wrote to him in 1595, became one of the leading writers against him during the Archpriest Controversy.[106]

The curious history of John Cecil (or Snowden, 1558–1626), which surfaces several times in Persons's correspondence, illustrates just how wide was the spectrum of English Catholic response to the regime. He was in effect the leader of the group of priests whom Persons took to Seville in 1590. They eventually made their way in various vessels and disguises to England in the spring of 1591. Tellingly, they bore letters to Spanish agents in France and the Netherlands. Cecil and his associate John Fixer (1562–post 1613) were intercepted at sea, and subsequently made a deal with Burghley to engage in spying activities in Flanders. He claimed that they stopped in Amsterdam in order to offer themselves to the governor of Brill in return for freedom of conscience.[107] John Cecil made a career of playing both sides: in 1593 he turned up in Valladolid with plans for collabora-

---

101. R. Doleman (pseud.), *A Conference about the Next Succession to the Crowne of Ingland* (Antwerp, 1595).

102. Persons to Standen, 8 September 1595 (B290).

103. Stephen Alford, *The Watchers: A Secret History of the Reign of Elizabeth I*, 2nd ed. (London, 2013), esp. 270–284 on John Cecil/Snowden.

104. See Ginevra Crosignani, Thomas M. McCoog, and Michael C. Questier, eds., *Recusancy and Conformity in Early Modern England: Manuscript and Printed Sources in Translation* (Toronto, 2010).

105. Peter Lake and Michael C. Questier, *The Trials of Margaret Clitherow: Persecution, Martyrdom and the Politics of Sanctity in Elizabethan England* (London, 2011).

106. *A dialogue betwixt a secular priest, and a lay gentleman: Being an abstract of the most important matters that are in controversie betwixt the priests and the Spanish or Jesuiticall faction* (Rheims, vere London, 1601; ARCR, 2: nos. 555–556), attributed to Mush by Persons in *A manifestation of the great folly and bad spirit of certayne in England calling themselves secular priestes* (Antwerp, 1602; ARCR, 2: no. 631), fol. 94v.

107. The record of their interrogation is to be found in *CSPD*, 3: 38–44.

tion between Spain and the Scottish Catholic earls, an operation known as the "Spanish blanks"; he was in Madrid again in December 1594 with similar plans, but Persons did not leave Seville to meet him. He also seems to have tried to draw Persons on the possibility of promoting Ferdinando, Lord Stanley (1559–1594), as a candidate for the succession. He may have been one of the few people who managed to deceive Persons; even in December 1595 Persons referred to him as a reliable source of information, but Richard Cowling, observing Cecil in Rome, was determined to undeceive Persons.[108]

The International Scene

If there was flux and unpredictability in the Catholic community in England, lay and clerical, the same could be said about the principalities and powers in Europe. The most significant changes took place in France and the Netherlands. Henry of Navarre's calculated conversion brought the French wars of religion to an end in March 1594 with his triumphal entry into Paris, causing the Spanish ambassador, Lorenzo Suárez de Figueroa y Córdoba, second duke of Feria (1559–1607) to withdraw in disgust. On 7 January 1595 the French Jesuits were expelled for refusing to take the oath of allegiance.[109] There was uncertainty about papal recognition and the lifting of excommunication, with Spain applying pressure on the papacy to try to prevent France from challenging her position as the preeminent Catholic power.

In the Netherlands, Spain's war with the Dutch republic continued, with military successes celebrated by both sides, until the death of the duke of Parma on 3 December 1592. After a succession of governors, the cardinal-archduke Albert of Austria (1559–1621) moved up a rank from viceroy of Portugal to succeed his brother Ernest at the beginning of 1596. Two years later, he married the infanta Isabella Clara Eugenia (1566–1633) and the long and relatively stable rule of the archdukes began. Relations with the English Catholic exiles were ambivalent. In earlier years, the English regiment in the army of Flanders, joined by Sir William Stanley (1548–1630), was aligned with Persons and the Jesuit cause. Hugh Owen, Parma's liaison, cemented this connection. Now Stanley was kicking his heels in Valladolid[110] while Owen and Holt no longer held unchallenged sway in Brussels. Even though their chief diplomatic opponent Malvasia was replaced as papal agent in 1596, his successor Ottavio Mirto Frangipani (1544–1612) kept his distance.

---

108. Persons to Richard Barret, 7 November 1590 (B86); Persons to John Cecil and John Fixer, 13 April 1591 (B102); John Cecil to Persons, 1 November 1591 and after 24 July 1594 (B126, B238); Garnet to Persons, 19 November 1594 (B249); Persons to Acquaviva, 15 May 1595 (B276); Persons to Idiáquez, 31 August 1593 and 6 December 1595 (B200, B302); Cowling to Persons, 13 February and 8 April 1596 (B315, B321).

109. Persons to Acquaviva, 2 and 9 December 1595 (B303); McCoog, *Building the Faith of St Peter*, 205–206.

110. See Persons's covering letter, 7 November 1590 (B85); Persons to Idiáquez, 4 April 1591 (B99); Memorial from Stanley, July 1593 (B192); Persons to Philip II, September/October 1595 (B293). On Stanley and Owen, see Loomie, *Spanish Elizabethans*, 52–93 and 129–181.

In Spain, these were Philip's declining years. He was preoccupied with cares of state and financial difficulties, continually worried about the fortunes of the treasure fleets from the Indies. It was no wonder that Persons rejoiced to watch one of them arrive safely in Seville in 1595.[111] At the Spanish court, the English Catholic interest was represented by Persons's associate Sir Francis Englefield (1522–1596), and after his death, Thomas Fitzherbert (1552–1640).[112] The king supported Persons's seminary projects with enthusiasm, and liked to meet the English missionaries, but his secretary Juan de Idiáquez, Persons's confidant and eyes and ears at the court, was fully aware of the caution with which he regarded his English dependants. There were frequent complaints about the non-payment of pensions to the exiles, especially when there was no longer an ambassador resident in Paris.[113] The king was reluctant to receive English converts into his service.[114] The *memorialista* controversy showed how nervous he was about trying to keep the Inquisition and the Spanish Jesuits happy while recognizing his responsibility to the Society as a whole. Persons had to use his utmost diplomatic skill to get what he wanted, or as much of it as possible. He also had to tread carefully when he got to Rome in 1597, being accountable both to the Spanish ambassador there, Antonio Fernández de Córdoba (1550–1606), fifth duke of Sessa, and to the court in Madrid, via Idiáquez. Spanish interests in Madrid and Rome were not always in harmony.[115]

Persons took a lively interest in preparations for a new armada to restore England to the Catholic faith. One of the few glimpses we have of him with his guard down is provided by a letter from the captured priest Thomas Palasor to William Waad, clerk of the Privy Council, in March 1597: "Touching any speeches either of F. Persons, or any other, touching Her Majesty or the conquering of the realm, I never heard them use any, but that F. Persons used sometimes to jest in the time of recreation which he very seldom kept."[116] As soon as he heard that Hawkins and Drake had sailed for the West Indies in late August 1595, Persons urged Philip II that it was an opportune moment for attack. He pressed the enterprise again in May 1596, following reversals for the English at Calais and Puerto Rico. Taking advantage of Philip's indignation at Essex's raid on Cádiz in June, he wrote further memorials to Martín and Juan de Idiáquez advising on the invasion and issuing instructions for Charles Tancard and other priests to join the fleet which was preparing in Lisbon. He recommended that a royal proclamation be drawn up for use when the troops landed. Although the 1596 Armada was disabled by storms in the channel, the fleet was repaired in the Galician port of Ferrol with a view to a further endeavour in October 1597, and Joseph Creswell prepared the proclamation which was printed to accompany the fleet.[117] Along-

111. Persons to Gonzalo del Río, 12 May 1595 (B275).
112. Loomie, *Spanish Elizabethans*, 14–51, 108–112.
113. Persons's speech to the scholars at the English college, 5 April 1597 (B361).
114. Persons to Idiáquez, 4 April 1591 (B99).
115. Persons to Idiáquez, 1 May 1597 (B371).
116. *Calendar of the Manuscripts of the Most Hon. the Marquis of Salisbury, K.G., &c. ... : Preserved at Hatfield House, Hertfordshire*, ed. Richard Roberts et al., 24 vols. (London: HMSO, 1883–1976), 6: 125.
117. Albert J. Loomie, "Philip II's Armada Proclamation of 1597," *Recusant History* 12.2 (April 1973): 216–225.

side the plans for military invasion, he devised various schemes to facilitate the restoration of the faith and the organization of the English church. He wrote several memoranda for setting up a council for English affairs in Flanders and appointing bishops in England and Flanders. These plans complemented and reinforced his campaign for the succession of the infanta.[118]

The papal court was another potential minefield. The death of Pope Sixtus V on 27 August 1590 was followed by a series of short reigns: Urban VII (1521–1590, r. 15–27 September 1590), Gregory XIV (1535–1591, r. 5 December 1590–16 October 1591), and Innocent IX (1519–1591, r. 29 October–30 December 1591). A few months after Niccolò Sfondrati (Gregory XIV) was elected with the support of the pro-Spanish cardinals, Persons wrote to his nephew, Paolo Emilio (1560–1618), the papal secretary of state, describing the new pope as one who sought to follow in the steps of his friend St Charles Borromeo.[119] Persons may have hoped to rehearse the productive relationship he had enjoyed with Gregory XIII's papal secretary, Tolomeo Galli (1525–1607), but the Sfondrati team proved to be unpopular and inefficient, upsetting the balance of papal policy towards France and Spain. Following this succession of popes, Clement VIII (Ippolito Aldobrandini, 1535–1605, r. 1592–1605) was consecrated bishop on 3 February 1592 to assume office as pope. He was determined not to be in the pocket of the king of Spain. His rapprochement with Henry IV of France and his cautious wooing of James VI (1566–1625, r. in Scotland 1567–1625 and in England 1603–1625) muddied the waters for Persons as he lobbied for a Spanish succession.

William Allen's death affected Persons's relationship with the papacy. Allen had written to Persons in January 1592, expressing his disappointment that Innocent IX, also a pro-Spanish pope, had reigned for only two months. Allen furnished Persons with a testimonial for his visit to Lisbon in 1593 and helped to ensure that Pope Clement VIII bestowed his blessing on the new seminaries. After his death in October 1594, the uncertainty who would succeed him as leader of the English Catholics in exile could not but affect the pope's attitude to Persons. Successive cardinal vice-protectors varied in stance towards the dissident students at the English College, Rome (a papal foundation), Sega backing the Jesuit establishment, Toledo sympathizing with the students. When he returned to Rome in 1597, Persons had to be careful not to appear to be a mere servant of Spanish interests. His most advantageous point of connection was with the cardinal-nephew Pietro Aldobrandini (1571–1621), a friend of Joseph Creswell, from his time as rector of the English college, and of Sir Francis Englefield.[120] Through Francisco de Peña, an official of the ecclesiastical court of the Rota, Persons scheduled regular meetings both with the Spanish ambassador and Aldobrandini. He cultivated cordial relations with the cardinal protector Enrico Caetani and the two candidates for vice-protector, Camillo

---

118. Persons to Philip II, September/October 1595 (B293); Memorial on present conditions in England, from Creswell, Englefield and Persons, 26 May 1596 (B326); Persons to Martín de Idiáquez, 30 August 1596 (two memoranda, B340–341); Persons to Juan de Idiáquez, 2 September 1596 (B342); memoranda and memorials in 1597 (appendix A, items BA 1 to BA 5). See Paul E.J. Hammer, *Elizabeth's Wars: War, Government, and Society in Tudor England, 1544–1604* (New York, 2003), 191–204.

119. Persons to Paolo Emilio Sfondrati, 18 April 1591 (B105).

120. Loomie, *Spanish Elizabethans*, 40–41, 213.

Borghese (1550–1621, later to succeed Clement as Pope Paul V in 1605) and Cesare Baronio (1538–1607), the eminent ecclesiastical historian. His letters from this period are sprinkled with references to prelatical coaches, gifts of wine, and visits to various cardinals as he canvassed support for his projects in Flanders and England. They mark the beginning of a new status and a new pattern of activity. Since Persons's only serious rival among English churchmen, Thomas Stapleton, was not in the end able to leave Louvain and come to Rome in response to the papal invitation, Persons's position as the leading source of information on English affairs was unchallenged, doubtless a source of further resentment amongst his detractors.

Controversy and Publicity

The years in Spain were not Persons's most prolific years as an author. But they witnessed the publication of two pseudonymous political works that became notorious: Persons's own *Elizabethae Angliae Reginae haeresim Calvinianum propugnantis, saevissimum in Catholicos sui regni edictum ... Cum responsione*, by "Andreas Philopater" (Antwerp, etc., 1592; ARCR, 1: no. 885) and *A Conference about the Next Succession to the Crowne of Ingland*, by "R. Doleman" (Antwerp, 1594 vere 1595; ARCR, 2: no. 167), which Persons compiled, edited and put into its final form. He was also responsible for another collaborative production, *Newes from Spayne and Holland* (Antwerp, 1593; ARCR, 2: no. 632), which, besides initiating his treatment of the succession, formed part of a programme of publicity for the new seminaries, seen in *A relation of the King of Spaines receiving in Valliodolid* (Antwerp, 1592; ARCR, 2: no. 634). A third strand of publication was martyrology, which involved collaboration with Joseph Creswell, Diego de Yepes (1529–1613), and Pedro de Ribadeneira (1526–1611). These works were addressed to varied readerships in Spain, Rome, France, Flanders, and England.[121]

Persons's works in Latin and English were published by his agent in Antwerp, Richard Verstegan, at the printing house of Arnout Coninx. But he was conscious of the value of publication in Spanish, to gain local support for the seminaries and the English Catholic cause in general. In Madrid, he relied on Pedro Madrigal, who had printed Pedro de Ribadeneira's *Historia ecclesiastica del scisma del reyno de Inglaterra* (1588; ARCR, 1: no. 993).[122] This was itself based on the text of Sander's *De origine ac progressu schismatis Anglicani* (Rome, 1586; ARCR, 1: no. 973), which Persons and Allen had edited and enlarged. Madrigal's first publication with Persons was a collection of martyrological narratives, *Relacion de algunos martyrios* (1590; ARCR, 1: no. 894), which included Persons's *Información que da el Padre Personio ... acerca ... del Seminario ... en Valladolid*, a copy of which he enclosed in a letter to Allen, 14 September 1589.[123] In 1592 Madrigal printed a Span-

---

121. For a recent analysis of Persons's output while in Spain, see Dominguez, *Radicals in Exile*.

122. *Pedro de Ribadeneyra's "Ecclesiastical History of the Schism of the Kingdom of England": A Spanish Jesuit's History of the English Reformation*, trans. Spencer J. Weinreich (Leiden, 2017).

123. Acquaviva to Persons, 2 September 1591 (B119); Juan López de Manzano composed a broadsheet on English martyrs from Rome and Rheims, *Breve Catalogo de los Martyres que han sido*

ish translation of the account of Philip's visit to the college, *Relacion ... de la venida de Su Magestad a Valladolid* (*ARCR*, 1: no. 899). After Madrigal's death, the English interest seems to have been taken up by Luis Sánchez, who published a larger collection, *Historia particular de la persecucion de Inglaterra, y de los martirios que en ella ha avido, desde el año del Señor, 1570* (Madrid, 1599; *ARCR*, 1: no. 284) under the patronage of Diego de Yepes, bishop of Tarazona. This included Joseph Creswell's *Historia de la vida y martyrio que padecio en Inglaterra, este año de 1595 P. Henrique Valpolo* which had been separately published by Madrigal in 1596 (*ARCR*, 1: no. 276).

Creswell was also involved in a salvo of Catholic responses to the English royal proclamation of October 1591 against seminary priests and Jesuits. Chief of these was the *Philopater*. Philip II sponsored the first edition, seen through the press in Antwerp by Richard Verstegan.[124] The work was printed also in Lyon, Rome, and Germany, with translations into French and German (*ARCR*, 1: nos. 886–892). Creswell's contribution was *Exemplar literarum, missarum, e Germania, ad D. Guilelmum Cecilium, consiliarium regium* (Rome, 1592; *ARCR*, 1: no. 275), and Thomas Stapleton, Philip's appointee to a chair at Louvain, weighed in with *Apologia pro Rege Catholico Philippo II* (Antwerp, March 1592; *ARCR*, 1: no 1141). These Latin works were designed to arouse indignation in Catholic Europe against the Cecilian commonwealth, with Persons in the *Philopater* also mounting a spirited defence of the seminaries which had been condemned by the proclamation as seedbeds of subversion.

It was also important to cultivate public opinion in England. Persons's collaborator in this was Richard Verstegan, who disseminated the *Philopater*'s message in two lively English pamphlets, published in Antwerp in the same year: *An advertisement written to a secretarie of my L. Treasurers of Ingland, by an Inglishe intelligencer as he passed through Germanie towardes Italie* (1592; *ARCR*, 2: no. 757), drawing attention to "an other booke newly written in Latin, and published in diverse languages and countreyes, against her Maiesties late proclamation," and *A declaration of the true causes of the great troubles, presupposed to be intended against the realme of England* (1592; *ARCR*, 2: no. 760), purporting to refute "sundry calumnies, there lately bruited, and spred among the people" by the proclamation. The following year, Persons incorporated an account of the founding of the seminary in Seville, probably by Henry Walpole, in *Newes from Spayne and Holland* (1593). The second part of this work described an imaginary dialogue in Amsterdam broaching the question of the succession.

It is notable that these English texts employed fictional narrators as a literary and propaganda device, rather like *Leicesters Commonwealth* (1584),[125] in which Persons also had a hand. Persons turned dialogue to great effect in *A Conference about the Next Suc-*

---

de los Collegios y Seminarios Ingleses (Valladolid, 1590), which was used by Ribadeneira; see *Pedro de Ribadeneyra's "Ecclesiastical History"*, trans. Weinreich, 48, 763–767 (appendix 5).

124. Persons to Acquaviva, 12 August 1592 (B153).

125. *The copie of a leter, wryten by a master of arte of Cambridge, to his friend in London, concerning some talke ... about the present state, and some procedinges of the Erle of Leycester* (Paris/Rouen, 1584; *ARCR*, 2: no. 31, attributed to Charles Arundell).

cession to the Crowne of Ingland. The *Book of the Succession,* as it was commonly called, was initially written in 1593, incorporating material from Sir Francis Englefield and William Allen, but publication was delayed because of fears that it would arouse hostility in England and provoke further persecution. Persons's opponents in Flanders wrote to Rome to warn against the book, and Acquaviva halted progress until he was more fully assured of its suitability.[126] The book was duly published early in 1595, with a dedication to Essex, and caused a considerable stir. Essex himself was temporarily embarrassed when the queen was shown a copy in November.[127] Persons presented Idiáquez with an abridged Spanish version,[128] and when he got to Rome, he gave the pope a Latin copy with an additional chapter asserting the pope's right to intervention in the succession.[129] Meanwhile, William Crichton wrote to Persons, protesting that the published work had provoked denunciation from pulpits throughout England.[130] Attempts to have the book read aloud in the refectory in the English College, Rome, met with hostility.[131]

The common charge was that the book simply promoted the claim of the Spanish infanta, Isabella Clara Eugenia (1566–1633, r. in the Netherlands 1599–1633). Persons excused himself by explaining that he was merely giving an impartial analysis of the various claims, on the understanding that mere proximity of birth did not confer an exclusive right of succession. From his point of view, *A Conference about the Next Succession to the Crowne of Ingland* was designed to promote unity among English Catholics so that they could rally around a single candidate. It can certainly be read as neutral or "indifferent" (in the sense then current), but by 1596 its endorsement of the infanta's claim was made explicit in a memorial prepared for Philip II by Persons, Creswell, and Englefield. It is generally accepted that Persons's *Memorial for the Reformation of England* was composed in that year for her consideration.[132] In the event, consensus was never achieved, and neither the Spanish court nor the infanta herself gave their full backing. Together with the failure of the 1596 Armada, this left Persons to his own devices in Rome.

---

126. Persons to Acquaviva, 10 March 1594 (B219); Persons to Idiáquez, 2 September 1596 (B342); Acquaviva to Persons, 1 August 1594 (B239); Memorial to Philip II, 26 May 1596 (B326). On the work in general, see Dominguez, *Radicals in Exile*, 153–179, esp. 171–178 on the response of Acquaviva and Allen, whose secretary Roger Baynes published *The Censure of C.A. Touching the Succession of England* (ACSA, series 2, Legajo 12, docs. 11–13).

127. On the dedication, and Essex's predicament, see Gajda, *Earl of Essex*, 135–140. On the authorship, see Peter Holmes, "The Authorship and Early Reception of *A Conference about the Next Succession to the Crown of England*," *Historical Journal* 23 (1980): 415–429, and Leo Hicks, "Father Robert Persons, S.J., and the Book of Succession," *Recusant History* 4 (1957–1958): 104–137.

128. Persons to Acquaviva, 4 and 16 June 1594 (B233).

129. Minutes of meetings with Francisco de Peña, 2 and 17 April 1597 (B360, B367).

130. Crichton to Persons, 20 August 1596 (B335); Persons to Crichton, 2 November 1596 (B347).

131. Agazzari to Persons, 27 August 1596 (B336); Kenny, "Inglorious Revolution," 84 (part 3).

132. Memorial to Philip II, 26 May 1596 (B326); on the *Memorial for the Reformation of England*, see above, n97.

The Correspondence Network

During his years in Spain, Persons was seldom in one place for very long, and letters sometimes had to chase him round the country. His three centres of operation were Madrid, Valladolid, and Seville, but besides shuttling between them, he signed letters from Alcalá de Henares, Toledo, Puerto de Santa María, Cordoba, and Marchena. He also recorded visits to Sanlúcar de Barrameda, León, Évora, Lisbon, and Medina del Campo.[133]

Understandably, Persons's chief correspondent during this period was Claudio Acquaviva, for whom he was carrying out a delicate diplomatic mission. Other frequent correspondents in Rome were Joseph Creswell, rector of the English college until he was transferred to Spain in 1592, and William Allen. In Spain, Persons corresponded with the king's secretary, Juan de Idiáquez, and the king himself, as well as fellow Jesuits and seminary priests on the move. The situation in Flanders called for him to write to William Holt, Thomas Stapleton, William Gifford, Charles Paget, and Olivier Mannaerts. Richard Barret wrote to him from Douai,[134] and he received regular despatches from Richard Verstegan in Antwerp, often forwarding news from England as well as retailing news of the war in the Netherlands. Later, despatches of this kind came to him in Rome, shared with Roger Baynes (1546–1623), formerly Allen's secretary and still furnishing the papal court with news on English affairs.

The logistics were complicated. There was not yet a fully developed postal system, but there was an *ordinario*, or regular courier, serving the main centres. The best connection appears to have been between Rome and Brussels, via Milan and Lyon.[135] The first part of this route was also used for some post from Rome to Madrid, but letters would more usually travel by sea via Genoa and Barcelona.[136] There was a well-established courier service from Madrid to Brussels and Antwerp, reinforced by express couriers to the commander of the Spanish forces in the Netherlands, such as the duke of Parma.[137] From Madrid the post radiated to Valladolid and Seville: even Persons's letters from Valladolid to Flanders would first go south to Madrid. There are frequent references to packets of letters and enclosures for other recipients, which made confidentiality difficult; consequently, some letters would be sealed separately and marked "soli," for the private attention of the addressee.[138]

A simple code of ciphers, with numbers assigned to personages, places and titles, as well as letters of the alphabet, was used by Acquaviva and Persons in some of their con-

---

133. See Victor Houliston, "Robert Persons on the Move in Spain, 1589–1596," forthcoming in Sheils, ed., *Writing the Catholic Past*.

134. These were edited by Penelope Renold, in *Letters of William Allen and Richard Barret, 1572–1598* (London, 1967).

135. Persons to Mannaerts, 12 April 1597 (B364).

136. Persons to Idiáquez, 3 July 1597 (B385).

137. See Nikolaus Schobesberger et al., "European Postal Networks," in *News Networks in Early Modern Europe*, ed. Joad Raymond and Noah Moxham (Leiden, 2016), 19–63.

138. Where possible, the status of letters from Acquaviva, who kept separate confidential registers, is indicated in the headnote.

fidential letters;[139] the same code appears to have been used by fellow Jesuits Henry Garnet and Edmund Harewood. There are references also to ciphers used by Persons's detractors in Flanders, Thomas Morgan, Charles Paget, and William Gifford.[140]

The nature of letters was much affected by these constraints. Many were written in haste, to catch the post, especially if a reply was expected by return. On one occasion, Acquaviva used Persons's letter itself as paper on which to draft his reply.[141] Letters were composed in advance and dated by the next courier, so that although letters to various personages in a particular province may bear the same date, they were in all likelihood composed at different times. Similarly, events might overtake the schedule, as, most strikingly, when Acquaviva's optimistic letter about the new pope, Urban VII, was postdated for a courier who only left after the pope had died.[142] Letters could take from three weeks to a month from Rome to Brussels or Madrid, or from Madrid to Brussels. On at least one occasion, two monthly posts from Madrid arrived in Rome on the same day.[143] It was unusual for a letter to take less than three weeks even from Rome to Louvain, as Stapleton commented when he received a letter from Persons, dated 15 June, on 4 July 1597.[144] As noted in the introduction to the first volume, this could lead to delays in decision-making and a greater reliance on the man on the ground. In most instances, letters crossed, so that Persons would only get a reply to a letter after he had written the next. Many letters went astray, so that the reader should be cautious in assuming that all letters recorded in Acquaviva's register actually reached their destination.[145] Thomas Stapleton expressed his frustration when his acceptance of an offer from the pope of a pronotariat did not get through to his would-be benefactors in Rome and he suffered the embarrassment of being asked again for a final answer. There was a certain irony in this, given his own stated policy of attending only to the most important mail.[146]

The letters were written variously in Latin, Italian, Spanish, and English. Latin was generally used for official correspondence with the papacy and for letters designed for several potential readers; this was to ensure that there would be no misunderstanding of the author's intentions. Persons resorted to this when furnishing reasons why he felt it was

---

139. Acquaviva to Persons, 12 June 1589, 22 January 1590 (B18, B47); Persons to Acquaviva, June 1592, 4 and 16 June 1594, 9 December 1595 (B147, B233, B304); Garnet to Persons, 19 November 1594 (B249); Persons to Garnet, 12 May 1596 (B324); Persons to Harewood, 12 June 1595, referring to Harewood's of 10 April (B280, B269). Some of the ciphers are preserved at ARSI, Fondo Gesuitico 678/21, item 3. On the ciphers used by the papal nuncios and the Spanish service, see Jerome–P. Devos, "La cryptographie espagnole durant la seconde moitié du XVIe siècle et le XVIIe siècle," *Miscellanea Historica in honorem Alberti de Meyer*, 2 vols. (Leuven, 1946), 2: 1025–1035.

140. Persons to Philip II, 26 March 1596 (B319); memorial on the faction of Paget and Morgan, 30 June 1597 (B383).

141. Acquaviva to Persons, 12 June 1589 (B18).

142. Acquaviva to Persons, 4 September 1590 (B75).

143. Acquaviva to Persons, 5 June 1595 (B278).

144. Stapleton to Persons, 6 July 1597 (B386).

145. Acquaviva to Persons, 6 June 1594 (B231).

146. Ibid.

not for God's greater glory that he should be made a cardinal.[147] Besides this, many letters in Italian and Spanish contain phrases in Latin, sometimes as quotations or allusions, but sometimes also because Latin seemed to come more naturally to the writer at a particular moment. On the other hand, Alfonso Agazzari normally wrote to Persons in Latin, but shifted to Italian for parts of his letters written in the autumn of 1596,[148] because his amanuensis was more versed in Italian. Italian was the natural language for Persons to address Acquaviva in, but once he got to Spain there was a gradual shift to Spanish.[149] Since Acquaviva was writing several letters for the same post to various provincials, rectors, visitors, and other superiors in Spain, he was used to discussing matters of common interest in Spanish, and soon he did so when writing to Persons as well, although for some time the confidential letters continued to be in Italian.[150] Persons gradually gained confidence in Spanish, and by 1592 used it almost exclusively in this correspondence. There was more overlap between the two languages then than now: a mark of confusion can be found in Persons's Italian letter of 26 June 1590 where words such as "Spagna" and "segnelato" have a diacritical mark above "gn" rather like the Spanish "España" and "señelato." In several Spanish letters the Italian "che" appears instead of "que."[151]

Partly because of the loss of material from the Venerable English College, Rome, at the suppression of the Society in 1773, there are significant gaps in the record. Most glaring is the absence of most of Persons's own letters from 1589 to 1592; these can only be pieced together from short notes by Grene and references in Acquaviva's replies. Of what must have been an extensive correspondence with William Holt, Persons's main contact in Brussels, very little has survived, and the record of correspondence with Garnet, as the superior of the Jesuit mission in England, is patchy at best. When Persons arrived in Valladolid in June 1593 after a long detour from Seville, for instance, he was faced with a great pile of letters, mainly dealing with persecution and difficulties in England, but we have no further record of them. It seems clear from the letters from Richard Cowling, Henry Tichborne, and William Warford that Persons kept in touch with many, possibly all, English Jesuits, especially as they completed their training and offered themselves to the mission.[152] We can assume, also, that Persons wrote frequently between Seville, Madrid, and Valladolid, but there is little trace apart from his letters to Gonzalo del Río. There are no letters from women correspondents, not even a fervent supporter like Luisa de Carvajal, nor the Bridgettine nuns in whom Persons took considerable interest as they relocated to Lisbon in 1594.[153]

---

147. Persons to Acquaviva, 20 February 1595; this may be compared with the Spanish letter of the same date (B257–258).

148. Agazzari to Persons, 27 August and 25 September 1596 (B336, B343); cf. the letters to and from Agazzari in volume 1.

149. Acquaviva to Persons, 24 December 1589 (B44).

150. Acquaviva to Persons (soli), 9 July 1591 (B112).

151. E.g., the document sent to Juan de Idiáquez, 4 April 1591 (B99).

152. Warford to Persons, 15 May 1591 (B108); Cowling (Collins) to Persons, 13 February and 8 April 1596 (B315, B321); Tichborne to Persons, 5 June 1596 (B327).

153. Luisa de Carvajal's connection with Persons can be inferred from her interest in the English Catholic community in Valladolid, where she hoped for an English Carmelite convent to

In this edition, we have endeavoured to reconstruct at least the outlines of the missing correspondence.[154] Many letters that are (to the best of our knowledge) no longer extant can be inferred from the surviving documents, not only from actual references but from the pattern of letters ordinarily included in the posts. As we have seen, Acquaviva wrote to several Jesuit superiors in each province by virtually every post. Persons's despatches to Rome commonly included letters to Acquaviva, to the rector of the English college, and to William Allen. Similarly, the Brussels packet would include letters to Paris, Saint-Omer, and Antwerp, and from Antwerp to London, although only a small proportion of these have come down to us. We are presented with a picture of Persons managing an extensive correspondence, receiving news and directing operations on a wide front. It is testimony to his extraordinary energy, despite several bouts of severe illness. There are, however, only hints of a more personal and pastoral dimension to his apostolate of letters.[155]

Archival Sources

The sources for Persons's correspondence are chiefly concentrated in two archives. The Jesuit archives in Rome (ARSI) contain Acquaviva's registers of copies and drafts of letters written by the general to the various provinces of the Society, with separate registers in some cases for open and confidential letters. Letters to Persons in Madrid are to be found in the register for the province of Toledo; to Valladolid, in the register for Castile; to Seville, for Andalusia, labelled as Boetica. ARSI also houses codices of letters received. These may be listed as follows:

Angl. 38/II, Daniello Bartoli's notes towards *Dell'istoria della Compagnia di Giesù l'Inghilterra* (Rome, 1667);
Tolet. 4, the general's register of confidential letters to the province of Toledo;
Tolet. 5/I and 5/II, the general's register of letters to the province of Toledo;
Baet. 3/I, from the general's register of letters to the province of Andalusia;
Hisp. 135, 136, 137, 138, 139, the general's collection of letters from the Spanish assistancy;
Cast. 6, from the general's register of letters to the province of Castile;
Hisp. 74, 75, 76, from the general's register of confidential letters to the Spanish assistancy;
FG, Fondo Gesuitico, documents returned to the Jesuit archives by Benito Mus-

---

be founded: see *The Letters of Luisa de Carvajal y Mendoza*, ed. Glyn Redworth, 2 vols. (London, 2012), 1: 42–48, 51–52, 72–73; there are some tantalizing references to Persons (1: 55, 262); on the Bridgettines, see the despatches for Philip II, 24 February 1594 (B218).

154. See Victor Houliston, "Puzzles and Posts: Reconstructing Robert Persons's Correspondence with Claudio Acquaviva, 1589–1592," *In Die Skriflig* 53, no. 2 (2019): 1–8.

155. See the letters from Harewood, Tichborne, and Worthington, 25 October 1595, 5 June 1596, and 10 January 1597 (B297, B327, B353).

solini, including the folder 651/640, chiefly containing documents relating to Persons.

In London, the Jesuit archives (ABSI) house the transcriptions, notes, and collections of letters and documents gathered by Christopher Grene, SJ (1629–1697) in the seventeenth century, formerly held at Stonyhurst College, Clitheroe, Lancashire. This is our chief source for letters to and from Henry Garnet in England and Joseph Creswell in Rome,[156] as well as letters and despatches from Richard Verstegan, Persons's agent in Antwerp.[157]

The archives of the Roman Catholic diocese of Westminster contain some codices of the Anglia series, as the result of an exchange with Stonyhurst.[158] In the Petyt Collection of the Inner Temple, London, are contemporary copies of letters intended for use in the appellant campaign (1598–1602) to discredit Persons and woo leading English Catholics into calling for the exclusion of the Jesuits. These were probably made for Richard Bancroft (1544–1610), bishop of London from 1597–1604 and then appointed archbishop of Canterbury.[159] Some letters intercepted by the English government's intelligence services can be found in the National Archive at Kew (TNA) and the Cecil Papers at Hatfield House (CP). There is a collection of letters connected with George Birkhead (or Birket, 1549–1614), who was appointed archpriest in 1608, in the Milton House archives (MH), now held at Georgetown University: this contains several letters from a slightly later period, and a few from 1597. Persons's dealings with the Spanish court, the Spanish ambassador in Rome, and the papal curia are reflected in letters and papers at the archives of the English College, Valladolid (ACSA), the State archives in Simancas (AGS) and the Vatican archives (AAV). A codex at the Vatican Library (BAV, MS Vat. Lat. 6227) contains letters, despatches and notes from 1597, when Persons met regularly with Francisco de Peña. It also contains several memorials and memoranda on English affairs, the succession, and ecclesiastical strategy, for the attention of decision-makers in Spain and Rome.[160]

---

156. Fr Leo Hicks's transcriptions and translations of letters from Persons and Garnet, also at ABSI, are acknowledged in the preface.

157. Most of these are to be found in *The Letters and Despatches of Richard Verstegan (c. 1550–1640)*, ed. Anthony G. Petti (London, 1959), to which may be added an entry in this volume for May 1593. Similar news reports were sent to Roger Baynes in Rome, and when Persons reached Rome these were perused by him and Baynes, and then passed on to interested parties at the Spanish embassy and the papal court. Where these despatches are in the nature of a personal letter to Persons, they are included in the present volume.

158. See esp. AAW, old series, VI. Many of these letters were printed by Mark Tierney in his edition of Charles Dodd (*vere* Hugh Tootell), *Dodd's Church History of England*, 5 vols. (London, 1839–1843), to be referred to as Tierney.

159. Most of these were edited by Thomas Graves Law in *The Archpriest Controversy*, 2 vols. (London, 1896–1898), to be referred to as Law, *Archpriest Controversy*.

160. These memorials have been collected in appendix A.

Dramatis Personae

José de Acosta, SJ (1540–1600), entered the Society of Jesus 1552; provincial of Peru from 1576 to 1581; returned to Spain 1587; Rome 1588; Madrid 1589 on diplomatic mission (with Persons) to King Philip II; visitor of the provinces of Andalusia and Aragon March 1589–1591; superior of professed house, Valladolid 1592; visit to Rome December 1592; Fifth General Congregation Rome December 1593–March 1594. Author of *De promulgatione evangelii apud barbaros, sive De procuranda Indorum salute* (Salamanca, 1588) and *Historia natural y moral de las Indias* (Seville, 1590). Claudio M. Burgaleta, *José de Acosta, SJ (1540–1600): His Life and Thought* (Chicago, 1999); Mary Elizabeth Baldridge, "José de Acosta (1540–15 February 1600)," in *Dictionary of Literary Biography, Volume 318: Sixteenth-Century Spanish Writers*, ed. Gregory B. Kaplan (Detroit, 2005), 3–7; J. Baptista (*DHCJ*, 1: 10–12); Fermín del Pino Díaz (*DBE*).

Claudio Acquaviva, SJ (1543–1615), superior general of the Society of Jesus from 1581 to 1615. M. Foes (*DHCJ*, 2: 1614–1621).

Alfonso Agazzari, SJ (1549–1602), rector of the English College, Rome 1579–1586 and 17 May 1596–25 May 1597.

Pietro Aldobrandini (1571–1621), created cardinal 1593; cardinal-nephew to Pope Clement VIII (Ippolito Aldobrandini, 1535–1605, r. 1592–1605). Elena Fasano Guarini (*DBI*).

William Allen (1532–16 October 1594), created cardinal 1587; founder of English College, Douai, 1568, and chiefly instrumental in the founding of the English College, Rome, 1579; president of Douai until 1585; with Persons to Rome 1585; leader of the English Catholics in exile. Author of *An Apologie and true declaration of the institution and endeavours of the two English colleges, the one in Rome the other now resident in Rheims* (Rheims, 1581), *A brief history of the glorious martyrdom of xii reverend priests* (Rheims, 1582), and *A true sincere and modest defence of English Catholics that suffer for their faith* (Rouen, 1584). Eamon Duffy, "William, Cardinal Allen, 1532–1594," *Recusant History* 22 (1595): 265–290, and in *ODNB*; Anstruther, 4–5.

Richard Barret (1544–1599), ordained in Rome 1580; president of English College, Douai, 1588–1599; sent students to Valladolid 1588; assisted with unrest at the English College, Rome, April 1596. Anstruther, 24–25; Michael E. Williams (*ODNB*).

Roger Baynes (1546–1623), secretary to William Cardinal Allen, Rome 1587; remained as English Catholic agent and adviser; administrator of property of English colleges at Douai/Rheims and Rome. Michael E. Williams (*ODNB*).

John Cecil or Snowden (1558–1626), priested Rome 1584; Valladolid 1589; Seville and Sanlúcar with Persons 1590; intercepted en route to England May 1591; entered Cecils' intelligence service; to Valladolid 1593 to promote plans of Scottish Catholic earls; Madrid December 1594; Rome 1595–1596, including sojourn at English college. Stephen Alford, *The Watchers: A Secret History of the Reign of Elizabeth I*, 2nd ed. (London, 2013), 270–284; Anstruther, 63–68; James Edward McGoldrick (*ODNB*).

Joseph Creswell, SJ (ca. 1556/7–1623), entered the Society of Jesus, Rome 1583; rector of the English College, Rome 1589–1592; Valladolid 1592; Seville 1593; procurator for English affairs, Madrid 1593–1613; Flanders 1613–1623. Author of *Exemplar literarum, missarum, e Germania, ad D. Guilelmum Cecilium, consiliarium regium* (Rome, 1592; *ARCR*, 1: no. 275) and *Historia de la vida y martyrio que padecio en Inglaterra, este año de 1595 P. Henrique Valpolo* (Madrid, 1596; *ARCR*, 1: no. 276). Loomie, *Spanish Elizabethans*, 182–229, and in *ODNB*; McCoog, *English and Welsh Jesuits*, 150.

William Crichton, SJ (ca. 1534/5–1617), entered the Society of Jesus, Rome 1562; consultations with Persons over Guise invasion plan Rouen 1582; captured en route to Scotland 1584; Tower of London 1584–1587; Brussels 1589–1598; Madrid January to August 1592; in charge of Scottish college at Douai (1593) and Louvain (1595). Francisco de Borja Medina, "Intrigues of a Scottish Jesuit at the Spanish Court: William Crichton's Mission to Madrid (1590–1592)," in *The Reckoned Expense: Edmund Campion and the Early English Jesuits*, ed. Thomas M. McCoog, 2nd ed. (Rome, 2007), 227–325; Mark Dilworth (*ODNB*); McCoog, *English and Welsh Jesuits*, 150.

Sir Francis Englefield (1522–1596), Privy Counsellor under Mary Tudor 1553–1558; Flanders 1562–1580; adviser on English affairs, Madrid, 1580–1596; died Valladolid 13 September 1596. Contributor to *Conference about the Next Succession* (1595). Loomie, *Spanish Elizabethans*, 14–51, and in *ODNB*.

Fernández de Córdoba y Cardona, Antonio (1550–1606), fifth duke of Sessa, Spanish ambassador in Rome from 1590 to 1604. Miguel Ángel Ochoa Brun (*DBE*).

Girolamo Fioravanti, SJ (d. 1630), rector of the English College, Rome, from 27 May 1594 to 17 May 1596.

Ottavio Mirto Frangipani (1544–1612), ordained bishop 1572, apostolic nuncio to Brussels, appointed 20 April 1596. Stefano Andretta (*DBI*).

Henry Garnet or Garnett, SJ (1555–1606), entered the Society of Jesus, Rome 1575; sent to England with Robert Southwell 1586; succeeded William Weston as superior of English mission August 1586; chiefly based in London; accused of complicity in the Gunpowder Plot and executed near Paul's Cross, 3 May 1606. Philip Caraman, *Henry Garnet, 1555–1606 and the Gunpowder Plot* (London, 1964) and *A Study in Friendship: Saint*

Robert Southwell and Henry Garnet (St Louis, 1995); Thomas M. McCoog (*ODNB*); McCoog, *English and Welsh Jesuits*, 188.

John Gerard, SJ (1564–1637), studied at Douai and Paris 1577–1583; imprisoned at the Marshalsea 1584; entered the Society of Jesus, Rome 1588; accompanied Edward Oldcorne on the English mission 1588; arrested in April 1594; transferred to Tower of London April 1597; escaped 5 October 1597; remained at large until 1606. *John Gerard: The Autobiography of an Elizabethan*, trans. Philip Caraman, 2nd ed. (London, 1956); Thomas M. McCoog (*ODNB*); McCoog, *English and Welsh Jesuits*, 311–312 *sub* Thompson, John.

Richard Gibbons, SJ (1547/1553–1632), entered the Society of Jesus, Rome 1572; travelled to Spain 1589; Lisbon and Valladolid 1590; Coimbra 1591; Valladolid 1593; returned to Rome 1594; transferred to Louvain 1597. Thompson Cooper (*ODNB*), rev. Thomas H. Clancy; McCoog, *English and Welsh Jesuits*, 190–191.

William Gifford, OSB (1557/1558–1629), ordained priest English College, Rome, 1581; related to Gilbert Gifford, spy; Rheims 1582; doctorate Pont-à-Mousson 1584; dean of Lille May 1595; expelled from Netherlands 1606; entered Benedictine order 1608, adopted the name Gabriel of St Mary; ordained bishop 1618; archbishop of Rheims 1623. Michael E. Williams (*ODNB*).

Gil González Dávila, SJ (1532–15 January 1596), entered the Society of Jesus Alcalá de Henares 1551; provincial of Andalusia 1585–1588; visitor to Castile (May 1589–August 1590) and Toledo (October 1590–March 1592); represented Toledo at fifth general congregation 1593–1594. M. Ruiz Jurado (*DHCJ*, 2: 1783–1784); Javier Burrieza Sánchez (*DBE*).

William Holt, SJ (1545–1599), entered the Society of Jesus, Rome 1578; English mission 1581; negotiations in Scotland 1582; arrested 1583 but protected by James VI; left Scotland for Rome 1586; rector of English College, Rome 1586–1588; chaplain to duke of Parma's army; active in Flanders, chiefly Brussels 1588–1598; to Spain via Milan 1599 and died in Barcelona. Albert J. Loomie (*ODNB*); McCoog, *English and Welsh Jesuits*, 210–211.

Juan de Idiáquez (1540–1614), personal secretary to King Philip II of Spain; secretary of the Council of State 1579–1587; responsible for foreign affairs as member of Junta de Noche until 1593; Junta de Gobierno 1593–1598; minister of state under Philip III. Juan Carlos Mora Afán (*DBE*).

Owen Lewis (1533–14 October 1595), archdeacon of Hainault and provost of Cambrai 1572; sent to Rome 1574–1580; befriended William Allen; involved in foundation of the English College, Rome 1578–1579, controversial because of supposed favouritism to

Welsh students; vicar-general to Charles Borromeo, cardinal-archbishop of Milan 1579; consecrated bishop of Cassano 1588; remained in Rome; proposed for elevation to cardinal after Allen's death October 1594. Godfrey Anstruther "Owen Lewis," in *The English Hospice in Rome* (Rome, 2012), 274–294; Michael L. Williams (*ODNB*).

Innocenzo Malvasia (1552–1612), monsignor, papal agent (often loosely referred to as nuncio) in Brussels September 1594–April 1596; associated with anti-Jesuit party in Flanders. Renato Sansa (*DBI*).

Olivier Mannaerts or Manare, SJ (1523–1614), entered the Society of Jesus 1551; assistant for Germany 1573–1580; vicar-general of the Society following the death of Everard Mercurian, 1580; rector of the Roman college, 1583–1585; provincial of Lower Germany 1585–1589; provincial of Belgium 1589–1594; allied with Persons during the 1580s, later more critical. G. Meessen (*DHCJ*, 3: 2495–2496).

Thomas Morgan (1543–ca. 1611), agent of Mary Stuart in Paris 1581; friend and collaborator of Charles Paget; imprisoned in the Bastille 1584–1587, but continued correspondence with Mary; removed to Flanders 1588; arrested by command of the duke of Parma 1590; released and banished 1592; canvassed for Owen Lewis's elevation Madrid 1594; expelled and returned to Paris. Leo Hicks, *Elizabethan Problem*; Loomie, *Spanish Elizabethans*, 112–115, 124–125; Alison Plowden (*ODNB*).

Hugh Owen (1538–1618), employed by prince (later duke) of Parma 1580 as liaison with the Spanish court and to create English Catholic intelligence network; collaborated with Richard Verstegan in providing news reports (*avisos*) for Persons. Loomie, *Spanish Elizabethans*, 52–93.

Charles Paget (ca. 1546–1612), brother of Thomas Paget, fourth Lord Paget (ca. 1544–1590); in exile in Paris and Rouen 1581–1588; collaborator with Thomas Morgan; secret visit to England 1583 ambiguously connected with Guise invasion plans; possibly a double agent involved in Babington Plot 1586; Brussels 1588; promoted opposition to English Jesuits, especially William Holt and Robert Persons; canvassed for elevation of Owen Lewis 1594–1595; Paris 1598; returned to England 1603. Hicks, *Elizabethan Problem*; Peter Holmes (*ODNB*).

Francisco de Peña Calvo (1540–1612), appointed auditor of the Roman Rota, highest ecclesiastical court of the Holy See 1588; dean 1604. Manuel Fuertes de Gilbert y Rojo, barón de Gavín (*DBE*).

Francisco de Peralta, SJ (ca. 1554–1622), rector of St Gregory's College, Seville, 1592–1607. Murphy, 142–162; Thomas M. McCoog, "Fostering Harmony and Respect: English Jesuits in Seville, 1592–1605," in McCoog, *And Touching Our Society*, 261–281.

Pedro de Ribadeneira, SJ (1526-1611), entered the Society of Jesus 1 September 1540; London 1557-1558; assistant for Spain and Portugal, Rome 1571-1574; Toledo 1574-1583; Madrid and Alcalá de Henares (chiefly at the retreat house at Jesus del Monte) 1583-1611. Author of *Vita Ignatii Loiolae* (Naples, 1572), *Historia ecclesiastica del Scisma del Reyno de Inglaterra* (Madrid, 1588), *Segunda parte* (Alcalá, 1593), *Tratado de la Tribulación* (Madrid, 1589), *Tratado de la Religión y Virtudes que debe tener el Principe cristiano* (Madrid, 1595). Spencer J. Weinreich, introduction to *Pedro de Ribadeneyra's "Ecclesiastical History of the Schism of the kingdom of England"* (Leiden, 2017); M. Ruiz Jurado (*DHCJ*, 4: 3345-3346); Armando Pego Puighó (*DBE*).

Robert Southwell, SJ (1561-1595), entered the Society of Jesus, Rome 1578; English College, Rome, 1580-1586; accompanied Henry Garnet on English mission 1586; sheltered by Anne Howard, countess of Arundel, in London 1587 until arrested 25 June 1592; incarcerated in Tower of London until February 1595; transferred to Newgate and put on trial; executed at Tyburn 21 February 1595; canonized as English martyr 1970. Author of *An Epistle of Comfort* (Paris, 1587-1588), *An Humble Supplication to Her Majestie* (London, 1595), *A Short Rule of Good Life* (London, 1596-1597), *S. Peters Complaint and Saint Mary Magdalens Funeral Teares with Sundry Other Selected, and Devout Poems* (Saint-Omer, 1616). Christopher Devlin, *The Life of Robert Southwell, Poet and Martyr* (London, 1956); Nancy Pollard Brown (*ODNB*); McCoog, *English and Welsh Jesuits*, 299; T. Clancy (*DHCJ*, 4: 3617-3618).

Sir William Stanley (1548-1630), knighted 1579 in recognition of service in Ireland against the earl of Desmond; joined Leicester's forces in the Netherlands with his regiment and seized Deventer 1586; as governor, handed Deventer over to the Spaniards January 1587; travelled to Spain 1589, remaining in Valladolid; returned to Flanders 1591 but found little employment. Loomie, *Spanish Elizabethans*, 129-181; Rory Rapple (*ODNB*).

Thomas Stapleton, [SJ] (1535-1598), fellow of New College, Oxford; went into exile 1559 and established himself in Louvain 1563; won high reputation as a controversialist in English, 1565-1567; doctorate, Douai University 1571; theological works in Latin, 1571-1590; entered the Society of Jesus, Louvain 1584; dismissed 1587; chair of sacred scripture at Louvain 1590 through patronage of Philip II; speculation about elevation to cardinal after Allen's death; invited to Rome 1596 but unwilling to travel. Translator of Bede's *History of the Church of England* (Antwerp, 1565); author of *A Counterblast to M. Hornes Vayne Blaste* (Louvain, 1567), *Tres Thomae* (Douai, 1588), *Promptuarium Morale* (Antwerp, 1591, etc.). Marvin R. O'Connell, *Thomas Stapleton and the Counter Reformation* (New Haven and London, 1964); McCoog, *English and Welsh Jesuits*, 303.

Francisco de Toledo, SJ (1532-14 September 1596), entered the Society of Jesus, Salamanca 1558; created cardinal 17 September 1593; persuaded Pope Clement VIII to accept sincerity of conversion of Henry of Navarre (King Henry IV of France); critic of

Claudio Acquaviva, close associate of José de Acosta; vice-protector of the English College, Rome, April to September 1596. J.P. Donnelly (*DHCJ*, 4: 3807–3808); Javier Burrieza Sánchez (*DBE*).

Richard Verstegan [Rowlands] (1548/1550–1640), secretly printed Thomas Alfield, *A True Reporte of the Death & Martyrdome of M. Campion* (London, 1581/2); agent and news reporter for Robert Persons, Antwerp 1587–1610; engaged in Anglo-Saxon scholarship, poetry and journalism. Producer of *Theatrum crudelitatum haereticorum nostri temporis* (Antwerp, 1587); author of *An advertisement written to a secretarie of My L. Treasurers of Ingland ... concerning an other booke written in Latin ... against Her Majesties late proclamation* (Antwerp, 1592), *A declaration of the true causes of the great troubles, presupposed to be intended against the realme of England* (Antwerp, 1592), and *Restitution of Decayed Intelligence in Antiquities* (Antwerp, 1605). *Letters and Despatches*, ed. A.G. Petti (London, 1959); Paul Arblaster, *Antwerp & the World: Richard Verstegan and the International Culture of Catholic Reformation* (Leuven, 2004) and in *ODNB*.

Henry Walpole, SJ (ca. 1558–1595), present at execution of Edmund Campion, 1 December 1581; enrolled at English College, Rheims 1582; English College, Rome 1583; entered the Society of Jesus, Rome 1584; priested Paris 1588; joined Stanley's regiment as chaplain but captured at Flushing 1589; ransomed January 1590; joined Persons in Spain 1592; St Gregory's College, Seville and St Alban's College, Valladolid; sent on English mission June 1593; assisted at Saint-Omer en route to England; captured at Kilham, Yorkshire, 7 December 1593 and incarcerated in York; removed to the Tower of London January 1594; interrogated and tortured; sent to York for trial 1595; executed at York 17 April 1595; canonized as English martyr 1970. Brother of Richard Walpole, SJ (ca. 1562–1607) and Michael Walpole, SJ (ca. 1570–1625). Part author of *Newes from Spayne and Holland* (Antwerp, 1593). Augustus Jessopp, *One Generation of a Norfolk House*, 2nd ed. (London, 1879); Antony Charles Ryan (*ODNB*); McCoog, *English and Welsh Jesuits*, 323; P.C. Barry (*DHCJ*, 4: 4009).

Thomas Worthington, SJ (1548/1549–1626), entered the Society of Jesus 1626; English College, Douai 1573; associate of Bible translator Gregory Martin (ca. 1542–1582); priested Cambrai 1577; returned to England 1579; arrested 1583 and kept in Tower of London; released into banishment January 1585; vice president of English College, Rheims but removed to Brussels; succeeded Barret as president at Douai, 1599. Chief translator of *Holie Bible*, 2 vols. (Douai, 1609–1610); author of *A Relation of Sixtene Martyrs* (Douai, 1601). Albert J. Loomie (*ODNB*); Anstruther, 387–388; McCoog, *English and Welsh Jesuits*, 339.

Thomas Wright, [SJ] (ca. 1561–1623), entered the Society of Jesus, Rome 1580; studied theology in Milan; priested Rome 1586; Genoa 1589 and 1593; St Alban's College, Valladolid, 1594; returned to England after dismissal from the Society 1595; enjoyed protection of earl of Essex; 1597 confined in house of dean of Westminster and instrumental in conversion of William Alabaster (1568–1640). Author of *Certaine articles or forcible reasons: Discovering the palpable absurdities, and most notorious errours of the Protestants religion* (Antwerp, 1600) and *The Passions of the Minde in Generall* (London, 1604). Ginevra Crosignani, "Thomas Wright and Occasional Conformity," *AHSI* 71 (2002): 149–156; T.A. Stroud, "Father Thomas Wright: A Test Case for Toleration," *Biographical Studies* [now *British Catholic History*] 1 (1951–1952): 189–219; Peter Milward (*ODNB*); McCoog, *English and Welsh Jesuits*, 340.

Valladolid, 1588–1592

B1 Instructions for Fr Persons, Rome, 31 October 1588

SOURCE: ARSI, Tolet. 4, fols. 41r–42r, preceded by instructions to José de Acosta.
HICKS: 73–75.

NOTE: Father General Acquaviva entrusted Persons with negotiations with Philip II about the state of the Society in Spain and the future of the English mission. He was to collaborate with José de Acosta, former provincial of Peru, on questions regarding the king's regard for the Society and the Inquisition's authority over it (see introduction, "The *Memorialistas*"). He left Rome on 6 November, accompanied by Brother Fabrizio Como (Astrain, 3: 480; Hicks, *Seminaries*, parts 1 and 2; Edwards, 129–135; and McCoog, *Our Way of Proceeding*, 260, and *Building the Faith of St Peter*, 97–99).

In these instructions, Acquaviva insists on the importance of the Society's Institute, or agreed "way of proceeding," which was subject to criticism from certain quarters in Spain. Acquaviva expected Persons to proceed to Flanders once the mission was complete.

Instruttione per il Padre Roberto Personio
datale in Roma l'ultimo d'Ottobre 1588.

Trattarà con la Maestà del Re Catholico, et con quelli de suoi ministri, che giudicherà spediente, del frutto dell'anime, che per gratia del Signore si fa, et della fedeltà con che la Compagnia s'affatticca, secondo il suo instituto dovunche si ritrova, nelle cose appartenenti al servigio di Sua Maestà Catholica —— A solo il Re proporrà il pregiuditio et danno che riceverebbe la Christianità in tutte le parti Settentrionali, se l'ordine ch'il Conseglio dell' Inquisitione ha dato, non si levasse, cioè, che nissuno della Compagnia di quei regni, possi andare in quelle parti ultramontane, essendo questo soccorso tanto necessario in quelle bande, tanto conforme alla carità Christiana, tanto proprio alla gratia della vocatione et instituto della Compagnia espresso, non solo nella sua Regola et bolla di confirmatione Apostoliche, ma dimostratosi per la Divina bontà da gl'effetti del frutto, et conversioni innumerabili che si sono seguite: ne essendosi visto, infin' ad hoggi, da che la Compagnia si fundò, inconveniente alcuno in questo. Oltre che simil prohibitione non è stata mai fatta, non solo a sorte alcuna de Religiosi, ma né anco a mercanti,[1] né a soldati, né a passaggieri, né a sorte alcuna di persone. Per il che si supplica a Sua Maestà vogli ordinare che si levi. Et quando tuttavia paresse di usare con la Compagnia il genere di

---

1. a mercanti] MS *obscure; possibly* a li mercanti

cautela, con altri non giamai usato, dovrebbe più tosto prohibirsi che li nostri non ritornerassero dà quelle bande senza licenza, o senza presentarsi al Santo Officio —— Tratterà con Sua Maestà et con i suoi ministri ciò che haverà dà trattare, conforme al nostro instituto, senza intromettersi in maneggi di guerra ——[2] Doppo ch'il padre Gioseppe d'Acosta haverà parlato a Sua Maestà le parli Vostra Reverentia et le dia la lettera nostra che in sua credenza porta, dicendole, che al detto Padre habbiamo data commissione de proporre alcuni, de quali Sua Maestà eleggesse un Visitatore per le provincie di Castella et Toleto; et hora per Vostra Reverentia le proponiamo il Padre Diego de Avellaneda, et l'istesso Padre Gioseppe d'Acosta, acciò Sua Maestà, se non trova inconveniente alcuno, elega un de loro per Visitatore delle Provincie de Aragone et d'Andalusia. Il che non ci parve di commettere al Padre Acosta insieme con l'altra nominatione che egli porta, per essere egli in questa uno de nominati, et non parere conveniente, né a lui, né alla cosa istessa che egli nominasse se stesso —— Se Sua Maestà non vuolesse eleggere, aviserà Vostra Reverentia il Padre Gioseppe d'Acosta, il quale in tal caso ha ordine di quello che doverà fare —— Al Padre provinciale di Toleto darà la nostra lettera, et lo potrà reguagliare del contento di quest' instruttione, in quel che a lei parrà che possi giovare. —— Finito che haverà di negotiare in Madrid, potrà andarsene in Fiandra, per la quale Missione porta anco patente, et un'altra acciò sia superiore delli nostri Anglesi, che sarano nell'essercito, et habbi superintendenza de quelli che sono in Inghilterra —— Informarà ancora Sua Maestà del grave danno che la Compagna in quei regni ha sentito sin' adesso, et sentirà maggiore, se egli non ni mette la mano; non potendo li superiori governare liberamente, né procurare l'osservanza della disciplina Regolare, perché ogni suddito ardisce di minacciare, etc. —— Le significherà ancora il mio sentimento che non si sia degnata Sua Maestà farmi dire; come più volte l'ho supplicata, quel che desidera da me o dalla Compagnia. Della quale si vede per gl'effetti che a Sua Maestà è fatta sinistra informatione, et se le cose si sapessero, se le potrebbe o dare sodisfattione con la verità, o emendarse, se ci sono cose che ricerchino emendatione, et che di questo la supplico instantemente per l'avenire; perché altrimenti ogn'uno sarà libero a dire in memoriali delle falsità, etc. essendo sicuro che prima faranno colpo, che la Compagnia si possa difendere o scolpare.

Translation

Instructions to Fr Persons
given to him in Rome on the last day of October 1588.

You are to discuss with His Majesty the Catholic king, and those among his ministers whom you consider suitable, what is to the advantage of souls (which is to be achieved by God's grace), and what will safeguard the loyalty which the Society, according to her way of proceeding, seeks wherever she is, in matters concerning our obligation to His Catholic Majesty.

2. [*in margin:*] A bocca gli si disse che bisognando, poteva parlare prima, senza trattare però de questa nominatione, sin che il Padre Acosta havesse parlato. *See commentary.*

With the king alone you should discuss the prejudice and harm that Christianity would suffer in all its northern lands if the order given by the Council of the Inquisition should not be withdrawn: that is, that no member of the Society coming from there[3] may travel to those ultramontane regions. For this type of succour is very necessary to those regions, very consistent with Christian charity, and very proper to the graces connected to the vocation and the explicit intention of the Society's way of proceeding – not only as these are expressed in its rule and bull of apostolic confirmation, but as they are shown by divine mercy through the effectual fruit and the innumerable conversions which have followed. To this very day there has never, since the foundation of the Society, been seen any such inconvenience in this regard. Besides, no such prohibition has ever been made, either with respect to religious, or to merchants, soldiers, travellers, or any other kind of persons. Therefore, you should plead with His Majesty that such orders be withdrawn. However, if it is thought expedient to use with the Society the kind of caution that has never been used with others, it should only be required that those of Ours who are without a licence, or have not appeared before the Holy Office, should return from those regions.

Whatever you have to discuss with His Majesty and his ministers, is to be handled in accordance to our way of proceeding, without meddling with military strategy.

After Fr José de Acosta has spoken to His Majesty, Your Reverence should speak and give him our letter of recommendation, and you will say that we have commissioned the said father to propose some names, from which His Majesty may nominate a visitor for the provinces of Castile and Toledo. Now, through Your Reverence we propose Fr Diego de Avellaneda[4] and the same Fr José de Acosta,[5] so that if His Majesty should find no objection, he may nominate one of them as visitor for the provinces of Aragon and Andalusia. This is something we did not want to commit to Fr Acosta together with the other commission he bears, because he is one of the two recommended; and it does not seem appropriate, either for himself or for the nature of the position, that he should nominate himself.

If His Majesty does not want to nominate them, Your Reverence should make that known to Fr José de Acosta, who has already been ordered what to do, if that should be the case.

---

3. I.e., specifically from Spain. This prohibition was issued by the king on behalf of the Inquisition in 1586 following the arrest of four leading Jesuits, including the provincial of Toledo, Antonio Marcén: see *Synopsis historiae Societatis Jesu*, ed. Franz Xaver Wernz, Ludwig Schmitt, and Johannes Baptist Goetstouwers (Louvain, 1950), an. 1586. Behind the measure were the malcontent Jesuits Dionisio Vázquez (1527–1589; see C. de Dalmases, in *DHCJ*, 4: 3911) and Enrique Henriques, 1520–1602; see Josef Wicki in *DHCJ*, 1: 177–178, *sub* Anrriques), leaders of the campaign for greater autonomy for the Spanish provinces of the Society.

4. It appears from Acquaviva's letter to Persons, 6 March, that the two initial nominees were, instead, Gil González Dávila (for Castile and Toledo) and Diego de Avellaneda (for Andalusia and Aragon). Avellaneda (ca. 1529–1598) was former confessor of the Spanish ambassador to Vienna (1570–1576) and visitor to the province of Castile from 1577–1580 (see José Martínez de la Escalera, in *DHCJ*, 1: 302–303). In the event, Avellaneda was unavailable and Acosta was nominated in his stead.

5. [*marginal note:*] In person he told him that he should not discuss the matter of this nomination until Fr Acosta had spoken first.

Please would you deliver our letter to father provincial of Toledo,[6] and acquaint him with the details of the present instructions, insofar as you think it will be productive.

As soon as you have concluded the negotiations in Madrid, you should proceed to Flanders, since you also hold a licence for the mission there, as well as another one appointing you superior of our Englishmen who are in training, as well as superior of those who are in England.

Please could you impress upon His Majesty, once again, how great is the harm the Society has been suffering until now in those lands. It will be even greater if he does not intervene, as superiors cannot govern freely, nor impose the discipline of the Rule, if any subject is entitled to threaten them, etc.

Would you once again, please, convey how I feel about the fact that His Majesty has not deigned to let me know – although I have often pleaded with him – what he wants either from me or the Society. The situation appears to have arisen from inaccurate information given to His Majesty. If things were brought into the open, they could either be set right by the truth, or by amendment, if there are things that need to be changed. This is what I utterly beseech for the future; otherwise, everyone will be free to make false claims in memorials, in the confidence that they will cause damage before the Society can defend or exculpate herself.

B2 Correspondence with Richard Barret at Rheims, 1588–1589

>SOURCE: More, 156–157.
>
>TRANSLATION: Edwards, *More*, 204.
>
>NOTE: Richard Barret succeeded William Allen as the president of the English seminary at Rheims (formerly Douai), being formally installed on 28 November 1588. The college was under financial pressure and in some physical danger, given the tension between King Henry III of France and Henry, duke of Guise, who was assassinated on 23 December 1588 (Edwards, *More*, 129).
>
>More's account is probably a summary of several exchanges. Blackfan refers to a letter written by Persons from Rome, which may have conveyed an initial failure to obtain further funding from Spain (*Blackfan Annals*, 2–4). Hicks refers to a letter written by Barret "shortly after Persons's arrival at Madrid," to which Persons replied after his audience with the king on 6 February (Hicks, *Seminaries*, part 2, 416–417; see also 410–412), reporting on the promised grant of 3000 crowns. The suggestion that some students could be sent to Spain may have been made later: three students were despatched from Rheims at the beginning of May, possibly in response to such a suggestion.

Eo tempore *Barrettus* qui in Rhemensis, seu dicas, Duaceni Seminarii curas successerat (occiso enim Guisio Rhemis Duacum rursus translatum est) *Personium* rogarat uti explicatis Regi & numero Alumnorum & impensarum angustiis impetraret incrementum illius pecuniae quam eius opera quotannis liberaliter Rex solvendam pridem constituerat. *Personius*, Regis pertentata mente, respondet difficulter ad vetera resarcienda inducendum,

---

6. Antonio Marcén, who had been imprisoned by the Inquisition since 1586.

novi operis gloria capi potius. Igitur cum numero gravaretur *Barrettus*, mitteret ad se decem aut duodecim bonae spei iuvenes; non dubitare quin eos esset collocaturus apud Praelatos sibi benevolos, virosque alios Principes, qui sumptum interea facerent dum certior ratio se ostenderet.

Translation

At that time Barret, who had taken charge of the seminary at Rheims, which is to say Douai (for with the death of the Guise, the college of Douai was transferred back from Rheims), had asked Persons to explain to the king the difficulties arising both from the number of students and the expenses involved, and to ask him for an increase in the stipend, which the king, through his efforts, had generously decided some years ago to pay. Once Persons had sounded out the king, he reported that it would be difficult to get him to increase the original allowance; he would more easily be attracted by the distinction of starting something new. Therefore, since Barret had more students than he could cope with, he should send Persons ten or twelve promising young men. He had no doubt that he could get them placed with prelates well-disposed to himself and with other men in leading positions, who would meet their expenses in the interim until a more permanent solution presented itself.

B3 To Claudio Acquaviva, Madrid, 31 January 1589

SOURCE: Acquaviva to Persons, 6 March 1589 (B6).
NOTE: From Acquaviva's reply, it appears that Persons reported on his safe arrival and relayed Acosta's query about nomination as visitor.

B4 To Claudio Acquaviva, Madrid, 17 February 1589

SOURCE: Acquaviva to Persons, 17 April and 12 June (B11, B18).
NOTE: Persons sent Acquaviva two letters on this date, most likely because he needed to keep some information secret. He reported on the audience with Philip II and mentioned his own ill health and need for an amanuensis. He also suggested that Acquaviva consult Allen, to whom he wrote by the same post.

On 6 February, Persons had a two-hour audience with Philip, in which he discussed English affairs and the state of the Society in Spain, as briefed by Acquaviva (Astrain, 3: 481–483). Persons had the first audience with the king (Hicks, *Seminaries*, part 2, 413, citing a letter of Fabrizio Como, 4 March 1589), but was expected to defer the question of Acosta's nomination as one of the visitors to the Jesuit provinces in Spain. Acquaviva wanted this to be an internal affair, in accordance with the Society's institution, or "way of proceeding," but Pope Sixtus V and Cardinal Gaspar de Quiroga y Vela, head of the Inquisition, had agreed that Jerónimo Manrique, bishop of Cartagena, should be appointed as external visitor, under the aegis of the Inquisition. The king assured Persons and Acosta that the Society could appoint its own visitors: Acquaviva authorized the appointment of Gil González Dávila for the provinces of Castile and Toledo, José de Acosta for the provinces of Andalusia and Aragon, and Pedro Fonseca for Portugal. González Dávila was well known to Persons because the Spanish Jesuit had taken care of him when he fell ill on his return from Lisbon and Madrid in 1582 (see A86).

Persons also had a lengthy interview either with the king's treasurer or, more likely, his secretary, and secured a grant of 3000 ducats for the college at Rheims, to be paid by the Spanish ambassador in France (Edwards, 136; Hicks, *Seminaries*, part 2, 414). Philip was concerned about the English Catholics not supporting his cause; hence his interest in the seminaries in Flanders and Rome (Edwards, 137; McCoog, *Building the Faith of St Peter*, 105–106). It seems likely that this was the business ("*negotio*") of William Cardinal Allen referred to in Acquaviva's letter of 15 May (B16; see the entry below for Persons's putative letter to Allen, B5). Both Hicks and Edwards question whether the amount was ever paid.

The account of the meeting is given in a letter by Fabrizio Como of 4 March, summarised by Bartoli: "P. Personio si trova a la corte di Spagna molto ben veduto dal Re, e corti giàni; tratta li negotii d'Inghilterra, e'l Re fá dare 3000 scudi al seminario di Rems in riguardo suo" (Fr Persons was at the court of Spain, welcomed by the king and the courtiers; he dealt with the affairs of England, and the king agreed to give 3000 crowns to the seminary at Rheims in response; ARSI, Angl. 38/II, fol. 40r).

B5 To William Allen, Madrid, probably 17 February 1589

SOURCE: Acquaviva to Persons, 15 May (B16).

NOTE: Persons reported the Spanish court's response to Allen's query – probably a request for funds for the seminary at Rheims (see Barret's letter to Persons, probably January 1589, B4) – namely, the grant of 3000 ducats.

B6 From Claudio Acquaviva, 6 March 1589

SOURCE: ARSI, Tolet. 4, fol. 49v.

NOTE: This appears to be Acquaviva's first letter to Persons after he left Rome, although he wrote to Acosta regularly from 28 November 1588 (ARSI, Tolet. 5/I, fols. 33v–34r, etc.). The hasty writing and despatch of the letter indicates the strength of Acquaviva's interest in Persons's welfare. He asks Persons to pre-empt Acosta's advising the king on an alternative appointee as visitor in view of Diego de Avellaneda's unavailability: Acquaviva wants Acosta himself in the role.

Madrid. P. Roberto Personio. 6 de Marzo.

Questa è solo per dire a Vostra Reverentia che casoché il Padre Gioseppe d'Acosta le dicesse che conviene nominare un Visitatore di più per Toledo et Castiglia, per esser mancato il Padre Deza che era nominato insieme col Padre Egidio. Vostra Reverentia facci l'ufficio con Sua Maestà nominando l'istesso Padre Gioseppe al quale per tal fine mandiamo la patente. Ne altro per questa, perché alla sua dell'ultimi di Genaro, rispossimo subbito per un straordinario. Rallegrandoci del buon arrivo ...

Translation

To Fr Robert Persons in Madrid, 6 March.

This is only to keep Your Reverence informed in case Fr José de Acosta tells you that we must nominate another visitor for Toledo and Castile, because Fr Diego, who was nominated along with Fr Gil,[7] is no longer available. Would Your Reverence please negotiate with His Majesty about nominating the same Fr José, to whom we are sending the licence for the same purpose. No more for the present, because we are responding in haste, by special courier, to your letter of the last day of January. Rejoicing in your safe arrival ...

B7 To Claudio Acquaviva, Madrid, 20 March 1589

SOURCE: Acquaviva to Persons, 15 May and 12 June (B16, B18).

NOTE: This letter and that of 30 March (B9) reached Acquaviva on 13 May, two days before he replied.

B8 From Claudio Acquaviva, 21 March 1589

SOURCE: ARSI, Tolet. 5/I, fol. 52r-v.

NOTE: Acquaviva is relieved by Persons's safe arrival in Madrid and urges him to persuade the king to intervene on behalf of the Society against the Jesuit malcontents who are challenging the authority of their superiors. He is particularly concerned about the way they appeal to the Inquisition and thus enjoy its protection.

P. Roberto Personio. Marzo 21.

Mi son molto consolato d'intender per quella de Vostra Reverentia il loro viaggio et arrivo con la cui brebità mi par che si recompense qualunche altro fastidio de mar et e terra. Sia ringratiato il Signore per tutto. Io aspetto con desiderio d'intender l'effetto del'uficio che la Reverentia Vostra et il Padre Acosta havranno fatto con Sua Maestà, che credo sarà de molta importanza et utilità per meglorar lo stato delle cose nostre le quale sono venute a tal termine che clamano per brebe rimedio. Della visita me persuado che siamo sicuri, benché li inquieti non cessano de spingerla, né anco di far uffici col papa per mezzo de memoriali assai più nocivi per la compagnia che saria la visita, ma io spero nel Signore che di tutto ci cavarà senza alcun danno. Vorrei che Vostra Reverentia in quella occasione che gli parere più opportuna suggerise al Re con un poco de caldezza quanto danno si fa alla disciplina regular,[8] come in questi miseri tempi con dolor nostro haviamo sperimentato, per ligar le mani alli superiori et dar animo et ardire alli inferiori discoli, che vedendosi sotto l'ombra et protettione de simili personaggi diventario tanto

---

7. Gil González Dávila, visitor to the Jesuit provinces of Castile and Toledo. The letter appears to suggest that Avellaneda, and subsequently Acosta, was the nominee for Castile and Toledo, but in fact Acosta became visitor to the provinces of Andalusia and Aragon.

8. regular] relagular *R, with* la *obscure, possibly deleted*

insolenti che col loro essempio si guastano anco l'altri in maniera che il superior non può remediar quello che se vede esser tanto degno de rimedio. Si che desidero che Vostra Reverentia si adopere in questo particular in modo che il Re possia intender che in questo metta della cocienza sua, che essendo lui si christiano et timorato. Credo sera de importanza. Alli Santi Sacrificii et orationi de Vostra Reverentia mi racomando. De Roma 21 de Marzo 1589.

[PS] Et si ben parrà a Sua Maestà che inporta per il buon esser de quel tribunal pillar la protection de quelli che adeso ricoreria (il che noi anco diciamo), ma bisogna proveder de protegere soto questo colore quelli che non[9] ricorrerò al Santo officio per cosa di quel tribunale, ma solamente per esser soto questo pretesto protepti, il che fa loro divenir così discoli et insolenti che ruinano se et le altri.

Translation

To Fr Robert Persons, 21 March.

I am very heartened to learn from Your Reverence's letter of your journey and arrival. Your speedy progress seems to me to have made up for all the other inconveniences on land and sea: may the Lord be thanked for everything. I am eagerly awaiting the outcome of Your Reverence and Fr Acosta's negotiations with His Majesty, which I believe will be of great importance and usefulness in improving the condition of our affairs. These have reached the point where they cry out for an urgent remedy. Concerning the visitation, I am sure that we are safe, even though the malcontents do not give up agitating, as well as making application to the Pope by means of memorials much more harmful for the Society than the visitation will be – but I hope in the Lord that everything will pass without any damage being done. I would like Your Reverence to take occasion, when the moment seems right, to advise the king, with some warmth, how much harm is being done to the regular discipline – as in these sad times, to our sorrow, we have experienced – by tying the hands of the superiors and giving spirit and ardour to the unruly subordinates: that others, seeing them becoming so insolent under the shadow and protection of similar personages, are so spoiled by their example that the superior is unable to put right what is evidently in need of remedy. Therefore I would like Your Reverence to do all you can in this particular to make the king understand that in this he should act according to his conscience, being himself Christian and God-fearing. I believe it will have an effect. To Your Reverence's holy sacrifices and prayers I commend myself. From Rome 21 March 1589.

[PS] And even if it should seem to His Majesty that it is important for the good of this tribunal to undertake the protection of those who are now appealing to it (something which we also say), nevertheless it is necessary to guard, according to this rationale, against those who are not appealing to the Holy Office about anything involving the tribunal, but are only using this pretext to protect themselves: something which makes them become so unruly and insolent that they destroy themselves and the rest.

9. non] *obscure R*

B9 To Claudio Acquaviva, Madrid, 30 March 1589

SOURCE: Acquaviva to Persons, 15 May and 12 June (B16, B18).

NOTE: In this or the previous letter, of 20 March (B7), Persons must have reported on the state of the English colleges in Rheims and Rome. He expressed a need to know something about the contents of letters from Cardinals Carafa and Allen to the king, and relayed Philip's desire for more information about the Society and how Acquaviva wanted to deal with the dissension. Antonio Carafa (1538–1591) was librarian of the Holy Roman Church and participated in the papal conclaves of 1585 and 1590.

B10 From Claudio Acquaviva, Rome, 17 April 1589

SOURCE: ARSI, Tolet. 5/I, fols. 58r (main text) and 58v (addition).

NOTE: Acquaviva is concerned about Persons's health and advises him to stay in Madrid to recover and also to continue negotiations with the king, until he can go to Jesus del Monte, the retreat house for Jesuits from Alcalá de Henares, for recuperation. Acquaviva suggests that he should wait until the end of the summer to make the journey to Guadalupe; Persons may have intended to make a pilgrimage to the royal monastery of Santa María de Guadalupe, whose monks also founded the monastery of El Escorial (Edwards, 137).

According to Persons's instructions (B1) it was intended that he should return to Flanders once the business with the king was settled, but it now appears that he planned a visit to Portugal and Andalusia in the south and west, evidently to begin canvassing for an end to the dissension caused by the *memorialistas*. McCoog suggests that at this time Persons and Acquaviva agreed that Spain should replace Flanders as the centre of operations for the English mission (McCoog, *Building the Faith of St Peter*, 138).

P. Roberto Personio. 17 abril.

Poiché la dimora de Vostra Reverentia costì è tanto utile et importante, come per diverse lettere mi fanno intender, sì per le cose della Compagnia, come ancho per quelle della patria, mi pare che non bisogna afretarsi nelli negotii, ma attender a rifar la sanità, et ristorar la testa che mi rincresce stia tanto debole come mi dice, et però converra che misure[10] le sue fatiche in maniera che insieme possia haver la cura necessaria de la persona sua, et questo senza haver niuna della partenza sua poi che il tempo mostrarà quando potrà commodamente partire;[11] et per la medesima[12] cagion non conviene che la Reverentia Vostra facia ausentia si lunga della corte come bisognarebbe farla se dovesse far il viaggio de Portugallo et quello d'Andaluzia. Vostra Reverentia per adesso si ferma costì,

---

10. misure] *obscure R; alternatively,* misura

11. The following text has been deleted in R: "per adesso gli mando un memoriale accioché secondo quello che esso contiene si adopere un poco col Re in agiutarci ma intanto bisogna provedere con la misura detta" (and for now I am sending a memorial so that, following what it contains, you will put a little bit of effort into helping us with the king, but in the meantime it is important to proceed with the aforementioned moderation).

12. medesima] *this ed.;* medema *R, without contraction mark*

et si adopere un poco in agiutarci secondo quello che contiene un memorial che con questa gli mando, ma sia con la missura sudetta.[13]

Potrà Vostra Reverentia al fine della state far il viaggio de Guadalupe come desidera, con ciò che alhora non occurra qualche bisogno della persona sua per li negotii de Madrid, et poiché desidera haver per compagno del suo peregrinaggio il fratello Bartolomeo de Sicilia, parle col Padre Provinciale che esso gli consolarà in quello che dimanda. Oltra ciò mi pare, che essendo l'area de Giesù del Monte sì buona gioverà per rifar la testa et sanità de Vostra Reverentia massimamente col riposo che in quella casa potrà pigliar, sì che quando gli parerà haverne tempo de goder quell' area, et la buona compagnia delli padri et fratelli che in quella casa passano la state. Potrà Vostra Reverentia andar dilla, avisando[14] prima al Provinciale che so gli consolarà in questo et in qualunche altra cosa bisognarà per la comodità sua.

Ho scritto al collegio di Graz, dando ordine che il fratello Brachenburio parta subito per Genova, acciò possia con la prima commodità andar in Spagna et aiutar a Vostra Reverentia. Delli altri duoi anchora non mancaro de far come Vostra Reverentia desidera.

Ho ragionato alla lunga col Signore Cardinale Alano come Vostra Reverentia nella sua lettera mi avisa, prego il Signore che per la sua divina bontà tutto riesca come desideriamo et conviene per la sua gloria et bene nostro. Non altro in questa che racommandarmi alle orationi et Sancti Sacrificii della Reverentia Vostra. De Roma a di 17 d'Aprile.

Añadido a la del Padre Personio:
Stando per solto scriver questa ho ricivutto una lettera del Collegio de Graz nella quale me avisano che il fratello Brachenburio morì, io ho avisato al Rectore del Collegio Inglese che veda un poco se trovanno qualche uno che possia servir alla Reverentia Vostra in quel che dessidera.

Translation

To Fr Robert Persons, 17 April.

Since, as I understand from various letters, Your Reverence's sojourn over there is so useful and important, both for the Society's affairs and those concerning your homeland, it seems to me we should not rush into business, but wait until you recover your health and clear your head, which I am sorry is as weak as you say. However, please agree to moderate your efforts so as to take good care of your person as well; nor should you be anxious about your departure, as time will show when it will be more convenient for you to leave. In the same vein, it is not expedient for Your Reverence to be absent from the court for such a long time as would be needed to make the journey to Portugal and Andalusia. Your Reverence should now stay where you are and help us a little bit [with the king] according to the instructions contained in the memorial that I am sending with the present letter, but please do so with the aforementioned moderation.

---

13. The following text has been deleted in R: "et peroche le cose nostre saràno speditte" (and since our affairs will be facilitated).

14. avisando] R, replacing chiedendo [deleted]

48 | *Valladolid, 1588-1592*

At the end of the summer, Your Reverence might make the trip to Guadalupe according to your wishes,[15] if you are not needed personally for business in Madrid. As you would like to have Fr Bartolomé de Sicilia for a companion on the journey, please speak to father provincial[16] and he will accommodate your requests. Aside from that, it seems to me that the air of Jesus del Monte, being as good as it is, will be beneficial for making your head feel better and for Your Reverence's health. This will improve especially with the repose you will be able to take in that house, as you will feel when you find the time to enjoy that area and the good company of the fathers and brothers who spend the summer in that house. Your Reverence might go there after first informing the provincial, whom I know will accommodate you in this as in any other thing you might need.

I have written to the college of Graz and given orders that Brother Brakenbury should depart immediately for Genoa, so that he will be able to reach Spain with the first available mean of transportation and help Your Reverence.[17] About the other two, moreover, I will not fail to do as Your Reverence wishes.

I have had a long conversation with Lord Cardinal Allen as you advised me to in your letter. I pray the Lord that by His divine goodness everything will turn out as we wish and conduce to His glory and our own good. Nothing else in this, except to recommend myself to Your Reverence's prayers and holy sacrifices. From Rome, 17 April.

Addition to the letter to Fr Persons:

Just as I was writing this, I received a letter from the College in Graz in which they advise me that Brother Brakenbury has died. I have asked the Rector of the English College to see if they can find someone who can serve Your Reverence's needs.

B11 From Claudio Acquaviva, Rome, 17 April 1589

SOURCE: ARSI, Tolet. 4, fol. 51r.

NOTE: Pleased with Persons's reception by the king, Acquaviva awaits news of Acosta's success.

Comparison of this letter with the previous item (B10), the open letter of the same date, indicates that the confidential letter was written slightly later (see the comment on dating in the introduction, "The Correspondence Network"). In the open letter Acquaviva reports that he had just written to Graz to instruct William Brakenbury (1560-1589) to proceed to Genoa and make his way to Madrid to serve as Persons's amanuensis. Brakenbury entered the Society of Jesus in early 1584 and was ordained priest while serving as a theologian in Graz. Acquaviva nevertheless calls him "brother." Before the packet of letters was despatched on 17

---

15. Guadalupe is situated in the province of Cáceres, southwest of Madrid, en route to Lisbon.
16. Gonzalo Dávila, provincial of Toledo, not to be confused with the visitor Gil González Dávila (see the Introduction, Dramatis Personae). In 1590 he approved Persons's first publication in Spanish, *Relacion de algunos martyrios* ... (see Persons to Allen, 14 September, B34, headnote).
17. Brakenbury had in fact died; see the addition below, and the headnote to the confidential letter of the same date (B11).

April, news came of Brakenbury's death on 27 March (ARSI, Hist. Soc. 42, fol. 106r), which is recorded in the main text of this letter but in an addition to the earlier one. Acquaviva sent William Flack in his stead (see his letter of 15 May, B16),

In the open letter, Acquaviva also promised another two assistants; here he discusses, as possibilities, Thomas Stephenson (1552–1624) and William Wright (1563–1639). Stephenson entered the Society in 1585 and was made professor of Hebrew in Vienna in 1588. Wright entered the Society in 1581 and was given permission to travel to Austria in 1585, where he later became professor of philosophy, being ordained priest about 1591. In the event, neither was thought suitable, or the Austrian provincial resisted their re-assignment, arguing how necessary they were for their colleges.

Madrid. P. Roberto Personio. 17 de Aprile.

Ricevei quelle due de Vostra Reverentia delli 17 di Febraro; ci siamo tutti molto consolati nel Signore della grata audienza che la Maestà del Re ha data a Vostra Reverentia et speriamo che haverà fatto qualche buon effetto. Stiamo aspettando che la resposta che Sua Maestà voglia accogliere al Padre Acosta.

—— Scrissemo subito in Gratz acciò venesse su a Genova il fratello Guillelmo Brakenburio, et poco di poi arrivo aviso come Domino Nostro Signore l'haveva chiamato a sé.

—— Habbiamo che il Padre Rector del Collegio Inglese ci ha nominato al Padre Thomaso Stefanone quale tiene 37 anni et sono soli tre che entro nella Compagnia et oltre che è di età matura studia il tertio anno di Theologia et pare conveniente che finisca per l'età che ha, sta in Viena come anco il fratello Guillelmo Wrightio di 27 anni, otto della Compagnia et studia Theologia ma non sapiamo come ha buona mano; andaremo pensando quale sarà più apposito.[18] In tanto scriviamo al padre provinciale che le dia aiuto mentre che di qua se le manda. De gli altri ancora si manderano col titolo che Vostra Reverentia scrive. Per sua consolatione se le manda copia d'una che ci ha scritto il Padre Ricardo Holtbeo il primo di febraro. Non altro ...

Translation

To Fr Robert Persons in Madrid, 17 April.

I have received Your Reverence's two letters dated 17 February; we are altogether much consoled in the Lord by the welcoming audience which His Royal Majesty gave to Your Reverence, and we hope that it will in fact have a correspondingly good outcome. We are still waiting for confirmation that His Majesty approves of Fr Acosta.

We had just written to Graz that Brother William Brakenbury should proceed to Genoa[19] when, soon afterwards, we received notice that God Our Lord had called him to Himself.

We understand that the father rector of the English college[20] has nominated Fr Thomas Stephenson, who is 37 years old. Although only three years have passed since his

---

18. ci ha nominato ... sará più apposito] *supplied at end of letter R*; un altro che fusse apposito per avisar Vostra Reverentia perché ben vediamo la sua gran necessitá *deleted R*

19. En route to Spain.

20. Joseph Creswell.

entry into the Society, he is of mature age and studying the third year of theology. So it seems convenient, given his age, that he should bring his studies to completion. He is staying in Vienna, as is Brother William Wright also, 27 years old, eight in the Society, studying theology, but we do not know how well he will succeed; we will continue to consider which of them will be more suitable. In the meantime, we are writing to father provincial so that he can offer his help until they are sent over here.[21] The others, again, will be provided with Your Reverence's written instructions. As an encouragement, I am sending you a copy of a letter written by Fr Richard Holtby on the first of February. Nothing else for the present ...

B12 To Joseph Creswell, Alcalá de Henares, 28 April 1589

SOURCE: ABSI, Coll P II 479, Grene's partial transcription.
HICKS: 76–77.
EDITION: Pollen, *Miscellanea* IX, 18–19.
NOTE: Recuperating in Alcalá, Persons writes to Creswell at the English College, Rome, about prospects for English Jesuits and priests in Spain, especially a group of four from Sicily who were bound for Andalusia. He hopes he will be provided with an assistant.
It is likely that Persons was not in Alcalá itself, but at the retreat house at Jesus del Monte about twenty miles away, as Acquaviva had suggested in his open letter of 17 April (B10). He mentions Pedro de Ribadeneira, who was resident at Jesus del Monte, in a letter dated 29 April (B15).

If Fr Gibbons and Charles come I shall help myself by one of them, &c.[22] — The provincial also of Andaluzia Fr Bartolomeo Perez will receave willingly them from Sicily,[23] as before I wrott that you should sollicit; and the two niew visitors of all these four Provinces are very well contented to receave two at least of our countrymen in every Province, &c. — I have bin this month in Alcala almost under hands of Phisicians; but now I hope within 3 or 4 daies to be well, and to returne to Madrid, &c. —

B13 To Cardinal Antonio Carafa, Alcalá de Henares, 28 April 1589

SOURCE: Acquaviva to Persons, 12 June (B18).
NOTE: Persons wrote to Carafa (1538–1591) at the papal curia to give his view on the dissension in the Society in Spain.

---

21. This is probably a reference to the provincial of Toledo, who will assist with those who are sent to Spain to assist Persons.
22. On Persons's need of an assistant, see Acquaviva's letter of 17 April (B11). Here he anticipates the despatch of Richard Gibbons and Charles Tancard from Rome; see Acquaviva's letter of 15 May (B16).
23. Grene notes: "nostros intelligit Anglos qui tum in Sicilia morabantur" (he means English Jesuits who were then remaining in Sicily).

B14 To Claudio Acquaviva, Alcalá de Henares, 28 April 1589

SOURCE: Acquaviva to Persons, 12 June (B18).
NOTE: Persons reported on Philip's approval of the appointment of the visitors to the Jesuit provinces in Spain and Portugal. He also relayed some matters raised by Pedro de Ribadeneira, who was residing at the Jesuit retreat house at Jesus del Monte: the question of Luis de Mendoza's appointment as superior, and an attempt by Dionisio Vázquez, a leading malcontent, to induce Ribadeneira to leave the province of Toledo.

B15 To Claudio Acquaviva, Alcalá de Henares, 29 April 1589

SOURCE: ARSI, Tolet. 4, fols. 54v–55v, holograph, with the remains of a seal.
NOTE: This note was written in haste to accompany a longer, missing letter of 28 April as well as a letter from Pedro de Ribadeneira. It has survived because Acquaviva incorporated its two sheets of paper into his register, using the address folio to write his draft reply of June 12. The ciphers have been decoded in a different hand, interlined above.

Persons writes of himself in the third person and in code about letters shown to him by Ribadeneira. It appears that they had similar views on the internal divisions in the Society, and that both wrote to Carafa at the papal curia accordingly (see Acquaviva's letter of 12 June, B18).

Molto reverendo in Christo padre
Dopo haver servato il plico Ribadeneira [172] gli è stato con Personio [108] et gl'ha monstrato tre letere che manda per questo ordinario a P. Generalis [105]. Credo che gli piaceranno et a Vostra Paternità ancora perché mi paiono molto a proposito et toccano al punto sopra che egli et io havemo spesso ragionato, egli sta molto contento, et così spero che confirmara. 29 April 1589.

Vostra Paternità conosce il charattere.
[*Addressed*:] Al padre Claudio Aquaviva, Preposito Generale di Compagna di Jesu, Roma.
[*Endorsed*:] Toledo.[24]

Translation

Very Reverend Father in Christ
After finding the packet, Ribadeneira was with Persons and showed him three letters that he is sending to Father General by this courier. I think they will be pleasing both to him [Persons] and to Your Paternity; in fact, I think they are very much apposite and touch the aforementioned point that you[25] and I have often discussed. He [Persons] is very satisfied, and I hope you will confirm this. 29 April 1589.

Your Paternity knows the hand.

24. Persons was still recuperating at Alcalá, so this endorsement, if it is not in error, must refer to the Jesuit province of Toledo, not the city itself, which is on the other side of Madrid from Alcalá de Henares.
25. Either "he" or "you" since Persons addresses Acquaviva in the third person.

B16 From Claudio Acquaviva, Rome, 15 May 1589

SOURCE: ARSI, Tolet. 4, fols. 52r–53v.

NOTE: Responding to Persons's lost letters of 20 and 30 March (B7, B9), Acquaviva expresses his satisfaction with Philip II's handling of the conflict over the Society (that is, the question of nominating the visitors), but is still waiting for the lifting of the ban on Spanish Jesuits travelling to the north. Cardinals Carafa and Allen had also written to the king in commendation of the Society, but their letters may not have been delivered. Acquaviva wishes Persons to make sure that the king is well-informed about the Jesuit visitation and is able to make his will known to the visitors. He should explain to the king how Acquaviva intends to deal with the memorialists and why a change to the Institute of the Society, as requested by them, would not be suitable. In a postscript, Acquaviva asks Persons to deliver a letter of appreciation to the king, which would then afford him an opportunity to discuss these matters.

Persons was to remain in Madrid to complete negotiations with the king, but he was to have a companion and secretary, William Flack, because he was too ill to write himself. Other questions of deployment of Jesuits would also have to wait until the situation had stabilized. In a letter of the same date to the provincial of Toledo, Gonzalo Dávila, Acquaviva emphasizes how important it is to look after Persons's health, because "será de mucho provecho para todo" (he will be of great benefit in everything). He asks the provincial to welcome the newcomers with open arms (ARSI, Tolet. 5/I, fol. 60r): on 14 May he had given permission for the Jesuits Richard Gibbons (1547/1553–1632), Charles Tancard (1564–1599), and William Flack (1560–1637) to travel from Rome to Spain (McCoog, *Building the Faith of St Peter*, 108; Foley, 7: 299–300 and 761). They arrived in Madrid in July (Persons to Creswell, Madrid, 22 July 1589, B24).

It is an indication of the close relationship between Acquaviva and Persons that the general resorted to confidential letters to Persons by the posts of 15 May (B16) and 12 June (B18), resuming the open correspondence on 5 July (B21). The present letter ends with some pastoral advice, rare in this correspondence, on Persons's prayer life. On delicate personal matters, there is an allusion to tensions between Pedro de Ribadeneira and Fr Luis de Mendoza at Jesus del Monte. Acquaviva expresses his agreement, both here and in his confidential letter of 12 June, that Mendoza should not be appointed superior of the house. He wrote to Gonzalo Dávila, the provincial of Toledo, on this matter on 12 June (ARSI, Tolet. 4, fol. 56r).

Madrid. P. Roberto Personio. 15 de Mayo.
Di gran consolatione è stata nel Signore a tutti noi la buona et santa resolutione di Sua Maestà Catholica nelli nostri negotii, con la quale altro non ha fatto che[26] gettare a tutta la Compagnia una catena d'oro al collo, di nuovo obligo d'amore et di legame maggiore per servirla, et per[27] priegare, con maggior[28] instanza con la Divina Maestà per la

26. altro non ha fatto che] *interlined R*
27. per] *interlined R*
28. con maggior] *interlined R*

lungheza di vita et felice successo delle sante sue imprese. Della mente del Re, non potevamo dubitare, ma si[29] bene di quella d'alcuni de chi Sua Maestà s'informava. Et sarebbe un gran punto per il comun bene della Compagnia se la Maestà del Re havesse penetrato ch'in questi negotii[30] intravenivano alcune persone appassionate tanto della Compagnia come di fuori di quella, il che confido nella Divina bontà che gli lo darà ad intendere et non dubito che l'andata del Re grandamente ha aiutato a così favorevole risolutione per tutta la Compagnia; sia per tutto lodato il Signore[31] —

Con questa buona nuova può pensare Vostra Reverentia quanto ci siano state grate le sue delli 20 et 30 di marzo che venero insieme col corriere che arrivò a noi 2 giorni da questo et prorespondere.[32] Desidero ch'osservi quanto sia possibile la prohibitione che gl'hano fatto i medici di non scrivere di sua mano. Et poiché piacque al Signore chiamare a sé il fratello Guilemo Brakenburio,[33] li mandiamo per aiuto di Vostra Reverentia il fratello Guillelmo Flacco che sta a Loretto del quale[34] il Padre Provinciale di Roma mi da buona relatione. Hoggi partono di qua il Padre Riccardo Gibbone et fratello Carolo Tancardo, i quali passando per Loreto pigliarano il Flacco in sua compagnia. Il fratello Carolo ha data qui sodisfattione; desiderarei che in Alcalà finisse li suoi studii. Trattavasi di dar grado al Padre Ricardo, et attualmente era in Santo Andrea facendo il tertio anno di probatione: già sono otto mesi.[35] Come costi haverà data buona sodisfattione di sé, sì come quà l'habbiamo, ci potrano avisare per promoverlo —

Aspettiamo l'essecutione dell'ordine di Sua Maestà che sia levata la prohibitione alli nostri d'andare ad aiutare li paesi Oltromontanii, il che anco aiutarà accio li Signori Inquisitori intendano la buona mente di Sua Maestà et l'importanza di tal prohibitione impeditiva di gran servitio di Dio. ——

Mi rallegro dell'aviso havuto[36] per li Seminarii Anglesi. Quanto alli preparamenti di guerra, preghiamo il Signore dia felice successo et lunga vita ad Sua Maestà Catholica et per tal fine rinovaremo le solite nostre orationi et messe. Non conviene che Vostra Reverentia parta di costà finché questo gran negotio sia finito; col favor Divino.[37] ——

Fu mancamento non farsi di quà qualche saggio del contenuto delle lettere degl'Illustrissimi Cardinali Carafa et Alano per Sua Maestà. L'argomento era dare testimonio della Compagnia et del desiderio che habbiamo[38] di servire il Re, et che se niente desider-

29. Si] R; *properly* se
30. Negotii] *followed by* ci erano personi [*deleted*] R
31. et non dubito che l'andata del Re grandamente ha aiutato a così favorevole risolutione per tutta la Compagnia; sia per tutto lodato il Signore] *interlined, with* a così ... il Signore *supplied in the margin* R
32. che venero insieme col corriere che arrivò a noi 2 giorni da questo et prorespondere] *interlined, with* prorespondere *obscure* R
33. Et poiché piacque al Signore chiamare a se il fratello Guilemo Brakenburio] *supplied in margin* R
34. del quale *deleted in R but seems necessary for the sense*
35. già sono otto mesi] *interlined* R
36. havuto] *interlined above* che era proponessa a V.R. [*deleted*] R
37. col favor Divino] *interlined* R
38. habbiamo] bbiamo *interlined* R

ava Sua Maestà havrebbono modo di farle fare. Mi sarà caro che siano state date, altrimenti sarà meglio non darle, perché sarebbono molto antiche et non tanto apposito del tempo et stato de negotii,[39] secondo la quale avisandoci Vostra Reverentia del non essere date, faremo fare altre. ——

Mi par bene il pensiero di Vostra Reverentia di proporre al Re[40] in mio nome, che sebene la gratia che[41] a tutta la Compagnia ha fatta è grande, tuttavia perch'io desidero che la mente di Sua Maestà resti chiarita di quanto desideria intendere della Compagnia, il che ci sarà di[42] non minore gratia; e vere la supplo,[43] resti servita di nominare qualche persona alla quale li Visitatori diano conto delle cose che Sua Maestà vorrà più in particolare intendere, perché[44] dalla chiarezza delle cose nella mente di Sua Maestà pende senza dubio gran bene della Compagnia et conseguentemente del serviggio de Dio, poiché se ce sono cose dà emendare, con la notitia et[45] aviso di Sua Maestà s'emendarano; et se per rigore non sarano, restarà Sua Maestà consolata, la Compagna giustificata, et col suo favore aiutata a mettere freno[46] a quelli che l'hanno così malamente conturbata.

——

Ancora è bene raguagliare Sua Maestà di quanto quì si pretende negotiare con li memoriali quali è certo che sono pieni di bugie, come si vederà per le risposte[47] delli primi mandate al Padre provinciale di Toledo, Gonzalo d'Avila, et forse si mandarà col seguente corriero quella delli secondi. Ma quest'ufficio conviene facci Vostra Reverentia senza mostrare che temiamo mutatione de cose dell'instituto o governo, perché già Sua Santità ha scritto ad alcuni Prencipi che questo non lo farà, ma sibene fare capace al Re (come Vostra Reverentia scrive) che tale mutatione sarebbe certissima rovina della Compagnia et del frutto che per la gratia del Signore fa, et suggerirli, che se non al Papa, al meno vuolesse scrivere all'Ambasciatore[48] che dica a Sua Santità, come Sua Maestà resta sodisfatta della Compagnia et che la raccomandi a Sua Santità ordinando insieme alli Ambasciatori che per l'avenire per qualunche altra commissione generale havesse havuto prima, non facci officii con Sua Beatitudine in cose tocanti alla Compagnia senza nuovo et espresso ordine della Maestà sua et perché[49] alcuni dicono che Sua Maestà è male sodisfatta della Compagnia perché s'intromette in cose di stato, che egli facci fede al Papa et

39. stato de negotii] *interlined above illegible deletion R*
40. Re] *interlined above* S. M^{ta} [*deleted*] *R*
41. che] *followed by* ha [*deleted*] *R*
42. il che ci sarà di] *interlined above* ma [*deleted*]; di *inserted after* sarà; sarà *obscure, possibly* farà *R*
43. e vere la supplo] *obscure R*
44. perché *replaces* di qua senza dubio pende [*deleted*] *R*
45. *An illegible word follows in R*
46. freno a quelli ... conturbata] *supplied from a marginal addition marked* oo *R*
47. risposte *replaces* mandate [*deleted*] *R*
48. *Here in R the text* della mente di Sua Maestà quale sia intorno a (what His Majesty had in mind with regard to) *has been deleted, to be replaced with the section from* che dica *to* perché *below (see next note), which has been supplied from an addendum marked* F. *The addendum ends with an illegible contracted word, possibly* etc.
49. perché *is repeated here in R as the text resumes from the insertion.*

a che altro bisognerà di quanto Sua Maestà intende o crede interno a questa oppositione, et raccomandi le cose della Compagnia ——

Mostrai al Signor Cardinale Alano la risposta de Don Giovanni Idiaquez nel negotio di Sua Signoria Illustrissima di che resta consolata, et già per letera di Vostra Reverentia la sapeva. ——

Non accade tenere scropolo dell'hora dell'oratorie, anzi deve tenersi dall'eccesso che Vostra Reverentia forse fa stando come sta, il che gl'ordino che non facci,[50] ma si governi secondo che la debolezza di sua testa permette et non facci fatica d'oratione mentale, etiando dell'ordinaria senza consultarlo col suo confessore al quale dirà la mente nostra, che è che non si faticchi. Et finalmente la remetto in lei, come mi ricorderà.

Noi ancora desederiamo pacificare tutti sì come il Padre Soarez dice, ma nelle cose et modi che lecitamente si potrà, perch'il resto non è soavità, ma debolezza.

Del P. Rebadeneira et Mendozza io scriverò al Padre Egidio, a quest'ultimo non conviene farlo superiore; la fedeltà del padre ci piacerà d'intenderla, il che il tempo scuoprirà. ——

Il Padre Egidio et tutti[51] conascono Vostra Reverentia et sanno la nostra volontà et però se bene crediamo non essere necessario altra raccommandatione, tuttavia si fà caldamente[52] ——

La dispersione d'alcuni sarebbe buon rimedio, ma adesso non è tempo di tentarlo col Papa, et se per ora qua[53] si facesse sarebbe con disgusto delli signori Inquisitori et del Re, et cessando questo, sempre sarà in man nostra il farlo.

Sono stato a ringratiare il Signor Ambasciatore della buona resolutione di Sua Maestà al modo che Vostra Reverentia insinuava, nelle cui orationi.

Aggionto al fine di questa letera.

Con questa letera quella che scrivo al Re, quale desidero che Vostra Reverentia dia a Sua Maestà; le scrivio ringratiandola della gratia che ci ha fatta di restare servita deli nostri padri Visitatori, et la supplico a vuolersi informare de tutti tre Visitatori, cioè delli doi et del Padre Fonseca delle cose che sarà servita di vuolere, intendere conforme a quello ch'in questa ho scritto, et con questa occasione Vostra Reverentia potrà fare l'officio che di sopra ho detto.

Translation

To Fr Robert Persons in Madrid, 15 May.

The good and holy resolution of our affairs by His Catholic Majesty has given every one of us great consolation in the Lord, as the business did nothing but throw a golden chain around the Society's neck. This renews the Society's obligations to serve him with love and greater friendship, but also to intercede more insistently with the Divine Majesty

---

50. *The rest of the paragraph is inserted at the end of the letter, before the postscript.*
51. tutti] *followed by* sano le *deleted R*
52. Caldamente] *followed by* per che lei la dimanda (since you ask for it) *deleted R*
53. per ora qua] *obscure R*

on his behalf for a long life and the happy success of his holy enterprises. We could have no doubt about the king's intention, but rather of the motives of certain people from whom His Majesty received his information. And it would be of great advantage for the Society's common good, if the king's majesty had understood that among those who took part in this business were many men governed by passion, of whom some were members of our Society but some were not. I put my trust in the goodness of God, who will make him understand, and I have no doubts that the king's action has been of great help in bringing about such a favourable resolution for the entire Society: may the Lord be praised.

With such good news, Your Reverence can understand how grateful we were for your letters of the 20th and 30th of March which came together with the courier who reached us two days ago, and here is my reply: I would like you, as far as possible, to observe the physicians' prohibition of writing letters in your own hand. And since it was God's will to call Brother William Brakenbury to be with Him,[54] we are sending Brother William Flack to Your Reverence's aid. He is currently in Loreto and father provincial of Rome has provided me with a good report of him. Today Fr Richard Gibbon and Brother Charles Tancard are leaving from here, and they will go through Loreto and fetch [Brother] Flack to join them. Brother Charles has proved himself well here, and I would like him to finish his studies in Alcalá. The purpose is to help Fr Richard make progress: actually, he is currently in Sant'Andrea doing his third year of probation: it has been eight months already. Since up to now he has given a good account of himself, and we have him here [at the novitiate], we can rely on their advice about his promotion.

We await the carrying out of His Majesty's order that the ban might be lifted for Ours to go to help the ultramontane countries. This will also help the Lord Inquisitors to understand His Majesty's good intentions and the seriousness of that prohibition, as it was hindering the great service of God.

I rejoice at the report received about the English seminaries.[55] With regard to the preparations for war, we pray that the Lord will grant happy success and long life to His Catholic Majesty, and to that end we renew our accustomed prayers and masses. It is not expedient for Your Reverence to depart from there until this great business has come to a resolution, with God's favour.

It was a mistake, in this context, not to have given you some indication of the contents of the letters from the Illustrious Cardinals Carafa and Allen to His Majesty. The gist of them was to bear witness to the Society and to the desire we have to serve the king, so that they would somehow provide some means of overcoming any reluctance on His Majesty's part.[56] I will be satisfied if the letters have already been delivered: if not, it would

54. On William Brakenbury, see Acquaviva's letters of 17 April (B10, B11).

55. Persons had obtained a grant of 3000 ducats for Rheims (Persons to Acquaviva, 17 February, B4).

56. Here the Italian seems to be grammatically correct, but the meaning is obscure. Evidently Acquaviva had asked the cardinals to write letters to the king which he entrusted to Persons to deliver, without making it clear what they were about or when they should be passed on to the king. In his Spanish letter to Gonzalo Dávila of 15 May (see headnote), Acquaviva reflects: "Bien podra el Padre Personio dar al Rey las cartas de los Cardenales que para ninguna cosa dañarán,

be better not to release them [now] as they will be out of date, no longer appropriate for the time and the state of the business. So if Your Reverence advises us that they have not been delivered, we will have to order new ones to be made.

I approve of Your Reverence's intention of impressing on the king, on my behalf, that although the favour which he has bestowed upon the Society is great, it would be no less welcome to me if His Majesty found clarity about what he wants to know of the Society.

For now, I beg you to be content to nominate someone to whom the visitors might give account of the things His Majesty wants to know more particularly; indeed, the good of the Society and consequently of the service of God depends greatly on His Majesty's being clear in his mind about things. In fact, if there are things that need to be corrected, they will be through His Majesty's information and advice; and if through rigorous examination it is found there are not, His Majesty will be happy and the Society will be justified – and enabled, thanks to his favour, to put the brakes on those who have so grievously perturbed her.

It would be well to inform His Majesty how we wish to deal here with the memorials, which are certainly full of lies, as you will see from my responses sent to the father provincial of Toledo, Gonzalo Dávila with the first batch of letters this month (which perhaps will actually be sent with the next courier, the one carrying the second batch). But I would prefer Your Reverence to pursue this business without suggesting that we fear a change to our Institute or government,[57] since His Holiness has already written to some princes that he will not do it. All the same (as Your Reverence writes), it would be good for the king to realize that such an alteration would spell certain disaster both for the Society and for the fruit that she bears, by the grace of God. You should also suggest to him that he might write, if not to the pope, at least to his ambassador,[58] to tell His Holiness how His Majesty remains satisfied with the Society and commends her to His Holiness. At the same time, he could order the ambassadors that in any future general commission they have in hand, they should not treat with His Beatitude in matters concerning the Society without new and express order from His Majesty. And because some people claim that His Majesty is discontented with the Society for meddling in state affairs, he could make assurances that he will keep faith with the pope. He should say whatever else is necessary in connection with His Majesty's intentions and beliefs with regard to this opposition, and he should recommend the Society's affairs.

---

antes aprovecharan para todo. Si no las ha dado mejor será ya no darlas como al mesmo P. escrivo" (It would be a good idea for Fr Persons to give those letters of the cardinals to the king because they would do no harm but rather be of general advantage. If he has not given them, it would be better if he didn't do so; I am writing to the same father to the same effect).

57. The memorialists were dissatisfied with the Society's Institute ("way of proceeding") and centralized government in Rome.

58. Enrique de Guzmán, second count of Olivares, was Spanish ambassador to Rome, 1582–1591. See Michael J. Levin, *Agents of Empire: Spanish Ambassadors in Sixteenth-Century Italy* (Ithaca, NY, 2005), 112–123.

To my Lord Cardinal Allen I have shown Don Juan de Idiáquez's reply concerning His Eminence's business. He appeared to be happy with it, and already knew of it by Your Reverence's letter.⁵⁹

It is not necessary to be scrupulous about the hours of prayer – on the contrary you should abstain from excess (as Your Reverence might be guilty of, in spite of your health), which I order you to avoid: instead, you should be guided according to how much the weakness of your head allows, and should not weary yourself with mental prayer as well as with ordinary prayer,⁶⁰ without consulting your confessor first, with whom you should share our opinion, which is that you should not weary yourself. And in the last instance I refer the matter to you, as [I am sure] you will remind me.

We still want to create peace amongst everyone as Fr Suárez says, but only in matters and ways that remain within the bounds of what is permissible, for otherwise it is not graciousness, but weakness.⁶¹

I will write to Fr Gil about Fr Ribadeneira and Mendoza, that it is not fitting to make the latter superior; we will be pleased to learn of the father's loyalty, which (only) time will uncover.⁶²

Fr Gil, along with everyone else, knows Your Reverence and is aware of what we want; still, although we don't think any further recommendation is necessary, we offer it warmly.

The re-deployment of some would be a good remedy,⁶³ however now it is not a good time to broach that with the pope, and if it were done now, it would be to the greatest dissatisfaction of the inquisitors and the king; in any case, we can see to that once this is over.

I have gone to see my Lord Ambassador to thank him for His Majesty's good resolution in the direction that Your Reverence was pointing out, to whose prayers, etc.

[PS] With this letter I enclose one I have written to the king, which I want Your Reverence to give to His Majesty. I am writing to thank him for his favour shown towards our father visitors, and to encourage him to gather information about all three visitors, that is, the two and Fr Fonseca,⁶⁴ about everything he expects from them, in relation to

---

59. See the headnote to the missing letter to William Allen, 17 February (B5).

60. "Mental prayer" refers to the strict regular use of Ignatian methods, i.e. meditation according to the three faculties (memory, understanding, will), composition of place, and the like. "Ordinary prayer" refers to the saying of the divine office. See Joseph de Guibert, *The Jesuits: Their Spiritual Doctrine and Practice* (St Louis, 1986), 167–170.

61. Acquaviva means that there cannot be peace at any price; concessions can only be made within the framework of the Jesuit Institute. He may be appealing to a principle enunciated by Francisco Suárez, the eminent theologian and political theorist. Alternatively, this may be a reference to Juan Suárez, former provincial of Castile, a senior Jesuit whose opinions Acquaviva valued.

62. Gil González Dávila, as visitor to the province of Toledo, would have a say in the appointments at Alcalá and the retreat house at Jesus del Monte.

63. Acquaviva is referring to the possibility of transferring some of the *memorialistas*, an exigency to which he turned in the following months and years.

64. Pedro Fonseca was named visitor to the province of Portugal at the same time as the appointment of Acosta and González Dávila.

what I have written in this. This will give Your Reverence the opportunity to fulfil the commission outlined above.

B17 To Joseph Creswell, El Escorial, 26 May 1589

> SOURCE: ABSI, Coll P I 299, Grene's partial transcript.
> HICKS: 78.
> NOTE: Persons had recovered enough to return to Madrid and do some research at El Escorial. He refers here to the possibility of writing a Latin biography of Campion, including copies of his Latin works. Acquaviva later encouraged Persons to pursue this project (Acquaviva to Persons, 22 November 1593, B209).

I send you herewith the copy of an elegant oration of Fr Campians which I found heer. — I pray you to procure from Praga — the copies of all such orations, comedies &c. — in Latin as are there to be had, that if ever — we — sett — forth his life hereafter in Latin (as heer Luigi de Grenata has don largely in Spanish)[65] we may print diverse of his Latin works therwith.

B18 From Claudio Acquaviva, Rome, 12 June 1589

> SOURCE: ARSI, Tolet. 4, fols. 53v–54v.
> NOTE: Acquaviva is pleased about Philip's approval of the appointment of the Jesuit visitors, but is anxious that the king should make it clear that further agitation will not be welcome. He explains various measures that need to be taken to remedy the tensions in the Society in Spain: the king should write to the pope, endorsing current Jesuit practice, and obtain his support for disciplining the malcontents. This "medicine" should however be applied judiciously, at the right time and in the right place. The chief remedy would be to transfer some of the malcontents. The letter provides further evidence that Acquaviva relied strongly on Persons's influence with the king, rather than Acosta's. On this letter, see Edwards, 141 and McCoog, *Building the Faith of St Peter*, 135.
>
> In this draft, Acquaviva began by writing the name followed by the relevant cipher, and then changed to writing only the cipher with the name inserted above; in one case he evidently decided afterwards that a word ("*amici*") should go into cipher. He was responding to what appears to have been a long letter of 28 April (B14), and, needing more paper for his own reply, inserted a short confidential note from Persons, dated 29 April (B15), into the register, using the address leaf (fol. 54) to continue his draft.

Madrid o Valladolid. P. Roberto Personio 12 de Junio.

Ci siamo rallegrati nel Signore che l'elettione delli Visitatori sia stata generalmente grata, si come Vostra Reverentia per le sue dell 28 d'Aprile ci scrive, nelle quali la parti-

---

65. Luis de Granada, OP (1505–1588) was the author of several devotional works which were translated or adapted into English in the 1580s, mainly under Persons's direction (see vol. 1: 14). We have not traced a biography of Campion.

colare notitia che d'alcune cose ci dà non potrà se non aiutare. Il P. Joseph de Acosta [173] è più prudente et giudicioso et virtuoso che non è quell'altro de chi si dubita che lo tradiase et però no è periculo. L'essere egli et il P. Egidio [175][66] amici [20 18 29 22 29][67] con 177 aiutarà piú tosto, come speriamo nel Signore —

Con li perturbati [178] è bene andare con temperamento applicando le medicine a tempo et luogo; ma non già politicamente come dice [24 29 22 25] Porres [174]. Del dare governo [27 39 31 13 17 16] a Ludo [20 19 40 24 39] Mendoza [18 25 17 24 39 35 20] non c'è che trattare, perché non da quella sodasfattione di sé che noi desideravamo. Per de [24 25] Ribadeneira [171] lo raccomandaremo a Dio; credo bene che in questi nostri negotii haverà fatto de buoni uffici. Noi ancora giudichiamo speditamente che Porres [174] stia [12 11 29 20] in [38 17] Madrid [65]. Mi dispiace che Ribadeneira [171] dica che a [20] Dionysio [168] s'erano date molte occasioni [39 22 20 12 29 16 17 38] da [24 20] Roma [61] de dove non hebbe se non carezze *una excepta mutare ex Toletana habitum*, et fu necessaria per le cose che adesso sono al mondo palesi —

L'officio che Personio [108] fece con Acosta [173] et [25 11] Egidio [175] di prendere modo et conseglio per levare quella aversione ch'il Demonio va mettendo e alle [20 19 19 25] cose [22 39 12 25] di [24 29] Roma [61] è di molta importanza et non sarà difficile il persuadere la verità, poiché venendosi alli particolari tutte sono bugie.

Già per altre ho scritto la cura che desidero habbi Vostra Reverentia dalla sua sanità. Li tre compagni a quest'hora sono a Genova. Perché sono alcuni giorni che ci scrive il Rettore di Bologna ch'erano passi di là.

Quello che si pretendeva col officio che Personio [108] doveva fare con 82 era accio il Rè si chiarisse delle cose delli memoriali, mà lo faranno li Visitatori. Non si cercava da Sua Maestà lettera in favore dell'instituto se non che scrivesse al Papa che s'era informata delle cose nostre et che haveva sodisfattione di quelle et della Compagnia, et che però la raccommandava a Sua Santità et se questo si potrà havere soavemente, sarebbe bene altrimenti Dio Signor nostro risponderà per noi, come della sua infinita bontà. Speriamo, et in questo et anco nelle due cose che qua si trattano, tanto più che havendo scritto a Sua Santità da Germania parecchi principi del frutto che sì fa in quelle bande, et che sarebbe gran danno l'alterare l'instituto, come[68] intendevano che vuolevo fare, ha resposto Sua Santità che non vuol mutare cosa alcuna.

Non è necessario che quelli Padri gravi scrivano lettera mostrabile all' Illustrissimo Cardinale Caraffa, né il Papa si cura molto delli memoriali, né accade altro, basta quella che Vostra Reverentia et il P. Rebadeneira l'hano scritto. Più tosto dovendo scrivere, sarebbe meglio al Cardinale Deza, se bene non vego gran necessità.

Già per l'altre nostre haverà inteso Vostra Reverentia essersi ricevute le sue delli 17 di febraro 20 et 30 di marzo.[69]

Intendo per buona strada che gl'inquieti non esperano di dare nuovi memoriali perché hano sentito il caso ch'il Re sia sodisfatto de nostri Visitatori et perché se vede che cos-

---

66. Up to here, the ciphers are written after the name; from here on the names are inserted above the ciphers.

67. This cipher has been supplied in the margin.

68. come] *followed by* [*obscure word*] *forse dice che vi sia* [*deleted*] R

69. 17 di febraro 20 et 30 di marzo] *underlined* R

toro non vogliono cessare dall'inquietarsi (con tutto che Sua Maestà resti sodisfatto non pare pretendano il rimedio se non il turbarsi), dica Vostra Reverentia a Sua Maestà che la supplico metta il remedio davero perché altrimenti la Compagna ognidì andarà in maggior rovina: et esso consiste in due cose: l'una che facci intendere a costoro chiaramente che la Sua Maestà dispiaccino simili uffici, et che dopo di tanti memoriali mandati in Roma et dati costì in Spagna non quietarsi, ma ritornare à suscitare humori mostra bene che c'è della passione et malignità, et però che mettano fine a simili maneggi.

La seconda è che noi giudichiamo necessario, perché già si vede che costoro non si quietano di cominciare a mutarne alcuni de capi fuori di Spagna, ma che non vogliono tentare cosa alcuna senza intendere la mente di Sua Maestà la quale veda certo che altrimenti mai haveva la Compagna riposo in Spagna, con grandissimo danno della disciplina, se non si tolgono queste radici et se lo giudica bene, dia quell'ordine che sarà servita perché non siamo impediti che io all' insistere perché non potendo in questo altro che la pace darò la parola mia a Sua Maestà se così comanda di non procedere a castigo contro costoro, mà di trattar li con ogni soavità se già non dessero nuova occasione, ma solo domandiamo di mutarli di luogo perché non possino nuocere et lascino respirare coteste povere provincie. Questo negocio è dell'importanza che Vostra Reverentia vede, et però gli lo raccomando quanto posso, et lo raccomandarò particularmente al Signore come non dubito che Vostra Reverentia anco farà.

Translation

To Madrid or Valladolid, for Fr Robert Persons, 12 June.

We rejoice in the Lord that the choice of the visitors was generally welcomed, as Your Reverence writes to us by yours of 28 April, in which the specific news that you give us of certain things cannot but be of help. Fr José de Acosta is more prudent, judicious and virtuous than the other one,[70] on whom suspicion falls that he had betrayed the former; however, there is no danger. The fact that it is he and Fr Gil, friends of 177,[71] will be of some help, as we hope in the Lord.

Towards the malcontents it is good to act with moderation, by administering the medicine at the right place and time; but it is not politic now, as Fr Porres says.[72] As for putting Luis de Mendoza in charge, that is beyond dispute, for he is not as satisfactory as we had hoped for.[73] With regard to Ribadeneira, we will recommend him to God; I truly believe that in these negotiations of ours he will have offered good services. Again, we can easily gather that Fr Porres is in Madrid. I am sorry about what Ribadeneira says, namely, that many opportunities were offered him from Rome via Fr Dionisio: he could expect nothing but flattering advances from that quarter, on the sole condition that *he was*

---

70. I.e., Diego de Avellaneda, who had originally been proposed.

71. 177 may be Pedro Fonseca, the visitor to Portugal. Fr Gil is Gil González Dávila, visitor to Castile and Toledo.

72. Francisco de Porres (1538–1621), rector of the Jesuit college in Madrid (1585–1591), formerly vice provincial of Toledo.

73. On Mendoza's unsuitability for the position of superior at Jesus del Monte, Alcalá, see Acquaviva's letter of 15 May (B16).

to change his residence from Toledo – but that was inevitable, given the things that have now been disclosed to the world.[74]

The business that Persons undertook with Fr Acosta and Fr Gil, of discussing a way to eradicate that aversion which the devil has been insinuating towards things to do with Rome, is of great importance and it will not be difficult to show the truth – in fact when it comes to the details, they are all lies.[75]

I have already mentioned through other letters how much I want Your Reverence to take care of your health. The three companions are by now in Genoa.[76] In fact, it has been a few days since the rector of Bologna wrote to inform us that they had passed through there.

The mediation that Persons was required to perform with the king was meant to enable the king to get clarity about the things contained in the memorials; however, the visitors can take care of that. No one expected a letter from His Majesty in favour of the Institute,[77] but only that he should write to the pope that he had gathered information about our business, that he was pleased by the Society, and would indeed recommend it to His Holiness. It would be good if this could be obtained without difficulty, but in any case, God Our Lord will answer for us, as we have come to expect from His infinite goodness. We are hopeful, both in this as in the two other things that we are dealing with here; all the more because as a result of many princes writing to His Holiness from Germany of the harvest that has come forth in those lands, and of the great harm that would come from altering the Institute as they understand I wanted to do, His Holiness has replied that he does not want to change anything.[78]

It is not necessary for those grave fathers to write a letter to be shown to Cardinal Carafa, nor does the pope care much about the memorials: nothing else is needed besides what Your Reverence and Fr Ribadeneira have written. Rather, if something is to be written, it had better be to Cardinal Deza,[79] although I do not see any great need.[80]

---

74. The manoeuvres of the malcontents against their Jesuit superiors were conducted in secrecy. It appears that Dionisio Vázquez (d. 28 March 1589) had tried to win Ribadeneira over.

75. Acquaviva refers to the suspicion that the malcontents harboured against the Jesuit curia in Rome, and their attempts to spread it.

76. Flack, Tancard and Gibbon: see Acquaviva's letter of 15 May (B16). By 22 July they were in Madrid.

77. The Society's "way of proceeding," under attack from the *memorialistas*.

78. Evidently there was some confusion in Jesuit circles about Acquaviva's intentions with regard to the Institute of the Society ("our way of proceeding"). On the one hand, he sought Philip's endorsement of Jesuit practice in Spain; on the other, the German princes were apprehensive that he would change the Institute.

79. Cardinals Pedro de Deza (1520–1600) and Antonio Carafa (1538–1591).

80. Three letters from Ribadeneira are mentioned in Persons's letter of 29 April (B15). Cardinals Carafa and Deza were influential in the papal curia in Rome: Carafa was prefect of the Sacred Congregation for the Execution and Interpretation of the Council of Trent, and Deza the grand inquisitor of the Roman Inquisition. He had been president of the Council of Valladolid but was now resident in Rome.

From our other letters Your Reverence must have gathered that we received yours of 17 February, and 20 and 30 March.[81]

I hear from a good source that the malcontents are not hoping to submit fresh memorials, since they have heard that the king is satisfied with our visitors. And because it is evident that they have no intention of giving up their agitation – in spite of the fact that His Majesty has made up his mind, it seems that they contemplate no remedy except to continue agitating – would Your Reverence please tell His Majesty that I implore him to provide for a remedy, otherwise day by day the Society will fall into more ruin: and this consists of two aspects: the first is, that it should be communicated to them that His Majesty is highly displeased with this type of business, and that it is now clearly evident – given that in Spain they are still not satisfied, after sending so many memorials to Rome, but rather continue to excite their feelings even more – that they are driven by passion and malice, so they should put an end to these kind of intrigues.

The second [aspect of the remedy] is one we believe necessary, because it is clear now that although they will not give up their idea of changing some of the leaders outside of Spain, they will not attempt anything before understanding His Majesty's intention: consequently, he should acknowledge that the Society will never find peace in Spain, with the greatest harm to its discipline, if this business is not taken out by the root. If he thinks it wise, then, he should sanction the arrangement by which we will not be prevented from standing firm;[82] for my part, since in this situation I can't but work towards peace, I will give His Majesty my word that if such are his orders, they will not be punished, but will actually be treated in the gentlest manner (so long as they do not look out for another opportunity [of causing unrest]), and only be sent to another location where they can cause no harm and from where they will let these poor provinces breathe. Your Reverence can see just how important this business is; indeed, I will pursue it as much as I can, and I will particularly commend it again to the Lord as I am sure Your Reverence will.

B19 To Joseph Creswell, [Madrid], 24 June 1589

> SOURCE: ABSI, Coll P II 479.
>
> HICKS: 79.
>
> EDITION: Pollen, *Miscellanea IX*, 19.
>
> NOTE: Persons's invitation to Creswell to send students from the English College, Rome may be the first mention in this correspondence of a plan to found an English college at Valladolid. For more details, he refers Creswell to Allen, who was concerned about the precarious state of the college at Rheims and may have been party to the decision to make new provision in Spain. He also asks for four Jesuits to be sent from Sicily to Andalusia.[83]
>
> Most likely in response to a letter from Persons written to Richard Barret, president of the English college at Rheims, after his audience with the king on 6 February (see the head-

---

81. See Acquaviva's letters of 17 April and 15 May (B11, B16).
82. Acquaviva wished to remove some of the malcontents in order to defuse the situation.
83. On this unidentified group, see also Acquaviva's letter of 4 September (B31).

notes to the putative letters to Allen and Barret, 17 February, B2, B5), three English students, Henry Floyd, John Blackfan and John Bosvile, left Rheims on 8 May. They sailed from Nantes to Bilbao, and travelled overland to Valladolid via Burgos, where they were briefly imprisoned. On arrival at Valladolid, they began attending lectures at the university and the Jesuit College of St Ambrose (*Blackfan Annals*, 4–13). Persons himself records these events in *A relation of the King of Spaines receiving in Valliodolid and in the Inglish College of the same town* (Antwerp, 1592), 9. See Hicks, *Seminaries*, part 3, 497–498; Williams, *St Alban's College*, chapter 1; and Edwards, 138–139.

Touching your schollers in the end of this sommer I could be content you sent either all or the principall of them this way —. All things goe wel here, though slowly. I know not how the affaires of the Society goe there, for that none write to me of it, and so I know not whether anything be further to be dealt heer with 101[84] or noe, with whome they tell me that I may perchance speake ere many daies. These distractions of Portugal, and some indisposition of the king's person, have hindred all other businesse heer for this month past. I pray you sollicit the despatch of those four of Ours in Sicily for Andaluzia &c. —. The rest you will understand by my good Cardinal &c. — Jun. 24, 1589.

You know the hand.

B20 To William Allen, Madrid, 24 June 1589

SOURCE: Persons to Creswell, 24 June (B19).
NOTE: This contained a more detailed account of Persons's activities and interests than was given to Creswell.

B21 From Claudio Acquaviva, 5 July 1589

SOURCE: ARSI, Tolet. 5/I, fol. 67r.
NOTE: This concerns the request of Richard Blount to join the Society of Jesus: Acquaviva sends him to Spain for Persons to decide. Blount, a student at the English College, Rome, since 1584, was ordained priest on 1 April 1589. Persons sent him to the English mission in late 1590 (see Persons's letters to Creswell and Barret, 4 and 7 November 1590, B84 and B86, and John Cecil's letter to Persons, 1 November 1591, B126), and he finally joined the Society in 1596. Blount and Richard Banks were the first two secular clergy admitted into the Society and allowed to complete their novitiate training in England. Acquaviva's reluctance to allow novices to complete their novitiate in England may explain why someone so interested in the Society did not enter until 1596 (Persons to Acquaviva, 19 March 1595, B264). On suspicions that the Society was recruiting the best students, see Leo Hicks, "The English College, Rome, and Vocations to the Society of Jesus, March, 1579–July, 1595," *AHSI* 3 (1934): 1–36. Blount later established himself at Scotney Castle, Sussex, and was appointed provincial in 1623. See Anstruther, 41; Foley, 3: 481–488; McCoog, *English and Welsh Jesuits*, 122; Morris, 1: 187–215; Murphy, 55.

84. Grene identifies this as the king of Spain.

This is one of only a small handful of letters Acquaviva sent to Spain in early July. Writing to the provincial, Gonzalo Dávila, Acquaviva notes (fol. 67v) that the courier bearing the letters from Spain written on 27 May had not yet arrived, and he appears to have taken advantage of Richard's departure to send this letter and four others to Madrid.

Al Padre Personio a 5 de Julio 89.

Il Rettore del Collegio Inglesse mi ha parlato intorno a Richardo lator della presente che parechi giorni serio desidera esser admesso nella Compagna et havendose il sudetto Rettore inclinato a mandarlo in Spagna accio possa esser recivutto dove alla Reverentia Vostra parera, mi è parso mandarlo de lei con una mia littera per il Padre Igidio Gonzalez, nelle quale gli advertisco che havendo prima il parer et information della Reverentia Vostra gli potrà ricever in una de coteste due provincie secondo che Vostra Reverentia giudicarà. Io ho fatto che Ricardo sia essaminato secondo la bulla di Sua Santità et mando a la Reverentia Vostra il parer del Rettore del Santo Andrea che gli ha examinatto. Vostra Reverentia lo potrà communicar al Padre Igidio, et insieme informarlo, et perché il Rettore del Inglesse scrivirà a Vostra Reverentia piu longo non dico altro che racomandarmi &c.

Translation

The Rector of the English College spoke to me about Richard, bearer of the present, that for several days he has earnestly desired to be admitted to the Society. Since the aforementioned Rector was inclined to send him to Spain so that he can be received where you see fit, it seemed wise to me to send him from here with a letter of mine to Father Gil González. In it, I tell him that once he has received Your Reverence's opinion and advice he will be able to receive him in one of these two provinces, as Your Reverence decides. I have made sure that Richard has been examined according to the bull of His Holiness, and I am sending Your Reverence the opinion of the Rector of Sant'Andrea, who has examined him. Your Reverence may communicate it to Father Gil, and at the same time inform him [of your decision]. And since the Rector of the English College will write to Your Reverence at greater length, I say no more except to commend myself [to your prayers and sacrifices].

B22 From Joseph Creswell, 5 July 1589

SOURCE: Acquaviva to Persons, 5 July (B21).

B23 To Claudio Acquaviva, 22 July 1589

SOURCE: Acquaviva to Persons, 4 September (B31).
NOTE: In this letter Persons reported on his successful audience with the king on 13 July, which reduced further the danger of external visitation (i.e., by non-Jesuits) of the Society in Spain and also authorized the founding of an English seminary in Valladolid (Hicks, *Seminaries*, part 3, 499).

B24 To Joseph Creswell, Madrid, 22 July 1589

> SOURCE: ABSI, Coll P II 484 (G) and 479 (G1), an abbreviated version.
> HICKS: 80.
> EDITION: Pollen, *Miscellanea IX*, 19.
> NOTE: The king has approved the founding of a seminary at Valladolid, and Persons is about to travel there to handle the enterprise. Tancard, Gibbons and Flack have arrived in Madrid.
>
> In accordance with Acquaviva's instructions in his letter of 17 April, William Flack immediately began working as Persons's amanuensis, for Grene notes that this letter was originally written in his hand.

Pax Christi.

It is not for want of health — Our friends be arrived hither, as you may see by this hand, in perfect health. I have sent the relation of the successe of the English army to my Lord Cardinal — Upon the 13th of this month I had very gratious audience of His Majesty. I have also obteined of the king letters in favour of the niew[85] Seminary to be founded att Valladolid, as also of other noblemen, who all greatly do favour that enterprize.[86] God prosper it to his honour. I am likewise to goe shortly to Valladolid about the founding of the saide Seminary — / — Madrid, 22 July 1589.

B25 To William Allen, Madrid, 22 July 1589

> SOURCE: Persons to Creswell, 22 July 1589 (B24).
> NOTE: Amongst other news, Persons gave Allen a report on English military successes. In May and June 1589, forces of the "English Armada" under Sir John Norris had modest success at Corunna and Puente del Burgo. In the Netherlands, Sir Francis Vere assumed successful command of the English army. These developments would have been of concern to Allen because of their likely effect on the condition of the English college at Rheims. See Hicks, *Seminaries*, part 3, 497.

B26 To Thomas Marshall, Madrid, 22 July 1589

> SOURCE: ABSI, Coll P II 479.
> HICKS: 81.
> EDITION: Pollen, *Miscellanea IX*, 19-20.
> NOTE: Persons added a postscript to a letter to Marshall from Charles Tancard, who wrote that "he had happily arrived in Madrid with his companions and was to be sent to Alcalá." Marshall had originally been designated as a companion to William Weston in 1584 but was sent to Rome instead. Grene notes, citing More, 21, that Marshall died in Rome on the very day this letter was posted (Anstruther, 220; McCoog, *English and Welsh Jesuits*, 239).

---

85. niew] G1; *not in* G

86. Blackfan mentions the duchess of Feria and Sir Francis Englefield (*Blackfan Annals*, 12-13).

My little father I most hartily salute you and all your good chickens there, you know whome I meane, &c. —

B27 To Don Juan Ruiz de Velasco, Valladolid, 5 August 1589

SOURCE: AGS, Est. Leg. 166, holograph, with the remains of a seal (= S).
HICKS: 82–85, with English translation.
NOTE: Juan Ruiz de Velasco (d. 1605), a member of the prominent Velasco family, to the main branch of which belonged Luis de Velasco (1511–1564), viceroy of New Spain, and the constables of Castile, was one of the king's valets or chamberlains. He is described as presenting the king daily with his books of devotion and portable oratory (Parker, 81). Persons wrote to him again in August 1593.

As a result of Persons's audience with the king on 13 July (see Persons to Creswell, 22 July, B24), the English students were given permission to reside in Valladolid, at the hospice of Saints Cosmas and Damian. The abbot-president of the parent monastery of St Clara, Don Alfonso de Mendoza, was initially opposed, but Ruiz de Velasco wrote to him from the royal court on Persons's behalf (Hicks, *Seminaries*, part 3, 499; Williams, *St Alban's College*, 7–8).

Alfonso de Mendoza's opposition was based on fear of the spread of heresy (*Blackfan Annals*, 13–14); later, he recorded the dreams of Lucrecia de León, an employee of Jane Dormer, duchess of Feria, a generous patron of the foundation at Valladolid. From 1590–1595 Lucrecia was put on trial by the Inquisition in Toledo. See María V. Jordan, "Competition and Confirmation in the Iberian Prophetic Community: The 1589 Invasion of Portugal in the Dreams of Lucrecia de León," in *Dreams, Dreamers, and Visions: The Early Modern Atlantic World*, ed. Ann Marie Plane and Leslie Tuttle (Philadelphia, 2013), 72–87.

When Persons arrived in Valladolid, accompanied by Brother Fabrizio Como, he found the students "in a truly unsuitable lodging, in the upper part of some house beneath the tiles in the blazing summer heat" (*Blackfan Annals*, 12–13, dating the arrival mid-August). As this letter makes clear, he hoped to be able to transfer them to the hospice, but the fears of the brothers there that this would threaten their livelihood led him to abandon this plan, even though the abbot was now in support, and he "ordered that another more appropriate residence be acquired". He had also to convince the city authorities that the English students were not infected with heresy, as the local inquisitor, Vigil, feared (Hicks, *Seminaries*, part 3, 500, citing Persons's *Informacion* of 1 September; see Persons to Allen, 14 September, B34).

The original three students from Rheims, Floyd, Bosville, and Blackfan, had been joined by Henry Sherrat and John Gillibrand, who decided to stay in Valladolid rather than continue on their intended journey to the English College, Rome. Also of their company were the English priests William Cowling and Francis Lockwood, and possibly also Gerard Clibburn, passing through Valladolid on their circuitous route from Rheims and Douai to England. See *Valladolid Registers*, xiii–xvii, 1–8; *Blackfan Annals*, 12–17; McCoog, *Building the Faith of St Peter*, 106–107; Edwards, 141.

The text is notable for the inclusion of several Italianisms, such as "termine" for "termino" and "holgosi" for "holgose".

Muchas gracias rendo a Vuestra Merced por las cartas que me embió con mi Compañero, y por tantos otros favores que no les puedo dezir. El termine de los negocios nuestros por acá, Vuestra Merced intenderá por carta del mismo Abad, el qual holgosi mucho con la di Vuestra Merced, y nos si ha mostrado muy favorable en esto negocio, aunque los confradres del Hospital de St Cosimus, donde ordinó Su Magestad que fuessen ricevidos los clerigos y estudiantes yngleses, le han hecho y hazen grandes contradictiones, por miedo como dize él, que no viniessen los yngleses con tiempo a participar de los fructus,[87] que ellos aora comen; aunque nosotros no pretendemos esto, se no solamente habitacion por algun tiempo para estudiar y para servir a los mismos Confradres en la eglisia, y a los pobres en el Hospital quando vernan (porque aora no les hai, ni tampoco[88] cama alguna para receivirles) con lavarles los pies y hazerles otras obras de caridad que sí suelen hazer[89] en los buenos hospitales. Pero los dichos confradres son tan agenos de esto, que no lo quieren oyrlo, y assi nosotros que no queremos plitear ni hazernos odiosos acá con esta contradiction, huvieramos dexado todo el tratado del dicho Hospidal, se no fuera que el Abad queria enformar primero Su Magestad de lo que passa, y nosotros deseamos una sola de dos cosas, con bien saber, o que Su Magestad, vistas las razones del Abad, ordeni de nuevo que no ostante la contradiction de los Confradres, se nos dé la habitacion que hai en el dicho Hospital riservando solamente por los Confradres los aposientos que parescieren necessarios al Abbad o al presidente, o a él y al Abad juntamente, por los ministerios de la Confradia; o, se a Su Magestad paresciere mejor por las razones ya dichas y por haver paz,[90] que dexemos el Hospital, que entonçes si encomiende al Abad que nos[91] ayude por un'otra via, que él mismo[92] ha escripto al Señor Garcia Loaysa, y es, darnos parte de los fructus que sobran cada año[93] de diversos Hospidales y confradias acá, por qualquiera maniera que fuera, bastaría a estos siervos de Dios, que fueren ayudados a sostentarsi por algun tiempo.

    Y con esto, no offereceiendosi otro per aora, acabaré con rogar Dios nuestro Signor, que conserve siempre Vuestra Merced en su santissima gracia, supplicandole que en lo que huviere lugar nos[94] ayude para procurar breve determinacion y rispuesta en esto negocio nuestro, que no suffre mucha dilacion por la necessidad que padecemos de casa.

    Valliadolid al 5 de Agosto 1589.
        Rob. Personio.

    [*Addressed:*] A Juan Ruiz de Velasco de la camera del Rey nuestro Sgr Sto Lorenzo

---

    87. fructus] S; *properly* fructos
    88. tampoco] *interlined* S
    89. hazer] *interlined* S
    90. y por haver paz] *interlined* S
    91. que nos] *interlined above* de ayudarnos [*deleted*] S
    92. mismo] *interlined* S
    93. cada año] *interlined* S
    94. nos] *interlined* S

Translation

I am very grateful to Your Grace for the letters which you sent with my socius[95] and for other favours too numerous to mention. The position our negotiations here have reached, Your Grace will gather from the letter from the abbot himself. He was much mollified by Your Grace's letter, and has shown us much kindness in this affair, though the brethren of the hospice of St Cosmas (in which His Majesty gave orders that the English clerics and students were to be received) have raised and are raising great opposition to it, being afraid, according to him, that in the course of time the English might come to share in the revenues which they now enjoy. We however have no pretensions of that sort, but wish only for a place to dwell in for a time in order to study and to serve the brethren themselves in the church and the poor in the hospice (when they come there; for at present there are none of them, not even a bed prepared to receive them) by washing their feet and doing the other charitable offices that are usually done in good hospitals. But the said brethren are so averse to this that they won't hear of it; and so, as we do not wish for contention or to make ourselves unpopular here in consequence of this rebuff, we would have given up having anything to do with the said hospice if it were not that the abbot desired to report the state of affairs to His Majesty. We for our part desire only one of two alternatives, namely: either that His Majesty, in view of the abbot's representations, should give express orders that despite the opposition of the brethren we are again to be given what accommodation there is in the hospice, reserving for the brethren only the rooms which the abbot or the president, or both jointly, think necessary for carrying on the work of the brotherhood; or else, if His Majesty thinks it better that we leave the hospice for the reasons mentioned above and for the sake of peace, that in that case he should direct the abbot to assist us by another method. What this is he has himself written to Señor García Loaysa:[96] it consists in giving us a share in the revenue which is left over each year from various brotherhoods and hospices here. In any case it would be sufficient if these servants of God were helped to support themselves for a time.

And now as nothing else suggests itself for the moment I will end by beseeching God, our Lord, ever to preserve Your Grace with His most gracious favour, and begging

---

95. A Jesuit term for official companion and assistant, i.e., Brother Fabrizio Como.

96. García de Loaysa y Girón (1534–1599) was tutor to the prince Philip. Following the royal visit to the English college in Valladolid in August 1592, he was entrusted with a souvenir manuscript of emblems and poems connected with the visit, to be presented to the prince: see the speech to Philip II (B150). In 1598, as the recently appointed archbishop of Toledo, he administered the last rites to King Philip II (Kamen, 314–315; see Persons to Jiménez, 18 May 1597, B377). He commissioned the writing and publication of Juan de Mariana's *Historiae de rebus Hispaniae* (Toledo, 1592) and assisted in the publication of Mariana's *De rege et regis institutione* (Toledo, 1599); see Domínguez, *Radicals in Exile*, 194, who relates Mariana's ideas on church and state to Persons's *Memorial for the Reformation of England under her Next Catholic Prince*.

you, in so far as you have opportunity, to help us to get a quick decision and answer about this affair of ours, so that it may not suffer much delay, seeing that we are in such need of a place to live.

    Valladolid, August 1589.
        Robert Persons

[*Addressed:*] To Juan Ruiz de Velasco of the chamber of the king our lord, San Lorenzo.[97]

B28 From Claudio Acquaviva, Rome, 7 August 1589

    SOURCE: ARSI, Tolet. 5/I, fols. 72v (main text) and 74r–v (addition).

    NOTE: Acquaviva is surprised that Persons has not written by either of the last two posts, i.e., 26 May and 24 June (when he wrote to Creswell from El Escorial and from Madrid): the most recent letter to Acquaviva was that of 29 April (B15), to which Acquaviva replied on 12 June (B18). This would also explain why there is no letter from Acquaviva to Persons in July. Another letter is promised, of which no copy appears to have survived.

    A likely reason for Acquaviva's agitation is his anxiety over the continued threat of an external visitation: the possibility that the Society in Spain would be investigated by the Inquisition rather than the Society's own visitors, whom the king had endorsed. He instructs Persons to thank the king for approving of the Jesuit visitors and to plead with him not to allow the visitation to become a public scandal. In the additional note he asks Persons to preempt any adverse influences on the king in this regard.

    Unusually for this open register, textual additions (in a different hand) have been supplied in the margin; the translation should be treated with caution.

P. Roberto Personio. Agosto 7.

    Mi son maravigliato che la Reverentia Vostra non mi havia scritto né con questo ordinario, né col passato; con tutto ciò intendo che per gratia de Dio si trova bene, et so anchora che non manca di fare alla giornata li buoni ufficii che bisogna. Adesso occorre di far uno con Sua Maestà il che farà senza comunicarlo con niuno. La Reverentia Vostra havrà intesso quello che delli nuovi visitatori mi é stato scritto: hora secondo questo vorrei che se la cosa sta secreta, Vostra Reverentia solamente dica a Sua Maestà, che havendoci favorito de contentarsi che li nostri Padri visiteno la compagnia si serva anchora di fare come loro intendano la mente sua, et quello che desidera et comanda, acciò che loro meglio possino far la voluntà sua, et anchora dargli quella informatione che esso vorrà delle cose che li visitatori forastieri fano, et rimediano. Ma se la cosa delli visitatori fusse scoperta gli potrà agiungier che io mi protesto abanti'l tribunale et giudicio de Dio del gravissimo danno che con questa visita si farà in tutta la compagnia, et scarico la conciencia mia con haverlo representato alla Maestà Sua tante volte, et poiché insino a qui ha mostrato tener sodisfatione di quello che la compagnia ha fatto por il servitio suo, et rimedio delle cose, si deve contentar di lassarci proceder con quella pace et quiete che hormai cominciano ad haver le cose nostre fin qui tanto piene di turbatione et inquietudine et con tante firme de tute le provincie.

---

    97. The royal site of El Escorial.

Non altro in questa che racomandarmi alle orationi et Santi Sacrificii della Reverentia Vostra. De Roma 7 d'Agosto 1589.

[PS] adelante tiene otro capitulo que se anadio a esta.

Añadido al Padre Personio Agosto 7:

Et si altri di fuora come confessor o altri voglero farlo a Sua Maestà il contrario con dire che è obligato in concienza a farlo passar inanzi,[98] pare che assai possia scaricar la sua concienza con credere che noi cognosciamo meglio lo stato della Compagnia che maneggiamo le cosse de dentro che non fa il confessore o altri che le sanno per sugestione de quatro tentati; et si per prima non le havessemo conosciuto,[99] almeno è certo che da potanti rumori et depoi di haver noi dichiarato Visitatori almeno le andariamo discoprendo, et trovatoli non siamo di così grosse conscienze, ne si preme cosi poco il ben della Compagnia che nolle havessimo a rimidiar. Vostra Reverentia non lassi di dirlo a Sua Maestà con quella humildà et reverenza che conviene si bene, ma con molta ciareza perché rialmente yo temo che si pur va inanzi, il che non credo, sia qualche judicio di idio [come] acade delle cose di numerar il populo, nulla quale per molto che Joab dicesse il Rey David volse andar inanzi, et Dio lo permisse perché era sdenato et voleva castigar il populo. Vostra Reverentia sia più leberal di scriverci tanto più che spero havere[100] habuto l'ayuto de mei charissimi.

Translation

To Fr Robert Persons, 7 August.

I am surprised that Your Reverence has not written to me either by this courier or by the last. Nevertheless, I assume that by the grace of God all is well, and I am sure that you do not fail to perform daily those tasks that are needed. Now there is another that needs to be carried out concerning His Majesty, which you should please do without communicating it to anyone. Your Reverence will have been informed in the mean time what was written to me about the new visitors – now in accordance with this, I would prefer that if the matter is to remain secret, would Your Reverence please tell His Majesty only that since he has granted permission to our fathers' proposed visitation, we reserve the right to act according to what they understand of his desires and instructions, so that they may, as far as possible, do his will, and also give him whatever information he wants about what the external visitors are doing, and deal with queries. But if the affair of the visitors were to be made public you have my permission to add that I am protesting both to the tribunal and to divine justice about the very grievous damage that may be done to the entire Society by this visitation, and I discharge my conscience by having explained this to His Majesty so many times. And as up to now he has shown his satisfaction with what the Society has done in his service, and in putting things to right, he should be content to let us proceed with that peace and tranquillity which our affairs, so long full of such turmoil and restlessness, now begin to enjoy, and so much good will coming from all the provinces.

    98. inanzi] *this ed.*; inanze *R*
    99. non ... conosciuto] *this ed.*; no ... conoscuto *R*
    100. havere] *this ed.*; havre *R*

Nothing remains for this letter except to commend myself to Your Reverence's holy prayers and sacrifices. From Rome, 7 August 1589.

[PS] Another item to be added to this will follow.

Added to the letter to Fr Persons, 7 August:

And if others from outside, such as a confessor or others, try to influence His Majesty to do the opposite by saying that he is obliged in conscience to let [this measure] go ahead, it seems that he would discharge his conscience better by believing that we have a better understanding of the state of the Society: that we handle matters from within, unlike a confessor whose knowledge is based only on a few persons who have been corrupted. Even if we had not been aware of these problems at first, at least it is certain that from powerful rumours and then from having appointed visitors we will be able to unveil them. Once we have exposed them, our consciences are not so crude, nor is the well-being of the Society of so little account, that we would not seek to remedy them. Your Reverence should not hesitate to say as much to His Majesty, with all due humility and reverence, but with great clarity, because I fear that if it goes forward (which I do not think), it is some divine judgement, as occurred in the case of numbering the people: despite Joab's words,[101] King David went ahead with it, and God persuaded him because he was tired of his people's behaviour and wanted to punish them. Would Your Reverence be so kind as to write to us even more, I hope to have obtained the help of my most beloved.

B29 To Claudio Acquaviva, Valladolid, mid-August 1589

SOURCE: Acquaviva to Persons, 2 October 1589 (B35).

NOTE: Persons informs Acquaviva of the initial tensions in Valladolid over the establishment of an English seminary. See Persons to Juan Ruiz de Velasco, 5 August (B27), headnote.

B30 To Joseph Creswell, Valladolid, mid-August 1589

SOURCE: Persons to Creswell, 14 September 1589 (B33).

NOTE: In his letter of 14 September, Persons mentions that he had written by the previous post.

B31 From Claudio Acquaviva, Rome, 4 September 1589

SOURCE: ARSI, Tolet. 5/I, fol. 76v.

NOTE: Acquaviva has now received news of Persons's successful audience with Philip on 13 July, presumably from a (now lost) letter probably written on 22 July (B23).

Acquaviva once again urges Persons to make the king aware of the likely dangers of sanctioning an external visitation of the Society, especially if it should encourage the malcontents. He hopes that Persons will be able to facilitate the transfer of some of these.

101. 2 Sam. 24.

P. Roberto Personio Settembre 4.

    Mi son molto consolato d'intendere per quella di Vostra Reverentia la buona audienza che ha havutto de Sua Maestà, che essendosi portata la Reverentia Vostra con la prudenza et efficaci ragioni che vego per la relatione mandatami da lei, non dubito che per tutti sia stata molto a proposito et certo io penso che li visitatori fuorastieri non siano per darci più nissun fastidio, perché altramente non havrebbe detto il Re che etiam dio[102] per l'avenire saria consolata la Compagnia, con tutto ciò poiché la cosa delli visitatori è di già tanto publica. Vorrei che la Reverentia Vostra come nella passata gli scrisse, parlase con Sua Maestà et con poche parole gli refrescasse la memoria con le ragioni già allegate per mostrare li gravi danni et inconvenienti che sarà per la Compagnia esser visitata per forastieri, massime in questa occasione che con beneplacito di Sua Maestà hano cominciato a visitare li nostri visitatori, ma in caso che per esser cotesta visita delli vescovi commune all'altre religioni non giudicasse il Re che la nostra fusse eccetuata, Vostra Reverentia facia instanza con Sua Maestà accioché la Compagnia non sia sola ne la prima ad essere visitata, poiché attese le cose passate sareve per essa gran nota, et cagione di non picola infamia: non vego per che il illustrissimo Cardinale se possia lamentare del'uficio fatto col Re acciò si toglia la prohibitione fatta alli nostri, pur mi pare che la Reverentia Vostra ha, prudentemente acomodandosi a cotesti padri, che come la cosa riesce[103] importa poco, che sia per ordine del Re, o per beneplacito de cotesti signori del sant'uficio.

    Si scrive che vengano quanto prima quelli padri de Lorena et quelli ancho de Sicilia, et procurarò che con ogni brebità si spediscano. Dio ci dia la buona ocasione che Vostra Reverentia dice acciò possiamo mutare alcuni de quelli che meglio[104] starebbeno fuera che non dentro de Spagna. Non altro per questa che racomandarmi alla sue orationi et Santi Sacrificii. De Rome 4 de Settembre.

    [PS] Yo escrivio al Reverende Visitator quanto favorisca le cose del seminario in tutto quello che potrà, e credo che lo fara, perché nelle lettre che lui me scrive vego io che affetione che porta a la Reverentia Vostra et alle cose de Inglaterra.

    [PPS] Mi dicharo più in quello che di mano mia et anco in quando gli scrivo intorno all'ufficio che sia da[105] far con Sua Maestà et è che prima faccia l'ufficio acciò il Visitatori forastieri non ci visitano, et di questo procuri cavar parola et certezza di Sua Maestà. Ma quando questo non riesca all'hora procuri che noi non siamo li primi, ne soli ad esser visitati.

    [*Addressed in margin*:] P. Roberto Settembre 4.

Translation

To Fr Robert Persons, 4 September.

    I am very heartened to learn from Your Reverence's letter how well your audience went with His Majesty: that Your Reverence acted with the prudence and sound reasoning which I recognize from the account sent to me. I have no doubt that in everything you were very

---

102. etiam dio] R; *possibly Italianization of* etiam diu; *modern Italian* exiandio
103. riesce] *or* riesca R
104. meglio] *this ed.*; meglo R
105. sia da] *obscure* R

apropos and I think for sure that we are unlikely to be troubled by external visitors for the present, because otherwise the king would not have said that the Society should take comfort for the future as well, given that the business of the visitors is already so public.[106] I would like Your Reverence, as I wrote to you in my last letter, to speak with His Majesty and in a few words refresh his memory with the reasons already alleged to show the grievous harms and inconveniences which would arise if the Society were visited by outsiders, especially on such an occasion when our own visitors have already begun their visitation, with His Majesty's blessing. If, however, given that the visitation carried out by the bishops is something common to other religious orders,[107] the king might feel that our own should not be made an exception, would Your Reverence please urge His Majesty that the Society should not be the only one or the first to be visited. That is because, based on what has happened in the past, this will be widely noticed, and occasion no little disgrace. I do not see how His Eminence the cardinal[108] can possibly decry the fact that we have negotiated with the king, to take away the prohibition laid on Ours: it seems to me that Your Reverence has prudently settled it with the very same fathers, and that it is of little consequence how this matter has been resolved, whether by order of the king, or the blessing of those same lords of the Holy Office.

I have it in writing that those fathers from Lorraine and those also of Sicily are coming as soon as possible,[109] and I will make sure that they are sent with all haste. May God provide a good opportunity, as Your Reverence says, to be able to transfer some of those [malcontents], that they should rather stay outside Spain than within her borders. Nothing else remains for this letter except to commend myself to your prayers and holy sacrifices. From Rome, 4 September.

[PS] I have written to the Reverend Visitor[110] how much he should favour the affairs of the seminary in all that he can, and I believe that he will do so, because in the letters that he writes to me I can see the affection that he feels towards Your Reverence and all the affairs of England.

[PPS] I will say more of the matter in hand in addition to what I have written about your brief with His Majesty: and it is that first you urge the necessity that the external visitors should not visit us, and in this regard obtain the word and assurance of His Majesty. But if you do not succeed, at least ensure that we are not the first, nor the only ones to be visited.

B32 To Claudio Acquaviva, Valladolid, 14 September, 1589

SOURCE: Acquaviva to Persons, 31 October 1589 (B38).
HICKS: 86.
NOTE: This letter, presumably responding to Acquaviva's of 7 August (B28), contained news of the improved state of the seminary at Valladolid since the initial tensions with the hos-

106. This appears to mean that the Jesuit visitation had already become common knowledge, since Acosta and González Dávila had begun to tour the provinces.
107. I.e., an additional general visitation of religious orders envisaged by the Inquisition.
108. Probably Cardinal Gaspar de Quiroga y Vela, the head of the Inquisition.
109. There are several references to Jesuits travelling from Sicily to Andalusia in 1589.
110. Gil González Dávila.

pice. John Cecil had joined the group of students sent from Rome by William Allen. The first members of the college were admitted on 1 September.

B33 To Joseph Creswell, Valladolid, 14 September, 1589

> SOURCE: ABSI, Coll P II 484, Grene's partial transcript.
> HICKS: 86.
> EDITION: Pollen, *Miscellanea IX*, 20.
> NOTE: About to return to Madrid from Valladolid, Persons reports on the progress of the seminary at Valladolid, and the postings of Tancard, Flack, and Gibbons. William Flack was already acting as Persons's amanuensis and would take up a position at Valladolid. Richard Gibbons was posted to Portugal but was recalled to Valladolid later in the year to serve as prefect of studies (*Valladolid Registers*, xvii; see also *Blackfan Annals*, 22–23, and McCoog, *Building the Faith of St Peter*, 108, 110).

I wrott to you by the last ordinary — Since which we have nothing more then this, that the Seminary niewly begunn is now setled, albeit not without great adoe, as you shal understand by a certain *Relation*,[111] which I am sending to my Lord Cardinal. — I intend to departe tomorrow morning towards the Court, and from thence to Madrid, there to despatch some businesse, and see what further good may be done amongst good folkes for the better sustentation and help of this our Seminary &c. — Charles[112] is att Alcala — to end his Divinity. William Flack is to be heer in Valladolid for Minister in the English Seminary; and F. Gibbons, who goeth with me from hence to Madrid, shal from thence — goe — into Portugal &c.

B34 To William Allen, Valladolid, 14 September 1589

> SOURCE: Persons to Creswell, 14 September (B33).
> NOTE: Persons sent Allen a copy of a work he calls "a certain *Relation*." This may refer to the *Informacion que da el Padre Personio ... acerca ... del Seminario ... en Valladolid*, dated 1 September, which was printed at the end of Persons's *Relacion de algunos martyrios* (Madrid, 1590; *ARCR*, 1: no. 894). Persons may have sent Allen a manuscript version of the *Informacion*, or an advance copy of the longer *Relacion*. To publicize the foundation, he recounted the history of the seminaries founded by Allen, explained the reason for the arrival of the students from Rheims, and answered objections to the new foundation. See Berta Cano Echevarría and Ana Sáez-Hidalgo, introduction to *The Fruits of Exile: Emblems and Pamphlets from the English College at Valladolid* (London, 2009), xxix–xxxi; Pollen, *Miscellanea IX*, 2; Hicks, *Seminaries*, part 3, 501–502; and Williams, *St Alban's College*, 7–8 n26.
> Alternatively, the text sent to Allen may be a separate work, of which traces may be found in Persons's *A relation of the King of Spaines receiving in Valliodolid* (Antwerp, 1592), 9–12. It is also alluded to in the *Relacion de un Sacerdote Ingles ... de la venida de Su Magestad al colegio*

---

111. See headnote to the next item.
112. *G inserts in brackets* Tancard

de los Ingleses (Madrid, 1592), abbreviated in D. Yepes, *Historia particular de la persecucion de Inglaterra* (Madrid, 1599), 746–764. Persons's *Relation* seems also to have been used by Henry More in his account of the founding of the college in his *Historia*, 156–159 (Edwards, More, 203–208). Cf. *Blackfan Annals*, 14–15.

B35 From Claudio Acquaviva, Rome, 2 October 1589

SOURCE: Tolet. 5/I, fols. 85v–86r.

NOTE: This is addressed to Valladolid, presumably responding to a letter written in mid-August; although Persons left for Madrid on 15 September (see his letter to Creswell of 14 September, B33), he was back again on 25 October and travelled frequently between the two cities. Acquaviva responds to news of the initial difficulties with accommodation and approves of the decision to rent a house for the seminary instead of remaining at the hospice where they were not welcome. He has written to González Dávila, as visitor to Toledo and Castile, to provide additional staff.

This letter, written in Italian amongst other letters in Spanish, appears to have been particularly badly copied, and then corrected and augmented. The postscript shows the importance Acquaviva attached to the diplomatic work Persons was doing.

P. Roberto Personio in Vagladolid, Ottobre 2.

Non havrei voluto che la cosa del seminario cominciasse con lite et contraditione, massimamente non essendo quel luogo del[113] hospidale tanto commodo, et io per me credo che per adesso et ancho per l'avenire saria meglio pigliar al affitto qualche buona casa come Vostra Reverentia dice che vuol fare, et sarà più commoda stando tanto apresso del nostro collegio.

Benché qua si trova dificoltà in pigliar carico de governar il seminario come Vostra Reverentia dimanda pur ci o'parso de non mancar a la natione et al Signor Cardinale[114] in questo particolare, ma fare quello che esso commanda et Vostra Reverentia desidera,[115] si per esser tale la presente necessità, et l'opera tanto degna d'esser favorita, come per intender ha Sua Maestà gustarà che li nostri havino la cura come Vostra Reverentia dice, onde io scrivo al Padre Egidio Gonzalez che in questo agiute dando duoi o al più tre delli nostri che attendano a governar il seminario nella maniera che alla Reverentia Vostra pararà: che questo numero mi pare che bastarà servendosi de forastieri per altri ufficii come ancho si fà qui[116] nel seminario Inglesse. Non altro in questo che racomandarmi alli Santi Sacrificii et orationi della Reverentia Vostra. De Roma, 2 d'otobre, 1589.

[PS] Noi non manchiamo[117] poi con le provinciali di tener racconto al Signore i negotii che Vostra Reverentia tratta, et i comuni; piaccia alla Sua Divina Bontà di darci presto et desiderato comperimento.[118]

113. del ... cominciasse ... del] dil ... comincasse ... dil R
114. Sor Cardinale] *interlined above* Pre Personio [*deleted*] R: *apparently an example of careless copying*
115. commanda et V.R. desidera] *interlined below* vuole [*deleted*] R
116. qui] *followed by* in Roma [*deleted*] R
117. manchiamo] *replaces* mancaremo R
118. *Postscript added in the same hand as the earlier corrections in R.*

Translation

To Fr Robert Persons in Valladolid, 2 October.

I would have preferred that the business of the seminary should not begin with strife and contradiction, particularly since the place is not very well suited to accommodation; for my part I feel that both for now and the future it would be better to rent the decent kind of house Your Reverence says you have in mind, and it will be more convenient, being located so close to our college.[119]

Although you are finding it difficult to undertake the burden of governing the seminary there as Your Reverence would want, in such a way as not to fail to meet the needs of the nation and the Lord Cardinal in this particular,[120] still, let us do what he instructs and Your Reverence desires, such is the present necessity, and the work is so greatly worthy of favour – as it is clear that His Majesty would prefer that Ours have the responsibility, as Your Reverence says. Consequently, I am writing to Fr Gil González to ask him to help in this by providing two or three of Ours to attend to the running of the seminary in a manner that seems good to Your Reverence. It seems to me that this is a sufficient number of foreigners[121] to serve in various functions, such as are also performed here in the English seminary. No more in this, except to commend myself to Your Reverence's prayers and holy sacrifices. From Rome, 2 October 1589.

[PS] Through our provincials we shall not fail to keep the Lord [Cardinal] updated about the business which Your Reverence is dealing with, and also that which is of common interest. May it please His Divine Goodness speedily to grant the outcome we desire.

B36 To Claudio Acquaviva, El Escorial, 14 October 1589

SOURCE: Acquaviva to Persons, 27 November (B41).
NOTE: In this letter, Persons may have suggested that the correspondence could now be conducted in Spanish since he had mastered the language.

B37 To Joseph Creswell, El Escorial, 14 October 1589

SOURCE: ABSI, Coll P I 305, Grene's note.
HICKS: 87.

[*Grene writes:*] From the Escurial 14 October 1589 to F. Cresswell, Rome and many other letters this same yeare containe matters only about the seminary of Valladolid &c.

119. Persons rented a house in the Calle Don Sancho, close to the Jesuit college of St Ambrose.

120. Acquaviva seems to allude to the conflicting interests affecting the seminary, between the needs of the Spanish nation and the expectations of Cardinal Allen, whom Persons hoped would be given oversight over the seminary (see his letter to Joseph Creswell, 9 December 1589, B43). Alternatively, "nation" (here, *natione*), often used to denote a local community of foreigners, could refer to the English nation in Valladolid and possible tensions with a Spanish cardinal. Similarly, it is not clear which Spanish cardinal is referred to in the postscript.

121. I.e., non-English Jesuits (priests or lay brothers).

B38 From Claudio Acquaviva, Rome, 31 October 1589

SOURCE: ARSI, Tolet. 5/I, fol. 88r.

NOTE: This appears to be a reply to Persons's letter of 14 September (B32). Acquaviva is relieved that the initial tensions in Valladolid have been resolved but asks Persons to provide guidance to the visitors in their dealings with the king.

P. Roberto Personio, Ottobre 31.

Mi son molto consolato d'intender per quella della Reverentia Vostra che la cosa del seminario havia si bene riuscito, del[122] che non si potea dubitare poi che quantunche fallere delle contraditioni, col favor de Sua Maestà et l'agiuto de tanti Signori si doveano superare, et io penso che sia più commodo perseverar nel sito et casa che hanno pigliato a pisione, che non contrastar col hospedale, ma in questo mi remetto all Reverentia Vostra che da vicino[123] meglio vederà quello che conviene.

Molto importa che li nostri visitatori dieno sodisfatione a Sua Maestà, et gli facino intender quel che fano come io aviso loro, dando loro un poco d'instructione, perché altrimenti non si cavarebbe dalla loro visita che li visitatori forastieri non mettano la mano nelle cose nostre. La persona per il cui mezzo questo si deve far conviene sia Vostra Reverentia per esser sì grato a Sua Maestà, et per altre cause. Si che desidero che in questo la Reverentia Vostra si adopere con ogni diligenza et solicitudine quando li visitatori gli darano aviso de quello che convenga fare, poiché vede quanto alla Compagnia importe. In quello che al Padre Ricardo toca mi remetto al parer della Reverentia Vostra, nelli cui sacrifici et orationi mi racomando. De Roma. 31 d'ottobre.

[PS] Si ben io intendelo quello che la Reverentia Vostra mi scrive del Padre Egidio, nientedimeno ho havuto de intenderlo per letra sua, et certo è che la persona del sudetto &c. sia de grande importanza, come Vostra Reverentia dice, et della sua fidelità et amore verso di me non dubito punto, anzi so bene quanto la persona del Padre Egidio ci importa in coteste bande.[124]

Translation

To Fr Robert Persons, 31 October.

I am much encouraged to learn from Your Reverence's letter that the state of the seminary has improved, such that there can be no further doubt but that, although it may encounter setbacks, with His Majesty's favour and the support of such great lords it ought to succeed. I think that it will go forward more agreeably in the site and house which they

---

122. del] dil R
123. vicino] *replaces* prossima R
124. This additional material is entered in the margin following the first paragraph of the main text.

have taken for boarding, which avoids a clash with the hospice – but in this I defer to Your Reverence who can see close at hand what is suitable.

It is very important that our visitors give satisfaction to His Majesty, and make him understand what they are doing, according to my advice; I am giving them a little instruction because otherwise he would not grasp, from their visitation, that the external visitors should not meddle with our affairs. It would be best if the person by means of whom this should happen were Your Reverence as you are so well liked by His Majesty, and for other reasons. I would like Your Reverence in this instance to use all diligence and solicitude when the visitors advise him what is best for him to do, so that he sees just how important this is for the Society. As for what concerns Fr Richard,[125] I leave that to Your Reverence, as seems best – to whose sacrifices and prayers I commend myself. From Rome, 31 October.

[PS] I hope I have a good understanding of what Your Reverence writes to me about Fr Gil,[126] even though I had to infer it from your letter; still, it is certain that the aforesaid person is of great importance, as Your Reverence says, and of his faithfulness and love towards me I have not the slightest doubt; indeed I well know how important for us the figure of Fr Gil is in these particular regions.

B39 To Claudio Acquaviva, Madrid, 11 November 1589

SOURCE: Acquaviva to Persons, 24 December 1589 (B44).

NOTE: Persons returned to Valladolid on 25 October, in company with Bartolomé de Sicilia, who was to be the first rector of the new college. By 1 October John Fixer, Thomas Stillington, and Thomas Lovelace had arrived in Valladolid from Rheims as potential professors. Persons then travelled back to Madrid, to consult the king.

B40 To Joseph Creswell, Madrid, 11 November 1589

SOURCE: ABSI, Coll P II 498, Grene's partial transcript, introduced "de Urbe Madrito."
HICKS: 87, with English translation.
EDITION: Pollen, *Miscellanea IX*, 20.
NOTE: Grene concludes with the comment "parvi momenti" (insignificant), illustrating how little he was interested in the seminary.

[*Grene writes:*] Aliquid scribit de Seminario Valisoletano, quod adhuc satis tenuem habet fundationem; et de modo agendi P. Cresswelli non admodum grato de quo alias saepe, de viaticis &c.

Translation

He has something to say about the seminary at Valladolid, which as yet has somewhat slender means of support: also about Fr Creswell's way of doing things, which do not

125. Richard Blount (see Acquaviva to Persons, 5 July 1589, B21) or Richard Gibbons.
126. What Persons might have implied about González Dávila is obscure, but perhaps he was diffident about involving the visitor in the details of the new foundation.

please him too well and about which he often writes in other letters: and about travelling expenses &c.

B41 From Claudio Acquaviva, Rome, 27 November 1589

SOURCE: ARSI, Tolet. 5/I, fol. 101v.

NOTE: Probably in response to the missing letter of 14 October (B36), Acquaviva feels Persons is ready to receive letters in Spanish. He is confident now that the danger of external visitation has receded, but wants Persons to persuade the king of the necessity of transferring some of the malcontents. He also needs Persons to ensure that the visitors report truthfully to the king (see Acquaviva's letter of 20 March 1590, B54, when the report was imminent).

This letter reflects Acquaviva's fear that the college at Valladolid would remove Persons from Madrid, where he was so badly needed. He hopes that Gil González Dávila, to whom he had written at the beginning of October (Acquaviva to Persons, 2 October, B35) and again by this very post (Acquaviva to Gil González, 27 November, ARSI, Cast. 6, fols. 55v–57r), would, as visitor to Castile (May 1589–August 1590), provide a rector for the college. Gil González may already have intervened, because Pedro de Guzmán replaced Bartolomé de Sicilia on 26 November.

De Sicilia may have been recalled to Madrid because of court politics. It appears, from an obscure reference at the end of the letter, that the inquisitor Francisco Dávila y Guzmán (1548–1606; created cardinal 1596) had laid a charge against him ("lo de Sicilia"). According to Blackfan he was a royal favourite, "brought up at court before he entered the Society," and there "he shone with no little brilliance." In subsequent years he was to create trouble by campaigning vigorously for the college (Acquaviva to Persons, 8 June 1592, B145), and there may be some hint of aggression in the report that on arrival in Valladolid on 25 October he had brought royal letters instructing that the hospice be handed over to the English: an exigency that Persons decided not to pursue (*Blackfan Annals*, 18–19).

P. Roberto Personio. Noviembre 27.

Vuestra Reverencia se muestra tan aprovechado en la lengua española que tiene raçon de querer que le escrivamos en ella. Mucho he consolado de entender por la copia de la del Padre Gil Gonçalez[127] quanto dios nuestro Señor ayuda las buenas diligencias de Vuestra Reverencia como lo veo por el buen sucesso que tienen todas las que hizo con Su Magestad que por ser de tanta importançia para la Compañia las estimamos en lo que es raçon y le agradecemos mucho el zelo, fidelidad y cuydado con que a esta acude y segun la respuesta de Su Magestad. Pareçeme que ay muy bastante raçon para creer que las visitas de los nuestros podran continuar sin temor de que se les atajen.

Yo aviso al Padre Gil Gonçalez que provea el Seminario de un buen rector y que en todo lo posible sea ayudado de los nuestros, porque quanto aquello menos necessidad tubiere de la presencia de Vuestra Reverencia más asistencia podra haçer en Madrid. La qual deseo[128]

---

127. por la copia de la del Padre Gil Gonçalez] *added in the margin*
128. deseo] *this ed.;* de R *(truncated at the end of the line)*

que sea las más continua y ordinaria que sea possible, especialmente que yo he dado orden a los visitadores que, haviendo de dar notiçia a Su Magestad de lo que haçen en la visita para que se satisfaga de que se proçede con verdad, embien a Vuestra Reverencia los recaudos para que haga este ofiçio con el Rey, y porque entre las demás cosas de que deven dar cuenta a Su Magestad una será de algunas personas que es necessario las conozca y sepa quien son, dentro que Vuestra Reverencia en la ocasion que más conveniente le pareçiere[129] con las buenas raçones que para ello ay procure darle a entender que para la quietud y buen ser de esas provinçias me importa mucho sacar dellas algunos sujetos, sin lo qual no espero que de las demás diligençias ternan el efecto que Su Magestad quiere y todos deseamos, y que por esto sería bien que yo tubiere[130] en esto su consentimiento porque sin él no lo hare, ni lo intentaré, pues intentarlo y no salir con ello sería de mayor inconveniente. Vuestra Reverencia por charidad en esto no pierda la ocasion que hubiere de haçer ofiçio porque es de suma importançia en las cosas[131] y cierto que se le puede significar a Su Magestad el peligro de censura[132] que en ello ay, que creo no es pequeño.

Quando Vuestra Reverencia informare como es la instruction le aviso de lo de Siçilia, deseo que con buen modo signifique a Su Magestad que Don Francisco de Avila Inquisidor no es nada aficionado a nuestras cosas, y podria ser que hablase al Rey cargandonos esto de Sicilia, porque a él toca informar de esto a Su Magestad.

Translation

To Fr Robert Persons, 27 November.

Your Reverence, it appears, has so improved in the Spanish tongue that it seems reasonable to ask that we write in it. I am greatly comforted to learn, from a copy of the letter from Fr Gil González, how much God our Lord assists Your Reverence's skilful dealings, as appears from the good success achieved through those you have transacted with His Majesty. We esteem this to be of such great importance for the Society, as is only reasonable, and we thank you very much for the zeal, faithfulness and care with which you have attended to this, given His Majesty's response. It seems to me that already there is more than enough reason to believe that the visits of Ours may continue, without fear of anything preventing them.

I advise Fr Gil González to provide the Seminary with a good rector and to be helped by Ours as much as possible, because that would obviate the need to have the presence of Your Reverence. This would allow you to be of more assistance in Madrid, which I should like to be as continuous and regular as possible, especially since I have given order to our visitors who have to report to His Majesty what they have done in the visitation: then you can be satisfied that he is dealt with truthfully. I am sending Your Reverence on these errands so that you can perform this office with the king and because amongst others, account must be made to His Majesty about certain people whom he needs to know

129. pareçiere] *followed by obscure word, possibly deleted* R
130. tubiere] *obscure in* R
131. cosas] *obscure abbreviation* R
132. censura] cens^a R

and be aware of who they are. On this matter would Your Reverence, when the moment seems opportune, please use the relevant good reasons to make sure to give him to understand that for the peace and good of those provinces it is very important to me to transfer some particular individuals. Unless I do this, I do not hope that those other matters will turn out as His Majesty desires and we all wish for. Consequently, it will be good that I obtain his agreement in this, because without it I will not do it, nor even try it. If we keep on trying without achieving our goal, it will be very inconvenient. Would Your Reverence of your charity please not lose any opportunity that presents itself to perform this task because it is of the greatest importance in these matters. It is certain that you will be able to show His Majesty the risk of incurring censure, which I believe is not small.

When Your Reverence informs [the king] about the course of action I am advising you to take about that Sicilia, it is necessary that you politely indicate to His Majesty that Don Francisco Dávila, the inquisitor, is not at all well-disposed to our interests, and it is possible that he would speak to the king blaming us for that Sicilia, because he is in charge of reporting to His Majesty about him.

B42 To Claudio Acquaviva, Toledo, 9 December 1589

>   SOURCE: Acquaviva to Persons, 22 January 1590 (B47).
>   NOTE: Acquaviva's reply mentions two letters arriving by a recent post, without specifying the date of despatch. At least one of them coincides with Persons's letter to Creswell, 9 December (B43). Persons had again dealt with the king and had had some dealings, while in Madrid, with Lord Francis Dacre, who was at this time probably in Rome (see Acquaviva's letter of 22 January 1590, B47).

B43 To Joseph Creswell, Toledo, 9 December, 1589

>   SOURCE: ABSI, Coll P II 498, Grene's partial transcript.
>   HICKS: 87.
>   EDITION: Pollen, *Miscellanea IX*, 20.
>   NOTE: Persons gives news of the death of Thomas Warcop on arrival in Spain, and about the precarious state of the seminary at Valladolid, in need of a constitution; he hopes that Allen will be given oversight over the seminary.

— I have bin these 9 or 10 daies in Toledo. — F. Thomas Warcop dyed att Alicante the same day that he landed there.[133] Since the last Ordinary I spake againe with the king about our affaires of the Society, and what successe I had you shal easily learne at the Casa.[134] — I pray you faile not to send me an authentical copye of the Constitutions of

---

133. Thomas Warcop, from Carlisle, studied at Douai and Rome, and was ordained priest in December 1584. In 1587 he joined the Society of Jesus but was sent to Spain before he had completed his novitiate, and died on arrival in Alicante, 9 October 1589 (Foley, 7: 814; McCoog, *English and Welsh Jesuits*, 324). He may have been one of the group from Sicily mentioned in earlier letters.

134. The professed house in Rome.

your College there. — We have a family of about 20 persons in our Seminary of Valladolid, and noe lawes or constitutions as yet &c. — And if that[135] point might be procured, which I wrot to you before, to witt, that the head government as well of this seminary as of others might be in our Cardinal, I think it would be good &c. — God already beginneth to help this Seminary diverse waies, though hitherto the king hath not given but one hundred crownes &c. —

B44 From Claudio Acquaviva, Rome, 24 December 1589

SOURCE: ARSI, Tolet. 4, fol. 59r-v. There is no letter to Persons in the batch of open letters dated 25 December.

NOTE: Acquaviva replies confidentially to Persons's (untraced) letter of 11 November (B39), presumably advising the general of his visit to Madrid. Here Acquaviva is concerned to ensure that the visitors report regularly to Philip II, so that there is no room for misunderstanding about the treatment of the Jesuit malcontents. There is a suggestion here that someone in high office, possibly from the Inquisition, tried to block Acquaviva's negotiations with the king.

The manuscript is obscure in places and the readings should be treated with caution where indicated.

Madrid. P. Personio. 24 de dicembre.
Mi rallegro delle buone nuove del seminario che Vostra Reverentia ci scrive per la sua de gl' xi del passato. Al P. Egidio scriviamo che provega de un'altro de nostri che sono[136] quatro. Non habbiamo ricevuta quella relatione che ci accusa dell'ufficio fatto con Sua Maestà intorno alli nostri conturbanti, et così fu buona providencia il duppicarà la con questa [illegible contraction] sua.[137] L'ufficio è stato importantissimo, né dubitavamo della mente di Sua Maestà per il che tanto più speriamo nel Signore il buon effetto et successo. Alli Padri Visitatori, si è già[138] scritto, et di nuovo si scrive, che diano ogni almeno ogni quatro mese raguaglio a Sua Maestà di quel che fano et pervegono ivi[139] et che faccino diligenti informationi contra l'inquieti et glele diino et al fine delle loro visitatione lo raguaglino del tutto, perché di qua pende la liberatione de altre Visite et così la pace et quiete di coteste provincie, come credo che Vostra Reverentia haveva fatto li anco sapere; a quale priego dal Signore[140] le buone feste.

[Addressed in margin:] Madrid P. Personio 24 de xbre.

---

135. that] the *Pollen*
136. sono] syno R
137. duppicarà] *followed by* la conquesta [*illegible contraction*] sua R
138. è già] *obscure* R
139. ivi] *obscure, possibly* etc. R
140. come credo che Vostra Reverentia haveva fatto li anco sapere; a quale priego dal Signore] *interlined below, replacing* con che per fine priego il Signore da a Vostra Reverentia [le buone feste].

Translation

To Fr Persons in Madrid, 24 December.

I rejoice at the good news of the seminary which Your Reverence conveyed to me in your letter of the 11th of the past month. Fr Gil has been informed that he should provide for one more of Ours, in order to make a total of four.[141] We have not received the document which accused us of negotiating with His Majesty with regard to the troublemakers of Ours, and so it was providential that you made a copy – please send it with your next post.[142] The business was of the greatest importance, nor did we have doubts about His Majesty's intentions, since we put even more hope in the Lord for its good outcome and success. To the father visitors, instructions were given in writing, and have again been put in writing, that they should report what they are doing, and what they have found out there, to His Majesty at least every four months; that will provide some steady information with regard to the discontented party. This they will do, and at the end of their period of visitation they will give him a comprehensive summary report; in fact, the freedom to make further visitations depends on these men, as well as the peace and tranquillity of these provinces, which I believe Your Reverence has also impressed upon them; and so, I pray to the Lord that [he will give Your Reverence] happy feast days.

B45 To Claudio Acquaviva, Madrid, probably 7 January 1590

SOURCE: Acquaviva to Persons, 19 February (B51).
NOTE: Persons reported on an audience with the king.

B46 To Joseph Creswell, Madrid, 7 January 1590

SOURCE: ABSI, Coll P II 477 (reference) and 498, Grene's partial transcript.
HICKS: 89.
EDITION: Pollen, *Miscellanea IX*, 21.
NOTE: Grene transcribed only a few items of business, including a proposal to print "The story of the martyrs," probably *Relacion de algunos martyrios ... en Inglaterra* (Madrid, 1590), a collection of martyrological narratives, some written and some translated by Persons, including *Relacion de quatro martyrios ... hechos en la villa y universidad de Oxonia*, written or translated by Persons following the execution of the priests Thomas Belson and Richard Yaxley, as well as the gentleman George Nichols and his servant Humphrey ap Richard in Oxford on 5 July 1589. Joseph Creswell sent a copy of the latter work to Robert Bellarmine, who had it translated into French (*ARCR*, 1: no. 895). An Italian translation was also published in 1590 (*ARCR*, 1: no. 897): Questier, *Catholics and Treason*, 197–200, esp. 200 n92.

It seems likely that Persons cultivated a relationship with the printer, Pedro Madrigal, who also printed a Spanish translation of *A relation of the King of Spaines receiving in Valliodolid* (1592),

---

141. González Dávila had been asked to supply the seminary with two or three Jesuits; he is now being asked for a fourth (see Acquaviva to Persons, 2 October 1589, B35).

142. See textual note: this is only an approximate meaning.

and Pedro de Ribadeneira's *Historia ecclesiastica del scisma del reyno de Inglaterra* (1588), which was loosely based on Persons's edition of Nicholas Sander's *De schismate Anglicano* (Rome, 1586). On Persons's publishing enterprises in Spain, see Dominguez, *Radicals in Exile*.

I pray you pay to F. Thomas in Genua ten crownes.[143] I pray you remember to procure from Praga all that may be had of F. Campians doings, whereof I wrot to you before &c.[144] — I hope that by this day our Lord Cardinal is Archbishop of Machlen[145] &c. — The story of the martyrs we shal print here, if it like us &c. —

B47 From Claudio Acquaviva, Rome, 22 January 1590

SOURCE: ARSI, Tolet. 5/I, fol. 108r.

NOTE: Acquaviva commends Persons for his successful intervention with the king regarding Portugal (presumably the appointment of Pedro Fonseca as visitor to Portugal) and is hopeful that the discontent will come to an end. There is agreement between Philip and Cardinal Allen, probably over support of the colleges. He has again asked González Dávila to give every assistance to the new college in Valladolid.

P. Roberto Personio, enero 22.

Dos de Vuestra Reverencia he recevido con este ordinario y con cada una dellas particular consuelo, porque çierto el oficio que Vuestra Reverencia haçe y en este el particular delo de Portugal ultimamente hiço con Su Magestad y los que ha hecho y va haçiendo con esos señores son de gran servicio del Señor, de gran bien para la Compañia, y para mí de singular consuelo por ver que con esto se abre camino para que se entienda la verdad que de acá tratamos, el buen fin que tenemos y las siniestras pretensiones de los que nos inquietan. Vuestra Reverencia por amor del Señor continue que si Su Magestad se entera bien será facil el remedio de todo. Tambien estimo en mucho los buenos avisos que en la otra suya me da, del secreto esté seguro, y del remedio se terná cuydado que con ocasion de las visitas se podra bien poner.

He mi consolado que Su Magestad se aya acordado del Señor Cardenal y çierto merece todo el favor que se le hiçiere, y yo deseo que el Rey se le haga grande, porque todo su ser, su diligencia, y buenas partes los emplea y endereza en servicio de la yglesia.[146] En lo tocante al Seminario me huelgo que Dios le ayude tan copiosamente[147] el

---

143. [Grene writes:] plurima de re pecuniaria hoc omitto ("I omit much material here about financial matters"). On Thomas Wright, now apparently living in Genoa, see Persons's letter to Creswell, 26 May 1590 (B62).

144. See Persons's letter to Creswell, 26 May 1589 (B17). On Campion in Prague, see Gerard Kilroy, *Edmund Campion: A Scholarly Life* (Farnham, Surrey, 2015), 93–130.

145. [Pollen writes:] Allen was nominated to the see of Malines/Mechelen (Knox, *Allen*, cxv–cxvii).

146. porque todo ... en servicio de la yglesia] *added in the margin* R

147. copiosamente] *followed by* y de mi parte no faltará de acudirle en todo lo que pudiere, y aora escrivo al visitador que acuda a lo que V.R. pidiere para su buen gobierno, porque mi voluntad es que en esto no se falta [*deleted*] R

quarto sujeto que Vuestra Reverencia pide ya con el passado avise al Padre Gil que se le diese y lo hago de nuevo con el presente, escriviendole tambien que acuda a todo lo demas que Vuestra Reverencia juzgare ser necessario para su buen govierno y progresso, por que mi voluntad es que en esto no se falte sino que de gente y de lo demas que pudiessemos esté bien proveido. No más en esta de encomendarme, etc.

Translation

To Fr Robert Persons, 22 January.

I have received two letters from Your Reverence with this post and found particular comfort in each one of them,[148] because of the work which Your Reverence is performing and particularly your recent intervention with His Majesty concerning Portugal; what you have done and are doing with those lords is of great service to Our Lord, the great good of our Society, and of singular comfort to me: to see how this opens the way for everyone to understand the truth of what we are saying here, the good purpose we have, and (on the other hand) the sinister pretensions of those who are causing disturbance. Would Your Reverence please, for the love of Our Lord, persist, so that if His Majesty has a good understanding of the case, everything will be easily remedied. I also greatly appreciate the good advice which you give in the other; rest assured that it will be kept secret, and the remedy will be well taken care of through the visitations.

I am greatly relieved that His Majesty is now in agreement with my Lord Cardinal. For sure, he deserves every reward for doing so, and I wish to magnify the king, because he employs and puts his whole being, all his diligence and good parts, into the service of the church. With regard to the seminary I am delighted that God is aiding it so abundantly.[149] As for your fourth request, I have already advised Fr Gil by the last post that was sent, and I am repeating it also in my present despatch, writing to him to assist in everything else that Your Reverence judges to be necessary for its good management and progress, because it is my will that in this we must make sure that we are well provided not only with personnel and everything else. That is all for the present except to entrust myself [to your prayers and holy sacrifices], etc.

B48 From Claudio Acquaviva, Rome, 22 January 1590

SOURCE: ARSI, Tolet. 4, fols. 60v–61r.

NOTE: Acquaviva is concerned about the support the dissident Jesuits appear to be receiving from the Inquisition, but leaves the managing of the situation to Persons. Persons had met Lord Dacre in connection with the dissident Spanish Jesuits Luis de Mendoza and Sebastián Hernández (see Persons to Acquaviva, June 1592 and 2/9 December 1595, B147, B303).

148. Letters probably written in early December 1589.
149. The deleted text reads: "And for my part I will not fail to support you in everything, and to write to the visitor to support you in all your good government, because I would like nothing to be left out" (the gist is inserted at the end of the letter).

Francis Lord Dacre was the brother of Leonard Lord Dacre (d. 1573), who was active in the northern rebellion of 1569. He fled from London to Scotland in 1587, and after some time at the Scottish court travelled to Spain via Rome, where he found favour with Allen. He reached Valladolid in 1592 after a spell of imprisonment in San Sebastián on the northern coast of Spain, near Bilbao, and his later activity aroused suspicions on all sides (Loomie, *Spanish Elizabethans*, 105-107). It is likely that he met Persons, possibly in Madrid, late in 1589.

In the manuscript, the ciphers are written with the name following, underlined, as here, and other words and phrases have been underlined, possibly for encoding.

Madrid. P. Roberto Personio, 22 di Genaio.

Fu importantissimo l'ufficio che Vostra Reverentia fece col Signor Dacres informandolo del modo di procedere di Luigi de Mendoza.[150] Et dall'essere anco stato talvolta con lettera di 82 impagarsi in simili maneggi poco convenghe a Religiosi et anco raguagli altro delle singolarità degl'altri che hanno appoggi de secolari. Dio vuolesse che questi Signori lasciassero tali mezzi et modi et dessero braccio a superiori; spero bene, come Vostra Reverentia dice, che col tempo si potrà rimediare — è buon pensiero quello di Vostra Reverentia di fare processi[151] non solo a conturbanti [178] ma ancora a quelli che probabilmente si vede che sono maxima potentia da[152] per essere tali et così di questi si scrive adesso a Acosta [173] et Egidio [175] come già s'era scritto di quelli &c. —

Non so che il Padre Sebastiano Hernandez[153] possi pretendere causa alcuna di lamento o querella. Et perché non così facilmente occorrerà occasione di dare a Vostra Reverentia l'ordine che ricerca in particolare di poterli communicare alcune cose, glilo diamo in generale per farlo di quelle cose che la parerano, ma vadi cauto et così li potrà dire d'haverlo. Quanto al come dire del suo modo di trattare e toccare, bisogna andare con destrezza; aspettaremo l'aviso di quel che di più Vostra Reverentia potrà intendere, il meglio sarebbe che quelli Signori da loro stessi se ne vadino staccando di lui, o che si faccino intendere &c.

Translation

To Fr Robert Persons in Madrid, 22 January.

It was a most important office that Your Reverence performed with the Lord Dacre by informing him how Luis de Mendoza was going about things – and also at the same time dealing with the letter of the king about getting involved in similar matters unsuitable to religious,[154] and finding out more, too, of the irregularity of the others who have the support of the seculars. May God grant that these lords would leave such means and

150. Luigi de Mendoza] *underlined R*
151. processi] *underlined R*
152. da] *alternatively* di *R*
153. che il Padre Sebastiano Hernandez] *underlined R*
154. Possibly the king warned Dacre to detach himself from the dissident Jesuits, especially Mendoza.

methods and lend a hand to the superiors; I hope, as Your Reverence says, that things will sort themselves out with time. I approve of Your Reverence's plan to take action not only against the malcontents but also those who seem most likely to be such; and please explain to Acosta and Gil[155] what has already been written about those men.

I do not believe that Fr Sebastián Hernández has any reason to make any complaint or quarrel. And since perhaps an occasion will not so easily arise to give Your Reverence the specific authority you need to communicate various matters in particular, we give you general permission, in these matters, to do what seems wise; but please proceed with caution and speak to him when occasion serves. As much as we deplore his method of wheeling and dealing, we need to act strategically. We look forward to learning what Your Reverence intends to do further. It will be better that you keep those gentlemen at a distance, until they have made their intentions clear.

B49 To Claudio Acquaviva, Madrid, 26 January and 3 February 1590

SOURCE: Acquaviva to Persons, 24 March (B55).

NOTE: Clearly these letters contained a great deal of business: Acquaviva was only able to answer partly, in haste, on 24 March.

B50 To Joseph Creswell, Madrid, 3 and 24 February 1590

SOURCE: ABSI, Coll P II 477 (reference only) and 498, Grene's notes.
EDITION: Pollen, *Miscellanea IX*, 21.

NOTE: Grene writes: "Many other letters of Father Persons this yeare are about matters concerning the Seminary of Valladolid: privileges to be obtained at Rome for it &c. — de re pecuniaria &c. *viz.* one of Feb. 3 and 24" (Coll P II 498).

B51 From Claudio Acquaviva, Rome, 19 February 1590

SOURCE: ARSI, Tolet. 5/I, fol. 114r–v; Tolet. 4, fol. 61r, an addendum added in haste and entered into the general's private register.

NOTE: This letter contains advice and instructions for Persons's audiences with Philip II, and the provincial congregations of the Society, called to deal with the controversy over the *memorialistas*. It is most likely a response to a letter from Persons written in early January (not extant). Acquaviva is determined that the congregations should not be held with a royal appointee presiding.

In a confidential addendum, recorded in the private register, Acquaviva addresses the problem of the vocation of Luis de Morales, who has been asked to go to Japan. Evidently this matter needed to be referred to the king because of the prohibition on movement of Jesuits from Spain (see also Acquaviva's letters of 20 March and 15 May, B54, B61).

---

155. The visitors José de Acosta and Gil González Dávila.

P. Roberto Personio, hebrero 19.

Mucho quisiera que Vuestra Reverencia huviera hecho el oficio con Su Magestad sin pedir consejo ni parecer de nadie, porque yo confiava mucho que entendiendo Su Magestad lo que sentiamos de la persona que él nombraba, desistiria y hecharia mano de otra mejor y más a proposito para que salga bien como se pretende. Acá no estava el negoçio tan adelante como a Vuestra Reverencia dixeron, pues ni aún se havia propuesto al papa. Del Hermano Fabricio me parece bien que si por allá no ha de ayudar con consuelo y contento que se venga con los procuradores, o con otra ocasion. Del seminario aviso al padre visitador como Vuestra Reverencia lo pide.

Deseo que Vuestra Reverencia haga en otro particular oficio con Su Magestad, pero sea sin dar parte dello a nadie, porque importará para que las congregaciones provinciales se hagan con la paz que conviene: y es que Vuestra Reverencia con el mejor modo que le pareçiere le signifique que estos conturbantes no se quietan con nada sino que siempre buscan nuevos modos de inquietar, como aora se sospecha y no sin fundamento que ellos procuran que en las congregaciones presida algun personaje en nombre de Su Magestad. Vuestra Reverencia le persuada a no permitirlo, ansi por la nota de la Compañia y desunion de la Compañia,[156] como porque hará con esto que la congregacion no sea legítima, y porna el procurador a peligro de que con estraño sentimiento de todas las demas naciones[157] en la congregacion de procuradores no sea recevido.

Y entienda tambien Su Magestad que alli no haçe más que elegir un procurador y esto por votos secretos, de suerte que no determinan ni pueden estableçer cosa alguna. En las &c.

Añadido a una del Padre Personio de 19 de Hebrero registrada en registro comun.

Y ansi es necessario hazer con su Majestad todavia el Officio de la manera que yo escrevi a Vuestra Reverencia y añadir que despues de averse procurado que este Padre Luys de Morales se recogiese algunos dias a más oración. Ha salido con padre muy resolutamente que se le dé licencia para pasarse a otra Religion, de lo qual aunque no está determinado si conviene o no, avisamos a su Majestad para que entienda la disposicion del sugeto, y le supplicamos que esto tenga secreto, porque de otra manera él vendria a saberlo, y de eso mismo formaria quexa para pedir la licencia con más color.

Translation

To Fr Robert Persons, 19 February.

I should very much like Your Reverence to carry out the commission with His Majesty without asking advice or opinion from anyone,[158] because I have every confidence that once His Majesty understood how we feel about the person he nominated, he

---

156. y desunion de la Compañía] *added in the margin R*
157. con estraño sentimiento de todas las demás naciones] *added in the margin R*
158. Alternatively, Acquaviva may mean: "It was very much to my liking that Your Reverence carried out the commission", etc.

would desist and choose another, more suitable, and so things will proceed as intended. Here the business is not as well advanced as they told Your Reverence, because it has not yet been proposed to the pope. As for Brother Fabrizio, it seems good to me that if he is unable to assist you contentedly and with consolation over there, let him come with the procurators, or on some other occasion.[159] With regard to the seminary, I will advise father visitor as Your Reverence requests.

I would like Your Reverence to broach another particular matter with His Majesty, but without disclosing it to anyone, because it is important for the provincial congregations to proceed as peaceably as one could expect: and it is that Your Reverence would convey to him, in the best way you can find, that those agitators are not content with anything except always finding new ways of causing disruption: as it is now suspected, and not without good grounds, that they are trying to ensure that someone nominated by His Majesty should preside over the congregations. Would Your Reverence please persuade him not to allow this, because it will affect the reputation of the Society and break down its unity: it will undermine the legitimacy of the congregation and expose the procurator to the risk of not being accepted in the congregation of procurators because of the distrust of all the other nations.

And also, His Majesty should understand that no more needs to be done there than choose a procurator and that by secret ballot, otherwise it may be that they will not be able to decide or determine anything. To your, etc.

Addendum to Fr Persons's letter[160] of 19 February (which was recorded in the open register).

And indeed, it is necessary to raise the matter with His Majesty, just as I wrote to Your Reverence; and in addition, after you have accomplished that, please ask Fr Luis de Morales to devote some days more to prayer. Greater resolution has been reached with the father that he should have freedom to move to another religious order,[161] but it has not yet been determined if it is appropriate or not. We are keeping His Majesty informed, so that he can understand the disposition of this person, and we beseech him to keep it secret, because otherwise he [i.e., Morales] would come to know it, and for that very reason would be likely to complain more vehemently about getting the licence.

B52 To Claudio Acquaviva, Madrid, 24 Febuary or 3 March 1590

NOTE: Persons presumably wrote to Acquaviva on either or both of the days on which he wrote to Creswell (B50, B53).

---

159. Fabrizio Como seems to have been perennially dissatisfied, according to Acquaviva's letters.
160. The language is ambiguous, but he is presumably referring to his own letter to Persons.
161. R reads "Religion," which would mean joining another religious order; but the issue was that of a transfer to another province, possibly Japan (see Acquaviva's letter of 24 March 1590, B54), so this may be an error for "Region."

B53 To Joseph Creswell, Madrid, 3 March 1590

SOURCE: ABSI, Coll P II 477, Grene's notes.

NOTE: Grene mentions that Creswell was now rector (of the English college) in Rome (see appendix B).

B54 From Claudio Acquaviva, Rome, 20 March 1590

SOURCE: ARSI, Tolet. 5/I, fol. 118r. This batch of letters, originally intended for the courier of 16 March, was delayed until 24 March (fol. 115v).

NOTE: Acquaviva would like Persons to accompany and assist Acosta when he reports to the king at the end of April, thus completing his brief. Persons would be of great value in this.

P. Roberto Personio. 20 de Marzo.

Aunque para con Vuestra Reverencia no havia necesidad de este aviso con todo eso nos ha parezido escrivirle estos renglones para que en la ocasion que aqui diré acuda como en las demas lo ha hecho, y es que el Padre Joseph de Acosta luego como aya acabado su visita que será para fin de Abril, vendra a esa Corte a dar quenta a Su Magestad de lo que della quisiere saber, y no obstante que el dicho padre es tan conocido en esa Corte y a muchas personas della sea grato, con todo eso nos ha parezido que será de grande efecto para el buen despacho de lo que aý huviese de tratar que se ayude de Vuestra Reverencia en todo lo que se le ofreciere y ansi se le escrive de nuestra parte. Deseo mucho que venido que sea Vuestra Reverencia con su charidad se le ofrezca y ayude asi con Su Magestad como con qualquiera otra persona que el dicho Padre huviese de tratar para que desta manera unidos y ayudandose su venida a esa Corte tenga el efecto que se desea.

El Padre Gil González me da muy buenas nuevas del Seminario de Valladolid. El Señor lo augmente y conserve para gloria suya – en sus oraciones, etc.

Translation

To Fr Robert Persons, 20 March.

Although with Your Reverence there is no need of this information, altogether it seemed a good thing for us to write these lines to you so that on this occasion you can help as you have done on others. This is the matter: that when Fr José de Acosta has finished his visit (which will be towards the end of April) he should go to the court to give an account to His Majesty of what he would like to know. Although the said father is well-known at the court and many people in that court like him, all the same it seemed to us that it would be very effective in handling what is to be dealt with there if he has the help of Your Reverence in all that he needs – and that is the purpose of this letter. It would be very much appreciated if Your Reverence of your charity would offer and assist in this way with His Majesty or with any other person whom the said father has to deal with, so that in this way, with your support and assistance, his coming to that court will have the desired effect.

Fr Gil González gives me very good news of the seminary at Valladolid. May Our Lord increase it and preserve it to his glory – to your prayers, etc.

B55 From Claudio Acquaviva, Rome, 24 March 1590

SOURCE: ARSI, Tolet. 4, fols. 61v–62r.

NOTE: To catch the courier, this confidential letter deals in haste with several matters of business, as the multiple corrections and insertions attest: appointments and movements of Jesuits in Spain; the need for the visitors to consult with the king; the replacement of Pedro de Guzmán as rector of the college in Valladolid. Acquaviva advises caution in dealing with the reluctance of Spanish Jesuits to allow English seminarians of Protestant parentage to enter Spain, especially in view of the attitude of the Inquisition (McCoog, *Building the Faith of St Peter*, 109). The letter refers to the Inquisition several times, reflecting Acquaviva's frustration with its power and influence.

Madrid P. Personio 24 di Marzo.

Si sono ricevute quelle di Vostra Reverentia, una[162] delli 26 di Genaio et due delli[163] 3 di Febraro. Questi corrieri indugiano tanto a venire, et arrivati poi[164] partono così presto, che non[165] ci dano tempo di rispondere se non a poche lettere a proportione di quelle che restano senza risposta sino al seguente.

— Quel che di qua si scrisse che si procurasse costì il beneplacito di Sua Maestà per potere cavare di costà alcuni de capi de conturbanti: fu perché di la ci scrissero parecchi[166] Padri che era tempo di ricercarlo. Ma mi par bene che s'aspetti la venuta de Padri visitatori per quale spero sarà in buena.

— Poiché la cosa del Padre Luys de Morales è andata tanto inanzi non accaderà farne altra instanza à Sua Maestà. Io detto a questo Padre[167] seria et dissertamente che non lo voglio impedire in modo alcuno. Se cotesti Signori no lo crederano, non posso far' altro, il[168] commandarglilo. Non mi pare di poterlo fare con buona conscienza;[169] egli sempre m'ha detto che in modo alcuno non vuol andare àl Giapone[170] et quanto più instanza li vien fatta,[171] lo vego più fermo in questa risolutione, né a persone prudenti

---

162. una] *interlined R*
163. due delli] *interlined R*
164. poi] *interlined R*
165. non] *preceded by* ci [*deleted*] *R*
166. parecchi] *followed by* de primi et più confacenti [*deleted*] *R*
167. a questo Padre] *interlined R*
168. il] *interlined R*
169. mi pare di poterlo fare con buona conscienza] *interlined above* lo fare [*deleted*] *R*
170. al Giapone] *interlined R*
171. li vien fatta] se [li] fa *deleted*, vien fatta *interlined R*

sarà difficile[172] d'intendere che tale dignità in tal luogo et tempo non è altro che una buona croce[173] di pericoli et travagli grandi, la quale chi non si movesse ad abracciarla per servizio de Dio et desiderio della salute dell'anime, sta chiaro, che non è appetibile naturalmente.

— Fece bene Vostra Reverentia à mandarci gl'avisi del fratello Tancardo per nostra notitia benché gl'humori già si sanno.

— Et per qualche secreto di queste cose tocca Vostra Reverentia stia sicura[174] che ne manco al Padre Alarcone si communicheranno, con tutto che a lui sicuramente si può confidar' ogni cosa.

— Mi rallegro molto che in Madrid si sia messa in piede la disciplina.

— Fece benissimo Vostra Reverentia a non concorrere nel colore pavonazo per il vestito de Collegiàli Inglesi,[175] più tosto a tutti, ma a loro particolarmente conviene il lugubre et lamentevole.

— Il Padre Egidio mi scrive che avisarà il Padre Pietro Guzman; et se questo non basterà che[176] lo mutarà; con la quale occasione li raccomando[177] il provedere bene di rectore[178] a sodisfattione di Vostra Reverentia. Lei potrà scrivergli et proporgli chi li parerà caso che manco con gl'avisi riesca il Guzmán.[179] Raccomando anco caldamente[180] a lui et al Padre Viceprovinciale le cose del qual[181] Collegio, &c.

— L'officio che Vostra Reverentia fece col Padre Roggiero, fu molto a proposito, egli mi scrive che viene. Non credo che cotesti Signori l'impedirebbono il venire a render conto al suo superiore delle cose della nostra Religione in quelle bande,[182] né Sua Maestà il permetterebbe, si come non permesse ch'il Padre Alonso Sanchez fusse impedito.

— Ho avisato li Padri visitatori che con la brevità possibile[183] procurino per sé stessi raguagliare prevamente il Re. Spero che Sua Maestà ne resterà sodisfatta.

— Il rispetto et consideratione che costì hanno li nostri a non ricevere[184] figliuoli d'heretici[185] non è dubio alcuno se non che è conforme alla[186] raggione et prudenza per

 172. ne a persone prudenti sarà difficile] et [a persone prudenti] non [sarà] facil [difficile] *deleted* R

 173. una buona croce] *follows* croce [*deleted*] R

 174. Et per qualche secreto di queste cose tocca Vostra Reverentia stia sicura] *replaces* Del segreto di questo V.R. ci scriva, *with a series of deletions and* Et ... tocca *supplied in the margin. The previous paragraph,* Fece bene ... si sanno *is also supplied in the margin* R

 175. il vestito de Collegiàli Inglesi] *replaces* li Collegiàli [*deleted*] R

 176. che] *possibly deleted* R

 177. con la quale occasione li raccomando] *replaces* et con questa occasione gli raccomando R

 178. rectore] *interlined, followed on the line by* et il collegio istesso [*deleted*] R

 179. caso che manco con gl'avisi riesca il Guzman] *supplied in margin* R

 180. caldamente] *interlined* R

 181. qual] *interlined* R

 182. in quelle bande] *interlined* R

 183. possibile] *followed by* danno ogni sodisfa[ttione] [*deleted*] R

 184. a non ricevere] *replaces* nel ricevea in [*deleted*] R

 185. d'heretici] *followed by* senza quale ha prevencione dà farsi con li Signori delegati [*deleted*] R

 186. conforme alla] *replaces* secondo la [*deleted*] R

le circostanze del tempo et luego, etc. Et però mi pare che[187] senza fare qualche preventione con li Signori del Santo Officio non devono riceversi in modo alcuno; ma più tosto quando si giudicassero atti[188] per apuntare altre provincie si potrebbono poi avisare delle loro qualità li[189] provinciali de quelle, et poi se li accettarano, mandarglili. Ma perché questo sarebbe scommodo, et rimedio per pochi, Vostra Reverentia tratti col Padre Porres et Padre Ribadeneira parendo a loro che[190] si debbi informare il Cardinale et gl'altri Signori di quel che dice la nostri confrere quando sono de paesi infetti,[191] potràno loro stessi et il Padre Provinciale quando vi farà,[192] fare tal officio d'recordarglilo Vostra Reverentia da partenza[193] et contentadosi quelli Signori del tribunale si potràno ricevere &c. Et così Antonio Skimero[194] in Andalusia, del che Vostra Reverentia havutosi il beneplacito delle Signori Inquisitori, potrà scrivere al Padre Bartolomeo Perez provinciale.

Translation

To Fr Persons in Madrid, 24 March.

We have received your letters, one of 26 January and two of 3 February.[195] These couriers linger so much on the way, that they arrive no sooner than they have to depart almost immediately, which does not give time to answer the letters except in part; the rest will have to remain unanswered until the next post.

— Whatever we wrote from here to obtain His Majesty's assent for removing some of the chief troublemakers from there – that was because several fathers[196] wrote from there that it was time to obtain it. But I would prefer that we await the arrival of the father visitors, through which I hope things will turn out well.

— As the matter of Fr Luis de Morales has advanced so much already, it would be redundant to put another request to His Majesty. I have said to this father, seriously and solemnly, that I do not wish to impede him in any way. If these selfsame lords do not believe him,[197] the only option I have is to command him. I do not think I can do so with a good conscience; he has always said to me that he has absolutely no desire to go to Japan, and the more he is urged, I see, the firmer he is in this resolution. Neither will it be difficult for any wise man to understand that taking up such a role, in such a place and time, is none other than taking up a heavy cross, of dangers and great travails. And if there

187. che] *followed by* quando si giudichera [*deleted*] R
188. atti] *followed by* si potrebbono per mandare [*deleted*] R
189. delle loro qualità li] *supplied in margin, replacing* i [*deleted*] R
190. parendo a loro che] *replaces* se parendo che [*illegible word*] [*deleted*] R
191. infetti] *followed by* et parendo che se [*deleted*] R
192. farà] *alternatively,* sarà
193. d'recordarglilo Vostra Reverentia da partenza] *obscure, interlined* R
194. Skimero] *followed by* mi pare bene che [*deleted*] R
195. B49.
196. The deleted phrase reads, "the principle and best suited."
197. This term ("cotesti signori") seems to refer to the Inquisition which may not license Morales' departure. Acquaviva is reluctant to pursue the matter further, given Morales' resistance to the idea.

is no intention to embrace it for the service of God and desire for the saving of souls, clearly it cannot be caused by natural inclination.

— [*marginal addition*] Your Reverence has done well to bring information of Brother Tancard to our attention, although the general mood is already known.[198]

— And with regard to some of the secrets involved in these matters, Your Reverence may rest assured that not even Fr Alarcón will be acquainted with them,[199] even though anything can be safely entrusted to him.

— I am delighted that the discipline is being implemented in Madrid.

— Your Reverence has done very well not to agree with the choice of purple colour for the clothing of the students of the English college. This would be true for anyone, but to them especially something mournful and sorrowful is appropriate.

— Fr Gil[200] has written to me that he will notify Fr Pedro de Guzmán; and if this is not enough, he will transfer him. As this occasion presents itself, I recommend that you consider who would be best as rector, to Your Reverence's satisfaction. You could write to him and propose whoever you please, if the news from Guzmán is not very helpful.[201] I also warmly commend the affairs of that college to him and father vice provincial.

— The agreement that Your Reverence made with Fr Ruggiero was very much apropos. He has written to me that he is coming. I do not believe that those selfsame lords will prevent his coming and rendering account to his superior of the matters of our religion in those parts, nor would His Majesty allow that to happen, just as he would not allow Fr Alonso Sánchez to be held back.[202]

— I have advised the father visitors to take the first opportunity of reporting briefly to the king, as expeditiously as they can. I hope that His Majesty will be content with that.

— Regarding the dutiful reluctance which Ours observe over here, about not receiving the children of heretics,[203] there is no doubt at all that it conforms to reason and pru-

---

198. Charles Tancard, a scholastic, was completing his studies at Alcalá. As a minister later at Valladolid, he proved to be somewhat temperamental (McCoog, *Building the Faith of St Peter*, 216–218). Acquaviva seems to be referring to the general opinion in Rome about how to deal with Tancard.

199. García de Alarcón was [later] visitor to Castile and Toledo (Persons to Acquaviva, 2 and 9 December 1595, B303). It is unclear whether this paragraph is linked to the previous one about Tancard.

200. Gil González Dávila.

201. Guzmán was replaced by Juan López de Manzano in July 1590 (Hicks, *Seminaries*, part 3, 503).

202. On Sánchez, see Persons to Acquaviva, 22 March 1593 (B173). Philip permitted him to be summoned to Rome in 1587, after his return to Madrid from the Philippines, despite the restrictions on the movements of Spanish Jesuits. Ruggiero was presumably another Jesuit whom Acquaviva wished to come to Rome.

203. Acquaviva addresses the question of admitting English Jesuits and students to Jesuit institutions and provinces, given that they come from an "infected" region. In Rome, due caution is observed; in Spain, there is the added complication of the Inquisition. He suggests that Persons, currently in Madrid, discuss the situation with Francisco de Porres, rector of the Jesuit college in Madrid, and Ribadeneira, also residing in the province of Toledo. A particular instance [*continued*]

dence, given the circumstances of the time and place. However it seems to me that in order to avoid any kind of disfavour with the lords of the Holy Office, it is best not to receive them at all; rather, if they were considered suitable to be assigned to other provinces, the provincials of those [provinces] might be notified of their qualities, and then, if they agree, they could be sent over there. But because this might be inconvenient, and a remedy for only a few, could Your Reverence please discuss it with Fr Porres and Fr Ribadeneira, explaining to them that the cardinal and the other lords should be informed of what our constitutions say about those who come from infected areas. The very same men and father provincial, when occasion serves, will be able to perform that service, that is, Your Reverence may agree to their departure, and if those lords of the tribunal are satisfied, they shall be received, etc. And just so Antonio Schimero in Andalusia, for whom Your Reverence has had consent from the lords of the Inquisition, will be able to write to Fr Bartolomé Pérez the provincial.

B56 To Claudio Acquaviva, Madrid, 31 March 1590

SOURCE: Acquaviva to Persons, 15 May (B61).
NOTE: Persons reported that Luis de Morales had finally decided to decline the appointment in Japan.

B57 To Joseph Creswell, Madrid, 1 April 1590

SOURCE: ABSI, Coll P 477, Grene's notes.

B58 From Claudio Acquaviva, Rome, mid-April 1590

NOTE: On 24 March Acquaviva promised to reply more fully to Persons's letters of 26 January and 3 February (B49). It seems likely that in the meantime a letter or letters from Persons from the end of February would have reached Acquaviva and the general would have replied to these too, at about this time. There is no letter to Persons in the batch of 17 April (Tolet. 5/I, fols. 120r–125r).

---

is that of Antonio Schimero, a pious gentleman who wishes to enter the Society in Andalusia, who should be referred to the provincial, Bartolomé Pérez. From Bartoli's notes it appears that Schimero, or Schinelli, assisted the English Catholics in Rome and Naples: "Il P. Personio raccommanda al P. Cresuello il Sig. Antonio Skimero, che voleva entrare nella Compagnia" (Fr Persons recommends Sir Antonio Schimero, who wished to enter the Society, to Fr Creswell; ARSI, Angl. 38/II, fol. 78r, item 11), and "Pietro Antonio Skinelli. Fa fare molte divotioni nelle congregationi dell Cittá, e Regno di Napoli, per gli Catolici d'Inghilterra perseguitati" (Pietro Antonio Schinelli has performed many devotions among the congregations in Rome, and in the kingdom of Naples, on behalf of the persecuted Catholics of England; fol. 92v). Anthony Skinner was a servant of William Allen, who was arrested and condemned to death in 1592 but apostatized: see Verstegan to Persons, 6 August 1592 (B152) and his despatch of 3 August 1592 (Petti, 57–62, esp. 61 n5). He appears to have carried letters from Creswell to Brussels in April and May 1591 (Walpole to Creswell, 28 June 1591, in *Letters of Henry Walpole*, ed. Augustus Jessopp [Norwich, 1873], 28–30).

B59 To Claudio Acquaviva, Madrid, 17 April 1590

SOURCE: Acquaviva to Persons, 9 July (B68).
NOTE: This letter may have taken longer than usual, since Acquaviva does not mention it in his letter of 9 June (B64).

B60 To Joseph Creswell, Madrid, 28 April 1590

SOURCE: ABSI, Coll P 477 and 498, Grene's notes.
EDITION: Pollen, *Miscellanea IX*, 21.
NOTE: Many were urging Persons to consider founding a seminary in Lisbon, and especially in Seville: including the English priests John Cecil and William Warford (whom Persons had sent to Andalusia to beg alms for the college at Valladolid), and the provincial of Andalusia, Bartolomé Pérez – see Pollen, *Miscellanea IX*, 2–3; Hicks, *Seminaries*, part 4, 27; and Murphy, 5, who mentions John Fixer. Fixer and Cecil proved to be double agents (see the introduction, "The English Mission").

[*Grene writes, Coll P 498:*] in qua multa de Collegio erigendo in Lusitania, Hispali &c.

Translation

In which much is to be found about the establishment of a college in Portugal and Seville.

B61 From Claudio Acquaviva, Rome, 15 May 1590

SOURCE: ARSI, Tolet. 4, fol. 65v.
NOTE: Acquaviva expresses his hope that González Dávila will provide a good rector for Valladolid. Since Luis de Morales has declined to be transferred to Japan, there is no need to trouble the king, but Acquaviva is concerned about the requirements of the province of India. Once again, he has to write in haste because of the urgency of the courier service.

Madrid P. Roberto Personio 15 de Mayo.
Son bene quelle che Vostra Reverentia dice per la sua delli 31 de Marzo, scrivero che non si facci altro officio con Sua Maestà del Padre Morales, poiché egli ha recusato. Mà non sarà se non bene come Vostra Reverentia scrive[204] e se il Re[205] intenda quanto importa il prendere tali informationi dà chi[206] si deve et le sà; come anco il procurare che il provinciale dell' India non ci sia levato.[207] — Scriviamo di nuovo al Padre Egidio che vega di provedere il Seminario Anglese di buon superiore et speriamo che lo farà. Questo corriere non ci dà tempo di scrivere più che tanto perché essendo[208] arrivato huc, l'altro parte hoggi. Et però faccio fine col raccomandarmi &c.

204. come Vostra Reverentia scrive] *supplied in margin* R
205. il Re] *replaces* S. M^{ta} R
206. chi] *followed by indecipherable deletion ending in* et R
207. *Followed by one and a half lines of indecipherable material, deleted* R
208. perché essendo] *replaces* essendo R

Translation

To Fr Robert Persons in Madrid, 15 May.

What Your Reverence suggests in your letter of 31 March is commendable: I shall write that no further office need be performed with His Majesty on behalf of Fr Morales, as he has recused himself. But there is no harm in doing so, as Your Reverence writes, and the king should understand that he should gather such information from reliable persons; as also to make sure that the provincial of India is not removed from his office. — We are writing again to Fr Gil who is ready to provide the English seminary with a good superior and we hope that he will do so. This courier does not give us time to write more than this because he has just arrived, while the other one leaves today. And so I make an end, commending myself, etc.

B62 To Joseph Creswell, Madrid, 26 May 1590

SOURCE: ABSI, Coll P II 477, Grene's notes; cf. Coll P II 477.
EDITION: Pollen, *Miscellanea IX*, 21.
NOTE: Persons updates Creswell on the whereabouts of Thomas Wright (ca. 1562–1623). Wright joined the Society on 3 February 1580, was ordained priest in 1586, and spent the next few years working in northern Italy (McCoog, *English and Welsh Jesuits*, 340 and 354 n197). He joined Persons in Valladolid in November 1593.

[*Grene writes*:] in qua apparet quod P. Thomas Wrytus habitabat tunc Genuae &c.

Translation

In which it appears that Fr Thomas Wright was then living in Genoa.

B63 To Claudio Acquaviva, Madrid, 26 May 1590

SOURCE: Acquaviva to Persons, 9 July (B68).

B64 From Claudio Acquaviva, Rome, 9 June 1590

SOURCE: ARSI, Tolet. 5/I, fol. 128v (main text) and 129v (addition).
NOTE: Acquaviva laments the loss of two priests, but hopes to be able to replenish the mission. He refers an enquirer to the rector of the English college, Joseph Creswell. In the addendum, he thanks Persons for his intervention with the king, which should ensure peaceful proceedings with the congregations, and assures him that Gil González will supply him with a suitable rector for the college in Valladolid.

P. Roberto Personio Junio 9.
Pues Dios nuestro Señor ha querido lastimarnos con la muerte de aquellos dos buenos padres que se ahogaron,[209] procuraremos que vayan otros dos de los que quedan

209. ahogaron] *possibly a scribal error for* ahorcaron *("hanged")*

en Françia, verdad es que el Padre Estero no sé si podra ir porque creo lee Teologia pero irá otro en su lugar y avisaremos que sea qual conviene. Ya ha llegado aqui aquel gentilhombre que desea ser recevido, y será consolado, pero en este particular me remito a lo que escrivira el padre Rector del Inglés. No más en esta de encomendarme, etc.

Anadiose a la del Padre Personio. Junio 9.

El buen ofiçio que Vuestra Reverencia ha hecho con Su Magestad ha sido de mucha importançia, y su respuesta tal como haviamos menester y se devia esperar de pecho tan christiano, con esto creo que las congregaçiones se havran hecho con paz y quietud: dios pague a Vuestra Reverencia el cuydado y solicitud con que acude al bien comun de las cosas de la Compañia.

Yo he encomendado mucho al Padre Gil Gonçalez lo del seminario de Valladolid, y en particular que le provea de un buen superior; aora lo hago de nuevo. Vuestra Reverencia le hable y de los que conoçe y le pareçe serian a proposito le proponga alguno que si no estuviere tan prendado de otra cosa que no le pueda quitar de la ocupaçion que tiene, él le dara.

Lo del Padre Vasconçelos tiene al presente una dificultad que es estar él en la corte ocupado en negoçios de tanta importançia como Vuestra Reverencia save, los quales no se podran dexar sin grave detrimento, pero en acabandolos yo holgaré que atienda a lo que Vuestra Reverencia pide, y se lo encargaré, y el Padre Manuel Rodriguez tanbien gustará de que ayude a la naçion inglesa en eso y en lo demas que se pudiere. No otro &c.

Translation

To Fr Robert Persons, 9 June.

Since it has pleased God our Lord to afflict us with the death of those two good fathers who were drowned,[210] we will try to arrange that another two may go who are still in France. The truth is that I don't know whether Fr Estero will be able to go because I believe he is reading theology,[211] but another may go in his place, and we advise that this will be just as suitable. A certain gentleman has arrived here who desires to be received, and he has yet to be satisfied,[212] but in this particular I will wait to see what the father rector of the English [college] writes. No more in this except to commend myself, etc.

Added to the letter to Fr Persons, 9 June.

The good office that Your Reverence has performed with His Majesty has been of great importance, and his response is what we needed and should be expected from such a Christian breast. As a consequence, the congregations will proceed with peace and

---

210. This may refer to the seminary priests Francis Dickenson and Miles Gerard, who were hanged, drawn, and quartered at Rochester on 30 April 1590. See textual note.

211. This may refer to Thomas Lister (entered the Society 1583), at this time a student at Pont-à-Mousson. Later he joined Garnet in England. Another Jesuit in France was Thomas Owens (ca. 1556–1618).

212. This may be the same Antonio Schimero mentioned in Acquaviva's letter of 24 March (B55).

quiet. May God repay Your Reverence for the care and solicitude with which you further the common good of the affairs of the Company.

I have strongly commended the Valladolid seminary to Father Gil González, and in particular to provide it with a good superior; now I am doing it again.[213] Would Your Reverence please speak to him, and kindly propose someone from those you know and consider suitable. Unless this person is so engaged with other things that he cannot be removed from that occupation, he will grant him.

The choice of Father Vasconcelos currently presents a difficulty, which is that he is in that court busy with business of great importance, as Your Reverence knows, which cannot be left without serious detriment. But as soon as he finalizes that business, I will be content for him to attend to Your Reverence, and will commission him accordingly. Father Manuel Rodríguez will also appreciate it if he would help the English nation in that and in whatever else he could. No more [for the present except], etc.

B65 To Joseph Creswell, Valladolid, 24 June 1590

> SOURCE: ABSI, Coll P II 477 and 498.
> HICKS: 89.
> EDITION: Pollen, *Miscellanea IX*, 21.
> NOTE: Persons had been in Madrid from November to the end of May; returning to Valladolid, he noted the building operations and also the unsuitability of the rector, Pedro de Guzmán (see Acquaviva's letter of 24 March, B55).

I repose myself a little now after a most painful winter past in Madrid, though heere alsoe there want not labour enough — in building &c. — More concerning this house you may reade in my lettere to Dr Barret, which I pray you send to him — *Praesens rector parum idoneus*[214] &c. —

B66 To Richard Barret, Valladolid, 24 June 1590

> SOURCE: Persons to Creswell, 24 June (B65).
> NOTE: Persons enclosed this in a letter to Creswell, for forwarding.

B67 To Claudio Acquaviva, Valladolid, 26 June 1590

> SOURCE: ARSI, FG 651/640, item 25, holograph.
> NOTE: Acquaviva responded to this letter on 7 August (B72). Persons reports on the progress of the seminary at Valladolid: building plans, the interest of the king, the dowager empress Maria of Austria, and the cardinal of Toledo. Philip II provided funding but also stipulated that Valladolid should be the centre for all English priests in Spain. Arrangements are being made to replace Pedro de Guzmán as rector.

213. See Acquaviva's letters to Gil González, 9 July 1590 (Tolet. 5/I, fols. 133r–136v, at 134v). On Fr Vasconcelos, see Acquaviva's letter of 4 September (B75).

214. The present rector is not very suitable.

Persons reports on a disappointing discussion with Idiáquez, who could only give a general assurance that the king wanted all Jesuits to adhere to the Society's "way of proceeding." Gil González Dávila, supported by Francisco de Porres, recommends caution: Acquaviva's plan to transfer the leaders of the memorialists in order to subdue the provinces of Spain should be postponed until the visitation to Toledo is completed, because neither the king nor the Inquisition would sanction the transfers. In the meantime, González Dávila would prepare some memorials for the king's attention, and explain more fully in person after the visitation of Toledo.

This is the only letter from Persons to Acquaviva to have survived between 29 April 1589 (which is interleaved in the general's private register, B15) and June 1592 (B147). A curious feature is the contraction mark placed over words such as "segnalato" and "Spagna," and the altering of "trattado" to "trattato," suggesting some confusion between Italian and Spanish.

Molto Reverendo in Christo Padre nostro
Pax Christi.
Con l'ordinario passato scrissi a Vostra Paternità da Madrid quello que per alhora me s'offerse intorno le cose nostre, dipoi me parti de là alli 10 di questo per venir qua a Valladolid et passai per Escurial dove trattai de espacio con Don Juan Ideaquez et hebbi risposta di Sua Maestà, circa alcune cose di questo Seminario, al quale Sua Maestà ha segnalato per questi principii, 140 scudi per il mese, et l'ha stabilito sopra le sue rente reali nel Medina del Campo con promessa di più per l'avenire, con la qual pensione che monta a 1680 per anno, et 800 altri per anno che danno l' imperatrice, il Cardinale de Toledo, et altri, teniamo de fermo 2500 Δ per l'anno, con buone speranze d'altre cose; di maniera, che già possiamo con l'aiuto di Dio nostro Signor, et di Vostra Paternità, cominciar a metter in ordine questo Seminario, il qual benché sia stato comminciato con molto deboli principii, tuttavia mi persuado che con tiempo riuscerà a esser grande, et conforme a questa speranza andiamo mettendo già in ordine buona casa, perché il sito che teniamo è molto excellente et vicino al Collegio della Compagnia, l'orto grande et bello quatro vuolte come quello di cotesta casa. L'habitatione non è molto grande[215] ma comoda, et bastante per 24 persone, che al presente stiamo in essa, et di più tiene comodità per far una chiesola bella a basso circa la portaria. Et tutto questo già sta comprato et pagato, con 2000 ducati. Ma più di questo, v'è una casa quasi una vuolta et mezzo magior di[216] questa congionta con l'orto nostro,[217] la qual con un corritor si può molto commodamente congiongersi con questa casa, la qual casa vicina[218] hoggidì havemo pigliato per nuove anni, et il provinciale non desidera altro se non che la compriamo anchora, et come sta vincolata con un censo de 50 misse ogni anno, non si provender senza licencia particular del Re, et egli[219] pensa che noi potremo più facilmente procurar quella licencia che altri, et così[220] credo che col tiempo ci verrà più commodamente.

215. grande] *interlined with caret R*
216. magior di] *interlined, replacing* con *R*
217. nostro] *interlined with caret R*
218. vicina] *supplied in margin R*
219. egli] *interlined with caret R*
220. et così] *interlined with caret R*

2. Ma in questo mentre tendremo bastante habitatione per ottanta persone, quando le rente bastassero per tanti. Vero è che per accomodar queste due case a nostro uso, particularmente questa prima che è comprata (della qual una parte va cascando verso l'orto) et per far il corritore et accomodar l'ecclesia serà necessario spender 500 overo 600 ducati, li quali tengo già, et alcuni altri di[221] più per comprar cose necessarie in casa et perché Sua Maestà vuol che tutti li sacerdoti Ynglesi che stanno in Spagna siano di questo Seminario et che[222] tenghino dependencia d'esso, benché[223] per alcuni servitii stan[n]o fuora (como alcuni stanno nella Colletta altri con alcuni Signori particulari che l'hanno dimandato). Vostra Paternità vedrà nella lista che[224] le mando, che siano trenta quatro in tutto[225] benché actualmente ressidino[226] qui (come ho detto) solamente 24. Et perché nel fine di queste estate, la magior parte delli sacerdoti si partiranno da qui, o in missioni, overo per star in Ebora o Sivilla dove ci offeriscono principii d'altri Seminarii, io ho mandato[227] a Rhemis per vinti altri scholari, et che 6 o 8 di loro siano theologi, et l'altri per comminciar il[228] corso de philosophia poiché li nostri padri qui haverebbono molto a charo[229] di cominciar a legger un corso di philosophia con questo pretesto et ragione, alla quale l'università non potrà contradit per esser l'Ynglesi raccomandati alla Compagnia dal Re[230] per loro institutione nelle fere,[231] etc.

3. Et perché habbiamo trovato per esperienza già[232] che questo buon Padre Pietro Gusman non è sufficiente per quello che qui è necessario per il governo di dentro, et fuorestieri, et per le[233] correspondenze di fuora con li ministri del Re et altri prelati et Signori ni l'applica a esso, si non a studiar solamente et a[234] predicar; per questo ho trattato[235] con il Padre Visitator che avanti che[236] si parta da qui, stabilisca un Rettor sufficiente, con un confessore per le cose spirituali, oltra li quali non sarà necessario altro della Compagnia, se non fusse un fratello più con tiempo[237] per Compagno del Rettore, di maniera che al summo fussero sei, li quali bastaranno, benché il Seminario crescesse a tener ottanta studianti, supplendo con garzoni seculari quello che mancarà, li quali faranno molte cose di casa meglio che non li nostri fratelli particularmente qui in Spagna dove li fratelli congiuntori d'ordinario sono tanto delicati et cavallieri, che non si può

221. altri di] *interlined, replacing illegible deletion* R
222. che] *interlined with caret* R
223. benché] *interlined, replacing illegible deletion* R
224. nella lista che] *replaces* che R
225. che *and* in tutto *interlined with carets* R
226. ressidino] *interlined, replacing* siano R
227. Paragraph no. 2 placed here in margin.
228. il] *interlined with caret* R
229. charo] *interlined, replacing* car R
230. dal Re] *interlined with caret* R
231. nelle fere] *this ed.;* nelle le fere R
232. già] *interlined with caret* R
233. per le] *interlined with caret* R
234. a] *interlined with caret* R
235. trattato] *corrected from* trattado. *Paragraph no. 3 placed here in margin* R
236. che] *possibly deleted* R
237. con tiempo] *interlined with caret, using Spanish spelling* R

espettar da loro ningun servicio, se non sia la superintendencia de algun negocio, et così ci dicono chiaramente, di maniera che in luogo di Fabricio che desidera tornar a esser mio Compagno, ho procurato suo nepote Ambrosio Lissio Italiano che pare un[238] fratello di molto travaglio et grandemente desidera star qui. Tutto il resto circa questo Seminario Vostra Paternità l'intenderà dalle letere del Padre Visitatore et d'altri.

4. In quanto alli negotii della Compagnia ho trovato qui il Padre Egidio Visitatore di parere, che non convenga per adesso dimandar da Sua Maestà che si mutino li capi delli conturbanti, ni che si der a Sua Maestà processi personali poiché contra la magior parte di loro, dice che[239] non ce ne son tali, delli quali li ministri di Sua Maestà, usati a casi gravi, faranno molto conto et poiché tutti già di questa provincia promettono emendatione si Vostra Paternità li vuol abbrachiar, et dall'altra parte sarebbe farli desperati se non s'admettessero, è di parere che convenga provar si questo medio riuscirà, almanco fin' al fine d'altera Visita de la provincia de Toledo, nella quale molte cose si trovaranno intricate con quelle di questa provincia, et così le une non si potranno fini bene senza l'altre.

5. Di più è di parere, et in questo anco viene il Padre Porres, che pendente la visita delle altre provincie,[240] il Re mai consentirà che si faccia alcuna mutatione di persone, n'anco il Santo Officio, al che anco io più facilmente m'incline a credere[241] (nonostante le buone parole del Re) perché trattando io con Don Juan della necessità del remedio per questi perturbanti, lui se mostrà molto[242] fervoroso in esso, ma quando io fra altri mezze gli[243] proposi come per principale, il mutarli le persone, egli mi rispose, che si pratticassero l'atri mezzi fuora del mutarli, et quando a questo io replicai molte ragioni, non mi rispose niente, fuora che dirmi che il Re gustaria grandemente che questi et tutti l'altri se compellissero a osservar la disciplina della Compagnia essattamente.

Per queste ragioni et altre ch'il Padre Visitatore scriverà a Vostra Paternità di suo pena.[244]

6. Io vengo ancho a sperar che il modo che Sua Reverentia sta determinato di tener con Sua Maestà riuscerà, molto bene, et, a consolatione di Vostra Paternità; et il modo che pensa tener è questo, che darà[245] a Sua Maestà tre memoriali, il primo historiale[246] del stato della provincia quanto alle persone, all'officii, alle cose temporali et alle letere. Il secondo delli capi principali delli memoriali trattando anco a bocca di questi capi più largamente che non delle cose del primo memoriale. Il terzo memoriale sarà delle vere cause et delli progressi di queste turbationi, della intentione delli conturbanti, delli mezzi ch'hanno usato, et altre cose simili, le quali Sua Reverentia potrà explicar molto più larga-

---

238. pare un] *interlined with caret, replacing* é un R
239. dice che] *interlined with caret* R
240. delle altre provincie] *interlined with caret* R
241. m'incline a credere] m'incline *interlined with caret,* a credere *supplied in margin, replacing indecipherable single word* R
242. molto] *interlined, replacing* anchora R
243. gli] *interlined with caret* R
244. di suo pena] R, *possibly in error for* di sua pena *or* di suo pugno
245. darà] *interlined, replacing* dava R
246. historiale] *interlined with caret* R

mente et particularmente a Sua Maestà che non lasciar in scritto, et così conviene a mio parere, benché sia anche necessario lasciar alcune cose in scritto, per sodisfattione delli ministri di Sua Maestà delli[247] quali alcuni[248] saranno forse più curiosi in questa materia che non amici, benché a quelli che sono confidenti sarà bien dir tutto, se non fusse cosa alcuna che al Re solo si ne dicesse.

7. Questo è il desegno che tiene il Padre Visitatore, et poiché per le ragioni già dette et altre che egli scriverà a Vostra Paternità non è di parer[249] che si devono far per[250] adesso le due cose ex professo[251] che altre vuolte s'è trattato, cioè, dar al Re processi personali contra li capi, et dimandar licencia per mutarli di qua, tuttavia ha promesso di farle tutte due[252] incoative, cioè, parlando al Re sopra il terzo memoriale delle cause di queste turbationi, dirà le cose più gravi che sa contra 170[253] et qualche altro a bocca, et dipoi havendo mostrato il male et la necessità di remedio, dirà che il più efficace et presente remedio saria divider questa gente et mutarli, ma como loro offeriscono emendatione et Vostra Paternità è desiderosa di provar tutti l'altri mezzi possibili prima che venir a questo, andarà supportando qualche più tempo si Sua Magestad[254] così l'ordena, però con speranza che si loro non se emendino né cessano d'esser inquieti, che Sua Magestad non solamente permetterà ma anco darà brachio per mutarli, etc.

8. Questo modo di preparar la strada (supposto che al presente non si può far alto) mi parerebbe a proposito per obligar il Re che almanco nel fine dell'altra visita della Provincia di Toledo (nella qual anchora se deve ...) [*incomplete*][255]

Translation

Our Very Reverend Father in Christ
The peace of Christ.

By the last ordinary post, I wrote to Your Paternity from Madrid whatever occurred to me about our affairs,[256] and then I left there on the 10th of this month, to go from there to Valladolid. I passed through El Escorial, where I spent a good deal of time dealing with Don Juan de Idiáquez; I had a response from His Majesty concerning some matters of this seminary, to which His Majesty has assigned 140 crowns a month for the time being, basing this on his own royal revenue in Medina del Campo,[257] with promise of

247. delli] *replaces* che R
248. alcuni] *interlined with caret* R
249. di parer] *this ed.;* di parver R
250. per] *interlined with caret* R
251. ex professo] *initially placed after* adesso, *interlined with caret and deleted* R
252. tutte due] *interlined with caret* R
253. 170] Abreo *interlined* R
254. Sua Magestad] *abbreviated* sua Mg^d *in this paragraph only* R
255. Some of the letters, and not simply those by Robert Persons, in *FG* have been lost. The collection was never bound, nor the folios numbered sequentially. Thus, some letters have disappeared – perhaps as collectors' items – and others have been misfiled. See also Persons to Acquaviva, 12 August 1592 (B153).
256. 26 May (B63); see also Acquaviva to Persons, 9 July (B68).
257. Medina del Campo is situated some 45 km from Valladolid.

more to come. With this pension, which amounts to 1680 per annum, and 800 more per annum from the empress, the cardinal of Toledo,[258] and others, we can count on 2500 ducats per year, with good hopes of the rest; to the extent that we can now, with the aid of God our Lord, and of Your Paternity, begin to get this seminary in order. Although it has begun on a very shaky footing, I am, nevertheless, fully persuaded that in time it will succeed to great things. In keeping with this hope, we have already begun getting our house in order, because the site which we occupy is most excellent and near the college of the Society, with a large and beautiful garden four times as large as the house itself. The residence is not very large but it is comfortable, and enough for the twenty-four people who are staying in it at present; moreover, it has room for a beautiful chapel below near the entrance. And all of this has already been bought and paid for, for 2000 ducats. But besides this, there is a house, almost one-and-a-half times bigger than this, abutting on our garden, which could be very conveniently joined with this house by a corridor; this house nearby we have now taken for nine years; and the provincial wants nothing else but that we go ahead and purchase it. It is bonded to a requirement of 50 masses per annum, so it cannot be sold without a particular licence from the king, but he[259] thinks that we could obtain this licence more easily than others, and therefore I think that in time things will work out most conveniently.

2. But in the meanwhile we will stretch the accommodation to eighty persons, when our income is sufficient for so many. The truth is that to adapt these two houses to our use, especially that first one which has been bought (of which one part overhangs the garden), and to make the corridor and create the chapel, it will be necessary to spend five or six hundred ducats, which I already have in hand, and some more to purchase necessities for the house – also because His Majesty desires that all the English priests who are in Spain should belong to this seminary and depend on it, even if they remain outside because of various commitments (for instance, some stay in the offertory, some with certain particular gentlemen who have requested them). Your Paternity will see in the list which I am sending you that there are thirty-four in total, although only twenty-four are actually residing here (as I have said). And because at the end of this summer most of the priests will depart from here, either on missions, or to stay in Évora or Seville[260] where they teach the rudiments at other seminaries, I have sent to Rheims for twenty more scholars, six or eight of them to be theologians, and the others to begin the course of philosophy, as our fathers here greatly desire to begin to read a course of philosophy, with this pretext and reason: that the university will not be able to prevent them, just because they are English, from being recommended to the Society by the king for their ordination on feast days.

3. And because we have found by experience already that this good Fr Pedro de Guzmán cannot cope with what is necessary here for the management, both internal and external, and for the external dealings with the ministers of the king and other prelates and

258. Cardinal Gaspar de Quiroga y Vela (1512–1594) was archbishop of Toledo and patron of the painter El Greco. The empress Maria of Austria (1528–1603), widow of Charles V, was living in retirement in a convent in Madrid.

259. I.e., the provincial, Pedro Villalba.

260. This suggests that English priests spent time in Seville and other cities in Spain to help with the teaching in schools and colleges.

noblemen in matters relating to it – quite apart from the studies and preaching – I have therefore consulted with father visitor, who before we leave here will supply a capable rector, with a confessor for spiritual matters. Besides this, there will be no need for another from the Society, except perhaps for a brother for the meantime as *socius*[261] to the rector. So there will be six at most, who will be enough, even if the Seminary grows to take eighty students – if they make up what is necessary with secular youths, who do many things better than our own brothers, especially those here in Spain, where the associated brothers are ordinarily so delicate and cavalier that you can't expect any service from them, except to supervise some business, and that is what is said openly. Consequently, in place of Fabrizio, who wishes to return as my *socius*,[262] I have procured his nephew Ambrosio Lissio, an Italian, who seems a brother of great industry and greatly desires to be here. All the rest about this seminary Your Paternity will learn from the letters of father visitor and others.

4. As far as the business of the Society goes, I have found here that Fr Gil the visitor believes this is not the right time to ask of His Majesty that the leaders of the dissidents be transferred, nor that you entrust actions against individuals to His Majesty, because in most of these cases, he says, they are not the kind of things that His Majesty's ministers, used to weighty matters of state, will pay much attention to. And since everyone in this province already promises to reform if Your Paternity will accept them, and on the other hand they will become desperate if they are not admitted, he is of the opinion that it is better to see if he can succeed by this means, at least until the end of the other visit (to the province of Toledo), in which many matters will be found to be tangled up with those of this province, and so neither will be able to be dealt with without the other.

5. Moreover, he is of the opinion (and in this Fr Porres is also in agreement) that, pending the visit of the other provinces, the king will never allow any transfer of persons to be made, nor will the Holy Office. I am more easily inclined to believe this (notwithstanding the fine words of the king) because when I was dealing with Don Juan about the need for a remedy for these dissidents, he showed himself very enthusiastic, but when amongst other means I proposed as principal, the transfer of persons, he answered me that he would try other means rather than transferring them, and when I opposed many reasons to this, he did not reply at all, except to tell me that the king greatly desired that these and all the others should be compelled to observe the discipline of the Society strictly: these reasons and others father visitor will write to Your Paternity, by his own hand.

6. I am also hoping that the method which His Reverence[263] remains determined to pursue with His Majesty will succeed, very well, and to the consolation of Your Paternity. And what he plans to do is this: to give three memorials to the king. The first will be historical, about the condition of the province with regard to persons, to offices, to temporal matters, and to letters. The second, about the main instigators of the memorials,[264] will deal (also by word of mouth) with these leaders more fully than with the matters of the first memorial. The third memorial will be of the true causes and developments of

---

261. Companion and assistant.
262. Brother Fabrizio Como was in Rome at this time; he returned only in 1592.
263. I.e., González Dávila.
264. I.e. the memorials drawn up by the *memorialistas*.

these perturbations, of the motives of the dissidents, of the means that they have used, and other similar matters, which His Reverence may explain much more fully and in detail to His Majesty than he can put in writing; and that is appropriate in my opinion, although it may also be necessary to put some matters in writing for the satisfaction of the ministers of His Majesty in some respects, who will perhaps be more curious in this matter than friendly, although with those who are trustworthy it will be good to confide fully, except for any matter which should be communicated only to the king.

7. This is father visitor's settled intention. For the reasons he has already given and others that he will explain to Your Paternity in writing, he does not believe that these two things ought to be done immediately at present but dealt with at another time – that is, to entrust the king with taking action personally against the leaders, and to ask for a licence to transfer them from there. Nevertheless, he has promised to perform these two outstanding matters: that is, when talking to the king about the third memorial, of the causes of these perturbations, he will tell him about the more serious charges that he knows against Abreo[265] and another individual by word of mouth. On top of that, having demonstrated the evil and the need for a remedy, he will say that the most efficacious and urgent remedy will be to divide this tribe and transfer them; however, since they offer amendment and Your Paternity is desirous to try all other possible means before resorting to this, he will go on allowing some more time if His Majesty should so ordain, but with the hope that if they do not amend themselves or cease to be unquiet, His Majesty will not only permit them to be transferred but even lend a hand.

8. According to this method of preparing the ground (supposing that for the present it is not possible to do more), I am inclined to think that, by way of obliging the king, [we should wait] at least until the end of the other visit to the province of Toledo (in which, again, it ought ...)

B68 From Claudio Acquaviva, Rome, 9 July 1590

SOURCE: ARSI, Tolet. 5/I, fol. 137v–138r.

NOTE: Acquaviva commends Persons for his further dealings with the king; entrusts the needs of the seminary in Valladolid to the visitor, González Dávila; expresses concern for Persons's health; and recommends that he deal firmly with Richard Gibbons, who had been recalled from Lisbon to assist at Valladolid.

P. Roberto Personio Julio 9.

Por la de 26 de Mayo me avisa Vuestra Reverencia de la grata audiencia que le dio Su Magestad y quam bien respondio a los puntos que le propuse, graçias a Dios nuestro Señor que todo lo govierna y endereza con providençia tan paternal como la que en nuestras cosas siempre ha mostrado, y a Vuestra Reverencia agradezco la charidad con que atiende a ayudarnos.

---

265. Francisco Abreo, a leading *memorialista*, was dismissed from the Society in 1588 but permitted to live independently within the Society until 1592.

En lo del seminario me remito a lo que con el passado escrivi, aunque veo al padre visitador tan deseoso de ayudar que no creo será necessario más que proponerle, pues él me escrive que antes de venir a la provincia de Toledo dexará acomodado el seminario de Valladolid.

Encargo a Vuestra Reverencia que mire por su salud, y si para ella fuere necessario que yo desde acá haga alguna diligencia a estos padres, me lo avise, aunque fío de su charidad que acudiran a Vuestra Reverencia como saben que es razon y yo lo deseo. Del buen despacho de los Ingleses me he consolado.

Bien es que Vuestra Reverencia dé algunos avisos y acuerdos al Padre Ricardo porque como él ama y respecta a Vuestra Reverencia creo le ayudará, y él los aceptará, y importa mucho que él se vaya a la mano en sus coleras porque si son con algun excesso algo impediran para su promoçion. Non otro en esta que encomendarme, etc.

Translation

To Fr Robert Persons, 9 July.

In your letter of 26 May[266] Your Reverence told me about the welcome audience that His Majesty gave you, and how good an answer he gave to the matters which you raised. Thanks be to God our Lord who governs everything and directs it with such fatherly providence, as He has always shown in our affairs, and I am grateful to Your Reverence for the charity with which you attend to our needs.

With regard to the seminary, I refer you to what I wrote in my last letter;[267] also, I see that the father visitor is so desirous to help that I do not think anything more will be necessary than he proposes; indeed, he writes to me that before he goes to the province of Toledo, he will leave the seminary of Valladolid well taken care of.

Be sure, Your Reverence, to take good care of your health, and if it is necessary for your health's sake that from here on I should make some appeal to those fathers, please let me know, although I trust their charity to come to the aid of Your Reverence as is only right, and I desire it.[268] I am much consoled that the English have been sent out safely.[269]

It would be good if Your Reverence gave some advice and suggestions to Fr Richard, because, as he loves and respects Your Reverence, I believe that should help, and he will accept them – and the fact that he takes his anger to extremes is a serious problem, because any such excess will stand in the way of his advancement. Nothing else for the moment, except to commend myself, etc.

---

266. B63.

267. 9 June (B64).

268. Acquaviva suggests that the Spanish Jesuits in Valladolid should aid Persons in his illness. See his letter of 4 September (B75).

269. The meaning of "buon despacho" is unclear: it may refer to some business that has been well done, to the resolute disposition of the English students and priests, or it may refer to the plans for the departure of John Cecil and his companions who spent time in Seville and left for England in May 1591.

B69 From Claudio Acquaviva, Rome, 9 July 1590

SOURCE: ARSI, Tolet. 4, fol. 71v–72r.

NOTE: In this confidential letter, Acquaviva expresses his pleasure over the news of the provincial congregations. He wants Persons to be entirely frank with him about the details. There is continued concern about the attitude of Sebastián Hernández, whose name is underlined here for encoding: clearly this was a sensitive matter.

Madrid. P. Personio, 9 di Luglio.

Si sono ricevute quelle di Vostra Reverentia delli 17 d'Aprile et 27 di Maggio. Ci siamo consolati molto nel Signore del buon successo delle Congregationi qual è grand' argumento della Divina assistenza[270] et benignità con che va preparando i cuori alla pace et unione fraterna. Il favore anco della Maestà del Re importa molto, del quale aspetto qualche buon risolutione[271] per mettere rimedio con la Divina grazia[272] alla disciplina della Compagnia poiché li Visitatori quali Sua Maestà aspettava, sarano costì a quest'hora.
—
Li punti di quella de 27 sono ottimi; né accade che Vostra Reverentia habbi scrupulo di scrivere cose molto particolari poiché la notitia di tutte quelle è[273] molto necessaria. Et particolarmente m'è stato caro intendere il particolare del Padre Sebastiano Hernandez.[274] Con che per fine di questa, &c.

Translation

To Robert Persons in Madrid, 9 July.

Your Reverence's letters of 17 April and 27 May have been received.[275] We are much consoled in the Lord by the good success of the congregations, which is a great argument of God's benign assistance in preparing hearts for peace and fraternal union. Also, the favour of His Majesty the king counts for a great deal, which leads me to expect just such a good resolution to apply a remedy, with the grace of God, to the discipline of the Society as the visitors whom His Majesty had been waiting for, must be there by now.

The points you make in your letter of the 27th are excellent; please would Your Reverence have no compunction to write in great detail, as the news of all these things is very necessary. And particularly I am very concerned to hear the particulars of Fr. Sebastián Hernández. With that I will end this.

---

270. assistenza] *initially placed before* Divina *and deleted* R
271. risolutione] *interlined, replacing* habere R
272. con la Divina grazia] *interlined with caret* R
273. la notitia di tutte quelle è] la notitia di *interlined and* quelle è *supplied in margin, replacing* tutte sono R
274. del Padre Sebastiano Hernandez] *underlined*
275. B59, B63 (dated 26 May).

B70 To Claudio Acquaviva, Valladolid, about 22 July 1590

SOURCE: Acquaviva to Persons, 4 September (B75).

NOTE: Persons sent an encouraging report on the seminary and the assistance of Gil González Dávila, the visitor.

B71 To Joseph Creswell, Valladolid, 22–26 July 1590

SOURCE: ABSI, Coll P II 500, Grene's partial transcript.
HICKS: 90.
EDITION: Pollen, *Miscellanea IX*, 21.

NOTE: Grene refers to this letter, and the two following, in a note on Coll P II 477. Possibly there was one letter written over several days. On the possibility of founding a seminary at Seville, see the headnote to Persons's earlier letter of 28 April (B60); see also Acquaviva's letter of 10 June 1591 (B109, McCoog, *Building the Faith of St Peter*, 113).

In the second extract, dated 23 July, Persons reports on the likely influx of students from Rheims and Eu. The English preparatory school at Eu, established under the auspices of Henry, duke of Guise, collapsed after the duke's assassination on 23 December 1588, but several students remained in the town. See McCoog, *Our Way of Proceeding*, 264, and Maurice Whitehead, *English Jesuit Education: Expulsion, Suppression, Survival, Restoration, 1762–1803* (Farnham, 2013), 22.

Pedro de Guzmán, rector of the college at Valladolid, died towards the end of June, to be replaced by Juan López de Manzano. The confessor, Rodrigo de Cabredo, was summoned from Cuenca, where he had been minister to the Jesuit community (*Blackfan Annals*, 26–27). He was later to become a very successful rector of the college.

No further details are given of what was written on 26 July.

[22 July]
I remaine here in Valladolid since the 15 of June, and am soe to doe until about the 15 of August, when I am to returne to Madrid, though — many — do make great instance that I goe presently to Sevil for the great hope there is given of a Seminary alsoe — but 'tis impossible to attend to so many things together — The present maintenance of this Seminary will amount to 2500 Δ.

[23 July]
Expectat pro illo Seminario 20 aut 30 alumnos Rhemis aut Augio &c. [—] ut in aliis literis scripserat[276] — Niew rector Juan Lopez Mançano, a most worthy man &c. [—] Fr Roderico Cabredo Confessour and most affectionat to our nation — the habitation fitt for 50[277] &c. —

276. "[Persons] is awaiting the arrival at this seminary of twenty students from Rheims and Eu, as he had written in other letters."
277. 50] G; 30 *Pollen*

B72 From Claudio Acquaviva, Rome, 7 August 1590

SOURCE: ARSI, Tolet. 4, fol. 72v–73r.

NOTE: Acquaviva is pleased with the increased funding for the college and is willing to be reconciled with the discontented Spanish Jesuits if there is genuine willingness to reform. But he is anxious not to leave the situation in the king's hands, and depends greatly on the visitor, Gil González Dávila.

Madrid P. Roberto Personio 7 d'Agosto.

Ho visto quanto Vostra Reverentia per la sua delli 26 di Giugno mi scrive; et mi rallegro della crescimento del seminario et lemosina datagli da Sua Maestà et d'altri Signori. Circa il non dimandare per adesso al Re che[278] li capi de conturbanti si possino mutare et disgregare, né manco dare a Sua Maestà i loro processi per le cause che Vostra Reverentia scrive. Già il Padre Egidio sarà costì, et però mi rimetto a quello che giudicherano[279] più ispediente, con questo però[280] che s'intenda essere totalmente[281] necessario assicurare la Compagnia che costoro non faccino il medesimo un'altra volta, né questo pensiero lascierò io mentre non si trova quello zelo[282] et forma di tal' assicurezza che altrimente se non il rimoverli o adesso, o poco dipoi.[283] Nel resto sono pronto ad abbracciargli et scordarmi del passato, se nell'avenire si mostreranno essere veramente mutati *in unum alterum melius*. Per il che[284] non mi pare che al Re si dica che si starà a vedere se c'è emendatione: prima perché[285] sebene io la desidero, conviene però[286] che questa si facci et s'aspetti dove se non riesce, non possino fare più dano.[287] Secondo perché se da un canto le Reverentie Vostre dicano al Re che staremo a vedere l'emendatione, et dall'altro giudicano che alli ministri del Re avezzi a maggiori delitti, parerano picuoli quelli della maggior parte di costoro, se adesso non s'insinua al Re questa necessità d'assicurarci col rimuovergli, potrà Sua Maestà dipoi dimandare che cosa habbino costoro fatta da questo tempo in poi, per la quale vogliano disgregargli, non havendolo fatto prima

---

278. al Re che] *preceded by the code* 20 19 82 22 28 25 *R* [= al Re che]

279. et però mi rimetto a quello che giudicherano] et però *interlined*, a quello, *etc. replaces* a loro; se *deleted before* giudicherano *R*

280. però] *interlined R*

281. totalmente] *interlined R*

282. quello zelo] *obscure R*

283. che altrimente se non il rimoverli o adesso, o poco dipoi] *supplied in margin R*

284. unum alterum melius. Per il che] unum alterum *obscure, possibly deleted*; Per il che *interlined with caret R*

285. prima perché] *interlined, duplicating* perché *R*

286. conviene però] ma *deleted before* conviene; però *interlined R*

287. At this point the figure refers the reader to a short passage inserted at the foot of the page, "per la quale vogliamo disgregargli non havendolo fatto prima," which is replaced at the head of the next page with the passage given in the text, "Secondo perché ... *necessario succumbemus*," incorporating the earlier insertion.

et non havendo all'hora in mano, come forse non havremo cosa di nuovo che sia di momento, *necessario succumbemus*. Questa potrà Vostra Reverentia mostrare al Padre Egidio[288] per cui fine mi raccommando.

Translation

To Robert Persons in Madrid, 7 August.

I have seen what Your Reverence wrote to me in your letter of 26 June;[289] and I rejoice in the growth of the seminary and the alms given by His Majesty and other noblemen. Consequently, for the present we will not ask the king that the leaders of the disturbances should if possible be transferred and dispersed, much less leave it to His Majesty to deal with the actions against them, for the reasons which Your Reverence writes. Fr Gil will already be there, and so I defer to his judgement on what is more expedient, with this proviso, that it is understood that it is absolutely necessary that they assure the Society that they will not do the same again. Nor do I think I should allow this matter to drop until there is clear evidence, both in zeal and outward form, of such an assurance; otherwise, they will have to be removed, either now or a little later. For the rest I am ready to embrace them and forget what is past, if when they come it is shown that they are truly changed for the better, one and all. Still, I do not think that the king should be told that we are waiting to see if there is any amendment: first, even though [reconciliation] is what I want, we must be sure that [amendment] has taken place, so that if it does not, they will not be able to do more damage. The second reason is this: if on the one hand Your Reverences tell the king that we are waiting to see if there is any improvement, and on the other you judge that these things for the most part seem insignificant to the ministers of the king (being accustomed to greater crimes) – then, unless the necessity of assurance and removal has by then dawned on the king, His Majesty may ask, later, what more these men have done in the meantime for you to want to break up their party, given that you haven't yet done it, and do not presently have it in hand. If at that point we perhaps have nothing new that is significant, we will have no choice but to give in. Your Reverence may show this to Fr Gil, to whom I commend myself.

B73 To Claudio Acquaviva, Valladolid, about 20 August 1590

SOURCE: Acquaviva to Persons, 2 October.
NOTE: It appears that the visitors were about to have an audience with the king.

---

288. Egidio] *followed by* accio nega [*deleted*] R
289. B67.

B74 To Joseph Creswell, Valladolid, 20 August 1590

SOURCE: ABSI, Coll P II 477, Grene's note, and II 500, partial transcription.
HICKS: 90.
EDITION: Pollen, *Miscellanea IX*, 22.
NOTE: The letter records a donation, likely to be annual, from Francisco Sarmiento de Mendoza (1525-1595), bishop of Jaén, in the province of Granada.

Scribit plura de seminario Vallisoletano.[290] — Our Seminary here goeth forward very well: since my last unto you the Bishop of Jaén sent us a bill of 600 Δ the year &c. &c.

B75 From Claudio Acquaviva, Rome, 4 September 1590

SOURCE: ARSI, Tolet. 5/I, fol. 150r.
NOTE: Following the death of Sixtus V on 27 August, Acquaviva hopes the election of a new pope will be advantageous to the Society and will limit the actions of the troublemakers in Spain. Urban VII, however, only reigned from 15 September until his death on 27 September. The letter is preceded by a common letter to the visitors and provincials, which concludes with an addition concerning the coming conclave and the prospects for the election of a pope favourable to the Society: "Nuestro Señor sabe bien con la sua eterna providencia, a quien a de poner en este cargo en tiempo tan travajoso. Pero de cinco, o seis, Cardinales que estan en opinion de poder la tener cada uno es tan aficionado a las cosas de la Compañia que espero en la bondad divina podremos rehazer los daños" (Our Lord, in his eternal providence, well knows to whom to entrust this responsibility in a time of such difficulty. But there are five or six cardinals each of whom is believed to have a care for the affairs of the Society, through whom I hope in the divine goodness we will be able to repair the damage).

Replying to a letter probably written in late July (B70), Acquaviva expresses his satisfaction with developments in the college, appreciating the efforts of the visitor, Gil González Dávila, and the new rector, López de Manzano. He leaves the decision about an assistant to Persons as the man on the ground, deferring also to the judgement of Pedro de Fonseca, visitor to the Portuguese province.

P. Roberto Personio Septiembre 4.
Particular consuelo recivo de entender que las cosas del Seminario vayan tan adelante como entiendo por la de Vuestra Reverencia. Yo escrivo al visitador agradeciendole la voluntad y diligencia con que atiende a ayudarle y le encargo que ansi lo continue. Tanbien escrivo al nuevo Rector significandole quanto yo gusto de que con toda su diligençia procure el bien spiritual y temporal de aquel Seminario, y animandole a emplearse todo en esto. Espero en el Señor que todo lo mejorará y amparará con su misericordiosa mano.
Yo deseo como escrivi a Vuestra Reverencia que el padre Vasconzelos ayude en lo que Vuestra Reverencia pide, pero por buenos respectos no conviene que yo le inte-

---

290. He writes much about the Seminary at Valladolid.

rrumpa el hilo de sus negoçios. Si el padre Fonseca por alguna via entendiese, como Vuestra Reverencia dice,[291] que otro sería más grato para negoçiar con los oydores, ese sería buen medio para que desocupado él pudiese acudir a lo que Vuestra Reverencia desea. Tratenlo alla, que de acá importa que dexemos haçer a los inmediatos.

Ya Vuestra Reverencia havra sabido la muerte del Papa. Espero en el Señor que quando esta llegue a sus manos, nos havra dado un tal successor que nos ampare con más[292] voluntad que el pasado, y con cuya sombra podamos vivir sin los temores que los tiempos passados causavan, de suerte que los conturbantes no tengan tanta liçençia para perturbar la disciplina religiosa, etc.

Translation

To Fr Robert Persons, September 4.

I take special comfort in learning that the affairs of the seminary progress so well, as I understand from Your Reverence's letter. I am writing to the visitor thanking him for his willingness and diligence in endeavouring to help you, and I am charging him to keep it up. I am also writing to the new rector, indicating how much I appreciate the way he is using all his diligence to further the spiritual and temporal welfare of the seminary, and encouraging him to do all he can in this regard. I hope in the Lord that He will enhance and succour everything with His merciful hand.

As I wrote to Your Reverence, I would like Fr Vasconcelos to assist in what you ask, except that for good reason it is not suitable that I interfere with the thread of your business.[293] If Fr Fonseca in any way should feel (as Your Reverence says) that another would be more welcome in negotiating with the judges, that would be a good means of employing him in assisting with whatever Your Reverence wishes. Please could you deal with the situation there, as from my point of view it is important to leave the matter to those in immediate proximity.

Your Reverence must already know of the death of the pope. I hope in Our Lord that by the time this letter comes to hand, He will give us such a successor as will protect us with more goodwill than the past one, and that we can live under his protection without the fears which the past times have brought about, so that the troublemakers will not have so much freedom to disturb religious discipline, etc.

B76 From Claudio Acquaviva, Rome, 4 September 1590

SOURCE: ARSI, Hisp. 74, fol. 29v–30r, from the general's register of confidential letters to the Spanish assistancy.

NOTE: This is the private letter, in Italian, accompanying the open letter (B75) of the same date, in Spanish. Acquaviva is clearly very anxious that the king should endorse the

291. como Vuestra Reverencia dice] *supplied in the margin* R
292. más] *this ed.;* mal R
293. See Acquaviva's open letter of 9 June (B64) about intervening on Persons's behalf. Vasconzelos was presumably one of the Spanish Jesuit fathers in Valladolid.

Jesuit visitors: the marginal note, that the original was written in the general's own hand, seems to confirm the impression of great agitation. The phrasing is frequently obscure, suggesting scribal errors.

Al Padre Personio. Septembre 4.[294]

Già scrisse a Vostra Reverentia quel che mi occoreva che dicesse a Sua Maestà in mio nome intorno alla cosa della visita ma non replicherei adesso altro se i nostri de carta[295] per varie bande non mi facessero la cosa molto periculosa. Io voglio credere che essendo il Re informato da noi et nominatosi con suo beneplacito i nostri visitatori, et molto più doppo l'havere ultimamente detti a Vostra Reverentia in questa materia parole molte amorevole, non faci questa resolutione pure quando le cose non fussero secure. Vostra Reverentia torni a fare l'uficio et veda de pigliar parola certa asicurando Sua Maestà che queste suspensioni fanno tanto danno col dare ardire a discoli, et disanimando i superiori, che realmente è obligato in coscienza, per no distrugger afatto la disciplina religiosa che in coteste provincie ogni giorno va peggiorando, di dichiararsi,[296] et torre la speranza a nostri tentati di riuscir con questi suoi desegni, mostrando[297] che anzi s'offenda di loro et che piutosto farà che i superiori le cognoscano et emendino se non vogleno tacere. Vostra Reverentia si ricorda quel che io gli disse qui più volte che mi dava[298] più dolore per le cose publiche temendo qualche flagello alla armata, che per le nostre, vedendo così vessar la Compagnia. L'essito mostrò che li mei timori non erano vani; dico adesso di nuovo *coram domino* che temo qualche gran flagello se vanno così rovinandoci per persuasione de quatro tristi et d'alcuni pochi malevoli le quali copriranno[299] pur la cosa come vogleno che *deus non irredetur*. Vostra Reverentia facci più l'uficio in mio nome alla libera che stimo che sia gran servitio de Dio et del Re stesso al quale molto pochi ardiscono dire la verità, et *dominus erit nobiscum*. Alle orationi, etc.

Translation

To Fr Robert Persons, 4 September.

I have already written to Your Reverence what I feel should be said to His Majesty in my name about the matter of the visitation, but I would give no reply for now, except that Ours, operating in various regions,[300] undeniably consider the affair to be very dangerous. I would like to believe that since the king has been kept informed by us and our visitors have been nominated at his good pleasure, the only reason this resolution has not been made is that things are not yet settled – even more so, once he has exchanged very loving words with Your Reverence on this matter. Would Your Reverence please return

294. [*marginal note in R:*] Scrisse nostro Padre de mano propria (Our father wrote this in his own hand).
295. carta] *obscure; possibly* costa R
296. dichiararsi] *obscure, possibly* dichiararli R
297. mostrando] *followed by* chiaramente se [*deleted*] R
298. mi dava] R; *possibly a scribal error for* non dava *or* mi non dava R
299. copriranno] *obscure* R
300. Obscure: see textual note 295.

and carry out this mission, and see that you find the right words to impress upon His Majesty that these delays are causing great damage by giving encouragement to the undisciplined, and discouraging the superiors, so that truly he is in conscience bound, if he is to avoid the complete destruction of religious discipline, which in these particular provinces is getting worse every day, to take a stand,[301] and remove the hope of Ours that their attempts will succeed thanks to these plans of his, showing, indeed, that he is offended by the dissenters and that it would be much better if the superiors would recognize them and set them right, if they do not want to keep quiet. Your Reverence will remember what I told you so many times here, that it grieved me more for public affairs, fearing some blow to the armada, than for our own concerns,[302] seeing how it troubles the Society. The outcome has proved that my fears were not vain. I say now, again, before the Lord, that I fear a very great blow if they continue to ruin us by persuasion of four miserable men[303] and a few evil-wishers, who may cover up the whole thing as much as they like, but "God is not mocked." Would Your Reverence please feel free to use my name in carrying out this commission, which I regard as a great service to God and to the king himself, to whom very few wish to speak the truth – and may God be with us. To your prayers, etc.

B77 To Joseph Creswell, Valladolid, 7 September 1590

SOURCE: ABSI, Coll P II 477 and 500, Grene's notes.
NOTE: Grene notes "*similiter*," i.e., similar to the previous letter, of 20 August (B74).

B78 To Claudio Acquaviva, El Escorial, 14 September 1590

SOURCE: Acquaviva to Persons, 29 October (B83).
NOTE: Persons had anticipated Acquaviva's request, made in the letter of 4 September, to go to Madrid to monitor the king's audience with the visitors: see his statement of intent in his letter to Creswell, 22 July (B71). He remained there, it appears, until 4 November.

B79 To Joseph Creswell, El Escorial, 14 and 15 September, 4, 12, 14, and 26 October 1590

SOURCE: ABSI, Coll P II 477 and 500, Grene's notes.
NOTE: These letters were probably despatched with letters to Acquaviva.

---

301. Alternatively, adopting the reading *dichiararli*, "to denounce them." Cf. Acquaviva's letter of 7 August (B72), where he cautions against allowing the king to interfere in the disciplinary processes of the Society. Grateful thanks to Prof. Luigi Robuschi and Dr Marco Rinaldi for assistance in interpreting this passage.

302. It seems more likely that Acquaviva meant: "[The loss of the armada] grieved me no more than [this trouble for the Society]." See textual note.

303. Acquaviva seems to refer obscurely to four ringleaders.

B80 From Humphrey Shelton, Rouen, 26 September 1590

SOURCE: Persons to Shelton, 7 November (B87).

NOTE: Shelton was an English gentleman living in exile in Rouen, employed by William Allen to conduct correspondence with England (Loomie, *Spanish Elizabethans*, 57, 257–258). The letter was brought to Persons by one of ten students who arrived in Valladolid from Rheims in early November (*Blackfan Annals*, 24–25), after Persons's return from Madrid.

B81 From Claudio Acquaviva, Rome, 2 October 1590

SOURCE: ARSI, Tolet. 5/I, fol. 153r.

NOTE: Acquaviva is eager to know how the visitors have fared with the king. He hopes for improved conditions under the new Pope, Urban VII. The pope had in fact already died, but the letter would have been drafted in advance and dated for the next scheduled courier. In a letter to Fr Porres of the same date, Acquaviva writes: "Ha nos dado el Señor por successor de Sixto Quinto, a Urbano Septimo que ansi se llama el que ante era Cardenal Castano que V. R. conoceria Nunçio en esa corte, ha commençado con tales prinçipios, que da esperanza de grandes efectos en bien della iglesia, dios le conserve por muchos años, que la compañia no perdera nada en su Pontificado" (The Lord has given us, as successor to Sixtus V, Urban VII, who as a matter of fact was previously known as Cardinal Castano, whom Your Reverence knows was nuncio at that court. He has begun on such principles which give hope of many good effects in the church: may God keep him for many years, that the Society may incur no damage in his pontificate).

In the latter part of the letter Acquaviva discusses the question of whether the English college should subsidize the Spanish Jesuits in Valladolid; see also his letter of 29 October (B83). According to Jesuit practice, a professed house is intended for the common life and practice to which the Jesuits aspired, including preaching, hearing confession, and spiritual direction, and was to be funded entirely by alms, in accordance with the ideal of poverty proposed by the Constitutions. See Javier Burrieza Sánchez, *Valladolid, tierras y caminos de Jesuitas: Presencia de la Compañía de Jesús en la provincia de Valladolid* (Valladolid, 2007), 88–93; Martin Chase, "Professed. Professed House," in *The Cambridge Encyclopedia of the Jesuits*, ed. Thomas Worcester (Cambridge, 2017), 652–653; and Íñigo Arranz Roa, "Las Casas Profesas de la Compañía de Jesús: Centros de actividad apostólica y social; La Casa Profesa de Valladolid y Colegio de San Ignacio (1545-1767)," *Cuadernos de Historia Moderna* 28 (2003): 125–163.

The professed house in Valladolid was founded in 1566, following the second general congregation of the Society (1565), which elected Diego de Laínez as superior general. It was housed in the college of St Antony, founded in 1545 after the visit of Antonio de Araoz and Pierre Favre. Teaching was entrusted to a new college, St Ambrose, which later gave assistance to the English college.

P. Roberto Personio. Otubre 2.

Deseo tengo que ayan hablado los visitadores a Su Magestad y entender como le satisfacen, Vuestra Reverencia me informará de todo lo que huviere passado, como por la suya se ofrece de haçerlo, que si Su Magestad se satisface, con su favor y con el que espero ternemos en el buen Papa que dios nos ha dado, podremos mejor poner en orden algunas cosas que con los tiempos estan muy caidas.

El Señor prospere las cosas de ese Seminario como yo deseo, que cierto me consuelo del buen ser que va tornando, yo escrivo al rector animandole como tambien le escrivi con el passado, y le toco las dos cosas que Vuestra Reverencia me avisa. Y en lo de acompañarse con los alumnos yo no hallo dificultad si alla no ofende, y ansi lo remitto al padre visitador, porque siendo tan pocos los nuestros que en el seminario estan, pareçe[304] que con dificultad se podra haçer menos.

Historia[305] me pareçe no muy justificada[306] la de los 300 ducados que los padres de la casa de Valladolid pidieron a Vuestra Reverencia segun que lo escrive un padre de Valladolid a otro de esta casa, no sé cómo ellos los pudieron pedir ni Vuestra Reverencia dar, pues saven que[307] conforme a las constituciones ni aun un collegio de la Compañia puede ayudar a la casa profesa, quanto menos podra ayudarse de las limosnas de un seminario que no es nuestro: yo escrivo al visitador lo que desto me pareçe. En su, etc.

Translation

To Fr Robert Persons, 2 October.

I trust that the visitors have spoken to His Majesty and would like to know how he feels about it. Would Your Reverence please inform me about everything that has happened, as you have offered to do: whether His Majesty is satisfied. With his favour, and with the hope we entertain in the good pope whom God has given us, we will be able to put in better order some things which have fallen away in recent times.

I hope the Lord will prosper the affairs of that seminary just as I wish; it surely comforts me that things are turning out so well. I am writing to the rector[308] to encourage him just as I wrote to him last time, and I am mentioning the two matters which Your Reverence raised with me. As to the question of being accompanied by the students I have no objection if it gives no offence, and rather I leave this to father visitor:[309] given that there are so few of Ours at the seminary, it seems that it would be difficult to manage with fewer.[310]

There seems to me no justification in the business of the 300 ducats which the fathers of the professed house of Valladolid demanded of Your Reverence, according to what one father at Valladolid wrote to another of the same house. I do not know how they could ask Your Reverence to make a contribution, nor why you should give it to them; they know that according to the constitutions not even a college of the Society

---

304. pareçe] *followed by* necessaria cosa [*deleted*] R
305. Historia] *preceded by* graçiosa [*deleted*] R
306. no muy justificada] *interlined* R
307. saven que] *followed by* ni a leer se puede [*deleted*] R
308. López de Manzano.
309. González Dávila.
310. Edwards, 143, takes this to refer to Persons's intention of taking Charles Tancard and four other priests with him to Seville and sending them on their way to England (see his letter to Creswell, 4 November, B84), thereby depleting the Jesuit contingent at the college in Valladolid.

should give assistance to the professed house: how much less should they expect assistance from the alms of a seminary which is not our property. I am writing to the visitor with my opinion in this regard. To your [prayers and sacrifices], etc.

B82 To Claudio Acquaviva, Madrid, 12 and 14 October 1590

> SOURCE: Acquaviva to Persons, 24 December (B89).
>
> NOTE: The letter refers to weariness and continued difficulty with the Spanish Jesuits. Nevertheless, Persons was extremely active in the next few months, returning to Valladolid, making an excursion to Palencia, and accompanying priests to Seville via Madrid (see headnotes to his letters to Creswell, 4 November, B84, and Barret, 7 November, B86).

B83 From Claudio Acquaviva, 29 October 1590

> SOURCE: ARSI, Tolet. 5/I, fols. 159v–160r, from the general's open register of letters to the province of Toledo.
>
> NOTE: Acquaviva refers to an appeal from the rector of the English college at Valladolid, López de Manzano, to Cardinal Allen about conflict with the local Jesuits over a subsidy (see his letter of 2 October, B81). Allen was at this time attending the papal conclave of 8 October to 5 December which resulted in the election of Cardinal Niccolò Sfondrati as Pope Gregory XIV.

P. Roberto Personio. Otubre 29.

Recevi la de Vuestra Reverencia escrita a 14 de Septiembre y deseo ya ver el successo que tiene la audiencia de nuestros visitadores, y con que gusto y resoluçion queda Su Magestad porque de esto depende en gran parte nuestra quietud. Espero en el Señor y en el christiano zelo de Su Magestad que de satisfará y holgará de ayudarnos.

Por la que el rector del Seminario escrive al Cardenal Alano he entendido el embarazo que han tenido en Valladolid con ocasion de la Compana, daremos relaçion dello al Cardenal quando salga del conclave, pero tengo por mejor que con paz y buenos medios se rematan cosas semejantes, pues como Vuestra Reverencia save para entrar con más aprobaçion y beneplacito de la gente con quien han de vivir y de quien han de depender, es mejor padeçer un poco y llevar la cosas por buenos terminos: bien creo que Vuestra Reverencia con su prudençia havrá soldado estos negocios: no otro en esta que encomendarme, etc.

Translation

To Fr Robert Persons, 29 October.

I have received the letter Your Reverence wrote on 14 September[311] and I wish I could already see the outcome of the audience of our visitors, and what His Majesty's inclination is, and how he is disposed to act, because on this our tranquillity largely

---

311. B78.

depends. I put my hope in the Lord and in the Christian zeal of His Majesty to be satisfied and pleased to help us.

From the letter which the rector of the seminary wrote to Cardinal Allen, I understand the awkward situation they face in Valladolid in dealing with the Society, and we will give an account of it to the cardinal when he leaves the conclave, but it seems better to me that issues like this should be dealt with peacefully and in an appropriate way, since, as Your Reverence knows, to win the approval and blessing of the people with whom you have to live and on whom you have to depend, it is better to put up with a little trouble so as to bring things to a satisfactory conclusion: I truly believe that Your Reverence with your prudence will have settled these matters: no more in this except to commend myself, etc.

B84 To Joseph Creswell, Valladolid, 4 November 1590

> SOURCE: ABSI, Coll P II 500, Grene's partial transcription.
> HICKS: 90.
> EDITION: Pollen, *Miscellanea IX*, 22.
> NOTE: Persons returned from Madrid on 31 October, met a group of ten students who had arrived from Rheims ten days previously (see his letters to Humphrey Shelton, 7 November, and to Creswell, 12 November, B87–88), and was now preparing to travel to Seville with a party of priests on their way to England. Grene's dating of this letter is doubtful; the fragment transcribed here may actually be part of the letter of 12 November, since Persons evidently left Valladolid on the 13th (see below: "To-morrow or next day after"). Either this letter or that of 12 November may have broached the possibility of a renewed Spanish invasion attempt: see Persons to Emilio Paolo, Cardinal Sfondrati, 18 April 1591 (B105).
>
> According to the *Blackfan Annals*, 24–27, Persons visited Palencia (about 50 km north of Valladolid) at the end of October (more likely early November), in company with Richard Blount and John Bosvile. There they were entertained by the college's benefactor Don Francisco de Reinoso y Baeza (1534–1601), later (1597–1601) bishop of Cordoba, and obtained an annual allotment of twenty loads of grain from the cathedral chapter. See Gregorio de Alfaro, *Vida de don Francisco de Reynosso obispo de Cordoba* (Valladolid, 1617), chapter 23 (fols. 51–53).

To-morrow or next day after,[312] we are to depart hence towards Sevill, Charles Tancard and I, with the 4 priests that goe to imbark there for England &c. —

B85 To Unidentified Addressee, Valladolid, 7 November 1590

> SOURCE: TNA, SP 15/31/161, holograph, with a pencilled note "pinned together for probable inclosures," probably added at the time of the compiling of *CSPD*.
> HICKS: 94–95.
> NOTE: This covering letter enclosed several letters to Persons's connections in Rheims and Rouen, which were intercepted when the bearers, John Cecil and John Fixer, were cap-

---

312. In fact, Persons was still in Valladolid on 12 November.

tured at sea (see headnote to the letter to Barret, B86). Besides his letters to Richard Barret and Humphrey Shelton (B86–87), there were two letters by Thomas Stillington (1558–1597). Stillington's letter to James Vavasour, priest at Rheims, contains an account of the movement of priests similar to that given in Persons's letter to Barret; the other provides interesting information about the state of affairs at Valladolid (see Stillington to Barret, TNA, SP 15/31/159): "Delay of letters. I will do what I can to serve you. I am sorry His Majesty's pension is stayed from Fr Parsons. I will try to aid therein. At first the fathers here wanted nobody but themselves and their scholars in this college; and now I think I had better go but will stay if Father Parsons thinks it best. Thanks for your offer of a place in your college, but you want no readers there. My Lord, the father, and you shall dispose of me. For public affairs, we are wearied with uncertainties. In the college, our chief difficulty will be in the schools, for in three lessons a day, in four years, a scholar will not learn a third part of his divinity. There has been much sickness, but our scholars are all well. Sir William [Stanley] is come to winter here, until His Majesty give order to stir. For the college, we have two large houses, with a garden between; but we shall be put to stabling if you send us any more. The habit is a black cloth gown, such as you wear; for, without a habit, no college in Spain can stand."

Sir William Stanley had been the leader of the English Catholic regiment in the Netherlands in support of Spain, following his controversial surrender of the town of Deventer to the Spanish forces in 1587. He came to Spain from Flanders early in 1590 in company with Hugh Owen and was now in Valladolid (Loomie, *Spanish Elizabethans*, 56, 129–182; see also Persons to Shelton, 7 November, B87). According to John Fixer, presumably wishing to curry favour with Lord Burghley, Stanley was treated with little respect by the Spaniards: "They observe Caesar's saying, 'love the treason and hate the traitor'" (*CSPD*, 3: 38–44).

References to Thomas Fitzherbert and Richard Hopkins, as well as the enclosed letter to Humphrey Shelton, indicate Persons's involvement in the intelligence networks of Philip II and William Allen (Persons to Charles Paget, 20 December 1597, B428). Fitzherbert was sent to Rouen as an agent of Philip II in 1590; Shelton also operated there. Richard Hopkins was Cardinal Allen's agent in Paris. In 1593, when stationed in Antwerp, he was involved in secret negotiations over toleration for English Catholics in the event of peace between France and Spain (Knox, *Allen*, 348–351). In the 1580s he had been engaged in the translation of works by Luis de Granada (*ARCR*, 2: nos. 439–445), evidently in close association with Persons, whose *First booke of the Christian exercise* was largely based on Granada. See Loomie, *Spanish Elizabethans*, 57 and 109.

My loving frend for that I am streytened of tyme and do send yow the inclosed for Mr President, open that you may read them. This only shal be to[313] salute yow and to let yow understand that Mr Fizharbert imbarked a good whyle gone in Bilbo to come towardes yow and he borrowed of me xxx crowns in particular to be repaid ther to Rhems, but I doubt he wil not be able to discharge it in hast, Our Lord help him. If Mr Hopkyns be alyve I pray yow commend me to him: I have seene nothinge from yow or him synce the begynning of June last: more I have not the time[314] to wryte now. Our Lord be with yow.

313. to] *not in SP, supplied by Hicks*
314. time] *not in SP, supplied by Hicks*

Valliodolid[315] this 7 of November 1590.
Yow know the wryter[316]
[PS] To the nephew Robert[317] a thousand commendations if he be with yow and many thousandes to the old father yf yet he be *in rerum natura*.
[*Endorsed*:] 7 November 1590. Parsons the Jesuit, to [*blank*]

B86 To Richard Barret, Valladolid, 7 November 1590

SOURCE: CP, 167: no. 113, contemporary hand (= *CP*).
HICKS: 91–93.
EDITIONS:

1. "Cecil Papers: October 1590," in *Calendar of the Cecil Papers in Hatfield House: Volume 4, 1590–1594*, ed. R.A. Roberts (London, 1892), 65–70, at 69, an abbreviated transcript, beginning, "[It] be not sufficient to pass them from hence."

2. *CSPD*, 12: 315: "Notes from most of the intercepted letters calendared above, and also from others now missing [5 pages. *Endorsed*, Jan. 1591; *probably the date when the intercepted letters arrived in England*]," a summary.

NOTE: This letter illustrates the development of the missionary route to England from the colleges at Rheims and Rome, via Spain. Persons identifies eight priests who are about to go on the English mission, by two separate routes: north via Biscay and Galicia, and south via Seville in Andalusia (see also Persons to Creswell, 12 November, B88). He commends them for the way they have completed their formation in Spain and plans to invite more from Rome, although he is concerned about the sufficiency of the *viaticum*. He also insists that those who are sent from Rheims should be well-disciplined men.

Persons left Valladolid with Charles Tancard on or about 13 November, accompanying John Fixer, Richard Blount, Richard Dudley (b. 1563), and James Younger (b. 1563). Fixer came to Valladolid from Rheims in 1589, the other three from Rome (*Valladolid Registers*, 7–8). They had an audience with Philip II in Madrid, stopped frequently on the way to seek alms by giving speeches to noblemen and cathedral chapters, and finally joined John Cecil in Seville: see Pollen, *Miscellanea IX*, 15 n, citing *Relacion de un Sacerdote Ingles ... de la venida de Su Magestad ... al colegio de los Ingleses* (Madrid, 1592); Hicks, *Seminaries*, part 4, 28–29; and Persons to Creswell, 12 November (B88). There Persons rented a house for the priests and considered the possibility of founding a college (see the headnote to a letter from Puerto de Santa María, January 1591, B91).

Bearing the letters and possibly planning to stop at Rheims before proceeding to England, Cecil and Fixer sailed for Amsterdam in April, accompanied by Blount, Dudley, Younger, and other English priests, including John Roberts (b. 1560), Oliver Almond (b. 1561), and William Warford (d. 1608). To reduce the risk of detection, the priests grew their hair and beards, used various disguises, some as galley slaves, and travelled in three ships (Anstruther, 6–7, 41, 106, 292, 370, 391–393; Pollen, *Miscellanea IX*, 14–15).

315. Valliodolid] *preceded by* Madrid [*deleted*] SP
316. Yow know the wryter] *preceded by* R [*deleted*] SP
317. Possibly a reference to Robert Southwell; see Southwell's letter of 18 April 1591 (B104).

Cecil and Fixer were taken when their ship *The Adulphe* was intercepted by HMS *Hope*, and were subsequently held at Burghley's house in the Strand. Hoping for employment as a government agent, Cecil (Snowden) claimed that Persons was sending priests to drum up support for a Spanish invasion, and to send falsely encouraging reports to Spain (*CSPD*, 3: 38–44; Alford, 270–283 and 360). This may have contributed, as claimed in the *Blackfan Annals*, 28–29, to the issuing of the proclamation of 18 October 1591, "Establishing commissions against seminary priests and Jesuits" (33 Elizabeth I, in Paul L. Hughes and James F. Larkin, *Tudor Royal Proclamations*, 3 vols. (New Haven, CT, 1964–1969), 2: 86–87), which Persons attacked in his "Philopater," i.e., *Elizabethae Angliae Reginae haeresim Calvinianum propugnantis, saevissimum in Catholicos sui regni edictum ... Cum responsione ad singula capita* (Antwerp, 1592): see Allen to Persons, 7 January 1592 (B133) and Persons to Acquaviva, 12 August 1592 (B153), headnote. Cecil's letter to Persons of 1 November 1591 (B126) gives his report of the success of this, Persons's first mission from Spain (see headnote for the fortunes of the other priests).

Francis Lockwood, Henry Rook, and Thomas Salway took the northern route and presumably undertook missionary work in England: Lockwood was one of the founding members of the college at Valladolid. Henry Rook studied at Rheims and Verdun; by 1596 he was in Flanders. Thomas Salway studied at Rheims, was ordained at Soissons in 1588, and was admitted to the college at Valladolid on 10 January 1590 (*Valladolid Registers*, 4, 8; Anstruther, 211, 295, 298).

In the text below, punctuation has been regularized and abbreviations expanded for ease of reading.

Thos which are presently to go in missions are Mr Cicil, Fixar, Yonger, Blunt, Dudly, Lockwod, Rooke and Salloway, and al do go with the faculties which they brought from Rome and Rhemes with them, gyven them ether by my Lord Cardinal or by your self at ther departure; only Mr Fixar hath a doubt whether yow gave him any or no, but yet, presuminge that your intention was to gyve him as to other preestes yf he went into Ingland, and that yow wil actually confirme the same presently upon the recept of this (which I pray yow to do), he is lyke to persiste and to excercyse the faculties that other preestes do, assuring him self both of your satisfaction[318] and my Lord Cardinal, who yf he first see[319] this petition then your self I hope wil confirme the same, and so I do beseech his grace. Thes preestes have wel behaved them selves heer and have wel reposed them selves, and donne them selves much good many wayes by this years staying heer, for they have had tyme to revewe ther bookes and learne both the language and the maners of this nation, and now att ther departure do they edifie them muche and accredite our Seminaries by the missions, wherunto they shew so great desyre and corage – God be thanked for his sweet providence in all. Three or fower of them shal go by the portes of Viscay and Galicia and the rest with me to Andaluzia, and in the way shall see the king and his counsel and have occasions to make speeches to dyvers great personages, Chapters and the lyke, which wil much notifie and justifie our cause[320] that was utterly unknowen hereto-

318. satisfaction] ratification *ABSI transcript*; *CP obscure*
319. see] *CP obscure, possibly* s[econ]de
320. cause] *CP obscure, possibly* course

fore. And yf they dyd send me an other such mission of preestes from Rome that would stay heer and repose them selves for some monethes and lyve in discipline as thes have donne I would take them and help them from hense and adde to the *viaticum* which they bringe from Rome if it be not sufficient to passe from hense, as we have donne to thes, who I thinke veryly would never have passed over into Ingland the halfe of them, nor with that allacritie as now they do, if they had not come this way, for that their *viaticum* would have byn spent longe before they came to the sea syde and so some would have shronke in Italy, other in France and Flanders, and others would have layne upon yow as soe many doe. Wherfore when the subjectes be good and able men and capable of disciplyne, I will offer to the rector of Rome that if he wil send 3 or 4 a yeare this way with the same *viaticum* that he sendeth them to France that I will receave them hear and cherish them and after some monethes refreshinge send them hence with much more commoditie of sure passage to Ingland then they can have from France or Flanders, and so we shall hold them in the spirit of ther vocation and put them safely into Ingland and by ther experience of this country make them more able men to serve and together edifie wel thes people, but this is to be understood: that they be learned and of good lyfe and that they come with this moderation as I have said and not in clusters or disorderly, nether would I have this animate your preestes ther that yow send into Ingland, to take ther course hither without order as some have done before, for in no case may we receave them and heer wil they be[321] put to extreme necessitie, excepted alwayes if any man perforce should be thrust hither, in which case wee should not want to help him in what we might.

I am right glad that yow hold together in such unitie, love and consort in thes trublesome dayes. Our Lord continew it, and I pray yow to commend me to al our frendes ther with yow, namely to Mr Dr Webb, Mr Dr Worthington, Mr Dr Gifford and Kellynson and the rest.[322] And so our Lord God be with yow al, amen. Valliodolid this 7 of November 1590.

    yow know the wryter

[*Addressed:*] To the right worshipful Mr Dr Barret president of the Inglishe College in Rhems.

[*Endorsed:*] Parsons the Jesuite from Valliodolid[323] to Doctor Barrett at Rheims.

B87 To Humphrey Shelton, Valladolid, 7 November 1590

SOURCE: TNA, SP 15/31/160, contemporary hand with postscript holograph.

HICKS: 96–98.

NOTE: Persons reports on the arrival of ten students from Rheims: Thomas Green, Thomas Brown, Edmund Gervase, Walter Owen, John Bennett, Robert Drury, John Worthington, John Thomson, Francis Kemp, and Matthew Silisdon (Bedingfeld). They were

321. be] *om. CP;* supplied *in ABSI transcript*

322. Thomas Worthington (ca. 1548–1626/7) was vice president of the college at Rheims; William Gifford taught theology at Rheims from 1582; Matthew Kellison (1561–1641) came to Rheims from Rome in 1589 to teach theology (Anstruther, 387–388, 132–33, 193–94).

323. Valliodolid] Valliodid *CP*

admitted to the college on 24 October, having left Rheims on 17 September (*Valladolid Registers*, 9–11). Bedingfeld died on 31 October, the very day when Persons arrived back from Madrid. John Worthington (ca. 1572–1652), nephew of the vice president of the college at Rheims, entered the Society of Jesus on 27 October 1598. Drury was put to death at Tyburn on 26 February 1607, wearing a Benedictine habit: see James E. Kelly, "The Contested Appropriation of George Gervase's Martyrdom: European Religious Patronage and the Controversy over the Oath of Allegiance," *Journal of British Studies* 57 (2018): 253–274, and Anstruther, 104–105.

Persons asks Shelton, a Spanish agent in Rouen (Loomie, *Spanish Elizabethans*, 57) to ensure the speedy despatch of his books, presumably left in Rouen on his departure for Rome in 1585. Many of these are now to be found in the library of the English College, Valladolid: see *La misión de Robert Persons: Un jesuita inglés en la antigua corte de Valladolid; Robert Persons Mission: An English Jesuit in the Old Court of Valladolid*, ed. Javier Burrieza and Peter Harris (Valladolid, 2010), 97–115.

The letter was dictated, with Persons adding the postscript in his own hand. The main body of the letter is punctuated with full stops, which seem to indicate pauses as he dictated. In this edition these have generally been replaced with commas.

Right wourshipfull

I have receavid your letter of the 26 of September by one of thos ten which be arrivid heare, who have hadd good and spedy passage both by sea and after that they came into Spayne for they weare no more but ten dayes upon the sea; and as many mo in comming hether to Valladolid from the place whear they toke land. They be also all (prased be God) in very good health, save only one Mathew Bellingfild,[324] who by the way toke a fluxe and died of the same a ten dayes after that he arrived heare, and both he and I weare very glad to see one a nother befor his deathe, for it chansid that I cam hether from Madrid the self same day that he departid this life, and arrived not tow oures befor his death, at the which time notwithstanding he had perfete judgment, and truly he died so well that he showed many synes of his proper salvation. Thos 90 crownes which you ordeyned that they should take of Mr Giles weare not all payed them for he gave them only in thear purse 30 crownes. And other thirty he bestowed in ther provision, which was marvelous evel, and other thirty they should have recoverid at the Ferrol, which, because they arrivid not at that port they could not have, and it is to be affraid that they shalbe lost.[325] As for my bookes which should come into Spayne, I request you good Sir that you will take particular care to send them with the spediist and securist commodity. And as concerning your necessityes in the which I understand you to be in, I hopp that God will provid for all, as hitherto he hath done, and, thus desiring you to be of good courage I commit you to God, who presearve us all in his holy grace. From Valladolid 7 of November 1590.

324. Matthew Bedingfeld, alias Silisden, was the son of John Bedingfeld, of Redlingfeld, and Margaret Silisden, his wife; he arrived in Rheims on 21 December 1588 (Knox, *Douay Diaries*, 222).

325. Ferrol is a port city in Galicia, north-west Spain. See appendix A, item BA 1, "Memorial on the State of English Affairs," n16.

I pray yow pardon me that I wryte by an other mans hand at this tyme, for I have not comoditie to wryte with myn owne. Sir William Stanly and al the rest ar in health heer and salute yow. VIII preests do pass hense presently for the missions into Ingland. Our Lord God be with yow.

Yow know this last yvel letter[326]

[*Addressed:*] A monseur Hemfry Shelton, Roan

[*Endorsed in a later hand:*] 7 Nov 1590 from Valladolid / To Mr Humfriy Shleton at Roan

B88 To Joseph Creswell, Valladolid, 12 November 1590

SOURCE: ABSI, Coll P II 477 (reference) and II 500, Grene's partial transcription.
HICKS: 99.
EDITION: Pollen, *Miscellanea IX*, 22.
NOTE: This letter repeats material from Persons's letters to Barret and Shelton of 7 November (B86–87): the arrival of students from Rheims and the departure of priests for England.

I coming to Valladolid to putt certain of our English Missioners in order, found that there were arrived here 10 schollers from Rhemes whose names be these: Thomas Grene, Edmund Gervis — Robert Drury — all in good health, although they were spoiled thrice of Vandome's souldiers[327] — in France, and so came hither all naked.[328] Those which are to go into England be these: Mr Sicil, Fr James Yonger, Fr Fixer, Blunt, Dudley, Lokwood, Rook, Thomas Salway.[329] The 3 last shal goe towards Gallicia & Biscaia to embark: the other 4 shal goe to Sevill, where they shall meete with Sicill, and theer shall they take shipping.

B89 From Claudio Acquaviva, Rome, 24 December 1590

SOURCE: ARSI, Tolet. 4, fols. 78v–79r.
NOTE: Acquaviva hopes the king will deal firmly with further agitation by the *memorialistas*, referring perhaps to a memorial presented by Juan Bautista Carrillo in September 1590, in which the Society's "way of proceeding" was held up to scrutiny (Astrain, 3: 505–510).

He is looking for assistance from Francisco de Porres, provincial of Toledo (Acquaviva to Persons, 24 March 1590, B55), who had already shown his loyalty to the general by resisting the appointment of visitors from outside the Society: in 1587 he refused to accede to the appointment of Jerónimo Manrique, bishop of Cartagena, as the head of a papal visitation of

326. I.e., poor penmanship.

327. Of the ten students who were admitted to the college on 24 October (see the letter to Shelton, B87), Persons names only the three who were robbed by the soldiers of Henry of Navarre, duke of Vendôme and later King Henry IV of France.

328. [*Grene's marginal note:*] Rob. Drury, Rich. Blunt.

329. [*Grene's marginal note:*] P^a Missio in Anglia ex Sem^o Vallisol (The first mission to England to leave from Valladolid).

the Jesuits (Edwards, 132). Acquaviva reassures Persons of González Dávila's assistance in his controversies with the Spanish Jesuits in the Province of Castille (see his letter of 2 October, B81).

On a personal note, the general compassionates Persons's weariness and is making arrangements for him to have rest and time for reflection. Blackfan remarks: "It is astonishing how Father Persons threw himself into such hard work and worry" during the following year (*Blackfan Annals*, 29).

Acquaviva laments the death of Urban VII (27 September) and can only hope that Gregory XIV (elected on 5 December) will be sympathetic to the cause. He is optimistic about the founding of a seminary in Seville.

Madrid P. Roberto Personio 24 de Decembre.

Ho visto quanto Vostra Reverentia per le sue delli 12 et 14 d'Ottobre mi scrive. Del modo di mettere rimedio all'importuna estimatione de conturbanti si vederà come fu dura provedere, quando la Maestà del Re havea data risposta di mandarle de Visitatori. Ma io sto[330] sempre fermo in non lasciare passare le cose, senza sanarlo da orddire con la divina gratia, se potrò,[331] così è che la ragione de questi mali et ambitione, humore antico in alcuni di coteste provincie lasciarano il seme in cotesti suoi discipoli.

Mi maraviglio che al Padre Porres possi venire. Pensiero de che l'habbiamo per deludente; poiché et a lui stesso quale et ad altri habbiamo scritto lo[332] certificatoli che tal'ombra o pensiero no habbiamo et che di questo stia sicuro; io le scrivo adesso[333] una buona lettera, et oltre che l'ho più volte raccommandato al Padre Egido, daremo qualch'ordine per il Padre Procuratore. —

Dio paghi a Monsignor Mellino la sua molta carità verso la Compagnia. Dio ci ha tolto il buon Urbano, speriamo che Gregorio XIIII ci ascoltarà.[334] Spero che il seminario di Sevilla haverà buon'essito. Ho compassione alle fattiche di Vostra Reverentia. Col Padre Bartolomé Pérez potrà trattare del riposo et raccoglimento che per qualche mese lei desidera. Con che ...

Translation

To Fr Robert Persons in Madrid, 24 December.

I have seen what Your Reverence wrote to me in your letters of 12 and 14 October. As for finding a remedy for the importunate demand of the troublemakers, it is yet to be seen how hard it will be to provide, since His Majesty the king has given a favourable reply on the question of the visitors. But I remain still adamant not to allow these matters to pass, without rectifying them by taking control of them, by divine grace, if I can; that is, what is the reason for these evils and ambitions, why the old humour in some of those provinces has contaminated their followers.

330. sto] *preceded by* sono [*deleted*] R
331. The rest of the paragraph has been added in the margin.
332. scritto lo cerificatoli] scritto lo *and* li *interlined* R
333. adesso] *interlined, replacing* aora *or* aça R
334. ascoltarà] *followed by indistinguishable word* R

I am surprised that you were able to approach Fr Porres: I was worried we had reason to be disappointed, so much so that I wrote both to him and to others to assure them that we have not the shadow of a thought except to ensure their security in this matter. I am now writing an appreciative letter to him, and as regards the other matters which I have recommended many times to Fr Gil, we shall give order via father procurator.[335]

May God repay Monsignor Millino for his great love to the Society.[336] God has taken away the good Urban; we hope that Gregory XIV will listen to us. I hope that the seminary of Seville will turn out well. I am very sorry that Your Reverence is exhausted. You will be able to deal with Fr Bartolomé Pérez[337] about the rest and reflection that you desire during the coming months. With that ...

B90 From Joseph Creswell, 24 December 1590 or January/February 1591

SOURCE: Persons to Emilio Paolo, 18 April 1591 (B105).

NOTE: Creswell notified Persons that Acquaviva had shown to the newly-appointed papal secretary a confidential letter from Persons to Creswell (probably 4 or 12 November, B84, B88).

B91 Possibly to Claudio Acquaviva, Puerto de Santa María, January 1591

SOURCE: ABSI, Coll P II 477, Grene's note.

NOTE: In Seville, Persons rented a house for English priests, including Simon Swinburne and William Cowling, and, bearing in mind the encouragement of the provincial of Andalusia, Bartolomé Pérez (Persons to Creswell, 28 April 1590, headnote, B60), contemplated founding a seminary. He decided, however, to wait until Valladolid was more settled.

Downriver, Persons then attended to the needs of the English prisoners in the galleys at El Puerto de Santa María, opposite Cádiz. He also took an interest in the English community in Sanlúcar de Barrameda, a little further up the coast, where he renewed the chapel with a grant from the duke of Medina Sidonia and the king, finalized on 29 April 1591. Besides the Church of St George, which was the centre of the merchant community, there was also the Church of St Francis, established by Henry VIII for English sailors on behalf of Catherine of Aragon. Persons set up an English residence there, with Thomas Stillington as provost of the church and Martin Array, George Ambler, and William Seborne as chaplains; see Pollen, *Miscellanea IX*, 4–5. The residence served as a waystation for students passing through to the colleges at Valladolid and, later, Seville. See Hicks, *Seminaries*, part 4, 30–35.

Although Grene does not specify an addressee, this is likely a letter to Acquaviva, whose letter of 20 March (B95) may have been written in response.

---

335. The procurator was the province's representative in Rome.

336. Pietro Millino was papal nuncio in Spain at this time. See McCoog, *Building the Faith of St Peter*, 127 n115.

337. Provincial of Andalusia, with oversight over Seville, where Persons was resident.

B92 Possibly to Claudio Acquaviva, Puerto de Santa María, 19 February 1591

SOURCE: ABSI, Coll P II 477, Grene's note; Persons to Swinburne, 20 February (B93).

NOTE: Grene notes a letter of this date "of the conversion of 90 English slaves in the Gallies of Spaine & of 16 or 18 boyes" (see Persons to Idiáquez, 4 April, B99). Again, Grene does not specify an addressee, but Acquaviva's letter of 13 May (B107) might have been written in response to this.

B93 To Simon Swinburne in Seville, Puerto de Santa María, 20 February 1591

SOURCE: TNA, SP 12/240/41, a deciphered copy.
HICKS: 101–102.

NOTE: Remaining in Puerto de Santa María, Persons had to try to manage the arrangements for securing the passage and lines of communication to Amsterdam and London. This letter, with its information about possible safe houses in London, was an addendum to some communication with Cecil of the previous day. The most likely interpretation is that Cecil came to Puerto de Santa María to confer with Persons and left on 19 February. The following day Persons wrote hastily to catch the post to Seville with additional instructions, addressing his letter to one of the English priests there. When Cecil sailed at the beginning of April, he would have taken with him the original of this letter, which was seized and decoded by the English authorities (see Persons to Barret, 7 November 1590, headnote, B86).

In the State Papers the letter is filed with letters from February 1592 and there is a later endorsement 1591/2 Feb. 20. However, Cecil had left for England in April 1591. Deciphered phrases are underlined in the copy. Punctuation is editorial.

Simon Swinburne (1562–1638) entered the Society of Jesus in Rome in 1586. He appears to have remained in Seville until February 1595 when he was replaced by William Baldwin because of the harshness of the Spanish climate (Persons to Acquaviva, 18 April 1594, B226; McCoog, *Building the Faith of St Peter*, 191).

Pax Christi.

I pray yow good Father to tel Mr Sicil that I had forgotten to request him yesterday to wryte to me from Holland & to settle some man and howse ther to which I may send my lettres for him, & under what name: that is, what name I shal use to Mr Sicil[338] and to what man to direct them with a cover[339] in Holland. And of the first I pray Mr Sicil to advertise me from Ayemouth[340] & of the second from Holland. Whence also he must appoynt some howse in London wher letters may be sent to hym. And let him not fear for the first letters; lett hym not doubt, for they shal be of trifles and marchandise so that if they should be intercepted it should be no matter until our intelligence be settled. Any Catholique howse in London were sufficient to appoynt wher a letter from hence might

---

338. Sicil] *underlined*
339. man to direct them with a cover] *underlined*
340. Ayamonte; see the letter from John Cecil, 5 April 1591 (B100).

be left until Mr Sicil came[341] & asked for it & so could it be no inconvenience in the world: as, Thomas Payns howse haberdasher[342] just over agaynst the Counter in the pultry,[343] or the lyke. Let Mr Sicil wryte me his mynd in this with his name, & so we may wryte not only by Holland but immediately also for Ingland. I can wryte no more; the post passeth. *Valete* this 20 of February.

[PS] An other Catholique is James Tayler grosser[344] right over agaynst the conduit in Fleete Street. Let Mr Sicil chuse one of these & send me his name and perhaps he shal fynd my lettres ther for him.

[*Addressed:*] Al Padre Simon Swinborn Yngles de la Compañia de Jesus, Sivilla.

[*Endorsed:*] 20 Febr. 1591. Persons the Jesuet to Swynborn. Thomas Payn haberdasher. James Tayllor.[345]

B94 To King Philip II, Puerto de Santa María, March 1591

SOURCE: Persons to Idiáquez, 4 April (B99).

NOTE: In his letter of 4 April, Persons refers to a letter he wrote to the king "a few days ago" about the conversion of the galley slaves.

B95 From Claudio Acquaviva, Rome, to Persons, 20 March 1591

SOURCE: ARSI, Tolet. 4, fol. 82v.

NOTE: Acquaviva confidentially discusses the posting of Richard Gibbons, presently prefect of studies at Valladolid, whom Persons found difficult to deal with (Acquaviva to Persons, 9 July 1590, B69; Edwards, 141).

Madrid. P. Roberto Personio. 20 di Marzo.

Intendo ch'il Padre Richardo Gibbono no ha altro occupatione in Coimbra che di Ministro, havendo egli così buoni talenti et a impiegarsi meglio;[346] et perché le provincie Oltramontane spetialmente quelle di Francia hanno gran bisogno d'aiuto, habbiamo pensato che sarebbe bene impiegato a mandarglo in quelle bande. Però ne se Vostra Reverentia non ha di lui qualch'altro bisogno o dissegno, lo faremo avisare che venghi in Francia,[347] quando haverano la risposta di lei. Nelle cui orationi ...

---

341. Mr Sicil came] *underlined*

342. Thomas Payns howse haberdasher] *underlined*

343. Counter in the pultry] *underlined*. The Counter in the Poultry was a London prison where many Catholics were held, including (later) John Gerard.

344. James Tayler grosser] *underlined*

345. Hicks records that the endorsement is by Burghley, who "underlined the underlined words."

346. havendo egli così buoni talenti et à impiegarsi meglio] *supplied in margin R*

347. Francia] *followed by indecipherable deletion R*

Translation

Madrid.[348] To Fr Robert Persons, 20 March.

I understand that Fr Richard Gibbons has no other occupation in Coimbra except for that of minister, but he has such good talents that he could be better employed; and because the ultramontane provinces, especially those of France, have great need of help, it has occurred to me that he would be well employed if we send him to those regions. So, unless Your Reverence has some other need or plan for him, we would recommend that he goes to France – when I have received a response from Your Reverence. To your prayers [I commend myself] ...

B96 To William Holt in Brussels, n.d. 1591

SOURCE: ABSI, Coll P II 477, Grene's note.

NOTE: Persons was hoping that Holt might be transferred from Brussels to Spain to assist him (cf. Acquaviva to Persons, 9 July 1591, B111).

Personius ad P. Holtum Bruxellis ut veniat in Hispaniam.

Translation

Persons [writes] to Fr Holt in Brussels that he should come to Spain.

B97 To William Cowling, Puerto de Santa María, March 1591

SOURCE: Persons to Cecil and Fixer, 13 April (B102).

NOTE: Illness has prevented Persons from returning to Seville in time for the departure of Cecil and Fixer on 1 April. He writes accordingly to Cowling, one of the English priests he had brought to Seville in connection with the possible founding of a college.

William Cowling (1557–1592) left Rheims for Spain with Francis Lockwood in November 1588 and reached Valladolid via Lisbon (*Valladolid Registers*, 4; *Blackfan Annals*, 12, where he is named Cook). Earlier, when he passed through Rheims on his way to England in May 1582, William Allen described him as bilious or choleric (Knox, *Allen*, 136, 154; Anstruther, 91–92).

B98 To King Philip II, Seville, 4 April 1591

SOURCE: Persons to Idiáquez, 4 April (B99).

NOTE: Persons follows up an earlier letter with a further appeal to the king to respond more enthusiastically to the offers of service from English converts at Puerto de Santa María.

348. Persons had passed through Madrid on his way to Seville.

B99 To Don Juan de Idiáquez, Seville, 4 April 1591

SOURCES:
ABSI, Coll P I 246–247 Grene's transcript, "copyed out of F. Persons owne wryting," and II 477 (reference) = G;
ARSI, Angl. 38/II, fol. 80, item 12 (reference, "Copie d'una lettera del P. Personio de i 4 d'Aprile. Sopra soldati sudd^i convertiti").
HICKS: 103–113, with English translation.
EDITIONS: Knox, *Allen*, 329–332.
TRANSLATIONS: Knox, *Allen*, cxiii–cxv; Ethelred L. Taunton, *History of the Jesuits in England 1580–1773* (London, 1901), 139–42 (dating the letter 21 April).

NOTE: Despite his illness, Persons seems to have made his way back to Seville by early April. The letter concerns the conversion of the English prisoners working as slaves in royal galleys at El Puerto de Santa María, across the bay from Cádiz; see Pollen, *Miscellanea IX*, 3; Hicks, *Seminaries*, part 4, 29–30. An account of their reception into the church is given in *Newes from Spayne and Holland* (Antwerp, 1593): "Every one being first confessed of all his life past, and afterward al together in solemne procession were caried to the great church of the port, and there hard masse together ... and that ended, the Adelantado ... had them all home to his owne house, and gave them a ryall dinner, himselfe serving them at the table" (fol. 2r). The Adelantado (military governor) of Castile was Martín de Padilla (1540–1602).

Despite his warm reception at Puerto de Santa María, Persons is dismayed at the attitude of the Spanish, who were reluctant to take the English into the king's service, although he understood the need for precautions. Indeed, according to one of Burghley's spies, some of the converts ran away, "to Persons's great shame" (TNA, *SP* 94 [Spanish], 4 [1591–1594]: "A Well-wisher to Burghley, 27 Dec/6 Jan 1591/2"). Persons wishes to impress upon the king the necessity of cultivating a Spanish party within England, if there is to be any hope of restoration. He goes so far as to lament the likely fate of Catholics in England if there were a successful Spanish invasion unless they are treated as allies.

Persons asks Idiáquez to mediate his letters on this subject to the king. Hicks comments on "the independent tone which [Persons] adopted when dealing with the great officers of the Spanish crown" (*Seminaries*, 30).

Copia de la carta para Don Juan de Ideaquez
sobre los soldados convertidos a 3 de Março 1591.

Tras lo que escrivi los dias passados sobre la reducion de los Yngleses en las galeras, torno a escrivir alcunos[349] renglones aora a Su Magestad de las señales que ay de que esta conversion aya sido muy verdadera, y esto por las causas que Vuestra Señoria ya sabra, o las diré a Vuestra Señoria a la buelta y aunque bien sé que Su Magestad monstrará la misma carta a Vuestra Señoria toda vía he querido embiar el traslado para mayor seguridad.

En la substancia del negocio, no tengo que añadir más a Vuestra Señoria sino fuere dezirle llanamente con la confiança que suelo presumir con Vuestra Señoria que me he

---

349. alcunos] G; algunos *Knox*

espantado de la tibieça con que si ha recebido la volundad de los Yngleses que ellos an offerecido con tanto amor y con tan grande riesgo y perdida suya.

Muy buena obra si les hará en quanto a lo temporal en mandarles bolver a su tierra en veniendo su riscate que si aguarda, y en lo espiritual tambien confio en Dios que por donde quiera que vayan la mayor parte dellos quedarán siempre constantes en la fe, que es la sola cosa de mi interes, si parte alguna tengo en esta riducion que será muy poca. Pero si esto será mejor por el servicio de Su Magestad si deve mirar y yo por mí lo tengo por muy cierto que si el enemigo tubiere tal occasion de honrar a se y de haçernos daño con gente nuestra, no lo dexaré passar ansi sin servirse della con mayor cuydado y demonstracion.

Una cosa muy cierta es, que pensar poder prevalecer en Ynglaterra sin tener parte de dientro, es engaño muy grande, y pensar tener esta parcialidad sin procurarla y conservarla es tambien engaño; ni hai cosa tan contraria a esto, como la disconfiança la qual hasta aora si ha muestrado con los Yngleses aun Catholicos en todas las occasiones las quales podrei cuentar a Vuestra Señoria en particular: pero bastará por todas la del tiempo de la Jornada quando si manifesto a todo el mundo, pues teniendo Su Magestad más menester entonces que nunca de sirvirse de su parcialidad, ningun caso si hizo della, ni si hizo confiança alguna de persona viviente de la naçion dientro o fuera del reyno, aunque avia muchas que pudieren aver ayudado y avian offerecido sus vidas antes en servicio de Su Magestad.

Esto sintieron mucho todos los buenos de la nacion pareciendoles que su volundad fedelissima a Su Magestad no merecia una disconfiança[350] tan notoria a todo el mundo. Mucha pena tambien les dava entender que algunos ministros principales de Su Magestad dezian (y esto sé yo que es verdad) que ellos no entendian que avia Catholicos en Ynglaterra; y si algun dixiere que él lo era, muy bien se recatarian en creerlo, y si quesieren[351] reduzirse no se admiterian sino con recato &c.

En esta manera Vuestra Señoria vee lo que succediere a los pobres catolicos si la victoria estubiere de nuestra parte y esto era forçoso succederles no solamente por la poca noticia y amor que llevavan los ministros, pero tambien y principalmente por la disconfiança que tubieren de todos los buenos de la nacion, los quales les podian dar luz de los demas, y porque intiendo que Dios no quiso que a sus siervos si hiziessen tantos estragos por mano de los nuestros, despues aver padecido lo que an padecido de los hereges, dio el successo que emos visto, ni tengo esperanza de mejor, hasta que si toman medios más proporcionados al santo fin de la sincera reformacion de aquel reyno que si pretende que no si tomaron la otra vez, aunque no si duda de la buena intencion de Su Magestad.

Esto escrivio a Vuestra Señoria con la occasion de la disconfiança que si ha muestrado aora de recibir al servicio de Su Magestad los Yngleses reducidos en las galeras, ni lo dixo para que no si mire muy bien para toda siguridad, antes deseo esto sobre todas las cosas: pero con esto dixo que tan poco si deve creer a los que para parecer prudentes y cuydadosos quieren poner dudas y suspechas en todos los estrangeros; porque esto no es siempre prudencia ni piedad, antes muchas vezes es enfermidad, y nasce de nuestra

350. disconfiança] *Knox*; disfiança G
351. quesieren] G; *Knox suggests* quisiesen

casa y es causa di muy grandes males, particularmente de enemistadas, pues adonde hai suspecha y disconvenienza, no[352] hai amor ni fidelidad; ni hai cosa nel mundo que más haçe desesperar a los hombres que recebir disconfiança en paga di buena volundad, y quanto más universal[353] fuere o nacional, tanto peor.

Y porque he commençado hablar en esta materia, diré tambien esto particular que en los 30 años que ha reynada Isabella en Ynglaterra an venido al servicio de Su Magestad en Flandes y otras partes muy grande número de Yngleses Catholicos que ubieren podido hazer grandes cosas y grandes daños a la reyna y muchos dellos eran hombres de calidad y perdieron lo que tenian para acudir a esta parte, y otros quedavan alla a la mira para seguirles si les succediere bien: pero nunca si ha hecho confiança dellos en cosa alguna de importancia y assi an perecido todos in effeto, y no solamente los hombres particulares sino las compañias y regimientos tambien de soldados, y esto por el poco amor y cuydado che dellos toman los ministros para tratarles bien y conservarles aunque los de la parcialidad de nuestro Morgan y Pageto an querido attribuirlo a principio más alto que es a la disconfianza que Su Magestad y toda esta nacion tiene de los mismos catolicos de Ynglaterra en lo qual si les ha hecho la contradicion por el Cardenal y otros que Vuestra Señoria en parte sabe, *et hic fons discordiae extitit*.

Más he escrito de lo que pensava en esta materia aunque no más de lo que importa la consequencia deste negotio de los reducidos; el qual como es caso nuevo y nunca antes accaecido y muy notorio por todas las partes ansi si advirterá mucho la demonstracion que en el hará Su Magestad; y si poco caso si hiziere destos no aya miedo Vuestra Señoria che otros siguiran a su exemplo ni que los de Ynglaterra aguardaran mejor tratamiento en llegando Españoles alla y intiendo que esto solo pondra más disconfiança y disesperança en los amigos de alla que qualquiera otra cosa que hasta aora ha succedido. Dios encamine todo por lo mejor.

En lo universal no ay que escrivir más ni de que cansar más a Vuestra Señoria con más papeles pues sobran los que emos escripto. Vuestra Señoria me dixo en Escurial que o este año, o nunca, y ya estamos en lo primero, y veo tan poco aparejo que me haze pensar que por ventura Dios quiere lo segundo: *fiat voluntas eius sicut in coelo ita et in terra*. Una sola cosa tengo de supplicar muy encarecidamente a Vuestra Señoria que si Su Magestad no tiene en que emplear de presto el Coronel Stanley que se le de licencia para bolver a Flandes o Francia donde Su Magestad fuere servido occuparlo en algo; pues esto seria darle vida y mucho consuelo, y al contrario tenerlo acá sin hazer nada es martyrizarlo de mil muertes, y pues intiendo que esto otro será servicio de Su Magestad y grande contiento por el buen cavallier, el qual lo merece por su fedelissima volundad a Su Magestad torno a supplicar a Vuestra Señoria que si haga con effetto con quanta instancia puedo pedirlo &c. — Dios guarde a Vuestra Señoria siempre. Sevilla, 4 Abril 1591.

Rob. Personio.

---

352. no] ne G
353. universal] *interlined* G

Translation

Copy of the letter to Don Juan de Idiáquez about the soldiers converted on 3 March 1591.[354]

After what I wrote a few days ago about the conversion of the Englishmen in the galleys, I am writing a few lines again now to His Majesty to tell him what signs there are that this has been a very genuine conversion; and I say this for reasons of which Your Excellency will be already aware, or at any rate I will tell them to Your Excellency on my return;[355] and though I am well aware that His Majesty will show Your Excellency the letter itself, still I have thought well to send you a copy for greater security.

As to the substance of the affair I have nothing further to say to Your Excellency except to tell you frankly, with the confidence which, I trust, exists between us, that I am appalled by the coolness with which the desire [to convert], offered by the English with such love and at such great risk and loss to themselves, has been received.

It will be doing these men very great service, so far as their temporal needs are concerned, to have them sent back to their native land when their ransom arrives; and spiritually too, I trust in God that, wherever they may go, the greater part of them will always remain constant in the faith, which is the only thing that interests me, if I have had any role – and it is a very small one – in their conversion. But whether it would be better for them to remain in the service of His Majesty is something to be considered; and for my part I take it to be certain that, if the enemy had a similar opportunity of winning prestige for themselves and doing us damage by means of *our* own people, they would not let it slip in this fashion, without taking advantage of it more assiduously and with great fanfare.

There is one thing very certain, that to imagine that we can prevail in England without having a party within the realm is a very great illusion; and to imagine that we can have such a party without seeking it out and fostering it is no less an illusion; nor is there anything that works so much against this being achieved than the distrust with which the English, even the Catholics, have been treated on every occasion. I could give Your Excellency instances of these, but it will cover them all if I mention what took place at the time of the Armada, when this lack of trust was made manifest to all the world; for, although His Majesty had more need than at any other time to take advantage of their favour, they were entirely ignored, nor was confidence placed in any living person of our nation either within or without the kingdom, although there were many who could have been of assistance and had previously offered their lives in the service of His Majesty.

This was deeply regretted by all the well-disposed people of our nation, for it seemed to them that their loyalty and affection towards His Majesty did not deserve a lack of trust that was so notorious to the whole world. They were saddened also to note that some of His Majesty's principal ministers were in the habit of saying (and this I myself know to be

---

354. Persons had already mentioned these conversions in a letter of 19 February (B92). The date 3 March may refer to their reception into the church or, alternatively, to the date of the previous letter.

355. I.e. to Madrid.

true) that they were not aware that there were Catholics in England, and that if any one were to claim that he was one, they would be reluctant to believe it, and if any should wish to be reconciled, they would not receive them except with considerable reserve, etc.

Thus Your Excellency can see what would happen to the poor Catholics if the victory were on our side; and this would necessarily have happened to them not only on account of the slight notice taken of them and the little love shown for them by the ministers, but also and principally because of the distrust shown to all of the good people of our nation who were in a position to enlighten them about the rest; and, I think, it was because God did not wish that such destruction should be inflicted on his servants by our own people, after having suffered as they have done from the heretics, that He allowed the expedition to meet with the fate we have witnessed. And I have no hope of any better result until means are adopted better proportioned to the holy purpose we have in view of the genuine reformation of that kingdom, than those which were employed on the former occasion; though no doubts are cast on the good intentions of His Majesty.

My writing this to Your Excellency is occasioned by the reluctance which has been shown at the present moment to take the Englishmen who were converted in the galleys into His Majesty's service. I am not saying it to prevent precautions being taken for complete security; on the contrary, I desire that above everything; but I say it for this reason, that little credence should be given to those who, in order to appear prudent and careful, seek to sow doubts and suspicions of all foreigners.[356] For this is not always a case of prudence or piety; often it is an infirmity, rather, and springs from our attachment to our own homeland; and is also the cause of great evils, especially of enmities; for where there is suspicion and discord, there is neither love nor fidelity. Nor is there anything in the world which makes men despair more than to receive distrust in return for their goodwill, and the more universal or national this is, the more serious is it.

Since I have begun to speak on this subject, I will mention this also in particular: that during the thirty years that Elizabeth has reigned in England, a large number of English Catholics have come to join His Majesty's service in Flanders and elsewhere, who might have done great things and inflicted great losses on the queen. Many of them were men of rank and sacrificed what they had in order to come over here; others remained there, watching out to follow if all went well with them. But they have never been treated with confidence in any matter of importance and so nothing has come of them. This applies not only to private individuals but also to companies and regiments of soldiers, and it is due to the little love the ministers have for them or care they have taken to treat them well and preserve them; though those who belong to the faction of our Morgan and Paget have sought to assign this to a deeper cause: that is, the distrust which His Majesty and all your nation have of the Catholics of England; an opinion indeed which has been refuted by the cardinal and others, as Your Excellency is partly aware, and which has been a very wellspring of discord.

I have written more on this subject than I intended, though not more than the importance of this affair of the converted English deserves. As it is an unprecedented

---

356. The verbs "write" and "say" in the first two sentences are third person singular in the Spanish text, possibly an oversight in Grene's transcription.

event, which has never happened before, and is very notorious on all sides, great attention will be paid to what His Majesty will do in the matter; and if little account is made of these men, Your Excellency need have no fear that others will follow their example, or that those in England will expect any better treatment when the Spaniards get there. I am assured that this alone will cause more distrust and despair in your friends there than anything else that has happened till now. May God direct everything for the best.

As regards matters in general there is no need to write more, nor to weary Your Excellency further with additional papers, for those which we have written are more than enough. Your Excellency said to me in El Escorial that it would be either this year or never.[357] We are already well into the first, but I see so little preparation made, that it makes me think that perhaps God wills the latter. *His will be done on earth as it is in heaven.* One thing only I have to beg Your Excellency very earnestly, namely, that, if His Majesty has no pressing employment for Colonel Stanley, he might be granted leave to return to Flanders or France, where His Majesty may be pleased to find him some employment.[358] This would be to give him a new lease of life and much consolation; while on the contrary, to keep him here in idleness is to inflict a thousand deaths on him. And I am sure that to do this will be of great service to His Majesty and will greatly content the good soldier, who deserves it for his loyalty and goodwill to His Majesty: and so again I beseech Your Excellency with all the urgency I can muster, that effect be given to this request, etc. ... May God protect Your Excellency always. From Seville, 4 April, 1591.

Robert Persons.

B100 From John Cecil, Ayamonte, 5 April 1591

SOURCE: Persons to Cecil and Fixer, 13 April (B102).
NOTE: Cecil and Fixer left Seville on 1 April, but were able to get no further than Ayamonte, a port on the estuary of the Guadiana River, the border with present-day Portugal.

B101 To Joseph Creswell, Seville, 8 April 1591

SOURCE: ABSI, Coll P I 305, Grene's note, and II 477 (reference).
HICKS: 114.

From Sivill 8 April 1591 and this same yeare divers other letters from Valladolid about the two seminaries & little else.

---

357. In the event, further armadas sailed only in October 1596 and October 1597 (see introduction, "The International Scene").

358. William Stanley had been in Valladolid since early in 1590 (see the covering letter of 7 November 1590, B85, headnote).

B102 To John Cecil and John Fixer, Seville, 13 April 1591

SOURCE: CP 168, a contemporary copy, signed by Persons but with heading and marginal notes in another hand = CP.

HICKS: 120a–121.

EDITION: "Cecil Papers: April 1591," in *Calendar of the Cecil Papers in Hatfield House: Volume 4, 1590–1594*, ed. R. A. Roberts (London, 1892), 102–108, at 104.

NOTE: Cecil and Fixer were delayed for some weeks in Ayamonte, enough time for Persons to reply to their letter of 5 April (B100). The letter, which came into the hands of the authorities after their capture, contains hints of a scheme to approach Ferdinando Stanley (ca. 1559–1594), Lord Strange, about his claim to the succession. Stanley became fifth earl of Derby on the death of his father on 25 September 1593 but died in 1594 under circumstances giving rise to suspicions of Catholic plots. When Cecil and Fixer offered themselves to Burghley in May, Fixer claimed that Persons was looking to Lord Strange as an alternative candidate for the succession if Spanish invasion failed, partly because John Gerard's brother was close to Strange (*CSPD*, 3: 38–44).

My loving bretherin and frindes

By reason of my indisposition whearof I writ to Mr Couling,[359] I can not writ this with my owne hand. I receaved Mr Sicil letter of the fifth even now, and very sory I was of your disapoyntment in Aymont, but yit the certayne hopp which Mr Sicil giveth me of your present and prosperous dispache from thence, did comforth me greatly agayne, and I besiche Christ Jesus to assist you thearin, and in all your actions, to his glory. Fr Warford[360] departed the third of this present,[361] with commoditye and company greatly to his contentment, and I thinke [you] shal heare of his passage by the place whear unto you goo. Fr Oliver[362] for that he found no passage directly to Ingland, with good commodity also of safe landing, upon good consultacion tooke the same, and is ether gonne or to go presently.[363] I pray you bothe to have great care to advertise me by the first, and by as many ways as you can ether by Holland, Yerland, St Malos or Flanders.[364] What you find in the mane my cousin, whearof Mr Sicil and I talked so muche in the grine before St Francis in the po ...[365] that it may be advertised better, or to Rome for my better satisfaction, what hopp thear be of him every way, and that you keep the matter only to your selves for his most safty, eccept it be only to tell Fr Garnet or Fr Southwell[366] of it. The forme in which you may advertise me, may be this, and I pray you note it: Your cousin the baker is well inclined, and glad to heare of you and meaneth not to give over his pre-

359. William Cowling.
360. [*in margin:*] One of them that are come oute of Spayne.
361. On William Warford, see his letter from Amsterdam, 15 May (B108).
362. [*in margin:*] Oliver Almond another.
363. On Oliver Almond, see the headnote to Persons to Barret, 7 November 1590 (B86).
364. [*in margin:*] By these wayes passe men in and out of unto Spayne; & for that he wishith to [be] advised hearof quicly. *Editorial punctuation.*
365. CP is defective here. The Plaza de San Francisco was the main public square in Seville.
366. [*in margin:*] Garnet and Suthwill Jesuites in England.

tence to the old bakehouse you knowe of, but rather to put the same in sut when his ability shall searve.³⁶⁷ To John Garret³⁶⁸ you may commend me by tokin, that at his last departure from me, he gave me a littill *vulto Salvatoris* for my diurnal inamled upon the print, and tow letteres under for his name.³⁶⁹ Agayne I request you that my cousin³⁷⁰ matter be delt in secresy least it may turne the poore man to hurt, but great desier I have to heare truly and particularly of his estat. And thus having nothing else to writ, but only to do my harty commendacions to Mr Peares Harborne your good guide,³⁷¹ I take my leave of you this 13 of April 1591.

    Your owne ever during lyfe³⁷² and after
        Robert Persons.

[*Headed:*] This letter I browght of purpose that yow myght see hyt was no matter framed of myne owne heade that which they pretende of my Lord Strange.

B103 To Claudio Acquaviva, Seville, 18 April 1591

    SOURCE: Acquaviva to Persons, 10 June 1591 (B109).

    NOTE: From Acquaviva's reply, it appears that Persons was in two minds about the suitability of Seville for an English seminary.

B104 From Robert Southwell, London, 18 April 1591

    SOURCE: Madrid, Real Academia de la Historia 9/3689 (13), olim Papeles de Jesuitas, vol. 116, no. 13 (2), fols. 33–34: "Copia de carta del P. Suelo de la Compania de Jesus a Roberto su amantissimo padre sobre asuntos de religion en aquella nacion. Londres 18 de abril 1591" (Copy of a letter of Fr Southwell, SJ, to Robert his beloved father on matters of religion in that country): a Spanish translation (= *M*), included in a collection of newsletters from England, 1591–1592.

    NOTE: Southwell writes passionately about the sufferings of the English community, which is struggling to hold its defences against the attacks of the enemy. They are earnestly hoping and praying for military aid from Spain, and trust in Persons to aid them. Grateful thanks to Martin Murphy for alerting us to this letter and for his interpretation of it. Punctuation is editorial and should be treated with caution.

Este mensajero mio G. M.³⁷³ que esta dara a Vuestra Reverencia ha muchos años que es muy conocido mio, y de quien me e ayudado en muchas cosas tocantes a mi mission de

---

    367. [*in margin:*] By baker & bakehouse is understoode my Lord Strange and the title they would have hym pretende when her Majestie dieth.
    368. [*in margin:*] John Garret a priest in England.
    369. John Gerard landed in England in November 1588. He parted from Persons in Rome before leaving for England in August: see Gerard, *Autobiography*, 6.
    370. [*in margin:*] By his cousin is meant my Lord Strange.
    371. Unidentified.
    372. [*scribal note:*] These words and signature in Persons's hand.
    373. [*marginal note:*] Guilielmo Masfildio

suerte que puedo ser siempre testigo de la fee y entereça con que en ellas se a mostrado ansi conmigo como con las demas personas con quien a tratado porque de muchas y muy calificadas ha alcansado una grande loa de su ynocençia y piedad. Ha muchos dias que tiene gran deseo de ir a esas partes y ocuparse en el estudio de aquellas letras que Vuestra Reverençia con su prudençia jusgare que le seran más convenientes y asi si por pedirlo yo a Vuestra Reverençia y prinçipalmente por el amor de Christo nuestro Señor le ayudaré Vuestra Reverençia de suerte que pueda conseguir su deseo dejaranos perpetuamente obligados a él y a mí[374] y a todos los demas que despues cogeran el fruto de sus trabajos y espero que nuestro Dios y Señor no se olvidará jamas de este benefiçio y de todos los demas que Vuestra Reverençia a esta persona hiziere que es solo como yo creo lo que siempre a movido a Vuestra Reverençia con deseo de agradar siempre a Su Magestad. Los demas compañeros suyos que con él van son dignisimos de la misma loa por su piedad y virtudes que se pueden pedir y desear en ellos en esta sazon como me a certificado uno de mis charisimos hermanos a quien sé que puedo dar siguramente fee y ansi hallará de cierto Vuestra Reverençia que ninguno de todos ellos será menos acto para qualquiera cosa que este mi G. A quien siempre casi entre todos hallé Actissimo para qualquiera cosa y ansi pido y Ruego a Vuestra Reverençia que tambien los reciba y acoja paternalmente como suele por pedirmelo encareçidamente. Aquel charissimo hermano mio de quien arriba dixe que de esta manera haziendo siempre bien y a tantos se añadira un grande colmo a los mereçimientos de Vuestra Reverençia con nuestros.

La familia[375] de Vuestra Reverençia y todos sus hijos sino son los que an acabado con glorioso fin como ya Vuestra Reverençia por muchas vias abrá oydo biven. Pero qué pueden hazer con tanta perfidia, fuerça y hurtos de los vezinos?[376] Mucha parte dellos padeçen gran neçeçidad [sic] por aver perdido toda su hazienda siendo despojados de estos vezinos que no paran aqui sino pasan a poner muchas açechanças[377] a su sangre y vida. La qual sangre uvieran dias a derramado si nuestro summo Dios por las causas que él sabe no se lo uviera estorvado. Muchas vezes an procurado quitarles la vida con averles ya quitado todo lo demas que tenian: sus rentas sus campos sus bienes y su libertad y ansi todos los demas temen no sin mucha razon el mismo fin de sí y de todas sus cosas si Dios nuestro Señor no detuviere y refrenare el furor de estos hombres porque la crueldad de estos vezinos no se disminuye antes creçe más en todas partes cada dia con ancia de fieras ni jamas en todos los tiempos pasados llegó al punto que a llegado este año pasado y el en que estamos y no me quejo agora de nuestros poderosos enemigos de cuya crueldad y robos[378] saben ya todos en los quales prosiguen aún mucho más desenfrenadamente que solian porque es más intolerable lo que diré que se an hallado y hallan en todas partes muchos hombreçillos de la hez de la plebe que todo lo escudriñan[379] sacan y roban de grandes medianos y pequeños, y de aquellos que avian estado hasta agora encubiertos. Esto es lo que más behementemente nos lastima estos días y lo que siempre

374. y a mí] *this ed.*; y an M, *damaged in margin*
375. [*marginal note:*] Los Catholicos de Inglaterra.
376. [*marginal note:*] herejes
377. *Cf.* achecancas Murphy (*hand-written correction*)
378. [*marginal note:*] consejeros [de] la Reyna
379. escudriñan] *this ed.*; escrudiñan M

nos lastimará y aun nos despojará y herira, mientras que a los nuestros les quedare algo en que estos cruelesimos hombres tengan en que hazer presa y que robar. Y ansi padre mio deseo que Vuestra Reverencia sepa y con su prudençia considere que facilmente somos oprimidos los huerfanos y biyudas y lo seremos mientras nuestros padres y procuradores estuvieren lejos de nosotros porque si de los sectos aunque sean grandes altos y muy densos se quitan de raiz las espinas facilmente de qualesquier animales pueden ser rompidos y entrados. Con todo eso defienden todos aquel derecho y verdad que de sus padres y varones les fue dexado hasta la muerte y esto vemos perpetuamente que lo hacen animosisimamente toda suerte de gente de entranbos sexos grandes y pequeños y tienen tan grande fee y confiança en la dotrina escrita y palabras que de sus mayores recibieron formadas[380] y selladas que por ninguna via les puede nadie persuadir que riban alguna novedad lo qual tienen muchos tan asentado que aunque cada dia los tientan con esto estan fuertes. Y, por dezirlo en una palabra, me pareçe que podemos ser comparados a los sercados[381] que cada ora estan en peligro de su enemigo y en cada asalto reciben en lo esterior gran daño; pero en los animos estan siempre fortissimos de manera que en ningun tiempo temen los asaltos de los enemigos ni piensan por flaqueça rendirsele. Sean dadas a Dios infinitas gracias pues este ánimo fuerças y voluntad es suya concedida a nosotros liberalisimamente; y tenemos confiança que con la presencia de Vuestra Reverencia y de los amigos podra ponerse remedio[382] a todos estos daños pagando la deuda con que se obligaron a los acreedores de que de espacio y claramente nos veriamos este dia aguardamos[383] y esperamos que llegará presto no nos faltando la buena yndustria de Vuestra Reverencia y las ayudas de los que no suelen faltar. Plega a la Magestad de Dios que guarde a Vuestra Reverencia salvo y sano hasta este tiempo, a quien tambien suplicamos intensamente que açelere esta hora como a su eterna sabiduria pareciere más conviniente asi para la eterna gloria de su sancto nombre, como para la salud de todos nosotros. Él guarde a Vuestra Reverencia.

De Londres a 18 de abril de 1591 años.

[*Addressed/endorsed:*] P. Suelo de la Compañia, a Roberto su Amantissimo Padre. En Londres 18 de Abril de 1591.[384]

Translation

My courier William Mansfield who will deliver this to Your Reverence has been known to me for many years, and is the one who has assisted me in many things related to my mission – so I am always able to testify to the loyalty and integrity which he has shown in them, both to me and to others he has dealt with, because he has attracted much praise for his innocence and piety from many people who are well qualified to judge. For a long

380. formadas] *M, i.e.,* firmadas
381. sercados] *M, i.e.,* cercados
382. [*marginal note:*] venir con un buen ejercito a Inglaterra que se a prometido a los Catholicos (to come to England with a good army, which the Catholics have been promised).
383. aguadarnos *Murphy*
384. Father Southwell of the Society [of Jesus], to Robert his most beloved Father. In London, 18 April 1591.

time he has had a great desire to go to those parts and occupy himself in the study of such letters as Your Reverence in your prudence should judge to be most suitable for him. And so, if by my intercession to Your Reverence, and mainly for the love of Christ our Lord, you could help him to fulfil his desire, you would keep us all eternally obliged to you: him, me, and all those who will reap the reward of his labours. And I hope that our God and Lord will never forget this benefit and all the rest that Your Reverence will do for this person – which is no more, I believe, than Your Reverence has been moved to do with your constant desire to please His Majesty. The other companions who are going with him are similarly the most worthy of praise for their piety and virtues that you could ask for or desire of them at this time, as one of my dear brothers has assured me, whom I know I can certainly believe; and Your Reverence will find for sure that not one of them all will be less suitable for anything than my William who almost always is the most capable amongst them all in any matter. So I ask and pray Your Reverence that just as you receive and welcome them in a fatherly manner so you will ask the same of me at any time. The same very dear brother of mine I mentioned above will add greatly to Your Reverence's merits by always doing good to so many.

Your Reverence's family and all your sons[385] are alive except for those who have accomplished a glorious end, as Your Reverence must have already heard by many different means now. But what can they do in the midst of such great treacherous violence and stealing from their neighbours? The majority of them [the English Catholics] suffer great need because they have lost all their property, despoiled by those same neighbours who do not stop until they set snares for their very blood and their life – which blood would have been spilled some time ago if Our God on high for reasons of His own had not prevented it. Many times they have tried to deprive them of their lives, having already deprived them of all else: all the rest that they possessed – their incomes, their fields, their goods and their freedom, and everything else; and they fear the same end for themselves, not without good reason, and all their possessions if God Our Lord did not curb and contain the rage of those men, because the cruelty of those neighbours is not lessened but rather increases more, daily, in all parts, with the fury of wild beasts, even more than in all times past. It has come to the point which it reached in the past year and that in which we are now. I do not complain now of our weighty enemies whose cruelty and depredations we have all known and which continue, only much more unbridled than usual, because what I am saying about what has been and is being found in all parts is quite unbearable. Many striplings of the lowest sort of people scrutinize everything and pillage and steal from everyone of great, middling, and little account. For those [of us] who have kept under cover until now, this is what most cruelly damages us these days and will always damage us and even spoil and harm us, as long as our people still have anything left for those most cruel men to pillage and plunder. And so, my father, I would like Your Reverence to be aware of this and to consider in your wisdom how easily we orphans and widows are oppressed and will continue to suffer as long as our fathers and procurators are kept away from us, because if the thorns even of great, high and very thick hedges are removed at the root, the hedges can be broken by any predators so that they can force an

---

385. I.e., the Catholics in England, as the rest of the paragraph makes clear.

entry. Despite all this the right and the truth is defended unto death which they inherited from their fathers and forefathers, and perpetually we see that they do so resolutely. All kinds of people, of both sexes, great and small, keep such great faith and loyalty to the written doctrine and the words which they have received from their forefathers, signed and sealed, that by no means can anyone persuade them to prefer some novelty. They are so steadfast, that although they are tempted by it every day, they remain firm, and, just to say one word, it seems to me that we can be compared to fences which are in hourly danger from their enemies, outwardly damaged in each assault; yet their souls remain fortified, such that at no time do they fear the assaults of their enemies nor do they think that through weakness they will give in. Countless thanks should be given to God, as this courage, strength, and determination is His favour, bestowed on us all so generously. We are confident that with the presence of Your Reverence and our friends a remedy will be found for all these injuries, a payment of that debt which our creditors promised we should shortly expect. We should see clearly this very day approaching and we hope that it will reach us soon, Your Reverence's good industry not failing us nor the help of those who do not usually fail, God's Majesty willing. He has kept Your Reverence safe and whole up to this time, and we earnestly beseech Him that the hour will come as quickly as seems in His eternal wisdom most fitting for the eternal glory of His sacred name and the salvation of us all. May he keep Your Reverence safe.

From London, 18 April 1591.

B105 To Paolo Emilio, Cardinal Sfondrati, Seville, 18 April 1591

> SOURCE: AAV, Segr. Stato, Spagna 38, fols. 420 and 422, holograph.
> HICKS: 115–120, with English translation.
> NOTE: Sfondrati (1560–1618) was nephew of Pope Gregory XIV and had recently been made a cardinal and appointed papal secretary (see introduction, "The International Scene," and McCoog, *Building the Faith of St Peter*, 140–141). Persons reminds Sfondrati of their meeting in Milan when Campion and Persons passed through on their way to the English mission in 1580 and begs him to lend his weight to the appeal for military intervention in England. He also mentions that he has asked the new pope for special faculties for the ordination of priests in Valladolid.

Illustrissimo et Reverendissimo Signor

Se ben mi serve la memoria, viddi Vostra Signoria Illustrissima nel palazzo del Cardinal Borromeo in Milano con Sua Santità ch'è adesso, nell'anno 80, quando il Padre Campiano et io con altri sacerdoti Inglesi passassimo a Inglaterra et fummo hospeti per alcuni giorni di quel Santo Cardinale che sta in gloria.

Dipoi habbiamo sempre inteso per il mondo, li passi di santità che l'Illustrissimo Cardinale Sfondrata faceva all'imitatione dell'altro santo, et mi ricordo che s'intese sua promotione al Cardinalato con grandissimo contento delli Catolici in Ingleterra, però infinitamente più sarà stata adesso la consolatione loro della sua sublimatione al pontificato, et la speranza grandissima ch'han conceputo del aiuto che tutti li buoni trovaranno in Vostra Signoria Illustrissima che s'ha allevata nella casa e schola d'un tanto grande zio et maestro. Deo Nostro Signor augmenti siempre a Vostra Signoria Illustrissima suoi santissimi doni et gratie, accioché in questo alto luogo nel qual l'ha posto, Vostra Signoria Illustrissima le vada procurando molto grande aumento di sua divina gloria nella terra, et a lei medessima grande tesoro di richezza nel cielo.

Il padre Cresuello rector del Collegio Anglico in Rome, m'ha scritto come per ordine del Reverendo Padre nostro Generale della Compagnia communicò con Vostra Signoria Illustrissima una letera mia, la qual scrissi a lui solo, ma dipoi no pensato che fu particular providenza di nostro Signor che venisse anco alla vista di lei, poiché me scrive, che Vostra Signoria Illustrissima si degno di mostrar molto grande et piissimo affetto alli negozii trattati in quella letera, dalla qual cosa io n'ho conceputo multa speranza che Dio ha de servirse molto di Vostra Signoria Illustrissima in questa grande opera, da dove pare a tutti che considerano bene il nigotio, et il tiempo in che ci troviamo con l'altre circumstanze, che dipende più il rimedio universale della Christianità che da ninguna altra cosa che si può pensar, poiché tutti l'altri rimedii non sono efficaci per rimediar alla radice del male si non solo questo.

L'Illustrissimo Cardinal d'Ingleterra principalissima pietra in questa opera, et il Padre rector diranno a Vostra Signoria Illustrissima quanti anni andiamo già travagliando per procurar questo rimedio, et per confesar la verità io di mi parte mi trovo al presente assai debole et stracco, non solamente di forze corporali per le fatighe, ma anco d'animo con veder le dilationi di principi che s'han usate, et le grandi opportunità che si son perse con le quali tutto s'haveria potuto rimediare facilmente, ma al fin habbiamo de conformarci con la volontà di Nostro Signor et chi sa si Nostro Signor lo ha riservato per la grande corona di questo pontificato, etc.

Questa è cosa certa a parere di tutti che intendono meglio le cose di quella professione che non è così difficile la speditione di questo negotio come alcuni le fanno, et si quello che si spende in altre parti et in altre opere pie senza multo frutto, in duoi anni, si spendesse qui sobra questa opera in un anno, tutto si potria rimediare.

Li medessimi son di parere, che si come il negotio è propriamente della Chiesa, et della Sede Apostolica, così, si non si indrizza et si incamina per essa, pigliando suo vigore et spirito da essa, non haverà l'effetto che si desidera ni bastarà che da costi venga solamente concorso et conformità, ma che tutto il calore, stimulo, indrizzo, et altri parti vitali influiscano costi, altrimente poca speranza c'è per le raggioni che al Padre rector ho scritto. Vostra Signoria Illustrissima le vedrà et farà come suo santo zelo in tutto le dettarà, et io non mancarò da tiempo in tiempo di avisar le cose che[386] s'offeriranno per questo medessimo mezzo del rector il qual m'assicura che sarà con il secreto che converrà.

Il medessimo rector informarà Vostra Signoria Illustrissima del progresso delli nostri sacerdoti Inglesi in queste parti, et quanti siano andati nella loro missione d'Inglaterra. Supplicava[387] anco a Sua Santità per la facultà di dar'ordini sacri alli Alunni del Seminario di Valliodolid *sine titulo patrimonii*, senza la qual facultà, non potrà passar più inanzi quel seminario poiché non tiene più sacerdoti già, come Vostra Signoria Illustrissima vedrà dal memoriale che mandiamo. Confidiamo molto nel aiuto particular di Vostra

---

386. che] V; preceded by p without space or contraction
387. supplicava] V; possibly supplicarà

Signoria Illustrissima con Sua Santità per questa opera, poiché siempre si ha visto suo favore pronto per simili opere del divino servigio. Dio Nostro Signor conservi siempre Vostra Signoria Illustrissima nella sua santissima gratia, et dia felicissimo pontificato a Sua Santità come noi altri tutti suoi siervi et capellani indegni preghiamo Sua Divina Maestà. Seviglia alli 18 d'Aprile 1591.
    Di Vostra Signoria Illustrissima et Reverendissima
        Servo humilissimo
            Roberto Personio.

[*Addressed:*] All Illustrissimo el Reverendissimo il Signor Cardinale Sfondrata Nepote del Santissimo Domino Nostro Papa Gregorio 14°.[388]

[*Endorsed:*] 1591 Siviglia 18 April P. Roberto Personio: le cose di Inghelterra se si abbracciano no sono così difficili come paiono y supplica per la facoltà di dare gli ordini sacri a gli Alumni del Seminario di Valladolid *sine titulo patremonii*, non potendo caminar più avanti questo seminario no havendo più sacerdoti et manda memoriale sopra di ciò.[389]

[*At foot of the page:*] Al S. Cardinale Lanulletti.[390]

Translation

Your Most Reverend Eminence

If my memory serves me well, I saw Your Eminence in Cardinal Borromeo's palace in Milan together with His Holiness now reigning, in the year '80, at the time when Fr Campion and I with other English priests were on our way to England, and we were for some days the guests of that holy cardinal who is now in glory.[391]

Since then, we have heard, always and everywhere, of the steps in holiness which His Eminence Cardinal Sfondrati was making in imitation of that other holy man, and I recall how very pleased the English Catholics were to learn of his promotion to the cardinalate. But now that he has been elevated to the papacy, their consolation will have been infinitely greater, and great indeed the hopes they have conceived of the aid which all good men will find in Your Eminence, brought up as you were in the household and school of your uncle, who was so great a man and teacher. May God our Lord ever increase his holy gifts and graces to Your Eminence, so that in this lofty position in which he has placed you, Your Eminence may continue to gain for Him a great increase in His divine glory on earth, and for yourself rich treasure in heaven.

Fr Creswell, rector of the English college in Rome, has written to me that by command of the reverend father general of our Society, he showed Your Eminence a letter of

---

388. Addressed to "the Very Reverend His Eminence Cardinal Sfondrati, nephew of our most holy father Pope Gregory XIV".

389. Endorsed: "From Fr Robert Persons, Seville, 18 April: If they undertake the enterprise of England matters will not be as difficult as they seem. He asks for the faculty to bestow holy orders on the students of the seminary of Valladolid without title of patrimony, because the seminary cannot make further progress unless they have more priests. He sends a memorial on this issue."

390. Possibly Scipione Lancellotti (1527–1598), cardinal priest of San Salvatore in Lauro.

391. Cardinal St Charles Borromeo died on 3 November 1584.

mine, a confidential letter for himself alone:[392] but I have since thought that it was a special providence of Our Lord that it also came to your notice, for he tells me that Your Eminence deigned to show the greatest and most charitable interest in the business I dealt with in that letter. Thanks to this I have conceived great hopes of the use that God is going to make of Your Eminence in this great work. And it is clear to all who consider well the undertaking and the times in which we are living, and other circumstances, that the restoration of Christianity throughout the world depends more on this than on anything else imaginable, seeing that no other remedy is capable of curing the root of the evil, except this one.

His Eminence the cardinal of England, who is the cornerstone of this work, and father rector will tell Your Eminence for how many years we have now been labouring to obtain this remedy; and, to confess the truth, for my part, I find myself at present rather weak and weary, not only in bodily strength owing to fatigue, but also in spirit, when I see how sluggishly the princes have acted, and the great opportunities lost whereby all could have been remedied with ease. But in the end we must submit to Our Lord's will, and who knows whether our Lord has not reserved this matter to be the chief crown of this pontificate.

In the opinion of all who are more skilled in this profession, we can be sure that the carrying out of this enterprise is not as difficult as some make out; and if what is spent without much fruit in the space of two years on pious works in other places were spent here on this work in one year, everything could be set to rights.

The same persons are of opinion that, since the business belongs properly to the church and the Holy See, it will not have the desired effect, unless it is directed and set in motion by her, deriving its energy and spirit from her, nor will it be enough for that side merely to collaborate and agree, but all the warmth, inspiration, guidance, and other vital elements must flow from there: otherwise there is little hope, for the reasons which I have written to father rector. Please would Your Eminence see him and act in all things as your holy zeal directs; and I shall not omit to inform you from time to time of anything that suggests itself to me, by means of this same rector, who assures me that it will be done with due secrecy.

The very same rector will acquaint Your Eminence with the progress made by our English priests in these parts, and how many are gone on their mission to England. I have also asked His Holiness for faculties to bestow holy orders on the scholars of the seminary of Valladolid *without right of patrimony*;[393] without these faculties that seminary will

---

392. This may refer to Persons's letter to Creswell of 4 November 1590 (B84), which mentioned the prospective departure of John Cecil and other priests for England and may also have dealt confidentially with plans for a further Spanish invasion attempt, as hinted at in this paragraph: there were reports of a naval buildup in Santander, Ferrol, and Bilbao: Paul E.J. Hammer, *Elizabeth's Wars: War, Government, and Society in Tudor England, 1544–1604* (Basingstoke, 2003), 161–162. Creswell would have shown such a letter to Acquaviva and was then asked to show it to Sfondrati, appointed papal secretary on 19 December 1590. Creswell would then have written to Persons by the same post as Acquaviva's letter of 24 December (B89).

393. The letter encloses a copy of the ruling about ordination without patrimony: "Licet Concilium fol Tridentinum in Sess. 21, cap. 2° statuerit, ne Clericus secularis possit ad Sacros

not be able to make further progress, for it no longer has any priests, as Your Eminence will see from the memorial we are sending. We rely greatly on Your Eminence's special help with His Holiness towards carrying on this work, since you are well known to have always been prompt in supporting similar works in the service of God. May God, our Lord, ever preserve Your Eminence in His holy grace, and grant a most happy pontificate to His Holiness, as all of us, his unworthy servants and bedesmen, beseech His Divine Majesty. Seville, 18 April 1591.

Your Eminence's most humble servant
Robert Persons.

B106 To Claudio Acquaviva, Madrid, May 1591

SOURCE: Acquaviva to Persons, 9 July 1591 (B111).

NOTE: In this letter Persons reported that he had returned to Madrid and explained what his plans were for Andalusia in general. He hoped that William Holt could be released from his responsibilities in Brussels, possibly to relieve Creswell in Rome and allow him to come to assist Persons in Spain. He would likely have corresponded with Holt and Walpole about this; see his letter to Walpole, 18 July 1591 (B115).

B107 From Claudio Acquaviva, Rome, 13 May 1591

SOURCE: ARSI, Tolet. 5/I, fol. 188r.

NOTE: Acquaviva sends two priests from the English college to Persons for reception and placement in the Society in Spain: Richard Walpole (1562/4–1607) and Ralph Pickard, who died on the journey at Saragossa (Anstruther, 276). Walpole was admitted to the college at Valladolid on 1 November 1591; in 1592 he welcomed Philip II to the college in Valladolid in Greek. He joined the Society on 6 March 1593, after aborting his journey to England at Seville, where he later became prefect of studies. See introduction, "The Seminaries," Anstruther, 276 and 369–370; *Valladolid Registers* 16; McCoog, *English and Welsh Jesuits*, 324.

P. Roberto Personio Mayo 13.

Los portadores de la presente son dos sacerdotes deste seminario que como Vuestra Reverencia entendera dellos desean entrar en la Compañia en esas partes, llamanse Ricardo Valpolo, y Rodolfo Picardo, Vuestra Reverencia los vea hable y examine que yo

---

Ordines promoveri, nisi possideat beneficium Ecclesiasticum, vel nisi ordinetur ad Titulum patrimonij, vel pensionis, secundum formam ibi traditam; Tamen Papa solet concedere facultatem ordinandi, absque dicto Titulo patrimonij, et benef[ic]ij, prout concessit Alumnis Collegij Anglos de Urbe" (Although the Council of Trent in session 22 chapter 2 decreed that a secular priest could not be promoted to holy orders unless he was already possessed of an ecclesiastical benefice, or was ordained to an entitled patrimony or a pension, according to the form that was customary there, nevertheless the pope is accustomed to allow a faculty of ordination without the said title of patrimony, and has done so in the case of students of the English college in Rome). This may have been appended by Persons, or attached to the record.

me remito a su pareçer ansi en el reçevirlos como en la Provincia donde mejor le pareçiere que sean recevidos y esten. En sus oraciones, etc.

Translation

To Fr Robert Persons, 13 May.

The carriers of this present letter are two priests of this seminary who, as Your Reverence will learn from them, wish to join the Society in those parts: namely, Richard Walpole and Ralph Pickard. Please would Your Reverence be sure to meet them, talk to them, and examine them. I leave it to you to judge whether to receive them and in which province they should best be received and placed. To your prayers, etc.

B108 From William Warford, Amsterdam, 15 May 1591

SOURCE: ACSA, Series II, Legajo 1, item 7 (five fair copies of a Spanish translation, all in the same hand) = *Vd1, Vd2, Vd3, Vd4, Vd5.*

NOTE: William Warford (ca. 1560–1608), of Oxford and Rheims, served Allen until 1588, then went to Spain and left Seville for the English mission on 3 April 1591 (see Persons to Cecil and Fixer, 13 April, B102; Anstruther, 370; Murphy, 133). He entered the Society of Jesus in Rome in 1594 and died in Valladolid in 1608 (McCoog, *English and Welsh Jesuits*, 325–326). This report was sent to Persons en route. It describes Warford's good fortune in finding passage to London and makes recommendations about directing missionaries and material through Amsterdam. It ends on a light-hearted note about archiepiscopal drinking habits.

It appears that the copyist refined the translation progressively, probably in the order in which the copies appear in the collection. *Vd5* has therefore been adopted as the copy text, with errors and omissions corrected from earlier versions. Only significant variants have been recorded in the apparatus. From the multiple copies, Williams infers that there was wide interest in the contents.

Copia de una carta de Guliermo Warfordo sacerdote Inglés, escrita en Amsterdam de Olanda a 15 de Mayo al Padre Roberto Personio Inglés de la Compañia de Jesus. Partio Guliermo de España para yr a predicar la santa[394] fee Catholica en Inglaterra a primero de Abril 1591.

Ayer estando yo en Harlem tres leguas desta çiudad tuve aviso como la nave que yo tenía concertada aqui en Amsterdam[395] para pasar en ella a Naucastel en Inglaterra, avia de partirse luego, y asi escrivi a Vuestra Reverencia una carta larga de cosas que me parecio Vuestra Reverencia más deseava más saver y la ymbié por la via de Anversa, en la qual di quenta a Vuestra Reverencia de los peligros que he tenido en este mi viage, y la miseri-

394. la santa] nuestra santa *Vd1*; la *Vd2 Vd3*; nuestra *Vd4*
395. aqui en Amsterdam] *om. Vd5*

cordia de Dios nuestro Señor en librarme dellos y particularmente de Ingleses hereges que topé de camino en los puertos y lugares por donde pasé; y juntamente di en ella algunos avisos que me parecian necesarios para los hermanos que han de seguir este mismo camino y viage, cómo se han de aver con estos Ingleses,[396] y qué vestido han de traer que no paresca ser de España, y que pasen con nombre de Irlandeses, Escocés, Alemanes, Polacos, o de otra qualquiera nacion antes que de Ingleses,[397] porque este nombre pone mucha atencion en los que lo oyen, pues todos los Ingleses se tienen o por grandes hereges, o por muy determinados Catholicos y lo uno o lo otro destas dos cosas tiene su peligro consigo[398] en estos caminos.

El maestro de la nave que me ha de llevar es catholico y[399] save tambien mi profesion y juntamente el peligro que corre en llevarme[400] a Inglaterra, si se descubre: todavia se ha determinado de haçerlo. Y pareçe que Dios va poniendo algun calor a las personas que hemos menester. Dize que conoce algunos Catholicos en Neucastel y me nombró al Señor Selby, cuya muger murio catholicamente y por esto diçe que no la quisieron enterrar los hereges. Y esto de conocer él alla alguna casa de Catholicos nos viene muy a proposito para que me ponga luego en cobro, si Dios no aya ya permitido que me cojan en el puerto. Y si esto fuere, *sicut voluntas fuerit in cœlo, sic fiat*. De más desto me ha dicho este maestro que estando los dias pasados en Neucastel, oyo dezir que los hereges avian martyrizado pocos dias antes[401] algunos Jesuitas, pero yo entiendo que eran sacerdotes de los seminarios, que suelen los hereges ponerles este nombre por haçerlos más odiosos como Vuestra Reverencia save. Y yo no he savido que algun Padre de la Compañia residiese en aquellas partes. Y pues alla van tan baratas las coronas de martyrio, grandissimo deseo tengo de verme en Inglaterra y Christo mi Señor me lo conceda, si me vee digno; y si una vez pudiere llegar a donde Vuestra Reverencia desea, le ymbiare luego la instruction cumplida que hemos concertado para ymbiar y recibir cartas de alla. Y si me prendieren en el puerto, dello[402] llevará nuevas el maestro de la nave o alguna gente suya.

La comodidad que hemos descubierto acá en Olanda para al pasage de nuestros hermanos y para ymbiar y recibir avisos[403] me pareçe muy buena y segura y que ha sido particular providençia de Dios Nuestro Señor averla descubierto, porque en las casas que apunté en la otra mia destas dos villas de Harlem y Amsterdam (aunque el govierno universal de las villas[404] sea por manos de hereges), hallarán muy buen acogimiento de Catholicos, mucha virtud, fidelidad y cuydado para ayudarles en la execucion de sus buenos propositos.

---

396. Ingleses] *Vd3 adds* hereges
397. antes que de Ingleses] *Vd1 Vd3 Vd5*; y no de Ingleses *Vd2 Vd4*
398. tiene su peligro consigo] *Vd5*; tiene su peligro *Vd2 Vd3 Vd4*; se trae consigo su peligro *Vd1*
399. y] *Vd5*; que *Vd1 Vid2 Vd3 Vd4*
400. llevarme] *Vd4 adds* consigo
401. pocos dias antes] de pocos dias a esta *Vd1, which then inserts* padres
402. dello] *Vd2 Vd4 Vd5*; desto *Vd1 Vd3*
403. avisos] *Vd1 Vd4 Vd5*; cartas *Vd2 Vd3*
404. de las villas] *Vd5 only*

La casa en que al presente quedo es de un sacerdote muy Catholico y devoto llamado Dominus N. y tiene un hermano Doctor en Medicina y[405] hombre de bien y muy letrado, cuyo nombre es N. A qualquiera destos dos o al señor Cornelio N. se puede ymbiar seguramente qualquiera carta o persona, porque aunque ellos no esten en casa, todos los de sus familias son Catholicos y recibiran de buena gana qualquiera cosa de Vuestra Reverencia de quien tienen ya buena noticia. El sobrescrito de las cartas ha de venir en flamenco en esta manera: *E ersamen goode etc.* Y sepa Vuestra Reverencia que ay muchos Catholicos en esta ciudad de Amsterdam y entre los demas ay una calle entera dellos que cierran sus tiendas publicamente todos los dias de fiestas de precepto por la yglesia[406] y no se les da nada de que los hereges se enojen dello.

En Harlem tambien aunque no aya mayor número de sacerdotes que en Amsterdam, todavia ay mucha mayor libertad para bivir catholicamente, de manera que ay gran número aún de monjas y escuelas de estudiantes que se crian catholicamente; y si uviese algunos seminarios para sacar esta gente y perficionarla por alla, y hombres de zelo y maña que los encaminasen, seria yncreyble el bien que en pocos años se podria haçer para la reduction destas provincias perdidas, las quales sera dificultosissimo de reducir por armas temporales y para esto otro poco bastaria y antes las mismas obras[407] y superfluydades de pocos hombres serian bastantissimas. Las cartas para Harlem han de venir en esta forma: *E ersamen etc.* en casa del señor N. o de su hermano Dominus N. que es sacerdote letrado y pio.

Aviendo escrito esto me han venido a ofrecer otra comodidad muy grande de una nave que va derecha a Londres y el maestro della es buen catholico y conoce unos Alemanes tambien Catholicos que moran en Londres, en cuya casa me pondra luego con grande seguridad. Esto Padre mio nos viene del cielo y me anyma mucho de que avemos[408] de haçer alguna cosa buena en servicio de Nuestro Señor pues nos ayuda por tantas vias. Luego dexaré el pasage para Naucastel y tomaré esto[409] de Londres que es más cerca y más a proposito. Y con esto no tengo duda sino que asentaremos para cartas presto un camino muy bueno y seguro. Vuestra Reverencia se acuerde de nosotros en sus sacrificios como bien sé que lo haze &c.

Pésame de no tener tiempo para escrivir dos renglones a mi señor el Arçobiscopo de Ebora, aunque no es tanta la falta de tiempo como de materia digna, pues no juzgo cosa alguna ser digna de su señoria *si non fuerit a torcularibus*. Guarde Dios a Vuestra Reverencia. De Amsterdam 15 de mayo 1591.

  R.W.[410]

[PS] En este ynstante han entrado acá dos navios flamencos bien armados que dizen averse escapado de Cádiz, donde estavan embargados por el Adelantado. Traen alguna artilleria de Su Magestad que llevaron de ay.

 405. y] *Vd5 only*
 406. de precepto por la yglesia] que la yglesia Romana manda guardar *Vd1*; de guardar por la Iglesia *Vd2*; de precepto *Vd3*; por la Iglesia Romana *Vd4*
  407. mismas obras] nuestras sobras *Vd1*
  408. avemos] hemos *Vd1*
  409. esto] este *Vd5*
  410. R.W.] *evidently a copyist's error for G.W. although it is in all copies*

Translation

A copy of a letter by William Warford, English priest, written in Amsterdam in Holland on 15 May to Fr Robert Persons of the Society of Jesus. William left Spain to go to preach our holy Catholic faith in England on 1 April 1591.

Yesterday being in Harlem three leagues from this city, I received notice that the ship in which I had arranged to take voyage from here in Amsterdam to Newcastle in England, would leave later, and so I have written Your Reverence a long letter about the things which I thought Your Reverence ought to know, and have sent it via Antwerp. In it I give an account of all the dangers I experienced on my journey and the mercy of our God in saving me from them and particularly the English heretics whom I encountered on the way, at the ports and places I passed through. And together with that I have given some notice of what seems necessary to me for my fellows who will follow this same path and journey: how they should deal with these Englishmen, and that they should not dress as if they came from Spain and how they should go by the name of Irish, Scots, Germans, Poles, or any other nation rather than English, because this name causes a great stir among those who hear it, because all the English are considered either great heretics or very determined Catholics, and either the one or the other of these two brings its own danger on this journey.

The master of the ship carrying me is a Catholic who knows my vocation and also the danger which he incurs by carrying me to England, if he is discovered; nevertheless, he decided to take me. And it seems that God is prompting those people we need. He says he knows some Catholics in Newcastle, and he named Mr Selby whose wife died in a Catholic way. Because of this, he says, the heretics did not want to bury her. And so it is known that there is a house of Catholics, and it is very much to the purpose for me to be concealed, if God should still permit me not to be caught at the port – may His will be done here as it is in heaven. Furthermore the master has told me that, being in Newcastle a few days ago, he heard tell that the heretics had martyred some Jesuit fathers a few days before, but I understand that they were seminary priests, since the heretics use that name which they regard as most hateful, as Your Reverence knows.[411] For I do not know that any father of the Society dwells in these parts; but since the crown of martyrdom goes so cheaply there, I desire very greatly to see myself in England and may Christ my Lord vouchsafe this to me, if I am found worthy. And if I could once get there, would Your Reverence be pleased to send me the completed instruction we agreed on for sending and receiving letters from there. But if they take me at the port, the master of the ship will bear the news of that, or one of his men.

---

411. Despite the chronology, he may mean Edmund Duke, Richard Hill, John Hogg, and Richard Holiday, seminary priests hanged, drawn, and quartered at Durham, 27 May 1590: *The Catholic Martyrs of England and Wales: A Chronological List of English and Welsh Martyrs Who Gave Their Lives for Christ and His Church During the "Penal Times" (A.D. 1535–1680)* (London, 1979), 37.

The convenience which we have experienced here in Holland with regard to the passage of our men and the sending and receiving of messages seems to me very good and secure, and discovering it has been a particular providence of God Our Lord, because in the houses that I mentioned in my other [letter] in the two towns of Harlem and Amsterdam (even though the overarching government of those towns may be in the hands of heretics), there will be found much good reception of Catholics, much virtue, faithfulness, and care in assisting them and the fulfilment of their good purposes.

The place where I'm currently staying belongs to a very Catholic and devoted priest called Master N. and he has a brother, a doctor of medicine and a very learned and good man, whose name is N. To each of these two or to Mr Cornelius N. it is possible to send any letter or person securely, even if they are not in the house. Their whole families are Catholics and will willingly receive anything from Your Reverence, because they already have good references of you. The superscript of the letters should be in Flemish thus: *E ersamen goode etc.*[412] Your Reverence should know that there are many Catholics in this city of Amsterdam and amongst others there is a whole street of them who close their shops publicly on all the feast days which the Roman church stipulates should be kept and they do not care that it makes the heretics angry with them.

In Harlem, although with no greater number of priests than in Amsterdam, they still have much more freedom to live in a Catholic fashion, in that already a large number of nuns and schools of pupils are being brought up in a Catholic way; and if they had some seminarians to serve the people and improve them, men of zeal and skill who would direct them, it is hard to believe what good they could do in a few years in the reduction of those lost provinces, which are very difficult to reduce by temporal arms, while not much would be necessary by this other means. And soon the same actions[413] and a few highly capable men will be more than enough. Letters to Harlem should be addressed in this form: *E ersamen etc.* to the house of Mr N. or his brother Master N, who is a learned and pious priest.

While I was writing this there has come to me the offer of another very great opportunity of a ship that is going directly to London, and its master is a good Catholic and knows of some Germans, also Catholic, who dwell in London, in whose house I can find a lodging with great security. My father, this seems to be providential and has encouraged me much to do something good in the service of our Lord, who helps us in so many ways. Then I will put aside the passage to Newcastle and take the one to London because it is closer and more to the purpose and with that there is no doubt but that it will speedily establish a route for letters, good and secure. Would Your Reverence please remember us in your sacrifices just as we do, etc.

I am sorry not to have time to write two lines to My Lord Archbishop of Évora,[414] although it is not time I lack so much as suitable matter, because I do not regard any-

---

412. This means, roughly, "together goods."

413. *Vd1*'s variant yields: "our additional [men]."

414. Teotónio de Bragança (succeeded 7 Dec 1578, d. 29 Jul 1602), brother of the duke of Braganza, of a powerful family in Portugal, was a member of the Society of Jesus until dismissed as a troublemaker in 1555. See William V. Bangert, *Jerome Nadal, SJ, 1507–1580*, ed. and completed Thomas M. McCoog (Chicago, 1992), 99–101.

thing to be suitable to His Lordship unless it came from the winepresses. God save Your Reverence. From Amsterdam, 15 May 1591.

R.W.

[PS] Just this moment two Flemish ships have entered the harbour, well armed, which claim to have escaped from Cádiz, where they had been held by the governor. They are carrying some artillery of His Majesty's that they took from there.

B109 From Claudio Acquaviva, Rome, 10 June 1591

SOURCE: ARSI, Baet. 3/I, 3-4, from the general's register of letters to the province of Andalusia.

NOTE: Acquaviva tries to rouse Persons's spirits, torn between the needs of Valladolid and Seville. He applauds Pérez's help, as provincial of Andalusia, with developments in Seville, hoping that Gil González Dávila, as visitor to Castile, will help Persons with choosing a new rector for the college at Valladolid, possibly Cabredo, in place of Manzano.

P. Roberto Personio, Junio 10.

Recevi la de Vuestra Reverencia escrita a 18 de Abril, y aunque por lo que en ella me escrive veo quanta raçon ay para tenerle compasion pues por una parte le da cuydado lo de Castilla, por otra lo de Sevilla no sale tan bien como se desea, con todo eso no quiero consolar a Vuestra Reverencia porque sé el buen pecho que para todo le da nuestro Señor, y que save que las grandes cosas no se acaban sin gran trabajo y dificultad. Yo aviso a Padre Bartolome Perez lo mucho que Vuestra Reverencia reconoçe, y agradeçe[415] su voluntad y la buen acogida que en él halla, y deseo que la mesma halle en los demas, el provincial[416] de Castilla se lo encargó, y en ocasiones lo hará con otros como el Padre Bartolome Perez me lo dice que lo haga. Vuestra Reverencia esté de buen ánimo que su empresa es de Dios y todos le ayudaremos en lo que para ella pudieremos: ya el visitador me ha escrito las vezes[417] que el Rector del Seminario no da la satisfaction que se desea, y yo le he respondido, y de nuevo le respondo que le quite y ponga otro que sea más a proposito, y que si le pareçiere que era sufiçiente el Padre Cabredo lo vea, y haga como le juzgare convenir, Vuestra Reverencia lo puede tratar con él con ocasión desto etc.

Yo escrivo a Vuestra Reverencia y vean quién será mejor para hazer este oficio, especialmente que aora que no corre el impedimento de los illegitimos ternan más padres[418] para escojer y si otra cosa fuere necessario, Vuestra Reverencia con toda libertad me avise que yo en lo que pudiera no fallaré. En sus oraciones etc.

---

415. agradeçe] *obscure, alternatively* agradera R

416. el provincial] *in R, an indecipherable word precedes* provincial, *possibly denoting* vice, *as reflected in the translation*

417. las vezes] *obscure, possibly* dos vezes *or* diziendo R

418. padres] *obscure, possibly* personas R

Translation

To Robert Persons, 10 June.

I have received Your Reverence's letter written on 18 April, and although from what you wrote in it I can see how much reason there is to sympathize with you, since you are concerned about Castile on the one hand and on the other you are not so sure about the outcome in Seville as you would like, nevertheless I am not going to try to comfort Your Reverence, because Our Lord gives you good cheer for everything, and he knows that great matters cannot be accomplished without great effort and difficulty. I am advising Fr Bartolomé Pérez how much Your Reverence recognizes and appreciates his good will and the strong support you find in him, and I wish that one could find the same in the rest of them, as the [Vice] Provincial of Castile has charged them,[419] and that sometimes others would behave as Fr Bartolomé Pérez tells me he has done. Your Reverence should be encouraged in your enterprise, and God's, and we will aid you in it in every way we can. The visitor has now written to me to say that the rector of the seminary does not give the satisfaction he desires, and I have answered him, and I am answering him again, that he should remove him to appoint another more suitable. If it appears that Fr Cabredo would meet the case, and does as seems appropriate to you, Your Reverence may deal with it as occasion serves, etc.

I am writing to Your Reverence to see who will be better to undertake this task, especially now that the obstacle no longer exists of the illegitimate ones, so that more fathers are eligible for promotion,[420] and [to consider] whether something else is necessary. Your Reverence should feel completely free to advise me how to avoid making a mistake in this. To your prayers, etc.

B110 From John Gerard, probably July 1591, via Henry Walpole

SOURCE: Henry Walpole to Joseph Creswell, 22 August 1591; ABSI, Anglia A1, no. 58.

NOTE: Walpole's letter to Creswell enclosed "two blanks from Mr. J[ohn] Gerard, the one for yourself, the other for Mr. Per., that is Peckam," whom Jessopp identifies as Persons: *Letters of Henry Walpole*, ed. Augustus Jessopp (Norwich, 1873), 37 n4. Gerard had been at large in England since 1588.

B111 From Claudio Acquaviva, Rome, 9 July 1591

SOURCE: ARSI, Tolet. 5/I, fol. 195r (main text) and fol. 195v (addendum).

NOTE: Responding to a letter probably written in May, Acquaviva is encouraged by developments in Seville and reassures Persons about Gil González Dávila. He is in agreement that Richard Gibbons need not go to Coimbra but to Flanders instead (see his letter of 20 March, B95). In the event, Gibbons was transferred to Coimbra. In this open letter, Acquaviva is careful not to be specific about his plans for William Holt. Acquaviva suggests that

---

419. The reading is obscure; see textual note.
420. The reading is obscure; see textual note.

Henry Walpole might replace Holt in Brussels and that Thomas Wright might also go to Flanders in another capacity.

In an addendum, Acquaviva asks for advice about an English Jesuit in France who wants to return to England, presumably John Curry (see Verstegan's despatch, 7 June 1593, B182, where the name is given as "Correo," here "Crureio").

P. Roberto Personio en Madrid, Julio 9.

Yo me consuelo que Vuestra Reverencia sea vuelto a Madrid, y que dexe lo de Andaluzia en el buen término que por la suya me avisa. Ya he significado al Padre Bartolome Perez quan agradeçido le está Vuestra Reverencia y lo que yo gusto de que él acuda como lo haçe a favoreçer las cosas que Vuestra Reverencia trae entre manos. Lo de Valladolid entre el padre Gil Gonzalez y Vuestra Reverencia lo podran facilmente reparar poniendo allí otro superior como he escrito al Padre Gil que lo haga.

No importa que el Padre Ricardo sea ayudante del ministro en Coimbra, que si él no quadra con castellanos ni españoles, embiar le hemos a França donde no le faltará en que ocuparse.

Del Padre Holto yo tengo el buen concepto que Vuestra Reverencia por la suya me escrive dél, y avisaremos al Padre Oliverio que nos embíe la informacion solita para tratar de su promocion, y pues su persona en Flandes no es tan necessaria que no se pueda passar sin él. En otra parte le emplearemos donde será bien necessario, y en su lugar bastará que este el Padre Valpolo: pues Vuestra Reverencia me escrive que para lo que aora es necessario él será sufiçiente, que el Padre Tomas Hurit[421] no creo que es a proposito para encargar de aquello, aunque lo será para emplearse en Flandes en luego en semejantes ministerios. De lo demas escrivo en otra. En los etc.

Añadido al Padre Personio, 9 de Julio.

Escrivenme de la Provincia de Francia que Tomas Crureio[422] que está en ella desea bolver a Inglaterra, pero aquellos padres no juzgar que conviene porque demás de no tener dél tanta satisfacion como quisieran, una de las razones que a él le ponen deseo de Inglaterra, es tratar no sé qué negocios de los suyos. Vuestra Reverencia me avise si ese sugeto la será en esos Provincias de España de utilidad y alguna ayuda porque si le quisiere se le embiarán.

· *Translation*

To Robert Persons in Madrid, 9 July.

I am relieved that Your Reverence has returned to Madrid and that you are leaving Andalusia with such a good outcome as you inform me of in your letter. I have already indicated to Fr Bartolomé Pérez how grateful you are to him, and how pleased I am that he is assisting – as he is – to promote the matters which Your Reverence has in hand. The disagreement in Valladolid between Fr Gil González and Your Reverence you can easily repair by appointing another superior, as I have written to Fr Gil to do.

421. Cf. "Vrit" in Acquaviva's letter of 20 January 1592, ad finem.
422. Possibly a transcription error for Curreio: see headnote.

It is not important that Fr Richard should be assistant to the minister in Coimbra. If he does not fit in with Castilians or Spaniards, we shall send him to France, where he will not find himself without occupation.

I have the same favourable view of Fr Holt which Your Reverence expresses in your last letter, and I am suggesting to Fr Olivier[423] that he send us the usual information about handling his promotion, given that his person is not so necessary in Flanders that they could not do without him. We will employ him in another region where he is truly necessary, and in his place Fr Walpole will suffice, since Your Reverence writes to me that he will be able to fulfil the present need. As for Fr Thomas Wright,[424] I do not believe that he is suitable to take over that responsibility, although he would be suitable in Flanders in charge of similar ministries. For the rest I will write in another. To your [sacrifices], etc.

Added to the letter to Fr Persons, 9 July.

They write to me from the Province of France that Thomas Currey, who is in it, wants to return to England, but those fathers do not judge that it is convenient, because in addition to their not being as satisfied with him as they would like, one of the reasons why he wished to be placed in England was to deal with some or other business of his own. Would Your Reverence please let me know if that individual will be useful to you in those Provinces of Spain and of some help, because if you want, he will be sent to you.

B112 From Claudio Acquaviva, 9 July 1591

SOURCE: ARSI, Hisp. 74, fol. 31, from the general's register of confidential letters to the Spanish assistancy.

NOTE: This is the confidential letter accompanying the previous item. Acquaviva advises that he is recalling William Holt from Flanders to replace Joseph Creswell as rector of the English College, Rome. Creswell will join Persons in Spain. In the event, Holt remained in Brussels. See Persons to Walpole, 18 July 1591 (B115), and McCoog, *Building the Faith of St Peter*, 116–117.

Al P. Personio, 9 de Julio 1591.

Con el pasado escriví a Vuestra Reverencia que el estado presente del colegio Inglés me tenía con algun cuydado por ser muchos los que en él no tienen con el padre Rector tanta union como yo quisiera. Hemos hablado sobre ello el Señor Cardenal Alano y yo y nos ha pareçido que será bien llamar al padre Holto que venga de Flandes y tome el cargo deste colegio. Conforme a esto pues Vuestra Reverencia me escrive en esta última que para lo de Flandes por aora será suficiente el padre Henrico Valpolo, él se quedará allí y a Vuestra Reverencia le embiaremos al padre Joseph Crisuelo, pues siente y será a proposito para lo que aý es menester y al padre Holto le daremos el cargo deste colegio, etc.

---

423. Olivier Mannaerts, provincial of the Belgian Province.
424. See Acquaviva to Persons, 20 January 1592 (B134).

Translation

To Robert Persons, 9 July 1591.
 In my last letter I wrote to Your Reverence that I am concerned about the present state of the English college, particularly that there are many in it who do not keep as much concord with father rector as I would desire. We have spoken to my Lord Cardinal Allen about it, and together we felt that it would be good to call Fr Holt to come from Flanders to take charge of that college. Accordingly, since Your Reverence writes to me in that last letter that Fr Henry Walpole would suffice to handle things in Flanders for the present, let him remain there; meanwhile we will send Your Reverence Fr Joseph Creswell, since he is well-disposed and will be suitable for what is needed there while we give Fr Holt responsibility in this college.

B113 To Joseph Creswell in Rome, El Escorial, 17 July 1591

> SOURCE: ABSI, Coll P I 305, Grene's note, and II 477 (reference).
> HICKS: 122.
> EDITION: Pollen, *Miscellanea IX*, 22.
> NOTE: Persons is about to leave Madrid for Valladolid.

The number of our Seminary in Valladolid wil quickly come to 60. I am to depart this night from hence thither.

B114 To Claudio Acquaviva, Madrid, 18 July 1591

> SOURCE: Acquaviva to Persons, 2 September (B119).
> NOTE: Evidently Persons also informed Acquaviva that he was departing for Valladolid, since the general addressed his next letter to that city.

B115 To Henry Walpole, 18 July 1591

> SOURCE: Henry Walpole to Joseph Creswell, 22 August 1591; ABSI, Anglia A1, no. 58.
> EDITION: *Letters of Henry Walpole*, ed. Jessopp, 34–36.
> NOTE: Walpole reports that "Even while I am writing these I receive yours of the 29th July and Father Parsons' of the 18th. I suppose I have written to Father General of the matter which was in consultation" (Jessopp, 36). The matter in question was whether Walpole would be able to take on William Holt's responsibilities in Brussels if Holt were called to Rome to take charge of the English college there. See Acquaviva to Persons, 9 July 1591 (B111).

B116 To Joseph Creswell in Rome, Valladolid, 27 July 1591

> SOURCE: ABSI, Coll P I 305, Grene's note, and II 477 (reference).
> HICKS: 123.
> EDITION: Pollen, *Miscellanea IX*, 22–23.
> NOTE: Soon after Persons's arrival in Valladolid an epidemic afflicted the college; the rector, Fr López de Manzano, retired to the professed house and Persons withdrew to St Ambrose, the Spanish Jesuit College, and then to León to recuperate.
> Here Persons gives Creswell advice about rebellious students, urging him to deal plainly with them (cf. Mush to Persons, 24 March 1595, B266). He doubts the efficacy of placing the students in separate rooms.

I am sorry to see your troubles there with those ingratefull youths — I doubt whether division of chambers brought in[425] by this occasion, wil remedy the matter or no — for all signes of diffidence make Englishmen more distrusters and canvessers,[426] as you know, &c. — and therfore my opinion is that plaine and confident dealing with them & letting passe all things already don, is the best way[427] of ending this matter — & assure yourself that many defects must be winked att and not pursued in a multitude;[428] and for spyeries and sentinels — is the way to marr all &c. —

B117 To Claudio Acquaviva, Valladolid, possibly 22 August 1591

> SOURCE: Acquaviva to Persons, 28 October (B125).
> NOTE: In this letter Persons evidently complained about the way the local Spanish Jesuits dealt with the epidemic at the English college. Although Acquaviva's reply does not specify a date for this letter, his letters despatched to other recipients in Spain on 28 October refer to letters from Spain dated in late August.

B118 To Joseph Creswell in Rome, Valladolid, 22 August 1591

> SOURCE: ABSI, Coll P II 477, Grene's note.

B119 From Claudio Acquaviva, Rome, 2 September 1591

> SOURCE: ARSI, Tolet. 5/I, fol. 204v.
> NOTE: Acquaviva felicitates Persons on the success of his audience with the king. He hopes that the rector at Valladolid, Juan López de Manzano, is recovering, but considers replacing him with Cabredo or perhaps another, in consultation with the visitor, Gil González Dávila.

---

425. in] *obscured in A by show-through*.
426. canvessers] *A*; canvassers *Pollen, ABSI ts*: persons who criticize destructively (*OED*, s.v. canvass, *v*. 3b).
427. way] *A*; may *Pollen*
428. semi-colon *Pollen*

Padre Roberto Personio en Valladolid, Septiembre 2.

Recevi la de Vuestra Reverencia de 18 de Julio con particular consuelo del entender por ella que la audiençia de Su Magestad aya sido tan a gusto y satisfaccion de Vuestra Reverencia y con tan buenos efectos como el buen despacho de los que esperavan en la corte, el Rey lo haçe como tan christiano, y los provee como tan piadoso con gente pobre. En particular me he consolado de la buena ayuda que les ha dado para el Seminario que todavia con eso respirará y se animarán todos viendo que eso es tan favorecido de Su Magestad. Yo escrivo al Padre Juan Lopez que supuesta su poca salud es bien que mude ayre, y dexando ese trabajo del colegio atienda a repararse. En el entretanto me pareçe bien que como Vuestra Reverencia diçe prueve el Padre Cabredo, y si satisfaçe prosiga, sino saliere tomen el que a Vuestra Reverencia y al Padre Gil mejor pareçiere que de acá no les quiero señalar ninguno sino que de los tres y de los demas escojan el que juzgaran ser más a proposito. En su etc.

Translation

To Fr Robert Persons in Valladolid, 2 September.

I received Your Reverence's letter of 18 July and was particularly comforted to understand from it that the audience with His Majesty went off so well and to Your Reverence's satisfaction, and with such good effect and despatch from those who waited in court, the king acting in so Christian a manner, and so piously supporting the poor. I am especially encouraged by the good aid he has given to the seminary, which will bring some [financial] relief and cheer everybody, seeing that it is so favoured by His Majesty. I am writing to Fr Juan López that given his poor health, it would be good for him to have a change of air, leave the work of the college and devote himself to his recovery. In the meantime, it seems good to me, as Your Reverence suggests, to try Fr Cabredo, and if he is satisfactory, let him stay. If he does not turn out well, choose the one who seems better to Your Reverence and to Fr Gil; from here I would not want to indicate anyone except to choose from those three and the rest one who seems more suitable to you. To your [prayers, etc.]

B120 To Claudio Acquaviva, Valladolid, 12 September 1591

SOURCE: Acquaviva to Persons, 28 October.

NOTE: Persons reports favourably on the state of the seminary but is concerned about the health especially of the rector, Juan López de Manzano.

B121 To Joseph Creswell, Valladolid, 12 September 1591

SOURCE: ABSI, Coll P II 477, Grene's note.

B122 To Joseph Creswell, Valladolid, 1 and 9 October 1591

SOURCE: ABSI, Coll P II 477, Grene's note.

B123 To Claudio Acquaviva, Valladolid, 1 or 9 October 1591

SOURCE: Acquaviva to Persons, 25 November (B129).

NOTE: Persons reports on the kind treatment he had received at the Spanish college of St Ambrose. The date of this letter is uncertain, because Acquaviva may have been responding to a letter written for the mid-September post or one in early October – possibly both. Acquaviva's reply (B129) indicates that the letter was inscribed by an amanuensis.

B124 From William Allen, Rome, 26 October 1591

SOURCE: Allen to Persons, 7 January 1592.

NOTE: The letter advised Persons of the anti-Jesuit faction's intentions to negotiate with the authorities in England.

B125 From Claudio Acquaviva, Rome, 28 October 1591

SOURCE: ARSI, Cast. 6, fol. 105r-v, from the general's register of letters to the province of Castile.

NOTE: Acquaviva expresses concern about the illness of Juan López de Manzano, and the way he has been treated by the local Spanish Jesuits. He has written sternly to the vice provincial and to the rector of the Spanish college of St Ambrose.

In the second part of the letter Acquaviva addresses the problem of replacing Creswell as rector of the English college in Rome (see Persons to Creswell, 27 July, B116). Holt was considered too valuable in Flanders to be released, and it was hard to find another suitable candidate. Acquaviva felt that Creswell would be better employed as Persons's assistant in Spain and planned to send him there once Brother Fabrizio Como arrived in Rome and could accompany Creswell to Valladolid.

P. Roberto Personio, Otubre 28.

Aunque por una parte me consuela Vuestra Reverencia y no poco con las buenas nuevas que me da del seminario, y próspero progreso que en todas cosas tiene, por otra siento que algunos de los nuestros no acudan en algunos particulares como yo deseo y devrian haçerlo segun que tantas veçes se lo he encomendado. Çierto he sentido pena de lo que ha pasado en el negocio del Padre Juan Lopez y ansi lo escrivo con palabras serias al Viceprovincial y al Rector del colegio de Valladolid, porque me pareçe que poco a poco se nos va disminuyendo la charidad que segun raçon devria abrazar no solo los proprios, pero aun los muy estraños: pero Vuestra Reverencia tenga buen ánimo que si unos faltaren otros lo supliran, y al fin ya savemos que la divina providencia ha compartido las cosas de manera que en unas nos falte y en otros se supla, para que en todos aya algo que nos lleve a Dios en quien todo lo hallamos y nada nos falta, yo aviso de nuevo al provincial[429] y al Rector del colegio, pero en lo que necessario fuere, Vuestra Reverencia me avise que yo dare orden que se le provea. Tambien escrivo al Padre Gil que le dé al Padre

---

429. provincial] *preceded by* vice [*deleted*] R

Gaspar Alonso para confesor de los alumnos y confiar⁴³⁰ al Padre Rodrigo Cabredo por Rector como Vuestra Reverencia pide y le embío la patente, aunque para Rector de seminarios no se suele dar.

    He me consolado⁴³¹ de ver al buen coronel que me pareçe muy buen cavallero. No le sacaremos al Padre Holto porque diçe es muy necessario en Flandes, acá buscaremos alguno que poner por Rector en el colegio Inglés y embiaré a Vuestra Reverencia el Padre Cresuelo, aunque çierto tiene dificultad en hallarle un successor como conviene y yo deseo que sea. El Hermano Fabriçio hasta aora⁴³² no ha venido a Roma quando venga vere su disposicion y procuraré que vuelva con el Padre Cresuelo. El lavandero que Vuestra Reverencia pide no le ay pero aunque le huviera no solemos permitir que ninguno de nuestros hermanos lo sea en seminario de forasteros, ni conviene que se haga. El hornero le embiara de buena gana si le tuviera, pero desto ay acá tanta necesidad que para esta casa hanselo⁴³³ forçados a tomar un forastero por algunos meses por no tener quien supliese por el hermano Antonio que estava indispuesto. En las etc.

Translation

To Fr Robert Persons, October 28.

    Although on the one hand Your Reverence comforts me, and not a little, with the good news you give me of the seminary, and of the prosperous course which it holds in all matters, on the other hand I feel that others of Ours are not proceeding in some particulars as I expect – and they ought to follow in all ways as I have recommended. I have truly been pained by what has happened in the business of Fr Juan López and I have conveyed this with grave words to the [vice] provincial and to the rector of the college of Valladolid,⁴³⁴ because it seems to me that little by little charity is waning in us, which according to reason ought to embrace not only our own but especially outsiders. But Your Reverence can take comfort in the fact that if one falters the others will make up for it, and in the end we know that the divine providence has ordered matters in such a way that in some things we fall short, in others we are provided for, so that everybody has something that leads us to God, in whom we find everything and we lack nothing. I am once again reporting to the provincial and the rector of the college; but as to what is necessary in this, please would Your Reverence advise me what order I should give for this to be provided. Nevertheless, I am writing to Fr Gil that he should take Fr Gaspar Alonso as confessor for the students and appoint Fr Rodrigo Cabredo as rector as Your Reverence asks, and I am sending him the patent, even though it is not customary for the rector of a seminary.

    430. confiar] *obscured in margin* R
    431. consolado] *followed by a contracted word, possibly* mucho, *probably deleted* R
    432. aora] *obscure, alternatively* acá R
    433. hanselo] *obscure* R
    434. The vice provincial of Castile was either Alonso de Montoya or Francisco Galarza. The rector of the Spanish college of St Ambrose, Valladolid, was Juan Suárez (see Acquaviva's letter of 25 November 1591, B129).

I am encouraged to take note of the good colonel, who seems to me a good knight.[435] We are not removing Fr Holt because he says he is very necessary in Flanders, but we are looking for someone to appoint as rector of the English college. I will send Fr Creswell to Your Reverence, although for sure I am finding it difficult to choose a suitable successor to my liking.[436] Brother Fabrizio has not yet arrived[437] in Rome: when he does, I will gauge his disposition and arrange for him to return with Fr Creswell. There is not a launderer, as Your Reverence requests; but even if there were, we do not usually allow any of our brothers to be in a seminary of foreigners, nor is this desirable. I would be glad to send you a baker if I could,[438] but the need is so great here that in this house we have no choice but to use a foreigner for a few months because there is no one to supply the place of Brother Antonio, who has been indisposed. To your [prayers and holy sacrifices], etc.

B126 From John Cecil (*alias* Snowden), possibly at Rheims, 1 November 1591

SOURCES:

ABSI, Coll B 65 (English) and 31 (Spanish) = B;

ABSI, Coll M fols. 195v–197r (olim 166–167), Grene's transcription of a Spanish version "coppyed out of F. Persons own-hand-wryting, gathered by him out of letters received from London" = M.

ACSA, Series II, Legajo 6, item 4, a contemporary Spanish version = Vd

EDITION: Pollen, *Unpublished Documents*, 199–203, material relating to martyrs only.

NOTE: Cecil's letter exists in various recensions. A very similar letter was addressed to Joseph Creswell in Rome, 20 September 1591, and equivalent letters from England dated 1 October were combined into a Spanish newsletter for distribution in Spain. The present letter is more personally addressed to Persons. The text below presents the English letter, followed by the Spanish compilation, using B as the copy text for both.

Cecil's letter to Creswell appears in Spanish translation (or, more properly, adaptation) in Pedro de Ribadeneira, *Historia ecclesiastica, segunda parte*, chapter 7 (Weinreich, 588–591); there is also a partial transcription of the Latin text in ABSI, Coll M fol. 187r (see Weinreich, appendix 4, 762). The marked differences between the incomplete Latin text and Ribadeneira's version strongly suggest editorial embellishment, as indicated in Weinreich's notes.

Because the final page of the English letter itself is missing, we cannot be certain of the date; Persons endorsed it twice, once with the date 1 November 1591, and again with the date June 1592, from Cecil in Italy. The opening paragraph implies that Cecil had left England, with the knowledge of Garnet and Southwell, and was travelling in France and the Netherlands, in contact with Barret at Rheims and Allen in Rome. Since his letters to Creswell

---

435. Sir William Stanley, currently in Valladolid (see the covering letter of 7 November 1590, B85, headnote).

436. Creswell was replaced by Muzio Vitelleschi.

437. Alternatively, "not arrived here." See textual note.

438. A non-English lay brother was perforce being used in the English College, Rome, as there were no Englishmen to fulfil that role. On the laundry and bakery, see Acquaviva's letter of 23 December 1591 (B131).

and Persons were written after he had become Burghley's agent, the information in them should be treated with due caution. Playing a dangerous double game, he evidently wanted to publicize his account widely amongst Catholics as a sign of his loyalty to the faith. Accordingly, Pollen argues that his treatment of martyrdom lacks "true sympathy" (Pollen, *Unpublished Documents*, 200 n ✠).

Cecil reports on the fortunes of the priests who left Spain with him in April 1591 (see the intercepted letters of Persons, 7 November 1590, B85-87), as well as other priests and laymen martyred in England in the summer of 1591. The letter continues with local news of the kind relayed to Persons by Verstegan from 1592 onwards (Petti); this may explain the later date given in the second endorsement. Of the priests who left Seville in April 1591, four (John Roberts, Richard Dudley, Richard Blount, and James Younger) sailed together from Calais and were arrested at Portsmouth, while Cecil and Fixer, sailing separately, were intercepted at sea and taken to Burghley's house in the Strand. There they wrote statements which were forwarded to Burghley at Theobalds and interested him sufficiently to employ them as double agents. Some time after July 1591 they travelled abroad but returned and were captured once more, perhaps as a ruse. Cecil subsequently went to meet Cardinal Allen in Rome in 1592 (Alford, 270-283).

James Younger wrote a lively autobiography in August 1592; he tarnished his reputation by informing on many of his fellow priests and Catholics. Of John Roberts, little is known except that he was said to be "of a reasonable stature, a little blackish beard." Richard Dudley operated in Lancashire and the border region for several years, Oliver Almond mainly in Oxfordshire (Anstruther, 6-7, 106-107, 292, 391-393). On Richard Blount, see Acquaviva to Persons, 5 July 1589 (B21).

Ryght Reverend and my very lovinge Father

I have at last allbehyt with greater dyffycultues in one respecte then I supposed performed that diligence that I thowght one myghte dooe personally to be donne for the conversion of my poore parentes. I lefte the best order thearin I coulde and ame returned for the accomplyshemente of those my vowes yow only *in re* and substaunce are privye.[439] Sone I mynde to followe my Lord Cardinals direction altogether thearin with whome I hope to be shoartlye and from thence of my particuler I wyll wryte more att large. Only this I woulde advise yow that my cominge is so secrete that besydes Fr Garnet and Fr Sowthwell no one in England and besydes my Lord and Fr Rector none of this syde are acquaynted thearewith; yf yow please to keape hyt to yowr selfe tyll yow heare from me or see me I thinke for divers respectes hyt wyll not be amysse. And because perhappes yow have not herde precisly what successe yowr last and fyrst Spanyshe myssion hadde as also of our late martyrdomes in Englande my badde penne and shorte tyme and hastye uturince[440] wyll not permytte me to dwell uppon evry perticuler as I know yow woulde reqyre.

Of your Spanyshe myssion, the fyrst that wente from Calez weare all taken at Portchemowthe and sente to the Counsel. In the waye one fayned hymself sycke, viz.

439. The sense seems to be: "the vows to which you alone are privy, both in fact and substance." The phrase "in re" is obscure in B.

440. Utterance.

Robertes, and soe his companion Dudly was lefte to folowe the rest for theyre reward to the Counsel: the other 2 Blunte and Younger weare caryed to the Admiral and after 2 or 3 dayes examination weare rewarded and dismissed.[441] Mr Fixer and my self weare taken by the Queanes shippes over agaynst Dover by Sir Henry Palmer,[442] and by hym sent joyntely to the Admiral and Treasurer, who beinge both owte of the waye the one at sea the other at his howse at Tibalds with the Queen,[443] we weare kepte at a manns howse of his in Westmester, and theare hadde sent us certen interrogatoryes of martial men and warrlike affayres of the King's intentions and preparations and suche like. After 5 or 6 dayes I only was caryed to the Treasurer, and by worde demaunded the same questions, which in writynge weare tendered us, and so we weare dysmissed, of the particularity wheareof moore heareafter either from Rome or in presence. Mr Fixer was like to have byne taken twyse sythence that time, once they tooke his horse and rapyer. Mr Warforde, Mr Oliver and all the rest are placed and in coler, as also Coffin and Bell and the last myssion from Rome, and Mr Bisshope owte of France.[444]

In Easter and Whitson tearme weare martyred at Yorke, to whose executions Toply the torturer wente, a pryest and a clerke, viz. Robert Thorpe and Thomas Watkinson.[445] At Winchester the lyke, viz. Roger Dickonson and Ralph Mylner,[446] who desyringe the judges to be good to his wyffe and 8 or 9 smal children he hadde was answered thus: "Goe to churche foole and looke to thy children thye self" who replyed that the losse of

---

441. The Lord Admiral was Charles Howard, baron Howard of Effingham, later earl of Nottingham. The verb "reward" seems to be used here in the sense of "punish" or "chastise" (*OED*, s.v. reward, *v.* 4a).

442. Sir Henry Palmer (ca. 1550–1611) was a senior naval commander who took part in the battle against the Spanish armada. He was later appointed comptroller of the navy.

443. Queen Elizabeth was enjoying a ten-day visit to Theobalds House, Hertfordshire, a residence of Lord Burghley; in 1607 James I acquired it from Sir Robert Cecil as a royal palace. Burghley's townhouse, Exeter House or Burghley House, was located on the north side of the Strand, Westminster.

444. Henry Bell (b. 1563), William Bishop (1553/5–1624) and Thomas Coffin (b. 1568) arrived in England from Rheims in May July 1591; in 1623, Bishop was appointed bishop of Chalcedon, the first new episcopal appointment in England since the beginning of Elizabeth's reign (Anstruther, 29, 36–38, 82). On William Warford and Oliver Almond, see the headnote to Persons's letter to Barret, 7 November 1590 (B86) and Warford's letter from Amsterdam, 15 May 1591 (B108).

445. Robert Thorpe (named Church in the Spanish version) and Thomas Watkinson were hanged, drawn, and quartered at York, 31 May 1591 (Anstruther, 353–354; Foley, 3: 746–750). In the letter to Creswell, Cecil wrote that Thorpe "ended his race with the greatest joy"; Watkinson was "his partner in life and death and in the glory of martyrdom, who had greatly aided his labors in the vineyard of the Lord" (Weinreich, 588–589, 762; see also Questier, *Catholics and Treason*, 206–07). "Toply" is Richard Topcliffe (1531–1604).

446. On Roger Dickenson, Ralph Milner (or Miller), executed on 7 July 1591, and the eight or nine women (seven, in the letter to Creswell), see Anstruther, 103; Foley, 3: 297–298; Pollen, *Acts of English Martyrs*, 83–97; and Questier, *Catholics and Treason*, 207–208.

his sowle was to hye a pryce and[447] so smale and vile a comoditye,[448] and so he dyed blessedly *in Domino*. With them weare condemned 8 or 9 younge damsels but not sentenced, the which with open owtcryes and exclamations urged the judges most constauntly that, as they weare al culpable of the same crime, viz. of hearinge masse, releaving a pryest, confessinge theyre synnes and servinge theyre Saviour after the ryte of the Catholique churche, so they myght drynke al of the same cuppe, with such fervor and vehemense that they made the whole assembly astonyshed.[449]

At London weare martyred George Beasely and Monford Skotte of whome Topely sayde that he hadde that daye donne the Queen a singler peace of service, in ryddinge the realme of suche a prayinge and fastinge papist as hadde not his peare in Europe.[450]

To make Mr Bysely the moore odious, after most exquisite tormentes exercised uppon hys inocente members, they proposed this most barbarous and blody question, what he woulde doe in case the pope shoulde commaund hym to kyll the Queen. He answered that he thought hyt a meritorious acte, beinge so commaunded.[451] Mr Por-

447. and] B; to pay for *Pollen*

448. Pollen compares Cecil's version of this answer unfavourably to that given by an old man in similar circumstances: "He answered that he hoped to do them as much good where he went as if he were with them. Having the halter about his neck, his son asked his blessing, which he gave him in the following manner, 'I pray God send thee no worse end than thy father,' and so he was cast off the ladder." See Pollen, *Acts of English Martyrs*, 96–97, from ABSI, Coll M fol. 195r.

449. In the letter to Creswell, Cecil elaborates: "And they hoped in God that as he had given them the spirit to do what they had done, he would also give it them to die gloriously for their holy Catholic faith. O ladies, no ladies at all; O manly, valiant hearts; O human frailty and divine strength!" (Weinreich, 589–590). Weinreich, 66–67, quotes the apostrophe "O ladies, no ladies at all ..." to introduce a discussion of the treatment of women in Ribadeneira's *Historia ecclesiastica*; most likely, it is Ribadeneira's addition.

450. On George Beesley (b. 1562) and Montford Scott, see Anstruther, 28–29, 303–304, and Peter Holmes, "Beesley, George" (*ODNB*). A more circumstantial account is given in Cecil's letter to Creswell (Weinreich, 590): "In London of the same month, two other priests died with wonderful joy and constancy, to the edification of their brothers. One was named George Beesley; before they killed him, he was tortured with exquisite torments to make him tell them which Catholics he had met and by whom he had been received and supported. But however much they badgered him, they could never get a thing out of him. Alongside Beesley, the priest Montford Scott, a wise and holy man, endured his martyrdom with such perfect calmness of spirit and gentleness that even the heretics were frightened, such that the commander of the queen's troops later boasted that he had done the realm a huge service in ridding it of so devout a papist, so worn out with penances, fasts, and vigils." Henry Walpole intended to send particulars to Creswell (Walpole to Creswell, 22 August 1591, in *Letters of Henry Walpole*, ed. Jessopp, 34–37). See also Pollen, *Acts of the English Martyrs*, 299–304, and Questier, *Catholics and Treason*, 207.

451. Cecil's record has a bearing on the vexed question of priestly treason, and should not be accepted uncritically: cf. the Spanish version, below, and the Latin text of his letter to Creswell (Weinreich, 762): "Respondit Papam tale quid non iussurum, verum si iuberet meritorium esset si exequeretur" (He replied that the pope had ordered no such thing, but if he did order it, it would be meritorious to carry it out). The term "bloody question" was used by Edmund Campion at his trial in 1581.

molothe was taken summ xx dayes befor I departed, fyrst commytted to Brydewel and then hadde to Topelyes howse, and men stood in feare of his confession.[452]

The Erle of Essex departed into Fraunce, with 6000 and hadde summe litle overthrowe of 200 Cumberlandes menne most sycke and the newes of his 2 shyppes lost. New preparations for sea and Drake sente for to the corte.[453]

Sir John Parrat accused by an Iryshe pryest for wrytinge to the Prince of Parma and the King of Spayne may escape that bruyte[454] but uppon the takine of on[e] Ororke an Iryshe L. that favored the Spanyardes and drewe the queens picture or statua at his horse tayle for correspondence hadde with hym he is lyke to paye for hyt.[455]

Sir Thomas Fitzharbert accused by his owne nephewe in the tower for receavinge a pruest desyreth rather to dye a martyre then a confesser beinge abowte 80 yeare oulde.[456] Al the recusantes are at libertye and they that best may doe lest good to pryestes.[457] The meaner poorer sorte are they that helpe us owte withal dyfficultye.[458]

452. The seminary priest Thomas Pormort, a friend of Robert Southwell, escaped after his arrest on 25 July but was taken again in the last week of September. He was put to death on 21 February 1592, after a trial in which he revealed Topcliffe's sexual fantasies about the queen; see Anstruther, 280–281, and Richard Rex, "Pormort, Thomas" (*ODNB*).

453. Essex was allowed to take a force of 4000 men to Normandy to assist Henry of Navarre (King Henry IV) in his struggle against the Catholic League. He landed at Dieppe on 2 August 1591. "Cumberlands men" refers to troops drafted in Cumberland. Sir Thomas Coningsby, in his *Journal of the Siege of Rouen in 1591*, ed. John Gough Nichols (London, 1847), relates how on 25 October "Our generall brought him to see our armye, which was drawne out into the fields, where he showed him 2,000 and upward brave men by the head, besides iii^c [300] sicke in the strawe" (30). Drake returned from an abortive naval expedition to the Azores in July 1590 and was summoned to the Privy Council to explain his failure. He was sidelined for the next five years (Hammer, *Elizabeth's Wars*, 159–160).

454. I.e., rumour. Sir John Perrot (1528–1592) was lord deputy of Ireland from 1584 to 1588. He was put on trial for high treason in 1592, accused of corresponding with the duke of Parma, William Stanley, and Philip II via the Irish priest Dennis O'Roghan. He was also accused of instigating O'Rourke to rebellion. See *A Complete Collection of State Trials and Proceedings for High Treason and Other Crimes and Misdemeanours from the Earliest Period to the Year 1783*, ed. Thomas Bayly Howell et al. (1816), 1: 1315–1333, esp. 1326, and John Turvey, "Perrot, Sir John" (*ODNB*).

455. Brian O'Rourke (ca. 1540–1591), lord of West Breifne, challenged English rule in Ireland. He fled to Scotland in 1591, was arrested in Glasgow, imprisoned in the Tower of London, and executed on 3 November 1591. In the complex arguments surrounding his arraignment for treason, he was accused of dragging an image of the queen in the mud. See Hiram Morgan, "Extradition and Treason-Trial of a Gaelic Lord: The Case of Brian O'Rourke," *Irish Jurist*, n.s., 22 (1987): 285–301, esp. 293–294.

456. Sir Thomas Fitzherbert (1513/4–1591).

457. pryestes] *preceded by* Catholiques [*deleted*]

458. Cecil's letter to Creswell, as relayed by Ribadeneira, concludes with two paragraphs of consoling news about conversions to Catholicism as well as increasing division and conflict among the Protestants and Puritans: "But just as a troubled river is a blessing to the fishermen from the many fish that gather, so in the midst of these turbulent waters of the persecution of the Catholics, God our Lord consoles us with the abundant catch we win." But since, as Weinreich notes (591), this is based on the Spanish proverb "A rio revuelto, ganancia de pescadores," it is probably Ribadeneira's embellishment.

Theare are divers menne of importaunce that woulde be fully certifyed of there intention; of which argumente moore at our meatinge. The E. of C. is so farre from the manne he hoped for that he is knowen nether to be in religion indifferente nor for his owne honor valiaunte nor in his greatest affayres secrete.⁴⁵⁹ He is exceadinge timorous and hathe and dothe persecute as mutche as in hym lyethe. He braggeth to his companions that on this syde in al owr masses he is by name remembred: in fyne by al mens judgementes he is no subjecte fytte to make eny sounde foundation.

Huntington hath forsaken his puritans or rather they hym. Arbella is now moste looked at. L. Nor. and Sowth. may easely be dealte with. Worcest. for the presente is a notorious temporizer but he hathe given me certen propositions to deliver to his good frendes heare that in fyne may turne to summe purpose.⁴⁶⁰

The Counsel is divided into the Cauncellers faction, viz. the Arch B. of Cant., Bukehurst, Walls. and Foscewe – and the Treasurer, with Knowles, Cobbam, the Admiral and the rest.⁴⁶¹ Likewyse the martial men are in partyes to wytte the L. Willoughby, Sir Frauncys Veare, Bascavile on the one bande and Norice and his complices on the other.⁴⁶²

---

459. Since the abbreviation "E. of C." is obscure (possibly "E. of E."), this could refer either to Essex (who was more likely to boast about his popularity among Catholics) or to George Clifford (1558–1605), third earl of Cumberland, whose fleet suffered losses at the battle of the Berlengas islands off the coast of Portugal in July 1591.

460. The earl of Huntingdon was president of the Council of the North. For an appraisal of his treatment of Catholics, see Claire Cross, *The Puritan Earl: The Life of Henry Hastings, Third Earl of Huntingdon, 1536–1595* (London, 1966), 159–269. Arbella Stuart (1575–1615) was a grandchild of Margaret Tudor, Henry VIII's sister, and thus also had a claim to the succession. Henry Percy (1564–1632), ninth earl of Northumberland; Henry Wriothesley (1573–1624), third earl of Southampton; and Edward Somerset (ca. 1550–1628), fourth earl of Worcester, were believed to be Catholic sympathizers.

461. Sir Christopher Hatton (1540–1591) was created Lord Chancellor in 1587. His allies in the Privy Council are listed here as John Whitgift (ca. 1530–1604), archbishop of Canterbury from 1583; Thomas Sackville (1536–1608), Lord Buckhurst and later (1604) earl of Dorset; Sir Francis Walsingham (ca. 1532–1590), the queen's secretary, by this time deceased; and Sir John Fortescue of Salden (ca. 1531–1607), chancellor of the exchequer from 1589–1603. The other faction is that of William Cecil (1520–1598), first baron Burghley, Lord Treasurer: including Sir Francis Knollys (ca. 1511–1596), treasurer of the royal household; William Brooke (1527–1597), tenth baron Cobham, Lord Warden of the Cinque Ports; and Charles Howard, Baron Howard of Effingham, Lord Admiral. In the version prepared for distribution in Spain (see below), religious differences are mentioned, as well as the welcome possibility of a resultant collapse of the regime.

462. The prominent military commanders mentioned here are Peregrine Bertie (1555–1601), thirteenth baron Willoughby de Eresby, who fought in the Netherlands and France; Sir Francis Vere (1560/1–1609), who distinguished himself against the duke of Parma at the siege of Knodsenburg near Nijmegen in July 1591; and Sir Thomas Baskerville (d. 1597), who served under Willoughby and participated in the siege of Rouen under Essex in November 1591. Sir John Norris (ca. 1547–1597) was celebrated for his feats in Flanders and Ireland.

One which cauled hymself King of the Worlde a puritan was apprehended and putt to death in July. He sente his propettes into Fleete streate and Cheapesyde[463] who preatched that the queen was an heretique but showlde not be damned for that she was seduced, that Hatton Whitegyfte and Sackevile weare archetraytors, that they woulde have al the Counsel deposed, that my L. Graye showlde be E. of Sowthhampton, & Davis showlde be protector, that the C. of Cumberlande was a prophytes and that of Bedforde an evangelist;[464] in fine, Christ uppon earth with his disciplis was taken and dyed blaspheminge, caulinge for Elias byddinge a pop[e] and a plauge on them al his disciples dyed in pryson one of them a manne of fayer livinge.

In the tower at white haule buylte a raven which mad owr mystres afrayde as prodigious towardes her.[465]

Rawley hath sett upp a newe religion of athistes and hathe many folowers: the new testamente they deny and of the oulde they make a jest and not[e] the contradicions, and make accompte of Moyses as of a shrewde hedde and saye they confesse theare is a Godde but not such a God as we make hym and runne uppon this poynt with the revivinge of al the oulde philosophers opinions his prophet is on Heriette[466] a converte and they are as gladde when they canne gette eny younge gentleman to theyre opinion as we are to gayne a sowle to heale.

[*First endorsement by Persons:*] Mr Sicils advices, 1 Nov. 1591.

[*Second endorsement by Persons:*] Mr Sicils lre wryten in Italie in his iourney to Rome mense Julio 1592. He telleth of the martyrdomes of Thorpe, Watkingson, Dickenson, Milner, Bisly and Scotte and of the apprehension of Pormort.

463. See Verstegan to Persons, 29 October 1592 (B160). Puritan extremists Edmund Coppinger (ca. 1555–1591) and Henry Arthington, a Yorkshire gentleman (fl. 1569–1609), mounted a cart in Cheapside on 19 July 1591 to announce the arrival of the Messiah in the person of William Hacket (d. 1591), a maltster from Northamptonshire. Hacket was found guilty of treason, and was executed on 28 July. Coppinger died in Bridewell twenty-four hours later after an eight-day hunger strike. Arthington recanted as soon as he heard of Hacket's death; his confession was published as *The Seduction of Arthington by Hacket especiallie, with some tokens of his unfained repentance and Submission* (London, 1592); see Southwell's report of 8 August 1591 (ABSI, Coll P II 507–508, in Pollen, *Unpublished Documents*, 332–333), Milward, 101–102, and Alexandra Walsham, "'Frantick Hacket': Prophecy, Sorcery, Insanity, and the Elizabethan Puritan Movement," *Historical Journal* 41 (1998): 27–66.

464. Arthur Grey (1536–1593), fourteenth Baron Grey de Wilton, was notorious for the massacre after the siege of Smerwick (1580); Sir John Davies or Davis (1560/3–1625) was an associate of Essex; Margaret Clifford (1560–1616), countess of Cumberland, renowned for her learning, was courted by Puritan writers; Bridget Hussey Russell (1525–1601), countess of Bedford, was known for her Puritan sympathies. Margaret Clifford was stepdaughter to Bridget Hussey (see the Spanish version, which describes them as mother and daughter).

465. The raven is treated as an omen in Shakespeare's *Othello*, 4.1.20–22: "O, it comes o'er my memory / As doth the raven o'er the infectious house / Boding to all." Ravens are traditionally associated with the Tower of London rather than the palace of Whitehall.

466. Thomas Harriot (ca. 1560–1621) was an astronomer and mathematician. On Persons's treatment, in his *Philopater*, of Raleigh's supposed school of atheism, led by the "wizard Earl" of Northumberland, see Ernest A. Strathmann, "Ralegh and the Catholic Polemicists," *Huntington Library Quarterly* 4 (1945): 337–358.

Avisos de Ynglaterra de primero de Otubre 1591

Ya Vuestra Reverencia avra sabido como acá han llegado a salvo todos los ocho sacerdotes yngleses que aý se embarcaron en Andaluzia y estan repartidos por el reyno y juntamente casi al mismo tiempo llegaron otros de los seminarios de Roma y de Rhemis de los quales a uno llamado Pormorto prendieron la semana passada y está en la casa de Topeli donde se entiende que passará[467] muy rigurosos examenes, pues el Topely es el más cruel perseguidor y verdugo de los Catholicos que los hereges tienen en estos reynos.

Este verano ha avido muchos martirios de Catolicos en este reyno, porque en la ciudad de Yorke martirizaron a dos: el uno era sacerdote llamado Roberto Churche, el otro su clerigo llamado Thomas Watginson, y para darles más crueles tormentos ymbiaron a Yorke desde Londres (que seran más de cinquenta lleguas) al sobredicho Topely para este effeto: sus muertes fueron de muy grande edificacion.

En la ciudad de Vintonia llamada Winchester hizieron lo mismo, porque martirizaron a un sacerdote cuyo nombre era Rogero Diginson hombre de grande virtud, el qual avia servido a los catolicos que estan presos en las carceles desta ciudad mucho tiempo proveyendoles de todo lo que avian menester en lo temporal y espiritual. A este siervo de Dios llevaron preso y atadas[468] manos y pies a Londres y sentenciado a muerte lo bolvieron a Winchester para martirizarlo y pusieron espias para prender a todos los catolicos de aquella provincia que viniessen a su martyrio.

Con este padre murio juntamente un lego hijo suyo espiritual llamado Rodulfo Milnero porque avia estado con este sacerdote y rehusava andar a las yglesias de los hereges y assi quando los Jueçes conforme al costumbre de Ynglaterra le pronunciaron la sentencia de muerte en público con la solenidad y pregones que alli se usan, este la recibio con rostro muy allegre y les dixo que una sola cosa les avia de pedir que tubiessen quenta con su muger y con ocho o nueve niños chiquitos que tenía pues ellos no tenian parte en este delicto de lesa magestad que se le imputava. Ellos respondieron que en su mano estava remediarlos todos y de salvar aun su vida si quisiesse andar a sus yglesias y conformarse en esto con las leyes del reyno. Pero él les replicó que esto sería en prejuycio de su alma y que no queria comprar tan caro el remedio temporal de sus hijos que Dios era poderoso de remediarlos: y con esto fue alegremente a la muerte.

Con estos dos varones fueron tambien condenadas a muerte ocho o nueve donzellas por los mismos delictos de averse confesado con sacerdotes y oydo misas y pensaron los Jueces (como parece) que con sola la condenacion se espantarian y bolvieran atras, pero quando las vieron constantes y muy animosas[469] dilataran la sentencia pública que se suele dar, para consultar el negocio con la Reyna y su consejo, como se puede creer, pero quando las donzellas oyeron la sentencia dada contra el sacerdote y el lego, y no contra ellas, començaron a llorar y dar vozes a los Juezes que no las apartasen de aquel Padre y hermano; pues ellas tambien estavan ya condenadas por los mismos delictos que

467. passará] B Vd; passava M
468. atadas] B; atado M; attado Vd
469. animosas] B; animadas M Vd

los otros dos, con que toda la multitud de la⁴⁷⁰ gente quedó attonita, y los Juezes mandaron las bolviessen a la carcel.

En Londres martyrizaron en el mismo tiempo a dos sacerdotes llamados Jorge Bisly y Monfredo Scoto, al primero por ser hombre animoso y averles respondido con mucha libertad le dieron muy grandes y rigurosos tormentos y despues para hacerlo más odioso a la gente lo sacaron en público para examinarlo de nuevo, y le preguntaron qué le parecia se devia hacer si el Papa mandasse a alguno que mattase a la Reyna, a lo qual él respondio que si el Papa lo mandase, sería con mucha justicia y circumspection y asi le parecia que sería meritorio cumplir la obediencia, con lo qual los hereges quedaron muy enojados.

Del otro que era hombre muy manso y de grandes penitencias, el Topely dixo en la corte el mismo dia que lo avia martirizado que entendia aver hecho el mayor servicio aquel dia a la Reyna que le⁴⁷¹ avia hecho en muchos dias antes por aver liberado el reyno de un papista hypocrita de los mayores ayunos y de las más largas plegarias que avia en toda Europa.

El Puritano que se llamó a sí mismo Christo y señor del mundo fue ahorcado en la plaça mayor de Londres a siete de Agosto. Murio blasfemando y llamando a Elias para fuego del cielo, y dio su maldicion a todos diciendo que el papa y la pestilencia los consumiesse; dixo que la Reyna era herege, pero engañada de otros y por esto que su castigo sería temporal; dixo que se avia de deshacer todo el Consejo de Estado y nombró a otros de su secta para aquel officio; dixo que Dios avia embiado para reformacion de Inglaterra las dos Condesas de Bedforda y de Cummerland madre y hija que son de su secta de Puritanos, la primera para Evangelista y la segunda para profetissa.⁴⁷² Sus profetas de Justicia y Misericordia murieron en la carcel y no si sabe si de garrotes &c.

El consejo de estado de la reyna está dividedo entre sí en cosas de Religion pero tambien en las demas; la cabeça de una faccion es el Chanciller y con él el Arcobiscopo de Cantuaria, Buguehurst, Wolly, y Fortescu, de la otra es el Tesorero, el Almirante, Cobbam, Cuenols y otros. En la misma manera estan divididos en dos vandos los capitanes principales del reyno porque de una parte es my lord Willoby, Francisco Vear, Bascovil y otros, y de la otra parte contrarios a estos estan Juan Noris, my lord Grey y los suyos. De manera que se podría esperar que reyno tan dividido entre sí vendra presto a disolucion sino que todos se hacen a una contra los catolicos por el miedo que dellos tienen. Dios haga lo que fuere para mayor gloria suya y guarde siempre a Vuestra Reverencia. De Londres a primero de Otubre 1591.

Translation

Reports from England 1 October 1591

Your Reverence will already know that all eight priests who recently set sail from Andalusia have arrived here safely and have been dispersed through the kingdom. Almost at the

---

470. la] *om. M Vd*
471. le] *B; no M Vd*
472. la primera para Evangelista y la segunda para profetissa] *B Vd; om. M*

same time others arrived from the seminaries at Rome and Rheims, one of whom, called Pormort, was taken last week. He is being kept in the house of Topcliffe, where it is understood he has endured very rigorous examination, since Topcliffe is the cruellest persecutor and executioner of the Catholics that the heretics have in these realms.

This summer has seen many martyrdoms of Catholics in this kingdom, for in the city of York they martyred two: one was a priest named Robert Church, the other was his clerk named Thomas Watkinson. To increase the cruelty of their torture they were sent from London to York (which is more than fifty leagues)[473] to the said Topcliffe to this purpose: that their deaths might cause greater edification.

In the city of Wintonia, called Winchester, they did the same, for they martyred a priest named Roger Dickenson, a man of great virtue, who had ministered to the Catholics imprisoned in that city for a long time, providing them with whatever they needed, both temporal and spiritual. This servant of God was taken prisoner, tied hand and foot, to London, and being sentenced to death they returned him to Winchester to martyr him and set spies to catch all the Catholics of that region who came to his martyrdom.

Alongside this father died a layman, his spiritual son called Ralph Miller, because he had been with this priest and refused to go to the churches of the heretics. When the judges, according to the English custom, publicly pronounced sentence of death, with the solemnity and street cries which are used there, he received it with a very cheerful countenance, saying that he had but one thing to ask them, that they might take into consideration his wife and the eight or nine dear children he had, since they had played no part in this crime of *lèse majesté* which they imputed to him. They replied that the remedy was in his hand, to save all of them and his own life too, if he was prepared to go to their churches and conform according to the laws of the land. But he replied that that would endanger his soul and he would not purchase at such a high price the worldly remedy for his children, whom God was mighty to save. And with that he was speedily put to death.

With these two men, eight or nine maidens were also condemned for the same crime of going to confession with priests and hearing masses. The judges seemed to think that it was only by condemning them they could frighten them and make them change their mind, but when they saw how constant and very cheerful they were, they delayed giving the public sentence until they had consulted the queen and her council, as you can imagine, but when the damsels heard sentence given against the priest and the layman, and not against them, they began to cry out and exclaim to the judges not to separate them from the priest and his companion, since they had been convicted of the same crime as the other two. With that, the whole crowd of people were stunned, and the judges ordered them to return to their cell.

In London at the same time they martyred two priests called George Beesley and Montford Scott; because the former was a spirited fellow and responded to them very freely, they applied very great and rigorous tortures, and then, to make him more hateful to the people they took him out to be examined again in public, and asked him what

---

473. I.e., over 150 miles; in fact, it is over 200. For commentary on this Spanish text, see the English version above, where the details coincide.

he felt he ought to do if the pope ordered anyone to assassinate the queen. To this he replied that if the pope gave such an order, he would do so with much justice and circumspection, and so it seemed to him that it would be meritorious to offer his obedience, [an answer] which irritated the heretics very much.

As for the other, who was a very meek man and performed great penances, Topcliffe told the court, the very same day that he had been martyred, that he believed he had done greater service to the queen that day than he had done for many days, to free the kingdom of a papist hypocrite who made the greatest fasts and the longest prayers in all Europe.

The Puritan who called himself Christ and Lord of the World was hanged in the main square of London on 7 August. He died blaspheming and calling on Elijah to bring down fire from heaven. He laid his curse on everyone, calling on the pope and the plague to consume them all. He said that the queen was a heretic, but because she was deceived by others her punishment would be temporal. He said that the entire council of state should be disbanded and other of his sect should be appointed to that office. He said that God had sent the countesses of Bedford and Cumberland, who were the first woman evangelist and prophetess of the sect of the Puritans, for the reformation of England. His prophets Justice and Mercy died in jail and it is not known whether by execution.[474] Etc.

The Privy Council is divided against itself in matters of religion but also in other matters. The head of one faction is the chancellor and with him the archbishop of Canterbury, Buckhurst, Walsingham,[475] and Fortescue; on the other, the treasurer, the admiral, Cobham, Knollys, and others. In the same way the chief captains of the kingdom are divided into two bands, because on one side are My Lord Willoughby, Francis Vere, Baskerville, and others, and on the other opposing them are John Norris, My Lord Grey, and their followers. Consequently, it could be expected that such a divided kingdom would soon come to ruin,[476] except that they are all united against the Catholics because of the fear they have of them. May God's will be done, to His greater glory and may He always protect Your Reverence. From London, 1 October 1591.

B127 To Claudio Acquaviva, Valladolid, 6 November 1591

SOURCE: Acquaviva to Persons, 23 December (B131).

B128 To Joseph Creswell in Rome, Valladolid 7 November 1591

SOURCE: ABSI, Coll P II 477, Grene's note.

... he writeth expecting him, Fr Creswell, to come to Spaine.

---

474. The Spanish term "garotes" is taken here to mean "a method of execution."
475. Presumably indicated by "Wolly."
476. Mk 3:25.

B129 From Claudio Acquaviva, Rome, 25 November 1591

SOURCE: ARSI, Cast. 6, fol. 108r, from the general's register of letters to the province of Castile.

NOTE: Acquaviva rejoices in the kindness shown to Persons by Fr Juan Suárez (1528–1599; see Manuel Ruiz Jurado in *DHCJ*, 4: 3657), former provincial of Castile and now rector of the college of St Ambrose, Valladolid, hoping this will signal better relations between the English and Spanish colleges. Acquaviva wrote appreciatively to Suárez by the same post (fol. 107v).

P. Roberto Personio, Noviembre 25.

Recevi la de Vuestra Reverencia con harto consuelo de que Dios le aya dado salud para podernos escrivir aunque sea de mano agena, porque çierto su indisposicion me causava mucho sentimiento y en siendo tan peligrosa, por las muchas raçones que Vuestra Reverencia vea que ay para desearle la vida y la salud, desela el Señor para que a gloria suya la emplee en ayuda y amparo de esa buena gente. El Padre Juan Suarez me ha dado gran contento con lo que a hecho y yo le escrivo agradeciendose lo y le digo que con esto compensa la falta que en la pasada le adverti, y que continue porque importa para el buen exemplo de los demas. Vuestra Reverencia atiende a su salud y modere las ocupaçiones hasta tornar a las fuerzas pasadas, porque las enfermedades deste año suelen rebolver con reveses muy peligrosos. En sus oraçiones &c.

Translation

To Fr Robert Persons, 25 November.

I was much heartened to receive Your Reverence's letter, God giving you health to write, even though by another's hand. Your indisposition has certainly caused me much distress, being so dangerous, given the many reasons that there are, as Your Reverence can see, to wish you life and health. I pray the Lord will give you health, to use you for his glory and the aid and protection of his good people. Fr Juan Suárez has given me great happiness by doing what he did, and I am writing to him to thank him and tell him that with this he has made up for the fault which I drew his attention to in my last letter, and that he should continue, because his good example makes such an impact on the others. Your Reverence must attend to your health and keep business to a minimum so as to regain your past strength, because the infirmities of this year usually return with even more dangerous setbacks. To your prayers, etc.

B130 To Claudio Acquaviva, 6 December 1591

SOURCE: Acquaviva to Persons, 20 January 1592 (B134).

B131 From Claudio Acquaviva, Rome, 23 December 1591

SOURCE: ARSI, Cast. 6, fols. 109v, 113r, from the general's register of letters to the province of Castile.

NOTE: Rejoicing in Persons's recovery of health, Acquaviva encourages him not to be downcast in the face of resistance from the local Jesuits. Creswell is about to leave Rome for Spain, with Acquaviva attempting to supply him with books. He is pleased that Cabredo is proving an excellent new rector at Valladolid.

In a confidential annotation to Persons, recorded in the register for 20 December, Acquaviva alludes to a change involving the provincial of Andalusia, Bartolomé Pérez, apparently to smooth the way for a foundation at Seville. Pérez had written to Persons in 1590 urging the project; see Persons to Creswell, 28 April 1590 (B60; Hicks, *Seminaries*, part 4, 28).

P. Roberto Personio, Decembre 23.

Recevi la de Vuestra Reverencia de 6 de Noviembre y pues el Señor le ha dado salud viva consolado, que lo que toca al Seminario se le proveera de todo lo necessario siempre que fuese menester, esos padres con su charidad lo haría, porque la tienen para eso y para más, y porque yo se lo he encomendado seriamente. Y quando ellos faltasen, Vuestra Reverencia no dude sino que de acá se remediará, y no le dé fastidio ni le cause encogimiento ver que algunos de los nuestros no muestran a eso tanta voluntad y afiçion, que eso mesmo viene de la divina providencia que juzga convenir que en todas cosas aya un poco de amargo y cruz, pero el Señor lo allanará todo como ha allanado otras mayores dificultades que huvo en la erection y principios de ese Seminario. El Padre Crisuelo partira presto, y de lo que por la suya pide que de acá le proveamos no faltaré en lo que pudiere, aunque de los hermanos que pide para el horno y bugata ya le escrivi que el[477] no los ay, ni lo de la bugata conviene aunque le tuvieramos. Yo me consuelo que el Padre Cabredo lo aya hecho y haga tambien para que el colegio tenga el Superior que ha menester. Ya creo que tambien les havrá embiado el Padre Visitador al Padre Gaspar Alonso, porque yo se lo escrivi dias ha. Ens.

Añadido al Padre Roberto Personio. 20 de Diziembre.

A solo Vuestra Reverencia escrivo lo que a ninguno de esos Provinciales se ha escrito ni conviene escrivir por ahora, y es que por ventura hazemos alguna mudanza del Padre Provincial de Andaluzia avisolo para que antes de hazerla Vuestra Reverencia quiere prevenirse haziendo en aquella Provincia algo de lo que con ayuda del Provincial presente piensa se podra mejor executar que no con otro que por ventura non será tan favorable. Lo haga luego, pero encargole que esto no salga de su pecho, ni lo comunique con superior ni inferior alguno ni con el mesmo Provincial de Andalucia porque podria tener inconveniente.

---

477. el] *followed by* uno [*deleted*]

Translation

To Fr Robert Persons, 23 December.

I have received yours of 6 November,[478] and since the Lord has given you health, you should feel comforted. As for what concerns the seminary you will always be provided with all the necessities that you lack: those fathers will do so out of charity, because they have it for one and for more, and because I have charged them with it again and again. And should they fall short, Your Reverence should have no doubt but that it will be remedied from here, so do not be worried or discouraged if you see that any of Ours does not show as much goodwill and affection. For this very thing is governed by divine providence which rules that in all things there should be some bitterness and cross to bear, but the Lord will make it all smooth as he has smoothed other greater difficulties which there have been in the foundation and beginnings of this seminary. Fr Creswell will soon depart, and we will not fail to provide him with everything possible that he asks for himself, except for the lay brothers he requests for the bakery and for laundry: concerning which, I have already written to him that there is none of the former available, and of the latter it is not suitable even if we had. I am encouraged by what Fr Cabredo has already done and continues to do, so that the college has the superior it needs. I believe that father visitor has sent him Fr Gaspar Alonso,[479] because I wrote to him about it some days ago. Etc.

Addendum to Fr Robert Persons, 20 December.

I am writing privately to Your Reverence what I have written to none of those provincials for the present, nor should I: that peradventure we are making some transfer of the provincial of Andalusia. I am alerting you so that, before making it, if Your Reverence wants to get started with carrying out something in that province which with the assistance of the present provincial you think could be achieved better than with another [i.e., the new appointee] who will perhaps not be so favourable, you should do so, but please ensure that you keep this close to your chest, and do not communicate this either to a superior or inferior, not even to the same provincial of Andalusia, because he may not like it.

B132 To Claudio Acquaviva, Valladolid, late December 1591 or early January 1592

SOURCE: Acquaviva's reply of 17 February 1592 (B136).

NOTE: Persons reassures Acquaviva of the support received from the local Spanish fathers.

---

478. B127.
479. Alonso became one of the college's consultors (McCoog, *Building the Faith of St Peter*, 210).

B133 From William Allen, Rome, 7 January 1592

SOURCE: Persons, *A briefe apologie, or defence of the Catholike ecclesiastical hierarchie* (Antwerp, 1601/2), fols. 39–40.

EDITION: Knox, *Allen*, 338–340.

NOTE: Allen laments the brevity of the reign of Pope Innocent IX (Giovanni Antonio Facchinetti, reigned 29 October to 30 December 1591); repeats his earlier report of the dealings of Paget, Cecil, and Fixer with Burghley and the Privy Council; reports on the news of the royal proclamation against seminary priests and Jesuits; and comforts Persons in his illness.

The proclamation "Establishing Commissions against Seminary Priests and Jesuits," 18 October 1591, elicited a flurry of responses from the Catholic exiles, most notably Persons's own *Philopater*: see his letter to Acquaviva, 12 August 1592 (B153), and Verstegan's advice of 12 December 1591 (Petti, 34–38). A second proclamation of the same date was entitled "Specifying Questions to be Asked of Seminary Priests" (*Tudor Royal Proclamations*, ed. Hughes and Larkin, 3: 86–95). Robert Southwell sent Verstegan an extended critique of the proclamation in late November or early December (Petti, 1–33), and Richard Holtby included an account of the proclamation in his report on increased persecution in the north (Morris, 3: 105–219, esp. 152–153): see Questier, *Catholics and Treason*, 208–215 and 224–228.

My good father

God is angry with us, as yow may perceave, and we do feele by the open taking from us our head and Pastor, for now is *Innocentius* also (in whome for his great prudence, learning and vertue, we had great hope) taken unto God, after he had byn in the seat only 2 monethes, &c. And now we are to enter the 10 of January into the *Conclave* againe; God send grace and mercy and avert his wrath from us, &c. And this for that.

Now for our English matters I wrote to yow I thinke by one of myne upon the 26 of October last past, how N. N.[480] had written hither from Flanders to some of the Inquisition, that the Counsel of England offered him a pasport and safe conduct to passe and repasse especially with C. and H. who wil he saith become Catholikes, by which yow may see what kind of practises these goodfellowes (of the faction) have in hand, and with whome they deale.[481] Moreover I had warning 2 or 3 moneths agoe, and wrote to yow of the same, how the two companions N.N. N.N. were with the treasurer,[482] and were suspected to have discovered all they knew, and perhaps added somwhat of their owne more then they knew, since which the former of them hath byn heere, as yow ere this knowe.

480. [*Persons's marginal note:*] This is a cheefe piller of the faction.
481. Knox suggests that the bracketed words are Persons's comment. Glyn Parry, "Occult Philosophy and Politics: Why John Dee Wrote His *Compendious rehearsal* in November 1592," *Studies in History and Philosophy of Science Part A* 43 (2012): 480–488, identifies Charles Paget as the person offered safe conduct, and Hatton and Whitgift as the two likely converts (484).
482. John Cecil (Snowden) and John Fixer. See the headnote to Persons's covering letter of 7 November 1590 (B85).

But now we are further advertised that they have betrayed all indeed, &c., by whose advertisments, & I know not by what other meanes or surmises, they have lately set forth a proclamation of an entended invasion by the king of Spayne, wherin particularly they set downe his practises, and how he procured me for my treasons to be made Cardinal, & other things to bring us and all priests into hatred of the people, and I thinke yow be named in the said proclamation, and the way how the priests are sent out of Spayne to prepare (as they say) the way to the said invasion, and so followeth in the said proclamation most strayte order and provision for prevention of the said fayned invasions with very cruel provision against priests and Catholikes:[483] the poore wretches are more afrayd then we know cause, *sed Deum non invocaverunt ideo trepidaverunt, &c.*[484] And Dr Dee their conjurer or Astrologer is said to have put them in more doubt, for that he hath told the Counsel by his calculation, that the Realme indeed shalbe conquered this Somer, beleeve him who wil.[485]

If it should come to his Majestie or other superiors eares, that those priests should betray the Catholike cause, or be occasion of this proclamation, it would be very scandalous, especially there in Spayne. I trust we shal have a copy of the Proclamation shortly; I doubt me your way of entercourse betwene England and Spaine and contrary wise, is now by the said companions discovered. Gods wil be fulfilled and save us *a falsis fratribus.*[486] I hope yow be before this perfectly recovered, have a good hart in God, for by him we shal overcome all. Thus much for a farewel before I enter the *Conclave*, adew my deare Father my comfort in these tribulations & temptations this 7 of January 1592.[487]

B134 From Claudio Acquaviva, Rome, 20 January 1592

SOURCE: ARSI, Castell. 6, fol. 111v, from the general's register.

NOTE: Acquaviva rejoices in Persons's improving health, following a sojourn in León (about 125 km north of Valladolid), and hopes that Creswell will be a support. He sanctions the movement of missionaries through Spain, but argues that neither Henry Walpole nor Thomas Wright would be suitable to replace Holt in Brussels. It had been proposed that Walpole should leave the employ of the duke of Parma and replace Holt, but Olivier Mannaerts, provincial of the Belgian province, had reservations. Following Acquaviva's suggestion here, Persons called for him to be sent to England via Spain. Wright was in Genoa (Persons to Creswell, 26 May 1590, B62; Persons to Holt, n.d. 1591, B96).

---

483. [*Persons's marginal note:*] A most cruel proclamation against priests and Catholikes 1592.

484. Adapted from Ps. 52:6 (Vulgate, following Septuagint): "They have not called upon God: there have they trembled for fear, where there was no fear."

485. The eminent mathematician and astrologer Dr John Dee (1527–1608/9) dined frequently with Burghley and Robert Cecil. Parry, "Occult Philosophy," argues that Dee was being used by Burghley to counter those in the Privy Council, such as Hatton and Whitgift, who favoured greater toleration for Catholics.

486. "From false brethren" (2 Cor. 11:26).

487. [*Persons's marginal note:*] Confidence betwixt the Card. and F[r] P[ersons].

P. Roberto Personio, Enero 20.

Recevi la de Vuestra Reverencia de 6 de deciembre con particular consuelo de entender que su salud esté tan reparada como me significa, y que para ello aya ayudado la jornada de León. Vuestra Reverencia la conserve, que harto deseo yo para este efecto embiarle presto al Padre Crisuelo que de algo le descargue, pero no hallo lo que querria para suplir suficientemente su lugar, en esto andamos; dios nos descubra uno que sea a proposito.

El hermano Fabriçio propone su poca salud; y no le veo tan inclinado a volver como conviene para que con alegria esté y se emplee, por esto he dado orden que de la provincia de Andalucia vaya otro en su lugar.

Yo escrivo de nuevo encargando a los Provinciales la execucion de lo *de ratione studiorum*. Creo que aprovechará este recuerdo porque les digo que espero me avisen de lo que se haçe.

No he podido hablar con el Señor Cardenal, aora está en el conclave, a mí me pareçe bien que las misiones se hagan por España como Vuestra Reverencia diçe, que en esto yo me remito a su pareçer, el rector del inglés tiene en ello alguna dificultad, él avisará.

El Padre Oliverio no muestra tanta satisfaction del Padre Henrrico Valpolo que se deva embiar a Ingalaterra; del Padre Tomas Vrit Vuestra Reverencia save que no es a proposito; tengamos paciençia, y empleemos los que nos da dios tales quales conviene, que pocos y buenos haran mucha labor. En las &c.

Translation

To Fr Robert Persons, 20 January.

I have received Your Reverence's letter of 6 December, learning – quite to my comfort – that your health has been restored as you indicate, and that in this respect the journey to León was of help. Would Your Reverence please look after your health, which I heartily desire. For that reason, I am sending you Fr Creswell soon, who may relieve you of some of your burden, but I have not found someone suitable enough to replace him; that's what we're trying to resolve – may our God reveal someone who will be appropriate.

Brother Fabrizio informs us about his poor health; and I do not see him so inclined to return as would be advisable if he were to be cheerfully employed, and therefore I have given instruction for someone else to go to the province of Andalusia in his place.[488]

I am writing again to the provincials asking for the implementation of the book *De ratione studiorum*.[489] I believe that this reminder will be beneficial because I am asking them to let me know when it has been done.

488. In fact, Brother Como left Rome in April, and waited in Genoa to be joined by Creswell (Acquaviva to Persons, 13 April, 11 May, and 8 June 1592, B141, B144–145).

489. This refers to a document circulated in 1591, following the comments elicited by a trial *Ratio* issued in 1586. The final document, *Ratio studiorum* (1599) regulated Jesuit education in schools. See Maurice Whitehead, *English Jesuit Education: Expulsion, Suppression, Survival and Restoration, 1762–1803* (Farnham, Surrey, 2013), 13–15, and *The Ratio Studiorum: The Official Plan for Jesuit Education*, ed. Claude Pavur (St Louis, 2005).

I have not been able to talk with my Lord Cardinal, as he is now in the conclave. I think it will be all right for the missions to go forward to Spain as Your Reverence says; in this I defer to your opinion. If the rector of the English college has any difficulty with it, he will notify us.

Fr Olivier does not seem very convinced that Fr Henry Walpole should be sent to England. As for Fr Thomas Wright, Your Reverence should know that he is not suitable. Let us have patience, and employ those whom God gives us as being more suitable, as a few good men will do much work. To your prayers, etc.

B135 To Claudio Acquaviva, Valladolid, January/February 1592

SOURCE: Acquaviva's reply of 13 April (B141).

NOTE: Persons reports on his improved relations with the local Spanish Jesuits.

B136 From Claudio Acquaviva, Rome, 17 February 1592

SOURCE: ARSI, Cast. 6, fol. 114r, from the general's register of letters to the province of Castile.

NOTE: Acquaviva continues to be encouraged by the support Persons is receiving at the seminary, both from the rector of St Ambrose, Juan Suárez, and the provincial of Aragon, Francisco Galarza (see his letters to them, fols. 113r–114r, expressing appreciation). He rehearses his hopes that Creswell's arrival will lessen the burden on Persons.

Acquaviva consults Persons about the Annual Letter of the Society, a compilation of reports from each province; the *Annuae litterae Societatis Iesu* for 1592 (Florence, 1600) contains reports on the English colleges in Rome (9–12), Valladolid (160–161) and Seville (169–170). Here Acquaviva seems to be concerned about delicate aspects of the 1591 report.

P. Roberto Personio, Hebrero 17.

Bien esperaba yo de la charidad de esos Padres que quando huviesen entendido mi voluntad, y quanto yo deseo que todos favorescan las cosas de ese seminario, lo havien de haçer con las buenas muestras que Vuestra Reverencia me diçe, que dan, y yo me consuelo dello y se lo agradezco al Provincial y al Padre Juan Suarez en las que aora les escrivo.

Razon tiene Vuestra Reverencia de notar lo que en la Anua se diçe deste seminario, que aquello mejor fuera callarlo, y no sé cómo se dieron aquellos puntos entre los demas para hazer el Anua, procuraremos se remedie en lo por venir.

Deseo y procurare embiar presto al Padre Joseph Cresuelo, el Señor Cardenal Alano tambien lo desea, y me solicita. Vuestra Reverencia diga al Padre rector que reçevi la suya en respuesta de la qual tenga esta por propria, pues con esto que digo del Padre Crisuelo respondo a lo que en la suya pide respuesta. En sus &c.

Translation

To Fr Robert Persons, 17 February.

I had good hopes of the charity of those fathers that when they realized how I felt, how much I wish that they would all favour the affairs of the seminary, they would do so, with those fine instances that Your Reverence tells me they give. And I am encouraged by that and I have expressed my appreciation to the provincial and to Fr Juan Suárez in what I am writing to them now.

Your Reverence has reason to note what is said in the Annual Letter about this seminary, which it would be better to keep quiet about, and I do not know how you have managed to deal with those matters along with everything else to be included for the Annual Letter, but we will try to remedy this in the future.

I would like to ensure Fr Joseph Creswell's early departure; the Lord Cardinal Allen also desires this, and urges me to do it. Your Reverence should tell father rector that I have received his letter. He may treat this letter as a reply to him personally, since what I say here of Fr Creswell is by way of answer to him, who asked for a reply in his letter. To your [prayers], etc.

B137 From Richard Verstegan, Antwerp, 21 February 1592

SOURCE: Verstegan to Persons, 5 March 1592 (B138).

B138 From Richard Verstegan, Antwerp, 5 March 1592

SOURCES:
ABSI, Coll B, 37–42, holograph letter, with "avisos" in Spanish translation (= G_1);
ABSI, Coll M 95 (olim 67), Grene's short extract (= G_2);
ACSA, Series II, Legajo 6, item 5 (= Vd).

EDITIONS: Petti, 39–48; Pollen, *Unpublished Documents*, 208–209 (part of the English letter); part of the Spanish "avisos" was adapted by Pedro de Ribadeneira in *Segunda Parte de la Historia Ecclesiastica* (1593), book 3, chapter 10, trans. Weinreich, 599–600.

TRANSLATION: Extract from Spanish news despatches, translated into English in Thomas Ellison Gibson, *Lydiate Hall and Its Associations* (Edinburgh, 1876), 260.

NOTE: As was his custom, Verstegan sent news to Persons in the form of a letter as well as a despatch (translated into Spanish for the information of local Jesuits and the Spanish court). The despatch duplicates much of the material in the letter, but is not a close translation of it, and contains a more personal note at the end. Both are included here to illustrate the nuances influenced by the different target audiences. The most significant change is the attribution of new measures not to the "Cecillian Inquisition" but to the queen: the Spanish court would be less concerned about the distinction between Elizabeth and her "evil counsellor." In some cases, the Spanish follows the English closely; in others, details are given which are not in the English letter, and some paragraphs are rearranged. One paragraph, "There is not any Chauncelor made as yet," relating to the death of Hatton and other news about English personages which might not be of interest to the Spanish court, is omitted in the Spanish text.

Right Reverend,

In the end of my last letter unto your fatherhoode dated the 21 of February, I signified the Arryvall of a Catholik gentleman at this towne, since which tyme there is another arryved here and for the same cause fled oute of England, to witt, for the receyving of priestes.[490] It seemeth by them that very many more shall shortly be forced to followe, yea, priestes aswell as others, so extreme and great is the present persecution, which albeit I do otherwise understand, yet had I rather write uppon the relation of thease two gentlemen beeing knowen and of credit then uppon other reportes of lesse certainty. First you shall please to understand that by the new Cecillian Inquisition[491] there are certaine comissioners ordayned in every shyre to take the examinations of Catholiques, and thease comissioners do in every parish apoint 8 persons, of which number must be the minister constable and churchwardens. Thease 8 do once a weke (or every day in the weke yf they please) go from house to house and examyne those[492] they fynde of what religion they are, and whether they do go to the Churche, and as they fynd them doubtfull in their answeres, they do present them to the further examination of the comissioners; the servantes of recusantes they do eyther perswade[493] by flattery, or compell by torture in hanging them up by the handes, to betray their masters, in discovering what preistes he dothe relieve, what persons do frequent the house, and the lyke.[494]

There were executed aboute Christmas 3 priestes and 4 laymen for receiving them: the names of the priestes were Mr Jeninges, Mr Eustace Whyte, and Mr Paule Blasden. 2 of the laymen were gent[lemen], the one named Swithin Welles, the other Bryan Laycie; the other twaine were servingmen, whose names I have not,[495] since which tyme there hathe bene a priest executed at Norwich, and one Mr Grey in whose house he was taken, is sent unto the towre.[496]

490. Lawrence Mompesson (see n497 below).
491. The phrase "Cecillian Inquisition" is underlined. In the Spanish despatch, the persecution is attributed to the queen rather than Cecil: see the paragraph beginning "Jamas pienso que se a visto tal rigor de persecucion."
492. those] *followed by* of [*deleted*] G1
493. perswade] *followed by* them [*deleted*] G1
494. The following three paragraphs were included by Pollen, *Unpublished Documents*, 208–209.
495. [*marginal note in G1:* Mr Jenings Eustace White Polidor Plasdin Priests martirs.] Grene transcribes most of this sentence. Polidore Plasden (b. 1563), Eustace White, and Edmund Gennings were executed at Tyburn on 10 December 1591; their host Swithin Wells was hanged outside his house in Gray's Inn Fields, where they had been taken by Topcliffe during mass (Anstruther, 128, 278–279, 378–379). Petti identifies the two servingmen as John Mason and Sydney Hodgson, and comments that 10 December (o.s.) was close to Christmas in the Gregorian calendar. See *The Life and Death of Mr Edmund Genings, Priest* (Saint-Omer, 1614) and the documents gathered by Pollen under "The Martyrdom of Edmund Gennings and Companions" (*Unpublished Documents*, 204–208); also, Questier, *Catholics and Treason*, 214–217.
496. [*marginal note in G1:* In ye Catalogues I finde no such martyr.] Pollen concludes that the unnamed priest-martyr of Norwich was Thomas Pormort, who was executed in London, 21 February 1592 (Anstruther, 280–281), but Petti, 42–43, referring to Verstegan's letter to Roger Baynes, 6 June, 1592 (49), identifies him more convincingly as Nicholas Fox and his alleged host as Robert Grey of Marton in the diocese of Norwich (Anstruther, 123–124).

The last moneth was one Mr Patteson a priest executed at Tyborne, for receyving of whome one of the gentlemen before mentioned is fled away.⁴⁹⁷ This Mr Patteson, the night before he suffred, beeing in a dungeon in Newgate, with 7 prisoners that were condemned for fellony, he converted and reconsyled 6 of them, to whom also he ministred the Sacrament, which the seaventh, remayning an heretike, in the morning uttered:⁴⁹⁸ they were all executed together: the 6 died Catholik which made the officers to be the more fierse and cruell unto the priest who was cut downe and bowelled beeing perfectly alive.

No priestes are suffred to speak at their deathes but so soone as they are dead Topclif in an oration unto the people faineth the cause to be for assisting the intended invasion of the realme and to that end he fixeth also pages⁴⁹⁹ uppon the gallows or gibbett. The aflicted state of Catholiques was never such as now it is and therefore it is highe tyme to solicite the redresse thereof. Some other things I would signifie, which for want of more secure meanes of writing I will omitt.

There is not any Chauncelor made as yet nor none lyke to be.⁵⁰⁰ The Treasurer meaneth to mak himself *dictator in perpetuum*; and beeing discended of princes, it wilbe no disparagement in blood to mak up his intended match betwene Sir Thomas Cecills eldest sonne beeing his grand child, and the Lady Arbella. The yonge youth is as pretely instructed in Athisme as the Lady Arbella is in puresy,⁵⁰¹ for he will not stick openly to scof at the Byble; and will folkes to spell the name of God backward. I cannot thinck that there was half so great iniquitie in Sodoma as is now in England, besydes the shedding of innocent bloud which daily crieth for vengeance and may give us most hope of our countries recoverie, Our Lord send due consideration thereof in the myndes of such as have the best meanes to remedy this great evill, which I can assure your fatherhoode was never at such rypenesse as now it is.

There dothe passe among Catholiks divers foxes in lambes skinnes, with protections in their bosomes from the Treasurer: by which meanes they go invisible among the inquisitors.

The old recorder called Fletewood is oute of his office. The cause I thinck was only slacknesse in proceeding against Catholikes, for another hathe it that is of a more whoter spirite.⁵⁰² The aforesaid recorder meeting of late with a gentlewoman asked her what kin

497. William Pattenson was seized in Clerkenwell, in the house of Lawrence Mompesson, and put to death at Tyburn on 22 January. Mompesson fled the country with his wife and settled in Brussels (Petti, 43; Anstruther, 270–271; Questier, *Catholics and Treason*, 218–220).

498. Grene's extract reads: "the seventh remayning heretick, in the morning discovered."

499. pages] papers *Petti*

500. Sir Christopher Hatton, Lord Chancellor, died on 20 November 1591, and the position was not formally filled. This paragraph has no equivalent in the Spanish text.

501. puresy] *G1*; Petti suggests it may be an archaic but unrecorded form of "purity", or may refer to Puritanism. As a coinage, combining "puritan" and "heresy," "puresy" may reflect Verstegan's philological interest and resourcefulness.

502. William Fleetwood (ca. 1525–1594) was replaced as recorder of London by Edward Coke (1552–1634); in Verstegan's view, this was because Coke was more fervent in proceeding against Catholics. In July 1588 Fleetwood recommended that Catholic clergy should be more closely examined to distinguish those with traitorous intentions: Questier, *Catholics and Treason*, 182. For Justice Richard Young, see Verstegan's letter of mid-August 1592 (B154).

another was unto her, whome he then named. Marry, quoth the gentlewoman, she is my aunt. I assure you quoth hee yf she were my aunt as she is yours, I would forthwith send her woord that Justice Yong dothe meane to search her house this night for a priest, by meanes whereof the gentlewoman did asmuch for her aunt as the recorder would have donne for his.

Thus having troobled your fatherhoode with a long letter, I will for the presente tak my leave and comitt you to Godes tuition.[503] Antwerp, this [blank] of marche 1592.

  Your fatherhoodes
    assured servitor
      R. Verstegan.
        5 of march.

I have expected now thease 3 dayes past to heare from F. S.[504] but the wynde seemeth to have bin contrary to passe over.

Mr Covert comendeth him to Your Fatherhoode.

[*Addressed*:] Al molto Reverendo in Christo Padre il Padre Roberto Personio della Compagnia di Giesu a Validolid or Madrid.[505]

[*Endorsed by Fr Persons*:] Mr Verstingham of the martyrs, 5 Martii, 1592.

[*Endorsed at the head of the letter*:] Mr Vestigannes of the martyres the 5 of march 1592. Mr Eustace White Polidor Plasdin & Willm Pattison

[*The enclosed news report*:]

Avisos de Anveres de 5 de Março de 1592. De las cosas de Inglaterra.

Esta semana han llegado aqui dos cavalleros de Ingalaterra Catholicos que han huido de alla por causa de ser la persecucion que ay contra los Catholicos intolerable y grandissima despues de el postrero edicto de la Reyna que se publicó el mes de Noviembre passado en el qual los declara por sabidores y fautores de la invasion que ella diçe que el Rey de España pretende hacer en aquel Reyno el verano que viene.

El uno de estos Catholicos trae consigo tambien su mujer para tenerla aqui con él en su destierro y el otro quisiera haçer lo mismo sino que le ataxaron los pasos y le pusieron en grand aprieto y peligro de prenderle en que yva su vida porque su delicto fue auer recevido en casa un sacerdote del seminario de Rhemis llamado patison al qual martiriçaron en Londres en el mes pasado de Hebrero y lo mismo hicieran a este cavallero por auerle sustentado si le prendieran.

La noche antes que martiricassen a este saçerdote lo hecharon en un calaboço muy hondo de la carçel de neugat de Londres donde estava y lo pusieron entre siete ladrones condenados tambien a muerte la qual avian de padesçer el día siguiente con él. Y fue nuestro señor servido dar espiritu a este su siervo de predicarles con tal efficacia que convirtio seis de los siete que todos eran hereges los quales el día siguiente saliendo a morir se confessaron por Catholicos y murieron con mucha paciencia y edificacion de los buenos

  503. Care, guardianship.
  504. Robert Southwell was sending reports to Verstegan (Petti, 44 n19).
  505. della Compagnia di Giesu a Validolid or Madrid] *this ed.*; della Comp *suppl. Petti*; or Madrid *has been added in a later hand*

confessando su fee y con grande enojo de los herejes los quales para vengarse de el sacerdote por auerles convertido le abrieron vivo con cuchillos y le hicieron quartos con gran crueldad.

Al mes pasado martiriçaron tambien otro sacerdote en la ciudad de Noruico al qual predieron en la casa de un cavallero llamado gray al qual tienen preso en el castillo de Londres y se piensa que tanbien le arán martir presto.

En el fin de diçiembre martiriçaron en Londres a siete juntamente de los quales tres eran saçerdotes de los seminarios de Rhemis y de Roma cuyos nombres eran Juan Jeningo Eustacio Vito Paulo Plasdeno los otros quatro eran legos dos cavalleros llamados Suithen Wello y Brianto Laceyo por aver tratado con los dichos saçerdotes y los otros dos eran criados suyos todos fueron presos juntamente estando oyendo missa en la calle de Holborn en Londres.

Jamas pienso que se ha visto tal rigor de persecucion porque la Reyna ha enbiado a todos los condados de el Reyno que son quarenta un juez y comisario particular para inquirir contra los Catholicos y estos an señalado en cada perrochia y provincia[506] a ocho personas de las más malas y herejes para examinar continuamente a todas las personas que con cada parrochia viven o pasan por ella y tienen sus espias en cada casa y meson y estan obligados a juntarse todos una vez cada semana para dar quenta de lo que han hecho.

Offreçen a los hijos y criados de Catholicos premios y danles tormentos para que descubran a sus padres y amos.

No se permite ya a ningun sacerdote hablar palabra al pueblo quando salen a morir sino que luego despues de la muerte el Juez que está presente y la manda executar haçe a la gente una larga arenga sobre las causas de las muertes diçiendo mil mentiras y disparates de las conspiraçiones que les imponen que avian hecho con el Rey de España para la conquista de el Reyno y luego van divulgando lo mismo en cartones por todas las plaças y puertas de las çiudades.

Plega a dios de Remediarlo presto y de mover los coraçones de los principes Catholicos que tienen fuerças para concurrir en esto pues entiendo que su divina magestad no permitira yr muy adelante una crueldad tan fuera de toda christiandad y raçon. Él guarde a Vuestra Reverencia siempre. De Anveres, a 5 de Marco de 1592.

Translation

Two gentlemen have arrived here this week from England who were forced to flee because of the unbearable persecution of Catholics intensified by the queen's recent proclamation, published last November, in which she declares that they are informants and supporters of the invasion which, she claims, the king of Spain plans to launch against her kingdom next summer.

One of these gentlemen has also brought his wife to live with him here in exile. The other would have done the same, except that his efforts were thwarted and he ran the risk of arrest. He faced sentence of death on the charge of receiving a priest from Rheims,

---

506. provincia] pila *G1*

by name of Patterson, into his house. The priest was martyred in London in the month of February past, and if they had captured this gentleman, they would have done the same to him for succouring him.

The night before they martyred this priest, they put him in a very deep dungeon of the prison of Newgate in London where he was being held, placing him among seven condemned thieves with whom he was to suffer the next day. Our Lord afforded grace to this his servant to preach so effectively that he converted six of the seven, all of them heretics. When they went to their death the following morning, they professed themselves Catholics, and died with exemplary resignation and constancy in the faith. This edified good people and vexed the heretics to the extent that they disembowelled the priest while he was still alive, as a return for converting them, and quartered him with every cruelty.

Last month they also martyred another priest, in the city of Norwich, who was taken in the house of a gentleman by the name of Gray. They keep him prisoner in the Tower of London, where it is believed they will soon make a martyr of him, too.

At the end of December they martyred seven men in London at the same time: three were priests from the seminaries at Rheims and Rome, named John Gennings, Eustace White, and Paul Plasden; the other four were laymen: two gentlemen, called Swithin Wells and Brian Lacey, with their servants, for having dealings with these priests. They were all arrested together while attending mass in Holborn in London.

I do not think such a rigorous persecution has ever been seen before. The queen has sent a judge and a special commissioner to each of the counties of the kingdom (forty in number) to investigate the Catholics. In every parish and district these officials have nominated eight of the most flagrant heretics to subject every person living there to unrelenting examination. They keep spies in every inn and household, all of whom are required to meet once a week to report on their findings.

May God remedy this soon and move the hearts of the Catholic princes that have armies, to join together in this matter, since we believe that His Divine Majesty will not permit such cruelty to continue, beyond all Christianity and reason. May He always protect Your Reverence. From Antwerp, 5 March 1592.

[*Endorsed, in a contemporary hand*:] Advises from London the 5 of march 1592.

B139 To Claudio Acquaviva, 28 March 1592

SOURCE: Acquaviva's reply of 11 May (B144).

NOTE: Persons queried Creswell's movements, whom he was expecting to join him in Spain. There is no evidence of any letters to Acquaviva between now and June: Persons spent some time in Madrid in connection with what he calls "the greater business of the general," i.e., the agitation for a general congregation and the report by the visitors (see his confidential letter tentatively dated June, B147). He also had dealings with William Crichton, who was in Madrid sounding out the possibility of Spanish collaboration with Catholics in Scotland (see Persons to Idiáquez, 31 August 1593, B200, and to Acquaviva, 12 May 1594, B230; Yellowlees, 119–123).

With the college in Valladolid badly in need of funds, Persons approached several notables for help, but had success only with the archbishop of Toledo, Gaspar de

Quiroga, who made a bequest of a thousand gold pieces a year, and Philip II, who gave him a licence to import cloth, which he sold on for four thousand gold pieces (*Blackfan Annals*, 36–38). He also persuaded the king to obtain from the pope a document, dated 25 April, placing the seminary at Valladolid directly under the authority of the papacy (Edwards, 152).

B140 From William Allen, 13 April 1592

SOURCE: Valladolid, II.1, item 12; original holograph, with twentieth-century typescript.
EDITION: Renold, *Letters of Allen and Barret*, 217–218, with English translation.
NOTE: Allen agrees to provide a pension of 50 gold pieces per annum, to be paid out of his episcopal income to the rector of the College at Valladolid. Allen was to be Cardinal Protector of the College (Edwards, 152).

R. Patri Personio.

Reverentia Vestra petat, quaeso, a D. Aulestio meo illic procuratore, singulis annis quinquaginta aureos, quos potest de mea pensione super episcopatum Palentinum subducere, atque rectori Collegii Anglicani qui pro tempore fuerit, ad beneplacitum nostrum, pro meo servitio, per duas mediates secundum terminos in quibus eiusdem pensionis colatio fieri solet, hoc est pro festo Natalis Domini 25 et pro festo Nativitatis S. Joannis Baptistae totidem numero, incipiendo a festo Natalis proxime praeterito ante datum presentium. Quem colationem et de pensione praedicta subductionem gratum ac ratum per presentem schedulam mea manu scriptam et subscriptam me habiturum spondeo. Datum in Urbe 13 Aprilis anno 1592.

Gulielmus Cardinal Alanus

[*Endorsed:*] Literae Ill[mi] Card. Alani ad Dominum Aulaeum pro solutione 50 scutorum singulis annis in sustentatione etc.

Translation

To Reverend Fr Persons.

Would Your Reverence please ask Mr Aulest my procurator there, for 50 gold pieces per year, which he may deduct from my pension for the bishopric of Palencia,[507] and pay it to the rector of the English college so that, according to circumstances, it might be available for our gracious purpose as my service. This is to be paid in two equal half portions, according to the appointed days on which my pension is normally paid: that is, before Christmas and the Feast of the Nativity of St John the Baptist,[508] to just that amount, beginning on the Christmas nearest to the date of this document. This withdrawal and the deduction from the aforesaid pension I hereby promise that I will regard that contri-

---

507. It appears that Allen had been granted a pension from Palencia, as he had from Pavia (Knox, *Allen*, 373–74); the bishop of Palencia was a benefactor of the English college at Valladolid (Persons to Creswell, 4 November 1590, B84, headnote). The name and location of the procurator in question remain obscure.

508. 24 June.

bution and the deduction from the aforesaid pension as acceptable and ratified by the present schedule, which was written and signed by my own hand. Rome, 13 April 1592.

William, Cardinal Allen

B141 From Claudio Acquaviva, Rome, 13 April 1592

SOURCE: ARSI, Cast. 6, fol. 119v, from the general's register of letters to the province of Castile.

NOTE: Acquaviva is pleased with the effect his letters of admonishment have had on the Spanish Jesuits who have not been fully supportive of Persons's enterprises (see his letter of the same date to Francisco Galarza, provincial of Aragon, fol. 119r–v). Despite Acquaviva's previous reservations (see his letter of 20 January 1592, B134), Fabrizio Como is on his way to help Persons, via Genoa. Creswell can leave Rome shortly since a successor has been found: Muzio Vitelleschi (1563–1645; see Mario Fois, in *DHCJ*, 2: 1621–1627, *sub* "Generales"), who succeeded Acquaviva as sixth superior general of the Society of Jesus in 1615.

P. Roberto Personio, 13 de Abril.

Yo me consuelo de entender por la de Vuestra Reverencia que mis cartas ayan hecho en esos Padres el buen efecto que yo deseava, y el que conviene para que esa obra se promueva, escriveme el Provincial ofreçiendose de favoreçer y ayudar en todo lo que pudiere, y yo le respondo quan agradeçido está Vuestra Reverencia a su charidad, y como aqui el Señor Cardenal Alano me ha hablado agradeciendo lo mesmo, espero que ellos lo haran muy bien. Avisado he que el hermano Fabriçio espere en Genova para que vaya en compañia de uno de los Padres que de aqui van a España. Llegado alla, él acudira a Vuestra Reverencia y podra servirse dél. El Padre Crisuelo tambien partira en brebe, que ya le hemos dado por sucesor al Padre Muçio Vitelesqui, que espero satisfara, y estos Señores Cardenales estan muy satisfechos dél. En sus ...

Translation

To Fr Robert Persons, 13 April.

I am relieved to learn from Your Reverence's letter that my letters have had that good effect on the fathers which I desired, with the welcome result that this work may be promoted. The provincial has written to me offering his support and assistance in whatever he can. And I have replied to him how grateful Your Reverence is for his charity, and similarly the Lord Cardinal Allen has expressed the same gratitude to me. I hope that those men will put this to good effect. I have been advised that Brother Fabrizio should wait in Genoa in order to proceed in company with one of the fathers who is going to Spain from here. When he has arrived there, he will go to Your Reverence and you will be able to make use of him. Fr Creswell also will leave in a short while, whom we have replaced with Fr Muzio Vitelleschi as his successor here. I hope he will be satisfactory, because those Lord Cardinals are very satisfied with him. To your ...

B142 To Juan de Idiáquez, 22 April 1592

SOURCE: Idiáquez to Persons, 27 April (B143).
NOTE: Evidently Persons had looked over a document for Idiáquez, and commented on it.

B143 From Juan de Idiáquez, probably to Persons, Madrid, 27 April 1592

SOURCE: ARSI, FG 651/640, item 26, a hastily written note.
NOTE: Idiáquez commends Persons for his attention to a document, and the reasons he has put forward. It appears to be about the new arrangement, procured by the king, for the college at Valladolid to be placed under the direct authority of the pope: see the "Brief of Pope Clement VIII Confirming the Erection of the English College, Valladolid," dated 25 April 1592, in *Valladolid Registers*, 246–251 (appendix 1).

El folio que vino con la carta de Vuestra Paternidad de 22 deste buelve dentro desta y el cuydado y obra que ha tomado Vuestra Paternidad a pechos es muy de su zelo y prudencia, y harto buenas las razones porque se ha movido, el secreto se guarda excepto con quien no se ha de cubrir nada que es su Majestad y el vernos podra ser en San Lorenzo con más comodidad de todos que en otra parte. Yo avisaré a tiempo para quando podra venir Vuestra Paternidad alli &c. Encomiendenos a Dios y él le guarde y cumpla desseos pues son tan de Su Magestad &. De Madrid a 27 de Abril 1592.

Don Juan de Idiaquez.

Translation

I am enclosing herewith the folio which came with the letter from Your Paternity of the 22nd of this month. The attention and effort which Your Paternity has bestowed on it speaks much of your zeal and prudence, and there are very good reasons to justify the decision. It is being kept secret except for the one from whom nothing should be concealed, namely His Majesty. We will be able to see each other, maybe, in San Lorenzo[509] more conveniently for all than elsewhere. I will advise the time when Your Paternity may come there. Please commend us to God; may he keep you and fulfil your desires as they are the same as His Majesty's, etc. From Madrid, 27 April 1592.

Don Juan de Idiaquez.

B144 From Claudio Acquaviva, Rome, 11 May 1592

SOURCE: ARSI, Cast. 6, fol. 120r, from the general's register of letters to the province of Castile.
NOTE: Vitelleschi had been appointed to replace Creswell as rector of the English College, Rome, and this seems to have quietened the unrest; he remained in office until 1594,

---

509. I.e. San Lorenzo de El Escorial.

when he was replaced by Girolamo Fioravanti. On 30 April Creswell left Rome for Genoa, where Brother Fabrizio Como was waiting to accompany him to meet Persons at Valladolid. Acquaviva is having to change his mind about replacing the provincial of Andalusia, but this need not affect Persons's plans.

P. Personio, 11 de Mayo.

Recevi la de Vuestra Reverencia de 28 de Marzo y en lo que toca al Padre Cressuélo no digo más de rogar al Señor le dé bueno y breve viage como espero que le terna. Partio de Roma último de Abril y en Genova le esperava Fabricio para hazerle compañia que no poco he gustado de embiarle para que ayude a Vuestra Reverencia como por sus cartas me ha mostrado que lo desea. Las cosas del Collegio Inglés ahora estan muy quietas con el nuevo rector que es el Padre Mutio Viteleschi y espero que continuarán con la mesma paz, porque la prudencia y mansedumbre del rector prometen qualquiera buena esperanza. De la mudanza del Provincial de Andalucia no sé lo que haremos ni quando porque depende de otras cosas que conforme a ellas havremos de tomar la resolucion, pero como quiera que se haga el Señor que hasta aqui ha ayudado a Vuestra Reverencia le ayudará en lo por venir. En sus oraciones, &c.

Translation

To Fr Persons, 11 May.

I have received Your Reverence's letter of 28 March.[510] With regard to Fr Creswell, I will say no more than to pray that the Lord will give him a safe journey. He left Rome on the last day of April, and Fabrizio was waiting for him to join him in Genoa. I was not a little delighted to send him to help Your Reverence, as you have indicated in your letters to be your desire. The affairs of the English college are now more settled with the new rector, who is Fr Muzio Vitelleschi, and I hope that their peace will last, because the prudence and gentleness of the rector promises good hope to all. Concerning the new appointment of the provincial of Andalusia, I do not know what we are doing or when, because it depends on other matters which will resolve the issue. But whatever happens, the Lord who has helped Your Reverence up to now will assist you in the future. To your prayers, etc.

B145 From Claudio Acquaviva, Rome, 8 June 1592

SOURCE: ARSI, Cast. 6, fol. 124r, from the general's register of letters to the province of Castile.

NOTE: Acquaviva is anxious that Creswell and Fabrizio Como should reach Persons soon, to help shoulder the burden. He advises that Persons should find a better time to found a seminary at Seville, given the current financial constraints on the Spanish people and the overzealous begging of Bartolomé de Sicilia.

510. B139.

P. Roberto Personio, Junio 8.

Espero que el Padre Crisuelo estara presto por alla porque nos dieron nuevas dias ha de no sé qué buen pasaje que se iba poniendo en orden. Deseo su brebe llegada porque pueda en algo aliviar a Vuestra Reverencia que çierto temo su salud entre tanta carga de ocupaçiones. El Hermano Fabriçio siente poca inclinacion a tener cuydado o officio alguno en el seminario por la poca ayuda que esto le es para su superior pero de muy buena gana acompañará a Vuestra Reverencia y acudira a todo lo demas en que le empleare.[511]

Entiendo que Vuestra Reverencia trata de fundar en Sevilla otro Seminario, y no ay duda sino que alli estara muy bien, y el Provincial presente ayudará bien, pero supuestas las desgraçias que estos años han tenido las flotas, y que por esto la gente estara algo apretada, y supuesta tambien la presençia y ocupaçión del Padre Siçilia, vea Vuestra Reverencia si esto será impedimento para el buen successo del seminario, y si será mejor dilatarlo algunos meses, que no digo esto para impedirlo, si no solo para que Vuestra Reverencia considere bien el tiempo y coyuntura más a proposito para que salga bien. En sus &c.

Translation

To Fr Robert Persons, 8 June.

I hope that Fr Creswell will soon be there because these past days we had news about an opportune passage. I wish for his early arrival because he can bring some relief to Your Reverence, as I surely fear for your health under such a burden of occupations. Brother Fabrizio feels little inclination to undertake any care or duty in the seminary, because (as he says) his work is of little help to his superior, but he will very willingly accompany Your Reverence and attend to everything else in which you can use him.

I understand that Your Reverence is trying to found another seminary in Seville, and there is no doubt that this will be a very good thing there, and the present provincial will be very helpful, but in the light of the misfortunes which the fleets have had in these years, and the constraint that the people feel as a result, and also the alleged presence and activity of Fr Sicilia, Your Reverence will judge whether this will be an impediment to the good success of the seminary, and whether it would be better to delay this for some months. I say this not to hold you back except that Your Reverence should reconsider what time and occasion would be more favourable to a happy outcome. To your [prayers], etc.

B146 To Claudio Acquaviva, Valladolid, June 1592

SOURCE: Acquaviva to Persons, 3 August (B151).

NOTE: Persons asks for letters of authorization for the proposed seminary in Seville and also reports on further tensions between the English and Spanish Jesuits in Valladolid.

511. This sentence added in the margin.

B147 To Claudio Acquaviva, possibly Valladolid, June 1592

SOURCE: ARSI, FG 651/616, fol. 1r–v, holograph with the remains of a seal indicating "soli," a private letter.

NOTE: Here Persons reports confidentially on the pressure building in Spain for a general congregation of the Society. After submitting their report at the end of 1591, the visitors Acosta and González Dávila waited for a reply from Acquaviva and were now growing impatient. Acosta had now taken up the position of superior at the professed house in Valladolid, where his brother Jerónimo was also resident (Astrain, 3: 520–521). Acosta was trying to recruit Philip II and his chief advisor the count of Chinchón, Diego Fernández de Cabrera y Bobadilla (1536–1608), in support of his demand for a general congregation where the memorialists' grievances might be aired. In his letter of 9 September (B156) Persons claims he was unconvinced, and that Acquaviva's reply confirmed his reservations about the wisdom of calling a general congregation at this time.

The letter is undated, but clearly belongs to the period after the submission of the visitors' reports and the calling of the general congregation. McCoog, *Building the Faith of St Peter*, 135, assigns it to June 1592. In the manuscript, the ciphers have been decoded in another hand above the line and are here recorded after the decoded names.

No he escrito los dias passados cosa de los negoçios mayores del General [de 105] por no aver sabido nada de importancia, por aver estado absente de Madrid [65] y de los viejos [177] y perturbantes [178] si^{512} algunos ay, como aora me an dicho algunos en Madrid [65] aún los ay, Dios remedie a todo. Tanbien no queria escrivir cosa de pesadumbre al General [a 105] a la qual no supiesse dar algun medio para remediarla, pues bien me imagino los cuydados que tiene particularmente de las cosas de España y me lastiman el coraçon más ciertamente que otra cosa en esta vida, aunque me assiguro que nuestro Señor no faltará con su ayuda y consuelo por ser la causa tan suya como es. Quando me parti para andar a Madrid [65] traté largamente con Joseph Acosta [173] et despues de mucha plática mostro estar discontento de que el General [105] non hizo nada de aquello que él y Gil [175] propusieron al fin de sus travajos, y me dixo que Gil [175] quedava tan bien assi; y que attribuýanlo a lo que el General [105] creýva demasiado a Marcen [172], y a lo que el avia negociado con el General [105] y Alarcon [166], quando estava en Roma [61]. Al fin quiso persuader a Personio [108] que escriviesse, como de suyo muy encarescidamente al General [a 105] persuadiendo que llamasse Congregacion general [22 16 17 27 13 25 27 26 11 29 39 17 37 27 37 17 25 13 20 19 37], porque sin duda otramente lo harian los Procuradores [19 39 12 18 13 16 22 31 13 20 24 39 13 25 12] con la primera comodidad y porque en llegando a Madrid [65] el Provincial [176] mi dixo con mucha efficacia las mismas palabras, añadiendo más que si el General [105] non lo hazía de suyo que el Rey [82] lo pidiria y el Conde [86] de [24 25] Chinchon [22 28 29 17 22 28 16 17] le avia ya comunicado ablar en ello, no sé *quorsum ista dicebantur* benché de las buenas intenciones de Joseph Acosta [173] y del Provincial [176] y Personio [108] no puede dudar, toda via porque le pidian entrambi que lo escri-

512. perturbantes si] *obscured by damage* R

viesse al General [a 105] en su proprio nombre, parecio dar quenta de todo. En Madrid [65] hallé mucha disunione todos casi contra il Rettore [29 19 13 25 22 11 16 13 37] y entre los demas a Porres [174] hecho ya de los viejos [177]. Sebastian [180] está malissimo tanto con il Rettore [29 19 13 25 22 11 16 13 37] quanto el Provincial [176]. En el camino de la buelta toppé con Joseph Acosta [173] que yva para hallar a Luys de Mendoça [82][513] y me dixo llamado, aunque en la casa donde salia dexó otra voz. Pareciale que podia ser para las cosa de Aragon [20 13 36 27 16 17] donde yo le dixe que ya Sebastian [180] no yva por la contradicion que el Provincial [176] le avia hecho en esto, que entonces me dixo Joseph de Acosta [173] que si Luys de Mendoza [82] quesiere llevar[514] a él con sigo yria, y no ha buelta hasta aora. Más no me se oferece por aora y esto es demasiado *in hoc genere*. Dios nuestro Señor consuele y esperançe al General [a 105] y entonces no dudo si no que todo yrá finalmente bien.

    De la Vuestra Paternidad
        hijo indegno
            Roberto Personio.[515]

[*Addressed, not in Persons's hand*:] Al molto R[do] in Xto P. N. Claudio Aquaviva Preposito Generall della Comp[a] di Giesú.

[*Endorsed*:] Madrid/[516] P Roberto Personio.[517]

Translation

I have not written the past days of the matter of the greater business of the general because I had learnt nothing of importance, for I was absent from Madrid and from the veterans[518] and the troublemakers (if there are any, as I have now been told there are still some in Madrid); may God put everything right. Also I did not want to write something that would cause concern to the general without knowing how to provide any remedy, since I can well imagine how many things you have to worry about, especially in relation to Spain: and for sure, my heart grieves me over this more than any other matter in this life. Still, I rest assured that our Lord will not fail with his help and comfort, its being so much his very own cause. When I left to go to Madrid, I consulted José de Acosta and after much discussion he showed himself to be discontented that the general had not done anything about the thing which he and Gil González proposed at the end of their assignments. He told me that Gil remained of that opinion, and that he put it down to the general's excessive trust of Fr Marcén, and to what he had negotiated with the general and Fr Alarcón when he was in Rome. In the end he sought to persuade Persons to write, independently as it were, very forcibly to the general, to urge him to call a general con-

    513. 82 is normally the cipher for the king.
    514. llevar] R *damaged*
    515. The salutation has decayed.
    516. R *damaged*
    517. R *damaged, with one word obscured, followed by largely illegible Spanish summary.*
    518. Presumably Persons means established Spanish Jesuits who might obstruct Acquaviva's plans for reform.

gregation, because otherwise the procurators would doubtless do so at the first opportunity. Also, when the provincial[519] came to Madrid he very earnestly told me exactly the same thing, adding moreover that if the general did not do it himself the king would demand it – and the count of Chinchón had already commissioned him to speak to that effect. I do not know if *these things were said*, although of the good intentions of Acosta and the provincial and Persons there could be no doubt; still, because they both asked that he write to the general in his own name, that seems to have accounted for everything. In Madrid there is much disunity, as almost everyone is opposed to the rector's wishes, including amongst others Fr Porres and the elders. Sebastián is just as evilly disposed towards the rector as the provincial.[520] On my way back I met Acosta, who was going to find Luis de Mendoza, and he left me a message,[521] although in the house he was leaving, he left another one. It seems that it could be about the matter of Aragon, in relation to which I told him that Sebastián did not plan to contradict what the provincial had done about this: at that time Acosta told me that Luis de Mendoza asked him to go with him, and he would go. Nothing else occurs to me to say for the present and this is already too much *of this kind*. May God our Lord console and give hope to the general and so I do not doubt but that all will turn out well in the end.

Your Paternity's unworthy son,
Robert Persons.

B148 From Claudio Acquaviva, Rome, possibly 5 July 1592

> SOURCE: Persons to Acquaviva, 9 September 1592 (B156).
> NOTE: This letter, about Acosta, seems not to have survived, but it may have been sent with the batch of 5 July, recorded in Tolet. 5/I, fols. 305v–306v, where letters have been summarized rather than copied or drafted in full; a letter to Persons may have been overlooked. Acquaviva wrote to Acosta on 6 July (ARSI, Cast. 6, fol. 125v).

B149 From Richard Verstegan, Antwerp, 24 July 1592

> SOURCE: Verstegan to Persons, 6 August 1592 (B152).
> NOTE: In this letter, which does not appear to have survived, Verstegan acknowledged receipt of a bill of exchange.

519. Gonzalo Dávila, provincial of Toledo.
520. Evidently there was debate amongst the Jesuits in Madrid relating to the rector of the Jesuit college (Juan de Sigüenza) and to the province of Aragon (where the provincial was Pedro Villalba). Francisco de Porres replaced Gonzalo Dávila as provincial of Toledo (including Madrid) in 1593; on Sebastián Hernández, a prominent local Jesuit who seems to have given Acquaviva much difficulty, see Acquaviva to Persons, 22 January 1590 (B48), 9 July 1590 (B69), and 31 August 1592 (B155), and Yepes to Persons, 9 October 1596 (B346).
521. Luis de Mendoza, an early member of the Society, was named as one of the *inquietos* in the visitation of Gil González Dávila. He was renowned for his indiscipline at the college in Madrid (Astrain, 3: 503, 612, 620–621).

B150 Speech to Philip II, Valladolid, 3 August 1592

SOURCES:
    ABSI, Coll P I 248–51, "Ad regem Hispaniae Oratio P. Personii ... recitata ab Alumno transcripta ex autographo" (Fr Persons's speech to the king of Spain ... declaimed by a student, transcribed from his own handwriting") = G

    Robert Persons, *Relacion de un sacerdote Inglés ... en la qual le da cuenta de la venida de Su Magestad a Valladolid, y al Colegio de los Ingleses* (Madrid, 1592), fols. 32–40 (Latin, with Spanish translation) = M

    Robert Persons [or Joseph Creswell], *A relation of the King of Spaines receiving in Valliodolid, and in the Inglish College of the same towne, in August last past of this yere 1592* (Antwerp, 1592), 27–31 (incomplete, with English summary) = Antwerp

SPANISH TRANSLATION: Diego de Yepes, *Historia particular de la persecucion de Inglaterra* (Madrid, 1599), 759–762, a reprint of the Spanish translation in *Relacion de un sacerdote Inglés* (above).

NOTE: This speech was composed, supposedly by Persons, for delivery by one of the students on the occasion of the king's visit to Valladolid, along with his son Philip and daughter Isabella Clara Eugenia. In *A relation of the King of Spaines receiving in Valliodolid*, 27–30, the speaker is described as "a youth of verie gratefull aspect, and commelie action. ... he uttered [the speech] with such good grace and hartie affection, and with so effectual words and speech in the Latin tongue, as greatlie pleased all men, and made deepe impression in the hearers, especiallie to such as knew the speaker (whereof also his Maiestie was partelie advertised by a father that stood neere him) to be the son of a worshipfull gentleman of our contrie, that dyed in prison for his religion, and that the youth himself being then but 14 yeares of age had bin twise or thrise imprisoned in Ingland for confession of the catholique faith, with two of his brethren, before they came into theis parts." Despite a discrepancy in dates, this would appear to be John Worthington (1573–1652), son of Richard Worthington of Blainscoe, who died in prison on 25 September 1590. His brothers Laurence and William came to Valladolid in 1594 and 1595 respectively (*Valladolid Registers*, 10–11, 29, 37–38). The sufferings and exploits of the Worthington brothers are recounted in Foley, 2: 75–135. John Worthington transferred to the English college in Seville in November 1592, and delivered another oration penned by Persons (B164; Murphy, 6–7, 104).

    Further speeches were made in many languages, expounding selected verses from Psalm 71 (72), beginning (as translated in *A relation*) "O Lord geve judgement unto the King, and justice unto the Kings son." The speech in Hebrew was delivered by Thomas More (b. 1565/1566), great-grandson of the martyr (*Valladolid Registers*, 16–17). Banners were displayed to exhibit the students' devotion to learning and piety, and a souvenir manuscript of poems and emblems, *Epigrammata Serenissimo Excellentissimoque Hispaniarum Principi Philippo 3º*, was entrusted to the prince's tutor, García de Loaysa y Girón. *Blackfan Annals*, 32–33, assigns the date 1591.

    The occasion is discussed by Berta Cano Echevarría and Ana Sáez-Hidalgo (introd.), *The Fruits of Exile: Emblems and Pamphlets from the English College at Valladolid* (Valladolid,

2009), xxxix–li. The volume includes reprints of the two pamphlets, an edition of the manuscript and reproductions of selections from the manuscript. On the event, see also Loomie, *Spanish Elizabethans*, 191; Williams, *St Alban's College*, 11; and McCoog, *Building the Faith of St Peter*, 112–113. Dominguez, *Radicals in Exile*, 104–111, treats the speech as supporting the diplomatic purposes of the royal progress through Castile into Aragon, "partlie (as is supposed) the better to appease and remove some litle difficulties raised there [in Aragon] by the evil humors and practises of some few unquiet persons" (*A relation*, 15).

Persons's English record of the event, printed in Antwerp, prints only the first two paragraphs of the Latin text and provides an English summary of the rest. The *Relacion de un sacerdote Inglés* differs from the English account in some respects, most notably in that it provides a complete text of the Latin oration, along with a Spanish translation.

The variants in the manuscript and print versions suggest that the speech was composed by Persons and then adapted for performance and publication. The text as it appears in the *Relacion* (*M*) was revised to address the king's two children and to enhance the compliments to the king, omitting a lengthy comparison of the king's hospitality to that of the Shunamite woman who provided for Elijah. *M* has been used as the copy for this edition, because, along with its Spanish translation, it appears to offer the most complete representation of the performance and arguably has more historical value. It is not certain, however, that *M* records the speech as delivered, as the sample of text given in the *Relation* (*Antwerp*) is closer to the manuscript version (*G*). A full critical apparatus is supplied to enable the reader to reconstruct the other versions.

Oratio habita ad Philippum Hispaniarum Regem potentissimum in Collegio Anglicano Vallisoletano

Singulari beneficio contigisse mihi arbitror hodierno die, potentissime, piissimeque Rex, quod cum caeteri mei socii, patres, fratresque corona hac circumfusi, conceptam animis laetitiam, cordiumque gaudium ex hac Maiestatis tuae, et serenissimorum Principum gratissima praesentia plenissime cumulatum,[522] oculis tantum, et vultu testentur; mihi soli inter caeteros sors haec[523] gratissima obtigerit, ut gestientis animi exultationem verbis quoque eloquar. Quod summam sane[524] mihi iucunditatem parit: non quod ego melius quam caeteri praestare hoc possim, sed quod exuberanti cordis affectui commodius hac oratione[525] satisfaciam, quam reliqui, qui erumpentem mentis ardorem vocis silentio premere coguntur.[526]

Quanquam ex altera quoque parte, summam profecto eloquendi mihi difficultatem facit, tum[527] temporis huius, tum sermonis etiam circumscriptio, qua iubeor esse brevissimus. Quid enim, quaeso, immensum illum ingentemque factorum tuorum nobilissi-

522. ex hac Maiestatis tuae, & serenissimorum Principum gratissima praesentia plenissime cumulatum] *M Antwerp*; ex desideratissima hac Maiestatis tuae praesentia cumulatum *G*

523. haec] *M Antwerp*; ista *G*

524. sane] *M Antwerp*; certe *G*

525. oratione] *G*; ratione *M Antwerp*

526. Paragraph break in Antwerp.

527. tum] *M*; cum *G Antwerp*

morum campum ingredienti, gloriosissime Monarcha, quid innumerabilia laudum tuarum encomia animo percurrenti, magis adversum, aut[528] incommodum cogitari potest, quam temporis angustiae et orationis praescripta brevitas? Idque multo magis mihi[529] hoc primo aditu ad Maiestatis tuae conspectum, quo, ut caetera omnia taceam, et silentio involvam, aliquid certe de Anglia nostra, vel tua potius[530] dicendum mihi fuerat: nonnulla de nobis ipsis,[531] filiis, alumnis, et hospitibus tuis: multa de Hispania dulcissima matrice[532] nostra: plurima vero de te, tuisque maximis, et infinitis in nos beneficiis. Quae omnia, cum vel omittere prorsus, vel in huius tantilli temporis angustias indecore plane compingere cogor, permolestum certe videbatur;[533] quamquam, ut verum fatear,[534] eo uno interim me solabar plurimum, quod tantam esse scirem Maiestatis tuae prudentiam, et in omni rerum genere, et nostrarum maxime cognitionem, usum, et singularem, felicissimamque memoriam,[535] ut quicquid ego dicturus sim, aut dicere his de rebus[536] possim, id tu ex unico nostrum[537] intuitu animo praeconciperes,[538] et benignitatis tuae assensu, sive dicentem me, sive gratulantem, sive gratias agentem, vel etiam supplicantem anteverteres.[539] Nota enim iam diu est[540] Maiestati tuae conditio nostra, nota causa, prospectae[541] difficultates, cognitum propositum, audita desideria, intellectae spes, non ignota studia: quibus omnibus cum tu, pro singulari tua pietate, et Regia[542] clementia, ac munificentia tantopere[543]

528. immensum illum ingentemque factorum tuorum nobilissimorum campum ingredienti, gloriosissime Monarcha, quid innumerabilia laudum tuarum encomia animo percurrenti, magis adversum, aut] *M*; immensam illam ingentemque factorum tuorum nobilissimorum sylvam ingredienti (gloriosissime monarcha) quid innumerabilia laudum tuarum encomia animo percurrenti, magis adversum, aut *Antwerp*; per ingentem illam factorum tuorum nobilissimorum sylvam ingredienti (gloriosissime princeps), quid laudum tuarum praeconia immensa animo percurrenti magis adversum et *G*

529. mihi] *M Antwerp*; not in *G*

530. vel tua potius] *M G*; not in *Antwerp*

531. de nobis ipsis] *M Antwerp*; etiam de nobis *G*

532. dulcissima matrice] *M*; dulcissima nutrice *Antwerp*; nutrice *G*

533. cogor; permolestum certe videbatur] *M*; cogar; permolestum sane videbatur *G Antwerp*. *G*'s use of the subjunctive after *cum* is more correct.

534. ut verum fatear] *M Antwerp*; not in *G*

535. et in omni rerum genere, et nostrarum maxime cognitionem, usum, et singularem, felicissimamque memoriam] *M*; et in omni rerum genere (nostrarum maxime) cognitionem, usum, ac singularem, foelicissimamque memoriam *Antwerp*; ac sapientiam, tantam rerum omnium et nostrarum maxime cognitionem, memoriam atque experientiam *G*

536. his de rebus] *M Antwerp*; not in *G*

537. In both *M* and *G*, but not in *Antwerp*, the word "nostr[um]" is contracted, and may represent "nostrorum." See commentary to the translation.

538. praeconciperes] *M Antwerp*; praeconcipis *G*

539. sive gratulantem, sive gratias agentem, vel etiam supplicantem anteverteres] *M Antwerp*; vel gratulantem vel gratias agentem vel supplicantem antevertes *G*

540. Nota enim iam diu est] *M G*; Nota est enim iamdiu *Antwerp*

541. prospectae] *M*; perspectae *G Antwerp*

542. Regia *M Antwerp*; regali *G*

543. tantopere *M Antwerp*; tam paterne *G*

faveas, ac patrocineris; non ista nobis tam commemorare necesse est, quam gratis animis prosequi, quam memoria sempiterna complecti, quam⁵⁴⁴ extensis manibus, oculis, cordibusque (quod certe⁵⁴⁵ facimus) ad coelum usque quotidie transmittere: ubi tantae beneficentiae praemium et remuneratio tibi futura est sempiterna.⁵⁴⁶

Nam si Abdias ille, vir potens, et timens Deum, ut inquit Scriptura, tantum gloriabatur apud Heliam prophetam, et merito,⁵⁴⁷ quod centum Dei servos protexisset, persequente Jezabele, et mortem inferente; quid hic dicemus, ubi omnia sunt ampliora? *Nunquid non indicatum est tibi domino meo,* inquit Abdias ad Heliam, *quid fecerim, cum interficeret Jezabel prophetas Domini? Quod absconderim de prophetis Domini centum viros in speluncis,*⁵⁴⁸ *et paverim eos pane, et aqua?* At ego dico: Nonne manifestum est, et celebratum in universo Orbe, quid fecerit Rex Hispaniarum Philippus cum Jezabel Anglicana sacerdotes Dei, et Catholicos eiiceret, persequeretur, et ad caedem quaereret? Quod non tantum centum viros, sed multas centurias internecioni eripuerit: neque absconderit speluncis,⁵⁴⁹ sed palam potius,⁵⁵⁰ civitatibus, ac domibus suis acceperit:⁵⁵¹ nec pane tantum, et aqua paverit, sed honorifice, liberaliter, ac munificentissime sustentaverit? Quae aetas, quod saeculum, quae hominum memoria, aut posteritas de his conticescet?⁵⁵²

544. quam] *M Antwerp*; quam Deo offerre *G*
545. certe] *M Antwerp*; not in *G*
546. praemium & remuneratio tibi futura est sempiterna] *M*; praemium certissimum ac remuneratio tibi futura est sempiterna *Antwerp*; pretium ac remuneratio certissima tibi futura est *G*. *Antwerp* breaks off here; hence the editorial paragraph break.
547. merito] *M*; merito quidem *G*
548. Vulgate reads (3 Rg 18:13): centum viros quinquagenos et quinquagenos in speluncis
549. speluncis] *M*; eos in speluncis *G*
550. potius] *M*; potius urbibus *G*
551. acceperit] *M*; exceperit *G*
552. Paragraph break in *G*, followed by a passage omitted in *M*: "Testantur divinae litterae gratissimam fuisse Deo mulieris illius Sunamitidis cogitationem et orationem ad virum suum, qua perspecta Elizaei exulantis et faciem Jezabelis fugientis necessitate, dixit quidem piissime, *Faciamus homini Dei caenaculum parvum et ponamus ei in eo lectulum et mensam et sellam et candelabrum ut cum venerit ad nos, maneat ibi.* Non faciam hic comparationem ullam, non enim sumus nos Elizaei neque ullo modo cum illo componendi, cum longissime absimus ab illius viri sanctissimi meritis ac virtute, hoc unum tamen confidenter dicam, nos eidem Deo caeli servire cui ille, nec admodum dissimilem esse causam aut disparem exilii conditionem, cum ille Jezabelis Idololatrae nos Isabellae hereticae iracundiam furorem et persecutionem declinamus. In te vero, Rex nobilissime, omnia longe illustriora cernuntur quam in pia illa Sunamitide quae singularem tamen accepit a Deo remunerationem: Tu enim non parva illa caenacula sed ampla potius Seminaria et ornatissima bonarum tuarum ac virtutum domicilia nobis condis, neque alia illa necessaria parva et humilia quae piissima mulier pro tenuitate sua commemorat subministranda nobis, sed omnia potius pro magnitudine tua grande et munificentissima: victum nimirum et vestitum, habitationem, studia, praeceptores, caeteraque omnia his consona et conformia, ut si remunerationum divinarum magnitudo ex operum humanorum praestantia et dignitate expectanda est (ut certe est) non dubitamus ingentem gloriae cumulum Maiestati Tuae in caelis quoque esse repositum ob egregiam hanc tuam in istos miseros benificentiam; non enim indignitas nostra meritorum tuorum magnitudini officiet, sed proderit potius, cum tanto clarius solius Dei causa fecisse te constet, quanto minus nos ut causa nostra faceres, mereri potuimus." For English translation, see the commentary below.

Et certe video pientissimum Deum, cum populum Israeliticum[553] ob sua flagitia in exilium Babylonicum extrusisset, placata tamen ira, tanti aestimasse reditum eius in patriam ut ad eam unam rem, Cyrum regem potentissimum excitandum, et summis beneficiis afficiendum, annis plusquam ducentis[554] praedixerit per Isaiam prophetam, quam ille nasceretur. *Haec*, inquit Isaias, *dicit Dominus christo meo Cyro, cuius apprehendi dexteram, ut subiiciam ante faciem eius gentes, et dorsa regum vertam, et ante te ibo, et gloriosos terrae humiliabo, et dabo tibi thesauros absconditos, et arcana secretorum, propter servum meum Jacob, et Israel electum meum: vocavi te nomine tuo, accinxi te, et non cognovisti me.* Haec ille. Quod si propter Israeliticum populum, et semen Jacob aedibus restituendum propriis,[555] tanta Deus beneficia in Principem Ethnicum, qui ipsum non cognoscebat, effudit; quanta erunt merita tua, religiosissime Rex, qui et maiora his praestas, et pietatis causa, et[556] intuitu praestas? Et si ineffabilis Dei bonitas, amor, et misericordia, tanta animi solicitudine Cyrum redemptorem populo Israelitico providit;[557] cur etiam et nos[558] aliquando ab immensa eius bonitate idem non speremus? Cur non existimemus te nobis, Philippe, Cyrum esse datum, qui patriae nostrae nos aliquando reddas ad cultum Dei antiquum renovandum? Cur non cogitemus ideo Dominum apprehendisse manum tuam in tot rebus magnis et mirabilibus quas fecisti, ideo tot gentes, et infideles, tot haereticos[559] ante faciem tuam, tuorumque[560] subiecisse, ideo tot dorsa regum vertisse, ideo tot gloriosos terrae humiliasse, et monarchiam tuam, frementibus licet haereticis, et impiis omnibus, tantopere extulisse;[561] ideo denique thesauros absconditos Indiarum, et arcana secretorum aliorum regnorum longissime positorum tibi uni pandisse;[562] ut hoc tandem semen dispersum Jacob, hos electos quos vides Israelis filios, hos sacerdotes, hos levitas, hos Catholicos Anglicanos patriae suae aliquando[563] restituas? hoc opus grande, difficile,[564] et gloriosum diebus tuis perficias: ad quod te vocatum, et divina providentia praeordinatum confidimus.[565]

Et quia hoc uno verbo complexus sum omnia, et vereor, ne longius progressus sim ardore dicendi,[566] non dicam amplius. Hoc unum tantum praetermittere, aut silere[567]

553. pientissimum ... Israeliticum] *M;* misericordissimum ... Hebraeum *G*
554. ducentis] *M;* quadringentis *G*
555. aedibus restituendum propriis] *M;* terrae suae restituendum *G*
556. religiosissime Rex, qui et maiora his praestas, et pietatis causa, et] *M;* princeps religiosissime, qui maiora his praestas, et pietatis causae atque *G*
557. providit] *M;* providit, ut in libertatem restitueret *G*
558. etiam et nos] *M;* nos quoque *G*
559. tot haereticos] *M; not in G*
560. tuorumque] *M;* tuorum *G*
561. frementibus licet haereticis, et impiis omnibus, tantopere extulisse] *M;* tantopere (frementibus licet haereticis et impiis omnibus) sublimasse *G*
562. longissime positorum tibi uni pandisse] *M;* longinquorum tibi dedisse *G*
563. patriae suae aliquando] *M; not in G*
564. difficile] *M;* et difficile *G*
565. Editorial paragraph break.
566. dicendi] *M;* dicendi quam debebam *G*
567. Hoc unum tantum praetermittere, aut silere] *M;* unum hoc tamen omittere *G*

nullo modo possum, quod fratres isti mei, sociique tanquam fidei commissum uno ore, ac animo vehementer mihi commendatum, Maiestati tuae[568] offerendum, suoque nomine spondendum voluerunt: ut cum tantis hisce Maiestatis tuae beneficiis nulla alia ratione[569] pares esse possint, gratissimos tamen se fore semper pollicentur: adeo ut quicquid sint in praesenti, vel futuri[570] sint aliquando, sive in hac vita, sive in alia, id Maiestati tuae serviturum perpetuo. Itaque omnium nomine, ac postulatione offero hic quicquid possumus, valemus, sumus, aut erimus. Offero animos, offero vires Maiestati tuae: trado in manus nostrorum omnium conatus, studia,[571] vitas, mortesque, neque nostra tantummodo, sed et parentum[572] etiam nostrorum, amicorum, necessariorum, Catholicorum omnium, qui in Anglia sunt. Quae omnia, licet parva sint,[573] et Maiestatis tuae magnitudini non necessaria; ab eadem tamen magnitudine non est alienum, parva, magno animo, et amore oblata, boni consulere. Quod Maiestatem tuam facturam non dubitamus. Quam Deus Optimus Maximus[574] diutissime nobis, et universae reipublicae Christianae conservet.

Spanish translation from Relacion de un sacerdote Ingles, *fols. 35–40*

Oracion hecha a la Magestad del Rey Catolico en el Colegio Inglés de Valladolid

Por singular merced y beneficio tengo el dia de oy, poderosissimo, y piissimo Rey, que quando todos los demas padres, y hermanos compañeros mios, que en este teatro estan, testifican solo con los ojos, y con el rostro la grande alegria de sus animos, y el gozo de sus coraçones, que de la gratissima presencia de Vuestra Magestad y Altezas han concebido, a mí entre todos me aya cabido esta dichosa suerte, que diga con palabras el contento que el ánimo regozijado tiene. Lo qual en grande manera me alegra; no porque yo pueda hazer esto mejor que los demas, sino porque desta manera podre más comodamente satisfazer al copioso afecto del coraçon, quando los demas detienen con silencio, como forçados, la fuerça con que sale el ardor de sus animos: aunque por otra parte me causa summa dificultad para poder hablar, assi este tiempo en que hablo, como la brevedad de lo que tengo de dezir; pues se me manda que sea brevissimo. Porque pregunto, gloriosissimo Monarca, qué cosa más adversa, ni incommoda podria ofrecersele al que entra en aquel inmenso, y grande campo de los nobilissimos hechos de Vuestra Magestad al que va passando por su ánimo, para explicar fuera, los inmensos titulos de sus alabanças; que la estrechura del tiempo, y la brevedad señalada de la oracion? Y mucho

568. Maiestati tuae] *M*; et Maiestati vestrae *G et sic infra* Maiestati/-s vestrae
569. tantis hisce Maiestatis tuae beneficiis nulla alia ratione] *M*; nulla alia ratione tantis vestris beneficiis *G*
570. semper pollicentur: adeo ut quicquid sint in praesenti, vel futuri] *M*; semper, adeo ut quicquid sint in praesentia, aut futuri *G*
571. studia] *M*; studia, orationes, sacrificia *G*
572. nostra tantummodo, sed et parentum] *M*; nostrorum solum modo, sed parentum *G*
573. licet parva sint] *M*; etsi parva sunt *G*
574. Optimus Maximus] *M*; Dominus Noster *G*

más a mí en esta primera entrada, que hago a la presencia de Vuestra Magestad en la qual, callando otras muchas cosas, y embolviendolas en silencio, era cierta razon que dixera algo de nuestra Inglaterra, o por mejor dezir, no nuestra sino de Vuestra Magestad que dixera algunas cosas de nosotros mismos, como de hijos, alumnos, y peregrinos acogidos de su Real clemencia: que dixera muchas de España, que como dulcissima madre, y tierna ama nos cria: y muchissimas de Vuestra Magestad y de los infinitos, y grandes beneficios que nos a hecho, y haze. Lo qual todo como me sea forçoso, o dexarlo, o no hazer más que tocarlo, no con el decoro que querria; no pudo dexar de parecerme cosa trabajosa quando se me encargó; aunque de otra parte, para dezir verdad, me consolava mucho el saber quan grande es la prudencia de Vuestra Magestad, quan grande su sabiduria; quan grande conocimiento y esperiencia tiene de todas las cosas, y singularmente de las nuestras; quan singular y felicissima memoria: de suerte que todo lo que yo dixesse destas cosas, y pudiera dezir, lo concibiria[575] Vuestra Magestad de una sola vista con que nos mirasse, y assi prevendria con el benevolo assenso de su benignidad todo lo que yo dixesse, aora fuesse congratulandome, aora dando gracias, aora supplicando algo a Vuestra Magestad. Porque ya, señor, es sabido de Vuestra Magestad nuestro estado, sabida nuestra causa, vistas las dificultades, conocido el proposito, oydos los desseos, entendidas las esperanças, no desconocidos los cuydados. A las quales cosas todas como Vuestra Magestad por su singular piedad, y Real clemencia, y liberalidad tanto ayude y favorezca, no es tan necessario que contemos estas cosas, quanto que con gratos pechos las agradezcamos, que con memoria eterna las tengamos como abraçadas, que con las manos levantadas, con los ojos, con los coraçones, como lo hazemos cada dia, las remitamos al cielo, donde tendra Vuestra Magestad el premio certissimo, y eterna paga de tal beneficio.

Porque si aquel Abdias varon ilustre, y temeroso de Dios, como dize la Escritura, tanto se gloriava, y con razon, hablando con Helias profeta, de aver guardado cien siervos del Señor persiguiendolos Jezabel, y dandoles la muerte: qué diremos aqui, donde todo es muy más aventajado? Por ventura no te han contado, señor mio, dixo Abdias a Helias, lo que yo hize quando matava Jezabel los profetas del Señor, que escondi cien dellos en cuevas, y los sustenté alli con pan, y agua? Pero yo digo: No es ya sabido, y celebrado en el mundo universo lo que a hecho el Rey de las Españas Filipo, quando la Inglesa Jezabel echa los sacerdotes, y Catolicos de su Reyno, quando los persigue y busca para quitarles la vida? que no solo a cien varones, sino a muchos centenares a librado de la muerte; ni los a escondido en cuevas, sino que los a recebido publicamente, y puesto en sus ciudades; dádoles casas, y sustento, no solo de pan, y agua, sino honradissimo, liberalissimo, y magnificentissimo? Qué edad, qué siglo, qué memoria de hombres, o qué posteridad podra jamas de tal hecho olvidarse?

Y cierto, que considerando esto me parece que veo a aquel piadosissimo Dios, que aviendo echado al pueblo de Israel por sus pecados en el destierro de Babilonia, aplacada su ira, estimó tanto que aquel pueblo bolviesse de aquel destierro a su patria, que para ello solo se determinó de escoger, y levantar a Cyro Rey poderosissimo,

---

575. concibiria] M; entendiera M var.

haziendole muchos beneficios y mercedes, y prometiendole por el profeta Isaias dozientos años antes que naciesse, que assi dize Isaias, *Esto dize el Señor a mi christo Cyro, cuya mano diestra he tomado para que se arrodillen delante dél las gentes, y los Reyes se le rindan; iré delante de ti, y humillaré los gloriosos de la tierra; darete los tesoros escondidos; descubrirte he los secretos más cerrados por mi siervo Jacob, y por mi escogido Israel; he te llamado por tu nombre; he te escogido, y tú no me has conocido.* Esto dize alli. Pues si por el pueblo de Israel, y por bolver la decendencia de Jacob a su patria hizo Dios tan grandes mercedes y beneficios a un Principe Gentil, que no le conocia; quan grandes seran los merecimientos de Vuestra Magestad Catolico y religiosissimo Rey, que haze mayores cosas que no Cyro, y las haze movido de piedad, religion, y virtud. Y si la inefable bondad de Dios, y su amor, y misericordia tuvo tanto cuydado de proveer que Cyro fuesse librador de su pueblo; porqué no esperaremos nosotros esto mismo de su inmensa bondad? porqué no pensaremos que nos a dado a Vuestra Magestad por Cyro nuestro, que nos restituya, y buelva a nuestra patria, para renovar el antiguo culto, con que Dios alli solia ser honrado? porqué no pensaremos que por esto a tomado el Señor la mano de Vuestra Magestad para hazer tantas cosas grandes, y admirables como con ella a hecho; y que por esto a sujetado delante de Vuestra Magestad y de sus gentes tantos pueblos, y naciones infieles, y hereges; y que por esto a puesto a sus pies tantos Reyes, a humillado tantos gloriosos de la tierra, y levantado tanto su monarchia, por más que los hereges, y los malos ayan bramado; y que por esto a dado a Vuestra Magestad los tesoros escondidos de las Indias, y descubierto los secretos de los otros Reynos por más apartados que esten; para que compadeciendose desta semilla de Jacob esparcida, destos hijos de Israel que aqui vee, destos sacerdotes, destos levitas, de estos Catolicos Ingleses, los restituya algun dia a su patria, y acabe en sus dias esta grande empresa, dificil, y gloriosa; para lo qual confiamos que la divina providencia le ha llamado y escogido.

Y porque en esta palabra he abraçado todo lo que tenía que dezir, y temo de no aver passado más adelante de lo que devia, con la fuerça, y el ardor que me ha hecho hablar, no diré más: pero esta sola cosa no puedo dexar, ni callarla, que estos hermanos y compañeros mios que aqui estan, como fideicommisso me encomendaron instantemente con una misma boz, y ánimo para ofrecerlo, y consagrarlo en su nombre a Vuestra Magestad que pues no pueden en manera alguna agradecer como deven estos beneficios, que de mano de Vuestra Magestad han recebido, ofrecen de ser eternamente agradecidos como pudieren; de manera que todo lo que aora son, y seran en algun tiempo en esta vida, o en la otra, servira siempre a Vuestra Magestad y assi ofrezco aqui en nombre y boz de todos, todo lo que podemos, somos, y seremos; ofrezco los animos; ofrezco las fuerças; pongo en manos de Vuestra Magestad todos nuestros conatos, desseos, vidas, y muertes; y no solo de nosotros, sino tambien de nuestros padres, amigos, y parientes, y de todos los Catolicos de Inglaterra. Las quales cosas todas aunque son pequeñas, y parezcan a la grandeza de Vuestra Magestad no necessarias; pero no es ageno dessa grandeza tener a bien las cosas pequeñas que con grande ánimo y amor se ofrecen: lo qual no dudamos que hará Vuestra Magestad a quien Dios nuestro Señor guarde muchos años para bien nuestro, y de toda la Republica Christiana.

Translation

An oration delivered before Philip, most powerful king of the Spaniards, in the English College, Valladolid

I consider that I have been favoured with a singular benefit this day (most powerful and pious king), in that while all my other friends, fathers and brothers, surrounding me in this multitude, testify as much by their eyes as their countenance the happiness they have conceived in their minds and the joy of their hearts made absolutely perfect by the most welcome presence of Your Majesty and Your Most Serene Highnesses,[576] that most welcome lot has fallen upon me alone, amongst the others, also to utter in words the exultation of my eager spirit – something that truly fills me with the most intense joy: not because I am better able than the rest to perform this, but because I may better satisfy my heart's overflowing feeling in this oration than the rest, who are forced to suppress the vehement ardour of their minds without giving it voice.

On the other hand, what makes it particularly difficult for me to speak out is that I am bound to the very briefest compass both of time and speech. For what, I beg, could be imagined more contrary or distressing to the heart, entering that immense, great plain of your most noble deeds (most glorious prince), or rushing through the boundless expanse of your praises, than to be restricted to narrow limits of time and brevity of speech?[577] All the more for me, when, being for the first time admitted to Your Majesty's presence, to pass over everything else, and cover it up in silence, I ought to say something, for sure, about our England (or yours, rather), as well as a few things about ourselves, your sons and students and guests, many things about Spain our sweetest mother,[578] and more indeed about you and your great and infinite benefits to us. To be compelled to pass over all these things completely, or to compress them in a clearly unsuitable way into this tiny narrow space of time: that seemed troublesome indeed. But all the same, to tell the truth, I comforted myself in the meantime with one thing above all: that I know Your Majesty's prudence to be so great – your understanding, memory and experience of affairs of every kind, and especially ours, and your unique, most happy way of calling them to mind[579] – that whatever I am about to say or could say on these matters, you would have already conceived in your heart by your

---

576. The manuscript version addresses the king only.

577. The printed version embellishes the tribute to the king's achievements by replacing the manuscript's *sylvam* ("forest") with *campum* ("plain"), emphasizing the expanse rather than the diversity of the king's deeds, and by replacing *praeconia* with *encomia*, preferring a word associated with a life's work rather than a single public proclamation.

578. The more elaborate *dulcissima matrice* (literally, "very sweet nursing mother") replaces the manuscript's *nutrice* ("nurse").

579. The phrase *singularem, felicissimamque memoriam* ("unique and most happy calling to mind") is an addition made in the printed version to enhance the description of the king's knowledge, flattering what many commentators have referred to as his obsessive attention to detail; see, for example, Parker, 61–79.

particular regard for what is ours,⁵⁸⁰ and by the assent of your favour have anticipated my speech and my congratulation and my thanksgiving and my supplication: for our condition has been well known to Your Majesty for a long time now, and our cause; you have anticipated our difficulties,⁵⁸¹ been cognisant of what we propose and given ear to our desires. You have understood our hopes, and our studies are not unknown to you: to all of these you give such great⁵⁸² favour and patronage, in accordance with your singular piety, regal clemency, and munificence. And so we need not bring these very things so much to mind, as to pursue them with grateful hearts, to hold them fast eternally in our memory, to commit them to the heavens, stretching out our hands and eyes and sinews (which we do), even daily, when the prize⁵⁸³ and reward for such great beneficence will be yours for ever.

For if Obadiah, that mighty and God-fearing man, as Scripture says, boasted so much to Elijah the prophet (and with justice) that he had protected a hundred servants of God when Jezebel was pursuing them and threatening them with death, what shall we say here when all the circumstances are intensified? "Hath it not been told thee, my lord (said Obadiah to Elijah), what I did when Jezebel killed the prophets of the Lord, how I hid a hundred men of the prophets of the Lord, in caves, and fed them with bread and water?"⁵⁸⁴ But I say: is it not manifest and celebrated in all the world, what Philip, king of the Spaniards, did when the English Jezebel threw out the priests of God and the Catholics, persecuted them and sought their ruin: that he snatched not just a hundred men, but many hundreds from death, nor did he hide them away in caves, but openly rather, received them in his cities and homes, nor fed them with bread and water alone, but sustained them honourably, liberally, and munificently? What age, what century, what memory or posterity of men could keep silent about these things?⁵⁸⁵

580. Alternatively, "regard for Ours", i.e. members of the Society of Jesus.

581. The manuscript version has *perspectae*; the change to *prospectae* suggests that the king not only understood, but had foreseen their difficulties.

582. *Tantopere* ("so greatly") may be a mistake. The manuscript reads *tam paterne* ("so fatherly').

583. *Praemium* replaces the manuscript's synonymous *pretium* ("prize, reward, recompense").

584. 1 Kgs 18:13; the Latin text of the letter quotes the Vulgate verbatim, except for the phrase "by fifty and fifty [in caves]." Cf. Loomie, *Spanish Elizabethans*, 191.

585. In the manuscript version, a lengthy comparison follows, between the king and the Shunamite woman (2 Kgs 4): "Holy Writ testifies how very acceptable to God was the regard and the language of that Shunamite woman towards His servant, who, having seen the need of Elijah while he was in exile and fleeing the face of Jezebel, said most piously: 'Let us make a little chamber for the man of God, and put a little bed in it for him, and a table, and a stool, and a candlestick, that when he cometh to us, he may abide there.' I would not make any comparison here, for we are not Elijahs nor must we be compared with him in any way, since we come very short of the virtue and merits of that holiest of men; but this one thing I may say with confidence, that we serve the same God as he, nor is our cause altogether dissimilar nor our condition of exile unlike his, since we are avoiding the rage and fury and persecution of the heretic Elizabeth as he did that of the idolater Jezebel. But in you, most noble king, all those things are much more eminently apparent than in that pious Shunamite woman, who nevertheless received a singular reward from God. For you are

And surely I see that our most just and merciful God,[586] after sending the Israelite people into exile in Babylon because of their outrageous sins, nevertheless valued their return to their native land so highly that, once His wrath was propitiated, He proclaimed, by the prophet Isaiah, more than two hundred years before Cyrus was born, that that most powerful king would be incited to that one purpose and moved by the greatest inducements.[587] "Thus (says Isaiah) says the Lord to my anointed Cyrus, whose right hand I have taken hold of, to subdue nations before his face and turn the backs of kings: I will go before thee and will humble the great ones of the earth, and I will give thee hidden treasures and the concealed riches of secret places, for the sake of my servant Jacob and Israel my elect; I have even called thee by thy name, I have girded thee: and thou hast not known me."[588] That is what he said. And so, if for the sake of restoring the Israelites and the seed of Jacob to their very own homes and land God poured out such great benefits on a pagan prince who did not even acknowledge him, how much more do you deserve, most religious prince, who are performing greater things than these, and excel in the inner knowledge and cause of piety? And if God's inexpressible goodness, love and pity, with such great solicitude of spirit, provided the people of Israel with Cyrus as their redeemer,[589] why should we not also sometime hope for the same out of his boundless goodness? Why should we not regard you, Philip, as our Cyrus, given to restore us to our native land one day, to renew the ancient worship of God? Why should we not suppose that this is the reason why the Lord has taken hold of your right hand in the many great and marvellous things you have done, why He has subdued so many nations and infidels and heretics before your face and the face of your people, why He has turned the backs of kings, why He has humbled so many of the great ones of the earth, and so greatly raised[590] your monarchy (let the heretics and all the impious grind their teeth),

---

founding, not those small cells but rather ample seminaries for us, and richly embellished dwelling places of your gifts and virtues: we do not need to be supplied with all the other small and modest necessities which in accordance with her scant means that most pious woman calls to mind, but rather all according to your most munificent and excellent greatness: food, to be sure, and raiment, habitation, studies, teachers, and all other things consonant and conformable with these, so that if an abundance of divine rewards can be expected for the dignity and excellence of human works (as certainly is the case) we do not doubt that a great weight of glory is laid up for Your Majesty in heaven also, on account of this exceptional beneficence of yours to those pitiable people; for our unworthiness will not stand in the way of the magnitude of your merits, but rather increase it, since the less we are able to deserve your doing this for our sake, the more clearly it is certain that you have acted for God's sake alone." The printed version omits the passage, possibly because the comparison was deemed less than flattering to the king.

586. The printed version replaces *misericordissimum* with *pientissimum*, a variant of *pietissimum*, stressing that God's mercy is bound up with his justice.

587. The printed version replaces *quadrigentis* ("four hundred") with *ducentis* ("two hundred").

588. Isa. 45:1–5, with omissions.

589. The manuscript comments: "to restore them to liberty," which may have been omitted in error.

590. The more energetic *extulisse* replaces the synonymous *sublimasse* ("raise up") given in the manuscript.

and finally, why He has laid open[591] the hidden treasures of the Indies for you alone, and the concealed riches of other remote, widespread kingdoms: that at length you may at some time restore to their native land this scattered seed of Jacob, these elect sons of Israel whom you see, these priests, these Levites, these English Catholics, that you may perfect this great and difficult and glorious work, to which we believe you have been called and preordained by divine providence in your time?

And since I have summed everything up in this one word, and I fear that out of the passion of my speaking I have continued too long, I shall not amplify my theme any further. But this one important thing I may in no wise pass over in silence,[592] which those brothers and companions of mine in the faith, as it were, have commissioned with one voice and heart, and vehemently commended to me, desiring it to be offered to Your Majesty and pledged in their name: that since they are not able to match such great benefits as yours in any other way, nevertheless they will always be most grateful, such that whatever there may be in the present, or at any time in the future, whether it be in this life or the next, that will be put to Your Majesty's service for ever. And so, in the name of all of them and by their request, I offer here whatever we are able, whatever we have strength for, whatever we are or will be; I offer our hearts, I offer our strength to Your Majesty; I place in your hands all our studies, our efforts,[593] lives and deaths, and not only ours alone, but those of our parents and friends, relatives, and all Catholics who are in England; although all of these are small and not indispensable to the greatness of Your Majesty, nevertheless it is not foreign to that same greatness to think well of such small things offered up with great love and spirit, which we do not doubt Your Majesty will perform, whom may God, the greatest and best,[594] preserve very long for us and the whole of Christendom.

B151 From Claudio Acquaviva, Rome, 3 August 1592

> SOURCE: ARSI, Cast. 6, fol. 127v, from the general's register for the province of Castile.
>
> NOTE: Acquaviva will provide letters of authority for Persons to go to Seville and found a college there. There are some delicate questions about the teaching in the English seminary at Valladolid and the neighbouring college of St Ambrose; wisdom is needed in deciding how best to manage this.

P. Roberto Personio, Agosto 3, en Valladolid.

Las cartas que Vuestra Reverencia pide para el viaje de Sevilla y empresa del Seminario, y las copias dellas se le embiarán con el ordinario que viene de manera que estén

---

591. *Tibi uni pandisse* ("laid open to you alone") replaces the manuscript's simpler *tibi dedisse* ("given you").

592. *Praetermittere, aut silere* ("pass over or remain silent about") adds a flourish to the manuscript's *omittere*.

593. The manuscript includes *orationes, sacrificia* ("prayers, sacrifices") which may have been overlooked in error when the printed version was prepared.

594. The more exalted appellation, *Deus Optimus Maximus*, replaces the manuscript's *Deus Dominus Noster*.

alla al tiempo que diçe le seran menester. El Señor le dé en todo el buen successo que todos deseamos.

Siento mucho que entre nuestros Maestros no aya la union que conviene, por que demas de ser en sí mesma cosa de mucho inconveniente, redunda en daño y poca edificaçion de los oyentes. Para lo que toca a ese seminario yo escrivo con este ordinario al Padre Gonzalo de Avila que procure darles a Gaspar Alonso aunque sea dandole en Castilla algun trueque, Vuestra Reverencia le soliçite, que creo lo hará.

Los remedios que me diçe Vuestra Reverencia ha puesto el Rector del Seminario para evitar los inconvenientes que se han començado a experimentar tienen otro digno de consideraçion, y es que no queda el Seminario del todo sujeto en cosas de letras, al Colegio, como saben Vuestra Reverencia y el Padre Cabredo que lo estan los Seminarios de aqui al Colegio Romano. Lo de las lectiones que tienen en casa para suplir lo que falta en el colegio puede pasar, aunque sea con dispensacion,[595] pero en lo otro deseo que miren, y me avisen, lo que sienten. En sus &c.

Translation

To Fr Robert Persons in Valladolid, 3 August.

The letters which Your Reverence asks for the journey to Seville and the project of the seminary, I will send, along with copies of them, with the next courier so that they will be there by the time that you say you will need them. May our Lord grant you good success in everything, as we all desire.

I am very sorry that there is not that unity amongst our teachers which there ought to be, because apart from being a very bad thing in itself, it causes harm and little edification to those who hear about it. With regard to the seminary, I am writing by this courier to Fr Gonzalo Dávila[596] so that he will see to it that they are given Gaspar Alonso,[597] even at the expense of bartering him for someone in Castile; should Your Reverence ask, I believe he will do it.

Besides the measures that Your Reverence tells me the rector of the seminary has implemented to avoid the inconveniences which have emerged, there is another worth considering: and that is that the seminary should not remain entirely dependent on the college for the teaching of letters[598] – as Your Reverence and Fr Cabredo know is the case of the seminaries here with the Roman college. You may allow lectures to be held in the house to supply those that are not available in the college, even if it involves a dispensation. But I would like you to look into the other, and let me know how you feel.

---

595. aunque sea con dispensacion] *supplied in margin* R
596. Gonzalo Dávila was provincial of Toledo.
597. Gaspar Alonso, consultor and confessor at Valladolid (McCoog, *Building the Faith of St Peter*, 210)
598. The neighbouring Spanish Jesuit college of St Ambrose.

B152 From Richard Verstegan, Antwerp, 6 August 1592

SOURCE: ABSI, Coll B, 57–58.
EDITION: Petti, 63–66, decoding the ciphers given in square brackets.
NOTE: Verstegan reports the arrest of Southwell and gives news on the state of the war between the Catholic League and Henry of Navarre, now King Henry IV of France.

Right Reverend

In my last unto you dated the 24 of the last moneth I acknowleged the receit of yours with the bill of exchange, which is promised to be paid the 16 of this present beeing two monethes after the date.

I am right sory to send you the ill newes of Fr Southwell his apprehension, who is now in combat with his mortall enemyes. Our Lord graunt him strenght to go forward as he hathe resolutely begun. And so shall he remain perpetuall victor. So much as hetherto I have understood thereof I have written in a sheete of paper enclosed in this pakett unto Sir Fraunces[599] but that paper is unsealed to the end he may send it with the other things therein conteyned, because I would save the labour to write it twice. Yett yf you see any inconvenience in this course you may please to let me understand it. Here are letters from London of the 28 of July by the which I understand that Navarr his ambassador is either departed, or uppon the point to departe but withoute either mony or men.[600] There are not any forces in levying for Navarr in Germany, and in Fraunce his meanes is very much decreassed espetially since the deathe of the Marshall of Biron,[601] so that he is almost brought unto[602] a very desperate state and I trust wilbe driven to great extremity when Our Duke shall enter with his forces.[603] Whereby it may please God some good oportunity may fall oute for victory [208], yf the occasion be taken hold on. And in my slender judgment it were good that the Spanish convoy [7 m 14 p me 20] that cometh from[604] the West Indies [38] having delivered their chardge in Spain [20] might foorthwith come into France [54] which may fall oute to espetiall good purpose yf some things do succede in England [25] that I shall not nede to name. I beseech you to consider hereof.

Thease late letters from England before mentioned do still signify the generall discontentment of the people, all marchandise and necessary comodities beeing very scarse, yet are victualls resonable cheape, which may procede of want of mony. And corne is[605]

---

599. Sir Francis Englefield, who attended at the Court in Madrid until just before his death in 1596 (Loomie, *Spanish Elizabethans*, 14–51).

600. Navarre's ambassador, Nicolas de Harlay, seigneur de Sancy (1546–1629), negotiated with Elizabeth for assistance in the war against the League.

601. Marshal Biron, killed at the siege of Epernay, 26 July 1592.

602. unto] into *Petti; unclear A*

603. Alessandro Farnese, Duke of Parma, died on 3 December, before he was able to intervene again on behalf of the League.

604. from] *replaces with* [deleted] A

605. is] *interlined with caret* A

so very aboundant that thease twenty yeares there was not such store, nor the same so good cheape.[606]

We heare not as yet of any pay, and that is the 11[607] moneth that we had nothing but the third parte of one monethes pay.[608] I do not directly perceave your fatherhoodes meaning touching the 230 florins which you have appointed me to receave over and above the 80^ld[609] for Mr Barcrofte[610] but I shalbe enforced to use thereof by reason of this great extremity, to the end I retaine my creditt here and content such as I do deale withall for intelligence, etc.

I sent of late unto Southwell [197][611] before I hard of his absence but I trust my letters will come to Garnet [195] his handes whose answere I expect the next weke. More for the presente I will not trouble you with but comitting your fatherhoode to God I humbly take my leave. Antwerp this 6 of August 1592.

      Your very assured servitour
         R. Verstegan.

[PS] We heare from Germany that the yong duke of Saxony, and the heire to the counte palatine of the Rhene are with the Emperour at Prage and bothe brought up under Catholike tutors.[612]

[Addressed:] Al molto R^do in X° Padre il P. Roberto Personio della compagnia di Giesu a Validolid.

[Endorsed by Persons:] Verstenghan[613] advises and accomptes Augusti 6 1592.
[Endorsed at letter head:] Vestingames advises Augusti 6 1592.

B153 To Claudio Acquaviva, 12 August 1592

SOURCE: ARSI, FG 691 (missing).

NOTE: See Acquaviva to Persons, 28 September (B158). The letter is cited by Albert J. Loomie, "The Authorship of 'An Advertisement written to a Secretarie of M. L. Treasurer of England ...'," *Renaissance News* 15 (1962): 201–207, but appears to have been mislaid (see the note to Persons's letter to Acquaviva, 26 June 1590, B67). Loomie refers to the funding of

---

606. good cheape] A; Petti interposes [and]. See OED, s.v. cheap, n.¹ 8a; cf. Dutch "goedkoop."
607. 11] with + interlined above A
608. On the unreliability of pensions for the English exiles in the Low Countries, see Loomie, *Spanish Elizabethans*, 26–40.
609. 80^ld] A; 80 li. Petti
610. Petti identifies this as Thomas Barcroft (Anstruther, 20), who was operating in Lancashire up to Whitsun 1592; he and Verstegan were at the English College, Rome, in 1584. A may read "Barrett," i.e., Richard Barret, president of the English college still at Rheims.
611. Or "Garlick"; see Garnet's letter of 26 July enclosed in Verstegan's despatch of mid-August (B154).
612. Christian II (1583–1611) succeeded his father as elector of Saxony in 1591; Frederick IV (1574–1610) succeeded his father Louis IV as elector Palatine in 1583, but only began his personal rule in 1592 after the death of his uncle and tutor John Casimir. The Holy Roman Emperor Rudolph II (1552–1612) held court in Prague.
613. Verstenghan] A, obscure; Verstenghan's Petti

Persons's *Philopater*. Persons enclosed an order to Thomas Fiesco, the factor general of the Hazienda, 11 August (ARSI, FG 651/640, item 27), for a payment of 500 escudos to Persons's agent in Antwerp, presumably Richard Verstegan, who was probably the author of two related English tracts and also arranged for the printing of the Antwerp edition of the *Philopater*. Persons informed Acquaviva that he had circulated the MS of the *Philopater* to José de Acosta, William Crichton, Rodrigo de Cabredo, and Sir Francis Englefield, for their comments and approval.

Persons's *Elizabethae Angliae Reginae ... in Catholicos sui regni edictum ... cum responsione*, published under the pseudonym Andreas Philopater, was first printed in Antwerp by Joannes Faber at Philip II's expense; in 1592 it was also printed in Lyon by Joannes Didier, in Rome by Aloysius Zannetti, and also in Germany; French and German translations were published in 1593 (*ARCR*, 1: nos. 885–892). See Victor Houliston, "The Lord Treasurer and the Jesuit: Robert Persons's Satirical *Responsio* to the 1591 Proclamation," *Sixteenth Century Journal* 32 (2001): 383–401; Harro Höpfl, *Jesuit Political Thought* (Cambridge, 2004), 104–105; Peter Lake, *Bad Queen Bess* (Oxford, 2016), 337–375; and Dominguez, *Radicals in Exile*, 121–127.

It is likely that Persons used the opportunity of the royal visit to the English college at Valladolid to secure funding for the *Philopater* and the proposed college at Seville. He also requested letters of recommendation for Seville (see Acquaviva's letters of 28 September and 24 November, B158, B162).

B154 From Henry Garnet via Richard Verstegan, Antwerp, mid-August 1592

SOURCE: ABSI, Coll B, fols. 35r–37v (olim pp. 49–51; formerly AAW, IV, 305), in Verstegan's hand.

EDITIONS: Petti, 67–71; Foley, 1: 352–354.

NOTE: Verstegan included a copy of Garnet's letter to him, along with some notes on other letters by Garnet and others, in his despatch to Persons. Garnet's letter, which is mainly concerned with the arrest of Southwell, is notable for its use of the merchant pretence, as well as the ironic references to papists.

> The copy of his letter to Verstegan [181][614]
> dated in London 26 of July 1592 *stylo novo*

After my harty comendations, I sent you letters of late which I hope are come to your handes concerning our merchandise, and manner of writing which I would willingly understand of. We are lyke to have heare a very plentifull yeare so that we may make great comoditie of corne, yf we be secret in our course whereof you shall know more by the next oportunitie. We would willingly understand some of your newes for all forreyne matters are here concealed. All our newes here is of taking of Jesuytes and priestes with great hope of discovery of highe treasons, but mountaines many tymes prove molehilles.

Of late even the fyfth of July beeing Sounday, at one Mr Bellamyes house 8 myles from London was apprehended one Southwell, a Jesuyte, a man by reporte very learned

614. I.e., Henry Garnet's letter; see Persons's endorsement.

and one that for many good and rare partes in him had setled a generall good lyking in all that either knewe him or but hard of him. The manner of his taking I have hard delivered in this sorte:[615] he rode to the said house on Sounday morning and there said masse purposing the next morning a further jorney. In the meane,[616] by some meanes (whereof the certainty is not knowen) his beeing there was discovered to some in aucthoritie and aboute midnight, thether came Mr Topclif (a Famous persecutor of Papistes) accompaned with one Mr Barnes a Justice and dwelling neere the place, also yong Mr Fitzherbert and divers others, and so besett the house that none could escape.[617] Then comaunded he the dores to be opened, which donne he entred, and first bound all the men in the house, then called for the gentlewoman, for he himself (I meane Bellamy) was not at home, and presently willed her to deliver him one Mr Cotton (for so was he there[618] named, that came that day to her house), which she at first very stoutly denyed. In fyne either overcome with[619] threates, or as she sayeth her secret place whereinto[620] she had conveyed him beeing betrayed, she yeilded to deliver him, which she performed speedely fetching him thence, whome as soone as Topclif had sight of, he offred to run at[621] with his drawne rapier, calling him traytor which he denying, he demaunded what he was. He answered, A gentleman. Nay, saithe he, a Priest and a traitor. He bad him proove it, whereat he would againe have run at him with his rapier, urging him that he denyed his priesthoode. He said no, but, quothe he, it is neither priest nor treason[622] that you seeke for, but only blood, and yf myne will satisfy you, you shall have it with as good a will as ever any ones, and yf myne will not satisfy, I do not doubte but you shall fynd many moe as willing as my self, only I would advise you to remember there is a God, and he is just in his judgment[623] – and therefore blood will have bloode,[624] but I rather wishe your conversion, or some lyke[625] speech to lyke effect. This doen, Topclif despatched Fitzherbert to the courte to tell what good service he had doen, and so fell to searching of the house fynding there much massing stuf papisticall bookes and Pictures, all which he caused to be laid in a carte which was redy provyded and sent to his loging,[626] at Westminster, whether also by 6 of the clock in the morning he had brought the said Jesuyte. And so the rumour thereof came presently unto us marchants from the courte, where there was bothe joy and I thinck some sorrowe for his taking.

    615. sorte] *A Petti*; state *Foley*
    616. meane] *A Petti*; meantime *Foley*
    617. Thomas Fitzherbert, nephew of Sir Thomas Fitzherbert (d. 1591). John Barnes, JP, is mentioned in the entry for 6 April 1593 in "Middlesex Sessions Rolls: 1593," *Middlesex County Records: Volume 1, 1550–1603*, ed. John Cordy Jeaffreson (London, 1886), 211–219: British History Online, accessed January 26, 2019, www.british-history.ac.uk/middx-county-records/vol1/pp211-219.
    618. there] *A Petti*; then *Foley*
    619. with] *A Petti*; by *Foley*
    620. whereinto] *A Petti*; whereunto *Foley*
    621. run at] *A Petti*; run at him *Foley*
    622. treason] *A Petti*; traitor *Foley*
    623. judgment] *A Petti*; judgments *Foley*
    624. Cf. the final line of "Thomas of Woodstock, Duke of Gloucester," in *The Mirror for Magistrates*, ed. Lily B. Campbell (Cambridge, 1938), 99.
    625. lyke] *A Petti*; om. *Foley*
    626. loging] *A Petti*; lodgings *Foley*

All that day he remained in Topclifes house and the next night he was conveyed[627] close prisoner to the gatehouse. He hathe bene examyned divers tymes by Topclif and others: as by Mr Killigrew, Mr Wade, Mr Bele, and Mr Yonge by order from the Consaile, bothe jointly and severally.[628] In all which examinations, they can get nothing but that he is a priest and a religious man true to the queene and state, free from all treasons, only doing and attending his function.[629]

It is reported by some and very credibly that he hathe bene tortured: as by beeing hanged up by the handes, put in irons, kept from sleepe and such lyke devyses to such men usuall, but hereof there is no certainty. I write this long discours because I knowe you shall fynde many his favourites there that will reporte it more plausable to the Papistes and therefore I thoughte good to advertise the sole[630] truthe as farr as I could any way learne. And what I shall learne further you shall be certified of, either by my self or John Falkner whome you may creditt. London is at this season so whot[631] that for my health I meane to take the country ayre for a season, uncertaine of my tyme of returne. But you may hold on your course; I will leave some one in trust to receave and answere.[632] I wrote how my marchant was arrested, but his elder brother hathe undertaken his busynesse who with all other frendes are well. And thus troobling you with this tedious and unnecessary[633] newes I pray your patience and committ you to God.

    Your assured[634] frend and partner,
        John ——, Marchant.[635]

[*Verstegan's notes:*]

[1.] This parties other[636] letter beeing of an elder date briefly signifieth how his marchant was arrested for debt etc.

And also how Mr Skinner and Mr Ashton were condemned for adhearing to the king of Spaine etc.[637]

627. conveyed] *Foley*; coveyed *A Petti (with note)*
628. Justice Richard Young was appointed to a special commission to deal with imprisoned recusants on 8 January 1592 (G.B. Harrison, *An Elizabethan Journal: Being a Record of Those Things Most Talked of During the Years 1591–1594* [London, 1974], 100); the Cornish diplomat Sir Henry Killigrew (ca. 1528–1603) was evidently also involved; Robert Beale (1541–1601) and William Waad (1546–1623) were clerks of the council.
629. his function] *A Petti*; to his functions *Foley*
630. sole] *A Petti*; real *Foley*
631. whot] *A Petti*; wet *Foley*
632. receave and answere] *A Petti*; write and answer *Foley*
633. and unnecessary] *A Petti*; om. *Foley*
634. assured] *A Petti*; om. *Foley*
635. Referring either to his supposed occupation (a common trope in the missionary letters) or to an assumed surname (Foley, 4: 38; Petti, 71 n14).
636. other] *interlined with caret A*
637. Roger Ashton was hanged, drawn, and quartered at Tyburn, 10 July 1592; Anthony Skinner, a former servant of William Allen, escaped execution, possibly by becoming a spy. See Acquaviva to Persons, 24 March 1590 (B55), and Verstegan's despatch of 3 August (Petti, 57–62).

[2.] The later letter which is written by John Falkner (a yonger brother to your partner),[638] dated there the 4 of this presente signifieth that the marchant that was arrested continued[639] still in his distresse till of late that his father by his frendes hath laboured that he is not now used in the extremest manner as he was.[640]

Mr. Garlyke[641] the fishmonger was oute of towne but he saith he will very shortly be ther and give order for our affaires. This is the chief effect of the last letter.

[*Endorsed by Persons:*] f. Garnetes lettere of f. Southwels taking. London 26 Julii 1592.[642]

B155 From Claudio Acquaviva, Rome, 31 August 1592

SOURCE: ARSI, Cast. 6, fol. 130r, from the general's register of letters to the province of Castile.

NOTE: Acquaviva is thankful for the arrival of Creswell; he is also sending Walpole from Flanders to Valladolid, to relieve Persons's burdens. James Archer is to go to Salamanca, to help with the founding of an Irish college there. Walpole and Archer had been chaplains to Parma's army. They arrived in Seville in January 1593.

An Irish priest, Thomas White, had established a small community of Irish students in Valladolid. During Philip II's visit to the English college, the king promised support for a college in Salamanca: see Acquaviva's letter to Acosta of the same date (ARSI, Cast. 6, fol. 129v), and McCoog, *Building the Faith of St Peter*, 119–120.

P. Roberto Personio, Agosto 31.

Hemonos consolado del buen viaje que el Señor a dado al Padre Crisuelo, porque esperamos podra ayudar mucho por alla, y quien no hiçiere más que aliviar a Vuestra Reverencia algo de sus muchas ocupaçiones estaría muy bien empleado. Buen corte se dio en lo del Seminario de Salamanca procurar sea que vaya a aquel colegio el Padre Jacobo Archero, y tambien se escrivira a Flandes que embien a Vuestra Reverencia el Padre Valpolo, y a Portugal se avisa que embien a Valladolid el Padre Ricardo Gibonio, Vuestra Reverencia podra dexar alli orden de lo que con él se ha de haçer.

Se avisa al Provincial que no quite de la lectura al Padre Padilla porque sería con desconsuelo suyo y daño de aquellos estudios. Lo del Padre Martinez es de más consideraçion, el tiempo dira.

---

638. Neither Falkner nor Garlyke has been identified; the names are probably aliases and the occupation (as with "merchant") a cover. Nicholas Garlick, priest and martyr, was put to death on 24 July 1588 (Anstruther, 126–127).

639. arrested continued] *Foley Petti*; arresteth continued *A corr*.

640. See also Verstegan's letter to Roger Baynes, 22 August and his despatch of 15 October (Petti, 72–73, 79–82).

641. Garlyke] Carlyle *Foley*

642. At the head of the letter the endorsement, in another hand, reads "Mr Garnetes letter ... ."

No havrá ayudado nada para el futuro seminario de Sevilla, la demanda del Padre Siçilia, pero dios ayudará, y en lo que pudieren aquellos Padres no se faltará. Las cartas para ellos irán con otro. En las &c.

Translation

To Fr Robert Persons, 31 August.

I am very pleased by the favourable passage the Lord has given to Fr Creswell, because we hope he will be able to help much over there, and even if he does no more than relieve Your Reverence of some of your occupations, he will be very well employed. A good measure has been taken in the case of the seminary of Salamanca; we must try to ensure that Fr James Archer goes to that college, and I shall also write to Flanders that they send Fr Walpole to Your Reverence, and to Portugal to advise that they send Fr Richard Gibbons to Valladolid.[643] Your Reverence may make your own arrangements there about what you would like to be done.

I have advised the provincial not to relieve Fr Padilla of lecturing because that would increase his desolation and do harm to those studies. The question of Fr Martínez is another consideration. Time will tell.[644]

Fr Sicilia's requests have been of no help to the future seminary of Seville, but God will aid, and help will not be lacking from those fathers in what they are able. The letters for them will come with the next. To your, etc.

B156 To Claudio Acquaviva, Valladolid, 9 September 1592

SOURCE: ARSI, FG 651/640, item 28, holograph, a confidential letter (*soli*).

NOTE: Following the discussion with Acosta which he reported to the general in his letter of June 1592, Persons is persuaded that it is best not to call a general congregation to deal with the questions raised by the Spanish dissidents. He questions Creswell's attribution of troubles at the English College, Rome, to the nature of the English students. This is the first extant letter to Acquaviva by Persons since 26 June 1590 (B67), possibly responding to letters sent to the province of Castile, 6 July (Cast. 6, fols. 125r–126v, wrongly dated 6 June, including a letter to José de Acosta, fol. 125v), or Toledo, 5 July (Tolet. 5/I, fols. 305v–306v).

---

643. Richard Gibbons had previously been in Lisbon (1589) and at the college at Valladolid (1590); evidently, he had subsequently spent some time in Flanders and was now being recalled to Valladolid. In 1592 he was transferred to Coimbra.

644. Antonio de Padilla, SJ, formerly a count, was one of the first to welcome the English students at Valladolid; he was a popular teacher, but was weighed down by other responsibilities. In 1595 he clashed with the new rector, Gonzalo del Río, over a thesis. See Persons to Acquaviva, 4 December 1593 (B210) and 9 December 1595 (B303). Martínez (possibly Francisco Martínez, former rector of the university of Alcalá) was a lecturer at St Ambrose whose approach to St Thomas alienated the English students (Edwards, 139, 181; McCoog, *Building the Faith of St Peter*, 209–211).

Molto Reverendo in Christo Padre Nostro
Pax Christi.

Molto mi rallegro che Vostra Paternità se ne contentasse havergli scritto io quello che me disse 173[645] intorno alla congregatione generale, et io facilmente me persuadeva prima et molto più adesso che Vostra Paternità et li Reverendi padri Assistenti, tenghino buonissime raggioni per non trattar per adesso di congregatione generale, et piacci addio che tutti quelli che la desiderino tanto, habbino così retta intentione come credo senza dubio[646] che molti n'habbino, benché siano ingannati nelle raggioni che allegano. Ma a tutti quelli che non hanno altro fine che il maggior bene della Compagnia basta, que il Capo et membri principali che stanno al governo universale et vedono più ch'altri la dispositione di tutto il corpo, siano di parere che non convenga, et per me, s'io havesse havuto altra opinion prima, per le ragioni che alcuni m'han detto (como in verità mai h' trovato ni m'han quadrato molto le ragioni), bastantissimo argumento saria questo, como ancora un' altro, di non menor momento, appresso di me, et è, che li principali ch'han desiderato questa Congregatione, sono stati de' tentati ne me s'offerisce altro per adesso, quando intenderò altra cosa d'importanza, ne dare aiuto a Vostra Paternità con la confidanza che sempre qui non mi parla nissuno delle cose nostre della Compagnia, né conviene dimandarli, né tengo tempo fra tante occupationi, per esso,[647] solamente dico a Vostra Paternità che non ho perduto l'occasioni che si son offerte mentre stava qui la corte, d'informar bene[648] le persone principali circa Sua Maestà nelle cose della Compagnia, et particularmente con occasione delle cose de questo seminario.

Ho visto et letto questi giorni li discorsi larghi del Padre Cresuello sopra l'inclinationi et nature delli alunni suoi Inglesi, nelle quali cose penso che il buon Padre s'ingannasse molto attribuendo quello alla[649] natura, o naturale inclinatione che nasce d'altri principii et cause, como altre vuolte ho scritto a Vostra Paternità e come proviamo qui dove tenendo le medessime nature, non esperimentiamo l'effetti, perché non habbiamo le medessime cause estrinsiche.

Iddio rimediélo tutto et conserve Vostra Paternità. Valladolid alli 9 le Settembre 1592.

    Da Vostra Reverentia
        figliuolo indegno
            Roberto Personio.

[*Addressed*:] Al molto Reverendo in Christo Padre il Padre Claudio Aquaviva, Proposito General della Compagnia di Giesù, Roma.

[*Endorsed*:] Valladolid. P. Roberto Personio. 9 de 7bre.

---

645. 173] Joseph de Acosta *interlined by recipient* R
646. dubio] *inserted in margin with caret* R
647. per esso] *interlined with caret* R
648. bene] *interlined with caret* R
649. alla] *interlined, replacing short deletion* R

Translation

Our Very Reverend Father in Christ
The peace of Christ.

I am very pleased that Your Paternity approves of my having written of what José de Acosta said to me about the general congregation. I was easily persuaded, then, and even more now, that Your Paternity and the reverend fathers serving as assistants[650] have the very best reasons not to consider holding a general congregation for the time being. Please God that all those who desire it so much, have such right intention as I believe many have, no doubt, although they are deceived in the reasons which they allege. But to all those who have no purpose other than the greater good of the Society it is enough that the head and the principal members who are responsible for worldwide affairs and can see more of the disposition of the whole body, are of the opinion that it is not appropriate. As for me, even if I formerly had another opinion on the matter, for the reasons that some had given me (although in truth I never found myself in full agreement with those reasons), this will be more than enough argument. There is also another, of no less moment, as I see it, and that is, that whereas the principals who desired this congregation have been trying to offer me more reasons at present, I regard it as more important to support Your Paternity with the assurance that nobody ever speaks to me here of the affairs of our Society. It is not appropriate to ask them, either, and take time for that from such great occupations:[651] I will simply tell Your Paternity that I have not lost occasions as they have presented themselves while I am at court, to inform the principal personages around His Majesty of the matters of the Society and particularly, on occasion, of the matters of this seminary.

In the past few days, I have seen and read Fr Creswell's lengthy discussions about the inclinations and natures of his English students. On these matters I think that the good father has deceived himself greatly by attributing to nature or natural inclination something which derives from other principles and causes, as I have written at other times to Your Paternity, and as we prove here, where, dealing with the very same natures, we do not experience the same effects, because we do not have the same extrinsic factors.

May God set everything to rights and preserve Your Paternity. Valladolid, 9 September 1592.

Your Paternity's unworthy son,
Robert Persons.

B157 To Richard Verstegan, Valladolid, 9 September 1592

SOURCE: Verstegan to Persons, 29 October (B160).

650. At the time four assistants advised the superior general: for Spain, Germany, Portugal and Italy.
651. This appears to mean that he refused to entertain any further discussion, so that Acquaviva could be assured that the notion was not being extensively canvassed.

B158 From Claudio Acquaviva, Rome, 28 September 1592

SOURCE: ARSI, Cast. 6, fol. 133v, from the general's register of letters to the province of Castile.

NOTE: Acquaviva wants to be diplomatic about the conditions of royal support for Persons's seminaries.

P. Roberto Personio, Septiembre 28.

Para muchas cosas havrá servido (como Vuestra Reverencia diçe en la de 12 de Agosto) la ida de Su Magestad a ese Seminario: pues como cosa bien vista y favoreçida por él, lo será tambien de otros muchos, de manera que esperamos en el Señor irá esa obra muy adelante. Bien es que en lo de los privilegios se acomoden a lo que alla conviene y puede passar sin ofension de los ministros del Rey. Acá se porna diligencia de nuestra parte si nos avisaren que en algo es necessaria. Las cartas para lo de Sevilla iran con otro; en el interim se escrive un buen capítulo al Provincial y otro al Preposito de Sevilla, en las que con este ordinario se le embian. En sus &c.

Translation

To Fr Robert Persons, 28 September.

In many respects (as Your Reverence says in his letter of 12 August)[652] His Majesty's visit to the seminary will prove useful; just as the matter was approved and favoured by him, so it will also be by many others, so that we hope in the Lord that this work will go forward very fruitfully. It would be well that as to their privileges you accommodate yourself to what is appropriate and may take place without offence to the ministers of the king. Here we will do everything as diligently as we can on our part if you advise us of anything that is necessary. The documents concerning the seminary at Seville will come with the next courier, and in the meantime, I have written a favourable report to the provincial and another to the superior of Seville, which I have sent by this ordinary.[653] To your, etc.

B159 From Claudio Acquaviva, Rome, 27 October 1592

SOURCE: ARSI, Cast. 6, fol. 137v, from the general's register of letters to the province of Castile.

NOTE: Acquaviva expresses gratitude to the king for all that is going forward at Valladolid; he sends letters for the ecclesiastical powers in Seville to aid in the foundation of the seminary there, and he alludes to the possible transfer of Thomas Hunt to Valladolid. Hunt (1552–1626) was currently prefect of the church and library at Innsbruck, as well as confessor.

652. B153.
653. The provincial of Andalusia, Bartolomé Pérez. The superior of the professed house at Seville was Esteban de Hojeda (Murphy, 7).

P. Roberto Personio, 27 de Ottobre.

Favoreze tanto Dios nuestro Señor los buenos trabajos de Vuestra Reverencia que con razon devemos esperar que su divina Magestad quiere sacar dellos muy copioso fructo. Gran consuelo es entender el buen progresso del Seminario de Valladolid en spiritual y temporal y no ay duda sino que para que en todos crezca la estima de los Alumnos y de lo que aquello es havra importado mucho el favor y limosna que la Magestad del Rey les ha hecho. Obligacion particular tienen de rogar a Dios por sus largos dias y buenos sucesos.

Con este ordinario se embian las cartas para los Padres Provincial Preposito y Rector de Sevilla sobre lo del Seminario y con esta se embia a Vuestra Reverencia la copia de todas tres. Esperamos que hallará mucha caridad y ayuda en todos.

Quanto a la yda del P. Huncto a Valladolid se consultará venido que sea nuestro provincial y se avisará de la resolucion que se tomare. En las oraciones etc.

Translation

To Fr Robert Persons, 27 October.

God our Lord has so much favoured Your Reverence's good work that we have good reason to hope that His Divine Majesty wishes it to bring forth even more abundant fruit. It is very encouraging to observe the good progress of the seminary at Valladolid, both spiritual and temporal, and there is no doubt but that the reputation of the students is growing in everybody's estimation and in all that, the favour and alms which His Majesty the king has given them must have been of great importance. These have created a particular obligation to pray to God for length of days and good success.

With this courier I am sending the letters for the father provincial, the superior, and the rector of Seville,[654] concerning the seminary, and I am also sending Your Reverence copies of all three. We hope that you will find much charity and help from all of them in everything.

As for Fr Hunt's coming to Valladolid,[655] there will be consultation when our provincial has come, and you will be informed about the resolution which he takes. To your holy prayers, etc.

B160 From Richard Verstegan, Antwerp, 29 October 1592

SOURCE: ABSI, Coll B 61–62, holograph, with note at letter head: "Advises from Vestigane [sic] of 29 October 1592."

EDITION: Petti, 86–91.

NOTE: Verstegan sends Persons news of his books in press, the English military expedition to Brittany, the persecution (both of Catholics and dissenters) in England, and developments in the Netherlands.

---

654. The rector of the college of St Hermenegild.
655. Thomas Hunt, SJ (1552–1626) was serving in Innsbruck at this time.

Right Reverend, good father

In my last unto you beeing of the 15 of this presente I acknowleged the receit of yours of the 9 of September.

The latin booke goeth forward with so much spede as I can bring the printer to make.[656] The fourthe leaf is at this presente in hand and the whole as he gesseth wilbe aboute 16 leaves. When he began this, he had some other woorck in doing which will shortly be ended and then shall our woorck go forward with more expedition.

The relation in English of his majesties beeing at Validolid will shortly be printed and had bene don eer this had I not stayed a litle for an other printers leasure.[657]

I sent unto your fatherhoode long since, an hereticall pamphlet entituled a triall of truthe,[658] because I supposed your fatherhoode had a woorck in hand of lyke tytle wherein I could wish that[659] the untrue triall of this vaine pamphlet were confuted, because the foolish thing carieth some credit among Protestants.

By letters of the 15 of October from England I understand that such men as were embarcked to passe into Bretany and said to be departed, were not yet gon and in lyke sorte the 2000 English from Holland and Zealand are kept back by contrary wynde and ly still embarcked neere unto Flushing.

Sir Robert[660] Sidney the governour of Flushing hathe of late bene distracted of his wittes and hathe burnt almost all his bookes, and still cryed oute that he was damned. Some ministers have bene busy with him to put him oute of this humour, and some reporte that he is somwhat more quiet, howbeit he still retayneth some degree of frensie.[661]

Sir John Norris is sent with expedition into Britany but hathe left his forces behynde; it is thought that they of England were afrayd to send them over having had entelligence that their were in that province 11,000 Spaniardes.[662]

---

656. On Persons's *Philopater*, see Persons to Acquaviva, 12 August 1592 (B153), headnote. The sixteen "leaves" presumably means sixteen gatherings.

657. Persons's *A relation of the King of Spaines receiving in Valliodolid, and in the Inglish College of the same towne, in August last past of this yere, 1592* (Antwerp, 1592).

658. *The Trial of Trueth; or, A Treatise wherein is declared who should be Iudge betwene the Reformed Churches, and the Romish* (London, 1591), a translation by Richard Smith of a Hungarian work, *Oratio de constituendo judice controversiarum religionis pontificiae atque reformatae* (Basle, 1591); see Peter Milward, *Religious Controversies of the Elizabethan Age* (London, 1978), 129–130.

659. I could wish that] *interlined with caret A*

660. Robert] *preceded by* Phyll [*deleted*] *A*

661. Sir Robert Sidney (1563–1626), brother of Sir Philip Sidney and later Viscount Lisle and Earl of Leicester, was appointed Governor of Flushing in 1588. He was charged with sending Dutch troops from Flushing to Brittany, but the operation was delayed both by the weather and the rumour of an enemy fleet assembled at Dunkirk. See Hammer, *Elizabeth's Wars*, 177–180.

662. The transportation of Norris's forces to assist Essex's expedition to Brittany against the Catholic League was delayed until early November; see his letters of 19, 20 and 27 October (*CSPD*, 3: 280–281, nos. 42, 43, 49; *Acts of the Privy Council*, 23: 298), and to Burghley, 8 November (SP 78/29, fol. 296).

Generall musters are made throughoute England. The plague encreaseth still bothe in London and other places. The Lord Montacute is recovered of his daungerous sicknes.

The Queene cometh to lye at Hampton courte for this winter.

The fury of the inquisition is aswaged and men do passe reasonable well up and downe the country withoute beeing examyned at their Innes or otherwise.

Sundry English Catholiques are gon over into Ireland where for the tyme they are at more quiet then yf they were in England, and by reason that the country hathe now some yeares together bene withoute warres ther is very great aboundance of victualls and corne so plentifull that this year great quantitie hathe bene transported to other countries.

The Queene hathe bene very depely lurched in this late East Indian prize and therefore by a new Proclamation hathe made it felony for any man to have any of the goodes that were of it, yf he do not reveale them to her officers.[663]

Ardington one of William Hacket his prophetes hathe set foorthe some monethes since his submission to the Queene and recantation of his opinion wherein a man shall see strang stuf. I expect the booke shortly for having hard of four pointes thereof, I have sent for it.[664]

When Hacket was executed, Copinger one of his prophetes died raging in prison. This[665] (as is said) was in daunger of death and reported to be dead but he yet liveth.

From thease partes I can send your fatherhoode litle newes. There[666] is an uncertane reporte that the new Duke of Muscovia hathe sent his obedience to the Pope but my owne letters from Rome speak not of it.[667]

The Duke of Parma is in Bruxells, and in health entending to go into France.[668] The Counte de Fointes is very shortly expected in this courte.[669] Fr Holte Sir William and all

---

663. The 1600-ton carrack, a prize worth up to £500,000 was taken off the Azores in July 1592. The queen's indignation at the "lurching" ("pilfering," OED, s.v. v.¹ 3) of a great deal of the treasure by the crew and officers who seized the vessel led to a royal proclamation issued on 23 September 1592. See Verstegan's despatch of 15 October (Petti, 79–82; Hammer, *Elizabeth's Wars*, 168).

664. William Hacket's two "prophets," Edmund Coppinger ("Mercy") and Henry Arthington ("Judgement") died in jail; see John Cecil to Persons, 1 November 1591 (B126).

665. Petti supplies [man] and suggests that Verstegan now reverts to Arthington.

666. There] A, obscure; Here Petti

667. During the reign of the incompetent Tsar Feodor I, grand duke of Muscovy (1584–1598), his brother-in-law Boris Gudanov (the future tsar, reigned 1598–1605) acted as regent. After the death of Feodor's half-brother Dmitri Ivanovich under suspicious circumstances on 15 May 1591, the question of succession intensified, and this may have given rise to rumours of the kind relayed here.

668. The governor-general of the Spanish Netherlands, Alessandro Farnese, duke of Parma, was wounded at the siege of Caudebac (April–May 1592) and escaped to Brussels, but did not recover his health. He died in Arras, France, on 3 December, within a month of leaving Brussels.

669. Pedro Henríquez de Guzmán de Azevedo y Toledo (1525–1610), count of Fuentes de Valdepero, arrived in Brussels on 23 November with instructions for Farnese from Philip II.

frendes are well in Bruxells.⁶⁷⁰ 185 is yet in 22 or on his returne.⁶⁷¹ Mr Haselwode is departed this world at Liège: our lord have mercy on his soule.⁶⁷²

181 dothe thinck it best to stay for a fewe weekes to send any 239 to any 139 in 25 because Mr 9 m 12: dothe here by 227 meanes very much seek to understand which way and how 181 dealeth, insomuch that some of the parties he hathe enquyred of have told it to 181 which maketh him the more wary, there is no one of all our nation, now 179 is gone that⁶⁷³ dothe kepe such a do. I pray God he may do himself good and other men no hurte.

I am in some doubt that Fr Walpole and Fr Archer are still attending the wynde for their passage.⁶⁷⁴

Your brother and my self have bene at Bruxells aboute our sute, but nothing is don in it as yet.⁶⁷⁵ Fr Holte hathe promised to solicite Signor⁶⁷⁶ Cosimo: meane whyle your brother is returned to Doway because his wyf was neer lying downe⁶⁷⁷ and I thinck afterward will returne hether againe. More for the presente I have not, but with most harty thanckes I humbly take my leave. Antwerp this 29 of October 1592.

    Your fatherhoodes ever
        assuredly to comaund
            R. Verstegan.

---

670. William Holt and Sir William Stanley.

671. Petti deciphers tentatively: 22 [Italy]; 181 [Verstegan]; 239 [letter]; 139 [priest]; Mr 9 m 12 [possibly Robert Poley]; 227 [?spying] 179 [Thomas Morgan]. 185 is not identified. The notorious agent Robert Poley was involved in intelligence work in the Netherlands and France. On 30 May 1593 he was present in Deptford Strand at the murder of Christopher Marlowe, who was arrested by Sir Robert Sidney in Flushing in January 1592. See Charles Nicholl, "Christopher Marlowe" (*ODNB*). Verstegan was evidently afraid that Elizabethan agents would uncover his routes for correspondence and missionary priests.

Thomas Morgan was expelled from the Netherlands in June 1592, at William Allen's request: see Knox, *Allen*, 320–329; *CSPD*, 3: 244 dated 12 July; Leo Hicks, *An Elizabethan Problem: Some Aspects of the Careers of Two Exile-Adventurers* (London, 1964), 78, 190, 197; and Robert Lechat, *Les réfugiés anglais dans les Pays-Bas espagnols durant le règne d'Élisabeth 1558–1603* (Louvain, 1914), 163–164.

672. Henry Haselwood, a young gentleman from Northamptonshire, is mentioned several times in Knox, *Douay Diaries*, 1579–1580.

673. that] *interlined with caret above* & [*deleted*] A

674. See Acquaviva to Persons, 31 August 1592 (B155). Walpole and Archer were at Calais, awaiting passage to Spain.

675. Verstegan and George Persons enlisted Holt in their suit for their royal pensions (30 crowns per month) to be paid, and also approached Parma's secretary Cosimo Massi, but to no avail. Philip II wrote to Parma on 15 August 1592 and wrote to the Brussels court again, more successfully, in March 1594; see Loomie, *Spanish Elizabethans*, 256, 262.

676. Signor] A, *obscure abbreviation*; Secretary *Petti*

677. Near giving birth to a child.

[PS] Your fatherhoode may please to do my very harty comendations to good Fr Creswelle.[678]

Since the wryting of this letter I understand that Sir R. Sidney is put oute of his frantike humour.

Since the tyme that his majesties letter were delivered to the Duke and Counte we have had no answere; only we lyve in hope. We are now entring into the fourteenth moneth since we had any pay, except one succours long since.

Some of the books your fatherhoode wrote for I will send by the first good comoditie that I can fynde; and the others that yet I have not gotten into my handes, so soone after as I can.[679]

[*Addressed:*] Al muy R^{do} in X^o Padre il P. Roberto Personio de la compagnia de Jesus, Validolid.

[*Endorsed by Persons:*] Advises from Verstenghan of 29 8$^{b.}$ 1592.

---

678. Creswell, rector of the English College, Rome, since 1589, was transferred to Spain and named procurator of the English college at Seville when it opened on 25 November 1592 (McCoog, *Building the Faith of St Peter*, 115; Loomie, *Spanish Elizabethans* 190–193).

679. A consignment of books was sent the following year: see Verstegan to Persons, 2 October 1593 (Petti, 187–188).

Seville, November 1592–October 1594

B161 From Claudio Acquaviva, Rome, 24 November 1592

SOURCE: ARSI, Baet. 3/I, 89.

NOTE: Acquaviva confirms that he has sent the letters requested in Persons's letter of 12 August for the foundation of the seminary at Seville and is hopeful of the outcome. There is a further reference to the possibility of bringing Thomas Hunt to Valladolid from Innsbruck; evidently, the provincial of the Austrian province (Bartholomé Villerius) has approved. On both these, see the letter of 27 October (B159).

P. Roberto Personio, 24 Noviembre.

Ya con el pasado se embiaron las cartas que Vuestra Reverencia pedia para el Provincial de esa Provincia y para los Padres Preposito y Rector de Sevilla. Espero que havrá hallado en ellos toda caridad y buena acogida y que en lo que se ofreciere le ayudarán como de acá se les encomendo. Plega al Señor que la erection de ese Seminario salga tal como Vuestra Reverencia y todos deseamos que con las buenas ayudas que[1] el Rey va dando con cartas y dineros y siendo la obra en tanto servicio de la divina Magestad podemos esperar un buen progresso. En lo que pide por la suya de 8 de setiembre de que le embiemos el P. Huncto, se procurará que vaya y para este efecto le embiaremos a llamar pues juzgan que aý será de tanto provecho. En las oraçiones etc.

Translation

To Fr Robert Persons, 24 November.

The letters which Your Reverence requested for the provincial of that province, and for the superior father and the rector of Seville were sent with the last post.[2] I hope that you have found them most charitable and welcoming, and that they will help you as occasion demands, as they were asked to do from here. Please God may the foundation of this seminary turn out according to Your Reverence's wishes and ours, since with the king's strong support in letters and funds, and seeing that the work is in the great service of His Divine Majesty, we may hope for good progress. As for what you ask in your

1. que] *followed by* su [*deleted*] A
2. Cf. Acquaviva's letter of 28 September (B158), referring to the provincial (of Andalusia) and the superior (of the professed house); here he refers also to the rector of the Jesuit college of St Hermenegild, Melchor de Castro.

letter of 8 September about sending Fr Hunt, we will try to send him, and to that effect, we have summoned him because it is felt that he will be very profitable. To your prayers, etc.

B162 To Pope Clement VIII, Seville, 1 December 1592

SOURCE: AAV, Fondo Borghese III, 124 g.2, fols. 3–4, holograph.
HICKS: 124–125, with English translation.
NOTE: Persons seeks the pope's interest in obtaining the support of the cardinal archbishop of Seville for the establishment of an English seminary in Seville. Clement VIII (elected 30 January 1592 and consecrated on 3 February) had previously, as Ippolito Aldobrandini, been the Cardinal Protector of England and could thus be expected to take a special interest in the prospects of the English mission.

Rodrigo de Castro Osorio (1532–1600) was archbishop of Seville from 1581 and created cardinal in 1583; despite his association with the Inquisition, he founded the magnificent Jesuit College of Our Lady of Antigua in the Galician city of Monforte de Lemos in 1592/3, while recuperating from a serious illness. Persons had already obtained a letter from Philip II requesting the archbishop's discreet support, possibly banking on de Castro's experience in England during Mary I's reign.

Noble patrons of the foundation at Seville included the dukes of Arcos, Béjar, and Medina Sidonia, the marquises of Priego and Ayamonte, and the marchioness of Tarifa (Persons to Acquaviva, 12 June 1595, B279, n194; Murphy, 6).

At the very end of his life, Persons wrote his own account of the foundation at Seville, "Annales seminarii seu Collegii Anglorum Hispalensis ab anno 1591" (ARSI, FG 1616/6/3/1–3 and ABSI, Coll P II 344–349), published in Pollen, *Miscellanea IX*, 6–10.

Beatissimo padre

Aunque la obligacion antiqua que yo tenía a Vuestra Santidad, quando era grandissima por los muchas favores y mercedes que Vuestra Santidad me hazía, mientras estubi en Roma, y tenía cargo del Collegio Ynglés, del qual Vuestra Santidad era por entonces protector; todavia, siendo andado Vuestra Santidad a la silla de San Pedro, y al govierno universal de la yglesia de nuestro Señor, no me atrebi escrivir a Vuestra Santidad, sabiendo las muchas occupaciones gravissimas que avrá tenido en estos principios, hasta que el padre Joseppe Cresuello il qual me succedio en el cuydado del Collegio Anglico, llegando por acá; nos dixo de la benignissima memoria que Vuestra Santidad es servido tener de nos duos indignos hijos, y siervos suyos, y del singular amor que muestra a la obra de la conversione de Ynglaterra que llevamos entre los manos, de la qual, no será necessario que yo escriva muy largo quan prosperamente va adelante en estas partes por medio destos seminarios, ni tan poco las esperancas grandes que tenemos de la breve reducion della, por esta via, pues el dicho padre Joseppe lo ha tomado por su assumpto de dar quenta particular a Vuestra Santidad dello, solamente tengo con esta de besar muy humilmente a los sagrados pies de Vuestra Santidad y supplicarla que nos dé su santa benedicion, y el favor para con este Cardinal Arçobispo de Sevilla que el padre Joseph apuntado tiene en su carta con el qual favor de Vuestra Santidad confío en nuestro Señor que

el buen Cardinal nos hará mucha merced, y que Dios llevará muy adelante esta obra para su gloria. Él guarde siempre a Vuestra Santidad. Sevilla a primo da Decembre 1592.
  di Vuestra Santidad
    [indegno siervo
      Roberto Personio.]
[*Addressed, in Persons's hand:*] A la Santidad de nuestro Señor, Clemente Octavo.
[*Endorsed:*] Seviglia 92 / primo di Decembre. Rob. Personio.

Translation

Most blessed Father

 Despite my long-standing obligation to Your Holiness for the many favours and kindnesses which Your Holiness bestowed on me while I was in Rome,[3] in charge of the English college, Your Holiness being at that time its protector, when Your Holiness was raised to the chair of St Peter and the government of the universal church of our Lord, I did not have the audacity to write to Your Holiness – for I knew how many grave affairs you would have to occupy you in those first days – until Fr Creswell, my successor in the care of the English college, on his arrival here, told us of Your Holiness's gracious and most kindly remembrances of us both, your unworthy sons and servants, and of the special love also which you show to the work of England's conversion which we are taking in hand. And in this regard, it will not be necessary for me to write at great length how successfully it goes forward in these regions thanks to these seminaries; nor yet of the great hope which we have of the speedy reduction of the country by this method. For the above-mentioned Fr Joseph has taken on himself the task of giving Your Holiness a special report on this subject.[4] So there only remains for me to kiss Your Holiness's sacred feet very humbly and to beg you to give us your blessing and to use your good offices for us with the Cardinal Archbishop of Seville here of whom Fr Joseph has spoken in his letter. With this support from Your Holiness, I trust in our Lord that the good cardinal will give us much support and that God will give great success to this work, for His glory. And may He ever preserve Your Holiness. Seville, 1 December 1592.
  Your Holiness's
    unworthy servant
      Robert Persons.

B163 To Claudio Acquaviva, December 1592

  SOURCE: Acquaviva to Persons, 15 February 1593 (B165).
  NOTE: Persons reported on the foundation of the seminary at Seville on St Catherine's Day, 25 November, when Persons, Creswell, and fourteen students took up residence in the Plaza de San Lorenzo (Murphy, 6).

 3. I.e., when he was cardinal protector, as Ippolito Aldobrandini.
 4. In a letter to Acquaviva of 9 September 1592 (B156), Persons somewhat sceptically describes a report by Creswell on the state of the English college in Rome.

B164 A Sermon Delivered at the English College, Seville, on the Feast Day of St Thomas of Canterbury, 29 December 1592

SOURCES: The opening paragraph and the conclusion are reproduced and translated in Robert Persons, *Newes from Spayne and Holland* (Antwerp, 1593) (= N), which is the earliest witness to the sermon. Christopher Grene transcribed it twice:
  AVCAU Libro 1422, from Grene's Collectanea F = C
  ABSI, Coll P I 273–80, Grene's transcription, copied from C = G

NOTE: The founding of St Gregory's College, Seville, was celebrated with an elaborate ceremony to mark the feast of St Thomas (Becket) of Canterbury of 1592, attended by the cardinal archbishop Rodrigo de Castro Osorio and several noble patrons. Mass was sung by Alonso de Columna, a canon of the cathedral, who was probably related to a branch of the Italian family Colonna that had strong bonds with the Habsburgs. The sermon in praise of the saint, reproduced here, was preached during mass, after the gospel, by John Worthington, one of the students, nephew of Thomas Worthington (Anstruther, 385). As an hour-long performance, entitled "oratio," it is chiefly addressed to the local dignitaries, with a view to attracting funds and support, although it also appeals to the students to emulate the martyr's life and devotion. The celebrations at Seville resembled those at Valladolid on the occasion of Philip II's visit in September. See Pollen, *Miscellanea IX*, 8–9; Murphy, 6–7.

St Thomas was venerated with special fervour in the post-Reformation English Catholic community because of the spoliation of the shrine at Canterbury by King Henry VIII and because he affirmed the supremacy of the pope over the monarchy. Surprisingly, this is not mentioned in the sermon, despite the popularity of works like Stapleton's *Tres Thomae* (Douay, 1588), but the sermon dwells on his persecution, exile and martyrdom, familiar themes for the exile community. See Victor Houliston, "St Thomas Becket in the Propaganda of the English Counter-Reformation," *Renaissance Studies* 7 (1994): 44–70, and Ana Sáez-Hidalgo, "*E Duobus Elige*: The 'Devise' of Thomas Beckett and Queen Elizabeth's Spanish Dilemma," forthcoming.

The account of Becket's life appears to be largely based on the biographies by Edward Grim, Herbert of Bosham, and John of Salisbury; see *The Lives of Thomas Becket*, ed. and trans. Michael Staunton (Manchester and New York, 2001), and Frank Barlow, *Thomas Becket* (London, 1986), which are frequently cited in the notes below.

The text of the sermon survives in two successive copies made by Grene in the seventeenth century. The second (G) contains some corrections imported from N and some which are presumably Grene's editorial interventions. The introduction and conclusion were translated in *Newes from Spayne and Holland*, published in Antwerp early the following year. This translation is given separately below.

The authorship of the sermon is unclear: a note on the cover page of the copy at the English college in Rome reads "scripta est haec oratio a B.P. Henrico Walpole martyre et composita a R.P. Roberto Personio" (this oration was written by Blessed Father Henry Walpole, martyr, and composed by Rev. Father Robert Persons). The copy at ABSI bears the legend "Oratio Personii" in a marginal note next to the title, and an endnote adds "uti hic adnotavit P. Nathanael Sotuellus," i.e., Nathaniel Southwell (*vere* Bacon, 1598–1676), who was ordained in Rome in 1622 and professed there in 1634 (McCoog, *English and Welsh Jesuits*,

299). The style is more florid than Persons's usual manner, so it is likely that "composita" means "prepared in outline." See W.F. Rea, "The Authorship of 'News from Spayne and Holland' and Its Bearing on the Genuineness of the Confessions of the Blessed Henry Walpole, S.J.," *Biographical Studies* (now *British Catholic History*) 1 (1951): 220–230, esp. 223.

Oratio Habita in Festo D Thomae Cantuariensis
in Collegio Anglicano Hispalensi anno Domini 1592[5]

Bonus Pastor animam suam dat pro ovibus suis.[6]

Dicturus hodie de praeclarissimo ecclesiae Catholicae lumine divo Thoma Cantuariensi (illustrissime cardinalis, clarissimique auditores), illud saepe mecum ad solatium cogitare soleo, nihil me dicturum in hac tanta frequentia, quod ad omnes fere non pertineat, cum nemo fortasse sit ex universa hac nobilissimaque hominum corona, qui aliquid suum in gloriosissimo hoc Dei servo non agnoscat. Dicturus enim sum[7] de cive apud cives, de senatore apud senatores, de iudice apud iudices, de regni cancellario apud conciliorum praesides, de religionis assertore apud religionis vindices, de pastore vigilantissimo apud animarum duces, de regularis vitae professore apud regularis vitae observantissimos, de archiepiscopo apud archipraesulem, de universi regni primate apud universalis ecclesiae purpuratum antistitem: de martyre denique apud martyrii cupidos, si Dominus eos dignos invenerit. Itaque cum omnium partes in praesenti celebritate reperiantur, quid ni omnium quoque votis, omniumque precibus ad communem omnium Dominum recurramus,[8] ut dicentem me hodierno die, vel narrantem vel perorantem vel supplicantem, vel lamentantem etiam et complorantem (si id vel temporum vel rerum Anglicanarum necessitas postulabit) divina sua gratia comitari dignetur? et in primis beatissimam eius matrem (quam summa semper religione Archiepiscopus Thomas venerabatur) omni contentione imploremus, ut dextram porrigat dicenti, et fluentem orationis meae cursum ad fili sui gloriam plentissime dirigat.[9]

Faciam autem dicendi initium ab eo potissimum, quod omnis dictionis atque orationis esse debet[10] fundamentum, ut nimirum nihil allaturum me hoc loco de vita Sancti Thomae promittam, quod non certum, indubitatum, exploratumque habeatur, et ipsorum etiam litteris contestatum, qui totius fere negotii spectatores fuerunt. Habet enim huius sancti vita hoc prope singulare, ut per eos, qui una vixerunt, et rebus ipsis plerumque interfuerunt, litteri consignaretur, quo veritas certior, maiorque autoritas totius narrationis existeret.

Fuit igitur (ut hinc exordiar) sanctus hic Christi martyr patria quidem civis Londinensis genere vero tum nobilibus tum locupletissimis etiam ortus parentibus, unde et

    5. Oratio Habita in Festo D Thomae Cantuariensis in Collegio Anglicano Hispalensi anno 1592] *C*; Oratio Habita in Collegio Anglicano Hispalensi in Festo D Thomae Cantuariensis anno Dni. 1592 *G*
    6. [*marginal note:*] Ioan. 10
    7. sum] *C N*; om. *G*
    8. recurramus] *C N*; recurram *G*
    9. *N leaves off here, resuming at* [Atque haec dicta sunt] ut hinc etiam intelligamus *below*
    10. esse debet] *C*; debet esse *G*

facultates ei ad omnem vitae rationem, quam ipse vellet sequendam non deerant, quod vero optimam in tanta copia secutus[11] sit, id perexcellenti Dei gratiae tribuendum censeo. Accedit autem quiddam singulare in Thomae natalitio, ut quo die nimirum ederetur in lucem, eo ignis ex domo paterna incerto casu egressus, magnam civitatis Londinensis partem incenderet, quod ego profecto (fratres mei dilectissimi) vos enim caeterorum auditorum ornatissimorum venia, hortandi causa subinde alloquar, ad nos potissimum interpretabor pertinere, qui concives et contribules sanctissimo huic martyri secundum carnem sumus; ad nos (inquam) pertinere hunc Thomae ignem existimabo, ut eo ad omnem eiusdem imitationem pro ecclesia Dei defendenda incendamur. Quanquam sane si ad universalis reipublicae Christianae statum, qui plusquam quadringentis abhinc annis miserrimus plane, et perturbatissimus erat, oculos coniiciamus, intelligemus fortasse non tantum civibus suis Thomam, i, Anglis, sed totius etiam orbis Christiani incolis propositum fuisse exemplum, et tanquam signum quoddam in gentibus et nationibus sublatum, quo mortales omnes officii sui admonerentur, et ardentiora inserviendi Deo proposita ex inflammato Thomae igne conciperent.

    Nam si temporum illorum memoriam repetamus[12] ex annalibus, quibus haec gerebantur, quae de clarissimo hoc martyre dicturi sumus, calamitosa rerum facies apparebit (auditores) et ignis caelestis indigens, quando omnia fere frigerent, et laethali quodam torpore Christiani fervoris ardor propemodum extingueretur. Quid enim miserabilius, quid calamatosius dici fingive potest, quam quod de aetate illa, qua vixit Thomas, referunt historiae? Omnia bellis, omnia seditionibus, omnia cupiditatibus, odiis, luxuriis plena humana perturbata, divina subversa. Romae sedebat Alexander Tertius Pontifex sanctissimus atque fortissimus, sed quatuor sibi repugnantes Antipapas habuit. In Cicilia Guilielmus rex contra ecclesiam Romanam tumultuabatur, in Italia et Germania Fridericus imperator dictus Aenobarbus[13] armis cruentis eam ubique dirissime persequebatur. In Graecia Emanuel Imperator cum Andronico de imperio orientis decertabat, uterque ecclesiae Romanae inimicus, quo factum est, et Graecorum simul in Latinos odio, ut Joannes cardinalis ab Alexandro papa cum legatione Constantinopolim missus immanissime trucidaretur, ac[14] per vicos urbis contumeliosissime raptaretur. Hierosolimis rex Balduinus Christianus affligebatur a Turcis; in Aegipto sultanus cum Saladino pugnabat; in Hispaniis Sanchius Tertius et Ferdinandus Secundus reges Catholicissimi confligebant cum Mauris. In Gallia Ludovicus Septimus, In Anglia Henricus Secundus, in Scotia Macholomis reges tum domi iam suis tum foris etiam inter se dimicabant, ac collidebantur. Praetereo Venetorum bella cum Hungaris de principatu Dalmatiae, Germanorum cum Henrico Saxoniae Duce, Boemorum cum Polonis, aliaque plurima, quibus universus orbis (ut recte annotavit Cromerus episcopus) sub Alexandro Tertio Pontifice concutiebatur: adeo ut non solum litterarum ac virtutum studia iacerent sed omnis etiam Christianae pietatis ardor pene extingueretur, furta, latrocinia, homicidia dominarentur, omnia manarent sanguine, et sanguis sanguinem, quod inquit propheta tangeret.

    11. secutus] G; secutas C
    12. repetamus] C; repetam G
    13. Aenobarbus] C; Aenobardus G
    14. ac] C; et G

Huic tanto malorum diluvio, ut Deus optimus maximus pro summa sua benignitate aliquo modo mederetur, excitavit hoc ipso tempore nonnullos viros praeclarissimos qui mundo praelucerent et muros se opponerent pro domo Dei tuenda. Ac pro litteris quidem restaurandis, cum multos nominare possem, satis sit Petrum Lombardum episcopum Parisiensem, theologiae scholasticae architectum, Gratianum quoque monachum, sacrorum canonum[15] et decretorum collectorem, Petrum etiam Comestorem historiae ecclesiasticae authorem perinsignem nominasse. Pro virtutis vero excitando studio, mundique contemptu inducendo praeclarissimi duo ordines religiosorum virorum Carthusianorum nempe et Carmelitarum, sub hoc ipso Pontifice Alexandro emissi sunt. Ordines etiam militares S^{ti} Jacobi, et Calatravensium in Hispania Sancho Rege procurante et Alexandro approbante exorti. Mitto (quod primo loco dicere debueram) Divum Bernardum, qui omnis virtutis, religionis, eruditionis atque sanctitatis speculum fuit, qui hoc ipso tempore cum Sancto Thoma Cantuariensi vixit, et centum quadraginta monasteria sui ordinis exaedificavit, et paulo ante mortuus est, quam D. Thomas martirio affectus, et uterque singulare spectaculum Deo, angelis et hominibus facti sunt, et ambo ab eodem Papa Alexandro in sanctorum numerum relati.

Non igitur sine causa hoc ignis praesagium in D. Thomae exortu datum est, ut inde constaret universam rempublicam Christianam, tum vitae tum mortis eius exemplo ad omnem divini famulatus ardorem incendendam fore.

Atque de vitae quidem genere, ut primum dicamus, fuit illa certe ab ipsa adolescentia in omni honorum, divitiarum et dignitatum cursu, per omnes enim officiorum gradus subvectus ad illud tandem pervenit Thomas, quod summum ac supremum est in Anglicano regno, et regi proximum, ut totius nimirum regni Cancellarius fieret. Quo in magistratu administrando, ut singularem prudentiam, sagacitatem, diligentiam, iustitiam etiam sua sponte ipse exercuit, ita ne ex summa illa potentia, facultatum copia, vitae ornatu, splendore atque fastu evanesceret Thomas, aut in vitia difflueret, providit ei divina bonitas potentissimum quendam aemulum Rogerium Archidiaconum Cantuariensem, qui postea archiepiscopus Eboracensis quoque factus per universam vitam viro huic Dei pertinacissime restitit, et summa contentione in quibuscumque potuit, contradicebat, divina providentia sic ordinante ut per huius aemulationem Thomas ad omnem vitae perfectionem erudiretur.

Accidit deinde, ut decedente Theobaldo viro magno ac prudentissimo vacaret sedes Cantuariensis, quae totius insulae metropolis est, quam cum Henricus Rex diu multumque cogitasset, cuinam hominum potissimum deferret neminem reperit ullo modo cum Thoma comparandum. Ille igitur archiepiscopus constitutus, cum regni se patrem ex iudice factum cerneret, paternos omnino mores imitandos, paternos affectus induendos censuit, quod ut melius praestaret arctius se Deo coniungendum statuit. Itaque statim post inaugurationem, quae summa celebritate ac[16] splendore Cantuariae fiebat, dilapsa iam hominum turba, quae infinita pene confluxerat, solus sibi factus Thomas et Deo, praesens coepit animo revolvere, quisnam esset, quid egisset, quem in locum pervenisset, quantum oneris in se suscepisset, quae ratio reddenda, quae officia praestanda

15. canonum] *this ed.*; canonem C G
16. ac] C; atque G

caeteraque istiusmodi, quae divina gratia suggerere hominibus ad vitam praeordinatis solet. Quae omnia cum serio mente perlustrasset sua, et illud D. Gregorii in memoriam revocasset, tanto esse debere quemque humiliorem, et ad Deo serviendum promptiorem ex munere, quanto se obligationem conspicit in reddenda ratione, plane decrevit vita saeculari relicta, religiosam ingredi, et ordini canonicorum regularium, qui singulari sanctitate per id tempus in Anglia florebat, se adiungere, quod et re ipsa statim emisso voto praestitit, licet ad vulgi laudes fugiendas, et ne quis aliorsum rem interpretaretur atque ipse sentiebat, saecularem habitum retinendum sibi ad tempus iudicaret. Itaque rem quidem ipsam expetebat, et explebat, nomen vero dissimulabat, vigilias, chorum, ieiunia, penitentias amplectebatur, externum habitum iustis ut sibi videbatur de causis differebat. Quae tamen prudentiae humanae moderatio Deo minus probari visa est: quadam enim nocte vir quidam aspectu plane terribilis cuidam e domesticis archiepiscopi apparuit praecipiens ei, ut Thomae renunciet habitum quoque sibi[17] mutandum esse, sin autem minus inimicum se illum perpetuo habiturum. Qua ille voce accepta, dici non potest quantum vir Dei horruerit, et quam intimis sensibus commotus fuerit, adeo ut a Deo profectam vocem illam minime dubitaverit. Itaque ex hac ipsa hora post uberrimos lachrimarum imbres, totum se Domino consecravit, totum se tradidit, et quanquam Pontificiam dignitatem, quam assumpserat, non reliquit, neque externum apparatum et splendorem, qui autoritati illi debebatur, repudiavit, mira tamen sunt, et plane stupenda (auditores) quae de interiori huius hominis vita litteris tradiderunt ii qui oculati testes esse potuerant; mira de victus parcimonia, de vestitus asperitate, de ieiunorum frequentia, de vigiliarum perseverantia, de orationis assiduitate, de eleemosinarum maximarum ingenti copia, et quod in illa vitae condicione magis adhuc admirandum est, de perpetua severissimaque corporis castigatione, de quo uno litteris prodidit vir venerabilis Robertus Meritonensis archiepiscopi capellanus, et individuus vitae comes, et qui eodem fere cubiculo semper dormiit, nullum diem praeteriisse, plane nullum, ex eo tempore, quo factus est archiepiscopus usque ad mortem, in quo quinquies, aut quater, aut saltem ter, graviter flagello in se non animadverteret.

O mirum et pene inauditum Christianae severitatis exemplum! quis non mirabitur, quis non obstupescet (auditores) si illa tempora cum nostris componat? si istiusmodi sanctorum incensa studia cum praesentis aetatis tepiditate conferat? atque hoc quidem de verbere. De cilicio vero quid dicam, quod amplum asperrimumque cum esset, nunquam fere a carne sua dimovit, neque die, neque nocte, neque domi, neque foris, neque in itinere, neque quiescens, neque pro tribunali, neque in ecclesia, neque in his ipsis etiam festis Domini natalitiis, quibus immaniter trucidatus fuit. Demortuo enim repertum est sic intrarens carni cilicium ut inspectantes omnes ad horrorem impulerit. Quid igitur de vita hac D. Thomae dicemus (auditores) quae tam admirabili combinatione connexa fuit, ut pontificia simul dignitati, et religiosissimae quoque severitati satisfaceret, et foris quidem blanda, intus vero aspera, foris splendida, intus squallida, foris copiosa, intus egentissima, ita ut et religionem cum dignitate, et disciplinam cum ornatu, et humilitatem cum amplitudine, et inopiam cum copia, et solitudinem cum frequentia, et monasterium denique cum aula coniungeret.

17. quoque sibi] C; sibi quoque G

His passibus currentem Thomam voluit Dominus tentatione quoque probare, ut impleretur illud angeli ad Tobiam: *Quia acceptus eras Deo, necesse fuit ut tentatio probaret te*,[18] iuxta illud etiam Sapientis: *certamen forte dedit illi Deus, ut vinceret.*[19] Ecce enim Henricus Secundus Angliae rex, vir bellicus et efferati animi, qui praeter summam potentiam, qua ad insolentiam Principes facile incitantur, plurima quoque beneficia in Thomam contulerat, quibus deberi sibi putabat, ne voluntati in re ulla reluctaretur suae. Ab impiis adulatoribus misere deceptus leges quasdam sancire voluit immunitatibus ecclesiasticis penitus adversas quibus tum Clericorum, tum rerum etiam ecclesiasticarum iudicia fere omnia ad sua tribunalia revocabat, quibus cum initio ab omnibus fere[20] repugnaretur, quod iniquissimae essent, tandem tamen partim vi et metu, partim adulatione et muneribus, et ipso quoque regio nomine (quod potentissimum esse solet), non solum proceres omnes laicos in suam sententiam traxit, sed magnam etiam episcoporum et cleri Anglicani partem inflexit, solus archiepiscopus, ut erat caeterorum pater pastorque ita pro omnium salute resistendum regiae cupiditati existimavit. Quod cum alter aegerrime ferret, mille adhibuit machinas, ut hominem Dei expugnaret, quas hoc loco recensere longum esset, satis sit dixisse, nihil praetermissum esse, quod vel ars, vel fraus, vel adulatio, vel minae, vel authoritas, vel potentia usurpare potuerunt: amicorum hortationes, inimicorum argutiae, necessariorum preces, cognatorum lachrimae ad flectendam martyris constantiam adhibitae, sed nihil valuerunt. Qua re eousque exarsit regis iracundia, ut aperta vi agendum sibi ratus convocatis totius regni comitiis archiepiscopum ad tribunal suum evocat, et quia statim morbo gravi impeditus non venisset, magna pecuniae summa mulctandum curat. Postera vero die Thomas, ut nihil eorum praetermitteret quae in se essent, regem supplex adit, petit, ut suae salutis et publicae aedificationis rationem habeat, sed exclusus a rege, et ad comitia reiectus domum rediit, et Deo causam suam ardentissime commendat. Interim fit certior multa in comitis contra ipsum agitante rege calumnosissima tractari seque statim tanquam rebellem regi et publicae pacis perturbatorem condemnandum fore, et castigandum; quo ille intellecto appellat ad pontificem Romanum, eaque re maior adhuc tumultus factus est, et regis animus longe exasperatior. Cumque iam ad manifestam vim ac[21] caedem res spectaret, erant ex amicis, qui domi Thomam suorum manu muniendum contra praesentem regis furorem suaderent, at ille remit, affirmans lateribus non parietibus hanc causam Dei tuendam esse. Alii ad placandum regis animum, abdicandum se statim magistratu, et archiepiscopatum in manus regias resignandum consulebant. At ille *Pastor* (inquit) *bonus animam suam dat pro ovibus suis, mercernarius autem, et qui non est pastor videt lupum venientem, et dimittit oves et fugit et lupus rapit et dispergit oves,*[22] non (inquit) ea lege episcopatum coepi, ut ingruente periculo regi eum tradam, sed solum Christo, a quo illum accepi, vel eius vicario, vel meipsum pro illo defendendo impendam. Itaque totam illam noctem, qua multi eum occidendum credebant, vir Dei intrepide vigiliis, orationibus, verberibus transegit. Postera vero luce post sacrum magna lachrimarum copia peractum stola indutus et crucem manu

18. Tob. 12:13.
19. Wisd. 10:12 (adapted).
20. ab omnibus fere] C; fere ab omnibus G
21. ac] C; atque G
22. John 10:11–12, omitting "cuius non sunt oves propriae" (whose own the sheep are not).

gestans regis palatium in quo erant comitia adit, concilium ingreditur, rationes multas, quare regis voluntati in legibus illis admittendis quae sacris ecclesiae canonibus contrariae essent, assentiri non possit, modestissime proponit, petit ut res ad Pontificem Romanum, qui omnium iudex est, devolvatur. Interim eos admonet de perpetrato scandalo, quam iniquum esset, se archiepiscopum et Angliae primatem ad illud tribunal saeculare in rebus etiam ecclesiasticis[23] compelli, quam indignum se patrem a filiis, praesulem a subditis, pastorem ab ovibus condemnari; qua oratione tamen cum nihil proficeret, sed altercatio ad noctem usque produceretur, exiit tandem vir sanctus ex medio eorum multis conviciis impetitus opprobiisque affectus, alio alium ex ministris regiis incitante, et plebem concitante, ita, ut iam in transeuntem virum Dei sordes quoque proiicerent, et parum abfuit, quin discerperetur nisi episcopi quidem verentes censuras ecclesiasticas si ni eorum conspectu trucidari illum permisissent, authoritatem suam apud regem interposuissent, ut archiepiscopus domum salvus dimitteretur.

Sed domum veniens reperit familiam peritus dissipatam, et omnes pene famulos ex metu regis diffugisse. Contulit ergo se ad monasterium vicinum cumque monachos quoque tristes timidosque cerneret, *Eia* (inquit) *Deus adhuc in caelo regnat, non deiiciamur animo.* Convocari autem statim iubet ex plateis magnam copiam pauperum quibuscum coenaret, eorumque precibus negotium suum commendat. Illisque dimissis parari sibi lectulum retro post altare petit, ut sive capiendus, sive occidendus ea nocte fuerit (quod omnes existimabant) id ei iuxta Dominum suum accideret. Atque haec in civitate Northamptoniae gesta sunt, media fere hieme, cum imbres maximi et ingens frigus urgerent. Thomas autem dimissa turba solus ante altare se provoluit, immensis lachrimis, suspiriis, atque singultibus petit consilium, auxiliumque a Domino, incertus plane quid ageret, quid concilii caperet. Nam ex una parte pastoralis officii constantia, ovium suarum defensio, ardens martirii desiderium, et exigua spes, quae fugae supererat, vehentissime ipsum ad permanendum incitabant; ex alia vero parte volvebat animo res eo loco iam esse suas, ut ipse in Anglia nihil ultra posset prodesse, apud pontificem fortasse nonnihil, concilium esse et exemplum etiam Christi, posse aliquando pastores periculis se subtrahere, idem constare de apostolis, de Athanasio etiam, Hilario, aliisque episcopis, quare ut paucis rem absolvam, convocatis ad se duobus sanctissimis monachis, et uno famulo, mutata veste, socium illis se adiungit, et intempesta nocte cum plueret copiosissime, maximaeque essent tenebrae, pedites egrediuntur, Deoque duce fugae se[24] tradunt.

O sanctum coetum, O foelix consortium! Videte, fratres mei, archiepiscopum vestrum, patriae parentem, columen reipublicae nostrae, ducem, magistrum, antesignanum huius nostri exilii, videte illum eiectum domo, exclusum civitate, nudatum bonis, spoliatum dignitate, desertum a suis, proditum ab alienis, exagitatum ab omnibus. Videte, praesules, fratrem vestrum, coepiscopum vestrum, ordinis vestri ornamentum, et decus, media nocte errantem, per devia reptantem, luce latitantem, ut pontificiae dignitatis integritatem conservaret. Videte, caelites, alumnum vestrum, clientem vestrum, pugilem vestrum, qui ob hierachiae vestrae, et ecclesiae defensionem, cum tot inuriis, incommodis, et calamitatibus conflictatur. O caelum! o terram! quo me vertam ut audiatur vox

---

23. in rebus etiam ecclesiasticis] C; om. G
24. fugae se] C; se fugae G

ploratus mei? An sol unquam facinus indignus vidit? aut si sol non vidit, quia nocte gestum est, an unquam Christianae aures ab hominibus Christianis rem atrociorem perpetratam audierunt? Quid agis Henrice rex? quid furis? quid debaccharis? quid tantis te inferni sceleribus ingurgitas? quid tantopere iam expetis, quod tanto dolore sis postea defleturus? quid modo concupiscis, quod tanta penitentia sis postea redempturus? O caecas hominum cupiditates, o furiosam iracundiam, o effrenatam ambitionem, o periculosam principum conditionem, qui tantum possunt, quantum volunt, tantumque saepe volunt, quantum ira, libido cupiditasque suggerunt. O stultum hominis iudicium! an quicquam felicius dici potest (auditores) quam Thomas, qui haec suffert? An quicquam miserius fingi potest, quam Henricus, qui haec infert? Etiam[25] Thoma, securus Deo duce, angelisque comitantibus, beatam illam terram, quae te recipiet, ingratam, quae dimisit, miseram,[26] quae eiecit. Totum me sentio commotum (auditores) hoc summo patriae meae scelere, et multa quidem occurrent, quibus illud deplorem, nisi temporis brevitas solicitam finiendi celeritatem imperaret.

Transeo igitur cum D. Thoma mare Gallicum navigio[27] vecto piscatoris, ubi expositus in arenam, cum ob corporis imbecillitatem pedes progredi non possit, impositus iumento sine freno, et ephippio, ut Christi magis figuram exprimeret, ductus est Audomaropolim Artesiae Belgicae civitatem, quo cum pervenisset, et sperasset se iam securum esse, ecce nova pericula. Comes enim Flandriae ab Henrico rege praeoccupatus archiepiscopum minabatur in Angliam remittere, sed opera Episcopi Tornacensis ereptus, Senonas tandem ad pontificem pervenit, ubi licet Henricus iam per oratores suos multa de illo questus fuisset, et nonnullos etiam in partes suas pertraxisset, ut existimarent servum Dei maiori zelo, quam prudentia voluntati regis restitisse, pontifex tamen audita causa secundum Thomam iudicavit. E duobus etiam sancti viri postulatis, quorum alterum erat, ut archiepiscatum se exoneraret, alterum, ut colligendi sui causa ad monasterium aliquod diverteret, primum abnuit pontifex, secundum concessit. Dixit enim Alexander se hominem episcopatum digniorem in ecclesia Dei non cognovisse: sed quoad res tamen eius cum Henrico componerentur, permissum ei esse, ut ad monasterium Pontinacense ordinis Cisterciensis animi sui oblectandi causa deflecteret. Quo secundo laitissimus factus Thomas, dum festinato gressu eo properaret, ecce nova turbatio, novumque certamen occurrunt, enim ei in itinere omnes amici, cognati, necessarii ex Anglia eiecti, vexati, spoliati, et bonis omnibus exuti per Henricum, qui omnes cum importunis vocibus virum Dei implorarent, ut eorum misertus, voluntati regiae se accommodaret: ille daemonis strategema hoc esse intelligens, mirabili fortitudine affectui carnis restitit. Litteris enim tantum commendatitiis ad proceres Galliae eos dimittens ipse animo pacatissimo ad Eremum suam fruendam cucurrit.

In monasterio Pontinacensi positus, quid egerit, quantam vitae suae admirationem omnibus excitaverit, festinanti mihi difficillimum fuerit explicare. Testis sit inter caetera[28] fluvius ille monasterium alluens, in quem Dei martyr hiberno tempore sui cruciandi causa descendere consueverat, quousque nervi corporis rigore contraherentur. Testes sint

25. Etiam] this ed.; obscure in C and G
26. ingratam ... miseram] C; ingrata ... misera G
27. navigio] C; vestigio G
28. caetera] C; caeteros G

asperitates illae stupendae, quas in monasterio Sancti Columbae (eiectus e Pontinacensi Henrici minis) in corpus suum per annos quoatuor, quotidie exercebat, quas referre sine horrore vix quisquam potest. Ultra cilicium enim et verbera, de quibus ante iam dixi, humi semper dormiebat, lapidem capiti supponebat, tertiam noctis partem flexis genibus transigebat, oleribus tantum vescebatur, ieiuniis largissimis se macerabat, aliisque corpus affligebat, spiritum inflammabat, seque ad futurum martyrii bravium praeparabat, quod Christus hoc ipso tempore ei apparens clarissima voce futurum praedixerat, promiseratque,[29] ut hinc etiam intelligamus (fratres mei charissimi) quae vita martyrium antecedere debeat quantoque disciplinae ac sanctitatis studio hoc summum in terris bonum a Domino sit comparandum.

Thomae vero pro singulari hac[30] vitae praestantia non est mirum si singulare genus[31] martyrii concessum fuerit; de quo, cum iam mihi ingrediendum esset, ut pro rei dignitate nonnulla dicerem, video me exclusum tempore, ut ne facti quidem narrandi locus detur. Sit igitur satis uno quasi verbo summatim quae sequuntur perstrinxisse: Henricum scilicet ficta pace Thomam in Angliam post septem annorum exilium revocasse, quo cum venisset et sedi sua restitutus fuisset, novas calumnias statim excogitatas, veteres inimicitias resuscitatas esse. Regi in Normandia degenti, verba quaedam per iracundiam excidisse, quibus gratum ei putabatur fore, si vir Dei de medio tolleretur: advolasse statim in Angliam aulicos quosdam e[32] regia familia, qui his istis festis natalitiis salvatoris Cantuariam ruentes, virum Dei nec fugientem, nec repugnantem, nec se defendentem cum possit,[33] nec fores claudi sinentem, sed orantem, et ante altare in genua procumbentem, gladiis nefandis (proh facinus) transverberasse. Testis est qui adfuit, qui vidit, qui historiam scripsit, qui martyrem Christi ulnis amplexus brachium in certamine amisit amputatum ab homicidis; testis (inquam)[34] est Thomam in martyrio ne gemitum quidem edidisse, nec in quatuor gladiorum ictibus qui capiti eius inferebantur unquam manus aut brachia sustulisse (quod homines naturae ductu et consuetudine facere solent) ut caput tueantur,[35] sed haec tantum verba aliquoties ingeminasse: *Pro Christo Domino et ecclesia libenter morior*. O virum admirabilem, o vocem divinam! Videte (fratres mei) ducem praestantissimum viae vitaeque nostrae, videte magistrum, intuemini praecursorem. *Pro Christo Domino* (inquit) *et ecclesia libenter morior*. Quae vox fortior? Quae sanctior? Quae praesule Christiano dignior? Quae vox Deo ad gloriam, Angelis ad laetitiam, inimicis ad confusionem, daemonibus ad terrorem, nobis ad imitationem, omnibus ad exemplum, ipsi martyri ad triumphum cogitari potuit illustrior? *Libenter* (inquit) *morior*, et quidni libenter Thoma, cum mors pro Christo,[36] non sit mors, sed initium potius vitae, arrha regni, sigilum gloriae, porta aeternitatis, et beatitudinis complemen-

29. N *resumes here, introducing the text with* Atque haec dicta sunt [ut hinc etiam intelligamus]
30. singulari hac] C G; hac singulari N
31. singulare genus] C G; singulare quoque genus N
32. e] C N; om. G
33. possit] C G; posset N
34. N *places bracket after* est
35. tueantur] C G; tueretur N
36. N *inserts* sumpta *after* pro Christo

tum? O sanguinem bene impensum, qui[37] pro Christo impenditur, quidni excitemur (fratres mei), quidni animemur hoc exemplo? Vidimus labores huius martyris breves illos quidem, sed gloriam sempiternam, et gloriam quidem, quae vera gloria est, qua ille iam plusquam quadringentis annis in caelis fruitur, nondum vidimus. Has umbras gloriae, quae in terris habentur, vidimus Thomae mirabiliter multiplicatas: gloriam nimirum miraculorum, gloriam sepulchri, gloriam devotionis, et concursus omnium gentium, sed inter caetera omnia, nihil ei tam gloriosum in hoc mundo accidit, quam quod persecutorem suum Henricum virtute caelesti ad tantam penitentiae humilitatem adegerit, ut nudis pedibus gemebundus[38] ad sepulchrum eius venerit et infinitis effusis lachrimis gemitus, suspiria et lamenta ediderit, humi etiam prostratus veniam petierit a sancto martyre, et penitentiam ab episcopo pro delictis,[39] denique post integram noctem vigiliis, et verberibus transactam, humo nuda residens, omnes ad commiserationem sui[40] spectaculo commovit. Quae maior gloria? Quae martyris vis divinior?

O Domine Jesu, vita virtusque martyrum, utinam placitum esset in oculis tuis hanc gratiam persecutoribus quoque nostris Anglicanis facere, ut ad te convertantur, et quod Henrico concessisti unius Thomae martyris tantum[41] exoratus precibus, id Henrici filiae concedas, plusquam centum testium tuorum ab illa occisorum placatus intercessione. O quam laeti tibi ageremus gratias de hoc beneficio? quam sollicite laudes tuas ubique descantaremus? Verum si iustitiae tuae severitas hoc forte non permittat, humiliter tamen te obsecramus, ut vires saltem nobis et fortitudinem[42] tribuas ad praeliandum praelia tua in hoc agone quem nobis proposuisti, ita ut neque vitae cupiditas a certamine, neque metus a periculis, neque ignavia a labore nos unquam retardet, sed omnia impendentes in tuam gloriam, patriaeque salutem, superimpendamus etiam nos ipsos[43] si opus fuerit, ut sic aliquo modo saltem respondeamus vocationi nostrae et infinitis beneficiis a te acceptis: de quibus *Gloria tibi et gratulatio et gratiarum actio in aeternum.* Deo gratias.[44]

[*Note on cover page of C:*] scripta est haec oratio a B.P. Henrico Walpole martyre[45] et composita a R.P. Roberto Personio.[46]

[From *Newes from Spayne and Holland*]

Having to speake this day (most excellent and renowmed cardinall,[47] and you the rest most honorable auditors) of that right famous and noble light of Christs Catholique

37. qui] *C N*; quo *G*
38. gemebundus] *C G*; gemibundus *N*
39. delictis] *C G*; delicto *N*
40. sui] *C G*; tanto *N*
41. tantum] *C G*; om. *N*
42. et fortitudinem] *C G*; om. *N*
43. nos ipsos] *C G*; nosmetipsos *N*
44. Deo gratias] *C G*; om. *N*
45. martyre] *interlined with caret*
46. "This oration was written by Blessed Father Henry Walpole, martyr, and composed by Rev. Father Robert Persons."
47. Rodrigo de Castro Osorio, cardinal archbishop of Seville. See Persons to Pope Clement VIII, 1 December 1592 (B162), headnote.

church S. Thomas of Canterbury, one point am I well to remember for my comfort, that I shall speak nothing this day in this noble audience which in some sorte pertayneth not to all that are present, seing there is scarse any man in my opinion in this most ample & honorable assembly which may not acknowledge some parte of his estate, calling or condition to be resembled in this most glorious servant of our Saviour. For if you consider wel, my speech must be of a citizen unto cityzens,[48] of a senator unto senators,[49] of a judge unto judges,[50] of a head and chancelor of a kingdome unto the heades and presidents of honorable counsels,[51] of a defendor of religion, unto them that by office do protect religion;[52] of a vigilant pastor unto those that are captaines in guyding soules,[53] of him that professed reguler life, unto such as are most observant of regular austerity,[54] of an archbishop to an archprelate, of the primate of an universal kingdome, to a cardinal of Christs universal church,[55] and finally of a martyr to them that are desirous of martyrdome,[56] if God shall finde them worthy of so great a dignity. Wherfore, seing al that are present have there parts in this holy celebrity, what remayneth but that with the prayers of al we make recourse to him that is master and Lord of al, beseching His Divine Majestie to accompany me this day with his holy grace, while I in this sermon shal recount, declare, persuade, implore, cry out, complaine or weepe in your presence, according as the consideration of these tymes or the most afflicted state of our desolate country shal enforce me to do. And first of al, let us begin with our humble recourse unto his glorious mother the blessed virgin Marie, whom S. Thomas ever honored with special devotion, desiring her with al instance to assist me in this action for the directing the course of this my spech, unto the honor & glory of her sonne, our Saviour.

[...]

These things of S. Thomas his great austeriti in life, I have recounted (deare brethern & countrimen) to the end that therby also we may understand partly, what manner of life ought to goe before martyrdome,[57] and with how great indevour of discipline and holynes, this supreme benifit and privilege to be a martyre is to be procured at Gods handes here uppon earth: and for that S. Thomas did excell in this kynde of holynes (as now I have declared), no marvail if according to the excellency of life, so excellent a kind of death was graunted him also. Of which sacred death and martyrdom, wheras now I would begin to say somewhat, I see my selfe so strayghtned in tyme, as there is not space to recount the very fact, wherfore let it be sufficient to touch the rest that followeth in one worde, to witt, that King Henry after al these troobles, made feigned peace with the good

48. [*marginal note:*] Citizens.
49. [*marginal note:*] Councelours.
50. [*marginal note:*] Judges.
51. [*marginal note:*] Presidentes of concelles.
52. [*marginal note:*] Inquisitores.
53. [*marginal note:*] Pastors & preachers.
54. [*marginal note:*] Monkes & fryers.
55. [*marginal note:*] Archbishopes Cardinales.
56. [*marginal note:*] Inglish schollers dedicated to martyrdom.
57. [*marginal note:*] A good life is needfull before martyrdom.

archbishop, and restored him to his country and sea of Caunterbury agayne, after he had bine seven yeares abroad in banishment; where he was no sooner aryved, but presently new quarels and calumniations were devised and raysed agaynst him agayne; and theruppon the king being then in Normandy incensed with coller, spake in his rage certaine doubtfull woords, wherby it was conceaved that it should be grateful unto him, if the archbishop by violence were made away: by which conceat, certayn wicked courtiors of his owne family, departing from thence and rushing into Canterbury, even in this festival dayes of holy Christmas (good hearers)[58] set uppon this servant of God, who nether fled nor resisted, nor defended himselfe as he might, nor suffred the dores of the church to be shutt: but praying and casting himselfe before the high alter, on his knees, suffred himselfe most innocently to be slaine by wicked caytifes. Witnes wherof, is he among others, that was present when the act was done, he that saw it with his owne eyes, he that wrote the story, he that held the blessed martyr in his armes, while he was slayne, and had his owne arme cutt of by the murtherers for his labour.[59]

This man, I saie, is witnesse under his own handwriting, how that S. Thomas in al his marty[r]dome, never gave out so much as one grone or sigh, nor in fower blowes stryken at his head, wherby his braynes were beaten on the pavement, he never so much as lifted up his handes or armes to defend his head (as men by natural instinct in such cases are wont to doe), but only repeated once or twise these wordes, *I dye most willingly for Christ and for his church*. O admirable man, O heavenly speach, behold heere (my loving brethren of this colledg), behold here a most excellent captaine of this our life and course that we are to follow: behold our master, behold our forerrunner: what spech more valiant, what voice more holy? What wordes more worthy of a Christian prelat? What sentence more excellent can be imagined, eyther to the glory of God, or to the joy of angels, or to the terror of divels, or to the confusion of his enymies, or for our imitation, or for the example of al posterity, or for the edification of the universal world, or for the endles triumph of this martyr himselfe?

I die most willingly (sayeth he) *for Christ and his church*. O holy martyr, O blessed Thomas, thow hast great reason to die willingly in such a cause, for that death suffred for Christ thy master, is no death at all, but rather a beginning of a longer life, an earnest peny of an everlasting kingdom, a seale of glory, a gate of eternity, & the very complement of al felicity. O blood wel spent that is spent for Christ, why should not we stir up our selves (deare bretheren), why should not we be animated and inflamed with this example? We have seene the labores and toyles of this martyr, though great, yet short and sone ended, but his glory is everlasting. And yet the true glory which he hath enjoyed now above foure hundreth yeares in heaven, which only indeede is to be called glory, we have not yet seene. These shadowes only of glory, which on earth are to be seene, we have beheld most wonderfuly multiplied unto S. Thomas: I meane (good hearers) the glory uppon earth of his infinite miracles, the glory of his sepulcre throughout al Christendome, the glory of the universal concourse and devotion of al nations unto him. But among al other glories and glorious accidents happned unto him, no one thing was ever

---

58. The oration was delivered on the feast day of St Thomas of Canterbury, 29 December.
59. Edward Grim.

more glorious or admirable, then that soone after his death, by vertue from heaven, he procured to King Henry his persecutor such grace and humility of repentance, as that he came barefooted with many sighes and sobbes unto his tombe, and ther prostrating himselfe uppon the ground with fluds of teares, asked pardon of the blessed martyr and penance of the bishop for his offences, and so after a whole night spent in watching prayer and bearing of him selfe, and lying uppon the bare ground he departed, leaving al the lokers on most deeply moved with his harty repentance. What greater glory, what more heavenly force of a Christian martyr then this?

O Lord Jesu, which arte the life and vertue of al martyrs, would it might please Thy Divine Majestie and infinite mercy to give this grace also to our Inglish persecutors, wherby they would repent and turne unto thee: and that which thow didest graunt unto King Henry by the only prayer of thy martyr Sainct Thomas, that his sinnes might be forgiven, thow wouldest graunt the same unto King Henryes daughter at the intercession of above an hundreth of thy glorious martyrs whom she hath slayne, that she might not perish. O how joyful should we render thankes unto thee, for this so singuler and desired a benefite! Oh how chearefull should we singe every where thy prayses for the same! But if perhaps the severity of thy justice do not permitt this, yet most humbly we do besech thee, to give unto us thy unworthy children, here present, so much strenght and hevenly fortitude as to fight manfully and hold out chearfully in this combat which thow hast prepared for us, so as neyther desire of life may stay us from this batail, nor feare of death from perill, nor slouth from labour in this thy cause, but that we bestowing our selves wholy unto thy glory and to the salvation of our owne selves and of our country, we may give our soules up also, and pay our blood in this holy work, if need require, and therby in some sort be answerable unto our vocation, and to the infinite benifits which of thee we have receaved, for which *both praise, glory, gratulation and thankesgiving be unto thee for al eternity*. Amen.

Translation

An Oration Delivered at the English College of Seville
on the Feast Day of St Thomas of Canterbury, 1592 AD

"The good shepherd giveth his life for his sheep."

Faced with the prospect of speaking today about that brightest shining light of the Catholic church, St Thomas of Canterbury (Your renowned Eminence, most distinguished hearers), I have frequent recourse to this comforting thought: there is nothing I am about to say in this great concourse which does not relate to almost everyone present, since it is unlikely that anyone amongst this whole, most noble assembly of people does not recognize something of himself in this most glorious servant of God. For I am to speak of a citizen, amongst citizens; of a senator before senators; of a judge in the presence of judges; of a royal chancellor in front of the leaders of councils; an upholder of the faith amongst the appointed guardians of the faith; of a most watchful shepherd amongst directors of souls; of a devotee of the religious life amongst those who keep the rule of life most observantly; of an archbishop before a prelate; of the primate of a whole kingdom to a cardinal prince of the universal church: and finally, a martyr in the presence of those who seek martyrdom, if God should find them worthy. And so, since every one of these titles is to be found in this congregation, why do we not also turn to the common Lord of all with the vows and petitions of all, that as I speak today, whether I recount or declare or plead, whether I lament or mourn (if either the necessity of the times or of English affairs should demand it), I may be worthy of God's grace accompanying me? And first, let us implore our most holy mother (whom Archbishop Thomas always venerated with the deepest devotion) with all our might, to stretch out her right hand to aid my speech, and guide the flow of my discourse to the highest glory of her son.

But, as best I can, I shall make the starting-point of my speech what ought to be the foundation of every speech and oration: that I promise truly not to mention anything in this place of the life of St Thomas which is not affirmed to be certain, unquestioned and fully proved, and attested in writing by those very same people who were eyewitnesses of virtually the whole business. For the life of this saint has this almost unique character, that it was put in writing by those who lived alongside him and were for the most part present at the events themselves, so that the whole account may come forth with more assured truth and greater authority.[60]

To start on this basis, therefore, this holy martyr of Christ was no less than a London citizen of our native race, born of parents both noble and extremely wealthy to boot. Consequently, he lacked no opportunity to pursue whatever course of life that he himself might wish: that indeed he followed the best, among such a store, I judge to be attributable to the sovereign grace of God. But something out of the ordinary occurred on Thomas's birthday, that on the very day when he was brought into the light, a fire broke out from his father's house, who knows whence, and burnt down a large part of the city of London.[61] With the permission of the other most distinguished hearers (my most beloved brothers) I shall go ahead and recount it as an encouragement to you. I shall interpret it, as far as possible, as it pertains to us, who are, according to the flesh, fellow citizens and of the same tribe with this most holy martyr. I shall consider that this fire of Thomas's touches us, I say, that by it we should be set on fire to imitate him in every thing he did to defend God's church. Besides this, of course, if we cast our eyes on the state of the whole of Christendom, which for more than four hundred years since then has certainly been most unhappy and very greatly disturbed, we will perhaps recognize that Thomas has been brought forth as an example not only to his English fellow citizens (come now!), but also to the inhabitants of the whole Christian world, and as a kind of sign set before the peoples and nations, by which all mortals may be reminded of their

---

60. Several of Thomas's clerks wrote eyewitness accounts of his death: Edward Grim, Benedict of Peterborough, William of Canterbury, and William Fitzstephen. John of Salisbury and Herbert of Bosham also wrote biographies. See *Lives of Thomas Becket*, ed. and trans. Staunton, 6–10 and 182–219, esp. 195–203 (Edward Grim's account of the murder).

61. On Becket's early life and career, see Frank Barlow, *Thomas Becket* (London, 1986). The fire on Thomas's birthday is mentioned on page 15. See also *The Lives of Thomas Becket*, ed. and trans. Staunton, 40–42, where other "omens of future greatness" are recounted.

duty and may conceive more ardent purposes of serving God, from the flame ignited by Thomas.

For if we recall the memory of those times from the chronicles of the years in which these things took place that we are about to tell of this most renowned martyr, the outward appearance of things will seem calamitous (hearers) and standing in need of fire from heaven. Virtually all things were then gone cold, and the ardour of Christian passion was very near to being put out by a deadly torpor. For what could be told or imagined more wretched or more calamitous than what the histories recount of the age in which Thomas lived? All that was human was disturbed by war, sedition, ambition, hatred, and luxury: everything divine, turned upside down. At Rome sat Alexander III, a most saintly and powerful pope, but faced with four antipopes challenging him. In Sicily, King William was in an uproar against the Roman church; in Italy and Germany, the emperor Frederick, called Barbarossa, was persecuting her most sorely everywhere with blood-stained arms.[62] In Greece the emperor Manuel was contesting the imperial power of the east with Andronicus, both of them hostile to the Roman church. Hence it came about, especially with the antipathy the Greeks felt towards the Latins, that Cardinal John, sent with a delegation to Constantinople by pope Alexander, was most savagely murdered, and dragged most outrageously through the streets of the city.[63] The Christian king of Jerusalem, Baldwin, was under attack from the Turks; in Egypt the sultan was fighting with Saladin.[64] In Spain the two most Catholic kings Sancho III and Ferdinand II were in conflict with the Moors.[65] The kings of France (Louis VII), England (Henry II), and Scotland (Malcolm) were at war with their own people at home and also abroad amongst themselves, and clashed together.[66] I pass over the wars of the Venetians against the Hun-

---

62. Pope Alexander III (r. 1159–1181), supported by France and England, was opposed from the very start of his reign by Victor IV, and his successors Paschal III, Calixtus III, and Innocent III, who had the backing of the emperor, Frederick Barbarossa (r. 1155–1190). The Latin word, "Aenobarbus" means "copper bearded."

63. The authority of the Byzantine emperor Manuel I Komnenos (r. 1143–1180) was threatened by the escape of his cousin Andronikos (r. 1183–1185) in 1164–1165. An attempt by Pope Adrian IV (r. 1154–1159) to secure a papal-Byzantine alliance in 1155 was unsuccessful in the long term.

64. Baldwin IV (r. 1174–1185), called the leper, waged war with Saladin (r. 1174–93), sultan of Egypt and Syria, for several years. Saladin had to defend his position against supporters of the Fatimid Caliphate, which he had abolished.

65. Sancho III (r. 1157–1158), king of Castile, and his brother, Ferdinand II (r. 1157–1188), king of León, reached an agreement regarding lands they expected to take from the Moors, by the treaty of Sahagún (May 1158). Sancho's successor, Alfonso VIII, married Eleanor Plantagenet (daughter of Henry II of England), who was instrumental in disseminating a very early devotion to Becket in Iberia (e.g., the Church of St Thomas of Canterbury in Salamanca, built in 1175).

66. Louis VII (r. 1137–1180), king of France, faced opposition from Theobald II of Champagne and Geoffrey V, count of Anjou (the father of King Henry II of England), and was in conflict with Henry II of England during the 1150s. Malcolm IV (r. 1153–1165), king of Scotland, had to deal with a succession of rebels and neighbouring princes, including Ferchar, mormaer of Strathearn, Somerled, king of Argyll, and Fergus, lord of Galloway. He had an uneasy relationship with Henry II, who knighted him at the siege of Toulouse in 1159.

garians over the principality of Dalmatia; the Germans against Henry, the duke of Saxony; the Bohemians against the Poles; and many others besides, by which the whole world (as Bishop Cromer rightly remarked) was convulsed under Pope Alexander III – to the point where not only was the pursuit of learning and virtue laid aside, but also all zeal for Christian piety was almost extinguished.[67] Thieving, robbery, and homicide held sway, everything dripped with blood, blood touched blood, as the prophet said it would.[68]

To cure such a great deluge of evils, God, as the greatest and best of all, of his surpassing benevolence, at this very time raised up several men of outstanding character who lit up the world and set themselves up as fortifications to protect the house of God. And indeed, to restore learning, although I could mention many, it will suffice to name Peter Lombard, bishop of Paris, architect of scholastic theology, also the monk Gratian, compiler of the *Decretum* of canon law, and also Peter Comestor, the preeminent author of ecclesiastical history.[69] But for zeal in promoting virtue and inducing contempt for the world, two very famous orders of religious men were commissioned by this same Pope Alexander: namely, the Carthusians and the Carmelites. Also, the military orders of St James and Calatrava rose up in Spain with the support of King Sancho and with the approval of Alexander.[70] I pass over the one I ought to have spoken of in the first instance: St Bernard, who was a mirror of virtue, religion, learning, and holiness, who lived at this same time with St Thomas of Canterbury, and founded one hundred and forty monasteries of his order.[71] He died not long

---

67. Marcin Cromer, prince-bishop of Warmia (in office 1579–1589), wrote extensively on Polish history. In *De origine et gestibus Polonorum libri XXX* (Basel, 1558), mentioning several of the conflicts detailed here, he writes "Ac totus tunc fere orbis Christianus mutuis bellis collidebatur" (And virtually the entire Christian world was crushed by mutual wars) (chapter 6, p. 158).

68. Hosea 4:2.

69. On Peter Lombard (1090–1160), bishop of Paris from 1159, author of the four books of *The Sentences*, which became a standard textbook throughout the middle ages and attracted innumerable commentaries, see Marcia L. Colish, *Peter Lombard*, 2 vols. (Leiden, 1994) and Philipp W. Rosemann, *Peter Lombard* (Oxford, 2004). On the *Concordia discordantium canonum* or *Decretum Gratiani*, similarly the standard textbook for students of canon law, see Anders Winroth, *The Making of Gratian's Decretum* (Cambridge, 2000) and Wilfried Hartmann and Kenneth Pennington, eds., *The History of Medieval Canon Law in the Classical Period, 1140–1234: From Gratian to the Decretals of Pope Gregory IV* (Washington, DC, 2008). The *Historia scholastica* of Peter Comestor (1100–1178) is concerned with Biblical rather than ecclesiastical history; see Beryl Smalley, *The Study of the Bible in the Middle Ages* (Oxford, 1941) and Mark J. Clark, *The Making of the "Historia scholastica"* (Toronto, 2016).

70. The order of Calatrava was founded during the brief reign of King Sancho III to allow the lay brothers of the monastery at Fitero to act as knights to defend the castle of Calatrava la Vieja. The order was confirmed by Pope Alexander III in 1164. The order of St James was founded in León in about 1170 in order to protect pilgrims to the shrine of St James at Compostela.

71. St Bernard of Clairvaux (1090–1153), founder of the Cistercian order, was canonized in 1174. See Étienne Gilson, *The Mystical Theology of St Bernard*, trans. Alfred Howard Campbell Downes (London, 1940), Jean Leclerq, *The Love of Learning and the Desire for God: A Study of Monastic Culture*, trans. Catharine Misrahi (New York, 1961), and Gillian R. Evans, *Bernard of Clairvaux* (New York, 2000).

before St Thomas suffered martyrdom, and both were made remarkable spectacles before God, angels, and men,[72] and both were numbered among the saints by the same Pope Alexander.

It is not without reason, therefore, that this presage of fire was given to mark the birthday of St Thomas, so as to leave no doubt that the whole Christian commonwealth would be fired up by the example of his life as much as his death, to every kind of ardour for divine service.

And indeed to speak first of his manner of life: from adolescence itself it certainly followed every course of honours, riches, and dignities: Thomas swept through every rank of officialdom until at length he reached that which is highest and supreme in the English realm, and closest to the king, so that he became no less than chancellor of the whole kingdom. In fulfilling that magistracy, as he himself instinctively acted with singular prudence, wisdom, diligence, and even justice, precisely so as not to be swallowed up by that supreme power, by his wealth of opportunities, by the outward show, splendour, and vaingloriousness of his life, or should be dissipated in vice, the divine bounty provided him with a certain very powerful rival, Roger, archdeacon of Canterbury, who also later being made archbishop of York most stubbornly resisted this man of God throughout his whole life, and made every effort to contradict him in whatever he could.[73] In this way divine providence ordained that Thomas, through the rivalry of this man, should be seasoned to every perfection of life.

Then it came to pass, with the decease of Theobald, a great and most prudent man, that the see of Canterbury became vacant, which is the metropolitan of the whole island. When King Henry had thought long and hard about the question on whom, amongst men, he should best confer it, he found no one to be compared with Thomas in any way. When therefore, being constituted archbishop, he realized that he had been made father of the kingdom after being its judge, he came to the realization that the customs of the forefathers should be altogether imitated and their dispositions adopted. For he decided that he would fulfil his role better if he united himself to God more strictly. And so, immediately after his inauguration, which took place at Canterbury with consummate splendour and ceremony, when the almost countless throng of people who had flocked together had dispersed, and he was left alone with himself and with God, Thomas seized the moment to begin turning over in his mind who he was, what he had done, to what place he had come, how great a burden he had taken up, what reckoning would have to be made, what duties he had to fulfil, and other matters of this kind, which divine grace customarily intimates to those who are predestined to life. When he had seriously reviewed all these things in his mind, and recalled to mind the saying of St Gregory, that one ought to be that much humbler, and more ready to serve God as a duty, according to the obligation one recognizes for oneself in rendering one's account, he fully resolved to leave secular life behind and enter into religion, and attach himself to the order of reg-

72. 1 Cor. 4: 9, quoted by Edmund Campion on the scaffold.
73. Roger de Pont Lévêque (ca. 1115–1181) was archdeacon of Canterbury from 1148 and consecrated archbishop of York in 1154. He and Becket were at odds in the household of Theobald of Bec, archbishop of Canterbury (r. 1139–1161); see Barlow, *Thomas Becket*, 37–38, and *Lives of Thomas Becket*, ed. and trans. Staunton, 46–47.

ular canons, who flourished with particular holiness in England at that time. He performed this in reality immediately after uttering the vow, even though, to avoid the praises of the common people, and to preempt anyone understanding the matter differently from what he himself felt, he judged it wise to retain the habit of a lay person for a time. And so he strove for the thing itself, and carried it out, but concealed his name. He embraced the vigils, choir, fasts, and penances, but deferred the outward habit for good reasons, as it seemed to him. However, this moderation born of human prudence seemed less acceptable to God: for one night a certain man truly ghastly to behold appeared to one of the archbishop's servants and warned him that he should report to Thomas that he should change his habit also, and if he did not, he would forever treat him as an enemy. When he heard that message, it is impossible to say how much the man of God was struck dumb with fear, and how he was disturbed in his most inward feelings, to the point where he hardly doubted that that voice had come from God. And so, from that very same hour, after shedding a great storm of tears, he consecrated himself entirely to God and fully surrendered himself, and although he did not give up the pontifical rank which he had taken up, he did renounce the outward show and paraphernalia which belonged to that rank. The things they have passed on in letters of the inward life of this man are marvellous and quite stupendous (listeners) – those who were able to be eyewitnesses! Wonders about his meagreness of diet, his roughness of dress, the frequency of his fasts, his perseverance in vigils, his persistency in prayer, the huge quantity of his alms, exceedingly great; and – something which in that condition of life is even more to be admired – his continual and very severe punishment of the body. On this one subject, the venerable man Robert Merton, the archbishop's chaplain and inseparable life companion, who always slept in virtually the same room, relates in a letter that he allowed no day to pass, hardly any, from the time when he was made archbishop, right until his death, in which he was not to be seen flagellating himself severely five, four, or at least three times.[74]

O wondrous and almost unheard-of example of Christian asceticism! Who will not be amazed, who will not be struck dumb (listeners) to compare those times with our own; or to contrast the burning intensity of saints of such a kind with the lukewarmness

---

74. On Thomas's transformation from chancellor to archbishop, including his dress habits and his increasing asceticism, see Barlow, *Thomas Becket*, 74–87, and *The Lives of Thomas Becket*, ed. and trans. Staunton, 66–69. Several of Becket's early biographers, including William of Canterbury and Herbert of Bosham, dwell on his change of habit, invoking the idea of putting on the new man, but I have not been able to trace the anecdote about the apparition. William of Canterbury mentions a related vision: "Nam a quodam coenobita Cantuariensis ecclesiae, sanctissimae conversationis, acceperat, cui Dominus in visione locutus fuerat, quod si monachum indueret, Dominum in negotiis propitium et coadjutorem mereretur" (For he understood, from a certain monk of the church at Canterbury, to whom God had spoken in a vision, that if he donned the habit of a monk, he would earn God's favour and assistance in his affairs); see William of Canterbury, *Vita, Passio, et Miracula S. Thomae Cantuariensis Achiepiscopi* 1.10, in *Materials for the History of Thomas Becket*, ed. James Craigie Robertson (London, 1877), 1: 10. Ronald E. Pepin, *Anselm & Becket: Two Canterbury Saints' Lives by John of Salisbury* (Toronto, 2009), 13–14, notes that Becket was associating himself with the tradition that the Archbishops of Canterbury were appointed from the monastic orders.

of our present age? And so much for his scourging. But what shall I say about his hairshirt, which being extensive and extremely harsh, he hardly ever removed from his flesh, neither by day nor by night, at home or abroad, on a journey or resting, in the court or in the church, not even during these very feast days of our Lord's nativity in which he was cruelly murdered. For after his death it was reported that the hairshirt was so embedded in his flesh that it drove all those who saw it to horror. What therefore shall we say of the life of this St Thomas (listeners), which was so wonderfully and wholly integrated that he was able to satisfy both his pontifical rank and also the most religious asceticism at the same time? Outwardly, indeed, his life was amiable, but inwardly strict, splendid in show but plain in spirit, outwardly wealthy, inwardly most needy, such that it combined religion with high rank, discipline with adornment, humility with grandeur, poverty with riches, solitude with society: in short, the monastery with the palace.

While Thomas was spurring himself thus, the Lord wished to test him with a temptation as well, so that what the angel said to Tobias should be fulfilled: "Because thou hast been acceptable to God, it was necessary that temptation should prove thee,"[75] alongside that other text from Wisdom: "God gave him a strong conflict, that he might overcome."[76] For look, Henry II, king of England, a bellicose, brutal-minded man who, besides the supreme power, by which princes are easily provoked to arrogance, showered Thomas with an abundance of favours in addition, by means of which he thought to put him under an obligation not to oppose his will in anything. Pitifully deceived by wicked flatterers, he wanted to sanction certain laws utterly hostile to ecclesiastical immunities, by means of which he reappropriated to his own courts virtually all jurisdiction over the clergy, and even ecclesiastical matters. In this he was opposed from the start by almost everyone, because these laws were extremely unjust, but at length, partly through force and fear, partly through flattery and gifts, and also by virtue of his royal name itself (which used to be the most powerful), he not only drew all the lay nobility to agree with him, but even turned the greater part of the bishops and the English clergy. Only the archbishop, seeing he was the father and pastor of the rest, considered that he should put up some resistance to the king's greed, for everyone's safety. The other, taking this very hard, employed a thousand devices to overcome the man of God. It would take a long time to review them all in this place; suffice it to say that nothing was left out that art or fraud or flattery or threats or authority or power could exert: the urgings of his friends, the subtlety of his enemies, the pleading of his connexions, the tears of his relatives were brought to bear, to bend the martyr's constancy, but they had no effect at all. As a result, the king's rage increased to the point where, considering that he should proceed with open force, he convened an assembly of the whole kingdom and summoned the archbishop to his court, and because he did not come immediately, being prevented by a serious illness, the king saw to it that he should be forced to pay a great sum of money as a penalty. But on the next day, Thomas, neglecting nothing that was in his power to do, came to the king as a suppliant, and begged that he would give some thought to his own salvation and the public advantage; but being refused admittance by

---

75. Tob. 12:13.
76. Wisd. 10:12; in the Vulgate, the agent is Wisdom, altered here to God.

the king and referred back to parliament, he returned home, and very fervently submitted his cause to God. Meanwhile he was informed that many very scandalous things would be said about him in parliament, on the instigation of the king, and he would be straightway condemned as a rebel against the king and disturber of the common peace, and punished. Realizing this, he appealed to the Roman pontiff. Consequently, an even greater uproar ensued and the king was greatly exasperated in his mind. Since the business was heading for manifest violence and murder, there were some of his friends who urged Thomas to fortify himself at home with a band of his supporters against the present fury of the king, but he sent them away, affirming that this cause of God's would not be protected by brick walls. Others advised him to appease the king's feelings, abjure his office immediately, and resign his archbishopric into the royal hands. But he said, "'The good shepherd giveth his life for his sheep, but the hireling, and he that is not the shepherd, seeth the wolf coming, and leaveth the sheep, and flieth: and the wolf catcheth, and scattereth the sheep.' I did not take up the episcopate on the principle that the moment danger appeared I would hand it over to the king, but only to Christ, from whom I received it, or his vicar – or devote myself to His defence." And so the man of God fearlessly spent that whole night, when many believed he would be killed, in watchings, prayers, and flagellation. But when dawn came, he celebrated Mass with a great quantity of tears, donned his stole, and carrying a cross in his hand arrived at the king's palace where the parliament was, entered the council chamber and very restrainedly set out the many reasons why he could not submit to the king's will in accepting those laws that were contrary to the holy canons of the church. He asked that the matter be referred to the Roman pontiff, who is the judge of all. Meanwhile, he rebuked them for the scandalous act they had committed: how unjust it was that he, the archbishop and primate of England should be forced to attend that secular tribunal, especially in matters ecclesiastical, and how unworthy that he as a father should be condemned by his sons, a prelate by his subjects, a shepherd by his sheep. But when he achieved nothing by this speech, but the argument was stretched out right into the night, the holy man eventually went out through the midst of them, assailed by many reproaches and goaded by insults, one royal minister inciting the other, and egging on the people until they threw mud at the man of God even as he was passing through, and it nearly got to the point where he would have been torn to pieces had not the bishops, in fear of ecclesiastical censure if they allowed him to be assassinated under their very eyes, asserted their own authority with the king, so that the archbishop was sent home safely.

But when he got home he found his household had been utterly dispersed, and almost all of his servants had fled, out of fear for the king. So he repaired to the nearby monastery. When he saw that the monks, too, were frightened and sorrowful, he said, "God still reigns in heaven; let us not be cast down." But he straightway instructed that a great crowd of poor people should be summoned from the streets so that he could dine with them and commend his matter to their prayers. When they had left, he asked for a humble reading-couch to be prepared for him behind the altar, so that if he was to be captured or killed that night (which everyone considered likely), it should happen to him next to his Lord. And these things took place in the city of Northampton, almost in the middle of winter, when very great showers of rain and a sharp frost were bearing down on them. But Thomas sent the crowd away and prostrated himself before the altar alone, seeking counsel and aid from God with floods of tears, sighs, and sobbings, quite unsure what to do, what plan to follow. For on the one hand the constancy demanded by his pastoral duty, the protection of his sheep, his ardent desire for martyrdom, and the meagre hope that remained for flight urged him very powerfully to remain; but on the other hand, he was exercised by the fact that his affairs had already reached such a pass that he himself could achieve nothing further in England, perhaps nothing with the pope. He considered that it was the counsel and example even of Christ, that formerly pastors were able to withdraw themselves from danger, that the same applied to the apostles, to Athanasius even, Hilary, and other bishops. And therefore, to sum it up briefly, he summoned two of the most holy monks and one servant, changed his clothes and joined them as a companion. On a stormy night, when it was raining heavily, and the darkness was at its most intense, they set out on foot and, God being their guide, took flight.[77]

O holy band, O happy company! Behold, my brothers, your archbishop, the one on whom our native land is founded, the support of our commonwealth, the leader, master, standard-bearer of this our exile: you see him thrown out of his house, barred from the city, deprived of his goods, stripped of his rank, abandoned by his own people, betrayed by outsiders, censured by all. Behold, prelates, your brother, your fellow bishop, the ornament of your order, and the flower, wandering in the middle of the night, creeping along byways, hiding from the light, to keep his pontifical dignity intact. Behold, angels, your fellow, your ally, your champion, who, to protect your hierarchy and the church's, is distressed by so many injuries, inconveniences, and calamities. O heaven! O earth! Where shall I turn so that the voice of my complaint may be heard? Has the sun ever seen a more shameful act? Or if the sun did not see it, because it was performed by night, have Christian ears ever heard of anything more savage perpetrated by Christian men? What are you doing, King Henry? Why are you angry? Why are you out of control? Why are you gorging yourself on such great hellish crimes? Why do you now pursue so earnestly what you will weep over with such great sorrow hereafter? Why do you now covet what you will later pay for with such great penitence? O blind desires of men, O frenzied wrath, O unbridled ambition, O perilous condition of princes, who can get whatever they want, and often want whatever anger, lust, and greed suggest. O foolish judgement of men! Can anyone be said to be happier (hearers) than Thomas, who suffers these things? Or can anyone be imagined more miserable than Henry, who instigates them? Even so, Thomas, secure with God as your guide, and accompanied by angels, blessed is that land which receives you; wretched, that which has sent you away; miserable, the one that has cast you out! I am conscious that I am utterly distressed (hearers) by this consummate crime committed by my native land, and many things occur to me indeed, which would make me wail bitterly over it, if lack of time did not require that I bring things swiftly and suddenly to an end.

With Thomas, then, I cross the French sea in a fisherman's sailing vessel. There he was deposited on the beach. When he was not able to proceed by foot, because of the frailty of his body, he was mounted on a mule without a bridle or saddle, so that he pre-

---

77. For the trial at Northampton (6–12 October 1164) and Thomas's subsequent flight, see Barlow, *Thomas Becket*, 109–116, and *The Lives of Thomas Becket*, ed. and trans. Staunton, 100–119.

sented rather the image of Christ, and led into Saint-Omer, a city in Artois in Belgium. When he arrived there, and hoped that he would now be safe, behold! new dangers arose. For the count of Flanders had been previously engaged by King Henry and warned the archbishop to return to England. He was, however, rescued through the help of the bishop of Tournai, and at last he reached the pope at Sens.[78] There, although Henry had already lodged many complaints about him through his envoys, and had won quite a few to take his part, so that they came to the view that the servant of God had opposed the king's will with more zeal than prudence, the pope nevertheless heard the case and judged in Thomas's favour. Of two requests made by the holy man – the first, that he would relieve him of his episcopacy, and the other, that he might go to some monastery in order to recover himself – the pope refused the former but granted the latter. For Alexander said that he had never known a man in the church of God more worthy of the episcopacy; but until his dispute with Henry was settled, he would be permitted to move to the monastery of the Cistercian order at Pontigny for the sake of refreshing his soul. Thomas was greatly gladdened by this support, but while he was hastening there with hurried step, behold! a new confusion and a new struggle presented itself, for on the journey he was met by all his friends, relatives, and connexions who had been thrown out of England, harassed, robbed, and deprived of all their goods by Henry, who all begged the man of God with persistent voices to take pity on them and accommodate himself to the royal will: he, recognizing this to be a stratagem of a demon, resisted his natural affection for them with astonishing fortitude. For he only sent them with letters of recommendation to the noblemen of France while he himself, with great serenity of spirit, made haste to enjoy his monastic retreat.[79]

What he did, once he was settled in the monastery at Pontigny, how much wonder his life aroused in everyone, it would be very difficult for me to describe hastily. One witness, amongst the rest, would be that river flowing next to the monastery, into which God's martyr used to descend in wintertime, for the sake of mortifying himself, until his nerves were contracted from corporal rigour. Witness those stupefying acts of harshness, which he exercised on his own body daily for four years in the monastery of St Columba's (after he was expelled from Pontigny by Henry's threats), which hardly anyone could recount without horror.[80] For besides the hair shirt and the flagellation about which I

78. Crossing the channel in a small craft, Thomas landed at the beach of Oyes, near Gravelines, on 2 November 1164. At Saint-Omer, he received an equivocal welcome from Philip of Alsace, acting count in the absence of his father on crusade, and was assisted by Milo II, bishop of Thérouanne (seventy miles west of Tournai), to meet his clerks at Soissons. He then proceeded to meet Alexander III at Sens, the pope's residence-in-exile, a few days after Henry's envoys. See Barlow, *Thomas Becket*, 116, 119–124, and *The Lives of Thomas Becket*, ed. and trans. Staunton, 120–134. Saint-Omer and Tournai would have had resonances with the English exiles, Saint-Omer because Persons would arrange for the founding of an English seminary there in 1593, and Tournai because Persons visited the English Catholic soldiers there in the prince of Parma's camp in 1584.

79. The word *eremum* ("desert') is used here to symbolize the eremitic monastic life. An alternative translation would be "hermitage."

80. For Thomas's sojourn at Pontigny and then St Columba's (near Sens), see Barlow, *Thomas Becket*, 124–142, and *The Lives of Thomas Becket*, ed. and trans. Staunton, pp. 136–149.

have already spoken, he always slept on the ground, supporting his head on a stone. He spent one-third of the night on bended knee, he ate mainly vegetables, tormented himself with extended fasts, and afflicted his body in other ways while he inflamed his spirit and prepared himself for the prize of martyrdom that lay ahead, which Christ, appearing to him at this very time had foretold and promised him in a very clear voice.

From this we may understand, my most beloved brothers, what kind of life ought to precede martyrdom, how much devotion to discipline and holiness is needed, to obtain from the Lord this, the highest boon there is on earth. Given that nothing could surpass Thomas's life, however, it is no wonder that he was granted a unique kind of martyrdom. Since I have already undertaken to say something about the worthiness of the thing itself, I see that time prevents me from recounting the actual event. So, it will have to be enough to condense what follows as it were summarily in one word: that is, that first pretending to make peace with him, Henry summoned Thomas to England after seven years of exile. When he got there and was restored to his see, it was not long before fresh calumnies were fabricated against him and the old hostilities revived. The king, now based in Normandy, let slip some words in his anger which created the impression that he would be pleased if the man of God were taken away out of their midst. Immediately, certain courtiers from the royal household took off for England and stormed into Canterbury on these very days of Our Saviour's nativity. The servant of God did not flee or resist nor defend himself as he might have. He did not allow the doors to be closed, but threw himself down on his knees before the altar to pray, and there – oh, such wickedness – they ran him through with their unrighteous swords. Our witness is one who was there, who saw it happen, who wrote down the story, who, cradling the martyr of Christ in his arms, lost his arm in the action, cut off by the murderers; he is our witness, I say, that Thomas did not so much as utter a groan while he was being martyred, nor did he raise his hands or arms to protect himself against the blows of the four swords aimed at his head (something which in such cases men naturally do by instinct and habit). Instead, all he did was to murmur these words repeatedly: "I give my life freely for Christ my lord and the church." Oh, he was a man to be wondered at, and his speech was divinely inspired! My brothers, behold the most excellent leader of our journey and our life; behold our master, fix your gaze on the one who goes before you. "It is for Christ our Lord" (he said) "and the church that I freely give my life." What speech could be more valiant or more holy? What more worthy of a Christian prelate? What words could we imagine more luminous in bringing glory to God, joy to the angels, confusion to our enemies, and terror to the demons, for us to imitate, for all people to follow his example, and to bring the martyr himself to triumph? "Freely" (he said), "I lay down my life." And why not freely, Thomas, since to die for Christ is not death, but rather the entry into life, an earnest of the kingdom, the seal of glory, the gate of eternity and the perfection of bliss? Oh, that blood is well spent, which is spent for Christ: why are we not roused up (my brothers), why are our spirits not kindled by this example? We see how brief are those sufferings of this martyr, whereas his glory is eternal, and yet we have not seen that glory indeed which is true glory, which he has already enjoyed for over four hundred years in heaven. We see only those shadows of glory which are to be had on earth, wonderfully multiplied to Thomas: that is, the glory of his miracles, the glory of his tomb, the glory of the devotion and concourse of all nations, but amongst all the rest, nothing so glorious happened to him on this earth as when through his heavenly power he drove his own persecutor, Henry, to such great humility and repentance that the king approached his tomb barefoot and moaning, wept countless tears, uttered sighs and lamentations, and having stretched himself out on the bare earth, begged pardon of the holy martyr and penance from the bishop for his misdeeds. Finally, he moved all to pity at the spectacle as he lay naked on the ground, after spending the whole night in vigil and flagellation. What glory could be greater? What martyr's strength more divine?

O Lord Jesus, the life and strength of martyrs, if only it would be pleasing in thy sight to give this grace to our persecutors in England also, that they may be converted unto thee, and what thou didst grant unto Henry, urged by the prayers of Thomas the martyr alone, be pleased to grant the same unto Henry's daughter, through the intercession of more than a hundred of thy witnesses whom she has put to death. Oh, how joyfully we would give thee thanks for this benefit! With what full hearts we would sing thy praises everywhere! But if the strictness of thy justice perhaps would not allow this, nevertheless we humbly beseech thee that thou wouldst give us at least the strength and courage to fight thy battles in this struggle which thou hast set before us, such that love of life may never hold us back from the contest, nor fear from the dangers, nor faintheartedness from the suffering, but that sacrificing everything for thy glory and the salvation of our homeland, we may spend our very selves, if need be, so that thus we may at least go some way towards fulfilling our calling and making recompense for the countless benefits we have received from thee: for which "Glory and honour and thanksgiving be unto thee for ever." Thanks be to God.

B165 From Claudio Acquaviva, Rome, 15 February 1593

SOURCE: ARSI, Baet. 3/I, 100.

NOTE: Acquaviva expresses his satisfaction with the news about the founding of the seminary in Seville and the choice of rector, Francisco de Peralta. William Baldwin (1562–1632) has been sent to Flanders, possibly to replace Henry Walpole (Acquaviva to Persons, 31 August 1592, B155). After a short spell in Brussels, Baldwin became professor of theology at Louvain (McCoog, *English and Welsh Jesuits*, 110).

P. Roberto Personio, 15 febrero en Sevilla.

Mucho me he consolado con las buenas nuevas que Vuestra Reverencia por la suya me da de los felices principios de su Seminario. Espero en el Señor que lo llevará adelante con mucho augmento. Yo significo a los Padres que en esto han ayudado la notiçia que Vuestra Reverencia dello me da, quán agradecido se muestra, y quánto yo estimo lo que han hecho y les encomiendo prosigan, como creo lo haran, y siempre que Vuestra Reverencia me avisare de qualquiera cosa en que yo de mi parte pueda ayudar lo haré con toda voluntad.

La disposiçion del govierno del Seminario me parece muy buena y gusto mucho que el Rector dé la satisfaction que Vuestra Reverencia me avisa. De los demas Padre

Valpolo &c. haga como juzgase convenir. El Padre Balduino partio para Flandes y supuesto que el Padre Valpolo salio de alli parece necessario que este Padre asista.

Vuestra Reverencia salude en mi nombre al Padre Crisuelo y le diga como reçevi la suya y el libro que con ella venía. No más en esta de encomendarme &c.

Translation

To Fr Robert Persons in Seville, 15 February.

I am much encouraged by the good news which Your Reverence gives me in your letter about the happy foundation of the seminary. I hope in the Lord that he will favour it with much increase. I am sharing the information which Your Reverence has given to me about it with the fathers who have helped in this: how obliged you have shown yourself to be to them, and how much I esteem you for this achievement. I encourage you to continue, as I believe you will, and assure Your Reverence that whatever you advise me, on whatever matter in which I for my part can help, I will do it with all my heart.

The arrangement of the management of the seminary pleases me greatly, and I am much gratified by what Your Reverence tells me of your satisfaction with the rector. For the rest – Fr Walpole, etc. – please do as you deem fit. Fr Baldwin has left for Flanders, and given that Fr Walpole has left there it seems necessary that that father should supply his place.

Would Your Reverence please greet Fr Creswell in my name and inform him that I have received his letter and the book which came with it. No more in this. I commend myself, etc.

B166 From William Allen, Rome, 15 February 1593

> SOURCE: ABSI, Coll M 138 (olim 109), Grene's notes.
> EDITION: Renold, *Letters of Allen and Barret*, 229–230.
> NOTE: John Arden, younger brother of the Jesuit Robert Arden, appears to have acted as a would-be intermediary between Allen and the English authorities, including Burghley, Privy Counsellor Sir Thomas Heneage (1532–1595), and the queen herself, in connection with Anglo-Spanish peace initiatives. See Allen to Arden, 21 March and 4 September 1593, in Renold, *Letters of Allen and Barret*, 230–231 and 235. At this time, Robert Arden was confessor at Loreto but was dismissed from the Society on 13 November (McCoog, *English and Welsh Jesuits*, 106 and 179 n7).

Arden Fr Roberts brother that was with you last yeere in Spaine is now come hither &c. (*tum multa de eo narrat ex quibus videtur colligi quod esset explorator* &c.—).[81] Now he goeth to his brother who is at the present in Loreto &c.—

---

81. "Then he gives a long account from which it can be surmised that he was a spy."

B167 To Claudio Acquaviva, Madrid, 16 February 1593

SOURCE: Acquaviva to Persons, 12 April (B174).

NOTE: It appears that Persons travelled to Madrid at this time, to consult Acosta and to approach the king about funding for the college at Valladolid and the new seminary to be founded at Saint-Omer. See Persons to Acquaviva, 22 March (B173), headnote.

B168 To William Allen, Madrid, 16 February 1593

SOURCE: Allen's testimonial for Persons, 15 March (B170).

B169 To Claudio Acquaviva, Madrid, 27 February 1593

SOURCE: Acquaviva to Persons, 12 April (B174).

NOTE: In his next letter, 22 March (B173), Persons reminds Acquaviva that in this letter he had explained his reasons for coming to Madrid.

B170 Testimonial for Robert Persons, by William Allen, Rome, 15 March 1593

SOURCES:
  ACSA, Series II, Legajo 1, item 16;
  ARSI, Angl. 38/II, fol. 81r, item 2, Bartoli's notes on Allen's letters.
EDITION: Knox, *Allen*, 346–347.
NOTE: Persons planned to return to Valladolid from Seville via Évora and Lisbon, where he had some necessary business (see his letter to Acquaviva, 16 June, B233), so the churchman to whom the testimonial was addressed may have been Miguel de Castro (1536–1625), cardinal archbishop and patriarch of Lisbon, who assisted in the establishment of an English residence there.

Scripserat ad me diebus praeteritis P. Robertus Personius Societatis Jesu cum Hispalim proficisceretur, se istac in reditu per Dominationem Vestram Illustrissimam transiturum, ut manus vestras osculetur et benedictionem accipiat, resque Anglicanas cum Dominatione Vestra Illustrissima[82] tanquam cum patre amantissimo fideique Catholicae defensore acerrimo zelosissimoque (id enim a multo tempore intelleximus iam omnes) fiducia multa communicaret. Quod et ego satis quoque mihi causae esse existimavi, ut has statim literas exararem, quibus et tantam pietatis famam ex animo Illustrissimae Dominationis Vestrae gratularer, et patri Personio testimonium praestarem quod eius virtus et prudentia religioque merentur. Fuit enim mihi a multis iam annis fidelissimus semper in hac communi patriae nostrae ac Dei causa sustinenda, et contra hereticos propugnanda, coadiutor, maximosque labores et pericula subiit pro Dei gloria. Quo etiam Dominus usus est instrumento, ad seminaria gentis nostrae istic in Hispaniis instituenda, e quibus

82. Illma] *Vd, with contraction for* Illmam *deleted*

cum insignem Dei honorem, tum ingens etiam patriae nostrae afflictissimae solatium et immortalem nationis istius laudem emanaturam confido. Ipse coram explicabit rerum nostrarum statum et condicionem, eique in omnibus tanquam mihi ipsi fidem prestari cupio. Dominus Jesus Illustrissimam Dominationem Vestram incolumem semper salvamque[83] conservet. Romae, Idibus Martiis 1593.
        Illustrissimae Dominationis Vestrae
           Servus indignusque frater
              Gulielmus Cardinalis Alanus.

Translation

Fr Robert Persons of the Society of Jesus wrote to me some days past, when he was setting out for Seville,[84] that on his return from there he would be passing through Your Eminence's diocese, to kiss hands and receive your blessing, and to communicate the affairs of England faithfully to Your Eminence as to a most loving father, a most keen and zealous defender of the Catholic faith (for all of us have known that from very long ago). I judged this to be sufficient reason also to write this letter straight away, in which I could both heartily pay tribute to such a great reputation for piety as that of Your Eminence, and provide Fr Persons with the testimonial which his virtue, prudence, and religion deserve. For he has always been most faithful to me as my partner from many years ago in supporting this common cause of God and our fatherland, and combating the heretics, undertaking the greatest labours and danger for the glory of God. Our Lord has even used him as his instrument in establishing our nation's seminaries in Spain, from which God's signal honour will proceed, I trust, as well as great comfort to our most heavily afflicted country and undying praise for that nation. He will explain the state and condition of our affairs in person, and I desire that in everything trust will be shown to him as if it was to me myself. The Lord Jesus keep Your Eminence always safe from harm. From Rome, the Ides of March, 1593.
        Your Eminence's
           unworthy servant and brother
              Cardinal William Allen.

B171 To Richard Verstegan, Madrid or Toledo, 19 March 1593

SOURCE: Verstegan to Persons, 30 April 1593 (B179).
NOTE: Persons enclosed a large packet and 500 crowns for William Holt in Brussels, who was to be involved in the founding of the seminary for English Catholic boys at Saint-Omer.

---

83. salvamque] *Knox*; salvaque *Vd*
84. Persons must have written from Madrid by the post of 16 February, intending to set out for Seville, but had progressed no further than Toledo by 22 March.

B172 To Ralph Emerson, Madrid or Toledo, possibly 19 March 1593

SOURCE: Emerson to Persons, 25 April 1593 (B177).
NOTE: In this letter Persons evidently informed Emerson that he had been delayed in Madrid or Toledo.

B173 To Claudio Acquaviva, Toledo, 22 March 1593

SOURCE: ARSI, Hisp. 135, fols. 147–49 (olim 44–46), holograph.
HICKS: 131–145, with English translation.
NOTE: Persons reports in detail on a satisfactory audience with the king immediately after his arrival in Madrid, about the foundations at Seville and Valladolid. Philip II also approved the plan to set up a seminary at Saint-Omer. Persons records his concern over the indigence and importunity of the English exile community, and notes that Fr Cabredo, rector of the college at Valladolid, has come to Madrid to consult him, since he would not be in Valladolid until later in the year.

The letter continues with an account of three crucial meetings: a conference with González Dávila and Alonso Sánchez (1547–1593) in Alcalá de Henares, during the carnival recess, followed by further audiences with the king and the count of Chinchón and then another discussion with his Jesuit colleagues. All of these were prompted by the news that Acquaviva had reluctantly agreed to call a general congregation of the Society. Sánchez, procurator for the Philippines, had arrived in Madrid from Rome in September 1592, briefed by Acquaviva to support the visitors and impress on the king the importance of the role of the superior general of the Society (Acquaviva to Persons, 24 March 1590, B55; Astrain, 3: 532–553; F. Zubillaga, *DHCJ*, 4: 3486–87; Lourdes Díaz-Trechuelo y López-Spínola, Marquesa de Spínola, *DBE*). Following discussions with him and González Dávila, Persons had an extended interview with the king, trying to persuade him to uphold the regular principles of the Society against the Spanish Jesuit dissidents. He had a similar but less satisfactory conversation with Diego Fernández de Cabrera, third Count of Chinchón (d. 1608), a prominent member of the king's Junta Grande (or, with Zúñiga, the Junta de Noche).

When Persons returned to Alcalá, he discovered that Chinchón had been coached by José de Acosta, because his response echoed a letter from Acosta to Pedro de Ribadeneira. In the event, as recorded in Persons's next letter, 19 April (B176), Sánchez later spoke to the king and Chinchón along the same lines, cautioning them about the role being played by Acosta, who had made an unofficial visit to Rome to lobby for a general congregation.

Molto reverendo in Christo padre mio
Pax Christi.
Con l'ordinario passato scrissi a Vostra Paternità le cause della mia venuta a Madrid, et la grata audienza che da Sua Maestà hebbi nel Prado[85] subito che venni, con le speranze di breve speditione nelli negotii. La qual pur h'havuto, benché non con la brevità che desiderava, perché in fin son stato sforzato star in Madrid più che un mese.

85. Prado] *ABSI ts*; pardo R

Ma li dispacii non son mali, poiché habbiamo ottenuto tre cedule reali, la una paraque si paghen senza più indugio li 4000 Δ che Sua Maestà c'assignato nel mese d'Agosto passato para el Collegio Yngles de Valladolid, et l'altra per 300 Δ de renta per il Collegio Inglese in Sevilla. Et la terza per 1920 Δ de renta in Flandes per comminciar un Seminario di putti Inglesi in Sant Omer,[86] a ragion di dece[87] ducati per ogni un el mese di sedeci persone che Sua Maestà vuol che a sua costa si sostentino, con promessa di magior sostento quando sarà magior el numero delli studianti. Et certamente è stato cosa per lodar molto nostro Signor, veder con quanto affetto, il Re, l'Imperatrice, l'Infanta, il Principe et tutta questa corte habbiano approvato et abbrachiato questa opera, lodando li travagli della Compagnia in queste cose. Sua Maestà vuol che la Compagnia tenga cargo di questo Seminario tanto per la buona educatione delli scolari, quanto anco per la sodisfattione della città, la qual per esser frontera ne fece alcuna difficultà di lasciar Inglesi starvi, ma perché qui non hano di star si non putti, come dissi, fra 10 et 18 anni d'età, et perché la Compagnia ha di dar conto di loro, si scrive al Marchese de Warambon governatore della provincia de Artoys che ogni cosa sarà sigura. Ha gustato qui bien Sua Maestà che il padre Gulielmo Flacco ch'è stato ministro questi anni passati nel Seminario di Valladolid vada con meco adesso a Seviglia accioché veda ancora quel Seminario et di la s'imbarchi per Cales e Sant'Omer perché havendo visto le cose di qua potrà darci miglior correspondenza et così spero che farà, et preghiamo la Paternità Vostra che scriva subito al padre provincial di Fiandra accioché proveda a questo Seminario de la gente dela Compagnia che sarà bisogno avanti che parta per la Congregatione Generale. La qual cosa facilmente se può far poiché non haveremo bisogno più che un buon Rettor della natione Fiaminga per adesso con un fratello, perché il padre Henrico Broy[88] Inglese potrà far l'officio del ministro, et il padre Nicolao Smith del maestro delli[89] studii, et il padre Gulielmo che va da qui potrà attendere alle cose spirituali et alle missioni, et il padre Gulielmo Holt stando in Bruxellis potrà negotiar le cose della corte che saran necessarie per questi principii et benché il Re qui non c'habbia dato niente per cominciar, di presente, fuora delle letere per l'intrata che Vostra Paternità vedrà per le copie che riceverà[90] con questa, tuttavia io ho mandato 500 Δ con questo ordinario al padre Holt raccolti d'alcune persone particulari della corte chi l'offerirono per principiar la cosa, et oltra di questa farò le spese del viagio del padre Flacco et ne darò alli agenti da tiempo in tiempo accioché possino passar fin a tanto che cobrino l'intrata che il Re l'ha assignato, la qual come ho ditto, spero che sarà certa, et così con quello et con l'agiuti che li putti porteranno con sico d'Inglaterra potrà sustentarsi come spero questo Seminario, specialmente considerando che potrà il Rettor andar discargando sempre sua gente sobre l'altri Seminarii, et quando tutto questo mancasse me pare che l'altri Seminarii haverebbono di contribuir a sustentar questo, poiché ha d'esser la fonte di tutti in quanto a mandar li sugietti atti per studiar philosophia, delli quali già sentiamo molta carestia et non si potrà rime-

86. Edwards, 156 and 159, gives 1720 scudi, referring also to Persons's letter to Acquaviva, 19 April (B176).
87. dece] R *obscure: could be* due
88. Broy] R; Bivy *Hicks*
89. delli] R *obscure; could be* delle
90. riceverà] ricevera; vi cederò *Hicks*

diar si non per questa via. Et mal siguro[91] nigotio saria che tutti l'altri Seminarii che stanno sotto la Compagnia dependessero[92] in questo punto principale da'seculari che governano il Collegio di Rhems, ma per questa via si renderà tutto siguro;[93] le quali cose tutte considerate, spero che Vostra Paternità favorirà a questo nuovo Seminario come a cosa molto principale et fondamento dell'altri Seminarii tutti, et haec de his. Vostra Paternità vederà si sarà bene mostrar questo capitolo al padre Mutio Vitaleschi Rettor nostro costì.

2. Fu necessario ch'il padre Cabredo Rettor nostro di Valladolid venisse per alcuni pochi giorni a Madrid per conferir meco sopra cose de suo Collegio poich'io haveva di tornarme a Seviglia, et così venne et sua venuta fù di molta importanza per molte cause, ma particularmente per stringere questi Signori della corte che non lo lasciassero[94] partirse senza sua cedula di 4000 Δ come s'è detto. È vero che alcuni due o tre padri del Collegio di Madrid lo sentirono molto che tanti Inglesi vi si trovassero insieme, ma non si poteva far altrimenti, et diessimo la priezza ch'era possibile, et pagassimo molto voluntieri al Procuratore per tutti li giorni che stettimo là, come è giusto che sempre si faccia, et procuraremo che non avenga questo altra vuolta, et prometto a Vostra Paternità ch'io sento tanta ripugnanza di vederme in Madrid che voy allà come al Purgatorio per molte cause, et particularmente per non veder le necessità et miserie delli poveri Inglesi che vi sono senza rimedio, et per no udir li clamori di tanti che mi scrivono subito che sanno che sto lì, et così piacendo a Dio fugerò quanto posso Madrid, benché alcuna vuolta non si potrà senza danno grandissimo de la causa che trattiamo, et occurrendo tal necessità desidererei (si fusse possibile) che ninguno si contristasse di mia venuta, perché Dio sa che desidero far servitii a tutti, et offendere nissuno, et così intendo ch'il padre Rettor et il padre provinciale et tutti li superiori gustano di questo, come m'han detto, et credo lo medessimo dell'altri, si no sia di due or tre delli Consultori che non sanno la necessità né l'importanze delle cose che si trattano; il padre Cabredo me urgò che ne scrivesse queste due parolle di questa materia, benché a mi, apena pareva cosa degna. Il detto padre fa suo officio molto bene et così fa ancora il padre Francisco Peralta in Seviglia. Dio ne sea lodato per tutto.

3. Nel tempo di Carnivale quando non si poteva nigotiar nella corte andai insieme con il padre Alonso Sánchez a Alcalá per vederme con il padre Gil Gonzales et fra l'altre cose, tutti due li padri furono di parer che saria bene ch'io cercasso occasione a la despedida di parlar qualche cosa al Re circa la Congregatione Generale; et così feci, et fu con buona comodità et gusto di Sua Maestà, come pareva. La substanza fu, dar conto breve et particular a Sua Maestà di mia andata a Andaluzia et di là a Castilla si fusse possibile, per hallarme en la Congregatione provinciale, li mezzi che s'usavano di oratione continua, misse, digiunii et altre penitenze per ottener l'assistenza del Spirito Santo in questo nigotio, et che molto più nella Congregatione Generale s'usarebbono, et si moltiplicarebbono li detti mezzi, che per questi mezzi tutti speravano buono successo della detta Congregatione per il servicio di Dio y ben universale di questa sua povera famiglia: solamente quello che si poteva dubitare e timere, era, che alcuni inquieti, delli quali già Sua

91. siguro] R; signo Hicks
92. dependessero] R; dependessen Hicks
93. siguro] R; signo Hicks
94. lasciassero] R; lasciassen Hicks

Maestà haveva notitia, non cercassero con questa occasione di turbar le cose, et torcher il camino dritto, et procurar violenza per mezzi inordinati, lo qual saria di grandissimo inconveniente et offensa di nostro Signor; et così come la Compagnia haveva isperimentato sempre Sua Maestà per grande protettore suo, et tutto il mondo conoscia la sua prudenza et pietà religiosa, per tutte due cause si sperava, che Sua Maestà in questa occasione così importante, mostraria l'uno et l'altro, come io le supplicava molto instantamente da parte di tutti li buoni figliuoli et disapassionati della Compagnia, et per amor di Christo nostro Señor institutore d'essa, che lo facesse assigurando a Sua Maestà che, oltre il grande merito che con questa opera acquistarebbe con nostro Signor, gli serià mena[95] molto honor en il mondo, et molto utile servigio per tutti suoi stati, che come così grande monarcha tenia fuora di Spagna, dove pare che quelli della Compagnia hanno occasione di servir più a Sua Maestà (come altre vuolte gl'haveva dichiarato) che non qui, dove per la abondanza d'altre religioni, pareva che la Compagnia non poteva servir a Sua Maestà tanto come nelli altri regni, donde v'erano manco religiosi; et più d'humori et emulationi contra la grandezza di questa monarchia, et che non avia gente più dissapassionata in questo particulare che quelli della Compagnia, i quali per intender che la defensa dela religione Christiana Catolica dependeva principalmente da Sua Maestà, opponevansi molto a questi humori d'altri, et li templavano, et servivano molto fidelmente et utilmente a Sua Maestà nell'occasioni che si offerivano. Et per continuar questo affetto delli padri d'altre nationi, saria di grande importanza che Sua Maestà defendesse la libertà della Compagnia in questa Congregatione Generale, acciochè li detti padri tornassero a sue terre consolati, et animati a servir a Sua Maestà, et edificati della sua prudenza et pietà in non lasciarsi mover dalle passioni particulari d'alcuni pochi inquieti et turbatori di sua religione etc.

Questa fu la substanza del discurso che habbi con Sua Maestà benché molto più largamente et me ascoltò Sua Maestà attentamente, et dipoi me rispose che se avia holgado entendere tutto questo et li mezzi in particulare che s'usavono per acertar nelle Congregationi et che erano molto buoni et santi, et conforme a questo si deveva sperar molto buoni fini di tutto per il ben publico, et quello della Compagnia che importava molto alla Christianità, et che suo aiuto non mancaria in tutto quello che potrebbe far et particularmente in quello ch'io gl'haveva raccomandato, et che ben vedeva li buoni officii che la Compagnia gli faceva in altre nationi, alli quali egli corresponderebbe sempre con amor et con li favori che potesse. Il mismo discorso quasi passai depoi con il Conde di Chinchón in sua casa, si non che con costui entrai più in particular, pregandolo molto strettamente che considerasse ben da quali huomini della Compagnia pigliasse informationi, poiché era cosa certa,[96] ch'alcuni che gli venivano con pretensioni del ben publico della Compagnia, intendevano suoi interessi particulari, et si conoscerebbono con questo, si cercavano mezzi straordinarii per ottener quello che pretendevano, come al contrario, quelli che desideravono che la congregatione procedesse liberamente secondo li mezzi spirituali et proprii che tiene, et secondo l'instituto della Compagnia, era segno che no potevano tener mala intentione. Me rispose il Conde buone parolle benché non mi contentavano tanto come quelle del Re che parevano uscir dal cuore; il tempo dirà. Ben

95. mena] *R*; mena di *Hicks*
96. certa] *Hicks*; serta *R*

mostrò il Conde d'esser stato informato di grandi et urgentissime necessità che vi siano en la Compagnia di questa Congregatione, le quali io gli mostrai che non erano tante come gl'havevano voluto pintarle. Le medessime parolle quasi viddi dipoi in una letera del padre Joseppe de Acosta al padre Ribadeneyra, que le necessità d'Italia erano ancora magiori che non queste di Spagna, benché grandissime. Però molto ben certamente gli responde il padre Ribadeneyra con questo ordinario, perché mi mostrò la letera en la qual gli dice che egli era stato sempre di parere che una Congregatione Generale con le conditioni che ivi pone, saria di molta utilità della Compagnia, tuttavia sempre ancora era di opinione, che una congregatione forzata saria ruina della Compagnia, et per questo sconguira al padre Acosta, se[97] vuol che con Dio et con il mondo si scarichi delle cose che si suspettano di lui per questa sua jornata a Roma, procuri con tutte le sue forze che vi sia summa libertà nella Congregatione, né che vi si tratti di mezzi straordinarii o violenti, y certamente digo a Vostra Paternità che la carta me sia contentado y edificado. Dio nostro Señor guye todo a sua magior gloria, et ci conservi Vostra Paternità per molti anni per suo magior merito, bien della Compagnia, et consolatione di tutti li figliuoli vostri d'essa, li quali non dudo, si no che mostraranno in questa Congregatione il cordial amor et respetto che portano a Vostra Paternità non obstante la malignità et ingratitudine di pochi discoli, huomini animali, senza spirito. Et così Vostra Paternità per amor di Dio si anime, *quia si Deus nobiscum quis contra nos,*[98] *ipse consoletur Vestrae Paternitati semper. In cuius sanctis sacrificiis et benedictione humiliter me comendo.* En Toledo stando de buelta para Sevilla a 22 di Marco 1593.

    Di Vostra Reverenda Paternità
        indegno figliuolo et siervo
            Rob. Personio.

[*Addressed:*] Al molto Reverendo in Christo padre nostro il padre Claudio Acquaviva preposito de la Compagnia de Giesu, Roma.

[*Endorsed:*] P. Roberto Personio, Marzo 22. [*with summary of contents*]

Translation

My Very Reverend Father in Christ
The peace of Christ.

By the last post[99] I wrote to Your Paternity explaining the reasons for my coming to Madrid and about the satisfactory audience which I had with His Majesty in the Prado as soon as I came, as well as of my hopes of expediting our business, which, in the event, had a positive outcome, though not as quickly as I was hoping, for eventually I was forced to stay in Madrid more than a month.

However the despatches are not bad,[100] for we have obtained three royal letters patent, one for payment to us without any further delay of the 4000 ducats which His

---

97. se] *this ed.*; si R
98. Rom. 8:31 (slightly adapted); from here to "humiliter me comendo" Persons switches to Latin.
99. 16 February.
100. These may be despatches of the kind the Persons sent on behalf of the king, 24 February 1594 (B218).

Majesty assigned to us in the month of August last for the English college of Valladolid, another for a rent of 300 ducats for the English college in Seville, and the third for a rent of 1920 ducats in Flanders to start a seminary of English boys in Saint-Omer, on the basis of ten[101] ducats a month each for sixteen persons whom the king wishes to be supported at his charge, with promise of larger support when the number of students increases. And certainly, it has been something for which to give great praise to our Lord, to see the enthusiasm with which the king, the empress, the infanta, the prince, and the entire court have approved and taken this cause to their hearts, by praising the labours of the Society in these matters. His Majesty wishes the Society to have charge of this seminary,[102] as much for the sake of the scholars getting a good education as to satisfy the concerns of the city, which, being on the frontier, made some difficulty about letting Englishmen stay there. But as it is here only a case, as I told them, of boys of between ten and eighteen years of age staying there, and seeing that the Society is to be responsible for them, a letter is being written to the marquis de Varambon, governor of the province of Artois,[103] assuring him that everything will be quite safe. His Majesty here has thoroughly endorsed my plan that Fr William Flack, who has been minister these past years in the seminary of Valladolid, should go with me now to Seville, so that he may see the seminary there also, and embark from there for Calais and Saint-Omer. For after seeing those establishments, he will be able to conform to our ideas better, and I hope he will do so. We beg Your Paternity to write at once to father provincial in Flanders[104] to make the necessary provision of men of the Society for this seminary before he leaves for the general congregation. This can easily be done, for we shall not have need of anything more than a good rector of Flemish nationality for the present, and a brother, because Fr Henry Broy, an Englishman, can undertake the office of minister, Fr Nicholas Smith prefect of studies;[105] and Fr William, who is going from here, will be able to look after spiritual matters and the missions, and Fr William Holt, being in Brussels, will be able to manage the negotiations at court which will be necessary in these early stages. And although the king here has not given us anything to make a beginning with so far, beyond the letters of introduction (copies of which will be delivered along with this letter for Your Paternity to see), I have nevertheless sent Fr Holt 500 ducats by this post,[106] which I have collected from some particular individuals of the court who offered it to get the project going. In addition to this, I will bear the expense of Fr Flack's journey and make payments to the agents from time to time to enable them to carry on until they collect the revenue which the king has

101. Or two: the MS could read *due* or *dece*.
102. I.e., at Saint-Omer.
103. Marc de Rye (d. 1598).
104. Olivier Mannaerts.
105. Henry Broy, SJ (b. 1550) moved from Tournai to Saint-Omer in 1593 and remained there until his death in 1598; see Henry Chadwick, "Father Bray, Jesuyte," *Biographical Studies* 1 (1951): 125–127. Nicholas Smith, SJ (1558–1630) was at this stage subminister in Brussels but was minister at Saint-Omer by 1594. From 1621 he was superior of the Society in England (McCoog, *English and Welsh Jesuits*, 130, 296–297).
106. I.e., the simultaneous post to Flanders; see Persons to Verstegan, 19 March and 30 April (B171, B179).

assigned to them. This, as I have said, I hope can be relied on, and so with that, and with the contributions which the boys will bring with them from England, this seminary, I trust, will be sustainable; especially when one takes into consideration that father rector will be able to keep passing his charges on to the other seminaries. And should this fail, it seems to me that the other seminaries would have to contribute to the support of this one, for it is destined to be the source of supply for them all, inasmuch as it will send students to them to study philosophy. Of such students we are already experiencing a great dearth, which can not be remedied except in this way. It would be a poor thing for all the other seminaries which are in the Society's care to depend in this important respect on the seculars who govern the college of Rheims; but in this way everything will be quite secure. When all these considerations are weighed, I hope that Your Paternity will show favour to this new seminary, as being a matter of outstanding importance and the basis for the well-being of all the other seminaries. So much for that. Your Paternity will judge whether it is advisable to convey this section to Fr Muzio Vitelleschi, our rector over there.[107]

2. It was necessary for Fr Cabredo, our rector at Valladolid, to come to Madrid for some few days to consult me about matters concerning his college. I was obliged to return to Seville, so he came here, and his coming was a matter of great importance for many reasons, but especially in bringing pressure to bear on these courtiers not to send him away without his warrant for the 4000 ducats I mentioned. It is true that some two or three fathers of the college at Madrid were disconcerted by so many Englishmen being there at the same time, but it could not be managed otherwise, and we gave what we could afford and paid the procurator very willingly for all the days that we were there, as it is just that we should do always. We will take care that this does not happen again, and I assure Your Paternity that I feel such a repugnance to paying a visit to Madrid that I go there as though it were to purgatory; this for many reasons, and especially because I have to see the hopeless want and misery of the poor Englishmen who are there, and attend to the clamours of those who write to me in such numbers as soon as my presence is known.[108] And so, please God, I shall flee Madrid as fast as I can, although at times it will not be possible without very great injury to the cause in which we are engaged. When the need to go arises I should desire no one to take offence at my coming (if it were possible), for God knows that it is my desire to do service to all and cause offence to no one. And indeed, I understand that father rector and father provincial and all the superiors are pleased with this business, as they have told me, and I believe the same is true of the others, except for two or three consultors who do not know the urgency and importance of the matters with which we are dealing. Fr Cabredo urged me to write these few words on this subject, although for my part it hardly seemed worth mentioning. The said father performs the duty of his office very well, as does also Fr Francis Peralta in Seville. Praise be to God for it all.

3. At carnival time, when dealings with the court were not possible, I went to Alcalá, along with Fr Alonso Sánchez, to pay a visit to Fr Gil González. Among other things, both fathers were of the opinion that it would be a good thing if I were to seek an opportunity, when taking my leave of the king, to say something about the general congrega-

107. Vitelleschi had taken over as rector at the English College, Rome, after the departure of Creswell in 1592.
108. This importunity is confirmed by a comment in Verstegan's letter of 30 April (B179).

tion. This I did, and it was very opportune and to the liking of His Majesty, as it seemed. The gist of what I said was as follows: I gave His Majesty a short and detailed account of my proposed journey to Andalusia and if possible from there to Castile, so as to be present at the provincial congregation; I told him of the means that were being used, by continual prayer, masses, fasts, and other penances, to obtain the assistance of the Holy Spirit in this matter, and said that the same means would be used even more, and multiplied, in the case of the general congregation. Through these means all were hoping that the said congregation would turn out well for the service of God and the general welfare of this poor family of His. The only thing that could cause doubt and was to be feared was that some disaffected persons, whom His Majesty already knew about, might seek to take this opportunity to create a disturbance, turn away from the straight path and use improper means to get their way. That would be a very serious inconvenience and an offence to our Lord, and therefore, both because the Society had always found by long experience that His Majesty was their great protector, and also because all the world knows his prudence and devotion to religion – for both these reasons – it was hoped that His Majesty would prove himself true in both respects, on such a serious occasion as this; and I begged him very urgently on behalf of all the good and peaceful sons of the Society and for the love of Christ our Lord, its founder, to do so; assuring His Majesty that, besides the great merit he would acquire by this action in the sight of our Lord, it would cause him to win much prestige in the eyes of the world and would be a very useful service to all his domains which, being a great monarch, he possessed outside of Spain. It was in these that the men of that Society seem to have greater opportunity of giving service to His Majesty (as I had declared to him on other occasions) than they have here, where on account of the great number of other religious orders it seemed that the Society could not serve His Majesty so much as in other realms where there were hardly any religious orders. In those places there was more dislike and jealousy of the greatness of this monarchy, and no people more fair-minded in this regard than the members of the Society. They recognized that the defence of the Christian and Catholic religion depended chiefly on His Majesty, and so they were very much opposed to this kind of feeling in others and would restrain it. They were serving His Majesty very faithfully and usefully where opportunity offered. In order to retain the goodwill of the fathers of other nationalities, it is of the greatest importance that His Majesty should defend the freedom of the Society in the general congregation, so that the said fathers would return to their countries consoled and encouraged to serve His Majesty, edified by his prudence and compassion in not allowing himself to be influenced by the individual grievances of a handful of disaffected men who made trouble in their order, etc.

This was the gist of the case I made to His Majesty, though it was of much greater length. His Majesty heard me with attention, and at the end replied to me that he had been glad to learn about all this, and especially of the measures which were being taken to safeguard the congregations. They were very good and holy ones and, being so, they could hope for very good results from it all for the public good and the Society, which had a very important role in the cause of Christianity. His help would not be wanting in anything that he could do and particularly in the matter which I had suggested to him; he acknowledged the good offices which the Society has used on his behalf with other nations, and these he would always reward with affection and all possible favours. I repeated almost the same statement later to the count of Chinchón at his house, except that in his case I entered into more detail. I implored him very earnestly to consider the sort of men in the Society from whom he was getting his reports, for it was quite clear that some of those who came to him under pretext of the general welfare of the Society had their own private interests in view. They could be recognized in this way: if they were found to be seeking irregular means of accomplishing their aims. On the other hand, those who were anxious that the congregation should proceed in freedom according to the proper spiritual means which belong to it, and according to the Society's Institute,[109] gave proof thereby that they could not have any evil intention. The count answered me with fair words, but they did not give me the same satisfaction as those of the king, which seemed to proceed from his heart. Time will show. The count gave sure indications that he had received reports of the great and urgent need that we have in the Society for this congregation, and I showed him that this was not so great as people had wished to represent to him. Afterwards, I saw almost the very same words in a letter of Fr José de Acosta to Fr Ribadeneira: namely, that Italy's need for a general congregation was still greater than Spain's needs, very great as these are. In truth, however, Fr Ribadeneira answers him very much to the point by this post, for he showed me the letter: in it, he tells him that he had always taken the view that a general congregation would be of great advantage to the Society, if it were held under the conditions that he outlined;[110] yet he maintained that a congregation that was forced on them would be the ruin of the Society; and for this reason he begs Fr Acosta, if he would clear himself in the eyes of God and of the world of the suspicions caused by this expedition of his to Rome, to use all his efforts to ensure that absolute freedom should reign in the congregation and that there be no question of irregular or violent measures. And truly I can say to Your Paternity that I was pleased and edified by the letter. May God our Lord direct everything for His greater glory and preserve Your Paternity to us for many years, for your greater merit, for the good of the Society, and for the consolation of all your sons who belong to it; and I doubt not but that they will give proof in this congregation of the heartfelt love and respect which they bear to Your Paternity, notwithstanding the malice and ingratitude of a few quarrelsome ones, dull men, driven by instinct rather than reason. And so, let Your Paternity take courage through the love of God, *for if God be for us, who can be against us?*[111] *May he ever console Your Paternity. To your holy sacrifices and to your blessing I humbly commend myself.* At Toledo, on my way back to Seville, 22 March 1593.

    Your Reverend Paternity's
        unworthy son and servant
            Robert Persons.

---

109. "Our way of proceeding," the agreed approach of the Society.

110. Ribadeneira set down the regular conditions for the calling of a general congregation, rather than the unusual pressure which the Spanish dissidents were bringing to bear on the matter.

111. Rom. 8: 31.

B174 From Claudio Acquaviva, Rome, 12 April 1593

SOURCE: ARSI, Tolet. 5/I, fol. 292r.

NOTE: Acquaviva refers to two letters from Persons, dated 16 and 27 February, and congratulates him on his plans for Saint-Omer. He is consulting Olivier Mannaerts, Belgian provincial, about the level of support that can be expected from the local Jesuits. He confirms the transfer of Persons's *socius* William Flack to Flanders and depends on Persons to make up for the delinquency of many other Jesuits.

P. Roberto Personio, 12 de Abril.

Dos de Vuestra Reverencia he recibido de 16 y 27 de febrero con particular consuelo de las buenas nuevas que me da del Seminario. Sea el Señor bendito por la muestra que a todos nos haçe que por proprio y como tal agradezco al Señor la que en esa Cuidad ha recibido esa Juventud y su nacion. Del viage de Madrid me parece muy bien que lo haya hecho. Plegue al Señor sea en todo con los buenos efectos que desea. Carga sentiran los de St Omer si se les da el cuydado del Seminario. Yo escrivo al Padre Oliverio encargandole mire lo que se puede hacer y me avise de su parecer porque no es justo encargarselo, sin entenderlos primero pero yo espero de la caridad de aquellos Padres que no faltarán en lo que pudieren. Del Padre Guillermo ya he escrito a Vuestra Reverencia que le embiamos a Flandes.

De lo que toca a la persona y caridad de Vuestra Reverencia estoy yo bien cierto que nos ayudará como dice en todas las ocasiones que pudiere especialmente en tiempo que se deven más mostrar los que son fieles hijos de la Compañia pues no faltan otros que deviendolo ser no lo hacen. En sus ...

Translation

To Fr Robert Persons, 12 April.

I received Your Reverence's two letters of 16 and 27 February,[112] taking particular comfort from the good news you give me of the seminary. May our Lord be blessed for showing His favour to us all. I am personally grateful to the Lord for the city's welcome of this nation and its youths. As for your journey to Madrid, I am very pleased that you made it. May the Lord bring to fruition all that you desire. Those of Saint-Omer[113] will feel burdened if they are given charge of the seminary. I am writing to Fr Olivier, charging him to see what can be done and let me know what he thinks, because it is not right to burden them with this without listening to them first, but I hope that of their charity those fathers will not fail to do what they can. As for Fr William, I have already written to Your Reverence that we will send him to Flanders.

With regard to Your Reverence's own person and charity, I am fully assured that you will help us, as you say, on all occasions that you can, especially at a time when those who are faithful members of the Society should make their presence felt even more, for

---

112. B167, B169.
113. I.e., the local Jesuits.

there will not fail to be others who will not carry out their duty. To your [prayers and sacrifices] ...

B175 To Pope Clement VIII, Seville, 15 April 1593

> SOURCES:
> ABSI, Coll P I 327–29; cf. Coll P II 477;
> ARSI, Angl. 38/II, fol. 81r, item 3.
> HICKS: 146–153, with English translation.
> EDITION: Knox, *Allen* 453–454.
> NOTE: Persons enclosed a copy in a letter to Acquaviva, who passed it on to Allen to present it to the pope (see Acquaviva's letter of 7 June, B183). He may have been prompted by reading José de Acosta's letter to Ribadeneira (Persons to Acquaviva, 22 March, B173) which forcibly reminded him of Acosta's attempts to influence the pope.
> Besides reporting on the state of the two seminaries, Persons appeals to the Pope to support Acquaviva in resisting the demand for de-centralization amongst Spanish Jesuits, presumably by using his influence in the general congregation. Bartoli's note reads: "Lettera del P. Personio al Papa. Gli da ragguaglio de i seminarii fondati in Spagna, delle loro entrate, e limosine fatteli dal Re, et altri Principi. Gli raccommanda la Compagnia contro i persecutori di quella. E lo prega in fine a voler castigare esemplarmente il Decano di [*blank*] da lui chiamato a Roma per i suoi delitti scandalosi &c." (A letter from Persons to the pope. He gives an account of the foundation of seminaries in Spain, of their initiation and the alms provided by the king and other princes. He commends the Society against its persecutors. And finally, he asks him please to punish, as an example, the dean of [blank] summoned by him to Rome on account of his scandalous behaviour.) Although the letter below does not specify the delinquent personage, it describes the dissidents generally.

Beatissimo Padre

Benché l'obligatione —— Ma dipoi che il P. Gioseppe Creswelo che fu Rettore di cotesto collegio Inglese in Roma, arrivò qui nelli mesi passati e m'ha detto tante cose della benignità singolare di Vostra Santità verso di noi, e del zelo suo santissimo per la conversione della nostra patria, et il Cardinale Alano et il nostro Padre Generale ci han scritto altre tante, non ho potuto differir più di ringratiar humilissimamente la Santità Vostra — et in particolare per il Breve che con l'ordinario passato Vostra Santità fu servito di scrivere a questo Cardinale Arcivescovo di Seviglia in favore del nuovo seminario, che in questa città Nostro Signore ci ha dato, del quale e di alcune altre cose nostre darò breve raguaglio a Vostra Santità in questa, come a padre et signore amantissimo, con tutta confidenza.

Penso che sia stata providenza molto particolare di Nostro Signore che in questi 4 anni passati, nelli quali li heretici ci han voluto dare la maggiore stretta che già mai, et il seminario Rhemense ha corso pericolo di esser disfatto, ci habbia Iddio aperto una porta così grande in Spagna, che per questa via teniamo già tre altri seminarii, uno in Valladolid — l'altro qui in Seviglia — et il terzo in Sant'Omer di Fiandra, che la Maestà di questo buon Re ha ordinato che si faccia adesso, per ricevere immediatamente li figliuoli più piccoli delli Catolici Inglesi. ———

Questi altri due seminarii posti in Spagna vanno bene inanzi per la grazia e favore molto particolare di Nostro Signore. Vi stanno in essi più di 100 persone, et ogni dì va crescendo il numero, con molto fervore e meravigliosa resolutione degli alonni di offerire le vite loro in questa impresa, alla quale vanno di qua ogn'anno con maggior animo et alegrezza, di quel che si potrebbe credere, se non lo[114] vedessimo con gli occhi proprii. Iddio ne sia sommamente ringratiato e glorificato, poiché è un beneficio che pare che ad altra natione in questi nostri tempi non sia concedvto, e così che lo potiamo pigliare per segno di sua grandissima misericordia verso Inghilterra e che non l'habbia d'abbandonare totalmente. ——

La maggior parte del sostento di questi due seminarii in Spagna dipende dalla carità et elemosine de particolari, benché a quello di Valladolid Sua Maestà contribuisce 1700 Δ[115] ogn'anno — a questo di Siviglia Sua Maestà non da elemosine; però il favore e patrocinio di Sua Maestà è quello che da animo a tutti li altri di favorirci, e così in effetto tutto si deve attribuir a Sua Maestà, e conforme a questo preghiamo humilissimamente la Santità Vostra di riconoscere e ringratiar la Maestà sua di tanta e tanto singolare pietà.[116]

Di altre cose poco ho da scrivere &c. —— Quanto la nostra povera Compagnia debbia a Vostra Santità facilmente potremo pensare qui, benché non ci scrivessero tante cose da Roma, come fanno; e ben m'assicuro che *retribuetur Sanctitati Vestrae in retributione iustorum* e molto mi rallegro ancora che Iddio habbia dato maggior occasione di obligare tutta la Compagnia a Vostra Santità che a nissuno delli suoi predecessori doppo la sua fondatione, poiché nel Pontificato di Vostra Santità, s'ha da fare la prima Congregatione Generale, che ha havuta[117] la Compagnia in vita del Generale, e forse la più importante *simpliciter* di tutte in rispetto delli dissegni e machinationi di alcuni contro l'instituto d'essa, le quali diconsi esser tante e tanto artificiose, che — darebbono molto timore alli figliuoli veri di questa religione, se non stessero molto confidati dell'aiuto certissimo di quel Signore — che la fondò, e del favore e patrocinio di Vostra Santità non solamente come Pontefice di quella santa sedia che fondò e stabilì detta Compagnia e la ricevette in un modo così particolare sotto la sua protettione, ma ancora come padre amantissimo d'essa, e pastore sapientissimo che sappia et habbia visto et esperimentato quanto importino alla chiesa di Dio le fatiche di questi suoi figliuoli, le quali il demonio vorrebbe adesso turbare con varii pretesti di riformationi e ben publico. Dico il demonio perché *in rei veritate et coram Deo affirmo* che in questi 4 anni e più che sono stato in Spagna ho considerato il meglio che ho potuto e con ogni indifferenza le pretensioni di alcuni pochi inquieti della medesima Compagnia che disconsi esser cause di queste turbationi e quel ch'ho potuto giudicar è stato questo; primo poco spirito ordinariamente nelli pretensori e poco essempio di vita religiosa, poi segnali evidenti d'ambitione in alcuni, e dopo questo emulatione manifesta contro la natione Italiana per esser il Nostro P. Generale di quella; et ultimamente poca affettione anzi ripugnanza chiara contro la dipendenza e subordinatione di Roma; e con quest'ultimo per esser ancora cosa toc-

---

114. lo] *om. Knox*
115. scudi *Knox*
116. *Knox ends here.*
117. havuta] *this ed.*; hauta *A*

cante raggion di stato pare che habbino fatto più impressione appresso alcuni personaggi di governo — persuadendoli che questo governo così absoluto da Roma potrebbe esser pregiudiciale: il quale argomento Vostra Santità ben vede dove tira, e che per certa conseguenza potrebbe tirar ancora a cose maggiori. Basta haver detto questo a Vostra Santità *cum omni veritate et simplicitate,* e prego humilmente la Santità Vostra che questo sia per lei sola. La persona del nostro P. Generale Vostra Santità deve già conoscere meglio che molti altri, e non dubito, se non che stando li Padri congregati vedrà Vostra Santità testimonio universale di suo buon governo, il quale è tale che nissuno può giustamente riprendere; ed io di certa scientia posso dire che non ho visto fin qui buon religioso nissuno di qualsivoglia natione che non dia infinite grazie a Nostro Signore per tal padre. Quel che tutti desiderano adesso è che questa Congregatione si faccia con la libertà et altre circonstanze che conviene, acciochè Iddio vi concorra, e che non vi entrino prattiche e negotiationi di fuora per violentar le cose, perchè questo sarebbe non solamente per escludere l'assistenza dello Spirito Santo ma ancora per screditare tutto quello che si conchiuderà, e rimandare tutti li Padri sconsolatissimi a casa, e così confidiamo che Iddio e Vostra Santità non lo permetteranno. —— &c.

Translation

Holy Father

Although the obligation ——[118] But after Fr Joseph Creswell, who was formerly rector of the English college there in Rome, arrived here a few months ago and told me so much of Your Holiness's singular benevolence towards us and your most holy zeal for the conversion of our country (and Cardinal Allen and our father general have written in the same strain), I could not wait any longer to return very humble thanks to Your Holiness — and especially for the brief which Your Holiness was so good as to send by the last post to the cardinal archbishop of Seville here, in favour of the new seminary which our Lord has given us in this city.[119] And about this and some other matters that concern us, I am going to give Your Holiness a brief report in this letter, in full confidence, as to a most loving father and master.

I think it was a very special providence of Our Lord that in the course of these last four years, during which the heretics have tried to suppress us even more than they have ever done before, and the seminary at Rheims has been in danger of collapse, God has opened a door to us in Spain so wide that thereby we already possess three other seminaries, one in Valladolid — another here in Seville — and a third which His Majesty here, in his great goodness, has now ordered to be set up at Saint-Omer in Flanders, so as to receive, without delay, the younger sons of the English Catholics. ——

These two other seminaries situated in Spain are making good progress, thanks to the grace and very special favour of our Lord. There are more than a hundred persons in them and the number goes on increasing every day, along with much zeal on the part of

---

118. Cf. the similar opening to Persons's previous letter to the pope, 1 December 1592 (B162).

119. The cardinal archbishop of Seville was Rodrigo de Castro Osorio (B162).

the students and wonderful determination to offer their lives in this enterprise, to which they go from here every year with greater courage and gladness than could be believed if we had not witnessed it with our own eyes. Glory and thanks be to God above all for it, for it is a benefit that does not seem to have been bestowed on any other nation in these days; and so it seems we can take it as a sign of His very great mercy towards England, and that He does not intend to abandon her completely. ——

The upkeep of these two seminaries depends chiefly on the charity and alms of private individuals, though His Majesty subscribes 1700 Δ a year to the one at Valladolid. —— His Majesty does not give any alms to this one at Seville, but it is his favour and patronage which inspires all others who befriend us, and so His Majesty should in fact be given the credit for everything. In this regard we very humbly beg Your Holiness to express acknowledgements to His Majesty and thank him for this great and singular act of piety.

There is little that I have to write about other matters, etc. —— The great indebtedness of our poor Society to Your Holiness we should easily be able to recognize here, even if they did not write from Rome of as many instances of it as they do: and I am fully assured that *Your Holiness will be recompensed when the just receive their reward.*[120] I greatly rejoice also that God has provided an occasion for the whole Society to become more indebted to your Holiness than to any of your predecessors since it was founded; inasmuch as it is in Your Holiness's pontificate that the Society is to hold the first general congregation that it has held in the general's time. And, *to speak plainly*, it may be the most important one of all, when we consider the schemes and machinations of certain persons against her Institute. These, they say, are so extensive and so cunningly devised —— that they would cause great fear in the true sons of this order, if they did not place their confidence fully in the most certain help of that master —— who founded it, and in the favour and patronage of Your Holiness: and this not merely because you are the occupant of that holy see which founded and established the said Society and took it especially under its protection, but also because you are a most affectionate father to it, and a most wise pastor, who knows and has seen and had experience what great advantage ensues to the church of God from the labours of these her sons, whom the devil now seeks to perturb under various pretexts of reforms and of the public good. I say the devil, because *in all sincerity and before God* I declare that in the course of these four years or more that I have been in Spain I have weighed in my mind as best I could and with complete impartiality the aims of some few dissatisfied members of this Society who are said to be the source of these broils; and the conclusion I have been able to come to is this: first, that as a rule there is not much of a spirit of piety in the schemers, and little evidence of a religious life; next, there are clear signs of ambition in some of them, as well as blatant jealousy of the Italian nation because our father general belongs to it; finally, there is little liking, rather there is obvious dislike, of being subject to and under the orders of Rome. With this last appeal, in so far as it is also a matter that touches reason of state, it seems that they have made a greater impression on certain personages in the government —— persuading them that this all but absolute government from Rome could be prejudicial to their interests. Your Holiness can easily see where this argument is head-

---

120. Lk 14: 14.

ing, and that its inevitable result will be to lead on to more serious things. It is enough to have said this much to Your Holiness *in all truth and candour*, and I humbly beg Your Holiness to prevent it from going any further. Our father general's character should by now be more familiar to Your Holiness than to many others, and I doubt not that, when the fathers are assembled, Your Holiness will perceive that there is universal testimony to his good government, which is of such a kind as no one can justly find fault with it; and I can state from certain knowledge that I have not so far come across any good religious of any nation whatsoever who does not give unbounded thanks to our Lord for such a father. What everybody is anxious for now, is that the congregation may be characterized by freedom and all other convenient circumstances, so that God may cooperate with it, and no schemes and plots from outside for violent courses gain entry; for this would not only have the effect of inhibiting the help of the Holy Spirit but also of discrediting all the decisions reached, thus sending all the fathers home in the utmost dejection. And so we trust that God and Your Holiness will not permit it —— etc.

B176 To Claudio Acquaviva, Seville, 19 April 1593

>SOURCE: ARSI, *Hisp.* 135, fols. 187–188, holograph, with remains of a seal.
>HICKS: 154–163 with English translation.
>
>NOTE: Persons responds to Acquaviva's letter of 15 February (B165) and gives further details of the condition and support of the new seminary in Seville. He elaborates on his earlier report on his audience with the king and the count of Chinchón about the coming general congregation, enclosing a copy of his letter to the pope on the same subject.
>
>Persons has been asked to attend the congregation of the province of Castile at Medina del Campo (about thirty miles south-southwest of Valladolid) in preparation for the general congregation. He is to travel via Évora and Lisbon.

Molto Reverendo in Christo padre mio
Pax Christi.

1. Da Madrid scrissi a Vostra Paternità con l'ordinario passato, quello che per alhora s'offeriva, et dipoi tornato qua hebbi la letera de Vostra Paternità delli 15 di febraro, et ne ringratio la Paternità Vostra molto humilmente, di che n'habbia scritto a questi Padri di Siviglia in riconoscimento delli loro favori fatti a questo nuovo Seminario Inglese perché per questo mezzo ci sarà più salda la carità loro, ch'è la cosa che più desideriamo et che ninguno ci sia contrario, come penso che ninguno sarà per molte cause, et principalmente per la molta pietà et religione che tutti tengono, et sin qui tutti ci favoriscono.

Questo Collegio lodato sia Nostro Signor va molto ben inanzi tanto nello spirituale come nello temporale, stanno 46 bocche in casa, hanno speso più di 2400 Δ in quattro mesi, et non penso che devono 200. Et quando la flota vendrà tengo grandi speranze già et promesse d'aiuti in grosso. Habbiamo accommodato questa casa in tal maniera che 80 persone potranno star et ce ne sono moltissime commodità d'essa fuora del sito, che è il miglior di tutta la città. Et quando questa casa non sarà assai capace, v'è un'altra vicina contigua la qual potremo pigliar et così habbiamo condotto questa per quattro anni et la potremo haver dipoi per quanto tempo vorressimo.

2. Il Padre Francisco Peralta fa molto bene l'officio de Rector, et il Padre Carlo Tancardo l'officio di ministro benissimo, il Padre Cresuello tene officio parte di Procuratore, et parte assiste nelli studii, et il Padre provincial c'ha dato un altro Padre chiamato Juan de Munnoz che fa l'officio di confessore, et assiste ancora in cose de studii perché fu necessario, et con questi quattro padri spero ch'il governo passarà molto bene.

Vi son tre fratelli della Compagnia qui, delli quali Fabricio Como è l'uno, et è la colonna della casa come il Rettor me dice, et sta molto contento et mi han fatto instanza di lasciarlo qui et così penso di far benché per altra parte n'haverei bisogno di lui.

[3.] Il Padre Gulielmo Flacco che fu ministro in Valladolid et venne meco qua, trovò subito una imbarcatione molto commoda per Cales, che fu il luogo dove massimamente desiderava andar, et così alli 8 di questo si partir da San Lucar. Al medessimo tempo si imbarco un altro sacerdote del Seminario de Valladolid per Inghilterra ma in nave differente. Menò seco il Padre Flacco un fratello coaiutore francese, ch'haveva vissuto alcuni mesi in questo collegio con grande edificatione di tutti, et Dio gl'haveva dato particular vocatione di sirvir in questa causa delli Inglesi. Spero ch'il Padre Flacco farà molto bene in Sant Omer, qui va una carta sua per Vostra Paternità che scrisse dal porto, è molto buon religioso et intelligente nelle cose agibili.

4. Nella passata diedi conto a Vostra Paternità di quello ch'il Re c'haveva dato per il nuovo Seminario di Sant Omero, che son 1920 ducati per l'anno, et benché la situatione sobre mercanzie Inglesi non sia cosa molto certa, con tutto ciò, mi parve ben pigliarlo al principio, perché quando per questa via non si potessero cobrar, sta più obligato il Re di provederli per altra, et quanto al bisogno presente, mandai là 500 Δ per letere di cambio d'alcune persone divote che me le dettero come nella passata scrissi a Vostra Paternità, oltre le spese ch'ho fatto del viaggio di questo padre et di suo compagno[121] et spero nel Signor che si ci da vita, non li mancarà. Et così priego la Paternità Vostra di raccomandar molto caldamente al padre Oliverio provincial di Fiandra questo nuovo Seminario acciochè gli provegga d'un buon Rettor y delle altre cose che gli saranno necessarie avanti che si parta per la Congregatione Generale, già io gl'ho scritto che il padre Henrico Broy servirà molto ben per ministro, et il padre Nicolo Smith per prefetto delli studii, et il padre Flacco per confessore et per incaminar le missioni si così a Vostra Paternità parerà. Tengo speranza che questo Seminario di Sant'Omer si va ben inanzi, sarà la cosa più importante per sostentar in piè et fornir tutti gl'altri seminarii di gente scelta che fin qui s'habbia trattato, et certo è che per esser questo Seminario di piccolini, tendrà più favore in questa corte che tutti l'altri insieme.

5. Di più scrissi nell'altra mia da Madrid il ragionamento che passe con Sua Maestà sobre le cose della Compagnia, et di questa Congregatione Generale, et quanto importava al servitio di Dio et ben di questa povera religione et al servitio di Sua Maestà in particulare che la congregatione si faccia con tutta libertà senza violenza di fuora, et fra altre ragioni, toccai quella del universal contento o discontento di tutti li padri più gravi della Compagnia che da tutte le nationi verrebbono a questa congregatione, et il servicio o disservitio che da questo punto potrebbe nascer alle cose di Sua Maestà massimamente nelli regni lontani, et oyò lo Su Magestad con attentione, et promesse tutto quello che possiamo desiderar, et lo medessimo fece dipoi il Conte de Chinchon benché algo più

---

121. compagno] *this ed.*; compagna R

freddamente che il Rey. Dipoi entiendo che il Padre Alonso Sanchez ha parlato più largamente a entrambas personas et più in particulare di maniera che mio parlar fu come una introductione solamente a quello del Padre. Faccia Nostro Signor che tutto approveche, come spero che fara facendo noi altri quello che da nostra parte convene.

6. Con questa Vostra Paternità vedrà quello che m'è parso scrivere ancora delle nostre cose al Papa con l'occasione del breve che ci mandò per questo Cardinale de Seviglia, si Vostra Paternità juzgarà che si convenga dar la carta, potrà Vostra Paternità darla al Cardinal Alano o altra persona che a lei parerà più a proposito, para presentarla a Sua Santità, et si non parerà ispediente darla, Vostra Paternità faccia in tutto et per tutto quello che in domino parerà meglio, et lo medessimo dice il Padre Cresuello della sua, perché in questo non desideriamo altro si non quello che Vostra Paternità juzgarà meglio, solamente voressimo esser avisati si se alertano[122] o no et per cui mano per conformarci meglio in altre letere nostre con quello che si fa di queste.

7. Il padre provincial de Castiglia la Vieja mi scrisse che desiderarebbe ch'io me trovasse in quella congregatione de Medina Campo etc. Et per sodisfar al buon Padre ho fatto tutto lo possibile qui per finir presto con il Padre Bartolome Perez et con questo Seminario et così me partirò fra tre o quatro giorni, ma perché mi necessita passar per Ebora et porventura ancora per Lisboa per alcuni nigotii forzati delli quali scriverò dipoi a Vostra Paternità non so si potrò llegar là a tempo, farò quello che potrò.

8. Non so si scrissi a Vostra Paternità nelle mie passate del Padre Richardo Walpolo et di due giovani Inglesi di molto buona abilità, che sono ricevuti qui nella Compagnia, ciò è li duoi postremi per coaiutori, et altri diversi vi sono delli migliori sugietti di questi due Seminarii che hanno propositi d'intrar con tempo, et così sarà necessario per la continuatione di questa opera et della missione d'Inghilterra, et qui non c'è inconveniente nissuno della loro entrata et così speriamo che Vostra Paternità ci favorirà sempre in questo, come in tutte l'altre cose fa, et tutto si farà ancora con la moderatione che convendrà, piacendo a Dio, il qual ci conserve sempre la Paternità Vostra, nelli cui Santi Sacrificii humilmente me raccomando. Da Seviglia alli 19 di Aprile 1593.

    Di Vostra Reverenda Paternità
        figliuolo et siervo endegno
        Rob Personio.

[*Addressed*:] A Nostro Padre Claudio Aquaviva Preposito General dela Compagnia de Jesus, Roma.

[*Endorsed*:] Sevilla. P. Roberto Personio. Abril 19 93. [*with summary of contents*]

Translation

My Very Reverend Father in Christ
The peace of Christ.

1. By the last post from Madrid I wrote to Your Paternity what there was to relate at the time,[123] and afterwards, on my return here, I had a letter from Your Paternity of the

---

122. alertano] *blotted in R, possibly* advertano
123. See Persons's letter of 22 March (B173).

15th of February.¹²⁴ I am very humbly grateful to Your Paternity for writing to the fathers here in Seville to acknowledge the favours they have bestowed on this new English seminary, because by this means their charity will be encouraged. This is what we are most anxious for: that no one may stand in opposition; and for many reasons I think that no one will, and this mainly on account of the piety and religious devotion which they all possess in good measure; and so far, all are showing us favour.

This college, praised be our Lord, is making very good progress both in spiritual matters and in temporal. There are 46 mouths to feed in the house; they have spent more than 2400 ducats in four months, and I do not think that they owe 200. They are already entertaining great hopes, with promises of substantial aid when the fleet arrives. We have fitted out this house in such a way that eighty persons can be accommodated, and it is convenient for us in a great many ways to be located on the outskirts of the town, being the finest area in the whole town.¹²⁵ And when this house becomes too small to hold us there is another neighbouring one, adjacent to us, which we can procure, and as we have arranged to have this one for four years, we shall be able to keep it for as long as we like in the future.

2. Fr Francisco de Peralta carries out the duties of rector very well, and Fr Charles Tancard those of minister excellently: Fr Creswell, besides holding the office of procurator, also assists with the studies; and father provincial has given us another father named Juan de Muñoz who performs the duties of confessor and helps also in the matter of studies, for this was necessary; and in the hands of these four fathers, I hope that the government of the house will be very well conducted.

There are three brothers of the Society here, including Fabrizio Como; and, according to what the rector tells me, he is the mainstay of the house. He is very contented, and they have pressed me to leave him here, and I think I shall do so, though I could make use of him elsewhere.¹²⁶

[3.] Fr William Flack, who was minister at Valladolid and came here with me, immediately found a very convenient vessel bound for Calais, where he particularly wanted to go, and so he left from Sanlúcar on the 8th of this month. At the same time another priest from the seminary of Valladolid embarked for England, but in a different ship. Fr Flack took with him a French lay brother who had been on a visit to this college for some months and had given great edification to all. God had given him a special vocation to serve in this cause of the English. I hope that Fr Flack will do much good at Saint-Omer. A letter of his is enclosed, which he wrote to Your Paternity from the port. He is a very good religious and a good man of practical affairs.

4. In my previous letter I gave Your Paternity an account of what the king had given us for the new seminary of St Omers, i.e., 1920 ducats a year; and although his levy on English merchandise is somewhat uncertain,¹²⁷ in spite of that I thought we should take

---

124. B165.

125. Murphy, 7, describes this as "cramped quarters in the Plaza de la Magdalena," beyond the city wall to the east. The college moved to the Calle de las Armas in 1594, a little closer to the centre.

126. This is in contrast with many other references to Como's restlessness.

127. Edwards, 159, thinks this arrangement is a touch of "wry humour" on the part of the king. Persons refers to his letter from Toledo, 22 March (B173).

it to begin with, because, when we are no longer able to collect the money by this method, the king is then under greater obligation to provide it from other sources. For present needs I sent them 500 ducats by bills of exchange which some devout persons gave me, as I wrote to Your Paternity in my previous letter, besides paying the expenses of this father's journey and of his companion; and I hope in the Lord that, if He gives life to our enterprise, they will not be in want. And so I pray Your Paternity to commend this new seminary very warmly to Fr Olivier, provincial in Flanders, that he may provide it with a good rector and with the other things it will need, before he leaves for the general congregation. I have already written to him that Fr Henry Broy will do very well as minister, and Fr Nicholas Smith as prefect of studies, and Fr Flack as confessor and to inaugurate the sending of missions, if Your Paternity approves. I am in hopes that this seminary of St Omers, if it makes good progress, will be the most effective way of keeping all the other seminaries going and for supplying them with picked men, such as we have dealt with until now; and we can be sure that this seminary, consisting as it certainly will of little boys, will receive more favour in the court here than all the others put together.

5. In my other letter from Madrid,[128] I also wrote about the discussion I had with His Majesty about the affairs of the Society and this general congregation: how important it was for the service of God and for the welfare of this poor order, and for the service of His Majesty in particular, that the congregation should be maintained in complete freedom with no compulsion from without; and among other arguments, I used that of the widespread satisfaction or dissatisfaction which would be given to all the fathers of most gravitas in the Society coming from all nations to this congregation, and the service or disservice that might ensue, from this course of action, to His Majesty's interests, especially in distant realms. And His Majesty listened to this attentively and promised all that we can wish for, and afterwards the count of Chinchón also did the same, though somewhat more coldly than the king. I understand that Fr Alonso Sánchez spoke at greater length to both of them afterwards, and in more detail, so that my conversation was as it were merely an introduction to that of the father. May our Lord cause all to turn out well, as I hope He will do, if we on our side do what is proper for us to do.

6. Enclosed with this Your Paternity will see what I thought well to write to the pope also about our affairs, taking the opportunity of the brief which he sent us through the cardinal of Seville here.[129] If Your Paternity decides that it is advisable to deliver the letter, you will be able to give it to Cardinal Allen, or to some other person who seems to you more suitable, to hand to His Holiness; and if Your Paternity does not think it expedient to pass it on, I would have you do in all things and for all things what you judge best in the Lord. Fr Creswell says the same about his letter, for we have no other desire in this matter than what Your Paternity judges to be best; only we would wish to be informed if they will be alerted or not,[130] and by whose hand, so that in our other letters we may conform better to what is done in regard to these.

---

128. This seems to be another way of referring to the letter of 22 March (B173), which deals with these matters as described here.

129. See Persons to Pope Clement VIII, 1 December 1592 (B162), headnote.

130. The verb here is conjectural: see the textual note.

7. Father provincial of Old Castile[131] wrote to me that he would like me to be present for the congregation at Medina del Campo and, to satisfy the good father, I have done all in my power here to finish my business quickly with Fr Bartolomé Pérez and this seminary; and so I shall be leaving in three or four days' time, but as I am obliged to go by way of Évora and possibly also by Lisbon, because of some necessary business which I will explain later to Your Paternity, I do not know if I shall be able to get there in time; I will do what I can.[132]

8. I do not know if I wrote to Your Paternity in my previous letters about Fr Richard Walpole and two very capable young Englishmen who have been received into the Society here: that is to say, the latter two as lay brothers; and there are several others from among the best of the students of these two seminaries who have the intention of entering in course of time; and so it will be necessary for them to do in order to continue this work and the mission in England. There is no difficulty here about their entering, and so we hope Your Paternity will always give us your support in this matter, as you do in all other things. Everything will be done, please God, with suitable moderation. And may He ever preserve Your Paternity to us. And to your holy sacrifices I humbly commend myself. From Seville, 19th April 1593.

    Your Paternity's
        unworthy son and servant
            Robert Persons.

B177 From Ralph Emerson, Gouda, 25 April 1593

SOURCE: CP, vol. 22.

HICKS: 164.

EDITION: "Cecil Papers: April 1593," in *Calendar of the Cecil Papers in Hatfield House*, vol. 4: *1590–1594*, ed. R. A. Roberts (London, 1892), 299–308, at 303–304.

NOTE: The right-hand margin of the letter has been torn, with the result that words are missing at the end of the lines. Where possible, these have been supplied in square brackets. Many of the details of the letter are also obscure because of poor translation.

Emerson, formerly Persons's assistant in France and the Netherlands, was a key figure in the contraband Catholic book trade. This letter from Gouda, probably a station on Emerson's smuggling route, was presumably intercepted by Burghley's intelligence network.

Since the letter was supposedly translated from Dutch, names, dates, and places are difficult to identify. The most likely interpretation is that Emerson wrote to Persons on 31 March asking him to confirm that his books (left over from his sojourn in France and the Netherlands during the 1580s) should be sent to him in Valladolid. The letter was despatched to someone in Rome, or more likely to Edward Kenyon at the college in Rheims (which was in the process of relocating to Douai), for forwarding along with a letter to a third party, Jacob (or James) Lutte, possibly an agent handling the correspondence to Valladolid. Meanwhile, Emerson learnt in a letter received on 12 April (and therefore probably despatched with a letter to Ver-

131. Gonzalo Dávila.
132. On the business Persons had in Lisbon, see Allen's testimonial, 15 March, headnote.

stegan on 19 March, B171–72) that Persons had been delayed in Madrid or Toledo: in fact, Persons was now in Seville.

On Persons's library at Valladolid, see *La misión de Robert Persons: Un jesuita inglés en la antigua corte de Valladolid; Robert Persons Mission: An English Jesuit in the Old Court of Valladolid*, ed. Javier Burrieza and Peter Harris (Valladolid, 2010), 95–115.

Emerson asks Persons to use his influence to gain the pope's support for the Catholic League rather than Henry of Navarre, now Henry IV of France, who has promised to convert. Henry was received into the Roman Catholic Church on 25 July 1593. Along with Persons's letter to Pope Clement VIII, 15 April (B175), Emerson's request implies that Persons may have been in regular correspondence with the papacy.

Reverend Sir.

I have written a lettre of the 31st of Ma[rch to] one Odwardius khi[133] to Rome, for I did understand that yow ... the letter was packet with Jacob Litius[134] letter to come the ... And by cause I know not, if yow have receaved it ... that I have your books by me packet in secret, there sh ... untill further relacion of yow. I have at Brother Shues comfort, if they will proceed against yow without ca[use] yow will use your self herin wisely.

I have receaved the 12th of April, your lettre of the [?19 March], theren understanding, how yow are hindereth to com[e. If] yow have receaved my writing, therby, yow maie ... untyll this commeth to yow also, &c.[135]

That yow saie yow troble me to much with your tinges, feigne not, or saie not so, for I would be con[tent yow] did use me, in much more, then in the same, therof assure your self.

I shall grete you from Brother Shueses, and John ... I make your writing not manyfest or openly kno[wne] should have many commendacions more of your f ... taunce. Mr Rettor doth aske me often, what yow ... me, and where yow are, and how it is with you, but he ... nothing of me from yow, then such thinges as are ... .[136] For conclusion is Mr. Odescalco arrived in Mylan, th ... and hath written to the governor of the five Canton ... should send them some body of our side, then would he ... to handle in the matter, but he doth not w... manner, therfor I would not ride my self to him, Belinger likewise, for

133. Odwardius khi] Gwardinski *Roberts*. This may be Edward Kenyon, who was in Rheims/Douai until transferred to Valladolid in May 1594. See Anstruther, 196–197, and Pollen, *Valladolid Register*, 28, where the surname is given as "chenion." If so, "Rome" must be an error for "Rems."

134. Litius] CP; Litig *Roberts; cf. Lutte* in the postscript.

135. It seems that Emerson wrote to Persons on 31 March, via a contact in Rome, enclosed with a letter to Jacob Lutte/Litte. Persons's books were in readiness for despatch, once they had news from him. Emerson had subsequently learnt, from a letter received on 12 April (probably despatched on 19 March, the same day as a letter to Verstegan), that Persons had been delayed, and would therefore read both letters at the same time. By "Yow have receaved my writing, therby," Emerson presumably means, "You will by then have received my letter of 31 March." The missing word may be "delay."

136. Emerson refers to the five central Swiss cantons that remained Catholic after the Reformation and had historic links with the duchy of Milan.

we[137] doubt he had not full ... would rather dispute, then to contract, or offer us a small somme, which would not be possible for us ... *Exitus acta probabit.*[138] I will with Godes help ... how it shalbe ended, if they will helpe us now will we take the rest, at such time, as we sh ... .[139]

Otherwise, Pater Roberte (I write this with grei ... eyes) if this contribucion, which the Duke of Savo ... wherin the holy father the Pope, and the Catholick K[ing] ... hended, from whom the money should come, being ... Savoy not able to paie it.[140] We doubt it will co[me] ... for he of Navarre declared by his Ambassador at Solotherne,[141] that he hath sent to his holynes, and desires mercy, and promised to be of the Catholick beleef, and to submit himself to his holynes, and desires thereupon to obtaine of his holynes the contribucion; but if it may not be obtayned, then will the Dukes and nobillity, which are with him, choose a Patriarch, and then desire likewise a contribucion for to cleere Fraunce, and tourne the warres into Italy. The Spaniardes do hinder this all, and would set there feete in Fraunce, which the Frenchmen mislike, and by cause the principall gentlemen and Catholick are yet by him of Navarre, and do proceed earnestly in these quarters or cantons; which hath moved them so farre, that he of Navarre shall sooner obtaine the contribucion or helpe, then they of the Holy League. And if they do not content us now, many captaines of our two regimentes will depart, that is for certaine, specially them of Lucerne will go to serve the other part, that is promised to us, except they helpe us now owt of our neede, then shall we returne againe to his holynes, and move others to come to us from the said Navarre, &c.[142] This is, pater Robert, the only way. It were good that his holynes truely were advised, that it might be moderated at the side of the League. For if Navarre should be furthered by the reason abovesaid, then should the warre be cast into Italy, for certainly the Frenchmen will agree in peace, as soone as the contribucion followeth. It is certaine that the Lutherish townes have promised helpe to send in Piemont to Desdiguides, for the Coronell Gailathe doth bring a great somme of money for this contribucion.[143] Pater Robert I meane it good, if they will not understand, hereafter with

---

137. we] *CP*; no *Roberts*

138. "The outcome will prove the deeds" (a tag from Ovid, *Heroides* 1.85, sometimes rendered "The end justifies the means").

139. Emerson seems to be referring to his negotiations to maintain, develop, and protect his lines of communication, i.e., the routes for movement of missionaries, books, and holy objects.

140. Emerson refers to the unreliable support of Charles Emmanuel I (1562–1630), duke of Savoy, for the Catholic League. The duke was in conflict with Henry IV (Navarre) over the marquisate of Saluzzo.

141. Jean de Vivonne, French ambassador to the Holy See, was dismissed in 1589, after which Navarre had only indirect diplomatic relations with the papacy. See De Lamar Jensen, "French Diplomacy and the Wars of Religion," *Sixteenth Century Journal* 5, no. 3 (1974): 23–46, at 37.

142. The syntax here is confused, but Emerson seems to be calling for papal reassurances which will keep officers of the English regiments serving in the Spanish army of Flanders from defecting to Navarre in sympathy with leading French Catholics who were backing Navarre against the Catholic League.

143. With the support of Protestant towns Navarre would be able to extend the war against Spain into northern Italy.

their tormoyle and if one maie prevent great harme with a small thing, and will not, the fault is his. The Canton cannot panic if it begin to take effect they sit warme, but if they should come 6 or 8 myles neere, or to Rome, as before hath hapned (which God prevent) then they should see *in quem tranfixerunt* & *sapienti pauca*.[144] God preserve yow. Gouda, at ... of April '93.

Your Rend ...
                    Rudolf.

[PS] I praie yow declare this newes to my frende Jacob Lutte, for he serveth yow and me much with the letters, and is true and secret.

[*Endorsed:*]—25 April 1593, Copie of a lettre translated owt of Dutch to Persons. Imperfect.

B178 From Henry Garnet, 26 April 1593

SOURCE: Persons to Acquaviva, 16 June.

NOTE: Garnet confirms that there is strong support in England for the establishment of a seminary for boys at Saint-Omer. He also emphasizes the need for more missioners.

According to Persons's letter to Acquaviva of 11 August (B196), Garnet wrote also in March and May. There appear to be traces of the missing letters in a digest of information from Richard Holtby[145] and a reminder from Henry Garnet that Persons had written to him "long since" about John Fixer's host in England (Garnet to Persons, 19 November 1594, B249).

---

144. "[They shall look] upon him whom they pierced" (Jn 19:37, quoting Zech. 12:10), and "a few words are enough for the wise." Emerson means that those who support Navarre will be betraying the Catholic cause.

145. "Out of Mr Holtby's letters the 12 of April 1593: At our last being togither I left a note in wryting with you, wherin I would have you to correct two thinges. The one was that Mistress Killingale could not obteine, being great with child, so much favour as to be delivered out of prison, untill she had layed her belly. The which I perceive did fall out otherwise before my returne againe, for shee was sent home soone after untill she was delivered, but I was enformed credibly that before it was denyed her. The other was that whereas I said that Mistress Rudderforth was found in a conveiance by meanes of one that hard her lament: it was otherwise, for her husband had escaped first out of their handes, & she alone went into the conveiance, where she remained so long untill partly with famin, & partly by the uneasines of the place, she was almost perished, having no meanes to gett forth. For Fenwick had putt all the servants out of the house, & kept it with his company wasting all with horse and man. Than at the last the gentleman her husband fearing the extremity of his wife, gott one to adventure to deliver her: & finding a time opened the place: but before he could gett her out, came in Fenwicke, & tooke her, being half gone, & now growen so stiffe, that shee could not move herselfe. So they layed her upon a bedd, to recover her. In the meane time, came in also the gentleman him selfe to save his wife: & so was also apprehended" ("The Apprehension of 2 Gentlewomen the 12 of April 1593," ABSI, Coll B 93: see also Tierney, 3: 105n).

B179 From Richard Verstegan, Antwerp, 30 April 1593

SOURCE: ABSI, Coll B 103–106, holograph, with two enclosures.
EDITION: Petti, 134–143.
NOTE: Verstegan reports on plans for a new Catholic ecclesiastical history of England, on the controversy over Puritanism, and on conditions in the Spanish Netherlands. Persons took good note of William Rainolds's suggestions, recorded here, and drew up a preliminary "Scheme for an English Church History," dated 1 September 1594. In 1598 he began compiling *Certamen ecclesiae Anglicana*, which was never published; see the selection edited by Jos Simons (Assen, 1965; the "Scheme" is reproduced in an appendix, pages 292–299). The four-volume manuscript is preserved at Stonyhurst College, Lancashire. In it, Persons incorporated material from Bede, Nicholas Harpsfield, and Nicholas Sander, as Rainolds proposed.

Right reverend.

I have receyved your fatherhoodes letter of the 19 of March, and therewith a great packet for F. Holte:[146] himself (as by his last letter unto me I understand) is now either at Namures or on his way to Tornay, wher the provinciall and sundry of the society do mete. I hold it best to send the packet unto him to Tornay by the rector of this towne who goeth thether, for himself beeing no further of, I do not thinck it requisyte that I should open the same.

In the meane tyme I have written unto him to signify what I have for him.

I moved Mr Reynoldes yesterday to write his answere unto your fatherhoode, Touching the setting foorthe of a generall Ecclesiasticall history of the Churche of England.[147] He answered that himself beeing not very well (as in dede he is not) and besydes that, somwhat busyed, and his answere not greatly requisyte to be so speedely given, he would for a whyle deferr it. I had some talke with him aboute this woorck, the methhoode whereof he lyketh to be thus: first the history of St Bede and Dr Harpsfeild to be joyned in one volume, and to continew from the first Christianity of our nation unto the revolt of king Henry the Eight. Then in a second volume, the Concertation which would make a volume greater then the first; and therein should be comprised so much of Dr Harpsfeild his history as since that revolt is continued; as also what Dr Saunders in his booke de Schismate Anglicano[148] hathe sett downe, and what els that oute of sundry writings and good notes may be gathered, and this beeing conferred together, should be made one intire pece of woorck, the first volume conteyning as it were the tyme of the peace of the churche and the second the troobles that have bene caused by Schisme and heresy.

I have receyved from our freindes in England [25] a discourse in writing conteyning 50+ sheets of paper beeing the confession of Mr Anthony Tirrell written by himself

---

146. See Persons's letters to Acquaviva, 22 March (B173), relating to Holt's role in negotiating the founding of a seminary for English boys at Saint-Omer.

147. William Rainolds (1544–1594), professor of divinity and Hebrew at Douai and Rheims and one of the translators of the Rheims New Testament.

148. Anglicano] *this ed.*; Anglicana *Petti; G appears to correct* Anglicana *to* Anglicano.

before his later fall, wherein there is very notable matter discovered to long here to be rehearsed,[149] and sundry copies of the treasurers letters (and others in aucthority) unto him: besydes divers articles and interogations, practizes of Walsingham and others, etc., which will yeild great light and matter unto your fatherhoodes intended woorck.

I have also gotten the late booke against the puritanes, sett foorthe by the aucthority of the Bishopes, and in my judgment there was never booke sett foorth by our English heretikes nor any other, more advantagious for us. Calvin and Beza are deciphered to be no better then seditious and rebellious spirites; their practizes, driftes, and sinister getting to credit and government in Geneva is displayd, and proved by their actes, consultations, and private letters to their fellow ministers – yea, Bezaes seditious letters to the puritanes in England, which we should perhapes never have come to the knowledge of, but that themselves have now layde open their owne Turpitude.[150]

One thing I cannot passe over which in this booke is sett downe and that is, that one beeing in Geneva did usually frequent the sermons of Calvyne, and would never come unto the sermons of Viretus, who did preach in another church at the same howre that Calvyne preached in his churche (either churche is named); uppon occasion one asked him why he did still heare the sermons of Calvine and would never heare any one of those of Viretus. I tell you, quoth this party, yf St Paule himself were alive and in Geneva and did preach at the same howre that monsieur Calvyne preachd, I would leave St Paule, and heare monsieur Calvyn.[151]

Another booke is sett foorth of some bignes also with lyke aucthorite and written against the puritaines by one Mathew Sutcliff (the same man that hathe lately written in Latin against Fr Bellarmyne and others, whereof I have alredy written unto you) and this fellow playeth uppon Calvyne and Beza in the same sorte as dothe the other, and hathe very many prety notes in him fitt for our purpose.

149. On the multiple apostate Anthony Tyrrell (or Tirell, d. 1615), see Anstruther, 361–363. After acting as an informer in relation to the Babington plot of 1586, he wrote the long recantation referred to here, but soon relapsed again, was protected by Walsingham, and became a Protestant clergyman. The holograph MS was sent from England to Verstegan, who passed it on to Persons in October 1593. Persons prepared it for the press, but it was not printed until the nineteenth century, in *The Troubles of Our Catholic Forefathers as Related by Themselves*, ed. John Morris, 3 vols. (London, 1872–1877), 2: 310–486. In his preface Persons mentions 56 sheets (p. 310); Petti gives 50, and the MS interlines "+" above "50."

150. Verstegan's enclosure reads: "The tytle of the booke against the puritanes sett foorthe by the direction and aucthoritie of the Bishopes. A Survay of the pretended holy discipline conteyning the beginninges, successe, parts, proceedinges, aucthoritie, and doctrine of it: with some of the manifold and materiall repugnances, varieties and uncertainties in that behalf; faithfully gathered by way of historicall narration, oute of the bookes and writinges of some principall favourers of that platforme. Imprinted at London by John Wolff 1593." See Richard Bancroft, *A Survey of the Pretended Holy Discipline* (London, 1593), esp. 50–60, for Beza's letters, and 372–373 for the preaching of Pierre Viret (1511–1571); see Milward, 102, and Patrick Collinson, *Richard Bancroft and Elizabethan Anti-Puritanism* (Cambridge, 2013), 8.

151. [*marginal note:*] I do not very well remember whether this tale be in the bishopes booke or in Sutcliffe but in the one of them I red it.

Amonge others: whereas the puritanes do say that papistes are more favoured then they are, he answereth them, that it "is a bold and impudent assertion, for it is well knowne that divers of them have bene executed, some *as* traitors, some *as* fellons, others have paid for it as recusants, whereas none of this faction have bene punished in lyke degree, save Hacket, albeit they deny her majesties supremacy, and many of them refuse to come to churche", etc. Thus far his owne woordes, for I have this booke also oute of the which I write it.[152]

I send at this present in Sir Frauncis his letter a paper of advices for your fatherhoode, as also an arraignment of certaine Brownistes,[153] the writing of the copy whereof I have paid for in 68, as also for thease books; and so do I for divers the lyk that a freind there sendeth me – I do not meane any 139,[154] but another – and thus much I ad to the end your fatherhood may partly knowe what charge I am at for thease things besydes the portage, which is also extraordinary.

I send your fatherhoode hereinclosed a copy of a letter written by some chief of the counsell to the comissioners of Lincolnshere, which was sent me from Fr Garnet [195],[155] as was also the discours of Mr Tirrells confession.

I send herewith also a letter sent unto me from my coosin Thomas Fitzherbert,[156] whose case seemeth unto me to be very hard. I perceave by entelligence from a frend in England [25] who is of this country, that my coosin hathe employed one their aboute some espetiall service and hathe bene at charges for the same, but the party is taken for beeing Catholic [225] yet hopeth for liberty, and as I am enformed dothe hold on his resolu-

---

152. Verstegan's enclosure reads: "The tytle of Mathew Sutclif his booke against the puritanes. An Answere to a certaine libell suplicatorie, or rather diffamatory, and also to certaine calumnious articles and interrogatories, bothe printed and scattered in secret corners, to the slaunder of the Ecclesiasticall state, and put foorthe under the name and title of a petition directed to Her Majesty; Wherein not only the frivolous discourse of the petitioner is refuted, but also the accusation against the disciplinarians his clients justified and the slaunderous cavills at the present government deciphered, by Mathew Sutcliffe at London imprinted, etc." For the quotation, see Matthew Sutcliffe (1550–1629), *An Answere to a Certaine Libel Supplicatorie* (London, 1592), 160. His *De Catholica, orthodoxa, et vera Christi ecclesia* (London, 1592) was a response to Robert Bellarmine's *Disputationes* (Rome, 1586). See Milward, 100 and 153–154.

153. For the account of the trial of Barrow and Greenwood, enclosed in a letter to Sir Francis Englefield, see Petti, 144–149. Henry Walpole wrote to Creswell on 25 July 1591 to say that he had collected some information about "the opinions of our Brownists" for Persons. As Jessopp points out, Walpole would have heard much about Brown's behaviour in Norwich from his family in Norfolk (*Letters of Henry Walpole*, ed. Jessopp, 33 and 34 n9).

154. Petti suggests "priest."

155. Fr Garnet] *interlined above* 195. For the letter from the Privy Council to the earl of Lincoln in November 1592, see *Acts of the Privy Council*, 23: 289.

156. Thomas Fitzherbert, appointed as agent of the king of Spain in Rouen, complained about lack of support from Bernardino de Mendoza; when Mendoza was replaced as ambassador by the duke of Feria, Fitzherbert became the duke's adviser and a member of his household (Loomie, *Spanish Elizabethans*, 110).

tion, and will do his busynesse so soone as he shalbe free. And by sundry letters that I have seene I do deeme him to be an honest man, and that he wilbe as good as his woord.[157]

The extreme misery of our nation here is wounderfull greate, and perswasion to patience hathe no force to resist hunger; their harts are even broken with sorrow considering that now almost in two yeares they have had no one pay. They in England rejoyce at it and proclaime it to the world.[158] Some here do murmur at the erection of new seminaries, aleaging that to be a meane to withdrawe his majesties benevolence from relieving the body of our nation. My self have argued with some that have bene very hot in this matter. Others do bothe say and write that it is intended by some either to starve us or to drive us away. Divers are sory of your fatherhoodes so speedy returne from Madrid and conceave litle hope of good successe by the solicitation of others.[159]

And touching the suing to Counte Mansfeild for our entertainments – I meane your brothers and myne in the Castels –[160] there is utterly no hope of it by him for he loveth not our nation, and Charles Paget [177][161] who hathe now gotten some credit with him, I suppose would rather crosse then further the same, and I thinck it would be a long sute to get his secretary to seeke up the kinges letter and to get afterwardes the Countes answere, for Paget [177] hathe got his creditt with the count by meane of this secretary.

Yf this Counte be to be removed from the government I suppose it best to see what may be don by the next. It is a grief to consider that after so great sute for his majesties letters, when they are once had, they are of no force; and some do say that by certaine privy marckes set downe in such letters the officers do know whether they are effectuall or not: els it were strang they should so litle regard the kinges owne writing.

I perceave that at the writing of your fatherhoodes letter of the 19 of Marche the letter of myne was not arryved touching a sute for the office of receit of the custome of Englishe clothes.[162] Whether any good may be don therein or no I know not, neither will I importunately urge your fatherhoode but leave it unto your consideration to do therein or in the former sute, as conveniently you may. And thus comitting your fatherhoode to

---

157. Petti suggests that Fitzherbert's agent may have been William Sterrell; he is mentioned in Persons's memorandum, below, "Principal Points to Facilitate the Enterprise," 30 August 1596 (B340), paragraph 17.

158. See Verstegan's report, 28 April, to the effect that the misery of Catholic exiles was the topic of pulpit oratory in England (Petti, 130).

159. This helps to explain Persons's weariness of being badgered by English exiles in Madrid over the question of their pensions (see his letter of 22 March, B173).

160. Count Pierre Ernst of Mansfeld, acting governor of the Spanish Netherlands following the death of the duke of Parma.

161. Petti suggests Charles Paget, who evidently was in Mansfeld's confidence: see the memorial prepared in 1594 for the archduke, Ernest, about the English exiles in Flanders, *Douay Diaries*, 401–408, at 408.

162. Verstegan appears to be hoping to obtain a licence (or passport) for importing cloth from England; he may have been encouraged by the fact that Persons had received such a licence from Philip II and then sold it on (*Blackfan Annals*, 37–38).

God I humbly take my leave. Antwerp this 30 or last of Aprill 1593, with right harty thankes for your good favour and affection towardes me.

    Your fatherhoodes most
        assured and redy servitor
        R. Verstegan.

[PS] Because the Latin booke of *Philopatris*[163] will not sell here, seeing so many editions hereabouts are printed, I do meane (as also your brother desyreth) to send more of them unto Spaine, and with those I will send the cronicles, Mr Tirrels confession, with divers other thinges.

[*Enclosure:*] Notes of bookes againste puritanes April 30 1593.

Yf my leasure a litle better served me and my mynde were more quiet and delivered from thease perturbations of want, me thinckes I could oute of sundry our late Englishe hereticall bookes (for I have licence to read them as also others[164]) drawe foorthe very espetiall matter to move any indifferent protestant to become doubtfull of the truthe in either the puritane or protestant religion. And this treatise I would intitule thus:

The second confusion of Babilon.
Wherein the repugnant speeches and actions of the buylders up of a pretended gospell are discovered, etc.

or I might call it, the confusion of Albion, and in the preface to the reader touch briefly how the one name conteyneth the very same letters of the other, one letter only doubled, for there is no letter in the one that is not in the other, nor no more nor lesse except the b. twice in the one and but once in the other.

Against the heretikes that would prove Rome to be Babilon and the Pope the whore of Babilon, I had once a toy in my head to have controled[165] that alusion and to have showed how Albion might by transposing the letters seme to be Babilon. The 7 hilles, saith the scripture;[166] are seaven kinges, *ergo* not seaven hills, and unto seaven kinges govermentes hathe Albion bene devyded, and Rome never. Also that the woman sat uppon a rose coloured beast and the rose is the Armes or banner of England. Moreover that the woman was druncken with the blood of sainctes, and said *Sedeo Regina et vidua*

    163. Philopatris] *Petti; possibly* Philopaters. The book was printed in Antwerp, Lyon and Rome: Verstegan sent a consignment of books to Persons on 2 October, including his own English abridgement, *An advertisement written to a secretarie of my L. Treasurers of Ingland* (Antwerp, 1592), but not the *Philopater* itself (Petti, 187–188).

    164. Henry Walpole obtained this concession for Verstegan in January 1590 by writing to Creswell in Rome. Protestant books were proscribed reading for Catholics except by special licence. The identification of Rome with Babylon or the whore of Babylon was a common trope in anti-Catholic propaganda, associated with the Antichrist in the *Apocalypse* or *Revelation of St John the Divine*. Albion is a legendary name for England. Verstegan argues that these Protestant works will harm England rather than Rome.

    165. Refuted.

    166. Several quotations or adaptations follow, from Rev. 17.

non sum, et luctum non videbo. And so dothe she sit as a Queene and is neither widow, wyf nor maid. But with all this I would not medle in the matter aforesaid, I only put it downe because it now came into my remembrance.

[*Addressed:*] Al molto Reverendo in Christi Padre, il Padre Roberto Personio della compagnia di Giesu, Sevilla.

[*Endorsed by Henry Walpole:*] Verstegan the last of April with advises 1593.

[*Endorsed by Persons:*] With a note of certayn books agaynst Puritans, and Mr Reynaldes answere about the *Concertation*.[167]

B180 From Claudio Acquaviva, Rome, 10 May 1593

SOURCE: ARSI, Baet. 3/I, fol. 115.

NOTE: Acquaviva refers to the seminary at Seville and the new plan for Saint-Omer; he has enlisted the support of Olivier Mannaerts, the Belgian provincial, and leaves it to Persons to discuss the question of location with Cardinal Allen. He hopes that the king will allow the provincial congregations to proceed undisturbed.

Both this letter, and the next (7 June) which Acquaviva addressed to Seville, were forwarded to Valladolid, where Persons received them (see his letters of 15 July and 11 August, B190, B196).

P. Roberto Personio, 10 Mayo, in Sevilla.

Desde Toledo me escrivio Vuestra Reverencia estando de vuelta para Sevilla y me console de entender el buen despacho de sus negoçios. Yo encomendaré al Provincial que los nuestros acudan con lo que fuere necessario para el nuevo Seminario de los moçicos que vienen de Inglaterra, pero segun me diçe el Señor Cardenal Alano havrase de haçer en Duai, donde tambien se traslada lo de Remis,[168] y no en San Omer; remitome en esto a lo que su Illustrisima escrivira a Vuestra Reverencia pero de nuestra parte procuraremos no se falte a esta buena obra.

Si todos los que vienen a Madrid viniese con tan justificada ocasion como el Padre Cabredo menos quejas havria de los huespedes; es bien ahorrar esta venida quando se puede, pero quando fuere necessario como sé que lo será siempre que Vuestra Reverencia le llamare, podra venir. De Vuestra Reverencia no digo nada porque es claro que podra venir y estar en Madrid el tiempo que juzgare convenir, pues los negoçios que de su diligencia y soliçitud penden toda esta libertad y licençia han menester, espeçialmente que estoy yo bien seguro de su modestia que nunca verna sino con necesidad forçosa.

Agradezco a Vuestra Reverencia el oficio hecho con Su Magestad, de cuya christiandad espero que havra dexado libres las congregaçiones, que si él una vez quedase con el entendimiento desengañado, de su voluntad no ay duda sino que es santa. En las &c.

---

167. See the paragraph beginning "I moved Mr Reynoldes" above.
168. donde tambien se traslada lo de Remis] *supplied in margin* R

Translation

To Fr Robert Persons in Seville, 10 May.

Your Reverence wrote to me from Toledo while on your way back to Seville, and it comforted me to learn of the happy outcome of your business. I will entrust the commission to the provincial to ensure that Ours assist with what is necessary for the new seminary for the young boys who come from England, but according to what my Lord Cardinal Allen tells me, it should be located in Douai (where the Rheims college has also moved), and not in Saint-Omer. In this respect I submit to what His Eminence will write to Your Reverence, but for our part we shall make sure that nothing is lacking for this good work.

If all those who come to Madrid came on such legitimate business as Fr Cabredo, we would have fewer complaints from the hosts; it is good to avoid such visits whenever possible, but when it is necessary, as will always be the case when Your Reverence summons him, let him come. With regard to Your Reverence, I have nothing to say because it is clear that you may come and stay in Madrid any time you think suitable, since the business which depends on your diligence and solicitude requires all freedom and licence, especially since I trust entirely in your discretion that you will not go [to Madrid] unless it is absolutely necessary.

I appreciate the work Your Reverence has done with His Majesty; of his Christian feeling I hope that he will have left the congregations free, because even if on this occasion he remains disenchanted, there is no doubt of the holiness of his will. To your [holy prayers and sacrifices], etc.

B181 From Richard Verstegan, Antwerp, 27 May 1593

SOURCE: ABSI, Coll B 47–48, headed "Verstigames advises the 27 of May 1592."
EDITION: Petti, 155–158.
NOTE: The letter is to be found among the despatches for 1592, because of the error in endorsement. The news relayed clearly marks the year as 1593, e.g. references to the parliament held from 19 February to 10 April 1593. Unlike many other despatches, this has a personal dimension and is thus included in this edition.

+

I have lately receaved from England the printed acts and statuts of the last parlament. The first acte entituled, To retaine the Queens subjects in their due obedience, dothe concerne the puritans as well as the Catholiks, for they must abjure the realme for recusancie, make a formall submission in the Churche, etc. The other acte, is to restraine popish recusantes to some certaine places of abode, and withall their is a forme of submission set downe which they must publykely make in the Church and it is somwhat different from that to be made by the puritanes. I would gladly have sent herewith the copies of thease two acts but neither tyme nor health would permitt and help I have none but must do all my self.

The acte touching the landes of Sir Francis Englefeild is also printed,[169] and sondry others concerning particuler persons are omitted, the tytles onely put downe.

Here are fowre Catholiks come over who are fled, to avoyd the severities of thease late Statutes, and they say that very many more will follow. Their names are Bellamy, Colford, Florian, and Gant,[170] and all are yonge men.

Their are above 10,000 strangers determyned this somer to depart from England, as well for that by this late parlament they are to pay very large subsidies and fifteenes, as also for feare of some comotion to be made by the comon people against them, for that on the gates of the[171] maire and shiriffes of London their were libells fixed threatning that yf they would not shortly take order to avoyde the citie of them, there should be order taken by other meanes to do it. The comon people do rage against them[172] as thoughe (for their sakes) so many taxes, such[173] decay of trafique, and their beeing enbrandled in so many warres did ensue.[174]

Here is no certaine newes from Fraunce. Many hard conceites are had of the Duke du Maine for that he did[175] admitt conferences with the comissioners for Navarr now[176] when the said Navarr is at the weakest. We heare further that Navarr will not stick at going to masse, yf therefore he may be admitted to the crowne.[177] Some do further reporte that the Catholiks (conditionally to admitt him) do require certaine strong places in possession as Rochell and such lyke, which in my opinion is to put themselves (in the end) in such state as the Huguenots stoode in the tymes of the late kinges.

In thease partes the Counte Mansfeild with about 15,000 men is even at the point to plant his artillery uppon the trenches of the enemy who remaineth at the siege of Gertremberg.[178] Yf the enemy be repulsed he will not be able to make head againe in

---

169. "An acte confirming the Queen's title to the landes of Sir Francis Englefield" (35 Eliz. I, c. 5), in *The Statutes of the Realm*, ed. Alexander Luders et al. (1810–1828), 4: 849–852.

170. Gant] *this ed.*; Gart *Petti*; A *obscure*. Richard Bellamy was the youngest son of Richard Bellamy of Uxendon; Gabriel Colford was a friend of William Byrd.

171. gates of the] *interlined with caret* A

172. them] *interlined with caret* A

173. such] *interlined with caret* A

174. For the measures taken by the Privy Council to protect the approximately 4000 foreigners in London from xenophobia, see *Acts of the Privy Council*, 24: 187, 200–201, 222.

175. did] *interlined, replacing* would [*deleted*] A

176. now] *interlined with caret* A

177. At a conference initiated by Charles of Lorraine (1554–1611), duke of Mayenne, and held at Suresnes late in April, Henry of Navarre announced his decision to convert to the Catholic faith. On Mayenne's outmanoeuvring of other League leaders, who opposed Henry's final succession, see Stuart Carroll, *Martyrs and Murderers: The Guise Family and the Making of Europe* (Oxford, 2009), 297–299.

178. The governor of the Spanish Netherlands, Pierre Ernst, count of Mansfeld, was unable to raise the siege of Gertruydenberg, commanded by Maurice of Nassau.

hast. This siege now having continued almost three monethes hathe cost the states infynitely, and I trust it wilbe cost lost.

From England there have not any forces bene sent unto thease partes of long tyme. More for the presente I have not.

[*Endorsed:*] Verstegans advyses 27 May 1592.

B182 Probably from Richard Verstegan, 7 June 1593

SOURCE: ABSI, Coll M fols. 187v–189r (olim 159–160), cf. Grene's reference, Coll P II 477.

NOTE: This appears to be a copy made by Persons of reports about England, possibly sent by Verstegan but not included in Petti. The reports concern the anti-Catholic legislation of the parliament of 19 February to 10 April (here recorded as 29 February to 20 April according to the Gregorian calendar). See vol. 1: 704 and Questier, *Catholics and Treason* 232–238.

Avisos de las cosas de Ynglaterra
(copyed out of a paper written in F. Rob. Persons hand) 7 Jun.
1593

En la corte o Parlamento que se començo en Londres a 29 de hebrero y acabó a 20 de Abril se an hecho y publicado hasta a 23 leyes nuevas, de las quales dos tocan solamente al negocio de la religion y contienen muchos capitulos muy rigorosos y prejudiciales contra los catolicos más principalmente los dos siguientes.

Lo primero que los catolicos declarados llamados Rechusantes porque rehusan andar a las yglesias de los hereges oltre los ochenta ducados que pagan ya por cada un mes de su rehusacion seran obligados sotto pena de la vida y perdimiento de todos los benes, de hallarse en sus casas donde suelen resedir de ordinario dentro de 40 dias despues de acabado el Parlamento y que han de registrar sus nomes y residencia por mano del magistrado público y no partirse de alla, oltre la distancia de dos lleguas sin licencia particular de la Reyna firmada por mano de 4 de su Consejo de estado sotto las mismas penas.

Lo segundo es que los Recusantes que no tubieron hazienda o bienes rayzes hasta a cierta quantidad en lugar a bolver a sus casas an de salir del Reyno y abjurar la patria y embarcarse en la nave y al puerto y dentro el tiempo que a cada uno dellos será señalado por el magistrado: y se rehusaren hacer esto o si bolvieren a Ynglaterra sin licencia de arriba seran ahurcados.

Otras leyes se han hecho tanto en universale contra tenientes criados y mugeres catolicas como tambien en particular una contra Don Francisco Ynglefild que vive en España dando poder a la Reyna para dishacer la succession de su sobrino y appropriar a la corona sus tierras y possessiones: pero los dos capitulos ya dichos son los más importantes y de mayor consequencia, los quales entiendese que an hecho con particular fine y malicia, el primero para que ubiesse lista y noticia muy particolar de los nombres hazienda y habitacion de los principales y más riccos catolicos, a los quales no pudiendo ellos partir de sus casas prender los hereges en qualquiera occasion de rebuelta sea de la muerte de la Reyna o otra y hallarles disarmados para mattarles a su placer.

El segundo capítulo tira a otro fine, y es que haviendo sabido los hereges en Ynglaterra la extrema pobreça y necessitades que an passado los catolicos Yngleses desterrados en Flandes los meses passados, an determinado de cargar tanto la mano en hechar de los catolicos más pobres de alla que vengan a causar a Su Magestad y a perecer todos de hambre.

En lo de la succession de la corona no ha querido la Reyna suffrir que se tratasse en estas cortes y a dos o tres hereges que començaron ablar y proponer algo sobre ello mandó hecharlos presos.

Se an concedidos en estas cortes a la Reyna para sus guerras de Francia y Flandes tres subsidios y seys quindenas de la hacienda de los llegos y seys diesmos del clero, y que todo se pague en 4 annos: cada un subsidio ordenario llega a ser la quinta parte de los bienes rayzes de los que los tubieron o la 7^a parte de los bienes muebles de los que no tubieren rayzes: pero los unos y los otros van estimados alla antica usanza del reyno y no al valor presente dellas.

Las quindenas son unas contribuciones de menor importancia, y los diezmos son la decima parte de todos los beneficios ecclesiasticos conforme que estan estimados en el registro antigo de la corona.

Contra los Puritanos tambien ha avido leyes nuevas aunque menos rigorosas que las contra los catolicos, toda vía se an justiciado dos o tres dellos por libros sediciosos que an publicado contra la Reyna y su gobierno, pero esto ha sido con grande peligro de rebuelta. Aguardamos más en particular las leyes con el P. Correo porque ya an llegado a Flandes.

Translation

News report on English affairs, 7 June 1593

In the court or parliament which began in London on 29 February and ended on 20 April, as many as twenty-three new laws were made and have been published so far; two of them are concerned exclusively with the business of religion, and contain many articles that are rigorous and prejudicial towards the Catholics, more especially the two following:

The first, in which the Catholics are named "recusants" because they recuse themselves from attendance at the churches of the heretics, besides the twenty ducats which they already have to pay on every month of recusancy, they are now required, on pain of death and loss of all their goods, to repair to their houses where they normally reside, within 40 days of the close of the parliament. They must register their names and addresses in writing with the public magistrate and are not to travel more than two miles without special licence of the queen, signed by four of the Privy Council, under the same penalties.

The second is that those recusants who have no property or goods up to a certain value, instead of going back to their homes, must leave the kingdom and renounce their native land, and embark on a ship at the port and within the time signified to each of them by the magistrate; and if they refuse to do this, or if they return to England without passport, they will be hanged.

Other laws have been made, both in general against custodians of Catholic properties, their servants and wives, and also in particular one against Sir Francis Englefield, who is living in Spain, empowering the Queen to disinherit his nephew and attach all his possessions and property to the crown.[179] But the two articles already mentioned are the most important and of greater consequence; they are believed to have been made with particular intention and malice: the first, because it lists and registers in full detail the names, property, and habitation of the chief and wealthiest Catholics, who, by not being allowed to leave their houses, can be arrested by the heretics on whatever pretext of sedition there may be, whether it is the death of the queen or some other; they will be found disarmed in order to kill them at will.

The second article tends another way, and that is that the heretics in England, realizing the extreme poverty and neediness which the English Catholics scattered in Flanders have suffered in these past months, have decided to intensify the persecution and impoverish the Catholics more, so that they come from there[180] to beg from His Majesty, and die of starvation.

On the question of the succession to the crown, the queen is unwilling to permit this to be discussed in those courts. She ordered two or three heretics who began to speak and make proposals about it to be thrown into prison.

In this parliament the queen has been granted three subsidies and six fifteenths from the treasury of the nobles and six tithes from the clergy for the wars in France and Flanders, and all to be paid over the next four years. Each ordinary subsidy will amount to one fifth of the real estate of those who have property, or one seventh of the movables of those who have none. But they are both estimated according to the ancient usage of the kingdom and not according to their present value.

The fifteenths are contributions of less value, and the tithes are the tenth part of all the ecclesiastical benefices according to the estimates in the ancient register of the realm.

They have also made new laws against the puritans, but less rigorous than against the Catholics, although two or three of them have been sentenced for seditious books which they published against the Queen and her government – but this is in view of a great danger of rebellion. We expect more particulars about the laws from Fr Curry because he has already arrived in Flanders.[181]

---

179. See Loomie, *Spanish Elizabethans*, 44–45.

180. I.e., from England.

181. Presumably the same as is mentioned in the appendix to Acquaviva's letter of 9 July 1591 (B111): John Curry, SJ (ca. 1552–1596), who arrived in England from Pont-à-Mouson in about 1589; he was involved in a raid on Baddesley Clinton (or Rowington Hall) in October 1592; see McCoog, *Building the Faith of St Peter*, 38–39, 46–47; Foley, 1: 396–397; and Caraman, *Henry Garnet*, 128–136.

B183 From Claudio Acquaviva, Rome, 7 June 1593

SOURCE: ARSI, Baet. 3/I, 119.

NOTE: Acquaviva expresses satisfaction with the developments with the seminary planned for Saint-Omer. In anticipation of the general congregation, Acquaviva will pass on to Allen the letter that Persons has written to the pope about the Society (Persons to Clement VIII, 15 April, B175). He hopes that Persons will be able to influence the provincial congregations, especially in the election of delegates to the general congregation. Finally, he entrusts the question of Richard Gibbons's posting to Persons's discretion.

This letter had to be forwarded to Persons as he was already in Valladolid by 17 June. He acknowledged receipt on 11 August (B196).

P. Roberto Personio, Junio 7.

Recevi la de Vuestra Reverencia de 19 de Abril, y me consuelo que el Provincial aya proveido el Seminario a gusto y satisfaction de Vuestra Reverencia porque con buen Rector y buenas ayudas podra passar bien, y es particular providencia del Señor que el Provincial de esa Provincia no solo acuda a eso por obediençia y charidad como los demas Padres, sino tambien por particular afiçion que él tiene a esa obra y a la nacion Inglesa.

Agradezco a Vuestra Reverencia la carta que escrive al Papa, que bien cierto estoy yo de su fidelidad y zelo que no faltará de acudir a qualquiera ocasion en que pudiere ayudar la Compañia. Yo di la carta al Señor Cardenal Alano para que la dé a su Santidad, espero que en tan sano pecho como el de su Santidad será de efecto.

Pareçeme bien que se reçivan esos sujetos que Vuestra Reverencia diçe porque siendo tales quales creo seran los que passaren por su mano, no ay duda sino que seran utiles para muchas cosas: esperando estamos saber los nombres de la buena gente que se havra elegido en esas Provincias, plegue al Señor sean qual conviene a la divina gloria y bien de la Compañia, ens.

[*in another hand, squeezed between these two paragraphs:*] De Inglaterra me escriven pidiendo licencia para recebir un adecuado sugeto que desea la Compañia. Yo respondolos con bien a Flandes que llegados allí los repartiremos.[182] ...

El Padre Ricardo Gibonio me escrive la ocupaçion que tiene en Valladolid y que en lo demas espera lo que yo de su persona resuelvo, yo le respondo que lo trate con Vuestra Reverencia a quien me remito. Si le pareçe que ayude donde aora está, bene, si le pareçiere que estara mejor, en Françia como los dias passados me apunto, le podra embiar, haga lo que in Domino le pareçiere más conveniente.

Translation

To Fr Robert Persons, 7 June.

I have received Your Reverence's letter of 19 April,[183] and I am glad to learn that the provincial[184] has already provided the seminary with his support, to the liking and sat-

---

182. allí los repartiremos] R, *obscure; final word possibly* repararemos
183. B176.
184. Olivier Mannaerts.

isfaction of Your Reverence, because with a good rector and good assistance things can go well, and it is a particular providence of the Lord that the provincial of this province supports the seminary, not only with the obedience and charity which he shares with those other fathers, but also with the particular enthusiasm which he has for this work and for the English nation.

I am thankful to Your Reverence for the letter which you wrote to the pope, whose faithfulness and zeal, I am quite sure, will not fail to come to our assistance on any occasion in which he is able to help the Society. I will give the letter to my Lord Cardinal Allen in order that he may give it to His Holiness. I hope that in such a sound heart as that of His Holiness it will be effective.

It would be a good thing, in my opinion, if those members be received whom Your Reverence indicates, because being of such a kind as I believe they will be who pass through your hands, there is no doubt but that they will be useful in many ways: looking forward to learning the names of the good people they have elected in those provinces: may it please the Lord they are such as tend to the divine glory and the good of the Society.

[I have received a letter from England asking for a licence to receive a suitable subject into the Society. I have written favourably to him in Flanders that once they arrive, they will be assigned where he has arrived. ...]185

Fr Richard Gibbons has written to me about the business which he is handling in Valladolid and that otherwise he is waiting for my decision about his personal future. I am writing to him that he should discuss it with Your Reverence, to whom I am delegating the matter. If you feel that he should help there for the present, good, but if you prefer to have him in France, as you indicated some days ago, you may send him there. Do as seems more appropriate to you in the Lord.

B184 From Joseph Creswell, Seville, June 1593

SOURCE: Persons to Acquaviva, 15 July (B190).

NOTE: Creswell read Acquaviva's letter of 10 May (B180), after Persons had already left for the congregation of the province of Castile, via Lisbon, and so forwarded it with a letter of his own.

B185 To Henry Garnet, probably June 1593

SOURCE: Persons to Acquaviva, probably 16 June 1593 (B186).

NOTE: At about this time, Persons wrote a long letter to Garnet about Southwell's imprisonment, presumably in response to the letter of 26 April (B178).

---

185. See textual note: this reading and translation are conjectural.

B186 To Claudio Acquaviva, probably 16 June 1593

SOURCE: ARSI, Hisp. 139, fol. 126r, an undated copy in a contemporary hand (possibly Persons's) of a confidential letter to the general, kept in the general's collection of letters from the Spanish assistancy and superscribed "1594 o prima."
HICKS: 129–130, with English translation.
NOTE: Persons relates how he has tried to console Garnet about Southwell's state of imprisonment. He also refers to the appointment of Francisco de Porres as provincial of Toledo, which took effect from 12 April 1593; Hicks dates the letter 1593.

[Soli.]

He escritto por dos vias largamente al Padre Henrico Garneto consolandolo et animandolo in questo apprietto della captividad del Padre Southwello, aunque se piensa que no han de martirizarlo y porque tengo un mercarder Flamenco, hombre siguro que abla perfettamente Ynglés, y connosce per alla a los Catolicos principales, y luego yrá alla, he dado orden tanto por via deste hombre como por otra via de Flandes, que den luego cien ducados al Padre Henrico y todo lo demas que tiene menester, porque él mismo me escrivia que tenía necessidad. Tan bien le he offereçido que dandome Vuestra Paternidad licencia para ello, le embiaré de acá más gente de la Compañia, si lo desea, y assi Vuestra Paternidad lo podra remitterlo a mí por todo lo que él tiene menester, si assi a Vuestra Paternidad parece, para que se le satisfaga siempre con más brevidad, pues él se quexa algo de lo contrario, et que si delatan mucho las respuestas a las suyas, aunque hasta agora ellos por alla, nunca an tenido buen modo en negociar, ni en escrivir sus cartas con claridad, pero agora teniendo nosotros esta correspondencia de Sevilla, le he dado una traça muy facil y sigura para toda la correspondencia que tiene menester. Y assi confio en Dios que yrá el negocio mucho más facilmente para lo venidero.

Todos de acá an sido de parecer que Vuestra Paternidad ha acertado mucho en haçer provincial al P. Porres para estos tiempos que corren, y que si aguardan. Dios avra guyado a Vuestra Paternidad como siempre en sus cosas. Él sea glorificado en todo y guarde siempre a Vuestra Paternidad.

R. Personio.

[*Addressed*:] Al Molto Reverendo in Christo Padre Nuestro il P. Claudio Aquavivo Preposito General della Compania di Giesu. Roma.

Translation

[Confidential.]

I have sent a long letter to Fr Henry Garnet by two different routes, consoling and encouraging him on the occasion of this distress which Fr Southwell's imprisonment has caused,[186] although it is thought that they are not going to martyr him. I am doing this by taking advantage of a Flemish merchant, a safe man who speaks English and knows the leading Catholics over there, and is due to go there at once. I have given instructions both

---

186. Southwell was arrested on 25/26 June 1592.

through this man as well as by the other route from Flanders for 100 ducats to be given to Fr Henry immediately, and everything else that he needs, because he himself wrote to me that he was in want. I have also offered, if Your Paternity gives leave for it, to send him a further supply of men of the Society from here, if he wishes it; and so Your Paternity will be able to refer him to me for all that he needs, if you think fit, so that his wants may be supplied with greater speed. For he complains a little of going without, and says that answers to his letters are very long in coming; it is a fact, however, that up to now people over there have never found a satisfactory way of doing business or of writing letters that were not obscure: but now, since we have this means of communication from Seville, I have given him a very easy and safe scheme for all the correspondence he needs. And so I trust in God that matters will go much more easily in future.

All here are of opinion that Your Paternity made a very happy choice of provincial in Fr Porres, both for the present times and in view of those that are expected. God will have guided you, as He does always in your affairs. Glory be to Him for everything, and may He ever preserve Your Paternity.

R. Persons.

B187 To Claudio Acquaviva, Valladolid, 16 June 1593

SOURCE: ARSI, *Hisp.* 135, fols. 306r–307v; holograph, with the remains of a seal.
HICKS: 165–172, with English translation.
NOTE: Persons arrived back in Valladolid on 15 June from Seville, Lisbon, and Medina del Campo. He reports on Philip's particular interest in the founding of the seminary at Saint-Omer. He is under pressure to speak to the king about the plight of the English Catholics in Flanders. The Belgian provincial, Olivier Mannaerts, has agreed in principle to the Society's taking charge of the seminary at Saint-Omer.

In Lisbon, Persons established an English residence, along the same lines as that at Sanlúcar, with the assistance of Cardinal Archduke Albert (viceroy of Portugal) and the archbishop of Lisbon. He decided against founding a seminary, in view of the existing Irish seminary, which was converted into a college in 1624. Persons may also have been considering Lisbon as a potential site for the Bridgettine nuns of Rouen, who felt under threat from the advances of Henry of Navarre (see his despatches for Philip, 24 February 1594, B218). Here he suggests that Richard Cowling might be transferred from Flanders to the residence at Lisbon; in the event, later in the year Cowling went to Rome instead, where he was attached to the penitentiary.

Acquaviva replied to this letter, as well as the following one, dated 15 July (B190), on 30 August (B197). He had evidently not received it by the time he wrote his letters to Castile on 2 August (ARSI, Cast. 6, fols. 161r–162v).

Muy Reverendo en Christo Padre Nuestro
Pax Christi.

En llegando ayer del viage de Sevilla y Lisboa algo cansado, hallé tanta multitud de cartas que me aguardavan, que no bastava todo ayer ni oy para leerlas, y mucho menos para responderlas, y eran las materias tan pesadas (pues todas ablavan de persecuciones y affliciones) que me quitavan buena parte, tambien del sueño de la noche passada solamente la carta de Vuestra Paternidad como siempre, me fue de consuelo, Dios se lo pague a Vuestra Paternidad en el cielo.

2. En lo del Seminario de Sant Omer el buen Provincial Padre Oliverio me ha respondido que en dandole licencia Vuestra Paternidad para ello, no avra difficultad en tomarlo a su cargo la compañia, pues emporta tanto al servicio de nuestro señor y el Rey gusta tan particularmente dello, y assi no dudo si no que Vuestra Paternidad en esto como en todo lo demas, nos favorecera. El Padre Henrico Garneto por la suya de 26 de Abril me escrive que será negocio de grandissima importancia que si haga este Seminario y que no le faltará gente de alla.

3. Me responde tan bien en lo que escrivi de embiarle más gente que en qualquiera manera holgará que se le embie uno, y nominalmente el Padre Cresuello si desea venir y si la condicion del tiempo no se alterará en peor, que avra menester de dos. Y aunque por ventura no será necessario hacer alguna mission por algun tiempo aún, todavia si Vuestra Paternidad lo remitira a mí, yremos disponiendo el negocio conforme al tiempo, y con la voluntad del Padre Cresuello o de otro que yrá; tan bien será necessario alguna vez hacer algun hueco de los yngleses en Flandes por acá para estos Seminarios, si parece a Vuestra Paternidad que con el parecer del Provincial de Flandes, si puede hacer, lo trattaremos, verbi gratia, ay en Flandes un coadjutor que desea venir por acá y tenemos bien en qué emplearle aqui, lo mismo es del Padre Nicolo Smith que no tiene salud por aý. Tan bien en San Roque de Lisboa desean un ynglés que supiesse las lenguas ynglesa, francesa y flamenca, y el Padre Guliermo Coulingo que está en Flandes las sabe y desea ser empleado en tal puesto, adonde ya tenemos una residencia de sacerdotes yngleses que confío en Nuestro Señor hara mucho frutto, y servicio a Nuestro Señor en hospedar a los destos Seminarios que an de entrar y salir por aquel puerto. Vuestra Paternidad me hara caridad de mandar escrivirme una palabra en respuesta destos puntos.

4. Estos dos Seminarios de Vallidolid y Sevilla estan muy bien gracias a Dios, solamente en Sevilla ha avido un poco de difficultad en accordar pareceres en algunas cosas entre el Rector y el padre Carlos Tancardo de una parte y el padre Cresuello, pero confío que todo yrá bien que si no, ya sabemos el remedio.

5. Por venir cansado deste largo viage, vengo con mucho deseo de discansar aqui, pues in utroque homine tengo menester pero las importunidades y clamores de todos los catolicos de la nuestra nacion en Flandes son tantos y tan continuos pidiendome que me vaya a la corte a ablar a su majestad para algun allivio de sus miserias que no sé, si se podra excusar, hare lo que pudiere para excusarlo, y lo trattaré primero por carta y memoriales. Y no dudo sino que Dios Nuestro Señor nos ayudará pues por su causa se padece. No puedo más por agora. En los santos sacrificios de Vuestra Paternidad muy humilmente me encomiendo. De Valladolid a 16 de Junio 1593.

De Vuestra Paternidad Reverenda
endegno hijo y siervo
Roberto Personio.

6. Despues de escrita ésta he entendido por una carta del Padre Provincial de Flandes que algun ha propuesto difficultades circa el lugar del Seminario Ynglés queriendo más presto que fuesse en Cortray, pero esto sería muy ageno de la intencion del Rey el

qual lo quiere en puerto de la mar, para mayor comodidad de embarcationes, y las dificultades que ponen contra S. Omer, son de ningun momento, y mucho menos el miedo que proponen de emulaciones, pues ninguna cosa importante se deve dexar por causa de emulaciones como más largamente tengo respondido a todas las dificultades en la que escrivo al Padre provincial. Vuestra Paternidad por amor de Dios mande dar calor al negocio porque será de grandissimo servicio de nuestro Señor y assi me escrive el Padre Henrico Garnet que todos sienten aý.

7. El padre Cabredo rector deste Collegio me ha dicho que suspecha que el Padre Ricardo Gibbonio aya pedido a Vuestra Paternidad de salir de aqui porque aqui ha dicho a algunos que presto será en Roma. Yo he dicho al rector que no le dé pena porque conosco bien al Padre Gibbonio y Vuestra Paternidad lo conosce mejor. Él me dice que está ya contentissimo y con todo esto puede ser que se lo aya pedido de salir porque agora me dice que se contentaria tornar a Portugal aviendome sollicitado tanto por cartas l'anno passado para que escriviesse a Vuestra Paternidad sobre el negocio. Él tiene de quando en quando algunos impetus, pero en fin passan presto y es muy buen religioso y aqui está muy bien y el rector sabe llevarlo muy bien y assi no se dé mucho a Vuestra Paternidad aunque aya pedido de salir porque ya pienso que será trocado su deseo, en todo lo demas haçe bien, y el Collegio va prosperamente gracias a Dios.

[*Addressed*:] Al muy Reverendo Padre Nuestro el Padre Claudio Aquaviva Preposito General de la Compañia de Jesus. Roma.

Translation

Our Very Reverend Father in Christ
The peace of Christ.

On my arrival yesterday after my journey from Seville and Lisbon, somewhat wearied, I found such a pile of letters waiting for me that the whole of yesterday and today was not long enough to read them, much less to answer them; and their contents were so weighty (for they all told of persecutions and vexations) that they deprived me as well of a good part of my sleep last night. Only Your Paternity's letter was, as always, a source of consolation; may God requite Your Paternity for it in heaven.

2. In the matter of the seminary of Saint-Omer, the worthy provincial, Fr Olivier, has replied to me that, if Your Paternity gives him leave for it, there will be no difficulty about the Society taking charge of it, since it is of so much importance for the service of our Lord and the king is so especially set upon it; and so I have no doubt that Your Paternity will give us your support in this matter as in all others. Fr Henry Garnet writes to me, in his letter of the 26 April,[187] that it is a matter of the greatest importance for this seminary to be started and that there will be no lack of boys from there to fill it.

3. As to what I wrote to him about sending him more men, he answered me also that he would be glad if I send him one man at least, and that one Fr Creswell, if he wishes to come; and, if the general situation does not alter for the worse, that there will be need for

---

187. B178.

two.[188] And though perhaps it will not be necessary to send any draft for some time yet, still, if Your Paternity would leave the matter in my hands, we will proceed with the arrangements as occasion permits, and obtain the consent of Fr Creswell or any other who is to go. It will be necessary also at some time to make some room in the seminaries here for the Englishmen in Flanders. If Your Paternity thinks that, with the approval of the provincial in Flanders, it can be done, we will take the matter up; for instance, there is a lay brother in Flanders who wishes to come here, and we are well able to find use for him here; the same thing applies to Fr Nicholas Smith, who is not in good health there. Also, at San Roque at Lisbon they want an Englishman who knows English, French, and Spanish, and Fr William Cowling who is in Flanders knows them and wishes to be employed in such a post.[189] We already have a residence of English priests there, which I trust in God is going to yield much fruit and do service to our Lord by supplying a lodging for the men of these seminaries who have to enter the country and leave it by that port. I shall be indebted to Your Paternity if you will have a brief reply sent to me concerning these points.

4. These two seminaries of Valladolid and Seville are in a very satisfactory state, thanks be to God; only in Seville has there been a slight difficulty in reconciling, in certain matters, the views of the rector and Fr Charles Tancard on one side with those of Fr Creswell; but I hope that all will go well, and if not, we already know the remedy.

5. Arriving weary after this long journey, I greatly desired to find some rest here, for I am in need of it for both elements of my being; but the importunity and clamour of all the Catholics of our nation in Flanders is so great and persistent, begging me to go to the Court and speak to His Majesty to obtain some alleviation of their distress, that I do not know if I can excuse myself from going. I shall do what I can to get out of going and deal with it by letter and memorials in the first instance. And I doubt not but that God our Lord will aid us, for our sufferings are in His cause. I cannot write any more for the moment. I commend myself very humbly to Your Paternity's holy sacrifices. From Valladolid, the 16th of June 1593.

    Your Paternity's
        unworthy son and servant
            Robert Persons.

6. After I had written this, I understood by a letter from father provincial of Flanders that someone has raised objections to the location of the English seminary, preferring rather that it should be at Courtrai. But this would be very foreign to the intention of the king, for it is his wish that it should be at a seaport for greater convenience of taking passage by sea. The reservations they have about Saint-Omer carry little weight, and still less the fear of jealousies which they allege as a reason, for no important thing ought to be given up on that account. I have answered all the objections at greater length in the letter which I have written to father provincial. I beg Your Paternity, for the love of God, to give instructions that the enterprise be warmly encouraged, for it will tend very greatly to

---

188. See the headnote to the lost letter from Garnet to Persons, 26 April (B178).

189. A mistake for Richard Cowling (see Persons's next letter, 15 July, B190). William Cowling died in 1592.

the service of our Lord, and Fr Henry Garnet writes to me that they are all of the same opinion there.

7. Fr Cabredo, the rector of this college, has told me that he suspects that Fr Richard Gibbons has petitioned Your Paternity to leave this place, because he has told some people here that he will shortly be in Rome. I have told the rector not to be put out, because I know Fr Gibbons well, and Your Paternity knows him better still. He tells me that he is now very contented, but, in spite of all this, it is possible that the petition to leave has been sent, for he tells me now that he would be very satisfied to return to Portugal, and last year he strongly importuned me by letter to write to Your Paternity about the matter. From time to time, he has fits of impetuosity, but in the end, they pass off quickly. He is a very good religious and is doing very well here; the rector knows very well how to deal with him. And so do not let Your Paternity take much notice, even though he has petitioned to leave, for I think he will change his mind. In every other way things are going well[190] and the college is flourishing, thanks be to God.

B188 To Olivier Mannaerts, Valladolid, 16 June 1593

SOURCE: Persons to Acquaviva, 16 June (B187).

NOTE: Responding to a letter from Mannaerts which may have been awaiting his arrival at Valladolid, Persons wrote to the Belgian provincial about the objections raised by the local Jesuits to the foundation at Saint-Omer.

B189 To King Philip II, after 16 June 1593

SOURCE: ABSI, Coll P II 500, a copy in Persons's hand.
HICKS: 173.

NOTE: As requested by Verstegan in his letter of 30 April (B179), Persons appeals to the king for succour for the English Catholics in Flanders, arguing that if they return to England this will demoralise the faithful. This is a good example of Persons's diplomatic manner.

Es tan grande la obligacion con que Vuestra Magestad nos tiene todos obligados los que somos de la nacion Ynglesa, con las muchas y continuas mercedes que Vuestra Magestad le haçe, que no me sería atrevido a ponerme por esta a supplicar a Vuestra Magestad otras, si las urgentissimas y lastimosas necessidades de todos los Yngleses entretenidos por Vuestra Magestad en Flandes no me forcassen, por ser tales y tantas que humanamente hablando no pueden passar más adelante sin algun remedio efficaz y breve de Vuestra Magestad; pues hombres graves an escritto de alla, que unos an perecido de hambre y falta del sustento necessario, y otros estaban para hacerlo; y otros constrenidos por la misma necessidad an tomado resolucion de bolverse a Ynglaterra y ponerse a la misericordia de los mismos hereges, con mucho sentimiento de los buenos Catolicos y detrimento de la causa pública de la fe, y pues ay esperança que estamos ya, plaziendo a Dios,

---

190. An alternative translation would be "You are doing well"; i.e., Persons appreciates Acquaviva's handling of matters concerning the seminary.

hazia el fin deste apprietto de la persecucion y Vuestra Magestad con su real clemencia y munificencia les ha amparado y entretenido ya tantos años, Dios Nuestro Señor me da mucha confiança que no permettera que Vuestra Magestad les desampare y dexe agora en esta suma afflicion que padecen, lo qual supplico muy humilmente a Vuestra Magestad por amor del mismo Señor, y que sea servido mandar poner remedio en esto con la brevidad que fuere possibile, pues la necessedad es tan precisa y Dios dello sera será tan servido y Vuestra Magestad merecera una grande corona en el cielo. El guarde la real persona de Vuestra Magestad por muchos y muy largos años como emos menester para el bien de su iglesia y consuelo.[191]

[*Addressed:*] Copia [three words lost: del mia carta?] al Re.
[*Endorsed:*] Videtur character Personii.

Translation

So great is the obligation we feel towards Your Majesty for all you have done for the English nation, for the great and continued gifts Your Majesty has made to us, that I would not dare to appeal to Your Majesty again, if the most urgent and dire necessities of all the English pensioners of Your Majesty in Flanders did not force me. These are of such a kind and so great that, humanely speaking, they cannot carry on any longer without some prompt and efficient remedy from Your Majesty; for grave persons have written from there that some have starved from lack of sustenance and others are about to do so; and others have been forced by the same necessity to resolve to return to England and throw themselves on the mercy of the heretics – to the great grief of the good Catholics and detriment to the public cause of the faith. And since there is still hope of an end to the harshness of the persecution, please God, and Your Majesty with your royal clemency and munificence has sheltered and accommodated them for so many years already, the Lord our God gives me much assurance that He will not permit Your Majesty to abandon them in this great affliction which they bear in this case; wherefore I most humbly beg Your Majesty, for the love of the same Lord, that you would be pleased to instruct that the situation be remedied with as much expedition as possible, since the necessity is so pressing – and God in turn will vouchsafe to reward Your Majesty with a great crown in heaven. May He protect Your Majesty's royal person as many years unfold, which we need for the good and comfort of his church.

B190 To Claudio Acquaviva, Valladolid, 15 July 1593

SOURCE: ARSI, Hisp. 135, fols. 372r–373v, holograph, with marks of a seal.
HICKS: 174–183, with English translation.
NOTE: In response to Acquaviva's letter of 10 May (B180), which was forwarded to him from Seville, Persons tries to finalize the location of the seminary at Saint-Omer. He has heard nothing yet from Allen but is confident he will approve the enterprise. He is concerned about Thomas Wright's future in the Society and suggests that he be transferred to Spain, as well as

---

191. The last line of the MS (*A*) has been torn away.

Richard Cowling. He also recommends that Creswell (currently in Seville) and Holt (in Flanders) should exchange places. Wright came to Valladolid via Seville later in the year, and Cowling was in Rome by December. Holt remained in Flanders.

Persons anticipates a meeting at El Escorial in September, along with Creswell, to concert the plans for the English nation. The king is well disposed to the Society's affairs but this may depend on Persons's influence.

Muy Reverendo en Christo Padre nuestro
Pax Christi.
Recibi la de Vuestra Paternidad de 10 de mayo, que me fue a buscar en Sevilla y con aquella occasion el Padre Cresuello tambien la vio y me la embió despues juntamente con la suya, y entrambos quedamos muy consolados, como siempre con lo que Vuestra Paternidad nos escrivio, y muy animados de llevar adelante esta causa, veendo que Dios Nuestro Señor mueve a Vuestra Paternidad de ayudarnos por tantas vias.

1. En lo del Seminario de Sant Omer ya tengo escritto dos otras veces a Vuestra Paternidad despues que llegué aqui que fue a 15 del passado, que al Rey y a los que le estan al lado parecio por muy particulares causas y raçones que sería bien poner el Seminario de los moçicos en Sant Omer, y en este parecer perseveran, y a nos otros y a toda esta causa importa grandemente que sea assi, y el Padre Henrico Garnetto me lo escrive de Ynglaterra con grandes encarecimientos, y per consequens, no es cosa más disputabile agora, y aunque aya algunos differentes pareceres de algunos que no entienden tanto las cosas en particular, o tengan differentes dictamines, no por esto si ha de dexar de proseguir y executar el orden de su Majestad, y conforme a esto tengo escritto al Padre Flacco que está en Sant Omer que quieren aquí que luego començe a congregar los moçicos que aý estubieren y sean aptos para ello, y assi no dudo si no que lo avra hecho, y él mismo con la ayuda del Padre Henrico Broy bastará por agora a tener el cuydado del Seminario hasta que el número cresca y el Padre Provincial tenga Padre a proposito para ser Rector[192] si a Vuestra Paternidad assi pareciere. Y en quanto al cuydado del sustiento, dexenlo a mi cargo por lo presente. El nuestro Cardenal Alano no me ha escritto cosa alguna hasta agora sobre este negocio aunque pienso que más presto se ayan perdido o detenido sus cartas pues nadie en España recibio carta suya por el ordenario passado, y no dudo si no que Su Señoria Illustrisima concorrera de buena gana en esta obra. Pues es de tanta importancia para el fin de la conversion de Ynglaterra que si pretende, y con esta escrivo tan bien largamente sobre esto a Su Señoria Illustrisima de manera que no queda otra cosa, si no que Vuestra Paternidad vaya encommendando algunas veçes el negocio en sus cartas a Flandes.

2. Escrivi tan bien por otra mia que pues avia algunos Padres Yngleses de la compañia en Flandes y otros aqui a los quales sería menester algunas veces mudar o trocar por bien destos Seminarios o su consuelo fuesse contento Vuestra Paternidad que quando res urgebat y no si podia commodamente aguardar respuesta de Roma, podiessimos acá con el parecer y beneplacito de los Padres Provinciales de acá y de Flandes a quienes más toccava, llamar o embiar alguna persona, dando quenta a Vuestra Pater-

192. Rector] *followed by* la proposito [*deleted*] R

nidad de todo despues, et Vuestra Paternidad sea servido mandar escrivirme alguna palabra de questo.

3. Escrivo por el ordenario passado tanto a Vuestra Paternidad como a Flandes, que tendremos menester por acá del Padre Ricardo Coulingo que está por ministro en Lila de Flandes si por alla no hiciesse falta. Pero despues con este ordenario me ha escritto el Padre Gulielmo Holto, que el Padre Tomas Wright que ha leydo teologia en Lovanio, no da la satisfacion a la Compañia que yo quisiere, y que estava en peligro de salirse, lo qual me ha dado mucha pena tanto por causa suya como tan bien de la Compañia que lo ha criado ya más de doçe años y en particular porque yo tubi alguna parte en su entrada y en la conservacion despues quando si trataba de su demision en la Provincia de Milano, por una melanconia que se le dio por una quebra con sus superiores, y por no perder este sujeto si sea possibile, he pensado, si sería bien provarlo un poco aqui en España, adonde por ventura yo podria hacer algo con él y podria estar muy bien en el Seminario de Sevilla y hacerles provecho si se accomodasse y si no, se podria despedir de aqui en más silencio y menor nota. Vuestra Paternidad lo mire, yo offeresco el viatico si viene y podria venir en lugar del Padre Coulingo, tengo tan bien escritta una palabra desto agora con este ordenario al Padre Viceprovincial de Flandes para que esté prevenido para quando Vuestra Paternidad le escriviere su resolucion en esto.

4. Otro negocio tambien ay, más importante circa estas mudanças de personas, y es, que el Padre Gulielmo Holto, parte por algunos disgustillos que le han passado con algunos soldados y cavallieros de la su nacion en Flandes, y parte por aver tenido mucha amistad por lo passado, con el Secretario Cosimo, y por no saber la lengua y modo de trattar con los ministros desta nacion española, no es tan grato, ni puede hacer lo que conbendria por la causa commun, en esta necessidad nuestra tan grande y universal, y demas está muy caydo de ánimo y deseoso de salir de alla, despues de tantos años de travajo, y me ha propuesto que el Padre Cresuello haria bien en su lugar pues le faltan todos los dichos impedimientos, y tiene ya la lengua Española y mucho uso y credito en esta Corte y en las personas principales della, y andando a Flandes podria llevar muy grandes recommendaciones del Rey y de otras personas principales en su favor, que sirvirian mucho para lo público, y a esto se añade, que fuera que él es persona muy sigura y religiosa, tiene talento particular para negociar, y por ventura mejor que para trattar en un collegio con muchachos como ya començamos a experimentar, y accordarnos algo de lo de Roma, y assi, si a Vuestra Paternidad pareciere, si podria haçer este trueco en octubre, y en este mientras se ha offerecido un negocio muy forçoso para que el dicho Padre e yo nos hallemos juntamente en el[193] Escurial en el mes de Septiembre, para assentar con su Majestad alguna resolucion en lo público de la nacion, y si nos saliere lo que tenemos pensado, si podra remediar de una vez todo lo que tocca al sustento tanto de todos los Seminarios quanto de los particulares de la nuestra nacion, y esto sin gasto ninguno de Su Majestad. Y despues de alla podra el Padre Cresuello (pareciendo assi a Vuestra Paternidad) partirse luego con sus cartas para Flandes, y el Padre Holto podria venir por acá en su lugar y enformarse de las cosas destos reynos y de los Seminarios, y tomar noticia de la Corte y si despues Vuestra Paternidad lo quisiere aý para la Penetenciaría, o dexarlo aqui, sería

193. en el] *this ed.*; en R

mucho más abile para todo, y ayudaria mucho a esta nuestra causa lo qual emos de llevar adelante por todas las vias possibiles, pues el Demonio y su ministros por tantas nos impugnan, y sin duda a mi quenta emos de tener la victoria más presto de lo que muchos piensan. Dios nuestro Señor conceda por su grande misericordia y nos guarde por muchos años a Vuestra Paternidad como emos menester. De Valladolid a 15 de Julio 1593.

   De Vuestra Reverenda Paternidad
     hijo endegno
      Roberto Personio.

 5. El Padre Gil Gonzales y Bartolome Perez me escriven con mucho contento del ánimo del Rey en las nuestras cosas y que importará que yo me sirva de las occasiones que ubiere, para conservar y confirmar a Su Magestad en ello, y no faltaré en lo que pudiere y si Vuestra Paternidad para Setiembre tubiere alguna cosa particular de mandarme en esta materia, ya estaré creo en el Escurial y sin esto no perderé las occasiones que se offereceran.[194]

 [*Addressed:*] Al molto Reverendo in Christo Padre Nostro il Padre Claudio Aquaviva Preposito Generale de la Compañia de Giesu en Roma. [With mark of a seal.]

Translation

Our Very Reverend Father in Christ
The peace of Christ.

 I have received Your Paternity's letter of the 10th of May, which went looking for me in Seville. Taking advantage of that circumstance, Fr Creswell read it as well and sent it on to me along with one of his own. We both feel much consoled, as we always are, by what Your Paternity wrote to us and much encouraged to press on with this enterprise, seeing that God our Lord is moving Your Paternity to help us in so many ways.

 1. In the matter of the seminary of St Omers I had already written to Your Paternity twice before my arrival here, which was on the 15th of last month, saying that the king and those who are close to him are of opinion that for very specific purposes and reasons it would be well to locate the seminary for the youths at Saint-Omer – and they persist in this opinion.[195] For us also and for this enterprise in general it is of the greatest importance that it should be so. Fr Garnet writes to me to this effect from England,[196] very emphatically, and consequently there is no place for further dispute on the matter: although different opinions are held by some persons who do not have as good an understanding of the state of the case, or who have a different perspective, that is no reason not to proceed to put the orders of His Majesty into execution. To this effect I have written to Fr Flack who is at Saint-Omer, telling him that their wishes here are that he should now begin to assemble such boys as may be there and are suitable for that purpose, and so I do not doubt that he has done so. For the time being he will be adequate to take

---

 194. [*Dated in margin:*] Julio 17
 195. See Persons's letters of 22 March and 19 April (B173, B176), from Toledo and Seville, reporting on visits to Madrid.
 196. Garnet to Persons, 26 April (B178).

charge of the seminary, with Fr Henry Broy's help, until the number of boys increases and father provincial has found a suitable father to be rector – supposing this to meet with Your Paternity's approval. And as for the burden of supporting them, leave it to me for the present. Our Cardinal Allen has not yet written me a word about this matter, but I think it is most likely that his letters have been lost or intercepted, for nobody in Spain received one from him by the last post. I have no doubt that His Eminence will gladly cooperate in this undertaking, because it is of such importance for the end we have in view, the conversion of England. Moreover, I am writing fully on this subject to His Eminence by this post,[197] so that it only remains for Your Paternity to keep pursuing the matter from time to time in your letters to Flanders.

2. In my other letter I also wrote that there are some English fathers of the Society in Flanders and others here whom it would be necessary at times to move or exchange for the advantage of these seminaries or for their own consolation.[198] I asked therefore if Your Paternity would be in agreement that, in cases of urgency and when it was not convenient to await a reply from Rome, we should have the power here, with the sanction of the fathers provincial here and in Flanders, who would be chiefly concerned in the matter, to summon an individual here or send him there. We would report everything afterwards to Your Paternity; and so I request Your Paternity to be so good as to let me have something in writing about this.

3. I wrote by the last post to Your Paternity and to Flanders as well, that we shall have need here of Fr Richard Cowling, who is acting as minister at Lille in Flanders, if he can be spared from there. But since then, Fr William Holt has written to me by this post that Fr Thomas Wright who has been teaching theology at Louvain is not giving the satisfaction to the Society that we should like, and that he is in danger of leaving it. This has caused me great concern, not only for his own sake but also for that of the Society which has nurtured him now for more than twelve years; more especially because I had something to do with his entering it and afterwards with his remaining in it, when there was a question of his dismissal in the province of Milan on account of a fit of melancholy caused in him by a clash with his superiors. To avoid losing him as a subject, if possible, I have been considering whether it would not be a good thing to give him a trial for a time here in Spain, where perhaps I could do something with him. He could very well be placed in the seminary at Seville and be of use to them if he were willing; and if not, he could be dismissed from here more quietly and with less publicity. Would Your Paternity please consider the matter. I offer to pay for his journey if he comes, and he could come instead of Fr Cowling; I have also written a few words about this to father vice provincial of Flanders[199] by this post, so that he may be forewarned when Your Paternity writes to him about your decision on this point.

4. There is also another matter of greater importance in reference to these movements of persons, namely that Fr William Holt is not as welcome as before, partly on account of some small unpleasantnesses that have taken place between him and some

---

197. I.e., Cardinal Allen.
198. Persons to Acquaviva, 16 June (B187).
199. George Duras.

soldiers and gentlemen of his nation in Flanders, and partly because he was very friendly in the past with the secretary, Cosimo,[200] and because he does not know the language or the way to deal with the ministers of this Spanish nation. Consequently, he is not able to do what he should do for the common cause in the face of our needs, which are so great and universal; moreover, he is very depressed and anxious to get away from there after so many years of labour. He has suggested to me that Fr Creswell would do well in his stead, because he is free from all the impediments I have mentioned: he knows Spanish, and he has much experience and credit with this court and with the principal persons belonging to it. If he went to Flanders, he could take very good credentials from the king and other persons in authority to assist him, and these would be a great help to him in public affairs. There is this to be said also, that besides being a very reliable and religious man, he has a special talent for negotiation, greater, perhaps, than for dealing with youths in a college – as we are already beginning to find out, bearing in mind some of your own experience of him in Rome. And so, if Your Paternity approves, this exchange could be made in October. In the meantime a matter has cropped up which makes it very necessary for the said father and myself to be present together at El Escorial in the month of September in order to collaborate with His Majesty in designing a certain policy for the public good of our nation; and if we are successful in our plans we shall be able at one blow to solve the whole difficulty of the support not only of all the seminaries but also of the private individuals of our nation; and this without any expense to His Majesty. And afterwards Fr Creswell (with Your Paternity's approval) could leave from there at once for Flanders with his letters of introduction, and Fr Holt could come here in his stead, and inform himself on the affairs of these kingdoms and of the seminaries, and get to know the court. If later on Your Paternity should wish to have him with you for the penitentiary, or prefer to leave him here, he would be much better qualified for any post, and would be of great help to this cause of ours, which we have to forward by all means possible, for the devil and his ministers work against us in so many ways. Nor is there any doubt in my mind that we are going to win the victory sooner than many people think. May God our Lord in his mercy grant it, and may He preserve Your Paternity to us for many years as we have need that He should. From Valladolid, the 15th of July, 1593.

        Your Paternity's
           humble servant
              Robert Persons.

5. Fr Gil González and Bartolomé Pérez write to me that they are greatly reassured by the king's disposition as regards our affairs and say that it will be a good thing for me to avail myself of any opportunities that offer to preserve and confirm His Majesty in that state of mind, and I shall not fail to do what I can. If Your Paternity should have any special instruction for me on this point for September, I shall then be at El Escorial I think, and in any case I will not lose any chances that offer.

---

200. Cosimo Massi (ca. 1537–1600), secretary to the duke of Parma (see Persons's letters to him, July 1585 to February 1588, A191, A196, A199, A218).

B191 To William Allen, possibly 15 July, 1593

SOURCE: Persons to Acquaviva, 15 July, 11 August (B190, B196).

NOTE: In his letter to the general, Persons speculates that letters from Allen about the new foundation at Saint-Omer have gone astray. He probably wrote to Allen by the same post, to explain the arguments for the location of the seminary, as noted in his letter of 11 August.

B192 Memorial from Sir William Stanley, July 1593

SOURCE: Walpole's confession, in Pollen, *Unpublished Documents*, 255.

NOTE: Persons forwarded this to Idiáquez with Henry Walpole, who had been minister at Valladolid since about February 1593 and was about to leave for Flanders and England (see next item). Cf. McCoog, *Building the Faith of St Peter*, 158. On Stanley, see the covering letter to an unidentified addressee, 7 November 1590 (B85).

[*Walpole confesses:*] Sir Willyam Stanley did send a memoriall to father Parsons to be presented to Don Juan D'Iddiaques, wherein he craved pay of his arrerages with some summe of money besydes, and then he would therewith enterpryse something against England, but Don Juan did geve no ear to his request and I caryed memoriall.

B193 From Richard Thorn, Madrid, July 1593

SOURCE: Walpole's confession, in Pollen, *Unpublished Documents*, 254.

NOTE: Thorn reports his lack of success in appealing to Idiáquez for royal alms for the seminary at Saint-Omer; Persons sent Walpole as more likely to succeed (see next item). Richard Thorn (d. Sanlúcar, 1597) entered the college at Valladolid in October 1589 and was subsequently priested (Anstruther, 351–352; cf. Pollen, *Unpublished Documents*, 260, 267).

[*Walpole confesses:*] being then one Thorn a prist at the court to sue for the kings second letters, for the almes to the Seminarye of St Omers, wherein the officers in flanders made delay, and the sayd Thorne, having written that he could not gett a good looke of don Juan and the rest ...

B194 To Juan de Idiáquez, Cristóbal de Moura and Juan Ruiz de Velasco, Valladolid, July 1593

SOURCE: Walpole's confession, in Pollen, *Unpublished Documents*, 254.

NOTE: Before leaving for Flanders and England, Walpole visited the court with letters of introduction from Persons to the king's ministers, requesting support for the seminary at Saint-Omer. He also brought the memorial from Stanley. He wrote to the rector at Seville, Francisco de Peralta, from El Escorial on 2 August, to confirm that he had received these letters and to apprise Peralta of Persons's plans (*Letters of Henry Wapole*, ed. Jessopp, 45–48).

After May 1594, as Philip's health declined, Cristóbal (Cristóvão) de Moura y Távora, first marquis of Castelo Rodrigo (1538–1613), and Juan de Idiáquez regularly drew up reports for the king on domestic and foreign affairs respectively, bypassing the council; Moura was regarded as the king's favourite, frequently deputizing for him and acting as his spokesman; see Kamen, 302–303, and Parker, 343–345. Later, he was viceroy of Portugal (1603, 1608–1612). On Ruiz de Velasco, see Persons's letter to him, 5 August 1589 (B27).

[*Walpole confesses*:] F. Parsons sayd that I being to go into England should be more gratefull unto them and therfore sent me with letters to Don Juan, Crestoval de Mora and the rest named before ...

B195 From Juan de Idiáquez, Madrid, August 1593

SOURCE: Walpole's confession, in Pollen, *Unpublished Documents*, 254.
NOTE: Walpole returned from the court to Valladolid, bearing a letter from Juan de Idiáquez.

[*Walpole confesses*:] Then I took my letters of all the forenamed[201] ... and none of them but Don Juan wrote to F. Parsons that I remember ...

B196 To Claudio Acquaviva, Valladolid, 11 August 1593

SOURCE: ARSI, Hisp. 136, fols. 14–15, holograph.
HICKS: 184–189, with English translation.
NOTE: Persons has finally received Acquaviva's letter of 7 June (B183), which was forwarded from Seville. He reports on satisfactory developments at Valladolid, on Henry Walpole's departure for Flanders and England, and on further royal support for the new foundation at Saint-Omer. There is evidence here of disagreement with Allen over the location of the seminary; see the headnote to Persons's putative letter to him tentatively dated 15 July.

Molto Reverendo in Christo Padre nostro

1. Con l'ordinario passato scrissi a Vostra Paternità quello che per alhora s'offeriva, et dipoi ricevetti la di Vostra Paternità delli 7 di Giugnio y quanto al Padre Gibbonio, già sta molto contento nelle occupationi che tiene in questo Collegio, et in verità non so per adesso dove egli potrebbe star meglio ni con più gusto suo o più frutto che qui, *consideratis considerandis*, suppuesto che *semper aliquid ferendum est de fratrum oneribus*. Ya se conoscen el Rettor et il Padre Gibbonio,[202] et sono grandi amici, et il Rettor fa molto bene suo officio et stanno tutti molto contenti di lui, et io in primis, perché ho trovato il Collegio tanto nel temporale como nello spirituale in buon stato, solamente me pare che habbino speso molto, ma non si ha potuto far altrimenti, et al presente per la gratia di Dio

201. I.e., Juan de Idiáquez, Cristóbal de Moura, and Juan Ruiz de Velasco.
202. In the lines preceding, Persons drops into Latin and Spanish before continuing in Italian.

habbiamo pagato li debiti, et c'avanzano poco manco di mille scuti liberi, non ostante le grandi spese delle fabriche passate, et delle missioni uscite a Inglaterra, como a Sevilla, et a Lisboa alla residencia che vi habbiamo, nostro Signor ne sia ringratiato sempre. Le bocche che habbiamo in casa sono più de cinquanta tre o 54.

2. M'han scritto già diverse vuolte li padri d'Inglaterra che haverebbono gran bisogno d'uno o due della Compagnia più, ma particularmente, il Padre Garneto per le sue letere di Marzo, Aprile et Maggio, m'ha tornato a pedirlo, agiongendo che già stava egli solo in quanto a negotii, poiché nissuno di quelli che allì stanno, lo possono giovar molto in quello particolare, et perché viddi che questo era così, et che si porventura il buon Padre venisse nelle mani delli nimici, non vi sarebbe ninguno che potesse darci correspondenza, mi parve necessario usar dela comission che Vostra Paternità me haveva dato et mandar il Padre Henrico Walpolo, il quale era molto desideroso, a molto tempore, di questo viagio, et mi parve assai a proposito per le buone parti che tiene, et la prudenza et esperienza di cose che qui ha pigliato. Un'altra causa anchora vi fu de su andata per adesso per consolar li catolici in questi nuovi stretti che l'ha dato il nuovo Parlamento passato, et alcuni avisi che habbiamo ricevuto di nuovo delli quali scrivo più al Cardinale nostro Alano, et così offerendosi una comodità grandissima d'un navio qual desiderar potessimo, andò il Padre a Escurial a dispedirse dove fu ricevuto con molto gusto di Sua Maestà, et subito dipoi si partì al porto per imbarcarsi. Egli lasciò la letra per Vostra Paternità che con questa vene, ma da Fiandra scriverà più largamente, perché il Re gustò che fusse per Fiandra, et procurasse di rassettar quello che tocca al Seminario de S. Omero, al qual Sua Maestà mostra di favorir molto, et n'ha scritto altre letre caldissime alli suoi ministri di Fiandra, acciochè subito et senza più dilatione et induggio faccino godere il Seminario di S. Omer, del sustento che Sua Maestà sennalò sopra le licenze delli panni, et che quando queste manchino Sua Maestà provederà d'altri mezzi di maniera che questo nigotio di S. Omero non potrà, piacendo a Dio, si non andar inanzi et esser di molto servitio di nostro Signor.

3. Et in quanto a quello che il Cardinale Alano disse a Vostra Paternità che saria meglio che questo Seminario fusse in Douay, già ho dato sodisfattione a su Signoria Illustrissima in questo, che non è possibile (almanco per adesso) perché Sua Maestà elesse il luogo di S. Omero per molte cause perticulari, et fra l'altre per star così vicino alli porti di Cales et Dunkerque, dove possino li sacerdoti che vanno a Inglaterra e a España star espettando le sue imbarcationi comodamente, il che non potrano in Douay o altro luogo discosto dalla mare.

4. Et per questo prego la Paternità Vostra molto humilmente che torni a raccomandar alli padri di Fiandra questo negozio di S. Omero, perché io ho dato ordine al Padre Flacco (il qual per adesso parendo così a Vostra Paternità podrà restar per superiore fin a tanto che la cosa venga a ser magior) come se potrà provedere de dinari bastanti per questi principii, sin a tanto che si cobre la venta senalada por Sua Maestà. Et perché la brevità del tiempo non permette più parolle per adesso, fo fine raccomandandome muy humilmente nelli Santi Sacrificii di Vostra Reverenda Paternità. Da Vallidolid a 11 de Augusto 1593.

Di Vostra Reverenda Paternità
    figliuolo et servo indegno
        Roberto Personio.

Translation

Our Very Reverend Father in Christ

1. By the last post I wrote to Your Paternity about the current situation, and afterwards I received Your Paternity's letter of the 7th of June. With regard to Fr Gibbons, he is now very contented in the employment which he is performing at this college; and in truth I do not know where he could be better placed at present, or more to his own liking and more productively than here, *all things considered – granting that we must always bear our brothers' burdens to some extent*. The rector and Fr Gibbons now are acquainted with one another and are great friends. The rector carries out the duties of his office very well and all are very satisfied with him, myself especially, because I have found the college in a good state in temporal matters as well as in spiritual; the only thing is, they seem to have spent a great deal of money, but it has not been possible to do otherwise, and by the grace of God we have paid our debts up to the present, and still have a little less than 1000 scudi left over, in spite of the heavy expenditure on the late building scheme and on the drafts despatched to England and likewise to Seville and the residency we have in Lisbon. May God be ever thanked for it. The mouths we have to feed in the house number 53 or 54 or more.

2. The fathers in England have already written to me several times that they have great need of one or two more of the Society. But Fr Garnet especially in his letters of March, April, and May has repeated this request, adding that he is now without help as regards business matters, for none of the men there is able to help much in that respect. And as I saw that this was the case and that if it happened that the good father fell into the hands of the enemy there would be no one there who could keep us in touch with things, I judged it necessary to make use of the authority which Your Paternity had given me and to send Fr Henry Walpole. He was very eager to make this journey and had been so for a long time, and he seemed to me to be quite suitable on account of his capabilities, his discretion, and the knowledge of affairs which he has gained here. A further reason for his going at this time was to console the Catholics afflicted by this fresh clampdown imposed by the recent parliament, and also some reports which we have received lately, about which I am writing further to our Cardinal Allen. And so, when the opportunity arose to take passage on a ship, just exactly suited to our needs, the father went to El Escorial to take his leave. He was received there very graciously by His Majesty and immediately afterwards left for the port to go on board.[203] He left the enclosed letter for Your

---

203. In his confession, Walpole claims that he returned to Valladolid from the royal court, and from there to Bilbao to take ship for Flanders, where "I looked after that business for some time, and frequently treated with the Secretary of State and other principal persons. Finally, hav-

Paternity, but he will write at greater length from Flanders, for it was the king's pleasure that he should go via Flanders and endeavour to settle matters pertaining to the seminary of St Omers. The king shows himself to be very well-disposed to this seminary and he has expressed the strength of his feeling in further letters to his ministers in Flanders, to the effect that they should at once, without further delay and procrastination, allow the seminary of St Omers to enjoy the maintenance appointed by His Majesty from the licences to import cloth, and telling them that when these fail His Majesty will provide other measures. Consequently, this project of St Omers, please God, cannot fail to go forward and to be of great service to our Lord.

3. With regard to what Cardinal Allen told Your Paternity, that it would be better for this seminary to be at Douai, I have already satisfied His Eminence about this matter, that that would not be possible (at any rate at present), because His Majesty chose the position of Saint-Omer for a number of specific reasons: among others, that its proximity to the ports of Calais and Dunkirk will allow the priests who are going to England and Spain to stay there conveniently while waiting to take their passage. They will not be able to do this at Douai or any other place at a distance from the sea.

4. In this connection I beg Your Paternity very humbly to commend this matter of St Omers again to the fathers in Flanders, for I have given instructions to Fr Flack (who for the present, if Your Paternity thinks fit, can remain as superior until further progress is made) how he can provide sufficient money for these first beginnings, until such time as we can collect the income appointed by His Majesty. And since time, being short, does not allow me to write more, I end my letter, commending myself very humbly to Your Reverend Paternity's holy sacrifices. From Valladolid, the 11th of August 1593.

    Your Reverend Paternity's
        unworthy son and servant
            Robert Persons.

B197 From Claudio Acquaviva, Rome, 30 August 1593

> SOURCE: ARSI, Cast. 6, fol. 163r–v.
>
> NOTE: In response to Persons's letters of 16 June and 15 July (B186–187, B190), the general encourages him to continue working on his behalf in Madrid in preparation for the general congregation.

P. Roberto Personio, Agosto 30.

En una de las dos que de Vuestra Reverencia he reçevido con este correo, me diçe la buena voluntad con que acudira siempre que en algo pudiere servir a la Compañia, y desto estoy yo bien çierto y seguro, por lo qual acordandome de los muchos Padres que por venir a la Congregaçion faltan en Madrid, donde en compañia de los que alli quedan,

---

ing obtained what I desired, I was permitted to see the king himself to return him thanks. Thence I immediately returned to Belgium, and handed to the Governor of that country the royal charter, and for some time solicited its execution." See Walpole's answer to the judges while in prison, January 1594, in Pollen, *Unpublished Documents*, 233–235, 254–255.

todos haçian muy buenos ofiçios, me ha pareçido, que si los negoçios de Vuestra Reverencia le dan lugar sería bien que asistiese en aquella corte para ayudar al Padre Rector y al Padre Sebastian Hernandez y a los demas que velan sobre nuestras cosas y acuden a informar los ministros de Su Magestad, que por ser el tiempo que es y estar nuestros negoçios como estan es necessario que tengamos alli personas fieles y diligentes que entre sí se ayuden y ayuden a la Compañia, y creo que lo podra Vuestra Reverencia haçer sin detrimento de sus negoçios, pues por cartas y por medio de algun otro padre podra desde Madrid suplir lo que se ofreçiese de esos y de los demas seminarios.

Yo escrivo al Viceprovincial de Toledo estas escrivo a Vuestra Reverencia esto, y que creo irá a residir en aquel colegio. En sus, &c.

Translation

To Fr Robert Persons, 30 August.

In one of the two letters I received from Your Reverence with this courier, you tell me of your readiness to assist at any time in anything which will be of service to the Society, something of which I am both sure and certain. This calls to my mind that so many fathers are missing in Madrid because they are coming to the congregation. In association with those who remain there, they all used to perform very good offices. It has occurred to me that if your commitments allow, it would be a good idea for you to assist in that court: namely, to help father rector and Fr Sebastián Hernández and the others who are keeping watch over our affairs and are helping to keep the ministers of His Majesty informed. Times being as they are, and our affairs standing as they do, it is necessary to have trustworthy and diligent persons there to help each other and help the Society. I trust that Your Reverence will be able to do this without detriment to your own affairs: both by letters and by means of some other father, you should be able to supply from Madrid what is necessary for this and for the other seminaries.

I am writing the same to the vice provincial of Toledo as to Your Reverence, and that I trust you will reside in the same college. To your [prayers and holy sacrifices], etc.

B198 From Claudio Acquaviva, Rome, 30 August 1593

SOURCE: ARSI, Cast. 6, fol. 163v.

NOTE: This is the second letter to be sent by the same courier. Acquaviva authorizes Persons to move English Jesuits from one posting to another as he sees fit. Thomas Wright, currently in Louvain (McCoog, *English and Welsh Jesuits*, 340), should not be sent to Spain but preferably be dismissed immediately; in the event, Persons prevailed on the general to allow Wright to come to Valladolid. Brother Fabrizio Como should be sent back to Rome.

P. Roberto Personio, 30 Agosto.

Yo me consuelo mucho que los seminarios vayan con tan buen passo como me escriven, y espero en el Señor que cada dia se augmentarán más, para lo de San Omer ya yo he dado facultad y los nuestros alli acudiran a tener el cuydado como Vuestra Reverencia pide. En lo tocante a las mudanzas y truecos de los sujetos Ingleses que Vuestra Reverencia en la suya me nombra, yo me remito a su pareçer y le doy facultad que en ello haga lo que entendiere ser más conveniente al divino serviçio y al bien de los negoçios que trae entre las manos. Solamente del P. Tomaso Writh no tengo por conveniente que pase en España. Vuestra Reverencia le dexe donde está que alli se verá lo que se deva hazer dél y esto es que sus cosas han llegado a traicion[204] que si a España fuese sería causar nuevos rumores y no dude sino que es hombre para turbarnos. Es mejor que donde ahora está le despidan porque cierto él no es para nosotros.[205] El Hermano Fabriçio entiendo que desea volver por acá donde le pareçe que se hallará más consolado; en la ocupaçion que aora tiene creo que haçe poco, y en otra fuera de aý hara menos, y ansi tengo por mejor que Vuestra Reverencia con la primera comodidad nos le embie, pues con qualquiera que aý le den se suplira suficientemente lo que él haçe. En sus oraciones &c.

Translation

To Fr Robert Persons, 30 August.

I am very pleased that the seminaries are progressing so well, as you write to me, and I hope in the Lord that they will increase more every day. Concerning that of St Omers, I have already given authority for Ours to be put in charge as Your Reverence asks. As for the movements and exchanges of the English members which Your Reverence mentions in your letter, I leave it to your discretion and I give you the authority to do what you judge to be most agreeable to the service of God and for the benefit of the business which you are conducting. Only, with regard to Fr Thomas Wright, I do not think it convenient that he should go to Spain. Would Your Reverence please leave him where he is, and there it will be decided what needs to be done with him: and that is because his behaviour borders on betrayal, and if he goes to Spain, it will cause new rumours and there is no doubt but that he is a man who will disturb us – it is better that he should be dismissed now because it is clear that he is not for us. I understand that Brother Fabrizio wishes to return over here where it seems he will find more consolation. In his present occupation I believe that he does not do much, and in the other place, even less, and indeed I think it for the best that Your Reverence send him to us at the first opportunity; really, anyone who is available there will be quite suitable enough to do what he is doing. To your prayers, etc.

B199 To Henry Walpole, Valladolid, August 1593

SOURCE: Walpole's confession, in Pollen, *Unpublished Documents*, 259.

NOTE: Walpole had left Spain in August and was now at Saint-Omer. Persons wrote to him about the arrival of John Cecil, who had evidently travelled from England via Saint-Omer and possibly met Walpole on the way.

[*Walpole confesses:*] F. Parsons wrote unto me once after my departure from Spayne unto St Omers, telling me that Mr Cicill a priest was with him there, who had bene in England.

204. a traicion] atr^n R
205. Solamente del P. Tomaso Writh ... para nosotros] *added at the end of the draft R*

B200 To Juan de Idiáquez, Valladolid, 31 August 1593

SOURCE: AGS, Sec. de Estado 839, fols. 76–77, holograph, enclosing a statement by Cecil. Both documents are summarized in *CSPS*, 4: 606–608, items 618–619.

HICKS: 190–197, with English translation.

NOTE: John Cecil (Snowden), volunteering for the service of Lord Burghley and Sir Robert Cecil, had left England for the Continent in the autumn of 1591 but was in Scotland by October 1592. He now returned to Spain to confer with Persons about renewed plans of the Scottish Catholic earls to combine forces with Spain against James's Protestant councillors and Queen Elizabeth. Cecil brought with him a "Statement of what happened in Scotland in the month of December last year, 1592, in consequence of the embassy which the Catholic lords of that country wished to send to His Majesty" (*CSPS*, 4: 603–606, item 617). This was an account of a previous, abortive conspiracy known as the "Spanish blanks," a scheme devised by William Crichton during his sojourn in Madrid from late autumn 1590 to August 1592, whereby the Scottish Jesuits would obtain signatures from the Catholic earls Huntly, Erroll, Angus, and Patrick Gordon of Auchindoun, on blank sheets of paper as earnest of their support for a Spanish invasion of Scotland and England. The blanks were intercepted on 27 December, before the courier, George Kerr, had left Scotland (Yellowlees, 117–129). To this account, Cecil added a memorial on the state of affairs in Scotland.

Persons now introduces Cecil to Idiáquez so that he can present his proposals to the Spanish court. He had been skeptical of Crichton's plan (Persons to Acquaviva, 12 May 1594, B230), but was now more confident. He spells out the advantages of allying with the Scots lords – Queen Elizabeth's vulnerability to invasion via Scotland, the effectiveness of foreign soldiers on Scottish soil, the potential deployment of English and Scots soldiers currently with the army of Flanders – and the risk of losing Scotland entirely to the Protestants if their offer is neglected. In his view, England and Scotland should be considered together in the development of Spanish diplomatic and military policy. He nominates William Bodnam (Bodenham) as a suitable agent to return with Cecil and verify his claims.

The letter encloses a document by Cecil outlining the advantages of his scheme: the safe port, the strong Catholic presence on the Scottish border, and the trouble it will cause to Queen Elizabeth. He also advises that a winter expedition will mean that the English troops will be impeded by the conditions. He has heard that the Spanish prince (the future Philip III) is sickly, but is encouraged to note his vigour. On the contrary, Crichton's interest in a Spanish succession waned because he found Philip "indecisive and sickly" (Yellowlees, 121).

Dios dé a vuestra Señoria salud y paciencia pues son menester para tantas occupaciones que se offerecen. No quesiera cansar a vuestra Señoria y a mí mismo con tantas cartas, pero no ay remedio. El portador desta, soldado de hábito, pero sacerdote de vocacion, trae un larga relacion de las cosas de Escocia y en ella unos punctos muy buenos como vuestra Señoria veerá. Lo demas dira a bocca. Vuestra Señoria puede fiarse dél, pues es hombre de bien, y siervo de nuestro Señor por cuya causa ha travajado muy bien, y puesto su vida al peligro del cucillo.[206]

206. cucillo] *S, obscure*

En quanto al negocio que viene a tratar de parte de aquellos señores de Escocia, vuestra Señoria se acordará que yo he dicho algunas veçes a vuestra Señoria que me parecia que las cosas de Escocia tomadas juntamente con las de Ynglaterra, serian de muy grande importancia para entrambos reynos, pero tomadas a parte, serian difficultosas a sustentar por causa de la vicinança de la Reyna de Ynglaterra. Mas a estas difficultades el padre trae las soluciones que vuestra Señoria veerá, y aquellos señores que estan *sul fatto* y han de arrisgarse más que nadie en la empresa la tienen por muy facil y sigura. Su Magestad lo considerará y mandará lo que fuere servido.

Grande punto es, averse reducido tantos señores a la nuestra santa fe catolica y con tantas veras como el padre dira, pues pocos años ay que apena avia uno. Importante tan bien es, querer ellos dar puerto en parte tan cómmoda y sigura como offerecen, y donde todo soccorro de tantas partes puede venirles sin que la Reyna pueda empedir. De momento estan bien lo de la condicion del Rey y de su Reyna, y de los de su corte; la vicinança de Britaña ayudará grandemente para el succorro y inteligencia, y la de Yrlanda que está llevantada contra la Reyna no hara poco.

Al fin, tres o quatro cosas me haçen a mí grande fuerça, y impression. La primera que estos señores Escoçeses estan ya reducidos a termine que si Su Magestad no les da succorro para servirse de las fuerças que tienen por alla, saldran de Escocia, de lo qual sigueran dos inconvenientes, el uno que cargarán por acá a pedir sustento, y el otro que dexarán a la Reyna de Ynglaterra el mando absoluto de toda la Escocia.

La segunda cosa es que por ninguna via del mundo si puede dar a la Reyna tanto travajo fuera de su reyno proprio, quanto por via de Escocia, ni hacer cosa que tanto le pigne, si se puede sustentar y mantener un golpe de soldados por alla como estos señores affirman, que assiguro a vuestra Señoria que es *tangere pupillam oculi eius*, por la vicinança, y intiendo que ninguna cosa le ha dado tanto pena por muchos años atras quanto vee esta mudança en Escocia, la qual ella attribuya a los seminarios y por consequens vuestra Señoria facilmente imaginará como les quiere.

La tercera cosa es, que yo he visto siempre por experiencia que los Reyes de Francia en todas las guerras que tubieron con los Yngleses tenian particular quenta con Escocia, y embiavan alla gente y deneros, y quando estavan appretadissimos en Francia sacavan de su gente armas y deneros para tener seis o ocho mil hombres en Escocia, y con estos hacian grandes diversiones a los Reyes de Ynglaterra y solian decir que cada mil Franceses en Escocia valian tres en Francia contra los Yngleses y assi no dudo si no que si estos tres o quatro mil hombres que piden los Escoceses, se les puede embiar, haran más que diez mil contra la Reyna en qualquiera otra parte, y enfrenaran a los hereges maravillosamente.

La quarta cosa es que Su Magestad tiene muchos Yngleses y Escoçeses en su servicio en Flandes donde le hacen poco, y con tal occasion como esta se podrian emplear approvechosamente, Su Magestad mirará lo que más conbiene a su real servicio y aquel de nuestro Señor. Si pareciere embiar alguna persona con este sacerdote a Escocia para averiguar o enformarse más de las cosas, como si propone en relacion, pienso que sería menester que fuesse persona plática, y que supiesse ablar alguna otra lengua fuera dela Española, porque otramente no podra andar por el reyno sin ser discubierto, y entre otras personas se me offrecido de accordar a vuestra Señoria de Guielmo Bodnam que sabe muchas lenguas y he oydo decir a Bernardino de Mendoça que es hombre de confiança y buenas partes. Vuestra Señoria lo conocerá mejor, yo solamente lo he querido apuntar porque no tengo mucha noticia de la persona, y por ventura vuestra Señoria tendra otras más a proposito si esto se resolviere de embiar alguno.

Finalmente esto solo supplico a vuestra Señoria que consuele a estos señores de Escocia y les anime en una manera o otra, y les despache presto al portador para que buelva, porque esto tanto a ellos como a él importa mucho, y por más secreto viene por aý en aquel su hábito de soldado para que sea menos conocido, Vuestra Señoria por amor de Dios le procure su despacho con brevidad, y por que con aver tardado en el camino más de lo que él pensava, y con traer con él tres estudiantes Yngleses, ha gastado todo lo que tenía, es necesario que Vuestra Señoria le procure con qué bolver a Escocia, y si el viatico que Su Magestad le será servido dar sea bastante para llevar tan bien otro sacerdote con él; que es muy a proposito para Escocia se lo daremos. Pero en una manera o otra supplico a Vuestra Señoria que buelva presto para que no se descubra por aý y no pierda su embarcacion que lo aguarda: y con esto remittiendome en lo demas a lo que él[207] dira a bocca beso las manos a Vuestra Señoria y supplico a nuestro Señor de guadarlo por muchos años. De Valladolid a 31 de Augusto 1593.

Roberto Personio.

[*Enclosed memo:*]

A la pregunta que su Señoria mi hizo lotra dia, por estar hablando de muchas materias, no pienso de haber dado entonces la respuesta tan complida, como la importança della requiria; y era que puesto caso que si diesse a Escoçia este socorro qué si resultaria de ello.

Digo agora más a la larga (y por escripto porque los muchos negoçios de Su Señoria y el estraneo hábito en que estoi, no dan lugar a muchas conferençias). Digo pero que con esta ayuda que piden estos Señores.

1°. Primeramente con este soccoro, si hallarán bastantes estos señores a forçar el Rey, alterar el estado presente, y restaurar la fe Catholica en aquel Reyno.

2°. El secundo es que estara siempre aquel Reyno a la devocion de Su Magestad.

3°. El tercero es que para refrenar la insolencia de la Reyna de Ynglatierra, y hazerla gastar más que tiene, y de disturbarla de sus otros pensamientos de Françia, Flandes y Indias no hai otro medio más efficaz deste.

4°. El quarto que hallandosi siempre en la impresa de Ynglatierra dos difficultades grandissimas: la una el peligro de hacer jornada por mar en aquel corriente de Ynglatierra, y la dificultad de tomar puerto. La otra cómo se podrian juntar los Catholicos con la gente del Rey. Entrambas si quitan con este poco gasto que en Escocia si haze: porque puertos daran estos señores a donde sin peligro si puede disembarcar y hacer fortalezas si fuere menester: y las provincias de Ynglatierra, adonde el golpe de los Catholicos si halla como Comberlande, Westmerland, Lancastria y otras provinçias de la Norte confinan con Escocia de manera que no hay mar, ny montes,[208] ny presidios ni fuerças algunas que les

---

207. él] S; om. Hicks
208. serras] *interlined, replacing* montes [*deleted*] S

pueden impedir a juntarsi con la gente de Su Magestad. Y antes de que la Reyna puede llamar su gente de Flandes y Françia, y inbiar una armada de Londres saran dos o tres meses.

A mi parescer expediente fuera que este socorro si diesse nel invierno, porque la tierra de Escoçia es secca y arenosa y por llevar la arteleria más cómoda que Ynglatierra y siendo invierno no puede una armada in Ynglatierra hacer camino, o si haze sará muy poco y con mucha difficuldad; mas en el mes de octubre hallarán la tierra llenissima de todos los bastimientos, la cosecha, el ganado gordissimo, el pescado ya puesto en barriles y todo lo demas para su sustiento.

Estas dias passadas vi el principe, para mi grandissimo consuelo, y no mi artaba de verlo, tanto más que he oydo en muchos cabos los hereges hablar mucho de su infirmidad, imbecilidad y (como dizen ellos) impossibilidad de viver muchos años y de las esperanças que tienen que muerto Su Magestad, por la pocidad del principe la monarchia de España si ha de dishazer que Aragona y Portugal si rebellaran, que en Italia cada uno tomará un bocado, y esta es la materia de sus libros, y sermones, sabiendo esto huelgomi infinitamente de ver con estos ojos como estan engañados estos siervos de Satanás. Siendo el principe como si ve tan habil, de tan prefecta complexion, tan buen puesto, y di tan buena salud, y tantas buenas prendas: huelgariami mucho que el vivo ritratto del principe fuera por buena mano sacado, y imbiado a vender por todos las partes para que pierdan los hereges estas sus mal fundadas esperanças. Atrevomi de abrir mis entrañas a Su Señoria porque ya si sabe que si Su Señoria bien sabe el zelo y fervor que tienen los Catholicos ynglesis a Su Magestad y todas sus cosas.

Suplico que su Señoria no mi dexa perder la comodidad que tengo aparexada por hacer mi vuelta, y por assentar las intelligençias que tanto desseamos y que no mi dexa de estar tantas dias sin poder servir a dios conforme a mi devoçion y vocaçion.

Si el negoçio de que tracto puede resultar al serviçio de dios y Su Magestad aquí estoi para riscar mi vida y todo quanto tengo y puedo en ello. Si no, si por agora no hai lugar suplico que mi dé licencia para volver a trabajar como antes *in vinea domini et animarum messe* y esto con brevidad por que por lo que he dicho a su Señoria, no puedo aguardar mucho.

        Criado y capellan de Su Señoria
        Juan Cecilio
        Alumno del seminario de Valladolid.

[*Endorsed*:] El Padre Personio con el disfraçado y la relacion que él haze de las cosas de Escocia y le que piden y con ello dize que se podria esperar.

Translation

May God our Lord give Your Excellency health and patience, for you have need of them for the great amount of work that comes your way. I should not wish to weary Your Excellency with so many letters, but there is no help for it. The bearer of this letter, by his dress a soldier but by his calling a priest, brings a long account of affairs in Scotland,[209] and in it are

---

209. *CSPS*, 4: 603–606, item 617.

some very good points, as Your Excellency will see. He will tell the rest by word of mouth. You can have confidence in him; for he is a trustworthy man, a servant of our Lord, in whose cause he has undergone many labours and exposed his life to the danger of the knife.[210]

With regard to the business of those Scottish lords which he comes to negotiate, Your Excellency will recall my opinion communicated to you on several occasions, that to deal with Scottish affairs conjointly with those of England might yield very great advantage to both kingdoms, but to deal with them apart would cause great difficulties owing to the proximity of the queen of England to Scotland.

To these difficulties, however, as Your Excellency will perceive, the father brings a solution. Those lords who take their stand on the facts of the situation and have more at stake than anyone else think the undertaking a very safe and easy one. His Majesty will consider it and order it as he thinks best.

It is a matter of great moment to have brought so many lords back to our holy Catholic faith, and with such fervour to boot, as the father will tell, for a few years ago there was scarcely one who was a Catholic. Their spontaneous offer to assign a port in a convenient and safe part of the country by which aid from so many places can reach them, without the queen being able to prevent it, is equally important: similarly, the disposition of the king and queen and of the gentlemen of his court. Moreover, Brittany, being so near, will be of great advantage for supplying aid and for keeping in touch with the state of affairs. The proximity of Ireland, which is already in revolt against the queen, will also be of no small benefit.[211]

Finally, three or four matters have forcibly impressed me. The first is that the state of these Scottish lords has reached the point where if His Majesty will not assist them with the forces they have there, they will leave Scotland. This will have two disadvantages: the one that they will be a burden here in seeking sustenance; the other that they will leave the whole of Scotland in entire control of the queen of England.

Second, in no other place in the world outside her own kingdom, as these lords assert, can the queen of England be put to so much trouble as in Scotland, to raise and maintain a sufficient force there. For I assure Your Excellency that owing to Scotland's proximity to England, this is *to touch the very apple of her eye*;[212] and I understand that nothing for many years has caused the queen so much distress as the consciousness of this change in Scotland which she attributes to the seminaries. From this Your Excellency will easily conceive what love she bears to them.

Third – and this is a point that past history has impressed on me – in all the wars waged against the English, the kings of France made great account of Scotland and sent men and money there. Even when France itself was in dire straits, they nevertheless took arms and money from their own people to furnish seven or eight thousand men in Scotland, and with this force made great diversionary attacks on the kings of England. They

---

210. The reading is obscure; see textual note.

211. The Nine Years War (1593–1603), waged by Hugh O'Neill of Tyrone and Hugh Roe O'Donnell of Tyrconnell.

212. Ironically quoting from Zech. 2:8, about the care of God for His people: "he that toucheth you, toucheth the apple of my eye."

used to say that against the English every thousand of French soldiers in Scotland was of as great service as three thousand in France itself. And so I have no doubt that if three or four thousand troops that the Scots ask for can be sent, they will have greater effect against the queen of England than ten thousand employed anywhere else, and will hamper the heretics to a surprising degree.

Fourthly, His Majesty has many Englishmen and Scots in his service in Flanders where they are not serving much purpose. On such an occasion as this, they might be employed with advantage; His Majesty should consider the matter and decide what is best for his service and the cause of Our Lord. Should His Majesty consider, as is proposed in this document, to send someone to Scotland with this priest to test the truth of his account and gather further information as to how matters stand, it is necessary, I think, that the person chosen be experienced and accomplished and able to speak some other language than Spanish; for otherwise he could not travel about the country without being discovered. Besides other persons suitable for the purpose, it occurs to me to draw William Bodnam to your attention.[213] He knows several languages, and I have heard Bernardino de Mendoza[214] say that he is a man to be trusted and of good parts. Your Excellency will know him better than I do. In naming him, I only wish to make a suggestion, because I do not have much information about him, and it may be that, if it is decided to send some one, Your Excellency will have others at your disposal who are more suitable.

To conclude, I have this one petition to make to Your Excellency: that you encourage these Scottish lords in some way or other and keep up their spirits, and settle the bearer's business quickly, so that he may return; for this is of much consequence both to them and to him. For greater secrecy he comes here dressed as a soldier, so that he may be less easily recognized. For the love of God, see to it, Your Excellency, that he returns soon; for he has already been longer on the journey than he expected. He has spent all his funds on bringing three English students with him. So Your Excellency will have to supply him with money for his return journey to Scotland. If His Majesty deigns to make that sum sufficiently large for him to take back with him another priest also, very suited for Scotland, we will assign him to that mission.

But I do beg Your Excellency to set him on his return journey quickly, one way or another, to avoid his presence here being discovered, and to enable him to catch his appointed vessel. And so, leaving all further matters for him to communicate by word of mouth, I kiss Your Excellency's hands and beseech our Lord to grant you many years of life. From Valladolid 31 August.

Robert Persons.

[*Enclosed memo from John Cecil:*]

It seems to me that the reply I gave Your Excellency the other day did not fully reflect the gravity of your question, because there were so many matters under discus-

213. On the Catholic family of Bodenham, based at Rotherwas, Herefordshire, see *Held in Trust: 2008 Years of Sacred Culture*, ed. Maurice Whitehead (Stonyhurst, 2008), 84–85.

214. Bernardino de Mendoza (ca. 1540–1604), former Spanish ambassador to England (1578–1584) and then France (1584–1591), was now living in Madrid.

sion. The question was: in case Scotland were given this aid, what would be the outcome?

Here I explain this more at length, and in writing because the many occupations of Your Excellency and the strange attire I am wearing are not very conducive to conversation. I say then that with the aid asked by these [Scottish] lords:

1st. With this help, enough lords will be found to force the king to alter the present state, and restore the Catholic faith in that kingdom.

2nd. That kingdom will always be obliged to his Majesty.

3rd. There is no other nor more effective remedy than this to restrain the insolence of the queen of England, and to make her spend more than she has, and to distract her from her other designs on France, Flanders and the Indies.

4th. The fourth is that the enterprise of England always runs into two difficulties: one is the danger of the journey in the currents of [the sea] of England, and the difficulty of making harbour. The other is how Catholics could get together with the king's forces. Both difficulties would be overcome with this small expense made in Scotland, because these lords will provide ports for us to disembark without danger and make fortresses if necessary. And the provinces of England where the majority of Catholics are, such as Cumberland, Westmorland, Lancashire, and other provinces in the North, border on Scotland, so that there is no sea, mountains, nor fortifications or military forces that will prevent them from joining His Majesty's forces. And two or three months will have passed before the queen can summon troops from Flanders or France and send an army from London.

In my view, it would be convenient to provide this help in the winter, because in Scotland the land is dry and sandy, which will make it easier to transport the artillery than in England. If it is winter time, an army in England will not be able to set off, and, even if it does, it will be with small progress and with great difficulty, but in October they will find the land very full of provisions, the harvest, full-grown cattle, fish in barrels, and everything else for their sustenance.

These last few days I saw the prince, to my greatest comfort, and I could not get enough of looking at him, particularly given that in many places I have heard the heretics talking about his illness, imbecility and – as they put it – the impossibility that he will live for many years, thus giving them hope that, once His Majesty dies, given the weakness of the prince, the Spanish monarchy will disintegrate, Aragon and Portugal will rebel, and in Italy everybody will take a piece. This is the topic of their books and sermons, and, knowing this, I greatly enjoy seeing with my own eyes how deceived these servants of Satan remain: the prince being, as is evident, so proficient, of such a perfect complexion, so fine looking, in such good health, and endowed with such physical and moral perfection that I would very much delight in having a live portrait of the prince done by a good artist, and have it distributed to be sold everywhere so that the heretics will abandon their groundless hopes. I dare to open my heart to Your Excellency because it is known that Your Excellency knows well the zeal and fervour that English Catholics feel for his Majesty and all his affairs.

I implore Your Excellency not to keep me waiting, as that will make me miss the opportunity to make my return, already arranged, and to secure the sources of information that we so much wish for. Every day that I am delayed will be a day that I am kept from serving God according to my devotion and vocation.

If the matter I am dealing with could bear fruit in the service of God and His Majesty, here I am to risk my life, and all I have and can put in it. Otherwise, if this is not the moment for it, I beseech you to give me leave to return to the work I did before in the Lord's vineyard and harvest of souls, and this as soon as possible for the reasons I have told Your Excellency, as I cannot wait for too long.

    Servant and chaplain of Your Excellency
      John Cecil
        Student of the seminary at Valladolid.

B201 To Claudio Acquaviva, 8 September 1593

SOURCE: Acquaviva to Persons, 28 October (B203).

NOTE: Persons requested that Oswald Tesimond (ca. 1563–1636), currently completing his studies in philosophy at Palermo, be sent to work in the colleges in Spain; Acquaviva agreed to send him to Seville to replace Simon Swinburne, once he had completed his course of studies, as requested by the provincial of Sicily, Bartolomeo Ricci (McCoog, *Building the Faith of St Peter*, 215–216).

B202 From Claudio Acquaviva, Rome, 27 September 1593

SOURCE: ARSI, Cast. 6, fol. 164v.

NOTE: Responding to Persons's letter of 11 August (B196), Acquaviva wishes Walpole well on his mission and approves of Persons's handling of affairs relating to Saint-Omer, hoping that Allen's support will influence the attitude of the local Jesuit fathers. He reminds Persons of his request that he should reside in Madrid for some months to take care of the affairs of the Society.

P. Roberto Personio, 27 de setiembre.
Recibi la de Vuestra Reverencia de 11 de Agosto y con ella me vino otra del P. Valpolo. Dios le dé buen viage y próspero suceso en su ocupacion. De lo tocante a Seminario se ha escrito a aquellos Padres y de nuevo se les encarga como Vuestra Reverencia por la suya pide, no dude sino que con su caridad acudiran a ayudar en lo que pudieren. En lo que toca al Rector sealo el padre Flaco pues ansi parece a Vuestra Reverencia. Con el pasado escrivi sería bien que fuese a residir a Madrid por algunos meses donde su estancia será util para la Compañia y ansi creo que esta mi carta le hallará ya alla. En sus oraciones --

Translation

To Fr Robert Persons, 27 September.
I have received Your Reverence's of 11 August, and with it came another from Fr Walpole. May God give him safe passage and a prosperous outcome to his enterprise.

With regard to the seminary, I have written to those fathers and charged them again as Your Reverence wishes; have no doubt but that with their charity they will come and assist as much as they can. As far as the rector goes, let it be Fr Flack, given that this seems to be Your Reverence's preference. With the last post I wrote that it would be good that you rather reside in Madrid for some months, where your presence will be useful to the Society, and in fact I believe this letter of mine will find you there. To your prayers ...

B203 From Claudio Acquaviva, Rome, 28 October 1593

> SOURCE: ARSI, Cast. 6, fol. 167r.
>
> NOTE: Acquaviva again expresses his satisfaction about the progress of the seminaries. He asks that Tesimond be allowed to stay in Sicily until he has fulfilled his teaching responsibilities (McCoog, *English and Welsh Jesuits*, 310): see Persons to Acquaviva, 8 September (B201).

P. Roberto Personio, otubre 28.

Reçevi la de 8 de Septiembre con particular consuelo de entender que continue y se augmente el buen progresso de los seminarios. El Señor los prospere en todo bien, como yo deseo, que en lo que de mi parte pudiere acudir no faltare.

Yo agradeçere aqui a los Provinciales la charidad con que ayudan las cosas de esos seminarios y de las personas de la Naçion.

El Provincial de Siçilia desea que Vuestra Reverencia les dexe al Padre Osoaldo Tesemondo hasta que acabe el curso que lee, que le rematará antes de la Pentecoste, por que no tienen quien con façilidad pueda suplir y satisfaçer. Si Vuestra Reverencia les haçe esta charidad ellos ternan cuydado de embiarsele con la primera enbarcacion que acabado el curso se ofreçiere. No más en esta de encomendarme &c.

Translation

To Fr Robert Persons, 28 October.

I received your letter of 8 September and was particularly comforted to learn how well the seminaries have progressed and grown. May our Lord prosper them in every good – as I wish. I will not fail to help as much as I am able.

I will express my gratitude to those provincials for the charity with which they assist the affairs of those seminaries and the people of your nation.

The provincial of Sicily desires that Your Reverence would allow Fr Oswald Tesimond time to finish the course he is lecturing (which he will complete before Pentecost), because he does not yet have someone with the facility to take his place satisfactorily. If Your Reverence would be so kind, he will take care to send him with the first passage that presents itself after has completed the course. I commend myself, etc.

B204 To Claudio Acquaviva, Valladolid, 2 November 1593

SOURCE: ARSI, Hisp. 136, fols. 107r–108v, holograph, with remains of a seal.
HICKS: 198–206, with English translation.
NOTE: Persons agrees to go to Madrid to keep an eye on things there during the fifth general congregation of the Society of Jesus, which opened on 3 November 1593, continuing until 18 January 1594.

The eminent Jesuit theologian and political writer Francisco Suárez (1548–1617) had passed through Valladolid and discussed prospects of printing his books there. It is possible that contact with him influenced Persons's political thinking, especially as shown in *Conference about the Next Succession*, which Persons compiled about this time. Similarly, Suárez's interest in English affairs, reflected in his *Defensio fidei Catholicae et apostolicae aduersus anglicanae sectae errores, cum responsione ad apologiam pro iuramento fidelitatis [et] praefationem monitoriam serenissimi Iacobi Angliae regis* (1613), may have been sparked by his visit to the college, where he left a copy of at least one of his books. See Eleuterio Elorduy, in *DHCJ*, 4: 3654–3656, and Francisco Gómez Díez, "Tyranny and the Usurpation of Spiritual Power: Pedro de Ribadeneyra, Francisco Suárez, and Robert Persons," in *Projections of Spanish Jesuit Scholasticism on British Thought: New Horizons in Politics, Law and Rights*, ed. Leopoldo J. Prieto López and José Luis Cendejas Bueno (Leiden, 2022), 213–234.

This letter is noteworthy for Persons's sympathetic discussion of the cases of Thomas Wright, the Jesuit theologian who had left Louvain under a cloud, and Fabrizio Como, the lay brother who had been Persons's *socius* for some years.

In the manuscript (R), many words and phrases have been underlined, as indicated.

Molto Reverendo in Christo Padre nostro
Pax Christi.

Due ho ricevuto da Vostra Paternità di 30 di Agosto, nella una delle quali me scrive che gustarebbe ch'io stesse per qualche tempo in Madrid per l'occorrenze de' nigotii della Compagnia che in queste occasioni della Congregatione generale et delle absentie delli Padri si potrebbono offerire, per la qual causa penso con la gratia del Signor sbrigarme con ogni diligentia dell'occupationi di qua per conpir quello che Vostra Paternità comanda et che molto presto me trovarò in Madrid.[215]

Ringratio humilmente la Paternità Vostra dela facultà che me da d'aiutar questa opera nostra delli Seminarii con il contracambio d'alcuni sogietti Inglesi della Compagnia fra questo paese et Fiandra quando serà necessario, et questa necessità s'offerisce alcuna vuolta molto urgente, come adesso il Padre Simone Swinborno ch'era ministro in questo Seminario restò così fiacco dela caldi dell'estate passata che li medici giudicarono che non gli sarebbe sicuro espettar li freddi dell'invierno et per questo loro parere fu che se n'andasse subito a Sevilla per questo inviervo, et che a la primavera passasse a Sant'Omer in Fiandra si no sitisse[216] notabile migliormente et così partì di qua la setti-

---

215. molto presto me trovarò in Madrid] *underlined R*
216. sitisse] *R, possibly in error for* sentisse

mana passata, et il Padre Carolo Tancardo ha de venir a Vallidolid in suo luogo perché non c'è altro qui che può far ben l'officio di ministro.²¹⁷

Già scrissi a Vostra Paternità nella passata il bisogno ch'habbiamo del Padre Osvaldo che sta in Palermo, et ha finito suo curso di philosophia, et n'ha mostrato desiderio di venir qui, si Vostra Paternità serà contenta, il che la supplico, perché senza alcun numero di Padri Inglesi, in questi Seminarii, no si può ben far le cose, et li Rettori lo desiderano molto et tengo speranza che sarà per molto servigio di nostro Signor. Da Palermo a Seviglia facilmente si può passar con li navi di frumento.²¹⁸

Quello che Vostra Paternità scrive del Padre Tomaso Wright, s'io l'havesse saputo avanti che scrissi a Vostra Paternità non haveria, credo, posto a rogar per lui, ma non seppi niente e li padri nostri di Fiandra me scrissero che sarebbe opera di pietà procurar suo rimedio con permettere che venisse a Espagna, et così li risposi che scriveria a Vostra Paternità, non pensando che ne sua causa havesse legado a quel termine che dipoi seppi, ni che lui vorrebbe così presto da Fiandra. Ma dipoi al medessimo tempo che ricevetti la letera di Vostra Paternità, hebbi altra del Padre da Sevilla dove già s'era arrivato amalato di calentura, et così è stato sempre dipoi. Sua letera era piena di buoni propositi con desiderio di vederse con meco, et così intendo che farà subito che l'infirmità lo permetterà. Et io penso di riprenderle molto asperamente et dipoi farò tutto quello di più che Vostra Paternità ordenarà, et si s'havesse di cacciar de la Compagnia, qui si potrà far con molto manco strepito et scandalo che non in Fiandra dove tutti le conoscevano. Qui ninguno lo conosce ni tratarà con persona che li potrà far mal, o ricever lo, et si fusse bisogno di mandarlo a Inglaterra o altra parte senza nota si può fare.²¹⁹

Ma poiché Vostra Paternità n'havuto tanta patienza con lui, e la Compagnia l'ha fatto le spese per tredeci anni già, si Vostra Paternità volesse sperarlo un altro anno evan-

217. *This paragraph underlined as follows*: <u>Ringratio</u> humilmente la Paternità Vostra <u>de la facultà</u> che me da <u>d'aiutar questa</u> opera nostra delli Seminarii <u>con il contracambio</u> d'alcuni sogietti Inglesi della Compagnia <u>fra questo paese et Fiandra</u> quando sera necessario, et questa necessità s'offerisce alcuna vuolta molto <u>urgente</u>, come adesso il Padre <u>Simone Swinborno</u> ch'era ministro in questo Seminario resto così <u>fiacco</u> ... <u>subito a Sevilla</u> per questo inverno, et che a la primavera passasse <u>a Sant' Omer</u> ... <u>Padre Carolo Tancardo</u> ha de venir <u>a Vallidolid</u> ... R

218. *This paragraph underlined as follows*: Già scrissi a Vostra Paternità nella passata <u>il bisogno</u> ch'habbiamo del <u>Padre Osvaldo</u> che sta <u>in Palermo</u>, et ha finito suo curso <u>di philosophia</u>, et n'ha mostrato <u>desiderio di venir</u> qui, si Vostra Paternità serà <u>contenta</u>, il che la supplico, <u>perché senza alcun numero di Padri Inglesi</u>, in questi Seminarii, no si può ben <u>far le cose</u> ... <u>li navi di frumento</u>. R

219. *This paragraph underlined as follows*: Quello che Vostra Paternità scrive del Padre <u>Tomaso Wright</u>, s'io l'havesse saputo avanti che scrissi a Vostra Paternità <u>non haveria, credo, posto a rogar per lui</u> ... <u>permettere che venisse</u> ... <u>Ma dipoi al medessimo tempo</u> che ricevetti la letera di Vostra Paternità, hebbi altra <u>del Padre da Sevilla</u> dove già <u>s'era arrivato amalato di calentura, et</u> così è stato sempre dipoi. Sua letera era piena di <u>buoni propositi</u> con desiderio di <u>vederse con meco</u>, et così intendo <u>che farà subito</u> che l'infirmità lo permetterà. Et io penso <u>di riprenderle molto</u> asperamente et dipoi farò tutto quello di più <u>che Vostra Paternità ordenarà</u>, et si s'havesse <u>di cacciar de la Compagnia, qui si potrà far con molto manco strepito</u> ... R

gelico anchora, *usque dum fodiam circa illum et mittam stercora*, sarebbe molto grande misericordia, et io lo riceberia per particular gratia, poiché fu il primo di tutti ch'io menai alla Compagnia. Et quanto a quello che Vostra Paternità scrive, che egli è huomo per conturbarci; si Vostra Paternità lo intende per l'occasione che può haver qui di trattar con Conturbanti, sepa Vostra Paternità che stando in questo Seminario, giamai tendrà occasione di conoscere o trattare con alcuno, perché qui non c'è comercio nissuno, et quando vi fusse, si lui non se emenda di tal manera, che ci liberi presto di questo sospetto, io non parlaria mai per lui, et stia sicura Vostra Paternità che presto *ponemus securim ad radicem et sciemus quid sit in homine*. Et si non sta saldo, Vostra Paternità presto lo saperà, et si egli si emendasse, potrebbe servir la Compagnia in molte cose, et particularmente in questi Seminarii, et al presente n'habbiamo grande bisogno d'un che legesse le controversie. Vostra Paternità poiché sta già qui sea contenta per amore de'Nostro Signor che lo proviamo per qualche giorno et si non riuscisse sarà la causa dela Compagnia tanto più giustificata *coram Deo et hominibus*. Y trovaremo modo di liberarci dà lui senza rumore et scandalo.

Quello che scrìsse il fratello Fabritio Como a Vostra Paternità di suo disgusto in Sevilla fu solamente per causa d'un altro fratello chiamato Peña, che stava nel Seminario con lui, et subito dipoi che haveva scritto la letera el hermano Fabritio al Padre Magio, accioché trattasse con Vostra Paternità per cavarlo di Spagna, pentito de lo ch'haveva fatto, ne scrisse una altra larga a mi, dicendome suo errore, et rogandome che lo impedisse, et che gustava di star tutta sua vita in questa opera delli Seminarii, et con molta ragione, perché senza dubbio sta molto commodamente et fa grande servitio al Seminario, et è molto amato in Sevilla et così prego la Paternità Vostra che non ci lo toglia perché in verità è molto necessario qui. Egli travagla molto, ma tiene anchora alcuni contrapesi che è bisogna alcuna vuolta haver molta patienza con lui, perché è di sua testa, et non si può per alhora con lui, ma passata quella passione, è buonissimo fratello, et il medessimo è di suo nepote Ambrosio Lissi, il quale se fece molto duro et intrattabile li mesi passati et così uscì di questo Seminario, ma dipoi repentito ha fatto le magiori instanze et humiliationi per tornarci che si può immaginare, et nunca c'ha lasciato riposar fin a tanto che sia già tornato, la qual cosa è stato documento ancho per suo tio Fabritio, et credo che sarebbe grande mortificatione a qualsivoglia d'essi, il cavarli da questi Seminarii, et alli Seminarii saria grande danno, perché non trovarèbbimo altri tali, et per questo prego la Paternità Vostra di consolarli più presto et animarli.

Qui passò la settimana passata il Padre Francisco Suárez et vedendo la buona comodità che c'è qui per stampare li suoi libri qui me ne parlo, et credo che ne scriverà algo a Vostra Paternità. Noi altri tanto per l'opera in si, quanto per la persona che è benemerita di tutti, et particularmente dela natione Inglesa, siamo promptissimi per farli tutta la carità che potiamo et che lui dimandarà, et credo che non trovarà in altre parti così buone comodità per questi effetti.

Ni se offerisce altra cosa per adesso; da Madrid scriverò a Vostra Paternità quello che trovarò, et non cessarò di cercare tutte l'occasioni per far li migliori officii nelle cose della Compagnia que potrò, assicurandome che nostro Signor non mancarà con suo aiuto

poiché tanto di quella si serve. Nelli Santi Sacrificii di Vostra Paternità molto humilmente me raccommando. Da Vallidolid a 2 di Novembre 1593.
    Di Vostra Paternità Reverenda
        figliuolo et servo indegno
            Roberto Personio.
[*Addressed:*] Al molto nostro in Christo Reverendo Padre il Padre Claudio Aquaviva, Preposito Generale de la Compagnia di Jesus. Roma.
[*Endorsed:*] Vallidolid. P. Roberto Personio. 2 de 9bre 93. [*with summary of contents*]

Translation

Our Very Reverend Father in Christ
The peace of Christ.

    I received two letters from Your Paternity of the 30th of August, in one of which you write that you would like me to stay in Madrid for some time, so as to be available for any business of the Society which might occur on this occasion of the general congregation, when the fathers are away. And for this reason, I intend with the grace of God to expedite the business I have to do here with all diligence, so as to comply with Your Paternity's commands, and I think that I shall be in Madrid very shortly.

    I humbly thank Your Paternity for the authority you give me to further this work of ours of the seminaries by transferring some of the English members of the Society between this country and Flanders, when necessary. The necessity for this sometimes occurs very urgently, as it has now in the case of Fr Simon Swinborne, who was minister in this seminary. He remained so debilitated after the heat of last summer that the doctors considered it would not be safe for him to stay for the cold of winter, and therefore they recommended that he should go at once to Seville for this winter, and that in the spring he should go on to Saint-Omer in Flanders if he did not experience a marked improvement in health. And so he left here last week, and Fr Charles Tancard is to come to Valladolid in his place, because there is no one else here who can fill the post of minister satisfactorily.

    I have already written in a previous letter[220] to Your Paternity of the need we have of Fr Oswald who is at Palermo. He has finished his course in philosophy and has shown a wish to come here, if Your Paternity is agreeable, as I beg that you will be, because we cannot well carry on without a certain number of English fathers in these seminaries. The rectors are very anxious for it, and I am in hopes that it will conduce much to the service of our Lord. One can easily cross from Palermo to Seville in the corn boats.

    With regard to what Your Paternity writes about Fr Thomas Wright, if I had known it before I wrote to Your Paternity, I would not, I think, have undertaken to intercede for him; but I was ignorant, and our fathers in Flanders wrote that it would be a work of piety to make an effort for his reform by letting him come to Spain, and so I replied to them that I would write to Your Paternity, having no idea either that his case had reached the stage I later discovered, or that he would be coming from Flanders so soon. But later, at the

---

220. Persons to Acquaviva, 8 September 1593 (B201).

same time that I received Your Paternity's letter, I got another one from the father [himself], from Seville, where he had already arrived, sick of a fever, and he has been in that state ever since. His letter was full of good resolutions. He wanted to pay me a visit, and I understand that he will do so as soon as his sickness allows. I intend to reprimand him very severely; and after that I will do whatever else Your Paternity may ordain; and if it should be necessary to expel him from the Society, it can be done here with much less commotion and scandal than in Flanders, where everybody knew him. Here no one knows him, and he will not have intercourse with anybody who will do him harm or take harm; and if it becomes necessary to send him to England or anywhere else, it can be done without attracting attention.

But, seeing that Your Paternity has had so much patience with him and that the Society has now paid for his support for thirteen years, if Your Paternity were willing to await the result for yet another year, according to the Gospel, *until I dig around him and put in manure*, it would be an act of great mercy and I should take it as a special favour, for he was the first of all the men I brought into the Society. And as for what Your Paternity writes about his being a man likely to stir up trouble for us, if Your Paternity means to refer to the opportunity he might have here of having dealings with disturbers of the peace, Your Paternity may rest assured that while he stays in this seminary he will never have any opportunity of getting to know or having any dealings with anybody; for here there is no intercourse with anybody and if there were, he would have to mend his ways so as to free us very soon of any suspicion of this sort, or I would never speak on his behalf again. And Your Paternity may rest assured that soon *we shall lay the axe to the root*[221] *and find out what there is in the man*. If he is not sound Your Paternity will quickly know it; but if he were to mend his ways, he could be of service to the Society in many directions, especially in these seminaries where at the moment we have great need of someone to lecture on controversy. As he is now here, let Your Paternity, for the love of our Lord, be content that we make trial of him for a few days and, if he should not turn out well, the Society's case will be all the more justified *before God and men*,[222] and we will find a way of getting rid of him without gossip and scandal.

What Brother Fabrizio wrote to Your Paternity about his being discontented at Seville was merely caused by another brother named Peña, who was stationed in the seminary with him. Immediately after Brother Fabrizio had written the letter to Fr Maggio asking him to treat with Your Paternity for his removal from Spain,[223] he repented of what he had done and wrote a second, long letter to me, telling me of his mistake and asking me to prevent its taking effect, saying that he was glad to remain all his life in the work of the seminaries; and with good reason, for he is undoubtedly very comfortably placed here and does great work for the seminary and is very much liked in Seville. And so I beg Your Paternity not to take him away from us, because truly he is very necessary here. He is a great worker, but he has also some faults to balance it, so that it is necessary at times to have great patience with him, for he is pigheaded and nothing can be done with him

221. Lk 13:8, Lk 3:9, Mt 3:10.
222. Acts 24:16.
223. Lorenzo Maggio, SJ (1535–1605), was at this time the general's assistant for Italy. This flurry of letters may have taken place before Acquaviva wrote to Persons about Como either on 8 June (B145) or 30 August (B198).

at those times, but when this mood has passed, he is an excellent brother. The same applies to his nephew, Ambrose Lissi. This latter became very stubborn and intractable during the past months and in that state walked out of this seminary; but afterwards he repented and has made efforts and abased himself more than you can imagine in order to come back to us. He would never leave us alone until he was permitted to return back, as he has now done. This has been a lesson also for his uncle Fabrizio. I believe it would be a great mortification for one and the other to take them away from these seminaries; and it would be a great loss to the seminaries, for we should not find other men like them. For this reason, then, I beg Your Paternity to be ready rather to console them and give them encouragement.

Fr Francisco Suárez passed by here last week and, seeing what great facilities there are here for printing his books, he spoke to me about it, and I think he will write something to Your Paternity on the subject too. We for our part having regard both to the merits of the work itself as well as to the person of one who deserves so well of all men, and especially of the English nation, are most ready to do for him any charitable service we can that he may ask of us; and I do not think he will find anywhere else such great facilities for these purposes.

There is nothing more to say at the moment; I will write to Your Paternity from Madrid how I find things there, and I will not cease to seek every opportunity for using the best offices I can in the affairs of the Society, being assured that our Lord will not be wanting in His aid for that Society of which He makes so much use. I humbly commend myself to Your Paternity's holy sacrifices. From Valladolid, 2 November 1593.

> Your Paternity's
> unworthy son and servant
> Robert Persons.

B205 To Mr Roger Baynes, Valladolid, 2 November 1593

> SOURCE: ABSI, Coll P I 305, a note by Grene.
> HICKS: 207.
> NOTE: Baynes (1546–1623) was William Allen's secretary, and the letter may be concerned with the location of the seminary at Saint-Omer, which Allen had queried (see Persons to Acquaviva, 11 August, B196). Grene's remark, "nothing of importance for my purpose," reflects his lack of interest in the seminary.

B206 From Henry Walpole, Saint-Omer, 13 November 1593

> SOURCE: AAW, IV, no. 24, 135–137; mentioned also by Grene, ABSI, Coll P II 583. The first part of the letter is missing, but has been supplied by translation from Diego de Yepes, *Historia particular de la persecucion de Inglaterra* (Madrid, 1599), 677–679.
> EDITION: Pollen, *Unpublished Documents*, 224–225.
> NOTE: Walpole left Valladolid for England via Madrid and Flanders in August 1593. He stopped at the college at Saint-Omer, from where he wrote to Cabredo and Persons. The letter is mainly about the teething troubles of the seminary. The ciphers in the text, which not

even Pollen was prepared to attempt to decode, reflect his concern about his own safety, since his journey has been publicized by "unsecrecy."

[Having written fully to Your Reverence from Antwerp, and thinking I could send it another way within five days along with the commission of students, who (please God) will go to Spain in a ship from Calais, as is already arranged, I could pass it over now in silence, except for the obligation which I have to Your Reverence, and I wish to make known to you all that is going on, so I will not waste the opportunity to write to you.

I trust in our Lord, that we will leave this new seminary in some reasonable condition. The governor does not seem to be opposed. The secretary, Ibarra,[224] is more inclined to favour us; the lower officials (both on the question of funding, and because we are foreigners) are difficult; however, since we know that it is acceptable to His Majesty, and approved by the prince,[225] I hope that it will turn out well. We already possess an order for the payment of three months. Your Reverence may commend it much to God, who will no doubt succour it, since it is greatly for His service. Young men are beginning to come from England in great numbers, and it is for the best, and no seminary could be of greater profit than this.[226]]

T & π remayne great with H who commendes him to you, and they desyre your N were in R^s place which they think more easily obteyned then for ⊃ his frend, T or other.

I remember your wordes, but would be glad to have had your opinion in particular if occasion should be, but cheifly I desire your prayers and holy sacrifices that I may bestow my tyme and life to Gods greatest glory, how and when it shall please his divine majestye to appointe.[227]

224. Esteban de Ibarra (ca. 1538–1610), secretary of the council of the Spanish Netherlands.
225. Either Pierre Ernst, count of Mansfeld, governor of the Spanish Netherlands, or the archduke Ernest, who was expected in Brussels at the end of the year. See Verstegan's despatch of 13 January 1594 (B213).
226. The text of the letter up to this point has been supplied by translation from Yepes. The Spanish text reads: "1 Aviendo escrito largamente a V. R. de Ambers, y pensando hazerlo otra vez dentro de quinze dias con la mission de estudiantes, que (placiendo a Dios) yran a España, en un navio de Cales, que está ya concertado, pudiera passar aora con silencio, sino que la obligacion que a V. R. tengo, y el desseo de manifestarle todas las cosas, no me dexan perder occasion de escrivirle. 2 Confio en nuestro Señor, que dexaremos este nuevo Seminario en algun estado razonable. El Governador no parece contario. El Secretario Yvarra muy inclinado a favorecernos: los oficiales inferiores, (aunque en materia de dineros, y para gente estrangera, sean dificiles) toda via, por saber que es tan a gusto de Su Magestad, y favorecido del Principe, espero que al fin acudiran a ello. Ya tenemos una librança para la paga de tres meses. V. R. lo haga encomendar mucho a Dios, que sin duda lo ha de socorrer, pues es de tanto servicio suyo. La juventud comiença a venir de Inglaterra en grande número, y de la mejor, y ningun Seminario ha de ser mayor, ni mas provecho que este." Yepes then skips from point 2 to point 5, omitting the discussion of Persons's *Book of Resolution* (*The Christian Directorie*, 1585) mentioned in the endorsement.
227. The Spanish text reads: "5 En quanto a mí, se me ofrecen cosas, en las quales desseara mucho el parecer particular de V. R. pero pues por agora esto no se puede aver, pido oraciones, y santos sacrificios a nuestro Señor, para que yo emplee mis acciones, mi vida, y muerte fielmente en su mayor servicio."

It hath bene told w y^t ff would be geuen T as dd or such like yf he would use it. If ℵ heare that w is great frendes with ω ☐ &c. I know he will like it well, and so do I desire he were with all men as St Paule sayth *pacem quam fieri potest habentes cum omnibus*.²²⁸ Some feared ℘ is ζ, some not.

By some mens unsecrecy, which I will not name, my journey is much known, which may breed daunger or rather infinite gayne to me, that goe in so happy a mission and message, though most unworthy, *legatione fungens pro χρο, ut per eundem obsecrem, et reconciliem Deo*,²²⁹ wherein if I employ my life, how can I wish to bestow it better. Wherefore, Reverend Father, I humbly thank you uppon my knees for so high a favour obteyned and graunted, and desyre you to demaund grace of God for me, that I may be thankfull to his divine majestye, and walk allwayes worthely in his presence, in whose busines I am now immediately to spend all the dayes to come of my life. I meane by our youthes²³⁰ to write to Sir Frauncis, both our rectors, Ministers and Fathers and frends of those Seminaryes so dear unto me. But if commodity of passage should offer itself before, I desire that these may signify my duty, love and most harty and humble commendations, beseeching them all to remember me in their holy sacrifices and prayers to God, as I hope to be mindfull of them for ever and ever. And thus Reverend Father I humbly crave your benediction, and commend you to the eternall love of Jesus.²³¹

After I had written thus farr father rector²³² cometh here and he sheweth himself altogether resolved to sett forward this work what he can, and for the number he sayth, on Gods name when there be meanes let them come an hundreth. And whereas some of the Magistrates have seemed backward, he will reprehend them to their faces and tell them their duty to the king, and how they should be ashamed to be more rude and uncivil or rather uncharytable then they in Doway, Fraunce, Spayne and Rome. And if that will

228. "If it be possible ... have peace with all men" (Rom. 12:18).

229. Cf. 2 Cor. 5:20: "We are ambassadors therefore on behalf of Christ, as though God were intreating by us: we beseech you on behalf of Christ, be ye reconciled to God."

230. Walpole expected to send letters to Persons, Englefield, and others with youths who were due to go to Valladolid and Seville.

231. The Spanish text reads: "Por el poco secreto de algunos en estas partes, mi viage está descubierto, con no poco peligro de pérdida, o por mejor dezir, de ganancia mia, que ando empleado en esta dichosa mission, *Fulgens legatione pro Christo, y per eundem reconcilier Deo*. [*marginal note*: 2. Cor. 5] En la qual si su divina Magestad fuesse servido que yo perdiesse la vida, quanta felicidad seria la mia. Y por esto, mi amantissimo padre, doy mil gracias de rodillas a V. R. por tan alto favor que me ha hecho, en emplearme en esta empresa. Y le pido por amor del mismo Señor, que me pida gracia para ser agradecido a tan alto beneficio. *Et dignè ambulare tanta vocatione*, delante de su divino acatamiento. Al Señor Francisco Inglefilde escrivire despues con la mission de los estudiantes, y al Padre Cresuelo, y los dos Rectores de essos Seminarios de España, para que me encomienden a Dios: Oraciones, Padre mio, y sacrificios he menester por aora, y no otra cosa. Yo soy vuestro, in secula seculorum. Et amor eterno de Iesu Christo sea con V. R. y con todos, y su santo Espiritu encamine todas las nuestras oraciones a su mayor gloria. De San Omer, a 13 de Noviembre 1593." Yepes's version names Joseph Creswell as one of those to whom he will write by way of the students' journey to Spain.

232. Jean Foucart, SJ (1550–1608), rector of the English college at Saint-Omer.

not serve, will cry out uppon them in the pulpitt in behalf of God. Some there be which had need be cryed at the fier of Lundane.

Also in your next it wilbe good presently to appoint to Fr Flack, Fr Smith and Fr Broy their severall charges under the new rector when he cometh, which they will better take from you then from any other, as I perceyve, and perhaps otherwise not be so at their contentment.

This is all which occurreth to me now, and the rest and much of this you shall have from others. Our Lord Jesus direct and blesse you and all your holy actions to his greatest glory. I pray you good Father pray for me. Saint-Omer this 13 of November 1593.

Yours all ever
H.W.

[PS] Before I had a messenger to send this away Fr Broy is returned from Newport bringing with him vij c. florens and a half, the half of the three moneths &c. They of Gandt deale not so well with us, who should pay the other half. Father rector desireth me again and writeth himself to you to move you in behalf of Mouns. Sovastre for the government of Bethuine a town here hard by.

We hope to have a house very commodious and large for 25^{li} by yeare at Candlemas by Fr rectors meanes with a gentleman his frend.[233]

[Addressed:] Al Padre Roberto Personio de la Comp^a de Jesus.

[Endorsed by Persons:] F. Hen. Walpole 13 Novemb. 1593 from S. omers.

[Endorsed in another contemporary hand:] fa. Henry Walpoles letter to fa. Persons of the 13 of Nov. 1593 concerning the beginning of St Omers Colledge, with the K's pension for 16, and with subordination to the Walon rector. About our having a Colledge for 25^l at Betuyne by Candle Masse by meanes of a friend. Of fa. Walpoles going in Mission to England and about fa. Persons booke of Resolution.[234]

B207 From Henry Walpole, Saint-Omer, 19 November 1593

SOURCE: Diego de Yepes, *Historia particular de la persecucion de Inglaterra* (Madrid, 1599), 678–679 [misnumbered 673], Spanish translation; mentioned also by Grene, ABSI, Coll P II 583.

NOTE: Walpole attributes his safe passage to the fact that he is reserved for martyrdom. He is concerned about the lack of resources for the college at Saint-Omer.

Tres o quatro cartas tengo escritas a Vuestra Reverencia despues que llegué aqui, por las quales avrá entendido aver sido sin fundamento su miedo de averme yo anegado en el camino. Confio en nuestro Señor me ha ordenado otra suerte de muerte para su mayor

---

233. M. de la Croix (Walpole to Persons, 19 November, B207). The contract was signed on 17 December: L. Hicks, "The Foundation of the College of St Omers," *AHSI* 19 (1950): 146–180, at 168–169.

234. *The first booke of the Christian exercise, appertayning to Resolution* (Rouen, 1582), revised as *A Christian directorie guiding men to eternall salvation* (Rouen, 1585), was Persons's most widely distributed work. Walpole was likely to take copies with him on his journey to England.

gloria: plegue a su divina Magestad, que²³⁵ yo dé consuelo a Vuestra Reverencia en toda mi vida, y gloria a mi Dios en la muerte, y que sea causa de algun bien a mi patria.

Aqui se trata de comprar una casa muy comoda para el Seminario, el que la vende es Monsiur de la Croyz, cavallero muy piadoso y catolico, y favorecera al Seminario en todo lo que pudiere. Lo que me ha lastimado, es, ver la necessidad temporal que aqui ay, por la qual se han despedido cinco o seys muchachos, los más lindos que he visto. Yo he dicho a los padres, que no pierdan ánimo: porque no podra faltar Dios a tal obra. Mucho nos favorece el buen secretario, Dios se lo pague. Por causa de la pestilencia en Londres, no ay comodidad de passage para alla: pero yo tomaré qualquier otro que se ofreciere. Mucho me he holgado entender que está el Padre Cresuelo con Vuestra Reverencia. Será grande consuelo, y ayuda: y lo mismo he recebido yo por acá del buen Padre Holto, y voy muy animado y confiado en las oraciones y santos sacrificios de Vuestra Reverencia y de los demas Padres y amigos. Y con esto me despido. La gracia y bendicion de Jesu Christo quede con Vuestra Reverencia siempre. De San Omer, a 19. de Noviembre 1593.

Translation

I have written three or four letters to Your Reverence since I arrived here, by which you will have understood that your fears that I would drown on the way were without foundation. I trust in our Lord that He has ordained another kind of death for me, to His greater glory. May it please His Divine Majesty that I may give consolation to Your Reverence through all my life, and glory to God in my death, and that it may be the instrument of some good to my fatherland.

Here they are busy with the purchase of a more capacious house for the seminary. The seller is Monsieur de la Croix, a very pious, Catholic gentleman, who gives support to the seminary in every way he can. What has grieved me, is to see the temporal need which prevails here, as a result of which five or six boys have been sent away, the finest I have ever seen. I have told the fathers not to lose hope, because it is not possible that God will abandon such a work. The worthy secretary²³⁶ shows us much favour: God will reward him. Because of the plague in London, there is no convenient passage there, but I will take whatever is available. I am very pleased to know that Fr Creswell is with Your Reverence. He will be a great help and encouragement; I have received the same here from good Fr Holt, and I am much inspired and emboldened by the prayers and holy sacrifices of Your Reverence and the other fathers and friends. And with that, I will say farewell. May the grace and benediction of Jesus Christ remain with Your Reverence always. From Saint-Omer, 19 November 1593.

B208 From William Flack, Saint-Omer, November 1593

SOURCE: Persons to Acquaviva, 4 December.

NOTE: Persons mentions encouraging letters from William Flack and Henry Walpole about the new foundation.

235. que] *this ed.*; quo Yepes
236. Probably Esteban de Ibarra: see Walpole's letter of 13 November (B206), n224.

B209 From Claudio Acquaviva, Rome, 22 November 1593

SOURCES:
ARSI, Tolet. 5/I, fol. 323r.
ABSI, Coll P I 314, Grene's summary.
NOTE: In instructing Persons to write the life of Campion, Acquaviva was partly responding to a letter from Richard Gibbons at Valladolid, written on 6 October, praising Persons as always ready to help and encourage, but self-effacing and needing to be prompted by the general (ARSI, Hisp. 136, fol. 93). Accordingly, Acquaviva insists that Persons should not omit anything about himself through modesty. Persons's unfinished biography of Campion (ABSI, Coll P I 76–169), has been published as "Of the Life and Martyrdom of Father Edmond Campion" in *Letters and Notices* 11 (1877): 219–242, 308–339, and 12 (1878): 1–68. See also Persons to Creswell, 26 May 1589 (B17).

P. Roberto Personio, 22 de noviembre.
Aunque las cosas de la Congregacion nos tienen tan ocupados que nos es bien necessario el tiempo para dar ricaudo a las forzosas de manera que a pocos podemos escrivir por ahora, no he querido dilatar lo que en esta diré a Vuestra Reverencia y es que algunos padres me piden ordene a Vuestra Reverencia que ponga en orden las cosas del buen padre y Martir Edmundo Campiano²³⁷ y pareceme que tienen razon pues no es justo faltar en la memoria de los hombres y más en la nuestra, el que está tan en la presencia de Dios coronado como fiel testigo de su fee. Vuestra Reverencia por amor del Señor emprenda este trabajo, pues será para gloria del Señor que con la gloria y honrra de sus santos es glorificado. ... Y será tambien para lustre de nuestra Religion que tal hombre tuvo y para animarnos a la cruz que tan glorioso hizo a este varon de Dios; y porque serrá posible que la historia fuese menos cumplida de lo que conviene queriendo Vuestra Reverencia callar algunas cosas que le tocan, le ordeno que en esto escriva todo lo que sabe y todo lo que pudiere con su diligencia hallar sin mirar que toque a Vuestra Reverencia o a otro sino con toda entereza y fidelidad que si algo despues pareçiere quitar verlo an los que para examinar la historia fueren señalados, desde acá le ayudaremos con oraçiones y con qualquiera otra cosa que le fuere necessaria. Espero respuesta de lo que en esto se haze. En sus oraciones &c.

Translation

To Fr Robert Persons, 22 November.
The business of the congregation keeps us so occupied that we are forced to yield to the necessity of the moment, so that we are only able to write briefly at present. However, I do not want to delay what I will tell Your Reverence in this letter, which is that some fathers are asking me to instruct Your Reverence that you put together an account of the career of the good father and martyr Edmund Campion, and it seems to me that they have reason. For we should not fail to keep his memory alive, and especially in our

237. en orden las cosas del buen padre y Martir Edmundo Campiano] *underlined R*

Society: he who stands as he does in the presence of God, crowned as a faithful witness to his faith. Would Your Reverence for the love of our Lord please undertake this work, for it is for the glory of the Lord, who is glorified by the glory and honour of his saints. ... On the one hand, it will add lustre to our religion,[238] which could boast such a man, and on the other, it will embolden us to take up the cross which made this man of God so glorious. Moreover, if Your Reverence leaves out any details about him, it could happen that the history would be less complete than is appropriate, so I am instructing you to write all you know about him, and all that you can find out by research, without regard to what concerns Your Reverence or another, but with all integrity and fidelity. If anything needs to be left out afterwards, leave it to those who are appointed to examine the history. From here we will help you with our prayers and whatever else may be necessary. I look forward to your response in this connection. To your prayers, etc.

B210 To Claudio Acquaviva, Madrid, 4 December 1593

SOURCE: ARSI, Hisp. 136, fols. 163–164.
HICKS: 208–217, with English translation.
NOTE: Persons has now arrived in Madrid to monitor the situation there on Acquaviva's behalf. Here he deals mainly with the posting and condition of English Jesuits, especially regarding the seminaries. A good start has been made at Saint-Omer, and funds are sufficient, but there are unresolved issues of governance.

In response to Acquaviva's enquiry, relayed to him indirectly, Persons commends Ribadeneira's writings, showing how important it is to alert the Spanish public to the state of English Catholicism. Philip II had ordered all copies of Ribadeneira's *Segunda parte de la historia ecclesiastica del scisma de Inglaterra* (Alcalá de Henares, 1593) to be recalled so that the wording of Elizabeth's royal proclamation of October 1591 could be revised (Weinreich, 48–51).

Molto reverendo in Christo padre nostro
Pac Christi.

Ho ricevuto quella di Vostra Paternità di 28 del passato, per la qual ho inteso la voluntà di Vostra Paternità intorno a differir la venuta del Padre Osvaldo sin'alla Pentecoste, ch'habbia finito suo corso di philosophia, con che resto molto contento, ringratiando molto humilmente la Paternità Vostra per questa cura paternale, che tiene di questi Seminarii li quali con il favore divino van ogni giorno in augmento, con universale consolatione di tutti et quello di Valliodalid lasciai in buonissimo stato, tanto nel temporale come nel spirituale et nella fabrica et edificio, et la dominica prima: di questo advento cominciarono primo a usar del refectorio nuovo, che è riuscito bellissimo et molto grande, et v'è habitatione commoda per cento persone. Il Padre Rodrigo de Cabredo fa su officio di Rettor benissime, et è molto grato a tutti li scholari. La gratia che tutti habbiamo di supplicar da Vostra Paternità è, che non permetta che per alcuna occasione ci se toglia perché sarebbe grandissimo danno di tutta questa causa, et non trovaressimo facilmente

---

238. Either the Roman Catholic Church, or the religious order of the Society of Jesus.

altro simile per questo effetto. Quello di Sivigla ciò è il Rettor fa bene suo officio ancora ma le parti del Padre Cabredo sono più eminenti.

2. Già scrissi a Vostra Paternità come per causa dela fiachezza del Padre Simo Swinborno, che era ministro in Vallidolid, si pigliò per ispediente mandarlo per questo invierno a Seviglia, con intentione di che habbia di passar a Fiandra per mudar l'aere nella primavera si non se hallasse miglior, egli ha fatto suo officio di ministro molto bene in Vallidolid, et lo farà anchora in Seviglia, et rimediarà un poco di inconveniente che comminciava a nascere, in Seviglia, por causa che molti seculari ch'havevano conosciuto il Padre Carolo Tancardo, nel tempo che andava con l'Adelantado gli frequentavano nel collegio ynglese dipoi, et non si potette rimediar così ben per altra via che non chiamar il detto Padre a Vallidolid dove farà molto bene con la gratia di nostro Signore.

3. Là s'è venuto ancora il Padre Thomaso Wright, et benché sua causa stia sospensa sin'a tanto che venga la resposta di Vostra Paternità, nientedimeno per non star ocioso, o dar matteria de'sospetti a altri, l'habbiamo occupato in una lettione di controversie, et mia speranza è, che la risposta di Vostra Paternità sarà tale per questa vuolta, che potrà continuarla, almanco per qualche tempo accioché si veda la emendatione che farà. Egli mismo scrive a Vostra Paternità et promette una mutatione molto cordiale, et la medessima cosa ha promesso a mi, il tempo mostrarà il compimento qual sarà. Confio in nostro Signor que sarà buono, et questo suo caso ya sta qui secreto fin qui et così restarà, si Vostra Paternità non comanda altra cosa.

4. Ringratio a Paternità Vostra molto humilmente per quello che promette di agradecer alli Padri provinciali di Spagna la loro carità verso la nostra natione, et raccomandarli questi Seminarii, sarà cosa di molta importanza, et particularmente si se li raccomanda il ricevere duoi o tre sogietti di quelli in ogn'una provincia, poiché per la gratia di Dio si trovaranno con il tempo molto atti, et al presente qui sono duoi nel Seminario di Vallidolid che lo dimandono con grande instanza, et il uno è sacerdote et ha finito suo corso di theologia scolastica, et è molto dotto, et virtuoso, et l'altro ha finito suo corso di philosophia, et è delle più rare parti in tutto, che vi sea nel collegio. Il Padre provinciale inanzi di partire, promettì di ricevere l'uno a la natività, ma il Padre Viceprovincial fa difficultà adesso per causa dela povertà temporale delli collegii ma con una raccomandatione calda di Vostra Paternità spero che tutto si renderà facilissimo.

5. Del Seminario di Santo Omero m'ha scritto il Padre Walpolo et il Padre Flacco letere di molta consolatione, perché dicono che già tengono una familia là di più di vinti persone, delle quali 14 sono scholari molto belli figluolini et che non mancaranno cento dentro d'un anno, et che li catolici da ynglaterra han congratulato molto questo Seminario sopra tutti l'altri, assicurandoli che non li mancarà gente, et dall'altra parte tengo firma speranza che non li mancarà sostento temporale, per quelli che Dio mandararli. Ancora trovo molto amore da questi Signori verso quella opera in particular, et così con questo ordinario li mando altri quatrocenti ducati, oltra li 300 che li mandai in Augusto et benché siano prestati, sono di gente che non li dimandaranno con fretta et dall'altra parte intendo che già il Padre Holto haverà ricevuto per sei mesi la pensione segnalata dal Re in Fiandra, che sarà intorno a mille scudi, di manera, che giongendo tutto questo con li 500 Δ che li mandai al principio, haveranno più che due mille scudi per comminciare, et sempre li scholari porteranno ancora di ordinario alcuna cosa con seco da Ynglaterra, di maniera

che Vostra Paternità ha di considerar questa opera, come cosa che ha di crescer molto in poco tempo, et conforme a questo far il dissegno di aiutarla, et non conforme al presente stato del negotio. Me han scritto da Fiandra che li Padri di là han giudicato che non se li dia nome di Collegio, ni di Rettor, si non *ut vocetur Praeses Seminarii et subsit rectori Collegii Audomarensis*; però no gustan qui di questo, anzi desiderano che sia Collegio, distinto como quello di Roma et questi duoi qui in Spagna, et che tenga suo Rettor particular et stia immediatamente debaxo del provincial, come l'altri Collegii perché questa altra forma non è durabile, et il Rettor et il Preses non staran d'accordo molto tempo, et il Rettor di Santo Omero bastante occupatione tiene nel suo collegio, et così però forza haverebbe di lasciar di far le diligentie necessarie per questo, et così supplico la Paternità Vostra sea contenta ordinarlo adesso per sempre, et raccomandarlo molto al provincial che sarà, et che non sea subordinato al Rettor di Santo Omero per l'inconvenienti che siguirebbono, et benché il Re nella prima sua cedula, a mia instanza pusò che si pagasse la pensione al Rettor di Santo Omero, tuttavia questo fu solamente per principiar il negotio, fin a tanto che s'ordinasse Rettor proprio il quale subito che sarà in possessione il Re mutarà il stilo.

6. Et quanto al Padre Guliermo Flacco io non lo dimandai che fusse Rettor si non per l'interim fin a tanto che Vostra Paternità ci desse altro sufficiente della natione Belgica, al qual il Padre Guliermo Flacco potrà assistere, come procuratore et penso che questa compositione et mescla sirvirà per la pace come vedeamo qui per isperienza. Solamente importa che la persona del Rettor sea sufficiente per il carico che presto sarà molto grande, et la procuratione et assistenza del Padre Flacco sarà ancora necessaria, parte per tener li conti di denari con Spagna che già sta prattico d'essi, et dipoi ancora per tener conti con li Padri et parenti d'alcuni scholari dentro d'Inglaterra, et acciochè il Padre Flacco possa attendere a questo, il Padre Henrico Broy ch'è altro sacerdote ynglese che sta in Santo Omero gli potrà aiutar nelle cose domestiche nelle quali il detto Padre Henrico è prattichissimo.

7. Mi rincresce haver straccato Vostra Paternità con una letera così verbosa ma volsi dar conto di tutto a Vostra Paternità accioché intenda le cose nostre. Delle cose della Compagnia non scrivo cosa particulare perché so che altri lo faranno et io son stato pochi giorni qui in Madrid per informarmi d'essecose, tuttavia il Padre Francisco Rodriguez dirà a Vostra Paternità alcuna cosa che gli scrivo, et alcuni officii già ho comminciato a fare, et andaremo faciendo altri segondo l'occasioni, et tanto più si Vostra Paternità ci comandarà in particular quello che si ha de far, de la qual cosa ho scritto più largo al Padre Rodriguez.

8. Alcuni me han detto che scrivesse a Vostra Paternità quello che siento del effetto che fanno li libri del Padre Ribadeneyra che ha scritto delle cose de Ynglaterra et senza dubbio penso che ci aiutado molto para informar la gente di questi regni e son molto stimati e lodati i detti libri. Ho inteso che il Re per informatione d'alcuna persona ordenò che si mutasse qualche poco nel stilo del edito et così se ha fatto e tutto sta accomodato, credo che animarebbe molto al Padre Ribadeneyra che Vostra Paternità le agradicesse sue fatighe in questa parte. Ni ho altro per adesso si non raccommandarmi humilmente nelli Santi Sacrificii di Vostra Paternità. La qual Dio nostro Signor ci conserve et prospere siempre. De Madrid a 4 de Decembre 1593.

 Di Vostra Paternità Reverenda
  figliuolo indegno
   Roberto Personio.

Translation

Our Very Reverend Father in Christ
The peace of Christ.

I have received Your Paternity's letter of the 28th of last month[239] and have learnt from it Your Paternity's wish that Fr Oswald's coming should be postponed until Pentecost, when he will have finished his course of philosophy. I am quite content with this, and I thank Your Paternity very humbly for this fatherly care you take of these seminaries. By the favour of God, they go on growing every day, to the universal satisfaction of everybody. I left the one at Valladolid in excellent condition, in temporal matters as well as spiritual, and with regard to the fabric of the building. On the first Sunday of Advent, they began to use the new refectory for the first time: it has turned out to be a very fine and spacious room with easy accommodation for a hundred persons. Fr Rodrigo de Cabredo does very well in his post as rector and is much liked by all the scholars. The favour we all have to ask of Your Paternity is that you will not allow him to be taken away from us on any account, for it would be a great injury to this entire project of ours and we should not easily find another like him for this purpose. The one at Seville – the rector,[240] I mean – carries out his duties well, but Fr Cabredo's talents are more outstanding.

2. I have already written to Your Paternity that because Fr Simon Swinborne, who was minister at Valladolid, was run down, it was considered advisable to send him to Seville for the winter, the intention being that he should go on to Flanders for change of air in the spring if he did not find his health improved. He has carried out his duties as minister very well at Valladolid, and he could do so also at Seville. This too will remedy a slight inconvenience that was beginning to arise at Seville from the fact that a number of laymen who had known Fr Charles Tancard at the time when he was attached to the governor of the province used to seek his company in the English college afterwards; and the best way to put a stop to this would be to summon the said father to Valladolid, and there with the grace of our Lord he will do very well.

3. Fr Thomas Wright has come there also, and although his case is in suspense until Your Paternity's answer arrives, nevertheless, to avoid leaving him idle, or arousing suspicion in others, we have employed him in a course of lectures on controversies, and it is my hope that Your Paternity's answer this time will be such that he will be able to continue it, at any rate for some time, so that we can see whether he is going to change his ways. He himself is writing to Your Paternity and promises a complete change of heart, and he has promised me the same. Time will show whether this will be fulfilled; I trust in our Lord that he will be satisfactory. This case of his is still kept confidential here, and it will remain so unless Your Paternity orders otherwise.

4. I very humbly thank Your Paternity for your promise to express your appreciation to the provincials of Spain for their charity towards our nation, and to commend these seminaries to their care. It will be particularly helpful if they could be urged to receive two or three students from them in each province, seeing that with God's grace they are

---

239. I.e., October, when Acquaviva wrote about Tesimond (B203); the present letter was probably composed a few days in advance of the post of 4 December.

240. Francisco de Peralta.

going to prove very capable men in the course of time.[241] At the present moment there are two here in the seminary of Valladolid who are pressing very strongly for it; one of them is a priest who has finished his course of scholastic theology and is a very learned and virtuous man; the other has finished his course of philosophy and is more exceptionally gifted in every way than anyone else in the college. Father provincial, before he went away, promised to receive one of them at Christmas, but father vice provincial is raising objections now on the score of the material poverty of the colleges;[242] however, with a warm recommendation from Your Paternity, I hope things will all be smoothed over.

5. Fr Walpole and Fr Flack have written very heartening letters to me from the seminary of St Omers, for they say that they already have a family of more than twenty persons there, fourteen of whom are scholars, very fine little boys: and that there will be no fewer than a hundred within a year. From England the Catholics have expressed great satisfaction at having this seminary, prizing it above all others, and they assure them that there will be no lack of students. And on the other hand, I have a firm hope that temporal support will not be wanting for those whom God sends there. Here too I find that noblemen show great favour to that particular work. And so, I am sending them another 400 ducats by this post, in addition to the 300 which I sent them in August. Although it is a loan, it is from people who will not be in a hurry to ask for it to be paid back. On the other hand, I understand that Fr Holt will by now have received six months of the income appointed by the king in Flanders, which will be round about 1000 scudi, so that adding all this to the 500 ducats which I sent him at the beginning they will have more than 2000 scudi with which to make a start; and as a rule, the scholars will also always bring something along with them from England. And so it is that Your Paternity should view this work as one that is going to increase rapidly, and make plans for assisting it accordingly, rather than in its present state. They have written to me from Flanders that the Jesuit fathers there hold the view that the seminary should not be given the status of a college nor have its own rector, but a superior, *with the title of president, subject to the rector of their own college of Saint-Omer*.[243] People here, however, do not like this and wish this to be a college, independent like the one in Rome and these two in Spain, and to have its own special rector and answer directly to the provincial like the other colleges. For the other arrangement is not one that can last; on the one hand, the rector and the president will not get on together for very long; and on the other, the rector of Saint-Omer has enough to occupy him in his own college and so would necessarily fail to take proper care of this one. And so, I beg Your Paternity to consent to decide the matter now, once for all, and to recommend strongly to the provincial that he, the president, should not be subject to the rector of Saint-Omer, on account of the inconveniences that would ensue. It is true that the king in the first letters patent instructed, at my suggestion, that the allowance

---

241. Persons would like the Englishmen interested in joining the Society to be able to enter novitiates in Spain. For success in this regard, see the postscript to Persons's letter to Acquaviva of 20 March 1594 (B221).

242. The provincial of Castile was Gonzalo Dávila (away at the general congregation); the vice provincial was Francisco Galarza.

243. Christian Dalmer, rector of the Walloon Jesuit college in Saint-Omer. Evidently the chief mover here was the vice provincial, Jean d'Heur.

was to be paid to the rector of Saint-Omer, but this was only with a view to giving the business a start until such time as a rector of its own should be appointed: as soon as one was in possession, the king would change the assignment.

6. And in regard to Fr William Flack, I only asked for him to be rector for the time being, until such time as Your Paternity should give us another competent one of Belgian nationality. Fr Flack will be able to assist the latter as procurator; and I think this arrangement and combination will conduce to peace as we find by experience here. Only it is essential that the rector be a person adequate for the office, which will soon be a very important one. The assistance of Fr Flack as procurator will also be a necessary element, in order to account for funds from Spain (with which he is already familiar), and also to keep in touch afterwards with some of the scholars' parents and relations in England. And to allow Fr Flack to attend to this matter, Fr Henry Broy, another English priest who is stationed at Saint-Omer, will be able to help him in domestic matters, in which the said father is very well versed.

7. I am sorry to have wearied Your Paternity with so wordy a letter, but I wanted to give Your Paternity an account of everything, so that you might understand how matters are with us. I am not writing detailed news of the Society's affairs, because I know that others will do so and I have had only a few days in Madrid to get information about these matters. Nevertheless, Fr Francisco Rodríguez will tell Your Paternity something that I am writing to him. I have already begun to make some moves,[244] and we shall do so further as opportunity offers, and all the more readily if Your Paternity will give instructions in detail what is to be done: I have written about this to Fr Rodríguez at greater length.

8. I have been told by some here to write to Your Paternity, giving my opinion as to the effect produced by the books Fr Ribadeneira has written about affairs in England. Undoubtedly in my opinion he has helped much to enlighten people in these realms, and the said books are held in high esteem and greatly praised. I have heard that, as a consequence of a report made by a certain individual, the king gave orders that a slight change should be made in the wording of the proclamation, and this has been done and all is satisfactorily arranged. I think it would cheer Fr Ribadeneira very much if Your Paternity were to thank him for his labours in this connection. And now I have nothing further to say except to commend myself humbly to Your Paternity's holy sacrifices. May God our Lord ever preserve and prosper us. From Madrid on the 4th of December 1593.

 Your Reverend Paternity's
  unworthy son
   Robert Persons.

B211 From Claudio Acquaviva, Rome, 20 December 1593

 SOURCE: ARSI, Tolet. 5/I, fol. 325r.
 NOTE: This bears reference mainly to the matters raised in Persons's letter of 2 November (B204): the discontents of Fr Thomas Wright and Br Fabrizio Como, Persons's *socius*.

---

244. I.e., in the Society's interests at court. On Rodríguez, Acquaviva's secretary, see the headnote to his (lost) letter to Persons of 13 February 1594.

Que es de particular consuelo las buenas nuevas que vienen de los seminarios[245] etc. Que el P. Osvaldo se le embiará en acabando el Curso que será para la Pentecoste, etc. En lo del Padre Tomas Urit[246] me contento de esperar la prueva de Vuestra Reverencia plegue a Dios salga mejor que hasta aqui porque sin duda el sugeto será dificil de amoldar.

En lo del Hermano Fabricio tambien me place que se quede aý pues está ya más quieto etc. En los sanctos sacrificios etc.

Translation

The good news that has come about the seminaries is of particular comfort, etc. That Fr Oswald will be sent there after completing his course at Pentecost. In the case of Fr Thomas Wright, I am content to wait for Your Reverence's confirmation: may it please God that he turns out better than before, because without doubt the matter will be difficult to set right.

As for Brother Fabrizio, I would also be pleased if he stays there, because he has quietened down, etc. To your holy sacrifices, etc.

B212 From Richard Cowling, Rome, 29 December 1593

SOURCE: ABSI, *Coll M* 138 (olim 109), Grene's notes.

NOTE: Richard Cowling (1562/3–1617/8) was the younger brother of William (Anstruther, 91; cf. McCoog, *English and Welsh Jesuits*, 142, *sub* Collins). He corresponded frequently with Persons, whom he would have met at the time of his ordination in Rome in August 1587. He entered the Society in Tournai in 1588 and remained in Flanders as minister at Lille until transferred to Rome. Earlier in the year Persons had suggested he be posted to Lisbon or Spain (see his letters to Acquaviva, 16 June and 15 July, B187, B190).

Richardus Coulinus scribit Roma ex Paenitentiaria ad P. Personium, Vallisoletum 29 Decembris 1593 proponens magnum suum desiderium Missioni Anglicanae vel Scotiae quam ambit, nihilque obstare nisi officium quo fung^r in Paenitentiaria.

Translation

Richard Cowling writes to Fr Persons at Valladolid from the penitentiary in Rome, 29 December 1593, setting forth his great desire to join the English or Scottish mission and entreating him to grant it; there was nothing standing in the way except his duties at the penitentiary.

---

245. las buenas nuevas ... los seminarios] *underlined* R
246. lo del Padre Tomas Urit] *underlined* R

B213 From Richard Verstegan, Antwerp, 13 January 1594

SOURCE: ABSI (formerly Stonyhurst), Coll B 151–154 (153 misnumbered 155), holograph, headed "Verstingames advises."

EDITION: Petti, 203–207.

NOTE: This despatch includes a personal note in the penultimate paragraph, warning Persons against the informer Roger Walton. It contains news about the imminent arrival of the archduke, military developments in the Netherlands, the execution of Hesketh, the imprisonment and release of the Catholic composer Peter Philips, and the supposed death of John Aylmer, bishop of London.

At Antwerp the 13 of January 1594.

The Archduke Ernestus we heare is at Trevers, and is expected at Bruxells the 20 of this moneth at the furthest; the Countes of Mansfeild and Fuentes are gon to mete[247] and to receave him.[248]

We heare that the towne of Covorden in Friesland is gotten againe, and so is also a forte which the enemy lately tooke by Bruges, which forte the enemy abandoned of himself.[249]

Uppon Christmas eve by extreme tempest 35 sailes of shippes with 600 mariners lying at ancor in Holland and attending the wynde to passe towardes Spaine were sunck and all the men drowned.[250] And we heare that aboute 60 saile are lost in the river of Burdeaux by tempest also.

The Counte Charles of Mansfeild is either departed from thease partes or presentely to departe towardes the frontiers of France with 8 or 10 thowsand men which perhapes Navarr expected not so soone, when he brake the truce now a fewe dayes past, for the enemy is well acquainted with Spanish delayes and dothe make his profitt of them, thoughe now by this extraordinary expedition I hope he wilbe deceaved.[251]

The States of Holland have sent an ambassador (whose name is Calovort and hathe a brother in this towne a broker unto the marchantes) unto the pretended King of Navarr to encourage him to maintaine that religion which in his harte and conscience he holdeth to be true, and he shall not want any assistance that they or any freindes of their can yeild him.

247. mete] *followed by* him [*deleted*] A
248. Archduke Ernest of Austria (1553–20 February 1595) replaced Pierre Ernst, count of Mansfeld (1517–1604), as governor-general of the Spanish Netherlands; in turn he was succeeded by Don Pedro Henríquez de Acevedo, count of Fuentes (1525–1610).
249. Coeverden, captured by the Dutch in September 1592, in fact held out against the Spanish commander in Friesland, Francisco Verdugo (1537–1595), until he withdrew in May 1594. Philip of Nasau led an unsuccessful Dutch attack on Bruges (Petti, 206 nn2–3).
250. Between forty and fifty ships were lost at Vlye, in the West Frisian islands, and about five hundred men drowned (Petti, 201 n10).
251. Count Charles was the son of Count Ernst of Mansfeld, under instructions from Philip II to assist the Catholic League in France against Henry of Navarre; Charles's forces took La Capelle in May 1594 (Petti, 201 n14).

By the last letters which arryved here from England beeing of the 12 of December one writeth to his frend as a Protestant thus: Thinges in Scotland do stand so ill that we heere have no will to talke of them nor I desyre to write of them, for that they seeme to stand enclyned to great trooble and to great alteration.

There was one Mr[252] Hesket executed aboute a month past, of whome there hathe gon so many variable reportes that untill I see some letters from particular freindes I can write litle certainty.[253] The mans name was Richard Hesket; he had bene somtyme a marchant, but was fallne in decay by dealing with Alcumistes. He was for some fewe monethes of Sir William Stanleys regiment, and by him as is thought sent with some message to the presente Earle of Darby, but whether he were by him detected or not, is uncertaine, for some reporte that the Earle is deprived of his liberty, but the said Hesket seemed to die a Protestant, and said he was sory that he had bene so long of our religion; and yf this be true and that he ment as he spake, there is no great losse of the man unlesse he had bene honester. He was there called by the name of the Cardinalls coosin for he was of those Heskets of Lancashire, and nere kin unto Mr Thomas Hesket nephew unto his grace.[254]

Peter Philippes the musitian that was prisoner in Holland is delivered and arryved here now at Christmas; he told me how one Roger Walton somtyme page unto the Earle of Northumberland that was slaine in the towre, beeing at Middelbourg caused him to be apprehended and accused him of many notable treasons before the counsell at The Hage whether they were bothe sent, all his accusations beeing such markable fixions of his owne hed as they[255] were soone discovered by the counsell who by the testimony of certaine Italian marchants (that to have his company and musick[256] perswaded him to that Jorney) were fully satisfied that he came not thether to passe into England to kill the Queene as the other affirmed: and he proved Phillipes intension thereto in this sorte, *videlicet*, that beeing some yeares past in Paris, when the Baricades were made, there was an Image made of the Queene of England and set uppon a great heape of fagots, and the king and all sorts of religious men coming in procession with burning wax candells did give fyre to those fagots, and so did the Lord Paget, Sir Charles Arundell and all the English, amonge whome this Peeter Phillipes was one. At this, Phillipes replyed that there was

---

252. Mr] *interlined with caret A*
253. certainty] *Petti; possibly* certainly *A*
254. Thomas Hesketh was related to William Cardinal Allen and took his surname after the cardinal's death (Acquaviva to Persons, 24 October 1594, B247). His uncle Richard Hesketh was executed on 29 November 1593 for approaching the earl of Derby about the succession to the throne; the earl, Ferdinando Stanley, Lord Strange, who succeeded his father Henry on 25 September 1593, handed him over to the Privy Council. It was alleged that Holt and Persons were scheming to promote the Derby claim in the Catholic interest. See McCoog, *Building the Faith of St Peter*, 149, and Petti, 200 n8, citing a letter from Holt to Allen, 6 January 1594, in John Strype, *Annals of the Reformation* (Oxford, 1824), 4: 206–208. Edwards, 146–147, conjectures that Burghley may have induced John Cecil to lure Persons into pursuing an interest in Lord Strange (Persons to Cecil, 13 April 1591, headnote).
255. as they] *interlined with caret A*
256. and musick] *interlined with caret A*

never any such thing don, and that the king at the making of the Baricades fled oute of Paris, and therefore went not in precession in Paris, and that such a publyke acte must nedes have many wittnesses besydes Walton. At this answere the Counsell began to looke one at another, and Walton in a great chaf said in English unto Phillipes: O Papist, Papist,[257] yf I had the in England I would make shorte woorck with the. Why, quoth the other, what would you do? Marry, quothe Walton, I would aske the yf the Queene were supreame head of the Churche or not, and what wouldes thow answere to that? I would, quoth Phillipes, say she were not. Then would I hange the, quothe Walton. Hereupon[258] Phillipes asked of the counsell yf they did understand what Walton had said. They said, no, but willed him to tell them. Then did he tell it[259] them in Dutche, whereunto their president for the tyme (for they change often) replyed that he knew well enoughe what the justice of England was, but it should not be so theare.[260] Then did one Gilpen who now is ambassador with the States in Bodleys place (for that Bodley is in England expecting Walsingams place) aske Phillipes yf he had not bene at confession with the Jesuytes. He answered, ye. Then said Gilpen, you were enjoyned to kill the Queene, for whosoever cometh to confession to them they do so enjoyne. But notwithstanding Phillipes answered them well to every thing and the litle proof they had against him, they detayned him untill letters came from England to certify bothe of him and of Walton, of whome the Earle of Essex wrote that of Philipes they never understood other then that he had followed his soorte of musyck, and for Walton that he was a poore fellow and had nothing els to live by but by such meanes. And by other letters it was signified that Walton did in England make an occupation of accusing men, and that he had brought 5 or 6 to the gallowes, as he would have don Phillipes yf he had had him there and the assistance of Topclif, which is not lyke he could have wanted.

Phillipes was in the end discharged, as is said, and Walton is yet in prison, and hathe bene racked aboute the cyphers that he had with Mr Paget. And it seemeth that, notwithstanding the counsell of Holland are ill enoughe themselves, yet they do abhorre such wounderfull monsters as our country in thease dayes dothe yeild; for many such compagnions do play their partes in England. And because this fellow was so discovered by heretykes themselves for a false accuser, I thought it not impertinent to write so much of this matter, which peradventure may serve to some purpose.[261]

    257. Papist, Papist] *interlined, replacing* Traitor, Traitor [*deleted*] A
    258. Hereupon] *this ed.;* hereunpon *A Petti*
    259. it] *interlined with caret A*
    260. that he knew ... it should not be so theare] *underlined A*
    261. Peter Philips was organist at the English College, Rome, until 1585, when he joined the entourage of Thomas Lord Paget (Persons to Hoffaeus, 6 June 1587; A214); see Lionel Pike (*ODNB*) and Petti, "Peter Philips, Composer and Organist, 1561–1628," *Recusant History* 4, no. 2 (1957): 48–60. Roger Walton was sent to France as Walsingham's agent in 1588, operating there and in the Netherlands for several years. Verstegan refers here to Henry Percy, eighth earl of Northumberland (d. 21 June 1585); the barricades erected in Paris on 12 May 1588; Sir Charles Arundell (d. 15 December 1587); Thomas Bodley, agent to the States General 1589–1596; his deputy George Gilpin (ca. 1514–1602); and Robert Devereux, earl of Essex (Petti, 206–207 nn9–17).

My Lord of Westmerland his wyf is dead in England. Elmar, whome Martin Marprelate used to call John a London is dead also.[262]

[*Addressed:*] Al Padre Personio.

[*Endorsed by Persons:*] Verstengham advises, 13 Jan. 1594.

B214 From Claudio Acquaviva, Rome, 17 January 1594

SOURCE: ARSI, Tolet. 5/II, fol. 326v.

NOTE: Acquaviva sympathizes with Persons's desire to keep Fr Cabredo as rector at Valladolid and repeats his assurance that Persons should use his own discretion with the difficult members in his community, especially Thomas Wright.

P. Roberto Personio, Enero 17.

Recevi la de Vuestra Reverencia escrita a 4 de Deciembre, y Vuestra Reverencia no dude sino que aora y siempre terné yo el cuydado que hasta aqui he tenido de ayudar las cosas desos Seminarios, esto digo por lo mucho que Vuestra Reverencia insta en que no le quitemos al Padre Cabredo,[263] yo le tengo por muy bien empleado en lo que haçe, y gusto de que en ello dé tanta satisfaction como Vuestra Reverencia dice.

En lo demas que toca a la disposiçion de los sujetos, yo me remito al parecer de Vuestra Reverencia como en otra le escrivi. Prueve con el Padre Tomaso, que no hara poco si lo saca qual conviene para quedar en la Compañia.

Translation

To Fr Robert Persons, 17 January.

I have received Your Reverence's letter of 4 December. Your Reverence can rest assured of the care which I have now, and always have held until now, to help the affairs of those seminaries; I say this because Your Reverence so often urges us not to remove Fr Cabredo. I consider him very well employed in his present occupation, and it pleases me that he gives as much satisfaction in that as Your Reverence expresses.

For the rest, as regards the attitude of those who are in your charge, I leave it to Your Reverence's judgement, as I wrote in my previous letter. Keep trying with Fr Thomas: it will be no small thing if you can find some suitable way to keep him in the Society.

B215 To Claudio Acquaviva, Madrid, 30 January 1594

SOURCE: Acquaviva to Persons, 14 March 1594 (B220).

NOTE: Persons, responding to Acquaviva's letter of 20 December (B211), changed his mind about exchanging Holt in Flanders for Creswell in Spain (McCoog, *Building the Faith of St Peter*, 234).

---

262. Jane Howard, daughter of Henry Howard, earl of Surrey, married Westmorland before 1564. John Aylmer, bishop of London from 1577, died only in June 1594.

263. no le quitemos al Padre Cabredo] *underlined* R

B216 From Claudio Acquaviva, Rome, 2 February 1594

SOURCE: ARSI, Hisp. 76, fol. 10r–v.

NOTE: The general entrusts Persons with the delicate brief of persuading the king to delay the return of Acosta to Spain until after the return of the Jesuits from the congregation. He asks him to work in concert with the Jesuits Diego de Avellaneda and Francisco Antonio (1535–1610), the empress Maria of Austria, and a cardinal, possibly Rodrigo de Castro, archbishop of Seville.

Unfortunately, Persons only received a copy of this letter in mid-April, too late to prevent Acosta's return later that month (Persons to Acquaviva, 18 April, B226). On Acosta's return and subsequent career, see Astrain, 3: 606–612. In the meantime, Persons had an important audience with the king on 6 February and travelled to Seville soon after writing to Acquaviva on 10 March.

P. Roberto Personio, 2 de hebrero 1594.

Aunque entiendo que Vuestra Reverencia terna alguna notiçia de las muchas cosas que aquí hemos passado con el Padre Acosta es cierto que ellas son más de las que alla se havran podido saber, pero a su tiempo las entendera especialmente quando quiera Dios que estos Padres con bien lleguen por alla. Ultimamente despues de la Congregaçion él me ha hablado ofreçiendose con indiferençia para lo que yo determinase de su persona y para volver o no volver a España, aunque bien se puede sospechar hara por alla ofiçios contrarios a esta indiferençia, pues aún acá dice y haçe al contrario de lo que conmigo mostro. Yo le respondi que creia sentiria Su Magestad que no voluiese a España, pero que pues él se ofreçia a todo lo que dél determinasemos, se consideraria.

Será necessario que Vuestra Reverencia hable con Su Magestad en nombre de la Compañia y le diga que por hallarse muchos inconvenientes en que él torne a esas Provincias, le suplica se sirva de oyr sobre ello[264] a estos Padres deputados de la Congregaçion para informar a Su Magestad,[265] y contentarse que en el entretanto que ellos llegan, y Su Magestad los oye, le entretengamos por acá, esperando su respuesta y resoluçion. Las raçones que Vuestra Reverencia de presente le podra alegar seran, que los nuestros de la Congregaçion han quedado tan escandalizados de su modo de proçeder, que sentirian gravemente que tornase por alla. Lo otro que si no vuelve a su govierno será para él y sus fautores ocasion de muchas quejas, y si torna superior, será de grande ofension y desconsuelo para esas Provincias y más para los sujetos que governare, demas de que como por acá de su parte ha[266] hecho entre los nuestros ofiçios bastantes para perturbar la paz y union, es de creer que por alla los continuará con grave daño de la paz y quietud de esas Provincias[267] y en general le puede certificar que en este particular de volver o no a esas Provincias ay cosas de tanto peso, que obligan a que Su Magestad a lo menos se sirva de

---

264. sobre ello] *supplied in margin* R
265. deputados de la Congregaçion para informar a Su Magestad] *supplied in margin, replacing* que mas por entero le podran informar (who will be able to inform you more in detail) R
266. ha] *followed by* su, *possibly deleted* R
267. demas de que como por acá ... con grave daño de la paz y quietud de esas Provincias] *supplied in margin* R

suspender hasta que llegados estos Padres los oyga. Y si acaso Su Magestad respondiere que Vuestra Reverencia le dé memorial, o le remitiere a otro con quien aya de negoçiar le diga que en esto no se pretende proceder con memoriales, ni por intermedias personas, si no solo entender su voluntad para executarla y acudir a todo lo que nos mandare: y que si no obstante lo que Vuestra Reverencia le representa todavia Su Magestad manda que este Padre vuelva luego *etiam* antes de esperar la llegada destos Padres, que luego le embiare:

Vuestra Reverencia procure breve respuesta de Su Magestad y me avise della, y aunque podra comunicar lo que aqui le escrivo con el Padre Rector, con el Padre Avellaneda,[268] y con el Padre Francisco Antonio a quien escrivo que sobre lo mesmo hable con la emperatriz, será conveniente que Vuestra Reverencia y los demas que lo supieren procedan con todo secreto. En sus &c.

Translation

To Fr Robert Persons, 2 February 1594.

Although I understand that Your Reverence will have some news of many things that have happened here with Fr Acosta, you can be sure that they are more than you could have known there, but you will learn them in time, especially when God wills that those fathers arrive there safely. Finally, after the congregation, he talked to me – making a show of indifference – offering to defer to my decision about his future, whether or not he should return to Spain. Still, one could well suspect that over there he would act contrary to that indifference;[269] indeed, even here he says and does differently from what he has indicated to me. I answered him that I believed that His Majesty would be sorry if he did not return to Spain, but that because he was in agreement with all the decisions that we made, [my decision] could be reconsidered.

It will be necessary for Your Reverence to speak to His Majesty on behalf of the Society and tell him that there are many disadvantages if he should return to those provinces. Beg him to be pleased to listen to those fathers deputed by the congregation to inform His Majesty and be satisfied. In the meantime, until they arrive, and His Majesty hears them, we will keep [Fr Acosta] busy for the present, awaiting [the king's] response and decision. The reasons which Your Reverence presents could make the claim that Ours of the congregation have been so scandalized by his mode of procedure that they would regard it as a serious problem if he should return over there. On the other hand, if he does not return to his position, there will be occasion for many complaints among his supporters; and if he returns as superior, there will be great offence and dissatisfaction among those provinces and more among the subjects he governs: furthermore, since he for his part has done quite enough over here amongst Ours to disturb the peace and unity, it is likely that over there he should continue with grave injury to the peace and quiet of those provinces. And in general, you can assure him that in this particular matter, to return or not to those provinces, there are such weighty considerations, which should

268. con el Padre Avellaneda] *supplied in margin* R
269. "Indifference" is a key term in Jesuit decision-making: to be free of inordinate attachments which could sway the decision.

persuade His Majesty at least to allow himself to wait until he can listen to those fathers when they arrive. And in case His Majesty answers that Your Reverence should provide a memorial, or refers you to another with whom to speak about the matter, explain that you do not intend to proceed with memorials, nor through intermediaries, but only to learn [what is] his will to put in execution and to perform what he has commanded: and that, if despite Your Reverence's representations, His Majesty orders that that father should return right now rather than await the arrival of those fathers, I will send him then.

Would Your Reverence obtain a brief response from His Majesty and advise me about it, and although you can communicate what I am writing here to father rector, to Fr Avellaneda, and to Fr Francisco Antonio,[270] to whom I am writing that he should talk on the same matter to the empress, it will be convenient for Your Reverence and the rest who know about it to proceed with all secrecy. To your holy sacrifices, etc.

B217 From Francisco Rodríguez, Frascati, 15 February 1594

> SOURCE: Persons to Acquaviva, 18 April (B226).
> NOTE: The subject of this letter is unknown; in his letter of 18 April, Persons merely notes that Rodríguez (ca. 1548–1627), Acquaviva's secretary, wrote it in the general's presence. Rodríguez handled much of Acquaviva's day-to-day business.

B218 Despatches on behalf of Philip II, 24 February 1594

> SOURCE: ABSI, Coll P I 248.
> HICKS: 219–220.
> NOTE: Grene records (Coll P II 477): "Anno 1594. Nullam epistolam invenio praeterquam quod habes fol. 248. a," and (Coll P I 248): "The following letter or account is copyed also out of F. Persons own hand wryting."
> This is an incomplete copy of the despatches which Persons made, on the king's behalf, about monetary arrangements for the colleges and the Bridgettine nuns. There is a dispute with Mendoza, Philip's ambassador in Paris, over the funds for Rheims and the Bridgettines. The funding for St Omers was now to come from levies at the port of Gravelines. The king also wrote to the bishop, governor, and magistracy of Saint-Omer to favour the new seminary there. Further details and developments on the funding of Rheims and St Omers are given in Persons's letter to Acquaviva, 10 March (B219). On the early days at Saint-Omer, see Leo Hicks, "The Foundation of the College of St Omers," *AHSI* 19 (1950): 146–180.
> From the king, Persons obtained an annuity for the English Bridgettines, who were about to transfer their convent to Lisbon. The Bridgettine community at Syon Abbey fled

270. Acquaviva's letter to Antonio follows immediately: "From Fr Persons Your Reverence should understand what to negotiate with His Majesty. I would like, truly on my part, that Your Reverence speak to the Infanta and entreat her that in this particular she speak with the Cardinal and that he arrange that in this he favour and aid us, as a matter of great import to the Society, as a matter which for the same and for the attendant consequences, will be of great advantage to the Society, if it should turn out as he desires, and of grave offence and harm if it does not succeed as we intend" (fol. 11r).

England in 1559 and migrated to and from various localities in the Netherlands until it settled in Rouen in 1580. Following the success of Henry of Navarre against the Catholic League in 1593–1594, they decided, under the newly elected abbess, Elizabeth Hart (d. 1609), to relocate to Lisbon, where they arrived on 20 May 1594. See Ann M. Hutchison, "Transplanting the Vineyard: Syon Abbey 1539–1861," in *Der Birgittenorden in der Frühen Neuzeit/The Bridgettine Order in Early Modern Europe* (Frankfurt, 1998), 79–107, esp. 97–98. See also Elizabeth Perry, "Petitioning for Patronage: An Illuminated Tale of Exile from Syon Abbey, Lisbon," in *The English Convents in Exile, 1600–1800: Communities, Culture and Identity*, ed. Caroline Bowden and James E. Kelly (Farnham, Surrey, 2013), 159–174, esp. 160–164.

Persons's interest in the Bridgettines probably dated from the time of Campion's arrest at Lyford Grange, where some of the nuns were resident, and would have been strengthened during his sojourn in Rouen when they enjoyed the patronage of John Leslie, bishop of Ross. Soon after their arrival in Lisbon, Persons wrote a Preface to *Relacion que embiaron las religiosas del Monesterio de Sion de Inglaterra, que estavan en Roan de Francia* (Madrid, 1594), based on information from the community's confessor general, Seth Forster (d. 1628), and materials collected with the aid of Sir Francis Englefield; the preface was subsequently translated into Spanish and included in Yepes, *Historia particular de la persecucion de Inglaterra*, 714–722. The English text can be found in "A Preface, Written by Father Robert Parsons, S.J., to the History of the Wanderings of Syon: From a Manuscript Preserved at Syon Abbey, Chudleigh," by Dom Adam Hamilton in *The Angel of Syon: The Life and Martyrdom of Blessed Richard Reynolds, Bridgettine Monk of Syon, Martyred at Tyburn, May 4, 1535* (Edinburgh, 1905), 97–113. See Ann M. Hutchison, "Syon Abbey Preserved: Some Historians of Syon," in *Syon Abbey and its Books: Reading, Writing, and Religion ca. 1400–1700*, ed. Alexandra Walsham and E. A. Jones (Woodbridge, Suffolk, 2010), 228–251, esp. 239–244.

The despatches which His Majesty hath commanded to be made
for the Seminaries of Rhemes and of St Omers
and for the nunns of Sion 24 February 1594.

After much adoe to make cleere the accompts of Rhemes what is owing to them and from what time, we have brought the time back from the last of May 1591 (unto what time upon D. Bernardinos words these yeares past the kings officers heer would needes force us to accept the pay) unto the end of October 1590, and this we have gotten at last under D. Bernardino's own hand, so as therin we have gotten 7 months which import us as good as 1200 crownes. Since which time one yeares pay only hath bin made by Tho. Fiesco[271] so as there is due the pay of other two yeares ended in October last 93: for which mony His Majesty hath promised out of hand to give us our librança,[272] when it shal be payd without delay and securely though he have not yet assigned wherin: but this day Don Juan[273]

---

271. Factor general of the Hazienda, responsible for disbursements in the Spanish Netherlands: see Persons to Acquaviva, 12 August 1592 (B153).

272. Order of payment.

273. Don Juan de Idiáquez, the king's secretary of state.

hath assured me that within these 4 daies I shal have it sure and sounde so as it may goe with the first extraordinary.

About the nunns of Sion we have had an other stirre also with D. Bernardino who sheweth heer acquittance of theirs of the 14 of May 1591,[274] which acknowledgeth that they are payd of all ordinary and extraordinary due to them from His Majesty until the last of May past[275] — two yeares pay His Majesty hath promised also presently, and if there be any error in this accompt, let the nunns informe &c. —

As for the pension granted to the Seminary of St Omers: after long toyle and much contradiction made, as well by — as also by the President[276] &c. — God almighty hath given as good a despatch, as we could desire, for in steede of 1920 ducats which the king assigned us before upon uncertain licences for the maintenance of 16 scholars, now the king hath appointed 2000 crownes of gold to be setled payd and receaved of the first and surest money of the —— passaportes of all kinde of merchandize that enter att Gravelin which passaports are rented in that towne for the present at above 10,000 crownes a yeare and if at any time they should faile, it is setled upon the surest and readiest rent that the king hath in Flanders. All this is granted by the king and the minute given to the Secretarie to be drawn-out, wherin the matter is earnestly commended to Ernestus:[277] and besides this three other letters are written by the king to the Bishop, Governor & magistrats of St Omers to protect and favour the Seminary as a thing principally esteemed and loved by His Majesty. Order also is given to pay presently all arrerages from the date of the kings first letters which are of the 13 of March 1593 &c. — which shal goe also by the next extraordinary.

B219 To Claudio Acquaviva, Madrid, 10 March 1594

SOURCE: ARSI, Hisp. 136, fols. 245–246.

HICKS: 221–227, with English translation.

NOTE: Persons elaborates on the funding of St Omers and Rheims (cf. the despatches of 24 February, B218): by order of the king, the arrears for Rheims has been made up and the limit on the number of students at Saint-Omer has been removed. He asks whether Cardinal Allen should proceed to Flanders, given the dispute with the local authorities in Saint-Omer. He plans to send Acquaviva a Latin translation of part of *Conference about the Next Succession*, a book he had already compiled but did not publish until early in 1595.

Although the king seemed, at an audience on 6 February, very favourable to the position Persons held on the Society, Persons was dismayed to learn that the Spanish ministers had acted very differently during the general congregation in Rome. He hopes that his discussions with the king will change their approach.

274. This seems to be in error for 1593; the date "14" is obscure, possibly "24." Bernardino de Mendoza resigned as Spanish ambassador to France in 1591.

275. Grene notes: "*aliquot lineas hic omitto circa rationes hasce*" (Here I omit several lines relating to the reasons for this).

276. On the insistence that the English seminary at Saint-Omer be a mere hostel with a president, under the rector of the Walloon Jesuit college, see Persons's letter to Acquaviva, 4 December 1593 (B210).

277. See the letter from Henry Walpole, Saint-Omer, 13 November 1593 (B206), n225.

Molto Reverendo in Christo padre nostro
Pax Christi.

1. Con l'ordinario passato, non scrissi a Vostra Paternità per le occupationi que haveva et perché non hebbi risolutione delli mei negotii alhora, ma dipoi Sua Maestà me dette dispacho di alcune cose di quelle che trattava, particularmente per il seminario de Sant'Omer s'ha havuto buon ordine poiché in luogo di 1920 ducati de diece reali, che Sua Maestà c'haveva assignato prima, adesso con la contradittione che ci nacque, Sua Maestà ha determinato de darci 2000 scudi d'oro in oro, et questi si son assignati sopra li passaporti di Gravelinga che vagliono diece mille scudi l'anno, et quando questi mancassero s'han de pagar degli migliori et più certi denari ch'il Re tiene in Fiandra, et più di questo ha ordinato il Re ch'il numero delli scolari non sia limitato come quelli di Sant Omer volevano, si non che s'admettino tutti quelli che si possino sustentar a giudicio delli padri della Compagna a cui cargo commanda Sua Maestà che questo seminario sia come vedrà Vostra Paternità presto per la copia della detta letera del Rey la qual farò traduire de Francese in Spañolo et la mandarò a Vostra Paternità. Dipiù di questa letra al Archiduca, scrive ancora Sua Maestà molto caldamente in favor deste Seminario al Vescovo, governatore et magistrato di Sant Omer, per tre litere separate, de manera che con questo pienso quel Seminario restarà assicurato, per molto servigio di nostro Señor.

2. Più di questo, m'ha dato qui una cedula real Su Maestà sobre el banco delli Malvendi per pagar in Anversa 4000 scudi d'oro subito al Seminario de Rhemis, per quello che se li deve per l'elemosina ordinaria di Sua Maestà per duoi anni passati, et credo che non serà difficultà ni dilatione nella paga, et con questi dinari respiraranno quelli di Rhemis per alcun tempo, et considerate le difficultà del tempo presente in materia di dinari, pare a tutti che Iddio c'ha aiutato molto in procurar tal summa insieme, benché non senza molti travagli et fatighe.

3. Altre cose ancora di manco importanza m'han dispachato, con le quali voy contento a Seviglia, benché non habbino fatto tanto come io desiderava, massimamente nelle cose publice, ma si ha da pigliare quello che si può. La determinatione d'andar o non andar el Cardinale nostro Alano a Flandes (la qual cosa ci par qui di molta importanza) si rimette a trattar et concludere costì fra Sua Santità et l'ambassiatore et il medessimo Cardinale. Dell'altre cose si trattarà quando io tornarò da Seviglia che sarà per la grazia de nostro Signor, nel principio de Maggio, et alhora mandarò a Vostra Paternità la parte del libro della Succession d'Inghilterra, che si va traducendo, et *si quid aliud erit dignum* etc.

4. Io haveva pensado di scriver una vuolta un poco distesamente quello che passò fra Sua Maestà et mi, in una audienza larga et molto grata che Sua Maestà me dette alli 6 di Febraio, al qual tempo parlai assai largamente a Su Maestà sopra le cose della Compagnia le quali cose tutte contai al Padre rector di questo Collegio et a nissun altro et può essere che Sua Reverentia n'habbia scritto qualche cosa a Vostra Paternità ma io non le scrissi parte perché erano quasi le medessime cose che altre volte haveva trattato con Sua Maestà, et scritto a Vostra Paternità; cioè, per quante vie et modi la Compagnia serviva et desiderava servire a Sua Maestà, et quanto importava al mismo servigio di Sua Maestà che da vero favorisse a la Compagnia, parte ancora perché stando io con speranza per causa delle buonissime risposte et promesse che Sua Maestà me dette, che si pigliarebbe altro camino con la Compagnia, sopragionse la nuova delle cose che passavano costì per

suoi ministri nelli nigotii della Compagnia, le quali per confessar la verità, mi diminuò molto la detta speranza, benché dall'altra parte considero che coteste cose di Roma si di qua[278] uscirono, fu avanti che questa corte ricevese la sodisfattione della Compagnia che adesso confessano haver ricevuto, de maniera che da cui inanzi si può sperar altra forma di procedere.

Una cosa me disse claramente Sua Magestad che nel nigotio del hospite[279] di Jesus del Monte et altri simili, egli mai hebbe animo di patrocinar ni di favorir, si non che la Compagnia procedesse conforme a sue regule et instituto con tutta libertà, et questo poi lo mantenette nel caso del hospite come Vostra Paternità haverà saputo.

Ni tengo altro che scrivere per adesso si non raccomandarme molto humilmente nelli Santi Sacrificii di Vostra Paternità. Da Madrid alli 10 de Marzo 1594.

    Di Vostra Paternità Reverendissima
        figliuolo indegno
            Rob. Personio.

[PS] Di mattina spero poterme partir per Seviglia da dove scriverò a Vostra Paternitá. Il Padre Osvaldo espettaremo che venga immediatamente da Sicilia a Seviglia come Vostra Paternità ci promesse la prima vuolta si halla buona commodità di passagio.

[Endorsed:] – Al molto R^{do} in Ch^{to} Padre nostro il Padre Claudio Aquaviva preposito Generale della Compagnia di [Giesu], Roma. [with summary of contents]

Translation

Our Very Reverend Father in Christ
The peace of Christ.

1. I omitted to write to Your Paternity by the last post,[280] because I was much occupied and also because my negotiations were still in progress. Afterwards, however, His Majesty concluded some of the matters with which I was dealing and in particular a good settlement has been made for the seminary of St Omers for instead of the 1920 ducats of 10 reales each, which His Majesty had assigned to us in the first instance, now, in view of the opposition that is springing up, His Majesty has decided to give us 2000 golden crowns in gold. This is charged on the dues of Gravelines, which are worth ten thousand crowns a year; and if these should fail, it is to be paid out of the best-secured and most reliable funds that the king possesses in Flanders. Besides this, the king has given orders that the number of scholars is not to be limited, as the authorities of Saint-Omer wanted, but that all who can be supported should be admitted, according to the judgement of the fathers of the Society to whose care this seminary is committed by the command of the king. All this Your Paternity will see shortly in the copy of the king's letter, which I shall have translated from French into Spanish and shall send to Your Paternity. Besides this letter to the archduke,[281] His Majesty is writing very warmly in favour of this seminary to

    278. si di qua] *interlined* R
    279. hospite] *identified as* [Bartolomé de] Sicilia, *interlined* R
    280. Presumably mid-February, since Persons had previously written on 30 January.
    281. Archduke Ernst of Austria, governor of the Spanish Netherlands, January 1594–February 1595.

the bishop, the governor, and the magistracy of Saint-Omer in three separate letters: consequently, I think that this seminary will be in a secure position to do great service for our Lord.[282]

2. In addition to this, His Majesty has given me here a royal warrant on the Bank of Malvendi to draw 4000 crowns in Antwerp immediately for the seminary at Rheims, in lieu of what is owing to them of His Majesty's customary alms for the last two years. I do not think there will be any difficulty or delay in getting payment; and with this money in hand those at Rheims will breathe again for some little time. Considering the present financial difficulties, all are agreed that God has helped us very greatly in obtaining such a sum as this all at one time: though it was not procured without much wearisome effort.

3. Other matters also of less importance have been concluded and accordingly I am going to Seville contented, though they have not done all I desired, especially as regards public affairs; but one must take what one can get. The decision whether our Cardinal Allen should go or not go to Flanders, which to us here seems a very important matter, is left to be debated and decided by His Holiness and the ambassador and the cardinal himself in Rome. Other matters are to be dealt with when I come back from Seville, which by the grace of our Lord will be at the beginning of May; and I shall send Your Paternity the portion of *The Book of the Succession of England* which is in course of being translated, and if there is anything else worth telling, etc.

4. I had intended some time or other to write in rather more detail about what passed between His Majesty and me at a long and very agreeable audience which His Majesty granted me on the 6th of February. On that occasion, I spoke to His Majesty at considerable length about the affairs of the Society. All these things I recounted to father rector of this college and to no one else. It may be that His Reverence has written something on the subject to Your Paternity, but I omitted to write to you, partly because the matters treated with His Majesty were much the same as I had dealt with on other occasions and written about to Your Paternity: namely, the many ways and means by which the Society was serving and was desirous to serve His Majesty, and how important it was in the interests of His Majesty's service itself that he should genuinely give his support to the Society; partly also because, while I was still in hopes – thanks to the very favourable response and promises which I had received from His Majesty – that a different course would be adopted with the Society, to my consternation news arrived of what was being transacted over there by his ministers as regards its affairs, and, truth to tell, it greatly diminished the hopes I have mentioned: although on the other hand I believe that if those transactions in Rome had their source here, it was before this court had received the vindication of the Society which they now acknowledge: and so henceforward we may hope that different methods of procedure will be adopted.

There was one thing which His Majesty told me plainly, namely that in the affair of the guest at Jesus del Monte and others like him he never had any intention of giving his countenance or support, but wished the Society to proceed in the matter with complete freedom in accordance with its rules and institute, and I know that he after-

---

282. This paragraph summarizes the despatches of 24 February. The bishop of Saint-Omer was Jean de Vernois, OP (in office 1591–1599).

wards persisted in this course in the case of the guest, as Your Paternity will have heard.[283]

And now I have no more to say, except to commend myself very humbly to Your Paternity's holy sacrifices. From Madrid on the 10th of March 1594.

    Your Paternity's
        unworthy son
            Robert Persons.

[PS] In the morning I hope to be able to leave for Seville. I shall write to Your Paternity from there. We shall expect Fr Oswald to come from Sicily to Seville immediately, as Your Paternity promised us, as soon as a good opportunity occurs for the crossing.[284]

B220 From Claudio Acquaviva, Rome, 14 March 1594

SOURCE: ARSI, Tolet. 5/II, fol. 330r.

NOTE: This letter is a reply to Persons's missing letter of January 30 (B215), querying the decision that Holt should be transferred to Spain. Originally Persons's plan had been to replace Creswell with Holt, but he changed his mind and designated Creswell as his assistant in Madrid. Acquaviva still wants Holt to go to Spain but approves of Creswell's appointment as resident English agent in Madrid.

P. Roberto Personio, Marzo 14.

Reçevi la de Vuestra Reverencia de 30 de Enero, y aunque Vuestra Reverencia siente que no convenga que el Padre Holto vaya a esas partes, teniendo la repugnançia que muestra, todavia tengo por más espediente que vaya, que no que en Flandes quede, y pues quando llegó esta de Vuestra Reverencia ya yo le havia escrito que quando Vuestra Reverencia le llamare vaya a España, y que si hallare alguna buena ocasion de ir *etiam* antes que Vuestra Reverencia le llame que no la pierda, sino que se sirva della, me pareçe que no será bien alterar este orden sino que le execute. De lo que toca al Padre Crisuelo Vuestra Reverencia haga como le pareçiere que ya yo le tengo remitida la disposiçion destos sujetos, y si le pareçiere que estara bien por operario y morador de Madrid como yo tambien lo creo, Vuestra Reverencia le haga venir aý, y dello avise al Padre Viceprovincial y al Padre Rector de Madrid, que ellos lo ternan por bien. En las &c. ...

Translation

To Fr Robert Persons, 14 March.

I have received Your Reverence's letter of 30 January. Although Your Reverence considers that it is not suitable for Fr Holt to go to those parts, given his evident unwillingness, nevertheless I maintain that it is all the more expedient that he should go, rather than remain in Flanders. Moreover, by the time this letter arrived from Your Reverence I had already written to him that Your Reverence would call him to go to Spain, and that

---

283. On the activities of Bartolomé de Sicilia, who was briefly rector of the English college at Valladolid, see Persons's letter of 20 March (B221).

284. Oswald Tesimond; see Acquaviva to Persons, 28 October 1593 (B203).

if he found any opportunity to go, even before Your Reverence called him, he should not let it go without taking advantage of it. It does not seem to me to be a good idea to change this order and not carry it out. As regards Fr Creswell, please do as Your Reverence sees fit – as I have previously left the disposition of those members to your discretion – and if it seems to you that he would be well suited to the position of agent and resident in Madrid, as I also believe, Your Reverence may go ahead and do so, giving notice to the vice-provincial and to the rector of Madrid, who will [doubtless] agree with it. To your [prayers and holy sacrifices] &c.

B221 To Claudio Acquaviva, Cordoba, 20 March 1594

SOURCE: ARSI, Hisp. 136, fols. 249r–250v, holograph: in Spanish, with postscript in Italian.

HICKS: 228–238, with English translation.

NOTE: Cordoba is on the Guadalquivir River, upstream from Seville. This letter was written *en route* to Seville, with Persons carrying letters of recommendation from the king to the civic authorities to favour the English college.

Here Persons repeats much of what was in the letter of 10 March (B219), especially about the funding of Rheims and Saint-Omer, in case the earlier letter went astray. He provides a little more detail of the audience with the king, and the decisions reached about the affairs of the Society in Spain. The king has explained more about the controversy over Bartolomé de Sicilia, who was a "guest" at Jesus del Monte (the retreat house of the Jesuits from Alcalá de Henares), apparently prevented from moving around freely, because of the king's displeasure over his methods of fundraising (see also the letter of 10 March, *ad finem*). Bartolomé de Sicilia had been rector at Valladolid for only one month, 25 October to 26 November 1589. See Astrain, 3: 612–617, and *Valladolid Registers*, xvii–xviii.

Persons recommends that a Spaniard be appointed in Flanders, to ensure better relations with the Archduke Ernst, and also repeats his suggestion (from 10 March) that William Allen might be transferred from Rome to Flanders, to support the English operations there, and especially the college of St Omers.

Muy Reverendo in Christo Padre nuestro
Pax Christi, etc.

Antes de salir de Madrid escrivi a Vuestra Paternidad y embié la carta en el pligo[285] del Embaxador, por un extraordinario, y en ella di quenta a Vuestra Paternidad de los despachos que tubi de algunos negocios, y de la necessidad que se avia offerecido para llegarme yo a Sevilla, y de lo que traté en la audiencia que tubi con el Rey sobre las cosas de la Compañia, las quales cosas, en evento que la dicha carta mia no llegasse, tornaré a toccar brevemente acá.

Dos negocios dexé muy bien acabados, que son los de los Seminarios de Sant Omer y de Rhemis, porque para Rhemis mi dio Su Magestad una cedula sobre los Malvendos

---

285. I.e., pliego.

que son banqueros muy principales para que paguen luego de contante, quatro mil escudos de oro en Anvers, lo qual considerada la saçon del tiempo que corre por acá, ha parecido favor extraordinario, pues es todo lo corrido que Su Magestad deve a aquel Seminario.

Lo de Sant Omer tan bien está muy bien despachado, pues en lugar de 1920 ducados el año que antes estavan señalados a raçon de diez ducados el mes para cada uno de diez y seis estudiantes, los quales ducados no querrian pagar en Flandes, si no a raçon de diez reales por cada ducado, agora estan señalados dos mil escudos de oro, situados sobre las rentas de los passaportes de Gravelinga cinco leguas de Sant Omer, los quales passaportes si arrendan al presente en más que trece mil ducados el año y, en falta de paga, en aquel partido se assentan sobre el más cierto y libre dinero que ay de las rentas del Rey en Flandes.

Mas, los que replicavan contra este Seminario de Flandes que eran los de las finanças, con parecer del obispo de Sant Omer, como en su carta dicen, mostravan poca affiçion a la nuestra Compañia, y querian más presto que estos muchachos yngleses que el Rey mandava entretener, fuessen criados en sus pedagogias o pupillajes de Flandes, o a lo menos que viviessen dentro el Collegio de los Padres, sin tener casa aparte, y que no fuessen en mayor número que los diez y seis que Su Magestad nombrava en la primera carta española a todo lo qual responde el Rey en carta francesa que es más autentica por alla, y manda que todo el gobierno y cuydado deste negocio se comette ala Compañia, y que Vuestra Paternidad ordene lo que le pareciere más a proposito y ponga Rector y otros Padres que son necessarios para el dicho gobierno, y que se reciben quantos muchachos se pudieren sustentar y que covra la paga desde el dia de la fecha de la primera carta de Su Magestad que fue a 13 de Março, y que la Compañia, respondera a la Justicia para todos los que apperteneçieren al Seminario, y otros puntos semejantes que Vuestra Paternidad avrá visto de la copia de la carta del Rey que embié con la mia en el dicho pligo del Embaxador, con lo qual se entende que no solamente, si effetuará lo que si pretende del Seminario, si no que tambien se accreditará la Compañia con la confiança que el Rey della haçe, y esto es menester para con aquellos ministros flamencos de poco espiritu. Escrive tan bien el Rey aparte al obispo, Governador y magistrado de Sant Omer, y encomienda encarecidamente la obra deste Seminario; de manera que esta contradicion nos ha hecho mucho provecho, como suele accaeçer en las cosas de Dios, él sea glorificado de todo.

El tercero negocio que era de la yda del Cardenal nuestro a Flandes para assistir al archiduque en las cosas de la patria y otras que se offerecieran, ha sido muy favorecido y sollecitado por la Emperatriz a respeto de las muchas utilidades que parece siguerian dello, y parece tan bien que Su Magestad y su Consejo estan muy bien en ello, y asi lo an remittido aý para que el Embaxador lo trate y concluya con Su Santidad y con[286] el Cardenal. Otras algunas cosas se an hecho tan bien pero estas son las principales.

En quanto toca a las cosas de la Compañia escrivi a Vuestra Reverencia[287], en la otra que en la audiencia que tubi de Su Magestad a 6 de hebrero que fue muy grata por el espacio de más de una hora, ablé largamente de las cosas de la Compañia monstrando el

286. con Su Santidad y con] *interlined* R
287. V.R.] *apparently in error for* V.P^d. R

grande deseo, que ella tenía de dar contento y gusto a Su Magestad en todo, y por todo, aunque fuesse con mucho incommodo suyo, como Su Magestad avia visto, por lo que la Congregacion avia luego decretado para la revocacion de los privilegios, aunque en algun dellos particularmente en aquel de los consultores, la Compañia avia tanta raçon de reparar como otras veces se avia representado a Su Magestad & yo torné a repetirlo,[288] y eso no solamente para la conservacion de la disciplina religiosa en la Compañia pero tan bien para mayor servicio de Su Magestad y del Santo Officio, y con todo esto entendiendo que sería gusto de Su Magestad que lo renunciassen, lo hicieron con aquella conformidad que Su Magestad avia entendido, pero con esperança que Su Magestad no permetteria que por esta via los de la Compañia viniessen a pretender que los discolos y inquietos se amparassen del Santo Officio ni de Su Magestad, mostrando los grandes inconbinientes que avian seguido y que siguerian desto, y que sería certissima ruyna de toda religion, virtud y disciplina[289] en la Compañia, y porque algunos exemplos frescos se avian offrecido, se los quente, y entre otros aquel del huesped del Jesus de Monte, a todo lo qual Su Magestad respondio largamente, y de suerte que no se puede desear más, si se cumple, como entiendo que el Rey lo desea, si los ministros no lo estorvan, y a lo del huesped, repitio Su Magestad[290] dos o tres veçes que no avia sabido nada de lo que de parte de Su Magestad avian dicho al Nuncio, que no saliesse de Madrid, y más dixo que aunque él se sentia servido de aquella persona en la substancia de lo que negociava, pero que el modo que el huesped tenía, no le contentava, anzi le scandalizava y asi que la Compañia le podia recoger (esta fue su propria palabra) en el mejor modo que le pareciera. Esta fue la substancia de la plática, la qual menos me ha consolado, despues que entendi lo que passó en Roma, aunque muchas destas cosas dependen de los ministros como dixi. Dios guye todo para su mayor gloria y congserve el ánimo y fortaleça que da a Vuestra Paternidad para suffrir y passar con todo.

 La necessidad que se offerecio de llegarme yo a Sevilla escrivi antes dos veces a Vuestra Paternidad de manera que no será menester repetirlo, Su Magestad me ha dado dos cartas en mi favor y confio en nuestro Señor que haremos algo en provecho de aquel Seminario, aunque no puedo quedar alli más que un mes y medio. De alli tornaré a escrivir, esto escrivo en el Camino para Cordova. En Sevilla aguardaremos al padre Osvaldo para el tiempo que Vuestra Paternidad ha prometido y si se offereciere buen passaje derecho por mar, sería mucho mejor que no venir por Roma que es camino largo y costoso. Vuestra Paternidad lo mirará como tan bien le supplico considerar de quánta importancia sería un padre grave y de autoridad de la nacion Española en Flandes con el Archiduque Ernesto en estos principios, y esto no solamente para las cosas y personas de aquella nacion si no tan bien de todas las demas, y para todos los negocios que alli se tratarán, pues más respeto le tendria Ernesto, siendo el dicho padre de la nacion española y persona grave y prudente, como he dicho, que a ningun otro, y no conosco yo padre de tanta importançia desta nacion que no sería más utilmente empleado en Flandes por agora estando las cosas como estan que no en qualquiera otro lugar o cargo. Dios nuestro Señor guyerá a Vuestra Paternidad en esto y en todo lo demas, a cuya santa providencia

  288. & yo torné a repetirlo] *interlined R*
  289. virtud y disciplina] *interlined R*
  290. Su Magestad] *interlined R*

lo dexo, y en los santos sacrificios de Vuestra Paternidad muy humilmente me encomiendo. De Cordova a 20 de Março 1594.

  De Vuestra Reverenda Paternidad
    hijo endiño
      Rob. Personio.

[PS] Li duoi padri Viceprovinciali de Toledo et Castiglia c'han fatto carità di ricevere duoi sugietti del Seminario de Valladolid nella Compagnia, son persone di molta virtu et talenti.

[*Addressed:*] Al muy Reverendo en Christo Padre Nuestro el Padre Claudio Aquaviva Preposito General de la Compañia de Jesus en Roma.

[*Endorsed:*] Cordova. P. Roberto Personio. Marzo 20. 94. [*with summary of contents*]

Translation

Our Very Reverend Father in Christ
The peace of Christ, etc.

Before leaving Madrid, I wrote to Your Paternity and sent the letter in the ambassador's confidential mail, by an extra post.[291] In it I gave Your Paternity an account of the outcome of some of the matters I was negotiating, and explained the necessity that had arisen for me to be present in Seville. I spoke also of the line I had taken, at the audience which I had with the king, about the affairs of the Society. In case my former letter did not reach you, I will briefly touch on those matters again in this one.

Two matters I left very satisfactorily concluded: the negotiations on behalf of the seminary of St Omers and Rheims. His Majesty gave me a warrant for Rheims on the Malvendi, who are very important bankers, to draw 4000 crowns in gold at Antwerp, immediately at sight. And considering the financial weather we are experiencing here, this seems an exceptional favour, for it is the total of the outstanding sum due to that seminary from His Majesty.

The business in connection with St Omers has also been resolved very much to my satisfaction. In place of 1920 ducats a year which had previously been assigned, on the basis of ten ducats a month for each of sixteen students (which they would only pay at the rate of ten reals to the ducat in Flanders), now 2000 golden crowns are specified, and charged on the receipts from the dues of Gravelines, which is five leagues from Saint-Omer. These dues are farmed out at present for over 13,000 ducats a year, and in case of default in that quarter, there is a charge on the best secured and most immediately available source of revenue which the king has in Flanders.

Moreover, those who, following the lead of the bishop of Saint-Omer (as they claim in their letter),[292] were raising objections to this seminary in Flanders, that is, concerning its funding, showed little affection for our Society and would have much preferred that these English boys, whom the king commanded to be entertained, should be brought

---

291. Persons to Acquaviva, 10 March (B219).
292. Jean de Vernois, bishop of Saint-Omer.

up in their Flemish schools and students' hostels, or at least that they should live within the college of the fathers and not have a separate house. They were unwilling that there should be a greater number of them than the sixteen which His Majesty mentioned in his first Spanish letter. To all this the king is answering in a letter in French, which carries more weight there, giving orders that the whole government and care of this business is to be entrusted to the Society, and that Your Paternity is to order things in the way that seems most suitable to you and appoint a rector and the other fathers required for the government of the house. As many boys are to be received as can be supported, and the payment is to be drawn according to the arrangements detailed in His Majesty's first letter, which was the 13th of March. The Society will be answerable to the magistracy for all those belonging to the seminary. There are other stipulations of a similar nature which Your Paternity will have seen in the copy of the king's letter which I sent along with mine in the ambassador's packet. This makes it clear that not only will our aims in regard to the seminary be fulfilled, but also the Society will gain much prestige from the confidence placed in it by the king; and this is required in dealing with those Flemish ministers who are rather lukewarm. The king is also writing separate letters to the bishop, the governor, and the magistrate of Saint-Omer, recommending the project of the seminary in the warmest terms. And so, in effect this disagreement has brought us much profit, as usually happens in the things of God. May He be praised for everything.

The third matter is the question of our cardinal going to Flanders to assist the archduke in the affairs of our country and in other business that may arise. The empress is much in favour of this and has begged that he should come, in view of the many advantages which she thinks would result from it. It seems that His Majesty and his council are strongly in favour, and so they have referred the matter to Rome so that the ambassador may treat the matter with His Holiness and the cardinal, and a decision can be made. Some other matters were dealt with too, but these are the principal ones.

With regard to the affairs of the Society, I told Your Reverence in my former letter that at the audience which I had with His Majesty on the 6th of February, which was a very gracious one and lasted for an hour, I spoke at length about the Society's affairs and pointed out how greatly it desired to satisfy and please His Majesty in everything and in every way, even at much inconvenience to itself. This, I said, His Majesty had seen in the decrees just made by the congregation for the surrender of our privileges, despite the fact that in the case of some of them – especially the one concerning consultors[293] – the Society had such good reasons for restoration, as had been represented to His Majesty on other occasions and as I repeated again. This was not only for the sake of maintaining religious discipline in the Society, but also because it tended to the better service of His Majesty and of the Holy Office. Yet in spite of this, because they understood that it would be pleasing to His Majesty if they surrendered it, they did so with that spirit of accommodation of which His Majesty had been informed, but with

---

293. This refers to the privilege of exemption from serving as consultors to the Holy Office. Other concessions made by the general congregation to the Spaniards wanting to appease the Inquisition were to waive the privilege of reading books on the *Index prohibitorum* and of absolving from heresy in the confessional (Edwards, 168–169).

the hope that His Majesty would not allow members of the Society as a result of it to aspire to that office (of consultor) or those who are unruly and disaffected to enjoy the protection of the Holy Office or of His Majesty; and I pointed out the great inconveniences that had resulted and would eventually result from such a development, and that it would be the certain ruin of all religious spirit, piety, and discipline in the Society. And as some recent instances had occurred, I told him about them and among others the case of the guest of Jesus del Monte. His Majesty made a long reply to all this and in such a way that it will leave nothing to be desired, if what he said is carried out; and this is what the king wants, as I understand, if the ministers do not prevent it. And in the matter of the guest, His Majesty repeated two or three times that he had been quite unaware of what they had said to the nuncio in his name, that is, that he was not to leave Madrid. He said further that, although he felt that that individual was doing him a service as regards the actual work that he was doing, yet he was not pleased with the methods used by the guest; even more, he was scandalized; and so the Society may call him to order (that was his own expression) in the way that seems best to them. This was the substance of the conversation. The consolation I derived from it has diminished since I heard what happened in Rome, though much of that is due to action by the ministers, as I said. May God dispose of everything for His greater glory and continue to give Your Paternity courage and fortitude to suffer and bear with it all.

Of the need that arose for me to be present at Seville, I have written to Your Paternity twice before, so I need not repeat it. His Majesty has given me two letters of recommendation and I trust in our Lord that we shall have some success in providing for that seminary, though I cannot stay there longer than a month and a half. I shall write again from there. This, I am writing on the road to Cordoba. At Seville we shall expect Fr. Oswald at the time Your Paternity has promised; if there is any chance of his finding a suitable passage to come direct by sea, it would be much better than the long and expensive journey via Rome. Please would Your Paternity look into the matter, and I beg you also to consider what an advantage it would be to have a grave and respected father of Spanish nationality with the Archduke Ernst in Flanders now at the beginning of things,[294] and this not only for the sake of the interests of that country and its nationals, but for the sake of all others as well and for all the business that is to be conducted there, since Ernst will pay more attention to this father than to any one else if he is of Spanish nationality, and a grave and discreet person, as I have said. And there is no father of that nation that I know of, however important where he is, who would not be more usefully employed, at the present time and under existing circumstances, in Flanders, in preference to any other place or office whatsoever. May God our Lord guide Your Paternity in this and everything else. I commit it to His holy providence, and commend myself very humbly to Your Paternity's holy sacrifices. From Cordoba on the 20th of March 1594.

    Your Reverend Paternity's
        unworthy son
           Rob. Persons.

---

294. The archduke had taken charge in February 1594.

[PS] The two vice provincials, of Toledo and Castile, have done us the kindness of receiving into the Society two students from the seminary of Valladolid; they are men of much virtue and talent.²⁹⁵

B222 From Claudio Acquaviva, 30 March 1594

SOURCE: ARSI, Tolet. 5/II, fol. 333v.

NOTE: Acquaviva halts the publication of *Conference about the Next Succession*; Antwerp was already holding back the publication; there was also a Spanish version with Idiáquez, but only of the second part.

P. Roberto Personio, 30 de Marzo.

Por acá he entendido que cierta persona que está en esa Provincia escrive un libro de la succession de Anglia [45] y porque se descubren en esto no pocos inconvenientes, deseo que Vuestra Reverencia en todo caso lo impida de manera que no pase adelante porque etian los naturales de Anglia [45]²⁹⁶. No creo que lo tomarian bien, digo no todos, que algunos pocos podria ser que sí, pero como quiera que sea pues la cosa en sí es ambigua, como cosa que depende de Historias que no del todo se puede averiguar, y cosa que toca y puede ofender a personages y Principes no tengo por conveniente que salga de los nuestros, pues aunque más se procure callar el autor, crea Vuestra Reverencia que se sabra, y sabido por ventura se impediran muchos bienes de los que ahora se hazen. Ansi que encargo a Vuestra Reverencia que en esto ponga cuydado hasta atajar esta escritura, porque yo lo tengo por muy expediente. En sus oraçiones, etc.

[PS] Si Vuestra Reverencia entendiere que por estar esta cosa muy adelante su diligencia no ha de ser de más efecto que causar ofension sin sacar el fruto que se desea será mejor no intentarla, pero si se pudiere sin esta ofension que se procure que yo en ello me remito a la prudençia de Vuestra Reverencia.

Translation

To Fr Robert Persons, 30 March.

From here I have learnt that someone who is in that province is writing a book on the English succession and because not a few inconveniences are found in it, I want Your Reverence to hold it back altogether in such a way that it does not go forward, because it will offend the native citizens of England. I do not believe that they would take it well: I don't say all would take it amiss, because some might approve, but whatever the case, given that the issue itself is ambiguous, as something depending on histories that do not yield final interpretation, and it is something that affects and could offend personages and princes, I do not consider it to be suitable to come from Ours, not even if you try to conceal the author. Your Reverence may believe me, it will eventually be known, and, once known, it may perchance hinder many good things that are now in train. I would

---

295. Persons expressed his hopes for this in his letter of 4 December 1593 (B210).
296. Deciphering from Persons's letter of 4/16 June.

rather charge Your Reverence to be advised to delay this writing, because I think that will be very expedient. To your prayers, etc.

[PS] If Your Reverence understands that because this thing is already so advanced in its composition, your diligence cannot foresee any other effect except to cause offence without obtaining the desired fruit, it would be better not to attempt it, but if it can be done without offence, it should be ventured; I leave it to Your Reverence's prudence.[297]

B223 From Juan de Sigüenza, Madrid, 16 April 1594

SOURCE: Persons to Acquaviva, 18 April.

NOTE: Juan de Sigüenza was the rector of the Jesuit College in Madrid, and confessor to Luisa de Carvajal (1566–1614), who lived nearby in a small community in the calle de Toledo, Madrid: Glyn Redworth, *The She-Apostle: The Extraordinary Life and Death of Luisa de Carvajal* (Oxford, 2008), 48. Acquaviva asked him to deliver a copy of a letter to Persons (dated 1 or 2 February, B216) about delaying Acosta's return to Spain. It appears that Sigüenza only relayed these instructions in April, by which time Persons had already left for Seville.

B224 To Juan de Sigüenza, Seville, 18 April 1594

SOURCE: Persons to Acquaviva, 18 April.

NOTE: Persons replied to Sigüenza, explaining that he would not be able to treat with the king directly but would write to Idiáquez instead. He forwarded copies of these letters to Acquaviva.

B225 To Don Juan de Idiáquez, Seville, 18 April 1594

SOURCE: Persons to Acquaviva, 18 April.

NOTE: Instead of returning to Madrid to treat with the king about Acosta, Persons wrote to Idiáquez.

B226 To Claudio Acquaviva, Seville, 18 April 1594

SOURCE: ARSI, Hisp. 136, fols 284–85, holograph.
HICKS: 239–248, with English translation.

NOTE: Persons reports on the encouraging developments in Seville since his return there: the city council, headed by the chief magistrate, Pedro Fernández de Córdoba, Marquis of Priego, responded very favourably to the king's requests for support for the English college. Persons was on the verge of procuring a very suitable, spacious, and well-positioned property for the college, near to the Spanish college of St Hermenegild, whose rector was Melchor de Castro (Francisco de Borja Medina, in *DHCJ*, 1: 710–711). Similarly, he was

---

297. This appears to mean that if the book is too advanced in its composition to be radically revised, Persons should use his discretion about taking the project any further.

very hopeful about Saint-Omer, especially if Mannaerts should return to Flanders as provincial. He believed that Saint-Omer would draw many men into the Society. Simon Swinborne was *en route* for Saint-Omer, possibly in exchange for William Baldwin or Nicolas Smith. Persons expected to travel to Valladolid soon, with Creswell, whose health was improving, but to return to Seville later in the year to ensure that there would be an English Jesuit to act as minister.

Persons explains how he has dealt with Acquaviva's instructions about Acosta's return to Spain. The matter had in fact already been resolved (see Persons to Acquaviva, 12 May, B230).

Muy Reverendo en Christo Padre Nuestro
Pax Christi.

Con cada ordenario escrivo a Vuestra Paternidad lo que passa por acá en nuestros negocios. Yo llegué a Sevilla a 22 del passado y truxi cartas de Su Magestad al Cabildo desta ciudad, y otras al Conde de Priego que es assistente, encomendandoles este Collegio y agradeciendo lo que avian hecho, y particularmente encargandoles que proveessen al Collegio de una buena casa y sitio, para su vivienda. Yo fui al Cabildo y les ablé, y hallé tanta volundad en todos para favorecer esta obra que bien parece cosa de Dios pues en otras cosas y demandas, ay tanta diversidad de pareceres de ordenario, como suele aver en tanta variedad de gente, y en tiempos tan apprettados, pero en esto no ubo un voto en contrario, antes pidiendoles yo solamente que a los 300 Δ que ya nos davan en cada año para pagar el alquiler de la casa, mandassen añadir otros 200 de manera que en todo fuessen 500, ellos consultado el negocio respondieron que pedia poco y assi señalaron 600 en cada un año, añadiendo demas que buscassemos buen sitio donde comprar o fabricar casa propria y que la ciudad nos ayudaria más adelante para ello, particularmente si una vez acabassen de arrendar del Rey el Almojarefasgo que es la dogana, de que al presente si trata con muchas veras. A este modo tenemos ya (gracias a Dios) renta bastante para alquilar qualquiera grande casa de Sevilla, que nos venga a proposito y si no fuesse que estamos attados al barrio del Collegio de St Hermenegildo por causa de no estar lexos de los estudios, hartas casas grandes hallariamos, pero en este circuito del Collegio de la Compañia no si halla hasta agora, si no una casa sola que andamos tras comprarla, y creo que, placiendo a Dios, saldremos con ello, porque aunque sea de mayorasgo, ya si trata de venderla con licencia del Rey la qual Su Magestad sin duda la dara más facilmente para este effeto que no para qualquier hombre particular, y aunque el Alguazil mayor desta Audiencia, la aya concertado de comprar para sí, y esto[298] despues que nosotros tratamos de comprarla, todavia entendo que la casa será nuestra, pues el Rey lo ordenará asi, y teniendo esta casa, estaremos muy accomodados en este particular, pues es casa muy grande, ancha, y en lindo sitio, muy circano al Collegio de la Compañia y al Rio, y al campo, etc. Vuestra Paternidad lo encomiende a Dios todo porque entiendo que si sirvira mucho deste Seminario para ayudar a Ynglaterra, son gente

---

298. y esto] *interlined with caret* R

muy escogida los que estan²⁹⁹ aqui y seran cada dia más y más con las lindas plantas que nos vendran de Sant Omer, sin inficion ninguna de malos humores que en otras partes se les suelen pegar, de manera que ni aqui ni en Valladolid no hay rastro de lo que se ha visto algunas veces aý en Roma y en Rhemis; si no grandissima union entre sí, y reverencia y amor cordial a las cosas de la Compañia y vocacion en los más principales dellos³⁰⁰ para entrar a su tiempo en ella.

2. Lo del Seminario de Sant Omer confio en nuestro Señor que yrá muy bien agora con la postrera carta y resolucion de Su Magestad que manda que sin réplica se les paguen dos mil escudos de oro en cada un año, y que les amparen y favorescan y se fien de la Compañia en todo toccante al dicho Seminario, como Vuestra Paternidad avrá visto por la copia de la dicha carta del Rey que de Madrid embié. Tan bien ayudará mucho para ello³⁰¹ la buelta del buen padre Oliverio si queda por³⁰² provincial, y si no, su informacion y recomendacion al successor, y mucho más la de Vuestra Paternidad que será muy necessaria, particularmente si caesse el cargo en el padre Juan Orano, el qual se ha mostrado el más frio en este negocio que en mi vida he visto, siempre poniendo difficultades, y disanimando a los que estan alla, ni con averle yo escrito tantas veces que no avria difficultad, ni de la parte de autoridad y amparo, ni de deneros y sustento, porque entrambas estas cosas yo tomaria en mí a procurar, y actualmente yba yo³⁰³ embiando deneros por cada ordenario, y lo mismo hago al presente, aunque entiendo³⁰⁴ que ya no avrá falta, todavia no he podido hasta agora darle ánimo. Anteyer partio de aqui el padre Simon Swinborn por mar para andar alla digo a Sant Omer, fue en una nave del Governador de Cales, y juzgaron los medicos que no sería bien aguardar otro verano aqui, pues su salud, despues de quatro años que ha vivido aqui, no podia suffrir más estos calores. Ha dado buena satisfacion aqui, de buen religioso y discreto, y bien entendido en letras, he pedido al padre Provincial de Flandes que nos embíe algun de los padres yngleses que estan alla, como sería el padre Balduin o el padre Nicolas Smith qual más les pareciere en trueco del padre Simon,³⁰⁵ porque en lo que es leer theologia en lugar del padre Balduin o que supplir qualquier otra occupacion que él tiene, muy sobradamente lo hara el padre Simon.

3. El padre Cresuello va convalesciendo y pienso que yrá con migo a Castilla para accabar a estar bueno, y alla si veerá lo que será mejor hacer, para más adelante, la falta que ay aqui es de un padre ynglés, por ministro en este Collegio³⁰⁶ pero por otra via lo supplimos por lo presente, y pues yo tengo (placiendo a Dios) de bolverme aqui en septiembre para acabar de assentar este Collegio en lo que es casa, y fabricar lo que avrá menester, en la que tratamos de comprar, despues de sacada la facultad del Rey, más facilmente si puede passar este verano, sin padre Ynglés de la Compañia aqui, aunque para adelante será³⁰⁷ necessario proveerlo.

    299. estan] *followed by illegible deletion* R
    300. dellos] *interlined with caret* R
    301. para ello] *interlined with caret* R
    302. por] *interlined with caret* R
    303. yba yo] *interlined with caret* R
    304. entiendo] *preceded by* acá [*probably deleted*] R
    305. en trueco del padre Simon] *interlined with caret* R
    306. en este Collegio] *interlined with caret* R
    307. será] *interlined with caret* R

4. El padre Juan de Seguenza me embió los dias passados el translado de una carta de Vuestra Paternidad de primo de hebrero, en la qual me mandó Vuestra Paternidad que trattasse con Su Magestad, sobre lo de la venida por acá del padre Joseph de Acosta, y el padre Siguenza, quiso luego que yo bolviesse a Madrid dexando todas las cosas començadas por acá, Vuestra Paternidad veerá su carta y mi respuesta, y el expediente que en aquel aprietto me parecio tomar que fue escrivir sobre ello a Don Juan de Idiaquez, todos los translados embió con esta para que Vuestra Paternidad vea lo que está hecho, y mande lo que más Vuestra Paternidad quiere que si haga. Yo más me he confirmado en lo que escrivo al padre Siguenza despues que he recebido una carta del padre Francisco Rodríguez de Frescata de 15 de hebrero, que estava[308] con Vuestra Paternidad y no dice nada de aquel negocio, y otros[309] aqui tienen ya cartas de aý, que el padre Acosta avia salido de Roma para bolver a su gobierno en Valladolid. Yo no dexaré en bolviendo a Madrid[310] de hacer todas las[311] diligencias, en este particular y todo lo demas, que pensaré ser más conforme al deseo y volundad de Vuestra Paternidad y para bien de la Compañia aunque no tubiesse commission particular para ello, como siempre he hecho estoy obligado, de hacer[312] y mucho más lo que Vuestra Paternidad mandará nominativamente, a quien Dios nuestro Señor nos guarde por muchos años. En sus santos sacrificios humilmente me encomiendo. Sevilla, a 18 de Abril 1594.

 De Vuestra Reverenda Paternidad
  endegno hijo y siervo
   Roberto Personio.

[*Addressed*:] Para nuestro padre General.
[*Endorsed*:] Roberto Personio Abril 18. 94. [*with summary of contents*]

Translation

Our Most Reverend Father in Christ
The peace of Christ.

 With this courier, I am reporting to Your Paternity on developments in our affairs in this region. I arrived in Seville on the 22nd of last month,[313] and carried letters from His Majesty to the corporation of this city, and others to the count of Priego, who is the assistant, recommending this college, thanking them for what they had done, and particularly charging that they should provide the college with a good house and location for its home. I went to the council to talk to them and found in all of them such willingness to support this enterprise that it really seems to be the hand of God. In other matters and questions, there is such great disagreement over everyday business, as usually happens amongst such a variety of people, and in times so constrained, but in this case, there was not a single vote against us. Quite the contrary, I only asked that, on top

 308. Que estava] *replaces* estando [*deleted*] R
 309. otros] *replaces* al p^e [*deleted*] R
 310. Madrid] *replaces* Valla[dol]id [*deleted*] R
 311. las] *interlined with caret* R
 312. de hacer] *interlined with caret* R
 313. From Cordoba: see his letter of 20 March from that city (B221).

of the three hundred escudos which they have given us each year to pay the rent of the house, another two hundred be given in addition, making five hundred in all. After discussing the matter, they answered that I had asked too little, and so they assigned six hundred for each and every year. They also recommended that we find a good location where we could buy or build a suitable house. The city will help us later in that, particularly once they have finished renting the Almojarifazgo, which is the customs house, from the king, concerning which negotiations are presently under way in earnest. In this way we already have (thanks be to God) enough income to rent any large house in Seville which is suitable for the purpose, and if it were not that we are limited to the neighbourhood of St Hermenegild, so that the students can attend their lectures, we would find many large houses, but in the part of the city around the Society's college there is only one to be found so far, and this we are trying to buy. Please God, we shall succeed in doing so, for, although it is entailed, there are already negotiations afoot for getting the king's leave for it to be sold; and doubtless His Majesty will be more inclined to allow it for this purpose than he would be for a private individual. And although the high constable of the court here has arranged to buy it for his own use – and this after we had entered into negotiations to buy it – yet I understand that the house is to be ours, for the king will give orders to this effect. If we obtain this house, it will suit our purposes very well, for it is very large and spacious and in a beautiful position, quite close to the Society's college and to the river and to the open country. I beg Your Paternity to commend the whole matter to God, for I believe that this seminary will be of great use in providing help for England. Those here are a very select body of men, and every day they will become more and more so with the coming of those splendid seedlings from St Omers; and they are free from the infection of evil humours which are wont to attack them in other places; and so it comes about that neither here nor at Valladolid is there a trace of the sort of thing that has at times made its appearance with you in Rome and at Rheims. On the contrary, there is the greatest spirit of unity among them and of respect and deep affection for the ways of the Society; and the best of them have vocations to enter it in due course.

2. I trust in our Lord that the affairs of St Omers will now proceed quite satisfactorily, thanks to His Majesty's decision and his last letter, which orders that his officials should pay them 2000 golden crowns without fail every year, protect and support them, and entrust to the Society everything that has to do with this seminary, as Your Paternity will have seen from the copy of His Majesty's letter which I sent from Madrid. Good Fr Olivier's return will also be a great help if he stays as provincial there, and, if not, the information and advice that he can give to his successor. Still more so will be that of Your Paternity, and it will be very necessary, especially if the office should fall to Fr Jean d'Heur,[314] who has shown himself colder about this business than anyone I have ever seen in my life, always raising objections and disheartening the people who are there; and in spite of my having written to him so often, telling him that there was no obstacle, of authorization and protection, or of money for its upkeep – for I would be responsible for procuring both of these, and as a matter of fact I was in the habit of sending money by every post, and I am doing the same at present although I don't think there will be

---

314. Olivier Mannaerts was succeeded by George Duras as provincial of Belgium in 1594. Jean d'Heur (1544–1603) was the vice provincial.

any shortage – still I have not been able so far to raise any enthusiasm in him. The day before yesterday Fr Simon Swinborne left from here by sea to go there, that is to say, to Saint-Omer; he went in a ship belonging to the governor of Calais; the doctors were of opinion that it would not be well for him to stay another summer here, as his health, after being here four years, was not strong enough to stand the heat here any longer. He has given great satisfaction here as a good and prudent religious and a very learned man. I have asked father provincial of Flanders to send us one of the English fathers who are there, such as Fr Baldwin or Fr Nicolas Smith, whichever they like, in exchange for Fr Simon; for as regards lecturing in theology in place of Fr Baldwin or undertaking any of his duties, Fr Simon will be more than capable of doing so.

3. Fr Creswell goes on improving in health, and I think he will come with me to Castile to complete his cure. When we are there, we shall see what it will be best to do in future; what is wanted here is an English father to be minister in this college; but we are making shift for the present otherwise. As I have to come back here, please God, in September to complete the establishment of this college with respect to the house, and to do the building that will be required in the one which we are trying to get the king's authority to purchase, it will be all the easier to carry on for this summer without having an English father of the Society here, but later on it will be essential to provide one.

4. A few days ago, Fr Juan de Sigüenza sent me the copy of Your Paternity's letter of 1 February, in which you instructed me to negotiate with His Majesty on the subject of Fr José de Acosta's coming here;[315] and Fr Sigüenza wished me to return at once to Madrid, leaving everything that I had in hand here. Your Paternity will see his letter and my reply. The best course I could adopt, I thought, in this exigency was to write to Don Juan de Idiáquez about it. I am sending copies of all the letters along with this, so that Your Paternity may see what has been done and instruct further. I have been confirmed even more in the views I expressed to Fr Sigüenza after receiving a letter from Fr Francisco Rodríguez from Frascati of the 15th of February.[316] He was with Your Paternity and he does not mention this affair; others here too have letters now from there which say that Fr Acosta had left Rome to return to his post of authority in Valladolid. When I return to Madrid, I shall not omit to take all measures in this matter and in every other which I think most conformable to Your Paternity's desires and good pleasure, and most for the advantage of the Society, even without any special commission to do so. This is what I have always done, and it is my duty to do so – and much more is it my duty to do what Your Paternity expressly commands. May God our Lord preserve you to us for many years. I humbly commend myself to your holy sacrifices. From Seville, 18 April 1594.

    Your Paternity's
        unworthy son and servant
        Robert Persons.

---

315. I.e., returning to Spain, to take up the position of superior of the professed house in Valladolid. The letter is dated 2 February in the general's register, but Sigüenza's copy may have borne a different date. Letters were dated according to the next available post, so the dates are approximate.

316. B217.

B227 To Henry Garnet, Seville, April 1594

SOURCE: Persons to Acquaviva, 10 May.
NOTE: Persons wrote to Garnet to ask for Southwell or Weston to be sent to Spain, possibly because of the lack of an English Jesuit to be minister at the college in Seville.

B228 From Claudio Acquaviva, Rome, 9 May 1594

SOURCE: ARSI, Tolet. 5/II, fol. 337r.
NOTE: This is more of a summary than a complete letter, addressing various topics raised in Persons's letters of 10 and 20 March (B219, B221): the transfer of Oswald Tesimond to Spain and the appointment of a Spaniard to be the Society's representative in Brussels. He also mentions the problem of the expulsion of Jesuits from France.

P. Roberto Personio, 9 de Mayo.
    Escriviosele que es consuelo ver la piedad con que el Rey favorece los Seminarios de Saint-Omer y Remis que ay toda satisfacion de que en qualquiera ocasion que se ofrezca apoyará con Su Magestad las cosas de la Compañia, etc. Que se desea muy en particular el augmento del Señor Cardenal Alano. Que acabado el Padre Osvaldo el curso yrá a España como se le ha prometido. Que se considerará lo que dice de embiar algun Padre español a Flandes. Que encomiende a Dios las cosas de Francia pidiendo a Su Magestad les dé el ser que más convenga a su gloria etc.

Translation

To Fr Robert Persons, 9 May.
    It was written to him that it is encouraging to see the piety with which the king favours the seminaries of St Omers and Rheims. This is altogether satisfying in that on every occasion which presents itself the interests of the Society will be supported through His Majesty, etc. That more particularly there is a desire to have Lord Cardinal Allen's support increased. That, once Fr Oswald has completed the course, he will go to Spain as he has been promised. That some consideration will be given to sending some Spanish father to Flanders. That the affairs of France may be committed to God's care, asking His [Divine] Majesty that they be disposed to his greater glory, etc.

B229 To Claudio Acquaviva, Seville, 10 May 1594

SOURCE: ARSI, Hisp. 136, fols. 316–317.
HICKS: 249–254, with English translation.
NOTE: Persons was about to leave for Madrid and then Valladolid, accompanied by Creswell and Arthur, a lay brother (*vere* Gregory Hoare, ca. 1573–1639). He reports that he has written to England for Southwell and Weston to be sent to Spain, is waiting for Tesimond to arrive from Sicily via Rome, and hopes that Robert Jones may be able to come with him.

Much of the letter elaborates Persons's feelings about Henry Walpole, captured almost immediately on arrival in England, and the likelihood of his martyrdom. He reflects on the fact that so few priests have been captured, and none martyred, since the suffering of Campion (1581) and Thomas Cottam (1582). On Walpole and the state of persecution in 1594, see Questier, *Catholics and Treason*, 250–258.

Muy Reverendo in Christo Padre nuestro
Pax Christi.

Mañana, placiendo a Dios, nos partiremos para Madrid el padre Joseph Cresuello e yo, llevo tan bien un Hermano ynglés de los dos coadjutores[317] que se an recebido en esta provincia y yrá a Valladolid, si llama Arturo y es muy bueno, y otro llamado Juan queda en Cordua, y da mucha satisfacion a todos; tres estudiantes tan bien se an recebido en las tres provincias de Castilla, Toledo y Andaluzia, dos son sacerdotes y un escolar theologo. Si Vuestra Paternidad no tubiera occupacion importante para el padre Roberto Jones, quando acabara su curso de artes (lo qual él escrive al padre Cresuello que será en el fin deste verano) creo que sería bien empleado tan bien aqui, y sería buen escalon para embiarlo despues a Ynglaterra quando tubiera un poco de[318] más experiencia pues él lo desea tanto, y por acá es el mejor camino de todos, porque ay embarcacion sigura y secreta, y para continuar la mission de Ynglaterra, es menester tener aqui gente apparejada, pues los padres que estan en Ynglaterra lo piden, y agora lo pideran más, veendo que Dios no les concedio el padre Walpolo, del qual no sabemos aún, de cierto, si está martyrizado o no, aunque aya algunos avisos dello, e yo lo tengo por tanto más probabile, por quanto vi que el padre yva con grande deseo dello y con disposicion para merecerlo de nuestro Señor. Yo he escritto a Ynglaterra que si nos pudiessen embiar acá el padre Southwello o el padre Vestono, les dariamos qualquiera otro cambio, pero no sé, si se puede hacer tan facilmente, y no dudo si no que en poco tiempo de los que aqui an entrado y entrarán, y de los que Vuestra Paternidad nos embiará, tendremos sugetos bastantes para suplir y mantener[319] aquella mission contra todas las fuerças de los hereges. Porque ya Vuestra Paternidad avrá visto por experiencia, que Dios quiere que el número de los presos y mucho más de los martyrizados, sea muy limitado, aunque muchos se enbien y más lo deseen y assi que en el espacio de 13 años que murieron los padres Campiano y Cotamo de la Compañia, ninguno ha sido martyr aunque diversos ayan sido presos, de manera que Vuestra Paternidad podra bien alargar la mano para esta mission y Dios nuestro Señor hara dellos lo que fuera servido. Si el padre Henrico Walpolo muere agora, entendo que no solamente su intenso deseo, si no tan bien las oraciones de sus dos hermanos aý en Sant Andres, y del tercero aqui en Montilla avran ayudado para ello. Si el padre Roberto Jones pudiera acabar su curso este año para venir con el padre Osvaldo, sería bien, y si no, podra venir despues pareciendo asi a Vuestra Paternidad. En cuyos santos sacrificios humilmente me encomiendo. De Sevilla a 10 de mayo 1594.

    De Vuestra Reverenda Paternidad
        hijo y siervo
            Rob. Personio.

317. coadjutores] *interlined with caret R*
318. de] *interlined with caret R*
319. y mantener] *interlined with caret R*

[PS] El padre Garneto me avisó de la mucha caridad de Vuestra Paternidad en darles licencia para embiar doce para ser recebidos de la Compañia, en complimiento de la qual licencia ha embiado otros[320] quatro los dias passados a Flandes, y no dudo que Vuestra Paternidad mandará disponer dellos *pro majori Dei gloria*. El mismo padre me embió la lista de los que ay de la Compañia alli en Ynglaterra, que en quanto me accuerdo, llega a 17 que para mi fue grande consuelo saberlo. Aqui tan bien sin duda entrarán de los mejores abilidades que ay en los seminarios, y ya lo muestran y lo desean que todo será para gloria de nuestro Señor, y ayuda de la affligida patria, y confusion de los hereges.

[*Addressed:*] Al muy Reverendo en Christo padre el padre Claudio Aquaviva preposito General de la Compañia de Jesus, Roma.

[*Endorsed:*] Sevilla. 94. P. Roberto Personio. Mayo 10. [*with summary of contents*]

Translation

Our Very Reverend Father in Christ
The peace of Christ.

Tomorrow, please God, Fr Joseph Creswell and I will be leaving for Madrid. I am taking an English brother also, one of the two coadjutors who have been received in this province,[321] and he is going to Valladolid; his name is Arthur and he is a very good fellow. The other, whose name is John, is remaining at Cordoba; he is giving great satisfaction to everybody. Three students also have been received in the three provinces of Castile, Toledo, and Andalusia; two of them are priests, and one is studying theology. If Your Paternity should have no important employment for Fr Robert Jones when he finishes his course in arts (and he writes to Fr Creswell that that will be at the end of this summer), I think that he also could be well employed here; and it would be a useful step towards sending him later on to England, when he has a little more experience, for that is what he needs most. To go by way of this country is the best route of all, for one can embark safely and secretly.[322] Then too, in order to carry on the English mission, it is necessary to have men here who are well equipped for it; that is what the fathers in England are asking for, and now they will be likely to ask it even more, seeing that God did not allow them to have Fr Walpole. We do not know yet for certain whether he has been martyred or not, though there are some reports to that effect; and I think it is all the more probable because I saw that the father went with a great desire for martyrdom and with the dispositions that would be likely to merit this favour from our Lord. I have written to England that, if they could send Fr Southwell or Fr Weston to us here,[323] we would give them someone else in exchange, but I do not know if this can be done very easily; and I have no doubt that in a short time, what with those who have now entered and are about to enter, and those whom Your Paternity will be sending us, we shall have sufficient men to supply and maintain the mission there against all the forces of the heretics. For Your

---

320. otros] *interlined with caret* R

321. Two lay brothers now in Andalusia: Gregory Hoare and John Collins (ca. 1573–1602).

322. In the event, Robert Jones was given leave to travel via Flanders, 11 October 1594 (McCoog, *English and Welsh Jesuits*, 219).

323. Both were in custody: Southwell in the Tower, Weston at Wisbech.

Paternity will already have seen from experience that it is God's will that the number of those who are taken, and still more the number of those who are martyred, should be very limited, in spite of so many men being sent there and so many more being anxious to go. And so it comes about that in the space of thirteen years since the death of Fathers Campion and Cottam of the Society, no one has been martyred, even though a number have been taken prisoners. Consequently, Your Paternity can well afford to be openhanded with regard to this mission, and God our Lord will deal with them according to His good pleasure. If Fr Henry Walpole dies now, I believe that not only his intense desire but also the prayers of his two brothers there at Sant'Andrea and of the third one here at Montilla will have helped him to his death.[324] If Fr Robert Jones could finish his course this year so as to come with Fr Oswald, it would be a good thing; if not, he can come later, if Your Paternity agrees. I commend myself humbly to your holy sacrifices. From Seville, 10 May 1594.

    Your Paternity's
        son and servant
            Robert Persons.

[PS] Fr Garnet told me of Your Paternity's great kindness in giving them leave to send twelve to be received into the Society; and taking advantage of this leave he has sent another four to Flanders in the last few days. I doubt not that Your Paternity will give instructions how to dispose of them for the greater glory of God. The same father also sent me the list of members of the Society who are there in England; and as far as I can recollect the number comes to seventeen. It was a great comfort to me to know it. Here too there is no doubt that some of the most capable men in the seminaries will enter;[325] already they show signs of desiring to do so. May all be for the glory of our Lord, the help of our afflicted country, and the confusion of the heretics.

B230 To Claudio Acquaviva, Marchena, 12 May 1594

    SOURCE: ARSI, Hisp. 136, fols. 318–19, holograph.
    HICKS: 255–264, with English translation.
    NOTE: En route to Madrid, Persons stopped at Marchena at the invitation of the third duke of Arcos, Rodrigo Ponce de León (ca. 1545–1630), a benefactor of the college in Seville (Murphy, 6).

    Persons accepts the general's decision that Creswell and Holt should exchange places, as Creswell was not making himself popular with the Spanish rectors. In Flanders, tension was building between Holt and William Crichton, who was complaining about the lack of a Scots seminary: Persons was shown a letter to this effect from Crichton to the Scotsman Colonel William Semple in Madrid. He explains how much he assisted Crichton during the latter's stay in Madrid, from January to August 1592.

324. Christopher Walpole (ca. 1570–1606) and Michael Walpole (ca. 1570–1625) were currently at the novitiate in Rome; Richard Walpole entered the Society in Spain 6 March 1593 (McCoog, *English and Welsh Jesuits*, 323–324); evidently, he was stationed at the Jesuit school in Montilla, south of Cordoba.

325. I.e., join the Society of Jesus.

The letter provides an intriguing example of Persons's complex response to authority within the Society of Jesus. He had recently received news of the outcome of the general congregation; possibly the relevant correspondence had followed him to Marchena, since there is no mention of it in the letter from Seville two days before. Decrees 47 and 48 prohibited "engaging in affairs of state and in politics" and discouraged "close friendships with princes"; decrees 52 and 53 excluded those of "Hebrew or Saracen" descent from entering the Society; and decree 54 censured "disturbers of the Society." For details, see John W. Padberg et al., *For Matters of Greater Moment* (St Louis, MO, 1994), 187–246.

On the subject of the status of men of Jewish descent, Persons was himself opposed to restrictions, and inclined to side with Acosta, who had voted against the decree. Here Persons explains how he has reluctantly agreed to abide by the decision: his loyalty lay with Acquaviva and the decisions of the Society in general congregation, especially given the sentiments at court. If he knew about Acosta's opposition to the decree against *conversos*, he would also have wanted to distance himself from him. On this question, see Robert Maryks, *The Jesuit Order as a Synagogue of Jews: Jesuits of Jewish Ancestry and Purity-of-Blood Laws in the Early Society of Jesus* (Leiden, 2010).

Persons was also perplexed by the decree that Jesuits should not be involved in politics – how could this apply in England? The question is canvassed by Thomas M. McCoog in "'Rendering to Caesar': Religion, Politics, and the Society of Jesus in Elizabethan England," in McCoog, *And Touching Our Society*, 349–369.

Muy Reverendo en Christo Padre nuestro
Pax Christi.

Con el ordinario passado di quenta a Vuestra Paternidad de lo que por entonces se offerecia y embié el translado de la carta del Padre Siguença, el qual con priesa me llamava a Madrid para el negocio del Padre Acosta, y juntamente la carta que yo le[326] respondi con las raçones que me movian de no[327] andar por entonces, si no de escrivir a Don Juan de Idiaquez, la qual resolucion parece que el tiempo ha mostrado que fue acertada pues en estas postreras cartas de Vuestra Paternidad de 14 de Março, no escrive Vuestra Paternidad cosa alguna de aquel negocio, y por otras partes estamos avisados que el Padre Acosta buelve a su gobierno de Valladolid. En Madrid pienso que toparemos los Padres que vienen de Roma y sabremos las cosas más de raiz, y si fuere menester alguna cosa de mi parte lo hare con la voluntad y cuydado que deva.

1. De presente estamos el Padre Cresuello e yo[328] en Marchena de buelta para Madrid. Fue necessario passar por acá para complir con el Duque y la Duquesa que son amigos y benhechores del Collegio Ynglés en Sevilla, el qual, gracias a Dios, dexamos en muy buen término, porque en 17 meses que ha durado ha gastado más de 6000 ducados, y con todo esto no tiene deudas, si no más de mil ducados sobrados aunque esto tenemos muy en secreto. Agora si trata de accomodarlo de una casa propria, muy buena grande y ancha, Vuestra Paternidad veerá por unos translados de cartas que el Padre Cre-

---

326. Le] *interlined with caret* R
327. no] *interlined with caret* R
328. e yo] *interlined with caret* R

suello embia al Padre Edmondo Harodo, la grande benevolencia de la ciudad de Sevilla al Collegio, y cómo nos han señalado una renta de 586 ducados en cada año para pagar la alquile de las casas que tenemos. Al presente he embiado tres sacerdotes a Ynglaterra y el Padre Simon Swinborn de la Compañia, a Flandes, por su salud, como en la otra mia escrivi, y aguardo la venida del Padre Osvaldo Tesemond en su lugar. La gente destos Seminarios es la mejor que si puede imaginar y libre totalmente de aquelos humores que por algunas causas particulares ha avido en esto Seminario de Roma.

2. El Padre Gulielmo Olto[329] vendra acá, pues assi parece a Vuestra Paternidad y cierto pienso que será para mucho servicio de nuestro Señor, para que quede enformado en estas cosas aqui, si yo faltasse, porque él, aunque sea algo de condicion secca, todavia *est homo probatae virtutis* y de buen entendimiento, y lo que importará mucho, para esta obra, es hombre conformabile con otros, en sus dictamines, en lo qual el Padre Cresuello hasta agora no ha dado mucha satisfacion a estos rectores por acá,[330] pareciendoles que sus dictamines son particulares y *non secundum usum communem*, por lo qual y porque les ha mostrado mucha resolucion en llevarlos adelante, dudan estos Padres que no podrian passar con el Padre Cresuello, si yo no estubiere aqui, aunque en lo demas confiessan que es muy buen religioso y de buen discurso y entendimiento, como en verdad lo es.

3. Me an escrito de Flandes que el Padre Criton y el Padre Olto no an estado los dias passados muy a una, en sus pareceres y actiones, y me ha pesado, porque solian estar muy grandes amigos, y puede ser que el Padre Olto con su seguridad aya dado alguna causa, pero tan bien veo por otra parte, por cartas que an parecido acá, que el buen Padre Criton está con algunas passiones, porque una carta suya leý yo que escrivio al Coronel Simple Escoces en Madrid y él me la mostro, en la qual deçia que pues yo[331] avia sacado al Rey un Seminario para muchachos ordinarios y pobres de Ynglaterra, a quenta de diez ducados por cada un el mes, más razon era que el Rey lo diera para muchachos nobles de Escocia, y todavia es cosa[332] evidente que la mayor parte de los que an venido a Sant Omer son hijos de cavalleros muy principales. Otro padre de la Compania de Flandes, me escrive que estando un dia con el Padre Criton a ablar al obispo de Sant Omer, el qual[333] no estava muy affecto por entonces al Seminario Ynglés, preguntó el obispo, la causa porque los Yngleses tenian tantos Seminarios y los escoceses ninguno: y le respondio el Padre Crito, que esto era porque los yngleses eran más importunos y yvan pidiendo por acá y por alla, y que los escoceses eran más modestos y nobles de condicion, y no suffrian esta baxeça y otras cosas semejantes, que el otro Padre se corria de oyrlas, tan bien Algunos me an escrito que el buen padre algunas veces no dexa de quexarsi de mi, como si yo no le ubiesse ayudado en sus negocios aqui en España y prometto a Vuestra Paternidad como religioso que si Vuestra Paternidad mismo ubiesse venido a España, no le pudiere yo[334] acudir ni servirle con mayor voluntad en todo lo que yo valia, offreciendole deneros, travajo, consejo y todo lo demas. Verdad es que en quanto a sus desiños del

329. Olto] *interlined with caret R*
330. por acá] *interlined with caret R*
331. yo] *interlined with caret R*
332. cosa] *interlined with caret R*
333. el qual] *interlined with caret R*
334. yo] *interlined with caret R*

Padre[335] que proponia para remediar a Escocia, yo le dixi siempre que no llevavan fundamento, ni que eran factibiles, y siempre le acconsejé que los dexasse, y se animasse a fundar un buen Seminario de Escoçeses en Flandes, assigurandole que para contentarle, y embiarle consolado[336] le darian aqui todo lo que sería necessario *in hoc genere* que era proprio de nosotros, pero el Padre nunca quiso dar memorial dello, hasta al tiempo de su partida y entonces no quiso tener paciencia de aguardar la respuesta ni tan poco de cobrar su viatico, y assi partio sin lo uno y lo otro, y agora lo trata por via de cartas que es medio[337] muy flacco para estos hombres frios y tardios, y porque no se le conceden deve turbarse el buen Padre, y quexarse de otros. Esto es la misma verdad, la qual deseo que Vuestra Paternidad sepa y no más.

4. Los decretos de la Congregacion han llegado aqui, y otros escriveran a Vuestra Paternidad lo que sientan y ablan dellos, todos parecen muy bien, en quanto yo veo y oyo de fuera[338] si no es el 3, *de genere Haebreorum*, porque contra esto ablan muchos, tanto de la Compañia como de fuera. Y los unos lo llevan por via de espirito diciendo que parece poca piedad escluyr alguna generacion de hombres Christianos (*quantum in nobis situm est*) de los medios dexados de Dios para salvarse que es la religion, si en el siglo curren peligro, y si todas las demas[339] religiones al exemplo de la Compañia, hicieren lo mismo, esta generacion de hombres no tendrian medios seguros de su salvacion. Otros lo llevan por via de buen gobierno, diciendo que será este decreto causa de mucha disunion en la misma Compañia en España, y de agenacion de mucha gente principal de fuera &c. Veremos lo que diran en la corte donde entiendo que será mejor recebido este decreto, que en otra parte, por ser conforme al humor dellos, y al modo de proceder del regno, y algunos ministros del Rey me an ablado algunas veçes significando que sería bien que se hiciesse tal decreto, e yo por entonces allegava muchas raçones *in contrarium*, pero agora bolveremos la hoja, y buscaremos las mejores raçones que podremos para defender lo que nuestra madre ha determinado, pues esto será lo más acertado y los hijos an de sugetar sus entendimientos.

5. Deseo saber la intension o interpretacion del 12 decreto, *ne quispiam publicis & saecularibus principum negotiis quae ad rationem status ut vocant pertinent, ulla ratione se immisceat* &c. porque con la gracia de nuestro Señor deseo observarlo muy puntualmente, ni tengo difficultad alguna para ello[340] si no es que parece que las cosas de la religion catolica en Ynglaterra estan tan unidas y mescladas con las del estado, que no si puede tratar las unas sin las otras,[341] pues no ay otro estado en Ynglaterra si no de hereges, y todo lo que tratamos en favor de la religion[342] es contra su estado, y aunque quesieremos separar las cosas de religion de las de estado en la[343] speculacion, todavia in la practica no

335. del p^e *supplied from margin* R
336. y embiarle consolado] *interlined with caret* R
337. medio] *followed by obscure decayed word* R
338. y oyo de fuera] *interlined with caret* R
339. todas las demas] *replaces* otras [*deleted*] R
340. ello] *interlined with caret* R
341. que no si puede tratar las unas sin las otras] *interlined with caret* R
342. en favor de la religion] *interlined with caret* R
343. la] *interlined with caret* R

si puede tratar las unas sin mesclar las otras, y assi tengo necessidad de alguna declaracion dispensacion o direcion de Vuestra Paternidad[344] en esto, y supplico a Vuestra Paternidad me la mande embiar y Dios nos guarde muchos años a Vuestra Paternidad por bien de la Compañia. En cuyos santos sacrificios humilmente me encomiendo. De Marchena a 12 de Mayo 1594.

   De Vuestra Reverenda Paternidad
     indigno hijo y siervo
      Rob. Personio.

[*Addressed*:] Soli. Al muy Reverendo en Christo Padre nuestro Claudio Aquaviva General de la Compañia de Jesus. Roma. [*with summary of contents*][345]

Translation

Our Very Reverend Father in Christ
The peace of Christ.

By the last post I gave Your Paternity the current news, and I sent a copy of Fr Sigüenza's letter, which summoned me urgently to Madrid about the affair of Fr Acosta, and with it the letter which I sent in reply giving the reasons which persuaded me not to go at the moment but to write to Don Juan de Idiáquez. Time seems to have shown that this decision was the right one, for in these last letters from Your Paternity of the 14th of March[346] you do not say a word about the matter, and from other sources we are informed that Fr Acosta is returning to his post of authority in Valladolid.[347] In Madrid I think we shall run across the fathers who are back from Rome and shall get more to the root of matters. If there should be any need for me to take action, I will do so with due carefulness and goodwill.

1. At the moment, Fr Creswell and I are at Marchena on our way back to Madrid. We had to come this way in order to satisfy the duke and duchess, who are friends and benefactors of the English college in Seville. The latter, thank God, we left in a very good state, for during the seventeen months of its existence it has spent over 6000 ducats, and in spite of this it is free of debt and has a surplus of 1000 ducats, although we are keeping this fact very secret. Negotiations are now in hand for providing it with a house of its own, a very fine one, large and spacious; Your Paternity will see from the copies of some letters which Fr Creswell is sending to Fr Edmund Harewood[348] the great generosity which the city of Seville has shown to the college, and how they have appointed us an income of 586 ducats a year to pay the rent of the houses we possess. I have just now sent three priests to England, and Fr Simon Swinborne of the Society to Flanders for the sake of his health, as I told you in my other letter, and I am expecting the arrival of Fr Oswald Tesimond in

---

344. V. P. *interlined with caret* R

345. Entered as "en el soli" on fol. 317v, immediately after summary of letter of 10 May (B229).

346. B220.

347. Persons repeats what he wrote to Acquaviva on 18 April (B226).

348. Edmund Harewood, SJ (1554–1597), was minister at the English college in Rome; see Persons's letter to him of 12 June 1595 (B280).

his place. The men in the seminaries here are of the best type imaginable, and entirely free from those humours which owing to certain special causes have existed in the seminary at Rome.

2. Fr William Holt will come here, since this is Your Paternity's wish, and I certainly think it will be greatly for the service of our Lord; for in this way he will be able to keep himself informed about matters here, in case I should have gone away. Although he is somewhat unsociable in character, still he is a man of tested virtue and good intelligence and – a thing which will stand him in good stead in this kind of work – he is a man who can accommodate himself to other people's views. In this respect Fr Creswell has not so far made himself very acceptable to the rectors here; for it seems to them that his views are peculiar to himself and not those that are ordinarily held; and for this reason and because he has shown how he insists on baiting them all the time, these fathers are doubtful if they could put up with Fr Creswell unless I were here; although in other respects they admit that he is a good religious, well-favoured, and intelligent, as indeed he is.

3. I am told in letters from Flanders that in these last days Fr Crichton and Fr Holt have not been much in sympathy with each other in their views and line of action; and this has grieved me because they used to be very good friends. It may be that Fr Holt with his assertiveness has given some cause, but on the other hand I see also, from letters which have appeared here, that good Fr Crichton is becoming agitated. I saw a letter he wrote to Colonel Semple, a Scotsman in Madrid, which the latter showed to me;[349] in this he said that, since I had wheedled a seminary out of the king for poor and undistinguished boys from England on the basis of ten ducats a head per month, there was all the more reason why the king should do the same for boys from Scotland who were of noble lineage. Yet it is well-known that the greater number of those who have come to Saint-Omer are the sons of gentlemen of very good position. Another father of the Society in Flanders writes to me that one day when he was with Fr Crichton in conversation with the bishop of Saint-Omer, who at that time had not much liking for the English seminary, the bishop asked why it was that the English had so many seminaries and the Scots none; and Fr Crichton answered him that this was because the English were more persistent and went begging far and wide, while the Scots were more reserved and of a more aristocratic temperament, and could not stomach that base spirit; and there were other similar remarks which the other father was ashamed to hear. Others too have written to me that at times the good father complains ceaselessly about me too, as though I had not helped him in his business here in Spain. Yet I promise Your Paternity, on my word as a religious, that if you yourself had come to Spain I could not have helped or served you with greater goodwill than I did him in every way I could, putting money, my labour, advice, and everything else at his disposal. It is very true that, in the matter of the schemes which the father proposed for curing the ills of Scotland, I always told him that they were not well-founded and were impracticable, and also that I advised him to give them up and to take courage and found a good

---

349. William Semple or Sempill (1546–1633) founded the Scots College in Madrid in 1627. See Glyn Redworth, "Between Four Kingdoms: International Catholicism and Colonel William Semple," in *Irlanda y la Monarquía Hispánica: Kinsale 1601–2001: Guerra, Politica, Exilio y Religión*, ed. Enrique García Hernán et al. (Madrid, 2002), 255–264.

seminary for Scotsmen in Flanders. I assured him that to satisfy his wishes and send him away comforted they would give him everything he needed here for this kind of project, which belongs to us in particular. But the good father would never present a memorial on the subject, until the time came for departure, and then he would not have the patience to wait for the answer, nor even to draw his travelling expenses; and so he went away without either: and now he is dealing with the matter by letter, a very ineffective method to use with people here, who are cold and dilatory; and because he does not get what he wants, the good father must get annoyed and complain of others. This is the exact truth, and I am anxious that Your Paternity should be well aware of it.

4. The decrees of the congregation have arrived here, and others will be writing to Your Paternity what is thought and said about them; they all make a very good impression, as far as I can see and hear as an outsider, except no. 3, "concerning the Hebrew race." There are many, both in the Society and outside it, who have something to say against this one. Some treat it on the spiritual plane and say that it scarcely seems a pious proceeding to exclude one race of Christians (as far as in us lies) from the means which our Lord left for their salvation, that is the religious life, if they are incurring danger in the world. If all the other religious orders were to follow the example of the Society and do the same, this race of men would be deprived of the sure means of their salvation. Others treat it from the point of view of good government, and say that this decree will be the cause of a great deal of discord within the Society itself in Spain and will tend to alienate many notable men outside it. We shall see what they say at court; I believe that this decree will be better received there than elsewhere, as it agrees with their humour and with the method of procedure in this country. Some of the king's ministers have spoken to me at times and intimated that it would be a good thing for a decree of this sort to be made, and at the time I brought forward many reasons against it; but now we will turn over a new leaf and seek the best arguments we can to defend what our mother has decided; for that will be the most proper thing to do: sons must submit their judgements to hers.

5. I should like to know the intention of, and the interpretation to be put on, the 12th decree: "Let no one on any account be involved in the public and secular affairs of princes which pertain to matters, as it is termed, of the state, etc.," because by the grace of our Lord I wish to observe it very scrupulously. I have no objection to this, except that it seems that the interests of the Catholic religion in England are so bound up and intermingled with those of the state that one cannot deal with the one without dealing with the other, since there is no government in England except that of the heretics, and everything that we attempt to do for the service of religion is in opposition to their government; and even if we wished to keep matters of religion separate from those of the state in theory, in practice it is not possible to deal with the one without bringing in the other. And so I feel the need of some sort of statement or dispensation or instruction from Your Paternity with regard to this matter, and I beg you to have this sent to me. May God preserve Your Paternity to us for many years for the good of the Society. To your holy sacrifices I humbly commend myself. From Marchena, 12 May 1594.

Your Paternity's
unworthy son and servant
Robert Persons.

B231 From Claudio Acquaviva, Rome, 6 June 1594

SOURCE: ARSI, Baet. 3/I, 155.

NOTE: Acquaviva is glad that Persons did not return to Madrid to discuss Acosta's situation with the king. He trusts that Mannaerts and Duras, the previous and current Belgian provincials, will be a great support to the new seminary at Saint-Omer. He informs Persons that Muzio Vitelleschi has been replaced as rector of the English college in Rome by Girolamo Fioravanti (who was named on 27 May).

On 10 August (B240) Persons wrote to say that he had not received a letter by the latest post but understood from Francisco Rodríguez that Acquaviva had written to inform him about Fioravanti's appointment. This suggests that this letter, addressed to Seville, did not reach Persons, who was now in Madrid, and warns us to be cautious about assuming that letters in the general's registers were in fact delivered.

P. Roberto Personio, Junio 6.

Vuestra Reverencia hiço muy bien de no volver a Madrid para tratar el negoçio que yo le encomendava tratase con Su Magestad, porque ni era mi intençion que volviese, pues en caso que estuviese ausente, iba la carta enderezada al Padre Avellaneda; el ofiçio se hiço como havrá sabido, pero no fue de efecto.

Doy graçias al Señor por la protection que tiene de esos Seminarios la qual bien manifiesta su divina bondad poniendo en todos tanta afiçion a esa obra y gana de promoverla. Lo de Flandes será ayudado con la presençia del Padre Oliverio, y con el cuydado del Padre Duras que le ha succedido en el ofiçio, como Vuestra Reverencia sabrá, y de mi parte se lo encomendaré yo con qualquiera ocasion. En lo demas que Vuestra Reverencia me diçe de algunos[350] sujetos, yo me remito a su pareçer como antes de aora le tengo escrito.[351]

Hemos mudado el Rector deste Seminario y en lugar del Padre Muçio que es Rector del Collegio de Napoles, hemos puesto al Padre Jeronimo Fierabante, que espero satisfara. En las &c.

Translation

To Fr Robert Persons, 6 June.

Your Reverence did very well not to come back to Madrid to deal with the business which I entrusted to you to handle with His Majesty, because it was not my intention that you should return, but that, in case you had already left, the letter was addressed to Fr Avellaneda: the business was dealt with, as you will be aware, but it did not take effect.

I give thanks to the Lord for the protection he provides for those seminaries. This clearly shows forth His divine goodness, imbuing everyone with such great enthusiasm for the work and such willingness to promote it. The seminary in Flanders will be helped by the presence of Fr Olivier, and with the care of Fr Duras who has succeeded him in his

---

350. algunos] *interlined with caret R*
351. en sus &c. *deleted R*

position,[352] as Your Reverence will know, and for my part, I will entrust it to him on every occasion. For the rest, on the other subjects that Your Reverence raises, I leave them to your judgement, as I have written to you before now.

We have transferred the rector of this seminary, and in place of Fr Muzio who is now the rector of the college of Naples, we have appointed Fr Girolamo Fioravanti, who I hope will be satisfactory. To your [prayers and holy sacrifices], etc.

B232 From Francisco Rodríguez, Rome, 6 June 1594

SOURCE: Persons to Acquaviva, 10 August (B240).

NOTE: In this letter Acquaviva's secretary informed Persons that Acquaviva had written about the appointment of Fr Fioravanti as rector of the English college in Rome. From the term "one of his [letters]" (Persons to Acquaviva, 10 August), it appears that Rodríguez may have corresponded regularly with Persons.

B233 To Claudio Acquaviva, Madrid, 4 and 16 June 1594

SOURCE: ARSI, Hisp. 136, fols. 362–363, a confidential holograph letter with ciphers decoded above the line.

HICKS: 265–276, with English translation.

NOTE: Persons responds to Acquaviva's request (B222) to suppress the *Conference about the Next Succession* for the present, until Allen has had a chance to look at it. He refers also to a Spanish version of the second part, currently with Idiáquez, who will be discreet. Persons then explains the rationale for the book, and its argument, and argues that it will advance, not hinder, the cause. On the Spanish version, *Raçonamiento y parecer de los letrados ingleses sobre el caso de la sucesion del Reyno de Inglaterra* ("The reasoning and opinion of the English lawyers about the succession of England": Madrid, Biblioteca Nacional de España, MS 23199), see Dominguez, *Radicals in Exile*, 157–161.

Ribadeneira has arrived from Jesús del Monte but on account of his illness does not want to take up the position of superior at the professed house in Toledo as requested by the general. The king's support for the college at Seville is a great help, and Valladolid, St Omers, and Rheims are all progressing well. Letters from the king, and those anticipated from Acquaviva, may encourage Jean d'Heur, acting provincial in Flanders while Mannaerts was away in Rome at the general congregation, to be more enterprising.

Muy Reverendo en Christo Padre nuestro
Pax Christi, &c.

1. La de Vuestra Paternidad de 30 de Março no llegó a mis manos si no oy 4 de Junio en la qual Vuestra Paternidad manda que procure atajar un libro que diçe aver entendido, que se ha escrito en esta provincia de la succession de Anglia [45], y aunque antes que Vuestra Paternidad escrivio esto, se avia dado orden al Agente en Belgia [47] que el

---

352. George Duras replaced Olivier Mannaerts as Belgian provincial after the general congregation.

translado Anglo [144] detubiesse con secreto [136] hasta que recibiesse otra orden y particularmente hasta que Alano [106] aviesse visto todo y dado su parecer. Todavia por cumplir más con la Obediencia, y con el parecer y gusto de Vuestra Paternidad se a tornado a escrivirle luego lo mismo. Y quanto al otro traslado Hispano [142] que está qui en poder de D. Iddiaquez [103] (digo de la segunda parte del libro solamente que es de las particulares pretensiones de cada un pretensor) aunque no está en mi mano de quitarselo, todavia puedo assicurar a Vuestra Paternidad que ellos usarán dél con el secreto y recato que conviene, y no lo communicarán si no es con el papa [80] y el Ambassador de España en Roma [150] y assi me han dicho, y esto es quanto si puede hacer en esto particular por agora y si yo ubiesse pensado, o conforme a mi discurso pudiere pensar que Vuestra Paternidad reparara en el negocio, hiciera yo diligencias para estorvarlo antes, aunque no dependia el negocio totalmente de mí, si no de otros 3 o 4 a lo menos que tuvieron su parte y parecer tambien en ello, y son de los más graves,[353] pláticos y de los que más pueden saber y jusgar en semejantes materias de la nacion, y fueron de parecer que no solo no si puede temer inconveniente deste tratado, si no mucho bien para los Catolicos y grande ayuda para la causa y que sea una de las cosas más importantes y necessarias que se aya hecha en provecho della hasta agora. Esto es su parecer y por ventura Vuestra Paternidad no jusgará muy differentemente quando avrá leido el traslado Hispano [142] que con estas galeras se embiará. Non embié el traslado Anglo [144] porque no se entendiera, ni podia Vuestra Paternidad enformarse de persona aý que entiende más en este negocio que los de acá, particolarmente D. Inglefeld [104] y otro de Hibernia [50] que sabe mucho en semejante materia. Y assi embié a Vuestra Paternidad solamente los capitulos, y agora para que Vuestra Paternidad se satisfaga más hasta a veer el libro que se embia, apuntaré aqui algunas cosas que appertenecen a este effecto.

2. Primeramente entrambos libros son unos discursos de dos letrados[354] escritos con todo comedimento y indifferencia en esta materia sin prejudicar a nadie, y el primero libro trata solamente este punto, que en las successiones de Reynos no se ha[355] de considerar solamente parentesco y proximidad de sangre, sino otras condiciones tambien, y principalmente la religion y culto de Dios, y esto tambien si muestra que entre los mismos gentiles se guardava.

Este puncto se tiene por muy necessario, para que los Catholicos, no curren ciegamente tras qualquiera persona, que pretende succession de sangre sin otra condicion, como se a visto en Inglaterra, dopo la muerte de la Reyna Maria, y despues en Francia, y pensaron que estavan obligados en consciencia.

El segundo libro propone las pretensiones de 5 Casas reales, y de diez o onçe personas que pretenden todas en primero lugar, sin que la una ceda a la otra, y las raçones que cada uno allega para sí y contra los demas, y esto sin hablar mal de nadie, ni de su pretension, y sin determinar el drecho de ninguno.

Este punto tambien pareció neçessario se discubriesse para obviar a aquella ley de los Herejes que ninguno hablasse en ello, por medio de la qual ley querrian tener todos ciegos en esta materia, para hecharles a cuestas despues el Rey que ellos quieren, pero con

353. graves] R; grandes Hicks
354. discursos de dos letrados] underlined R
355. ha] inserted by Hicks; not in R

esta luz muchos abriran los ojos, y los mismos herejes si devideran entre sí, y los Catolicos veeran que tienen paño de que curtar sin escrupulo de Consciencia, si los pretensores son Herejes. Y en quanto a Re de Scotia [82] [51] no si dice cosa contra él, ni si ni quanto heretico [138] ni asi tam poco porque egualmente se habla tanto por heretico [138] como por Catolico [137]. Ni si repara en esto, si no que a parte rei, si dicen las[356] raçones que ay para todos *pro et contra*. Y el mismo si entiende en el caso de Re de Scotia [82] [51] y de los Prencipes d' Spagna [83] [43] y de otros. Y pienso sin duda que será servicio de Dios y bien de Anglia [45] y sin justa offension de nadie. Y todavia se Vuestra Paternidad jusgará otramente, hare[357] de muy buena gana lo que en mí fuera para que *supprimatur liber*, o que si haga qualquiera otra cosa que Vuestra Paternidad gustará en cuyos santos sacrificios humilmente me encomiendo. De Madrid a 4 de Junio 1594.

[PS] Esto escrivi y embié a Vuestra Paternidad por un extraordinario a 4 déste, despues an succedido algunas otras cosillas las quales tengo escritto a la persona que dara a Vuestra Paternidad ésta.

[3.] Y estandome al presente para partirme a Valladolid, ha llegado aqui de Jesus del Monte el padre Ribadaneyra y me ha dicho la infermidad que tiene de piedra, y la muy grande repugnancia que tiene a la proposition que Vuestra Paternidad le ha encargado de la casa[358] profesa de Toledo por ser aquella ciudad muy contraria a su enfermidad, y la occupacion a su condicion, y esto me ha pedido significar a Vuestra Paternidad y supplicarle que le discargue desta pesadumbre que le ha de quitarle[359] la vida como dice y no approvechar a la casa. Vuestra Paternidad lo mirará con su grande caridad y prudencia.

4. Para Settiempre aguardo en Sevilla al padre Osvaldo como Vuestra Paternidad nos ha prometido pues será muy necessario para aquel collegio, aqui emos negociado racionablemente porque el consejo real nos ha concedido la facultad que pedia la ciudad de Sevilla para darnos 586 ducados en cada un año, y más desto ha decretado el consejo de la camera que si escrive una carta a Sevilla para informar a Su Magestad de la casa que ha menester el dicho collegio de comprar, de manera que confio en nuestro Señor que en poco tiempo quedaremos con buena casa para la salud, y de lo demas para el sustento tengo poco cuydado, lo de Valladolid va bien y doy muchas gracias a Vuestra Paternidad de que no se me quitó el padre Cabredo, él hace su officio bien, y aý se hara hombre, para mucho servicio de nuestro Señor y de la Compañia, y es aún moço y harto tiempo ay para emplearlo despues.

5. El padre Cresuello queda aqui por morador deste Collegio con gusto de todos, y no dudo si no que hara bien y procuraremos que no sea cargo al collegio si no de su comida solamente la qual merecera muy bien con lo que travajará, está racionable de salud aunque no totalmente aunque convalecido.

6. El seminario tan bien de Sant Omer va bien y me escriven que ay 35 personas en él y yrá creciendo cada dia, particularmente agora con la postrera carta del Rey en que assento muy bien la renta de 2000 escudos de oro.

356. las] *interlined with caret* R
357. haré] *followed by* facilm^te [*deleted*] R
358. casa] *followed by* de [*deleted*]
359. quitarle] R; quitar a *Hicks*

7. El padre Orano agora[360] provincial ha andado siempre encogido y estrecho hasta agora, mandandoles[361] resolutamente algunas cosas, que bien se podian remetir o alargar, agora confio mostrará más ánimo con las cartas del Rey, y con lo que Vuestra Paternidad le escrivera, y si parece a Vuestra Paternidad escrivirle que en las cosas que tocan a la nacion las quales él no puede saber tanto, si fie de los padres que estan alli y de nos otros[362] por acá que emos procurado y sustentado aquel seminario hasta agora, no tendra inconveniente, como lo haçen los provinciales por acá. Y que aquel seminario tenga su rector a parte sin dependencia del Collegio de la Compañia como el de Roma y este de acá, y esta tan bien es la intencion del Rey en su fundacion y es necessario para la union y para que no aya quebras, y si Vuestra Paternidad pudiesse[363] hacerme caridad de mandarme embiar acá la copia de la que Vuestra Paternidad escrivera en esta materia paraque todos nos conformemos al orden de Vuestra Paternidad recibire mucho consuelo en ello. Al presente tratamos muy de veras de comprarles la casa en la qual viven que es muy buena.[364] Confio en nuestro Señor que se hara.

8. El seminario tan bien de Rhemis que si ha retirado a Douay topó alli con la cédula de los quatro mil escudos que de acá les embiamos con lo qual quedan muy consolados. Y con esto y otros medios tengo esperança que Dios ha de sustentar esta causa, hasta que sea servido de usar más misericordia con Ynglaterra. Él guarde siempre a Vuestra Paternidad. Madrid 16 de Junio 1594.

    De Vuestra Reverenda Paternidad
       Hijo y siervo endigno
        Rob. Personio.

[*Addressed*:] Al muy Reverendo en Christo padre el padre Claudio Aquaviva preposito General de la Compania de Jesus en Roma.

[*Endorsed*:] Soli. Madrid. P. Rob. Personio 4 et 6 d'Giugno 1594. [*with summary of contents*]

Translation

Our Very Reverend Father in Christ
The peace of Christ, etc.

1. Your Paternity's letter of the 30th of March did not reach me until today, the 4th of June. In it, you instruct me to try to stop the publication of a book which, you tell me, you have been informed has been written in this province on the subject of the succession to the English crown. Even before Your Paternity wrote this, orders had been given to the agent in Belgium that the English version was to be held up and kept secret, pending further orders, and in particular until Allen had looked into the whole matter and given his approval. Nevertheless, in compliance with the duty of obedience and to defer to Your Paternity's will and pleasure, we have written to him again immediately with the

 360. agora] *interlined with caret R*
 361. mandandoles] les *interlined with caret R*
 362. otros] *interlined with caret R*
 363. pudiesse] prometiesse *Hicks; R obscure*
 364. buena] *followed by* en, *evidently in error R*

same message. And as to the other version, in Spanish, which is here in the hands of Don Juan de Idiáquez (I am speaking only of the second part of the book, which treats of the claim peculiar to each claimant), although it is not in my power to take it away from him, still I can assure Your Paternity that they will observe due secrecy and reserve in the use they make of it, and will show it to no one except the pope and the Spanish ambassador in Rome. This is what they have told me, and that is all that can be done about it for the time being. If I had thought, or, as I reasoned, had any cause to think, that Your Paternity would call a halt in the matter, I would have taken measures before to hold it up – though the matter was not entirely in my control. This matter was shared with at least three or four others who also had their part and voice in it: they are highly grave, experienced men, who have the best means of knowing and judging in matters of this kind concerning the nation. They felt that not only is no ill consequence to be feared from this treatise, but that much advantage can be expected from it for the Catholics, and great help to the cause; and they say that it is one of the most important and necessary things that have been done on our behalf so far. This is their opinion, and possibly Your Paternity's judgement will not be very different when you have read the Spanish translation which will be sent to you by the galleys going now. I did not send the English version because it would not be understood; nor was there any one there,[365] from whom Your Paternity could get information, who has more knowledge of the business than those who are here, especially [Sir Francis] Englefield and another man from Ireland,[366] who is very wise in such matters. And so I have sent Your Paternity only those chapters.[367] And now, in order that you may be better satisfied in the interval before you see the book which we are sending, I will jot down some points that are contained in that document.

2. In the first place, both books are dialogues by two lawyers, and have been written on this subject courteously and impartially, without prejudice to anyone. The first book deals with this point only: that in the succession to a kingdom, kin and proximity of blood is not the only thing to be taken into consideration, but other circumstances also, and especially religion and the worship of God. And it is shown also that this practice was observed even by heathen races.

It is considered very necessary to make this point in order to prevent Catholics from running blindly after any person who may happen to have a claim to the succession by blood, without any other consideration. This was what happened in England after the death of Queen Mary, and afterwards in France; they believed they were bound to it in conscience.

The second book sets forth the claims of five royal houses and of ten or eleven individuals who all have *prima facie* claims. Without preferring one claimant over another, it sets out the arguments adduced by each one in his own interest and against the others. This is done without speaking ill of any one or of his claim, and without drawing any conclusion whether the right stands with any one of them.

365. I.e., in Rome.

366. Richard Stanihurst (1547–1618) cultivated the friendship of Englefield and Persons when he was occupied in Philip II's chemical laboratory next to El Escorial from 1592 to 1595; see Colm Lennon (*ODNB*).

367. Hicks translates as "chapter headings", but it seems that Persons is explaining why he has sent only the translation of book 2.

This point also needed to be made clear in order to counteract the law made by the heretics forbidding mention of this subject. By means of that law, they wanted to keep everyone in darkness in this matter, so as to saddle them later on with the king they themselves wanted. But when this light has thus been thrown on the subject, many people will have their eyes opened, and even the heretics will be divided in opinion among themselves. The Catholics too will see that there is another alternative which can be used without scruple of conscience if the claimants are heretics. With regard to the king of Scotland, nothing is said against him on the score of his being a heretic; in fact, that is not the point at issue, for what is said applies equally to a Catholic as to a heretic; nor does it stop at that; but the arguments that apply to each of the contestants, *for and against*, are stated objectively. This applies to the case of the king of Scotland equally with that of the Spanish prince and others. And I think that it will undoubtedly tend to the service of God and the advantage of England, and will give nobody just cause of offence. Yet if Your Paternity comes to a different conclusion, I will very willingly do all in my power *to have the book suppressed*, or anything else that you like. To your holy sacrifices I humbly commend myself. From Madrid on the 4th of June 1594.

[PS] I wrote the above and sent it to Your Paternity by an extra post on the 4th of this month. Subsequently there have been some other trifling occurrences about which I have written to the person who will give you this letter.

3. Just as I was about to leave for Valladolid, Fr Ribadeneira arrived here from Jesus del Monte. He told me of the ailment he suffers from – the stone – and of the great disinclination he has to Your Paternity's proposal to put him in charge of the professed house at Toledo – that city is very unfavourably located for his ailment, and the position is unsuitable for his condition – and so he has asked me to pass this on to Your Paternity and beg you to relieve him of this burden, which will be the death of him, he says, and of no advantage to the house. Please would Your Paternity consider the matter with your great charity and prudence.

4. I am expecting Fr Oswald in Seville for September, as Your Paternity has promised, for he will be very necessary for that college. Here we have come to a reasonable arrangement: the king's council has granted the authorization asked for by the city of Seville to give us 586 ducats a year; and in addition, the council has decreed that a letter be written to Seville telling them to report to His Majesty on the house which the said college needs to purchase. Thus, I trust in our Lord that in a short time we shall be in possession of a house that is satisfactory from the point of view of health; and for the rest, in the matter of upkeep I have little anxiety. Things are going well too in Valladolid, and I am very grateful to Your Paternity for not depriving me of Fr Cabredo; he carries out his duties there well and it will make a man of him, resulting in much service of our Lord and the Society. He is still a young man and there is plenty of time to give him other employment later.

5. Fr Creswell is remaining here as an inmate of this College with the goodwill of all, and I have no doubt that he will do well. We will arrange that he is not a charge on the college except for his food only, and he will earn that very fully by his work; he is in reasonably good health though not entirely recovered as yet.

6. The seminary of St Omers also is getting on well. They tell me that there are thirty-five persons in it, and the number will continue to increase day by day, especially now after the king's last letter assigning us the very comfortable income of 2000 golden crowns.

7. Fr d'Heur, the present provincial, has hitherto always acted in a narrow and pusillanimous way, giving them uncompromising orders to do certain things which might well be let alone or deferred; I trust that now he will show more courage, after the king's letters, and what Your Paternity will write to him. If Your Paternity sees fit to tell him that in matters touching our nation, of which he cannot have so much knowledge as they have, he is to rely on the fathers who are there, and on us here (who have been the means of setting up that seminary and have maintained it till now), it will not be out of place; that is what the provincials here do. Let him be told also that the seminary should not be subject to the Jesuit college but have its separate rector,[368] like the one in Rome and this one here. This too was the king's intention when founding it, and it is necessary in order to ensure oneness of spirit and to avoid quarrels. If Your Paternity could be so kind as to send me here a copy of what you write about this, so that we may all conform to your orders, I should receive much consolation from it. At present we are trying very hard to buy them the house they are living in, which is a very good one, etc. I trust in our Lord that this will be done.

8. The seminary of Rheims also, which has been withdrawn to Douai,[369] unexpectedly found there the warrant for 4000 crowns, which we sent from here, and they are much encouraged by it. So, by these and other means I hope that God is going to support this cause, until such time as He vouchsafes to treat England with greater mercy. May He ever preserve Your Paternity. Madrid, 16 June 1594.

> Your Paternity's
> unworthy son and servant
> Robert Persons.

B234 Undated note, possibly June 1594

SOURCE: ARSI, FG 651/640, item 24, an undated note in Persons's hand.

NOTE: The ciphers from Persons's letter to Acquaviva, 4/16 June 1594 (B233) have been applied. The note appears to relate to the English succession.

In the Fondo Gesuitico, this precedes the letters from 1590. The ciphers in the Latin text have been decoded in the translation, as far as possible, from the previous letter (B233), with some tentative suggestions. Further research may clarify the position taken here by Persons.

Probabile est quod 123 expedietur brevi; hoc tamen valde 136. 82 non vult Anglia pro se ullo modo neque pertinebit ad 43, quod valde contenti sunt 137 142. Primi fere et praecipui 86 45, et qui non sunt adhuc plane 136, petunt amicitiam cum 82 et ut illis subve-

368. See Persons to Acquaviva, 4 December 1593 (B210).
369. The English college at Rheims moved back to Douai in 1593 because of pressure from the military forces of Henry IV (Navarre).

niant, valde pertesi sunt 83. Puto quod 45 erit pro 83 88 cum filia 82. Si transigatur de 123, valde probabile est fore necessarium ut 108 una hinc ad tempus proficiscatur, quamquam faciet quod in se erit ut maneat. Et haec est adhuc coniectura. Scribam caetera, ut accident. Hac omnino 136 esse debet, quasi 123, expediatur dissimilanter fiet, si aliquod hoc in negotio fiat infra tres vel quattuor menses fiet, itaque necesse erit breviter nobis detur responsum.

Translation

It is likely that 123[370] will soon be put in order, but this must be kept very secret. Philip II does not want England for himself in any way, neither will it concern Spain, because the Spanish Catholics are quite content. First and foremost, nearly, are 86[371] of England, and those who are not so far fully secret, seek friendship with Philip and the princes are very disinclined to come to their aid. I think that England will be for the prince of 88[372] with the daughter of Philip. If things are settled concerning 123, it is very likely that it will be necessary that Persons also should set out from here for the time being, although he will do what he can to stay. This is all guesswork so far. I will write the rest, as it turns out. On this matter, just as 123, complete silence should be maintained: it is expedient that it should be done in a dissembling way. If anything should happen in the business below, it will take place within three or four months, so it will be necessary to give us a response quickly.

B235 From Claudio Acquaviva, 4 July 1594

SOURCES:

ARSI, Tolet. 5/II, fol. 347v–348r.

Ang. 38/II, fol. 82, Bartoli's note.

NOTE: Once again Acquaviva rejoices in the news from the colleges, enjoining the students to respond to their welcome in Spain by applying themselves to their studies. He gives his approval for Robert Jones to be sent to Britain, and applies further pressure for William Holt to be winkled out of Flanders and sent to Spain. He appeals to Persons to support Crichton, despite the latter's incautious words.

In an annotation, responding to Persons's query in his letter of 12 May (B230), Acquaviva clarifies the decree of the general congregation enjoining Jesuits not to involve themselves in matters of state. See Edwards, 171, and McCoog, *And Touching Our Society*, 364–365, and *Building the Faith of St Peter*, 233–234, noting Antonio Possevino's querying of the decree.

370. This may refer to a further armada.
371. Possibly the English Catholic nobles or gentry.
372. This may refer to a possible match for the infanta. After the death of Henry III of France, it was proposed that she should marry a French prince and succeed to the throne of France, but Philip II was not in favour. Before his death in 1592, the prince of Parma might have been considered, with a view to succeeding to the throne of England.

P. Roberto Personio, 4 Julio, Madrid.

Dos de Vuestra Reverencia he recevido con este Ordinario, una de 10, otra de 12 de Mayo, y çierto que todos tenemos grande[373] obligaçion a los muchos que con palabras, y con tan excelentes obras se muestran afiçionados a esos seminarios, pagueselo Dios por quien lo haçen, que bien seguros estan de no perder el premio dello: y es çierto que para los mesmos alumnos será cosa que les dara consuelo y ánimo verse tan ayudados y amparados en tierras estrañas, y eso mesmo les hara entender quanta obligaçion tienen de ser diligentissimos en salir hombres de virtud y letras, quales los requiere el fin para que se enderezan. Yo me consuelo que en esas provincias se ayan reçevido los que Vuestra Reverencia diçe, y en ello havia yo dado orden a los Padres Provinciales antes que de aqui partiesen: bueno es el Padre Roberto Jonas, para lo que Vuestra Reverencia le quiere, y es mision que él la desea, y es sujeto para ella. Dexemosle acabar su curso que despues procuraremos que en esto se dé a Vuestra Reverencia la satisfaction que en lo demas. No creo que podra ir por alla el Padre Holto, porque el Secretario Ybarra le detiene, y a mí me ha escrito sobre ello, diçiendo que avisara a Su Magestad de la necessidad que dél ay en aquella tierra, y que hasta tener respuesta deste no le saquemos.

Bien creo yo que Vuestra Reverencia por su parte ayudaria al Padre Critonio quando aý estuvo, y no obstante lo que Vuestra Reverencia me avisa de algunas palabras que se la han escapado, deseo que ayude a su negocio en la manera que con su prudencia le pareciere convenir, como más en particular le escriviran algunos destos padres, especialmente el Padre Tirio, a ellos me remito.

[Añadido al Padre Personio Julio 4:]
En el particular que Vuestra Reverencia toca çerca del 12. decreto de la Congregaçion general, espero que Vuestra Reverencia se havrá tan prudente y religiosamente que non terná necessidad de dispensacion, ni conviene que yo la dé en cosa que tan uniformemente sintio y encargó la Compañia, pero declaro a Vuestra Reverencia para que con más luz en ello proceda, que no prohibe el decreto dar consejo en cosas del divino serviçio etiam que en ellos se mezclen cosas de estado. Lo que vieda[374] y manda es que[375] los nuestros no las soliciten por cartas, ni menos atiendan a la execuçion dellas.

[Bartoli:]
Si rallegra con esso de i favori acquistati da i Seminarii[376] di Spagna. Secondariamente gli ricorda a non ingerirsi in negotii di stato; non vietandogli pero il dare in ciò consiglio in cose di servitio di Dio.

Translation

To Fr Robert Persons in Madrid, 4 July.

I have received two letters from Your Reverence with this courier, one of 10 May, the other of 12 May, and for sure we are greatly obliged to those many people who show

373. grande] *interlined above* mucha [*deleted*] R
374. vieda] *followed by* es [*deleted*] R
375. que] *followed by* no [*deleted*] R
376. Seminarii] *this ed.;* Semianrij R

their support for those seminaries, both through what they say and through their excellent works; may God repay them, for whose sake they are doing these things, and who will ensure that they do not lose their reward. And it is certain that amongst those students themselves it will be something that will comfort and encourage them, to see themselves so aided and protected in foreign lands; and that same will make them understand how great an obligation they have to show themselves most diligent in becoming men of virtue and letters, such as the purpose demands on which they are embarked.[377] It is a consolation to me that in those provinces they are welcomed as Your Reverence says, and in that regard I gave order to those father provincials before they left here. Fr Robert Jones is good for that which Your Reverence requires, and it is the mission which he desires, and he is suitable for it. Let us allow him to finish his course; after that we shall endeavour in this to give Your Reverence the satisfaction as in other things. I do not believe that Fr Holt can go there,[378] because the secretary Ibarra is detaining him,[379] and Holt has written to me about him, suggesting that His Majesty might be advised of the necessity which exists for him in Spain, and until we get an answer to this, we should not get him out.

I well believe that Your Reverence for your part helped Fr Crichton when he was there, and despite what Your Reverence warns me about certain words which have escaped him, I want you to assist in his business in such manner as seems suitable to your prudence; I defer to what some of those fathers will write to you more in particular, especially Fr Tyrie.[380]

[Addendum to the letter to Fr Persons, 4 July:]
With regard to the particular matter which Your Reverence mentions, concerning the 12th decree of the general congregation, I hope that Your Reverence would act so prudently and religiously that there would be no need for a dispensation. It is not convenient that I should give such a dispensation in a matter where the Society feels and instructs so uniformly, but to clarify it so that Your Reverence may proceed with more light in this matter: the decree does not prohibit one from giving advice on matters concerning the Lord's service, even when they are mixed up with matters of state; instead, what is forbidden and made mandatory is that Jesuits should not solicit such matters by letter, still less be involved in their execution.

[*Bartoli:*]
He rejoices with him about the favours obtained for the seminaries of Spain. Second, he reminds him not to meddle in matters of state – without prohibiting advice in the service of God.

377. An important specification of the purpose of seminary training.

378. I.e., to Spain, as Acquaviva had insisted.

379. Esteban de Ibarra was the secretary of state for the Spanish Netherlands, to the court of which Holt had been assigned.

380. James Tyrie (1543–1597), a Scottish Jesuit, was the general's assistant for Germany from 1592.

B236 To Claudio Acquaviva, Valladolid, 12 July 1594

SOURCE: ARSI, Hisp. 137, fols. 24–25.
HICKS: 277–286, with English translation.
NOTE: This is Persons's comprehensive report on the state of the college, now that he has returned to Valladolid after his lengthy sojourn in Seville and Madrid. There is need for discretion in the appointment of a new rector of the Spanish college of St Ambrose, where the English students attend lectures; Persons requests that Cabredo, the successful rector of the English college, not be transferred to St Ambrose. He asks that the unpopular Martínez be replaced as lecturer, because of his inflexible teaching of Thomist philosophy; Antonio de Padilla is hamstrung by poor health and a distracting workload, but much respected as a lecturer (Persons to Acquaviva, 9 September 1592, B156). Richard Gibbons, who stayed at Valladolid at his own request, is now ready to move on and concentrate on his writing on St Paul's Epistles, while Thomas Wright can fulfil his duties as lecturer; so, Persons recommends that Gibbons migrate to Rome. The college in Seville is flourishing under Peralta, with the favour and encouragement of Pérez as provincial of Andalusia and Gonzalo Dávila as provincial of Castile.

At the end of the year, Cabredo was replaced by Gonzalo del Río, and Luis de la Puente (1554–1624) was appointed rector of St Ambrose. Puente was the spiritual director of the Brigittine nun Marina de Escobar (1554–1633) and author of *Meditations on the Mysteries of Our Holy Faith*, translated by Richard Gibbons and published in Douai in 1610.

Muy Reverendo en Christo Padre nuestro
Pax Christi.

Por aver escritto a Vuestra Paternidad de Madrid y de Escurial todo lo que se offerecia, poco me queda por agora. Hallo este Collegio y Seminario en buen estado, gracias a Dios, ay mucha salud, union, paz, y contento, los estudiantes hacen muy bien en letras y virtud, an venido cinco de nuevo del Seminario de Sant Omer, muy buenas abilidades; aquel Seminario prosperandolo Dios, como lo hace, será el fundamento de todos los demas, en lo de lo temporal andamos siempre con alguna difficultad, pero en fin Dios nos ayuda y no tenemos muchas deudas.

1. En Sevilla donde el Seminario depende mucho del amor y benevolencia de los Padres de la Compañia (y la emos hallado siempre más que en ninguna otra parte) el Padre Peralta me escrive que por ser los superiores nuevos, digo el provincial y Preposito de la Casa, importará mucho que Vuestra Paternidad nos haga caridad de escrivir dos palabras a cada un dellos, al Padre provincial agradeciendole lo que hiço siendo Viceprovincial, y al otro encomendandole de nuevo, porque dice el Padre Peralta que al passo que anduvieren los superiores, yran los demas de la Compañia, y por aver estado el Padre Bartolome Perez y el Padre Cordeses muy affectos a la obra, todos los demas an favorecido, y entiendese que Dios lo ha pagado muy bien a la casa professa, la qual ha prosperado más en un año despues que el Collegio Ynglés ha estado en Sevilla que en dos o tres antes, y escrivenme de siette mil ducados *de extraordinario* que la casa ha recebido en partidos grossos este año de limosna, y más hara Dios con ellos cada dia, por las buenas

obras que nos hacen alli. La carta de Vuestra Paternidad nos ayudó grandemente al principio y assi le tornamos a supplicarla agora para la continuacion.

2. Dos años avrá que Vuestra Paternidad me escrivio toccante al Padre Ricardo Gibbono quando estava en Portugal, que le podria encaminar o para Roma o para Francia, pues él deseava salir de Portugal por su salud, y despues contentandose él de quedar aqui por algun tiempo, Vuestra Paternidad me lo remitio tan bien, pero agora llegando aqui he visto que él no es más necessario para esta casa, por supplir lo que él hacía el Padre Tomas Wright, y por la otra parte, se ha puesto a començar a escrivir sobre las epistolas de San Pablo como Vuestra Paternidad avrá entendido por el principio que ha embiado a Roma con los correos passados, y por tener necessidad de muchos libros para proseguir esta obra que no si hallan aqui, ni si pueden aver, particularmente de los hereges, el Padre ha tenido deseo de venir a Roma y veerse con Vuestra Paternidad tanto para esso, como para tomar la direcion de Vuestra Paternidad y de otros Padres aý en la dicha obra, si se ha de proseguir, y porque entiendo que no faltará en qué emplear el dicho Padre en Roma o en otra parte[381] en esto o otra cosa, considerando los muchos buenos talentos que tiene, pareciome que podia sirvirme de la licencia que Vuestra Paternidad avia embiado antes, pero con todo esto quisi escrivir esta y aguardar la respuesta, si viene antes de las embarcaciones de Siettembre. De Francia no parece que es cosa de pensar por agora qué[382] se embie alla, considerando los travajos que ay, pienso que en la penitenciaria o Collegio Romano, hallará Vuestra Paternidad alguna buena occupacion para él y más a su gusto, como tan bien de provecho. Ya Vuestra Paternidad conosce su condicion, y yo tanto que pienso que se yo pudiesse quedar con él siempre en esta casa, no avria difficultad, pero estando absente succeden algunas cosas de pesadumbre.

3. El Padre provincial ha estado algun dia con nosotros aqui en esta casa y nos ha consolado, le he consultado esta yda del Padre Gibbono y le parece que es con razon, en cosas desta casa tubo poco que haçer pues andan muy bien como he dicho, y assi occupó lo más del tiempo mientras que estubo en cosas universales y consultas con los Padres, conferi con su Reverencia algo[383] sobre las cosas del Collegio de Sant Ambrosio, pues estamos los deste Collegio muy interessados en ellas que vayan bien pues aquel Collegio y este son como madre y hijo, o maestro y discipulo, y porque he visto aquel Collegio andar estos años atras muy abatido y discontento tanto en el gobierno como en lo de los estudios, rogue mucho al Padre provincial y lo mismo hago a Vuestra Paternidad que si tenga particular quenta con ellos para su consuelo.

4. En lo de los estudios parece cosa clara que mientras el Padre Martinez continúa a leer no avrá contento, porque es impossibile poner estima en los estudiantes de sus cosas, yo he hecho aqui con los desta casa todo lo possibile por via tanto de rigor como de suavidad, y no he aprovechado nada, no lo quieren oyr si no a pura fuerça. La causa dicen es, que todas sus leciones son, si es opinion de San Tomas o no, y si la proposision es probabile o no probabile, y si la raçon de San Tomas es demonstrativa o no, bien fundada o no, y este juizio no se les puede quitar, y los nuestros estudiantes de San Ambrosio quedan con lo mismo que es otra confirmacion destos nuestros yngleses, pero lo que

381. o en otra parte] *interlined with caret R*
382. qué] *interlined with caret R*
383. algo] *interlined with caret R*

más me discontenta es, que veen con esto[384] la grande disunion que ay entre los nuestros en cosas de letras y de[385] juizios y conseguentemente tan bien en las volundades, y assi parece que es cosa degna de remedio efficaz y presto.

El Padre Antonio de Padilla tiene poca salud y por los meses atras ha tenido[386] muchas occupaciones y distraciones de negocios, sermones y otros[387] embaraços y assi ha leydo muy poco, este año, que es otra quexa muy grande de los estudiantes, pero quando lee dan tanta satisfacion sus papeles que no si puede más desear, y es realmente la reputacion principal deste collegio, y creo que avria mucho inconveniente quando él lo dexasse, y assi si pareciesse a Vuestra Paternidad ordenar que si juntasse otro buen lettor con él como sería el Padre Siguença o el Padre Cobos, y que él se disocupasse de negocios y sermones, para attender más a sus leciones, pienso que quedaria muy bien remediado lo de los estudios, aunque no ubiesse tercero lector, como hasta agora ha avido con poco fruto, pero esto es, con que no quede aqui el Padre Martinez, porque otramente nunca havrá paz.

5. En lo del rector tan bien diçen que avrian menester de un hombre de partes para allentar el Collegio tanto en lo temporal y espiritual como en los estudios, y aunque el Padre Luys de la Puente que venía señalado sea hombre docto y santo, dicen que no tiene las partes que avria menester para esto, pues es muy encogido secco y pusillanime, mas les parece que el Padre Labata o el Padre Phillipe de Acuña, o el Padre Emanuel Rojas dexando de leer, le[388] darian contento. Se avia pensado de pedir a Vuestra Paternidad al Padre Bartolome Perez para el año que viene, y passar este año con algun Vicerector o con el mismo Padre Juan Suarez, pero ay duda que Vuestra Paternidad tiene otros designos del Padre Perez, pero quando Vuestra Paternidad lo pudiesse dar, no sería otro tal ni para ellos, ni para nosotros en este Seminario. Algunos avian pensado de[389] pedir a Vuestra Paternidad al Padre Cabredo para rector de San Ambrosio, pero yo les dixe que confiava que Vuestra Paternidad no lo concederia, pues me lo avia defendido en otra occasion más urgente (de que quedo a Vuestra Paternidad muy agradecido) y quando Vuestra Paternidad se les concediesse, sería disacomodar más a este Collegio Ynglés que no acomodar aquel de Sant Ambrosio, pues más facilmente se hallará rector apto para aquella casa que no para esta[390] y assi pienso que no ablarán en esto a Vuestra Paternidad; y si ablaren, bien me assiguro que el paternal amor de Vuestra Paternidad no nos faltará como nunca. Y no[391] tengo otro que escrivir por agora. En los Santos sacrificios de Vuestra Paternidad humilmente me encomiendo. De Valladolid a 12 de Julio 1594.

    De Vuestra Reverenda Paternidad
        siervo y hijo endegno
           Roberto Personio.

    384. con esto] *interlined with caret R*
    385. de] *interlined with caret R*
    386. ha tenido] *interlined with caret R*
    387. otros] *Hicks*; otras *R*
    388. le] *Hicks*; les *R*
    389. de] *R*; a *Hicks*
    390. esta] *suppl. Hicks; not in R*
    391. no] *suppl. Hicks; not in R*

[*Addressed:*] Al muy Reverendo en Christo Padre nuestro el Padre Claudio Aquaviva Preposito General de la Compañia de Jesus en Roma.

Translation

Our Very Reverend Father in Christ
The peace of Christ.

Since I wrote to Your Paternity from Madrid and from El Escorial all there was to be said, there is little that remains to be written now. I find the college and seminary here in a good state, thank God. Health is good, and there is great union of hearts, peace, and content. The students are making good progress in letters and virtue. Five have lately come from the seminary of St Omers, of very great abilities. If God prospers it, as He is doing, that college will be the foundation of all the others. In temporal matters we always have difficulties to contend with, but in the end, God comes to our assistance; and we have few debts.

1. Fr Peralta writes to me from Seville, where the seminary is very dependent on the charity and generosity of the fathers of the Society (and this we have always found greater there than anywhere else), to say that, as the superiors (that is to say, the provincial and the superior of the professed house) are newly appointed, it would be convenient if Your Paternity would be so kind as to write a few lines to each of them: to the provincial to thank him for what he did as vice provincial;[392] and to the other to commend the seminary to his care afresh; for Fr Peralta says that the rest of the Society will follow in the footsteps of the superiors, and that because Fr Bartolomé Pérez and Fr Cordeses[393] were very keen on this project, all the others showed favour to it; and it is well-known that God has repaid the professed house very well for this, for in one year since the English college was established in Seville it has prospered more than in two or three previously. And they tell me of 7000 ducats extra which the house has received in gross income from alms this year; and God will do more for them from day to day, in return for the favours they do us there. Your Paternity's letter was of great assistance to us at the beginning, and so now we beg you again to continue your help.

2. It will be two years ago that Your Paternity wrote to me about Fr Richard Gibbons, when he was in Portugal, saying that I could send him either to Rome or to France, since he wished to leave Portugal for reasons of health.[394] Afterwards as he was content to stay here for some time, Your Paternity left that to me also. Now that I have come here, I have found that he is no longer required for this house; Fr Thomas Wright is available for the work he was doing. On the other hand, he has started to write on St

---

392. It is unclear who is meant here: Bartolomé Perez, mentioned later, was provincial of Andalusia from 1589 to 1594; Cristóbal Méndez was appointed viceprovincial in May 1593 and provincial in 1596.

393. Antonio Cordeses was superior of the professed house in Seville from 1593–94; see Garnet to Persons, 6 September 1594 (B243). According to Peralta's account, he supported the work of the English college unreservedly, arguing that the professed house, so far from losing revenue because of the college, had been blessed by its establishment (Murphy, 159).

394. Acquaviva to Persons, 31 August 1592 (B155).

Paul's Epistles,[395] as Your Paternity will have learnt from the first beginnings which he sent to Rome by the last post. As he has need of a great many books in order to proceed with this work and they are not to be found here, and cannot be got, especially those written by heretics, the father has conceived a wish to go to Rome, where he can both get together with Your Paternity for that project and receive guidance on the said work from Your Paternity and from other fathers, if it is to be proceeded with. And as I feel sure that there will be no difficulty in finding employment for this father in Rome or elsewhere, in this or some other work, considering his excellent capabilities, I considered that I could avail myself of the leave Your Paternity previously gave me, but all the same I decided to write this letter and await the answer, provided it comes before the ships sail in September. From what I hear from France there seems no reason to think that he should be sent there at present, in view of the trouble there; I think that Your Paternity will be able to find him some useful occupation in the penitentiary or in the Roman college, which will be more to his liking, as well as being more productive. Your Paternity knows his character well: I think that if I were able to remain with him in this house always, there would be no difficulties, yet in my absence things take place which cause trouble.

3. Father provincial[396] has been with us here in this house some days and has given us much consolation. I have consulted him about the question of Fr Gibbons going to Rome, and he thinks it is reasonable. There was little for him to do as regards matters in this house, for, as I have said, they are going very well; and so, he occupied most of his time here in matters of general import and in consultations with the fathers. I had some talk with His Reverence about the affairs of the college of St Ambrose, for we here of this college are much concerned that they should go well, since that college and this are mother and child, as it were, or master and pupil. For some years back I have watched that college becoming very dejected and discontented, both in the matter of its government and of its studies, and so I begged father provincial earnestly, and I do the same to Your Paternity, to have particular care of them and afford them relief.

4. In the matter of the studies, it seems clear that, so long as Fr Martínez continues to lecture, there will be dissatisfaction, for it is impossible to instil into the students any respect for his methods. I have done all that I could here with those of this house, employing severity as well as persuasion, and have had no success. Force alone will make them listen to him. The reason, they say, is because all his lectures amount to asking whether St Thomas teaches this or not. Is the proposition probable or not? Is St Thomas's argument conclusive or not? Well-founded or not?[397] It is impossible to rid them of this estimate of him, and it is shared by our students of St Ambrose – which is a further corroboration of what our English students say. But what gives me greatest uneasiness is that in

---

395. *ARCR* records only translations by Richard Gibbons.

396. Gonzalo Dávila, provincial of Castile from 1593–1597.

397. Although Aquinas was the authority *par excellence* in Jesuit education, the *Ratio studiorum* allowed some flexibility; see Harro Höpfl, *Jesuit Political Thought: The Society of Jesus and the State, c. 1540–1630* (Cambridge, 2004), 168, citing Albano Bondi, "La *Bibliotheca Selecta* di Antonio Possino: Un progetto di egemonia culturale," in *La "Ratio Studiorum"*, ed. Gian Paolo Brizzi (Rome, 1981). From the description given here, it appears that Martínez used a dialectical approach.

this way they see the great lack of agreement that exists among Ours in matters of scholarship and in our opinions, and infer from it a conflict of will also; and so it would seem to be a matter that deserves sure and speedy remedy.

Fr Antonio de Padilla is in poor health. For some months now he has had much to distract him in the way of business affairs, sermons and other impediments, and so he has lectured very little this year. This is another cause of great complaint by the students; but when he does give lectures, they are successful beyond expectation; and it is he really who gives this college its name. I think it would be a great misfortune if he were to give up lecturing, and so, if Your Paternity should approve of some other good lecturer being associated with him, such as Fr Sigüenza or Fr Cobos,[398] and that he should be relieved of business and sermons, so as to devote more attention to his lectures, I think that the question of the studies would be solved very satisfactorily, even if there were not a third lecturer as there has been lately, though with little profit. But this is on the assumption that Fr Martínez does not stay here; if he does, there will never be any peace.

5. In the matter of a rector too, they say that it would be necessary to give them a man of parts to foster the temporal and spiritual welfare of the college as well as its studies; and though Fr Luis de la Puente, whose name has been mentioned, is a learned and holy man, they say he does not possess the qualities required for this, as he is very reserved and taciturn, and lacks initiative. They think that Fr Labata or Fr Felipe de Acuña or Fr Manuel de Rojas, if he gives up lecturing, would be more likely to suit them.[399] They had thought of asking Your Paternity for Fr Bartolomé Pérez for next year and continuing this year with someone as vice rector, or with Fr Juan Suárez himself; but it is suspected that Your Paternity has other plans for Fr Pérez; should you however be able to afford him, there is no one else who would be so welcome both to them and to us also in this seminary. Some had thought of asking Your Paternity for Fr Cabredo as rector of St Ambrose's, but I told them I was confident you would not grant it, because you had refrained at my request from doing so before on another more critical occasion (for which I am still very grateful to Your Paternity). If you were to let them have him, the result would be to disrupt this English college more than to benefit that of St Ambrose; for it will be easier to find a suitable rector for the latter house than for this. And so, I think they will refrain from speaking of it to Your Paternity. If they do, I feel quite certain that your fatherly love will not fail us, for it has never done so before. I have no more to say at present. I commend myself humbly to Your Paternity's holy sacrifices. Valladolid, 12 July 1594.

    Your Paternity's
        unworthy son and servant
        Robert Persons.

398. Antonio de Padilla, rector, Manuel de Rojas and Juan de Sigüenza, professors, are mentioned in an early document about "the adjustment of lectures, disputations, etc., with St Ambrose's College," in Williams, *St Alban's College*, 241. Sigüenza was rector of the college at Madrid until 1594. Cristóbal de los Cobos (provincial of Castile, 1605–1609) is also mentioned in Acquaviva's letter of 29 August (B242), as the *socius* to the provincial.

399. Padilla, Cobos, Puente and Juan Francisco Labata (ca. 1549–1631), amongst others, represented Castile at the general congregation (Astrain, 3: 206, 691–692). For Rojas, see previous note.

B237 To Claudio Acquaviva, Valladolid, 12 July 1594

SOURCE: ARSI, Hisp. 137, fol. 26.
HICKS: 287–292, with English translation.
NOTE: This is the confidential letter accompanying the previous item. Persons deals at length with delicate personal issues relating to three English Jesuits at Valladolid, recommending that Richard Gibbons be transferred elsewhere. He looks forward to making the Spiritual Exercises.

The letter makes mention of letters written by Persons to the rector, Cabredo, and the minister, Charles Tancard, and probably to Wright and Gibbons as well. Throughout his absence from Valladolid, from October 1593 to 1594, Persons presumably maintained a regular correspondence with Jesuits there, but the details cannot be reconstructed.

Muy Reverendo en Christo Padre nuestro

Lo que escrivo en la otra carta desta misma fecha a Vuestra Paternidad de la pax y contento que ay en este Seminario, se entiende de los estudiantes y de los demas tan bien de la nuestra Compañia, si no de los padres yngleses que aqui viven que son el Padre Ricardo Gibbono, el Padre Carlos Tancardo y el Padre Tomas Wright, en los quales he hallado alguna turbacion, causada principalmente de las choleras del Padre Ricardo, las quales son tantas y tan vehementes quando començas, que no ay quien pueda con él. Yo quando sali de aqui, lo dexé muy contento y bien puesto. Siempre me confessé con él, para poder assigurarle mejor por esta via, de imaginaciones y suspechas, que le suelen venir; déxele tan bien mi aposiento y libros, en mi absencia, serrando solamente algunos papeles secretos, de lo qual todavia, y porque escrivi una o dos veçes al Padre Carlos que es ministro, y no a él, en ciertos negocios de casa, commenço a turbarse, lo qual entendiendo yo le escrivi una carta amorosa para placarle, y poco despues offereciendome una necessidad forçosa de veer un papel que tenía serrado en la arca de mi aposiento, quisi hacer confiança del Padre Ricardo, y le embié la llava[400] para que me buscasse y embiasse a Madrid, pero él en buscando, halló una carta del Padre Cresuello de Sevilla, un poco aspretta de cosillas del Padre Carlos y de unas libertades suyas, por las quales fue menester mudarlo de alli, y esta carta no solamente la communicó el Padre Ricardo con el Padre Tomas, si no tan bien, la dio en mano del mismo Padre Carlos, con que él quedó muy turbado, y creo que escrivio una carta en aquella turbacion, al Padre Ludovico Maselli, offereciendole de yr más presto a Alemaña o otra parte que no quedar en este officio, porque en llegando aqui me mostro luego lo que entonces escrivio, y la causa fue esta.

Pero succedio despues otra turbacion mayor, porque veendo el rector que estos Padres yvan turbados, y que se apartavan siempre de los demas Padres y hermanos españoles me lo advirtio e[401] yo le respondi, lo que me parecia para el remedio hasta que yo bolviesse; y esto por una o dos solis, fuera de la carta commun que siempre se les leýa a todos, pero el Padre Ricardo suspechando que avia alguna soli, aguardando a veer el rec-

---

400. llava] Hicks; possibly llave R
401. e] R; y Hicks

tor occupado y descuydado fuera de su aposiento, fingio tener necessidad de sacar un tomo de San Chrysostomo, que el rector tenía, y pidiole su llave y con esta occasion buscó y halló aquella soli mia[402] y la llevó y transladó, y la mostro a entrambos los Padres, y porque yo avia escritto al rector en ella quanto mi discontentava aquel modo de proceder dellos, turbaronse más, no solamente con el rector, si no tan bien contra mí, aunque en llegando aqui, quitóseles totalmente la turbacion, y supi todo el negocio como avia passado, porque me lo dixeron, y el Padre Ricardo tan bien (aunque no sabe que yo tengo entendido todas las particularidades[403] dichas) todavia la substancia de todo me ha dicho y queda muy placado y se ha[404] offerecido a hacer todo lo que yo quiero, y realmente si yo pudiesse quedar siempre en este Seminario con él, no tendria dudar[405] de passarlo todo bien con él, pero no me atreveria dexarlo otra vez con el rector en mi absencia, ni tan poco bastaria al rector el ánimo de quedar con él pues la otra vez, tan que yo[406] fui a Sevilla, succedio otra turbacion aunque no tan grande, y dice que[407] aunque las cosas del Padre Ricardo son meramente niñarias, de manera que con una paja se gana y con una paja si perde, todavia son niñarias pasadas para quien no sabe entrar y salir con él, ni sacar en[408] a luz las causas de su[409] turbaciones quando succeden, y por esto, parecio forçosa la resolucion[410] que se ha tomado de embiarlo de acá, y sin duda entiendo que él será util en otras partes, apartado destas occasiones de los de su nacion, a los quales se buelve facilmente contra los de otras, y las pone suspechas donde no les ay ni fundamento para ellas, y con todo esto él en substancia es buen religioso y amigo de la virtud y fiel a la Compañia, aunque en sus turbaciones y choleras no sería bien que conversasse con tentados, porque facilmente se le pega qualquiera tentacion. Los otros dos Padres de la Nacion que quedan aqui Carlos y Tomas, partido el Padre Ricardo pienso que passaran bien, porque son de naturales mucho más blandos, quietos y tratables, bien quesiera yo un poco más ternura de espiritu en todos nos, y en[411] esto andamos por agora, y mañaña placiendo a Dios commencaré yo los exercicios y creo que otros sigueran. Dios nos dé su gracia, y Vuestra Paternidad su santa benedicion, en cuyos sacrificios humilmente me encomiendo. Valladolid a 12 de Julio 1594.

    De Vuestra Reverenda Paternidad
        hijo endegno
           Rob. Personio.

[*Addressed:*] Al nuestro muy Reverendo General soli.
[*Endorsed:*] Vallid P. Roberto Personio Julio 12 94. [*with summary of contents*]

---

402. mia] *interlined with caret R*
403. particularidades] *Hicks corr.;* particularides *R*
404. ha] *R;* he *Hicks*
405. dudar] *Hicks; possibly* dudas *R*
406. yo] *R; om. Hicks*
407. dice que] *interlined with caret R*
408. en] *R; om. Hicks*
409. su] *R;* sus *Hicks*
410. resolucion] *Hicks corr.;* resolucio *R*
411. en] *R; om. Hicks*

Translation

Our Very Reverend Father in Christ

What I have written to Your Paternity in my other letter of this same date concerning the peace and contentment which reigns in this seminary is to be understood as referring to the students and to those also of our Society, with the exception of the three English fathers who live here, namely, Fr Richard Gibbons, Fr Charles Tancard, and Fr Thomas Wright. I have found them somewhat discontented, and the principal cause is Fr Richard's fits of anger, which are so frequent and so violent that, once they begin, no one can do anything with him. When I went away from here, I left him very contented and well-disposed. I always made my confession to him, so as to reassure him and remove ideas and suspicions that are wont to occur to him. I also let him have the use of my room and books during my absence, only keeping some secret papers locked up. This, however, and the fact that once or twice I wrote to Fr Charles, the minister, instead of him, on certain business concerning the house, began to upset him. Learning of this, I wrote him an affectionate letter by way of placating him, and shortly afterwards, when it happened that I urgently needed to see a document which I kept locked up in the chest in my room, wishing to show my trust of Fr Richard, I sent him the key, so that he could look for it and send it to Madrid. However, in looking for it he came across a letter of Fr Creswell's from Seville, which was somewhat severe about Fr Charles's delinquencies and some liberties he had taken, on account of which it had been necessary to remove him from there. This letter Fr Richard not only showed to Fr Thomas, but he actually handed it to Fr Charles. The latter was very upset in consequence and I believe that he wrote a letter to Fr Luigi Maselli,[412] offering to go to Germany or anywhere else, sooner than remain in his post here; because when I arrived here, he presently showed me what he had written at that time, and this was the reason.

But there followed another more serious commotion; for the rector seeing that these fathers were upset and always kept themselves apart from the other Spanish fathers and brothers, called my attention to it, and I wrote back, suggesting the remedies that seemed suitable pending my return. This was done in one or two confidential letters, separate from the common letter which it was the custom to read to them all. Fr Richard however suspected that there was a confidential letter and, waiting till he saw that the rector was occupied and off his guard away from his room, pretended that he needed to get a volume of St Chrysostom, which was in the rector's possession; asked him for his key; and took this opportunity of looking for and finding this confidential letter of mine. This he took away and copied and showed to both the fathers; and as I had told the rector in it how dissatisfied I was with their behaviour, they were still more upset, not only with the rector, but also with me; though when I arrived here, they put their annoyance entirely to one side, and I heard the whole story of what had happened, for they told me about it. Fr Richard too (though he is not aware that I have been informed of all these details) has told me substantially the whole story and is now quite calmed down and has offered to do anything I wish; and as a matter of fact, if I were able to stay with him in this seminary

---

412. Luigi Maselli, assistant for Italy until 1604.

all the time, I should have no reason to doubt that all would go well with him; but I would not dare to leave him with the rector in my absence again – indeed, the rector would not have enough courage to remain with him, either. That is because on another occasion when I was in Seville, there was another incident, though not as serious; and he says that though Fr Richard's outbreaks are merely trifles which make him turn this way and that like a straw in the wind, nevertheless they are trifles that weigh very heavily on anyone who, when they occur, does not know how to humour him and draw out the cause of them. And so it seemed necessary to take the decision, as we have done, of sending him away from here. I have no doubt at all that he will be useful somewhere else where he is free of such interactions with his countrymen; for he is quick to turn to them in opposition to foreigners, making them suspicious as never before, without cause. And yet, after all, at heart he is a good religious, a lover of virtue, and loyal to the Society, though, when he is upset and has his fits of anger, it would not do for him to mix with those who are wavering; for he is easily led astray. The other two fathers of our nation, who will remain here, Fr Charles and Fr Thomas, will get on well enough, I think, when Fr Richard has gone, because they are milder in disposition, and more peaceful and tractable; I should greatly like to see all of us showing a little more generosity of spirit. And that is how things are with us at the moment. Tomorrow, please God, I shall begin the Exercises,[413] and I think that others will follow suit. May God give us His peace. I beg Your Paternity's blessing, and I humbly commend myself to your sacrifices. Valladolid, 12 July 1594.

    Your Paternity's
        unworthy son
            Robert Persons.

B238 From John Cecil, after 24 July 1594

SOURCES:
    ACSA, Series II, Legajo 1, item 20, a contemporary Spanish translation (*Vd*);
    ABSI, Coll M 189 (olim 160b), another copy (*G*).

EDITION: Pollen, *Unpublished Documents*, 285–286, with translation, following *G*.

NOTE: John Cecil sends Persons an account of the execution of the priest John Boste, emphasizing his courage and the sympathy of the onlookers. Cecil was operating as an agent for Burghley, so this letter may have been a smokescreen.

John Boste and John Ingram were caught up in a campaign headed by the president of the North, Lord Huntingdon, to counter English Catholic infiltration into Scotland (Questier, *Catholics and Treason*, 238–249; Morris, 3: 183–213). Boste (born about 1543) was chaplain to Lady Margaret Nevill, the earl of Westmorland's daughter, who was arrested with him in September 1593. He confessed to having made several forays into Scotland. John Ingram (1565–1594), chaplain to Sir Walter Lindsay of Balgavies Castle near Forfar, Scotland, was similarly associated with moves to pressure James VI into an alliance with the Catholic lords, such as George Gordon, earl of Huntly. He was arrested near Berwick while trying to return to Scotland, and tried with Boste at Durham on 24 July 1594. Boste was put to death on that

---

413. The Spiritual Exercises of St Ignatius Loyola.

day, while Ingram was executed at Gatehead two days later (Anstruther, 43–44 and 182–184).

> Relacion de algunas particularidades que passaron en la muerte y martirio
> del padre Juan Boste sacerdote de los seminarios embiado
> por el padre Juan Cicilio al padre Parsonio.

Aunque Vuestra Paternidad está bastantemente informado de lo que passó quando estavan sentenciados a muerte los siervos de dios Juan Boste y Juan Ingram sacerdotes de los seminarios,[414] con todo esto ay algunas particularidades que no puedo dexar de escrivirles para nuestra[415] edificacion y consuelo, y son, que quando llevaron al buen padre al lugar de su martirio, salieron a le siguir y acompañar más de 300 damas y mugeres principales que todas llevaron bonetes frenche hoodes de tercio pelo (la qual no llevan entre nosotros si no mugeres de cavalleros)[416] deste espectalulo espantados todos[417] los herejes, preguntaronles adónde yvan, respondieron a acompañar aquel cavallero aquel siervo de Dios al lugar[418] de su muerte como las Marias a Christo, pues que no puedemos hazer más.[419] Huvo un ministro que Dio al siervo de Dios grande[420] pesadumbre en el camino llamandole traydor etc. lo qual visto por un cavallero muy principal, llegó más circa y di al ministro un rimpuson y le dixo, andad por villaco,[421] por que el Señor Boste se ha muestrado un buen cavallero y buen hombre. Llegado a la horca, besó la escalera, y subiendo al primero grado dixo, *Angelus domini nunciavit Mariae*, etc.: al segundo, *et verbum caro factum est* etc. al tercero, *ecce ancilla domini* etc.

Volvendose al pueblo començava a predicar, y professar la fe Catholica, mas los herejes le taparon la boca diciendo que no vino alla a predicar, si no a morir.

A lo menos respondioles él, daran me licençia de dar gracias a estos señores y señoras que me an hecho esta honra y merced de acompañar me esta dia, y aunque me quitan agora esta libertad, con todo esto esta mi sangre y muerte y inocençia a de predicar in los coraçones de los que dios quiere llamar y recoger a su sancta yglesia catolica, y esta mi cabeça y mis quartos an de predicar cada dia en vuestras puertos y paredes la verdad

---

414. Juan Boste y Juan Ingram sacerdotes de los seminarios] *Vd*; Juan Ingram y Juan Boste Sacerdote *G Pollen, followed by*: que avia sido ministro de los hereges, y cómo convertieron a su ministro en el mismo tribunal, adonde recibiron su sentencia di muerte (who had been an heretical minister, and how they converted a minister while at the bar where they received judgement of death)
415. nuestra] *Vd G*; vuestra *Pollen*
416. *G omits* que todas llevaron bonetes frenche hoodes de tercio pelo (la qual no llevan entre nosotros si no mugeres de cavalleros) *and explains*: (all with black hoods which with us is a signe of gentlewomen)
417. deste espectalulo espantados todos] *Vd*; Desto spettacolo [*blank*] *G*
418. al lugar] *Vd*; om. *G*
419. pues que no puedemos hazer más] *Vd*; om. *G*
420. grande] *Vd*; om. *G*
421. en el camino llamandole traydor etc. lo qual visto por un cavallero muy principal, llegó más circa y di al ministro un rimpuson y le dixo andad por villaco] *Vd*; por el camino y vino un cavallero y le di al ministro un rimpason y le dixo Andad [*blank*] vellaco *G*

de la fe catolica: y ansi⁴²² se puso un rato en oracion, y casi dispertandose pidó licençia para rezar un psalmo de David que es el 114,⁴²³ y llegando aquel verso, *Convertere anima mea in requiem tuam quia dominus benefecit tibi* dava gracia a dios por todos sus beneficios in general, y in particular de averle hecho aquella tan señalada merced de morir por su sancta fe catolica, y llegando aquel verso, *Quoniam eripuisti animam meam a morte, oculos a lachrimis, pedes a lapsu*, alabava a dios por la constancia, paciençia y perseverancia que le avia dado que aviendo sido ministro hereje, tenido tantas tentaciones y comodidades del mundo, con todo esto dios le avia dado la gracia de dexar todo por satisfacion de sus faltas de morir con Xto, in Christo, y por Christo y por su sancta esposa la Yglesia Catolica Romana, fuera de la qual (creed me ————— hermanos, porque este no es tiempo ni de dissimular ni haçer mentiras) *impossibile est intrare in regnum caelorum.* Y dicho esto horcaronle y le hizieron pedaços.

Translation

An account of certain particulars of what took place
in the death and martyrdom of Fr John Bost, seminary priest,
sent to Fr Persons by Fr John Cecil.

Although Your Paternity is well enough informed of what happened when the servants of God John Boste and John Ingram, seminary priests, were sentenced to death, even so, there are some other particulars which I cannot omit to write for our edification and consolation:⁴²⁴ they are, that when they took the good father to the place of his martyrdom, more than 300 high-ranking ladies and women followed and accompanied him, who were all wearing velvet French hood bonnets (which no one wears among us except gentlewomen). This spectacle terrified all the heretics. When these women were asked where they were going, they answered: "To accompany this knight, this servant of God, to the place of his death, as the Marys did to Christ, because we can do no more." There was a minister who caused the servant of God great distress on the way, calling him traitor, etc. When this was seen by a gentleman of higher rank, he came closer, pushed the minister away, and said to him, "You are acting like a villain, because Mr Boste has shown himself to be a good knight and a good man." He was taken to the gallows, kissed the ladder, and mounting the first step, said, *The angel of the Lord brought glad tidings to Mary*, etc., at the second, *And the word was made flesh*, etc., at the third, *Behold the handmaid of the Lord*, etc.⁴²⁵

Turning himself to the people he began to preach and profess the Catholic faith to the people, but the heretics covered his mouth, saying he had not come there to preach but to die.

Nonetheless he replied to them, "Give me leave to thank those gentlemen and ladies who have done me this honour and favour, to accompany me this day. Although I am now being deprived of my liberty to speak – despite this, this blood and death and inno-

422. ansi] *Vd*; aun si *Pollen*
423. 114] *Vd*; 114 (Dilexi quoniam) *Pollen*
424. Both *Vd* and *G* read "our," although Pollen's "your" makes more sense here.
425. Phrases from the Angelus.

cence of mine will preach to the hearts of those whom God seeks to call and reclaim to his holy Catholic church, and this head of mine and my quartered limbs will preach every day on your gates and walls the truth of the Catholic faith." And then he spent a short while in prayer, and as if waking he asked leave to recite a psalm of David, namely the 114th,[426] and coming to this verse, *Turn, O my soul, into thy rest: for the Lord hath been bountiful to thee*, he gave thanks to God for all his benefits in general, and in particular because he had given him this signal reward of dying for his holy Catholic faith, and coming to this verse, *For he hath delivered my soul from death: my eyes from tears, my feet from falling*, he gave praise to God for the constancy, patience, and perseverance which He had given him, who had been a heretical minister, attached to the temptations and comforts of the world; despite this, God had given him grace to leave all for the satisfaction of his sins, to die with Christ, in Christ, and for Christ and for his holy bride the Roman Catholic Church, outside of which (believe me brothers ————— for this is not the time to dissimulate or to tell lies) *it is impossible to enter into the kingdom of heaven*.[427] And when he had said this, they hanged him and cut him into pieces.

B239 From Claudio Acquaviva, 1 August 1594

SOURCE: ARSI, Cast. 6, fol. 183r.

NOTE: Acquaviva responds cautiously to Persons's defence of the *Conference about the Next Succession* and accedes to Ribadeneira's request not to be appointed superior of the professed house in Toledo. Acquaviva recognizes the problems with the Belgian vice provincial Jean d'Heur and trusts that Mannaerts's return will ease matters. He also expects the new provincial, George Duras, will be an improvement on d'Heur. Later Duras was to be entrusted with the care of the English college at Douai, which was ailing because of continued religious conflict in France (McCoog, *Building the Faith of St Peter*, 235).

P. Roberto Personio, 1° de Agosto.

Recevi las de Vuestra Reverencia 4 y 16 de Junio y no dudo yo de la Religion y prudencia de Vuestra Reverencia sino que en todas las cosas que son del peso e importancia que aquel libro procede con el recato conveniente y con deseo de ajustarse[428] a lo que entiende ser voluntad de sus superiores. Ni yo pretendi con mi carta dezir que la obra fuese mala, porque me parece buena y necessaria para el fin y fines que Vuestra Reverencia dice, ni fue mi intencion que por su parte haga diligencia con los seglares que en él han entendido para que cesen de su obra, sino solo dezirle que podia haver inconvenientes de momento si esto saliese de los nuestros porque en cosas tales no ay que fiar del secreto que las partes prometen guardar que al fin todo se viene a entender y como lo que toca a la Compañia se suel; de lo demas no me parece mal en este particular.

He visto las razones que el P. Ribadeneira me alega para que no le carguemos del govierno y algunas dellas me hazen tanta fuerça que no me parece justo hazerle más

---

426. Verses 7 and 8 are quoted.
427. An echo of the dogma, *extra ecclesiam nulla salus*.
428. ajustarse] *this ed.*; ajutarse R

instancia sino que descanse y mire por su salud. Esto digo por lo que Vuestra Reverencia me escrive de esta materia.

Espero que el P. Duras lo hará en Flandes con más libertad que el P. Orano que como no era más que ViceProvincial no se atreveria a tanto, yo vere lo que se les ha escrito y de nuevo escrivire lo demas[429] que fuere necessario como Vuestra Reverencia en la suya pide y le avisaré de todo lo que alla se escriviere. Hasta ahora de Flandes me escrive en buenas nuevas del Seminario de Saint-Omer y para todo ayudala la buena presencia del Padre Oliverio. Etc.

Translation

To Fr Robert Persons, 1 August.

I have received Your Reverence's letters of 4 and 16 June,[430] and I have no doubt that in all the affairs which are of weight and importance in this book, Your Reverence's religious feeling and prudence will exercise due caution and a willingness to conform to what you understand is the will of your superiors. My letter was not intended to condemn the work, because in fact it seems to me good and necessary for the purpose and purposes which Your Reverence says, nor was it my intention that for your part you would ask the laymen to stop working on the book, except only to stipulate that there could be inconveniences for Ours if it should come out, because in such matters we cannot trust the promises people make to keep the secret: eventually everything gets to be known, and anything that concerns the Society is released. The rest does not seem to me bad in this particular.

I have seen the reasons which Fr Ribadeneira has put to me why we should not burden him with more government, and some of them are of such force to me that it does not seem just to insist anymore, but rather let him rest and care for his health. This is what I have to say concerning what Your Reverence has written to me about the matter.

I expect that Fr Duras will act in Flanders with more freedom than Fr d'Heur, who as he was no more than the vice provincial was much too reticent. I shall see what has been written to them, and will write again about whatever else is necessary, as Your Reverence demands in your letter, and keep you informed of everything that is sent from there. So far, he writes good news of the seminary of St Omers and how much the good presence of Fr Olivier helps there. Etc.

B240 To Claudio Acquaviva, Valladolid, 10 August 1594

> SOURCE: ARSI, Hisp. 137, fols. 118–119.
>
> HICKS: 293–298, with English translation.
>
> NOTE: This is a confidential letter about Richard Gibbons, who is now on his way to Rome. It has transpired that he was not much to blame for the incident described in Persons's previous confidential letter of 12 July (B237), so the general is asked to overlook it

---

429. demas] *interlined with caret* R
430. B233.

and welcome Gibbons unconditionally. News of Fioravanti's appointment as rector of the English college in Rome has come via Acquaviva's secretary Francisco Rodríguez, making Persons wonder if a letter from the general has gone astray. See Acquaviva's letter of 6 June (B231), headnote.

Muy Reverendo en Christo Padre nuestro
Pax Christi &c.

Con el ordinario passado escrivi a Vuestra Paternidad un soli, de las causas particulares por las quales parecio expediente sirvirse de la occasion que se offerecio, para embiar a Roma al Padre Ricardo Gibonnio suppuesta la licencia que se tenía antes de Vuestra Paternidad que si podiesse embiarle a Italia o a Francia quando no fuesse necessario por aqui, y aunque aquellas causas eran asi, y que el rector deste Seminario sintia mucha dificultad de quedar más con él aqui en mi absencia, por la condicion colerica, y mobile que tiene para incenderse y mudarse con occasiones muy livianas, todavia confiessa que es hombre en lo demas de la vida muy religioso, y fiel a la compañia, como en verdad lo es, y más desto he hallado despues que de aquellas cosas que passaron entre el rector y él sobre sacar sus cartas del aposiento y mirarlas, no nascio del Padre Ricardo primeramente si no de otros que por ventura en ello tubieron egual o mayor culpa que él, y asi supplico a Vuestra Paternidad muy humilmente que no se dé a entender al dicho Padre en llegando aý que Vuestra Paternidad lo sabe, ni que aya avido algun disgusto por aqui con él, porque el dicho Padre lo desea, y lo mismo supplicamos el Padre Cabredo y yo a Vuestra Paternidad pues como digo la culpa del Padre no fue tanto, pues fue una repentina mocion, por instigacion de otra persona, y el Padre despues arrepintiose del hecho, mucho y pidio con grande instancia que Vuestra Paternidad no lo supiesse, y pues Vuestra Paternidad es tan Padre de sus hijos que puede dissimular las faltas que ay, sealo en esto, para que quede el Padre Ricardo Gibbonio con gusto y consuelo y union con todos como salio de aqui, y[431] con extremo deseo de ser bien recibido de Vuestra Paternidad y empleado en alguna cosa de letras, como él tiene abilidad para muchas, y no dudo si no que avrá aý occasiones hartas para sirvirse Vuestra Paternidad dél, pues tiene tanta variedad de partes que en qualquiera cosa de escrittura, controversias, philosophia, mathematicas, lenguas, o semejante, puede sirvir, y en la penitenciaria por la nacion etc.,[432] y pues él tiene deseo de quedar por algun tiempo en Roma, Vuestra Paternidad nos hara caridad a todos de la nacion en concederselo, porque sirvira tan bien su presencia aý para las cosas nuestras que se offereceran de informar a Vuestra Paternidad o otras personas, particularmente las de acá, que las sabe bien.

Él se partio de aqui para Barcelona a primo de Agosto, porque se nos dixo que avrá galeras y el Padre deseava yrse luego para hallarse aý a los principios de los estudios; más no tengo que escrivir por agora. Todo aqui va bien gracias a Dios.

El Padre Cresuello haçe muy bien en Madrid y su[433] presencia por alli, nos ayudará en muchas cosas. Yo no he recebido carta alguna de Vuestra Paternidad por este ordenario aunque el Padre Francisco Rodriguez me dice en una suya que Vuestra Pater-

431. y] *followed by illegible word* [*deleted*] R
432. etc.] R; & Hicks
433. su] *followed by illegible word* [*deleted*] R

nidad avia escritto algo toccante al nuevo rector deste Collegio Ynglés, que es el Padre Hieronymo Fioravanti, de que no sé deçir otro se no⁴³⁴ contentarme mucho de todo lo que Vuestra Paternidad haçe, assigurandome que es con el amor paternal que siempre suele, y con mucho más luz y conicion de las personas y cosas que nosotros no tenemos aqui, y asi confio en nuestro Señor que todo saldra bien y para su mayor gloria y nosotros le daremos el⁴³⁵ consuelo y buena correspondencia de acá al dicho Padre que pudieremos, y procuraremos que se dé tan bien de otras partes, para que le sea menos pesada la carga, y teniendo a Vuestra Paternidad tan a la mano aý no dudo se⁴³⁶ no que le será facil cosa llevarla bien adelante. Dios nuestro Señor nos guarde por muchos años a Vuestra Paternidad como emos menester. En sus santos sacrificios muy humilmente me encomiendo. Valladolid a 10 de Agosto 1594.
        De Vuestra Reverenda Paternidad
           endegno hijo y siervo
             Rob. Personio.

[PS] En el mes que viene aguardo el padre Osvaldo en Sevilla⁴³⁷ como Vuestra Paternidad prometio, porque yo tan bien tengo forçosamente de llegar alla y estar este enbierno para establecer la compra de una casa propria, si será possibile, y despues entiendo no será más necessario llamar yngleses de otras partes para estos seminarios porque bastará la gente que aqui ha entrado y entrará en la compañia, y son sujetos muy caleficados.

[*Addressed:*] Soli. Al muy Reverendo en Christo Padre nuestro el Padre Claudio Aquaviva, preposito General de la Compañia de Jesus. En Roma.

[*Endorsed:*] Valladolid. S. P. Roberto Personio 94/Agosto 10. [*with summary of contents*]

Translation

Our Very Reverend Father in Christ
The peace of Christ, etc.

By the last post I wrote Your Paternity a confidential letter, telling you the special reasons why it seemed advisable to seize the opportunity offered to send Fr Richard Gibbons to Rome, relying on the permission which we had from Your Paternity before, to the effect that we might send him to Italy or to France, if at any time he should not be needed here. And though the reasons were as I said and the rector of this seminary was very loathe to have him here any longer during my absence, owing to his irascible and unstable temperament, which causes him to be moved to anger and upset at the slightest provocation, nevertheless he admits that in other respects he is a man of very religious life and loyal to the Society. This is certainly true; but besides that, I have since found out that in the incident involving him and the rector when he took some letters from his room and perused them, the initiative did not come from Fr Richard but from others, who were possibly equally or more to blame. And so I beg Your Paternity very humbly that when

    434. se no] *R*; si no que *Hicks*
    435. el] *interlined above* y [*deleted*] *R*
    436. se] *R*; si *Hicks*
    437. en Sevilla] *interlined with caret R*

the father arrives in Rome, he should not be made aware that Your Paternity knows about the incident or that he was the subject of any displeasure here; that would please the father himself, and Fr Cabredo and I too implore Your Paternity; for, as I say, the father's fault was not so very great, since it was a sudden impulse instigated by someone else. Afterwards the father utterly repented of what he had done and asked most earnestly that Your Paternity should not be told of it; and seeing that Your Paternity has such a fatherly heart that you are able to shut your eyes when faults occur, please do so in this instance, so that Fr Richard Gibbons may be assured of welcome and consolation and concord with everybody. It was in that spirit that he left here, and with a great desire that Your Paternity should receive him kindly and give him some sort of literary occupation, as he is a man of many parts; and I have no doubt that there will be plenty of opportunities for Your Paternity to make use of him, for he has such great variety of talents that he can be employed in any field: scripture, controversies, philosophy, mathematics, languages, or such like; and in the penitentiary for our nation, etc. And as he has the wish to stay in Rome for some time, by allowing him to do so Your Paternity will be doing a favour to all our nation; for his presence there will also be useful to us when information about our affairs is given to Your Paternity or to others, especially when it concerns our situation here, with which he is familiar. He left here for Barcelona on the 1st of August, because we were told that there will be galleys there, and the father was anxious to get away at once so as to be in Rome when the schools begin. I have nothing further to write about at present. All goes well here, thank God.

 Fr Creswell is doing very well in Madrid, and his being there will help us in many matters. I have not received any letter from Your Paternity by this post, although Fr Francisco Rodríguez tells me in one of his that Your Paternity has written something on the subject of the new rector of this English college:[438] that it is Fr Girolamo Fioravanti. And to this I can only say that I am very satisfied with everything that Your Paternity does, and am certain that it is done with the same fatherly love as ever, and with more insight and understanding of persons and things than we possess here. And so I trust in our Lord that all will turn out well and for His greater glory; and on our part we will give this father all the consolation and willing collaboration that we can here, and will try to ensure that he gets it in other quarters too, so that the burden of office may be less grievous for him. And as he has Your Paternity so ready to help him there, I doubt not that it will be easy for him to make a great success of it. May God our Lord preserve Your Paternity to us for many years, as we have need. I commend myself very humbly to your holy sacrifices. Valladolid, 10 August 1594.

  Your Paternity's
   unworthy son and servant
   Robert Persons.

[PS] Next month I am expecting Fr Oswald in Seville, as Your Paternity promised, for I too must necessarily get there and be there this winter so as to carry through the purchase of a house of our own, if it is possible. Henceforward I believe it will no longer be necessary to bring Englishmen from other parts of the world to these seminaries, since

---

438. Rodríguez was Acquaviva's secretary in Rome.

those who have entered or will enter the Society here will suffice and these are men who have very good qualifications.

B241 From Claudio Acquaviva, 29 August 1594

> SOURCE: ARSI, Hisp. 74, fol. 23r.
>
> NOTE: Responding to Persons's confidential letter of 12 July (B237), Acquaviva addresses the behaviour of Fr Gibbons in stealing a private letter. He has not yet seen Persons's second letter on the subject, dated 10 August (B240).

P. Roberto Personio Agosto 29.

En el particular de Gibonio hallo tres faltas de consideracion, una que engañó al Rector pidiendo la llave para sacar un libro &c. el otro notable atrevimiento en buscar las cartas y tomar el soli. La tercera que faz specie de zizania mostrarla a los demas padres. No me pareçe le devan passar sin demostracion. Escrivo al provincial que averigue estos casos y los castigue. Si Vuestra Reverencia assi lo juzgare, déle la carta,[439] y si le pareçiera dissimular aora no se la dé y aviseme lo que siente al padre Gibonio nos le podra embiar con la mucha[440] comodidad que acá le ocuparé mejor.

Translation

To Fr Robert Persons, 29 August.

With regard to Fr Gibbons in particular, I find there are three faults to take into consideration: the first in deceiving the rector by asking for the key to take a book, etc.; another notable one in daring to look for letters and take out the private one. The third was to sow discord by showing it to the other fathers. It does not seem to me that this should pass without notice. I am writing to the provincial, who will make enquiries into these matters and punish them. If Your Reverence judges it convenient, give him the letter, and if you think it more convenient to conceal it for now, do not give it to him, and let me know how you feel about it. It will be perfectly convenient for you to send Fr Gibbons to us, as I can occupy him better here.

B242 From Claudio Acquaviva, 29 August 1594

> SOURCE: ARSI, Cast. 6, fols. 185r and 187v.
>
> NOTE: Acquaviva promises to write to Seville in favour of the English college there. He offers support and advice for the college at Valladolid. He agrees that Martínez be transferred and that Padilla be confirmed. He asks Persons to consult with the provincial, Gonzalo Dávila, over the appointment of a new rector, since Cabredo is needed to replace Cobos as *socius* to the provincial.

---

439. carta] *followed by illegible deletion* R
440. mucha] *obscure* R

P. Roberto Personio, Agosto 29.

Dos de Vuestra Reverencia he reçevido escrita a 12 de Julio, y no dude sino que siempre sere él mesmo que hasta aqui para ayudar en lo que pudiere esos Seminarios. Verdad es que yo[441] pense y deseé consolar a Vuestra Reverencia y a ese Seminario con dexarles el Rector que hasta aora han tenido, pero son tantos los que le proponen para compañero del Provincial en lugar del Padre Cobos que por su salud no puede haçer el ofiçio (que aunque para ningun otro Collegio le quitara de ese, para lo que se pide por ser util de toda la Provincia),[442] será forçoso conçedersele. Vuestra Reverencia vea con el Padre Provincial si en su lugar será bueno Gaspar Alonso, y pongasele[443] por Rector y en caso que él no sea a proposito yo aviso al Padre Provincial que procure dar otro que sea qual conviene con satisfaction de Vuestra Reverencia y dese Seminario: y el mesmo Padre Cabredo con el nuevo ofiçio, podra tambien ayudar su parte al Seminario. Escrivire tambien al Provincial y Preposito de Sevilla encargandole favorezcan aquel Seminario, como espero que lo harán.

Yo he deseado lo mesmo que Vuestra Reverencia diçe que los estudios y cosas dese nuestro Collegio de Valladolid se asienten como conviene y espero se hará. Yo escrivo al Provincial que en todo caso dexe de leer el Padre Martinez aunque en el modo se vaya con la necessaria suavidad, y de la mesma suerte escrivo al mesmo Padre Martinez diciendole que ansi conviene, y espero que verna en ello. El Padre Padilla no conviene quitarle sino que como Vuestra Reverencia diçe lea y se le advierta si en algo falta, porque su lection es estimada, y porque en esta conyuntura de los Dominicos sería cosa de mucha nota, ni mereçe ser quitado quien tan bien lo haçe como él. En las &c.

Translation

To Fr Robert Persons, 29 August.

I have received two of yours written on 12 July.[444] You may be sure that I will continue to help in whatever may assist those seminaries, just as I have up to now. The truth is that I had hoped and wished to oblige Your Reverence and that seminary in your desire to avert the departure of the rector who has held the position up to now, but there are so many who propose him as companion of the provincial in place of Fr Cobos, who cannot keep that office because of his health, that we are forced to allow this: even though he would not be removed from that position for any other college, he is needed to be available for the whole province.[445] Would Your Reverence please discuss with father

---

441. Verdad es que yo] *interlined, and continued as "anadido" on fol. 187v, to* podra tam bien ayudare su parte al Seminario, *replacing* no le quitaremos al padre Cabredo, que se le hemos confirmado, con otro se podra suplir lo que él havia de haçer

442. *Parenthetic text supplied in margin of the added material, "anadido" R*

443. pongasele] *obscure R*

444. B236–237.

445. This is an intriguing instance of Acquaviva's changing his decision between the time of composing the letter and posting it. At first he wrote, "We will not take away Fr Cabredo, whom we have confirmed; we will replace the one we have with someone else," but deleted the sentence

provincial if Gaspar Alonso would be good in his place, and appoint him as rector; if he is not suitable I am advising father provincial to provide another that will satisfy Your Reverence and that seminary. And in the meantime the same Fr Cabredo, with his new responsibilities, can play his part in helping the seminary. I will also write to the provincial[446] and superior[447] of Seville to support and favour that seminary, as I trust that they will do.

I share the desire Your Reverence writes of, that the studies and arrangements of this our college of Valladolid may be settled as is fitting, and I hope that this will be done. I am writing to the provincial that in any case Fr Martínez should stop lecturing, although this should be done with necessary gentleness, and I am writing to the same Fr Martínez about that same outcome, telling him that it is better like that, and I hope he will see it the same way. It is not advisable for Fr Padilla to be removed; instead, he should continue lecturing, as Your Reverence says, with a warning not to allow himself to be found at fault, because his lectures are valued, and also because, given the situation with the Dominicans, it would cause scandal, nor does someone who does so well deserve to be removed. I commend myself to your prayers, etc.[448]

B243 From Henry Garnet, 6 September 1594

SOURCES:

ABSI, Anglia A 1, item 81 = A;

ABSI, Coll P II 549–50, Grene's excerpts = G;

ARSI, Angl. 38/II, fol. 171r–v, Bartoli's translation of extracts.

HICKS: Garnet, 193–198.

EDITION: Foley, 4: 45–48.

NOTE: This is by way of a newsletter, reporting on the conditions of correspondence (it is safer for Garnet to send than to receive letters); the growing strife at Wisbech castle; the arrest of Walpole, Cornelius, and O'Collun; the increased persecution in London; and public events like the trial of López and a possible French raid on Rochester. On the contention at Wisbech, see Arnold Pritchard, *Catholic Loyalism in Elizabethan England* (London, 1979), 78–101, and Renold, *Wisbech Stirs*.

Good Syr, — Amongst so many crosses which now every day more & more do oppress us, this is one of the greatest, that we have of late bene abridged of that commodity which hitherto hath[449] bene of wryting and hearing of you. I hope it be in parte already

---

and replaced it with the sentence beginning "The truth is that I," completed towards the end of the entry in the register for the same courier (see textual notes).

446. Bartolomé Pérez, provincial of Andalusia.

447. From 1593–1594 the superior of the professed house in Seville was the formidable figure of Antonio Cordeses (1518–1601; see Manuel Ruiz Jurado, in *DHCJ*, 1: 952–953), formerly twice provincial of Aragón, superintendent of the college at Coimbra, and provincial of Toledo; on his controversial affective approach to prayer, see Philip Endean, "'The Strange Style of Prayer': Mercurian, Cordeses, and Álvarez," in *The Mercurian Project: Forming Jesuit Culture, 1573–1580*, ed. Thomas M. McCoog (Rome, 2004), 351–397, esp. 352–360. In his letter to Acquaviva, 12 June 1595 (B279), Persons refers to him as "santo."

448. On Alonso, Padilla and Martínez at Valladolid, see Acquaviva's letters, 3 and 31 August 1592 (B151, B155).

449. hath] *A*; has *G*

amended:⁴⁵⁰ & doubt not but it⁴⁵¹ will continew for a whyle. Yet this I desyre you to consider, that the safety of sending letters from hence as it now falleth out is greater, than of receiving; & therfore it behoveth you to send with great warines, for it were no small prejudice unto us if any letter of yours should miscarry, as I heare I know not what rumour one hath of late, but I hope it be false. Wheras by our ordinary meanes of sending there hath bene no mischaunce, although we have bene constrained to forbeare them untill now. A fortnight ago I adventured to trye, & wrote unto my ffrend in Antverp,⁴⁵² who I doubt not but hath lett you understand of such occurrences as than I could adventure to wryte. In the meane season I prepared my selfe to send a full relation of this yeare, hoping to have some large discourse in readines before this time⁴⁵³ to send you.⁴⁵⁴ But being coursed by my creditours,⁴⁵⁵ I was constrained to leave all my notes of sundry matters of edification, neither have I any meanes to come either by them, or by my alphabet,⁴⁵⁶ until I see farther⁴⁵⁷ what will happen to the place of my abode. Yet to intertaine your stomacke, & to provoke your appetite against a full repast, I send you a dainty collation of Mr Cornelius his happy combatte, which I caused one of my ffrends to write as he heard it of those which were privy & present⁴⁵⁸ almost alwayes in the action. Another copy I send unto Claud.⁴⁵⁹

Letter of yours I received none since that which you wrote to meet with Mr Henry W.⁴⁶⁰ Wherin I am sory I gave you such occasion to dilate of my obscurity.⁴⁶¹ But I assure

450. amended] *A*; mended *Foley*
451. it] *A*; that it *Foley*
452. Verstegan.
453. time] *A G*; letter *Foley*
454. Grene's sidenote, "Pro Annuis," suggests that Garnet was planning to write the Annual Letter for the English mission.
455. Garnet probably means pursuivants, adopting the language of merchants common in letters about the English mission; as a verb, "course" means to chase or pursue (*OED*).
456. The terms "notes of sundry matters of edification" and "alphabet" are intentionally cryptic. They presumably refer to information needed for his Annual Letter report, as well as the cipher codes for encryption.
457. farther] *A*; further *Foley*
458. present] *A G*; pressed *Foley*
459. Acquaviva.
460. Walpole.
461. Bartoli notes at fol. 171v: "Omnes litterae R. P. Garneti (quas habeo in magno numero) plerumque obscurae sunt, adeo ut 6.° Septembris 1594 sic scribat. Doleo quod occasionem dederim vobis tam fusè querendi de mea obscuritate &c. — Notis Arithmeticis saepe (hinc inde) utitur loco characterum et cum aliquos ex Societate nominat, fictis nominibus utitur. Aliquando inscribit epistolas suas ad Signore Marco & aliquando Rudolpho Perino &c. quorum hic uti arbitror e[tiam] P. Rob. Personi[um]: ille aliquis alias P. Anglus" (All Revd Fr Garnet's letters, which I have in great number, are for the most part obscure, so much so that on 6 September 1594 he writes thus: "I am sory I gave you such occasion to dilate of my obscurity," &c. — Hence he uses arithmetical ciphers in place of characters and when he mentions other members of the Society, he uses fictional names. Sometimes he addresses his letters to Mr Marcus and sometimes to Ralph Perin, &c. which I consider Fr Robert Persons uses as well: he has another alias, Fr English).

you that alwayes I[462] wrote as plainly as I could apprehend;[463] & such thinges as I left out were altogether unknowen unto me, & as easy to be[464] ghessed by you as by me. Neither can we by any meanes know the circumstances of such matters as come unlooked for & even as it were by meere chaunce unto us. The like I say of my Cosin Williams company;[465] where I understand in generall by him, that thinges go[466] worse & worse, with no order, but confusion & daunger of great scandall. If you think it be not to late to seeke to remedy such thinges: you may take order, but in this I could say[467] no more than I have written already. No person may be named, or particulerly required in exchaunge, for that were to breede farther inconvenience[468] than we seeke to remedy: but it must be putte to the free election of such as desyre to leave their country for indisposition or other respects, & than will the other company procure that such shall desyre it as are fittest to be spared. Neither can this be propounded to the Counsell by any leve; but by those which desyre to be delivered from thence; which they must do by wryting to their owne ffrends by ordinary postes.[469] Briefly, you see the end which we desyre: you know to find the meanes.

Now Syr, to wryte yow in particuler of all our broiles here were an infinite labour, this yeare having bene so fertile of troubles. I had written largely in my letter which I had prepared in answer of your last: but my ffrend durst not carry it, & so brought it me againe. And in very truth it is a wonder to see how God hath protected our letteres of late; for I could wryte of 2 or 3 severall escapes almost miraculous, if I could declare it without revealing the meanes of my sending, which I would[470] be very loth should appeare in my letter, if it chaunce to be taken.[471] Yet now will I briefly touch the thinges of most importance.

About the same time in[472] which Mr Walpole was taken, Mr Cornelius was apprehended with divers others, as you shall fully perceave by the relation which you shall receave herewithall. Soone after followed the arrainment of Patricke Olone,[473] who was innocently condemned for intending the queenes death, in whose arrainment how Jesuits were malitiously slaundered I have already written, & caused others to wryte. The death

    462. alwayes I] *A G*; I always *Foley*
    463. apprehend] *A*; comprehend *Foley*
    464. be] *interlined with caret A*
    465. [*marginal note in A:*] to that your self must answer. "Cousin William" is William Weston, reporting on the state of affairs at Wisbech Castle, where leading Catholics, originally including laymen, had been incarcerated since 1579.
    466. go] *A*; growe *Foley*
    467. say] *interlined above* do [*deleted*] *A*; do *Foley*
    468. farther inconvenience] *A*; further inconveniences *Foley*
    469. postes] *A*; post *Foley*
    470. would] *A*; should *Foley*
    471. Bartoli translates: "mirabile ... omnino est videre quomodo Dominus protexerit litteras nostras, ne in haereticorum manus devenirent: possem enim duos aut tres casus narrare in quibus miraculoso paene modo salvatae sunt, nisi metuerem ne via qua litteras meas mitto innotesceret, si hae ipsae intercipiantur" (fol. 171r).
    472. in] *A G*; *om*. Foley
    473. Olone] *A G*; Collyn *Foley*. Patrick O'Collun, a soldier under the command of Sir William Stanley, was interrogated in the Tower of London in February 1594, accused of conspiring with William Holt to assassinate the queen. See Alford, 301.

of López, a supposed Jew,[474] although he shewed him selfe at his death of the queenes religion, is greatly derived to the discreditt of Catholicks: although most unjustly. Wherin this was most worthy to be wondered at, that it could not quitte him of his supposed treason that he had immediately after he was moved therunto revealed the case to the queen. The 2 Portugalles which died for the same cause[475] shewed great religion in their death.

The Friday night[476] before Passion Sunday,[477] was such a hurly burly in London as never was seene in mans memory: no not when Wiatt was at the gates. A generall search in all London, the Justices & chiefe citizens going in person. All unknowen persons taken & putte in Churches till the next day. No Catholickes found, but one poore Tailoures house at goulden lane end:[478] which was esteemed such a booty as never was gotte since this queenes dayes. The Tailour & diverse others there taken lye yet in prison & some of them have bene tortured. That mischaunce touched us neere. They were our ffrendes and chiefest instrumentes. Of this also you have I think heard already by my ffrend in Antverp. That very night had bene there Long Jhon with the little beard,[479] once your pupill, if I had not more importunately stayed him than ever before. But soone after he was apprehended, being betrayed we know not how.[480] He wilbe stowt, I doubt not. He hath bene very close, but now is removed from the Counter to the Clink, where he may in time do much good. He was gladd of Mr Homulus his company,[481] but he had him[482] taken from him, &[483] caried to Newgate, whence he hopeth to redeeme him again. Edward Jhons companion, was once taken in a garden in the country: but he shewed him selfe nimble, leaped into the house, shutte the dore, & escaped away.

Two moneths ago[484] were taken eleven youths going from Chester towardes Spaine; all in Bridewell hardly used.[485] A fortnight sithence 2 boates were gone[486] downe with 8

---

474. See Francis Edwards, "The Lopez Plot," in *Plots and Plotters in the Reign of Elizabeth I* (Dublin, 2002).

475. cause] u *interlined with caret* A

476. night] *interlined with caret* A

477. March 15.

478. at goulden lane end] *interlined with caret* A. On Golding Lane, Holborn, see Gerard, *Autobiography*, 54–55 and 228–29.

479. [*marginal note in* A:] Jhon Gerard ... it was he of whom I wrote severally the last winter

480. Bartoli translates at fol. 171r: "[In iisdem] feria [inquit] 6.ᵃ ante Dominicam Passionis, Londini noctu inquisitum est pro Catholicis maximo cum tumultu totius urbis, nec ulli Catholici inventi sunt praeter domum pauperis sartoris qui cum nonnullis aliis in carcere detinentur, et aliqui eorum equuleum passi sunt. Hoc infortunium nos pupugit, fuerunt hi amici nostri et praecipua instrumenta. [*in margin*: P. Tompson] Joannes Gerardi illa nocte ibi erat futurus, nisi ego illum importunius quam unquam alias detinuissem; sed paolo post is ipse captus est, proditus a nescio quo modo."

481. Brother Ralph Emerson, whose alias was Homulus, at the time a prisoner in the Clink.

482. him] A; bin G

483. &] *followed by* was [*deleted*] A

484. ago] A; since G

485. Bartoli translates: "Duobus abhinc mensibus capti fuerunt undecim adolescentes Cestriâ tendentes in Hispaniam, omnes nunc sunt in carcere (qui vulgo Brigittae fontes vocar) nebulonibus vagabundis praecipue dessinato [assigned to idle vagabonds]" (fol. 171r).

486. gone] *preceded by* going [*deleted*] A

passengers 2 of the which were wemen, & five boyes; but lying over long beneath Gravesend, & the wemen crying out for feare of tempest, they[487] were descryed and taken all, except one ould man, & a little wrynecked boy a charge of mine, of whom I wrote & had your consent to send him. Before that tumult of goulding lane, about the latter end of February, they had layed a plotte of these great stirres & prepared[488] the people's mindes by a proclamation, wherin they comanded straight watches to be made certain dayes in a[489] weeke every where, for Priests & Irishmen, whose late attempts to kill the queene had bene discovered; & all Irishmen not inhabitants in Townes & citizens, banished England;[490] & all persons[491] not belonging to some nobleman or courtier banished the court, & commanded, for whatsoever suite to repaire to certain officers in places appointed neere the court, & with their licence to enter the court; all passengers to be stayed, who were not knowen, or had not testimony to appertaine to some nobleman. This proclamation I had sent you in my letter which was burnt; now it is not to be found, neither hath it bene straitly executed: & now almost forgotten. Since Easter a commission was graunted to about 20 persons who are in London & 10 myles about, to search & enquire for coiners, Priestes & lurking Papists, & to use towardes them all forceable meanes for the disclosing of their daungerous practises; and this busieth them all the day long.[492] The statutes of the last Parliament are rigorously executed, save that many servants are still retained, because warning is not geven every where to their Masters according to the statute.[493]

The last weeke[494] was the storehouse of Rochester burnt, to the losse of 30 or 40 thousand pound.[495] Some say it was maliciously donne by 2 Frenchmen, who are taken; others think it was donne by chaunce.

One Yorke & Williams both capitaines were lately taken at Middelborough, & in the Towre. It is reported abrode that they meant to kill the queene.[496]

The ould woman is w[ell] but I have bene constrained to leave her for a whyle.[497] It is time now to have[498] for the second yeare, although I have not yet receaved all for the first; but I shall do[499] shortly; I pray you leave order at the place appointed.[500] I have

    487. they] Foley; the A
    488. prepared] A G; had prepared Foley
    489. a] A G; the Foley
    490. Not inhabitants in Townes & citizens, banished England] added in margin A
    491. persons] interlined above strangers [deleted] A
    492. and this busieth them all the day long] added in margin A
    493. The statute (35 Eliz. I cap. i) was chiefly aimed at the Puritans, but also affected Catholics. Anyone sixteen years of age and older who refused to go to church for a month, and attended any other religious meeting or assembly, was liable to imprisonment.
    494. The last weeke] A; This week Foley
    495. pound] A; pounds Foley
    496. See Francis Edwards, Plots and Plotters in the Reign of Elizabeth I (Dublin, 2002), and Alford, 301–304.
    497. The ould woman is w[ell] but I have bene constrained to leave her for a whyle.] A; om. Foley. A reference to Persons's mother.
    498. have] A; leave Foley
    499. do] this ed.; die Foley; A obscure
    500. appointed] A; om. Foley

layed out already all the second yeeres pension by reason that the young widow & her children have bene settled of late.

I pray you consider whether it were not convenient to have here some Scottish or Italian Jesuits[501] that could speake English, for such are not subject[502] to the law, & many would deale with them, which feare[503] us. The mony I promised I have in great part sent. More I cannot, for the Creditours are bankrupte.[504] I pray you see that what is sent, may be beneficial unto us, for there is great neede, & our purse is ever empty. Thus[505] with most lowly commendations, & ernest intreaty of your prayers, I cease, this 6 of Sept.

  Yours always to command
    Henry Garnet.[506]

[*Addressed*:] Al molto magnifico signore il signore Marco Tusinga en Vinegia.[507]

[*Endorsed*:] Fath. Garnett 6 7^{ber} 1594. About dyvers poyntes of persecution.

B244 To Claudio Acquaviva, Valladolid, 7 September 1594

  SOURCE: ARSI, Hisp. 137, fol. 164, holograph.
  HICKS: 299–302, with English translation.
  NOTE: Persons asks Acquaviva for some rulings on St Omers, and to endorse his authority in relation to the English college there. He accepts Acquaviva's ruling on plans for a Scottish college, in consultation with Bartolomé Pérez, provincial of Andalusia. He follows up his earlier letter, of 10 August (B240), with an appeal on behalf of Richard Gibbons.

Muy Reverendo en Christo Padre nuestro
Pax Christi.

No tengo otro que[508] escrivir a Vuestra Paternidad por agora si no embiarle esta copia de la carta que he escrito al Padre Juan Focart rector del Seminario nuestro en Sant Omer, sobre algunas difficultades que le an succedido con el Padre Gulielmo Flacco y los demas Padres yngleses que aý estan en materia de escrivir y recebir cartas de acá, y de quentas de deneros, y para que si evite toda occasion y raiz de disunion y disgustos en este principios supplicaria a Vuestra Paternidad fuesse servido mandar escrivir dos palabras de su voluntad en entrambas cosas para que quede con el rector por su direcion por lo avenir. Y más porque me an escritto diversas veçes de alli, que suelen preguntar qué orden o autoridad tengo de Vuestra Paternidad para tratar con ellos las cosas de aquel semi-

  501. Jesuits] *interlined with caret A*. Persons indicated a need for an Italian Jesuit in England in his letter to Agazzari, 5 August 1580 (A16).
  502. subiect] *A*; subjects *Foley*
  503. feare] *A*; leave *Foley*
  504. bankrupte] *A*; bankrupts *Foley*
  505. Thus] *A*; This *Foley*
  506. Foley's note: "The signature has been cut off by some pious thief." [*marginal note, with hand pointing:*] I never receaved the new alphabet.
  507. An alias for Persons, as noted by Bartoli: "ad D. Marcum, i.e. ad P. Personium" (fol. 171r).
  508. que] *R*; a *Hicks*

nario, desearé (pareciendo asi a Vuestra Paternidad) que si les diciesse que Vuestra Paternidad gusta que me oyan en lo que es ayudar a aquel seminario y unirlo con estos de aqui, para mayor bien de toda la obra, y para complir con la intension del Rey y de Vuestra Paternidad y esto será bastante para que yo les sirva en lo que pudiera, porque otra cosa no deseo, y a fin que sepamos el ánimo y resolucion de Vuestra Paternidad en este particular, receberia mucha caridad en que Vuestra Paternidad mandasse embiarme un traslado de lo que les escrive acirca deste negocio.

    Lo que Vuestra Paternidad me manda acudir al negocio del Seminario Escoçes, lo haré con muy intera voluntad y ya tengo tratado con el buen Padre Bartolome Perez en ello y daremos la mejor traça que si pudiera, y prometo a Vuestra Paternidad que si yo estubiere libre desta carga de los yngleses me emplearia con no menor gana en la de los Escoçeses, si no mayor, porque pensaria merecer más, pero todo que si pudiera se hará en lo uno y en lo otro. Oy emos enterrado un angel en este collegio pues verdaderamente fue su vida tal, y algo me tiene entristecido, pero no ay remedio y para Dios se crió y a él ha ydo. En los santos sacrificios &c. Valladolid 7 de Settiembre 1594.

    De Vuestra Reverenda Paternidad
        hijo y siervo
            Rob. Personio.

    [PS] De la yda a Roma del Padre Ricardo Gibbonio tengo escritto ya dos veçes a Vuestra Paternidad y las causas, confio en nuestro Señor que avrá sido provedencia suya y que el buen Padre sirvira aý muy bien en muchas cosas conforme a los talentos que Dios le he dado. Vuestra Paternidad *amore Dei* lo reciba con su accustumbrada benignidad paternal.

    [*Endorsed:*] Valladolid. P. Roberto Personio Septembre 7 94. [*with summary of contents and date of reply? October 24*]

Translation

Our Very Reverend Father in Christ
The peace of Christ.

    I have nothing else to write to Your Paternity about at the moment, except to send you this copy of the letter I have written to Fr Jean Foucart, the rector of our seminary of St Omers, about some difficulties that have arisen with Fr William Flack and the other English fathers there on the question of writing and receiving letters from here and about accounting for money. And in order to avoid all occasion and source of disagreement and unpleasantness in these first days, I would beg Your Paternity to be so kind as to furnish a few lines indicating your pleasure in both these matters, so that they may be on record for father rector's guidance in future. Also, as they have at various times told me, when writing from there, that it is frequently being asked what orders or authority I have from Your Paternity to discuss the affairs of that seminary with them, I should wish them to be told (if Your Paternity agrees) that it is your pleasure that they should take heed to what I have to say by way of assisting that seminary and keeping it united to the seminaries here, for the greater good of the whole project and in order to carry out the intentions of the king and of Your Paternity. That will suffice to enable me to serve them in so far as I can, for I desire no more than that. And in order that we may know Your Paternity's mind in the matter and your decision on the point, I should be very grateful if you would give instructions for a copy to be sent to me of what is written to them on this subject.

The orders Your Paternity sends me to give my support to the project of the Scottish seminary, I will carry out with all my heart. I have already discussed the matter with good Fr Bartolomé Pérez, and we will develop the best scheme we can. I promise Your Paternity that if I did not have the responsibility for these Englishmen, I would assume it no less willingly for the Scots – nay, more so, because I should think it more deserving. However, everything possible shall be done for both. Today we have buried an angelic youth in this college, for truly his life was angelic; and it leaves me rather saddened.[509] However, there is no help for it; it was for God that he was created and to Him he has gone. To your holy sacrifices, etc. Valladolid, 7 September 1594.

    Your Paternity's
        son and servant
            Robert Persons.

[PS] I have already written twice to Your Paternity about Fr Richard Gibbons's departure for Rome and the reasons for it. I trust in our Lord that what has happened will prove to be providential for him, and that the good father will do excellent service there in many fields in accordance with the talents which God has given him. I beg Your Paternity to receive him for the love of God with your wonted fatherly kindness.

B245 To Claudio Acquaviva, Valladolid, 2 October 1594

> SOURCE: ARSI, Hisp. 137, fol. 201, holograph.
> HICKS: 303–309, with English translation.
> NOTE: Troubled with the ague, Persons is going to Seville. Creswell is now in Valladolid. Persons is still trying to direct Thomas Wright in the ways of holiness but is unable to dissuade him from his determination to go to England; Acquaviva is left with the decision to approve the transfer or to dismiss him from the Society so that he can go to England on his own account.

Muy Reverendo en Christo Padre nuestro
Pax Christi.

Por estar mal tratado de una quartana que me dio al 13 del mes passado de septiembre aqui en Valladolid, y aguardo la accession en este mismo dia no puedo escrivir más largo. El Padre Cresuello que al presente ha venido acá a visitarme y conferir nuestras cosas escrivira más largamente.

A los medicos ha parecido que será provechoso mudar ayer para esta enfermidad luego al principio antes que haga mucho assiento, y más desto la necessidad del Seminario de Sevilla es grande de que yo llegue por alla en esta conjuntura quando han de comprar y mudar casa y assi, placiendo a Dios, mañana o esso otro dia pienso ponerme en camino, confiado en su divina[510] bondad, que me ha de dar fuercas para llegar alli, donde no dudo si no que[511] hallaré mejora.

    509. Samuel Bradford, probably the son of Thomas Bradford of Cirencester, was admitted on 1 July and died on 6 September (*Valladolid Registers*, 30).
    510. su divina] *interlined with caret R*
    511. que] *interlined with caret R*

El Padre Thomas Wright ha procedido bien aqui hasta a dos o tres meses passados, quiero decir, ha vivido pacificamente y sin offension, aunque siempre he deseado y procurado lo que he pedido, con occasion de las cosas passadas, que ubiesse un poco[512] más espiritu y sentimiento interior, pero no parece que haya modo por donde sacarlo ni pegarselo; de nuestro Señor ha de venir, quando a él parecera. El Padre me ha importunado estos tres o quatro meses que escriviesse a Vuestra Paternidad para que le diesse licencia de yr a Ynglaterra en la mission por causa de su salud, lo he differido hasta agora, persuadiendole con mil raçones que desistiesse deste pensamiento, pero no ay remedio, ni yo, ni el Padre Cresuello y el Padre Tancardo podemos sacarle dello, si no que si persuade que con andar a Ynglaterra estara bueno, en cuerpo y ánimo, yo pienso sin duda que él lleva buena intencion, pero no pienso que esto basta y le tengo dicho muchas veçes que va engañado en muchissimas cosas, y que correra muchos peligros que no piensa, pero toda via instat y ha venido a resolverse que no puede leer más controversias en esta casa, y que si Vuestra Paternidad no lo embiará como de la compañia, que a lo menos vaya fuera de la compañia por algun tiempo, *promittit mirabilia sed iam dixi illi, non sunt viae hominis in manu eius, et exempla proposui multorum* &c. Pero todo no basta y assi, la resolucion depende de Vuestra Paternidad. Si a Vuestra Paternidad parece hacerle gracia de embiarle como hombre de la Compañia será la cosa que él más desea, e[513] yo tan bien por su consuelo la desearia, aunque no me atrevo acconsejarlo ni supplicarselo a Vuestra Paternidad pues no le juzgo muy apto para aquella mission. Si a Vuestra Paternidad parece bien venir a lo segundo que es demitirlo, deseo que sea con secreto, por acá y en Flandes, e yo le procuraré viatico y escrivere a los Padres nuestros en Ynglaterra cómo va el negocio con él, y Vuestra Paternidad en la carta de demission puede mandarle que nunca se diga ser de la compañia en Ynglaterra, y en[514] esto tan bien[515] agora le tengo prevenido. En todo Vuestra Paternidad hará como nuestro Señor le guyará, y alguna resolucion de Vuestra Paternidad[516] es necessaria luego en esto, pues es menester proveer aqui[517] tan bien lo[518] que nos[519] faltan y assi aguardaré la respuesta desta en Sevilla, se Dios me lleva alla.[520] En los Santos Sacrificios de Vuestra Paternidad humilmente me encomiendo. De Valladolid a 2 de Octubre 1594.

  De Vuestra Reverenda Paternidad
    hijo endigno
     Rob. Personio.

[PS] El Padre Gibbonio sabe tan bien deste negocio, pues se trató antes que él se partio aunque no quise escrivir sobre ello entonces, pensando que con tiempo si podia remediar aqui.

 512. un poco] *interlined with caret R*
 513. e] y *Hicks; preceded by* aunq[ue] *[deleted] R*
 514. en] *interlined R*
 515. bien] *interlined with caret R*
 516. de V. P. *interlined with caret R*
 517. aqui] *followed by* de *[deleted] R*
 518. lo] *interlined R*
 519. nos] *followed by* en estos *[deleted] R*
 520. alla] followed by ar *[deleted] R*

[*Addressed:*] El muy Reverendo en Christo Padre Nuestro el Padre Claudio Aquaviva, Preposito General de la Compañia de Jesus, Roma.
[*Endorsed:*] Vallodolid. P. Roberto Personio Octobre 2 1594. [*with summary of contents*]

Translation

Our Very Reverend Father in Christ
The peace of Christ.

I contracted a quartan ague on the 13th of last month of September here in Valladolid – and today I am expecting an attack of it – and so I am unable to write a longer letter. Fr Creswell, who has just come here to visit me and to discuss our affairs, will write at greater length.

The doctors think that a change of air will be a good thing for this sickness, now at the beginning before it has taken much hold. In addition to that, the seminary of Seville has great need that I should get there at this critical moment when they are to buy another house and move into it; and so, please God, tomorrow or the next day I intend to set out on my journey, trusting to the divine goodness to give me strength to reach my destination, where doubtless my health will improve.

Fr Thomas Wright conducted himself well here until two or three months ago; I mean he has lived peaceably and without giving offence. At all times I have looked for and tried to discover what previous events gave me reason to expect – namely, that there might be a little more spirituality and interior life – but there seems to be no way at all of drawing that out of him or imbuing him with it; it has to come from our Lord when it seems good to Him. The father has pressed me these three or four months past to write and ask Your Paternity to give him leave to go to England on the mission for reasons of health. I have put it off up to now and tried to persuade him by a thousand arguments to give up the idea; but nothing can be done; neither I nor Fr Creswell nor Fr Tancard can get out of his head the idea that if he goes to England, he will have health of body and mind. I am quite convinced that his intentions are good; but I do not think that is enough, and I have told him over and over again that he is suffering from illusions in many matters, and that he will run many risks that he is not aware of. But still he insists, and he has now come to the conclusion that he cannot lecture on controversies in this house anymore, and that, if Your Paternity will not let him go [to England] as a member of the Society, he will leave the Society for a time and go in any case. He devises wonderful plans, but I have already told him: the paths that a man treads are not under his control; and I have set out many instances, etc. But it is all futile, and so the decision rests with Your Paternity. If you can see your way clear to granting him the favour of being sent as a member of the Society, that is what will please him best, and I too would desire it for the sake of giving him consolation. But I dare not advise it nor beg it of Your Paternity, because I do not consider him very suitable for the mission there. If Your Paternity prefers to adopt the second alternative, which is to dismiss him, I would ask for it to be done discreetly, both here and in Flanders. I will have his travelling expenses paid and will write to our fathers in England and tell them how matters stand with him. And Your Paternity, in the letters of dismissal, can order him never to say in England that he is a member of the Society. I have also already warned him about that. Please would Your Paternity act in the whole matter as our Lord guides you; some prompt decision is needed from you on this matter, for it is necessary also to fill the gap here, and so I shall wait for an answer to this at Seville, if God gets me there. I humbly commend myself to Your Paternity's holy sacrifices. Valladolid, 2 October 1594.

[PS] Fr Gibbon knows this business very well, because I explained it to him before I left, even though I did not want to write about it just at that time, thinking that it could be remedied here in time.

   Your Reverend Paternity's unworthy son,
    Robert Persons.

B246 Correspondence with John Mush, probably October/November 1594

SOURCE: Mush to Persons, 24 March 1595 (B266).

NOTE: Probably in response to Garnet's report on the situation at Wisbech castle, 6 September (B243), Persons wrote to John Mush (1552–1617), a former student at the English College, Rome, and received a hasty reply. Mush followed this up with a longer letter on 24 March 1595.

After Allen, 1594-1596

B247 From Claudio Acquaviva, Rome, 24 October 1594

SOURCE: ARSI, Cast. 6, fol. 191r and 192r (addendum).

NOTE: The letter chiefly refers to the death of Cardinal Allen on 16 October; Acquaviva will write some words in common to Creswell about the family's needs. Priests are on the move: Oswald Tesimond to Spain, Richard Gibbons to Rome, Robert Jones to Flanders.

The additional paragraphs and the addendum suggest that Acquaviva was agitated by resentment in Flanders over Persons's authority to direct matters concerning the English in that region.

P. Roberto Personio, Otubre 24.

Hemos perdido al buen Señor Cardenal Alano con mucho sentimiento mio, y de todos los que le conoçian, que cierto hara gran falta un hombre tan exemplar como él era, y a los de la naçion les ha faltado un gran padre y amparo, pero Dios que es padre de las misericordias[1] lo suplira todo.

Havrá diez dias que de aqui partio el Padre Osvaldo para la Provincia de Andaluçia donde creemos hallará a Vuestra Reverencia. Dios le dé bueno y breve pasaje. Venga el Padre Ricardo que yo torné cuydado con el particular que Vuestra Reverencia me encomienda aunque çierto su escapada mereçia otra suerte de advertençias. El Rector del Inglés hasta aora proçede con satisfaction de los nuestros, de los alumnos, y de los demas, espero que ansi será en lo por venir, pero quando no fuese qual conviene, ya Vuestra Reverencia save que con el cuydado que hasta aqui he mirado por lo que toca a estos seminarios, con el mesmo lo miraré de aqui adelante. Partio tambien para Flandes el Padre Roberto Jonas, Dios le encamine y endereze en su viage y empresa como todos deseamos en las &c.[2]

Ya llegaron aqui el Padre Ricardo y el Padre Enrrique: y con el Padre Ricardo se hace lo que Vuestra Reverencia pide. Yo avisaré a Flandes que aquellos Padres acudan a lo que Vuestra Reverencia les pidiere como a persona a quien yo he remitido lo que toca aquellos seminarios y a los sugetos de la nacion, y si no fuera por no perturbar el orden de los superiores facilmente. Les avisará que en aquellos particulares dependieran de Vuestra Reverencia.

1. misericordias] *doubtful reading; R has* mias *with contraction mark*
2. *The two paragraphs following were later inserted into the register; and there is also an addendum on a following page.*

Monseñor de Casano me hablado con deseo de que Vuestra Reverencia no le haga mal oficio. Sé que Vuestra Reverencia no le hara en lo que a su persona tocare porque ni él lo merece ni Vuestra Reverencia se mete en cosas tales en lo demas que fuere en orden a la nacion. Vuestra Reverencia sabra mejor lo que convenga.

[Añadido] Teniendo Vuestra Reverencia tanto amor a la buena memoria del Cardenal Alano parece que era escusado este oficio de encargarle yo lo que toca al servicio del Señor Thomas su sobrino y toda su casa pero por satisfacerme a mí y a la voluntad que tengo a toda su familia me ha parecido añadir estas dos palabras que seran comunes[3] al Padre Cresuelo.

Translation

To Fr Robert Persons, 24 October.

We have lost the worthy Lord Cardinal Allen with great grief to me and all who knew him, for certainly it is a great loss, such a paragon as he was, and those of his nation have lost a great father and protector, but God, who is Father of all mercy,[4] will supply everything.

It has been approximately ten days since Fr Oswald left here for the province of Andalusia, where we trust he will reach Your Reverence – may God give him a good and swift passage. Fr Richard may come, as I will take particular care with him as Your Reverence recommended; although certainly it was right that you should raise such concerns at his departure. The rector of the English college has until now managed satisfactorily with Ours,[5] the students, and the rest, and I have hopes for the future, but if it should not turn out suitably, Your Reverence already knows that I will watch what happens here with the same concern that I have shown hitherto for whatever relates to your seminaries over there. Also, Fr Robert Jones has left for Flanders; may God guide him and ease his journey and endeavours as we all desire. To your [holy prayers and sacrifices], etc.

Fr Richard and Fr Henry have already arrived here: and with regard to Fr Richard, what Your Reverence requested has been done.[6] I will advise Flanders that those fathers should perform what Your Reverence asks, as the person to whom I have entrusted what concerns those seminaries and the subjects of the nation, and that this should not easily disturb the order of the superiors. I will advise them that in these particulars they should depend on Your Reverence.

His Lordship the Bishop of Cassano has spoken to me expressing his wish that Your Reverence should not do him a disservice.[7] I know that Your Reverence will not do anything against him personally, because he neither deserves it nor will Your Reverence get

---

3. comunes] coes *with contraction mark R; see n1 above.*
4. See textual note: alternatively, "God of the sorrowful."
5. Girolamo Fioravanti had recently replaced Muzio Vitelleschi as rector.
6. See the correspondence of 12 July, 10 August, 29 August, and 7 September 1594 (B236–237, B240–243, B244).
7. Owen Lewis, bishop of Cassano, considered Persons to be a rival candidate to replace Allen as cardinal. See Mannaerts's letter of 24 November.

involved in such matters concerning the rest besides what has to do with the order of the nation. Your Reverence will know better what would be appropriate.

[Addendum] Your Reverence having such love to the good memory of Cardinal Allen it seems unnecessarily officious for me to request you to take care of that which concerns the service of Lord Thomas his nephew[8] and all his house, but to satisfy me and the goodwill that I have to all his family, I have thought fit to append these two words which will be common to Fr Creswell.[9]

B248 To Claudio Acquaviva, Valladolid, early November 1594

SOURCE: Acquaviva to Persons, 19 December (B253).

NOTE: Persons evidently decided to move to Seville, where the climate was better for his quartan fever.

B249 From Henry Garnet, 19 November 1594

SOURCES:
ABSI, Anglia A 1, num. 82, holograph, with ciphers decoded in another hand = A;
ABSI, Coll P II 550, Grene's extracts = G.

HICKS: Garnet, 199–202.

EDITION: Foley, 4: 48–50.

NOTE: Garnet reassures Persons that he is doing all he can to gather historical texts and information for him: this was presumably for the historiographical project represented by the MS *Certamen Ecclesiae Anglicanae* (see Joseph Simons, *Certamen Ecclesiae Anglicanae: A Study of an Unpublished Manuscript*, Assen, 1965). Of Garnet's news items, the most important for Persons would be the account of the Cecil/Fixer conspiracy and their connection with Lord Burghley, and the imprisonment of Gerard (in the Clink) and Southwell and Walpole in the Tower. Garnet also sends news of Persons's mother ("the ould woman"), who is in good health.

For ease of reading, the terms as deciphered on receipt have been inserted into the main text, with the ciphers given in square brackets in footnotes.

Good Syr.

About a fortnight ago we all mette, & every one desyreth to be remembered unto you. I have geiven every one charge for his parte to gett informations of historical matters, although they saye it is very hard, & that they have from time to time sent such thinges as they cannot learne againe. But what may be donne shalbe, & that will aske time, & I hope you will accept what we are able to compasse, the times being harder than ever, & we having no trusty ffrend which may shew his face, & so we live in as great ignorance of our owne affairs as youre selfe.

8. Thomas Hesketh, who now adopted the name Allen. For a list of members of Cardinal Allen's household at his death, see Knox, *Allen*, 374–377.

9. This may refer to the addendum.

I sent you of late a new copy of the chronicle, which I take to be the autors owne, togither with a great work of Dr Langdall wherin it seemeth he tooke great paines, but I never read it.[10] The note of bookes of Protestants & Puritanes are very hard to be gotten. I have used the best meanes I could devise,[11] & yet have no assurance.

Fr Cecil was this last spring by sea constrained to [the] western part of Ingland;[12] he said he was a Scot, & after information of the Concel, sent away, another Inglish being still in prison. His name is Randal.[13] He dwells at Dunkerk. This is certaine. This[14] other is probable, which I heard of one who sayde he hard[15] it of another honest man, who sayeth thus: I saw letters from Fr Cecill to the Tresurers sonne, where he acknowledged being in [the] west part of Ingland, that he came from Spayne to goe to Scotland, and that he was not yet fully fraught[16] but whan he was he should understand, & herupon he was sent away. The party sayde he knew Fr Cecills hande. This also is certaine, that the Tresurer inquired of Fixer's host (for how they two fell acquainted I wrote long since),[17] "How doth thy frende?" And he: "Well, but he is gone"; "And is he well gone?" sayeth the other, "I am very glad of it" – with other words of kindnes.[18]

   10. Alban Langdale was the author of *Catholica confutatio impiae cuiusdam determinationis Domini Nicolai Ridlaei* (Paris, 1556). The chronicle referred to here may be Holinshed, most recently published in 1588, including the *History of Ireland* by Richard Stanihurst, now in Madrid.
   11. devise] A; advise *Foley*
   12. John Cecil (Snowden) left Scotland early in 1594 and travelled to Madrid and Prague, affecting to be canvassing support for the Catholics of England. He reached Rome in November 1595 (Anstruther, 67).
   13. Randal] A; Raulippe *Foley*. William Randall is listed as held in the Gatehouse in 1594 by order of the Council, for treason beyond sea and other treasons (Pollen, *Miscellanea II*, 287).
   14. This] A; The *Foley*
   15. hard] A; had *Foley*
   16. Furnished, supplied or equipped (*OED*, s.v. fraught, *v*. 3). Foley reads "brought" or "taught."
   17. The information about John Cecil's associate John Fixer's sojourn in England, when he was seeking employment with Burghley, may have been given in a now-lost letter from Garnet, possibly 26 April 1593.
   18. F. Cecil [204] was this last spring by sea [448] constrained to western part of Ingl. [98]; he said he [404] was a Scot [330], & after information of the Concel [201], sent away, another Inglish [331] being still in prison [484] his name is Randal [51 62 34 26 21 61 40], he [404] dwells [21 16 63 40 52] at [61 18] Dunkerk [143]. This is certaine. This other is probable, which I heard of one who sayde he hard it of another honest man, who sayeth thus: I [402] saw [52 61 10] letters [470] from [410] F. Cecill [204] to [411] the Tresurers [247] sonne [290], where he acknowledged being in west part of Ingland [98] that [409] he [404] came from Spayne [78] to [411] goe [30 67] to [411] Scotland [75], and that he was not yet fully fraught [29 51 61 17 30 31 18] but whan he was he should understand, & herupon he was sent away. The party sayde he knew F. Cecills [204] hande [31 62 52 21]. This also is certaine, that the Tresurer [247] inquired of Fixer's [29 65 15 63 51 52] host [31 67 52 18] (for how they two fell acquainted I wrote long since) how [31 68 16] doth [21 67 18 31] thy [18 31 14] frende [315], and [401] he [404] well, but he is gone [30 67 42 63] and [401] is [65 52] he [404] well gone [30 67 42 63], sayeth the other, I am very glad of it, with other words of kindnes.

Here is no newes that I can learne, for we live all as it were in a wildernes. Her Maiesty hath bene in danger by a short sicknes, but thankes be to God well recovered, & was yesterday at the triumphes all in yellow, that it was comfortable to behould her so fressh and lusty.[19]

The mariage of the Lady Veere to the new[20] Erle of Darby is differred by reason that he standeth in hazard to be unerled againe, his brothers wife being with child, untill it see[21] whether it be a boy or no. The young Erle of Southampton refusing the Lady Veere, payeth 5000 li. of present payment.[22]

Sir Thomas Wilkes goeth into Flanders as it is thought for peace.[23] Wherupon[24] the arrainment of the three Jesuits, Southwell Walpole & Gerard is stayed. Gerard is in the Clinck somewhat free: the other two so close in the Tower that none can heare from them.

The Erle of Essex hath the reversion of the Master of Wardes.[25] Topcliff & Tom. Fitzherbert pleaded hard in the Chancery this[26] last weeke. For wheras Fitzherbert had promised & entred into bonds to geve 5000 li. unto Topcliffe if he would prosecute his father & uncle to death, togither with Mr Bassett: Fitzherbert pleaded that the conditions were not fulfilled, because they dyed naturally; & Bassett was in prosperity. Basset gave witnes what trecherous devices he had used to entrappe him, and Cooke the queenes Atturney,[27] gave testimony openly that he very well had proved how effectually Topcliffe sought to infourme him against them, contrary to all equity & conscience; so that all the Court flowting Topcliffe, the matter was putt over to secrett hearing: where Topcliffe had the upper hand.[28]

19. Caraman quotes from this paragraph as corroboration of Garnet's loyalty to the queen, as claimed by Gerard under interrogation in the Tower in 1597: Gerard, *Autobiography*, 112 n1.

20. new] *preceded by* late [deleted] A

21. see] A; is seen Foley

22. William Stanley (1561–1642) succeeded to the title of earl of Derby after his brother Ferdinando's death in April 1594. Ferdinando's widow, Alice Spencer, gave birth to a daughter, allowing the marriage of Lady Elizabeth de Vere (1575–1627) to the new earl to go forward on 26 January 1595. Her grandfather Burghley, as master of the court of wards, had previously negotiated a marriage contract between her and his ward Henry Wriothesley (1573–1624), earl of Southampton. See A.L. Rowse, *Shakespeare's Southampton: Patron of Virginia* (London, 1965), 54–57 and 102–103, who accepts Garnet's testimony but questions the size of the fine paid to release Southampton from the proposed match.

23. Sir Thomas Wilkes (ca. 1545–1598) was detailed to go to Brussels on a diplomatic mission in September 1594, in connection with the supposed conspiracy of Dr Rodrigo López (d. June 1594), but the mission did not in fact take place.

24. Wherupon] A G; Whereby Foley

25. The lucrative office of master of the court of wards and liveries had been held by Burghley since 1561; see Joel Hurstfield, *The Queen's Wards: Wardship and Marriage under Elizabeth I* (London, 1958).

26. this] *preceded by* that for [deleted] A

27. [*Foley's parenthetic gloss:*] Sir Ed. Coke

28. As a result of the scandalous court action reported here, Topcliffe was briefly imprisoned by order of the Privy Council.

I looke for priests from Rome shortly, wherof I am very gladd.

The ould woman is well.[29] Her children seeke almost all to be Catholiques, & some help of money[30] would further it.[31] And so having now no more to wryte, I cease to trouble you, ernestly craving your prayers, this 19 of Nov.

   Yours always to command —
      H.G.[32]

[*Addressed:*] Al molto mag.^{co} S.^{re} il S.^{re} Marco Tussinga, a Vinesia.[33]

[*Addressed, in another hand:*] for ff. Persons

[*Endorsed:*] f. Garnet, 19 9^{ber} about Cicil Fixar &c. 1594

B250 Letters from Sir Francis Englefield, late 1594

> SOURCE: More, 232.
>
> TRANSLATION: Edwards, *More*, 290
>
> NOTE: Englefield, whom Persons felt was himself eminently suitable to replace Allen as cardinal, was anxious that the king should know how Persons felt about the question of a successor. See Persons to Idiáquez, possibly January 1595 (B255), and Persons to Englefield, 10 May 1595 (B274).

Hic frequentibus literis rogarat Personium ut suam vellet Regi Catholico sententiam aperire de Cardinale in Alani demortui locum substituendo. ...

Translation

He himself [Englefield] wrote frequently to Persons asking him to make his mind known to the Catholic king about finding a successor to the deceased Allen. ...

B251 From Olivier Mannaerts, Brussels, 24 November 1594

> SOURCES:
> ARSI, Hisp. 139, fol. 98, a fair copy.
> ABSI, Coll N1 157, Grene's summary.
>
> EDITION: More, 229–230.
>
> TRANSLATION: Edwards, *More*, 287–288.
>
> NOTE: Mannaerts, Persons's senior and until recently the Jesuit provincial of Belgium, urges Persons to discourage his supporters in Spain from lobbying for him to succeed Allen

29. Persons's mother.
30. money] *ABSI ts; cipher incomplete and explanation decayed A*
31. I looke for priests [183] from [410] Rome [117] shortly, wherof I am very gladd. The ould woman is well. Her children seeke almost all to be Catholiques [319], & some help of money [4] would further it.
32. H.G.] *supplied by Foley*
33. A pseudonym for Persons; *Hicks* notes: "Persons in fact was not infrequently addressed as 'Mr Mark.'"

as a cardinal to lead the English Catholic exiles. In particular, he is concerned that they might induce Philip II to intervene. He points out how such an appointment would disable Persons's most valuable work, and is inclined to support the rival candidacy of Owen Lewis.

McCoog, *Building the Faith of St Peter*, 247–248, opines that Mannaerts was chiefly moved by his concern with the principle of promoting a Jesuit to the cardinalate. On the relationship between Persons and Mannaerts, see "The Opposition in Flanders" in the introduction, and vol. 1: 52–53, 84 and *passim*.

Persons probably received this letter in Madrid, *en route* to Seville, or in Seville itself, and enclosed it in his letters to Acquaviva of 20 February (B257–58).

Reverende in Christo Pater
Pax Christi, etc.

Iam tempus est ut Vestra Reverentia Societati universae, et orbi ipsi, testatam faciat integritatem suam, et fidem erga Societatem ipsam. Occasione obitus Illustrissimi Domini Alani, nihil non moliuntur Angli nostri, nobiles, sacerdotes, et seminaria ut capiti tuo imponatur diadema Cardinalitium. Hunc in finem obtinuerunt literas ab his proceribus, nominatim a Duce de Feria, et forsan ab ipsomet Archiduce, ad regiam Maiestatem, atque ad suam sanctitatem variosque Cardinales, ad quam ipsi variis ex locis suas etiam precatorias dederunt. Actum est quidem cum aliquibus a nostris ad inflectendum eorum animos potius ad Reverendissimum Episcopum Cassanensem, quod multo utilior sit opera Vestrae Reverentiae, Angliae, et particularibus ac seminariis in statu in quo nunc versatur simplici et religioso, quam ad Cardinalitiam dignitatem evecta; in qua minime posset tam libere versari cum omnibus Anglis, intelligere secreta, praescribere necessaria particularibus et secretis personis, sicut nunc, neque emendicare eleemosynas a principibus et nobilibus, a praelatis et ecclesiasticis, a civibus et mercatoribus Cardinalis effecta, sicuti nunc sub privato habitu et modestia religiosa apud omnes libere et sine offensione facit: non converteret a religione Catholica alienos, non catechizaret, non visitaret aegros in carcere, et privatis aedibus, neque adventantes Anglos in navigiis, in portibus variis, non administraret denique sacramenta, sicuti nunc facit, et haec praestat omnia summa utilitate,[34] et omnium aedificatione: sed totam solicitudinem cogeretur transferre ad negotia publica ecclesiae, et ad oeconomiam et curam domesticam, quae non potest non esse permagna, ubi proventus exigui sunt, domestici multi, pauperes et peregrini plurimi, desiderium omnes iuvandi ardens. Nam quid posset[35] conferre in seminaria auxilii aucta dignitate Cardinalitia? Haberet, inquam, proventus octo vel decem millium ducatorum: Quid illud esset ad opitulandum tam multis, ad succurrendum seminariis, et ad honestam necessariamque familiae sustentationem?

Haec, inquam, suggerimus, et ostendimus Dominum Cassanensem iam habere proventus certos et paratos, et maiores quam habuerit optimus Cardinalis Alanus: sed haec non eos movent, propter causas Vestrae Reverentiae notas, cuius candor, humanitas, rerum Anglicarum peritia, et in omnes caritas, sic eos rapit,[36] ut non intendant aliis

---

34. summa utilitate] R; summa cum utilitate *More*
35. posset] *More*; potest R
36. rapit] R; capit *More*

quam suis consiliis. Superest igitur ut Vestra Reverentia, quod factura erat me non movente,[37] valde generose agat, ne porta semel aperta laxetur magis, magisque pateat aliquorum ambitioni. Advigilet autem ne clam se cum Rege agant, et eius animum inducant in hanc persuasionem, quod licet Societati id[38] non expediat, expediat[39] tamen bono communi ecclesiae, et regni Anglicani; nam ut pientissimus est, verendum est ne sibi persuaderi patiatur. Illud autem persuasum habeo, nullum esse in Societate qui vel facilius vel efficacius amolliri possit a Societate hoc malum quam Reverentia Vestra.

Nudius tertius huc reverti ex Arthesia dissenteria affectus, sed Deo sit laus, licet adsit quaedam alteratio nulla tamen est febris, et sanguinis copia magna non est quae effluit, ut[40] sit in manu Dei sum, quem[41] precor ut Vestram Reverentiam conservet, cuius sanctis precibus multum me commendo. Bruxellis 24 Novembris 1594.

    Reverentiae Vestrae servus in Christo
    Oliverius Manaraeus.

Translation

Reverend Father in Christ
The peace of Christ.

    The time has come for Your Reverence to give evidence to the whole Society, and the world itself, of your integrity and loyalty towards the same Society. Following the death of Cardinal Allen, our English gentlemen, priests and seminaries are making every effort to ensure that you should receive the cardinal's hat. With this in view, they have obtained letters from these leading men – namely, the duke of Feria,[42] and perhaps the archduke himself – to His Royal Majesty, His Holiness, and various cardinals, to which they have added besides their own petitions to the Pope sent from various localities. A movement was also initiated with some of our men to change their support rather to the most reverend bishop of Cassano, because Your Reverence's efforts would be of much greater value to England, to particular individuals and the seminaries, if you should remain as you are, a plain religious, rather than be promoted to the dignity of cardinal. For in the latter case, you would be much less free to maintain contact with all types of Englishmen, understand secret affairs, and prescribe what is necessary for individuals, and those with secret commissions, than you are now; neither could you beg alms from rulers, nobles, prelates, ecclesiastics, burgesses, and merchants as a cardinal, as now, when you can do this freely without offence to any, as a private man and acting within the bounds of religious convention; you could not convert those estranged from the Catholic faith;

    37. movente] *R*; monente *More*
    38. id] *R*; om. *More*
    39. expediat] *R*; expediet *More*
    40. ut] *this ed.*; ut ut *R*
    41. *More reads*: quam ut Deus Dominus noster conservet precor, et Sanctis suis precibus multum me commendo. Bruxellis 24 Novembris 1594.
    42. The second duke of Feria, Lorenzo Suárez de Figueroa y Córdoba (1559–1607), was the son of Jane Dormer, duchess of Feria, whose husband, the first duke, died in 1571. At this time, he was Spanish ambassador to France, having previously served in Rome.

you could not catechize, visit the sick in prison or in private houses, or meet English people arriving at the various ports. Finally, you could not administer the sacraments as you do now, and discharge all these offices of the highest utility and to the edification of all. Instead, you would be forced to shift your whole attention to public church business and the responsibility of running your household, which because of limited income, numerous servants, and even more numerous poor people and pilgrims would be restricted, while you burned with desire to help everyone. What possible help would your being raised to a cardinal's dignity bestow on the seminaries? You would have, let us say, an income of eight or ten thousand ducats. What would that amount to in the way of supporting so many people, helping the seminaries, and maintaining a household with the proper decency?

These things, shall we say, we put before you for your consideration, and we point out that his lordship of Cassano already has a ready and certain income, greater even than the most worthy Cardinal Allen enjoyed. But these considerations do not move those men, for reasons well-known to Your Reverence. Your honesty, humanity, knowledge of English affairs, and charity towards all so carries them away that they will not listen to anyone's reasoning but their own. It therefore remains for Your Reverence to do what you would have done without my advice, and to act with complete selflessness, so that the door once opened would be pushed wider open and give greater scope to the ambition of others. Be careful, however, to see that they do not manage things surreptitiously with the king and bring him around to this conviction: that even if this does not help the Society, it would be for the common good of the church and the realm of England. For, given that his sense of duty is most strong, it is to be feared that he will allow himself to be persuaded. This however I hold as a certainty, that there is no one in the Society who can protect it from this misfortune more easily or effectively than Your Reverence.

It is now the third day since I returned here from Artois,[43] sick with dysentery, but praise be to God that although there has been no improvement in the fever, and the quantity of blood that has flowed out is not great,[44] still, I am in God's hands – whom I beseech to keep Your Reverence safe, to whose holy prayers I greatly commend myself. From Brussels, 24 November 1594.

Your Reverence's servant in Christ
Olivier Mannaerts.

B252 To Claudio Acquaviva, Seville, December 1594

SOURCE: Acquaviva to Persons, 16 January 1595 (B254).

NOTE: It is unclear when Persons arrived in Seville, exhausted from his journey and still suffering from his illness; Acquaviva's letter of 16 January may be a response to a letter written in early December, but Persons apologizes, in his letter of 20 February 1595 (B257), for his being a poor correspondent during these months, and Acquaviva's letter of 19 December (B253), sent to the province of Toledo, suggests that he expected Persons might still be on his journey.

43. Artois, now a county of northern France, was at this time part of the Spanish Netherlands; the Latin name is Artesia.
44. Referring to the medical practice of bloodletting.

B253 From Claudio Acquaviva, Rome, 19 December 1594

SOURCE: ARSI, Tolet. 5/II, fol. 377r.

NOTE: Acquaviva approves Persons's decision to travel to Seville to try to shake off the quartan fever; he writes to Madrid since Persons was likely to stop there on the way from Valladolid. He entrusts the question of Thomas Wright's future to Persons's discretion. See McCoog, *Building the Faith of St Peter*, 219.

P. Personio, 19 de Diziembre.

El poco tiempo que nos dio el correo pasado nos hizo diferir la respuesta de muchas cosas y entre ellas la del Padre Tomas Vrit, del qual no digo más de que la dilacion de su despedida havia a lo menos servido, de que ella sea con él y con los demas tan justificada como[45] Vuestra Reverencia ha visto. La peticion de yr a Inglaterra es tan fuera de lo que conviene como Vuestra Reverencia y esos Padres le han dicho, y él lo mira mal si tal desea, pues ver que se pone a grave peligro. De la Compañia en ninguna manera quiero que vaya sino que en caso que él no se quiete trataremos de executarlo,[46] lo qual antes se havia determinado y Vuestra Reverencia quiso se dilatase para probar si le podia acomodar y en la execucion y despedida suya Vuestra Reverencia use todas las prevenciones que le parecieren necesarias que yo me remito a su parecer.

Conforme al peligro en que me dicen ha estado Vuestra Reverencia podemonos contentar que aya parado en la quartana, que aunque sea molesta y peligroso, y ha sido acertado resolverse de yr a Sevilla, porque el temple de la tierra es más benigno para esa enfermedad que no Castilla. Espero que aý le dara el Señor más en breve la salud y lo que durare la quartana será menos molesta. El Señor guarde a Vuestra Reverencia y le enrriquezca con sus dones como Padres esos. En sus oraciones, etc.

Translation

To Fr Persons, 19 December.

The little time afforded us by the last post made us defer our response to many matters, and amongst them that concerning Thomas Wright, about which I can say no more than that the delay of his departure has at least served to confirm that both in his case and in others it has been justified, as Your Reverence has observed. His request to go to England goes beyond what is convenient, as Your Reverence and those fathers have told him, and he has adopted a mistaken approach if that is what he wishes for, because he is putting himself in great danger. I do not at all want him to leave the Society except that if he does not stop, we will arrange to put into practice what was formerly decided, which Your Reverence wanted to delay, so as to test whether you could accommodate him. In his expulsion and departure, Your Reverence may use all the precautions that seem necessary – which I leave to your discretion.

According to the danger I am told Your Reverence has been in, we must be content that the quartan has come to an end, although not without trouble and danger. You have

---

45. como] *this ed.*; com R
46. en caso que él no se quiete trataremos de executarlo] R, *supplied from margin with marker* F

made the right decision to go to Seville, because the climate there is more benign for that infirmity than Castile. May the Lord bring you more speedily to health there and grant you that the quartan will be less troublesome while it lasts. May the Lord keep Your Reverence and enrich you with his gifts, as also those fathers. To your prayers, etc.

B254 From Claudio Acquaviva, Rome, 16 January 1595

SOURCE: ARSI, Baet. 3/I, 192.

NOTE: Acquaviva suggests that all talk about Persons and the cardinalate should be stopped, especially in the Spanish court. His reference to Persons's state of health may be a response to a letter from Persons reporting on his arrival at Seville or simply an indication that Acquaviva understands why he has not written (see Persons's letter of 20 February, B257).

P. Roberto Personio, 16 de Enero.

Sentido he la poca salud con que Vuestra Reverencia se halla aunque como ha sido causada de la agitacion y cansacio del camino, espero que desta hora se havrá reparado con la quietud de la cama y con la caridad de esos Padres – ya creo que havrá llegado a su noticia lo que estara bien lejos de su pensamiento que es la diligencia que aqui hacen algunos de la naçion para suplir con la persona de Vuestra Reverencia la falta del buen Cardenal Alano. Bien sé que no es necessario avisar a Vuestra Reverencia de los inconvenientes que eso ternia[47] pues como persona a quien Dios ha dado tanta luz, vee muy bien lo que en esto ay; solo le quiero acordar que si por alla se hizieren oficios, procure de superior atajarlos como quien es tan hijo de la Compañia, que por acá quando necessario fuere, no faltaremos de hazer los que conviniere,[48] pero más facil cosa será atajarlos en su original; que es Su Magestad que es el que puede en esto darnos alguna molestia pero no quiero creer que lo aya de hazer pues le bastará entender la voluntad y parecer de Vuestra Reverencia, en cuyas oraçiones etc.

Translation

To Fr Robert Persons, 16 January.

I am sorry about the poor health in which Your Reverence finds himself. However, as it has been caused by the agitation and fatigue of the journey, I hope that by now it has been repaired by the quietness of bedrest and the charity of those fathers. And I suppose that there has come to your attention something that is far from your thoughts: the endeavours which some of your nation are making here to supply, with the person of Your Reverence, the loss of good Cardinal Allen. I well know that there is no need to warn Your Reverence of the inconveniences that would result – as a person to whom God has given so much light, you can very well see what this would entail; all I seek is to remind you that if manoeuvres are being made over there,[49] try to tackle them with your

---

47. [*in margin:*] de eius Cardinalata R
48. Conviniere] *preceded by illegible deletion* R
49. I.e., unwelcome moves taken in Spain in the direction of supporting Persons's appointment as cardinal.

superior as a son of the Society. What we need to do over here we will not omit, but it is easier to nip them in the bud: it is His Majesty who could create some hindrance, but I would like to believe that he will not do it if only he understands what Your Reverence believes is the right thing to do – to whose prayers, etc.

B255 To Juan de Idiáquez, possibly January 1595

> SOURCE: More, 232.
> TRANSLATION: Edwards, *More*, 290–291.
> NOTE: In response to Englefield's urging (see Englefield to Persons, late 1594, B250), Persons eventually wrote to the king's secretary.

Personius ... scriptis literis ad Dominum Ioannem Idiaques (virum in consilio regio fidentissimum) explicuit, quam id primum, eo praesertim tempore, esset necessarium, et quibus hominem oportebat esse dotatum ornamentis. Dein, si quinam essent futuri idonei quaereretur, remisit ad *Iosephum Creswellum*.

Translation

Persons wrote to Don Juan de Idiáquez, a most trusted member of the king's council, and explained to him how urgent and necessary it was [to find a successor to Allen], especially at that time, and what qualities the candidate should be endowed with. But on the next question, to name those who would be suitable, he deferred to Joseph Creswell.[50]

B256 To Thomas Wright, Seville, about 20 January 1595

> SOURCE: Wright to Persons, 20 February (B260).
> NOTE: In this letter Persons presumably conveyed to Wright (in Valladolid) Acquaviva's answer to Wright's request to be allowed to go to England for health reasons. See Acquaviva to Persons, 19 December 1594 (B253).

B257 To Claudio Acquaviva, Seville, 20 February 1595

> SOURCE: ARSI, Hisp. 138, fol. 143 (olim 246), holograph.
> HICKS: 310–311 (text), 314–316 (translation).

---

50. More explains the reasons why Persons relied on Creswell's discretion: "Tum quia sciebat hunc et instituti Societatis esse studiosissimum, et cum comperessit huiusmodi agitari inter principes viros consilia, atque in Personium coniecisse oculos, respondisse pro more suo quibusdam per parabolam, 'Non esse Deum aut opis aut consilii tam egenum, ut cum in animo esset vestem novam parare, eam sineret ex veteri et lacernoso confici pallio'" (Both because he knew that he was most observant of the Society's rules, and also when Creswell found out that counsels of this kind were being exchanged among the princes, and that their eyes had fallen on Persons, he replied with a comparison, as his custom was: "God is not so short of material or plan that when he wants to make a new suit He has it made from an old overcoat!").

EDITION: More, 231–232.

TRANSLATION: Edwards, *More*, 289–290.

NOTE: Persons, now in Seville, writes to clarify his position in relation to rumours that he should be made cardinal. This open letter, in Latin, reads like a response to Acquaviva's caution in his letter of 16 January (B254). It enclosed another, private letter in Spanish (see next item) and the letter from Mannaerts, 24 November 1594 (B251). Grene summarizes the letter, "He relateth how he had heard many of our nation seemed to endeavour to gett him made Cardinal, which he has much aversion to and desireth his Paternity to hinder it if any such matter should be," and comments, "'Tis a most modest and prudent lettere" (ABSI, Coll N1 157). Persons may have chosen to write in Latin so as to inform a wider audience of his position.

Admodum Reverende in Christo Pater noster
Pax Christi.

Quod rarius breviusque his praeteritis mensibus ad Paternitatem Vestram scripserim, in causa fuit, partim, valetudo adversa, partim etiam quod negotium nullum magni momenti occurreret, de quo scriberem. Nunc vero quando febribus nostris quartanis, Dei beneficio, magna ex parte levatus sum (licet non omnino liber) et negotium se offert gravissimum, copiosius mihi scribendum duxi.

Post mortem Illustrissimi Cardinalis Alani, rumusculi nescio qui, his in partibus spargi caeperunt, mihi impendere Cardinalitiam dignitatem, quod, etsi mihi eo tempore ridendum potius et contemnendum, quam resistendum videbatur, eo quod nullo certo fundamento aut authore niteretur, et eiusmodi esset negotium de quo ego sine verecundia vix loqui aut mentionem facere possem, ne quod dicitur, dum fumum conarer reprimere flammam viderer velle accendere; tamen cum postea Madriti etiam nonnullorum hominum sermone agitari rem comperi neque non Romae: magis me commotum sensi; postea vero cum ante biduum opinor aut triduum literas a Patre Oliverio Manaraeo acceperim, quarum exemplar ad Paternitatem vestram una cum his transmitto, quibus intellexi, serius[51] id negotium ab Anglis nostris in Flandria agi, vel saltem bonum Patrem sic existimasse (quanquam alii recentius contrarium scripserint) non amplius mihi tacendum omnino iudicavi saltem apud Vestram Paternitatem cuius praecipuam in me caritatem semper expertus sum, et cui ex officio paterni sui regiminis, tum mihi tum Societati etiam ipsi prospicere incumbit.

Primo igitur verissime Paternitati Vestrae affirmare possum, molestissimam mihi extitisse huius rei mentionem, nihil enim ab animi mei vel sensu vel iudicio alienius cogitari potest, quam ut ego ab hoc tranquillo vitae genere, in quo summa animi consolatione nonnihil in sanctum Dei servitium, et commune patriae meae afflictissimae subsidium per eiusdem Domini nostri gratiam conferre videar, ad aliud vitae exercitium tam longe dispar transferar, ad quod licet illustre et per se Sanctum et Venerabile, ego tamen nullam in me vel[52] aptitudinem vel vocationem vel inclinationem sentio,[53] nec vires habeo quibus illud expleam. Deinde etiam, ut quod vere sincereque in Domini nostri

51. serius] *R*; serio *Hicks*
52. vel] *R*; om. *Hicks*
53. sentio] *R*; om. *Hicks*

conspectu, re bene perpensa sentio, eloquar, omnino iudico, ea omnia verissima esse quae Pater Oliverius enumerat incommoda, quae causae nostrae publicae acciderent, si ego ab hoc vitae cursu removear, nimirum quod seminaria haec tum[54] hispanica tum ea etiam quae in Belgio sunt, detrimentum paterentur. Et si quid modo particularibus hominibus praesto, id minus praestare possem extra hoc vitae genus, utilioremque omnino esse operam meam patriae civibusque meis modo (si tamen utilis est) quam esset alio illo in genere quod aliqui mihi obtrudere vellent, non intelligentes incommodare se sibi ea in re, qua maxime prospicere et commodare cupiunt. Quod cum verissimum sit, Paternitatem Vestram humillime omnique quo possum affectu ob Dei causam precor, ut veri patris officium hac in re praestet, et periculum hoc, si quod impendeat (nihil enim adhuc certi habeo) avertere conetur; quibus autem[55] illud mediis fieri possit, Paternitatis Vestrae prudentia optime constituet, ego solummodo rem ipsam significandam, et Paternitatis Vestrae caritati proponendam iudicavi. Deus ipsam multos in annos incolumem nobis conservare dignetur cuius sanctis me sacrificiis humillime commendo. Hispali die 20 Februarii 1595.

        Paternitatis Vestrae Reverendae
           indignus filius et servus
              Robertus Personius.

[*Addressed*:] Admodum reverendo in Christo patri nostro p. Claudio Aquaviva preposito Generali [Societa]tis Jesu. Romae.

[*Endorsed*:] Sevilla. P. Roberto Personio hebrero 20. [*with summary*]

Translation

Our Very Reverend Father in Christ
The peace of Christ.

The fact that in these last months I have written to Your Paternity more infrequently and briefly,[56] has been partly due to my ill health, and partly also because it so happened that there was no business of great consequence to write about. Now however I have been largely relieved, by the goodness of God, from my quartan ague, though not entirely, and, as a very serious matter has cropped up, I thought I should write at greater length.

After the death of His Eminence, Cardinal Allen, faint rumours as it were began to spread in these parts that I was destined for the dignity of becoming a cardinal. Although at that time this seemed to me to call for laughter and derision rather than repudiation, since there was no definite foundation or authority underlying it – indeed, it was the sort of thing that I could hardly discuss or mention without embarrassment, in case, as they say, while trying to smother the smoke, I seemed to be trying to fan the flame – nevertheless, when I found out later that the idea was being bandied about in Madrid in the conversation of certain people, and even in Rome, I felt more perturbed; and afterwards when, two or three days later, I believe, I received a letter from Fr Olivier Mannaerts (a copy of which I am enclosing to Your Paternity), from which I gathered

54. tum] R; *om. Hicks*
55. autem] R; *interlined with caret*
56. It appears that Persons did not write at the beginning of January and February.

that this matter was being more seriously mooted by our English friends in Flanders, or at any rate that the good father had thought so (though others have subsequently written to me to the contrary), I came to the conclusion that I could no longer remain entirely silent, at least in Your Paternity's presence, since I have always experienced your extraordinary charity towards me, and also because you are duty bound by your office of paternal governance to take timely measures both for my good and the good of the Society itself.

In the first place, then, I can affirm to Your Paternity with absolute sincerity that I have been very deeply disturbed by the very mention of this matter; for I can imagine nothing more alien to my feelings and judgement than that from this peaceful kind of life, in which, to the great consolation to my soul, I would seem to be making some small contribution to the holy service of God and the general succour of my country in its most need, I should be transferred to another, such a very different sphere of life. And, although it is illustrious and in itself holy and worthy of respect, I nevertheless feel in myself no aptitude or vocation or inclination for it, nor have I the strength to fulfil its duties. And moreover, to explain honestly and truly, in the sight of our Lord, what I feel about it after due consideration, I am entirely persuaded of the validity of all those inconveniences enumerated by Fr Olivier and that they would indeed weaken our common cause if I should be removed from my way of life here; that is to say, that the seminaries here in Spain as well as those in Flanders would be adversely affected. And if I am now of any service to private individuals I should be less able to give that service if I were removed from this kind of life, and I think that my help is altogether more profitable to my country and to my fellow citizens now (if indeed it is profitable) than it would be in that other kind of career which some would like to impose upon me, not realizing that they will inconvenience themselves by the very thing they want to turn to their advantage as they look to the future. This being the undoubted truth, I beg Your Paternity most humbly and with all the earnestness of which I am capable, for God's sake to fulfil the role of a true father in this matter and make every effort to ward off this danger – if indeed any is impending, for I have no definite information so far. However, Your Paternity in your discretion will decide for the best how this can be done; it has only been right, as I see it, to acquaint Your Paternity with the matter and hand it over to you to deal with charitably. May God vouchsafe to preserve Your Paternity to us in safety for many years, and to your holy sacrifices I humbly commend myself. From Seville, 20 February 1595.

    Your Reverend Paternity's
        unworthy son and servant
           Robert Persons.

B258 To Claudio Acquaviva, Seville, 20 February 1595

SOURCE: ARSI, Hisp. 138, fol. 142 (olim 245).
HICKS: 308–309 (text), 312–313 (translation).
NOTE: Here Persons comments on Mannaerts's letter of 24 November (B251), enclosing a copy for the general. He endorses Mannaerts's reasons for resisting any pressure to put himself forward for the cardinalate, and adds more of his own.

Grene comments that in this letter Persons "writeth ... most candidly how he had signified all the matters to some superiors and fathers there, and had and would dow all that they or Fr General should think fitting in the matter. The first letter in Latin was ostensible [i.e., open]." See ABSI, Coll N1 157.

Muy Reverendo en Christo Padre nuestro
Pax Christi.

Vuestra Paternidad veerá por la carta del Padre Oliverio lo que me escrivio toccante el negocio del Cardinalado, quando yo estava bien descuydado de que se avia de ablar más en ello. No puedo decir más a Vuestra Paternidad en mi conscientia de lo que escrivo en la carta mostrabile en latin que va con esta. Recebi anteyr la carta del Padre Oliverio y hasta entonces avia callado, por tener la cosa por ridicula y no poder yo ablar en ella sin verguença, esperando que con un poco de tiempo passaria la memoria della, pero en recebiendo la carta del Padre Oliverio, pareciome deber conferirla con el Padre Preposito y con otros cinco o seis Padres de los más graves. Fueron de parecer que yo escriviesse lo que escrivo a Vuestra Paternidad y tan bien a los Padres de Madrid, que hiciessen todas las diligencias que pudieren, y assi lo hago y hare tan bien de mi parte todo lo que será possible sin ruydo y sin avivar más el negocio. Escrivo una carta mostrabile tan bien a los Padres de Madrid, con instruciones particulares a parte. No parecio a los Padres que era aún tiempo que yo mismo escriviesse al Rey o a sus consejeros, pero esté Vuestra Paternidad segura que de mi parte no dexaré de hacer todo lo possible para estorvar el negocio, porque ansi lo siento conbenir in Domino, tanto por mi particular como por lo comune de la Compañia que amo más que a mí. Si a[57] Vuestra Paternidad se le offerece algun medio particular, nos hara caridad de avisar. Yo pienso y confio en nuestro Señor que no yrá más adelante el negocio, si no que morirá con el tiempo. Con todo esto estaremos aliertos para obviar a lo que entendieremos.[58]

Yo estoy mejor de mis quartanas aunque no totalmente libre. Anteyr concertamos de comprar una casa nueva para este Seminario en 7 mil ducados y tres mil más ha de costar ponerla en orden, pero será grande, capaz y hermosa. No tenemos cosa alguna aún[59] por la paga en denero contado aunque por otra via tenemos *spei multum, et aliquid etiam rei*. Tenemos 3 años de espacio para la paga y *interea temporis* pagamos solamente 200 ⁊ de renta. La casa vale más de 15 mil, pero es mayorasgo y el Rey no quiso dar faculdad para venderla a otros. Las oraçiones destos alumnos[60] son los que lo alcancaron de nuestro Señor, porque son virtuosissimos. En los santos sacrificios de Vuestra Paternidad humilmente me encomiendo. Sevilla a 20 de Febrero 1595.

 Indigno hijo y siervo
  de Vuestra Paternidad
   Roberto Personio.

[*Addressed:*] Al muy Reverendo en Christo Padre nuestro el Padre Claudio Aquaviva Preposito general de la Compañia de Jesus en Roma.

[*Endorsed:*] Sevilla. P. Roberto Personio. hebr⁰ 20. [*with summary of contents*]

57. Si a] *interlined with caret R*
58. *Editorial paragraph break*
59. aún] *R; om. Hicks*
60. alumnos] *interlined with caret R*

Translation

Our Very Reverend Father in Christ
The peace of Christ.

Your Paternity will see from Fr Olivier's letter what he wrote to me about the affair of the cardinalate, though I was then quite free of any fear that it would be mentioned again. I cannot conscientiously say any more to Your Paternity than I am doing in the open letter, in Latin, which accompanies this. I received Fr Olivier's letter the day before yesterday, and until then I had held my peace, because I considered the thing ridiculous and could not mention it myself without shame, and I hoped that in a short time all memory of the matter would pass away. When, however, I got Fr Olivier's letter, I thought it was my duty to consult the father superior and five or six of the most respected fathers about it. They were of the opinion that I ought to write (as I am) to Your Paternity, and also to the fathers in Madrid, asking them to bring all the influence they can to bear, and this I am doing; and I also for my part will do all that is possible without arousing talk and reviving the matter. I am writing an open letter separately to the fathers in Madrid also, with special instructions.[61] The fathers did not think the time had yet come for me to write to the king or his councillors myself, but Your Paternity may rest assured that for my part I shall leave nothing undone to put a stop to this business, because I think that in the sight of our Lord this conduces most both to my own private good and to the general good of the Society, which I love more than myself. If anything in particular occurs to Your Paternity that can be done to achieve this, you will be doing us a favour by letting us know. I think and trust in our Lord that the matter will not go any further but will die out as time goes on. All the same, we will be on the watch to counter whatever steps we hear are being taken.

I have recovered from my quartan ague, though not entirely free of it. Before leaving we arranged to buy a new house for this seminary for 7000 ducats, and it will cost 3000 more to put it in condition; but it will be large and spacious and a fine house. We have no ready money to pay for it yet, although on the other hand we are very hopeful and have had some encouragement. We have a period of three years in which to pay, and in the meantime we are paying a rent of only 200 escudos. The house is worth more than 15,000, but it is entailed, and the king would not give permission to sell it to anyone else. The prayers of the students here are what helped to obtain this favour from our Lord, for they are very virtuous. I humbly commend myself to Your Paternity's holy sacrifices. Seville, 20 February 1595.

    Your Paternity's unworthy son and servant
    Robert Persons.

---

61. See Persons to Acquaviva, 12 June (B279).

B259 To Juan García, Seville, 20 February 1595

SOURCE: Persons to Acquaviva, 20 February and 12 June 1595 (B258, B279).

NOTE: Persons wrote to the fathers in Madrid, under their rector, about the agitation for him to become cardinal, in much the same terms in which he wrote to Acquaviva. They found it unnecessary to take the matter further.

B260 From Thomas Wright, Valladolid, 20 February 1595

SOURCE: ARSI, Hisp. 138, fol. 147, a contemporary fair copy.

NOTE: In response to a letter from Persons, Wright renews his request to be sent to England for his health; faced with the dilemma of forfeiting his membership in the Society if he should be allowed to leave, he proposes that he be given two years to prove himself in England. Persons enclosed this copy for the general's attention in his letter of 19 March (B264).

Reverende in Christo Pater
Pax Christi, etc.

Literas Reverentiae Vestrae simul cum exemplari illarum quas ad ipsam Nostram Patrem Generalis dedit, recepi: ambae in eandem conspirarunt sententiam, et hanc solam, nulla me ratione in Angliam mittendum, tanquam Societatis legitimum filium: sin autem ab ea mittendum. Gravis haec visa est mihi sententia: ex una enim parte valetudinem amitto, sine qua quicquid ex studiis supellectilis comparavi tot annorum laboribus amitto: ex altera vero Angelorum societatem desero, quo quid luctuosius? in medio positus quo me vertam? utrumque possidere impossibile, alter utro carere molestissimum; hinc inde angustiae.

Sed tandem subiit[62] animum illud consilium ut spero saluberrimum quod Vestrae Reverentiae paucis exponam, cui incumbit ex charitate negotium absolvere. Procuret mihi quaeso Nostri Patris Generalis literas dimissorias ad biennium quo tempore et virtutis et valetudinis dabo experimentum quo peracto ad pristinum statum redibo.

Quod si nec istud concedere dignabitur, absolute concedat, novi enim patris ingenium, novi prudentiam, novi charitatem, pro certo enim habeo, quod modo negat, concessurum postea; si tales proventus ex Anglicano agro colligam, quales germanum societatis decet filium.

Vestra ergo Reverentia huic petitioni ne quaeso obsistat, sed quod in multos distulit menses ne dicam annos tandem absolvat. Sat scio illam me diligere, ac ea de causa quae speciem aliquam incommodi prae se ferunt conaturum[63] prorsus avertere: sed parcat precibus, indulgeat importuno, animat postulatis: videbit spero brevi fruitus non paenitendos, cognoscet se corpori et animae consuluisse. Plura non scribo, quia haec forte videbuntur multa,[64] sed cogit necessitas, urgent angustiae. Hoc solum adiungam ut cito

---

62. subiit] *interlined with caret* R
63. conaturum] R, *possibly in error for* conaturam
64. multa] *preceded by* nimis [*deleted*] R

expediat ne calores inveniant quem cito expediant. Vale mi Pater; Deus Vestram Reverentiam diu conservet incolumem, cui ad altare[65] me commendare dignetur. Vallesoleti. 20 Feb 95.

  Vestrae Reverentiae
    servus in Christo
      Thomas Wrightus.

Translation

Reverend Father in Christ
The peace of Christ, etc.

 I have received Your Reverence's letter, together with a copy of the one which you gave to our father general; both letters concur in the same judgement, and that one only: that I should by no means be sent to England, as a legitimate son of the Society: otherwise I would have to be expelled from it. This seems to me a hard choice: for on the one hand, I sacrifice my vigour, without which I lose whatever accomplishments I have gained from my studies in the labours of so many years; on the other, I leave the society of angels indeed – what could be more lamentable than that? Placed in the middle of this, which way should I turn? I cannot possess both; to lose either one of them would be most troublesome; there are hardships on either side.

 But at length I have set my heart on a resolution that I hope would be the most practical to explain to Your Reverence in a few words, since it falls to you to settle the business, of your charity: I am asking you to obtain letters of dismissal from father general for two years, in the course of which I shall make every effort to restore my strength and health to its former state by the time the period has expired.

 If you should only vouchsafe to make this concession, please could you make it without restriction, for I know father's acumen, I know your prudence, I know your charity, for I am assured, what you deny now, you will allow in the future – if I should gather such crops from the English field, as is worthy of a true son of the Society.

 So, reverend father, I ask you not to stand in the way of this request, but settle, finally, what you have deferred for many months, not to say years. I know well enough that you love me, and for that reason you will try to avert entirely whatever things would bring me any kind of harm. Be favourable to my prayers, indulge my importunity, give life to what I have asked; you will shortly see, I hope, fruits that will lead you not to regret this, you will know that you will have consulted the interests both of body and soul. I will write no more, since even this will seem much, but necessity compels me, hardship urges me. Let me add just this one thing, that you despatch me swiftly, so that the fever does not find someone to despatch quickly. Farewell, my father; may God keep Your Reverence long unharmed, to whose altar be pleased to commend me. Valladolid, 20 February 1595.

  Your Reverence's
    servant in Christ
      Thomas Wright.

---

 65. altare] R, *possibly in error for* altarem

B261 From Gaspar Alonso, Valladolid, February/March 1595

SOURCE: Persons to Acquaviva, 19 March (B264).

NOTE: Alonso, the confessor of the seminary, wrote to Persons about the urgency of dismissing Thomas Wright from the Society.

B262 From Gonzalo Dávila, February/March 1595

SOURCE: Persons to Acquaviva, 19 March (B264).

NOTE: Dávila, provincial of Castile, wrote to inform Persons that he had appointed Gonzalo del Río rector of the English college.

B263 From Henry Garnet, London, February/March 1595

SOURCE: Persons to Acquaviva, 19 March (B264).

NOTE: Garnet urged the case of Richard Blount, one of the priests who left Seville for England in April 1591, who now sought to join the Society. See Persons to Barret, 7 November 1590 (B86), headnote.

B264 To Claudio Acquaviva, Seville, 19 March 1595

SOURCE: ARSI, Hisp. 138, fols. 184–85, holograph.
HICKS: 317–322, with English translation.

NOTE: Persons continues to subdue talk about his promotion to the cardinalate. He deals from a distance with questions relating to the college at Valladolid, Creswell's position as procurator in Madrid, and Richard Blount's request to join the Society.

Grene describes the letter (see ABSI, Coll N1 157): "Repetit de Cardinalatum et laudat P. Bluntum petitque ut possit recipi in Anglia, &c." (He returns to the subject of the cardinalate and praises Fr Blount and asks that it be possible for him to be received [into the Society] in England, etc.)

Muy Reverendo in Christo Padre nuestro
Pax Christi.

1. A la de Vuestra Paternidad de 16 de Enero, no será necessario escrivir mucho, pues a lo principal contenido, que fue del capelo, respondido ya tenía a Vuestra Paternidad antes que esta recibi. Tengo hecho por acá todas las[66] diligencias que a los Padres con quienes lo consulté, parecio necessario o expediente se hiciessen, y tengo prevenidos los Padres de Madrid que me manden avisar quando otra cosa convenga hacer, y assi me esfuerço de no pensar ni saber más dello, pero quando no se acabasse el negocio con esto (como yo tengo esperança que se acabará), confio en nuestro Señor que Vuestra Paternidad me hallerá siempre fiel hijo de la Compañia y muy lexos destos pensamientos.

2. Con el Padre Tomas Wright he hecho todo lo que he podido, para que buelva in sí y desista de sus pretensiones de yr a Ynglaterra pero no si hace nada con él; enbío a Vuestra

66. las] *interlined with caret R*

Paternidad su postrera carta que me escrivio, y no se si será possibile detenerle hasta a la respuesta de Vuestra Paternidad y el Padre Gaspar Alonso confessor del Seminario, me escrive que la delacion de su dispedida no hace provecho en aquela casa, Vuestra Paternidad nos hara caridad de embiarla luego, y si en este mientras, será necessario dexarle andar, usaré de la facultad que Vuestra Paternidad me dio la suya de ordinario passado y avisaré de lo que avrá.

3. Al fin, el Padre provincial de Castilla nos ha señalado un rector para Valladolid. Devia hallar difficultad en los sujetos. Escriven que será muy a proposito, si llama el Padre Gonzalo del Río. Vuestra Paternidad le conoscera mejor, y el tiempo lo monstrara. El Collegio tendra tanto más necessidad de buen rector por agora, porque parece impossibile que yo puedo partirme de Sevilla por estos 9 o 10 meses hasta dexar acabada la fábrica de la casa y yglesia nueva, que emos comprado, y ya estamos en la obra muy mettidos y sin duda saldra muy cómoda y a proposito para el fin del Seminario.

4. No me accuerdo si escrivi en la postrera a Vuestra Paternidad de la necessidad que tenía el Padre Cresuello de un compañero en Madrid, para seguyr los negocios de entrambos Seminarios y de la nacion, a lo menos por algun tiempo, y porque el Padre provincial ponia mucha difficultad en ello, pienso que todos escrivieron a Vuestra Paternidad. Se ha offericido de pagar cien ducados en cada año al Collegio por la comida sola de los dos, y realmente importa tanto a estos Seminarios y a la causa nuestra publica que el Padre Cresuello acuda a sus tiempos a los negocios (lo qual no podra hacer sin compañero proprio como ya por la experiencia si ha visto) que por falta dello se ha padecido harto, y pues para una provincia sola, si permeten procuradores particulares, confio que Vuestra Paternidad mandará tan bien que si tenga cuenta con un reyno y con[67] una nacion intiera tan necessitada como es[68] esta, pues al Collegio no ha de ser pesada, a mi parecer. El Padre provincial dio licencia que un hermano fuesse con el Padre Cresuello hasta la respuesta de Vuestra Paternidad, la qual no dudo sino que será en favor.

5. Escrive de Ynglaterra el Padre Henrique Garnet de un sacerdote alumno que fue deso Seminario de Roma, y despues aqui en España moró por espacio de dos años. Es de rara virtud, gracia y letras, y de casa noble en Ynglaterra. Si llama Ricardo Blunto, y tiene las mayores dotes de prudencia y ciencia, que he visto de los del Seminario en muchos años. Pide con grande instancia y el Padre Henrique tan bien por el que Vuestra Paternidad lo admitta en la Compañia, estando él en Ynglaterra, pues su obra es muy util por aý, por algunos años, particularmente para reducir a sus parientes, que son gente principal y ninguno fuera dél puede tratar con ellos con la misma efficacia para reducirles. Si a Vuestra Paternidad parece hacerle esta gracia, como se ha hecho ad algunos otros, será tan bien mucho consuelo para el Padre Cresuello y mí, y si no, él se resolverá de romper con todo y bolver acá, donde de buena gana lo receveran, con licencia de Vuestra Paternidad y pido a Vuestra Paternidad que se responda a este capitulo. En los santos sacrificios de Vuestra Paternidad muy humilmente me encomiendo. Sevilla a 19 de Marco 1595.

    De Vuestra Reverenda Paternidad
        indigno sirvo y hijo
            Rob. Personio.

67. con] *interlined with caret R; not in Hicks*
68. es] *interlined with caret R*

[*Addressed:*] Al muy Reverendo en Christi Padre Claudio Aquaviva, Preposito General de la Compañia de Jesus en Roma.

[*Endorsed:*] Sevilla 95. P. Roberto Personio Marzo 19. [*with summary of contents*]

Translation

Our Very Reverend Father in Christ
The peace of Christ.

1. There is no need to say very much in answer to Your Paternity's letter of the 16th of January, because I had already given you my answer to its main concern, the question of the cardinal's hat,[69] before I received this letter. Here I have taken all the measures that the fathers whom I consulted thought necessary or expedient to take, and I have warned the fathers in Madrid to have word sent to me if there should be anything else that can be usefully done. And beyond this I will not allow myself to give any further thought or attention to the matter. If, however, these measures do not put a stop to the business (as I hope they will do), I trust in our Lord that Your Paternity will still find me a loyal son of the Society, and far from having any such designs.

2. I have made every effort that I could to induce Fr Thomas Wright to come to his senses again and give up his project of going to England, but nothing has any effect on him. I am sending Your Paternity the last letter he wrote to me;[70] I do not know whether it will be possible to make him wait for your reply. Fr Gaspar Alonso also, the confessor of the seminary, writes to say that the delay in dismissing him is doing no good in that house. Your Paternity will do us a favour if you send letters of dismissal at once, and if in the meantime it becomes necessary to let him go, I will avail myself of the authority Your Paternity gave me in your letter by the last post, and I will inform you what happens.

3. Father provincial of Castile[71] has at last appointed a rector for us at Valladolid. He must have encountered difficulties on the part of the Jesuits there. They write that he will be a very suitable person; his name is Fr Gonzalo del Río. Your Paternity will know him better than I do, and time will show. The college will have all the more need of a good rector just now, because it does not seem possible for me to leave Seville for the next nine or ten months, until the building work on the new house and church that we have bought is close enough to completion for me to go. We are already very busy with the project, and there is no doubt that it will turn out to be very convenient and suitable for the purpose of the seminary.

4. I do not remember whether in my last letter to Your Paternity I mentioned Fr Creswell's need for a companion in Madrid to enable him to carry on the business of the two seminaries and of our nation, for some time at any rate, because father provincial[72] was making it very difficult for him to do so. I believe they have both written to Your Paternity. We have offered to pay the college 100 ducats a year for food alone for the two of them. It is really so necessary, in the interest of these seminaries and of the general

69. See Persons's two letters of 20 February (B257–258).
70. B260.
71. Gonzalo Dávila.
72. Francisco de Porres, provincial of Toledo 1593–1595.

good, for Fr Creswell to attend to his business in good time (and this he will not be able to do without a companion of his own, as we have already found out by experience), that harm enough has been done by his not being able to do so. And since individual procurators are allowed for single provinces, I trust that Your Paternity will order it so that our claims receive some attention – the claims of a kingdom and an entire nation in such straits as ours; for as I see it, this will not place any burden on the college. Father provincial has given leave for a brother to be attached to Fr Creswell, pending Your Paternity's reply, which I have no doubt will be favourable.

5. Fr Henry Garnet writes from England about a priest, a former student of the college in Rome, who afterwards stayed here in Spain for the space of two years. This is a man of rare virtue, well favoured and learned, and born of a good family in England, by the name of Richard Blount.[73] He has greater gifts of prudence and learning than I have seen in men of that seminary over many years. He begs with great insistence, and beseeches Fr Henry also to ask on his behalf, that Your Paternity will accept him into the Society while he is still in England, since he has very useful work to do there for some years to come. This consists especially in trying to convert his relations, who are important people; and no one but himself can deal with them with the same prospect of converting them. If Your Paternity thinks well to grant him this favour, as has been done in the case of a few others, it will be a source of much consolation to Fr Creswell and me too; if not, he will decide to break off all his work and return here, where they will very willingly accept him with Your Paternity's permission. I beg Your Paternity for a reply to this section of my letter. I commend myself very humbly to Your Paternity's holy sacrifices. Seville, 19 March 1595.

> Your Paternity's
> unworthy son and servant
> Robert Persons.

B265 To Gonzalo del Río, Seville, probably after 19 March 1595

SOURCE: Persons to del Río, 12 May 1595 (B275).

NOTE: Del Río's appointment, by the provincial of Castile, is noted in Persons's letter to the general, 19 March (B264), and Persons would very likely have written to him almost immediately (and possibly even before his letter to the general) to offer advice. His letter to del Río of 15 May refers to two previous letters, but the endorsement to that letter states that it is his second to del Río.

B266 From John Mush, London, 24 March 1595

SOURCE: ABSI, Anglia A I 179.

NOTE: Following earlier correspondence about Wisbech, Mush deals here at length with the troubles at the English college, Rome, where he had been a student from its inception in 1579. Mush is critical of Persons for not responding to the students' pleas, and urges tolerance

---

73. On Richard Blount, see Persons to Barret, 7 November 1590 (B86), headnote.

and understanding. He protests that he is writing in a spirit of friendliness to the Jesuits, commending their educational methods and deprecating Claudio Acquaviva's request for the Society to be relieved of the charge of the college. On the troubles at the English college, see Kenny, "Inglorious Revolution"; Arnold Pritchard, *Catholic Loyalism in Elizabethan England* (London, 1979), 102–119; Maurice Whitehead, "'Established and Putt in Good Order': The Venerable English College, Rome, under Jesuit Administration, 1579–1685," in *Jesuit Intellectual and Physical Exchange between England and Mainland Europe, c. 1580–1789*, ed. James E. Kelly and Hannah Thomas (Leiden 2019), 315–336; and Lake and Questier, *All Hail to the Archpriest*, 58–72. On Mush, see "The English Mission" in the introduction.

For ease of reading, in this letter ampersands have been expanded.

Good Sir

At the receipt of your letter the tyme was so shorte and our frend Mr Francis maid suche haist to departe, that I had no tyme to reade over what I had written, and in post I answered you, as then I could. But being ever synce greivd with the evyl newes of your letter, I longed tyll I writt againe. For the matters belonging then of Wisbitch: I pray you lett yt trouble[74] nether you nor them what idle heades or evyll disposed parsons talke and jangle thus or so: tyme and patience, and the good mens weldoyng at home, wyll consume and overcome thes factions and troublesome humors. Lett bothe sydes when they heare evyll take it as a penance and satisfaction for their faultes (for in like discords and garboile, the best wyll hardly scape fault and blame) and be more warie they give no suche cause of scandal hereafter. None surely that haith either witt or grace wyll I hope nowe intermedle or laboure by indiscrete babling to revive that which the blessed men have buried, with so greate charitye. But who is he that can escape ungratious toungs? With humilitie patience and charitie we must overcome all, and not muche regard what men prattle but make ourselves as straight as we may with God.

The matter and untowardliness of the house whence I came[75] is a thing of exceding greife and continewally to be lamented – and, yf yt be possible, to be helped before all be undone. You aske what I thinke. Alas, Sir, I tender bothe partyes but darr I presume now (after so foule a checke and rebuke given me for my frendly advice) to committ the same fault againe,[76] and speake my mynd? You and yours be wise ynough, and nede no fooles advice, or simple mens counsel. Yet the cause now urging, and you demaunding my opinion, I wyll dread the fire wherwith I was burned no more, tho for my paines I receive an unworthy checke againe and be reproved of sawsiness and folly.

You have sene how often in thes few yeares the Devil haith laboured to overthrow, and dislove[77] that house and so haith prevayled many tymes, that he haith had yt even[78] at the pinche banke. Yett ever God by the wisdome and authoritie of our great frend dead[79] kept yt up, and saved yt not onely from subversion, but from any great discredit or harme

74. trouble] *interlined with caret A*
75. The English college in Rome.
76. againe] *interlined with caret A*
77. I.e., dissolve.
78. even] *A, possibly* ever
79. William Allen.

also. They have loved youres[80] and youres them. What? shall the enimie now prevaile so mightely, that the frowardness of them shall make yours flye, and forsake the unrulye sheepe, and give over their weldoyng, and so great a meritt? Tho they be disordered and stubborne, yett they be Christes sheepe surely, and not to be forsaken for any vexation or importunitie they bring to youres. I have alwaies bene perswaided verely, that ther is no education to be found so good as that, nor that our people can have any to traine them up and make them so fitt for our countrie as yours can do every way; they have taken paines hytherto. Yf for God they undertooke the charge, and respected no humaine remuneration, lett them for the same good lords sake continue still. He wyll not defraud them of their waige, but augment the same according to the increase of their toile in the foulest weather. In mens opinions, all the good turnes and benefitts we have received from them hitherto, wylbe lost and forgotten, yf now for their owne ease and quiet, they cast us of, yea our poore countries comforth taken in their favours and cares over yt, and their assistance and travels not at home onely but every where also abrode to reduce yt to that anciant happiness in religion, must now be turned into greife and hevyness, yf Claud suite take place. Rather lett him thinke him selfe an unfortunate man, yf this ruine happen in his daies. Turne of this, and the rest wyll follow er yt be longe. Write theirfore good Sir, that in no wise he procede in that course, but kepe fast his charge. Yt wylbe no credit for him to seke his owne ease and quiet, with our so great losse and discredit. As I knowe[81] this mischiefe would not have hapned yf you had gyven eare to your frendes advice when they foreseying what was likely to faule, besought you to prevent yt in tyme, and you contemned to heare. So verely I doubt not by Godes grace but this tempest wyll sone overblowe and never mo rise againe,[82] yf you have patience awhile, and reforme some trifles which may be cause or occasion to weaklinges of murmur and discontentment. What should not yours beare with and tollerate? What frailties and imperfections should they not overse and condescend unto (so that regard be had, that necessarie discipline be ever kept) that the common peace may stand saife, and no particular member be lost or broken? Yea verely (my deare Sir) what should they not do to preserve the credit of our Nation in that place? What should they not suffer (being men by holy profession *mortui mundo, quibus mundus crucifixus est, et ipsi mundo*,[83] and suche as alredy have with extraordinarie fervour of charitie bestowed them selves upon us, every where indevoring to benefitt us and singularly above all other orders accompaning us in all difficulties and dangers of our bloudye warfaire) rather than suche foule garboiles and dissentions and breaches should appeare emong them. Young men entring and undertaking suche a course, could never resolve theron, but by the extraordinarie motion and grace of God. They be of[84] divers constitutions. All arte surely is to be used by youres, that none of them whom God haith sent and put under their charge, perishe, that none be

    80. The Jesuits, whose government of the English College, Rome, was resented by many students.
    81. knowe] *replaces* doubt not [*deleted*] A
    82. never mo rise againe] *interlined with caret A*
    83. Cf. Gal. 6:14: "But God forbid that I should glory, save in the cross of our Lord Jesus Christ; by whom the world is crucified to me, and I to the world."
    84. of] *interlined with caret A*

altogether broken, bycause they can not ply and bend as is to be wisshed. Some by natures framyng ar swete and tractable as can be desired, some contrariewise are stearne and rough. Some ar quiet and flexable to any thing, some againe ar busie headid, restles, and stubburne. Some approve and like well any order, some againe can hardly brooke any at all. Some, do and say what you wyll, ar no whitt offendid. Some others take scandall and are disquiet at almost every occasion. God you se sendeth of all sortes. In this poynt then, all the captaines grace, all his skill, all his wyttes and pollicies should be imployed, that every souldier be trayned up, tollerated, and delt with in all occasions as is best agreable with his nature, that so they may albe brought to good, and none through evyl guiding maid to miscarie in their tyrocinie.[85] But what? am I become a teacher? or presume I to instruct men of singular graces, skill, government and experience and vertu? or judge I them ignorant or careless in thinges belonging their charge? No my dearest Sir, what I say, is, for the good affection and honor I beare to youres, and their children, yea and wisshing (for the common good of all, that[86] either by speache or silence I might do good, and se[87] all as they should be) I were therfore *Anathema inter fratres*:[88] wo to me, if I ayme at any privat interest; wo to me if I emulate in evyll sorte the weale, and credit of other. Wo to me, yf for any cause, I wishe not, as becommeth me to everye one. I can not my selfe shapp well a garment, yett after the counnyngest tailer of them all haith made up his worke, an unskilful foole may spie a fault. The exactest painter standing neare his worke commonly discerneth not the errors which a simple man beholding farther of, espieth. Many tymes as you knowe that house haith bene in danger of subversion. Some cause ther is[89] hereof. What may yt be? or in whome is yt? In the youthes no doubt resteth the greatest part, but not all verelye, as not I onely, but the best of our nation, and suche as most affected youres have ever noted. Why do not yours perceive their owne[90] error, if yt be so? I will not examine that.

1. Contynewall experience haith proved, that to deale sharpely and roughly with hard, hautie, and stubberne natures undoes them, and extremely disquieteth[91] bothe superiour and subject. And by that indiscrete dealing aversion once taken on bothe parties, inconveniences growe more and more dalye; then factions and partakinges[92] increase, complaintes ar multiplied, and of a litle error on bothe sides in the beginnyng, commeth shortely too to[93] greate tumult and[94] harme. The orders be swete as may be, and no whitt burdenous to the good natured, yett they be not in religious staite, but voluntarily submitt them selves under order for a time. Yf hevnly[95] natures frame to do any

85. tyrocinie] *ending of the word obscure in A (tirocinium* (Lat.): *experience of raw recruits).*
86. that] *followed by* so, *interlined with caret, and deleted A*
87. se] *A, obscure*
88. "Anathema amongst the brethren": Mush calls down the curse ("anathema") upon himself if he speaks in his own interest rather than for the common good.
89. is] *followed by* not [*deleted*] *A*
90. owne] *interlined with caret A*
91. disquieteth] *this ed.;* disquiethe *A*
92. partakinges] *followed by* growe [*deleted*] *A*
93. to] *interlined with caret, possibly a correction of* too *A*
94. and] & *followed by* dis[sension] [*deleted*] *A*
95. hevnly] *A, obscure*

whitt like, yt is well, make of them what may be, with courtesie, the rest referr to God, for the houses peace.

2. When one of thes ar out and disordered, to be jelious and suspitious of any other that converse with him, and to use the same partie hardly or unfrendly therfore, maketh the matter in worse case and discontenteth them that ar verye good, and which without that kind of usage would never have entred into factions.

3. Againe to sett spials (otherwise cauled *Angeli custodes*[96]) over any, to sound their affections, and to prye into their conversation, and to accuse them secretly of faults, or evyll meanynges, haith ever bene a most odious device, *vastans nequidem etiam iustorum & infirmorum malorumque adaugens mirum in malum perversitatem.*[97]

4. What tumults and confusion haith ever bene raised ther, by the zeale of them that perswaid and intice the youthes to religion?[98] This I knowe haith bene a principal blocke[99] wherby the house haith bene in hassard many tymes, and ever greately disquieted. But this is lawful, therfore *scandalum phariseorum.* Be it so. Yett *omnia quae licent non expediunt.*[100] And farr better yt were, and more to the credit of yours, that you had none of them by that meanes, than to gett some with so muche disturbance of common peace. Without that meane, God no doubt wyll caul, and move sufficiently, youres can not faile to have of them now and then as it pleaseth God to move their hartes; suche offensive and troublesome occasions should not be used. They ar in a commendable way alredye; perfect them, and furnishe them sufficiently to the end they came for, and they can not accuse you, that you seke rather your selves, then the charge you have committed to you. Besides yf we consider wel, we shall se that seldom any gotten by that indiscrete meanes have good proofe. And so muche[101] haith and is this an hartesore amonge them of that house, and so greately yt distempereth them, that not onely the most profitt less in vertu and learning, in the practice therof, but by this occasion[102] divers also upon stomake and discontentment rushe to other religions[103] which other wise they would not have once thought upon. And wearye of that staite also after a while returne againe to worse[104] caise than they were before.

5. Againe when yt is once knowen that some which alredye ar resolved to religion abide yett in the house to[105] they have endid their courses, yt bredeth no litle quarrel and greife in contentious heades, and by litle and litle bringeth evyll conceipts and murmur to many.

96. The "guardian angels" were a much resented method of surveillance introduced by Harewood.

97. "Destroying indeed the just and the infirm and the evil, adding wonder upon wonder to the evil perversity" (source untraced).

98. I.e., pressure to join the Society of Jesus.

99. blocke] *followed by* to [*deleted*] A

100. "A [mere] stumbling-block for the Pharisees" (a tag from St Thomas Aquinas); "not everything that is lawful is expedient" (cf. 1 Cor. 6:12).

101. so muche] *interlined with caret* A

102. by this occasion] *interlined with caret in the margin* A

103. I.e., other religious orders, notably the Benedictines.

104. worse] *followed by* stai[te] [*deleted*] A

105. I.e., until.

6. And finally (for I have said too muche unless thinges would be amendid) the extraordinarie favours and partialities which at all tymes have bene used towards them esspecially which either were desired, or were of them selves inclined to religion (yf they were good wittes or of gentrie cheifly) haith ever bene a fier brand of discord, discontentment, contempt of superiours and rebellion.

Thes vi be the most (good Sir) which either my selfe have noted or have hard other complaine upon, against yours in that house, to[106] be the causes of trouble or[107] disquietness or harme, or evyl government. But what? Do I condemne yours as guiltye of thes? Be they not rather surmises and quarrels proceding from[108] a mynd evyl affected to our[109] companye? How I am affected to yours, God and I knowe, tyme and occasion must trye. Sure I am since I first knewe them, I have receyved verie manye benefitts from them. Yf I be not answerable in all frendliness againe, to my best abillitie, bothe sinne and shame wyll befaule me. In dede I wishe as to my owne harte yours were every way irreprehensible and sackless,[110] and that they were conceipts and fantasies of an idle head, rather than tru experiences. But yf they be false, the most harme is, that many your good frends ar deceived. Your charities wyll easely pardone their error[111] and the merit is yours. And yf they be truthes, no discredit can touche your Companie, when, hearing them, they studye to reforme them. When particular members of a Company or private younge men, through indiscretion or want of skill or extraordinary grace requisite for him that must governe well and hitt a right[112] everye mans particular vaine under him, committ an error or oversight, no disgrace nor blott of credit can faule to his Companye therby, unless for too muche affection and high conceipt of them selves and their order, they either wyll not have that in theirs[113] to be a fault, which in dede is one, or neglect to reforme yt when yt is tould them, and every man seeth yt.

To end then, I beseche you write most earnestly to Claud, that in no wise he faile us now, but kepe still his charge and by his prudence and fatherly[114] compassion compose and streight all againe, and take order to prevent thes outragious tumults as well as may be. I doubt not but yf yt pleased him to reforme what may be amisse in the foresaid points all would go wel for tyme to come. And for Gods sake pardon you my bouldness for yt is more agreable to my nature to deale thus plainely, rather than to shake the head, and say I dare not speake my mynd, for they wylbe offendid, as I se some of no smale accompt do. Jesu kepe you. Pray for me. Commend me to Mr Thomas.[115] This 24 March 1594.[116]

   Your assured frend
    M J Nat. Wharton.

106. to] *replaces* yt [*deleted*] *A*
107. or] *interlined with caret A*
108. from] *interlined with caret A*
109. Possibly a mistake for "your," as Mush was not a Jesuit; alternatively, used to mean "the one we are discussing."
110. Beyond reproach.
111. error] *followed by full stop and* God ys; & *interlined and deleted A*
112. a right] *interlined with care A*
113. in theirs] *supplied from margin A*
114. fatherly] *replaces* charitable [*deleted*] *A*
115. Possibly Thomas Wright.
116. 24 March 1595 new style, since the letter refers to the death of Allen in October 1594.

[*Addressed:*] To my verye good frend Roberts thes.

[*Endorsed:*] Mr Mushes letters to me a yeare ago, about the Societies geving over the College. 1594.

B267 From Richard Verstegan, Antwerp, 30 March 1595

SOURCE: ABSI, Anglia A II, no. 3, fols. 23r–24v.

EDITIONS: Petti 228–230, Foley, 1: 377–378.

NOTE: Apart from miscellaneous news, this letter (which sounds a personal note in the opening paragraph) contains an account of Southwell's execution and the capture of William Baldwin, whom Persons had called to Spain in 1594. Ciphers were decoded above the line, possibly by Persons himself.

Another advice dated 25 March (fol. 26r, Petti, 223–227) was incorporated into the present letter: divergences are footnoted where appropriate, including differences in the encoding.

In Antwerp the 30 of march 1595 stylo novo

Having lately receaved 2 severall letters from two frendes in England the one of the 4 the other of the 10 of this present, I do here send your fatherhoode the contents of them bothe together. By their next I am promised more particulers the which (yf so soone I attaine unto them) I will imparte in my next unto you.

The second of this present according to the niew style, F. Robert Southwell was arraigned and condemned of highe treason at Westminster, for beeing priest and coming into the realme contrarie to the statute.[117] The morrow after being Saterday and the 3 of this monethe he was executed at Tybourne: he had beene tortured ten severalle tymes, two yeares and three quarters imprisoned,[118] for the most parte in the tower of London, and now nothing but priesthood was to be laid to his charge. He was suddenly by the instigation of bloudy Topclyf (and secretly as such an action might be[119]) thus

---

117. 27 Eliz. I cap. 2; see vol. 1, appendix 1: "Anti-Catholic Legislation." For Southwell's trial and execution, see Christopher Devlin, *The Life of Robert Southwell: Poet and Martyr* (New York, 1969), 305–324, drawing on letters by Garnet to Acquaviva, 22 February, 7 March, and 1 May 1595 (the letter of 22 February is translated in Foley, 1: 376–377); "A Brefe Discourse of the Condemnation and Execution of Mr Robert Southwell" (by an anonymous eyewitness; ABSI, Anglia A II, no. 1, transcribed in Foley, 1: 364–376); and "Leake's Relation" (Pollen, *Unpublished Documents*, 333–337). Petti, 225 n2, discusses the discrepancy in the dates: 3 March according to the Gregorian calendar corresponds to 21 February, the day on which his feast is celebrated, but it was a Friday, not a Saturday.

118. Petti, 225 n4, quotes "Leake's Relation," where Southwell is said to have exclaimed at his trial: "I am decayed in memorie with long and close imprisonment, and I haue bene tortured ten times: I had rather haue endured ten executions. I speak not this for my self, but for others; that they may not be handled so inhumanelie to drive men to desperation if it weir possible" (Pollen, *Unpublished Documents*, 335).

119. On the secrecy both of the trial and execution, Petti, 225 n5, quotes from Garnet's letter to Acquaviva of 22 February: "By cunning contrivance, his enemies secured that the smallest audience possible should be present" (Foley, 1: 377).

used, to the admiration of all beholders, who were[120] moved with great compassion (seeing so many good partes to be in him and how with all patience and myldnes he endured this tragedy), and seemed much to repyne at thease proceedinges. Beeing come unto the place of execution he their died with great comendations of all[121] because he prayed for the Queene and realme, and made such a mournefull speech as caused many weeping eyes; he hanged untill he was dead throughe the crye of the people, who would not suffer him sooner to be cutt downe, so great an impression his death did make within them.[122] I have used in this relation the only woordes of our frendes letters.

Certaine yong schollers[123] beeing taken on the seas in passing from St Omers towardes Spaine have beene kept prisoiners in the Bishop of Canterbury his house, yong Mompersons only yelding in religion is with his freindes,[124] Woorthington, the most resolute of all, hathe made an escape oute of the Bishop his house, and cannot be heard of.[125]

Fr Baldwin [6 r 12 8 & 20 14], bearing himself as one borne in Italie [22] was by meanes of mony [237] gotten oute of their handes and is with Fr Garnet [195].[126] This pointe for some respects is to be concealed.

One Fletcher now Bishop of London is in great disgrace for marying with the Lady Baker a woman of ill fame, sister unto Mr Doctor Gifford. All other ladies repyne at her base choise, and have incensed the Queene against him, whereuppon he is comaunded prisoner to the Bishop of Canterburies.[127] It seemeth to me strange that her choise is reputed base seeing shee beeing but a lady hathe maried with a lord; but by this we may

---

120. The syntax of the earlier report is changed by the insertion (with caret) of "were" here and "&" before "seemed much to repyne."

121. The advice of 25 March has, in addition "and was lamented of all."

122. Petti, 225 n6, quotes from "A Brefe Discourse" (see ABSI, Anglia A II, 11): "One of the officers proffered there three tymes to have cut him downe [alive], but the people cryed: 'Staye, stay,' and the Lord Mountjoye forbad him lykewise. ... The people were so much moved with his charitable endinge that no one of them (contrary to theire accustomed wont) did speake any evill word againste him."

123. The advice of 25 March specifies "Inglish."

124. The earlier advice uses the term "kindred."

125. Persons summoned William Baldwin to Spain in 1594 (Persons to Acquaviva, 18 April 1594, B226; for Persons's further dealings related to him, see his letter to Acquaviva, 10 July 1595, B283). On his capture and subterfuge, see McCoog, *Building the Faith of St Peter*, 191–192, and Foley, 3: 502–520, esp. 502–505. Baldwin used his Jesuit alias, Ottaviano Fuscincelli, which was confirmed by John Gerard, so that he was released for a ransom of 200 gold pieces. The students were later identified by John Copley, one of their number, as William Worthington, John Iverson, Thomas Garnet, James Thompson, and Henry Montpesson (Foley, 1: 186–189, at 187). All were subsequently released; see Petti 225–226 n7.

126. The ciphers, deciphered above the line in the MS and here in brackets, are different in the earlier report: 40 20 48 42 56 46 49 (Baldwin), 142 (Italy), 114 (Garnet); "money" is not encoded, and "in 137 [England] still" follows 114; "is to be concealed" is rendered "must be secret", immediately following "this pointe."

127. John Whitgift (ca. 1530–1604), archbishop of Canterbury from 1583.

note what reputation thease Lordes do cary, when such a lady as this, dothe debase her self to marry with one of them.[128]

In Ireland[129] the Earle of Tirone, Odonell and others do muster and make great preparations for warr. The Inglish [215] Catholics [225][130] do stand[131] in expectation to see what assistance they shall have from Spain [20] and will measure their owne hopes by [the] king of Spain [146] his tymely furtherance for thease affaires.[132]

Drake will be redy to go forthe aboute the end of Apprill.[133]

By reason of exceeding great rayne and snowe, there have bene wounderfull inundations in Holand; some of their fortes by force of the floodes cleane taken away and the men drowned, and the artilery sunck into the mudd. The principall of thease fortes was one called Skinok Sconce, and which stoode on the ryver of Rene; and another called Creve Ceur, which was neere unto Bolduke. Thousandes of cattell and many men are drowned (soldiers and others); divers of their causses and banckes, which held oute the water, broken thorow, insomuch that it is thought they will not be able in many yeares to repaire thease losses. The element of water hathe heretofore served their tiurnes, and now they are thereby punished.[134]

The towne and castle of Huy are gotten againe, the towne by force, the castle by composition.[135]

The Bishop of Liège is to pay unto the kinges soldiers three monethes payes, and then the Spaniardes are to leave the castle unto him, for as yet they remaine in itt.[136]

128. On Richard Fletcher (1544/5–1596), see Brett Usher, *ODNB*. As dean of Peterfield he officiated at the execution of Mary, Queen of Scots, and following the death of John Aylmer in 1594 obtained the bishopric of London thanks to Essex's patronage. Against Elizabeth's wishes, and contrary to his own declaration of intent, he married Mary (*née* Gifford, sister of William Gifford), the widow of Sir Richard Baker of Sissinghurst, Kent. Elizabeth treated this as a broken promise, and he was suspended from episcopal functions from 23 February until July 1595. He had a reputation as an outstanding preacher.

129. The earlier advice precedes this with "from Scotland I heare nothing." Hugh O'Neill, earl of Tyrone (ca. 1550–1616) allied with Hugh Roe O'Donnell (1572–1602) in resistance against the English in the Nine Years' War (1595–1603). O'Neill ambushed an English force near Clontinbret, County Monaghan, in May 1595.

130. In this paragraph, the earlier report encodes only "Catholics" [94].

131. From this point the MS (A) has been largely obscured, and Petti's readings have been followed where necessary.

132. The earlier advice contains the sceptical comment: "God graunt they [leane not onto a backe staf] ... ."

133. On 25 March the expected date was the middle of April. In the event, Drake sailed in August. The MS (A) reads "foothe," here corrected.

134. This paragraph is not in the earlier report. For "tiurnes," Petti reads "turmes."

135. The earlier advice, which ends here, puts it more graphically: "some dayes after was yeilded by the sold[iers], only to have their lives saved." The siege of the town of Huy, in the province of Liège, took place between 7 and 20 March, following the brief ascendancy of the Dutch, who captured the town and castle about 20 February. A Walloon Jesuit college was established here in the seventeenth century.

136. The prince-bishop of Liège was Ernest of Bavaria (1554–1612), also elector-archbishop of Cologne.

The Turck hathe caused all his brethren to be murthered, beeing 19 in number.¹³⁷

The king of Polonia who is also king of Swethen hathe caused all protestant churches to be shutt up in all Polonia, and intendeth to bring Jesuytes into all cities.¹³⁸

From France we have litle of certainty.

The Count Fuentes giveth much hope of very effectuall proceeding against the enemy.¹³⁹

[*Addressed*:] All Padre Personio.

[*Endorsed, probably by Persons*:] Verstengh advises 30 Martii 1595.

[*in another hand*:] Of f. Southwells martyrdome.

B268 From Claudio Acquaviva, 10 April 1595

> SOURCE: ARSI, Baet. 3/I, 209–210.
>
> NOTE: Responding to a letter of 20 February (B257), Acquaviva approves of Persons's attitude to the cardinalate, that he does not support the campaign for his promotion and indeed actively opposes it, and asks him to make this clear to Philip II.

P. Roberto Personio, 10 Abril.

Las de Vuestra Reverencia rescebi de 20. de hebrero y en ambas dize muy bien y toca las razones que yo por acá he dicho algunas vezes, porque es cierto que ampara el bien de la naçion, que se pretende no era ayuda sino ympedimento la mudança que algunos pretendian en la persona de Vuestra Reverencia. Acá hemos hecho el Officio necesario, qual aya de ser el que alla conviene Vuestra Reverencia lo verá, que a mi juicio es que Su Magestad y sus ministros entiendan las veras con que Vuestra Reverencia está ageno de lo que pretenden los de su nacion, y que sepan que aunque ellos lo negocian Vuestra Reverencia jamás ver¹⁴⁰ ello sino que lo contendria con todas las maneras y vias

---

137. Mehmed III, who succeeded Murad III as sultan of Turkey in January 1595, had his nineteen brothers strangled and buried next to their father. Shakespeare's allusion to this event, in 2 *Henry IV*, 5.2.47–49, was the subject, in 1958, of a controversy about anachronism, based on the mistaken dating of this event to 1596. See Richard Hillman, "'Not Amurath an Amurath Succeeds': Striking Crowns into the Hazard and Playing Doubles in Shakespeare's Henriad," in his *Intertextuality and Romance in Renaissance Drama* (New York, 1992), 26–57.

138. Sigismund III Vasa (1566–1632), crown prince of Sweden, was elected king of Poland in 1587 after the death of his uncle Stephen Bathory, and on 19 February 1594 was also crowned king of Sweden. He invited the Jesuits to establish schools throughout Poland and was much influenced by his court preacher Piotr Skarga, SJ (1536–1612), an active supporter of the English Jesuits: see Mirosława Hanusiewicz-Lavallee, "Recusant Prose in the Polish-Lithuanian Commonwealth at the Turn of the Sixteenth Century," in *Publishing Subversive Texts in Elizabethan England and the Polish-Lithuanian Commonwealth*, ed. Teresa Bela, Clarinda Calma, and Jolanta Rzegocka (Leiden, 2016), 11–27, at 20–24, and Urszula Augustyniak, *Informacja i propaganda w Polsce za Zygmunta III* (Warsaw, 1981).

139. Don Pedro Henríquez de Acevedo, count of Fuentes (1525–1610), succeeded Archduke Ernest of Austria (d. 20 February 1595) as the governor-general of the Spanish Netherlands.

140. ver] *obscure, possibly* res, *followed by illegible word* R

que pudiere¹⁴¹ que de lo que toca a su ánimo y verdad, no ha menester satisfacerme pues yo lo sé tantos años ha. No tengo en esta más de encomendarme etc.

Translation

To Fr Robert Persons, 10 April.

I have received your letters of 20 February. In both you express yourself very well, dealing with the reasons which I have already detailed several times. For it is certain that you are protecting the good of the nation [when you say] that the promotion that some are proposing for Your Reverence's person would not be a help but a hindrance. Here we have taken the necessary action, in accordance with what I would like Your Reverence to attend to: what I have in mind is that you should help His Majesty and his ministers understand the truth that Your Reverence is not involved in what those of your nation propose. They should know that even if they manage it, Your Reverence would never consent¹⁴² and would resist it in every way and with all the means you can. As for your disposition and trustworthiness, it is not necessary to reassure me, since I am already fully aware of them [and have been] for years. I have no more to say in this except to commend myself, etc.

B269 From Edmund Harewood, Rome, 10 April 1595

SOURCE: Persons to Harewood, 12 June (B280).
NOTE: Harewood, minister at the English College, Rome, wrote to Persons about the disturbances under the new rector, Fioravanti.

B270 To Claudio Acquaviva, Seville, mid-April 1595

SOURCE: Persons to Acquaviva, 15 May (B276); Acquaviva to Persons, 5 June (B278).
NOTE: On 15 May Persons advised that he was writing by every post; on 5 June, Acquaviva acknowledged receipt of letters coming by the posts of March and April. Persons would have written a letter in between 19 March and 15 May.

B271 From Gonzalo del Río, Valladolid, 1 May 1595

SOURCE: Persons to del Río, 12 May 1595 (B275).
NOTE: In his reply, Persons refers to two letters, one dated the first of the month, the other brought by four students the previous week. Del Río may have been replying to a letter by Persons sent after 19 March. Given the time it would take to travel from Valladolid to Seville, it seems likely that the letter brought by the students was composed some time before 1 May.

---

141. y que sepan ... vías que pudiere] *supplied in margin* R
142. This reading is conjectural; see the textual note.

B272 Letters from Charles Tancard, Oswald Tesimond, and Gaspar Alonso, about 1 May 1595

SOURCE: Persons to Acquaviva, 15 May (B276).

NOTE: These three Jesuits, concerned about the new rector's approach, wrote to Persons in Seville. His response was to write firmly to del Río, inform Acquaviva, and refer the matter to the general's assistant for Spain.

B273 From Cristóbal Méndez, 9 May 1595

SOURCE: Persons to Méndez, 20 May (B277).

NOTE: Méndez, who replaced Bartolomé Pérez as provincial of Andalusia in 1594, was concerned about the financial threat posed to the local Spanish Jesuits by the English college.

B274 To Sir Francis Englefield, Seville, 10 May 1595

SOURCE: More, 232–234.
HICKS: 323–328, with English translation.
TRANSLATION: Edwards, *More*, 291–292.

NOTE: This letter was written in response to Englefield's request not to be named in connection with the appointment of an English cardinal to succeed Allen. It provides an insight into Persons's scrupulous use of the Ignatian examen to try to determine God's will in the matter of his own possible elevation.

Nunc vero quoniam occaepi tecum clare his in literis et cum omni fiducia agere, progrediar aliquanto ulterius, et quod ad hoc negotium spectat, totum effundam animum meum, et quidquid intus in me sentio, sive iudicii, sive propensionis aperiam in conspectu Dei, sine ulla simulatione post multam apud me et Deum meum deliberationem, cum quanta potui indifferentia et summo desiderio et voto cognoscendi divinam voluntatem.

Primum igitur, ut tu probe nosti, licet salus totius mundi penderet ab hac mea promotione ad dignitatem quam tu mihi optas (quod quam sit incertum Deus novit, et eventus ipsi mire varii nos commonent, uti in quibus quotidie fallimur sive nostras inspiciamus sive aliorum rationes), ego tamen neque directe possum, neque indirecte praetendere, aut ambire hanc promotionem, quoniam voto adstringor ut ne ambiam: quod votum ut inviolatum custodiam det mihi, obsecro, Deus suam sanctam gratiam, atque vitam istam mihi auferat potius quam voluntatem illum non offendendi hoc in genere; et hoc fateor, unicum est ad quod ex voto obstringor, non ambire videlicet directe vel indirecte.

Secundo; licet ambitu seposito, posset quis sibi placere in huiusmodi promotione, vel eam etiam desiderare, gratias tamen Deo meo, sentio me ab utroque (uti confido) liberum: etsi enim speciosae multae rationes se offerant quandoque de rebus magnis quae praestari possent ab homine in illa dignitate constituto, sincere tamen dico, quod quando cogitatione penitus ingredior in deceptiones quas secum ferunt huiusmodi longe positarum rerum imagines, atque in eventus incertos, et in pericula molestiasque quae mihi in ista atque in futura vita possent oriri; et animo deinde verso conditionem hanc vivendi securam et plenam consolatione in qua dego, utiliorem etiam mihi fortasse et aliis; ista inquam, dum mihi ante oculos statuo, et quaedam praeterea quae mihi a multis retro annis sunt proposita, per oppida, scilicet, et vicos in Anglia discurrendo tradere Christianae doctrinae praecepta, si Anglia meo tempore reduceretur, ab alio illo vitae genere, tam me sentio alienum, ut ne cogitare quidem de illo sustineam, multo minus ut cupiam: quapropter liber sum (uti spero) ab omni tali desiderio; et quod amplius est, his argumentis et spirituali quodam sensu et affectu ducor in hanc sententiam, ut omnino iudicem hanc esse Dei voluntatem, non vero illam. Ista non clare quidem rem evincunt fateor: si enim evidenter evincerent, iam non esset in me locus deliberationi, quantumvis videri res posset aliis aut utilis aut necessaria.

Attamen tertio hinc sequitur (quod et tu facile dabis) quod cum non sciam esse Dei voluntatem ut promovear, dubitem vero plurimum propter rationes positas, teneor, et tenebor semper, non solum non desiderare promoveri, aut praetendere, sed animo esse semper in contrarium inclinante; atque si altior potestas (quaecunque demum illa sit) vellet mihi istud imponere, obsistere debeo, et rationes afferre cur contra sentiam. Idque non solum ut quod vovi praestem, et fidum me probem Religioni meae, quae detrimentum pateretur ex tali promotione; sed ut animae meae periculo caveam, quae mihi carior esse debet quam orbis universus etsi plures essent. Quandoquidem ingressus in huiusmodi dignitates solet esse iucundus et blandus, exitus molestus et luctuosus; quod in ultimo nostro bono Cardinale nemo fortasse me attentius observaverit.

Denique post haec omnia diligenter in conspectu Dei perpensa atque agitata, et quae a me fieri possent cuncta accurate praestita ad Dei voluntatem cognoscendam quoad fugam huius promotionis, si per auctoritatem cui resisti non posset imponeretur (quod spero nunquam futurum) posset equidem eo eventu sperari illam esse divinam voluntatem, et (quod consequitur) daturum illum gratiam sufficientem ad onus sustinendum pro eius gloria; et quo magis sincere conatus fuerit quispiam onus declinare, eo maiora praestiturum suscepto onere, quemadmodum multis et magnis Dei servis olim contigisse legimus. Atque hic habes, quidquid aut dicere aut cogitare possum in hoc negotio, non aliter scriptum quam si ad pedes confessarii mei essem Deo redditurus confestim animam. Quod apud te, quaeso, serva reconditum, quoniam tua solius importunitate victus haec scripsi, ut tibi satisfaciam; nisi ex intimis aliquis particeps tuo iudicio fieri debeat, qualis est Fitzherbertus etc. Deum tibi rogo esse propitium, decimo Maii anni 1595.

Translation

But now, since I have begun to deal with you openly and with complete confidence in this letter, I will proceed a little further and, as far as this affair is concerned, open my mind entirely and confess in the sight of God exactly what are my inmost feelings, whether of judgement or inclination, without any pretence – after deliberating at length with myself and my God, with all the indifference I could muster and with overwhelming desire and devotion to know the divine will.

First of all then, as you have rightly supposed, even if the salvation of the whole world depended on my being promoted to the rank which you seek for me (because God knows how uncertain things are, and the wondrous way that things themselves turn out so variously is a warning to us that, being deceived every day as we are about them, we should examine both our own arguments and those of others), still, I cannot directly or indirectly aspire to or seek to obtain this promotion, since I am bound by vow not to strive for it. And this vow I pray God to give me His holy grace to keep inviolate, and to take away my worthless life rather than my determination not to offend him in this respect. To this one thing only, I confess, I am bound by vow: that is, not to seek promotion, either directly or indirectly.

In the second place, assuming that, setting ambition aside, it would be possible for a man to take pleasure in a promotion of this sort, or even to desire it, yet, thanks be to my God, I feel that I am free (as I trust) from either of these impulses. For although many specious arguments suggest themselves in its favour at one time or another – about the great actions that could be performed by a man placed in such a high rank – yet I declare in all sincerity that when on the one hand I enter into deep consideration of the deceptions which fantasies of this kind bring with them, of things set aside long ago, and the uncertainty of the outcomes, and the dangers and inconveniences that could arise for me both in this life and the next, and then on the other hand turn my thoughts back to the way I pass my time in this present way of life, so free of care and full of consolation, more profitable too for myself and (perhaps) for others also – when I set these things, I say, before my eyes and certain other things besides, which for many years I have wanted to do: that is, to travel through the towns and villages of England expounding the precepts of Christian doctrine, if England should be converted in my life time – I feel myself to be so averse to that other kind of life that I cannot bear even to think about it, far less wish for it. Therefore I am free, as I hope, from all such desire; and, what is more, I am led by these arguments, and a certain spiritual motion and inclination, to this conclusion: that I am firmly persuaded that this is God's will, and not that. These things indeed do not settle the point entirely, I admit as much; for if they manifestly prevailed, there would be no further need for deliberation on my part, however useful or necessary the idea might seem to others.

All the same – in the third place – it follows from this (and even you will easily grant this) that, since I do not know that it is God's will for me to be promoted but doubt it very much, for the reasons stated, I am bound, and at all times will be bound, not merely not to desire promotion or aspire to it, but always to set my mind against it. And if a higher authority (whatever form that may take) should wish to impose it on me, I should resist it, and furnish reasons why I oppose it. This would be not only to fulfil my vow and prove my faithfulness to my order, which would suffer harm from such a promotion, but also to protect my soul from danger, which ought to be dearer to me than the whole world, however many there may be. However much the entry into dignities of this kind may usually be pleasant and soothing, leaving them is troublesome and grievous; and perhaps no one has observed this, in the person of our late beloved cardinal, more attentively than I.

Finally, if, after all these considerations have been carefully weighed and pondered in the sight of God, and all possible means diligently applied by which I could find out God's will in regard to rejecting this promotion, it were to be imposed by an authority which could not be resisted (which I hope will never be the case), in that event, indeed, it might be hoped that it was the will of God, and (what follows) that He would give sufficient grace to bear the burden for His glory's sake; and the more sincerely one had tried to escape the burden, the more aid would He give when the burden was undertaken. This we read of as having happened in the past to many great servants of God. And so, here you have all that I am able to say and think about this affair, written down just as I would do if I were at the feet of my confessor, on the very point of rendering my soul to God. I beg you to regard it as confidential, since I have written it only because I was overcome by your insistence, so as to satisfy you – unless in your opinion any of your intimate friends ought to be participants in it, such as Fitzherbert, etc.[143] I pray that God may be merciful to you, 10 May 1595.

B275 To Fr Gonzalo del Río, Seville, 12 May 1595

SOURCE: ACSA, Series II, Legajo 1, item 22, a fair copy, headed (in a different hand from the body of the letter) "Copia dela carta del padre Personio al padre Gonzalo del Río."

HICKS: 329–343, with English translation.

NOTE: As tactfully as he can, Persons explains what is wrong with Fr del Río's handling of the seminary, as the new rector. He refers to two previous letters, neither of which is extant, but the letter is endorsed "my second letter to Gonzales [sic] del Río." According to the address lines, copies of this letter were kept for Persons himself and for Rodrigo de Cabredo, former rector of the college.

Persons was so concerned about del Río's actions that he felt it necessary not only to mention the problem to Acquaviva in his letter of 15 May (B276), but to refer it to Acquaviva's assistant for Spain, Antonio de Mendoza, forwarding copies of this letter as well as others from Charles Tancard, Oswald Tesimond, and Gaspar Alonso.

Pax Christi.

Con este ordinario recebi la de Vuestra Reverencia del primero deste mes, y otra me traxeron los quatro estudiantes que llegaron la semana passada, los otros tres que venieron de Douay para este seminario aguardaremos tanbien que Vuestra Reverencia ha hecho muy bien en dexarles discansar por aý por algunas dias que bien menester devian tener conforme a lo que me escriven de uno dellos que tiene la pierna tan[144] lastimada que no podra venir a pie con los demas, Vuestra Reverencia, podra embiarlo despues con algun harriero. El padre rector deste collegio escrivera más particularmente de todo esto, y del viatico que es justo que se pague de acá pues vienen embiados de Flandres nominadamente para esta casa; solamente temo que los dos muchachos veniendo tan largo camino de más de cien leguas a pie y sin lengua y compañia, podran padecer mucho, ma-

143. Thomas Fitzherbert.
144. tan] *Hicks*; tam *Vd*

ximamente, si se les diere por aý tan estrecho viatico como a los otros quatro que les falto al medio del camino, y harto quesiere que se ubiesse hecho alguna buena combinacion o reparticion entre los siette (pues toparonse todos juntamente en esse collegio) por ayuda en el camino, mesclando algunos de los grandes que sabian algo de la lengua Española con essos novicios, como siempre se ha accustumbrado, pero por ser las primeras missiones que Vuestra Reverencia ha hecho desso su collegio, no me maravillo, lo que el padre rector e yo tenemos que reñir se alguna cosa no succediera bien, será, con el Padre Gaspar Alonso y con el Padre Carlos como hombres platicos ya y los más antigos consultores dessa casa.

En lo que Vuestra Reverencia escrive que recibio summo consuelo con mi carta de avisos acirca las mudanças que Vuestra Reverencia proponia, y que recibera muy grande caridad todas las veçes que yo le diga llanamente mi parecer, confiesso a Vuestra Reverencia que me edifica, y obliga mucho tanta bondad y modestia de Vuestra Reverencia y de mi parte me esforçaré de corresponder en todo lo que pudiere, y cierto deseara con todo mi coraçon poder escrivir siempre a Vuestra Reverencia cosas de consuelo y gusto, particularmente toccante a esso govierno del seminario, y Dios sabe la poenitentia que me ha sido el escrivir lo que tengo escritto en las dos cartas postreras, y no dudo si no, que, si Vuestra Reverencia e yo ubiessimos estado juntos por algunas dias al principio, todas las cosas avrian ydo con summo gusto de entrambos al mismo hilo que andavan antes en tiempo del Padre Cabredo y andan acá en el gobierno del Padre Peralta, muy a contento de todos y al approvechamiento de los collegios; pero como yo estava tan enfermo aqui quando la obediencia nos[145] quitó el Padre Cabredo, y despues la misma enfermedad y negocios urgentissimos no me han dado lugar de veer me con Vuestra Reverencia no es maravilla que entre hombres tan distintos,[146] y en una empresa tan nueva a Vuestra Reverencia entreveniessen pareceres differentes.

Y para antevenir a esto, rogue mucho al Padre Cabredo que enformasse largamente y muy a menudo a Vuestra Reverencia del modo del govierno que se avia de tener en los seminarios, y más escrivi a los Padres Gaspar y Carlos como a los consultores más platicos, que assistiessen a Vuestra Reverencia con todo amor y cuydado dandole luz en las cosas particulares de casa que se offerecieren y particularmente les rogue que a poco a poco induciessen a Vuestra Reverencia en el modo de gobernar del Padre Cabredo por aý que fue muy acertado, y del Padre Peralta por acá que es lo mismo, y nunca ha acontecido entre estos padres y mí por su mucha virtud y discrecion dellos, cosa minima de disgusto o de dispareceres en materia de negocios gobierno o de otras cosas, y assi confio tan bien que será con tiempo entre Vuestra Reverencia y mí, tomando Vuestra Reverencia (como confio que tomará) el mismo modo de proceder que ellos, el qual conciste principalmente (despues del amor entrañable a la obra) en consultar bien y a menudo las cosas de casa, con los consultores della, y mostrar gana de ser enformado y aconsejado por ellos, y por las cosas que otros an hecho antes, porque como ya tengo escritto, otras veçes y Vuestra Reverencia mejor sabe, es muy natural inclination a qualquier hombre que entre a nuevos gobiernos, de mudar cosas y haçer novidades, si no se rige algo por lo que hallan hecho, y los collegios de la Compañia an padecido su

---

145. nos] *this ed..*; no *Vd*
146. distintos] *Vd, obscure, possibly* dissintos

parte en muchas provincias por la libertad de algunos rectores en esto, y en otras religiones es cosa tan vedada que suelen quitar a un superior por pocas cosas que haga deste género. Pero en ninguna parte se ha de proceder con más recate y circunspeçion en este particular que en los seminarios donde estamos a la mira de tantos siglares, que presto nos notarán, si andamos mudando las cosas el uno del otro, y gastando la hacienda que no es nuestra, sin necessidad.

No quiero responder más por agora a la raçon que Vuestra Reverencia allega para aprobacion de aver mudado a los moços el lugar de comer fuera del refectorio, diciendo que no convenia a todos quantos picaros de la plaça entrar en refectorio, porque no creo que no es necessario que los moços dessa casa o los más dellos sean picaros, ni lo an sido ni lo son al presente, y quando la necessidad truxera algun picaro para servir en cosas baxas por algun tiempo, este podria comer a parte, y aunque Vuestra Reverencia dice que lo hiço con buenos paraceres, a lo menos entiendo que no eran los de sus consultores de casa, si no de algunos Padres de fuera, los quales, aunque otramente prudentissimos, no podian juzgar lo de casa sin oyr las raçones en contrario, y con essa raçon sola de picaros o semejante que Vuestra Reverencia les allegaria juzgarian conforme al parecer y gusto de Vuestra Reverencia contra toda[147] la custumbre de todos los seminarios y particularmente contra lo que dos veçes se avia assentado en esso collegio por raçones muy urgentes que essos Padres Consultores devian deçir a Vuestra Reverencia aunque no approvechó, pero dexaré al Padre Peralta de escrivir una apologia larga sobre este negocio de comer los moços a la tercera mesa en el refectorio, porque aunque él tan bien al principio por falta de experiencia de la cosa no lo approvava, agora confiessa que no ay cosa más acertada en todo el gobierno de los seminarios ni que más bien haga a los moços y que dé más quietud a la casa, como al contrario Vuestra Reverencia veerá que los muchos repartimientos que Vuestra Reverencia ha hecho de comer en la cosina, dispensa, portaria y panoderia, dara mucho embaraço y inquietud y particularmente aquella clausula que Vuestra Reverencia añade en la suya que los moços yngleses comen aparte y los Españoles en otra parte, porque esto pondra zelos y suspechas y emulaciones nacionales que con todo cuydado se avian de evitar, pues destos participarán luego los estudiantes y hermanos de la Compañia cada un por su nacion como si suele y es cosa peligrosa la qual yo he procurado siempre que no ubiesse rastro della en estos seminarios a donde necessariamente an de vivir entrambas naciones, y gracias a dios hasta agora no ha avido, *et haec de his*.

En lo del pan y panadaria, ya tengo escritto a Vuestra Reverencia lo que siento; nos costó más de ducientos ducados de poner la panadaria en casa, y nos ahurroles en el primer año, y ansi no veo porqué las emos de lapidar *de bono opere*, y hechar la de casa, pues otros collegios de por acá y particularmente este seminario de Sevilla piensa de proverla muy presto en casa aunque sea con harto gasto. En quanto al pan escrivi a Vuestra Reverencia que me contentava se mejorasse con que fuesse la moderacion que combiene a la pobreça de la casa, aunque los passados passaron bien con el pan passado, entiendo que está ya mejorado en el quinto, de manera que con cinco anegas se hace agora el pan que antes con quatro, lo qual en 50 boccas importa el pan de diez o doçe

147. toda] *Vd*; om. *Hicks*

personas que es más de cien anegas de pan el año, pues 500[148] anegas apenas bastavan antes por aquela casa, y agora no bastaran 600 pero todo se ha de passar para dar contento, y ansi lo passaré yo de buena gana con que no se vaya más adelante en apurar la harina, porque sería demasiado gasto, pues el que ya si hace más que antes, nos quitará el sustento de dos o tres estudiantes lo qual los que han de buscar de comer para estos collegios saben lo que importa y lo mucho que les costa hallar sustento para uno solamente, y ansi pido a Vuestra Reverencia en toda caridad como antes, que mire mucho para la hacienda de su collegio, por acá se ha decho no se qué de conbites en esso seminario, despues de la venida de Vuestra Reverencia mucho más frequentamente y regaladamente que no en tiempo del Padre Cabredo, y algunos de los mismos conbidados[149] an dicho y escritto en essa materia como si suele; ya Vuestra Reverencia sabe los avisos que el nuestro Padre General suele embiar acirca desto para los collegios de la Compañia, pero mucho más en los seminarios conbiene andar recate en ello, por no ser la hacienda nuestra, y por estar nosotros no solamente a vista de siglares si no tanbien sugetos a dar quienta a ellos de lo que se gasta, y la reputacion facilmente se pierde con los estudiantes quando ay excesso, yo cierto Padre mio, deseo sumamente dar gusto a todos y nunca me pesará de que los rectores a su arbedrio hagan en esto, lo que les pareciere, ni escriviere palabra a Vuestra Reverencia dello,[150] si no ubiere visto que más de dos de la Compañia que aman mucho a Vuestra Reverencia han reparado en ello; tan bien digo que la puerta que Vuestra Reverencia ha començado a abrir en recibir huespedes de la Compañia que vienen a Valladolid por negocios a pasar en el seminario, en ninguna manera deve passar adelante por infinitos inconvenientes que ay en ello, y nuestro Padre General nunca ha gustado que se haga en los seminarios, por la mal edificacion que siglares dello tomarán, y otros daños que el Padre Cabredo dira a Vuestra Reverencia que lo emos tratado muchas veçes con harto deseo de admittir algun en algunas occasiones, pero *nullo modo expedire videbatur*, y los mismos superiores de la Compañia siempre an jusgado esto, y ansi no dudo si no que lo haran por lo venir tanbien si Vuestra Reverencia les da las raçones que ay para ello. Todo esto escrivo a Vuestra Reverencia con llaneça y confiança en este principio paraque que[151] no aya en que reparar despues, ni tengo otra cosa que decir ni avertir a Vuestra Reverencia porque si la tubiera la dixiera aqui con lo demas, y ansi confio en nuestro Señor que para adelante no avrá menester de escrivir si no cosas de gusto y consuelo, como siempre se ha hecho hasta agora en otros tiempos y se hara con Vuestra Reverencia placiendo a dios el qual guarde a Vuestra Reverencia. De Sevilla a 12 de Mayo 1595.

    Roberto Personio.

    [PS] Todos embian de aqui sus grandes encomiendas a Vuestra Reverencia. Estan todos con salud y contentos con la llagada de la flota, faltan dos o tres navios, solamente de plata, y se aguardan, la nuestra coseja tan bien va en ella, y cogida esta y[152] confirmada

    148. 500] *Vd, obscure, possibly* 300
    149. conbidados] *this ed.*; conbidades *Vd*
    150. dello] *Vd, obscure, possibly* della
    151. que] *Vd; om.* Hicks
    152. y] *Vd; om.* Hicks

un poco más la salud confio de veer presto a Vuestra Reverencia y a sus hijos por aý a los quales Vuestra Reverencia dara mis intimas saludes.

[*Addressed:*] (1) Al Padre Rodrigo de Cabredo de la Compañia de Jesus.
[*Addressed:*] (2) Al Padre Personio, Sevilla.[153]
[*Endorsed by Persons:*] my second letter to Gonzales del Río.

Translation

The peace of Christ.

By this post I received Your Reverence's letter of the first of this month and another was brought to me by the four students who arrived last week; we are also awaiting the arrival of the other three who have left Douai to join this seminary. Your Reverence was well advised to let them rest with you for a few days; they must have been in great need of it, judging by what they have written to me about one of them who has injured his leg so badly that he will not be able to proceed on foot with the others. Your Reverence can send him later with one of the carriers. Father rector of this college will write in more detail about all this and about the travelling expenses, which it is fair should be paid from here since they were sent from Flanders assigned specifically to this house. The only thing I am afraid of is that the two boys, coming on such a long journey of more than a hundred leagues on foot and without knowing the language and no one with them, will be liable to suffer a good deal, especially if they are given as meagre provision for the journey as was given to the other four there; for it ran short when they were in the middle of the journey; and I should have been glad if there had been some proper arrangement for combining or forming better parties from the seven of them (since they all met together at the college there) so as to help them on the journey, some of the older ones who had some knowledge of the Spanish language being put with these novices, as has always been the custom. But as these are the first drafts Your Reverence has sent from your college, I am not surprised; the fault which father rector and I will have to assign if anything should go wrong, will be the responsibility of Fr Gaspar Alonso and Fr Charles, as being men of practical experience now and the oldest consultors in your house.

With regard to what Your Reverence writes, that you took much encouragement from my letter of advice about the changes you were proposing to make, and that you will take it as a great act of charity at all times if I give you my views frankly, I confess to Your Reverence that such good temper and modesty on your part edifies me and puts me under great obligation; and for my part I shall make an effort to meet your wishes in every way I can. And truly I should wish with all my heart to be able to write comforting and pleasant things to Your Reverence at all times, especially with regard to your government of the seminary; and God knows what a penance it has been to me to write what I have written in my last two letters, and I have no doubt that, if Your Reverence and I had been together for a few days at the beginning, everything would have proceeded with the great-

---

153. The addresses are in different hands, both of which differ from that of the letter itself. There are the remains of two seals, the first (opposite the first address) being the same as that used on Persons's original letters.

est satisfaction to us both, along the same lines as things went previously, in Fr Cabredo's time, and do proceed here, under Fr Peralta's government – with great contentment to all parties and profit to the colleges; but I was very ill here at the time when holy obedience deprived us of Fr Cabredo, and afterwards the same illness and very pressing business have given me no opportunity of paying Your Reverence a visit, and so it is no surprise if, between men so far away from one another and concerning an undertaking that is so new to Your Reverence, differences of opinion should have intervened.

It was to forestall this that I earnestly begged Fr Cabredo to keep Your Reverence informed, fully and often, about the method of government that should be used in the seminaries; and I wrote besides to Fr Gaspar and Fr Charles, as being the most experienced consultors, asking them to assist Your Reverence with all charity and solicitude, and to enlighten you on details connected with the house where necessary, and I asked them especially to bring Your Reverence by degrees to adopt the method of government used there by Fr Cabredo, which was very successful, and by Fr Peralta here, which is equally so. For in the case of these fathers, owing to their great virtue and discretion, there has luckily never been the smallest instance of annoyance or difference of opinion between them and me on questions of business, government, or other matters; and so I trust in time will also be the case between Your Reverence and myself, if you adopt (as I hope you will) the same method of procedure as they do. This consists mainly (in addition to a deep-seated love for their work) in consulting well and often about the affairs of the house with the consultors of the house, and in showing both a willingness to receive information and advice from them and learn from what other people have done before; for – as I have written before on other occasions, and Your Reverence knows it better than I do – there is a very natural tendency in any man who comes to a new post of authority to make changes and introduce novelties, unless he guides himself somewhat by precedent. For their part, colleges of the Society in many provinces have suffered thanks to the recklessness of certain rectors in this respect, and in other religious orders it is a thing so strictly forbidden that they usually get rid of a superior after one or two instances of this kind. Nowhere however is it necessary to proceed with such discretion and circumspection in this matter as in the seminaries, where the eyes of so many laymen are upon us who will be quick to notice if we keep changing things from one [rector] to another one, and spending the money which does not belong to us, unnecessarily.

I do not wish to make any further reply to the explanation Your Reverence offers for approval of your having moved the servants' mess outside the refectory, saying that it was not suitable that every sort of scamp from the street should enter it, because I do not think it necessary for the servants of your house or the majority of them to be rogues:[154] nor have they been, nor are they at present; and should necessity bring some scoundrel to serve in menial occupations for a time, it would be possible in this case for him to eat apart. And although Your Reverence says that you did it on good advice, nevertheless I understand it was not the advice of the consultors of the house but of some fathers outside, who, though in other respects very prudent men, could not judge of a

---

154. The word used here, "picaro," refers to a sly or roguish young fellow of the servant class, not to be trusted; it has generated the literary term *picaresque*.

matter concerning the house without hearing the arguments on the other side; and for this single reason – that they were knaves or such like, which Your Reverence would represent to them – would give their judgement in agreement with your opinion and desire, though it was contrary to the custom observed in all the seminaries and expressly opposed to what had twice been agreed to in your college for very pressing reasons. These your father consultors would have mentioned to Your Reverence, even if you had not taken them into consideration. However I am going to leave it to Fr Peralta to write a full explanation of this policy of the servants dining in the refectory at third table, because, although at first through lack of experience in the matter he too was not in favour of it, he now admits that there is nothing that has been more successful in all the government of the seminaries or has done such good to the servants or that gives such peace in the house; and Your Reverence will see on the other hand that the proliferation of places allotted by you for their meals, such as the kitchen, the storeroom, the porter's lodge, the bakehouse, will cause much confusion and discontent. So in particular will that little matter which Your Reverence also mentions in your letter, namely that the English servants have their meals by themselves and the Spanish ones somewhere else; for this will give rise to jealousy and suspicion and factions between the nationalities, which should have been most carefully avoided; for presently the students and brothers of the Society will join in them, each according to his nationality, as is always the case. It is a dangerous thing and I have always made it my endeavour that there should be no trace of it in these seminaries where both nations have necessarily to live together, and, thank God, so far there has been none. So much for that.

Concerning the bread and the bakery I have already explained my views to Your Reverence in writing. It cost us more than two hundred ducats to install the bakery, and it saved us as much in the first year; and so I do not see why we should cast stones at it when it is a good piece of work and do away with it;[155] in fact other colleges in this area, and the seminary at Seville in particular, are thinking of installing one very shortly, in spite of its being a rather expensive item. With regard to the bread, I wrote to Your Reverence that I was in agreement with its being improved, provided that economy suitable to the poverty of the house were observed, even though former students have found no fault with it in the past. I hear that it is already improved by one fifth, that is to say that five measures are now used for the quantity of bread formerly made with four measures. This in the case of fifty mouths means bread for ten or a dozen persons, that is, an increase of one hundred measures of bread per year: for five hundred measures hardly sufficed for your house before, and now six hundred will not be enough. Still, this should all be passed, so long as it gives satisfaction, and so I will give in with good grace, provided nothing further is done in the way of refining the flour, for it would be too great an expense. The present increase over what we spent before will cost us what would be the upkeep of two or three students; and those whose task it is to seek the means of livelihood of these colleges know what that

---

155. Possibly a subliminal reference to Jn 10:33, "Responderunt ei Iudaei: De bono opere non lapidamus te" (The Jews answered him: "For a good work we stone thee not"), which is echoed in the Spanish, "lapidar de bono opere."

means, and the great effort it costs them to find the support for even one. And so I beg Your Reverence in all charity, as I did before, to take great care of the patrimony of your college. There has also been comment here about the entertainment of guests at your seminary since Your Reverence's coming, as being much more frequent and on a grander scale than in Fr Cabredo's time: some of the guests themselves have talked and written on the subject, as one would expect. Your Reverence already knows what advice father general is accustomed to send to the colleges of the Society about this matter, but in the case of the seminaries there is even more need to act discreetly in that matter, since the patrimony is not our own: not only are the eyes of laymen upon us but we are bound to render them an account of our expenditure. Our good name with the students too is easily lost when there is any extravagance. I assure you, my dear father, that I have the greatest wish to satisfy everyone, and it will never distress me if rectors do at their discretion what they think best in this matter, nor would I write Your Reverence a word about it if I had not perceived that more than two of the Society, who love Your Reverence very much, have commented on it. Also I say, in regard to the precedent Your Reverence is setting[156] by taking guests of the Society, who come to Valladolid on business, as guests to stay in the seminary, that this should by no means proceed any further, because of the infinite number of inconveniences to which it gives rise. Our father general has never liked it to be done in the seminaries, on account of the scandal caused to laymen, and other damage in consequence. Fr Cabredo will tell Your Reverence that we have often discussed it, being quite desirous at times to allow someone to come, but it did not seem to serve any good purpose, and the superiors of the Society themselves have always taken that view; and so I have no doubt that they will continue to do in future, even if Your Reverence gives them the arguments there are in its favour. I am writing all this to Your Reverence plainly and frankly, now at the beginning, in order that there may be no need to mend things later on; and there is nothing further that I have to say or call Your Reverence's attention to; if there were, I would say it now along with the rest. And I trust in our Lord that in future there will be no need to write anything but pleasant and consoling things, as has always been the case up until now at other times, and will be in the case of Your Reverence, please God. May He protect Your Reverence. Seville, 12 May 1595.

    Robert Persons.

[PS] All here send Your Reverence their kind remembrances. All are in health and pleased at the arrival of the fleet.[157] Two or three ships are missing, carrying silver only; and they are waiting for them to come. Our harvest also depends on that; and when it is gathered and I am a little stronger, I hope to visit Your Reverence and your sons there soon: please would Your Reverence give them my affectionate regards.

---

156. Literally, "the door you are opening."
157. See headnote to Persons's letter to Acquaviva, 15 May (B276).

B276 To Claudio Acquaviva, Seville, 15 May 1595

SOURCES:
ARSI, Hisp. 138, fols. 264–265, holograph;
ABSI, Coll P II 477 (a brief mention, dated 14 May).
HICKS: 344–351, with English translation.
NOTE: There have been significant developments in Seville: in particular, the purchase and furnishing of buildings for the English college, large enough to accommodate 150. There are sixty at present and would be more but for the loss of twenty students captured at sea in two separate incidents. For an account of the capture of William Baldwin and six students bound for Seville, see Verstegan to Persons, 30 March 1595 (B267).

The treasure fleet has finally arrived safely, to great rejoicing. Persons has celebrated the Feast of St George (23 April) at Sanlúcar, at the church of St George he restored in 1592. The patron of the church, the duke of Medina Sidonia, much gratified by the present festivities, has offered to supply water to the English college in Seville.

John Cecil arrived in Madrid in December 1594 to lobby for support for the Catholic earls in Scotland: Yellowlees, 139–145, and McCoog, *Building the Faith of St Peter*, 242–244. Persons, possibly drawn into an earlier scheme in 1593 (see his letter to Idiáquez, 31 August 1593, B200), again wishes his enterprise well but is relieved to use the state of his health, though much improved, as an excuse not to travel to Madrid to meet the Scottish delegation.

Francisco de Peralta is doing excellent work as rector of the college in Seville, but the situation at Valladolid is cause for concern. The new rector, Gonzalo del Río, has disregarded Persons's advice and is following his own fancy. See the letter to del Río (12 May, B275).

Muy Reverendo en Christo Padre Nuestro
Pax Christi.

1. Con todos los ordenarios escrivo algo a Vuestra Paternidad para darle quenta de las cosas de acá, aunque no se offerescan negocios de mucha importancia, el de más gusto y alegria desta ciudad, es por agora la venida de la flota, prosperamente aunque muy peligrosamente por aver sido dispercidos los navios con un temporal muy reçio de manera que ayan entrado por acá y en algunos puertos de Portugal, muy apartados y mal tratados, y sin duda si los yngleses ubiessen salido a la mar, por tiempo, conforme a sus preparaciones, avrian llevado grande parte del denero, *sed Deus occaecavit illos, et consolatus est nos, adiutor in opportunitatibus, ipse sit benedictus in aternum.*

2. Este Collegio anglico va muy bien adelante gracias a Dios, y da grande edificacion a toda la ciudad, estamos más de sessenta, y si Dios no permitiera que dos quadrillas de estudiantes que venian por acá, fuessen presos por los hereges y llevatos a Londres en este año (los unos que tomaron en la mar de Yrlanda y los otros en el canal de Ynglaterra) ya tubiessimos otros veynte porque tantos eran los que a dos veçes nos han cogido los navios de la Reyna, todo será para mayor gloria de dios. Uno de los treçe que se prendieron en Yralanda y fueron llevados cargados de cadenas a londres, escapó despues fuera de la carcel, y está al presente en este Collegio, y nos quenta los tratamientos, que es grito y lástima de oyrlos; los postremos seis que se prendieron en el canal juntamente con el Padre Balduino, eran del Seminario de muchachos de S. Omer como Vuestra

Paternidad estava ya avisado, y por ser tales, y todos gente principal y de grande expectacion, nos ha dado grandissima pena pero estamos ya accustumbrados algo a semejantes olas de quando en quando, en esta nuestra navigacion, no ay otro remedio, si no abaxar la cabeça y passar adelante, *Dominus est, quod bonum fuerit in oculis suis, hoc faciat.* En hartas otras cosas nos consuela y ayuda, *et si bona recipimus de manu eius, quare etiam non*[158] *mala?*

3. Yo me siento libre de las quartanas, gracias a Dios, aunque no de algunas reliquias y effectos dellas, que son unos dolores y hinchasones de piernas, que se yran tan bien quando Dios fuera servido, y estos dias me han servido de muy buena defensa para liberarme de un viaje a Madrid, que harto me han importunado de alla, que me fuesse, particularmente los dos Señores Escoçeses que estan alli de parte de los Condes catolicos juntamente con Juan Sicilio sacerdote ynglés que Vuestra Paternidad conoçe los quales por venir encaminados a mí de aquellos Señores, an procurado por todas las vias de traerme a Madrid pero las malas piernas me an ayudado, y les he servido a ellos por otra via lo que he podido, que es, con cartas, Dios les dé el successo que yo deseo, temo que las largas desta corte por nuestros peccados an de hechar a perder todo.

4. Yo estoy al presente en la casa nueva que emos comprado para este Seminario, con tres o quatro hermanos de la compañia, y otros tantos moços y más de treynta officiales para labrar lo que falta de habitacion y officinas, y accomodar lo demas, quatro mil ducados gastaremos en accomodar la casa y otros tantos seran menester para la fábrica de la yglesia, y tres para comprar algunas otras casillas que estan juntas, los quales todos, con los siette mil que pagamos para la casa principal, seran dieçeocho mil ducados, y más valdra la casa quando será acabada de treynta, porque será el más hermoso collegio que avrá en muchas leguas, y más de 150 personas cabaran en ella.

5. A 23 de Abril fui a San Lucar de Barrameda para veer celebrar la fiesta de San Jorge en la yglesia de su invocacion que emos reparado y accomodado aý con dos mil ducados que el Rey me dio en Valladolid para esto, quando Su Magestad estubo por alla es hermosa cosa, y la casa muy grande y capaz con tiendas de fuera que rentaran quingientos ducados en cada un año para el sustento del preposito y capellanos que al presente alli estan. El duque de Medina Sidonia estuvo en la fiesta, y con muchos otros cavalleros, y veendo comulgar a una media doçena de estudiantes que yo llevé alla, deramó muchas lagrymas, y nos embió muchos regalos de comer el dia de la fiesta y el dia siguiente me dio una paja entera de agua de sus casas en Sevilla, para esta nueva del Seminario la qual por estar tan circa, nos vale más que mil y quingientos ducados. Dios se lo pague en el cielo, fue mucha nobleça y Christianidad.

6. El Padre Francisco de Peralta rector de aqui hace muy bien su officio, y estamos todos contentos dél. El Padre Gonzalo del Río rector nuevo del Seminario de Valladolid, no parece que toma hasta agora el camino derecho[159] para dar contento y approvechar su casa porque escriven de alla que es muy incapaz de consejo, y que consulta solamente sus cosas de fuera de casa, y no con sus Consultores, quiere hacer y dishaçer de su cabeça y entroducir mil novidades, y quando los Padres de casa le acconsejan lo contrario se dis-

---

158. non] *this ed.;* no R
159. derecho] *this ed.;* drecho R

gusta, muchas mudanças me propuso luego en entrando en el gobierno y porque yo no las approvava, parece que lo tomó mal y algunas hiço de hecho, que fuera mejor averlas dexado, parece grande gastador, y particularmente en combites, como todos tres Padres de casa me escriven que son el Padre Gaspar Alonso, el Padre Carlos Tancardo, y Osvaldo, embío al Padre Antonio de Mendoça las postreras cartas que me escrivieron con la que yo tanbien le escrivi al rector, tengo alguna esperança aún de alguna enmienda[160] con los avisos que le he dado y yre dando, y con la ayuda que procuro se le dé por los Padres que estan con él, y por medio tan bien del Padre Cabredo a quien escrivo todo que passa, para que de su parte tan bien assista, cree Vuestra Paternidad que la Compañia no tiene obra de mayor importancia por las manos en España que ésta de los Seminarios, ni que más luzga en los ochos[161] de todos, y con todo esto todos no lo entienden, y no es cosa facil hallar hombre por el gobierno dellos que sea a proposito, ni puedo yo llevarlos adelante si no es con rectores que sean para ello; yo obedeci llanamente y sin réplica como era raçon, quando Vuestra Paternidad mandava quitarme al Padre Cabredo, aunque veýa el grande daño que se nos haçia en ello, y que en ningun puesto podra el Padre sirvir más a Dios y a la compañia que en esta obra, Vuestra Paternidad como tan padre della mirará por su bien, y nos ayudará en lo que fuera necessario, quál esto será el tiempo nos dirá, e yo yre avisando a Vuestra Paternidad de tiempo en tiempo. Nuestro Señor nos guarde a Vuestra Paternidad por muchos años como emos menester, en sus santos sacrificios muy humilmente me encomiendo. Sevilla a 15 de Mayo 1595.

        De Vuestra Paternidad Reverenda
            hijo y siervo
                Rob. Personio.

[*Addressed*:] Al muy Reverendo en Christo padre nuestro el padre Claudio aquaviva preposito de la [Compañia de] Jesus.

[*Endorsed*:] Sevilla 95 P. Roberto Personio. Mayo 15. [*with summary of contents*]

Translation

Our Very Reverend Father in Christ
The peace of Christ.

1. I write something to Your Paternity by every post, so as to give you an account of things here, even if there are no matters of much importance to tell. What has caused most pleasure and rejoicing in this city at the moment is the successful arrival of the fleet, despite much danger because of the ships having been driven apart by a very severe storm. As a result, they have come in here and to some ports in Portugal scattered far apart and much battered. And there is no doubt but that, if the English had put out to sea for a time, as they had prepared to do, they would have carried off a large part of the treasure; but *God blinded their eyes, and consoled us, may He be blessed for ever, our help in times of need.*

    160. enmienda] *this ed.*; emienda R
    161. ochos] R, *i.e.* ojos

2. The English college here makes very good progress, thanks be to God, and gives great edification to all the city. We are more than sixty souls and if God had not allowed two parties of students, who were on their way here, to be captured and carried off by the heretics during this year (one party which they took in the Irish Sea, and the other in the English Channel) we should now have another twenty; for that was the number of those whom the queen's ships seized on those two occasions; all will be for the greater glory of God. One of the thirteen who were taken in Ireland and carried off to London loaded with chains escaped later out of prison and is at the present moment in this college.[162] He tells such a story of their treatment that there are groans and lamentations on hearing it. The last six, who were taken in the channel along with Fr Baldwin, were from the seminary for boys at St Omers, as Your Paternity was informed before, and because of this and because they were all of high rank and great promise, it has caused us very great grief. Still, we are somewhat accustomed now to rollers like this from time to time, in the course of our voyaging. There is no other remedy but to bow our heads and go on: *It is the Lord, let Him do what is good in His eyes.*[163] In plenty of other things He consoles and helps us, and *if we accept good from His hand, why not evil also?*[164]

3. I feel that I am free of the quartan ague, thank God, though not of some of its aftereffects, which consist of pains and swelling of the legs; these too will pass when God pleases. In these past days they have served as a very good pretext to excuse me from a journey to Madrid, where I was put under some pressure to go, by people there and especially by the two Scottish gentlemen who, together with John Cecil, an English priest whom Your Paternity knows, are there on behalf of the Catholic earls. These men, having come with a commission to me from those lords, have tried by every means to get me to come to Madrid; but my bad legs have helped me, and I have been of service to them in other ways so far as I could be, that is by letters. May God give them the success which I desire, but I am afraid that the dilatory methods of this court, for our sins, are bound to ruin everything.

4. I am at present in the new house which we have bought for the seminary here, along with three or four brothers of the Society and as many more servants and more than thirty workmen, in order to construct the remaining rooms and offices, and adapt the rest of it. We are going to spend four thousand ducats on adapting the house, and the same amount will be needed for the building of the church and three for buying some other small structures connected with it. All this, with seven thousand we paid for the main building, will amount to eighteen thousand ducats; and the house, when finished, will be worth more than thirty thousand, for it will be the finest college for many a league. There will be room for more than one hundred and fifty persons in it.

162. According to Murphy's directory, alumni of the English college in Seville who arrived in 1595 include Henry Almond, two Briant brothers, Edmund Cannon (June), William Davies, John Evans, John Hall (via Valladolid), Matthew Holmes, Thomas Holmes (via Ireland and Valladolid), Richard Humphrey, Edward Hutton, William Jessopp, George Johnson, Henry Mailer (ca. 1594), Richard Pentreth, Thomas Pole (via Valladolid), John Reynolds, Nicholas Rock, and Thomas Travers (ca. 1594).

163. 1 Sam. 3:18.

164. Job 2:10.

5. On 23 April I went to Sanlúcar de Barrameda to see the feast of St George celebrated in the church dedicated to him which we have restored and furnished with the two thousand ducats which the king gave me for the purpose when he was in Valladolid. It is a beautiful sight. The house is very large and ample, with shops on the outside which will bring in five hundred ducats a year for the support of the priest in charge and the chaplains who are there at present. The duke of Medina Sidonia was at the celebration and many other gentlemen with him; and, seeing communion given to half a dozen students whom I took there, he shed many tears and that same day he sent us many gifts of food, on the day of the feast, and on the following day he gave me an entire canal from his houses in Seville for this new seminary building. Being so close at hand, this water supply is worth more than fifteen hundred ducats to us. May God reward him in heaven; it was a very noble and Christian act.

6. Fr Francisco de Peralta, the rector here, carries out the duties of his office very well, and we are all very satisfied with him. Fr Gonzalo del Río, the new rector of the seminary at Valladolid, seems not to be taking a satisfactory course so far, one that would get the best from his house; for they write from there that he is quite incapable of taking advice: he consults about his affairs outside the house only and not with the consultors. He wants to do and undo things at his own whim and to make a thousand innovations; and when the fathers of the house advise a course opposed to his views, he is annoyed. At the time when he took up the position, he proposed many changes to me and it seems that he was offended because I was not in favour of them. Some changes he actually made which he should rather have omitted; he seems to be a great man for spending money, especially on entertaining; so three fathers in the house write to me, namely Fr Gaspar Alonso, Fr Charles Tancard, and Oswald.[165] I am sending the last letters they wrote to me to Fr Antonio de Mendoza,[166] along with one which I also wrote to the rector. I still have hopes of some improvement resulting from the advice that I have given him and which I shall go on giving him, and from the help which I am endeavouring to have given him by the fathers who are with him, and also by means of Fr Cabredo to whom I am writing all that happens, so that he also may assist on his part. Your Paternity believes that the Society has no work on its hands in Spain of greater importance than this of the seminaries, nor any that should be more resplendent in the eyes of all. And in spite of everything it is not everyone that understands this, and it is not an easy matter to find a man who is suitable to govern them, and I can only work for their advancement using what rectors there may be for the purpose. I obeyed simply and without question, as was proper, when Your Paternity ordered that I was to be deprived of Fr Cabredo, although I perceived the great harm that was being done to us thereby, and that there is no position in which the father will be able to give greater service to God and to the Society than in this work. Would Your Paternity, who has such a fatherly care for it, please watch out for its welfare and aid us where necessary; what this necessity will be, time will reveal to us, and I shall go on reporting to Your Paternity from time to time. May our Lord preserve

---

165. Tesimond.

166. Antonio de Mendoza (ca. 1545–1596), was appointed Acquaviva's assistant for Spain after the general congregation of 1593–1594.

Your Paternity to us for many years in accordance with our need. I commend myself very humbly to your holy sacrifices. Seville, 15 May 1595.

>Your Reverend Paternity's
>>son and servant
>>>Robert Persons.

B277 To Cristóbal Méndez, Seville, 20 May 1595

>SOURCE: ARSI, Hisp. 138, fol. 281, contemporary copy.
>HICKS: 352–358, with English translation.
>NOTE: The copy is headed "Copia de la carta que Padre Personio escribio a el Padre Cristobal Mendez provincial de la Andalusia." It is a contemporary copy with the mark indicating that it has been seen.
>The letter is a significant testimony to the tact required in dealing with the Spanish Jesuits in the Seville region. Méndez had recently replaced Pérez as provincial of Andalusia, and Persons had yet to develop a sympathetic relationship with him. Persons explains why he does not write more frequently to the provincial: Fr Peralta, rector of the English college, has been performing this function. He hopes that Méndez will do them the honour of visiting the college when passing through, especially now that water is being supplied by the duke of Medina Sidonia.
>Tensions have arisen between the local Jesuits and the English college over alms collecting (see Persons's letter to Acquaviva, 12 June, B279). Persons assures Méndez that Brother Fabrizio Como's trespassing on the Spanish fathers' begging territory has ceased. There are also suspicions that the fathers at the seminary are benefiting unduly from alms given for masses. This raises the delicate question of who should certify that the masses have been said. The formula of the certificate, dated 10 June, was presumably sent later and appended to the copy of the letter.

Pax Christi.

No escrivo a Vuestra Reverencia tan a menudo, por las muchas occupationes que ay de escrivir a otras partes, y de fábrica y otros negocios, y por las que Vuestra Reverencia deve tener de muchadumbre de cartas tanbien, y porque el Padre Peralta para alliviarme en esto particular, ha tomado a su cargo de avisar a Vuestra Reverencia en nombre de entrambos, de todo lo que passó por acá, y grande consuelo fuera para mí, hallarme presente quando Vuestra Reverencia estubo en Sevilla, aunque de passo, y nos hiço caridad de veer la casa nueva, la qual va se accomodando bien, aunque la falta de deneros nos haçe caminar a poco a poco, confio en nuestro Señor que la ha de acabar, pues cierto, es cosa necessaria para su Santo servicio. El Padre Peralta avrá avisado ya a Vuestra Reverencia la limosna y liberalidad del Duque de Medina Sidonia, que nos hiço de una paja de agua que será grande consuelo desta casa, va se traendo y pienso que dentro de 5[167] dias estara ya en casa placiendo a Nuestro Señor.

---

167. 5] R; or 13 or 15 Hicks

La de Vuestra Reverencia de 9 deste recibi, y en quanto a las dos cosas que manda nuestro Padre General remediar a circa deste seminario la primera pienso que ya está remediada muchos meses ha, desde que Vuestra Reverencia estando por acá, avisó al Padre rector della, digo de no pedir más el hermano Fabricio para este seminario en la manera que se dixo por entonces y que apunta nuestro padre, porque aquela quexa, nacio de una salida que hiço al Hermano Fabricio a la Cerasa conbidado (como él dixo) de algunos cavalleros de Sevilla para procurar alguna azeite, y creo que cayo en algunas casas adonde tan bien se pedia para la Compañia, y ansi se la vedó luego, y no se ha hecho despues, y crea Vuestra Reverencia que se anda con toda circunspicion (como me dice el Padre rector) y se yrá siempre de no impedir ninguna la limosna de la Compañia aunque minima, y es muy justo pues tanta caridad nos haçen los padres en todo, e yo de mi parte aunque quiero mucho a esta obra, por servirse mucho della nuestro Señor toda via quiero y devo mil veçes más a mi madre la Compañia y consequenter por donde ha de perder la Compañia no deseo que esta obra gane pero mi esperança es en la bondad y misericordia de nuestro Señor, que la Compañia no ha de perder nada si no más presto de ganar muchissimo *in benedictionibus tam celestibus quam terrenis*, por medio destos Seminarios, y que Dios que es ricquissimo, ha de proveer para la una y para la otro, como hasta agora, y sacar mucha gloria suya dello.

La segunda cosa que es firmar el Padre rector algunas veçes que tantas missas se han dicho en el seminario por los alumnos, tiene algun difficuldad mayor para remediar, pues los que embian cien missas, *verbi gratia*, a decir en el Seminario quieren la firma del superior de que estan ya repartidas y dichas, y lo que el Padre haçe, no es más que dar testimonio como superior de aquella casa que los alumnos del collegio ynglés han dicho las dichas missas y esto se pone con tanta claridad y distincion, que no pueda aver ningun género de duda o suspecha que algun hombre de la Compañia saque provecho de las missas, toda via, sabida la verdad del hecho, si a nuestro Padre General o a Vuestra Reverencia parecen aver inconveniente en el modo, en el qual ninguno hasta agora ha reparado, se podra provar el otro que nuestro Padre General apunta que es fermar algun alumno, aunque entiendo que parecera cosa muy nueva y de menos autoridad, y que los que suelen embiar missas al seminario no se contentarán dél, y ansi deseo que se pondere el uno inconveniente y el otro, pues importa mucho al pobre seminario, por ser buena parte de su sustento las missas de los alumnos. Vuestra Reverencia como tan padre desta obra la mirará con su accostumbrada caridad, y nos hara todo buen officio con nuestro Padre General que tan bien lo es mucho destos seminarios. En los santos sacrificios de Vuestra Reverencia mucho me incomiendo. Sevilla a 8 de Mayo 1595.

Roberto Personio.

[PS] De Ynglaterra no ay cosa nueva por estas dias fuera de las que escrivio el Padre Peralta a Vuestra Reverencia de la prision de los seis estudiantes y del Padre de la Compañia, dicen, que la armada ha parado y no se sabe porqué, porventura por suspechas que tiene la Reyna, de que el Rey ayudará a los catolicos de Escocia, plegue a Dios que no se engañe.

[PPS]168
Modo de dar fee de las missas que dicen los alumnos inglesses.

Digo yo el Padre Francisco de Peralta de la Compania de Iesus rector del collegio inglés de Sevilla que en este seminario los sacerdotes inglesses alumnos del dicho seminario an dicho cien missas por la intencion de N. que pidio se dixesen, y el seminario ha recebido 200 Reales de limosna. Porque es assi lo firmo (de mi albedrio). Fecho, 10 de Junio de 95 años.

   Francisco de Peralta.

[*Endorsed:*] Copia de la carta que el Padre Roberto Personio escribio a el Padre provincial sobre las dos cosas, &c.

Translation

The peace of Christ.

I do not write to Your Reverence so very often, on account of my time being much occupied in writing to other places and in connection with building and other transactions, and because Your Reverence's time also must be occupied with an abundance of correspondence. Moreover Fr Peralta, with a view to relieving me in this respect, has taken on the responsibility of keeping Your Reverence informed in both our names of all that happens here. It was a great consolation to me that I happened to be in Seville at the same time as Your Reverence, even though you were only passing through, and you did us the kindness of inspecting the new house. Good progress is being made in fitting it up, although lack of funds makes us proceed little by little. I trust in our Lord that he is going to complete the work, for assuredly it is a thing that is necessary for His holy service. Fr Peralta will have informed Your Reverence already of the generous alms which the duke of Medina Sidonia made us in granting us a sluiceway; it will be a great relief to this house. The water is being channelled, and I think that within five169 days it will have arrived at the house, our Lord so willing.

I received Your Reverence's letter of the 9th of this month,170 which dealt with the two matters concerning this seminary which our father general orders us to put right. As to the first matter, I think it has already been attended to many months ago, since the time when Your Reverence was here and told father rector about it: I mean about Brother Fabrizio not begging anymore for this seminary, in the way you mentioned, for the time being and as long as our father general ordains. For that complaint arose out of an expedition which Brother Fabrizio made to La Cerasa,171 on the invitation, as he said, of some gentlemen of Seville, to procure some oil. I understand that he approached some houses where it is has been customary to beg also for the Society. For that reason, he was for-

  168. In another hand, probably Peralta's.
  169. Or thirteen or fifteen. See textual note. Hicks translates "paja de agua" as "apportionment," i.e., water sluiced off at regular intervals to supply an agreed amount.
  170. B273.
  171. Possibly La Cereza, a region in the Extremadura, west of Madrid, best known for its cherries.

bidden to do so at the time and it has not been done since; and Your Reverence may rest assured that we are proceeding with all caution (so father rector told me) and will always take care not to interfere in any way with the alms received by the Society, even in the slightest degree. And this is indeed only fair, because the fathers are so charitable to us in every way. For my part, very devoted as I am to this work because our Lord will have much profit from it, still I am more devoted and have a thousand times more obligation to my mother, the Society, and consequently I have no wish that this work should make profit if it is going to cause loss to the Society. My hope however is in the mercy and goodness of our Lord, that the Society may lose nothing but rather gain exceedingly *in blessings both for heaven and on earth* by means of these seminaries, and that God who is abundantly rich will take care both of the one and of the other, as He has done up to now, to His greater glory.[172]

The second matter, that is the certification by father rector from time to time that so many masses have been said in the seminary by the students, is somewhat more difficult to put right, because the persons who commission, say, a hundred masses to be said in the seminary, like to have the superior's certificate that they have been allocated and said. What the father does is no more than to bear witness as superior of the house that the students of the English college have said the above-mentioned masses. This is put so clearly and distinctly that it is impossible for there to be any sort of doubt or suspicion that some member of the Society is drawing benefit from the masses. Still, if, as the truth of the matter is known, it appears to our father general or to Your Reverence that there is something untoward in the method – which no one has noticed so far – the other one which our father general suggests can be tried: that is, certification by one of the students – though I believe it will be considered a great novelty and of a lesser authority, and that people who are concerned to commission masses at the seminary will not be satisfied with it. I should wish therefore the one inconvenience to be weighed against the other, because it is a matter of great importance to the poor seminary, the masses of the scholars being a large item in their means of support. Since Your Reverence has so fatherly a feeling for this work, please would you regard the matter with your accustomed charity and use your best offices for us with our father general, who also has a very paternal love for these seminaries. I commend myself much to Your Reverence's holy sacrifices. Seville, 20 May 1595.

    Robert Persons.

    [PS] There is no news from England these days except what Fr Peralta wrote to Your Reverence about the capture of the six students and of the father of the Society,[173] and that the expedition has been stopped,[174] no one knows why, possibly on account of

---

172. Literally, "and will have much glory from it," an allusion to the Jesuit motto, AMDG.

173. William Baldwin; see Persons's letter to Acquaviva, 15 May (B276).

174. An expedition planned by Drake and Hawkins to gain possession of Panama was delayed because of a Spanish raid on Cornwall, raising fears of vulnerability to attack, but Elizabeth ordered it to go ahead in August following reports that a Spanish treasure ship was stranded at San Juan, Puerto Rico. See Paul E.J. Hammer, *Elizabeth's Wars: War, Government, and Society in Tudor England, 1544–1604* (New York, 2003), 190–191.

the queen's having suspicions that the king will give aid to the Catholics in Scotland. Please God she is not mistaken.

[PPS *In another hand at the end of the letter:*]
Formula used for certifying masses said by the English students.

I, Fr Francisco de Peralta of the Society of Jesus, rector of the English college at Seville, declare that in this seminary the English priests, students of the said Seminary, have said 100 masses for the intention of N., which he asked should be said; and the seminary has received an alms of 200 reals. In witness whereof I sign my name (of my own free will). Dated and signed, 10 June in the year '95.

Francisco de Peralta.

B278 From Claudio Acquaviva, 5 June 1595

SOURCE: ARSI, Baet. 3/I, 220.

NOTE: Acquaviva washes his hands of Thomas Wright. He undertakes to have del Río replaced as rector at Valladolid if necessary, and to provide Creswell with a companion. He is pleased with the pastoral work of Peralta as rector at Seville and agrees to allow Richard Blount to be received into the Society as a novice in England, provided that he can be moved to Belgium as soon as possible, preferably within a year. See McCoog, *Building the Faith of St Peter*, 190 n.

P. Roberto Personio, Junio 5.

Dos de Vuestra Reverencia he recevido con los dos ordinarios de Marzo y Abril que llegaron juntos quinçe dias ha, por el successo que ha tenido Tomas Vrit,[175] havrá visto Vuestra Reverencia que mis sospechas eran con bastante fundamento de pensar que él no duraria, vaya con la bendicion de Dios, que Vuestra Reverencia lo ha hecho muy bien de darle su dimisoria y embiarla con gusto.

Pésame que no salga bien el Rector del seminario de Valladolid, yo escrivo al Provincial una palabra, y Vuestra Reverencia esté a la mira, y si viere que no se mejora avise al Provincial que ponga otro, que él lo hara, y yo se lo escrivo.

Desde que Vuestra Reverencia me escrivio la primera vez que el Padre Cresuelo havia menester compañero, avisé yo al Provincial de Toledo que se le diese, y ahora me escrive que se le ha dado.

Vuestra Reverencia dé mis encomiendas al Padre Francisco Peralta y le diga recevi la suya, y consuelo de entender por ella, que tan de veras le aya entrado la devoçion de los Ingleses, que para su tiempo serán buenos los deseos que tiene.

Dias ha que el Padre Cresuelo me escrivio lo que Vuestra Reverencia dice de Ricardo Blunto, y yo le respondi que viniendo él a Flandes, o otra provincia, será luego reçevido, pero reçevirle alli y que luego sea operario, aora sé que tiene sus dificultades, especialmente que el Padre Garneto no[176] en todos los que con liçençia reçivio ha tenido el

---

175. el successo que ha tenido Tomas Vrit] *underlined R*
176. no] *followed by illegible deletion R*

acierto que convenia, mas ya que Vuestra Reverencia y los demas padres tanto alaban a Ricardo, Vuestra Reverencia avise a padre Garneto que le pruebe por un año, y esté a la nuestra[177] como procede, y avise a Vuestra Reverencia porque si procediera con satisfaction, le daremos liçençia que le reçiva. En las etc.

Translation

To Fr Robert Persons, 5 June.

I received two letters from Your Reverence with the two ordinary posts of March and April, both of which arrived at the same time fifteen days ago.[178] As for the outcome you have had with Thomas Wright, Your Reverence has seen that I had good grounds to suspect that he would not last the course. May he go with God's blessing. Your Reverence has done the right thing giving him his dismissal and sending him on his way rejoicing.

I am very sorry that the rector of the seminary of Valladolid has not started off well, and I will write a word to the provincial; Your Reverence should keep a lookout, and if you see that things do not improve, tell the provincial to replace him with another, which he will do, on my written authorization.

Since the first time Your Reverence wrote to me that Fr Creswell had need of a companion, I advised the provincial of Toledo that he should give one to him, and now he has written that he has done so.

Would Your Reverence please give my compliments to Fr Francisco de Peralta and tell him that I have received his letter and am encouraged to understand from it how deeply he has become devoted to the English, that his disposition will be helpful when the time comes.

Some days ago, Fr Creswell wrote to me what Your Reverence says about Richard Blount, and I answered him that when he comes to Flanders or another province, he would be welcome, but now I realize that there may be certain difficulties about receiving him there and having him operate there, especially given that in Fr Garnet's experience, not all those who have been received with licence have had the success which we should like. But since Your Reverence and the rest of the fathers have already praised Richard so much, would Your Reverence please advise Fr Garnet that he should try him for one year, and see if he fits in with the Society as he proceeds,[179] and then inform Your Reverence if he has given satisfaction, so that we may give him the licence to admit him. To your [holy prayers and sacrifices], etc.

B279 To Claudio Acquaviva, Seville, 12 June 1595

    SOURCE: ARSI, Hisp. 138, fols. 299–301, holograph.

    HICKS: 359–373, with English translation.

    NOTE: Persons is relieved that the agitation for him to be put forward for the cardinalate has died down, thanks to Mannaerts in Flanders and the Jesuit community in Madrid. There

---

177. nuestra] *this ed.*; nutra R

178. Persons's letters of 19 March and mid-April (B264, B270, not extant). The earlier post must have been delayed.

179. This reading is conjectural: see n177.

is no further need for intervention, except that he has consulted with Idiáquez, who may act on his behalf to suppress the idea.

Despite the disappointing outcome of Persons's attempt to raise funds following the arrival of the Spanish treasure fleet, the college in Seville is in sound financial order.

This letter is notable for the evidence it provides of the tensions between the English colleges and the Spanish Jesuits in Seville, Valladolid, and Madrid. In Seville, questions have been raised about competitive fundraising, even though the chief benefactors of the English college are not those who support the Spanish fathers. Fortunately, Pérez as the former provincial and Cordeses as superior of the professed house have helped to smooth things over, even though the present provincial, Cristóbal Méndez, is less understanding (see Persons's letter to him, 20 May, B277). In Valladolid, envy has also surfaced, with Cabredo suspected of soliciting alms to the detriment of the Spanish fathers. It seems that José de Acosta and his brother have been writing from there to the former superior of the professed house in Seville, Esteban de Ojeda (ca. 1568–1614; superior 1587–1593; see Murphy, 7), to complain. However, Persons asks Acquaviva not to intervene.

Joseph Creswell's position in Madrid has become fraught with difficulties. The Spanish court does not trust him to deal with English affairs, and at the Jesuit college he has been deprived of the support of his lay brother assistant, torn between obedience to Creswell and Juan García, who succeeded Juan de Sigüenza as rector in 1594 (Astrain, 3: 316). Unable to pay his own way, he is becoming a burden on the college, with García treating him with great reserve. In concert with Gil González Dávila, Persons recommends that Creswell be appointed procurator in charge of English affairs, and that he be supported financially by the English seminaries in Seville and Valladolid. See McCoog, *Building the Faith of St Peter*, 223–224.

Muy Reverendo in Christo Padre nuestro
Pax Christi.

1. Me he consolado mucho con entender por la de Vuestra Paternidad de 10 Abril que las diligentias que hiçi por cartas en Roma Francia y Flandres sobre lo de no mudar estado parecieron bien a Vuestra Paternidad y confio en nuestro Señor que les ha de dar el successo que deseamos para su mayor gloria y siguridad de mi pobre ánima que eligio la vida de la compañia por medio de su salvacion, *et in eo uno acquiescit, timendo et aversando* todo lo demas. El buen Padre Oliverio tan bien me escrive agora cartas da mucho consuelo, *nimirum* que mis cartas y raçones an obrado bien con muchos, y *quod multum refrixerit negotium etc.* Por acá en España despues de lo que escrivi a los Padres nuestros de Madrid conforme a lo que escrivi a Vuestra Paternidad no he hecho otra diligencia, por parecer a ellos y a los Padres tan bien de acá, que no era necessario, y a mí lo mismo, para no despertar y continuar la memoria de lo que io deseo tanto que se olvide. Solamente me parecio que con el Señor Don Juan de Idiaquez, como amigo íntimo y espiritual que bien entiendo que me quiere bien *in Domino et propter Dominum*, y es capaz de raçones espirituales, fuere de las de estado y del servicio del Rey – con este, digo, he hecho algun officio efficaz, encargando tanto a su consciencia y supplicandole encarecidamente que me haga amistad verdadera en esto, que entiendo sin duda que me lo hara aunque hasta agora no me ha respondido; y es hombre de tanta verdad, devocion y secreto que bien si-

guro estoy que no nos disaprovechará esta diligencia, y con esto me consuelo y callo, y ni ablo ni pienso más en ello.

2. En lo demas haçemos lo que podemos, yo ando en la obra desta casa nueva, con más ánimo que deneros; y aunque aya venida la flota, por venir algo manco, y por pedirse a los mercaderes venias y gastos muy grandes, estan los animos de los hombres muy encogidos. Yo fui un dia solamente a la Casa de la Contratacion con un o dos cavalleros de Sevilla y llevamos quatro estudiantes recien venidos pensando que sacaria algo para la compra y fábrica desta casa, y fue tan poco que me disanimó, y los cavalleros se corrieron y ansi no bolvi más, si no más algunos cavalleros particulares y mercaderes affectos a esta obra juntaron en secreto lo que pienso bastará para poner en estado raçonable esta casa y habitacion por agora, que es lo que yo avia forçoso menester, y no dudo si no que nuestro señor yrá remediando tan bien lo demas a sus tiempos.

3. Lo que a mí más cuydado da en toda esta obra de los Seminarios, no es las graves difficultades que se offerecen de la parte del enemigo, y de la gente y de su sustento, gobierno, missiones, etc. si no de la parte de los nuestros de la Compañia,[180] a los quales no queria dar un minimo disgusto, et con todo esto los reçelos son tantos por causa de las limosnas, que muchas veçes es cosa travajosa dar satisfaction en todo. Aqui en Sevilla los benhechores principales desta obra son el Rey,[181] el obispo de Juan, los Duques de Arcos, Alcala, Vejar, Medina Sidonia, y los marqueses de Priego, Ayamonte, Alcala, Tarifa, el Cardinal y Cabildo de la Yglesia, la ciudad o regimiento de Sevilla, y algunos particulares que nunca, creo, han dado ni darian blanca de limosna a la Compañia, y se tiene summo cuydado de no pedir a los que dan a la Compañia, y con todo esto ay tantos reçelos como digo, llevantados por lo demas por hermanos que ablan lo que no saben, y ay tantos avisos sobre esto al rector, embiados[182] de la casa professa, que realmente si el rector[183] no fuera muy buen hombre y llano, se cansaria; pero él passa con todo y en dando su raçon de los yerros que se levantan, todo se acalma. Toda via[184] bien facilmente hecho a veer que si la provedencia de Dios no ubiera puesto aqui un Padre Bartolome Perez por provincial, y a un santo Padre Cordeses por preposito de la casa al principio, quando se assento esta obra, fuera impossibile averla assentada, porque aunque los Padres provincial y Preposito que son agora nos haçen mucha caridad y son hombres santos, no entienden la importancia de la obra como los otros, ni son para romper por las dificultades etc. Pero con el amparo de Dios y de Vuestra Paternidad todo yrá suavemente, placiendo a su divina Magestad, ni digo esto por via de quexa alguna, si no para que Vuestra Paternidad entienda lo que passa, y con su solita caridad paternal nos ayuda en las occasiones, y mande untar la rueda algunas veçes donde avrá menester, con su santa prudencia y discrecion, para que corra adelante y no pare en algunas difficultades que naçen más presto de la nuestra estrechura de coraçon y entrañas[185] que *nos ipsi coarctamus et angustiamur*

180. de la Compañia] *interlined with caret R*
181. *All the names following have been underlined in R*
182. embiados] *interlined with caret R*
183. el Rector] *interlined with caret R*
184. via] *interlined with caret R*
185. entrañas] *this ed.;* entrañcas *R*

invicim que no de la cosa en sí. Ni digo esto para que[186] Vuestra Paternidad mande escrivir algo a Sevilla, antes la supplico que no se diga ni se escriva nada porque ya todo está compuesto y convenido entre el Padre Preposito y el rector, y el Padre Preposito le ha pedido el rector que no diga nada esto a mí, y ansi passamos con muy grande amor y paz y será siempre placiendo a Dios.

4. Más siento que dicen por acá, que de quando en quando ay cartas de algunos de los nuestros en Valladolid que quexanse de las limosnas del Seminario ynglés por alla, siendo verdad que de quatro o cinco mil ducados que aquel Seminario ha gastado hasta agora en cada un año, no salien[187] más de dieceocho ducados el año de la villa de Valladolid y todo su distrito, quando yo estava alla, pero despues o poco antes llegó a vivir a Valladolid, un cavallero llamado Don Francisco de Manriquez y por no tener hijo, offerecio al Padre Cabredo, que era su amigo, de sustentar un estudiante en el Seminario, y aunque no sé si platicava mucho en la compañia este cavallero o les dava limosna porque vivia muy lexos de alla y muy circa el Seminario, nos ha costado hartas murmuraciones esta limosna y muchos me profetizavan que no nos avia de durar mucho el Padre Cabredo en el officio de rector, por averse suspecha dél que[188] procurava destas limosnas, y por cierto no me accuerdo que nos procurasse otra que esta en todo el tiempo que fue rector, todavia siguio la penetencia al Seminario, de perder su rector, aunque a Vuestra Paternidad no devia pasar por pensamiento esta consideracion, quando lo mudó, pero ha sido la mayor herida por aquella pobre casa que se podia acontecer, pues con el largo interregno que ubo y con la poca applicacion y aptitud deste nuevo rector como parece ay hasta agora, mucho ha padecido el Seminario *in utroque homine*, y lo que más me pesa es que no ay union en casa. Yo daré la priesa que la salud y negocios por acá daran lugar para llegarme alla, y entonces escriveré a Vuestra Paternidad lo que ay de rayz, y hasta entonces, tan poco deseo que si escriva algo de parte de Vuestra Paternidad por alla, antes combiene que no se sepa nada de lo que yo escrivo aqui para que no se pongan las cosas en peor estado. Suspecho que los escriven de alla de los nuestros fuera del Seminario, son el Padre Hieronimo Acosta y el padre Preposito su hermano, al Padre Ojeda de acá. Del padre Hieronimo soy cierto por lo passado, pero no dudo si no en llegando yo alla se dara satisfacion a todos de todo, y quedaremos como siempre muy grandes amigos. El buen Padre Joseph de Acosta me hiço carga dos o tres veçes de que yo avia escritto tan bien contra él a Vuestra Paternidad quando yva en sus negocios, pero decistio despues diciendo que lo dicia de burla, como tan bien que le avia hincado la lancea (como él dixo) con el Rey.

5. Lo que me es forçoso supplicar a Vuestra Paternidad que mande poner algun remedio luego en lo de Madrid, donde está el Padre Cresuello tan affligido y cansado de las difficultades que le cargan con el poco favor de los superiores immediatos que no puede passar adelante. Él tiene a cargo los negocios de quatro Seminarios dos en España y dos en Flandres y más desto los de los reynos de Ynglaterra Escocia y Yrlanda que no son pocos en aquella corte, y al presente estan dos cavalleros Catholicos de Escocia y otros de Yrlanda y Don Juan de Idiaquez que es con quien al Rey quiere que todos los nego-

186. paraque] *this ed.*; parnque R
187. salien] *this ed.*; salian R
188. Cabredo en el officio de Rector, por averse suspecha dél que] *underlined* R

cios de los reynos ultramontanos se traten, no quiere recebir informacion si no por mano de quien conoçe; me han hecho grandissima instancia y al mismo Don Juan que yo me llegasse alla, pero yo me he escusado fortissimamente, y a él y a ellos por muchas raçones, y el padre Cresuello suple por mí en todo, y digo a Vuestra Paternidad que es tan forçoso que él o otro hombre tal esté alli que sin esso no es possibile passar adelante, y si por los negocios de una provincia sola, tienen aqui su procurador en la corte con tener alli otros tantos de su nacion, piense Vuestra Paternidad lo que es forçoso para tantos Seminarios y reynos. Vuestra Paternidad ordenó a mi peticion el año passado que el padre Cresuello quedasse en Madrid por morador para attender a los negocios de su nacion sin gasto, pero luego se hechó a veer que sin compañero para salir a sus tiempos, no podia hacer nada, y ansi se supplico a Vuestra Paternidad que pudiesse tener compañero, y para quitar toda difficultad con el rector, se concerto que pagarian los Seminarios para él y su compañero, cien ducados en cada un año para la comida sin vestidos y esto se acceptó por entonces, hasta que Vuestra Paternidad respondiesse; pero despues en occasion de un orden que ubo que a los huespedes si trocassen los compañeros, le quitaran tan bien a él su compañero que se le embió de Valladolid, y le an embaraçado de tal manera que ni puede proseguir negocio a su tiempo, ni él ni su compañero, que es hermano ynglés novicio, muy bonissimo, pero tan affligido y embaraçado con las dos obediencias differentes del padre rector y del padre Cresuello por los negocios, que está en peligro de perderse, como me ha escrito el padre Gil Gonçales y el mismo hermano por su carta, la qual embío juntamente con la del padre Gil Gonçales, para que Vuestra Paternidad vista la necessidad ponga remedio en ellio, que será (conforme al parecer de los Padres más graves de Madrid) que attenta la necessidad de las cosas de ynglaterra y de todos estos Seminarios, mande Vuestra Paternidad assentar el padre Cresuello por procurador particular dellos, con su compañero aparte, que no se empleó en otra cosa que en attender a ayudar al padre y que de aqui de los Seminarios podamos mudarselo quando fuera menester, y con esto y con pagar los Seminarios el gasto de entrambos enteramente en Madrid (lo que haremos de muy buena gana), si podra passar adelante con paz y suavidad, y no otramente, y que este orden dure hasta que los cosas de ynglaterra quedaren con su necessidad de recurso a aquela corte que al presente tienen, y quanto más presto Vuestra Paternidad nos hiciere caridad deste assiento tanto mejor será.

6. Lo que yo he escritto al padre rector de Madrid sobre este negocio veerá Vuestra Paternidad por la copia de la carta que embío con esta[189] y lo que le digo de las limosnas y recelos dellas, es mucho verdad, pues es certissimo que el Padre Cresuello no ha procurado hasta agora un ducado en Madrid para los Seminarios con averles gastado más de ciento, y con todo esto entiendo que esta suspecha de limosnas es la rayz fundamental de toda la estrechura del padre rector con él, y por esto desea darle un compañero que le diga despues dónde, y con qué gente y de qué cosas aya ablado, lo qual haçe al compañero tan curioso muchas veçes que quiere saber cosas de los negocios que no combiene, suppuesto el poco secreto que ay de ordinario, y quando se abla en ynglés, toma suspechas, ni puede ayudar al Padre en[190] escrivir ni trasladar cosas, y salen estos hermanos de tan

---

189. esta] *interlined with caret R*
190. en] *interlined with caret R*

mala gana y tan despacio[191] que si pierden las conjuncturas de audienças con las personas de occupacion y respeto, y despues en casa se abla de los negocios sin risguardo. Pardone Vuestra Paternidad que le escrivo tan largo, esto negocio nos es de mucha importancia y ansi confio que Vuestra Paternidad lo assentará de una vez por siempre, y es necessario que el orden venga a nuestras manos para que tratemos con efficacia con el padre provincial y rector para el assiento. En los santos sacrificios de Vuestra Paternidad muy humilmente me encomiendo. Sevilla a 12 de Junio 1595.

    De Vuestra Paternidad Reverenda
        Indigno hijo y siervo
            Roberto Personio.
[*Endorsed:*] Sevilla. P. Roberto Personio. [*with summary of contents*]

Translation

Our Very Reverend Father in Christ
The peace of Christ.

    1. I am very encouraged to hear from Your Paternity's letter of 10 April[192] that the steps which I took by writing letters to Rome, France, and Flanders on the subject of avoiding a change in my state of life had the approval of Your Paternity. I trust in our Lord that He will give them the outcome that we desire, for His greater glory and for the safety of my poor soul, seeing that I chose life in the Society as the means of its salvation, and *in that alone does it rest content, fearing, and abrogating* everything else. Good Fr Olivier has also written very consoling letters to me now, *namely* that my letters and arguments have had a good effect on many people and that *the affair has largely died down*, etc. Here in Spain, after I had written to our fathers in Madrid in the same vein in which I wrote to Your Paternity, I have taken no further steps because it seemed unnecessary, to them as well as to the fathers here, and I felt the same, in order to avoid awakening and prolonging the recollection of a thing which I am so desirous should be forgotten. Only in the case of Don Juan de Idiáquez – as being an intimate friend and a spiritually minded man who, I know well, wishes me well *in the Lord and for the Lord's sake* and is open to arguments of a spiritual nature apart from those concerning the state and the service of the king – with him, I say, I have taken some effective steps, laying it so much on his conscience and begging him so earnestly to act as my trustworthy friend in the matter, that I entertain no doubt that he will do me this favour, though up to now he has not answered me. He is a man of such sincerity, loyalty, and discretion that I am fully assured that he will not deny us his support, and I am consoled by this, and keep silence, and neither speak nor think of it anymore.

    2. For the rest, we are doing what we can, and I am carrying on with the work on this new house with more enthusiasm than money. Although the fleet has come in, it has arrived somewhat depleted, and very large dues and payments are being demanded from the merchants, so that people are not inclined to be very generous. I went to the Casa de

---

191. despacio] *this ed.;* deespacio R
192. B268.

Contratación[193] on one day only, with one or two gentlemen of Seville, and we took four students who had lately arrived, thinking that we would come away with something towards the purchase and building of this house; but it was so little that it disheartened me, and the gentlemen were ashamed, and I did not go again, except that some private gentlemen and merchants who are interested in this work secretly subscribed what will I think be enough to put this house and the living quarters in reasonable order for the time being. That is what I needed urgently, and I have no doubt but that our Lord will proceed to remove our other difficulties as well, in His own good time.

3. What causes me most anxiety in all this work of the seminaries is not the grave difficulties which present themselves from the enemy – and in connection with the nation, its support, government, and missions, etc. – but rather, those which are made by Ours of the Society. I would not want to give them the slightest cause for displeasure, but in spite of all this there is so much jealousy in the matter of alms that often it is very hard to give satisfaction in everything. Here in Seville the principal benefactors of this undertaking are the king; the bishop of Jaén; the dukes of Arcos, Alcalá, Béjar, Medina Sidonia and the marquises of Priego, Ayamonte, Alcalá, Tarifa; the cardinal and chapter of the church; the city or municipality of Seville; and some private persons who, I think, have never given nor would ever give a farthing in alms to the Society.[194] The greatest care is taken not to beg from those who give to the Society, and in spite of this there is all this suspicion, as I say, stirred up for the most part by brothers who talk of things they know nothing about. The rector receives so many reports about this, sent from the professed house, that really, if the rector were not a very good man and very good tempered, he would be worn out. But he puts up with everything, and when he gives his explanation of the mistakes which arise, everything is smoothed over. All the same, it is easy to see that, if God's providence had not placed a Fr Bartolomé Pérez here as provincial, and a saintly Fr Cordeses as superior of the house, at the beginning, when this work got under way, it would have been impossible to have got it going; for although the present father provincial and father superior are very charitable to us and are holy men,[195] they do not realize the importance of the work as the others did, nor are they concerned to overcome the difficulties that arise, etc. However with the support of God and of Your Paternity all will go smoothly, if it please the divine majesty; I do not say this by way of making any complaint but so that Your Paternity may understand what is going on and with your accus-

---

193. This is the Casa de Contratación de las Indias in Seville, which controlled trade between Spain and its American possessions.

194. The bishop of Jaén was Francisco Sarmiento Mendoza (1525–1595; appointed 1580). The other notables listed here are the duke of Arcos (see Persons to Acquaviva, 12 May 1594, B230), the duke of Medina Sidonia, Alonso Pérez de Guzmán (1550–1615), and his cousins, Francisco Diego de Zúñiga y Mendoza (ca. 1560–1601), fifth duke of Béjar, and Francisco de Zúñiga (d. 1604), fourth marquis of Ayamonte; and a second group, related to Fernando Enríquez de Ribera y Portocarrero, second duke of Alcalá de Gazules (1517–1594), father-in-law both to the widowed marchioness of Tarifa, Ana Téllez-Girón (1555–1625), and Pedro Fernández de Córdoba y Figueroa, fourth marquis of Priego (1563–1606). The cardinal archbishop of Seville was Rodrigo de Castro Osorio.

195. Cristóbal Méndez, provincial of Andalusia, and Pedro Bernal, who succeeded Cordeses as superior of the professed house in Seville in 1594.

tomed paternal charity may help us as occasion offers, and keep the wheels turning sometimes when needed, using your holy prudence and discretion, so that they may run on and not halt when any difficulties arise, which do so rather from the narrowness of our hearts and affections – *which we ourselves overcrowd so that we are in turn constricted* – than from the nature of the work itself. Nor do I say this in hopes that Your Paternity will get something written off to Seville; rather I beg you not to say or write anything, because at present everything has been settled and agreed between the father provincial and the rector; and father superior has begged the rector not to say anything about this to me, and so we are proceeding very lovingly and peacefully, and please God it will always be so.

4. I am more concerned that they say here that from time to time there are letters from some of our fathers in Valladolid complaining of the alms given to the English seminary there; the truth being that out of four or five thousand ducats, which this seminary has spent each year up to now, not more than eighteen ducats a year came from the town of Valladolid and all its neighbourhood, when I was there; but afterwards or shortly before I left, a gentleman named Don Francisco de Manríquez came to live in Valladolid and, as he had no son, he offered Fr Cabredo, who was a friend of his, to sponsor a student in the seminary; and, although I am not aware whether this gentleman had much converse with the Society or gave them alms, because he lived very far from them and very close to the seminary, this alms has cost us all these murmurings; and many people predicted to me that Fr Cabredo would not last us very long in the post of rector, given the suspicion that he was soliciting these alms. Certainly, I have no recollection that he obtained any other for us during all the time he was rector,[196] apart from this; nevertheless, this meant the seminary was punished by losing its rector. Even though no consideration of this sort would have passed through Your Paternity's mind when you transferred him, still, it has been the greatest injury that could happen to that poor house, for what with the long interregnum that ensued and the lack of diligence and aptitude in this new rector, as it seems so far, the seminary has suffered much *by reason of each of these men*. What weighs on my mind most is that there is no unity of spirit in the house. I am going to make haste, as much as my health and business here will allow, to get there and then I will write to Your Paternity what is at the root of the matter. And till then I would prefer that nothing be written to them on Your Paternity's part: rather it is desirable that nothing be known of what I am writing here, in case the situation deteriorates further. I suspect that those who are writing from there, amongst those of Ours outside the seminary, are Fr Jerónimo Acosta and the superior, his brother, to Fr Ojeda. About Fr Jerónimo I am certain from what has gone before, but I have no doubt but that, when I get there, everything will be sorted out to the satisfaction of all, and that we shall remain the great friends we have always been. Good Fr José de Acosta charged me two or three times with having written unfavourably of him also to Your Paternity in the initial stages of his enterprise, but he stopped afterwards, saying that he had said it in jest; as also that I had poked him with a lance (as he expressed it) as regards the king.

5. There is something I am obliged to beg Your Paternity to have some remedy assigned at once, and that is the case of Madrid, where Fr Creswell is so distressed and

---

196. 1591–1593.

worn out by the difficulties that oppress him because he finds so little favour with his immediate superiors, that he cannot make any headway. He is charged with the affairs of four seminaries, two in Spain and two in Flanders, and those of the kingdoms of England, Scotland, and Ireland besides, which are not inconsiderable in that court. At the present moment two Catholic gentlemen from Scotland and others from Ireland are there, and Don Juan de Idiáquez, who is the man with whom the king wishes the business of all the ultramontane kingdoms to be conducted, will not receive reports except from the hand of someone he knows. They have very strongly insisted, and Don Juan himself, that I should betake myself there, but I have excused myself very firmly both to him and to them for many reasons, and Fr Creswell acts for me in everything. I can tell Your Paternity that it is so essential that he or another such man is there that otherwise no progress is possible; and if for the affairs of one province alone they have their procurator here at the court, despite having so many other men of their nation there, Your Paternity can imagine what is required in the case of so many seminaries and kingdoms. Last year Your Paternity ordered, at my request, that Fr Creswell should remain permanently at Madrid to look after the affairs of his nation, without expense to them; but presently it became evident that he could achieve nothing without a companion to go out with him when he needed; and so a request was made to Your Paternity that he might be allowed to have a companion, and, to remove all difficulty with the rector, it was agreed that the seminaries should pay one hundred ducats a year for food for him and his assistant, not including clothing. That arrangement was accepted for the time being, pending Your Paternity's reply; but later, on the occasion of an order being given that the companions of guests should be changed, they also took away from him the assistant who was sent to him from Valladolid, and they have hampered him to such an extent that he cannot even pursue his business when he needs to, neither he nor his *socius*. The latter is an English lay brother novice,[197] a very good fellow, but he is so hindered and distressed by the two conflicting obediences due to father rector and to Fr Creswell in business matters, that he is in danger of collapse, as Fr Gil González has written to me, and the brother himself in his letter, which I am sending along with Fr Gil González's so that Your Paternity may see what the need is, and assign a remedy. This will be (in the opinion of the most respected fathers at Madrid) that, taking into account the needs of English affairs and of all these seminaries, Your Paternity would approve Fr Creswell's appointment as procurator exclusively for them, with a separate assistant who will not be employed in anything else but be available to help the father; and that we, from the seminaries here, should be able to transfer him if necessary. In this way and with the seminaries paying the entire expenses of both of them in Madrid (which we will very willingly undertake), it will be possible, and not otherwise, for matters to proceed peacefully and smoothly. This order should have force as long as it remains necessary for English affairs to be referred to this court, as is the case now; and the sooner Your Paternity does us the kindness of making this settlement the better it will be.

197. The lay brother has not been identified, but Creswell employed Francis Fowler, brother of the prominent English Catholic printer John Fowler (1537–1579), as his secretary from 1594 to 1605 (Loomie, *Spanish Elizabethans*, 194).

6. What I have written to father rector of Madrid about this affair, Your Paternity will see in the copy of the letter which I am sending with this. What I tell him about the alms and the jealousies they cause is very true, for it is quite certain that in Madrid Fr Creswell has not obtained one ducat for the seminaries up to now, whilst he has spent more than a hundred on them; and in spite of all this I understand that this suspicion about alms is the root cause of all father rector's reserve towards him. It is on this account that he wishes to assign him an assistant who will report to him [the rector] afterwards where, and with whom, and on what matters he has spoken. This makes his assistant so often very curious that he wants to know details of the negotiations which are not appropriate, considering how little confidentiality ordinarily prevails: and when English is spoken, he becomes suspicious; nor is he able to assist the father with writing and translating. And these brothers sally forth so unwillingly and at such a leisurely pace, that appointments for audiences with people who are busy and entitled to respect are missed; and afterwards in the house there is indiscreet talk about the business. I pray Your Paternity to pardon me for writing at such length; this matter is of great importance to us, and so I trust that Your Paternity will settle it once for all; it is necessary too that the order should come to our hands so that we can deal effectively with father provincial and the rector and settle the matter. I commend myself very humbly to Your Paternity's holy sacrifices. From Seville, 12 June 1595.

    Your Reverend Paternity's
        unworthy son and servant
            Robert Persons.

B280 To Edmund Harewood, Seville, 12 June 1595

SOURCES:

    ARSI, FG 651/640, item 29, a contemporary copy (= A);

    item 30, containing only the second and last paragraphs (= A1).

NOTE: Edmund Harewood, SJ, was minister at the English College, Rome, i.e., the priest charged with running the day-to-day affairs of the college. This letter is Persons's response to his letter of 10 April (B269) about the unrest at the college. Although Harewood's letter was obscure, Persons has learned more from Sir Francis Englefield.

Following the death of William Allen, a party amongst the English Catholic exiles wished to prefer Owen Lewis, bishop of Cassano, to the cardinalate. This led to division in the English college, with Lewis's supporters strongly condemning Persons and Creswell, who had been rector himself until April 1592. Harewood took Persons's part, but the current rector, Girolamo Fioravanti, was very defensive. Two years later, Harewood's unpopularity among the students led to his being removed (Edwards, 199).

Persons reproaches Harewood for trying to conceal the strife, and is indignant about Fioravanti's attitude. He professes neutrality about Lewis's claims to preferment and asks for more information about the students who have attacked him.

The Latin text is difficult to interpret in places and may be corrupt.

Exemplar literarum ad P. Edmundum Harevardum scriptarum a
Reverendo P. Personio die 12 mensis Junii 1595.

Vestrae Reverentiae literae datae 10 Aprilis hisce diebus elapsis ad manus meas pervenerunt, et quamvis Vestra Reverentia habeat ciphram, et via quam servat mittendi sit satis secura, ita tam breviter et obscure scribit ut nullus illam intelligat; sed magis clare et apte scribunt alii[198] de rebus vestri collegii et aliorum, quas Vestra Reverentia ex parte intelligere posset per hoc summarium Equitis Domini Francisci quod ad me nuper transmisit ex suis ultimis literis Roma missis, quod legat et reservet sibi et Patri Rectori, et Domini Baynes; et non permittat ut ipsi, qui scripserunt de rebus vestris Romanis, intelligant exemplar suarum literarum Romam reversum esse, hanc enim mihi licentiam non concessit Eques Dominus Franciscus.

Meo sane iudicio nec Pater Rector nec Vestra Reverentia bene fecerunt ita dissimulare sicut fecerit tumultus vestri collegii, quia fortassis, hinc a nobis aliquod auxilium vel consilium accepissetis. P. Cresuellus etiam[199] secutus est similem modum procedendi, donec tumultus toti mundo innotesceret. Credo hoc factum esse, ut non daretur mihi hinc causa doloris, vel ne hoc attribuetur errori regiminis, quod nunquam[200] fecissem, nam omnes laudant rectoris regimen, et sola causa huius est quod sollicitentur a factiosis extra collegium, quod quacumque via et ratione potestis rescindere debetis,[201] nec in hoc negotio ullum timere. Si Dominus Throgmortonus se ultima commotioni inmiscuit, ut aliqui scribunt, iuste meruit ut prohiberetur illi a Protectore accessus ad collegium, et sciat pro certo Vestra Reverentia quod hoc et ipsum et novam ipsius rempublicam mortificabit.

Sed haec scribo Vestrae Reverentiae et Patri Rectori tamen: rogo Vestram Reverentiam ut se melius explicet et scribet ad nos in particulari qui erant, qui se obtulerunt opponere Personio et Cresuello, et aliquid mali contra illos machinari, et an erant Angli et ex Societate an non; et quod scribit Vestra Reverentia P. Hieronymum Floravantium rogatum fuisse ut se gereret negative tantum, cum viderit et Cresuellum et Personium tam male quam ipsum se gessisse, et ipse P. Floravantius, credo, et Vestra Reverentia optime norunt et respondere poterunt pro Personio qui numquam in vita sua offenderit P. Floravantium, quo non igitur possibile est aliquod malum officium a Personio contra ipsum fuisse praestitur; scribat quaeso apertius, quid cogitabat isti aggredi contra Cresuellum et Personium, et cum quibus, et in quo genere, et quare etc.

Quantum ad Episcopum Cassanensem et id quod ipse praetendit, quamvis Personius non curaverit inmiscere se huic negotio pro aut contra, quia[202] ipsemet Personius[203] contra suam voluntatem fuit introductus[204] in hanc scenam, intelligat tamen Vestra Reverentia quod Personius nunquam fuerit huius opinionis quae hoc cederet in Dei servitium

---

198. alii] *interlined with caret A*
199. etiam] *interlined with caret A*
200. nunquam] *A*; nunquam sane *A1*
201. potestis rescindere, debetis] *A*; possetis, rescindere debetis *A1*
202. quia] *A*; cum *A1*
203. Personius] *A*; et *A1*
204. fuit introductus] *A*; introductus sit *A1*

ut in bonum publicum; et quantum ad collegium et curam quam habet P. Floravantius,[205] pro certo sciat quod totum everteret; et quicquid iam fit vel hactenus factum fuit in Anglia ab hominibus Personio similibusque omnino perverteret.[206] Et secundum hoc Personii iudicium Vestra Reverentia procedat in omnibus suis actionibus ibi.[207] Novitiani quatuor in literis Domini Baynes, de quibus Vestra Reverentia cogitet inter reliquos. Tempus iam non permittit plura scribere. Dominus Jesus Vestram Reverentiam semper conservet. Hispali die 12 Junii 1595.

    Novit scriptorem.

[*Endorsed:*] Hispali. 1595 Jun. 12. P. Rob. Personio ad P. Eduardum Hervodum.

Translation

Your Reverence's letter of 10 April came to hand a few days ago, and although Your Reverence might use cipher, and the route which you used for the post is safe enough, still you wrote so briefly and obscurely that no one could understand it. But others write more clearly and suitably about the affairs of your college and others. Your Reverence will be able to understand these in part, through this summary made by his lordship Sir Francis from the latest letters sent from Rome, which he sent to me recently. Please read it, and keep it to yourself, along with father rector and Mr Baynes: do not allow those very people who wrote about your matters in Rome to be aware that a copy of their letter has been returned to Rome: for his lordship Sir Francis did not give me that permission.

    To be sure, in my opinion neither father rector nor Your Reverence have done well to conceal in this way the fact that such a tumult had happened in your college, because perhaps you would have received some help or advice from us here. Fr Creswell also followed a similar mode of proceeding, until the riot was known to all the world. I believe that this was done so that I should be given no reason for grief over here, or that this should not be attributed to any defect in the management. I would never have done that, for everyone praises the government of the rector: the sole cause of this trouble is the interference of factions outside the college, which you ought to cut off by whatever means and stratagem possible; nor should you fear anything in this process. If Mr Throckmorton has involved himself in the latest commotion, as some report, he justly deserves to be denied access to the college by the protector, and Your Reverence may be quite sure that this will be the deathblow both to himself and to his own new republic.[208]

    But I write these things to Your Reverence and to father rector and also to ask Your Reverence to explain himself better and to write to me in particular who they were who put themselves out to oppose Persons and Creswell, and to scheme some evil against them, and whether they were English or of the Society or not. And as for what Your Rev-

    205. Floravantius] *A*; Rector *A1*
    206. ab hominibus Personio similibusque omnino perverteret] *A*; ab hominibus meae professionis perverteret *A1*
    207. *A1 ends here.*
    208. Thomas Throckmorton was a leading promoter of Owen Lewis's candidature.

erence writes about Fr Girolamo Fioravanti, that he had been asked whether he acted negatively[209] only because he saw that both Creswell and Persons had acted as badly as he himself – both Fr Fioravanti himself and Your Reverence, I believe, know very well and are able to answer for Persons, who has never in his life offended Fr Fioravanti, so he could not possibly pretend that any evil office has been done to him by Persons. I beg you to write more openly what you thought of the attack on Persons and Creswell, and with whom, and of what kind, and why, etc.

As far as the bishop of Cassano[210] is concerned, and what he aspires to, although Persons did not care to involve himself in this business for or against, because Persons himself was introduced into this scene against his own will, Your Reverence should understand, all the same, that Persons was never of the opinion that this would turn out to the service of God and the public good. And as far as the college is concerned and the charge which Fr Fioravanti holds, he should know for certain that he is turning everything upside down, and that he is utterly ruining the state of things now in England as well as whatever has been done up to now by Persons and men like him.[211] And Your Reverence should proceed in all your actions there in accordance with this judgement of Persons. Four novices are mentioned in the letter of Mr Baynes, to whom Your Reverence should give some thought, among others. Time does not permit me to write more. May our Lord Jesus Christ always take care of you. Seville, 12 June 1595.

You know the hand.

B281 From Richard Cowling, Rome, 1 July 1595

SOURCE: ABSI, *Coll M* 138 (olim 109), Grene's notes.

NOTE: Cowling (or Collins) evidently wrote to Persons frequently from Rome, very likely about the troubles in the English college.

P. R. Coulinus qui supra scribit iterum ex Penitentiaria Roma 1[212] Jul. 1595 ad Personium de Anglo combusto in Campo Flore ob sanctissimum sacramentum pugno percussum dum in processione deferretur. Idem P. Coulinus fuit in Collegio Anglo Romae 13 Febr. et 8 Apr. 1596 ut apparet ex epistolis.[213]

---

209. The Latin phrasing, "rogatum fuisse ut se gereret negative," translates "had been asked to act negatively" but the sense seems to require an indirect question, "asked whether he had acted negatively."

210. Owen Lewis.

211. *A1* reads: "He should altogether overturn whatever has been done in England by men of my profession."

212. 1] *A*, obscure, possibly 8

213. Grene concludes: "Obiit in Anglia 16 Aug. 1617. Fuit in Missione annis 22 in Societate 32." (He died in England on 16 August 1617. He was 22 years on the mission, and 32 in the Society.)

Translation

Fr R. Cowling (mentioned above)[214] again wrote to Persons from the penitentiary in Rome on 1 July 1595,[215] about an Englishman who was burnt in the Campo de' Fiori for striking the most Holy Sacrament with his fist while it was being carried in procession.[216] The same Fr Couling was in the English college in Rome on 13 February and 8 April 1596, as appears from his letters.[217]

B282 From Claudio Acquaviva, Rome, 3 July 1595

SOURCE: ARSI, Baet. 3/I, 225.

NOTE: Acquaviva advises that Persons, once fully recovered, should return to Valladolid to deal with the inadequacies of the rector there. He reports on the splendid graduation ceremony of Gervase Pole (ca. 1572–1641), who joined the English college in Rome in August 1593, was ordained in Rome at the Church of Santa Mario in Aquiro in 1598, and entered the Society of Jesus in 1607 (Anstruther, 280; see also McCoog, *English and Welsh Jesuits*, 268–269).

P. Roberto Personio, Julio 3, en Sevilla.

Reçevi la de Vuestra Reverencia escrita a 15 de Mayo, con particular consuelo de entender que las cosas de ese Seminario[218] vayan en lo temporal y spiritual con tanto augmento. Lo de Valladolid,[219] creo que tambien proçede con buen passo, aunque el Rector no les dé tanta satisfaction, ni él está muy gustoso con el ofiçio, creo es porque deve de haver entendido el desgusto[220] que tienen con su govierno. Yo le escrivo que se acomode y siga en todo la direction de Vuestra Reverencia. Déle la que le pareçiere convenir, y quando eso no bastare se podra poner derecho.

Havrá ocho dias que sustentó sus conclusiones en el colegio Inglés un alumno llamado Polo, fueron muy solemnes, y por respecto del Señor Cardenal Farnesio muy autoriçadas con doce Cardenales, salieron muy bien, como más en particular escriviran a Vuestra Reverencia los padres de aquel Colegio.

Gracias a Dios que ha librado a Vuestra Reverencia de las quartanas,[221] quien destas le libró le sanará tambien de las reliquias dellas, que bien havrá menester la salud para lo

---

214. See Cowling to Persons, 29 December 1593 (B212).
215. Pope Pius V commissioned the Society of Jesus to provide confessors, in various languages, to St Peter's in 1569. Shortly thereafter Francis Borja established a community for the confessors, a "college." See Philip Caraman, "Ministerio de la Confesión," *DHCJ*, 1: 897–898.
216. A Londoner of about thirty years of age struck the host out of the hands of a priest in a procession; his hand and tongue were cut off, and he was burnt with fiery torches: Joseph Mendham, *The Life and Pontificate of Saint Pius V* (Duncan, 1832), 120.
217. Possibly letters written to Persons with these dates (B315, B321).
218. ese Seminario] *underlined R*
219. Lo de Valladolid] *underlined R*
220. desgusto] *R, final letters obscured in margin*
221. V. R. de las quartanas *underlined R*

mucho que ay que haçer, no sería malo dar una vista[222] a lo de Valladolid que con su presençia se podrian mejor asentar las cosas. En su etc.

Translation

To Fr Robert Persons in Seville, 3 July.

I have received your letter written on 15 May,[223] and was particularly comforted to know that the affairs of that seminary are proceeding with such great spiritual and temporal growth. I believe that the seminary at Valladolid is progressing at a similar pleasing rate: even if the rector does not give much satisfaction, nor is he very pleased with the job. I believe that it is because he must be aware of the dissatisfaction that you feel about his government. So I am writing to him that he should settle down and follow Your Reverence's guidance. Give him the direction you find most suitable, and if he does not measure up, you can put him right.

It is eight days since a student at the English college, called Pole, made his formal defence. It was very solemn, and on account of Cardinal Farnese,[224] highly approved by twelve cardinals, it went off very well, as the fathers at the college will write to Your Reverence in more detail.

Thank God He has freed you from your quartan fever; just as He has freed you of these, He will heal you of the traces of them, as you will need your health for all that needs to be done. It would not be a bad thing for you to visit Valladolid, so that you can help things along better with your presence. To your [holy prayers and sacrifices], etc.

B283 To Claudio Acquaviva, Seville, 10 July 1595

SOURCES:
ARSI, Hisp. 138, fols. 339–341, holograph;
ABSI, Coll P II 477 (a brief mention).
HICKS: 374–386, with English translation.

NOTE: Gradually a better understanding has developed between the English seminary in Seville and the local superior, chiefly thanks to Peralta's furnishing Bernal with an account of the finances of St Gregory's. But in Madrid, Creswell is resented as a burden by the rector of the Jesuit college, Juan García, and Persons would like him to be appointed procurator for English affairs, fully funded from the English seminaries. The death of the Bishop of Jaén, Francisco Sarmiento Mendoza, a major benefactor to the English seminaries, has been a blow. This increases anxiety about the seminary in Valladolid, where the new rector, Gonzalo del Río, is not expert in dealing with finances. There are also strong differences in opinion amongst the lecturers over modern Jesuit theologians such as Francisco Suárez (1548–1617) and Luis de Molina (1535–1600). The close relationship between del Río and Acosta, the

---

222. vista] R, probably in error for visita
223. B276.
224. Odoardo Farnese (1573–1626), second son of Alessandro Farnese, duke of Parma, was made cardinal in 1591.

local superior in Valladolid, has aggravated the tensions. Persons will be able to assess the situation better when he gets to Valladolid in person and restores friendship with Acosta.

In a postscript, Persons recommends that Garnet withdraw from England temporarily to regain his strength. Robert Jones and William Baldwin had recently arrived in England to reinforce the English mission (see McCoog, *Building the Faith of St Peter*, 190–192).

Muy Reverendo in Christo Padre nuestro
Pax Christi.

1. No dexo de cansar a Vuestra Paternidad casi por todos los ordenarios, pues nunca faltan negocios, y quanto más adelante anduviere esta obra de la reducion de Ynglaterra, y acircare más a su fin, tanto más creciendo tendra en que Vuestra Paternidad nos haga caridad ayudandonos y facilitando las difficultades, las quales por lo más no son tantas *a parte rei*, como de la parte de algunos que no entienden la importancia de la obra, y por consequens, no afficionandose demasiado (que cierto son bien pocos) tienen coraçon estrecho y medroso en lo que es subsidio temporal y limosnas, pareciendoles que todo lo que Dios reparte a los Seminarios, aunque no sea nada por su medio, ni toque de lexos a la Compañia, se quite todavia a ellos. Pero vanse ya desingañando y yran cada dia placiendo a Dios más y más, particularmente el buen Padre Vernal, Preposito de aqui (que cierto lo es, muy buen hombre y santo, *licet angusti pectoris*) despues que el Padre Peralta, rector deste Seminario, le ha dado en secreto y con toda confiança cuenta particular, digo,[225] al padre Preposito (el qual no quiso en manera alguna que sus temores se communicassen conmigo) de como esta obra se sustenta, y quan poco se saca de Sevilla para ella[226] respeto a lo que nos viene de Señores de fuera, y que esto mismo que Dios nos da en Sevilla, es casi todo de personas que nunca dan, ni davan a la Compania (los nombres escrivi a Vuestra Paternidad en la postrera mia). Está muy sussiegado y satisfecho el buen Padre y ha dicho que durante los dos años que le quedan de su prepositura, no hablará más palabra en ello, y ansi quedamos con grandissima paz y amor; y Domingo passado estubieron aqui conmigo en la casa nueva el dicho Padre Preposito y una doçena de otros Padres graves de la casa professa a hacer penetencia y veer la obra, y otros tantos del Collegio de Sant Hermengildo el Domingo antes, y todos aman y muestran mucha caridad a este Seminario y reciben dél muchissimo consuelo.

2. Esto pasa por acá, pero no sé si el Padre Juan Garcia, rector del Collegio de Madrid, se hara capaz tan facilmente, de que, el estar el Padre Cresuello por alla, no le quita a su Collegio limosnas, porque escrivenme Padres graves como el Padre Gil Gonçales, Bartolome Perez y Cabredo que los dias passados estuvo en Madrid con su provincial, y trató este punto largamente con el rector, que aunque sea muy buen hombre el rector,[227] toda via por no conoçer otra cosa que España, y no estender sus pensamientos más que al sustento de aquel su Collegio, no le entra facilmente consideracion de estrangeros, ni de effectos universales de reducion de reynos, y por esto se estrecha tanto con el Padre Cresuello y con su compañero, como en la passada escrivi

---

225. digo] *interlined with caret R*
226. para ella] *interlined with caret R*
227. el rector] *interlined with caret R*

a Vuestra Paternidad y otros pienso tan bien han escritto: y no querira él[228] que los Yngleses tubiesssen procurador en Madrid, lo qual toda via es tan justo y necessario (siendo el reyno en los terminos que se sabe, y quatro Seminarios grandes dependentes totalmente desta corte), que no se puede escusar: y es certissimo (como escrivi a Vuestra Paternidad la otra vez) que el Padre Cresuello en todo el tiempo que ha estado en Madrid, no nos ha procurado un real de limosna, que yo sepa, y nos ha costado más de ciento y cinquenta ducados por sus gastos, y los de su compañero, de manera que confio que Vuestra Paternidad ha de mandar assentar este punto una vez por siempre, que los Yngleses puedan tener su procurador en Madrid con su compañero como las provincias particulares de España tienen, pues es tan forçoso, y que estara sin gasto alguno del Collegio de la Compañia, y esto ha de constar por alguna carta mostrabile de Vuestra Paternidad al Padre Cresuello, para que no aya pleyto cada dia sobre ello. Los Padres Gil Gonzales y Avellanedo escrivieron cartas a Vuestra Paternidad algunos meses ha en esta materia, y las embiaron a mí, para que yo las encaminasse con las[229] mias, y no sé dónde ayan tardado en algun Collegio por el camino. Las embío agora *quia praestat sero quam nunquam*, aunque entiendo[230] que para Vuestra Paternidad no eran necessarias.

3. La muerte del buen obispo de Jaen nos ha affligido mucho por ser como era Padre tiernissimo destos Seminarios, que nos dava mil ducados de limosna muy bien pagados en cada un año, los quales perdemos agora totalmente, y aunque escriven que los Padres nuestros en Valladolid ayan publicado que nos dexó dos mil ducados en denero, entre entrambos Seminarios, toda via por acá no ay tal cosa aunque se aya hecho mucha diligencia para saberlo. El santo hombre no devia tener nada sobrado por causa de sus grandes y muchas limosnas. *Retribuatur ei in resurrectione iustorum.* Interim nosotros lloramos y meritamente, y aunque a entrambos Seminarios hace grandissima falta; toda via la siento más por el de Valladolid, tanto[231] por ser la limosna mayor que dava, que fueron 600 en cada un año, y por ser el sustento de aquel Seminario muy limitado, y de ciertas personas de las quales no si puede cobrar sin trabajo y cuydado, quanto por ser el nuevo rector poco cuydadoso y applicado en este particular, y gastador en cosas escusadas, como de alla me van escriviendo, no obstante todos los avisos y ruegos que[232] en esta materia le tengo escrito, de lo qual, y de una escarapela de nuevo que ha acontecida en aquel Collegio entre el rector y el Padre Antonio de Padilla, y los nuestros[233] Padres del Seminario sobre un acto de Theologia que defendio un sacerdote estudiante del dicho Seminario, por no cansar a Vuestra Paternidad, he embiado una relacion escrita de mano del Padre Gaspar Alonso, confessor, consultor y admonitor del rector, al Padre Antonio de Mendoça, como de persona, entre las demas que me han escrito la historia, muy indifferente y dispassionada, se yo no me engaño. La cosa fue harto pública como me escriven,

228. él] *interlined with caret* R
229. las] *interlined with caret* R
230. entiendo] *this ed.;* entendo R
231. tanto] *interlined with caret* R
232. que] *interlined with caret* R
233. nuestros] *interlined with caret* R

y de bien poca edificacion para los estudiantes de casa, y para los de fuera que la supieron. Lo que más me pesa es, que siendo de poco momento en sí, deve aver accrecentado la disunion en casa, y fatigado tan bien al rector, pues no me escrive palabra dello ni tan poco de algunas otras cosas graves y urgentes que avia de escrivir toccante a missiones y disposicion de sujetos, recien venidos, y otras cosas semejantes, en las quales calla todalmente. *Ex altera parte res summopere urgeat* que aya alguna resolucion.

4. El fundamento destas quebras en Valladolid, o grande parte dellas, suspecho que sea la estrecha amistad y dependencia que tiene el Padre Gonçalo del Rio (como de alla escriven) con el Padre Preposito Joseph de Acosta, el qual sé de cierto, que no está bien (en cosas a lo menos de letras) con el Padre Antonio de Padella ni con el Padre Rojas, ni tan poco con Suarez, Molina, y los demas theologos nuestros neotericos y moços como él me ha dicho algunas veçes. Y los años passados aviendo ganado para sí y para el Doctor Martinez a un prefecto de estudios en el Seminario Ynglés, que fue el Padre Gonçalo de Ormaz, que ponia mal a los estudiantes Yngleses con la doctrina destos sus maestros neotericos (aunque poco approcho con ellos), el Padre Acosta trató vehemente conmigo para que juntandome yo con él y con los otros dos[234] sustentassemos esta parte con Vuestra Paternidad, pero temendo yo el mal que sigueria de la disunion, lo disuadi al Padre y procuré luego[235] por via del Padre Cobos y otros amigos, que suavemente y con buen pretexto se quitasse el Padre Ormaz del Seminario, *et sic cessavit tempestas*. Pero agora teniendo el Padre Acosta el rector del Seminario a su devocion, como parece, y estando yo absente, no me maravillo, si ha siguido alguna turbacion en estas cosas, pero confio en nuestro Señor que en llegando yo por alla (que será con toda la brevidad que podre) se podran accomodar bien las cosas, porque no obstante que[236] entiendo que el Padre Acosta tubo alguna suspecha tan bien de mí en sus negocios passados,[237] pues me dixo dos o tres veçes ryendo, que yo tan bien le avia hincado la lance (que Vuestra Paternidad sabe lo contrario pues nunca me pusi en sus cosas del Padre más que avisar algunas veçes, y esto muy pocas, lo que entendia por acá ser de obligacion), toda via, pienso que está[238] ya satisfecho de la verdad, y que en llegando por alla seremos grandes amigos como antes, aunque es cosa certissima, y la prudencia de Vuestra Paternidad facilmente lo concibera, que si el rector de aquel Seminario no tiene el secreto de su casa para sí, y para los de su casa, si no lo communica y depende de qualquiera persona de fuera, nunca faltarán suspechas, quexas, y quebras, y para evitar estos inconvenientes, es menester primero grande amor a la obra, y despues prudencia, descretion, secreto, y mucha confiança y union con los que le assisten en la misma obra, y no sé quanto destas partes tiene el rector que agora está. Despues aver llegado por alla y visto las cosas, lo escrivire a Vuestra Paternidad, a quien nuestro Señor nos guarde por muchos años. En los santos sacrificios muy humilmente me encomiendo. Sevilla a 10 de Julio 1595.

        De Vuestra Paternidad Reverenda
            hijo y siervo endiño
                Roberto Personio.

234. y con los otros dos] *interlined with caret R*
235. luego] *interlined with caret R*
236. que] *interlined with caret R*
237. tan bien de mí en sus negocios passados] *interlined with caret R*
238. está] *interlined with caret R*

[PS] 5. Me ha parecido proponer a Vuestra Paternidad que pues el Padre Henrique Garneto ha estado mucho tiempo en Ynglaterra y ha travajado mucho y que el Consejo anda muy solícito en buscarlo, y ha escapado los dias passados casi milagrosamente, y que ya an llegado por alla juntos los Padres Balduino y Roberto Jones, si sería bien dar algun discanso al buen Padre, aunque él por su grande zelo de martirio, no lo pida, y que buelva por acá, pues yo podria procurarle por ventura buena commodidad de salir y venir acá, y sería su venida muy a proposito para informarnos de algunas particularidades que importarian, y luego podria passar a Roma a veerse con Vuestra Paternidad, si ansi Vuestra Paternidad mandare, y juntamente llevaria buenos avisos de cosas por acá. Si a Vuestra Paternidad contenta la proposicion se sirva darme comission e yo se lo escrivire por via segura y con cifra que con él tengo, y no conviene que salga de alla sin algunos avisos y estruciones de acá, ni combiene que él lo communique con persona de alla, si no despues de estar fuera. El venir acá por via de Yrlanda es el más seguro, aunque yo tengo otra via tan bien. Combiene que quede muy secreto por aý, lo que Vuestra Paternidad resolviere en este caso. El mismo padre[239] sabra mejor a quien de la Compañia aya de dexar por superior en su lugar, si Vuestra Paternidad le manda venir, pues él tiene probado la virtud de cada un. Vuestra Paternidad me hara caridad mandar avisar de su voluntad en este negocio, pues conforme a la resolucion de Vuestra Paternidad yre yo tan bien disponiendo de cosas por acá.

[*Addressed:*] Al muy Reverendo en Christo Padre nuestro el Padre Claudio Aquaviva preposito General [de] la Compagna de Jesus en Roma.

[*Endorsed:*] Sevilla 95. P. Roberto Personio. Julio 10. [*with summary of contents*]

Translation

Our Very Reverend Rather in Christ
The peace of Christ.

1. I do not cease to weary Your Paternity by nearly every post, because business is ceaseless; and the more this work of the conversion of England goes forward and approaches completion, the more will it provide increasing opportunities for Your Paternity to do us kindness by helping us and smoothing over our difficulties. These arise for the most part not so much *from the work itself* as from certain individuals who do not understand the importance of the work, and consequently are not too well disposed to it (but assuredly these are very few) and so are mean-spirited and timorous when it comes to our temporal support and alms. They think that everything that God bestows on the seminaries, though it is in no way their own doing and does not affect the Society at all, nevertheless takes something away from them. But they are already beginning to be undeceived – increasingly so, every day, please God; more especially good Fr Bernal,[240] the superior here (who is without doubt a good and holy man, *although somewhat ungenerous*) now that Fr Peralta, the rector of this seminary, has given him, secretly and absolutely in confidence, an exact account – to the superior, that is (and the latter was extremely anxious that I should not be told of his misgivings) – of the way this work is supported, and

---

239. padre] *interlined with caret* R
240. Pedro Bernal, superior of the Jesuits in Seville.

has shown him how little is raised for it in Seville, compared to what comes to us from gentlemen elsewhere; and that even what God gives us in Seville comes almost entirely from persons who never give and never have given to the Society. Their names I gave Your Paternity in my last letter.[241] The good father is now very much relieved and satisfied, and he has stated that during his remaining two years as superior he will not say another word on that subject. And so, we are going to be in a state of very great peace and charity. Last Sunday the father superior and a dozen other grave fathers of the professed house were here with me in the new house, to do penance and see the work; and with as many more from the college of St Hermenegild[242] on the Sunday before that. They all love the seminary and are showing it great kindness, and receive very great consolation from it.

2. That is how things are here; but I do not know whether Fr Juan García, rector of the college of Madrid, will be so easy to convince that Fr Creswell's being stationed there will not deprive his college of alms. For I hear from some grave fathers, such as Frs Gil González, Bartolomé Pérez, and Cabredo, that he was in Madrid a few days ago with his provincial,[243] who discussed the matter at length with the rector. And although the rector is a very good man, yet, as he has no experience except in Spain and his outlook is limited to the upkeep of that college of his, he does not easily take foreigners into consideration, or the wider effects of the conversion of kingdoms; and it is this which makes him so narrow-minded in regard to Fr Creswell and his companion, as I told Your Paternity in my last letter, and others also I think have written to this effect. He would not be in favour of the English having a procurator in Madrid, even though this is so just and necessary (the kingdom being in the condition you know and four large seminaries being entirely dependent on this court) that it cannot be dispensed with. And it is an absolute fact, as I told Your Paternity once before, that Fr Creswell has not obtained one real in alms for us, as far as I know, in all the time that he has been in Madrid, and he has cost us more than one hundred and fifty ducats for his expenses and those of his companion. Consequently, I trust Your Paternity will have this point settled once for all: that the English can have their procurator in Madrid, with a companion of his own, just like the individual provinces of Spain, for this is so necessary; and that it is to be without any expense to the college of the Society.[244] This should be set down in some sort of open letter from Your Paternity to Fr Creswell, to avoid wrangling over the matter every day. Fr Gil González and Fr Avellaneda wrote letters to Your Paternity on this subject some months ago and sent them to me to enclose with mine; they must have been delayed, in one of the colleges on the way, I suppose. I am sending them now *because it is better late than never*; although I know that, as far as Your Paternity is concerned, they were not necessary.

3. The death of the good bishop of Jaén has caused us much grief on account of his being as it were a most fond father to these seminaries; for he used to give us a thousand

---

241. 12 June (B279).

242. The Spanish Jesuit college in Seville, named in honour of the local saint and martyr St Hermenegild (Murphy, 4).

243. This appears to refer to a discussion between Creswell and García's superior, Francisco de Porres, provincial of Toledo.

244. That is, the Spanish Jesuit college in Madrid.

ducats in alms, paid very punctually every year. Now we shall lose this altogether; and though they write that our fathers in Valladolid have announced that he left us two thousand ducats in cash, between the two seminaries, yet nothing is known of it here, despite the great pains we have taken to find out. The holy man could not have had much left, given the extent of his almsgiving. *May he be rewarded at the resurrection of the just.* In the meantime we who are left weep, and with reason. Although both seminaries have sustained very great loss, yet I am more concerned for that of Valladolid, not only because the alms he gave it was larger, amounting to 600 a year, and because the support given to that seminary is very limited and derived from certain individuals from whom payment cannot be obtained without trouble and anxiety, but also because the new rector is not very thrifty, and pays little attention to this aspect of affairs. He is prodigal in superfluities (so they keep writing to me from there), despite all the representations and requests I have sent him on this subject. I do not want to weary Your Paternity about this matter, and also about a recent fracas which has taken place in that college between the rector and Fr Antonio de Padilla[245] and our fathers in the seminary over a thesis in theology which was defended by a student priest of that seminary. So I have sent a report from the pen of Fr Gaspar Alonso, the confessor, and a consultor and admonitor of the rector, to Fr Antonio de Mendoza,[246] as from an individual who, amongst all the rest who have written me an account of the affair, stands out as being very impartial and unprejudiced, if I am not mistaken. The incident took place somewhat publicly, as they inform me, and was not very edifying to the students in the house, or to those people outside who learned about it. What distresses me most is that, though the thing has slight importance in itself, it must have increased the tension in the house, and worn out the rector too, for he has not written a word to me about it nor about some other grave and urgent matters which he should have broached, concerning the missions, the posting of members, the recent arrivals, and other similar matters; about these he is completely silent. *By reason of this second circumstance, the affair would seem to have urgent need* of some solution.

4. The root cause of these outbreaks at Valladolid, or of a great many of them, I suspect to be Fr Gonzalo del Río's close friendship with the father superior, José de Acosta, and the deference he pays to him (as they write from there). I know also for a fact that the latter is not in agreement (in matters of scholarship at any rate) with Fr Antonio de Padilla or with Fr Rojas,[247] nor for that matter with Suárez, Molina, and our other modern young theologians, as he has told me several times. And having in past years won over to his side, along with Dr Martínez, a prefect of studies in the English seminary, namely Fr González de Ormaz, who took a dim view of the English students' being taught the doctrine held by their masters of the modern school (though I am far from associating myself with their views), Fr Acosta tried very hard to get me to join with him and the other two in upholding this attitude with Your Paternity. But, as I was afraid that harm would result from the estrangement this would cause, I dissuaded

245. Antonio de Padilla (rector), Manuel de Rojas, Cristóbal de los Cobos, and Martínez, mentioned below, were on the teaching staff of the Spanish Jesuit college of St Hermenegild. See Persons to Acquaviva, 12 July 1594 (B236).
246. Acquaviva's assistant for Spain.
247. Manuel de Rojas, a lecturer at St Hermenegild.

the father from that course, and in due course, through Fr Cobos and other friends, I managed to have Fr Ormaz removed from the seminary, kindly and with a good pretext; *and so the storm ceased.* But now that Fr Acosta has the rector of the seminary as his devoted follower,[248] as it seems, and I myself being away, I am not surprised that some trouble has ensued in these matters. But I trust in our Lord that when I arrive there (which will be as soon as I possibly can) it will be possible to settle matters satisfactorily; for, notwithstanding my awareness that Fr Acosta was a bit suspicious about me too, in connection with his past dealings – since he said to me two or three times with a smile that I also had had my knife in him (which Your Paternity knows is quite the contrary, for I never interfered with the father's business, except to report occasionally, and that very seldom, what I understood here to be my duty), I think nevertheless that he is now convinced of the truth, and that when I get there we shall be good friends as we were before. All the same, it is a matter of certainty – and Your Paternity in your prudence will be quick to realize it – that, if the rector of that seminary does not keep the affairs of his house secret, for his own sake and that of its inmates, but communicates them to some other person outside and defers to him, there will be no end to suspicion, complaints, and quarrels. To avoid these inconveniences there is need first of all for a great love for the work, and then prudence, discretion, reticence, and great confidence in and concord with those who are assisting him in the same work. I do not know how far the present rector has these qualities. After I have arrived there and looked into things, I will write to Your Paternity about it. And may our Lord preserve you to us for many years. To your holy sacrifices I commend myself very humbly. Seville, 10 July 1595.

    Your Paternity's
        unworthy son and servant
            Robert Persons.

[PS] 5. I have thought it well to suggest to Your Paternity that, as Fr Henry Garnet has been in England a long time and has laboured very hard, and as the Council is taking great pains to search for him, and he escaped a few days ago almost miraculously, and since Fr Baldwin and Fr Jones have arrived there together, it would be good to give the good father a break for a time – even though he is so zealous for martyrdom that he does not ask for it himself – and that he come back this way, since I could possibly find him a good means of getting out of the country and coming here. His coming would be very opportune because he could give us information on any particular points that might be necessary. In due course he could go on to Rome and have an interview with Your Paternity, if you should so command, and at the same time he could take some useful information about matters here. If my proposal finds favour with Your Paternity, please give me authority, and I will write to him by a safe route and in the cipher that I use with him. It would not be appropriate for him to leave there without some information and instructions from here, and he ought not to tell anybody there about it, until after he is out of the country. The safest way to come here is by Ireland, although I have another route available as well. Whatever Your Paternity decides about this should be kept very secret in

---

248. Hicks translates, "in his pocket."

Rome. The father himself will know better who of the Society should be left as superior in his place, if Your Paternity orders him to come, because he has proved the virtue of each one of them. Please would Your Paternity have the goodness to let me know what your pleasure is in this matter, for in accordance with Your Paternity's decision I also shall proceed to make arrangements here.

B284 To Claudio Acquaviva, Seville, 15 July 1595

SOURCE: Acquaviva to Persons, 25 September 1595 (B296).
NOTE: Either in this or his next letter to the general, Persons mentioned a church building project.

B285 From Claudio Acquaviva, Rome, 31 July 1595

SOURCE: ARSI, Baet. 3/I, 228–229, 231.
NOTE: Acquaviva supports Persons in his struggle with local Jesuits, who have accused him of rival alms-seeking, and in his determination to free Creswell from the control of the rector at Madrid, Juan García.

P. Roberto Personio, Sevilla, Julio 31.

Reçevi la de Vuestra Reverencia de 12 de Junio, y pesame que no les ayan salido las esperanças que tenian en la venida de la flota, pero Vuestra Reverencia tiene ya suficientes prendas para esperar del Señor que no les faltará en lo porvenir, pues les ha sido tan favorable en lo passado:[249] y no les dé pena la que piensa tienen algunos de los nuestros por que les impiden las limosnas, porque estos son unos zelos dificiles de remediar; bastará dar les satisfaction de los particulares que ocurrieren, como veo que lo hacen, en lo demas no ay que tener cuydado.

Vuestra Reverencia dice muy bien que es necessario tenga el Padre Cresuelo su compañero[250] desocupado, para no perder ocasion ninguna en los negocios que entre manus tiene. Yo lo escrivo al Rector de Madrid, y ansi se hara. Vuestra Reverencia vea qué compañero será a proposito para ayudar al Padre porque segun entiendo no es suficiente el que tiene, ni siendo tan noviçio pareçe conveniente meterle en tanto trasiego de negocios. Embiele el que le pareçiere más conveniente que ese le ayudará.

Vuestra Reverencia dé mis encomiendas al Padre Francisco de Peralta y le diga recivi su carta en respuesta de la qual tenga ésta por propria, y Vuestra Reverencia se la lea, porque en la suya me habla destas mesmas cosas y que en el modo que usa de dar fee de las missas que dicen los alumnos, no veo[251] inconveniente, puede proseguir en caso que no se contenten sus partes con firma de otro que de Rector. Ens.

---

249. pues les ha sido tan favorable en lo passado] *underlined R*
250. tenga el Padre Cresuelo su compañero] *underlined R*
251. y que en el modo ... no veo] *supplied in margin R, suggesting a line was missed in the copying*

[*A later addition:*]²⁵²
P. Roberto Personio, 31 de Julio.

Por entender que los Padres del Collegio Inglés informarán a Vuestra Reverencia más por menudo la poca quietud que algunos de los Alumnos tienen y han communicado a los demas, no sere²⁵³ yo largo en esto. Solo digo que como hombre que ha dias que prevee estas cosas y tiene portion de otras tales, no tome pena, porque ni de mi parte se faltará en tal con ellos lo que hasta ahora se ha hecho, ni de poner el remedio que pide la presente ocasion, y por ventura Dios le ha permitido para que se ponga el remedio de veras no solo para ahora sino para adelante. El Señor Cardinal Caetano y yo estuvimos con su santidad, él nos remitio el negocio. Procuraremos con la posible suavidad acabarle; aunque nos será forzoso despidir algunos del Collegio. El Señor les dé la luz que han menester para que conozcan su yerro. En las oraciones &c.

Translation

To Fr Robert Persons in Seville, 31 July.

I have received Your Reverence's letter of 12 June, and I am sorry that your hopes have been disappointed about the arrival of the fleet,²⁵⁴ but Your Reverence has already had enough signs to be able to trust in our Lord, who will not fail you in the future, as he has been so gracious in the past; and please do not grieve over those who hold some of Ours responsible for impeding alms, because these are jealousies difficult to remedy. It is enough to give them a satisfactory explanation of what happens in particular, as I see is being done, and for the rest there is no need to be anxious.

Your Reverence says very truly that it is necessary for Fr Creswell to keep his companion²⁵⁵ free from entanglements, so as not to lose any opportunity for any business that comes to hand. I have written accordingly to the rector at Madrid, and it will be done accordingly. Please would Your Reverence see to it that the companion is suitable to assist the father, because, as I understand, the one he keeps is inadequate, given that it seems inappropriate to engage such a novice in such great work of business; please send him someone who seems more suitable to help him.

Would Your Reverence please commend me to Fr Francisco de Peralta and tell him that I have received his letter; he may take this present letter as a reply to his. Your Reverence may read it to him, because in his he relates the same things. As for the method he uses to issue a certificate for the masses said by the students,²⁵⁶ it is not at all inappropriate: he may continue with the practice, in case the parties concerned are not satisfied with someone else's signature, other than the rector's. To your [holy prayers and sacrifices] ...

252. A later hand has annotated in the margin (*R*): "Turbae Col. Angl. in urbe" (Disturbances in the English college, Rome).

253. no sere] *this ed.; R obscure*

254. The diminishment of the treasure fleet affected the level of alms-giving to the college in Seville (see Persons's letter of 12 June, B279).

255. I.e., his *socius*.

256. See Persons's letter to Méndez, 20 May 1595 (B277).

[*A later addition:*]
To Fr Robert Persons, 31 July.

I will not go into the question of the restlessness which some of the students feel and have communicated to the others, on the understanding the fathers of the English college will report it to Your Reverence in more detail. I will only say that you, as a man who has foreseen these things for days and has experience in others like it, should not feel any compunction, because for my part I will not fail to deal with them as the situation has been handled in the past, nor to apply the remedy which this present occasion requires. Perhaps God has allowed this in order to find a remedy, not just for now but for the future. The Lord Cardinal Caetani[257] and I were with His Holiness; he put the business in our hands. We will try to proceed with all possible gentleness, although we shall be forced to expel some from the college. May the Lord give them what they need so that they will learn their mistake. To your prayers, etc.

B286 To Claudio Acquaviva, Seville, 7 August 1595

SOURCE: Acquaviva to Persons, 25 September 1595 (B294).
NOTE: This is the second letter referred to by the general, who is disappointed that Persons has said nothing about the delinquent Fr Simon Swinburne.

B287 To Claudio Acquaviva, Madrid, 18 August 1595

SOURCE: Acquaviva to Persons, 23 October 1595 (B296).
NOTE: Persons had travelled to Madrid to confer with the king, and evidently intended to continue to Valladolid to try to deal with the problem of the rector there. It seems that instead he returned to Seville in late September.

B288 From Claudio Acquaviva, Rome, 28 August 1595

SOURCE: ARSI, Baet. 3/I, 233.
NOTE: Acquaviva promises Persons support in his proposed visit to Valladolid to deal with the problems at the college, especially the attitude of the rector. The visitor, García de Alarcón, can be relied on to assist where necessary.

P. Roberto Personio, Sevilla, 28 de Agosto.
Pues Vuestra Reverencia como me diçe en la de 10 de Julio piensa ir a Valladolid[258] presto podra entonçes con su presençia, y con la ayuda del Padre Garça que estara alli, acomodar las cosas de aquel seminario, quando segun entiendo requieran que Vuestra Reverencia las dé una vista y ponga en buen orden; y si le pareçiere que se mude el Rector lo podra haçer, que ya yo se lo he escrito al Provincial y hallandose alli el padre Garçia

---

257. Enrico Caetani (1550–1599), cardinal protector of England, with special oversight of the English college.
258. piensa ir a Valladolid] *underlined* R

no será necessaria más diligencia de mi parte, pues él como Vuestra Reverencia sabe ama la nacion y sus cosas, y las ayudará[259] en lo que pudiere.

En lo de aquel Padre que Vuestra Reverencia desea salga de donde está para que repare[260] un poco, y supla en su lugar otro de los que han ido, no sé quánto esto convenga hasta que los que de nuevo han entrado o alguno dellos tenga la prática necessaria, la qual hasta aora no tienen, creo que será mejor esperar algunos meses. En los &c.

Translation

To Fr Robert Persons in Seville, 28 August.

Since Your Reverence, as you tell me in yours of 10 July, is planning to go to Valladolid soon, you will then be able, with your presence and the help of Fr García, who will be there, to settle the affairs of that college, if (as I understand) it should become necessary that Your Reverence review them and put them in good order. If you think it best to change the rector, you can do that; I have already written about it to the provincial, and with Fr García being there it will not be necessary for me to take any further action, since, as Your Reverence knows, he loves the nation and its affairs, and will assist with them as far as he can.

With regard to that father whom Your Reverence wishes to extract from his present location to relieve him so that he can recover,[261] and to put in his place another of those who have gone there, I do not think this will be very appropriate until those who have newly entered, or one of them, has the practical experience – which they do not yet have, but I believe there will be more to hope for in a few months. To your [holy prayers and sacrifices], etc.

B289 To Claudio Acquaviva, Madrid, 5 September 1595

SOURCE: Acquaviva to Persons, 23 October (B296).
NOTE: There is no clear indication, from Acquaviva's reply, of the topic of this letter.

B290 To Anthony Standen, Madrid, 8 September 1595

SOURCE: ABSI, Coll P I 310–311, Grene's summary and partial transcript.
HICKS: 387–389.
NOTE: Sir Anthony Standen (ca. 1548–ca. 1615) was a Catholic exile and informer who was at this time in the service of the earl of Essex (see Paul E.J. Hammer, *ODNB*). The letter may indicate that Standen tried to draw Persons out on the succession, following the scandal of the publication of *Conference about the Next Succession*, dedicated to Essex. Copies of the book reached the English court in May 1595. McCoog, *Building the Faith of St Peter*, 258 n174, invites further reflection on Persons's correspondence with Standen; see also Edwards, 182.

259. ayudará] *this ed.*; ayadara R
260. repare] *this ed.*; R *defective*
261. Probably a reference to Garnet (see the postscript of Persons's letter to Acquaviva, 10 July, B283).

September 8 1595, from Madrid to Mr Standen.

He treateth of the many competitors to the Crowne of England & of great danger of civill warrs therefore. The letter containes two sheetes of paper; most part of the matter is more largely treated in the book of Dolman concerning Succession. He bringeth very many reasons to shew how improbable it seemeth that the king of Scotland wil be ever admitted to the crowne of England and that he wil finde more difficulty herein then any one of all the other competitors: first in regard of his tytle which was cut-off in his mother by the oath and statute of association — if she were rightly executed for the crime pretended, & if that Parliament had authority to determine in that matter, as few I think will deny. 2nd in regard of his religion (Puritanisme). 3rd of his little power. 4th in regard that few either Scotts, English, Danes or others desire the union of both kingdomes but have great cause to abhorre it. Finally in regard that the puritan faction in England seemeth wholy addicted to Huntington: the protestant either to Hartford or the others in England. The Catholick though it be not yet known on whome he maketh head since the death of the Scottish Queene, yet certaine it is that it can not be to her sonne in respect of his religion &c.

haec omnia fuse Personius et deinde subdit:[262]

Finally his extreme ingrate and unnaturall dealing towards his mother and such a mother, as she was to him, by whome he receaved all title of dignity that he hath or pretendeth (which dealing was no better then betraying her & consenting to her death, as abroade in the world it is commonly believed), maketh every man of good nature, of what religion so ever he be, to have aversion to be under his government. For what may others expect at his hands who to her that bare him & made him a king was so unkynde? And that there is good groundes to believe this there are alleaged 3 arguments among other that are very pregnant in all mens sight: first the small demonstration he hath made since of his greef & displeasure for that fact. 2nd the open confession of his Embassador the master of Gray[263] that is evidently known to have betrayed her in England and layeth for his excuse to all his friends that he did nothing in that action without expresse order and consent of the King: which thing is the more easily believed for that the very day, when the niewes of his mothers slaughter came into Scotland (and this is the 3rd argument) he shutt himself up into a chamber (as those that were present of his own nation do report) together with his Chancelor the greatest enemy his mother had in all Scotland and there passed the day in such laughter for the prosperous atchieving of this treachery as the chancellor and some other of his faction were faine to put him in mynde to forbeare so great demonstration of joy and somewhat better to dissemble the matter. All which being well knowen in England, & experience being had of this mans nature, not only in the overthrow of his mother, but alsoe before in the death of the Earle of Murton[264] and some others of his friends of his own religion, whom cunningly he sent to the slaughter, when yet he was but a little lyon, and began but to learne to catch his prey, I doubt not

262. "All these things Persons [wrote] copiously, and then added at the end ... ." The rest of the letter is in Persons's own words, with omissions marked.

263. Patrick Gray, sixth Lord Gray (died 1612); see vol. 1, *passim*.

264. James Douglas (ca. 1516–1581), fourth earl of Morton, regent of Scotland.

but as well those of the councell of England, howsoever now they give him fayre words, and much more all English pretenders to the crowne wil look well about them, before they putt him upon their heads, especially seeing his chief force and confidence of government must be (as before is touched and reason maketh it plaine) by the Scotts and Danes of whose good will & usage towards the English, each man can imagin what may be expected &c. &c. ——]

Post multa de iure successionis in genere et in particulari iterum subjungit:[265]
But howsoever these matters of tytles goe, which God only must determine — my conclusion shal be to your whole letter: that among such variety and perplexity of pretenders as now are for that crowne, it is enough for a Catholick sober man to have any prince admitted by the body of his realme and allowed by the authority of Gods Catholik Church, and that will defende the religion of his old noble ancesters, and without this nothing is sufficient nor should any reason in the world move us to yield him favour or obedience, though he were our father, son, or brother &c. ——— And soe — I committ you to Gods holy protection. From the place you know, the 8 September 1595.

B291 To Claudio Acquaviva, Madrid or Seville, 13 September 1595

SOURCE: Acquaviva to Persons, 15 January (B308).
NOTE: Persons, who may already have been back in Seville, recommended replacing del Río at Valladolid, preferably with Cabredo.

B292 From John Gerard, London, n.d. [September 1595]

SOURCE: Persons to Creswell, 28 October (B299).
NOTE: A new arrival at the English college at Seville brought notes for Persons from various prisons in London. Gerard had been captured in Holborn on 23 April 1594; at first, he was confined in the Counter in the Poultry, then transferred to the Clink, where he set up a chapel and conducted spiritual direction. He remained there until moved to the Tower in April 1597.

B293 To Philip II, Seville, September/October, 1595

SOURCE: AGS, Est. Leg. 2851, holograph fair copy.
HICKS: 390–393, with notes but no translation.
NOTE: On his return to Seville, following an audience with the king, Persons elaborated some ideas for invasion, urging action in the winter and allowing for a parliament of English Catholics to decide on a successor to Elizabeth. The king should take advantage of the absence of Drake and Hawkins, who had sailed from Plymouth for the West Indies on 24 August: this letter must therefore have been written towards the end of September at the earliest. The

---

265. "Following much material about the right of succession in general and in particular, he once again added ... ."

Drake/Hawkins expedition had been delayed precisely because of fears that this might weaken England's defences (see Persons to Méndez, 20 May 1595, B277, postscript.) Many of the points made here were later incorporated into memorials prepared for the king and his council the following year (see Persons to Idiáquez, 2 September 1596, B342). The letter is summarized by Edwards, 182–183, who comments, "Persons could only have supported [the scheme] as a desperation measure, being keenly aware that every week's delay might mean another martyr."

The recommendation of Milford Haven (in Pembrokeshire, Wales) as a likely place for the Spanish armada to make land may derive from documents, including maps, given to Persons in 1594 by Jonas Jones on behalf of N. Lambert, a mariner based in Cádiz (Dominguez, *Radicals in Exile*, 151).

+

Señor.

Aunque Vuestra Magestad me hiço merced de una benigna y larga audiencia, no pudi tocar todos los punctos que me se ofrecian acerca un negocio tan grave, como se trató, y ansi vengo a haçer esta breve recapitulacion por escrito, suplicando a Vuestra Magestad sea servido pasarla por sus ojos, pues importa mucho a su Real servicio.

1. Circumstancias del tiempo presente.

1. Juan Hauquins y Francisco Draque, dos de los mejores Capitanes por mar que la Reyna tiene, estan absentes, y Juan Nores que es el principal por tierra está embarçado en Irlanda, y con estos estan los mejores soldados, y marineros del Reyno, fuera, y muchos navios.

2. Irlanda y Escocia estan rebueltos, y Inglaterra con las parcialidades y las demas disposiciones que Vuestra Magestad sabe. Estas conjunturas no pueden durar mucho, sy Vuestra Magestad no se sirve dellas luego, porque la rebuelta de Irlanda se allanará como las passadas, y los Escoceses bolveran a su liga de Francia, teniendo ya Vandoma por Catholico, y los humores de los Condes de Inglaterra mudarse han con dilaciones.

3. Vandoma no puede impedir ny estorbar por aora, por no estar aún asentado y bien fortificado en su Reyno lo que será despues.

4. Vuestra Magestad una vez tiene la ventaja de estar armado en Flandres por tierra, y en España por mar, no teniendo la Reyna preparacion alguna de momento: Sy esta ocasion se dexar passar, no bolvera tam presto.

5. Está ya hecho grande parte del gasto de la jornada, y sin más costa, se puede agora acabar todo de una vez. Sy se dilata vendran nuebos embaraços, y quedará gastado el denero sin probecho. Y cada año naceran nuebos Draques, Corsarios y enemigos destos Reynos.

2. El tiempo y la forma.

1. El tiempo proprio de hacer el efecto, sería por todo este inbierno, quando la Reyna no nos aguarda, y la forma sería con un exército moderado – más presto que con una machina grande que tiene muchos inconvenientes.

2. El Abuelo desta Reyna, el Rey Enrique 7°, siendo Conde de Richmondia, entró en tiempo comodo con menos de dos mil franceses, y ganó el Reyno al Rey Ricardo 3°, y lo

mismo hiço antes dél Edouardo 4°, Duque de Yorque, con 4000 flamencos, y lo mismo antes dél, su Capitan Ricardo Conde de Salisbury, y le quitó el Reyno con 3000 soldados franceses, y lo mismo hiço antes destos Enrique 4°, Duque de Lancastre, con menos de 1500 soldados Bretones, y ninguno destos tubo tanta parcialidad dentro del Reyno, como nosotros al presente tenemos.

3. De quatro partes, van las tres en el tiempo y modo, pues mucho más haran diez[266] a tiempo comodo, que no quarenta en otro tiempo, quando se hiciese a la descubierta. Y por esto summamente convendria dar priessa antes que Draque se buelva de las Indias, y que la Reyna se pudiese armar.

3. De los Puertos para entrar.

1. Dos maneras ay para entrar immediatamente a Inglaterra. La una yrse a desembarcar en las Dunas de la provincia de Kent, y de alla yr drecho[267] a Londres, el qual camino se tiene por más breve, pero tiene más peligro por aver de passar grande parte del Estrecho con la armada y despues el Rio de Londres con el Exército.

2. Otro camino ay por el Puerto de Milford, por donde entró y ganó el Reyno Henrique 7°, y se tiene por mucho más siguro, y el mejor de todos.

3. Sy no quisieramos entrar primero a Inglaterra, ay los puertos de Escocia que los Cavalleros Escoceses ofrecieron, aunque son lexos y menos a proposito por causa de la sterilidad de la tierra por la qual se ha de passar para entrar despues a Inglaterra, y ansi más ha de servir Escocia por diversion entre sý mismos, que no para entrada de nuestro exército.

4. Fuera destos, ay los puertos de Irlanda que son muy buenos y cerca de España, y la tierra abundante de carne y pan. Y toda la gente enemiga a los Ingleses, y el passaje despues muy facil a diversas partes de Inglaterra y Escocia, y asy desta entrada, o del puerto del Milford, no ay difficultad ninguna, y al tiempo de la execucion, se podra escojer lo que paresciera más a proposito.

4. Del General.

Muchissimo va en esta jornada, qual sea la persona del general, pues el buen sucesso dependera, en grande parte de las voluntades ajenas y de los que le an de seguir, y ansi importa mucho que sea hombre piadoso, y lo haga por Dios, y que tenga valor, y ciencia en la guerra y particular noticia de las cosas de Inglaterra, y opinion y reputacion con la Nacion. Desta suerte quien sea, la prudencia de Vuestra Magestad sabe y lo mirará mejor que nadie. Yo veo el número reducido a tan pocos que sy ay uno que tenga estas partes, no hallo facilmente otro. Dios guiará a Vuestra Magestad en esta elecion como en todo lo demas.

266. diez] *this ed.*; deiz S
267. *sic* S

5. Del establecimiento de la Corona y Sucesion.

1. Lo que dixi a Vuestra Magestad del comun consentimiento de todos los Catholicos de remittir a Vuestra Magestad el nombrar y hacer Rey y Reyna de Inglaterra libremente, no obstante las proposiciones de los Condes, es tan cierto que yo me atrevo de assigurarlo, pues conosco el ánimo de las Cabeças principales, en este punto. Y todos los sacerdotes de los seminarios van a una en ello, por ser cosa en que ha de estribar toda la securidad de la Religion Catholica y buena reformacion de Inglaterra. Y por esto el buen Cardenal Alano quando vivia, y Francisco Inglefild y yo, y todos nuestros amigos, hemos tomado esto siempre por el punto principal adonde encaminar la proa de toda nuestra navigacion, y es cosa sin duda entre los Catholicos.

2. Solamente ay contra esto una cierta parcialidad, de Carlos Pajeto, Thomas Morgan y Thomas Throcmorton (como sabe ya Don Juan de Idiaquez), los quales por muchos años, an ydo recojendo los malcontentos que pudieron de la nacion Inglesa, contra la nacion Española, y contra las actiones del Cardinal Alano y de los seminarios. Tienen por cabeça al opispo de Cassano y por agente en Roma al dicho Throcmorton, el qual siendo sagaz procuró de ganar al Duque de Feria, y por su medio entraron algo, el Obispo de Cassano y él, con el Duque de Sesa. Y luego en muriendo el Cardinal Alano, revolvieron todo el seminario Inglés y alborotaron los estudiantes contra sus superiores los padres de la Compañia y el Cardinal Caetano su Protector, y les imprimieron humores muy malos contra esto que tratamos, y contra el servicio de Vuestra Magestad. Convendria atajar esta facion y parcialidad, y que Throcmorton no estubiese en Roma ny Pajeto en Flandres syno en Napoles o Sicilia, porque bien les conoce el Conde de Olivares.

3. El modo de asentar esto de la sucesion con suavidad y seguridad, sería que el General entrando y començando la guerra, no hablase de otra cosa syno de la restitucion de la Religion Catholica. Y dandole Dios la victoria, luego juntase los principales Catholicos en forma de Parliamento repentino, como muchas vezes se a hecho en casos semejantes, y se determinase, que por quanto ay tantas pretensiones a la sucesion, y tantos pretensores como en el libro nuebo publicado se veen, y que entre otros Vuestra Magestad y el Principe de España por la linea de Portugal y la señora Infanta por la linea de Bretaña tienen sus derechos muy claros. Por tanto para evitar dissensiones y guerras, y para agradecer el beneficio recebido de la reducion por mano de Vuestra Magestad remiten a Vuestra Magestad el señalarles Rey y Reyna, y establecerles la sucesion, y más de nombrar y señalar los primeros Obispos, conforme al previlegio de los Reyes de Inglaterra, para que se haga un Parliamento pleno para confirmar todo esto. Y entonces señalando Vuestra Magestad personas confidentes por obispos, segun la lista que dellos se podra dar, todo se hara a gusto de Vuestra Magestad y con suavidad, por ser los Obispos la parte más principal del Parliamento y que menean a los demas.

4. Se puede considerar tan bien en esta materia, sy será mejor llevar ya el consentimiento de Su Santidad y de Vuestra Magestad remetido al General de la jornada o al Archiduque Cardinal en Flandres, para nombrar y aprovar a estos Obispos luego despues de la victoria, y con esto assentar las cosas con brevidad, sin aguardar Bulas de Roma, las quales podran sacar despues de asentadas las cosas en Inglaterra, y importará mucho juntar luego y authorizar a este primero Parliamento.

6. De algunas prevenciones importantes.

1. La primera y principal parece que sería tener desde luego armadas algunas de aquellas naves que ay en Flandres, y que començacen[268] a haçer corerias para que a su tiempo con mayor dissimulacion passasen a Escocia los Condes Barones y Cavalleros Escoceses que estan desterrados, y juntamente los Ingleses con ellos, como son el Conde de Vestmerland y el Baron Dacres que tienen sus estados en Inglaterra, muy juntos a Escocia, y con su venida se levantaria mucha gente.

2. Tambien podria yr con estos el Coronel Guilielmo Estanleyo, su regimento de soldados, sy asy pareciere a Vuestra Magestad, o sy no, podria con dos o tres navios llegar a Irlanda, o al Puerto de Milford donde estubiera nuestra armada. Pero para que hiciese major servicio a Vuestra Magestad, y truxesse muchos otros a lo mismo, importaria, que Vuestra Magestad le honrasse con la encomienda que tubo Monseñor de la Mota, o otra, como algunas vecez se a suplicado a Vuestra Magestad.

3. A estos Cavalleros tornados a Escocia y llevantados, podra el General, que va de acá, embiar algun socorro de gente conforme a la necesidad para acomodar las cosas de Escocia, lo qual escusaria el cuydado de embiar gente de Flandres. Y sy estos salen del puerto de Dunquirque en todo el mes de Hebrero, no les pueden estorbar los navios de Flushelingas.

4. Otra prevencion sería tener Vuestra Magestad las cosas concertadas con el Papa, en quanto es necessario, para la jornada y para el primer asiento de las cosas de Inglaterra ya dicho.

5. Podriamos embiar desde luego algunas personas de confiança a Inglaterra con otro buen pretexto, sin que ellas mismas supiesen para qué fin se embian, como ya tengo comunicado con Don Juan de Idiaquez, y por esta via sabriamos más a menudo, como passan las cosas por alla, particularmente en quanto toca a las parcialidades y bandos que ay entre los mismos Erejes y Señores de la tierra, para servirse mejor dellas en las ocasiones.

6. Ultimamente torno a suplicar a Vuestra Magestad la merced y limosna que a boca supliqué para los seminarios que estan muy necesitados, y esta tambien será buena prevencion para animar a todos, y que los sacerdotes que agora se an de embarçar a Inglaterra, refieran a los Catholicos la singular piedad de Vuestra Magestad a estos seminarios, por la cuya próspera vida ruegan a Dios nuestro Señor continuamente.

Roberto Personio.

Translation

My Lord[269]

Although Your Majesty did me the favour of a kind and lengthy audience, I was not able to cover all the points that occurred to me, on such as serious business as we had in

---

268. començacen] S, i.e. començasen

269. A superscription signalled by a + commonly refers us to Jesus or Mary, in whose name the letter is written, but here "My Lord the King" might be what is meant.

hand, and so I would rather provide this brief resumé in writing, beseeching Your Majesty to be pleased to cast your eye over it, because it has an important bearing on your royal service.

1. Current circumstances.

1. John Hawkins and Francis Drake, two of the best sea captains the queen has, are away,[270] and John Norris, who is the principal commander on land, is occupied in Ireland. Along with them are the best soldiers and mariners of the kingdom, also absent, and many ships as well.

2. Ireland and Scotland are in rebellion, and England, with the factions and other divisions of which Your Majesty knows the circumstances, cannot be held for long. Your Majesty should not hesitate to take advantage of this, because the rebellion in Ireland will be pacified as in the past, and the Scots will return to their league with France, regarding Vendome as a Catholic,[271] and the affections of the English earls will change if there are delays.

3. Vendome cannot hinder or obstruct for now, because he is not established yet and is not as well fortified in his kingdom as he will be later.

4. Your Majesty holds the present advantage of being under arms by land in Flanders and by sea in Spain, and the queen has made no preparation for the moment. If this occasion is not seized, it will not arise again soon.

5. A great part of the expense of the expedition has already been met, and it will cost no more if everything can be finished in one blow. If it is delayed, there will be new obstacles, and the money will have been spent in vain. And every year new Drakes and pirates and enemies of the kingdom will appear.

2. The time and method.

1. The ideal time to put this into effect will be perfectly provided by this winter, when the queen is not watching out for us, and the method will be with a moderately sized army – it will be swifter than a large war machine, which entails many inconveniences.

2. When this queen's grandfather, King Henry VII, was earl of Richmond, he entered the realm at an opportune time with fewer than two thousand French and gained the kingdom of King Richard III, and Edward IV, duke of York, had formerly done the same, with 4000 Flemish, and previously his captain Richard, earl of Salisbury, had done the same, and took the kingdom with 3000 French soldiers, and before them Henry IV, duke of Lancaster, did the same, with fewer than 1500 Breton soldiers, and none of these had so great a party within the realm as we have at present.

3. Time and method make up three parts of four: it works better to have ten things done in good time than forty carried out over a longer period, because that would make

---

270. Both died during this expedition: Hawkins after 12 November 1595 and Drake on 23 January 1596, at Escudo.
271. Henri IV (Navarre).

it more exposed to discovery. And it would be best to make haste before Drake returns from the Indies and the queen is able to take up arms.

3. On the ports for entrance.

1. There are two ways of entering England immediately. One is to disembark on the downs of the province of Kent, and from there to go directly to London. This route is considered the shortest, but it is more dangerous because you have to cross a wide part of the Channel with the armada and then the river of London with the army.

2. Another route is through the port of Milford, where Henry VII entered the realm and conquered it. This is considered far more secure and best of all.

3. If we do not wish to enter into England in the first place, there are the ports of Scotland, which the Scottish nobles are suggesting, although they are remote and less suitable because of the barrenness of the land that needs to be crossed in order to enter England, and this way Scotland would serve rather as a mutual distraction than a way for our army to enter.

4. Apart from these, there are the ports of Ireland, which are very good and near Spain, and the land is abundant in meat and bread. And all the people are enemies to the English, and the passage from there to various parts of England and Scotland is easier, and so that entrance, or from the port of Milford, presents no difficulty, and at the time of carrying this out, you can decide which one seems more to the purpose.

4. On the general.

A very great deal is at risk in this expedition. Its good success will depend in large measure on what kind of person the general is, on the will of others, and on those who have to follow him; and so it is very important that he should be a devout man, who acts on God's behalf, and who has courage, and military knowledge, and particular awareness of the affairs of England, and be well regarded and reputed by the nation. Therefore, whoever it may be, Your Majesty in your prudence will know and will look into it better than anyone. I see the number reduced to so few that there is hardly one who has these qualities, nor can I easily find another. May God guide Your Majesty in making this choice as in all else.

5. On establishing the crown and the succession.

1. Concerning what I have told Your Majesty about the consensus among all the Catholics to defer the naming and creation of the king and queen of England freely to Your Majesty: despite the proposals of the earls,[272] it is so certain that I make bold to assure you of it, for I know the feeling among the principal heads in this matter. And all the priests of the seminaries are of one mind in that, since it is something on which depends all the safety of the Catholic religion and the good reformation of England. And

---

272. The Catholic earls who had made proposals via John Cecil.

in this regard, good Cardinal Allen, when he was alive, and Francis Englefield and I, and all our friends, have always taken it to be the principal point to which all our navigation steers, and it is a matter about which the Catholics have no doubt.

2. Only there is opposed to this a certain faction, of Charles Paget, Thomas Morgan, and Thomas Throckmorton (as Don Juan de Idiáquez already knows),[273] who for many years have been rallying the malcontents of the English nation against the Spanish nation, opposing Cardinal Allen and the seminaries. They take as their head the bishop of Cassano and the said Throckmorton as their agent in Rome, who is cunningly trying to win the favour of the duke of Feria, and through his means they have something in hand, the bishop of Cassano and, with him, the duke of Sessa.[274] And so when Cardinal Allen died, they stirred up the whole English seminary and agitated the students against their superiors, the fathers of the Society, and Cardinal Caetano their protector,[275] and they entrenched very hostile feelings against what we are planning, and against the service of Your Majesty. We should head off this faction and party and ensure that Throckmorton does not remain in Rome nor Paget in Flanders, but rather in Naples or Sicily, because the count of Olivares knows them well.

3. The way to settle the matter of the succession smoothly and safely is that when the general invades and begins fighting, he should only talk about the restoration of the Catholic religion. And if God gives him the victory, he should then gather the principal Catholics in a kind of parliament, as is so often done in situations like this. It can then be determined that – inasmuch as there are so many claims to the succession, and so many claimants, as can be seen in the recently published book,[276] and that amongst others Your Majesty and the prince of Spain, through the Portuguese line, and Her Grace the infanta through the Breton line have the most definite titles – they will, to avoid dissensions and wars, and in gratitude for the benefit received by the restoration at the hand of Your Majesty, concede to Your Majesty the right to appoint the king and queen, and establish the line of succession, and further to name and appoint the leading bishops, in accordance with the privilege of the kings of England, until a parliament is held to confirm all this. And so, when Your Majesty has appointed trustworthy persons as bishops, following a list that can be given on this score, everything will have been done to Your Majesty's satisfaction and with delicacy, because the bishops are the leading group in the parliament and give guidance to the rest.

273. See Persons to Idiáquez, 22 May 1597 (B378). Thomas Throckmorton, an associate of Morgan and Paget in Flanders, came to Rome to marry Allen's niece, and became a leader of the English community in Rome. He is not to be confused with Sir Thomas Throckmorton of Tortworth, Gloucestershire (1539–1607) or the recusant Thomas Throckmorton of Coughton, Warwickshire (ca. 1534–1615).

274. Owen Lewis, bishop of Cassano and the candidate favoured by Persons's opponents to succeed Allen as cardinal, died on 14 October 1595 (Godfrey Anstruther, "Owen Lewis," in *The English Hospice in Rome*, ed. John Allen [Rome, 2012], 274–294); many sources incorrectly give the date as 1594. The duke of Sessa, Antonio Fernández de Córdoba y Cardona (1550–1606), was the Spanish ambassador in Rome from 1590 to 1604.

275. Enrico Caetani, cardinal protector of the English nation.

276. *Conference about the Next Succession*.

4. It could also be considered, in this regard, whether it would be better to bring the consent of His Holiness and Your Majesty, delegating it to the general of the expedition or the cardinal archduke of Flanders, to name and approve those bishops immediately after the victory, and thus settle affairs briefly, without waiting for bulls from Rome, which can be published after the settling of things in England. It will be very important then to call together and authorize this first parliament.

6. On some important precautions.

1. The first and principal seems to be to make sure that some of the ships which are already in Flanders should be armed, and start to make incursions, so that in due course the exiled Scottish earls, barons, and knights can pass into Scotland under better cover, and together with them such Englishmen as the earl of Westmorland and baron Dacres[277] whose estates border most nearly on Scotland; and with their arrival a large host would rise up.

2. Also Colonel William Stanley could go with them, and his regiment of soldiers, if that seems good to Your Majesty; or if not, he could proceed with two or three ships to Ireland, or to Milford Haven, where our armada would be. But in order that he should render greater service to Your Majesty, and draw many others to the same, it is important that Your Majesty should honour him with the same commission as Monsieur de la Mothe or another,[278] as has often been requested from Your Majesty.

3. To those knights returning to Scotland and rising up in revolt, the general who is going from here can send some people in support, as needed, to manage the affairs of Scotland, which would obviate the need to send a force from Flanders. And if they set forth from the port of Dunkirk at any time during February, they will not be hindered by the ships from Flushing.

4. Another precaution will be for Your Majesty to handle these matters in concert with the pope, where necessary, for the expedition, and for the abovementioned settling of English affairs.

5. We should be able, at that time, to send some trustworthy persons to England on another good pretext, without their being aware of the reason for which they are sent, as I have already discussed with Don Juan de Idiáquez, and in that way we would more frequently have information about events as they occur over there, particularly as far as the parties and groups are concerned which exist among those very heretics and lords on the ground, to take advantage of this information when the occasion arises.

6. Finally I turn to Your Majesty to beseech your favour and alms, which I begged in person for the seminaries which are very needy, and this will also be a good provision to encourage them all, and that the priests who are now about to embark for England

---

277. Charles Nevill, earl of Westmorland (1542–1601); Francis Lord Dacre (d. 1633; see Acquaviva to Persons, 22 January 1590, B48).

278. An ironic reference to the former French ambassador to England, Bertrand de Salignac Fénelon, seigneur de la Mothe (1523–1589).

will relay to the Catholics the special favour Your Majesty has shown towards those seminaries, for whose prosperous life they pray continually to God our lord.

Robert Persons.

B294 From Claudio Acquaviva, Rome, 25 September 1595

SOURCE: ARSI, Baet. 3/I,237.

NOTE: Acquaviva is concerned about what to do with Fr Simon Swinburne, now in Flanders. He leaves the question of building a chapel to Persons's discretion. He explains how urgently he needs an experienced Englishman, Creswell or Holt, to assist in Rome, with Edmund Harewood (formerly minister at the English college) now occupied at the novitiate (see his letter of 25 October, B297). This letter only reached Persons early in December (see his letter of 2/9 December, B303).

P. Roberto Personio, 25 de Setiembre.

Dos de Vuestra Reverencia he recebido, la una de 15 de Julio la otra de 7 de Agosto, y estoy algo maravillado de que no me escrive cosa alguna de la falta en que cayo el P. Simon Suimborno, que no me parece es de las que se deven disimular. Vuestra Reverencia me escriva lo que siente della y lo que le parece que se deve hazer, porque havida su respuesta resolveremos lo que más conveniente pareciere.

En lo de la iglesia que quieren fabricar aquellos banqueros me remito al parecer de Vuestra Reverencia pero mire bien si es conveniente que siendo esa estancia de Sevilla de presente y por algun tiempo será bien hazer tanto gasto que despues se aya de dexar a quien no sabemos.

Los Ingleses que aqui ay son tan necessarios que por no bastar a lo que aqui es menester, querria que Vuestra Reverencia me diese el Padre Holto o al Padre Cressuelo, porque al novicio no conviene meterle en cosas que le disturben. El de la Penitenciaria tan poco puede faltar y el P. Edmundo es aqui del todo necessario, pues ningun otro tenemos que siendo necessario nos pueda dar noticia e informacion en las cosas de la nacion que cada dia ocurren, ansi que será forzoso que Vuestra Reverencia tenga paciencia. En sus &c.

Translation

To Fr Robert Persons, 25 September.

I have received two letters from Your Reverence, one of 15 July and the other of 7 August.[279] I am a little astonished that you have not written anything to me about the offence which Fr Simon Swinburne has committed, which does not seem to me to be something that should be concealed. Would Your Reverence please write to me what you think about this and what you think should be done about it, because from your response we will be able to decide what would be most suitable.

279. B284, B286.

In connection with the church which those bankers seek to build,[280] I leave it to Your Reverence's discretion, but make sure it suits your needs, since you are staying in Seville for the present and for some little while. It will be good to do so now that the expense has already been incurred, rather than leaving it later to someone we do not know.

The Englishmen who are already here are so necessary that indeed they are not as many as are required. I would like Your Reverence to give me either Fr Holt or Fr Creswell, because it is not appropriate that the beginner should be involved in things that disturb him.[281] With regard to the penitentiary, we have little to spare, and Fr Edmund[282] is absolutely necessary here, but we have no one else in the necessary role of giving notice or information on the affairs of the nation which happen every day, and so for now Your Reverence will just have to be patient. To your [holy prayers and sacrifices], etc.

B295 To Claudio Acquaviva, Seville, 2 October 1595

SOURCE: ABSI, Coll P II 477, Grene's note.

NOTE: Grene continues: "Item, Epistola quam scripserunt sacerdotes destinati ad Missionem ex Hispali ad Alumnos &c. Romae, data 2. Oct. 1595" (Also, a letter which the priests on their way to the mission wrote from Seville to the students at Rome, dated 2 October 1595), enclosed with Persons's letter to the father general.

[*Grene summarises:*] Oct. 2 is concerning the stirres in the seminarie at Rome.

B296 From Claudio Acquaviva, Rome, 23 October 1595

SOURCE: ARSI, Cast. 6, fol. 232r.

NOTE: Acquaviva deals with two controversial matters relating to the English college at Valladolid: whether servants and students should eat together in the refectory, and whether it is necessary to seek alms outside the city. It was del Río's innovation to make servants eat outside the refectory, to Persons's indignation (see his letters to Acquaviva, 19 March, 15 May, 10 July, and to del Río, 12 May, B264, B276, B283, B275). See McCoog, *Building the Faith of St Peter*, 210–211; Edwards, 178–179.

P. Roberto Personio, 23 de Otubre.

En el Collegio Inglés de Valladolid se repara en si conviene que los mozos de servicio coman en el Refectorio con los Alumnos, ha se respondido que se guarde el orden que Vuestra Reverencia diere ansi en esto como en lo demas, alla lo acomoden. Avisan nos que los Alumnos son tantos que no pudiendose sustentar con las limosnas de aquella ciudad, van a pedir limosna fuera della. Deseo que Vuestra Reverencia me avise el modo como se pide esta limosna y si van los de la Compañia a pedirla, porque haviendose esto

280. This may be the chapel endowed by Ana de Espinosa and completed in 1598 (Murphy, 8).

281. Acquaviva appears to mean that someone of experience is needed.

282. Harewood, minister at the English college in Rome.

prohibido a algunas casas professas por los inconvenientes que se hallan en que los nuestros anden solos pidiendo limosnas, no convendra ponerlos en estas ocasiones, pues sería menor inconveniente tener algunos Alumnos menos en el Seminario que no[283] usar deste medio. Si el pedir limosna es como significan yendo alguno de los nuestros a otras cuidades, y pedir alguna limosna a los obispos y eclesiasticos para ese seminario menos inconveniente tiene. En fin, se aguardará el aviso de Vuestra Reverencia para entender lo que esto es. En sus orationes, etc.

[PS] Hanse recibido la de Vuestra Reverencia de 18 de Agosto y la de 5 de Setiembre con el dupplicado y procuraré responder a ellas con la brevedad posible y podra ser que la respuesta llegue antes que esta o con ella.

Translation

To Fr Robert Persons, 23 October.

The question has been raised in the English college of Valladolid whether it is appropriate for the servants to eat in the refectory together with the students. To this I have replied that they should rather follow the order which Your Reverence prescribes, in this as in the rest: it should be dealt with there. We've been informed that there are so many students that they cannot be maintained by the alms of that city, and so need to go seek alms outside. I should like Your Reverence to let me know in what manner the alms are begged, and whether those of the Society go in search of alms, because having prohibited this to some professed houses, on account of the disadvantages which result from Ours spending all their time going about by themselves begging alms, I would prefer not to expose them to the same risks. It would be less problematic to keep fewer students in the seminary than to follow this method. If alms-begging is such that it means that one of Ours should go to other cities and beg alms from the bishops and ecclesiastics in this regard, it will cause the least inconvenience. In any case, I await Your Reverence's report so that I can understand the situation. To your prayers, etc.

[PS] I have received Your Reverence's letters of 18 August and 5 September[284] with the copies, and I shall attempt to answer them as quickly as possible. It may be that the reply will reach you before this or with this.[285]

B297 From Edmund Harewood, Rome, 25 October 1595

SOURCE: Persons to Acquaviva, 2/9 December 1595 (B303).

NOTE: The conflict at the English college had clearly escalated since Persons replied, on 12 June (B280), to Harewood's plea of 10 April (B269), and Acquaviva was now ready to relinquish Jesuit control of the college.

283. que no] *followed by* poner a los nuestros [*deleted*] R
284. B287, B289.
285. Acquaviva evidently replied promptly, on 29 October (B300), dealing with the urgent matter of the troubles at the English college in Rome. That letter, which was sent by special post, did indeed arrive before this one (see Persons's letter of 2/9 December, B303).

Harewood's attempts to counter manoeuvres among the students to promote Lewis's claim to the cardinalate culminated, in August, in a stormy confrontation during a visit to the college by the cardinal protector, Enrico Caetani. Pope Clement VIII then ordered a visitation of the college by Monsignor Bernadino Morra, notary of the Congregation for Bishops and Religious, and subsequently directed that Acquaviva relinquish administrative control of the college to Caetani. On Acquaviva's advice, Harewood retired to the novitiate of Sant'Andrea (see McCoog, *Building the Faith of St Peter*, 262–263).

B298 To Claudio Acquaviva, Seville, probably 28 October 1595

SOURCE: Persons to Acquaviva, 2/9 December 1595 (B303).
NOTE: Persons was about to leave Seville, with the seminary "in a reasonably good state." He arrived in Madrid in mid-November.

B299 To Joseph Creswell, Seville, 28 October 1595

SOURCE: ACSA, Series II, Legajo 1, item 24, a contemporary copy.
HICKS: 394–400, with English translation.
NOTE: Persons's departure from Seville has been delayed, allowing him to witness the blessing of the college chapel. He has been much encouraged by the arrival of four new seminarians, including two boys from a devout family of gentry in Dorchester whose story has moved all listeners to tears. Another arrival, an older man, has brought news of events in London and a letter from John Gerard.

Copia de una carta del Padre Roberto Personio de la Compañia de Jesus, al Padre Josefo Cresuelo de la misma Compañia de las cosas de Inglaterra.

Sino salgo de acá tam presto como Vuestra Reverencia desa y avrá menester, piense Vuestra Reverencia que no se puede más. Llega la familia a más que sesenta[286] bocas, y va cresciendo cada dia y es menester dexarles algun pan. Mucho tambien costa y ocupa la casa nueva, la qual toda via va en buen término, y todo el Seminario cabe en ella, y el domingo pasado se bendixo la yglesia, y dixose la primera missa.

Cinco nos ha llevado Dios para sí, y otro está muy de camino; murieron como avian vivido, que es como unos Angeles, o serafines abraçados de vivas llamas del amor de Dios nuestro Señor, pues no hablavan sino palabras de fuego en su muerte, diziendo que de ninguna cosa sentian pena, sino de que no morieron dispedazados por su Señor. Ha tenido el fiel Señor cuidado de consolarnos con la venida de otros en su lugar, porque anoche llegaron quatro de Inglaterra por via de Irlanda, de los quales los dos son de las más lindas y graçiosas criaturas que Vuestra Reverencia avrá visto en su vida. Son hermanos, el uno de 15, y el otro de 13 años, hijos de un Cavallero principal en la Provincia de Dorchestria, junto a Vaymoa. Su padre dellos estubo muchos años en la Carcel, por nuestra santa fee, y murio

286. sesenta] *this ed.*; sasenta *Vd*

en la misma Carçel; y en otra Carçel estubo tambien la Madre, que aún vive. Es una santa viuda, y no teniendo otro Suçesor que estos dos hijos, los ofrecio a Dios, y los embió con un mançebo cuerdo, que les ha sido maystro en la lengua Latina, y le mandó que me dijiese que más deseava ver a sus hijos saçerdotes y martires (si Dios fuesse servido), que no gozar del mayorazgo de la hazienda que les dexó su Padre, y que ella quedava con otras 3 hijas de tierna edad, las quales deseava sumamente trayerlas tambien a España y venir con ellas para entrarse todas quatro Monjas si fuesse posible, y que sin duda se arrojaria y aventuraria a la jornada, si yo le dava ánimo para ello. Vea Vuestra Reverencia lo que obra Dios por alla.

Ha movido muchas lagrimas por acá,[287] la vista destos dos niños, y realmente ver el ánimo y alegria con que vienen, y los quentos que quentan de sus trabaxos y persecuciones en Inglaterra, y peligros pasados in este vieaje, enterneçera a qualquier pecho humano.

El quarto que ha llegado, es hombre de 35 años, y ha gastado muchos dellos, en acudir a las carceles, y servir a los presos que padezen por la Religion Catholica, y asi en botones, çapatos, y otras partes más escondidas me traye muchas carticas de differentes carceles, una que es del Padre Juan Gerardo, escrita quando estava aguardo de ser martirizado; embío con esta por hazer en ella memoria a Vuestra Reverencia. Creo que han dilatado su martirio, por ser de casa tan prinçipal y sus deudos poderosos. Ha venido este buen hombre de Inglaterra con brevidad: traye con sigo 4 estudiantes[288] para estos seminarios, pero los dos fueron presos en el puerto de Chester, donde querian embarcarse la primera vez, y despues huyendo al puerto Bristol, fue preso el otro, y el quatro escapó, y éste sólo pudo embarcarse, por la suma vigilançia que usan los hereges, para que no venga esta juventud a España; toda via dize que vernan muchos.

No traye nuevas de importancia, si no la comun voz y fama de la salida de la armada de Draque para las Indias, y que la Reyna temia mucho una armada, que dezian publicamente que el Rey de España hazía contra Inglaterra, y que con esta sola voz mostravan aligria, no solamente Catholicos, sino tambien otros muchos que desean mudança. Que por falta de bastimentos en Londres, dos mil Aprendices, se avian armado un dia contra el Governador, y fueron apaziguados, y quatro, o çinco de los principales ahorcados, y hechos quartos. Que la Reyna avia dicho, que de aqui adelante usaria de más clemençia con algunos Catholicos, y esto a persuasion de Vandoma Rey de Françia, que le avia escrito, que convenia por raçon de estado, y asi luego se libraron muchos Catholicos de las carçeles, dando fianças que no huyerian. Que la gerra y movimientos de Irlanda[289] davan al Consejo de Inglaterra mucho cuydado, por averse[290] herido gravemente a Juan Nores y su hermano, y por temer que el Rey de España no se serviesse desta occasion de Irlanda y Escoçia asi rebueltas. Estas cosas y otras semejantes cuenta del progresso de la Religion Catholica en Inglaterra. Dios lo lleve adelante para su divina gloria, y salvaçion de las almas que tanto le costaron etc., y guarde a Vuestra Reverencia y a estos padres con salud. De Sevilla de donde pienso partir entre 5 o 6 dias. A los 28 de octubre, 1595.

    Roberto Personio.

    287. acá] *interlined with caret Vd*
    288. estudiantes] *this ed.;* estiantes *Vd*
    289. de Irlanda] *interlined in another but contemporary hand Vd*
    290. averse] se *interlined with caret Vd*

Translation

Copy of a letter from Fr Robert Persons of the Society of Jesus, to
Fr Joseph Creswell of the same Society, on the affairs of England.

If I fail to get away from here as soon as Your Reverence wishes and need requires, please would Your Reverence take it that I cannot do anything else. Our household here now consists of over sixty mouths to feed and keeps increasing every day; so it is necessary to provide bread for them. The new house also is also costly and takes up my time. Still, it is turning out very well, and there is room in it for the whole seminary. Last Sunday the church was blessed and the first mass was said.

God has taken five of our number to Himself, and another one is very likely to be taken. They died as they have lived, that is, like angels, or like seraphim on fire with living flames of love for God our Lord; for they spoke no words at their death except of fire, declaring that they regretted nothing except that they were not dying dismembered for their Lord's sake.[291] Our faithful Lord has taken care to console us by the arrival of others to replace them; for last night four arrived from England by way of Ireland. Two of them are the most handsome and graceful creatures Your Reverence could have seen in your life.[292] They are brothers, one fifteen and the other thirteen years of age, sons of a leading gentleman in the borough of Dorchester, close to Weymouth. Their father was in prison for many years for our holy faith and died also in prison. The mother too was in another prison and is still alive. She is a devout widow and, though she has no one else to succeed her but these two sons, she offered them to God and sent them in the charge of a discreet young man, who has been their instructor in the Latin tongue. She instructed him to tell me that she was more willing to see her sons priests and martyrs (if it were God's will) than for them to enjoy the succession to the entailed estate left to them by their father. She had three daughters as well, of tender years, and wished above all things to send them to Spain too, and to come with them, so that all four of them could enter a convent to be nuns, if that were possible. There was no doubt but that she would make the effort and venture the journey if I gave her any encouragement in the matter. See, Your Reverence, what God is working over there!

The sight of these two young boys has moved many here to tears, and in truth to see the courage and joy with which they have come and to hear the stories they tell of their labours and persecution in England and the dangers they have passed through on their journey here would melt any human heart.

The fourth person who has arrived is a man of thirty-five years who has spent many of them in attending prisons and being of service to prisoners who are suffering for the Catholic religion; and so he brings me, concealed in buttons, shoes, and other more secret places, a number of notes from different prisons, and one of them is from Fr John Gerard, written when he was in expectation of martyrdom; I am enclosing it because he men-

291. Two students, Robert Waller and Thomas Egerton, died in 1595 from excessive ascetic practices (Murphy, 8–9); see the account by the rector, Francisco de Peralta, in Diego de Yepes, *Historia particular de la persecucion de Inglaterra* (Madrid, 1599), 852–854.

292. The two boys have not been identified: see Edwards, 184 n29.

tions Your Reverence kindly. I believe they have postponed his martyrdom on account of his belonging to such a leading family and his relations being people of influence. This good man has made a swift passage from England; he was bringing with him four students for these seminaries, but two were captured at the port of Chester, where they initially intended to embark; after that they fled to the port of Bristol, where another was captured, although the fourth escaped. Only this man, then, succeeded in embarking, owing to the exceeding vigilance employed by the heretics to prevent these young men coming to Spain. Nevertheless, he says that many will come.

He brings no news of importance except of the general talk and rumour about the departure of Drake's expedition to the Indies; also, that the queen was in great fear of an armada which it was popularly claimed the king of Spain was preparing against England, and that the mere rumour of this gave rise to rejoicing not only among Catholics but many others as well who long for change. For want of provisions in London, two thousand apprentices had taken up arms one day against the Lord Mayor. Order was restored and four or five of the leading spirits were hanged and quartered. The queen had stated that from now on she would treat some of the Catholics with greater clemency – this at the persuasion of Vendome, king of France, who had written to her that it was advisable for reasons of state;[293] and as a consequence many Catholics were presently let out of the prisons, giving sureties that they would not flee the country. The war and disturbances in Ireland were causing the English council great concern, on account of John Norris and his brother having been seriously wounded, and for fear lest the king of Spain should take advantage of this opportunity when Ireland and Scotland were in such a rebellious mood.[294] These and other such things he relates in regard to the progress of the Catholic religion in England. May God further it for the sake of His divine glory and the salvation of souls, which cost him so much, etc. And may He keep Your Reverence and the fathers here in health. From Seville, which I hope to leave in five or six days time, 28 October 1595.

Robert Persons.

B300 From Claudio Acquaviva, Rome, 29 October 1595

SOURCE: Persons to Idiáquez, 6 December (B302); Persons to Acquaviva, 2/9 December 1595 (B303).

NOTE: The letter, which arrived by a special post, evidently dealt with the troubles at the English college, Rome. Persons replied on 9 December.

293. Jesuits were generally cautious in admitting "reason of state" as a legitimate political motive; see Harro Höpfl, *Jesuit Political Thought: The Society of Jesus and the State, c. 1540–1630* (Cambridge, 2004), 112–185.

294. In June 1595 London apprentices rioted on Tower Hill to protest to the Lord Mayor against food prices. Sir Francis Drake and Sir John Hawkins sailed for the Spanish Indies from Plymouth on 28 August 1595. John Norris (or Norreys, ca. 1547–1597) served in Ireland under Sir William Russell from May 1595. He and his brother were wounded at the battle of Mullabrack, 5 September 1595.

B301 To Richard Barret, December 1595

SOURCE: Barret to Persons, 10 April 1596 (B322).
NOTE: Richard Barret succeeded William Allen as president of the English college in Douai. He was about to travel to Rome to assist with the difficulties at the English college there and clear his name, in view of accusations that unsatisfactory students were being sent from Douai to Rome (Kenny, "Inglorious Revolution," 25 [part 2]; 78 [part 3]). Persons evidently wrote to ask him for an analysis of the contributory causes.

B302 To Don Juan de Idiáquez, Madrid, 6 December 1595

SOURCE: AGS, Est. Leg. 965 (unnumbered, in medio), autograph, enclosing a memorial "de los puntos que emos menester que Su Magestad mande escrivir al Duque de Sesa tocante el Collegio ynglés en Roma."
HICKS: 428–432, with English translation.
NOTE: After Persons had written, but not posted, his letter to Acquaviva of 2 December (B303), he received letters from Acquaviva (29 October, B300) and Harewood (25 October, B297) detailing the troubles at the English college in Rome. Acquaviva wished to relinquish Jesuit control of the College. So sick with worry was Persons that he was unable to leave the house and had to send Creswell to meet Idiáquez in his place.

The letter begins with an expression of gratitude to Philip II for the donation of a relic of St Alban (mentioned in the Annual Letter: ARSI Cast. 32 I, fol. 48r, English College 1596). The king was an enthusiastic collector of relics and possessed more than one relic of St Alban's. This one in particular was probably "un pedazito de carne" (a piece of flesh) given to him by Alessandro Farnese, duke of Parma: see the contemporary testimonial letters, entrega 6, fol. 40, nos. 11–12, printed in *Las reliquias del Real Monasterio del Escorial*, ed. Benito Mediavilla Martín and José Rodríguez Díez (San Lorenzo de El Escorial, 2005), 1: 442.

In this letter Persons asks Idiáquez to advise the king to write a letter to his ambassador in Rome, Antonio Fernández de Córdoba y Cardona, duke of Sessa (1550–1606, ambassador from 1590 to 1604), to assure Acquaviva of Spanish support and to call on Pope Clement VIII to assist, so that the college can remain under Jesuit government. A memorial is attached, to this effect. He recommends that the ambassador consult Allen's former secretary Roger Baynes, John Cecil, and Richard Haydock (Haddock) for information on the troubles. Roger Baynes, formerly Allen's secretary, continued to be an important source of information on English affairs. Richard Haydock (ca. 1551–1605), a seminary priest, had played an important role in the conflicts at the time of the foundation of the college in 1578–1579, was a member of Allen's household in 1594, and was regarded as a supporter of the establishment at the college (see A8; Anstruther, 159–160; McCoog, *Building the Faith of St Peter*, 266, 384; Knox, *Allen*, 375). He was of great assistance to Henry Piers, who arrived in September 1595, helping him to a place as a lay student in the English college. See *Henry Piers's Continental Travels, 1595–1598*, ed. Brian Mac Cuarta (Cambridge, 2018), 77–81.

Quedé tan consolado ayer con la merced que Su Magestad nos hacía de la reliquia de Sant Albano que bien aguardava alguna afflicion extraordinaria por contrapeso, y ansi me succedio una anoche tal que me ha quitado el sueño y rebuelto la cabeça en tal manera que no estando para salir he rogado al Padre Cresuello que no está tan poco aún bien convalecido que vaya esta mañana a tratarlo con Vuestra Señoria.

El caso es que la turbacion del Collegio Ynglés en Roma ha llegado tan adelante como supimos anoche por cartas del Padre General de la Compañia y de otros de 29 de Octubre que el dicho General con parecer de sus Assistentes está resuelto de dexar el govierno del dicho Collegio, pues la parte inquieta con la mano y instigacion de los que le ayudan de fuera se haçe tan porfiada y incorregible que an cansado ya y enfadado al General y a todos los demas; y aunque sea muerto el obispo Cassano parece que Andres Wise Yrlandes que se llama gran Prior de Ynglaterra ha entrado en lugar del obispo diciendo que ya él es cabeça de la nacion Ynglesa y juntandose con Ugo Grifin sobrino del obispo y Tomas Throgmorton y otros de aquela partialidad de Pageto y Morgano, hacen espaldas a los estudiantes alborottados para con Su Santidad y algunos Cardenales; y cansan al Rector, provincial y General de la Compañia, defendendo las libertades que piden los alborotados; y si el General dexa el gobierno como está determinado, queda perdido aquel collegio, y será un Seminario de libertades, dissençiones y de enemigos de las cosas de España y de Su Magestad, que es un fin principal que pretenden los cabeças de los[295] alborotadores, y presto vernan a dar tambien en estos Seminarios de España porque sin la ayuda y pia afficion del General será difficultoso sustentarlos.

Es tan grave y importante este daño que me obligará yrme con priessa a Roma y echarme a los pies de Su Santidad para el remedio, si otro no se hallare; y pensando en todo lo que puedo, no se me offerece otro efficaz que una carta buena de Su Magestad al Embaxador encargandole mucho que anime y assiste al Padre General y al Rector para con Su Santidad a que se ponga el collegio en paz y disciplina como antes, y que las cabeças de la rebellion y dissencion dentro el collegio se castiguen, y los de fuera se aparten, y que cree a los padres que gobiernan el collegio y a los buenos y quietos de fuera como son Rogero Baynes Secretario que fue del Cardenal Alano y entretenido de Su Magestad, y al padre Juan Secilio que Su Magestad embió de acá a Roma el verano passado y al padre Ricardo Haddoco sacerdote grave que está en Roma y no a los inquietos y alborotadores.

Supplico a Vuestra Señoria lo trate luego con Su Magestad para que siendo servido Su Magestad de escrivir como importa mucho por su real servicio y para todo lo que andamos tratando de Ynglaterra, la tenga luego la carta para embiarla antes que yo me parta, porque conviene embiarla nosotros con las nuestras al Padre General y a los confidentes que tengo nombrado para que ellos la den al Embaxador y con ella quedan consolados y animados a dishaçer la determinacion del Padre General de dexar el gobierno del collegio, lo qual dice que aguarda solamente la respuesta del padre Cresuello y mia para executarlo. Guarde Dios a Vuestra Señoria, etc.

  Roberto Personio.

[*Endorsed*:] Roberto Personio a. 6 de Diciembre 1595.

---

295. cabeças de los] *interlined with caret* S

[*Enclosed*:]
    Memorial de los puntos que emos menester que Su Magestad
    mande escrivir al Duque de Sesa toccante el Collegio ynglés
                            en Roma

1. Que por la edificacion y consuelo que Su Magestad ha reçebido de los seminarios yngleses por acá, en España, le ha pesado de entender de la Inquietud que le han dicho de aquel de Roma, y mucho más, de que aya llegado tan adelante, que el General de la Compañia de Jesus, aya pensado de dexar el gobierno del dicho Collegio.

2. Que esto sería grande Inconveniente, desamparar una nacion en Tanta necessidad, y assi que en ninguna manera conbiene, si no más presto que se curten las occasiones del mal, que se entiende ser la Comunicacion de la Juventud con algunos yngleses inquietos de fuera, de los quales conbiene apartar los estudiantes, y poner los demas remedios que conbendra.

3. Y que en esto y en todo lo demas que fuera en provecho de la paz y quietud y buen orden del Collegio, será servido Su Magestad que el Duque se Emplee con mucho cuydado, ora sea tratandolo con su sanctidad, y con el Cardinal Protector, ora con el General de la Compañia, al qual ha de dar ánimo para que en ninguna manera dexe el gobierno, y que avise a Su Magestad de lo que hiziere en esto.

[*Endorsed*:] Memª para la Carta al Duque de Sesa, tocante el Collº Inglés en Roma.

Translation

I felt so much consolation yesterday at the kindness of His Majesty in giving us the relic of St Alban that I quite expected some extraordinary counterbalancing affliction; and indeed last night I encountered one so great that it has deprived me of sleep and upset my mind to such an extent that I am not fit to leave the house, and so I have asked Fr Creswell, who is not himself as yet recovered in health, to go this morning and discuss it with Your Worship.

    The trouble is that the disturbance in the English college in Rome has reached the point – as we heard last night from letters of October 29th from the father general of the Society and others – where the said general with the approval of his assistants has resolved to give up the government of the said college, since the party in revolt, aided and instigated by its supporters outside, is becoming so contentious and incorrigible that it has now wearied out and vexed the general and everybody else. And, although the bishop of Cassano is dead, it seems that Andrew Wyse, an Irishman, who calls himself the Grand Prior of England,[296] has taken the bishop's place, saying that he is now leader of the English nation, and has joined with Hugh Griffin, the bishop's nephew, and Thomas Throckmorton and other members of the faction of Paget and Morgan in upholding the cause

---

296. Andrew Wyse (d. 1631), since 1593 grand prior of St John of Jerusalem in England, i.e., the remaining Knights of Malta ("A Knight of Malta: Portrait on View in Dublin," *Irish Times*, 29 July, 1933; cf. vol. 1: 652–654 on Richard Shelley; Edwards, 188; McCoog, *Building the Faith of St Peter*, 265).

of the rebellious students before His Holiness and some cardinals. They are wearying the rector and the provincial and the general of the Society by defending the demand for relaxations of discipline made by the rebels; but if the general gives up the government, as he is determined to do, the college is doomed and will be a seedbed of licence and dissensions, and of enemies of the interests of Spain and His Majesty. This is one of the chief ends which the leaders of the rebels have in view, and soon they will effect the ruin of these Spanish seminaries also, because, except with the aid and devoted interest of the general, it will be difficult to sustain them.

The harm that this will cause is so grave and of such consequence that it will oblige me to hurry to Rome at once and throw myself at His Holiness's feet to beg a remedy, if no other is to be found; and, after considering everything open to me, I can think of no other exigency likely to succeed except a strong letter from His Majesty to the ambassador, charging him urgently to encourage father general and the rector, and to give them his support with His Holiness, so that the college may be put in a state of peace and discipline as it was before, the leaders of the rebellion and of the quarrel within the college punished, and their supporters outside parted from them, and that he may give credence to the fathers who are governing the college and to good and peaceable men outside, such as Roger Baynes, the former secretary of Cardinal Allen and a protégé of His Majesty, and Fr John Cecil,[297] whom His Majesty sent to Rome from here last summer, and Fr Richard Haydock, a worthy priest who is in Rome, instead of to men who are turbulent and rebellious.

I beg Your Worship to discuss this immediately with His Majesty so that, if His Majesty is pleased to write such a letter – as it is very important that he should do for the sake of his royal interests and of all that we are attempting to do for England – I may have the letter immediately to dispatch before I leave; for it is better for us to send it along with our letters to father general and to the confidants I have appointed, so that they can give it to the ambassador and may take consolation from it and be encouraged to persuade father general to reverse his decision to give up the government of the college, which he says he only awaits an answer from Fr Creswell and myself before putting into execution. May God preserve Your Worship etc.

Robert Persons.

[*Enclosed:*]

A Memorial of the points which we need His Majesty to ask the duke of Sessa to write, with regard to the English College in Rome

1. Because of the edification and consolation that His Majesty has received from the English seminaries here, in Spain, it is a matter of concern to him to learn of the restlessness that he has been informed about in the one in Rome, and even more, that it has come to the point where the General of the Society of Jesus has thought of leaving the government of the said college.

297. Persons was taken in by Cecil (Snowden), who was acting as a government informer for Burghley.

2. That this would be a great inconvenience, abandoning a nation in such need, and thus in no way convenient, unless it would expedite a cure for the occasions of evil, namely (as it is understood) the communication of the young men with some dissident Englishmen from outside. It would be sensible to separate them from the students and apply other appropriate remedies.

3. And that in this and in everything else that would benefit the peace and quiet and good order of the college, His Majesty would be pleased if the duke would use great care in dealing with this matter, whether by treating with His Holiness, and with the Cardinal Protector, or with the General of the Society, to whom he should give encouragement so that he does not leave the government in any way. And he should notify His Majesty of what he does in this regard.

B303 To Claudio Acquaviva, Madrid, 2 and 9 December 1595

SOURCES:
ARSI, Hisp.139, fols. 122r–125v, holograph;
ABSI, Coll N I, 158, Grene's partial transcript from the register of the professed house in Rome, III, 76;
ABSI, Coll P II 477: "2 Xmbr about malcontents against the Soc^y. Hispali" (Grene's note).

HICKS: 401–426, with English translation.

NOTE: This long letter was extended when the post did not leave for Rome as expected on completion of the initial letter on 2 December.

Persons left Seville and arrived in Madrid in mid-November; the letter of 2 December reports on three strategic meetings in locales near Madrid.

At Alcalá, Persons consulted the visitor of the provinces of Castile and Toledo, García de Alarcón, about the unsatisfactory new rector at the English college in Valladolid, Gonzalo del Río; the visitor agreed to make a change when he visited the town. It was not, however, until September 1596 that a new rector, Alonso Rodríguez de Toro, took office.

At Jesús del Monte, Bartolomé de Sicilia, notorious for his aggressive fundraising and general bossiness, promised Persons to remain there until order was received from Rome. Back in Madrid, Persons spoke to the adelantado, Martín de Padilla, and his wife the countess of Santa Gadea, about Sicilia, confirming the reservations they had about him.

Persons then visited the royal palace of El Pardo, a few miles outside Madrid, and had a long, intimate audience with the king about the French Jesuits who had been made to feel unwelcome in Spain. The Jesuits were expelled from France on 7 January 1595 over the question of the oath of allegiance to Henry IV, who was still technically under the excommunication of 1585 (see McCoog, *Building the Faith of St Peter*, 205–206; Edwards, 184–185). The attempt on the life of the king by Jesuit-educated Jean Châtel on 27 December 1594 was a contributing factor. The coolness of Spanish Jesuits to their French confréres, Persons argues here, exposes the xenophobia of those who have not travelled more widely: the question of permission for Spanish Jesuits to travel to northern Europe was one that Acquaviva asked Persons to broach with the king in 1588. In the event, despite reluctant support from the provincial and his assistant, little was achieved for the Frenchmen, but the king was much more forthcoming with funds for the college in Seville: a grant of seven thousand ducats (see Acquaviva's letter of 11 February 1596, B314).

Turning to questions relating to English Jesuits, Persons defends Creswell, now at the college in Madrid, against the suspicions of the local Jesuits. He also asks Acquaviva for a decision on money left by Nicholas Smith's father, which could be applied at St Omers, where Smith is stationed.

The letter of 9 December chiefly concerns the continued disturbances at the English college in Rome, as reported in letters written in late October by Acquaviva and Edmund Harewood, minister at the college (B297, B300). Persons advises against the Society's relinquishing the college, suggesting instead that a new rector be appointed, in place of Girolamo Fioravanti. The rest of the letter deals with business in England and Spain. Creswell, Garnet, and Weston, as well as Brother Ralph Emerson, are ready to be professed (i.e., take their final vows as Jesuits). Papal signature is required for two documents relating to the English residence at Sanlúcar de Barrameda. Persons also asks for approval to create a new position, that of prefect of the missions in the English seminaries in Spain. These two documents have not come to hand.

Muy Reverendo en Christo Padre nuestro
Pax Christi.

A mediado Noviembre llegué aqui en Madrid y dexé el Seminario de Sevilla en raçionable buen estado, como de alli escrivi en el correo passado. Y porque la necessidad grande del Seminario de Valladolid me llama con priessa fui luego a veerme con el Padre Visitador en Alcalá, y conferi con su Reverencia las cosas que todos me escrivian de Valladolid del mal gobierno del rector. Pareciole que sería forçoso mudarlo, pero esto será despues en llegando su Reverencia por alla, y en este mientras yre yo y accomodaré las cosas lo mejor que podre; pero temo de hallar el Collegio en muy mal estado, no solamente en lo temporal si no tan bien en la falta de disciplina y union del rector con los nuestros, aunque entiendo será cosa facil remediarlo con la mudança, si nos buelvan a Cabredo, de que tengo esperança, y ningun otro vendra tan a proposito para el trueco sin nota del Padre Gonçalo del Rio, pues parecera que buelve el Padre Cabredo al officio antico, acabado el trienio del provincial, y que el otro estava alli solamente de prestado.

2. Mucho contento da a todos tener tal Visitador como es el Padre Alarcon,[298] grandissimo siervo de Dios, y muy prudente y discreto en su officio. Desean todos que commençasse presto. Él aguarda algunos dispachos de Vuestra Paternidad y ya son quatro meses acabados que no tenemos carta ninguna de Roma por via ordenaria. Hallé al buen Visitador con cuydado de alguna novidad que el compañero del Padre Sicilia avia escritto de Jesus del Monte, casi en secreto y confiança, toccante las cosas del Padre y de su[299]

298. Grene's transcription reads: "A mediade. Noviemb. llegue acqui en Madrid y dexi el Seminario di Sevilla en raçionable buen estado como de alli escrivi con el correo passado, y porque la necessidad grande del Seminario de Valladolid me llama con priessa fui luego a veerme con el P. Visitador en Alcala y conferi con su Reverenza las cosas que todos me escriven de Valladolid del mal govierno del rector ... Mucho contento da a todos tener tal visitador como es el P. Alarcon ... ."

299. su] *interlined with caret* R

estar por alla. Y assi por orden del Padre Visitador fui a veer al Padre Sicilia en Jesus del Monte, y le hablé muy claramente en sus cosas y hallé que todo lo que avia escritto el compañero, fue por concierto entre ellos, y me prometio absolutamente el Padre, que se accommodaria de aqui adelante y que no saldria de Jesus del Monte para Madrid, hasta que venga el orden que aguarda de Vuestra Paternidad. Y llegando despues acá, ablé al Adelantado y a la Condesa juntamente, con la misma claridad y confiança[300] en las cosas del Padre Sicilia, en[301] quanto toccan a ellos, y me confessaron en secreto llanamente que la Compania tenía raçon en hacer con el Padre lo que[302] hacía, y que no les contentava su modo de proceder con disgusto de su religion, y que bien sabran que él, teniendo los enemigos que tenía, no les avia ayudado nada en sus pleytos y cosas, si no solamente con el Presidente de Castilla, de manera que aunque ellos exteriormente haçen demonstracion de amistad y agradecimiento por lo que el Padre les[303] ha mostrado voluntad de hacer para ellos, toda via no les pesará de[304] que Vuestra Paternidad desponga dél a su modo, antes entiendo por algunas señales, que si el Rey empleasse al Adelantado en alguna jornada, como el verano passado si dicia (y realmente parece que Su Magestad por agora no tiene otro), pienso que no descontentaria al Adelantado que el Padre Sicilia fuesse in Ytalia, o que no tubiesse licencia de yr con él, pues su libertad en mandar y el aborecemiento que por esto los capitanes en las galeras le tienen, no pueden dar gusto al Adelantado, pero esto ha de ser en secreto.

3. En llegando que llegué a esta villa, el Padre Gil Gonzales y el Padre Visitador me dixeron del negocio de los padres franceses, como se avia perdido la occasion y conjuntura de pedir la merced del Rey para ellos, parte por el yerro que truxe la carta de Vuestra Paternidad para el Rey[305] a este Collegio, y no al Padre provincial, y parte porque el provincial no tomó el negocio con alguna demostracion de calor, lo qual me pesó mucho, y assi luego en veniendo el provincial por acá, que fue dos dias despues, le hablé en ello y le animé y le dixe quánto importava el negocio por muchas causas, y más offereci de avivar la causa con Don Juan[306] de Idiaquez el dia siguiente en El Pardo, y assi lo hiçi, y lo hallé de muy buena disposicion, y se lo dixe al Padre provincial, y preguntándome su Reverencia como se avia de guyar el negocio, o por via de Don Juan o de Don Christoval, mi parecer fue que por ninguno de los dos, si no, que ablasse su Reverencia al Rey mismo, y dexandole memorial juntamente con la copia de la carta de Vuestra Paternidad veesse a quien el Rey lo remetteria, y con esso acabarlo. Fue el Padre al Pardo con el Padre Sebastian Hernandez, y no podiendo hablar al Rey dexaron la copia de la carta sin memorial con el principe, el qual no attiende aún a negocios, y solamente platicaron a Don Christoval y a Don Juan para que favoriçiessen, pero andando yo despues al Pardo tres o quatro dias tras esto, para hablar al Rey,[307] aunque ninguno me avia encomendado

300. y confiança] *interlined with caret* R
301. en] *interlined with caret* R
302. el Padre lo que] *interlined with caret* R
303. el Padre les] *interlined with caret* R
304. de] *interlined with caret* R
305. para el Rey] *interlined with caret* R
306. Juº *interlined with caret* R
307. para hablar al Rey] *interlined with caret* R

el negocio todavia[308] por ser cosa que toccasse al bien público y encomendada de Vuestra Paternidad resolvime de informarme del estado en que estava, y hallando mucha frialdad en los ministros, y mucha probabilidad de que el negocio no avia llegado aún a los oydos del Rey,[309] me determiné de ablarle en ello muy de proposito, y assi lo hiçi a 27 del passado, despues de comer teniendo más de una hora y un[310] quarto de audiencia muy grata y a solas, y di a Su Magestad muchas raçones para moverle a mostrarse liberal en esta conjuntura con los padres franceses, alabando mucha la carta piadosa que avia escrito a Vuestra Paternidad como cosa degna de tal monarca y Rey Catolico. Mostro gusto y me pidio memorial y que lo tratasse con Don Juan de Idiaquez y assi lo hiçi, y me prometio todo su favor y dio muy buenas esperanças.[311]

Y todo esto[312] se lo dixi luego al Padre provincial rogandole que no aya falta en sollicitarlo, pues a él viene la comission de Vuestra Paternidad. Yo tengo forçosa necesidad de partirme luego a Valladolid y tan bien tengo otros[313] negocios de sollicitar en servicio de los Seminarios, a los quales está el Rey tan affecto que,[314] aunque estos padres no lo saben, ni combiene por las suspechas que corren, me ha prometido[315] una merced agora[316] de un arbitrio en Sevilla de 7 mil ducados para repartir a los Seminarios y residencias[317] para pagar deudas, y si algunos destos padres y hermanos que tienen coraçones un poco estrechos lo supiessen, dirian luego que lo emos quitado a ellos, aunque sea cosa que ellos nunca pidieren y quando lo pidiessen el Rey por ventura[318] no se lo daria, pero desto poco que tengo dicho, de la remission[319] en sollicitar el negocio de los padres franceses, veerá Vuestra Paternidad[320] lo que[321] me an dicho tan bien con mucho sentimiento los Padres Gil Gonçales, Bartolome Perez, Ribadaneyra, Garcia Alarcon[322] y

308. todavia] *interlined with caret R*
309. aún a los oydos del Rey] aun *possibly deleted;* a los *interlined above illegible deletion;* del Rey *interlined with caret R*
310. un] *interlined with caret R*
311. *Editorial paragraph break, following Hicks's transcripts.* Grene's version reads: "The king gave him [Fr Persons] audience of above an houre and a quarter, promised to be liberal towards our French fathers and gave him 7 mil ducados to be distributed among the Seminaries and he counsaileth F. General to keepe in Rome half a dozen Spaniards students in Roman College which would help infinitly for the union &c. — and all this he writeth at large ... ."
312. esto] *interlined with caret R*
313. otros] *interlined with caret R*
314. en servicio de los Seminarios, a los quales está el Rey tan affecto que] *interlined with caret R*
315. me ha prometido] *interlined with caret R*
316. agora] *interlined with caret R*
317. y residencias] *interlined with caret R*
318. ventura] *interlined with caret R*
319. remission] *interlined above illegible deletion R*
320. Vuestra Paternidad] *followed by large interlined circle in R. This may indicate an intention to revise the material immediately following, since it is substantially repeated at the end of the paragraph (see n364 below).*
321. que] *interlined with caret R*
322. Garcia Alarcon] *interlined with caret R*

otros, que an estado fuera de España, y tienen coraçones más anchos, quanto poco affecto hallan aqui en[323] algunos, para[324] las cosas de estrangeros, y assi no es poco beneficio y consuelo tener aý a Vuestra Paternidad y a otros padres más universales, aunque, gracias a Dios, no faltan tan bien por acá muchos, y essos otros son para nuestro excercicio, y son muy buenos hombres, si no que no aprehenden más de lo que han visto, *et nemo amat quod non cognoscit*. Dios quiere que aya de todos para el[325] excercicio de todos, y assi Vuestra Paternidad me perdone por aver sido tan largo en esto, y yo por mi particular puedo decir con verdad que[326] en mi vida no he hallado ni más amor ni más amistad que en estos reynos, pero veo alguna[327] falta para las cosas universales, y ansi con esta occasion[328] a persuasion de los padres arriba dichos, vengo a representar a Vuestra Paternidad despues de escritta esta carta que sería de mucha importancia, para todas las cosas universales, y para mayor union con Vuestra Paternidad y con las cosas de Roma, y para que Vuestra Paternidad tubiesse siempre por acá personas conocidas y provadas por aý, y affectas a las cosas de aý, que ubiesse siempre en Roma a lo menos una media docena de estudiantes destas provincias, porque aunque sea algun gasto y algunos se enfermen y mueren, es tan notabil el provecho de los demas que buelven acá, que facilmente se compensa el daño, porque realmente *relucent et eminent inter caeteros*, como se vee en los Padres Gil Goncales, Bartolome Perez, Cabredo, Duarte y otros, y los que no an salido de España *non tam afficiuntur ad externa, nec ad res universales*.

4. En quanto a las cosas de Padre Cresuello con este Collegio, las he mirado y me he enformado tan bien de los padres que viven aqui y son indifferentes, y no hallo cosa chica ni grande, porque el rector y otros de casa le hiciessen aquellas molestias que Vuestra Paternidad avrá sabido, sino meras suspechas, y ansi el Padre provincial mismo me ha dicho que estava muy corrido del negocio, pues aviendo examinado el rector y todos los demas que dician que el Padre Cresuello les quitava las limosnas, no pudieron allegar ninguna cosa de fundamento, y es cierto que el Padre Cresuello no quita a este Collegio un real, pues pide a nadie, como mostre en particular al Padre provincial, y ansi entiendo que él y el Padre Visitador finiran facilmente[329] esta controversia, y assentarán un orden que se ha de siguir despues conforme a la entencion y cartas de Vuestra Paternidad y lo hare de la otra parte que el Padre Cresuello les dé toda la satisfacion que será possible a los Padres y hermanos de casa, de tiempo en tiempo, como él realmente desea y lo hace.

5. El Padre Gulielmo Flarque, Nicolas Smith y otros de los padres nuestros Yngleses en Flandes, me escriven que quando el Padre Nicolas Smith bolvio ultimamente a la Compañia despues que vino de Ynglaterra, se puso en las manos del Padre Oliverio siendo provincial, el qual applicó al collegio de la Compañia de Douay todos los libros y otras cosas que le apertenecian, y aviendose muerto despues su padre en Ynglaterra[330]

323. en] *interlined above illegible deletion* R
324. para] *interlined with caret* R
325. el] *interlined with caret* R
326. por mi particular puedo decir con verdad que] *interlined with caret* R
327. alguna] *followed by* alguna [*deleted*] R
328. The rest of this paragraph has been written vertically in the lefthand margin in R
329. facilmente] *interlined with caret* R
330. en Ynglaterra] *interlined with caret* R

dexó alguna manda de 300 o 400 ducados más o menos, como yo entiendo, a un doctor médico su hermano que es Catolico en Londres, para que fuesse embiando dellos[331] a Padre Nicolas conforme a su menester o voluntad, y entiendo que parte del denero[332] ha llegado ya a Flandes a las manos del Padre Olto aunque no lo saben los Padres Flamencos,[333] y que más se aguarda si el doctor quisiera,[334] y porque el Seminario Ynglés de San Omer está con mucha necessidad y el Padre Nicolas Smith vive en él, y vivio muy poco en el collegio de la Compañia de Douay, al qual todavia dexó sus libros, se enclinaria más su tio el doctor médico en Ynglaterra que se empleasse este denero o la mayor parte dél en el dicho Seminario, donde reside el Padre Nicolas, y los demas Padres Yngleses del Seminario lo piden, porque los de la nacion Flamenca no saben aún[335] nada, como dixi,[336] del denero que ha llegado, y el Padre Nicolas desea tan bien ayudar al Seminario si Vuestra Paternidad le diera licencia. El negocio para y esté en secreto hasta que Vuestra Paternidad determine algo en ello. Puedese embiar la resolucion al Padre Holto, y advertirme tan bien a mí de la voluntad de Vuestra Paternidad en el negocio para que se execute lo que Vuestra Paternidad mandará.

6. El Padre Cresuello está en la camma de un dolor de colica y assi pienso que no escrive por esta vez, y tanto más cartas me cargan a mí. Del remedio de los disordenes que ha avido en el Collegio Ynglés, no escrivo aqui por aver escrito a parte a Vuestra Paternidad mi pobre paracer en ello, y lo recibera Vuestra Paternidad con este correo. Tenía tan bien otros papeles para embiar toccante el establecimiento destos Seminarios por acá, pero estos yran con un extraordinario del Nuncio de aqui algunos dias. Llegó aqui quatro dias ha un sacerdote desso Seminario con la patente de Vuestra Paternidad y lo emos acogido y consolado, y yra presto conmigo a Valladolid. Parece bonito, y es raçon que regalemos a los que an sido fieles a sus superiores. Ni se offereçe otro por agora. Dios nos guarde a Vuestra Paternidad por muchos años. En cuyos sacrificios etc. Madrid a 2 de diciembre 1595.[337]

   De vuestra Reverenda Paternidad
    hijo y siervo
     Roberto Personio.

[PS] 7. No se partio este correo al dia que se señaló, por averse entendido que venian dos ordinarios de Italia, y el uno ha llegado y trae cartas de 25 de Settiembre, pero el otro[338] no aún. Tan bien llegó a noche un extraordinario que me truxo carta de Vuestra Paternidad de 29 de Octubre y el Padre Edmondo Harodo de 25, toccante las cosas desso Seminario Ynglés, cuyo gobierno parece que Vuestra Paternidad está muy inclinado a dexar, y no me maravillo, pues no saca la Compañia sino travajos hasta agora y di-

---

331. dellos] *interlined with caret R*
332. del denero] *interlined with caret*
333. aunque no lo saben los Padres Flamencos] *interlined with caret R*
334. si el doctor quisiera] *interlined with caret R*
335. aún] *interlined over* non [*deleted*] *R*
336. como dixi] *interlined with caret R*
337. Grene continues: "El P. Creswello esta en la cama de un dolor de colica ... he subscribeth De V.R. Paternidad hijo y siervo Roberto Personio."
338. otro] *interlined with caret R*

sagradecimiento de los que reciben el beneficio. Pero de la otra parte ay, que si la Compañia alza la mano de aquel gobierno, estando los tiempos, personas y cosas de Ynglaterra como estan, hase de perder totalmente aquela juventud sin remedio, porque hanse de entrar luego libertades y lo que dellas siguera, y no teniendo la nacion Ynglesa sacerdotes siglares bastantes para aquel gobierno, como no les tiene, todo ha de caer, y quando ubiesse otros para el Collegio,[339] los inquietos animados con esta victoria, o les haran concederles todo lo que quieren, o les atropelaran etc.

8. Más, será esse Collegio un Seminario perpetuo de libertades, bandos, odios y dissensiones contra la Compañia, y todos los demas Seminarios gobernados por la Compañia, de donde siguerian notables daños y inconvenientes, y quando quisiesse la Compañia toda via discargarse desse gobierno, no parece que sería buen tiempo agora para que los inquietos no triumfen y piense la gente de fuera que aya avido alguna falta de parte nuestra. Tan bien sería necessario en tal caso considerar a quien se entregasse el Collegio, porque si a la gente de por aý que an procurado o fomentado el mal se entregasse, sería *tradere agnos lupis*. Alguna persona virtuosa se avia de esccoger de la nacion, o porventura algun[340] estrangero *probatae virtutis* sería mejor. Y más desto, pues prueven tan mal los Yngleses en Roma, tanto en la salud como en la disciplina, sería por ventura considerabile, quando la Compania ubiesse de dexar poner el gobierno,[341] si sería mejor bolver a algunos sacerdotes graves de la nacion Ynglesa por capelanos de aquela yglesia y señarlarles la renta que bastasse, como antes que començo el Collegio,[342] y la demas gastarlas en los dos Seminarios de Flandes, donde se sustentaria más gente con ella que no en Roma, y se escusarian tan largos viages, y los estudiantes se conservarian en mayor humild, modestia y simplicidad natural que no en Roma, donde parece que con el ayre solamente y con la vista de tantos personages grandes[343] y con el recurso a tantos, y con la conversacion con tantos Yngleses siglares de fuera cobran unos espiritus de mucho atrevimiento y immodestia, y no salen tan[344] buenos despues ni para alla ni para Ynglaterra, como los alumnos de los demas Seminarios.

9. Luego supplico a Vuestra Paternidad por amor de nuestro Señor, que no piense la Compañia de dixar el gobierno del Collegio por agora, sino que se prueven una vez los otros remedios por algun tiempo y si estos no salieren efficaces, se puede venir a otra resolucion. Ponga Vuestra Paternidad un rector de pecho, que les gobierne con suavidad y llaneça, pero tan bien con prudencia y vigor,[345] acquiriciando los buenos y castigando los malos. Ygualmente ni sea con ellos demasiado doméstico ni familiar, ni de la otra parte demasiado menudo en reparar en menudencias, pero resoluto en[346] guardar disciplina y clausura sobre todo, curtandoles toda communicacion con los de fuera, y tan bien con los enquietos de dentro. No se muestre timido en castigar ni dispedir[347] quando es

339. quando ubiesse otros para el Collegio] *interlined with caret R*
340. algun] *interlined with caret R*
341. quando la Compania ubiesse de dexar poner el gobierno] *interlined with caret R*
342. como antes que començo el Collegio] *interlined with caret R*
343. grandes] *interlined with caret R*
344. salen tan] *interlined with caret*
345. pero tan bien con prudencia y vigor] *interlined with caret R*
346. en] *interlined above* y [*deleted*] *R*
347. ni dispedir] *interlined with caret R*

menester, ni duro en perdonar y olvidar quando ay emienda. No les permeta ninguna suerte de electiones de prefectos o officiales en casa, sino que todo dipenda dél. Tenga dos o tres Yngleses de la Compañia consigo en el Collegio, si los ay, porque le allanaran mil difficultades. El paroco y los repetidores de la nacion Ynglesa de que nos escriven en ninguna manera nos contentan por acá, porque[348] si los estudiantes salen con estas impertinencias suyas, cada dia pideran otras. El paroco avia de ser elegido por el rector de los mejores y más quietos de todos, y éste de que escriven, ha sido cabeça de los bandos. Parece indignidad insuffribile. No combiene que los repetitores sean[349] de los alumnos a mi parecer.

10. El Rey ha sentido[350] mucho la turbacion desse Seminario y escrive con calor a su Embaxador que ayude y anime a Vuestra Paternidad para aquietarlo, y que trate tan bien con su Santidad lo que conbiene para remedio efficaz, como veerá Vuestra Paternidad por la copia de la carta que yrá con ésta. A mí se offerece que no sería bien que el Padre Edmundo Harodo[351] se quitaria al Collegio a la instancia de los inquietos, si Vuestra Paternidad no vea otra raçon. Harta mundança será si Vuestra Paternidad pone otro rector, como me dixo el Padre Jacomo de Vicariis, que pensava y importa que sea hombre de nervio y confiera con el Padre Alfonso Agazari, que huelga nos mucho entender que aya venido a estar en Roma, porque en muchas cosas dara luz por la mucha experiencia tiene de las nuestras cosas.

11. La profession del Padre Cresuello se la accuerdo solamente a Vuestra Paternidad y tan bien propongo que se mire si avrá alguna manera de dar la profession al Padre Henrique Garneto y al Padre Gulielmo Westono en Ynglaterra y al hermano Rodulfo que está en carcel, pues todos an dado tan grande satisfaction en su vida, y son más de veynte años que los padres estan en la Compañia y el hermano deceseis.

12. Embío con este correo dos papeles que deseo mucho que se buelvan presto, por casos que se pueden succeder. El primero es para que su Santidad confirme los traspassos que an hecho los Mercaderes Yngleses de la Yglesia y casa de San Jorge en San Lucar de Barrameda, a los sacerdotes de los Seminarios, y juntamente facultad a mí para hacer leyes y ordinancas de bien vivir para los capelanos, y para que se assiente una vez esta residencia *quicquid de me fuerit*. Se desea mucho que su Santidad confirme lo que los confradres an ordenado en bien de aquela obra pia. Se encomienda el negocio a Rogero Baynes y a Juan Secilio que solliciten y procuren con la direction de Vuestra Paternidad.

13. El otro papel es acirca del officio del prefecto de las missiones en estos Seminarios Yngleses que no pueden passar sin él, como veerá Vuestra Paternidad por las raçones que pongo a parte, y aunque mientras que yo quedo aqui no avrá, creo, menester desta declaracion, porque todo lo que se pone en sus reglas, lo passo yo facilmente agora en la praxi, todavia bien veo que si yo faltare, no podrian passar adelante sin este prefecto que assiste a entrambos Seminarios y a los residencias fuera de los rectores, y ansi Vuestra Paternidad hara grande obra buena a estos Seminarios de mirar los apuntamientos que propongo para el dicho officio, y mandar mudar o confirmar lo que le pareciere, y

348. acá, porque] *interlined with caret R*
349. sean] *interlined with caret R*
350. El Rey ha sentido] *underlined R*
351. que el Padre Edmundo Harodo] *underlined R*

nombrar luego la persona a quien Vuestra Paternidad dara el dicho officio con facultad de substituir caso de muerte o absencia hasta que pueda avisar a Vuestra Paternidad.

Rogero Baynes mostrará a Vuestra Paternidad la copia del Rey que escrive al Embaxador sobre las cosas del Collegio. Dios guarde a Vuestra Paternidad como le supplicamos. E la [sus etc.] De Madrid a 9 de Deciembre 1595.

    De Vuestra Paternidad
        hijo y siervo
            Roberto Personio.

[*Addressed:*] Al Reverendo in Christo el Padre Claudio Aquaviva Preposito General de la Compañia de Jesus en Roma.

[*Endorsed:*] Madrid. P. Roberto Personio Dec. 9 95. [*with summary of contents*]

Translation

Our Very Reverend Father in Christ
The peace of Christ.

I arrived here in Madrid in the middle of November, having left the seminary at Seville in a reasonably good state, as I wrote from there by the last post.[352] And because the gravity of the situation at the seminary at Valladolid demanded my urgent attention, I went immediately to have an interview with father visitor at Alcalá,[353] and consulted His Reverence about the problems which everyone is writing to me about from Valladolid, concerning the bad government of the rector. He took the view that it would be necessary to replace him, but this is to be done later when His Reverence arrives there; in the meantime, I am to go and arrange matters as best I can. But I am afraid I shall find the college in a very bad state, not only in temporal matters but through lack of discipline and of sympathy between the rector and our fathers; though I understand that this will be easily remedied by the change of rector, if they give us back Cabredo – and of this I have hopes. No one else could come in exchange so appropriately, so as to avoid any slur on Fr Gonzalo del Río, for it will look as if Fr Cabredo were returning to his old post on finishing the three years of the provincial's term,[354] the other having been there only as a supply.

2. It gives us all great satisfaction to have a visitor like Fr Alarcón,[355] a very great servant of God and very prudent and discreet in his office. All are anxious for him to begin work soon. He is waiting for some despatches from Your Paternity, and now for four

---

352. Probably 28 October, from Seville (B298).

353. About 22 miles northeast of Madrid.

354. Cabredo had been serving as an assistant to the provincial, Gonzalo Dávila, provincial of Castile 1593–1597.

355. García de Alarcón, SJ (1534–1597), recently appointed visitor to the provinces of Castile and Toledo (1595–1597), which had opposed the anti-*converso* decree of 1593. He was from a famous *converso* family himself and at the end of his visitation expressed his criticism of the decree in a memorial dated 16 December 1597: Robert Maryks, *The Jesuit Order as a Synagogue of Jews: Jesuits of Jewish Ancestry and Purity-of-Blood Laws in the Early Society of Jesus* (Leiden, 2010), 190–211.

whole months we have not had any letter from Rome by the ordinary post.[356] I found the good visitor disturbed about something new that Fr Sicilia's assistant had written from Jesús del Monte, virtually secret and confidential, regarding that father's affairs and his being stationed there. And so, by the visitor's orders I went to see Fr Sicilia at Jesús del Monte and spoke very plainly to him about his affairs, and I found out that everything that his assistant had written had been settled between them. The father promised me faithfully that he would be accommodating from then onward and would not leave Jesús del Monte for Madrid until the order for which he is waiting comes from Your Paternity. On my arrival here afterwards, I spoke to the governor and the countess together, with the same frankness and confidence, about Fr Sicilia's affairs in so far as they affect them; and in confidence they fully admitted to me that the Society was right in dealing with the father as it had done, and that they did not approve of his way of carrying on, compromising his order. They well knew that, because of the enemies he had, he had been of no help to them in their disputes and affairs, except only in that with the president of [the council of] Castile; and so, though outwardly they make a show of friendship and gratitude for the willingness that the father has shown to act for them, yet they will not be put out if Your Paternity disposes of him in your own way; rather I gather from various signs that, if the king should employ the governor on some enterprise,[357] as it was said last summer that he would do – and it really seems that His Majesty has no one else now – I think that it would not be disagreeable to the governor that Fr Sicilia should either go to Italy or at least not be given a licence to go with him,[358] because the freedom with which he gives orders and the resultant dislike which the captains of the galleys have for him cannot but be distasteful to the governor. But this must be treated as confidential.

3. When I arrived, as I did, in this town, Fr Gil González and father visitor told me of the business of the French fathers and how the critical moment had been let slip for requesting the king's intervention on their behalf, partly on account of the mistake which had caused Your Paternity's letter to the king to be delivered to this college instead of to father provincial,[359] and partly because the provincial gave no signs of any warmth in the matter – a thing which grieved me much; and so afterwards when the provincial came here, which was two days later, I spoke to him about it and roused him and told him how

356. In fact, the ordinary post from September arrived a few days later.

357. Martín de Padilla y Manrique, Count of Santa Gadea (1540–1602), adelantado of Castile and commander in chief of the Atlantic fleet, defended the mouth of the Tagus against the English fleet in 1589; in July 1596, following Essex's raid on Cádiz, he tried to persuade Philip to retaliate boldly, and in October of that year was forced, against his will and judgement, to lead an abortive attack on Ireland. Evidently Philip II was already, in the summer of 1595, turning to him as potential commander of the enterprise (Kamen, 307–308; Parker, 344; Glenn Richardson and Susan Doran, *Tudor England and its Neighbours* [Houndmills, Basingstoke, 2005], 194; and John Lingard, *The History of England, from the First Invasion by the Romans* [London, 1838], 8: 333, 335, citing Thomas Birch, *Memoirs of the Reign of Queen Elizabeth, From the Year 1581 till her Death* [London, 1734], 2: 307–308).

358. I.e., the governor.

359. I.e., to the Jesuit college in Madrid, rather than to the provincial of Toledo (either Francisco de Porres, or Luis de Guzmán, who succeeded in December 1595).

important the matter was, for many reasons; and further I offered to reopen the case with Don Juan de Idiáquez at El Pardo the next day.[360] This I did, and I found him very well-disposed. When I told father provincial of this, His Reverence asked me how best to proceed in the matter: whether through Don Juan or through Don Cristóbal.[361] My opinion was that it should be through neither of these two, but that His Reverence ought to speak to the king himself and, after leaving him a memorial, together with a copy of Your Paternity's letter, should go and see the person to whom the king referred the matter and conclude the affair with him. The father went to El Pardo with Fr Sebastián Hernández[362] and, as they were unable to speak with the king, they left the copy of the letter, but not a memorial, with the prince – who does not deal with affairs as yet – and merely had a conversation with Don Cristóbal and Don Juan by way of winning their support. But when I subsequently went to El Pardo, three or four days after this, to speak to the king, I resolved to inform myself of how matters stood, as it was a matter that affected the general interests and Your Paternity had ordered action to be taken about it, even though nobody had authorized me to deal with the business yet. And as I found the ministers very lukewarm about it and that it was highly probable that the affair had not yet reached the ears of the king, I made up my mind to speak with him on the subject very plainly. And so I did on the 27th of last month after dinner and had an audience of over an hour and a quarter, a very pleasant one and quite private, and I gave His Majesty many reasons to induce him to show a generous spirit towards the French fathers on this occasion; and I praised very highly the pious letter he had written to Your Paternity, as being a thing that was worthy of so great a monarch and Catholic king. He showed pleasure at this and asked me for a memorial and told me to discuss the matter with Don Juan de Idiáquez, which I did, and the latter promised me to use all his influence and gave me very great hopes.

All this I presently told father provincial and begged him to be quite sure to press the matter, since it was to him that Your Paternity had entrusted it. I am absolutely obliged to leave for Valladolid in a short time, and besides, I have other business to urge on behalf of the seminaries. The king is so favourably disposed to these that, although the fathers here do not know it (nor is it appropriate that they should, given the suspicion that prevails now), he has promised me now a grant of 7000 ducats from an impost at Seville, to distribute among the seminaries and residences to pay their debts; and if some of the fathers and brothers here, who are so mean-spirited, were to know of it, they would say at once that we have deprived them of it, in spite of its being a thing they would never ask

360. In 1547 Charles V converted a royal hunting lodge at the small town of El Pardo, a few miles from Madrid, into a palace, designed by Luis de Vega, known as the Palacio Real de El Pardo.

361. After May 1594, as Philip's health declined, Cristóbal de Moura and Juan de Idiáquez drew up reports for the king on domestic and foreign affairs respectively, bypassing the council (Kamen, 302–303); Moura was regarded as the king's favourite, frequently deputizing for him and acting as his spokesman (Parker, 343–345). See also Persons to Idiáquez, Moura, and Ruiz de Velasco, July 1593 (B194).

362. Sebastián Hernández, SJ, confessor of Luisa de Aguilera, testified before the Inquisition in 1575; see Gillian T.W. Ahlgren, *The Inquisition of Francisca: A Sixteenth-Century Visionary on Trial* (Chicago, 2005), 173.

for, and if they were to ask for it the king would possibly not give it to them. But from this slight mention I have made of the tardiness in pressing the affair of the French fathers, Your Paternity will realize the truth of what has also been said to me with much feeling by Fathers Gil González, Bartolomé Pérez, Ribadeneira, García de Alarcón, and others, men who have been outside of Spain and who are broader in their sympathy: that is, how little concern they find here in some of the fathers for the affairs of foreigners. And thus it is no small advantage and consolation that we have Your Paternity and other fathers, with a more cosmopolitan vision, there in Rome; although, thank God, we are not without many such here too. Those others are sent to try us:[363] they are very good men, only they cannot grasp more than they have seen, and *no one loves what he does not know*. It is God's will that there should be men of all sorts for all kinds of calling; and so I beg Your Paternity to forgive me for having enlarged on this point. For my own part I can truthfully say that I have never in my life found greater love and friendship than in these realms, yet I see that there is some failure to see things in a broader perspective, and so I take this opportunity, at the suggestion of the abovementioned fathers, to represent to Your Paternity, now that I have written this letter, that it would be of great value, in furtherance of all our interests throughout the world, and with a view to bringing about greater union with Your Paternity and with our interests in Rome, and to enable Your Paternity to have here at all times men you had known over there, of proven worth and attached to our interests there – that there should always be in Rome at least half a dozen students from these provinces. For even though it may entail some expense, and some of them would get ill and die, the benefit derived from the others who return here is so marked that it easily outweighs the loss; for truly *they shine out and excel among the rest*, as can be seen in the case of Fr Gil González, Bartolomé Pérez, Cabredo, Duarte, and others, whilst those who have never gone out of Spain *are not so interested in things outside and have not so wide an outlook*.[364]

4. With reference to Fr Creswell's dealings with this college,[365] I have looked into the matter and have obtained information from the fathers who live here and are unprejudiced, and I do not find any reason, great or small, for the rector and others in the house to cause him those inconveniences of which Your Paternity will have been informed, except mere suspicions. And so father provincial himself has told me that he was very much ashamed of the affair, for after he had cross-questioned the rector and all the others who used to say that Fr Creswell was depriving them of alms, they could not produce

363. The less cosmopolitan Jesuits lack wider perspective, but they are good for religious exercise or activity.

364. See note to the Spanish text for the repetition in this paragraph. The Jesuits listed here as having a wider outlook are Gil González Dávila; Bartolomé Pérez de Nueros y Maynar (1548–1614; see Francisco de Borja Medina, in *DHCJ*, 3: 3092–3093), until recently provincial of Andalusia; Pedro de Ribadeneira (1526–1611; see Manuel Ruiz Jurado, in *DHCJ*, 4: 3345–3346), author; García de Alarcón, visitor to Castile and Toledo; Rodrigo (Jiménez) de Cabredo (1558–1618; see Javier Baptista, in *DHCJ*, 1: 592–593), formerly rector of the English college at Valladolid; and Francisco Duarte (1560–1601), rector of the college in Cordoba, who studied at the Roman College (Eduardo Moore, in *DHCJ*, 2: 1156–1157).

365. I.e., the Jesuit college of Madrid.

a single well-founded instance. And it is certain that Fr Creswell does not deprive this college of a single real, for he begs from nobody, as I pointed out particularly to father provincial. And so I understand that he and father visitor will easily bring this controversy to an end, and they are going to lay down a rule that is to be followed in future in accordance with Your Paternity's intentions and letters; and I on the other side will ensure that Fr Creswell gives all the satisfaction that is possible to the fathers and brothers of the house from time to time, as he really wishes to do, and does.

5. Fr William Flack,[366] Nicholas Smith,[367] and others of our English fathers in Flanders write to me that when Fr Nicholas Smith finally returned to the Society, after he came over from England, he put himself in the hands of Fr Olivier, as provincial,[368] and the latter allotted all his books and other property to the Society's college at Douai; afterwards his father in England died and left a legacy of 300 or 400 ducats more or less, as I understand, to a medical doctor in London, a brother of his, who is a Catholic, so that he should take some from it from time to time to send to Fr Nicholas according to his need or wish; and I understand that a portion of the money has already reached Flanders and is in Fr Holt's possession, though the Flemish fathers are not aware of it;[369] and that more is expected if the doctor so wishes. And, since the English seminary of St Omers is in great need, and Fr Nicholas Smith is in residence there, and lived very little in the Society's college at Douai (to which nevertheless he left his books), his uncle, the medical doctor in England, is more inclined that this money, or the greater part of it, should be used in the said seminary where Fr Nicholas resides. The other English fathers in the seminary ask for this, because those of the Flemish nation, as I said, know nothing so far about the money that has arrived. Fr Nicholas also desires to help the seminary, if Your Paternity gives him permission. The matter is on hold, kept secret until Your Paternity comes to some decision about it. The decision can be sent to Fr Holt, with advice to me too of Your Paternity's pleasure in the matter, so that your orders may be carried out.[370]

6. Fr Creswell is in bed, sick with the colic, and so I think he is not writing this time, and thus all the more letters fall to my lot. I am not writing anything here about how to cure the disorders that have occurred in the English college, because I have written my poor opinion on the matter to Your Paternity separately, and you will receive it by this post.[371] I also had some other papers to send, dealing with the establishment of these

366. William Flack, procurator of the English Jesuits at Saint-Omer.

367. Nicolas Smith (1558–1630) joined the Society of Jesus three times: in 1578, when he was forced to return to England for reasons of health (see Persons to Agazzari, 5 August 1580, A16); in 1582, in Paris, where again his health failed him; and finally in 1592–1594, when he became the first minister at St Omers (Anstruther, 320–321).

368. Olivier Mannaerts.

369. William Holt, liaison between the seminary of St Omers and the court in Brussels.

370. Grene's version reads: "He then desireth leave that the money (some 300 or 400 ducadoes) fallen to or sent to F. Nicolas Smith after his returne to the Society may be applyed to St. Omers, and not come into the hands of the Flemings and to Doway College of our Dutch fathers, where F. Manareo provincial hath placed F. Smith, as all F. Smiths books were applyed to that College a little before ... ."

371. See the postscript and Persons's confidential letter of 9 December (B304).

seminaries here, but these will go by an extra post of the nuncio's a few days hence.[372] Four days ago a priest arrived here from that seminary with a letter of introduction from Your Paternity, and we have taken him in and made him welcome, and he will shortly go with me to Valladolid. He seems to be a fine fellow, and it is reasonable that we should reward those who have been loyal to their superiors. Nothing else occurs to me at the moment. May God preserve Your Paternity to us for many years. To your holy sacrifices, etc. Madrid, 2 December 1595.

  Your Paternity's
    son and servant
      Robert Persons.

[PS][373] 7. This post did not go out on the day appointed, because we understood that two ordinary posts were arriving from Italy. One of these has come, bringing letters of September 25th, but the other has not yet arrived.[374] A special post also arrived last night and brought me a letter from Your Paternity of October 29th and from Fr Edmund Harewood of the 25th, dealing with the affairs of the English seminary there. It seems that Your Paternity is very much inclined to give up the government of it; and I am not surprised, because the Society has got nothing but trouble from it up until now, and the ingratitude of those who have benefited from it. But on the other hand there is this to be considered: that, if the Society relaxes its hold of the government there, in the present state of the times and persons and affairs in England, that band of young men will be completely ruined, beyond repair; for in that case licence is sure to creep in, with the consequences that ensue, and so, since the English nation has not enough secular priests capable of governing it, as indeed it does not, everything will collapse; and even if other men were to be put in charge of the college, the rebels would be encouraged by this success and would either make them concede all their demands, or would act in defiance of them.

8. Moreover that college will be a perpetual seedbed of licence, factions, enmity, and hatred of the Society and of all the other seminaries under the Society's government; and notable harm and inconvenience will result from this. Even if the Society should wish to be relieved of this government in any case, this does not seem to be a good time, if we are to prevent the rebels from being triumphant and people outside from thinking that there has been some fault on our part. It would also be necessary in such an event to consider to whom the college is to be handed over, for if it were to the people there who have instigated and fomented the evil, [that would be] *to hand the lambs over to the wolves.* Some

---

  372. Patriarch Camillo Caetani (1552–1602) was the nuncio to Spain.

  373. Grene's summary of the postcript reads: "The post not departing he addeth a long postscript of almost one whole sheet of paper dated Madrid 9 December 1595 ... wherin he useth many arguments to dissuade F. General from leaving the government of the English Seminary in Rome and proposeth many waies in order to remedy the inconveniences there ... he desireth the Profession for F. Henry Garnet. F. Weston and Brother Rodolfo Emerson que estan en el carcel, pues todos han dado tan grande sodifacion en su vida y ser más de veynte annos que los Padres estan en la Compania y el Hermano diez y seys. — he writeth of the residence of St Lugar given to the English, and desireth to have the gift confirmed by the Pope."

  374. Evidently the post of 23 October, q.v.

virtuous person would have to be picked out from the [English] nation, or perhaps some foreigner of proven virtue would be better. And furthermore, since the English fare so badly in Rome, both in health and discipline, it would perhaps be worth considering, if the Society has to relinquish the government, whether it would be better to bring back some reputable priests of English nationality to take charge of the college chapel and assign them a sufficient income, as in former days before the college started,[375] and to spend the rest of the income on the two seminaries in Flanders, where a larger number could be supported on it than in Rome. Such long journeys would thus be avoided and the students could be kept in greater humility, modesty, and native simplicity than they can be in Rome, where it seems that merely from the atmosphere and by reason of the sight of so many great personages and intercourse with so many people, and from conversing with so many English laymen from outside the college, they acquire a spirit of excessive boldness and forwardness, and do not turn out so well afterwards for employment either there or in England as do the pupils of the other seminaries.

9. I beg Your Paternity, therefore, for the love of our Lord, not to let the Society think of giving up the government of the College at present, but first let other expedients be tried for a time, and if these do not prove effective, a different decision can be taken. Let Your Paternity place as rector there a resolute man who will rule them with sweetness and mildness, but with prudence and firmness as well: cherishing the good ones and chastising the bad. Likewise let him be neither too intimate and familiar with them, nor on the other hand too scrupulous in taking notice of trifles, firm however in preserving discipline and, above all, seclusion, cutting them off from all intercourse with outsiders and also with rebellious spirits within the college. Let him show that he is not afraid to punish them or dismiss them, when necessary, nor so obdurate as not to forgive and forget when there is amendment. Do not allow them any kind of election of prefects or officials of the house, but let everything be kept in his own hands. Let him have two or three Englishmen of the Society with him in the college, if they are available, for they will smooth over a thousand difficulties. The *parrocus* and *repetitores* of English nationality, about whom they write to us, are not at all satisfactory from our point of view, for, if the students get away with their impertinencies of this sort, every day they will be making other similar demands.[376] The *parrocus* should have been chosen by the rector from the best and most contented of them all, whereas the one of whom they write has been the leader of the factions. This seems an insufferable outrage. It is not a good thing that the *repetitores* should be chosen from the students in my opinion.

10. The king has been much grieved by the disturbances in the seminary there, and he is writing with some heat to his ambassador, telling him to help and encourage Your

---

375. Prior to the foundation of the English college in Rome in 1579, it served as a hospice for English priests: see Anthony Kenny, "From Hospice to College 1559–1579," in *The English Hospice in Rome* (Rome, 2012), 218–273, and Persons to Good, after 19 March 1579 (A8).

376. *Repetitores* were senior students charged with hearing repetitions; *parrocus* means "parish priest" but in this context seems to refer to the college confessor: not, in this instance, Edmund Harewood, but a student who was given this office: Edward Bennet, one of the leaders of the rebellious students, was elected to this position after Morra's visitation; see Agazzari to Persons, 27 August 1596 (B336).

Paternity to reduce them to order and to consult with His Holiness as well, as to what is best to be done to provide an effective solution. This Your Paternity will see from the copy of his letter which will go with this.[377] It occurs to me that it would not be a good thing for Fr Edmund Harewood to leave the college under pressure from the rebels, unless Your Paternity sees some other justification. There will be change enough if you put another rector there. This Fr Jacomo de Vicariis told me was his opinion: he thought it was important that he should be a man of spirit and that he should consult with Fr Alfonso Agazzari. We rejoice to hear of his coming to stay in Rome, because he will be able to shed light on many matters owing to the large experience he has had of our affairs.[378]

11. Of Fr Creswell's profession I merely remind Your Paternity; and I suggest also that you should see whether there is any way of conferring profession on Fr Henry Garnet and Fr William Weston and on Brother Ralph who is in prison; for they have all given such great satisfaction by their lives for upwards of twenty years that the fathers have been in the Society, and the brother sixteen.[379]

12. I am sending two documents by this post which I am very anxious should be returned quickly, on account of certain eventualities that may occur. The first is that His Holiness may confirm the conveyances of the church and house of St George at Sanlúcar de Barrameda made to the seminary priests by the English merchants, and likewise faculties for me to make rules and ordinances for the good conduct of the priests in charge, so that this residence may be established once for all, *whatever might become of me*. It is very much desired that his Holiness will confirm what the brethren have arranged for the welfare of that pious work. This business is entrusted to Roger Baynes and John Cecil,[380] who should apply for the endorsement and obtain it, under Your Paternity's direction.

13. The other document is about the office of prefect of the missions in the English seminaries here. They cannot get on without one, as Your Paternity will see from the arguments which I am giving in a separate paper; and, although there will be no need, I believe, of this appointment while I remain here, since I find no difficulty at present in giving effect to all that is laid down in the rules proposed, still, I see quite well that, should I fall out, they would be unable to get on without this prefect, who would attend to the interests of the two seminaries and the residences, besides their rectors. And so Your Paternity will do a great and good thing for these seminaries by looking at the notes of

---

377. See Persons to Idiáquez, 6 December 1595 (B302).

378. Agazzari was appointed rector of the English college in 1579 and corresponded regularly with Persons.

379. By "profession" Persons means the taking of final vows; hence the term "professed house" for those who had done so. Final vows came after the completion of formation and after a few years of service. Priests could be professed of the three vows (spiritual coadjutor) or of the four vows (usually referred to as a professed father).

380. Both men were in Rome: Roger Baynes had been secretary to William Allen, and the secular priest John Cecil was ostensibly canvassing support for the Scottish Catholic earls of Erroll (Francis Hay, 1564–1631), Angus (William Douglas, ca. 1554–1611), and Huntly (George Gordon, ca. 1562–1636, created marquess 1599).

what I propose for this office. Please have changes made or approval given as you think fit, and then name the person to whom Your Paternity will entrust the said office, giving authority for a substitute in case of death or absence, until Your Paternity can receive notice of it.

Roger Baynes will show Your Paternity the copy of the letter which the king is writing to the Ambassador about the affairs of the College. May God preserve Your Paternity as we pray Him to do. To your [holy prayers and sacrifices, etc.] From Madrid, 9 December 1595.

>   Your Paternity's
>   son and servant
>   Robert Persons.

B304 To Claudio Acquaviva, Madrid, 9 December 1595

SOURCE: ARSI, FG 651/640, item 31, holograph (*soli*).

NOTE: This is a confidential letter, accompanying the double letter of 2 and 9 December (B303); some further confidential papers, one in cipher, are mentioned but are not to hand.

Persons is concerned about the government of the two colleges in his absence: he hopes that Cabredo will be reinstalled in Valladolid, and he asks Acquaviva to write to the provincial of Andalusia (Cristóbal Méndez) with the aim of bolstering Peralta's authority as rector in Seville. He asks for some English Jesuits, possibly Richard Cowling and William Warford,[381] to be sent from Rome to increase the presence of English priests at the colleges in Spain. In the event, both remained in Rome (see Cowling to Persons, 13 February 1596, B315).

The letter also deals with the conflicts developing in Flanders and Rome. There is tension between the Scottish Jesuit William Crichton and Persons's associate in Brussels, William Holt. Hearing of the death of Owen Lewis, Persons adds a further postscript. He feels that the Morgan–Paget–Gifford–Throckmorton faction is now without a head and that Acquaviva should go ahead and discipline the rebellious students in Rome and replace the rector, Girolamo Fioravanti.

Más suppuesto, lo que digo en el papelico, será forçoso que buelva el padre Cabredo al Seminario de Valladolid, para poder dexarle toda la carga si yo me absentasse, y parimente para tal caso, será necessario que Vuestra Paternidad escriva al Provincial de Andaluzia, y que luego la carta venga a mí abierta, en la qual Vuestra Paternidad diga que aunque aya mucha satisfacion del gobierno del Seminario de Sevilla del padre Francisco de[382] Peralta y que yo y el Padre Cresuello lo emos alabado siempre; toda via para praticar tan bien de quando en quando el canon de los trienios en los seminarios[383] ordena Vuestra Paternidad que se dé otro Rector al Seminario y que el padre Peralta por ser tan util

---

381. On Cowling, see his letter of 29 December 1593 (B212); on Warford, see the headnote to Persons's letter to Barret, 7 November 1590 (B86), and Warford's letter from Amsterdam, 15 May 1591 (B108).
382. Francisco de] *interlined with caret R*
383. en los seminarios] *interlined with caret R*

y amado en aquel collegio quede por Confessor y procurador dél, y que de tres o quatro que seran a proposito por el successor, que son, el padre Francisco Duarte, el padre Juan de Montes, Rector de presente del collegio de Sevilla, y el padre Augustin Lopez y el padre Melchor de Castro, lectores de theologia, Vuestra Paternidad nombre uno o dexe al padre provincial y a mí de excoger qual será más comodo, y con esto se accomodarán las cosas si aquel caso succediera, de mi absencia, y si no yo detendre la dicha carta y no la dare, porque sin duda aunque el padre Peralta es buen hombre, y assistiendole yo puede passar adelante toda via no tiene substancia bastante para sustentar la machina si yo me absentasse pero bien ayudaria a dicho, y assi supplicó a Vuestra Paternidad que se me embíe la dicha carta luego.

Para el mismo respecto y para dexar provision[384] bastante de gente de la nacion en estos seminarios en mi absencia, deseo que Vuestra Paternidad nos embiasse de alli el padre Coulingo y el padre Warfordo, si se puede commodamente y si no ay falta por aý déstos, o de otros dos que fuessen a proposito por acá, porque es cosa certissima y los rectores de aqui lo confiessen (aunque los desso collegio ynglés ayan tenido siempre differentes dictámines) que tener dos o tres yngleses de la Compañia en cada seminario si son buenos y fieles y de edificacion, es grande ayuda por los rectores y por la union y paz de casa y assi querria yo dexarles aqui si yo me parto, y los rectores como digo, lo desean mucho, y porque algunos an de yr necessariamente con migo[385] si me parto y otro ha de estar en este puesto de Madrid, querria tener alguna gente más hasta que se madure la gente que entrará aqui, que será mucha con tiempo y muy buena, pero todo esto sea con commodidad de aý, porque más querria veer las cosas bien assentadas aý, que[386] no aqui, donde no hai peligro de rebueltas ni de escandalo, con la gracia de Dios.

De la inquietud del buen padre Criton en Flandes y de su disgusto notorio contra las cosas de acá, escriven muchos tanto de su nacion como de otras, y dicen que imprime cosas y imaginaciones[387] bien escusadas en muchos tanto de la Compañia como de fuera, contra nuestras cosas de acá (digo del Rey),[388] y contra el padre Holt en Flandes, y se muestra mucho del bando de Pagetto y otros contradictores. Vuestra Paternidad conoçe mejor el hombre que nadie: es un santo colerico y repentino, y con el disgusto que recibo aqui, que realmente fue en gran parte fue por su culpa, considerado el modo de proceder destos de la corte, quedó implacabile. Es menester proveer que no siga escandalo en Flandes. Ni conbiene en mí algun quitar de alli por agora por lo que veerá Vuestra Paternidad en el papelico, si no que el padre Criton, se reconcilie con él, dúdase que el provincial está algo impressionado del padre Criton; Vuestra Paternidad lo ha de remediar.

Yo me partire luego dentro de 3 dias a Valladolid pero suspecho que no podre quedar alli mucho, yre escriviendo a Vuestra Paternidad. En los Santos sacrificios de Vuestra Paternidad humilmente me encomiendo. Madrid 9 de diecembre 1595.

    Roberto Personio.

  384. provision] *this ed.; R obscure*
  385. con migo] *interlined with caret R*
  386. aý, que] *this ed.;* ay que, *R*
  387. y imaginaciones] *interlined with caret R*
  388. digo del Rey] *interlined with caret R*

[PS] *Modo audio de morte episcopi Cassanensis et Throgmortoni. Deus illis parcat, mira Dei iudicia.*[389]

[*Addressed:*] Soli. Al muy Reverendo en Christo padre nuestro el padre Claudio Aquaviva preposito general de la Compañia de Jesus.

[*Endorsed:*] Soli. Madrid. 95. 9 d. diecembre. P. Roberto Personio.

[*on a separate folio:*]
Fuera de las cartas y papeles que tengo escrito a Vuestra Paternidad con este ordinario, que son muchos, pareciome tan bien añadir esta soli para algunas cosas más secretas y lo cifrado yrá a parte en un papellillo por si el padre Francisco Rodriguez tiene la cifra.

Suppuesto lo que se escrive en cifra y que yo podra porventura hacer alguna absencia de aqui, aunque procuraré lo possibile por no hacerlo, es necessario lo que escrivo del officio del prefecto de las missiones con autoridad substituir en absencia porque sin esto no podran durar estos seminarios de aqui ni aquel de Sant Omer, por lo que digo en las raçones en el papel aparte.

Con la muerte del obispo de Cassano que sea en gloria, se ha curtado la cabeça de aquella faction y partialidad que llaman de Escocia por pretender que desean llevantar al Rey de Escocia a la corona de Escocia o sea catolico o no, y escluyr a los Españoles, pero realmente aquella faction está fundada en passion y ambision de pocos contra todo el cuerpo de los catolicos de Ynglaterra, y agora quedan solamente quatro o cinco sin cabecca que son Pagetto y el Doctor Giffordo en Flandes, y Trogmortono en Roma y Morgano no sé dónde pues de aqui y de Flandes está desterrado, y destos dependen algunos otros apassionados o de poca virtud como Nicolas Fizherberto aý en Roma, y por ventura los dos sobrinos del Cardinal Alano y de Cassano, y el padre Friço dom[estic]o al fin a su tio.

La inbidia que tienen contra los de la Compañia particularmente los de la nacion ynglesa, es, por parecerles que no estan accreditados con ellos, y que pueden mucho; y que en sus malas[390] pretenciones les serán contrarios, y a este blanco querrian tan bien traer los estudiantes alborotados, pero en ninguna manera conbiene que la Compañia se canse con esto, pues es evidente obra del demonio, y se accuerde Vuestra Paternidad que el padre Natal dixo al padre Ximenez (como nos ha referido el padre Cresuello) que nuestro padre Ygnacio le dixo quando recibio en la Compañia el primero hombre que entró, que Ynglaterra era el reyno donde más avia de florecer la compañia que en ninguno otro, y vea Vuestra Paternidad cómo se va compliendo por lo que Dios haçe por la Compañia alli, y si se reduciera (lo que yo me assiguro que será, y podra ser presto) se complirá *ad literam in conspectu totius mundi.*

Vuestra Paternidad *amore Dei* mande castigar con resolucion los insolentes, y se tengan los demas en disciplina; y si quieren partirse vayan, yo offeresco de embiar otros mejores de aqui. No conbiene sufrir tantas insolencias sin castigo. He tenido siempre que el padre Fioravanti no era a proposito. Pienso que Vuestra Paternidad lo puso a instancia de otros. El padre Nanni ni dicen me algunos[391] que sería a proposito. Vuestra

389. iudicia] R, *possibly* indicia
390. malas] *interlined with caret* R
391. algunos] R, *possibly* algun

Paternidad veerá mejor lo que conbiene, pero yo no dexaria quedar por agora el padre Fioravante, ni partirse de alli al padre Edmundo.

Translation

In addition to what I have said in the other letter,[392] that it is necessary for Fr Cabredo to return to the seminary of Valladolid, so as to be able to leave him with the whole burden when I am absent, and be my equal in such an eventuality, it will be necessary for Your Paternity to write to the provincial of Andalusia (and that then the letter should be sent in the open mail for me to read), in which Your Paternity says that although there is also much satisfaction with Fr Francisco de Peralta's government of the seminary of Seville, and that Fr Creswell and I have always said so; yet in order to put into effect from time to time the principle of a three year term in the seminary, Your Paternity should give instructions for another rector for the seminary, while Fr Peralta remains for the present in that college as confessor and procurator, appreciated and loved as he is. Three or four should be proposed to succeed him, namely Fr Francisco Duarte, Fr Juan de Montes, present rector of the college of Seville, Fr Agustin López and Fr Melchor de Castro,[393] lecturers in theology; Your Paternity should name one or leave it to father provincial and to me to choose which one is most suitable. This should allow him to deal with things, in the event of my absence; otherwise, I shall keep the said letter and not present it, because without doubt also Fr Peralta is a good man and able to go ahead with my assistance, though still he does not have enough weight to keep the operation going if I am absent unless he is given help – and so I beg Your Paternity to send me the said letter soon.

For the same reason, and to provide enough men of our nation in these seminaries during my absence, I would like Your Paternity to send Fathers Cowling and Warford from there (if it can be done conveniently and there is no deficiency over there as a result), or assign another two who happen to be over here, because it is most certain – and the rectors over here acknowledge it (although they always have different opinions in that English college)[394] – that we should have two or three Englishmen of the Society in each seminary, if they are good and faithful and edifying. They are a great help to the rectors both for the unity and peace of the house, and so I would want to leave them here, if I leave; and the rectors, as I say, greatly desire them. And because some have necessarily to go with me if I depart and another to stay in this post in Madrid, I would like to keep some more men until the men who enter here have matured, which will happen in time, with good results. But let it all depend on your convenience over there, because I would prefer to see matters well settled there, rather than here, where there is no danger of riots or scandal, thanks be to God.

Concerning the discontent of good Fr Crichton in Flanders and his notorious dislike of our affairs here, many have written, both of his nation and others, and they say

392. See the opening paragraph of the open letter of 2/9 December (B303).

393. Melchior (or Melchor) de Castro (ca. 1555–1599) was a distinguished theologian attached to the Jesuit college of St Hermenegild, Seville. Duarte is mentioned also in the longer letter of 2/9 December (B303).

394. In Rome.

that he is printing quite unnecessary and fanciful things to many, both of the Society and outside, against our affairs here (that is, of the king), and against Fr Holt in Flanders, displaying an affinity with Paget and others of that faction. Your Paternity knows more of the man than anyone: he is a saint, hot-tempered, and impulsive. As for the offence that he takes here, which truly is in large part his own fault, considering his manner of proceeding in relation to the court, he has remained implacable. It is necessary to ensure that no scandal follows in Flanders. It is not suitable that anyone should leave from there at present, as Your Paternity will see in the other little letter,[395] unless Fr Crichton is reconciled with him. It is doubtful that this provincial will be able to make any impression on Fr Crichton; Your Paternity will need to find a solution.

I will leave soon within three days for Valladolid, but I suspect that I will not be able to stay there very long, and I will be writing to Your Paternity. I commend myself humbly to Your Paternity's holy sacrifices. Madrid, 9 December 1595.

    Robert Persons.

[PS] I have just heard of the death of the bishop of Cassano and Throckmorton. May God spare them. Marvellous judgements of God.[396]

[*On a separate folio:*]
Apart from the letters and papers which I have written to Your Paternity with this post (which are a lot!), it seemed to me a good idea, all the same, to add this private one about some matters more secret, and the ciphered one separately in a very small letter in case Fr Francisco Rodríguez has the cipher.[397]

Assuming what has been written in cipher, and that I could perhaps take a leave of absence from here, although I will try not to, what I have written is crucial: that the position of prefect of the missions should have the authority to substitute in my absence, because otherwise these seminaries will not survive, either here or at St Omers. I have written my reasons for that in a separate letter.

With the death of the bishop of Cassano (may he be in glory), the head has been severed of that faction and party which looks to Scotland, professing that they desire to raise the king of Scotland to the crown of Scotland,[398] whether he is Catholic or not, and to exclude the Spaniards, but really that faction is founded on the passion and ambition of a few against the entire body of the Catholics of England, and now only four or five remain, without a head: namely, Paget and Dr Gifford in Flanders, and Throckmorton in Rome, and Morgan (who knows where, since he has been exiled from here and from

---

395. In the long letter of 2/9 December (B303), Persons discusses the situation in Flanders in paragraph 4. However, "el papelico" seems to refer to another short paper mentioned in the opening paragraph of the separate folio below.

396. See n389. Different translations of the final phrase are possible: "Marvellous (*mira* as adjective) judgements (*iudicia*) or proofs/signs (*indicia*) of God"; "Marvel at (*mira* as imperative) the judgements/signs of God." They amount to the same thing: Persons sees the deaths of Owen Lewis on 14 October 1595 and Thomas Throckmorton as providential. Throckmorton had not in fact died.

397. Rodríguez was the general secretary of the Society, in Rome.

398. Presumably a mistake for "crown of England."

Flanders), and on these depend all the other hotheads or men of little virtue such as Nicholas Fitzherbert, now in Rome, and perhaps the two nephews of Cardinal Allen and Cassano, and finally, the servant of his uncle Fabrizio.[399]

The grudge they hold against those of the Society, particularly those of the English nation, is that they feel they are not given any credit by them, whereas they are very capable; and that in their own evil fancies they are opposed, and meanwhile they seek to draw the riotous students to this purpose: but in no way is it right that the Society should make common cause with them, since it is clear that their work is of the devil; and Your Paternity will remember that Fr Nadal told Fr Jiménez (as Fr Creswell has drawn to our attention) that our Fr Ignatius told him, when he received into the Society the first father who entered, that England was the kingdom where the Society was most likely to flourish, and no other,[400] and Your Paternity can see how all that God has done for the Society would be perfected over there, and if it were to be reduced (something which I am sure will happen, and that right soon), it will take place *literally before the eyes of the whole world.*

Would Your Paternity *for the love of God* please instruct that the rebels be resolutely punished, and the rest put under discipline; and if they ask to leave, let them go; I offer to send others who are better, from here. It is not appropriate to tolerate such disorder without punishment. I have always held that Fr Fioravanti was not suitable. I think Your Paternity placed him at the urging of others. Fr Nanni has not mentioned anyone to me who might be suitable.[401] Your Paternity will have a better idea what would be right, but I would not allow Fr Fioravanti to stay for now, nor should Fr Edmund leave from there.[402]

B305 From Richard Verstegan, Antwerp, late 1595

SOURCES:

ABSI, Anglia A II, no. 13, fol. 73r-v, holograph, headed "Mr Richard Verstegan's hand-writing";

ABSI, Coll N2, 5 (olim p. 4), item 2, a copy of the first half of the despatch.

399. These members of the Paget-Morgan faction may be identified as Thomas Throckmorton (whose supposed death is reported in the postscript above), Nicholas Fitzherbert (1550–1612, a long-standing resident in Rome; see Edwards, 24), Hugh Griffin or Griffith (nephew of Owen Lewis), and Thomas Hesketh, who adopted the name Allen after his uncle's death (Edwards, 277; Knox, *Allen*, 397). The reference to Fabrizio is obscure, possibly corrupt.

400. Diego Jiménez (ca. 1530–1608) was secretary of the Society of Jesus from 1583–1594. Jerome or Jerónimo Nadal (1507–1580) was an early member of the Society. To the best of our knowledge, no English father, i.e., priest, entered the Society during the lifetime of Ignatius: the Londoner Thomas Lith (b. 1536) entered in 1555 and was dismissed in 1557. A Thomas Natale (Noel or Knowle), who may have been a priest, entered a few months after Ignatius's death, but he was dismissed in 1558.

401. Probably Giovanni Bautista Nannini (1551–1605), at the time rector of the Greek College.

402. Edmund Harewood.

EDITION: Petti, 247–248; Foley, 3: 474.

NOTE: Verstegan gives an account of the martyrdom of John Cornelius, and refers to his previous narratives of Southwell and Walpole. John Cornelius (O'Mahoney, ca. 1557–1594) entered the English College, Rome, via Rheims in 1580. He left for the English mission in September 1583 and acted as chaplain to Sir John Arundell of Lanherne (the "Great Arundell," d. 1590) and his widow in Cornwall, London, and Dorset until arrested in April 1594 and put to death at Dorchester on 3/4 July. In prison, shortly before his death, he took Jesuit vows and declared himself a Jesuit at his execution. The witnesses to the vows reported to Garnet, who then asked Acquaviva permission to ratify vows made under these circumstances. It is not known for certain, therefore, whether Cornelius' vows were valid. He is consistently named in lists of English Jesuit martyrs. See Anstruther, 88–89; Foley, 3: 435–474; McCoog, *Building the Faith of St Peter*, 167; Garnet to Acquaviva, 9 August 1594 (ARSI, FG 651/624); Verstegan to Baynes, 11 June 1594 (Petti, 212–13).

On the publication of Southwell's martyrdom, see Christopher Devlin, *The Life of Robert Southwell: Poet and Martyr* (New York, 1969), 358–359; *A Brefe Discourse of the condemnation and execution of Mr Robert Southwell* (ABSI, *Anglia* AII, no. 1) was copied by Verstegan in 1595; the Latin MS *Narratio martyrii* by Southwell's friend John Deckers (1595) was based on it, and there is a brief Spanish account in Diego de Yepes, *Historia particular de la persecucion de Inglaterra* (Madrid, 1599), 642–649, which also includes (at 666–708) Joseph Creswell's *Historia de la vida y martyrio que padecio en Inglaterra, este año de 1595 P. Henrique Valpolo*, first published in Madrid in 1596. The martyrdom of John Cornelius was described in English in an anonymous "Letter from London" in 1594 and published in Spanish translation in Yepes, pp. 633–640. There were also two contemporary MS translations, one into Latin and the other into Italian. Dorothy Arundell composed an English biography of Cornelius after entering a Benedictine abbey in Brussels in 1598. This was later translated into Italian for use by Daniello Bartoli. The original English versions of both texts are no longer extant. See Elizabeth Patton, "Four Contemporary Translations of Dorothy Arundell's Lost English Narratives," *Philological Quarterly* 95 (2016): 397–424. Grateful thanks to Professor Patton of Johns Hopkins University for information and advice.

Certaine verses which Fr Cornelius a priest of the Societie of Jesus[403] did write oute of prison to his freind:

Alter ego nisi sis non es mihi verus amicus,
ni mihi sis ut ego, non eris alter ego.
Spernere mundum: spernere nullum: spernere sese:
Spernere se sperni: quatuor ista beant.
Christe, tuos, tua, te, gratis accepimus a te
ergo, meos, mea, me merito nunc exigis a me.[404]

403. In Coll N2, he is identified as "Fa. John Cornelius Martir."
404. "Unless you are my other self, you are not my true friend; unless you are to me as I myself, you will not be my other self. To spurn the world, to spurn nothing, to spurn oneself, to spurn even oneself spurning, these four are to be happy. Christ, we have freely received from you,

He was afterward executed in the west countrie. They could not get a caldron for any mony to boyle his quarters in, nor no man to quarter him, so he hanged till he was dead, and was buried beeing cutt in quarters first.

This I thought not good[405] to omitt of this martir, not willinge to leave oute any thing concerning such holy martirs as may come to my knowlege and is woorthy the memory.

I wrote long since into Spaine the manner of Fr Southwell his apprehension, and partly[406] how he was tortured by Topclif. It were good that his apprehension together with his arraignment and death were printed for the present by it self in the Spanish tongue: as also Fr Walpole his history when it cometh, and afterward they may be put together in Latin with others the lyke, and in the meane tyme it would move much to be in the vulgar tongue.

[*Addressed*:] Al Padre Personio.

[*Endorsed by Grene*:] Verses of F. Cornelius the martyr of the Societie of Jesus 1595.

B306 To Joseph Creswell, Valladolid, 24 December 1595

SOURCE: ABSI, MS Anglia A V 9, 329–330, headed "Creswellum fuisse semper, piae memoriae Patri Personio amicissimum: et nemini post Reverendum Patrem Generalem, secundum" (That Creswell had always been a very close friend to Fr Persons of pious memory, second only to Reverend Father General).

HICKS: 433–434, with English translation.

NOTE: In 1613 Acquaviva recalled Joseph Creswell from Spain as the result of controversy over his foundation of an English college in Madrid (Loomie, *Spanish Elizabethans*, 221–227). In his defence, composed in 1614, Creswell included extracts from letters to him by Persons; see also Persons's letter to him of 16 January 1596 (B309).

[Audiamus ipsius Patris Personii testimonium. Adhuc enim, casu, supersunt litterae, ipsius manu scriptae:]

Gratias ago (inquit) Reverentiae Vestrae (mi bone Pater) pro omni vestra benevolentia. Existimo mihi non esse possibile magis amare Reverentiam Vestram, quam semper amavi, postquam primo ipsam novi. Et tamen, mihi videtur, quod quoties ab ipsa discedo, invenio in me novam vim benevolentiae et cordialis amicitiae erga ipsam: adeo sese prodit, omnibus viis, confidentia Vestra et fidelitas, quotiescunque convenimus et conversamur simul: Deus vos secundet semper. Si alios tantum duos aut tres haberem in

---

your friends, your possessions, and you yourself; now, therefore, deservedly you demand from me my friends, my possessions, and myself." Foley and Petti refer to George Oliver, *Collections on the History of the Catholic Religion in Cornwall, Devon, Dorset, Somerset, Wilts, and Gloucester* (London, 1857), 37–38, to show that the last four lines were composed long before, being extant in an MS of Henry IV, and thus not by Cornelius, as Verstegan supposed. More, 165–166, quotes two of the lines thus: "Spernere mundum: spernere nullum: spernere sese, spernere se sperni: vita boni Monachi est."

405. good] *interlined with caret A*

406. partly] p[ar]tly *A*; particularly *Petti*

hoc modo similes amicos: videor mihi quod auderem et sperarem magna. Sed Deus nos iuvabit in hac sua causa: et sanctae ipsius benedictioni et protectioni Reverentiam Vestram commendo. Vallesoleti 24 Decembris 1595.

Translation

[Let us hear the testimony of Fr. Persons himself, for a letter written in his own hand happens to be extant:]

My good father [he says] I thank Your Reverence for all your kindness. I do not think it is possible for me to love Your Reverence more than I have always done, since I first knew you. And yet it seems to me that every time I part from you I find in myself a powerful renewal of goodwill and heartfelt friendship for you, your confidence and loyalty being manifest in every way, whenever we meet and converse together; may God prosper you always. If I had only two or three other similar friends of this stamp, it seems to me I could dare and hope for great things. But God will aid us in this His cause; and to His holy blessing and protection I commend Your Reverence. Valladolid, 24 December 1595.[407]

B307 To Claudio Acquaviva, Valladolid, 27 December 1595

SOURCE: Acquaviva to Persons, 11 March 1596 (B316).

NOTE: Persons once again asked for a resolution to the problem of the rector at Valladolid.

B308 From Claudio Acquaviva, Rome, 15 January 1596

SOURCE: ARSI, Baet. 3/I, 248–249, 251–252.

NOTE: Acquaviva agrees that del Río be replaced as rector of the seminary at Valladolid, preferably by Cabredo (McCoog, *Building the Faith of St Peter*, 212); he has written both to the provincial of Castile (Gonzalo Dávila), and to the visitor, García de Alarcón, to try to facilitate this. In a (partly illegible) addition squeezed in at the end of the series of entries for

---

407. Creswell then argues that Persons did not later change his attitude towards him, even though Persons insisted that Creswell be summoned to Rome in 1605 to explain his handling of a crisis at the English college in Valladolid (Loomie, *Spanish Elizabethans*, 217–219; Edwards, 310–317): "Haec de Creswello tunc Patris Personii opinio. Ipse vero, nullius sibi conscius est mutationis. Licet (fortasse) alter suspicatus sit, fuisse ex diminuta benevolentia, quod revera factum est, ex sincero amore: ex debita observantia et fide in Societatem: ex maioris boni intuitu: ex conscientia: et ex studio tuendae societatis in primitivo suo spiritu, qui (nisi ex ambitione et humanarum rerum inordinato appetitu) labefactari non potest" (This was then Fr Persons's attitude to Creswell. Indeed, he himself was conscious of no change towards him. But suppose [perhaps] someone else surmised that diminished benevolence caused what was in fact done out of sincere love, the observance that he owed to the Society and his faithfulness towards it, from awareness of the greater good, from conscience, and from his commitment to keep the Society in its original spirit, which cannot be overthrown except from ambition and inordinate love of mortal ends).

this date of despatch, Acquaviva expresses his concern about the state of affairs at the English college in Rome, suggesting that Creswell might need to come to Rome; ideally, Persons himself might deal with the problem personally.

P. Roberto Personio, Enero 15.

Mucho siento que el Rector de Valladolid dé tan poca satisfaction en su oficio como se vee por la de Vuestra Reverencia de 13 de Septiembre y por la del Hermano Ambrosio que con ella venía, y aunque ha dias (como avisé a Vuestra Reverencia) que yo escrivi al Provincial pusiese alli otro Superior a gusto de Vuestra Reverencia, toda via escrivio aora al Padre Garçia que si la necessidad que tienen del Padre Cabredo no fuese tan forçosa, se le dé por Superior a aquel seminario, y en caso que esto no se pueda que provea de otro que lo haya como conviene, pues ya que éste de acá va tan el reves de lo que deve se supla con, mantener esos de alla en el buen estado que hasta aora han tenido, de lo de acá no digo nada remitiendo al Rector del Inglés y a los demas Padres que escriviran lo que ay. En las etc.

P. Roberto Personio, 15 de Enero.

Yo crey que las cosas de este seminario fuere para que nadie ... padre superiore ... de la que a Vuestra Reverencia escrivi sobre dexar su cuydado y govierno pero cosas han llegado ... visita le ahora el Cardinal Sega que es Vice-Protector en lugar del Cardinal Caetano.[408] Espero aver si con esta visita y con la venida del Caetano se pone en mejorar[409] del que ahora muestra, porque si esto no fuere porventura avisaré a Vuestra Reverencia que él o el padre Cressuelo vengan a Roma pues será necessaria la presencia de uno de los dos y la de Vuestra Reverencia más ansi pone respecto que le ternan los suyos (bien que ahora a ninguno le tienen) como porque la informacion de Vuestra Reverencia será en qualquiera ocasion de más eficacia y menos sospechosa por ser Vuestra Reverencia de su nacion. En el interim negociamos con Dios orando y Vuestra Reverencia se acuerde de mí en sus oraciones, etc.

Translation

To Robert Persons, 15 January.

I am very sorry that the rector of Valladolid gives so little satisfaction in his duty, as appears from Your Reverence's letter of 13 September[410] and from that of Brother Ambrose which came with it. And although some days have passed (as I informed Your Reverence) since I wrote to the provincial that he might place another superior there more to Your Reverence's liking, still I have written to Fr García that if in fact the necessity for keeping Fr Cabredo was no longer as great as it was, he could be released to be superior of that seminary. And in case this is not possible, I asked him to provide another one who would be convenient. As the one [seminary] here is going totally backwards

---

408. visita le ahora el Cardinal Sega que es Vice-Protector en lugar del Cardinal Caetano] *underlined R*

409. con esta visita y con la venida del Caetano se pone en mejorar] *underlined R*

410. B291.

from what it should be, at least the ones there [in Spain] should be maintained in the good condition they have held up to now. Concerning the issues here, I may not speak but rather defer to the rector of the English and the rest of the fathers who have written to explain the situation. To your [holy prayers and sacrifices], etc.

To Robert Persons, 15 January.

I believe that the affairs of this seminary are in such a state that not one father superior ... concerning which I have written to Your Reverence above to give up its care and governance ... Cardinal Sega is visiting them at present, who is vice-protector, in place of Cardinal Caetani.[411] I hope that as a result of this visit and the arrival of Caetani things will be put in better order than has obtained up to now, because if this does not happen I will warn Your Reverence that either you or Fr Creswell should come to Rome. It may be necessary that one of the two should be present and also Your Reverence could swiftly gain the respect which your own followers show to you (which at the moment they do not show to anyone), because Your Reverence's understanding on any given occasion will be more penetrating and less prone to suspicion, Your Reverence being of their nation. Meanwhile, we wrestle with God in prayer. May the Lord keep Your Reverence. To your prayers, etc.

B309 To Joseph Creswell, Valladolid, 16 January 1596

SOURCE: ABSI, MS Anglia V 9, fols. 254–256, 259, from Joseph Creswell's "Responsio ad calumnias"; indexed in ABSI, Coll P II, 502.

HICKS: 435–438 (with English translation).

NOTE: The letter relates to the departure of del Río, the rector of the English college at Valladolid, and the hostility of some of the local Jesuits to the English. Creswell's introductory and concluding words are given in square brackets, Grene's comments in the notes; for the occasion of his quoting the letter, see the headnote to Persons's letter to him of 24 December 1595 (B306).

[Ipsum Patrem Personium audiamus quid de his rebus scribat 16 Januarii anno 1596 in haec verba:]

Heri (inquit) discessit Segoviam, rector, qui, procul dubio, si usque ad triennii sui finem permansisset, Collegium funditus avertisset. Non defuere zizaniarum principia: et si conciliari sibi potuisset vel unum aliquem sacerdotem aut laicum Hispanum aut Anglum domi qui seditionem institueret, nobis fecisset negotium: pertractis iam ad ipsius partes epulis et conviviis nonnullis ex nostris satrapis. Sed neminem invenit, qui pro ipso staret. Incredibile est quam abjecte se insinuaverit rector, tam mihi quam caeteris domesticis, ut manere potuisset. Visus est habere constitutum sibi huius administrationis

---

411. Filippo Sega was once again vice-protector of the English nation, with Enrico Caetani the cardinal protector from 1586 to 1599. Both had special responsibilities towards the English college in Rome. See Michael E. Williams, *The Venerable English College, Rome* (London, 1579), Appendix VI, p. 232.

scopum, dominari, convivari, et obambulare stipatus alumnis, tamquam affectis honarariis. —— Coeperat (inquit) nos accusare apud Patrem Generalem, uti ex ipsius responsis colligere licet. —— Iubet enim Pater, ut rector mecum agat de omnibus. Neque monet, ut quid rei sit ad illum perscribam etc.[412]

[Quid autem hac de re (consequenter) in iisdem litteris scribat Pater Personius, opere pretium est audire ...]

Hoc (inquit) exemplo constat quid futurum sit, post Seminaria necessariis reditibus instructa: nisi opportune provisum fuerit, et quotidiana experientia docet, quam necessaria sit authoritas Praefecti Missionis, quae interpositis salutaribus legibus, rectores cohibeat. Tam externi hi omnia statim everterent, si ipsorum Arbitrio res permitterentur. Et tamen, incredibile est, quantum ambiant dominari sine arbitris: et suspicor rectorem nostrum convenisse, cum quibusdam ex his Patribus Hispanis. Sed ubi expositas eius merces conspexerunt, conticuerunt prae pudore, et omnibus suffragiis est damnatus. Hac occasione scribam fusius ad Patrem Franciscum Rodriguez quaedam (per otium) Patri Nostro Generali communicanda; scribat enim Reverentia Vestra quae ipsi visa fuerint, adhibito soli.[413]

Translation

[Let us listen to Fr Persons himself, who writes about these matters on 16 January in these words:]

Yesterday the rector departed for Segovia; if he had remained till the end of his three years he would undoubtedly have ruined the College completely. Signs were not wanting that tares were beginning to appear; and if he had been able to gain the adherence of even one individual priest or of a single Spanish or English layman in the house to start a sedition, he would have made trouble for us, having already brought some of our officials over to his side by means of feasts and entertainments; but he found no one who would take his part. It is hard to believe how abjectly the rector has tried to ingratiate himself with me as well as with others in the house, hoping to keep his position. He seems to have set before himself, as the object of his administration, to be lord and master, to entertain his friends, to walk about with a retinue of students as though to do him honour. —— He had begun to make accusations against us to father general, as one can gather from the latter's replies. —— For the father orders the rector to consult me about everything. And he gives me instructions to write him a full account of what is happening.

[But it is worth taking the trouble to hear what Fr Persons writes about this matter further in the same letter ...]

From this example it is clear what will happen, once the seminaries have been furnished with the revenues they require, unless timely provision be made; and daily expe-

412. [*Grene's note:*] Fr Cresswell here dilates on the unwillingness of some Spanish Rectors to obey the rules of the Mission, etc.

413. [*Grene's note:*] Fr Cresswell then explains how in consequence of this hint of Fr Persons and of his subsequent experiences, he would not get the Colleges endorsed, lest the Rectors should become prouder. The Seminary in question was that of Valladolid.

rience teaches how necessary is the authority of the prefect of the mission to keep the rectors in hand by imposing healthy restraints. For these outsiders would immediately spoil everything if matters were left in the rectors' hands. And yet it is hard to believe how ambitious they are to rule according to their own lights. And I suspect that our friend the rector had an understanding with certain of the Spanish fathers here; but, when they saw his corruption exposed, they kept silence out of shame, and he was condemned by the verdict of all. I shall take the opportunity to write more at length to Fr Francisco Rodríguez,[414] giving him certain facts to communicate to father general, when he has leisure. Just so, please would Your Reverence write what you think advisable, marking your letter "private."

B310 From William Crichton, Louvain, 20 January 1596

SOURCE: Persons to Crichton, 10 May 1596 (B323).

NOTE: Crichton thanks Persons for seeking financial assistance for the Scottish college, struggling at Douai (see Persons to Acquaviva, 7 September 1594, B244; McCoog, *Building the Faith of St Peter*, 235–236; Edwards, 174–175), and comments further on his own support for the succession of James VI.

B311 To Claudio Acquaviva, Valladolid, 24 January 1596

SOURCE: Acquaviva to Persons, 8 April.

NOTE: Persons evidently wrote two letters, one about replacing the rector at the college at Valladolid, the other about the troubles at the English College, Rome.

B312 To John Cecil, Valladolid, 24 January 1596

SOURCE: ABSI, Coll P I, 305, Coll P II, 488, 502.

NOTE: Grene notes that this letter concerned the dissensions in the college of Valladolid. Cecil was in Rome at this time (see Persons to Idiáquez, 6 December 1595, B302).

B313 To Roger Baynes, Valladolid, 24 and 31 January 1596

SOURCES:
 ARSI, Angl. 38/II, fol. 194r, Bartoli's extracts;
 ABSI, Coll P II 488, Grene's note, dated 31 January.
HICKS: 434b, 440, 442–443, with English translation.

NOTE: It is unclear whether these were two separate letters, but they deal with discrete matters: Persons's frustration with the continued rumours about the cardinalate, and his desire to come to Rome to deal with the problems at the English college there. As former secretary to William Allen, Baynes would have had an interest in both.

---

414. Rodríguez was Acquaviva's secretary in Rome.

Intorno a quello punto, del capello Io non occorre scrivermi più. Lei cognosce la mia resolutione. Già ho fatto tutta la diligenza, che me parve necessaria, et che io doveva usare per non haverlo. Il resto raccommandarò a Dio solo, e lo pregharò che faccia quello che vuole Lui, e desidero che li amici non mi scrivino più niente di questa cosa.

[31 Jan] Cupit vocari Roman ut tumultus Collegii Anglicani sedet. El pare di havare in testa un modo o due molto soave per remediare tutto, se ho non m'inganno.

Translation

On this matter of the Cardinal's hat I do not think I have anything further to say. You are aware of my decision. I have already taken every step that seemed necessary to me, and that I was bound to take, so as to avoid receiving it. For the rest I will commend it to God alone and will pray Him to do that which He wills. And I would have my friends write nothing further to me on this subject.

[31 Jan] He wishes to be called to Rome to quell the riots in the English college.[415] I fancy he has in mind one or two plans that will put all to rights with much sweetness, if I am not mistaken.

B314 From Claudio Acquaviva, Rome, 11 February 1596

SOURCES:
ARSI, Cast. 6, fols. 237v–238r;
ABSI, Coll P II 488 (listed).

NOTE: Acquaviva responds to several matters raised in Persons's letters of 2 and 9 December (B303), notably his suggestions for handling the crisis at the English College, Rome.

P. Roberto Personio, Valladolid, 11 hebrero.

Tres de Vuestra Reverencia he recevido escritas en noviembre y deçiembre en una de las quales me apuntas las advertençias que le pareçe podran ayudar para el govierno desta Juventud, y son muy buenas si como deseamos se pudiesen poner en execucion, en esto entienden aora los señores Cardenales Gaetano y Sega que tratan desto con su Santidad, y es çierto que si no se da algun corte, el govierno no puede passar adelante como aora va, aunque como ya he escrito a Vuestra Reverencia Su Santidad no nos permite dexarle.

Mucho he gustado de entender el razonamento que Vuestra Reverencia tuvo con aquel Padre en Jesus del Monte, y si lo haçe como lo prometio, ganará mucho. Yo escribo al Provincial que aunque aya Jornada no vaya en ella, sino que aunque le pidan no le conçeda.

Aunque aya Jornada como se sospecha no me pareçe que al presente seran neçessarios más padres de los que bastarán para dar el acostumbrado recaudo en sus ministerios, y estos los Provinciales los daran. Los demas que Vuestra Reverencia desea, tan-

---

415. Grene translates: "He desireth to go to Rome to appease the tumults."

bien se daran a su tiempo que será segun el successo de la Jornada, y entonçes no dude Vuestra Reverencia sino que será consolado en lo que se pudiere.

El ofiçio hecho con Su Magestad en favor de los Padres françeses, le agradezco, si quiere Dios que nos salgan las esperanças que nos dan de ser restituidos, no será necessario molestar a Su Magestad.

El Padre Holto estara en Flandes como Vuestra Reverencia dice, y bien entiendo que el otro bendito Padre exçede un poco con el zelo de su patria, pero no creo que será cosa de daño.

Pareçeme bien que saliendo Vuestra Reverencia de España se ponga por Rector en el Seminario de Sevilla uno de los Padres que nombre, y el que aora es Rector quede por confesor, y ansi lo escrivo al Provincial de Andalucia. Para Valladolid ya escrivi a Vuestra Reverencia como avisaba al Padre Garçia que si podia ser les restituyese al Padre Cabredo.

Las raçones que Vuestra Reverencia nos embia para que aya un Prefecto sobre esos dos Seminarios son muy buenas, y sin ellas sola la experiençia muestra la necessidad que ay desto, Vuestra Reverencia si se ausenta le podra nombrar, y darle las Reglas que nos ha embiado, que pareçen buenas, y si algo se ofreçiere çerca dellas, con éste o con el primer ordinario se le avisará.

Es justo que se dé la profesion a los Padres que Vuestra Reverencia nombra en su carta del padre Cresuelo espero se nos embie la informaçion, que por lo que le conozco no dudo sino que será muy buena. Del Padre Garneto y de sus compañeros pensaremos el modo, que de la cosa no ay duda sino que la mereçen.

Pareçeme bien que se den al Colegio de San Omer aquellos 300 ò 400 ducados que su padre dexó al Padre Nicolas Smith, pero no veo inconveniente en que se le diga al Provincial antes se lo escreviremos de acá.

Por una copia de la que se escrive a los Provinciales la qual se embia al Rector,[416] verá Vuestra Reverencia el trabajo y afliction con que el señor ha querido exerçitar estos dias estos Padres y a mí, y nos ayudará a dar las devidas graçias a la divina Magestad por la singular merçed que nos ha hecho librandonos de tan lastimoso peligro. En [sus &c.]

Translation

To Fr Robert Persons, Valladolid, 11 February.

I have received three letters from Your Reverence, written in November and December, and one of them containing suggestions which may help with the government of these young men. It will be very good if they can be implemented as we wish. The cardinals Caetani and Sega, who are dealing with the subject with his Holiness,[417] understand this now, and it is true that if some concession is not made, the government cannot continue as it is at present, but as I have already written to Your Reverence, His Holiness will not allow us to give it up.

---

416. la qual se embia al Rector] *interlined, possibly in a different hand* R

417. Cardinals Enrico Caetani and Filippo Sega were respectively the cardinal protector of England and vice-protector.

I very much liked the discussion which Your Reverence held with that father at Jesús del Monte,[418] and if he has done as he promised, much will be gained. I am writing to the provincial that he should not go into the expedition, but even if they ask him for it, he should not grant the request.

Even if there is an expedition, as is suspected, I do not think that at the present it is necessary for there to be more fathers than will suffice to give the accustomed care in their ministries, and the provincials will provide these. The others that Your Reverence wants will also be provided in its time depending on how the expedition goes, and then Your Reverence can rest assured that you will be relieved as far as is possible.

I am grateful to you for interceding with His Majesty in favour of French priests. If it please God that we can be hopeful that they will be restored, it will not be necessary to disturb His Majesty.

Fr Holt will be in Flanders, as Your Reverence says, and I understand well that the other blessed father is somewhat excessive in his love for his fatherland,[419] but I do not believe that it will cause harm.

It seems good to me that when Your Reverence leaves Spain, there should be appointed as rector of the seminary at Seville one of the fathers that you mention, and the one who is now rector should stay as confessor,[420] and I am writing accordingly to the provincial of Andalusia. As for Valladolid, I have already written, as advised by Your Reverence, to Fr García[421] that, if possible, Fr Cabredo should be reappointed.

The reasons which Your Reverence sends us about a prefect only for those two seminaries are very good, and even without them our experience shows the necessity there is for this; if Your Reverence absents himself, you could appoint one, and give him the instructions which you have sent us, which look good, and if anything more suggests itself about them, you will be given word by this or the very next post.

It is fitting that Your Reverence should allow the fathers whom you mention in your letter to make their profession: concerning Fr Creswell, I hope, the information will be sent, which from what I know of him will be very good; of Fr Garnet and his companions let us think about a way of carrying this out; there is no doubt of the matter but that they are deserving.[422]

I agree that those 300 or 400 ducats which his father left to Fr Nicholas Smith should be given to the college of St Omers, but I see no objection to the provincial being told before I write to him about it from here.

From a copy of what I have written to the provincials, which I am sending to the rector, Your Reverence can see the travail and affliction with which our Lord has been

---

418. Persons had strongly discouraged Bartolomé de Sicilia from going to Madrid and involving himself in public affairs, despite support from the Jesuits there (Persons to Acquaviva, 2 and 9 December 1595, B303).

419. The Scottish Jesuit William Crichton.

420. Despite the excellence of Peralta's government of the college at Seville, Persons argued for a rotation of the office of rector.

421. García de Alarcón, visitor to the province of Castile.

422. Persons had also mentioned Father William Weston and Brother Ralph Emerson as ready to take their final vows as Jesuits.

pleased to put our fathers and companions to the test in these days, and help us render the thanks we owe his divine majesty for his particular mercy which has rid us from such pitiful danger. To your [prayers and sacrifices, etc.].

B315 From Richard Cowling, Rome, 13 February 1596

SOURCE: AAW, V, no. 38, holograph = W.

NOTE: After arriving in Rome late in 1593, Cowling was attached to the penitentiary; this is his third or fourth letter to Persons since moving to the English college, where he acted as confessor and consultor. In this letter he offers his perspective on the conflicts developing at the college during the time of the vice-protector Sega's visitation, specifying two leaders of the party opposed to the Jesuits: Robert Markham (brother of Sir Griffin Markham) and Edward Bennet (1569–1637; Anstruther, 30–31). He also mentions a third, Robert Shepperd, also known as Bayes, but later in the letter associates him with Richard Haddock, a friend of Persons and supporter of the Jesuits. In Cowling's next letter, 8 April (B321), it transpires that Shepperd/Bayes has been accused of spying for the queen. Sir Griffin Markham, too, was in contact with Cecil (Kenny, "Inglorious Revolution," 149 [part 4]).

Much of the letter concerns John Cecil (Snowden), who had come to Rome from Madrid, in connection with John Ogilvie of Pury's project of reconciling King James VI with the papacy (Persons to Acquaviva, 15 May 1595, B276; to Idiáquez, 6 December 1595, B302; and to Cecil, 24 January 1596, B312). See Yellowlees, 139–142, and the "Summary of Memorials Presented to the King of Spain, by John Ogilvy of Pourie and Dr John Cecil, 1596," in *Documents Illustrating Catholic Policy in the Reign of James VI*, ed. Thomas Graves Law (Edinburgh, 1893), 21–24. On the strength of Persons's recommendation, Cecil used the college as a place of recuperation, putting a strain on its resources, and then played both sides. In effect, he lent his support to the dissidents, betraying the confidence of the protector and, in Cowling's opinion, alienating all in authority, including the pope. He warns Persons against putting any more faith in the man.

The postscript passes on greetings from Henry Tichborne, who was attending the thesis defence of George Turnbull (1569–1633). In 1597 William Crichton unsuccessfully requested that Turnbull, a Scottish Jesuit, be posted to the Scots college in Louvain (McCoog, *Building the Faith of St Peter*, 374). On Tichborne, see his letter to Persons, 5 June 1596 (B327).

Admodum Reverende in Christo Pater
Pax Christi.
Spero ad Reverentiam Vestram perlatas binas aut ternas a me litteras ex quo veni ad hoc Collegium, in praesentiarum non reticendum putavi quam inique coeptis insistant malevoli, suis contra nos calumniis et mendaciis neminem magis ferientes quam seipsos; fabula plebis, et offendiculum urbis consequenter et orbis nunc facti sunt Angli, quibus aliquando speculum pietatis, faculamque devotionis praetulerunt. Exsibilant illos omnes boni, irridet (accidet) Curia, redarguit Illustrissimus Protector, condemnat Illustrissimus Visitator, reprehendit ipse Sanctissimus. Adhuc tamen constant audaciae suae, eiicere certi, vel eiici de Collegio. Mitto ad Reverentiam Vestram obiectiones illorum contra

nostros in Anglia, quibus refutandis perutilis erat opera P. Warfordi, ut etiam in informa[n]do Visitatore. Adiunctum est exemplar literarum D. Griffini Markami Sienna ad fratrem suum Robertum alumnum Collegii egregium politicum, factiosorum coriphaeum, quas litteras invenit P. Minister pro limine P. Eduardi Benetti, socii individui dicti Markami, insignis quoque politici, ducisque tumultuantium. Quibus addi potest tertius Robertus Shepardus, recto nomine Baius, cognatus D. Martini Nelsoni sacerdotis in Anglia. Habui in manibus, ad legendum tantummodo, ipsius informationes, vel potius deformationes ad visitatorem de Collegio; ex quibus descripsi ad verbum, quod tractans de nostris in Anglia, contra nos protulit. Providendum est, ne verificetur de eis; laqueus ruinae populi mei sacerdotes mali, cum iam fere facti sint domui Israel in offendiculum iniquitatis, sanctos putavi cum essem in Anglia et Francia etc. at Romae (sic sensim latens in herba anguis exserpsit) utinam homines, quibus mansuetum esse summum est proprium, invenirentur. Haec ille. Alia ex aliorum scriptis scriberem acerbiora sed parco insolescentibus iuvenibus. Incredibile est quam multa spargantur per urbem mendacia de Illustrissimo Protectore, P. Generale, P. Rectore et aliis nostris patribus a nostratibus, ut nisi quid certi a nostris acceperitis, non adeo tutum aut consultum videatur relationibus aliorum acquiescere, ita mutuis omnia flagrant odiis.

Venit huc D. Cicilius a Reverentia Vestra ut audivi plurimum commendatus, exceptus fuit hospitio pro Collegii tenuitate, liberalius certe, quam nunc temporis excipiantur hospites, per duos menses quibus aegrotavit. P. Rector mihi dedit in mandatas (plus propter commendationes vestras, quam commendati merita) ut omnia darentur illi quae praescriberet medicus, et ipse peteret, idque factum vidi satis exquisite; sed ipse revera finem non fecit petendi, exquisitiora voluit, quam Collegii paupertas suppeditare potuit, et cum patribus expostulavit de parva caritate, unde arrepta ausa factiosi accusarunt nostros apud visitatorem. Iam vero extra Collegium positus, dum a patribus nescio quae desiderat officiorum genera, valde parum se dicitur praebere officiosum. Eo enim nunc res devenit, ut Anglorum dictis non detur fides, praesertim, quando facta contrarium indicant dicentis animum, nec habetur amicus nisi qui se ostendit amicum. D. Cicilius parum satisfacit expectationem patrum, nimis abcondendo affectum erga nos suum, si quem habet. Nolo dissimulare cum Reverentia Vestra nam amo sinceram simplicitatem cum amicis, displicet D. Cicilius omnibus bonis in suo procedendi modo. Nam intimus est omnibus factiosis, quotidie conversatur cum illis, visitavit 7 Ecclesias cum Fitzherberto, cum Fratre Sasheverelle est assidius, et visitat factiosos scholares, et visitatur ab illis, denique illis ostendit se amicum; sed contra cum D. Hadoco aut D. Baius vix audet prodire in publicum. Alumni plerasque ex obiectionibus contra nostros in Anglia, ad Illustrissimum Visitatorem ab eius ore detulerunt, eoque nomine citatus, excusavit se, illa dixisse ad expiscandas intentiones alumnorum; quicquid expiscatus fuerit secretum habet; quod contra nos dixit sub iudice est. Hoc sciunt Patres nostri et agerrime ferunt, miranturque Reverentia Vestra quomodo sic crediderit inconstanti viro, utor ipsorum verbis, imo videat Reverentia Vestra ne dum alium exaltet, suam elevet existimationem apud alios. Melius fuisset ille in Hispaniis vobiscum, nam hic neminem curat, nec admonitorem patitur.

Quid quod ipse Cardinalis Protector notet hominem inconstantiae, et lenitatis, quod secreto dixerat illi, de expellendis aliquibus e Collegio, statim dicitur vulgatum inter factiosos, non sine stomacho Protectoris. Hoc etiam animadversum est, quicquid accipit ab altera parte, defert alteri, sicque utrique infidus, neutri gratus existit. Non est tempus iam claudicandi, oportet sequi vel Deum, vel Baal. Quo laudandi sunt DD. Hadocus et Baius probati nostri amici. Doleo profecto vicem Domini Cicilii, illique bonum opto, ut mihi metipsi. Sed nisi deponat dissimulationem, non est hic manendi locus. Valde enim sunt exasperati Patres omnes Romae, nec immerito, ut oderint dissimulatores, plusquam ipsos inimicos. Sed tamen non ostendunt exterius aliquam aversionem ab illo.

    Haec scribo non aliam ob causam, quam ut Reverentiae Vestrae candide rem ipsam, uti se habet, aperiam, ut ipsa postmodum faciat, quod melius in Domino iudicaverit. De reliquo me commendo Reverentiae Vestrae sanctis sacrificiis et orationibus. Dominus Jesus Reverentiam Vestram custodiat incolumem. Ex Collegio Anglicano 13 Februarii 1596.

    Reverentiae Vestrae
        servus in Christo
            Richardus Coulingus.

[PS] Frater noster Henricus Touchbornus plurimum salutat Reverentiam Vestram. Scripsisset ipse nisi disputasset in Collegio Romano hoc mane, contra Georgum Turnebulum Scotum defendentem suas Theologicas conclusiones, coram P. Generalem aliisque praesentibus.

Translation

Most Reverend Father in Christ
The peace of Christ.

    I hope that the second or third letter from me has reached Your Reverence since I arrived at this college. In the present one I have thought well not to be shy to show how unjustly the evil-spirited are continuing in what they have started, no one striking out against us more than they themselves, with their calumnies and lies. The English have as a result now been made the talk of the people, and a stumbling block to the city and the world, when previously they appeared to be a mirror of piety and a torch of devotion. All good people hiss at them, the curia laughs at them, His Excellency the protector repudiates them, His Excellency the visitor condemns them, even His Holiness reproaches them. All the same, they remain constant in their audacity, whether expelling or being expelled from the college. I am sending Your Reverence the criticisms they raise against Ours in England, which Fr Warford's works are most useful in refuting, as also in informing the visitor. I have attached a copy of a letter of Mr Griffin Markham to his brother Robert, a prominent intriguer among the students of the college and cheerleader of the dissidents. Father minister found the letter in the doorway of Fr Edward Bennet, an inseparable friend of the said Markham, also a notable schemer, and leader of the rebels. A third can be added to them: Robert Shepperd, actually Bayes by name, related to Mr Martin Nelson,[423] a priest in England. I have to hand, but only to read, his depositions,

---

423. Martin Nelson (ca. 1550–1625) apostatized in January 1595 and was granted a special pardon on 19 March 1596, but later resumed his vocation as a Catholic priest (Anstruther, 246).

or rather defamations, to the visitor about the college. From them I have written down, word for word, what he advances against us in what he has to say about Ours in England: "We must take care that the saying is not made good of them: *the evil priests are a snare of ruin for my people*, when they are virtually become *a stumbling block of iniquity to the house of Israel*; I thought them to be saintly when I was in England and France, etc., but in Rome – thus the snake lying in the grass crept out stealthily – if only men could be found whose highest quality is gentleness." That is what he wrote. I would write other things, even harsher, from the writings of others, but let me spare the insolent youths. It is hard to believe how many lies are spread by our people through the city about His Excellency the protector, father general, father rector, and other fathers of Ours, so that unless you receive something dependable from Ours, it would not seem at all safe or reliable to accept any one else's accounts: everything is aflame with such mutual hatred.

Mr Cecil has arrived here, much commended by Your Reverence, so I have heard. He has been entertained according to the small means of the college – more generously, for sure, than guests are entertained nowadays – for two months, while he has been ill. Father rector instructed me (more on account of your recommendation than the merit of the one commended) that he should be given everything that the doctor prescribes and he himself asks for, and I saw that this was done to the letter; but in fact he would not stop asking, and wanted finer things than the poverty of the college could supply, and when he complained to the fathers of their lack of charity, the dissidents took up his bold demands and laid accusations against Ours to the visitor. But now that he is resident outside the college, he demands who knows what kinds of services from the fathers, while it is said that he shows himself of little service. The affair has reached the point where no credit is given to what the English say, especially when the facts bespeak a contrary spirit in the speaker, nor is one regarded as a friend unless one proves oneself to be a friend. Mr Cecil scarcely meets the expectations of the fathers, by too much suppressing whatever attachment he may still have to us. I do not want to make any pretence with Your Reverence, for I love sincere openness amongst friends: Mr Cecil displeases all good men with his manner of proceeding. For he is thick with all the dissidents, he holds conversation with them daily, he has visited the seven churches with Fitzherbert, he cultivates Friar Sacheverell,[424] and he exchanges visits with the dissident scholars: in short, he shows himself to be their friend. But on the other hand, he hardly dares to be seen in public with Mr Haddock or Mr Bayes. He has been the students' mouthpiece in conveying most of their objections against Ours in England to His Excellency the visitor, and when called out on this, he has given the excuse that he said those things from the intentions which were to be gathered from the students; whatever he had inferred he keeps secret; what he has said against us is *sub iudice*. Our fathers know this and take it most grievously, and they are amazed how Your Reverence could give such credit to this inconstant man – I use their own words – and Your Reverence should rather be careful not to lower your own reputation among the others by speaking well of him. It would be much better if he were in Spain with you, for here he cares for no one, and can bear no reproof.

424. On John (William) Sacheverell (1568–1625), see Persons's *Relacion* of 22 May 1597 (B378).

What is more, the cardinal protector himself charged the man with inconstancy and unreliability: what he had told him in secret, about the need to expel some from the college, is talked about openly among the dissidents, not without offence to the protector. Indeed, it has been noticed that whatever he hears from one side, he blurts out to the other, and so he is unfaithful to both, and welcome to neither. This is not the time to hesitate: one must either follow God or Baal. So Mr Haddock and Mr Bayes are to be praised as our trustworthy friends. Truly I am sorry on Mr Cecil's account, and I wish him well, for my own part. But unless he puts aside his deceit, there is no place for him to stay here. For all the fathers in Rome are exasperated with him, and not unjustly, for they hate deceivers even more than enemies. But all the same they do not show any outward aversion to him.

I write these things for no other reason than to reveal the truth of the matter frankly, as it is, so that you yourself may act in future as you judge best in the Lord. For the rest, I commend myself to Your Reverence's holy sacrifices and prayers. May the Lord Jesus keep Your Reverence in safety. From the English college, 13 February 1596.

    Your Reverence's
        servant in Christ,
            Richard Cowling.

[PS] Our brother Henry Tichborne greets Your Reverence heartily. He would have written himself had he not been disputing this morning in the Roman college against the Scotsman George Turnbull, who was defending his theological theses in front of father general and in the presence of others.

B316 From Claudio Acquaviva, Rome, 11 March 1596

SOURCE: ARSI, Cast. 6, fol. 239v.

NOTE: Responding to Persons's (lost) letter of 27 December (B307), Acquaviva assures him that he has asked the visitor, García de Alarcón, to find a replacement for del Río as rector at Valladolid. He asks Persons to resolve the conflict over alms-seeking in Seville. The letter is addressed to Valladolid, but Persons, possibly anticipating this request, was already in or on his way to Seville.

P. Roberto Personio, Valladolid, 11 de Marzo.

Con lo que en las passadas he escrito a Vuestra Reverencia se remediará lo que en la de 27 de deçiembre me avisa del Rector de ese Seminario,[425] en cuyo lugar espero que el Padre Garcia havrá ya puesto o el Padre Cabredo,[426] o otro que sea qual conviene. Lo que en esto quiero deçir a Vuestra Reverencia es que los de Sevilla se quejan que para el Seminario de aquella çiudad piden limosna los nuestros y a los mesmos a quien se pide para la casa professa. Bien será que en esto ponga Vuestra Reverencia algun orden, de manera que no se lamenten con razon los de la casa. En s[us ...].

425. del Rector de ese Seminario] *underlined R*
426. el Padre Cabredo] *underlined R*

Translation

To Fr Robert Persons in Valladolid, 11 March.

With the most recent posts that I have written to Your Reverence, the matter you raised with me in your letter of 27 December about the rector of that seminary will be remedied. I hope that Fr García will already have placed Fr Cabredo in his position, or another who will suit. What I would like to say to Your Reverence is that those in Seville complain that Ours are seeking alms for the seminary of that city from the same people who are solicited for the professed house. It would be a good thing if Your Reverence could straighten things out so that the house has no reason to be dissatisfied. To your [prayers, etc.]

B317 To Alexander Seton, Prior of Pluscarden, Seville, 18 March 1596

SOURCE: ABSI, Coll P II 488.

NOTE: Grene provides no text, merely a note about a letter "from Sevill to my Ld Prior." Alexander Seton, first earl of Dunfermline (1555–1622), held the office of prior of Pluscarden Abbey in Moray intermittently from 1565 to 1595. In 1596, as one of the "Octavians," eight commissioners to manage royal finances in Scotland, he tried to arrange for the return of the Catholic earls-in-exile, Huntly and Erroll (McCoog, *Building the Faith of St Peter*, 298, 300–302).

B318 To Don Juan de Idiáquez, 26 March 1596

SOURCES:
    ACSA, Series II, Legajo 1, item 25 = *Vd*;
    Ushaw College, University of Durham, Ushaw Manuscript Collections, UC/M3/4, endorsed "Discurso a Su Magd de las Cosas de Inglatera," probably late seventeenth or early eighteenth century (Hicks) = *U*.

HICKS: 443a–452, with English translation, including the enclosed letter to the king.

NOTE: The authorship of this letter, and the memorial to Philip II which it enclosed, is uncertain, possibly Creswell. Hicks suggests it is by Englefield, and McCoog, *Building the Faith of St Peter*, 382–383, doubts whether the author was Persons, partly because of the opposition to the Scots College in Louvain (p. 558 below; cf. Persons to Crichton, 10 May 1596, B323). The letter is signed from Madrid, but Persons appears to have been in Seville continuously from March to June.

Copie to Don Juan de Ydiaquez the 26 Martii – 1596.[427]

Con esto embío a Vuestra Señoria, ciertos avisos por ser presentados a Su Magestad con la primera oportunidad que Vuestra Señoria tubiere;[428] los quales pareçen a mý muy necessarios y importantes assy por el servicio de Su Magestad, como por la causa comun

427. – 1596] *Vd*; an. 1596 *U*
428. tubiere] *Vd*; tubiesse *U*

de nuestra lastimada tierra: el provechio[429] o daño de los quales concurren tan uniforme, que de qualquiera manera que sea[430] provechoso o dañoso a la una, será no más ny menos a la otra; y presumiendo como presumo que Su Magestad no ha desviado su santa intencion de reformar aquel Reyno, assistiendo a los Catholicos dello, quando la opportunidad se offeresce,[431] conviene en toda manera que Su Magestad haga algo en el interim assy, por el consuelo y augmento de los que son fielmente afficionados al servicio y enterés de Su Magestad, como para refrenar y suprimir los insolentes trabajos de sus contrarios, o por los medios contenidos en esto discurso, o por otros mejores y más breves que pueden ser aplicados, sin lo qual como la parte de Su Magestad está ya muy enflaquescida assi en número como en valor, ansi cotidianamente[432] vendra a ser menos o brevemente ninguno por las excessivas diligencias de sus adversarios, el qual surmonta tanto al frio[433] consuelo que hasta aora se a aplicado a los fieles defensores del título y enterés de Su Magestad, que si el governador que es agora de Flandes no defiende y sustiente mejor al padre Holto y a Hugo Owen contra las falsas y secretas enformaciones que dellos se han dado (de lo quale no paresce author ninguno) que hizieron los governadores antepassados en la defensa de Godfrey Folgam y Richarte Hopquines (los quales murieron de pena por las manifestas injurias que los hizieron), Vuestra Señoria me puede creer que avrá pocos o ningunos entre los entretenidos de la nacion alli, que[434] ozará demostrarse mantener la parte de Su Magestad contra la faccion de sus contrarios.

Supplico a Vuestra Señoria, sea servido de avisarme con el portador déste si Su Magestad a sido servido de ver los dichos avisos, y si Su Magestad requiere más larga enformacion de las partes y particularidades, estoy muy presto y aparejado para ello; y assi confiando que Vuestra Señoria me hara merced como siempre, quedo, Rogando a nuestro Señor le dé muchos y muy largos años de vida. Madrid a 26 de Marzo de 1596 años.

Translation

I am sending Your Excellency, along with this letter, certain news reports for His Majesty's attention at the earliest opportunity Your Excellency can find. They seem to me to be equally necessary and important for the service of His Majesty and for the common cause of our distressed country; and these interests are so closely bound up with one another that what is profitable or damaging to one of them will affect the other just the same, neither more nor less. And assuming, as I do, that His Majesty has not faltered in his holy resolution to reform that realm by giving help to the Catholics in it when the time is ripe, it is entirely appropriate that His Majesty should take some action in the meantime which would comfort those who are sincerely attached to his service and interests, and add to their number – and also restrain and repress the impudent doings of his opponents. This can be done either by the methods contained in this memorandum, or

429. provechio] *Vd*; provecho *U Hicks*
430. sea] *Vd*; *om. U*
431. offeresce] *Vd*; offresce *U*
432. cotidianamente] *Vd*; cotidiamente *U*
433. frio] *interlined with caret Vd*
434. que] *Vd*; *om. U*

by any other better and more efficient means that may be employed. And unless this is done, His Majesty's party, already very much weakened both in numbers and confidence, will tend to diminish daily and soon be extinguished, thanks to the extraordinary efforts made by their adversaries: this on top of the cold comfort that up to now has been meted out to the loyal supporters of His Majesty's title and interests, to the point where, if the present governor of Flanders does not protect and support Fr Holt and Hugh Owen against the false accusations stealthily laid against them (which seem to be entirely anonymous) more effectively than previous governors acted in defence of Godfrey Fuljambe and Richard Hopkins (who died of grief at the injuries openly done them),[435] Your Excellency can take it from me that there will be few, or none among the pensioners of our nation there who will dare to show themselves supporters of His Majesty's party against the faction of his opponents.

I beg Your Excellency to be so good as to inform me by the bearer of this whether His Majesty has been pleased to look at the said news brief: and if His Majesty requires fuller information about parties and individuals, I am very ready and well equipped to provide it. And so, trusting that Your Excellency will oblige me as you always do, I remain ever praying to our Lord to give you many long years of life. Madrid, on the 26th of March in the year 1596.

B319 To Philip II, Seville, 26 March 1596

> SOURCE: As above for the covering letter to Idiáquez.
>
> NOTE: Here the author pleads for the creation of another English cardinal (unnamed) and proposes an invasion of Ireland to keep James (as Elizabeth's most likely successor) from holding on to Spanish territory. The reference to the author's previous recommendation about the creation of an English cardinal suggests that the letter was written by Englefield.

Coppie to his Majestie the 26 Martii de 1596[436]

Señor[437]

No obstante que es muy probable, que quandoquiera que la Reyna de Ingelaterra muriera, el Rey de Escotia pretenderá no menos al Papa y Catolicos de Ingelaterra (para conbidar y grangearlos a favorescer su título) que Vandoma a hecho a Su Santidad y a los Catholicos de Françia (y más porque essos dos Reynos de Francia y Escotia an usado yr por un nivel por su antigua liga y alliança) con todo esso por quanto d'esse Rey de Escotia ni ay ny avrá (conforme a juizio humano) mayor esperança de la exstirpation de heregias y reformacion d'el mal govierno de Yngelaterra, que vemos ya impeçado, y se puede presumir prosiguera en Françia por la absoluçion de Vandoma; pero antes que sus to-

---

435. For Richard Hopkins (d. in or about 1596), see the headnote to Persons's letter to an unidentified addressee, 7 November 1590 (B85). Godfrey Foljambe or Fuljambe was a Marian agent in Paris and elsewhere and is mentioned in correspondence in 1586 (see A202 and John Hungerford Pollen, ed., *Mary Queen of Scots and the Babington Plot* [Edinburgh, 1922], 7-8).

436. de 1596] U; 96 Vd

437. Señor] om. Vd

leraçiones politicas de todas las[438] religiones vendran a ser la irremediable corruption de entrambos essos Reynos, assy en heregia como en toda injustitia. Sea por esso Vuestra Magestad servido, con[439] su gran prudencia y experiencia de considerarlo con tiempo, y poner en execution los remedios que el tiempo presente conçede, y sus otros negocios permiten.

Entre los quales la creation y constitucion de un Cardinal ynglés tal qual Vuestra Magestad sabe ser profundamente informado y instruido en el título y enterés que[440] Vuestra Magestad y su real succession tiene a la corona de Yngelaterra, y esté sinceramente afficionado a ella, paresce necessario ser una de las primeras cosas que se a de poner en execution, y esso por las razones siguientes.

1. Primeramente, porque sin las fuerças y assistencia de la Corona de Espania no ay esperança ny apparentia (por razon humana) que el[441] mal govierno de Inglaterra podra ser reformado, o la heregia jamas exstirpada, o la libertad de la fe Catolica continuada; sin la qual la esperanca es tam poca de la recuperacion de França, Flandes, Escocia y Irlanda.

2. Lo segundo, porque por la falta de un tal Cardinal de la nacion Ynglesa, las dissentiones y facciones dessa nacion an incredibletmente doblado y cresçido despues de la muerte del Cardinal Alano: assy en su Collegio de Roma, como en los entretenidos en Flandes: y la parte parcial del Rey de Escotia muy augmentada entre ellos, por la diligentia y solicitud de los escoseçes que residen en Flandes y Roma; la qual aviendose añadida a la primera parcialidad de Carlo Paget y Thomas Morgan (de los quales Vuestra Magestad a sido ya informado) a augmentada[442] y esforçavala en tanta[443] manera, que an ya llegado a tal número y atreviemento que requiere algun presto freno y repression; porque an ya no solamente hurtado de un Impressor en Anveres la primera copia escrita del libro de la succession, pero assy mismo an avisado de lo que contiene (antes que la impression se publicasse) a Ingelaterra y al santidad del Papa por su postrer Nuncio Malvasia, tratando a Vuestra Magestad por terminos de aspirar ser Monarcha del mundo, *per fas et nefas*, y persuadiendo ser el libro maldito y pestifero, solo porque declara el título y enterés de Vuestra Magestad y de su Real succession entre los otros muchos pretensores a la corona de Ingelaterra; y en esto concurren no solamente con la faccion françese en el Collegio de Cardinales y noblesa Italiana (en su aversion y alienacion de la prosperidad de Espania) pero tambien con la Reyna y Consejo de Ingelaterra, adonde el libro está prohibido so grandes penas y todos los libros quemados que se pueden hallar.

3. Lo tercero, an tomado atreviemento de sollicitar por sus amigos en Roma la creation de algun Cardenal Ynglés, y prevenir que no sea tal que venga encomendado por Espania, an nombrado a Su Santidad Poole Hescote y otros mançebos semejantes muy inhabiles y inaptos para essa dignidad y vocation. Y en esto concurren tambien, no solo con Yngelaterra (que de su grado no queria a ninguno), pero assy mismo con la faccion Italiana arriba nombrada, persuadiendo a su santidad que será más beneficioso a la ygle-

---

438. las] U; om. Vd
439. con] Vd; en U
440. que] Vd; de U
441. que el] U; quel Vd
442. augmentada] *interlined with caret* Vd
443. tanta] Vd; tal U

sia dar a los Yngleses un Cardinal y Rey de su mano que alguno que sea encomendado por Espania.

4. Lo quarto, an trabajado y trabajan con toda arte y diligencia de sembrar discordia y division entre los padres de la Compañia, y los saçerdotes seglares de la nacion Ynglesa assy en Yngelaterra y Flandes como en el Collegio en Roma, y excluir a los dichos padres a todo govierno y autoridad sobre los clerigos y estudiantes Yngleses dentro del Reyno y fuera dél. Y en esto concurren tambien con la policia Inglesa, adonde aunque se dissimulan con muchos clerigos seglares, o los desterran, ningun padre de la Compañia puede escapar sin martyrio si le cojen, solamente porque los más de los dichos padres se hallan affiçionados al título y enterés de Vuestra Magestad a essa corona.

5. Lo quinto, an endereçado una petition a Roma para ser presentada[444] a Su Santidad, en nombre y de baxo de las firmas de 7 o 8 de los principales cavalleros de la nacion Ynglesa, entretenidos por Vuestra Magestad en Flandes, en la qual accusan expressamente (*tacitis tamen nominibus*) a todos de su nation que ellos diçen tienen credito con Vuestra Magestad en Espania y con su governador en Flandes, de aver engañado y enformado a Vuestra Magestad y su Governador y Consejeros al daño y affrenta de la noblesa y Cavallaria de su propria naçion, y que por esso no se les a[445] en ninguna manera de dar credito, ny son de estimar a ninguno de sus motivos o persuasiones por Vuestra Magestad en Espania, ny por su governador en Flandes; lo qual requieren ser informado a Su Santidad, y que por su autoridad se intime y persuade assy a Vuestra Magestad propria como a su governador y Consejo en Flandes.

Y esto siendo discuvierto por dos de sus[446] cartas escritas de Flandes: la una por el Doctor Giffordo, y la otra de Carlo Paget, al obispo de Cassano y Thomas Throckmorton en Roma (a quienes dios no permitio que viviessen y las recibiessen) Vuestra Magestad no puede dexar de echar de ver quan requisito es que las demas cyfras, cartas y papeles del dicho Doctor Gifford y Pageto se tomen y se vean por algunos de la nacion que son más lealmente affiçionados a la parte y enterés de Vuestra Magestad (como son el Padre Guilliermo Holt, Doctor Peres, Doctor Worthington, Don Guillermo Stanley y Hugo Owen) assy para más clara inteligentia de ciertas oscuras caracteres[447] y señales en las cartas las quales tenemos, como otras muchas más de semejante materia se puede probablemente presumir se hallarán[448] entre ellos, como se halló antes en poder de Thomas Morgan, por lo qual fue desterrado de los dominios de Vuestra Magestad en tiempo del Duque de Parma.

Y demas desto Vuestra Magestad a de considerar quan poco fruto cogerá Vuestra Magestad y su Real succession por la erection del seminario Escoses en Lovayno, o de las limosnas y entretenimiento que Vuestra Magestad da a los de essa[449] nation, y a essos Yngleses que son de su parte y faction en sus Paeses Baxos, cuios desvelos son promptos y trabajos diligentes para aventajar el título escoses, y abatir de Vuestra Magestad.

444. presentada] *Vd*; presentenda *U*
445. a] *interlined with caret Vd*
446. de sus] *interlined with caret U*
447. caracteres] *U*; caracteras *Vd*
448. hallarán] *Vd*; hallaren *U*
449. de essa] *U*; dessa *Vd*

Y aunque Vuestra Magestad tenga proposito (como todos los Catolicos confian que tiene) de remediar estos negocios con poder (quando otro camino no uviera), si consiente la parte Catholica de la nacion Ynglesa (a quien Vuestra Magestad solo consuele y sustenta) ser no tan solo enflaquescida y descayda, pero assy mismo pervertida a[450] afficionar sus contrarios por la importuna diligentia usada de la faccion[451] escosesa, mientras no ay nadie de la parte de Vuestra Magestad, que tiene poder o autoridad de contrastarlos. Su grande prudencia no dexerá de echar de ver que las difficultades de collocar algun Rey o Reyna en Ingileterra por su nombramiento, se doblarán, y seran excessivamente crescidas, quandoquiera que esto se intentará[452] por la muerte de la Reyna o otra via.

Conviene por esso (segun todo parecer humano) que Vuestra Magestad no[453] se detenga más en dar a los Yngleses un tal Cardenal qual se ha ya propuesto, por cuyo credito y autoridad la insolencia de la quadrilla Escosesa pueda ser[454] algo refrenada, sus juntas dispercidas, y sus consultas y sollicitudes[455] (que son importunas) menos estimadas entre los demas Catholicos; y assy mismo que no se descuyde de renovar a menudo a su governador en Flandes: orden y cargo particular de entretener las propositiones offreçidas a Vuestra Magestad de Yngelaterra en el año passado (de las quales avisó a Vuestra Magestad el Duque de Feria) que quandoquiera la Reyna de Ynglaterra se muriera, su successor nombrado por Vuestra Magestad sea el primero que se publicasse en Londres; lo qual por las promesas de paz y trato será grato a essa ciudad y no difficultoso de poner en execution.

Y finalmente porque el tiempo de la muerte de la Reyna es incierto, parece ser muy requisito, que para refrenar las frequentes molestaciones que ella da a Vuestra Magestad assy en sus Indias y Islas como en el continente de Portugal y Espania, que Vuestra Magestad no se detenga más de que con alguna fuerça bastante, echada en Irlanda tomar en su poder el govierno dessas ciudades y puertos de la terra que spontaneamente vendran en[456] expeller los governadores della[457] y admitir y recebir los de Vuestra Magestad, conforme al exemplo que de[458] mucho tiempo atras ella a dado, con tomar y guardar diversas partes de los dominios de Vuestra Magestad más ha de 20 años complidos; porque la impresa de Irlanda será un gran medio no solamente de hazerla bolver en sus dias lo que tiene usurpada de Vuestra Magestad, y offrescer tales conditiones de paz quales Vuestra Magestad puede accetar, pero será tambien motivo principal para inducir a la noblesa Inglesa (despues de sus dias) de accetar y establesser el successor que Vuestra Magestad les propondra y señalará. Pero quando Vuestra Magestad dara orden para essa[459]

450. a] *interlined with caret Vd*
451. faccion] U; faccio Vd
452. intentará] U; intantera Vd
453. no] U; ne Vd
454. ser] Vd; se U
455. sollicitudes] Vd; U adds ines [deleted]
456. en] Vd; om. U
457. della] *interlined with caret Vd*
458. de] Vd; om. U
459. essa] *interlined with caret Vd*

empresa, conviene y emporta mucho que se tenga gran consideracion y respeto en el aplicar de las fuerças, porque no ay menos odio y malicia entre la gente politica y salvaje de essa nacion,[460] que entrambos ellos tienen contra los Yngleses; de manera que si Vuestra Magestad endereça sus fuerças para unir con la gente savaje y barbara (que sola a tomada armas contra la Reyna) Vuestra Magestad podria por ello perdera[461] la voluntad y afficion de todas las ciudades y villas grandes, que son politicas y la más fuerte y próspera parte de toda la tierra; porque en el norte y parte barbara no tienen ciudades, caudal, ny trato urbano ny traje.

Y quando Vuestra Magestad empleará a alquien[462] por General para hazer algo en Irlanda será muy provechoso que lleve consigo a algunos de la nacion Inglesa que an estado en essa tierra, y son bien conoscidos de la noblesa y cavallaria alla; como Richard Hadocque el clerigo primo del Cardinal Alano (que está en Roma totalmente dedicado al servitio de Vuestra Magestad) y el Coronel Don Guillermo Stanley que está en Flandes; los quales dos en sus vocaciones diferentes, son bastantes y desseosos de hazer a Vuestra Magestad leal y importante servitio en essa tierra. Pero si Vuestra Magestad defierre y detiene el hazer algo por este camino hasta que el Conde de Tyron sea suprimido, como lo fue el Conde de Desmond, o forçado de componer y hazer pazes con la Reyna, como fueron compellido a hazer los Milortes Escoseses con su Rey, por falta[463] de los soccorros prometidos, las fuerças y gastos que agora seran bastantes, seran despues muy insufficientes, y el suceso muy más dudoso.

Y rojandome a los pies de Vuestra Magestad le supplico muy humilmente de no dexar passar la opportunidad que al instante se[464] offresce por la vacançia de los obispados de Cambray y Tornay, los quales en my consciencia Vuestra Magestad no puede emplear mejor por el servicio de Dios y de Vuestra Magestad, que el de Cambray al[465] ... quien tengo ya proponido a Vuestra Magestad de ser Cardinal de Yngelaterra) y el otro de Torney al doctor Thomas Stapleton professor de Theologia de Vuestra Magestad en Lovayno: porque en applicando a ellos essos[466] beneficios espirituales, Vuestra Magestad manifestamente vincera y confutera aquella fama y falsa opinion que la Reyna y Consejo de Yngelaterra llevantan a Vuestra Magestad, que su intention es[467] de conquistar aquel Reyno por fuerça, y de subduçerla a la Corona de España: quando todo el mundo verá que de suyo y en sus dominios se sierve de preferir y aventajar tales de la nacion, qual sus vidas y condiciones merescen, hasta que aya tiempo y comodidad de beneficiarlos en sus proprias tierras.

[*Endorsed*:] 26 Martii 1596 Discurso a Su Magestad de las cosas de Inglaterra.

---

460. de essa nacion] *this ed.;* dessa nacion *Vd;* de essa *U*
461. perdera] *Vd;* perder a *U*
462. alquien] *U;* algien *Vd*
463. falta] *interlined with caret Vd*
464. se] *interlined with caret Vd*
465. *followed by a blank of two or three words A U*
466. essos] *Vd;* estos *U*
467. es] *Vd; obscure in U*

Translation

My Lord

It is very probable that, at whatever time the Queen of England comes to die, the king of Scotland will make overtures both to the pope and the English Catholics with a view to alluring them and gaining them to favour his title; just as Vendome[468] has done to His Holiness and the French Catholics. This is all the more likely because those two kingdoms of France and Scotland have been in the habit of acting on parallel lines on account of the ancient league and alliance between them. Despite this, however, by any human reasoning we cannot expect, either now or in the future, from this king of Scotland, any greater eradication of heresies or reformation of evil government in England than we are seeing at the outset in France, and can be presumed to continue, thanks to Vendome's being absolved. But before this *politique* toleration of all religions results in the irremediable corruption of these two realms both by heresy and by every sort of injustice, I beg Your Majesty, with your great prudence and expedience, therefore to take these matters into consideration in good time, and to put in execution such remedies as the present times allow and your affairs elsewhere permit.

And among these the creation and appointment of an English Cardinal – one whom Your Majesty knows to be fully informed of and conversant with the title and claim which Your Majesty and your royal line holds to the crown of England, and who is sincerely devoted to it – would necessarily seem to be one of the first things that should be put in hand. This for the following reasons:—

1. First, because without the forces and help of the Spanish crown there is no hope or likelihood, humanly speaking, that the evil government of England can be reformed, or heresy ever eradicated, or the freedom of the Catholic faith preserved; and failing this there is very little hope of the restoration of France, Flanders, Scotland, and Ireland.

2. Second, because it is for lack of such a cardinal of English nationality that dissensions and factions have doubled in number after Cardinal Allen's death, and to a remarkable degree become accentuated, both in his college in Rome as well as among those who are receiving subsidies in Flanders. The party that favours the king of Scotland has also increased greatly among them, thanks to the zeal and importunity of the Scots who live in Flanders and Rome. This party has joined itself to the original faction of Charles Paget and Thomas Morgan (about whom Your Majesty has been already informed) and has increased it so largely and given it such strength that it has now become so numerous and bold as to need some speedy restraint and curb. For lately they have already not only stolen a copy of the original manuscript of the *Book of Succession* from a printer in Antwerp, but have even given information of its contents (before the book was printed) to England and to His Holiness the pope, through his last nuncio, Malvasia.[469] They speak of Your Majesty as though you were aspiring to be monarch of the world *by fair means or foul*, and they make it appear that the book is an accursed and baneful thing,

---

468. Henri IV (Navarre).

469. Innocenzo Malvasia was the papal agent (not formally the nuncio) in Brussels but was recalled late in 1595 at the insistence of Pietro Cardinal Aldobrandini, the papal secretary, because of his anti-Spanish sentiment (McCoog, *Building the Faith of St Peter*, 368).

merely because it states the title and claim of Your Majesty and your royal line among those of the many other pretenders to the crown of England. And in so doing they are acting in sympathy not only with the French faction in the College of Cardinals and the Italian nobility (in their dislike and disaffection of Spain's prosperity) but also with the queen and council of England, where the book is forbidden under heavy penalties and all copies of the book that they can find are burnt.

3. Third, they have had the temerity to urge through their friends in Rome that some Englishman be made a cardinal, and, in order to prevent his being anyone that has the recommendation of Spain, they have proposed to His Holiness the names of Pole, Hesketh, and other similar young men who are quite incapable and unfitted for the dignity of that office.[470] And in so doing they are working hand in glove not only with England (which of its own accord did not want anyone) but again with the Italian faction mentioned above, by impressing on His Holiness that it will be more beneficial to the Church to give the English a cardinal and a king of his own choice than one who happens to be recommended by Spain.

4. Fourth, they have laboured and are labouring with all skill and diligence to sow discord and divisions between the fathers of the Society and the secular priests of English nationality, both in England and Flanders as well as in the college in Rome, and to exclude the said fathers from all government and authority over the English clergy and students within the kingdom and without it. And by so doing they are colluding with the policy of England where, although they tolerate many of the secular clergy or only banish them, no father of the Society can escape martyrdom if they set hands on him, simply because most of the said fathers prove to be in favour of Your Majesty's title and claim to that crown.

5. Fifth, they have addressed a petition to Rome, to be presented to His Holiness in the name and over the signatures of seven or eight of the principal gentlemen of the English nation who are maintained by Your Majesty in Flanders, in which they expressly accuse (though not mentioning their names) all those of their nation who (according to them) are in the confidence of Your Majesty in Spain and your governor in Flanders, of having misled Your Majesty and your governor and councillors and made reports to them tending to injure and insult the nobility and gentry of their own nation. They say that for this reason under no circumstances should credit be given to what they say nor judgement be formed from it of anyone's feelings or inclinations towards Your Majesty in Spain or your governor in Flanders. This information they wish to be given to His Holiness, so that by his influence the facts should be made known and impressed on both Your Majesty and your governor and council in Flanders.

And, as this has come to light through two of their letters written from Flanders, one by Dr Gifford and the other by Charles Paget, to the bishop of Cassano and Thomas Throckmorton in Rome (whom God did not permit to live to receive them), Your Majesty cannot fail to perceive how necessary it is that the rest of the ciphers, letters, and papers of the said Dr Gifford and Paget be taken and examined by some of our nation who are more loyal than they are in their attachment to Your Majesty's party and interests

---

470. Gervase Pole (b. ca. 1572), who entered the Society of Jesus in 1607, and Thomas Hesketh/Allen, Allen's nephew.

(such as Fr William Holt, Dr Percy,[471] Dr Worthington, Sir William Stanley, and Hugh Owen) not only in order to get a clearer understanding of certain obscure characters and signs in the letters in our possession but also to get much other matter of a similar kind, which we may probably assume will be found in these papers in the same way as it was found on a previous occasion in the possession of Thomas Morgan, on account of which he was banished from Your Majesty's dominions in the duke of Parma's time.

In addition to this Your Majesty should take into consideration how little profit you and your royal line will reap from the foundation of the Scots college at Louvain or from the alms and subsidies Your Majesty is giving to the men of that nation and to those Englishmen in the Low Countries who belong to their party and faction and who are impudently ready and eager to work for the advantage of the Scottish claim and for the overthrow of Your Majesty's.

Your Majesty no doubt intends (and all the Catholics are confident that you do so intend) to put a stop to these intrigues by force, should there be no other way; but if the Catholic party in the English nation (which Your Majesty alone consoles and supports) allows itself to become not only weakened and discouraged but even so turned as to adhere to your opponents, owing to the perseverance of the Scottish faction in their efforts while there is nobody of power or authority on Your Majesty's side to gainsay them, Your Majesty's great foresight will not fail to perceive clearly that the difficulties in the way of Your Majesty's nominating and setting up any one as king or queen in England will be doubly great and enormously increased whenever the time comes for this to be attempted either at the queen's death or by some other means.

It is convenient therefore, according to all human judgement, that Your Majesty should delay no longer to give the English a cardinal of the kind suggested, whose influence and authority will be able to restrain the insolence of the Scottish gang somewhat, to break up its meetings, and to bring the consultations and intrigues, so persistent as they are, into disrepute with the rest of the Catholic body. And so too Your Majesty should not neglect to repeat your orders frequently to your governor in Flanders, expressly enjoining him to entertain the suggestions made to Your Majesty from England last year (of which the duke of Feria informed Your Majesty), viz. that whenever the queen of England dies, the person who is named by Your Majesty to succeed her should be the first name to be proclaimed in London:[472] this if accompanied by promises of peace and conciliation will be well received by that city, and it will not be a difficult thing to carry out.

Finally, seeing that the time of the queen's death is uncertain, it would seem to be very necessary, in order to restrain her from giving constant trouble to Your Majesty as she is doing by her attacks on the Indies and the Islands, as well as on the mainland of Por-

---

471. Although the MSS clearly read "Peres," it seems likely that Persons is referring to Dr William Percy (elsewhere "Pierse"; see the memorandum to Martín de Idiáquez, 30 August 1596, B340), who joined Thomas Worthington in writing a memorial to the cardinal protector, Caetani, fully supporting the Jesuit authorities at the English College, Rome (Kenny, "Inglorious Revolution," 77–78 [part 3]). Later Percy shifted allegiance to the appellant party (see Persons to Holt, 15 March 1597, B357).

472. See Persons to Philip II, Seville, September/October, 1595 (B293).

tugal and Spain, that Your Majesty should not delay any longer to throw a sufficient force into Ireland and take charge of the government of the cities and ports of that land; they will be quite ready to expel their own rulers and to admit and accept those sent by Your Majesty. This will be to follow the example set by her for a long time back of seizing and retaining various portions of Your Majesty's dominions for full twenty years past. For this Irish expedition will not only be a good means of making her give back in her lifetime what she has taken unjustly from Your Majesty and offer terms of peace such as Your Majesty can accept, but will also be a first-rate inducement to persuade the English nobility after her lifetime to accept and put in power the successor proposed and indicated by Your Majesty. When however you give orders for this expedition it is appropriate, indeed very important, that great circumspection and caution be exercised in the way the forces are used; for the hatred and ill will between the educated and savage elements of this race is no less than that which both of them bear to the English; with the result that if Your Majesty directs your forces so as to combine with the savage and uncouth elements (which alone have taken up arms against the queen) Your Majesty would be liable to lose thereby the good will and support of all the cities and large towns that are politically organised and are the most powerful and prosperous portion of the whole country; for in the north and in the wild parts of the country they have neither cities, nor property, nor civilized habits, nor clothes.

And when Your Majesty employs someone as general in order to take some action in Ireland, it will be very advantageous for him to take with him some men of English nationality who have been in that country and are well-known to the nobility and gentry there: such as Richard Haddock, who was the senior priest in Cardinal Allen's suite (he is in Rome entirely devoted to Your Majesty's service), and Colonel William Stanley, who is in Flanders. They are both in their different spheres competent men and are anxious to render Your Majesty loyal and important service in that country. But if Your Majesty defers matters and delays taking any steps in this direction, allowing the earl of Tyrone to be suppressed as the earl of Desmond was, or forced to come to terms and make peace with the queen as the Scottish lords were compelled to do with their king through failure of the promised succour, the forces and expenditure which are sufficient now will later on be quite insufficient and the issue much more doubtful.

And now throwing myself at Your Majesty's feet I humbly beg you not to let the opportunity pass which is offered at this moment by the vacancy in the sees of Cambrai and Tournai. I can conscientiously say that Your Majesty cannot make use of them better in the service of God and of yourself than by giving that of Cambrai to ...[473] (whom I have already suggested to Your Majesty to be the English cardinal) and the other one of Tournai to Dr Thomas Stapleton, Your Majesty's professor of theology at Louvain: for by conferring these spiritual benefices on them Your Majesty will overcome and refute before the world that evil report and erroneous opinion held by the queen and the council of England against Your Majesty, saying that it is your intention to conquer that realm by force and bring it under the dominion of Spain; for then the whole world will see that

---

473. [*blank in A and U*] The only names mentioned in the extant documents are Persons, Stapleton, and Owen Lewis. Since the last was dead, the blank here could be "Persons."

on your own initiative you are pleased to give preferment and advancement in your own dominions to such men of our nation whose lives and capabilities deserve it, until the time and opportunity comes to give them benefices in their own country.

B320 From Claudio Acquaviva, Rome, 8 April 1596

SOURCE: ARSI, Cast. 6, fols. 242v–243r.

NOTE: Acquaviva is satisfied that Persons and García de Alarcón, visitor to the province of Castile, will have dealt with the problems at Valladolid by replacing the rector. The situation at the English college in Rome has been complicated by the illness of Cardinal Sega and the departure of Cardinal Caetani, the cardinal vice-protector and protector of England respectively. Sega died on 29 May, and Caetani was called to Poland from 3 April 1596 to 23 June 1597. Richard Barret has arrived from Douai to assist the rector, Fioravanti, and Creswell and Tancard were expected. In fact, Tancard was sent to join Don Martín de Padilla's armada, while Creswell remained in Madrid (McCoog, *Building the Faith of St Peter*, 388–389).

Holt's position in Brussels continued to be controversial, and Acquaviva hoped that Creswell would be able to replace him.

P. Roberto Personio, Abril 8 en Valladolid.

Dos de Vuestra Reverencia he recevido escritas a 24 de Enero, y en lo que toca al Colegio de Valladolid no digo más, pues con haver quitado el Rector que tenía,[474] y haverle proveido de otro qual convenga, como creo que el Padre Garcia y Vuestra Reverencia lo havran hecho, estara aquello remediado. Lo de acá se ha dilatado con la enfermedad del Señor Cardenal Sega. Finalmente el Señor Cardenal Gayetano habló a su Santidad y le mostro el libro de la visita y informaçion hecha por el Señor Cardenal Sega. Quiso[475] que se le dexase, y esperamos la resoluçión. Daño nos hara la partida del Señor Cardenal Gayetano que va por legado a Polonia, ya llegó aqui el buen Barreto, y por su parte ha hecho lo que ha podido, no sé el successo que esto terná, que el estado presente no es bueno.

Vuestra Reverencia tiene raçon de no creer lo que le han dicho, del Padre Fierabante, porque no va por el camino que alla le han insinuado, más fundamento ay para temer que estos inquietos lo manchan todo, y de todos diçen.

Vengan en buena hora los Padres Cresuelo y Tancardo[476] que aqui serán bien reçevidos, y a su tiempo como Vuestra Reverencia diçe podra el Padre Cresuelo yr a suplir por el Padre Holto. Los dos saçerdotes que Vuestra Reverencia desea se acepten, me contento que sean reçevidos, y si los quisiera embiar acá, los reçeviremos aqui de muy buena gana.

Espero que Vuestra Reverencia nos embíe la relaçion del martirio del Padre Valpolo, pues diçe es más copiosa que la que tenemos acá.

No se le ha quitado al Padre Holto la mano y correspondencia con el Collegio de Saint-Omer, ni menos removido el superior de aquel Seminario sino que lo ha escrito el

    474. haver quitado el Rector que tenía] *underlined R*
    475. Quiso *preceded by* quido [*deleted*] *R*
    476. Vengan en buena hora los Padres Cresuelo y Tancardo] *underlined R*

Padre Holto acá y alla; porque temia se hiziese. Lo que se ha quitado ha sido que no pida ninguno de los nuestros sino algun Inglés la limosna que para aquel Seminario piden en la Corte de Bruxellas. En las orationes, etc.

Translation

To Fr Robert Persons in Valladolid, 8 April.

I have received two letters from Your Reverence, written on 24 January,[477] and as for that which concerns the college at Valladolid I say no more, for if the previous rector has been removed, and another suitable one has been provided, as I believe Fr García and Your Reverence will have done, things will have been set to rights. Here things have been delayed by the illness of Cardinal Sega. Finally, Cardinal Caetani has spoken to his Holiness and shown him the record of the visit and the information gleaned by Cardinal Sega. He asked to keep it,[478] and we await his reaction. The departure of Cardinal Caetani, who is going on a legation to Poland, will do us harm. Good Barret has now arrived; and for his part he has done what he could. I cannot tell how successful he will be: the present situation does not augur well.

Your Reverence is right not to believe what they have said about Fr Fioravanti, because he is not following the path they have implied. There is the more reason to fear that these restless ones will corrupt everything, and they speak ill of everybody.

Frs Creswell and Tancard are coming at an opportune moment; they will be very welcome here, and in time, as Your Reverence says, Fr Creswell will be able to replace Fr Holt. As to the two priests whom Your Reverence would like to be admitted, I am content for them to be received, and if they are sent here, we will receive them here very willingly.

I hope that Your Reverence will send us the relation of the martyrdom of Fr Walpole, which is said to be fuller than that which we have here.[479]

We have not taken away Fr Holt's control and correspondence with the college of St Omers, nor was the superior of that seminary removed,[480] but Fr Holt has been writing to people here and there, since he was fearful that this would be done. What has been altered, is that none of Ours should beg for alms except a certain English man who begs for that seminary at the court in Brussels. To your prayers, etc.

B321 From Richard Cowling, Rome, 8 April 1596

SOURCE: AAW, V, 46, holograph = W.

NOTE: Cowling has heard from Persons via Oswald Tesimond, SJ (ca. 1563–1636), prefect of studies at Valladolid. He explains why he has not been able to come to Valladolid, and provides further information about the situation at the English college: the cardinal protec-

---

477. B311.
478. I.e., to examine it for himself.
479. Creswell's *Historia de la vida y martyrio que padecio en Inglaterra este año de 1595 P. Henrique Valpolo* (Madrid, 1596).
480. Jean Foucart was the rector.

tor, Caetani, is distracted by his imminent departure for Poland, and the vice-protector, Sega, is seriously ill. Although Richard Barret has arrived from Douai, he seems too mild and diffident to make much of an impression on the dissident students. John Cecil (Snowden) appears to have become their champion (see Cowling's previous letter, 13 February, B315). An attempt has been made to have Robert Shepperd, alias Bayes, denounced as a spy (see Kenny, "Inglorious Revolution," 150 n42 [part 4]).

Caetani's mission was to intervene in a dispute in the Balkan regions that revolted against the Ottoman empire. The region of Wallachia (in modern-day Romania) was ruled by Michael the Brave (1558–1601), who formed an alliance with Sigismund Báthory, ruler of Transylvania, but Polish forces seized Wallachia briefly after his death. The Ottoman empire regained control in 1602.

There is a brief postscript from Alfonso Agazzari, who later replaced Fioravanti as rector of the college. He intimates that he shares the same understanding as Richard Barret, who wrote to Persons on 10 April (B322).

Admodum Reverende in Christo Pater
Pax Christi.

Gratias ago Reverentiae Vestrae quod suae erga me benevolentiae memoriam fecerit in litteris P. Oswaldi Vallisoleto scriptis; perlibenter venissem ad vos, et venirem adhuc si Reverendus Pater Noster de me sic disponeret; mihi namque ut nil gratius, quam locus pacis et tranquillitatis spiritualis, sic nihil infestius infructuosis istis tumultibus, intestinis bellis, victoribus ut victis aeque perniciosis, ibi praesertim, ubi desperatur de fine. Scripseram antea, fore brevi ut omnia componerentur, sed experientia iam didici nihil adhuc eorum quae Patres nostri intenderunt aut tentarunt ex voto successisse, ut in posterum nihil omnino pro certo audeam polliceri; Reverendus Pater Rector laborat strenue, multa promittit Protector, multa viceprotector, sed tantum promittere videntur. Declaratus est Illustrissimus Protector legatus Pontificis ad Dietam in Polonia, ut pacem constituat inter Polonum et Transilvanum de Vallaccia concertantes, hic ut retineat, ille ut eripeat; iamque dicitur Cancellarius Polonus Vallacciam occupare, cum interim Turca trecentis militum millibus cervicibus nostris immineat. P. Alfonsus Hispanus ille pater confessarius Principis Transilvaniae venit Romam ut agat rem sui Principis. Protector autem noster ita intentus est itineri, ut nihil cogitet de nobis, ut vereor facturum sicut alia vice, biduo ante discessum introducturum officiales et infecta omnia relicturum. Nec multum expectamus a viceprotectore Illustrissimo Segua quem gravis infirmitas compulit Tusculum incerta spe sanitatis. D. Barettus nobis adhaeret, nec quisquam vel mediocriter verecundus, aut veritatis amicus contrarium faceret, tanta est factiosorum insolentia. D. Cecilius aut egregie dissimulat, aut egregie traducitur hic a factiosis, faciunt illum suum Aristotelem contra Societatem praesertim contra nostros in Anglia, ipsius iniurias ibi a nostris illatas repetunt ad unguem. Dixit mihi D. Barettus quatuor aut quinque illorum dixisse, Cecilium illis affirmasse, bono patriae non esse melius consulturos, quam si quo modo Jesuitas inde curarent evocatos, longeque remotos. Dixit etiam D. Barettus quod puto verissimum, omnes nostratium factiones hic regnare inter alumnos, illam vero contra Societatem ex Flandria penetrasse sic alumnorum viscera, ut eradicari non possit, Hispanum vel Societatem[481] nostram, summo prosequuntur odio. Reverentiam Vestram, P. Holtum et P. Creswellum tanquam p—[482] insimulant, nec quicquam audiunt quamvis falsissimum in rem suam faciens, aut ——,[483] quod pro sua impudentia non erubescant asserere. Non defuerunt qui D. Banis conati sunt in vincula coniicere tanquam suspectum exploratorem Reginae, sed qui imprudentius, et incitatus ab aliis suspicionis dederat occasionem verba revocavit, et secreto veniam petiit a D. Banis. Hinc apparet quo sint affecti erga nos animo egregii isti zelatores Angliae; quoad reliqua omnia sunt ut scripsi tabellario supremo. Mitto ad Reverentiam Vestram Epitaphium Episcopi Cassanensis marmore incisum ad latus P[atris] Illustrissimi Alani. Ad verbum ut ibi habetur et eodem plane modo, etiam quoad errores, si quos inveneritis. Restat ut Reverentiae Vestrae precibus obnixe me commendem. Secundet Deus incolumitatem vestram. Ex Collegio Anglicano 8 Aprilis 1596.

    Reverentiae Vestrae
        servus in Christo Jesu
            Richardus Coulingus.

[PS] Padre mio amantissimo saluto. Vostra Illustrissima e le do le buone feste. Dal Dottore Barretto intenderà ciò che io potrei dire. Però a me basta salutarla et amarla. Jesus. Alfonsus Agazzarius.[484]

[*Addressed:*] Al Molto Reverendo in Christo Padre il P. Roberto Personio sacerdote della Compagna di Giesu a Vagliodoleto.

Translation

Most Reverend Father in Christ
The peace of Christ.

I thank Your Reverence for your kind greetings to me, conveyed in Fr Oswald's letter from Valladolid. I would very readily have come to you, and would have done so before this if our reverend father had been so disposed in my case; for nothing would be more welcome to me than a place of peace and spiritual tranquillity, just as there is nothing more distressing than these fruitless disturbances, internal squabbles, pernicious to the winners and losers alike, especially when they do not know what the end will be. I wrote earlier that it would not be long before everything would be settled, but I have learnt from experience that thus far nothing that our fathers proposed or tried out has taken place as desired, so that I would dare to promise nothing at all for certain in the future. Reverend father rector is working very hard, the protector promises much, and so does the vice-protector, but all we see are promises. His Eminence the protector has been appointed papal legate to the diet in Poland, to make peace between Poland and Transylvania, who are quarrelling over Wallachia, one to hold on to it, the other to seize it,

    481. vel Societatem] *this ed.; R obscure*
    482. *R obscure*
    483. *Text blotted in R, ending in* famiam
    484. *The postscript is in a different hand, presumably Agazzari's. The words* "amantissimo" *and* "però" *are obscure.*

and already it is said that the Polish chancellor is occupying Wallachia – when the Turk meanwhile is threatening our necks with three hundred thousand soldiers. The Spaniard Fr Alfonso, that confessor of the prince of Transylvania, has come to Rome to treat of the affairs of his prince. But our protector is so preoccupied with his journey that he gives no thought to us, so I am afraid that he will do just as on another occasion: on the second day before his departure he would introduce officials and leave everything unfinished. Nor do we expect much from His Eminence the vice-protector Sega, who has been forced by a serious illness to retire to Tusculum with little hope of recovery. Mr Barret is attached to us, but the insolence of the dissidents is so great that no one so diffident or friendly to the truth can do anything to oppose them.[485] Either Mr Cecil is extremely deceitful or he is egregiously misrepresented here by the dissidents: they make him their Aristotle against the Society, especially against Ours in England, and they keep on repeating every grievance he has about the way he was treated by Ours. Mr Barret told me that four or five of them had said that Cecil had affirmed to them that they could do no better to look after the welfare of their country than to ensure somehow that the Jesuits were recalled and removed far away. Mr Barret also said something which I believe to be only too true, that all the factions of our country are in the ascendancy here among the students; indeed, the one based in Flanders, which is hostile to the Society, has so penetrated to the innards of the students that it cannot be rooted out. They feel the greatest hatred to the Spanish as well as our Society.[486] They accuse Your Reverence, Fr Holt, and Fr Creswell as if [word blotted], nor do they hear anything, no matter how false it may be in itself or [words blotted] infamous, which they are not too impudent to broadcast without any shame. There have even been some who have tried to throw Mr Baynes into jail on suspicion of spying for the queen, but the one who too imprudently and incited by others gave rise to the suspicion took back his words and secretly sought pardon from Mr Baynes. From this it is apparent how hostile is the feeling towards us that possesses these men who are so extremely zealous for England. For the rest, it is just as I wrote by the last courier. I am sending Your Reverence the epitaph of the bishop of Cassano,[487] carved in marble next to Dr Allen: literally as it you have it here and virtually in the same manner, even in the case of errors, if you should find any. It remains for me to commend myself resolutely to Your Reverence's prayers. May God keep you unharmed. From the English college, 8 April 1596.

   Your Reverence's
     servant in Christ
      Richard Cowling.

[PS] I greet my most beloved father. I wish you and Your Eminence happy feasts. From Dr Barret you will gather just what I would say. But[488] for my part, it is enough to greet you and express my love for you. Jesus. Alfonso Agazzari.

 485. It appears that at first the rebellious students welcomed Barret as a likely sympathizer but were soon disillusioned (Kenny, "Inglorious Revolution," 78 [part 3]).
 486. Conjectural reading.
 487. Owen Lewis, who died on 14 October 1595.
 488. For "Your Eminence" and "But," see n484: possibly facetious.

B322 From Richard Barret, Rome, 10 April 1596

SOURCE: AAW, V, 48, holograph = W.

EDITIONS: Renold, *Letters of Allen and Barret*, 250–252; Tierney, 3: lxxiii–lxxv (modernised).

NOTE: In response to a letter written in December 1595 (B301), Barret gives a full analysis of the causes of the troubles at the English College, Rome, chiefly attributing them to the students' involvement in public affairs such as the appointment of a new cardinal. He also observes that those in the local English community who are friendly to the anti-Jesuit network in Flanders are hoping to gain control of the rents in the college and offer incentives to the ringleaders of the student movement. However, he makes it clear that Fioravanti needs to be replaced.

Barret reports on a meeting with Acquaviva involving Caetani, James Tyrie (as the general's assistant for all Europe north of the Alps), and Fioravanti. In conclusion, he alludes to his differences with the vice president of the college at Douai, Thomas Worthington (see Worthington's letter to Persons, 10 January 1597, B353).

Persons printed this letter in his *Briefe Apologie or Defence of the Catholike Ecclesiastical Hierarchie* (Antwerp, 1601), fols. 54b–55b, as part of his account and analysis of the troubles at the English college in Rome following the death of Allen. He omitted the last two paragraphs, in Tierney's view because he wanted to whitewash the government of the Society (lxxv n2; cited with skepticism by Kenny, "Inglorious Revolution," 78 [part 3]). The more likely reason is that Persons was reticent about presenting himself as fulfilling the desiderata Barret enumerates for the next rector of the English college in Rome. He may also have preferred not to draw attention to the gradual growth of opposition during the 1590s.

In the text below, the MS spelling "the" has been silently regularized to "they."

Loving father

The causes of these shamefull sturres I fynde to be these: *Imprimis*, that schollers weare permitted to deale in publick affaires, for a Cardinal, for faculties, etc., wherein being persuaded that the Societie was of a contrarie mynde, they conceaved an indignation and aversion as thoughe the fathers weare enemies to them, to theire cause and theire countrie and so the fundation of peace and unitie cleane overthrowen and a faction cunninglie brought in before the Rector suspected. Yea the Rector of ignorance was as earnest as the other untill they weare gone to farre that yt was to late to recalle them.

2°. Some of the same faction heare in Rome weare in hope to have goten the fingering of the rentes under the name of a congregation, and promised the heades of this troble in the College offices and roomes to their contentment and manie priveleges to the schollers.

3°. There is one vehementle suspected for a false brother sent of purpose.

4°. I fynd such heare as I expelled owt of Rheims.

5°. I fynd verie manie receaved at all adventure.

6º. During these troblesome broiles wheare nether studie of learning nor exercise of vertew kepeth them occupied, no mervell yf some yonge men would willing[489] looke back to the world and take anie occasion to be gone with the rest.

7º. I fynd theire heades full of false brutes and differences betwixt yours and ours in England: yea, the selfsame faction at Bruxells to be heare against the Spaniers, and such as take that waye.

8º. They are gone so farre and have committed so manie owtrages that they dispaire to go back ether in yelding heare or going hense and the multitude sworne together maketh them more bold.[490]

These causes and some other I shewed to His Holines in more ample maner then I can stand to wryte nowe and withall made yt plaine that manie of those youthes weare pittifulle deceaved, craving pardon most humblie for such as would come to acknowledg theire faultes and beseching also His Holines to have consideration of those that have bin brought up hearetofore or maye be hereafter in the College lamenting theire madnes, that under the colour of doing good to the College and our countrie, they tooke the readie waye to overthrow both this and all other Colleges; yea, and the worke so well begune in England. The which I shewed to consist in the concorde of the woorkemen and these men to make a division not onlie betwixt us and the fathers, but betwixt ourselves and concerning the first part I tould my mynd of the obligation and dutie wherewith for manie respectes we are most bounden to the Societie and could not breake with them withowt wonderfull shame and the undoing of Gods cause in our countrie. Concerning the second I declared to be against these same[491] factious heades the whole College at Dowaye, the Colleges in Spain and at St Omers, the preistes in England and generallie all our nation Catholike, a fewe onlie excepted by whose ill counsell these youthes were deceaved.[492]

This was the effect of my speach to His Holines, who answered much to my contentment, willing me to attend to the remedes, and to consult with the Cardinal Protector. And His Holines would allowe of that we should conclude. So upon Thursdaye last the Cardinal, Father General, Fr Tirius, the Rector and my self have agreed upon the remedies, expecting His Holines authoritie for the execution of the same. Thus yt standeth and within fewe dayes we hope for an ende.[493]

Well, Father, theire must needes be a Rector that is skilfull in the affaires of England and such a one as can and will gyve correspondence to the Colleges and your frendes abrod and besides he must be a man of gravitie, of countenance and authoritie and such as deale for matters of England and for the Colleges in Flanders must concurre with your frendes at Dowaye otherwise yt is not in me to helpe nor in all your frendes theare. O, but these be generalites. Well I fynd heare and theare manie particularities that must be amended whereof I meane to conferre with Father General whom I fynd most willing to heare me and you will concurre I hope. This Rector will never be able to rule in this place.

489. willing] *W*; willingly *Tierney*
490. *Editorial paragraph break, following Tierney*
491. same] *Renold*; fewe *Tierney*; *W obscure*
492. *Editorial paragraph break, following Tierney*
493. The extract in *Briefe apologie* ends here.

Many thinges I can tell you of that must be amended concerning this College in the maner of government and concerning better correspondence with the College of Dowaye or els you will never have peace. Trust those that be your trewe frendes although they wright not alwayes to your mynd and beware of those that speake faire and make all well and condemne all but them selves. Your letter in Decembre I have and, for Worthington you little knowe the man I see by your lettres, nor shall not know by me except we happ to meete.

Fare you well and remember the poore College at Dowaye from whense I want such lettres as Father Creswell required.[494] God graunt they do anie good. Rome, the xth of Aprill, 1596.

 Your own
  Richard Barret.

[*Endorsed*:] Doctor Barretes relation of the causes of the styrres in Rome x Aprilis 1596.

B323 To William Crichton, Seville, 10 May 1596

SOURCES:

ARSI, FG 651/640, item 32, a contemporary copy = R;

ABSI, Coll P I 316–318, a partial transcription = G;

CP, vol. 42, nos. 32, 33, dd. 10 July, with seal, 3 ½ pages = H.

HICKS: 456–466, with English translation.

EDITIONS: More, 122; "Cecil Papers: June 1596, 16–30," in *Calendar of the Cecil Papers in Hatfield House*, vol. 6: *1596*, ed. Richard Arthur Roberts (London, 1895), 216–239, at 233–236.

NOTE: Persons apologizes for his lack of success in finding financial support for the proposed Scottish college. There had earlier been some tension between him and Crichton over fundraising for the Scots college and the English seminary at St Omers (see Persons to Acquaviva, 12 May 1594, B230 and Persons to Philip II, 26 March 1596, B319; Edwards, 170–171).

He then reviews his attempts, since 1580, to secure a Catholic succession to the crown of England, explaining why he has now given up hope of James's conversion or support of the Catholic cause. He expresses frustration with Crichton's inconsistency on the matter.

Reverende in Christo Pater
Pax Christi.

Serius aliquanto redditae mihi sunt literae Reverentiae Vestrae scriptae Lovanii 20 Januarii, quod Hispalim me sint secutae. Quod agit mihi gratias Reverentiae Vestrae de subsidio quodam pecuniario procurato, animo certe meo debentur[495] ac desiderio, licet non operi, ob temporum difficultates. Egi quod potui agoque, sed duorum hic semina-

---

494. Barret confesses that he has not been able to provide the letters from Douai that Joseph Creswell had asked for.

495. debentur] G, H; debenter R

riorum pressus onere, quorum unumquodque ad septuaginta fere alit, quid aliis praestare possim,[496] Reverentia Vestra facile pro sua prudentia videbit.[497] Utinam Reverentia Vestra istius seminarii Scotici cum hic adesset opus ursisset,[498] aliquid sine dubio effectum fuisset: nunc autem de absentibus lentum negotium ac languidum nisi istic cum Serenissimo Cardinali aliquid confici possit:[499] quod ego adeo cupio, optoque, ut nihil sciam quod[500] libentius me totum impenderem quam in opus istud vestrum, si ab his duobus collegiis quae humeris meis hic incumbunt, liber essem, neque[501] exiguo mihi dolori est inopia vestra, cui levandae etsi impar omnino sum,[502] aliquid tamen ut conferam, hoc libentissime ex tenuitate nostra offero, ut si Vestra Reverentia sex habeat istic adolescentes Scotos, bonae indolis, qui ad studia philiosophica idonei sint,[503] atque Anglorum convictum non respuunt, eos in haec Seminaria admittemus,[504] omnique caritate complectemur,[505] et si hoc initium ex animo nobis successerit, fieri potest ut reliqua deinde sequantur ampliora; ego benevolentiae causa rem propono, vestro arbitrio totam[506] permitto. Caetera quae Reverentia Vestra petit, cum Episcopo Legantino et Domino Idiaquez in istius Seminarii usum agenda, habet ea valde commendata pater Cresuellus, qui Madriti moratur, quo etiam cum ipse venero (quod brevi futurum puto) partes quoque meae non deerint.[507]

Quod de alio negotio successionis regiae Reverentia Vestra scribit, nimium reprehendi se a nonnullis tanquam rationes humanas[508] secutum, quod Regis Scotiae iuri hereditario faveat,[509] vel non sit ex eis qui precoces sunt ad eum a successione *Angliae* excludendum (ut verbis utar Reverentiae Vestrae[510]), nescio sane quid respondeam vel[511] an quicquam hac in re respondendum sit, cum magis optarem de caelesti tantum regno et non de terreno tractandum[512] nobis foret, sed quia temporum iniquitate patriaeque nostrae extrema calamitate factum est, ut de salute ei procuranda, quae ex religionis Catholicae restitutione pendet, nulla ratione agere possimus, nisi etiam[513] de suc-

496. possim] G; possem R H
497. facile pro sua prudentia videbit] H; pro sua prudentia facile videbit R G
498. ursisset] R G; vidisset H
499. possit] H; posset R
500. quod] H; in quod R
501. liber essem, neque] R; at H; G omits nisi istic cum Serenissimo Cardinali aliquid confici possit ... liber essem
502. omnino sum] R; omnino sim G; animo sum H
503. sint] R, G; sunt H
504. admittemus] R, G; admittens H
505. omnique caritate complectemur] R H; om. G
506. totam] R; totum H
507. deerint] H; deerunt R; G omits ego benevolentiae causa ... deerint
508. rationes humanas] R; rationis humanae H
509. faveat] R; H reads faveant
510. R. V.] R; vestris H; G omits nimium reprehendi ... ut verbis utar R. V.
511. vel] R H; om. G
512. tractandum] R G; sperandum H
513. etiam] R G; om. H

cessore Catholico cogitemus, dicam hac occasione[514] Reverentiae Vestrae quicquid animo conceptum habeo.

Ego[515] ab anno octuagessimo quo primum in Angliam mandato superiorum appuli, Regis Scotiae studere commodis omni qua potui ratione coepi, et statim quidem Gulielmum Wates sacerdotem meis impensis[516] in Scotiam ex Anglia misi. Patrem deinde[517] Holtum submisi: et cum haec initia non male nobis succedere cernerem,[518] scripsi ad Reverendum Patrem Nostrum Generalem[519] ut aliquot viri Societatis e[520] gente vestra in Scotiam mitterentur; cumque statutum esset ut experiendi causa Reverentia Vestra[521] praemitteretur, facile recordabitur qua animi alacritate Rothomagi[522] ei adfui, adeo ut socium unicum quem habebam mihi ipse detraxerim ut Reverentiam Vestram in Scotiam sequeretur. Revertenti deinde Reverentiae Vestrae neque consilio neque opere,[523] neque re[524] defui: iter arduum ac difficillimum in Hispaniam, Olissiponem[525] usque suscepi, cum magno vitae periculo, neque cum minori aliud deinde in Flandriam,[526] ac tertium demum Romam usque. Atque haec omnia post Deum Regis Scotiae matrisque suae in gratiam, quibus licet ad cetera[527] quae cupiebantur non esset utilis opera mea, duabus tamen vicibus viginti quatuor aureorum millia a Rege Hispaniae in eorum usum impetravi, et a summo Pontifice Gregorio decimotertio quatuor millia: cuiusmodi nescio an alii praestiterint[528] officia, eorum[529] cogor mentionem facere ut eis opponam qui Regis[530] me Scotiae adversarium faciunt: ad quos refutandos nemo testis locupletior esse potest quam Reverentia Vestra quae haec omnia novit et meminisse poterit.[531]

Tandem vero[532] cum mortua Regina regem vestrum obfirmatum hearesis cursum tenere animadvertimus, fateor tam Alanum quam me, cum nondum esset cardinalitia

514. hac occasione] *R G*; om. *H*

515. [*marginal note in G:*] *Ab hoc loco usque ad illa verba Tandem vero habentur apud Morum p. 122. (More includes this paragraph only.)

516. impensis] *R H*; expensis *More*

517. deinde] *H, More*; om. *R*

518. nobis succedere cernerem] *R H*; succederent *More*

519. Reverendum Patrem Nostrum Generalem] *R H*; Reverendissimum Patrem Nostrum *More*

520. e] *R H*; ex *More*

521. experiendi causa Reverentia Vestra] *this ed.*; experiunde causa R. V. *R H*; R. V. experiendi gratia *More*

522. Rothomagi] *R H*; Rotomago *More*

523. opere] *More*; opera *R H*

524. neque re] *R*; unquam *More H*

525. Olissiponem] *R*; Olyssiponem *More*; Ulissiponi *H*

526. Flandriam] *R More*; Italiam *H*

527. cetera] *R H*; vota *More*

528. praestiterint] *R More*; praestiterunt *H*

529. eorum] *R H*; horum tamen *More*

530. Regis] *R*; Regi *H, More*

531. poterit] *R H*; potest *More*; *G* omits et statim quidem ... meminisse poterit. (More's text ends here.)

532. vero] *R G*; uno *H*

dignitate[533] praeditus, languidiores animo[534] in regis haeretici negotio promovendo nos exhibuisse, cum tamen Reverentia Vestra Romae nobis[535] dixerit anno opinor 86 saepiusque repeteret,[536] nihil certi statuendum esse, quoad firmum aliquod experimentum de Regis animo haberemus, quod se allaturum Reverentia Vestra promittebat, cum eo ipso tempore una cum aliis profectionem[537] in Scotiam pararet. Expectavimus libenter Reverentiae Vestrae reditum[538] qui cum aliquot deinde annis successisset, omnem plane spem nobis omnibus de Regis reductione eripuit: omni enim asseveratione affirmabat Reverentia Vestra tum alibi tum hic saepissime in Hispania, quod et alii quoque viri pii prudentesque nationis vestrae confirmarunt, nihil esse quod quisquam de Regis[539] ad fidem Catholicam conversione expectaret, quod reliqua etiam deinde secuta vehementer comprobant. Itaque fateor ex eo tempore Cardinalem Alanum meque alia omnia quam[540] de Rege Scotiae cogitasse, idque unum atque solum cogitationum nostrarum meta fuit, quis potissimum et prae ceteris competitoribus religioni Catholicae divinoque cultui in patria nostra restituendo atque stabiliendo opitulaturus videatur, cumque cogitando atque perscrutando,[541] eam praetensionum latitudinem praetensorumque varietatem perspiceremus[542] (quoad ipsum etiam succedendi ius haereditarium amoto omni religionis respectu), quam[543] Reverentia quoque Vestra ex edito nuper libro de hoc argumento vidit, quid viris bonis facere liceat[544] vel etiam incumbat addita religionis ratione, id est, an debeant[545] vel tuta conscientia possint praetensorem haereticum vel dubium saltem[546] sequi in praetensione quoque dubia, cum Catholicorum praetensorum copia sit, nemo piae mentis est qui non videbit.

Iam Reverentiae Vestrae dixi, verissimumque sane[547] est, vehementer[548] me cupere, ut haec ipsa de terrenis regnis, nihil quicquam ad nos pertinerent: sed cum nostra peccata id effecerint, ut prostrata omni republica nostra,[549] res politicae atque religionis adeo sint immixtae[550] atque perplexae, ut de unis restituendis sine aliis tractari non possit,[551] neque de religione Catholica stabilienda[552] sine principe Catholico, cumque tantum sit iam in

533. Cardinalitia dignitate] R G; dignitate cardinali H
534. animo] R G; omnino H
535. nobis] H; nos R; om. G
536. repeteret] R G; repeterit H
537. profectionem] R G; professione H
538. R. V^{ae}. reditum R G; vestrum reditum H
539. H duplicates de regis
540. quam] R G; quae H
541. perscrutando] R G; scrutando saepius H
542. perspiceremus] R G; prospiceremus H
543. quam] R G; qua H
544. liceat] R G; convenit H
545. debeant] R G; deberent H
546. saltem] R G; solum H
547. sane] R G; quod H
548. vehementer] R G; om. H
549. nostra] R G; mea H
550. sint immixtae] G; immixta R; sunt imixtae H
551. possit] R H; posset G
552. stabilienda] R H; restituenda G

priori laboratum, ut non solum laboribus magnis sed copiosissimo etiam sanguine constiterit, non possumus de secundo quoque non esse soliciti, ex quo caetera[553] omnia pendent. Itaque quod[554] Reverentiae Vestrae praesenti saepe praesens affirmavi (quod et piissimum Alanum nostrum fecisse quoque[555] memini) id iterum in[556] hac occasione repeto, id unum atque primo[557] omnium loco me intueri in futuro nostro principe, ut vere sit Catholicus, sit cuiuscunque alioquin nationis, gentis, vel linguae sub caelo, et si hoc in eo non sit, vel dubium sit, neque[558] patriam ego respicio, neque personam, neque ullum aliud iuris haereditarii praetensi genus, quod contra Dei causam admitti non debebit,[559] etiamsi alias validissimum esset. In Regis vero Scotiae praetensione quam sit infirmum[560] vel cum aliis commune ex eo quam[561] iam dixi libro edito apparet;[562] atque hoc quoque sensisse[563] Reverentia Vestra aliquando bene memini; et certe mirari satis non possum adeo mutatam[564] iam videre, ut scribat se non esse ex eis qui praecoces sunt ad regem Scotiae excludendum, cum nemo se neque praecociorem neque maturiorem ea in re ostenderit, aut efficacius illud nobis et aliis idque infinitis prope testibus persuaserit: quod si[565] aliqua in rege ipso subsecuta fuisset mutatio non adeo mirarer, quamquam[566] non ita facile quoque in re tanta crederem, sed his ipsis Reverentia Vestra scribit: De rege Scotiae pro certo habemus, eum ad partes Catholicas venturum si validiores essent, sed quid deinde futurum esset incertum est. Hic duo iam dicuntur, pro certum esse, regem ad partes Catholicorum qui apud Scotiam in armis sunt, si validiores fuerint, venturum, non disputo qua certitudine Vestra Reverentia id sciat. Sed ego quoque id sentio, non solum de illo, verum etiam de Regina Angliae, si res in discrimen veniret, partibus nimirum validioribus si liceat pro tempore adhaesuram, si res[567] enim non solum prudentiae est, sed etiam necessitatis.[568] Sed quod in secundo deinde adiicit[569] Reverentia Vestra, incertum est quid tunc fieret si Rex partibus se fortioribus adiunxerit, num scilicet[570] religioni Catholicae opem sit allaturus necne, plane indicat Reverentia Vestra nihil quicquam de voluntate Regis certum habere, quod ne tunc quidem eum religioni Catholi-

    553. caetera] *R H; om. G*
    554. quod] *R G; om. H*
    555. quoque] *R G; om. H*
    556. in] *R G;* iam *H*
    557. atque primo] *R G;* at primum *H*
    558. neque] *R G;* ne *H*
    559. debebit] *R G;* deberet *H*
    560. praetensione quam sit infirmum] *R G;* praetensionis iure aut [*possibly deleted*] infirmum *H*
    561. quam] *R G;* quem *H*
    562. apparet] *R G;* apperaret *H*
    563. hoc quoque sensisse] *R G;* idem quoque sentisse *H*
    564. mutatam] *R G;* mutatum *H*
    565. si] *R; om. H*
    566. quamquam] *duplicated in H*
    567. si res] *R;* hoc *H*
    568. etiam necessitatis] *R;* alicujus necessitates *H*
    569. adiicit] *R* adiiciat *H*
    570. num scilicet] *R;* si *H*

cae fauturum sciat, cum in Catholicorum fuerit potestate,[571] itaque stultos nos plane ac miseros si post tot exantlatos pro fide Catholica sustinenda labores, tot emensa pericula perpessaque martyria, velimus iam iterum in Regis haeretici vel dubii, omnia nostra, Deique ac reipublicae bona manibus deponere. Hoc est iudicium, hic sensus meus, Deo angelisque testibus, me nihil praeter divinam gloriam hac in re quaerere, neque minimae mihi curae esse, quis hominum regnis terrenis fruatur, modo celeste quaeramus aliisque procuremus. Reverentia Vestra haec aequo animo amicoque ut solet accipiat, reliquisque amicis nostratibus ac vestratibus quibus videbitur communicet, meque divinae misericordiae in sanctis suis sacrificiis commendet. Hispali 10 Maii[572] 1596.
   Reverentiae Vestrae
     servus in Christo
       Robertus Personius.

Translation

Reverend Father in Christ
The peace of Christ.
 Your Reverence's letter written from Louvain on January 20[573] was somewhat late in being delivered to me, as it followed after me to Seville. The thanks Your Reverence gives me for procuring you some assistance with funding are certainly deserved for my good intentions and desire, but not for carrying them out, given the difficulties of the time. I did what I could and am still doing so: but I am hampered by the burden of these two seminaries here, each of which maintains nearly seventy souls; and so Your Reverence with your accustomed discernment will easily see what position I am in to give help to others. It is a pity Your Reverence did not press[574] the cause of the Scottish seminary while you were here: without doubt something would have been done; but now your absence makes the affair proceed slowly and sluggishly; unless possibly where you are you can get His Eminence the cardinal to move in the matter.[575] I desire and hope for such assistance so much that I do not know anything I would wholly devote myself to more freely than that work of yours, if I were free from the care of these two colleges here whose burden I am shouldering. Nor does your necessity cause me little grief, and although it is quite out of my power to relieve it fully, yet in order to make some contribution I very willingly make you the following offer out of our slender means: if Your Reverence has six Scottish youths over there of good character, who are suitable to take the course of philosophy and who do not disdain to live with Englishmen, we will admit them to the seminaries here and embrace them with all charity; and if this first step turns out to our liking it may be that more will follow on a larger scale. This I propose as a testimony of my goodwill, and I leave the decision entirely in your hands. Your Reverence's

 571. G *omits from* quod si aliqua in rege ipso ... potestate
 572. Maii] R G; Julij H
 573. B3 10.
 574. H's reading would give "had not seen."
 575. The governor of the Spanish Netherlands, Archduke Albert of Austria, was cardinal archbishop of Toledo.

other requests to the legatine bishop and Don Idiáquez, for the use of that seminary of yours, have been strongly recommended by Fr Creswell, who is staying on in Madrid, and when I myself have arrived there, which I hope will be shortly, my efforts too will not be wanting.

As to what Your Reverence writes about the question of the succession to the throne, namely that you are very much criticized by some as being influenced by human considerations, such as favour the hereditary right of the king of Scotland or, to use your own words, because you are not of those who would prematurely exclude him from the succession in England – I do not know how to answer this, or whether any answer ought to be given in this matter; for I would much prefer that the kingdom of heaven and not any earthly kingdom were the subject of our discussion.[576] However, owing to the iniquity of the times and the extreme misfortune that has befallen our country, it has come about that it is impossible for us to do anything towards procuring its salvation, depending as it does on the restoration of the Catholic religion, unless we also take into account the question of a Catholic succeeding to the throne; and therefore I will take this opportunity of telling Your Reverence exactly what I think of the matter.

From the year 1580, when by command of my superiors I first landed in England, I began to study the interests of the king of Scotland in every way I could, and without more ado I sent William Watts, a priest, from England to Scotland at my own expense. Afterwards I secretly sent Fr Holt.[577] And when I saw that these first steps did not turn out badly, I wrote to our father general, asking for some men of the Society of your nationality to be sent to Scotland. And when it was decided that Your Reverence should be sent in advance to sound things out, you will have no difficulty in calling to mind how eagerly I assisted Your Reverence at Rouen: so much so that I gave up the only companion I had for myself, so that he could accompany you to Scotland.[578] Afterwards, when Your Reverence returned, I never failed you either in advice, effort or action. I undertook a trying and very difficult journey to Spain, going so far as Lisbon, with great risk to my life: and with no less risk I made another journey from there to Flanders, and finally a third to Rome. All this I did to please, after God, the king of Scotland and his mother; and though my assistance did not avail to procure the other things[579] we desired, still on two occasions I obtained 24,000 gold pieces from the king of Spain for their use, and also 4000 from the Supreme Pontiff, Gregory XIII. I do not know if any others have performed like services, but I am forced to mention them in order to refute those who make me out to be hostile to the king of Scotland. To refute these people, no witness can be more competent than Your Reverence, who knows all about these matters and can recall them.

Finally, however, after the queen's death we noticed that your king was obstinately pursuing his course in heresy, and I confess that both Allen and I, at a time when he did not yet enjoy the dignity of the cardinalate, did not disguise the fact that we were less enthusiastic about promoting the cause of an heretical king: although it is true that Your Reverence told us in Rome, in the year '86 I think, and used to repeat it quite often, that

576. Or, "the object of our hope" (see textual note).
577. See A44 and A81–188 (*passim*).
578. Ralph Emerson accompanied Crichton to Scotland in 1582; see A264–265.
579. Or, "wishes" ("*vota*" in More).

nothing ought to be definitely decided until we had some reliable proof of the king's state of mind; and Your Reverence promised to report on this, for at that very time you were preparing along with others to set out for Scotland.[580] We willingly awaited Your Reverence's return, which, taking place some years later, wholly removed from us every hope of the king's conversion: for Your Reverence declared very frequently, in the most emphatic terms, both here in Spain and elsewhere – and it was confirmed also by other pious and prudent men of your nation – that there were no grounds for anyone to expect the conversion of the king to the Catholic faith; and subsequent events have strongly confirmed this view. And so I confess that from this time forward Cardinal Allen and I had nothing further from our minds than the king of Scotland; this one and only question was the object of our deliberations: who seemed most likely, above all other claimants, to assist in restoring and establishing the Catholic religion and the worship of God in our country? And as a result of our consideration and thorough examination of the matter we came to perceive what a wide field of claimants there were and how diverse – as far as hereditary right of succession was concerned, leaving out any consideration of religion – and this is plain to Your Reverence too, from the book recently brought out on the subject. What good men may do and indeed ought to do, once the religious aspect is brought into account – that is to say, when it is asked whether they should or even may with a good conscience support a claimant who is a heretic or at least a probable one, and whose claim itself is also doubtful, where there is no lack of Catholic claimants – is plain for any man of pious disposition to see.

I have said to Your Reverence before, and it is indeed very true,[581] that I earnestly[582] wish that these matters concerning earthly kingdoms were outside the sphere of our interests. But since our sins have brought it about that, our whole commonwealth being prostrate in the dust, the interests of the state and of religion are so mixed up and intertwined that one cannot treat of the restoration of the one without the other, nor of the restoration of the Catholic religion except by means of a Catholic prince, and since we have already laboured so hard in the cause of religion that it has survived not only at the cost of great toil but also by a plentiful shedding of blood, we cannot fail to be concerned about the succession too, on which all the rest depends. And therefore what I have often declared to Your Reverence when we were face-to-face (and I also recollect that our most devoted friend Allen did so), I take this opportunity of again repeating, namely, that the one thing above all else that I have regard to in our future prince is that he should be a Catholic indeed; let him be of any nation, any race, any tongue under heaven. And if he should lack this qualification, or if there should be any doubt about it, I make no account of the nation to which he belongs nor of his personal qualities, nor otherwise of any kind of hereditary right which he may put forward – for that ought not to be admitted if it conflicts with the cause of God, even though in other respects it be entirely well founded. As regards the claim of the king of Scotland, it is shown in the published book which I have

580. Crichton met Persons in Rome in June 1587, after his release from the Tower of London (A212, headnote). They subsequently met in Madrid in 1592 (Persons to Acquaviva, 12 May 1594, B230, headnote).
581. Or, "what is very true" (see n547)
582. *H* annuls "earnestly" (see n548)

already mentioned, how weak it is or no better than others: and I well remember that at one time this was your opinion too. And certainly, I can only marvel exceedingly that you seem to be so changed as to say that you are not one of those who would prematurely exclude the king of Scotland; for no one showed himself more premature or hasty in that matter than yourself, or more effectually pressed this view on us and others, and that, moreover, before countless witnesses. If there has subsequently been some or other change in the king's attitude it would not much surprise me, although I should also not have believed it so easily in a matter of such great moment, but Your Reverence writes in these very words: "Of the king of Scotland we are certain he would come over to the Catholic side if its forces were to prove the stronger, but what would result from this is uncertain." Two things are said here to be certain: one, that the king would join with the Catholic parties who are in arms in Scotland, should they prove the more powerful. I do not question with what certainty Your Reverence knows this. But I, too, think it true not only of him but also of the queen of England, namely that if the matter came to the proof, she would adhere for the time being to the stronger side, if she is allowed; for this is not only a matter of prudence but even[583] of necessity. What Your Reverence adds in the second place (that it is uncertain what would be the result, if the king were to join with the stronger party, whether, that is, he would give support to the Catholic religion or not), clearly indicates that Your Reverence knows nothing for sure of the king's attitudes; for you do not know that he would favour the Catholic religion even if he were in the power of the Catholics. And so we should be entirely foolish and wretched indeed if after so many exhausting labours to uphold the Catholic faith, encountering so many dangers and enduring so many martyrdoms we should once again wish to place all our possessions, all our interests and those of God and of the state in the hands of an heretical king (or one who is suspected to be such). This is my judgement, this my feeling in the matter, and may God and the angels be my witnesses that in this matter I seek nothing but God's glory: and that it is completely indifferent to me which man enjoys the kingdoms of the earth so long as we may seek the heavenly one, and procure it for others. Would Your Reverence please take what I have said with your customary good temper and friendly spirit, and pass it on to our remaining friends, both our countrymen and yours, as you think fit. And I beg you to commend me to the divine mercy in your holy sacrifices. Seville, 10 May 1596.

  Your Reverence's
    servant in Christ
      Robert Persons.

B324 To Henry Garnet, Seville, 12 May 1596

SOURCE: AAW, IX, 50, holograph.

HICKS: 467–468.

NOTE: Persons would like Garnet to leave England and go to Rome, but the situation is delicate. The matter was raised again in February 1597 when Garnet finally received a letter

---

583. *H* reads "in some respects" (see n568).

from Acquaviva and replied in some bewilderment about Persons's intentions (Caraman, *Henry Garnet*, 234-235). He gives news of the victory of the Spanish fleet over the English near Cartagena, and of the death of Drake. The code here is different from that used in the letters of 12 June 1589 (B18) and June 1592 (B147) above. "Garth" refers to Garnet, as indicated in the address.

Loving brother

I have wryten dyvers letters to yow of late bothe by lande and sea & namely by the waye of 74 by which one Dowles [21 67 17 42 63 52] will come unto you together with 294 407 275 that is a priest [183], and the former of the two will offer to conduct Garth [273] by 74 to 123 but since his departure I have understod that albeit he be 338 yet is he not 337 & so I will not wish Garth [273] to adventure much upon him but rather as he maye be spared to go to Rome [117] in September [498] as I could wish that rather he went by 80 directely and[584] it is very probable that he shall meet Persons [275] with 204 but this must be very secret to 403 alone, and this is all I can wryte at this tyme.

Our newes heer are, that upon shost wesday[585] last the armada of Spayne met with that of Drake in the Indian sea not far from Cartagena – I mean ix shippes of Spayne with 14 of the Inglishe – and had a sharpe fyght untill the Inglishe havinge the worse[586] fled, & left only one shippe of 150 tune behynde them which was taken & 80 men in her, who report that as Sir Jhon Hawkyns dyed at Porto Ricco, so dyed Sir Francis Drake[587] of a fever at the nombre de Dios & this relation is certayne for I have seen it of them that were present at the fyghte.[588]

I pray yow commende me most hartely to the old woman[589] and tell her that I am in health, God be thanked, and ever synce those quartan agews left me I feele my self better than I was before and so will her nephew Jhon tell her when he come to her and yow; & this is all I have to saye now. Commende me to all frendes & if Garth [273] do not go to Rome [117] let hym wryte his answer to this, & sende it to your agent in Antwerpe to convey it unto Persons [275] wher so ever he be; & so adew this 12 of Maij 1596.

Yow know the hande.

[*Below the signature, in the same hand as the deciphering:*] It is true for it is Parsons.[590]

[*Addressed by Persons:*] To his lovinge brother Mr Henry Garth fishemonger &c London.

[*Endorsed in same hand as decipher:*] 12 Maij 1596 from Parsons to Henry Garth.

584. and] *W*; as *Hicks*
585. shost wesday] shoftwes day *Hicks*; *W* obscure. See the note below, referring to the date.
586. worse] *W*; worste *Hicks*
587. dyed Sir Francis Drake] this ed.; dyed Sir Francis Drake dyed *W*
588. The Spanish admiral Bernardino de Avellaneda y Leiva (1544–1629) routed Sir Thomas Baskerville's fleet near the island of Pinos on Monday 11 March 1596, in the second week of Lent. Both Hawkins and Drake had previously died of dysentery, on 12 November 1595 and 27 January 1596, respectively.
589. Persons's mother at White Webbs.
590. The deciphering also spells the name "Parsons."

B325 To Claudio Acquaviva, Seville, 13 May 1596

SOURCE: Acquaviva to Persons, 29 July (B331).

NOTE: From Acquaviva's reply, it appears that Persons was engaged in some delicate negotiation which required discretion.

B326 To Philip II from Joseph Creswell, Robert Persons, and Francis Englefield, Memorial on Present Conditions in England, 26 May 1596

SOURCE: ASG, Est. Leg. 967, fol. 100, a document in Creswell's hand with original signatures of Creswell, Persons, and Englefield, enclosed in a letter from Creswell to Idiáquez, 26 May 1596 (fol. 99).

HICKS: 453-455 (Spanish text only).

NOTE: This memorial marks the beginning of a more concerted drive to promote the infanta's claim to the English succession. The writers urge that the time is ripe for invasion, thanks to the influence of *Conference about the Next Succession*, and two military and naval setbacks for the English: the fall of Calais to the Spanish in April and the failure of the Hawkins/Drake expedition to the West Indies: see Paul E.J. Hammer, *Elizabeth's Wars: War, Government, and Society in Tudor England, 1544–1604* (New York, 2003), 190–198. At the same time, the king's support amongst the English in Rome and Flanders is dwindling, and James VI is of a mind to follow Henry IV's example and convert, to improve his chances of succeeding to the throne of England.

Lo que se ha sacado, tocante al estado presente de las cosas de Inglaterra, de diversas cartas escritas tanto de Inglaterra misma como de Flandres y Roma, a las personas infraescritas en estos ultimos meses passados de Março Avril y Mayo 1596.

Lo primero que el progresso de los Seminarios i el libro que se escrivio de la Sucession a la Corona de Inglaterra an hecho tal impression en los animos de todos que los Catolicos an avierto los ojos para veer el campo que tienen para escoger un Rey Catholico, y la obligacion que les incumbe de no admittir a ningun ereje. Y los erejes estan muy perplexos de lo que an de hacer y particularmente el Rey de Escocia comiença a descubrir que sin muestras de ser Catholico no podra tener esperança de la sucession y por esto se entiende que lo tratará como Vandoma.

Lo segundo que los Catholicos despues de leydo el dicho libro de la Sucession estan mui inclinados de abraçar aquel apuntamento que pone el libro de admitir a la serenissima Señora Infanta de España por Reyna – mayormente si se casara con su Altezza del Cardinal Archiduque de Austria del qual an concebido grandes esperanças antes y despues de su llegada a Flandres, parescendoles que por esta via se podra assigurar la religion Catholica i obviar a los grandes inconvenientes que temen de qualquier de los otros pretensores.

Lo tercero que aviendo el Rey de Escocia començado ya a descubrir su intencion de darse por Catholico a imitacion de Vandoma, y ganado una parcialidad de Ingleses, tanto en Flandres como en Roma y escrito cartas particulares a algunos de los principales dellos como al Conde de Vestmerland y a Carlos Pajet y a otros por el Baron Pury Ogleby que al presente está en esta corte y demas aviendo tratado dello con algunos principes de Italia poco aficionados a las cosas de España, y ganado como se piensa algunos Cardinales en Roma y principalmente las personas que estan más cerca de su Santidad, son de parecer y afirman los dichos Catholicos Ingleses por cosa muy cierta y sin duda, que passando adelante esta ficcion del Rey de Escocia, y veniendo en ella su Santidad, llevará consigo forçoçamente el corriente de los Catholicos, como en Francia se ha visto, no se le podra resistir pues el mayor impedimento que se oppone al Rey de Escocia (mirando solamente la descendencia del Rey Enrique 7°) es no ser Catholico.

Lo quarto. Affirman los mismos que el unico remedio de todo esto saria[591] que luego antes que prevalesca este tratado del Rey de Escocia Su Magestad hechasse mano de Inglaterra pues facilmente despues se averiguarian las cosas y Su Magestad podria disponer de todo suavemente conforme a su voluntad. Y si esto no se hace con brevidad y eficacia no le parece que despues quedará remedio.

Esto en efecto es lo que escriven fuera de algunos[592] particularidades que por otra via se diran: Lo qual attento parece que importa sumamente que Su Magestad mande tomar resolucion sin más dilacion pues las conjunturas que al presente se ofrecen son grandissimas y no pueden durar, como son la parcialidad que Su Magestad tiene en Inglaterra, la disposicion de Escocia y de Irlanda, las victorias del Cardinal Archiduque, el estar Vandoma pobre y embaraçado y la Reyna afligida con el mal sucesso de la armada de Draque y de la presa de Cales y otras circumstancias del tiempo presente.

Y porque el Vando de contrarios que se va haciendo en Roma y Flandres contra las cosas de Su Magestad a crecido mucho los meses passados por los grandes apoyos y espaldas que an hallado en personas poderosas poco aficionadas a Su Magestad y entradas con algunos ministros principales de aquellas partes, a sucedido que los aficionados al servicio de Su Magestad de la nacion Inglesa an sido talmente atropellados y perseguidos y desanimados que si no se pone remedio eficaz en ello, no podran resistir a la insolencia de los otros, ni avrá hombre que se atrieva muestrarse de la parte de Su Magestad y por esto lo proponemos como puncto de mucha importancia y consideracion.

            Joseph Cresuelo   Francisco Engelfild
                    Roberto Personio

[*Endorsed:*] Lo que escriven de ynglat^a para su. mag^d

Translation

A digest of matters concerning the present state of affairs in England, from various letters written to the signatories below, both from England itself as well as from Flanders and Rome, in these last months past of March April and May 1596.

First, that the progress of the seminaries and the book that has been written on the succession to the crown of England have made such an impression on the spirits of all that

---

591. saria] *S, i.e.,* sería
592. algunos] *S, i.e.,* algunas

the Catholics have opened their eyes to see the opportunity they have to choose a Catholic king, and the obligation incumbent upon them not to admit any heretic, while the heretics are much perplexed about what to do, and particularly the king of Scotland is starting to find that without showing himself to be Catholic he cannot have hope for the succession and to that end there is an expectation that he will act as Vendome did.[593]

Second, that the Catholics after reading the said *Book of the Succession* are much more inclined to embrace that position which the book sets out: to accept Her Most Serene Lady Infanta of Spain as queen – especially if she would marry His Highness the cardinal archduke of Austria,[594] of whom they have entertained great hopes before, and after his transfer to Flanders. It seems to them that by this means it would be possible to assure the Catholic religion and avoid those great inconveniences which they fear from each of the other pretenders.

Third, that because the king of Scotland has already begun to reveal his intention to put himself forward as Catholic in imitation of Vendome, and has won over a party among the English both in Flanders as well as in Rome, and has written particular letters to each of the chief men among them, such as the earl of Westmorland, Charles Paget, and a few others, through Ogilvie, the laird of Pury,[595] who at present is in this court, and moreover, has treated of the matter with certain Italian princes who are not very friendly towards the affairs of Spain, and won over (as is thought) some cardinals in Rome and principally those personages who are very close to His Holiness, the said English Catholics believe and affirm, as a matter very certain and without doubt, that this pretence of the king of Scotland gaining credence, and His Holiness believing it, the majority of the Catholics will believe it, as has been seen in France, so that it will not be possible to resist him, given that the major impediment which stands in the way of the king of Scotland (noting only his descent from king Henry VII), is that he is not a Catholic.

Fourth. The same persons affirm that the only remedy for all this is that before this pact of the king of Scotland prevails, His Majesty should take control of England, as soon as possible, before the business has been found out, and His Majesty could arrange everything smoothly according to his will – and if this is not done efficiently and with despatch, it is not likely that he will find remedy hereafter.

In effect this is what they write further of certain particulars which will be conveyed by other means: what we should take note of is that it seems of the highest importance that His Majesty should ensure that a decision is made without further delay, since the opportunities which are on offer at present are very great indeed and are not likely to last,

---

593. I.e., convert to Catholicism to gain the crown, like Henri IV of France. Persons's *Conference about the Next Succession* urged Catholics in England not to support a non-Catholic claimant to the English succession, which may have tempted James to give out signals that he was considering conversion. See Thomas M. McCoog, "A View from Abroad: Continental Powers and the Succession," in *Doubtful and Dangerous: The Question of Succession in Late Elizabethan England*, ed. Susan Doran and Paulina Kewes (Manchester, 2014), 257–275, esp. 259–264.

594. Archduke Albert was appointed governor-general of the Habsburg Netherlands in 1596.

595. John Ogilvie of Pury came to Rome in 1595, claiming to be James's ambassador. He supported Lewis's candidature for the cardinalate and presented a letter to the pope suggesting that James was ready to convert (McCoog, *Building the Faith of St Peter*, 240–243).

such as the favour which His Majesty enjoys in England, the good disposition of Scotland and Ireland, the victories of the cardinal archduke, the fact that Vendome is poor and embarrassed and the queen afflicted by the ill success of Drake's armada and the taking of Calais, and other circumstances of the present time.[596]

And because the band of enemies which is gathering in Rome and Flanders against His Majesty's cause has increased greatly these past months, thanks to the great support and backing found in powerful personages ill-disposed towards His Majesty who are influential with some principal ministers of those parts, the result is that those of the English nation who are devoted to the service of His Majesty have been pushed aside and persecuted and discouraged so much that unless an effective remedy is found for it, they will not be able to resist the insolence of the others, nor will there be a man who dares to show himself of the part of His Majesty, and this is why we present it as a point of much importance and consideration.

     Joseph Creswell Francis Englefield
       Robert Persons

B327 From Henry Tichborne, Rome, 5 June 1596

SOURCE: AAW, V, 60, a contemporary fair copy.

NOTE: Henry Tichborne (1570–1606) entered the Society of Jesus in Rome 1587, when he would have met Persons at the novitiate of Sant'Andrea. In 1596 he was tutor in logic at the English college in Rome but was transferred to Spain in 1599 and became confessor at St Gregory's college, Seville (McCoog, *English and Welsh Jesuits*, 314). This appears to be his first letter to Persons, informing him of Agazzari's appointment as rector, and tentatively offering himself for service on the English mission.

Tichborne sends Persons information about four Jesuits who have recently completed their training: Thomas Wiseman, alias Starkey (1572–1596) entered the Society of Jesus in Rome in 1592 and left for Saint-Omer, as Tichborne records, in May 1596, despite his bad health. He died there on 9 August. Joseph Pullen (ca. 1543–1607), William Warford (ca. 1560–1608), and Richard Griffith (ca. 1576–1607) all joined the Society in May 1594. Pullen was given permission to travel to Flanders on 14 September 1596. Warford had previously been on the mission to England (see his letter to Persons, 15 May 1591, B108), but returned to Rome and joined the Society of Jesus in May 1594. He enjoyed the confidence of Persons and of Cowling (Persons to Acquaviva, 9 December 1595, B304; Cowling to Persons, 13 February 1596, B315), and later transferred to Seville and then Valladolid. Griffith (ca. 1576–1607) remained at the English College, Rome, at least until 1599 (McCoog, *English and Welsh Jesuits*, 197, 273, 325–326, 336).

Reverende in Christo pater
Pax Christi.
  Nunc tandem incipio Vestrae Reverentiae literas dare, cum pacatiori rerum statu in collegio fruimur, licet enim me rem gratam Vestrae Reverentiae facturum arbitrabar si de

---

596. Drake had died in Puerto Rico in January 1596; this is likely a reference to his unsuccessful American campaign (see Persons to Philip II, September/October 1595, B293).

progressu factionis huius nonnumquam certiorem facerem, ut convenienti si fieri potest remedio occurreret, quia tamen alios non defuisse certo scivi qui omnia diligenter perscriberent, et difficile mihi erat quae gerebantur scribere nisi aliquorum offensionem incurrerem, hactenus scriptioni supersedendum putavi; imposterum quod erit officii mei, quodque Vestrae Reverentiae gratum fore cognoscam diligenter praestabo.[597]

Collegium regendum suscepit 18 Maii P. Alphonsus Agazarius (patriae nostrae parens optimus) Anglorum omnium summo solatio, huius ut spero collegio summo bono. Principium dedit reformando collegio quod plane difforme reperit, qui seditiosi sunt dissimulant exterius licet plane non quiescant, eos speramus optimi patris et mansuetudine et prudentia superandos et in Christo uniendos. P. Guilielmus Starkeius, alias Thomas Wisman hic graviter laboravit, et pene pthysicus Flandriam versus ante mensem discessit, tum diu distulit profectionem, ut vix credam illum vivum in Flandriam perventurum. P. Josephus Polinus, P. Guilelmus Guarfordus, et Richardus Grifinus finito probationis tempore nuncupatis votis ex Sancto Andrea in Collegium Romanum migraverunt; P. Josephus et Richardus dant operam casibus conscientiae, P. Guarfordus nulli adhuc certo addictus exercitio superiorum exspectat voluntatem. Ego iam sex mensibus in hoc collegio versor logicorum repetitionibus praefectus (metaphysicorum et physicorum repetitionibus praeficiuntur duo alumni). Annum ago aetatis 26, in Societate nonum, in Theologia tertium; sequenti anno studia Deo iuvante absolvam, quibus completis omnes et animi et corporis mei vires ad salutem animarum in Anglia procurandam offero, et in quocunque exercitio quod Reverentia Vestra magis ad hunc finem conducere indicabit libens collocabo, rogans interim Reverentiam Vestram ut libertati meae parcat (absentem enim et oculis ignotum ut patrem charissimum alloquor), obtestans etiam ut in suis sanctis sacrificiis et orationibus mei aliquando memoriam faciat, quo Dei fretus ope solitas vitae meae imperfectiones eradicem, eam virtutum suppellectilem preparem quae laborantibus in vinea Domini hoc calamitoso saeculo necessaria est. Salutat Vestram Reverentiam plurimum P. Richardus Coulinus. Vale. 5 Junii 1596. Romae in collegio Anglorum.

    Vestrae Reverentiae filius in Christo
        Henricus Tichburnus

[*Addressed:*] Reverendo in Christo patri P. Roberto Personio Societatis Jesu sacerdoti, Madriti.

[*Endorsed*:] Henricus Tichbornus 5 Junii 1596.

Translation

Reverend Father in Christ
The peace of Christ.

    I am at last setting out to write a letter to Your Reverence now, when we are enjoying a more peaceful state of affairs in the college; for even though I would think I was doing Your Reverence a favour if I were sometimes to inform you about the progress of this faction, so that you could counteract it with some suitable remedy if at all possible,

---

597. *Editorial paragraph break.*

nevertheless, because I knew that there has been no shortage of others who have reported everything in detail, and it was difficult for me to write what was taking place without causing offence to others, I thought I should refrain from writing until now; because it would be my duty afterwards, to set out carefully whatever I know Your Reverence would appreciate.

Fr Alfonso Agazzari (an excellent servant of our country) took charge of the college on 18 May, to the utmost relief of all the Englishmen, and, I hope, to the supreme benefit of this college. He made a start in reforming the college, which he found in a pretty bad state. Those who were in revolt put on an outward show: even though in reality they are not submissive, we hope that they will be overcome and be united in Christ through the excellent father's gentleness and prudence. Fr William Starkey, alias Thomas Wiseman, has worked hard here, and left for Flanders a month ago, almost in a consumption, until he had deferred his departure so long that I could hardly believe that he would reach Flanders alive. Fr Joseph Pullen, Fr William Warford, and Richard Griffith have completed their time of probation, have taken their vows, and have now migrated from Sant'Andrea to the Roman College; Fr Joseph and Richard are attending to cases of conscience, Fr Warford has still not been charged with any particular office and is awaiting the decision of the superiors. I have been engaged in this college for six months already as tutor in logic (there are two members who are in charge of metaphysics and physics). I am in my twenty-sixth year, the ninth in the Society, my third in theology; next year I will complete my studies, God being my helper. When these have been completed, I offer all my strength, both of soul and body, to achieve the salvation of souls in England, and in whatever role Your Reverence should indicate would conduce more to this object I will gladly place myself, asking Your Reverence in the meantime to excuse my taking this liberty (for I address you as the most loving father even though you are absent and I have never seen you), begging you to remember me sometimes in your holy prayers and sacrifices, that, relying on God's help, I may eradicate the habitual imperfections of my life and prepare that panoply of virtues which is necessary for those working in the vineyard of the Lord in this calamitous age. Richard Cowling sends hearty greetings to Your Reverence. Farewell. 5 June 1596. Rome, at the English college.

  Your Reverence's son in Christ
    Henry Tichborne.

B328 To Thomas Hesketh (Allen), Toledo, 26 June 1596

SOURCE: ABSI, Coll P I 305, II 488, 502, references only, "from Toledo to Mr Hesket."

NOTE: In Rome, Hesketh (or Allen) was one of those, along with Hugh Griffin and Nicholas Fitzherbert, who were expected to be opposed to the succession of the infanta (Edwards, 194); he took over the leadership of the English colony in Rome after Griffin's departure for Cambrai in 1597 (McCoog, *Building the Faith of St Peter*, 360, 387). The new rector of the English college, Alfonso Agazzari, hoped that Hesketh could be induced to change sides: see his letters of 27 August (B336) and 25 September 1595 (B343).

B329 To Claudio Acquaviva, Toledo, 11 July 1596

SOURCE: ARSI, FG 651/640, item 33.

NOTE: This letter is remarkable for the brevity of its reference to the Anglo-Dutch raid on Cádiz, 30 June–15 July 1596 (Kamen, 306–307). Persons hopes this will spur the Spanish people to support the next armada. A statue of the Virgin and Child, mutilated by the soldiers, was later presented to the English college in Valladolid by Philip III. The *Vulnerata*, as it is known, remains as the centrepiece above the altar in the chapel, a symbol of iconoclasm and enduring piety (Dominguez, *Radicals in Exile*, 181).

The main subject of the letter is the question of recalling Creswell, rather than Persons himself, to Rome, to deal with the problems at the English college there (see his letters of 15 January, B308, 11 February, B314, 8 April, B320, and 28 August, B338, and McCoog, *Building the Faith of St Peter*, 360; cf. his letter of 29 July, B331, which authorizes Creswell's transfer to Flanders to replace Holt). Persons has presented the reasons to the king as objectively as possible, and the king, aware of the threat posed to his interests by the disturbances, is anxious for Creswell to be depatched quickly, but discretion is necessary.

Persons also protests about del Río's refusal to cover the cost of carriage of letters. Acquaviva responded briefly to this letter on 28 August (B338).

Muy Reverendo en Christo padre nuestro
Pax Christi.

Por ser muy tarde y éste el primero dia que me ha faltado una calentura escrivo éste brevissimamente a Vuestra Paternidad y digo que pues Vuestra Paternidad en las postreras cartas parece que más inclina que el padre Cresuello veniesse a Roma yo tan bien hallé más raçones para ello, y assi lo propusi aqui con la indifferencia que me parecia convenir para no offender pero allegando las raçones, y Su Magestad vino en ello que fuesse más presto el padre Cresuello que no yo aunque le parecia bien que se callasse por agora y assi me parece tan bien y por esto no lo he dicho ni escrito a nadie de los nuestros si no en ésta solo a Vuestra Paternidad, parte porque podra aver alguna mudança por acá, y quando no, convendria que no fuesse sabida hasta el padre estubiere en Italia si se puede.

El Embaxador ha escrito muy bien al Rey de las causas verdaderas dessas turbaciones y el Rey reconoce que tiene a la Compañia en este particular y que la radiz es contra él, y contra el bien de la patria que sin duda pienso que Su Magestad busca sinceramente y queren esto los contrarios le hacen agravio, y mucho más a la patria que no tiene medio humano para ayudarse si no por via desta monarchia, no obstante todas las faltas que ay por acá, las quales todos las vemos y lloramos, *sed aliud est tenere nullum remedium, aliud defectivum.*

Mucho nos confunde por acá, lo que escrive a los padres procuradores de aqui el padre que cobra los portes de cartas aý, diciendo que el padre Rector del Seminario no quiere pagar porte alguno de las cartas, que viene de España, si no que los procuradores lo cobren de los Seminarios de aqui, pues no le escrivimos ni hacemos caso dél, yo puedo affirmar de mi parte que he escrito a su Rectoria mucho más veçes de lo que he recebido carta suya, más escriviera si tubiera de qué, y si él nos diera parte de sus cosas del collegio, pero él no solamente no quiso escrivir nada por muchos meses, quando podiamos porventura aver procurado más facilmente algun remedio, pero vedó tanbien al padre Edmondo que otros que no escriviessen, y todas las cartas o la mayor parte que se an escrito despues an sido en favor de su causa y del collegio, si él favorece a los quietos, como yo presumo que lo haçe, no obstante lo que creen y escriven otros, en nostro rubove, y assi no es Justo que rehuse de pagar los portes de las cartas que en su favor se an escrito, supplico a Vuestra Paternidad mande poner orden en éste porque sería escandalo que passasse adelante este encogimiento y disunion y si esso Seminario no quiere concorrer a los cosas comunes como otros hacen, nunca avrá paz ni union ni consuelo y assi es necessario que aya Rector aý que sea unido pero deste ordenerá Vuestra Paternidad despues; aora basta que como de suyo Vuestra Paternidad mande que el Seminario pague los portes aý como nos otros pagamos aqui de todos las partes. Muy sea con harto travajo, pero aora me ha parecido escrivir una carta al Rector del negocio la qual va con ésta para que Vuestra Paternidad la vea y mande dar y con ésta tome occasion de remediar la differencia, el principal cuydado de aquel collegio ha de acudir a la causa pública.

De la desgracia que aqui ha acontecida de la pérdida de Cadiz Vuestra Paternidad entendera de otros y yo no tengo tiempo, yntiendo con todo esto que ha sido providençia de Dios para despertar a esta gente. En los Sanctos sacrificios de Vuestra Paternidad muy humilmente encomiendo. Toledo 11 de Julio.[598]

  De Vuestra Reverenda Paternidad
    siervo y hijo
      Roberto Personio.
[*Endorsed*:] Toledo 11 di Luglio 96 P. Roberto Personio.

Translation

Our Very Reverend Father in Christ
The peace of Christ.
 Being very late and the first day that my fever has subsided, I am writing this briefly to Your Paternity to say that since Your Paternity in your most recent letters seems more inclined that Fr Creswell should come to Rome, I have also found more reasons for that, which I presented here with the indifference which I considered appropriate, so as not to offend but merely outlining the reasons. And His Majesty agreed that it would be quicker for Fr Creswell to do so, rather than me; he thought it would be good not to speak about it, and I agree. So, I have not talked or written to anyone of Ours except this private letter to Your Paternity, partly because there might be some transfers around here, and even if not, it is better that it is not known until the father is in Italy, if possible.
 The ambassador has written very well to the king about the actual causes of the disturbances, and the king acknowledges the rights of the Society in this particular and that what underlies it all is hostility to him, and the good of the country: which undoubtedly

---

598. FG has the penciled headnote "21 Luglio," but the signature and the endorsement give 11; Acquaviva's response gives 11 July; Coll P I 305, II 488 and 502 refer to a letter to Roger Baynes variously as 11 or 12 July.

indicates that His Majesty is sincerely well-intentioned; the opponents seek to do him wrong, and even more their country, which has no other means to find help except by means of this monarchy, despite all the faults that are here, which we all see and lament, but *it is one thing to have no remedy at all, another to have a defective one.*

We are very confused over here by what has been written to the father procurators from here by the father who deals with postage charges there, saying that the rector of the seminary does not wish to pay the charges for any of the letters that come from Spain, unless the procurators cover those of the seminaries from here, since we are not writing to him nor do we have any dealings with him; I can confirm for my part that I have written to His Rectorship many more times than I have received a letter from him.[599] I would write more if I had some information to discuss, and if he shared some of his affairs of the college, but not only did he not wish to write anything for many months, when we might perhaps have been able to obtain some remedy more easily, but he also instructed Fr Edmund[600] that no one else should write. And all the letters, or most of them, that have been written later, were in favour of his cause and the cause of the college, if he favoured the orderly ones, as I presume he has done, notwithstanding what others believe and write, to our shame, and thus it is not just that he should refuse to pay the charges for the letters which have been written in his favour. So I beseech Your Paternity to order that this be sorted out because it would be a scandal to let this constriction and disunion go forward. If that seminary does not want to contribute to the common matters as others do, there will never be any peace or union or encouragement, and therefore it is necessary that there should be a rector and that they should fall in line with the rest. But on this, Your Paternity will issue orders later; for now, it is enough that Your Paternity should instruct that the seminary should cover the expenses there, just as the rest of us pay for our costs over here. Even though the whole thing is difficult, for now it has seemed wise to write a letter to the rector about the business, which will go along with this, so that Your Paternity can see it, and take this opportunity to remedy the dispute: the chief care of the college should be to refer to the public good.

As for the disgrace which has occurred with the loss of Cádiz, Your Paternity will learn this from others, as I have no time. In my view, the providence of God has brought it about to wake these people up. To your holy sacrifices I commend myself humbly.

Your Reverend Paternity's
servant and son
Robert Persons.

B330 To Roger Baynes, Toledo, 11/12 July 1596

SOURCE: ABSI, Coll P I 305, Coll P II 488, 502; references only; the date is given as 12 July at Coll P II 502.

NOTE: Baynes had been Allen's secretary. Persons may have wished to sound him out on the question of the troubles at the English college.

599. Fioravanti may have wished to distance himself from Persons, even though, as Persons notes, he was writing in his favour.
600. Edmund Harewood.

B331 From Claudio Acquaviva, Rome, 29 July 1596

SOURCE: ARSI, Baet. 3/I, 278-279.

NOTE: A marginal note, in another hand, possibly Grene's, reads "Haec est ultima ad eum Epistola in hoc regesto" (This is the last letter to him in this register). Acquaviva mentions the continuing problems at the English College, Rome; makes arrangements for the appointment of a new rector at Valladolid; intervenes to alleviate the tension between the local Jesuits and the seminarians in Seville over fundraising; approves of the exchange of Creswell and Holt; and instructs Persons to assist with the founding of a Scots college in Louvain.

P. Roberto Personio, Julio 29.

Reçevi la de Vuestra Reverencia de 13 de Mayo, y consuelo de entender por ella las buenas nuevas que me da de esos seminarios. Yo no se las[601] podre dar tales del de acá, porque todavia entiendo ay alguna inquietud en esta gente, sin que baste la soliçitud del Señor Cardenal, y la merçed que les haçe. Para Valladolid proveera el Padre Garcia segun me escrive de un buen Rector. Para lo de Sevilla escrivo yo al Padre Mendez que hable con el Preposito y le diga que poco o nada perjudicará a las limosnas de la casa, si quien se pide para el seminario Ynglés, el de la Compañia va acompañado con un par de alumnos y declara que pide para el seminario, y que con esta limitaçion y temperamento, de que no vaya el de la Compañia con otro de los nuestros sino con alumnos, se quitará el inconveniente si alguno huviere.

El trabajo que dice Vuestra Reverencia ha hecho me pareçe que será muy util, pero es bien como diçe en su carta que no se comunique sino a qualquier confidente. Vuestra Reverencia se acuerde que le he escrito conviene executar el cambio del padre Cresuelo para Flandes, y del Padre Holto para España. Ens.

[PS] Encargo a Vuestra Reverencia ayude lo que pudiere para el seminario de Escozeses en Lovania.

Translation

To Fr Robert Persons, 29 July.

I have received Your Reverence's letter of 13 May,[602] and am encouraged to understand from it the good news which you give me about those seminaries. I'm not able to offer the same from here, because I still am aware of some unrest among that nation, and the diligence of the Lord Cardinal and the grace he showed are not enough. As regards Valladolid, Fr García[603] writes to me saying that he will provide for a good rector. As for Seville, I am writing to Fr Méndez[604] to speak to the superior and tell him that there is little or no prejudice to the alms of the house, if when anything is being asked for the English seminary, one of the Society goes accompanied by a couple of students and declares

601. las] R, with s possibly deleted
602. B325.
603. García de Alarcón, visitor to Castile and Toledo.
604. Cristóbal Méndez, provincial of Andalusia.

that they are asking for the seminary, and that with such restriction and moderation, so long as the one from the Society does not go with another of Ours but just with the students, all trouble will be removed, if indeed there was any.[605]

The work that Your Reverence says he has done will be very useful, it seems to me, but it is well, as you say in your letter, that communication should only take place with some confidant. I beg Your reverence to remember what I wrote about the convenience to put into effect the change of Fr Creswell to Flanders and Fr Holt to Spain.[606] To your [sacrifices, etc.]

[PS] I charge Your Reverence to help as far as possible with the Scottish seminary in Louvain.[607]

B332 To Claudio Acquaviva, Madrid, about 10 August 1596

SOURCE: Persons to Acquaviva, 18 August (B333).

NOTE: Persons wrote this letter a few days before his letter of 18 August suggesting a visit to Rome.

B333 To Claudio Acquaviva, Madrid, 18 August 1596

SOURCE: ARSI, FG 651/640, item 34, holograph, marked confidential.

NOTE: Persons is keen to return to Rome to see Acquaviva and consult with him on many weighty matters. For the present things seem to be under control in Spain, so he is likely to be able to leave things to Creswell. He is concerned about hostility to William Holt in Flanders but asks that the matter be held over until he reaches Rome.

The letter contains references to a recent letter Persons had written to Acquaviva, and to a confidential letter he plans to write, giving reasons for his visit which should be kept secret. Neither of these letters is extant, but they presumably had to do with the growing conflict with the anti-Jesuit party in Flanders and elsewhere. We have traced no record of these letters, or of Acquaviva's reply, possibly because of the need for discretion.

Muy Reverendo en Christo Padre mio

Por una mia los dias passados signifiqué a Vuestra Paternidad como por lo que Vuestra Paternidad en differentes cartas suyas avia apuntado que gustaria nos viessemos en Roma por un par de meses si fuera possibile, y por los muchos y graves negocios que yo tenía que conferir con Vuestra Paternidad despues de ocho años de absencia lo deseava tan bien en sumo grado, veerme con Vuestra Paternidad por algunos dias, toda via por las difficultades que se offerecian en tanto de parte delos Seminarios como de otras per-

605. Acquaviva wishes to safeguard the interests both of the local Jesuits and of the seminary by ensuring that donors to the seminary are aware that the Society has separate needs and that the seminarians, when seeking alms, are not outnumbered.
606. This exchange did not in fact take place.
607. On the 1594 dispute between Crichton and Persons over the provision for the Scots, see Edwards, 170–171, citing Persons to Acquaviva, 12 May 1594 (B230). See also Persons to Philip II, 26 March 1596 (B319), and to Crichton, 10 May 1596 (B323).

sonas, escriví a Vuestra Paternidad que entendia vendria el Padre Cresuello, pero aora parece que se an mudado algo las cosas, y allanado las difficultades, de manera que es muy probabile que yo vea a Vuestra Paternidad y reciba su benedicion por aý muy presto, digo en todo el mes de octubre, offreciendose commodidad de embarcacion. Lo he encomendado mucho a nuestro Señor y communicado con el Padre Visitador el qual está muy presto en ello por las raçones que entendemos contentarán tan bien a Vuestra Paternidad en oyendolas porque son muy importantes, y algunas urgentissimas, todo sea a gloria y servicio de nuestro Señor el qual guýe a todo. Harto se lo encommendado y se lo encomiendo todos los dias y si no ubiesse otro negocio si no veerme y descansarme un poco con Vuestra Paternidad y recebir su benedicion despues de tantos años de travajo y peregrinacion, me pareceria muy bastante causa deste viage, pero ay tan bien las cosas desos collegio ynglés, de Roma, y destos dos seminarios de España, y delos dos residencias y del Seminario de Sant Omer, y las missiones de Ynglaterra circa las quales cosas todas ay muchos apuntamientos para assentar para que duren y perseveren que no se pueden assentar ni acabar por cartas.

No se sabe aún por acá nada desta mi yda, ni conbiene que se sepa, ni por acá ni por aý si no quando estare de camino por las raçones que Vuestra Paternidad puede pensar, y assi escrivo ésta con in soli, por el secreto y no creo que puedo tener respuesta si no en llegando aý porque por medio septiembre se ha de partir de aqui. Sea servido nuestro Señor que halle a Vuestra Paternidad con mucha salud porque él solo sabe el consuelo que dello recibere y confio tan bien en nuestro Señor que Vuestra Paternidad quedará consolado con la visita y conferencia de emos de tener. Guarde Dios a Vuestra Paternidad como le supplico y emos menester. Madrid a 18 de Agosto 1596.

  De Vuestra Reverenda Paternidad
    siervo y hijo
      Roberto Personio.

[PS] He entendido como en Flandes algunos de la nuestra nacion haçen muchas diligencias para que el padre Holto salga de alli y aunque yo pienso que no se aquietará con esto y es tan passion contra el padre, todavia deseara que estubiesse el padre fuera por su quietud y él tan bien lo desea pero el tiempo presente. No es a proposito para ello, y pues la vista ha de ser tam presto supplico a Vuestra Paternidad que se detenga hasta que yo llegue a Vuestra Paternidad.

[Addressed:] soli. Al muy Reverendo en Christo padre mio Claudio Aquaviva preposito General.

[Endorsed:] soli. Madrid 1596. Ag° 18. P. Roberto Personio. del suo venire a Roma e del P. Holto in Fiandra.

Translation

My Very Reverend Father in Christ

By one of my letters the last few days I indicated to Your Paternity – as Your Paternity has pointed out in several of your letters – that I would like us to see each other in Rome for a couple of months if possible, and to confer with Your Paternity on the many and weighty matters that occupy me; after eight years of absence, I wanted very much, in the highest degree, to spend some days with Your Paternity; yet, because of the difficulties which present themselves both from the seminaries and other persons, I wrote to Your Paternity that I understood Fr Creswell would come; but now it seems that some things have changed, and have smoothed out the difficulties in a manner which makes it very probable that I will see Your Paternity and receive your blessing there very soon, that is, during the month of October, if I have opportunity to embark. I have committed it much to Our Lord and have communicated with father visitor,[608] who is very favourably disposed towards it, for reasons which we believe will very much satisfy Your Paternity to hear, because they are very important, and some very urgent: all be to the glory and service of Our Lord, who governs all things. I have entrusted it to Him abundantly, and I do so every day. And even if there were no other business except for me to see Your Paternity and to refresh myself with you and receive your blessing, after so many years of work and travelling, it would seem to me quite reason enough for the journey, but in addition there are matters concerning the English college in Rome and of the two seminaries in Spain, and of those two residences and the seminary of St Omers, and the missions of England; concerning all these matters there are many questions to consider so that they will last and persevere, which cannot be settled or concluded by letter.

No one here knows anything of my departure yet, nor is it convenient that they should know, neither here nor there, but only when I am on the road, for reasons which Your Paternity can imagine, and so I am writing this as a private letter, for secrecy's sake, and I believe I will only receive the reply when I arrive there, because I will be leaving here in the middle of September. May it please our Lord that I find Your Paternity in good health, because He alone knows the comfort I will receive from it; and I also trust in our Lord that Your Paternity will be encouraged by seeing me and conferring on the matters we need to discuss. May God preserve Your Paternity according to my prayers and our need. Madrid, 18 August 1596.

   From your Reverend Paternity's
    servant and son
     Robert Persons.

[PS] I understand that some of our nation in Flanders are doing all they can to get Fr Holt out of there, and although I think that things will not be pacified with this [measure], as there is strong feeling against the father, still, I wish that the father were stationed elsewhere for the sake of his serenity, and he also desires that at present. Although this is not to the purpose for the present, and since the time is so short before I see you, I beg Your Paternity that it be kept until I reach Your Paternity.

B334 To Claudio Acquaviva, Madrid, about 18 August 1596

  SOURCE: Persons to Acquaviva, 18 August (B333).
  NOTE: Although Persons mentioned, in his confidential letter of 18 August (above), that he would give reasons, in another confidential letter, why his departure from Spain should be kept secret, it is uncertain whether such a letter was ever written.

608. See n603.

B335 From William Crichton, probably Douai, 20 August 1596

SOURCE: ABSI, Coll P I 318.
HICKS: 469–470, with English translation.
EDITION: Knox, *Allen*, 384.
NOTE: Crichton explains his reservations about Persons's *Conference about the Next Succession*. This letter was sent via Colonel William Semple in Madrid (see Persons's reply, 2 November, B347, and Persons to Acquaviva, 12 May 1594, B230).

Pax Christi.
Accepi literas Reverentiae Vestrae datas 10 Maii mihi pergratas. Omnia quae commemorat Reverantia Vestra erga regem nostrum et nationem fateor esse vera. De libro Successionis parum habeo quod dìcam. Quod scripsi fuisse precocem, de publicatione libri erat praecipue intelligendum, quae mihi et multis visa est tempus non sine praejudicio multorum quibus Reverentia Vestra favet antevertisse. Quid fructus attulerit publicatio plane ignoro; quid vero damni certe scio etc. —— Est proverbium Gallicum leporem non esse capiendum tympano, in pulpitis tam Angliae quam Scotiae Ministri pulsant.

Translation

The peace of Christ.
I have received Your Reverence's very welcome letter of 10 May.[609] All that you say as regards our king and our nation, I confess, is true. Of the *Book of the Succession*, I have little to say. What I wrote of its being premature was to be understood especially of the publication of the book, for to me and many others its appearance has seemed to be premature – not without prejudice to many to whom Your Reverence favours. I am quite unaware of any benefit its publication has brought, but I am quite sure of the harm, etc. —— There is a French proverb: you don't catch a hare with a drum. Ministers are now beating it in the pulpits both of England and Scotland.

B336 From Alfonso Agazzari, Rome, 27 August 1596

SOURCE: AAW, V, no. 66, 215–218.
EDITION: Tierney, 3: lxxv, "Extract from the Original in my possession."
NOTE: Agazzari replaced Fioravanti as rector of the English College, Rome, on 17 May 1596, in hopes that he might be able to quieten the unrest there. After delivering a sermon to the students on obedience, he treated them to a party at the college vineyard at St Maria alle Fornaci. In a letter to Creswell dated 28 July he complained, "We have gained nothing so farr but an external appearance of peace and quiet, just enough to avoid scandal and offence to others" (Kenny, "Inglorious Revolution," 81–88 [part 3]).

Agazzari is disappointed not to have had any response from Persons to his two previous letters, and wryly anticipates congratulations on his appointment. He cautions that the divi-

---

609. B323.

sions are deep-seated, identifying Edward Bennet (1569–1637), Thomas Hill (1564–1644), and Edward Tempest (b. 1568) as leaders of the disaffected party (see Anstruther, 30–31, 167–168, and 348–349; Barret to Persons, 28 September 1596, B344; and Persons's *Relación* of the disturbances, 22 May 1597, B378). On Hill, see Kenny, "Inglorious Revolution," 250–251 (part 1).

Agazzari was in the habit of writing to Persons in Latin, but because this letter was dictated to his secretary, Henrico (probably Henry Tichborne), who was better conversant in Italian, he uses both languages (see the first paragraph of his letter of 25 September, B343).

Molto Reverendo in Christo padre
Pax Christi, etc.

Questa è la terza lettera ch'io scrivo a Vostra Reverentia doppo la mia venuta a questo collegio, et mi pare mill'anni d'haver qualche risposta da lei come spero col proximo corriero. Non dubito che anco ella se rallegrerà di questa mia buona fortuna, et di questa mia humiliatione sperando che da questa ne debbia resultare grand servitio di Dio, et grande quiete et pace in questo collegio; tali congratulationi m'hanno scritto altri da diverse parte, ma sappia padre mio caro che fin adesso non ci veggo altro guadagno che la mia humiliatione, et continua mortificatione, se pure ne saprò cavare quella utilità che vi sta nascosta, alche fare domando humilmente l'aiuto di Vostra Reverentia nelle sue orationi et sancti sacrificii. Et vero padre mio ch'io venne con un grand animo di fare grand facende, et di ridurre questo collegio al suo pristino splendore et con amorose exhortationi, et suavissimo modo di procedere diede principio al opera pensando di ritrovare quelche correspondenza, et che fussero hor mai stracchi di contradictioni et discordie, ma in vero ho trovato tutto il contrario pòi che eccetto alcuni pochi li quali se può dire che *sunt veri Israelitae* (se bene per li nostri peccati habbiamo persi il megliore di loro il P. Blondello, che assalito da un'acuta febre in otto giorni se n'andò al cielo) li altri tutti sono così obstinatamente convinti che non troverò modo ne de separarli, ne de'aiutarli, et quel ch'è pegio si sono talmente guadagnati la gratia del protectore che ottengono ciò che vogliano etiamdio contro a quello che havrò ordinato io. Non credo già ch'il protectore sia consapevole et partecipe dei lor desegni et pretensioni, ma credo che solo condescend' a loro per paovra de rumori et tumulti essendo il papa et i cardinali stracchi et stuffi di quei de l'anno passato, et il papa in particolare si godè et rallegra molto di sentire questa pace esterna nel collegio che sia levato quello scandalo et quella mala edificatione che gli scholari davano a tutta questa città et di questo si contentino, ne voluntieri sentano cosa in contrario, ma la verità è come ho detto di sopra che questa è una cosa superficiale, et che in collegio ci è una manifesta fattione, capi della quale sono gli Padri Benetto, Hillo, Tempestio, quali per quanto ho scoperto assai chiaramente si sono uniti et coniurati contro la compagnia, et mi hanno detto apertamente che noi altri non siamo buoni ne per questo collegio ne per Ingleterra per che habbiamo fine diverso da loro, per che essi pretendono il bene d'Ingleterra, et noi il bene et l'exaltatione della compagnia, et che sempre in ogni occasione praeferiremo questo a quello, ciò m'hanno detto *disertis verbis* Tempestio et Hillo; Benetto come vulpe astuta et che pretende ingannarmi non parla così chiaramente ma con li amici suoi dice questo, et pegio anzi ha detto che pensa un giorno esser superiore di questo collegio. Et questo è il secondo punto che questi factiosi pretendono, et se bene sono mancati loro duoi appoggi principali per questi loro desegni, come erano Cassano et Throgmortono, nondimeno non si perdono di animo per che et qui et in Belgio non gli mancano fautori, si che questa est factio Wallica, cui tamen (mirabile dictu) ipsimet Angli favent tantum enim odium in Societatem conceperunt, cui ut aversentur. Timeo quod etiam cum haereticis se coniungerunt sicuti Galli faciunt ut resistant Hispanis.

Tertium quod isti factiosi praetendere videntur est Regis Catholici conatibus se opponere, quod multa et satis aperta signa ostendunt; loquuntur enim saepius et mordaciter contra libellum de Successione ad coronam Angliae, et contra illius auctorem, nempe, ut ipsi existimant, contra P. Personium, cuius nomen vix aequo animo ferunt. Omnes de malis Hispanorum successibus, ut nuper apud Cadiz, laetari videntur; de bonis, ut paolo ante apud Caletum, tristantur, etc. Nescio an odio habent Societatem propter Hispanos, an e contra Hispanos propter Societatem, vel potius utrosque propter Scotum, vel Gallum, vel propter quid deterius. Deo qui videt in corde ista relinquo.

De remediis ut alias scripsi agendum esset, sed nullum video efficax praeter unum quod non est positum in manibus nostris. Essent enim seditiosi paulatim dimittendi et introducendi boni et quieti novitii, et imprimis esset dimittendus confessarius huius factionis caput. Aliud esset remedium bonum et securum licet non adeo efficax si protector coniungeretur mecum, et sequeretur meum confidium ni istis licet seditiosis regandis et tractandis, sed ipse habet principia meis omnino contraria, et cum non possimus convenire, illi ut par est acquiescere debeo. Expectandum est auxilium ex alto et bene sperandum, et interim sustendandum collegium quomodocunque ne corruat, sed opus est ut Vestra Reverentia videt magna patientia.

Dominus Barrettus parat discessum ad suos quotidie; et in istis turbis stetit, ut mihi videtur, candide et sincere pro parte nostra, hoc est, pro parte iustitiae et veritatis: et licet non multum effecerit, est tamen aliquid, quod habeamus testem omni exceptione maiorem de nostris et illorum actionibus. Vix enim homines in Gallia vel in Belgio crederent nobis attestantibus vel scribentibus ea quae ab ipsis seditiosis dicta, facta nesciunt praesertim cum ipsi suis literis suisque nunciis multa sparserint falsa, ipsemet Barettus hoc tabellario Vestrae Reverentiae plurima significabit de legato Hispaniae, de Hugonis pensione, de Heschetti conversione de quo bene sperare incipio, et bonum esset si hominem lucraremur. Barettus multum illi profuit, et multa mihi de illo promittit. Vestra Reverentia suis literis illud consoletur Heschettum, addat animum, et significet ex meis etiam literis Vestra Reverentia spem istam de illo concepisse. Ipse coepit etiam agere cum Fitzherberto ut ad meliorem mentem revocaret significans ille se quoque fuisse deceptum sed iam manifestissime intelligere istam esse factionem Wallicam contra Hispanos et Societatem; propterea cavendum esse ne et ipsi involvantur in isto turbine.

Ad Patrem Cresuellem nihil hoc tabellario. Vestra Reverentia mittat salutem plurimam meo nomine vel si placet hanc ipsam epistolam, et nos non solum precibus et sacrificiis, sed quod ad te mi pater exspecto maxime consilio et directione iuvate. Roma, 27 Augusti, 1596.

     Reverentiae Vestrae
       servus inutilis quidem
         sed amantissimus in Christo
           Alphonsus Agazzarius.

[*Addressed:*] Al P[re] Roberto Personio della Comp[a] di Giesù, Madrid.
[*Endorsed:*] P[e] Agazario 28 Aug[ti] al P[e] R[or] de Sevilla.

Translation

Very Reverend Father in Christ
The peace of Christ, etc.

 This is the third letter that I have written to Your Reverence since my arrival at this college, and it feels like a thousand years to wait for any response from you, which I expect with the next courier. I have no doubt that you too will rejoice in my good fortune, and in my humiliation, hoping that great service to God may arise from it, and great peace and quiet in this college. Such congratulations others have written to me on all sides, but know, my dear father, that up till now I see no other gain than my humiliation, and continual mortification, even if I know how to draw out that usefulness that is hidden there, to which I humbly beg the aid of Your Reverence, in your prayers and holy sacrifices. And for sure, my father, I have come with an intense desire to do great deeds, and to restore this college to its original splendour, with loving exhortations and the most gracious mode of proceeding. The work originated in the belief that such harmony could be recovered, and that they were rather weary of contradiction and discord, but in truth I have found quite the opposite, because apart from a few of such a kind as one might call them *Israelites indeed* (although as a result of our sins we have lost the best of them, Fr Blundell,[610] who was attacked by an acute fever and betook himself to heaven in eight days), all the rest are so obstinately convinced that I can find no way either to separate them or to help them, and what is worse, they have so earned the grace of the protector that they have got whatever they want for so long, against my instructions. I do not believe that the protector[611] has as yet been cognisant of and complicit in their designs and pretensions, but I believe that he has simply condescended to them for fear of the rumours and tumults, the pope and the cardinals being weary and fed up with them this past year. The pope in particular will be rejoiced to learn of this outward peace in the college, should that scandal be quietened and that evil reputation which the scholars had provoked throughout this whole city, and if they should be satisfied with this and do not actually feel the contrary; but the truth is (as I have said above) that this is a superficial matter, and in the college there is manifestly a faction, the leaders of which are Frs Bennet, Hill, and Tempest, whom I have found very clearly to be united in their sworn enmity to the Society. They have told me confidentially that the rest of us are of no good either for this col-

---

610. William Blundell (1568–1596).
611. Cardinal Francisco de Toledo (1532–1596), the vice-protector.

lege or for England because we have a different goal from theirs: they claim to be working for the good of England, and we for the good and elevation of the Society, and always, on all occasions, we prefer this to that, as Tempest and Hill have told me in so many words. Bennet, like the shrewd fox he is, thinking he can deceive me, does not say so explicitly, but this is what he says to his friends – and even worse, he has said that he aspires one day to be superior of this college. This is the second point that those of this party claim, and although they are lacking two principal supports of these their designs, namely Cassano and Throckmorton,[612] nevertheless they are not cast down because both here and in Flanders they do not lack supporters, and if that this …[613] is the Welsh party, whom nevertheless (marvellous to relate) the English themselves support, so great is the hatred they have conceived against the Society, that they are averse to it. I fear that they will even ally themselves with the heretics as the French do, in order to resist the Spanish.

The third thing which those dissidents seem to busy themselves with is to set themselves in opposition to the efforts of the Catholic king, which many, quite open signs demonstrate: for they speak often enough and cuttingly against the tract on the succession to the crown of England,[614] and against its author, namely, as they themselves reckon, against Fr Persons, whose name they can scarcely bear to mention without losing their temper. All of them seem to rejoice whenever the Spaniards suffer a reversal, as recently at Cádiz, and they lament their successes, as a little while ago at Calais.[615] I don't know whether they hate the Society on account of the Spaniards, or, on the other hand, the Spaniards on account of the Society, or, more likely, both on account of something Scottish or French, or even worse. I leave these things to God, who sees into the heart.

I have written variously what needs to be done to remedy this situation, but I see nothing likely to succeed except this, which is out of my hands: rebels should gradually be removed, while good and quiet novices should be introduced; and the first to be removed is the confessor, head of this party.[616] There would be another good and safe remedy, although not effective so far – if the protector would join with me and follow my advice not to allow these rebels to be ruled and treated with – but he himself has principles directly contrary to mine, and since we are not able to agree, I ought, as is just, to submit to him.[617] We must expect help from above and hope for better, and meanwhile the college must be maintained in whatever way we can so that it does not decay further; but Your Reverence will just have to view it with great patience.

Mr Barret is preparing daily for his departure to his own flock. In these broils he has remained, as it seems to me, candidly and sincerely on our side, that is, on the side of justice and truth. And although it has not achieved much, it is something all the same, if

612. See Agazzari to Persons, 25 September (B343).
613. The letter switches to Latin at this point, and the syntax seems fractured.
614. *Conference about the Next Succession.*
615. Essex raided Cádiz in June–July 1596; Spanish troops seized the citadel of Calais on 24 April 1596.
616. Edward Bennet was appointed confessor from the ranks of the students, following Morra's visitation.
617. This presumably refers to Francisco de Toledo, the vice-protector, since Caetani was still in Poland.

only because we have a better, unexceptional witness to their actions and ours: for the men in France and Flanders would scarcely believe us when we testify to or write about the things that are said by those rebels themselves. They know nothing about what has happened, especially because the rebels have spread many falsehoods in their own letters and notices. By this courier the selfsame Barret will tell Your Reverence many more things about the Spanish ambassador, Hugh's pension, and a change of attitude in Hesketh, of which I begin to have good hopes, and it would be good if we win the man over.[618] Barret has done him much good and promises me a great deal from him. Would Your Reverence please give Hesketh that consolation in your letters, and encourage him, and may Your Reverence convey to him, from my own letters even, the hope that we have conceived of him. He even began to deal with Fitzherbert[619] to recall him to a better mind, indicating that he also had been deceived but now knew most manifestly that that was the Welsh party against the Spanish and the Society; besides, that they need to take care not to get involved in that disturbance themselves.

To Fr Creswell nothing by this courier. Would Your Reverence please send him ample greetings in my name, or, if you like, send the letter to the man himself; and assist us not only with your prayers and sacrifices, but more than anything, as I expect from you, my father, with your advice and counsel. Rome, 27 August 1596.

  Your Reverence's
    servant, indeed useless,
      but most loving in Christ
        Alfonso Agazzari.

B337 From Richard Barret, Rome, 27 August 1596

SOURCE: Agazzari to Persons, s.d. (B336).

NOTE: Barret wrote by the same post about the Spanish ambassador, the pension of Hugh Owen and the hope that Thomas Hesketh, a lay supporter of the dissident students, would change his mind.

B338 From Claudio Acquaviva, Rome, 28 August 1596

SOURCE: ARSI, Hisp. 75, fol. 49r.

NOTE: Acquaviva reassures Persons over the issue of postal charges. He is anxiously awaiting Creswell's arrival, to assist with the problems at the English college in Rome. In the event, Persons went to Rome instead of Creswell.

P. Roberto Personio, Toledo, 28 Augusti 1596.

Questo solo sarà per accusar la ricevuta del solo di Vostra Reverentia delli 11 di Luglio, in risposta al quale poco ho che dire, poiché il negotio del quale Vostra Reverentia scrive circa il porto delle lettere da pagarsi dal Rettor di questo Collegio Inglese sec-

---

618. See headnote to Barret's letter.
619. Nicholas Fitzherbert, a lay supporter of the dissident students.

ondo l'usanza, non havrà difficoltà stando al governo del Collegio il P. Alfonso ch'è pratichissimo delle usanze, e noi ancora cene faremo dire una parola.

Del P. Cresuelo staremo aspettando che venga, e della radice di questi romori successi nel Collegio io non voglio giudicare d'onde nasca, se bene spero che nostro Signore non lasciarà di cavar bene che questi travagli per maggior gloria e servitio suo. Ne altro etc.

Translation

To Fr Robert Persons, Toledo, 28 August 1596.

This letter is only to advise you that I have received Your Reverence's private letter of 11 July.[620] I have little to say in reply, because the business Your Reverence raises, about the carriage of letters being paid by the rector of this English college according to custom, presents no difficulty as long as Fr Alfonso is in charge, since he is very practical in such usage, and we will ask him to add a word of his own.

We are still waiting for Fr Creswell to come. Concerning the root of these stirs that have occurred in the college, I do not want to make any judgement whence they arise, but I hope that Our Lord will not cease to draw good out of these troubles for His greater glory and service. No more [for the present], etc.

B339 To Martín de Idiáquez, probably 30 August 1596

> SOURCE: AGS, Leg. Est. 839, fol. 125, holograph.
> HICKS: 511–512, with English translation.
> TRANSLATION: *CSPS*, 4: 633 (item 649).
> NOTE: Persons asks for Council approval of his recommendations about a council or board to be set up in Flanders, and for a declaration to be made on the succession. This appears to be a covering letter for the following two items, which are collected with it in the bundle.
> Martín de Idiáquez (1558–1559), a nephew of Juan de Idiáquez, was a secondary member of the Junta de Noche, assisting with the king's correspondence (Juan Carlos Mora Afán in *DBE*).

Pues Vuestra Merced me promete de tener a su cargo las cosas que yo propusi en los papeles que se dexaron con Vuestra Merced domingo passado, le supplico que vaya accordando a essos Señores los puntos siguientes para que aya alguna resolucion en ellos luego pues assi conviene para el servicio de Su Magestad y de la causa misma.

1. Que se resuelva lo que se propone de la declaracion acirca de la succession de la Corona pues importa tanto como en el papel se dice.

2. Que se resuelva la Consulta que se ha de hacer en Flandes sobra las cosas de ynglaterra, pues desto dependen las demas cosas particulares, como es molestar y distraer la Reyna, establecer modo de tener avisos, negociar con la nobleça etc.

3. La yda de los Condes Escoceses para divertir la Reyna.

620. B329.

4. Los breves que se an de sacar del papa para Stapleton y otros porque si estas cosas no se hacen a tiempo, no se podran hacer despues. y perdone Vuestra Merced la importunidad porque veo el daño que ha de hacer la falta destos prevenciones si no se haçen a su tiempo. Guarde Dios a su merced.

El Senor Don Juan me prometio que se escriveria esta noche al Marques de Poça por la librança de la limosna ordinaria de Rhemis, supplico a Vuestra Señoria se lo accuerde.

Roberto Personio.

[*Endorsed*:] A Don Martin de Idiaquez Secret° de Estado de su Mg^ad

Translation

Since Your Excellency promises me to take charge of the proposals I made in the papers which were left with Your Excellency on Sunday last, I beg that you will proceed to negotiate with those gentlemen on the following points, so that there may be some decision on them soon, for this is to the benefit of His Majesty's service and of the cause itself.

1. That a resolution should be made regarding the proposal for making a declaration concerning the succession to the crown; for this is of such great importance, as is pointed out in the paper.

2. That a resolution should be made regarding a council to be set up in Flanders to deal with English affairs, since on this depend the other items, such as the harassment and distraction of the queen, the establishment of an intelligence service, negotiation with the nobility, etc.

3. Also to the expedition of the Scottish earls for the purpose of distracting the queen.

4. Also for the briefs to be obtained from the pope for Stapleton and others, for if these matters are not attended to in due course, it cannot be done later. I beg Your Excellency to pardon my impatience: it is because I see the harm that will ensue from the lack of these precautions, if they are not taken in due time. May God protect Your Excellency.

Don Juan has promised me that a letter should be written tonight to the marquis of Poza[621] for an order for the payment of the customary alms for Rheims. I beg Your Excellency to remind him of it.

Robert Persons.

B340 Probably to Martín de Idiáquez, 30 August 1596: Principal Points to Facilitate the Enterprise

SOURCE: AGS, Est. Leg. 839, fols. 126–128, holograph = S.

HICKS: 477–488; with typed transcript by Msgr E. Henson (former rector of the English College, Valladolid).

TRANSLATION: *CSPS*, 4: 628–633 (item 648).

NOTE: Persons deals with the religious justification of the armada and with military strategy, considering especially the role of the Scottish Catholic earls and the possibility of

---

621. The president of the Council of Finance: see Persons to Juan de Idiáquez, 2 September (B342).

commencing the invasion in Ireland. He makes mention of his manuscript work, *The Reformation of England under her Next Catholic Prince*, to suggest a postconquest policy of restitution of church lands. Dominguez, *Radicals in Exile*, 190–193, connects this with Spanish criticism of Philip's appropriation of ecclesiastical resources for his own purposes.

This memorandum was probably intended for the attention of Juan de Idiáquez and the Spanish council of state. Persons's recommendation for a royal proclamation to be prepared to justify and explain the armada is developed further in the memorandum to Juan de Idiáquez, 2 September 1596 (B342).

Puntos principales para facilitar y assigurar la Empresa de Ynglaterra.

Primero, considerando la importancia y difficultad del negocio y como todo depende de la mano de Dios, sería de muy grande momiento si Su Magestad a imitacion y exemplo de los Reyes santos antiguos, hiciesse alguna offrenda a nuestro Señor, como sería que en dando Dios la victoria, Su Magestad restitueria la yglesia de Ynglaterra a aquella libertad y a aquellos privilegios que tenía quando el Rey Henrique octavo apartose de la union de la Sedia Apostolica, y en particular, que Su Magestad hara lo que en sí fuera, para que se haga alguna restitucion o composicion competente de los bienes ecclesiasticos que se quitaron, para aplacar la ira de nuestro Señor, conforme a una cierta moderacion que se ha apuntado en un memorial que se ha escrito para la reformacion de este reyno, el qual libro Don Juan de Idiaquez ha visto, la qual composicion pide solamente restitucion de las rentas antiguas que no llegan a la tercera o quarta parte del justo valor de las possessiones, y con todo esto, sería raconable composicion, y con esto solo se persuaden los mayores siervos de Dios que yo he tratado de la nacion, que nuestro Señor se contentaria y se aplacaria, y daria buen successo, y por lo contrario piensan que en el tiempo de la reyna Maria por no averse dado buen orden en remediar este gravissimo sacrilegio, se perdio tan presto la religion, y si se entendiesse que Su Magestad ubiesse hecho algun voto o promessa a nuestro Señor en este particular, muchissima gente santa nos siguerian y conciberian esperanças certissimas de buen successo por este santo proposito solamente.

2. Lo segundo, para disminuir la enbidia y suspechas que los contrarios an llevantado contra la intencion de Su Magestad, diciendo, que quiere este reyno para sí, nos escriven desde Inglaterra los amigos y aficionados, que será de grandissima importancia que desde luego aya alguna declaracion del ánimo de Su Magestad en este punto, porque, aunque los más zelosos catolicos por mirar solamente a la causa de la religion, se contentarian de sotometerse a Su Magestad absolutamente, pero otros, de los quales el número y fuercas son mucho mayores, no querian que la Corona de Ynglaterra se uniesse con la de España, y para contentar a éstos y quitar suspechas a los demas principes de la Christiandad que tan bien temeran esto mismo, facilitaria mucho la Empresa que Su Magestad[622] dexasse entender su ánimo en esto, por el medio y modo que más conbeniente pareciesse. Y un modo sería harto efficaz para los yngleses, que algun tratadillo se escribiesse por alguna

622. que Su Magestad] *interlined* S

persona de credito de la misma nacion, en el qual como amigo del buen público de la nacion, pusiesse las raçones que ay para desear que toda esta controversia se compusiesse en la persona de la serenissima Señora Enfanta de España, y los bienes que dello resultarian para todas las partes. Y en este tratadillo, *quasi aliud agens*, podria el autor supponer que pues es cosa sabida y muy cierta que Su Magestad nunca ha pretendido, ni pretende este reyno para sí, raçon sería procurar que veniesse en esso otro medio y partido para la Señora Enfanta. Y para escrivir esto a la nacion Ynglesa se offerece entre otros el Señor Francisco Ynglefildo, si Su Magestad gustara dello, y a mí me parece su persona muy a proposito para ello por muchos respectos, y pues será cosa breve se puede traducir luego en otras lenguas y particularmente en Latino para su Santidad, el qual es la persona principal que despues de Su Magestad ha de venir en esto.

3. Lo tercero, que Su Magestad se serviesse de todo lo que nos puede aprovechar para este effecto en la misma nacion, y las comercanas, sea para enflaquecer al enemigo o para confirmar, animar y accrecentar a los amigos, y para enflaquecer y distraer al enemigo ayudaria mucho tener en pie a los Condes y otros Cavalleros catolicos en Escocia, pues la Reyna teme más mil hombres en Escocia por ser en su casa, que no[623] diez mil en otra parte, y con muy poco se sustentarian estos Escoceses, por la condicion de la tierra y tomarian yslas, y plaças fuertes en prejudicio y daño de la Reyna, y lo mismo digo de los salvajes de Yrlanda, que se avian de animar con algunos succorrillos de deneros y armas (pues gente no les falta) con lo qual tendrian la Reyna disasusegada aunque no tanto como los Escoceses, ni los teme tanto la Reyna[624] por ser apartados en otra ysla, y por ser de menos fuerças y traca que los Escoçeses.

4. Pero lo que más de todo disasusagaria y tormentaria a la Reyna, sería que los mismos Yngleses que biven desterrados en Flandes, hiciessen correrias continuas en inbierno y verano, con aquellos navios pequeños que ay por alla, a Ynglaterra, lo qual harian con poquissimo o ningun gasto casi de Su Magestad, fuera de los cascos de los navios, que estan pudriendose por alla, porque se sustentarian con las presas que tomarian como se vio ante diez o doce años quando los dos hermanos Cavalleros que se llamanan los Caryes, se sustentavan por mucho tiempo y hacian notables daños a la Reyna hasta que los governadores y officiales de los puertos de Flandes por enbidia de las presas que trayan les cansaron con molestias.

5. Entre otros grandes provechos que estas correrias de gente ynglesa sobre ynglaterra causarian, uno sería que fuera de cansar a la Reyna y molestar la tierra y llevar vastimientos y prender a los cavalleros en sus casas y impedir el comercio de mercaderos; se harian tan bien muchos muy buenos marineros y soldados juntamente, que sirvirian a Su Magestad para aquellos mares, y por saber que si se prenden no ay perdono por las vidas se harian muy enforçados, y otro provecho sería, que los que vienen de Ynglaterra se emplearian en este exercicio, sin pedir todos a Su Magestad entretenimiento, como aora haçen por no tener en qué emplearse, pero para empeçar y sustentar esto, es necessaria la junta que emos dicho en Flandes en la qual aya tan bien algunos confidentes de Su Magestad de la misma nacion Ynglesa para enformar bien de las cosas que succederan, y esto es para offender y enflaquecer al enemigo.

623. no] *interlined* S
624. la Reyna] *interlined* S

6. Para confirmar y accrecentar a los amigos, el medio más effecaz será reducirles a union y quitar las occasiones de division y parcialidad, lo qual se hara primero por la declaracion sobredicha del ánimo de Su Magestad acirca de la succession de la Corona de Ynglaterra, y lo sigundo con apartar de la Corte de Flandes, o empleandoles en otra parte a dos o tres personas que son de la parciacion[625] Escocesa y fomentan la disunion entre otros, y lo tercero que Su Magestad se sirva con alguna reputacion y confiança de los confidentes y conocidos, porque por esta via se animarán los otros, y se podra tratar y negociar con las nobleça y gente principal de Ynglaterra, con los Cavalleros que tienen plaças y lugares fuertes de Su Magestad en Flandes, Olanda y Zelanda, los quales veendo la Reyna vieja y sin successor, pondrian luego la mira en componer sus cosas con Su Magestad, si viessen probabilidad de buen successo, y que con alguna reputacion y secreto pudiessen tratarlo, y estar siguros de las promessas que se las haran, por lo qual y para mil otras cosas que de dia en dia sigueran en servicio de Su Magestad, importa sumamente ordenar la Consulta que se ha dicho en Flandes y que algunos cavallaros bien meritos, y sobre todos el Coronel Stanly, se tratasse bien, pues en él como persona tan noble y tan estimado entre ellos, y quien dio libremente sin pacto ninguno todo lo que tenía en esta vida a Su Magestad, todos tienen la mira.

7. A este punto tan bien de assignar y accrecentar los amigos pertinece y es de singular momento, que en la armada que Su Magestad embiará a Ynglaterra, Yrlanda, Escocia o otra parte para la reducion de Ynglaterra, vaya alguna persona ecclesiastica de credito y riputacion de la misma nacion (como sería el Doctor Stapleton, o otro que esté en Flandes) con autoridad tanto de Su Magestad como del papa, para componer cosas y assigurar la gente de su nacion de las entensiones de Su Magestad, las quales el enemigo no dexará de calumniar luego por mil vias y con mil mentiras, y a los ministros del Rey desta o otra nacion en tales occasiones no creeran facilmente, si no aya alguno de la misma nacion y de fidelidad conocida que les disengañe, y si leemos en el primer libro de los Macabeos que el Rey Demetrio resolvio de embiar con su exército contra los Judios a un sacerdote falso de su nacion que era Alcimo para engañarles[626] y traerles a su obediencia, y salio con su entento, quanto más hara un sacerdote y perlado verdadero, prudente y piadoso, en la causa de la religion, con los catolicos, y con muchos otros que aún no son, pero con todo esto, en tal ocasion estaran dudosos quál parte an de seguir, y propondran preguntas y será menester responderles, y resolver sus dudas, y mil destas occasiones se offereceran cada dia.

8. Mas desto si los catolicos veen que la armada de Su Magestad viene sin tal prelado de la nacion se confirmarán en las suspechas que los hereges y politicos an sembrado de que Su Magestad quiere conquistar el reyno, y que no hace confiança dellos, y más dudarán del ánimo del papa en quanto a la absolucion del juramento de la fidelidad que tienen hecho a la Reyna y assi algunos tendran escrupulo y otros usarán desta capa, ni avrá quien les saque de aqui de manera que importa muchissimo este punto, y es menester hacer caso dél, porque avrá muchissimos señores y personas poderosas que en tal tiempo querran tomar resolucion por medio de los sacerdotes que andan en Ynglaterra, con este personaje, a quien conbendra escrivir muchas cartas, y algunas veces emprimir

625. parciacion] *S Henson*; parcialidad *Hicks*
626. engañarles] *interlined S*

declaraciones etc. y para esto sería necessario que llevasse en el exército alguna emprenta qual se aparejó en Flandes para el año 88.

9. Conbendria tan bien que ubiesse alguna renovacion de la excomunion contra la Reyna por su Santidad, y que ubiesse alguna declaracion pública empressa qual hiço el Cardinal Alano para el año 88 aunque nunca se publicó e yo la tengo aqui y se puede tornar a imprimir quando será tiempo *mutatis mutandis*, y importa tan bien mucho qual sea el edicto y primero pregon que ha de publicar el General de Su Magestad en tomando tierra y conbiene que se resuelva y se vea por acá antes que se parta y que se ponga en differentes lenguas, a lo menos en española y ynglesa declarando qual sea el entento de Su Magestad en esta guerra de lo qual dependara mucho el successo de las cosas, pues a pura fuerca no yran bien sin duda.

10. Si pareciesse que avria difficultad en haçer Cardinal al Doctor Stapleton por agora o que se temiesse el ruydo, se podria supplir con hacerle obispo de algun grande obispado de Ynglaterra como sería de Duram, o de Ely, y este título le podria dar el papa en secreto por un breve y juntamente hacerle su Nuncio Apostolico con autoridad de legado, como hiço Gregorio 13 al Doctor Alano en al año de 83 quando por orden de Su Magestad yo fui a Roma desde Francia a pedirselo, quando se pensava de ententar algo por via de Escocia, y el breve quedó en poder de Juan de Taxis Embassador de Su Magestad en Paris y nunca se sirvio dél, y por esta misma via se puede sacar una doçena de breves de su Santidad en secreto para qualquier señor de Yrlanda, Ynglaterra o Escoçia para exortarle a concurrir fielmente en esta empresa dexando lugar en el breve para poner el nombre de quien conbendria, e yo saqué más de veynte breves del dicho Papa Gregorio en esta forma, y sin duda hicieran grandes effectos con algunas personas principales si la empresa fuera adelante entonces, y haran aora y assi conbendria tenerlos, y juntamente algunas cartas particulares y regaladas de Su Magestad para las personas que fuera más menester, porque muchissimo effecto haçe una carta de tales principes a señores particulares.

11. Al Doctor Tomas Stapleton se pueden añadir otro Doctor o dos, que estan en Flandes y son bien affectos al servicio de Su Magestad y son hombres de autoridad para con los de su nacion, y de mucha acion, el uno es el Doctor Thomas Woorthington y el otro es el Doctor Juan Pierse, y a éstos si podrian señalar otros dos obispados menores de Ynglaterra, para accompañar al Stapleton y assistirle en las cosas agibles y consultas más graves por no ser él muy[627] plático, como serian los obispados de Chester y Carleil, y esto se entiende si la armada ubiese de yr luego a Ynglaterra, porque al punto que llegasse a Cales, se podrian poner éstos en orden y passar con nuestra armada, pero si se ubiesse de yr la armada a Yrlanda, parece que sería más a proposito dar el titulo de Arçobispo de Dublyn en Yrlanda a un otro sacerdote grave de la nacion Ynglesa[628] que vive en Roma y es pariente del Cardenal Alano y ha vivido en Yrlanda muchos años y tiene muchos cavalleros parientes, y conocidos por alla, y en la provincia de Lancastria que es su patria y cae muy circa de Yrlanda. Este sacerdote se llama Ricardo Hadoque y es muy conocido del Embaxador en Roma por afficionadissimo al[629] servicio de Su Magestad.

627. muy] S; más Henson, *underlined, possibly for correction*
628. de la nacion Ynglesa] *interlined* S
629. al] S Henson; *not in* Hicks

12. Prevenidas las cosas en esta manera para ganar los animos que es de summo momiento, confio en nuestro Señor que haciendo Su Magestad alguna cosa con brevidad para reparar y cobrar la reputacion, o sea comencando con Yrlanda o Escocia o con Ynglaterra misma en la qual todo ha de parar, todo ha de succeder bien en quanto es hallar muchos amigos, y esto digo supponiendo que algo se aya haçer presto, para cobrar la reputacion, porque sin esto, y con la fama que correra luego por todas aquellas yslas y partes settentrionales, de la flaqueça de España y de los riccos despojos que an llevado los Yngleses se armarán veynte navios por uno y vendran como moscas, pues assi vimos[630] que vinieron antiguamente de las mismas partes settentrionales, toda aquella multitud de Hunos, Godos, Herulos, Alanos, Lombardos, y otros con la fama de que los primeros avian llevados algunos despojos, y nunca cessaron hasta a quebrar en pedaços la monarchia Romana, y lo mismo hicieron por la mar con Ynglaterra los Pictos y Daneses, hasta a[631] sojugarla y los Normanos con Francia, y los Saxones con Alemania que eran corsarios y nunca aquietaronse hasta a quedar señores de grandes pedaços destos reynos.

13. Si es mejor commençar primero con Yrlanda o Ynglaterra, ay raçones de entrambas partes, y la más poderosa y efficaz de todas es la possibilidad, porque si no ay possibilidad, para Ynglaterra, mucho mejor es haçer algo en Yrlanda para cobrar la reputacion, y tener alguna escalera para Ynglaterra al año que viene, que no haçer nada, porque aunque con esto, digo, con hechar Su Magestad guerra en Yrlanda muchissimos se armaran este enbierno contra Su Magestad para la primavera, pero assi lo haran sin esto, y mejor es tener algo ganado que nada, y muchissimas cosas pueden succeder en Ynglaterra, viendose la guerra tan circa en Yrlanda y mucha negociacion se puede tener y mucha diversion por via de Flandes y de Escocia si a ello se attende, por los medios que aqui se ha propuesto. Pero con todo esto si se pudiessen esforçar las cosas de tal manera, que en el mes de septiembre si pudiesse passar a Ynglaterra en el modo que se propuso en un memorial a Su Magestad, no ay comparacion si no que esto sería lo mejor por todos los respectos y entiendo que se ganaria Ynglaterra este año, con la quarta parte de gente, gasto y de otros aparejos que seran menester para otro año quando el enemigo estara apercebido de nuevo, y fortificado con la junta de muchos confederados, y el peligro será tan bien mayor, por lo que podian prevenirnos otra vez los dichos enemigos.

14. Pero en qualquiera manera que se resuelva, o de començar esta año con Yrlanda o con Ynglaterra, será de muchissima importancia que buelvan a Escocia los Condes que estan en Flandes y que los que en Escocia aguardan la voluntad de Su Magestad, tengan alguno soccorro de gente o de denero para hacer gente alli, porque si se commençasse con Ynglaterra sería grande diversion estar obligada la Reyna a tener su gente en las fronteras de Escocia que estan más de cien leguas de su persona en Londres, y si se hubiesse de commencar con Yrlanda, vendria muy a proposito tener los Escoceses llevantados porque cada dia darian mano los unos a los otros.

15. Si no ay comodidad de embiar gente con los Condes desde Flandes, me an dicho que bastaria embiarles a sus casas con algunos capitanes y con dos pagadores que quedassen: el uno con el Conde de Huntely en la parte settentrional y el otro con el

---

630. vimos] S; om. Henson
631. a] S; om. Henson

Conde de Anguis en la parte del poniente de Escocia y que llevasse cada uno denero para pagar mil y quingentos o dos mil soldados, en cada parte para seis o ocho meses a un año, y que ubiesse personas confidentes con los pagadores que mirassen que no se diesse dinero si no para paga de los soldados, a modo de la tierra de alla, y con esto solo ellos rebolverian a toda Escocia y tomarian las yslas contra la Reyna que an prometido, y al mismo Rey de Escocia se podria persuader que todo esto es en su favor que se hace por los Condes, para que él pueda complir mejor y sin miedo de la Reyna de Ynglaterra lo que su Agente ha prometido en su nombre, y si este camino se tomara, vease si sería mejor que su Agente bolviesse por Flandes o que fuesse derecho a Escocia.

16. Ultimamente para esto y todo lo demas y uno de los principales puntos, y que en primer lugar se ha de tratar es, tener muy buenos avisos de Ynglaterra de todo lo que va tratando y haciendo el enemigo, los quales por algunos años los tubo buenos el Principe de Parma y antes del Señor Don Juan de Austria, pero en estos años atras, parte por descuydo y parte por falta de un poco de denero, el qual avia escusado el gasto de otro mucho, se ha faltado en este particular, pero se puede tornar a assentarlo, porque el padre Henrique Garneto, superior de los de la Compañia escrive en esta materia que se puede hallar hombres confidentes en Londres que sacarán los avisos de las mismas fuentes de las cosas que passan en consejo, y que ellos mismos procurarán correspondentes en los puertos principales los quales yran avisando lo que se va haciendo de preparaciones, y pues la Reyna sustenta Chateau Martin por espia en San Juan de luiz y le da cien ducados en cada mes y más un por ciento de todas las mercaderias Ynglesas que entran que por alla, solamente para que avise las cosas y preparaciones de España, y más deste tiene el enemigo tantos espias en todos los puertos de España quantos ay mercaderes Olandeses, Escoceses, Bretones y Yrlandeses que tratan por acá, no es maravilla que tiene mejores avisos de las nuestras cosas que nosotros de las suyas, pero se puede facilmente remediar, y es negocio que pertenecera a la consulta de Flandes para entablarla. Ugo Oen y Ricardo Versteghen son muy a proposito para attender a establecerla, si se señale denero para ello.

17. Tan bien parece que sería a proposito que algun hombre fuesse a Ynglaterra a tratar con aquellos Condes que embiaron dos veçes su Agente Sterello a Flandes el inbierno passado para que se vea qué substancia ay en aquel tratado, y otro que se ha offerecido de nuevo para Fluselingas, y que las cosas no muriessen en esta manera si no que se diesse quenta de tiempo en tiempo a su Altezza del Cardenal Archeduque y a Su Magestad por la Consulta, ya dicha del progresso de semejantes negocios.

Translation

Chief considerations for facilitating and assuring
the enterprise of England

First of all, considering the importance and difficulty of the business, and as everything depends upon the hands of God, it would make a great difference if His Majesty, following the example of the holy kings of old, were to make some vow to our Lord, such as that he would, if God gave His Majesty the victory, restore the Church of England to that liberty and those privileges she possessed at the time when King Henry VIII severed the connection with the Apostolic See. In particular, His Majesty could vow to do all he could to make some restitution or proper composition with regard to the ecclesiastical property which was taken from the church, to appease the wrath of our Lord. This might be done in a gracious way, as is set out in a memorial which was written with regard to the reformation of England, which book Don Juan de Idiáquez has seen:[632] that work requires only that the original value of the revenues should be restored, which would not reach a third or quarter of their present value, but would still be a reasonable arrangement. The most godly men of the nation, with whom I have discussed the matter, agree that in this way alone will God be appeased and bless the undertaking. They think, indeed, that it was because no effective means was found to remedy such a grave sacrilege in the time of Queen Mary that religion so soon collapsed in England. If it became known that His Majesty had made some vow or promise in this particular, many devout people would join us and conceive most certain hopes of success for this holy enterprise alone.

2. In the second place, to diminish the jealousy and suspicion which our opponents have raised as to the intention of His Majesty, saying that he wishes to seize the country for himself, our friends and supporters write to us from England that it is of the utmost importance that a declaration should at once be made about His Majesty's design in this matter, because, although the more fervent Catholics, looking to the cause of religion alone, would be willing to submit themselves absolutely to His Majesty, a much larger and more powerful majority do not wish the crown of England to be joined to that of Spain. In order to please these, and disarm the suspicions of other Christian princes, who fear the same thing, it would greatly facilitate the enterprise if His Majesty were to allow his views on this point to be known, by whatever means or method he may consider most convenient. One way that would be very effective with the English would be for a little tract to be written by some reputable man of that nation, in which he, as a friend of the public good of the nation, might set forth the reasons why it would be desirable that the whole controversy should be resolved in the person of Her Highness the Infanta of Spain, setting out the benefits that would ensue to all parties. And in this tract the author might assume, "as a generally accepted fact," that given that His Majesty does not, and never has, claimed the crown for himself, it would be reasonable to ensure that they see in this another means and support for the Lady Infanta. Amongst the persons who might write such a tract addressed to the English people is Sir Francis Englefield, if His Majesty approves, and to me he seems a very fit person for the task in many respects. As it will be short, the tract might at once be translated into other tongues, and particularly into Latin, for His Holiness, who is the principal person, besides His Majesty, whose agreement is needed.

3. The third point is that His Majesty should take every opportunity that presents itself, in England itself and neighbouring countries, to weaken our enemies and strengthen, encourage, and increase the number of our friends. And to weaken and distract the enemy it would be very helpful to support the Catholic nobles and gentlemen

---

632. First published by Edward Gee as *The Jesuit's Memorial, for the Intended Reformation of England, under their first Popish Prince* (London, 1690), to support an anti-Jesuit campaign.

of Scotland, for the queen is more afraid of a thousand men in Scotland, where they are at home, than ten thousand elsewhere. It will cost very little to support those Scotsmen, given the nature of the terrain, and they will take islands and strongholds, to the queen's prejudice and harm. The same thing may be said of the Irish clansmen, who should be encouraged by some trifling help, in the form of money and arms (as they have plenty of men), and thus the queen might be kept uneasy. The Scots, however, can trouble her most, as the Irish are separated in a different island and are less strong and forbidding than the Scots.

4. What would disturb and torment her most of all, however, would be if those same Englishmen who are exiles in Flanders should make constant raids into England, summer and winter, with those little vessels they have there. This could be done with little or no expense to His Majesty, except the cost of the ships themselves, which are now rotting there, as the expenses would be covered by the booty taken, as was shown ten or twelve years ago when the two noble brothers named Cary maintained themselves for a long time and greatly injured the queen, until the Flemish port authorities and officials, jealous of the booty they took, wearied them with impositions.[633]

5. Amongst other great advantages of such raids by Englishmen on England, in addition to distracting the queen from harrying the land, confiscating goods, arresting gentlemen in their own houses, and hampering the trade of the merchants, one would be that they would gather a large number of good hardy sailors and soldiers, who would serve His Majesty in those seas. As they would know that if they were caught, there would be no pardon for them, they would be very desperate for their lives. Another advantage would be that those who came from England would be employed in this action, and they would therefore not all have to look to His Majesty for maintenance, as they do now because they do not have an employment. But to begin and sustain this business, the board of which we have spoken in Flanders is essential. There should also be some Englishmen in His Majesty's confidence there, to keep His Majesty informed of what goes on. And so much is intended for offending and weakening our enemies.

6. To strengthen and increase our friends, the most effective means would be to unite them, and take away the reasons for division and partiality, which would be achieved primarily by the abovementioned declaration of His Majesty's intentions with regard to the succession of the English crown. The second means would be to take away from the Flemish court, or employ them elsewhere, two or three persons who have Scottish leanings, and who foment disunion amongst our friends there. A third means would be that His Majesty should treat his confidants and friends with trust and respect, as in this way others would be encouraged.[634] This way, the nobles and gentry of England, who have property and fortresses in Flanders, Holland, and Zeeland, might be approached. Seeing the queen old and without an heir, they would soon think of arranging matters with His Majesty if things looked propitious, and if they could do so discreetly, without los-

---

633. The Cary (Carey) family of Clovelly and Cockington, Devon, included many seafarers. They were related to the barons Hunsdon.

634. Philip II's distrust of the English is a common theme of Persons's letters, e.g., Persons to Idiáquez, 4 April 1591 (B99).

ing reputation, and were sure of the fulfilment of the promises made to them. For this, and a thousand other reasons that arise from day to day in the service of His Majesty, it would be well to convene the already mentioned council in Flanders, and that some worthy gentlemen, especially Colonel Stanley, should be treated well, as everyone looks to him, being so noble and of high esteem among them, and having surrendered everything in the world to His Majesty.

7. Another way of recruiting and strengthening our friends is pertinent and of particular import, namely that in the fleet His Majesty sends to England, Ireland, Scotland, or any other region for the restoration of England, there should go some trustworthy and reputable ecclesiastic from the same nation (such as Dr Stapleton would be, or some other in Flanders), with authority, both from the pope and His Majesty, to settle matters, and assure the gentry of his nation of His Majesty's intentions, which the enemy never leaves off slandering in a thousand ways and with a thousand lies. Neither the ministers of the king nor of any other nation will be easily believed, unless someone of that same nation, of established credibility, should undeceive them, and if we read in the first book of the Maccabees that the King Demetrius decided to send, with his army against the Jews, a false priest of their nation, called Alcimus,[635] to trick them into submitting to his obedience, and he succeeded in his design, how much more will a true prelate priest, wise and devout, in the cause of religion, with the Catholics and with many others who are not yet Catholics. But in any case, in such an eventuality they are uncertain which side to take: they will ask questions, and will have to be answered, so as to resolve their doubts – and a thousand such opportunities will present themselves every day.

8. If, moreover, the Catholics see His Majesty's fleet arrive without such a prelate of their nation, they will be confirmed in their suspicion that the heretics and politicians have been telling the truth in saying that His Majesty wants to conquer the country and does not put any trust in them; and they will have more doubt of the pope's intention to absolve them from their oath of allegiance to the queen. Consequently, some will have scruples and others will use this as an excuse, and there will be no one to persuade them otherwise, so that this is a most important point and must not be lost sight of, as on such an occasion very many lords and influential people will seek to be guided in their course by priests who will accompany this personage in England. It will be appropriate to write many letters to such people; and in addition, declarations will have to be printed. Therefore, it will be necessary to carry a printing press in the fleet, such as was prepared in Flanders for the year '88.

9. It is also fitting that there should be some renewal of the queen's excommunication by the pope, with some such public printed pronouncement as was to be made by Cardinal Allen in '88, of which, although it was never published, I have a copy here, and it can be reprinted, *mutatis mutandis*, when time comes. The edict and first proclamation His Majesty's general publishes when he lands is also of the greatest importance; it should be designed and seen here before the fleet leaves. It should be put into various languages, at least in Spanish and English, and should clearly state His Majesty's intention in this war,

---

635. 1 Macc. 7–9; Demetrius I Soter, ruler of the Seleucid empire from 162 to 150 BCE, appointed Alcimus high priest in return for his help in his suppression of the Maccabaean revolt.

upon which the success of the war will largely depend, for by sheer force, it is very doubtful if it will succeed.

10. If there is any difficulty in making Dr Stapleton a cardinal at this time,[636] for fear of the clamour such an appointment might arouse, he could be made bishop of one of the great English sees, such as Durham or Ely, which the pope could give him by secret brief, and he might be made apostolic nuncio at the same time, with legatine authority, as Gregory XIII made Dr Allen in '83, when I went from France to Rome by order of His Majesty to urge it, and it was intended to make an attempt via Scotland.[637] The brief at that time remained in the hands of Juan de Tassis,[638] the king's ambassador in Paris, and was never used. In the same way a dozen briefs might be got secretly from his Holiness for any gentlemen of Ireland, England, or Scotland, to exhort them to support this enterprise, the names being left in blank. I got more than twenty such briefs from Pope Gregory in this manner, and doubtless they would have been highly effective on some great persons if the enterprise should have gone ahead then, and they will be now, and so we should have those briefs. At the same time, there would be a need for some favourable private letters from His Majesty for those persons for whom they would be more convenient, for letters from such princes to particular gentlemen are very efficacious.

11. It would be a good thing if one or two other doctors in Flanders might be joined to Dr Thomas Stapleton. They are well-disposed to the service of His Majesty, energetic, respected, and influential among Englishmen: one is Dr Thomas Worthington and the other is Dr John Pierse.[639] They might be appointed to another two minor English bishoprics, such as Chester and Carlisle, so as to accompany and assist Stapleton in things that need to be done and more grave matters, given his little experience. This is in the case of the fleet eventually going to England, so that as soon as it arrived in Calais they could be ready to join it, and cross with our armada. But if the fleet is to go to Ireland, it might be more suitable to give the title of archbishop of Dublin to another grave English priest, who lives at Rome and is a relative of Cardinal Allen. He lived in Ireland many years and has many gentlemen relatives and acquaintances there, and in Lancashire, his native province, which lies very close to Ireland. This priest is called Richard Haydock, and is well-known to the ambassador in Rome as being a very enthusiastic adherent of His Majesty.[640]

12. If matters are arranged in this way to conciliate people in what is of greatest moment, I trust in our Lord that, in case His Majesty undertakes something promptly to recover and restore his prestige, either by way of Ireland or Scotland first, or to England

636. Stapleton's name was frequently mentioned at this time as a possible alternative candidate to Owen Lewis or Persons for elevation to the cardinalate, but Stapleton expressed little interest: see his letter to Persons of 16 April 1597 (B366).

637. On the invasion schemes of 1582–1585, see A70.

638. Juan Bautista de Tassis (1530–1610), Spanish ambassador to France from 1581 to 1584, when he was replaced by Bernardino de Mendoza. Mendoza and Philip II judged that he was indiscreet in his handling of the Guise invasion plans. See A70 and José Miguel Cabañas Agrela (*DBE*).

639. Possibly William Percy (ca. 1550–post 1603); see Persons to Philip II, 26 March 1596 (B319) and the memorandum on creating a council in Flanders (August 1596, B341).

640. On Haddock/Haydock, see Persons to Idiáquez, 6 December 1595 (B302).

direct, which must be the main object, all will go well as far as finding many friends is concerned. I write this on the understanding that something should be done quickly to recover prestige, because otherwise, with the common talk in all those islands and regions of northern Europe of the weakness of Spain and the rich plunder captured by the English, twenty ships will be fitted out against us for every one before, and they will come hither like flies, as we saw in ancient times from those northern parts, that whole multitude of Huns, Goths, Heruli, Lombards, and others, famed for taking some spoils from the start, never stopped until they had broken the Roman empire into pieces, and the Picts and Danes did the same to England by sea until they subdued it, as did the Normans in France and the Saxons in Germany: they were raiders who were not content until they became lord of large tracts of those kingdoms.

13. Whether it is better to commence with England or Ireland, there is much to be said on both sides, but the most weighty and decisive of all is feasibility. If England is impossible, then it would be much better to do something in Ireland to recover prestige, and to have a place of vantage from which to attack England next year, rather than doing nothing. Even so, I say, if His Majesty attacks Ireland, many (ships) will arm against him this winter to be ready for spring; but they will do so in any case, and it is better for him to have gained something already than nothing, besides which, in the meanwhile many things may happen in England, seeing the war is so close in Ireland, much negotiation may be carried on, and much diversion effected in Flanders and Scotland, if that is taken care of by the means which have been proposed here. But despite it all, if it were possible to advance matters in such a way as to send the force to England in the middle of September, as was proposed in a memorial to His Majesty, it cannot be doubted that this would be the best course in all respects, and I understand that [by doing this] this year England could be won with a quarter of the force, expense, and gear that would be necessary next year, when the enemy would be freshly prepared and fortified with the addition of many allies, and the danger would also be greater, so that the said enemies could prevent us once again.

14. In any case, whatever is decided, whether to begin this year in Ireland or in England, it will be crucial that the earls in Flanders should return to Scotland,[641] and that the Catholics in Scotland, who are awaiting His Majesty's decision, should receive some help either in troops or in money to raise them there. For if we began with England, it would be a great diversion to force the Queen to keep her army on the Scottish border, more than one hundred leagues from her own person and from London. If it is decided that we commence with Ireland, it will also be very useful to have the Scots in arms, as they would help each other every day.

15. If no troops can be sent with the earls from Flanders, I am told that it would suffice to send them to their own houses, with some captains and two paymasters to keep: one with the earl of Huntly in the north, and the other with the earl of Angus in the west of Scotland, each one with enough money to pay 1500 or 2000 men in each place for six or eight months to one year. There should be sent some confidential persons with the

---

641. George Gordon (1561/2–1636), earl of Huntly; William Douglas (ca. 1554–1611), earl of Angus; and Francis Hay (1564–1631), earl of Erroll.

paymasters, to see that no money was used except to pay soldiers in the way customary in that region. This alone would enable them to put Scotland in turmoil and take over the islands against the Queen as they have promised, and the king of Scots himself might be persuaded that what was done by the earls was all in his interest, so that he would fulfil, without so much fear of the queen of England, what his representative has promised in his name. Consider (if this course be adopted) whether it would not be better for his agent to return by way of Flanders rather than direct to Scotland.

16. Finally, with regard to this and all the rest, one of the principal considerations, and one that ought to be considered first, is to obtain very good information from England of everything that is being done or said by the enemy. For some years the prince of Parma obtained excellent intelligence, as did Don Juan of Austria before him, but in recent years, partly from neglect and partly for want of a little money, which would have saved much other expense, things in this respect have fallen off. An attempt may now be made to amend matters, as Fr Henry Garnet, superior of those belonging to the Society, writes, in this connection, that trustworthy men may be found in London, who will get their information at the fountainhead in the Council, and they themselves will provide correspondents in the principal ports, who will keep advising as to the warlike preparations. Chasteau-Martin is maintained in Saint-Jean-de-Luz as a spy by the queen, who pays him one hundred ducats a month, and in addition one percent on all English merchandise entering there. This is only that he may inform on the matters and the preparations in Spain; besides him [Chasteau-Martin], the enemy has in every port in Spain as many spies as there are Dutch, Scots, British, or Irish merchants operating there.[642] It is no wonder she is better informed of our affairs than we are of hers. This, however, may easily be remedied, and is a matter which will appertain to the board in Flanders. To set the matter going and establish communications, Hugo Owen and Richard Verstegan are very fitting persons, if money be given to them for it.

17. It would also be good for some fitting person to go to England to treat with those earls who twice sent their agent Sterrell to Flanders last winter, and to see what foundation there is for that treaty, or for the new one offered at Flushing.[643] Matters should not be allowed to die out in this way, but information should be conveyed from time to time to the cardinal archduke, and to His Majesty, by the board, as to the progress being made in them.

---

642. According to Alford, 264–266, 310, Henri Chasteau-Martin (an alias for Pierre d'Or) operated from Bayonne, being paid 1200 escudos per quarter to provide intelligence to Burghley; he was executed in 1596 when the governor discovered he was being employed by Spain. Edmund Palmer was based in Saint-Jean-de-Luz.

643. William Sterrell was involved in various intelligence schemes as an adherent of the earl of Worcester, an agent of Thomas Phelippes (now in the service of the earl of Essex), and a correspondent of Verstegan and Owen in the Spanish Netherlands. See Patrick Martin and John Finnis, "The Identity of 'Anthony Rivers,'" *Recusant History* 26 (2002): 39–74, who refer to Verstegan's letter to Persons of 30 April 1593 (B179).

B341 Probably to Martín de Idiáquez, 30 August 1596, Memorandum on the Establishment of a Special Council in Flanders to Advise the Governor on English Affairs

SOURCE: AGS, Est. Leg. 839, fol. 129.
HICKS: 489–500, with English translation.
NOTE: Unlike the previous two documents, this memorandum is not in Persons's hand, although it is included in the same bundle with them. The authorship is uncertain, but Persons was invested in the project of setting up the council (*CSPS*, 4: 628 [item 647]). Loomie, *Spanish Elizabethans*, 119–120, suggests that Archduke Albert, the new governor of the Spanish Netherlands, was unable to implement the plan because of more pressing issues such as the continuing Dutch war.

> Las razones por las quales conbiene que aya alguna Consulta particular en Flandes cabo la persona del Governador para las cosas de Ynglaterra y los negocios principales que se han de tratar en esta Consulta.

1. Aviendo las cosas de Ynglaterra llegado a tal término que aquel Reyno por la vecindad, comodidad de navios y inquietud de los hereges ha de ser, o enemigo muy prejudicial a Su Magestad como hasta agora por los daños que nos causa, o amigo y dependente de lo qual seguerian los contrarios effectos de Paz, siguridad y provecho a los estados de Su Magestad; justo es que las cosas dél se tomen a pecho, y que se procure de entendarles y pensarlas bien, lo qual en ninguna manera se puede hazer sin que algunos hombres de confiança, prudencia y buen zelo attendan a ellos en particular y muy de ordenario y que tengan alguna mano para representarlas a su tiempo, y procurar que se executen, lo qual sin Junta, o Consulta particular donde las cosas se puedan proponer y disputar quando es menester y resolverse con efficacia, nunca tendra effecto alguno, porque por via de memoriales es cosa larga y imperfecta, y no se pueden examinar las cosas y son tantos y tales los negocios que no caben ni se pueden dispachar por este medio solamente.

2. Ay muchos Señores Principales en Ynglaterra que por veer la Reyna vieja y sin heredero y el negocio de la succession dudosa, y muchos Pretensores al Reyno querrian tratar con Su Magestad o con su Governador de Flandes por estar más circa algunos conciertos muy importantes y otros negocios gravissimos, si diessen algun buen medio para ello, y si ubiesse personas confidentes de su nacion autorizadas por Su Magestad para semejantes cosas, con los quales pudiessen tratar con seguridad del secreto y con esperança de effecto, y de que se les compleria lo que se les promette, lo qual agora no pueden resolverse de haçer, por faltarles los medios ya dichos.

3. Ay muchos Cavalleros yngleses que tienen lugares y plaças fuertes de Su Magestad como Fluselingas, Ostenda, Brila, Daventre y otras los quales Cavalleros por veer que sería su provecho concertar con Su Magestad mientras tienen estas plaças en su poder, pues se les pueden quitar por qualquiera occasion por la Reyna y los de su Consejo vendrian tan bien a tratar desto si ubiesse el medio conveniente que ya se ha dicho.

4. Otro effecto muy importante desta consulta sería, unir bien la nacion Ynglesa entre si (a lo menos a los Catolicos que seguerian luego la autoridad deste Consejo) en todas las cosas que tocan al bien universal de la patria y al servicio de Su Magestad donde por lo contrario estan al presente muy divididos por no tener cabeça ni subordinacion alguna entre sí ni reconocer el uno al altro, si no que todos queren ponerse en cosas públicas y de estado y disacreditar al compañero, y algunos pocos más inquietos y ambiciosos que los demas aborotan a todos y hacen bandos y parcialidades contra todas las pretenciones de Su Magestad y de los buenos de la nacion, y por ser estos muy parleros y tener comodidad de deneros para presentes, dadivas, combites, y otros semejantes medios, ganan a muchos y muchas veces a personas poderosas, las quales por ser estrangeros, y no saver los fundamentos secretos destas mañas se dexan engañar y hazen mucho daño, con pensar que hacen bien y los mismos ministros de Su Magestad quedan alguna ves con mucha raçon dudosos a quién se han de fiar, viendo tanta division y contradicion entre los mismos de la nacion, con lo qual se pierden los negocios y los buenos se encogen y se retiran disanimados y corridos de la contradicion y los inquietos por ser más atrevidos se animan con esto pues su fin no es otro que revolver cosas y cansar a otros, y impedir que no se haga nada, los quales daños o grande parte dellos se asensarian con esta consulta porque a estos solos o principalmente se daria credito y no a otros.

5. Otro effecto no menos importante desta consulta, sería reducir a todos los de la nacion Ynglesa a una cierta conformidad que se pretende circa la succession de la corona de Ynglaterra para la Señora Infanta de España. Lo qual todos los Catolicos buenos y más prudentes desean summamente por los grandes bienes y convenientes que dello siguerian, no solamente a Ynglaterra si no a toda la Christiandad, como parece por las raçones evidentes que por ello se allegan tanto en el libro de Dolman que se escribio de la succession, como en un papel que anda del parecer del Cardinal Alano en esta materia y contra esta conformidad, como contra todo lo demas que pertenece a España, andan haciendo bandos los dichos inquietos en Flandes y en Roma, de los quales son cabecas Carlos Pageto, Guillelmo Giffordo, Guillelmo Tressam, y algunos otros en Flandes y sus correspondientes – Ugo Grifidio, Tomas Hesquet, Nicolas Fitzharbert y otros en Roma los quales no tendrian crédito ni mano para hacer tanto daño, si esta consulta se les mostrasse contraria y siguiesse otro camino.

6. Otro effecto muy grande desta consulta sería enformar bien y con verdad a Su Magestad y a su Governador de Flanders de la calidad y meritos de los de la nacion ynglesa, que residen en Flanders y otros partes o que vinieren de Ynglaterra para que se tenga quenta con ellos conforme a sus meritos en lo qual hasta agora por falta desta informacion ha havido grandes yerros, que an causado grandes discontentos de muchos y disservicios a Su Magestad.

7. Tan bien pertenecera a esta consulta, procurar que se empleen todos los de la nacion conforme a sus estados y talentos, en cosas conbinientes para que no bivan ociosamente como al presente, que es causa de infinitas males discordias, murmuraciones, vandos y enemistades.

8. Otro effecto y fruto desta consulta y de los mayores sería, attender a hacer daño continuamente a la reyna y tenerla ocupada, y con cuidado agora con correrias desde Flanders, agora con levantamientos, y otras difficultades en Escocia y Yrlanda, aora con

tratados en Ynglaterra y buscando personas abiles y a proposito para este effecto, y ganando y entreteniendoles y referiendo al Governador de Flandes lo que ay y con qué passo van los negocios, procurar tan bien avisos ciertos y muy a menudo de las cosas que passen en Ynglaterra, tanto en el corte y en el consejo como de las preparaciones que se hicieran en los puertos de la mar, y más attender a coger los espias que la reyna embia continuamente a Flandes y discubrir las personas que con ellos traten, y finalmente este consejo o consulta sería una contramina contra las machinaciones del consejo de Ynglaterra y sería un castello fuerte contra aquella batteria de los hereges, y sería un altar contra otro altar que traeria asi grandissima parcialidad al servicio de Su Magestad contra la reyna la qual se canseria que se affligeria más con esto solo y los Catolicos y amigos nuestros más se animarian, que con ninguna otra cosa que hasta agora se ha hecho.

9. Por estos effectos facilmente se descubren los negocios importantes que en esta consulta se an de tratar, como es entender y ponderar bien las cosas de Ynglaterra, conoçer las personas, negociar con las nobleça, y con los que tienen plaças y lugares del Rey, unir la nacion en servicio de Su Magestad y particularmente en lo que toca a la succession de la corona; quitar vandos, facciones y dissenciones; restitir a las negociaciones que se haçen por los contrarios de Su Magestad, disponer de los yngleses que estan al servicio de Su Magestad conforme a los calidades, abilidades, y talentos que tienen, y procurar que otros vengan de Ynglaterra, y dejen a la Reyna: attender a offender, y a tener avisos de alla, y coger los espias que se embian por acá, y finalmente dar vida y espirito a la causa de los Catolicos, que hasta agora queda desamparada, en una cierta manera, pues no tiene quien de proposito mira por ella.

10. Las personas que an de entrar en esta consulta, han de ser de la nacion española, o, como pareçiera para que si uno faltara, otro assista y por la misma raçon otros han de ser de la nacion Ynglesa, y mientras no ay cabeça entre ellos, el qual escoja los más id[on]eos, los que al presente tienen más partes para ella, y que más conoccidamente son bien affectos al servicio de Su Magestad, son el Coronel Stanley, Ugo Oen, Gabriel Trehern, y los dos Doctores Tomas Worthington, y Guillermo Pierse, que estan disoccupados para ésta; y en cosas mayores al Padre Guillermo Holto, Ynglés de la Compañia de Jesus podra assistir, y esto es lo que en este negocio se puede decir, la essecucion mostraria el provecho y la importancia.

[*Endorsed*:] Raçones para ordenar una Consulta en Flandes para las cosas de Ynglaterra.

Translation

Reasons setting out the advantage of having a special council in
Flanders to advise the governor on English affairs, and the principal
matters that are to be dealt with by this council.

1. The affairs of England have reached such a pass that owing to its proximity, its supply of ships, and the restless activity of the heretics, that kingdom either must be hostile to His Majesty and damaging to his interests, as it has been up to the present by the losses it has inflicted on us, or it must be friendly and favourable, and from this will follow the

contrary effects of peace, security and advantage to his majesty's dominions. Hence it is fitting that its affairs be very much taken to heart, that we must make sure we understand them and consider them aright. In no way can this be realised unless men of trust, prudence, and earnest zeal devote their attention to these affairs in particular and very regularly, and have authority in due course to make proposals about them and see that they are put into execution, but these measures will never have the slightest effect without a special board or council in which matters may be proposed and discussed when necessary and effective decisions taken: for the method of dealing with these affairs by way of memorials is a protracted business and leaves much to be desired; the affairs cannot be properly examined, and they are of such a nature and so numerous that they are beyond the scope of this method and cannot be expedited by it alone.

2. There are in England many prominent gentlemen who, seeing that the queen is old and without an heir, and that the question of succession is undecided and that there are many claimants to the throne, would be willing to treat with His Majesty or with his governor of Flanders about entering more decidedly into certain very important agreements and other negotiations of the gravest consequence, if he could provide some good channel for this purpose, and authorize men of trust of their own nation to negotiate such matters, with whom they could treat, assured of discretion and confident that effective action would be taken, and that what is promised would be put into execution. At present they cannot undertake this step for lack of the means mentioned above.

3. There are many English captains who hold towns and fortified places that belong to His Majesty, such as Flushing, Ostend, Brill, Daventry, and the like. Since they could be removed from their command by the queen and those of her council at any moment, these captains would also come to these negotiations if they had some suitable channel such as has already been indicated, seeing that it would be to their own advantage to come to an agreement with His Majesty whilst they still hold these places in their power.

4. Another very important consequence of this council would be to bring about a solid union among the English – at least among the Catholics who would be immediately subject to the authority of the council – on all matters that relate to the common good of their country and the service of His Majesty. At present, on the contrary, they are very divided on these matters, for there is no one in a position of authority among them, nor is there any subordination; no one gives recognition to the position of another, but all seek to be prominent in affairs that concern the public and the state and to throw discredit on their neighbour. Some few of a more restless and ambitious disposition lord it over the others and raise parties and factions against the interests of His Majesty and of the well-disposed of the nation. And because they are more vociferous and have money at their disposal for gifts, grants, feasting, and such like devices, they gain many to their side – usually persons of influence, who being strangers and not understanding the hidden reasons for these artifices allow themselves to be deceived, doing much harm while they think they are doing good. Moreover, the same ministers of the king, seeing this division and enmity amongst the English compatriots themselves, remain at times in doubt – and not without reason – as to whom they should trust. The result is: dealings go by the board, the well-disposed lose heart and retire dispirited and confused by this contradiction, and the unquiet spirits, because they are more audacious, are encouraged

by it; for their aim is no other than to throw things into confusion, weary others and prevent any effective action being taken. These damages or a great part of them would be repaired by this committee, for its members alone or in the main would have authority, not others.

5. Another no less important effect of this committee would be to induce all the English to come to a certain desired agreement as regards the succession to the crown of England, namely, in favour of the Lady Infanta of Spain. All the well-disposed and more judicious Catholics have this very much at heart on account of the great benefits and advantages that would follow from it, not only for England but for the whole of Christendom. These have been made clear by the convincing reasons alleged in favour of her claim both in Doleman's *Book of Succession* and in a paper which is circulating with Cardinal Allen's opinion on this matter. Against this agreement and against all the other interests of Spain the abovementioned unquiet spirits are continually raising factions both in Flanders and in Rome. The leaders of this party are Charles Paget, William Gifford, William Tresham, and a few others in Flanders, and their opposite numbers in Rome: Hugh Griffin, Thomas Hesketh, Nicholas Fitzherbert, and others. These would have neither the credit nor the power to do so much harm if this committee showed itself opposed to them and followed a different path.

6. Another very great benefit of this committee will be to give full and accurate information to His Majesty and to his governor of Flanders on the character and merits of those of the English nation who reside in Flanders and in other parts or who come from England, so that they would be valued according to their deserts. It is owing to a lack of such information that up to the present time grievous errors have been committed in this respect, which has caused many to be discontented and done harm to His Majesty's interests.

7. It would also be the business of this committee to see to it that all the English are employed according to their position and talents in suitable tasks, so that they may not live in idleness as they do at present; for this is the cause of infinite evils, quarrels, grumblings, factions, and enmities.

8. The committee and its members would also have another valuable function in planning measures to do continual damage to the queen, and keep her in a state of commotion and anxiety, now by forays from Flanders, now by uprisings and other difficulties in Scotland and Ireland, again by opening up negotiations in England, seeking out suitable persons for this purpose, winning them over and sustaining them and keeping the governor of Flanders informed as to what is afoot and the rate of progress of these affairs. They would also procure sure and very detailed reports as to what passes in England, both at court and in the council chamber, as well as such preparations as are being made at the ports. Furthermore, they would take greater care to run to earth spies whom the queen is continually sending to Flanders, and to discover the persons with whom they treat. Finally, this council or committee would be a countermine against all the machinations of the English Council, a strong castle to withstand all the broadsides of the heretics, an altar raised against an altar, which would bring about great partisanship towards His Majesty at a great advantage over the queen: she would be worn out by it and

would be more troubled and tormented by this one thing, and Catholics and our friends more animated than by any other expedient that has been tried up to the present time.

9. From these effects the important tasks that the committee would be called on to perform can easily be recognized: such as to obtain a good understanding of English affairs and deliberate upon them; find out about persons; treat with the nobility and with those also who hold towns and forts belonging to the king; unite the nation in its service to His Majesty and particularly as regards the succession; remove parties, factions, and dissension; take countermeasures against all the negotiations undertaken by those hostile to His Majesty; find employment for all the English who are at the king's service according to their qualities, abilities, and talents, and induce others to come over from England and desert the queen; to plan offensive measures, obtain reports from over there, and seize the spies that are sent here; and finally, to put some life and spirit into the Catholic cause, which up to present remains to a certain extent destitute, because in a certain way there is nobody whose business it is to take thought for it.

10. There should be Spaniards appointed to the Committee – or some suitable arrangement determined upon – so that should one fall out, another may take his place. For the same reason there should be others of the English nation; and in defect of a leader to select the most suitable persons, they should be those who have more aptitude for the task and who are more surely known to be well-affected towards His Majesty's service, such as Colonel Stanley, Hugh Owen, Gabriel Traherne, and the doctors Thomas Worthington and William Percy, who are free to engage in this work.[644] In matters of greater moment, Fr Holt, an English father of the Society, will be able to attend. And this is all that can be said of this matter. Its utility and importance will become manifest once it is put into execution.

B342 To Don Juan de Idiáquez, Valladolid, 2 September 1596, Enclosing Instructions for Charles Tancard, 31 August

SOURCE: AGS, Estado 839, fols. 138–139, holograph; fol. 143 (fair copy of instructions, enclosed) = S.

HICKS: 471–476 (enclosed instructions) and 501–510 (letter), both with English translation.

TRANSLATION: *CSPS*, 4: 633–634 (item 650).

NOTE: Persons was now ready to return to Rome and was soon to leave for Madrid and Barcelona. He would have met Idiáquez in person in Madrid early in October to explain his reasons for travelling in more detail: to deal with English Catholic affairs and especially the problems in the English colleges (McCoog, *Building the Faith of St Peter*, 360, citing Philip II's letter to Acquaviva, Madrid, 10 October 1596).

Here Persons reports on Sir Francis Englefield's visit to the college and canvasses ideas about the armada. He encloses a memorandum from the duchess of Feria about the succes-

---

644. Gabriel Traherne is identified by Loomie, *Spanish Elizabethans*, 119, as a former merchant in Andalusia.

sion (fol. 140), another memorandum on the succession (fols. 141–142), and the instructions given to Charles Tancard on 31 August (fol. 143). He also refers to various items compiled by Joseph Creswell about a proclamation to be made by the commander of the armada, Don Martín de Padilla. Creswell wrote to Idiáquez on 12 September enclosing materials on this topic (fols. 134–137). Idiáquez collected both sets of documents with a summary (fol. 133). On further developments, see Albert J. Loomie, SJ, "Philip II's Armada Proclamation of 1597," *Recusant History* 12 (April 1973): 216–225.

Charles Tancard had previously been expected to join Creswell on a visit to Rome (Acquaviva to Persons, 8 April 1596, B320). With the armada in preparation under Don Martín de Padilla in Lisbon, Persons now sent Tancard and six other priests from Valladolid and Seville to join the fleet. His hopes for success were also reflected in his letter to Idiáquez on 2 September (B342). Earlier in the year, Acquaviva had resisted pressure to assign larger numbers of Jesuits to the fleet. See McCoog, *Building the Faith of St Peter*, 387–388.

Por estar el tiempo adelante y approssimar el término que Vuestras Señorias me señalaron para la buelta a San Lorenço he querido embiar este proprio para tomar más luz y dar quenta de lo que aqui se va haciendo, donde está conmigo el Señor Francisco Ynglefild que vino a visitar unos sobrinos suyos estudiantes deste Collegio que an llegado de Ynglaterra y nunca avian visto al buen viejo ni él a ellos, ni les veerá en esta vida, pues ya no vee como Vuestra Señoria sabe.

Yo tengo hartas occupaciones, parte en las cosas que toccan al Collegio, parte en poner en Latin el libro de la succesion para que su Santidad y quien él mandare, lo vean si fuera menester, y assi quanto más tiempo Vuestra Señoria me podiera dar aqui sin prejuicio de los negocios, y de la siguridad de las galeras tanto mejor será, aunque más querria yo tiempo sobrado, que falta dél, especialmente porque algunos dias me seran necessarios tan bien por aý, para tratar y procurar los despachos que seran necessarios, y assi por lo menos será menester un mes de tiempo para la yda a Barcelona y para la morada por aý y[645] en Madrid y conforme a esto Vuestra Señoria me hara merced de avisarme luego con este proprio, quándo le parece que avrá galeras y dónde, y si seran de aqui o vendran de Italia y lo que pidera secreto lo tendre, y supplico a Vuestra Señoria me mande avisar en particular lo que tengo de haçer y si la intencion de Su Magestad para mi yda se va confirmando o no.

Embío con ésta el memorial que dixe a Vuestra Señoria que escriverian la Duquesa y los demas de la nacion en el negocio de la Señora Enfanta, esté Vuestra Señoria muy seguro que de la parte de los catolicos no avrá difficultad, si no summo deseo y con mucha raçon, como veerá Vuestra Señoria por el papel de las raçones que va Juntamente, si yo tengo de yr a Roma, por ventura será mejor que yo lleve el dicho memorial y raçones conmigo para el Embaxador, o si Su Magestad mandare embiarselo antes que no lo comunique con su Santidad hasta que yo llegue y le able al Embaxador, en todo lo qual yo me remitto, solamente confiesso a Vuestra Señoria, que quanto más pienso en este negocio y proposicion de la Señora Enfanta, tanto más me parece que podra ser medio de infinito bien en la christianidad, y llegar a obrar una paz universal por todas las partes, como veerá

645. y] *interlined with caret* S

Vuestra Señoria por las raçones, pero más adelante yo he pensado que si el Papa entrasse bien[646] en ello, como es probabile que ha de entrar por su honra y enterés publico, proponiendoselo a poco a poco y con indifferencia y reservacion, quisa si le parecera medio efficaz no solamente para accomodar[647] las cosas de Ynglaterra, si no tan bien las de Francia por via de una buena paz entre aquel reyno y éste, por que más a cuenta viene al Rey de Francia que la Señora Enfanta tenga Ynglaterra que no el Rey de Escocia, y con renunciarle la señora Enfanta todos los derechos que tiene a Bretaña, Aquitania, Anjou, Normandia etc. por las raçones que en[648] el libro de la succesion se vee, y más todas las pretensiones que los Reyes de Ynglaterra tiene a la Corona de Francia con el título que de presente usan etc. serian grandes motivos para que el Frances renunciasse tan bien a todas las pretensiones y títulos del reyno de Navarra etc. y que por esta via se apacifigasse todo etc., éste es un pensamiento mio secreto que he querido contar con Vuestra Señoria para que tan bien lo vaya pensando para quando será tiempo.

En quanto a la Jornada del Adelantado aunque Vuestra Señoria no me dice nada, voy discorriendo que porventura Su Magestad queria que vaya a Yrlanda, y sin duda si no ay comodidad para ninguno de los otros caminos que yo dixe a Vuestra Señoria y los propusi tan bien a Su Magestad, éste de Yrlanda podra ser de grande effeto, dando Dios buen successo, lo qual concistera mucho en que el Adelantado lleve de aqui el recaudo que fuera menester, de gente armas y denero, y que se parta antes que entre el imbierno, y que la Reyna tenga aviso cierto de su intension, y para quando llegará por alla he puesto en un papel algunos advertimientos, que porventura le podran ser de provecho, y si assi pareciera a Su Magestad, se podran consultar con el Adelantado como mandare.

Tan bien he querido prevenir y encaminar para Lisboa un padre Ynglés de la Compañia que fue Vicerrector desta casa con otros seis sacerdotes deste Seminario y del de Sevilla hombres doctos y platicos embiandoles por differentes caminos con[649] color de que yran en sus misiones desde Lisboa y solamente con el padre de la Compañia que es discreto y muy[650] nobil en Ynglaterra, he conferido en secreto algunas cosas y dado enstruciones, para consultar con los demas en caso que se offreciese occasion de yr con la armada, y entiendo que estos sacerdotes valdran su peso de oro en llegando por alla, porque cada uno valdra por muchos, y assi no he querido dexar de haçer este officio sabiendo quanto importará aunque faltandome denero me fue necessario buscarlo emprestado para embiarles, pero poco importa esto a respeto de la cosa en sí, las instruciones que les di, comunicandolas solamente por agora con el Padre superior de los demas que he dicho, van tan bien con estas para que Vuestra Señoria entienda todo lo que haçemos, pensamos y deseamos en esta materia. *Et haec de his.*

El padre Cresuello me ha escrito de Madrid que el Memorial del Arbitrio para los Seminarios queda aún en poder del Marquez de Pozza, y los Seminarios en este mientras se cargan de tantas deudas que no podemos passar adelante, ni puedo yo en manera alguna bolver las espaldas sin veer el fin deste negocio del Arbitrio, el señor Don Chris-

    646. bien] *interlined with caret* S
    647. accomodar] *interlined with caret* S
    648. en] *interlined with caret* S
    649. con] *preceded by* y [*deleted*] S
    650. y muy] *interlined with caret* S

toval me prometio que lo haria despachar presto del Marquez. Supplico a Vuestra Señoria se lo accuerde al Conde, yo escrivo a su Señoria quatro palabras en esto solamente remittiendome en lo demas a esta que escrivo a Vuestra Señoria.

Estando en Madrid apunté algunas cosas[651] principales que se avian de poner en el pregon del General para qualquiera parte de Ynglaterra, Escocia o Yrlanda que llegasse y las dexé con el padre Cresuello para comunicar con Vuestra Señoria y assi si no lo ha hecho puede mandar Vuestra Señoria que se le embie si le pareciere, para que el negocio vaya bien mirado al Adelantado.

El Señor Francisco Ynglafild, aunque vee los officios importantes que se puede haçer en Roma si Dios nos ayudara toda via queda con grandes recelos y miedos de que los nuestros[652] contrarios han de procurar, que me detengan por alli, o me hagan peor, pero yo no temo por esto, *nec facio animam meam preciosiorem quam me* como dixo San Pablo en caso semejante. Dios nuestro Señor me ha librado de caminos más peligrosos que no éste y assi, está en lo platicado y manda que vaya yo yre muy allegremente y con confiança que Dios ha de ser servido y Su Magestad de la Jornada y al fin el Señor Francisco está tan bien convincido que los negocios que piden la yda, son de más importancia, que no el quedar aqui aunque fuesse la yda con algun manifiesto peligro, que placiendo a Dios no lo ay, y assi no queda otro si no que Vuestra Señoria manda bolver luego a este messajero y que con él tenga alguna luz de lo que tengo que hazer. Guarde Dios nuestro Señor a Vuestra Señoria como puede. De Valladolid a 2 de Sietembre 1596.

  Roberto Personio.

[*Addressed*:] A Don Juan de Idiaquez, Comendador mayor de Leon, etc.
[*Enclosed*:]

Instructiones pro Patre Carolo Tancardo Societatis Jesu et sociis proficiscentibus ad classem regiam, cui praeest Excellentissimus Dominus Martinus de Padilla Adelantatus major Castellae. 30 Augusti 1596.

Primum omnium, proposito sibi huius missionis fine, qui est ut in Anglia Scotia Hibernia, vel ubicunque appulerit classis regia, verae fidei ac pietatis, religionisque Catholicae cultus, repulsa haeresi restituatur, eo animo proficisci debent, quicunque ad hanc provinciam capescendam vel promovendam mittuntur, ut intelligant opus se apostolicum prae manibus habere, eaque de causa debere se huiusmodi animorum praeparatione munire qua legimus Apostolos ad missiones se muniisse oratione nimirum, humilitate, frequenti meditatione, mortificatione passionum, patiendi desiderio et super omnia ardenti in Deum proximosque charitate, et spe firma Deum affuturum conatibus qui pro ipsius gloria suscipiuntur.

Haec quisque tum in se experiri tum aliis etiam impartire atque imprimere studeat, praecipue vero militibus et classis ducibus suaviter haec ac prudenter instillare oportebit, bellum nimirum hoc sacrum esse ac proinde pie suscipiendum atque legitime prosequendum, amotis furtis, latrociniis, oppressionibus pauperum aliisque istiusmodi,

  651. cosas] *interlined with caret* S
  652. nuestros] *interlined with caret* S

quibus offensa Dei maiestas bellantes dissipat, atque confundit, quod eo certius hac in expeditione faciet si similia perpetrantur, quanto maiora Catholici Angli Hiberni atque Scoti pro defensione verae fidei ac pietatis passi sunt, neque patietur Deus ut iterum a nostris militibus indigna patiantur impune, et quia hoc punctum magni momenti est ad consequendam victoriam unusquisque sacerdotum paratus esse debebit, ut idonea afferat in hanc sententiam quacunque oblata occasione sive pro concione sive privatis in colloquiis.

Si in Angliam, Scotiam vel Hiberniam appulerint, id in primum curent nostri sacerdotes, ut primum suo exemplo alios aedificent, deinde ut quo modis possint, literis nimirum, libris, nunciis, vel edictis sparsis, incolas certiores faciant, se non hostiliter adventare sed ut oppressis tantum opitulentur, religionem Catholicam restituant, neminem laedant in resistentem, ceteraque istiusmodi quae ad pacem faciant; imprimis vero in id incumbant modisque nitantur omnibus, ut populum doceant informentque de recta piaque regis Hispaniarum intensione in hoc bello falsasque opiniones ab haereticis impressas ab hominum animis eximant, quo inteligant nihil nisi salutare ac paterni amoris plenum Maiestatem suam cogitare, pro commodis tum reipublicae tum etiam singulorum.

Si quis ex adversa parte ad nostrum exercitum confugerit, humanite in quantum fieri potest tractetur, et informetur de eo Dux exercitus, sed caute tamen et cum prudentia ne error accidat aut damnum inde sequatur quod in nostros deinde reiiciatur tanquam in suos nimium affectos, itaque valde moderate atque circumspecte hac in re procedendum est, neque nimium fidendum aut pro quocunque spondendum.

Cum superiori nostrorum in Anglia aliisque sacerdotibus maioris apud nos autoritatis tum in Scotia tum etiam in Hibernia frequens habeatur correspondentia, magnoque studio conservetur ab omnibus atque cum omnibus amicitia unio atque Concordia, hucque ad nos scribant quoties commode possint, ea quae scribenda duxerint, maxime quae ad aedificationem ac consolationem pertinebunt, vel quorum difficultates a nobis dissolvi aut levari poterunt continuisque precibus alter alterum in vicem sublevemus.

Omnes nostri qui ex Societate sunt ei praestabunt obedientiam qui reliquorum superior designatur, sacerdotes vero seminariorum durante expeditione, Patris Caroli directionem sequantur, si quis autem id facere recusaverit a reliquis amoveatur et suae ipsius curae relinquatur, sciat tamen se contra superiorum suorum voluntatem facere, quorum autoritas eousque in eum firma esse intelligitur quoad duraverit haec expeditio. Vallesoleti, 30 Augusti 1596.

Robertus Personius nomine Patris Visitatoris, suoque.

[*Endorsed by Persons:*] Instructiones pro missione classica.

Translation

As time has gone by and the appointed time is drawing near which Your Excellencies indicated for my return to San Lorenzo, I wished to send this message, in order to get more information and to give an account of what is being done here. Sir Francis Englefield is here with me; he came to pay a visit to some nephews of his who are students in this College. They have arrived from England and had never seen the good old man, nor he them; nor will he ever see them in this life, for he is now unable to see, as Your Excellency is aware.

I am fully occupied, partly in the business of the College, and partly in putting into Latin the *Book of the Succession*, so that his Holiness and whoever he may commission may examine it if necessary, and so the longer the time Your Excellency can allow me here without prejudice to the business and to the safety of the galleys, the better. For indeed I would prefer to have time to spare rather than not enough; especially as I shall also need several days there to deal with the warrants that will be necessary and get them adopted, and at least a month will be required for the journey to Barcelona and for my stay there and in Madrid. And this being the case, Your Excellency will be doing me a kindness if you will let me know by this messenger when you think there will be galleys and where they will be, and if they will be got here or will be coming from Italy. Whatever secrecy is demanded, I will observe; and I beg Your Excellency in particular – to advise me what I have got to do, and whether His Majesty's intention that I should go persists or not.

I am sending along with this the memorial which I told Your Excellency the duchess and others of our nation would write on the subject of the Lady Infanta; Your Excellency may rest assured that there will be no difficulty on the part of the Catholics, but rather intense desire for her; and this is quite reasonable, as Your Excellency will see from the paper, giving the arguments, which is going along with it. If I have to go to Rome, perhaps it will be better for me to take the abovementioned memorial and the paper with me to hand to the ambassador; or if His Majesty orders them to be sent to him in advance, that he should not show them to his Holiness until I arrive and have speech with the ambassador. In all this I submit to your judgement; only I confess to Your Excellency that, the more I think about this business and the proposal about the Lady Infanta, the more it seems to me that it may prove to be a source of infinite advantage to Christendom, and a means of bringing about a general peace everywhere; this Your Excellency will perceive from the arguments put forward. But furthermore, I have reflected that, if the pope were to take an active part in the scheme, as it is likely that he will do, for the sake of his honour and the public interest, if this course is suggested to him without hurry and with a discreet indifference, it will possibly seem to him to be an effective means of settling matters not only in England but in France as well, by bringing about a good peace between those two kingdoms. For it is more to the interest of the king of France that the Lady Infanta should hold England rather than the king of Scotland; and if the Lady Infanta were to renounce all the rights which she has to Brittany, Aquitaine, Anjou, Normandy, etc., the grounds of which are to be found in the *Book of the Succession*, and in addition were to renounce all the claims which the kings of England make to the crown of France and the style, embodying them, which they use at the present time, there would be every motive for the French king also to renounce all claims and title to the kingdom of Navarre, etc., and in this way bring about a general appeasement, etc. This is a secret thought of mine which I wished to communicate to Your Excellency so that you also may turn it over in your mind with a view to future action.

As regards the governor's expedition,[653] although Your Excellency says nothing to me about it, I am drawing the conclusion that His Majesty would perhaps wish him to go to Ireland; and undoubtedly, if it is not convenient to adopt any of the other routes which I mentioned to Your Excellency and also suggested to His Majesty, this one by way of Ireland could be very effective, if God gave it success. And this would depend largely on the governor's taking from here an adequate supply of men, arms and money, and on his setting out before the winter sets in, and before the queen has definite information of his intention; and for his use when he gets there, I have set down on paper some notes which may perhaps be of value to him. If His Majesty thinks they will be, they can be discussed with the governor as he shall command.

I wished also to give instruction and set on the road for Lisbon an English father of the Society, who has been vice rector of this College, and six other priests from this seminary and from Seville, men of learning and good sense. I am sending them by different routes, and giving out that they will proceed to the mission from Lisbon; and only with the father of the Society, who is a discreet man and of very good family in England, have I secretly discussed certain matters, and I have given him instructions to take counsel with the others, in case the opportunity should offer for accompanying the armada.[654] I believe that these priests will be worth their weight in gold when they get there, for each of them will be worth many men. And for this reason, I would not omit to do this good office, knowing its importance, in spite of its being necessary for me, not having any money, to seek a loan from someone in order to send them; but that is of small consequence so long as they go. The instructions I gave them, and made known for the present only to the father who is in charge of the others as I said, are being sent with this letter, so that Your Excellency may know all that we are doing, thinking, and wishing in connection with this affair. So much for that.

Fr Creswell has written to me from Madrid that the memorial concerning provision for the seminaries is still in the hands of the Marquis de Poza,[655] and in the meantime the seminaries are getting so loaded with debt that we can make no progress; and I cannot possibly turn my back on things here without seeing the finish of this matter of the provision; Don Cristóbal promised me that he would have it promptly signed off by the Marquis; I beg Your Excellency to remind the Count of this; I am writing to his Excellency a few words only on this subject, relying for the rest on this letter to you.

When I was in Madrid, I jotted down a few of the principal points that ought to be included in the general's proclamation, appropriate to whatever part of England, Scotland, or Ireland he reaches; and I left them for Fr Creswell to show to Your Excellency; so, if he has not done so, Your Excellency can give instructions for them to be sent to you, if you think well, so that the matter may be thoroughly examined before being passed to the governor.

653. Martín de Padilla; see n357.
654. See the instructions for Charles Tancard, below.
655. Francisco de Rojas y Enríquez (1546–1605), third marquis of Poza, was president of the Council of Finance. See Carlos Javier de Carlos Morales (*DBE*).

Although Sir Francis Englefield sees that important services can be rendered in Rome if God aids us, yet he has great forebodings and fears of what our adversaries are likely to attempt: that they may have me kept there or do me a worse turn. But I have no fear of that: *neither do I count my life more precious than myself,*[656] as St Paul said in similar circumstances. God our Lord has delivered me from journeys that were more perilous than this; and so, if it has been arranged and I am ordered to go I will do so with pleasure and in confidence that God and His Majesty will be served by the journey; and in the end Sir Francis also has come to the conclusion that the business that calls for a journey is too important to allow me to stay here, even though my going entailed some obvious danger, which please God is not the case; and so it only remains for Your Excellency to order this messenger to return at once so that through him I can get some light on what I am to do. May God our Lord preserve Your Excellency, as He is able to do. From Valladolid on the 2nd of September 1596.

    Robert Persons.

[*Enclosed:*]

Instructions for Fr Charges Tancard, SJ, and his companions on
their setting out for the King's fleet, commanded by His Excellency,
Don Martín de Padilla, governor-in-chief of Castille.

First of all, as the end proposed for this mission is to drive out heresy and restore Catholic religion and worship in England, Scotland, Ireland, or wherever the King's fleet makes a landing, such as are sent to engage in or promote this task must set out with this understanding in mind: that they have in hand an apostolic work, and should therefore strengthen themselves with such a preparation of souls, as we read the apostles did for their missionary journeys, by prayer, certainly, by humility, by frequent meditation, by mortifying of the passions, by desire for suffering, and above all by fervent love for God and their neighbours and a firm confidence that God will assist undertakings that are entered upon for his glory.

Such sentiments then let each one endeavour both to arouse in himself and communicate to and impress on others. In particular, it will be necessary to instill the soldiers and leaders of the fleet with such considerations in a prudent and gracious manner: that this is truly a holy war, and hence that they must enter upon it in a spirit of piety and pursue it with justice, avoiding all thefts and robberies and other such like oppressions of the poor; for the offended majesty of God scatters and confounds those who go to war. And He will the more assuredly bring this about in the present expedition if such outrages are perpetrated, the more the Catholics in England, Ireland, and Scotland have suffered for the defence of true faith and piety; nor will God allow further indignities to be inflicted on them at the hands of our soldiers with impunity. And because this point is crucial in obtaining a victorious issue, each priest will have to be ready, at every opportunity, to press home these considerations by suitable arguments, whether in public discourses or in private conversations.

656. Acts 20:24.

If they should land in England, Scotland, or Ireland, in the first place let our priests take particular care to edify others by their example; second, in as many ways as they can – doubtless by distributing letters, books, notices, and edicts – let them take pains to reassure the native people that they have not come in enmity, but only to help those who are downtrodden, restore the Catholic faith, and do hurt to no one who does not offer resistance, and do other things of this kind which make for peace. Above all, however, they should devote all their labour and strive in every way to instruct and inform the people of the just and pious intention of the King of Spain in waging this war, and eradicate from people's minds the false views instilled into them by the heretics, so that they may realize that His Majesty intends nothing save what is for their good, and what is inspired by his paternal love for them, to the benefit both of the state and of the individual.

If anyone from the opposing camp should flee to our army, he should be treated humanely as far as possible, and the chief of the army informed about him; but this must be done with caution and prudence to avoid deceit or loss – for which our men may subsequently be blamed for being too favourably disposed to their fellow countrymen. In this matter, therefore, they must exercise great moderation and circumspection: they should not be too trusting, nor should they make promises on behalf of anyone.

There should be frequent correspondence with the superior of Ours in England and with other priests of greater account amongst ours, both in Scotland and in Ireland, and every effort should be made to preserve friendship, union, and concord with all. They are to write to us as often as they conveniently can whatever they consider newsworthy, particularly such as makes for edification and consolation, or such difficulties that persons have as can be solved or mitigated by us; and let us support one another with our mutual continual prayer.

All Ours of the Society should observe obedience to their designated superior, but for the course of the expedition the seminary priests should follow the direction of Fr Charles. However, if anyone refuses to do this, he should be separated from the others and left to his own devices. He should know, however, that he is acting contrary to the will of his superiors, whose authority over him is understood to hold good so long as the expedition lasts. Valladolid 30 August 1596.

Robert Persons, in the name of father visitor and in his own.

B343 From Alfonso Agazzari, Rome, 25 September 1596

> SOURCE: AAW, V, no. 69, pp. 227–30.
>
> EDITION: Knox, *Douay Diaries*, 1: 386–389.
>
> NOTE: Agazzari is disappointed by Persons's silence: he has had no reply to his last three letters. He reports on a series of major recent developments: the deaths of the vice-protector (Cardinal Francisco de Toledo), the bishop of Cassano (Owen Lewis) and Thomas Throckmorton, all of whom were felt to be supporters of the dissident students at the English college, and the intervention of Richard Barret, president of the college at Douai, who has come to Rome to assist with the crisis at the college. He discusses the likely candidates to succeed Toledo, cardinals Cesare Baronio and Camillo Borghese (Borghese was appointed). He is relieved by the departure of Hugh Griffin, to take up his position as provost

of Cambrai, leaving Thomas Hesketh, formerly of Allen's household, as leader of the English colony in Rome.

This letter, like the previous one (27 August, B336) was dictated to Agazzari's secretary, Henrico, for whose sake he leaves off writing in Latin after the first paragraph, although Latin phrases are dispersed throughout the letter. It contains a puzzling indication of an estrangement between Allen and the Society of Jesus at the end of his life; McCoog, *Building the Faith of St Peter*, 201–203, discusses possible differences of opinion over the succession, the Spanish armada and the administration of the seminaries; see also Pollen, "Colleges in Spain," 62–65, and Knox's introduction to the *Douay Diaries*, xcviii.

Reverendo in Christo padre
Pax Christi.

Ecce iam quartam vobis scribo epistolam et nihil literarum istinc accepi, quas avidissime exspecto, praesertim Reverentiae Vestrae; et certe his temporibus non solum semel in mense, sed singulis diebus vestro consilio vestraque directione indigemus. Propter meam commoditatem et vestrum exercitium nostrique secretarii eruditionem in Italica lingua, malo Italice quam Latine scribere.

Sabbato passato fece otto giorni che passò di questa a[657] miglior vita, comme esperiamo, l'illustrissimo Card. Toleto, nostro Viceprotectore; per la cui morte da una banda si può temere qualche danno per questo collegio, per che nelle cose temporali, si come era di grande autorità appresso il Papa et questi ministri camerarii, così poteva aiutar molto, et già haveva comminciato a farlo. Haveva anco tanto credito et tanta autorità et talmente s'era guadagnato l'anime di questi alumni et massime de' più seditiosi et turbulenti che non solo con le parole, ma con un minimo cenno poteva far di loro quel che voleva. Dal'altra parte credo che sia stata una grande providentia di Dio per beneficio di questo collegio, per che più tosto era pericolo che questi seditiosi et particolarmente Benetto non lo tirassero a fare tutto quello che si volevano, come in molte cose di già havevan fatto, et in confessore si vantava che poteva ottenere di lui tutto quello che voleva, fino a farmi cacciar via da questo collegio, si io non mi portavo bene con gli scholari. *O audaciam inauditam*! Et certo, padre mio, mi par questo un grand indicio di sua Divina Maestà et un grand segno dell'amore che porta alla Compagnia, a questo collegio et alla causa d'Inghilterra, il vedere che quando mancano i mezzi humani egli quasi miracolosamente ci metta la sua divina mano. Mentre che Alano caminò bene in questo negotio con quella coniunctione et fedeltà alla Compagnia che faceva, Iddio Benedetto lo conservò, prosperò et exaltò; ma cominciando a lasciare questa strada fu in un subito troncato il filo de suoi desegni et della vita insieme. Et essendosi dipoi sveilliato un adversario molto più pericoloso, mentre che quasi era pervenuto al summo, fu l'anno seguente levato di questa vita, il Vescovo di Cassano; et duoi giorni doppo il medesimo avenne a Throgmortono, ardentissimo cooperatore de'medesimi pensieri. Ma adesso pareva a questa gente, così Romana come Belgica, d'havere un appoggio più forte di tutti gli altri passati, come apertamente si gloriavano, ma eccogli di novo inexspettatamente spogliati et privi di quest'esperanza. Si che, padre mio, non ci perdiamo di animo per che *Deus pugnat*

657. a] *suppl. Knox; not in W*

pro causa sua, et il sangue sparso di tanti martiri et la continua loro intercessione in cielo ci deve in ogni evento apportare grande fiducia, facendo però dalla banda nostra il debito.

Io il giorno della sepultura del Cardinale, o fusse per qualche fatica extraordinaria usata nella sua infirmità, nella quale di et notte fumo quivi assistenti, sempre quatro o cinque della Compagnia, o pure per altra causa fui supraiunto di certi dolori così gravi che non potevo manco voltarmi per il letto; da quali per gratia di Dio adesso son libero, et heiri stei tutto il giorno in palazzo per havere audienza del nostro Signore, ma sempre stette con lui il secretario della ambasciata per le cose di Spagna, a tal che nè io nè altro hebbe audienza; se bene il Papa, per[658] mezzo del padre Generale che duoi giorni fa hebbe longa audienza, mi fece intendere che volea parlarmi circa la elettione de il novo Viceprotectore. Spero che l'havrò hoggi o domane, et si l'habbia avanti il partito del corriero farò una postscripta a Vostra Reverentia.

Il signor Baretto, vedendo che io per la malatia non potevo andare da Sua Santità, andò egli tre giorni sono da Sua Santità, ma non hebbe tempo di trattare se non duoi punti; l'uno del Viceprotectore, et domandò in particolare il Cardinal Baronio, qual pensiamo che sarebbe molto a proposito per più rispetti, et doppo un lungo discorsetto ch'hebbero in questa materia, il Papa risolse che ci harebbe dato o Baronio o Bourghesio, che era l'auditor della camera, ma non volse risolver niente alhora. L'altro punto che trattò Baretto fu in persuader il Papa che in nissun modo levasse la Compagnia dal governo di questo collegio, et addusse molti et efficaci ragioni, fino a dire che, se ciò seguisse, oltre alli altri inconvenienti grandi che adduceva, non gli bastava l'animo di poter governare il suo collegio di Duaco. Trovò il Papa in questo punto molto dubioso, et disse che haveva ricevuto lettere da Inglesi molto principali che erano di contrario parere, et che gli scrivevano questi formali parole, che la Compagnia voleva tyranneggiare in ogni luogho, come faceva in Ingleterra et in Flandria, dove particolarmente intendeva esservi un padre che voleva dominare et tiranneggiare la natione; al che Baretto rispose tanto bene quanto havrebbe potuto fare il signore Hadoko o vero il signore Rogiero, fin a dire che haveva demonstrationi del contrario, et che questi che scrivevano tali lettere bisognava che fussero persone poco degni di fede, et che si Sua Santità s'informasse meglio intenderebbe ciò non esser vero. Disse anco il Papa che haveva animo di far venire Stapletonio a Roma (il che haveva detto prima anco il Cardinal Baronio) a che fine non se sa; Vostra Reverentia la può considerar lei et ponderar bene questo punto. Di qua si può vedere manifestamente che li nostri amici di Fiandria non dormono, et danno questi belli informationi al Papa; unde mi par necessario trovar mezzo che nostro Signore sia informato della verità, et che intenda quali sieno costoro che scrivano queste buggie, acciò per la venire non habbino credito appresso di sua Santità. Questo officio mi pare che propriamente et efficacemente lo potrebbe fare il Cardinal Archiduca con una sua lettera a Sua Santità, o vero all'Imbasciatore qui, che in nome del Cardinale informasse nostro Signore. Questo stesso ho detto al padre Edmondo et il signore Rogiero, che sabbatho scrivino in Fiandria al signore Stanleo et il padre Holto.

Hugo Griffidio avanti la sua partita ha voluto fare un bel colpo. Invitò l'altro giorno il signor Baretto a pranso, et dipoi lo ritirò in camera, et gli diede un assalto così impetu-

---

658. per] *interlined* W

oso et terribile che Baretto retornò a casa rauco et quasi ammalato, essendosi anco egli riscaldato in contrario, non potendo supportare l'insolentie et ingiurie che Griffidio diceva contro la Compagnia et i seguaci di quella, et particolarmente *invehebatur in ipsum Barettum tanquam in instrumentum Societatis contra scholares reliquos, et praesertim quia deceperat dominum Heschettum*, il quale veramente se porta molto bene, et ha, se non guadagnato, al meno fatto retirare dall'impresa di favorire i seditiosi scholari, Fitzherberto et Smithsono; a talché spero con la gratia dal Signore che, partito che sia Hugone, non ci resterà persona fuora dal collegio che favorisca i tristi; il che veramente si deve al signore Baretto, che s'è mostrato molto fedele alla Compagnia: che Vostra Reverentia lo tenga e lo ricognosca per tale, si come desidero ancora che faccia il padre Holto, del quale egli dubita un pocho: Vostra Reverentia procuri che gli sia levato questo dubio. Raccommando anco a Vostra Reverentia il signore Heschetto: lo consoli et gli dia animo con amorevoli lettere, perché lo merita, et spero che sarà qua un buon instrumento, et doppo la partita di Griffidio quasi tutti gl'Inglesi fuora del collegio dependeranno da lui.

Padre mio, sento particolar mortificatione di non poter scrivare di propria mano.[659] Henrico è fidele secretario. Quel punto di Stapletono importa; però Vostra Reverentia ci pensi, et procuri di remediare, facendo promover presto qualche persona che sia fedele alla corona, della quale non si possa dubbitare. Pensi al Signore Adocco, et cito, perché *periculum est in mora. Plura intelliges a P. Emundo*. Vostra Reverentia ci raccomandi al Signore, che ne habbiamo bisogno. Da Roma, a 25 di Settembre, 1596.

  Di Vostra Reverentia
   servo
    Alfonso Agazzari.

[*Addressed*:] Al padre Roberto Personio, della Compagnia di Giesu, a Madrile.
[*Endorsed*:] P. Alfonso, 25 7^{bris}, for F. Walpole, 1596.

Translation

Reverend Father in Christ
The peace of Christ.

See, I am now writing my fourth letter to you without receiving a single letter from over there. I desperately long for one, especially from Your Reverence. And for sure, these days we need your advice and guidance not only every month, but every day. For my convenience and your practice, and to suit my secretary's expertise in the Italian tongue, I prefer to write in Italian rather than in Latin.

Last Saturday was the eighth day since His Eminence Cardinal Toledo, our vice-protector, passed from this life to a better, as we hope.[660] As a result of his death, some damage is to be feared for this college, according to a certain faction, because in temporal matters he had such authority with the pope and his curia that he was able to assist

---

659. This paragraph in Agazzari's own hand.
660. On Francisco de Toledo, see the headnote to Barret's letter to Persons, 26/28 September (B344).

them a great deal and had already begun to do so. He also had such credit and such authority and had so won the favour of the students, and particularly of the dissidents and troublemakers, that not only by word but also by the slightest nod he was able to achieve what he intended. On the other hand, this has been a great act of divine providence for this college, because there was imminent danger that these dissidents and especially Bennet would not hold back from forcing him to do whatever they wanted, as in many cases they already had done, and to his confessor he boasted that he could obtain from him all that he wanted, even having me expelled from this college, unless I behave well to the scholars. *What unheard-of audacity!* And for sure, my dear father, this seems to me a great indication of His Divine Majesty and a great sign of the love he bears to the Society, and to this college and to the cause of England, to see that when human means fail, he stretches out his divine hand quite marvellously. So long as Allen kept to the right path in this business, with the attachment and loyalty to the Society that he used to have, our blessed Lord kept, prospered, and exalted him; but when he began to stray from the path the thread of his designs and his life together were suddenly cut off.[661] And thereafter when a much more dangerous adversary was awakened, the bishop of Cassano, just when he was about to reach the heights, was lifted from this life the following year. And two days later Throckmorton met the same fate, that most ardent coadjutor in the same designs. Only a little while ago, it appeared to people both in Rome and Flanders that they had a stronger supporter than all the previous ones, as they openly boasted, but see now how they have been unexpectedly despoiled and deprived of this hope. Therefore, my dear father, let us not despair, for God fights for his own cause, and the blood shed by so many martyrs, and their continual intercession in heaven, ought to bring great confidence: but our faction must still carry on with its duty.

As for myself, on the day of the burial of our cardinal, whether it was through the extraordinary fatigue resulting from watching at his deathbed, at which day and night we were always in attendance, with four or five of us of the Society, or maybe for some other reason, I was overwhelmed by such strong pains that I was unable even to turn over in my bed. Thanks be to God, I am now free of this, and yesterday I spent the whole day in the palace expecting to have an audience with our lord [the pope], but the secretary of the embassy on Spanish affairs was there the whole time, so that neither I nor anyone else could have an audience; however, the pope, by way of father general, who had a long audience two days ago, informed me that he wanted to talk to me about the election of a new vice-protector. I hope that I will meet him today or tomorrow, and if this happens before the departure of the courier, I will write a postscript to Your Reverence.

Mr Barret, seeing that because of illness I was not able to go to His Holiness, went himself to His Holiness three days ago, but he did not have time to deal with more than two points: one about the vice-protector, and he asked in particular for Cardinal Baronio, whom we think will be much more suitable in certain respects, and after a long discussion that they had on this matter, the pope decided that he was prepared to give us

---

661. In June 1593 Allen agreed to write to Philip II in support of Thomas Morgan's scheme to have the duchess of Feria, Jane Dormer, transferred to Flanders where, Morgan hoped, she would lend weight to Morgan's anti-Jesuit party (Loomie, *Spanish Elizabethans*, 116–118).

either Baronio or Borghese, who is the auditor of the chamber, but he did not want to make any decision immediately.[662] The other point which Barret dealt with was to persuade the pope that he should by no means remove the Society from running the college, and he adduced many powerful reasons, to the effect that if it should so turn out, besides all the other great inconveniences that would be brought about, he would not have the strength to be able to run his own college at Douai. He found the pope very uncertain in this matter, as he said that he had received letters from very important Englishmen who were of the opposite opinion, and these were the very words they wrote: that the Society wanted to tyrannize everywhere, as was done in England and Flanders in particular, where he acknowledged there to be a father who wanted to dominate and tyrannize over the nation.[663] To this, Barret replied just as well as he thought Mr Haydock or in fact Mr Roger could have done,[664] to the point where he said he had proof to the contrary, and that he needed to know that those who were writing those letters were not worthy of trust, and that if His Holiness were better informed, he would know that this was not true. The pope also said that he had it in mind to make Stapleton come to Rome (something of which Cardinal Baronio had informed him even earlier), to what end is not known. Your Reverence may consider this point and ponder it well. From this it can be plainly seen that our friends in Flanders are not sleeping, and are giving these good tidings to the pope; hence, it seems necessary to me to find means to have His Holiness informed of the truth, and that he should understand what kind of people these are who are writing such calumnies, so that they will no longer have any credit with His Holiness. This duty, it seems to me, the cardinal archduke could undertake most suitably and effectively in a letter to His Holiness, or rather to the ambassador here, who in the name of the cardinal can inform our lord. This is what I have said to Fr Edmund and Mr Roger,[665] who wrote to Sir [William] Stanley and Fr Holt in Flanders on Saturday.

Hugh Griffin wanted to make a bold stroke before his departure. The other day he invited Mr Barret to supper, and afterwards drew him into his chamber, where he gave him such an impetuous and fearful assault that Barret returned to his house hoarse and almost ill, having lost his temper as well, not being able to bear the insolences and injuries that Griffin spoke against the Society and her followers. In particular he inveighed against Barret himself as a tool of the Society against the rest of the scholars, and in particular because he had deceived Mr Hesketh – who actually is behaving very well, since even if he has not been won over to our side, he has at least convinced Fitzherbert and Smithson to withdraw from their enterprise of favouring the dissident stu-

---

662. Cesare Baronio (1538–1607), superior of the Congregation of the Oratory, the pope's confessor and Vatican librarian, was occupied in writing his *Annales ecclesiastici* (12 vols., 1588–1607). Camillo Borghese (1550–1621) reigned as Pope Paul V, 1605–1621. Both were created cardinal on 5 June 1596.

663. This appears to mean that the pope was sympathetic to the anti-Jesuit party's criticism of Holt.

664. On Richard Haydock, see the headnote to Persons's letter to Idiáquez, 6 December 1595 (B302). Roger Baynes, formerly Allen's secretary, continued to be an important source of information on English affairs.

665. Edmund Harewood and Roger Baynes.

dents;[666] so much so that I hope that, with the grace of our Lord, once Hugh has left, no one will remain outside the college who supports the complainers. All this can truly be said to be because of Mr Barret, who has shown himself to be very faithful to the Society; may Your Reverence believe and recognize him as such, as also Fr Holt, of whom he has some doubts. I also commend Mr Hesketh to Your Reverence: give him some comfort and encourage him with loving letters, because he deserves it, and I hope that he may be a good agent, because, after the departure of Griffin, it is as if all the English outside the college depend on him.

My dear father, I am particularly mortified that I am not able to write in my own hand, but Henry is a trustworthy secretary. The matter of Stapleton is important, but Your Reverence should think it over and find some remedy, putting forward, soon, someone who is loyal to the crown, of whom there is no possibility of doubt. Consider Mr Haydock, and quickly, because *he who hesitates is lost*. You will learn more from Fr Edmund. May Your Reverence commend us to the Lord, something we are very much in need of. From Rome, 25 September 1596.

Your Reverence's servant
Alfonso Agazzari.

B344 From Richard Barret, Rome, 26/28 September 1596

SOURCE: AAW, V, no. 70, 231–234.

EDITION: Knox, *Douay Diaries*, 1: 384–386; Renold, *Letters of Allen and Barret*, 253–255 (with English translation in place of the Latin parts of the text).

NOTE: With the death of the vice-protector Cardinal Francisco de Toledo, who had sided with the dissidents and wanted Barret replaced at Douai by William Gifford, Barret approached Pope Clement VIII with hopes of a change of policy. At an audience on 22 September, he pleaded with the pope not to allow Acquaviva to withdraw the Jesuits from the government of the college (Kenny, "Inglorious Revolution," 85–86 [part 3]; McCoog, *Building the Faith of St Peter*, 270–272, 356–359).

The letter is addressed to either Persons or Creswell, at Valladolid or Madrid, in case one of them had already left for Rome. Barret begs them to press for the payment of Spanish pensions to the English exiles, especially since the opposing faction is so well supplied with funds.

The date given at the foot of the first page of the letter is 26 September, whereas the signature and the endorsement give 28 September, although the hand is somewhat obscure.

Reverend and my loving father

The death of Cardinal Tolledo hath bin the cause of my longer abode, for that yt importeth much to have in his place such a one as wilbe content to understand our cause

666. Thomas Hesketh and Nicholas Fitzherbert had been members of Allen's household in 1594; also mentioned is one Giovanni Smazzone (Knox, *Allen*, 374–375), whom Anstruther identifies as John Smithson (ca. 1567–1596), one of the chaplains who sailed with the Spanish armada, either of November 1596 or of October 1597 (McCoog, *Building the Faith of St Peter*, 399–400; Anstruther 323–325); however, he was already in Valladolid in 1594 (*Valladolid Registers*, 21).

and the estate of our countrie and to concurre accordinglie. And these busie-headed fellowes beganne to conceave some hope of removing the fathers. Besides father generall made suite to His Holines to have the Societie delivered of this government. The which his request together with the inclination of His Holines and the desires of these schollers put me in greate feare lest His Holines would have graunted, seing both partes so willing thereunto. Wherefore having obteyned audience I spake and made supplication after this sorte:

> Post pedum oscula sanctorum et gratiarum actiones humillimas de beneficiis nuper acceptis tam in spiritualibus quam temporalibus ad sustentationem collegii vestri Anglorum Duacensis, placet Sanctitati Vestrae ut paucis verbis possim significare periculum maximum et manifestum in quo non solum Collegium Anglorum de Urbe, verum etiam reliqua omnia Seminaria quae pro Angliae conversione sunt instituta, etiam universa Ecclesia Anglicana hoc tempore versatur, nisi Sanctitas Vestra pro sua bonitate et prudentia dignetur quamprimum remedium adhibere.
>
> Periculum autem est istud. Reverendus Pater Generalis, propter frequentes molestias, contradictiones et insolentias quas sui patiuntur ab istis seditiosis, omnino statuit supplicare Vestram Sanctitatem ut sibi liceat curam hanc et gubernationem deponere. Quod si fiat, periculum est ne Collegium hoc, brevi vel nullum sit, vel, quod est peius, sit tantum habitaculum seditiosorum. Nam qui in praesenti boni sunt et obedientes statim recedent, si patres dimittantur. Ex Anglia vero ut quisquis erit bene dispositus ita ad reliqua Collegia sese conferent. Huc vero nulli nisi ut similes possint cum similibus congregari, et sic quasi altare contra altare conabuntur, idque Romae in conspectu Sanctitatis Vestrae, erigere. Scandalum vero quando isti boni simul discedent multo erit maius etiam hic Romae quam si inquieti illi et turbulenti fuissent dimissi. Et in Anglia quidem apud Catholicos nihil fere potest evenire quod eos magis affligeret. Nam inter rapinas bonorum et incarcerationes et alia incommoda quae libenter propter Christum et Sedis Apostolicae authoritatem patiuntur, hoc maxime eos consolatur quod habeant Collegia sub patrum gubernatione ad quae filios suos possunt transmittere. Hinc Hispali in Hispania 70, et Valiosoleti totidem erudiuntur; apud Sanctum Audomarum in Belgio 40 sub eadem Societate. Collegium vero Duacense, quamvis neque sit neque unquam fuerat sub eorum regimine, tamen semper fuit cum Societate iunctissimum neque sine eorum auxilio videtur mihi posse consistere. Quare humillime peto, Beatissime Pater, non meo solum nomine (nam hoc parum esset) sed nomine fratrum meorum qui in messe Anglicana cum patribus laborant et ad sanguinis usque effusionem decertant, nomine Catholicorum omnium qui ibidem versantur, nomine reliquorum omnium Collegiorum quae cum patribus sunt unitissima, etiam nomine Sanctorum martyrum qui ex Collegio Rhemensi et Romano plus quam centum prodierunt, nomine universae Ecclesiae Anglicanae peto ut Vestra Sanctitas non patiatur nos a patribus divelli, atque ut rationem habeat potius eorum omnium qui cum

patribus sunt coniuncti quam istorum paucorum qui sese non magis patribus quam reliquis collegiis opponunt."[667]

Having spoken thus much and in such sorte as His Holines well perceaved my greif and sorowe[668] and the daunger I tooke our countrie to be in, he stayed a litle before he answeared anie woorde. Then he said (I suppose to gyve me occasion to answeare the objections of others):

Putasne quod totus mundus periret, si Societas relinqueret gubernationem? Stapletonus non veniret, si ego mitterem pro illo?

667. "Now that I have kissed your holy feet and given most humble thanks for the benefits, both temporal and spiritual, recently received for the maintenance of your English college at Douai, may it please Your Holiness to allow me to indicate in a few words the very great and manifest danger facing not only the English college in Rome, but all the other colleges which have been established for the conversion of England – indeed the whole church of England – unless Your Holiness of your graciousness and prudence should deign to apply some remedy as soon as possible. The danger is just this: Reverend Father General, on account of the regular annoyances, contradictions and insults which his men suffer from those factious students, is altogether determined to appeal to Your Holiness to be allowed to lay aside this burden and government. If this should happen, there is a danger that in a short while the college would either come to nothing, or, what is worse, become nothing but a nest of rebels. For those who at present are good students and obedient will immediately depart if the fathers are dismissed. Indeed, whoever is well-disposed, coming out of England, will naturally gravitate to other colleges; none, indeed, to this one, except that those who are of like disposition will join with their fellows here and try to raise altar against altar, and that in Rome, in the sight of Your Holiness. But if those students whose conduct is good leave at once, the scandal here in Rome will be much greater even than if those discontented and turbulent students were to be dismissed. And indeed in England, amongst the Catholics, nothing could possibly happen to cause greater grief. For in the midst of the pillage of their goods, and the imprisonments, and other hardships that they freely suffer for the sake of Christ and the authority of the Apostolic See, this one thing brought them comfort, that they had colleges, under the direction of the fathers, to which they could send their sons. Hence seventy are being educated in Seville in Spain, and the same number in Valladolid, in Belgium forty in Saint-Omer, under the care of the same Society. As a matter of fact, the college of Douai, although it neither is nor has ever been under their control, has nevertheless always been very closely associated with the Society, and it seems to me that it could not survive without their help. Wherefore I most humbly beg, most holy father, not only in my own name (for that would carry little weight), but in the name of my brothers who are labouring with the fathers [of the Society] in the English harvest and carrying on the struggle even to the shedding of blood, in the name of all Catholics who are engaged in the same endeavour, in the name of all the other colleges most closely united with the fathers, in the name, especially, of the holy martyrs, more than a hundred, who have issued from the college at Rheims and the college in Rome, in the name of the whole church in England, that Your Holiness would not allow us to be separated from the fathers, and that you would attend to those who are in solidarity with the fathers rather than those few wretches who set themselves in opposition to the fathers just as much as to the rest of the colleges."

668. sorowe] sorere *Knox*; W *obscure*

Dicebam ad primum, Quo sit de toto mundo Sua Sanctitas melius possit diiudicare; de Ecclesia vero Anglicana me affirmasse et affirmare quod in conscientia coram Deo et Suam Sanctitam puto esse verum, et quicquid acciderit me in conscientia esse securum in eo quod exposuerim sententiam meam et fratrum meorum et Catholicorum in Anglia.

Ad secundum dicebam me non scire quid ipse esset facturus, quia habet ibi optimam conditionem et praeterea est senex et in literis totus versatus.

Accepi nuper literas (inquit) ex Belgio de quodam patre qui ibi dominatur et tyrannizat, et idem scribunt de patribus in Anglia.

Huic ego de patribus in Anglia dixi multa quae mihi sunt notissima, et contraria affirmavi esse suspitiones, aemulationes quorundam et calumnias. Excusavi etiam P. Holtum magis quam ipse facile putabit.

Secunda mea petitio fuit de Vice-protectore constituendo. Nominavit duos Cardinales, Baronium et Burgesium, et ex istis alterum promisit: et iam Burgesius est constitutus.

Tertia petitio, ut Protector futurus simpliciter et absolute significaret alumnis ut non cogitarent de patribus amovendis. Annuit. Quarta, ut severe admoneret ne sese immiscerent gubernationi. Hanc etiam concessit.[669]

Since, father rector[670] had verie gratiouse audience and hath wrytten to yow thereof. We are nowe in great hope that all wilbe well. This Benet is the greatest dissembler and most perilous fellowe in a communitie that ever I knewe.[671] Well I leave other thinges to father rector and Mr Baynes.[672] For Godes sake gett our pension and some certein ordere

669. "[The pope asked] 'Do you think that the whole world would perish if the Society should give up the government? Would Stapleton not come, if I sent for him?' I replied to the first point, that as far as the whole world goes, His Holiness could judge better, but in respect of the church in England, I had affirmed and still affirmed what in all conscience, before God and His Holiness, I believed to be true, and whatever happened I was at peace with my conscience in that I had explained my position and that of my brothers and the Catholics in England. To the second point I said that I did not know what Stapleton himself would do, because he enjoys an excellent situation there [in Louvain], and besides, he is an old man and utterly immersed in his studies. 'I have recently received letters from Belgium,' he said, 'about a certain [Jesuit] father who lords it over everyone and tyrannizes there, and they write the same about the fathers in England.' In response I said many things about the fathers in England which were very well known to me, and affirmed that the contrary opinions were some people's jealous suspicions and calumnies. I even excused Father Holt more than he would easily imagine. My second petition concerned the appointment of a vice-protector. He nominated two cardinals, Baronio and Borghese, and of the two he promised us one of the two: in the event, Borghese was appointed. My third petition was that the protector should simply and absolutely indicate to the students that they should not give any thought to the removal of the fathers. He assented. Fourth, that he would admonish them strictly not to interfere with the running of the college. Even this he conceded." On Borghese and Baronio, see Agazzari to Persons, 25 September 1596 (B343).

670. Alfonso Agazzari.

671. Edward Bennet. See Agazzari to Persons, 27 August 1596 (B336).

672. Roger Baynes, formerly Allen's secretary.

to have yt better payed. Our adversaries are well monied, and manteine their faction more by that meanes then anie thing els. Men followe such as are able to pleasure them. My canonrie is as good as lost.[673] Helpe me to some pension, yf yow can, to manteine my self and my man. I am loth to lyve of the college, yf I could otherwise provide. Fare yow well. Rome, the 28 of September 1596.

 Your owne
   Richard Barret.

[*Addressed*:] Admodum R^{do} in Christo patri, P. Roberto Personio, vel P. Josepho Creswello, Societatis Jesu presbyteris. Valiosoleti vel Madriti.

[*Endorsed*:] Doct. Barret, 28[674] 7^{bris}, 1596. His speech to the Pope.

B345 From Olivier Mannaerts, Brussels, 3 October 1596

SOURCE: Persons to Mannaerts, 10 January 1597 (B352).

NOTE: Mannaerts recommended that Holt be transferred from Flanders so as to defuse the conflict between the Jesuits and the Gifford/Paget group.

B346 From Diego de Yepes, San Lorenzo de El Escorial, 9 October 1596

SOURCES:
 AAW, V, no. 76, 253–256;
 ABSI, Coll P II 352a, 502;
 ABSI, Coll M 263h.

HICKS: 516a.

NOTE: Yepes was confessor to king Philip II. He refers to the executions of George Nichols, Richard Yaxley, Thomas Belson, and Humphrey Pritchard, in Oxford (not York) on 5 July 1589 (Anstruther, 250–252); they were beatified by Pope John Paul II in 1987. In the second paragraph Yepes refers to a commission Persons had given him, involving the bishop of Cuzco and Sebastián Hernández (on whom, see Acquaviva to Persons, 22 January 1590 [B48], 9 July 1590 [B69], and 31 August 1592 [B155], and Persons to Acquaviva, June 1592 [B147]).

La de Vuestra Paternidad me a sido muy agradable, a quien hago saver que estos dias e estado ocupado en leer aquella historia de Jorge martyr de Inglaterra y sus compañeros: y e me consolado tanto con ella que a hecho en mí el efecto que en el ladron de la Universidad de Oxonio: y muchos pedaços della he leydo mill vezes y en las manos tenía el libro quando llegó la carta. Deseo ver a Vuestra Paternidad antes que se vaya para suplicarle que no dexe de escrevir todas las historias que desta materia se ofrecieren, porque le hago saver que son de gran consuelo. Y e tomado ternissima aficion a los Catholicos de Inglaterra y gana de vivir entre ellos.

---

673. Barret, like Allen before him, was a canon at Rheims Cathedral (Renold, *Letters of Allen and Barret*, xix).

674. 28] 26 *Knox, Barret*; *W obscure*

En el particular del obispo del Cuzco hare todo lo que pudiere conformandome con el parecer de Vuestra Paternidad a quien suplico se acuerde de mí y de encomendarme a todos quantos Ingleses topare. Digo de los que fueren amigos de Vuestra Paternidad pues es çierto que seran sanctos, no va ésta de mi mano por el gran catarro que tengo, por cuya causa no vi al padre Sebastian Fernandez, al qual, suplico al padre dé mis encomiendas, y que por esta causa no le visité, y que deseo saver de su salud. Nuestro Señor guarde a Vuestra Paternidad como deseo. En San Lorenzo 9 de Octubre de 1596.
 Fr Diego
   de Yepes.
[*Addressed*:] Al Padre Roberto Personio en la compañia de Jesus de Madrid.
[*Endorsed*:] Fray Diego de Yepes Confessor de su Mag^d a 9 de octubre, De la historia de Ynglaterra. 1596.[675]

Translation

Your Paternity's letter was very agreeable to me. I would like you to know that these days I am busy reading that history of George the martyr of England and his companions,[676] and I am greatly encouraged by it, which has had the same effect on me as the thief of the university of Oxford;[677] some sections in it I have read a thousand times and actually I had the book in my hands when your letter arrived. I wish to see Your Paternity before you leave to beg you not to stop writing all the stories which come up related to this matter, because I can assure you that they give great consolation and have provoked a very eager fondness for the Catholics of England and a desire to live among them.

In the matter in particular of the Bishop of Cuzco,[678] I shall do all I can to conform with Your Paternity's view. Please keep me in your thoughts and commend me to all the English you meet (I mean those who are Your Paternity's friends); for I am sure they will all be saints. This letter does not come from my hands because of the great catarrh I am suffering from; for that reason, I did not go to Fr Sebastián Hernández; I have asked the father to pay him my respects, telling him the reason why I did not visit him, and that I wish to know of his health. May Our Lord bless Your Paternity as I wish. In St Lorenzo,[679] 9 October 1596.
 Fr Diego
   de Yepes.

675. A note at the foot of the page repeats the date: "9 Octob. 1596."

676. Persons's *Relacion de algunos martyrios que de nuevo han hecho los hereges en Inglaterra* (Madrid, 1590), fols. 21v–41v.

677. A "heretical youth named Arcot, an infamous thief and felon," imprisoned in Oxford, was converted thanks to the influence of Fr George Nichols: see Ribadeneira's *Ecclesiastical History of the Schism of England* 3.3, in the account of the martyrdom of Thomas Belson and George Nichols (Weinreich, 572), where it is presented as proof of Fr George's holiness.

678. Antonio de la Raya Navarrete (1536–1606), inquisitor apostolic of the kingdom of Granada, was ordained bishop of Cuzco, Peru, in November 1594. He left the English college in Seville a bequest of 4000 ducats (Murphy, 32 n16).

679. El Escorial.

B347 To William Crichton, Madrid, 2 November 1596

SOURCE: ABSI, Coll P I 318–320, a partial transcript.
HICKS: 514–520, with English translation.
EDITION: Knox, *Allen*, 384–386.
NOTE: Now in Madrid, soon to leave for Rome via Barcelona, Persons defends *Conference about the Next Succession* from Crichton's charge that it was premature and was doing damage to the English Catholic cause. Taking up Crichton's reference to the proverb about not beating a drum if you want to catch a hare, he argues that the drum is scaring off the wolf. See Victor Houliston, "The Hare and the Drum: Robert Persons's Writings on the English Succession, 1593–96," *Renaissance Studies* 14: 233–248, and McCoog, *And Touching Our Society*, 283–348.
In the text below, paragraph breaks are editorial.

Pax Christi.
Literas vestras 20° Aug. scriptas reddidit mihi hesterno die Colonellus Simplus, &c. —— Egi quoque apud Regem solicite Seminarii vestri causam, &c ——
Quod Reverentia Vestra addit tam copiose contra librum de iure successionis regiae; nollem hoc argumentum saepius inter nos tractari literis: video enim dispari affectu oculoque rem hanc nos intueri. Si una essemus, facilius fortasse in unam eandemque veniremus sententiam. Existimat Reverentia Vestra precocem fuisse libri illius editionem, dicitque ex proverbio Gallico non esse tympano capiendum leporem. Ad quod respondeo primum librum illum antequam ederetur perlectum fuisse saepius atque accurate a viris Anglicanae nationis prudentissimis qui in Hispania, Italia, Belgioque reperiebantur et fortasse et in Anglia neque illis precocem sed permaturam ac pernecessariam fuisse temporibusque accommodatissimam libri editionem visum est, adeo ut nihil hactenus scriptum fuisse utilius ad causam Catholicorum promovendam censuerint; atque si virorum nomina hic apponerem nihil eis exceptionis opponi posset.
Quod vero dictum est de tympano: si libri editionem tympanum esse Reverentia Vestra vult, dicerem tympanum hoc non esse positum ad capiendum leporem sed ad lupum potius arcendum, qui nocte cupit subingredi: cum enim lex haereticorum, qua sub laesae Maiestatis prohibetur poena ne quis aliquid decernat de successionis iure, eo pertineat ut haeretici suo tempore cum omnium iura sint obscura successorem nobis haereticum, ignorantiae huius nocte usi, obtrudant, tympani huius sonitu detegitur: Principes etiam Christiani ac Catholici hoc tympano excitantur ut videant quid cuique iuris competat, quid sibi quid reipublicae Christianae expediat praecipue vero omnium Summus Pontifex qui praeter universalem religionis tuendae causa datam ei a Domino potestatem, particulare quoque maiestatis ac supremi dominii ius in Angliam habet, quo uti legitime saluberrimeque poterit ad litem hanc difficillimam dirimendam, si omnium praetensionem iura actionesque intellexerit: Denique hoc tympano expergefient Catholici Angli ut cogitent quid sibi faciendum sit cum necessitas impulerit ut in unam alteramve partem se dent, ne res prius ad arma quam disceptationem perveniat, et praecipitare se suaque cogantur, antequam consilium de re tanta ineant. Itaque si tympanum liber hic appellandus est, non inconcinnum nec malesonorum videtur, qui tot habeat utilitates

publicas. Et quanquam Reverentia Vestra scribat de bono quod attulerit, se penitus nescire, de multis damnis certam esse: ego tamen de commodis has attulit rationes, testes etiam afferre possem locupletissimos ex Anglia qui affirmant prae caeteris libris hactenus scriptis vehementer profuisse, quod copiosius postea docebit tempus. De damnis vero nescio quid Reverentia Vestra afferat: nam quod de persecutione aucta affirmat, contrarium plane cernimus in Anglia, ubi post libri editionem, mansuetius multo actum est cum Catholicis.

De Scotia nihil amplius affirmare possum quam quod Reverentia Vestra scribit Patres duos Societatis per Regem liberatos esse, aliosque nonnullos benigne habitos: et res ipsa loquitur nam ante libri editionem Rex Scotiae Baronem Fentrium religionis Catholicae causa capite mulctandum curavit, post editionem vero libri neminem quod sciam. Neque sane est cur Rex Scotiae in Catholicos Scotos huius libri causa inhumanior fiat, qui eis non tribuitur &c. —— Fateor me cupere (regni) possessionem penes hominem notae fidei atque constantiae esse: haereticos dubiosve pro omni mea virili parte aversor. — Satis calamitatum perpessi iam sumus ob eum errorem quo Anglicani Catholici Maria regina mortua Elisabetham istam ob eam solam causam quod natione esset Angla (dubiae licet fidei) Mariae Franciae reginae Catholicae quod patria esset Scota praetulerint, quam postea tamen reginam Scotam vel capitum suorum periculis cum Angla hac commutare cupiebant. Itaque ne iterum in eundem errorem incidamus et ne iuxta evangelium posteriora fiant peiora prioribus, nullis lenociniis, nulli spei dubiae credendum iudico hac tanta in causa, sed quod summum ac praecipuum est, primo loco intuendum. Sit vere Catholicus, sit fidei probatae princeps et quacunque ex mundi parte veniat, parum refert, modo vires habeat tum adipiscendi tum etiam tuendi ac conservandi regni, Summusque Pontifex (cuius maxime omnium interest) calculo suo rem approbet: eius enim iudicium in re adeo dubia nobis regula praecipua esse debet, quid nobis quid reipublicae etiam Christianae ad maiorem Dei gloriam expediat, ad quam rem non exiguam puto lucem allaturum librum illum de quo iam diximus neque amplius habeo, quod hac de re scribam. Reverentiae Vestrae precibus etc. Madriti 2° Novemb. 1596.

Translation

The peace of Christ.

Colonel Semple[680] handed me yesterday your letter of August 20,[681] etc. —— I also pressed the cause of your seminary earnestly with the king, etc. ——

With regard to what Your Reverence goes on to say at such length against the book dealing with the right of succession to the kingdom, I would regret this matter's being discussed so often in our letters; for I see that we look at the matter with different sympathies and from a different point of view; if we were together, it would perhaps be easier for us to reach one and the same conclusion. Your Reverence thinks that the publication of that book was premature, and you quote the Gallic proverb: A hare is not to be caught

---

680. On Semple, see Persons to Acquaviva, 12 May 1594 (B230).
681. B335.

with a drum. To this I answer in the first place that, before the book was published, it had been read carefully at various times by men of English nationality, as prudent as were to be found in Spain, Italy, and Belgium and possibly in England too, and that in their opinion the book was not premature but overdue, and very much needed, and very suited to the times; so much so that nothing more useful for promoting the Catholic cause had been written up to then; and if I were to set down here the names of those men no exception could be taken to them.

Now as to what was said about a drum: if Your Reverence means to say that the publication of the book was beating a drum, I would say that the drum was not intended for the catching of hares but rather to keep off the wolf that desires to creep in by night. For that law of the heretics, whereby it is forbidden under pain of high treason for anyone to make any pronouncement about the right of succession, has this effect: that, since there is uncertainty about the rights of each one of the claimants, the heretics can take advantage of this night of ignorance and foist on us a heretic to succeed; and it is this fact that the noise of this drum exposes. Christian and Catholic princes too, by means of this drum, are stirred to examine what right resides in each of them, and what is expedient for themselves and for the Christian state; but above all else, the Supreme Pontiff, who, besides the universal authority given him by God for the purpose of guarding religion, has also in regard to England a particular right of sovereignty and supreme dominion, will be able to use this right legitimately and with much profit to decide this very difficult dispute about the succession, provided he has knowledge of the claims, rights, and proceedings of all the parties. Finally, at the sound of this drum the English Catholics will be roused to take thought what they ought to do, when necessity forces them to take one side or the other, so as not to find themselves in arms before the issue has been discussed, or be rushed into staking their lives and possessions before they can begin to take counsel about a matter of such gravity. And therefore, if this book is to be called a drum, it would seem not to be inopportune or an ill-sounding one, as it has so much general usefulness. And as for Your Reverence's saying that you are quite unaware of any good it has produced, but sure that it has done much harm – I on the other hand have gathered these conclusions as to its usefulness, and I could also produce witnesses of the highest credit from England who vouch for it that, beyond other books so far written, this one has helped exceedingly; and this time will teach us more fully. As to the harm it has done, I know not what instance you can give; for, as for what you say about an increase of persecution, we clearly see the opposite to be the case in England; for there, after the publication of the book, the Catholics were treated much more mildly.

About Scotland I can add nothing to the statement which Your Reverence makes in your letter: that two fathers of the Society have been set free by the king and some others treated kindly.[682] The facts speak for themselves; for, before the book was published, the king of Scotland had the Lord Fintry[683] beheaded on account of his Catholic faith, but no one, as far as I know, after the book was published. Nor indeed is there any reason

---

682. The Jesuits active in Scotland were Robert Abercrombie, Alexander McQuhirrie, William Murdoch, and George Elphinstone (Yellowlees, 143).

683. David Graham, laird of Fintry (ca. 1560–1592).

why the king of Scotland should become less humane to the Scottish Catholics on account of this book, as it is not laid to their charge, etc. —— I confess that I desire the possession of the kingdom to fall to a man of known faith and constancy; heretics or doubtful Catholics I abhor with all the strength of my manhood. —— We have already suffered enough misfortunes from the mistake which the English Catholics made at the death of Queen Mary when they chose this present Queen Elizabeth for the sole reason that she was an Englishwoman (though her faith was doubtful), and rejected Mary, the Queen of France, a Catholic, because Scotland was her native land. And yet after a time they were anxious to have the Scottish Queen, even at the risk of their heads, in place of this English one. Therefore, that we may not make the same mistake a second time and that, as the gospel says, our last state may not be worse than the first, it is my opinion that in this great cause we should put no trust in any blandishments, or in anyone of doubtful expectation, but look first of all to what is the main thing and of supreme importance: let him be a true Catholic prince, let him be of proved faith, and it matters little from what part of the world he comes, if only he has strength both to seize and also to protect and maintain the kingdom. Moreover, the voice of the Supreme Pontiff (whose interest it is above all others) should approve the choice; for in a matter that is so open to doubt the chief rule of conduct for us ought to be to follow his judgement as to what is best for us and for Christendom, for the greater glory of God; and to do so, I think that book of which we have been speaking will afford no little light. I have no more to say on this subject. To Your Reverence's prayers, etc. —— Madrid, 2 November 1596.

B348 To William Gifford, Madrid, 2 November 1596

SOURCE: Gifford to Persons, 20 March 1597 (B359).

NOTE: From Gifford's reply, it appears that Persons may have challenged him about his attitude to the troubles at the English college in Rome.

B349 From Camillo Caetani to Pope Clement VIII, Spain, 6 November 1596

SOURCE: AAV, Segr. Stato, Spagna 47, fol. 431, and 50, fol. 454.

HICKS: 521; "Personius commendatur a Nuntio" (referring to a handwritten note by Pollen and indicating that the document still needs to be copied).

NOTE: Patriarch Camillo Caetani (1552–1602) was the apostolic nuncio to Madrid. Evidently Persons asked him for a recommendation to the pope, before setting off for Rome later in the month; Creswell also wrote letters of recommendation to the pope and Cardinal Pietro Aldobrandini. Alternatively, this may refer to Caetani's decision to appoint Persons superior of the English residences at Lisbon and Sanlúcar on 29 November (McCoog, *Building the Faith of St Peter*, 402).

B350 To Richard Walpole, n.p., 14 November 1596

SOURCE: ABSI, Coll P II 488.
NOTE: Richard Walpole, Henry's brother, was currently at the English college in Seville. In August he had complained to Verstegan that the college needed a better library (McCoog, *Building the Faith of St Peter*, 402 n202).

[*Grene's summary*:] An et quousque liceat Anglis Catholicis bellare pro haereticis contra Hispanos.

Translation

Whether and to what extent it is lawful for English Catholics to wage war on the side of the heretics against the Spanish.

B351 To Henry Garnet, n.p., n.d. (1596/7)

SOURCE: Garnet to Persons, 10/11 June 1597 (B381).
NOTE: After his transfer from the Clink to the Tower on 12 April 1597, Gerard was interrogated about a packet of letters which he forwarded, via a middle man, to Garnet. He said they were about financial assistance to English Catholics on the continent. Caraman suggests that this was probably the cause of Gerard's transfer, that he was receiving intelligence from Persons: see Gerard, *Autobiography*, 106–107. Persons most likely sent these letters before leaving Spain.

Rome, 1597

B352 To Olivier Mannaerts, Barcelona, 10 January 1597

SOURCES:
AAW, VI, no. 4, 13–16, a contemporary copy;
ABSI, Coll P II 361, Grene's notes.
HICKS: 523–533, with English translation.
EDITION: Partly printed in Tierney, 4: lxxxiv–lxxxvi, "MS. copy in my possession, endorsed by Persons himself."
NOTE: By early January Persons had reached Barcelona, where he had a meeting with the duke of Feria, Lorenzo Suárez de Figueroa y Córdoba (1559–1607), formerly Spanish ambassador in France (1593–1595) and now viceroy of Catalonia.

Here Persons responds to Mannaerts's proposal that William Holt should be transferred from Flanders to Spain: he agrees that it is desirable for Holt's own sake and the benefit of the seminaries in Spain, but queries the wisdom of yielding to the wishes of those he regards as malicious enemies of the Society of Jesus. His portrayal of the anti-Jesuit party in Flanders anticipates much of the antagonism of the Archpriest Controversy, which would flare up the following year.

Admodum Reverende in Christo Pater
Pax Christi.

Breves a Vestra Reverentia litteras Bruxellis datas 3 Octobris accepi, longiores vidi ad patrem Cresuelum; ambas de eodem argumento, de dissidio nimirum nostratium qui istic vivunt, cui nonnullum fore remedium Reverentiae Vestrae videtur, si P. Holtus inde ad tempus amoveretur ut tempori hominumque importunitati cedamus. Ego vero tantum Reverentiae Vestrae iudicio notissimoque in nos affectui tribuo ut, si aliud nihil ad ipsum me induceret, hoc solum satis esset ad propensionem meam eliciendam, quod Reverentia Vestra ita iudicat; sed sunt praeterea alia quae a biennio iam et amplius hoc idem mihi suaserunt, et ut rem serio cum Reverendo Nostro Patre per litteras pertractarem impulerunt: — Primum, ut ipsius Patris Holti paci et quieti hac ratione consulatur desiderio etiam satisfiat, qui iam saepe idque vehementer petiit istinc educi; — deinde, quia vere eius opera valde egemus hic in Hispania, et utriusque seminarii rectorumque votis plurimum expetitur; — tertio quoque, quia cum Pater Cresuelus rerum Hispanicarum non exiguum iam usum comparaverit, linguamque calleat, neque desit illi suavitas illa agendi quam Vestra Reverentia requirit in Patre Holto, forsitan, ut Vestra Reverentia dicit, ad tempus aliquod gratior atque acceptior quibusdam videretur, quamvis nullo modo sperem illum pacis fructum secuturum apud eos qui Patrum Holtum amovendum curant, quem Vestra Reverentia sibi proponit, cum multorum annorum experientia certissimaque ratione mihi constet, istos non hunc vel illum patrem sed Societatem impetere; de quo postea.

Romae inquieti Patrem Edmundum Harodum Anglum, collegii confessorem, amoveri postulabant eaque re omnia fore pacata, sed eo amoto turbulentiora fuere omnia, quia inquieti palam in totam Societatem insurrexerunt. Nunc tantum aio me his causis motum de mutatione Patris Holti cum Nostro Patre et cum ipso Patre Holto diu tractasse atque statim iterum me tractaturum cum Romam venero; iam enim in itinere hoc scribo causamque itineris prioribus litteris Vestrae Reverentiae me significasse memini, voluntatem nimirum Reverendi Nostri Patris Generalis, horumque seminariorum Hispanicorum negotia quaedam necessaria quae, nisi cum Sua Sanctitate ac Nostro Patre rite transigantur, damnum patientur seminaria; spero me, Domino bene iuvante, brevi omnia confecturum ac in Hispanias rediturum; ea enim conditione hinc discedo, nisi obedientia superiorum aliud statuerit. Atque haec de his.

Et quanquam haec ita se habeant propositumque sit mihi serio rem, ut dixi, cum Reverendo Patre Nostro tractandi negare tamen non possum magnas se mihi difficultates in re exequenda offerre, hoc maxime tempore, quas Reverentiae etiam Vestrae proponam.

Prima est quod Dux Feriensis ac Stephanus de Yvarra, ministri regii qui nuper istinc e Belgio venerunt, mihi fassi sunt se in instructionibus vel advertentiis quas regis mandato serenissimo Archiduci Cardinali de statu Belgii reliquerunt id primo loco inter caetera affirmasse Societatem vehementer rebus regis utilem esse, ideoque expedire ut quacumque ratione promoveatur; deinde vero in rebus Anglicanis, quae maxime hoc tempore regis interest ut bene tractentur, Patrem Holtum prae caeteris omnibus audiendum esse, ob experientiam fidemque ac prudentiam in agendo, neque aemulos eius ulla ratione audiendos esse ut e Belgio amoveatur; atque id ipsum regi tum litteris tum sermone retulerunt; ex quo quid nobis difficultatis ad hanc mutationem accesserit, Vestra Reverentia facile videt.

Secunda difficultas etiam recens nata est, quod, ex sermone Summi Pontificis cum Doctore Bareto, seminarii Duacensis rectore, nuper intellectum est, istos ipsos qui amotionem Patris Holti apud Reverentiam Vestram, caeterosque patres nostros pacis specie sollicitant ad Sanctitatem Suam scripsisse, non tantum contra Patrem Holtum sed etiam contra omnes Societatis patres qui in Anglia versantur; affirmantes eos clero reliquo dominari, imo omnibus per tyrannidem imperitare (quod etiam de Patre Holto nominatim assuerunt), hacque ipsa de causa omnes esse amovendos, quod etiam istorum exemplo atque suasu scolares nonnulli Romani, ab istis eorumque complicibus ad rebellionem excitati, per memorialia petierunt atque affirmarunt maximo iniquissimoque mendacio; cum patres illi non nisi omnium commodis inserviant et horum etiam ingratissimorum inter caeteros et prae ceteris quod de Patre Holto vere affirmare possum qui suis litteris saepe ac vehementer causam eorum egit in curia Hispanica qui maxime eum impugnant.[1]

1. *Tierney omits from here to* Atque haec *below*

Sed haec Reverentia Vestra mirari non debet, in tanta enim causa quanta est Anglicani regni reductio, et in tanta penuria, egestate, libertate, ac otio hominum exulum ac afflictorum, atque in tanta astutia haereticorum qui per emissarios suos has lites fovent, non est mirandum si haec accidant; inter alias etiam nationes quae extra patriam vivunt, si multi sunt egentes, sui iuris et sine ulla subordinatione, aemulationes rixae ac dissidia quotidie oriuntur quia mendici de obulo dimicant, et qui animo amaro est facile ad querelas ac rixas inducitur, sed haec virum pium ac prudentem neque avertere neque decipere debent. Satis est ut videat quae pars rationem sequatur, quae vero passionem quod in nostra causa clarissimum est: ex una enim parte sunt omnes patres Societatis Anglicanae nationis valde uniti per Dei gratiam, fuit etiam Cardinalis Alanus dum viveret, sunt sacerdotes omnes seminariorum exceptis paucis discolis quos isti alii corruperunt, sunt Catholici meliores domi forisque, extant etiam opera erectio ac conservatio seminariorum plusquam sexcenti sacerdotes novi, martires plusquam centum et triginta confessores plusquam ducenti, haeretici conversi infiniti libri scripti plurimi; ex alia parte paucissimi sunt inquieto ingenio homines, sine spiritu, et quanquam Reverentiae Vestrae maior fortasse pars videantur eorum qui istinc Bruxellis resident, tamen si cum ceteris componantur qui vel per universum Belgium vivunt vel alibi morantur, exiguo valde numero sunt; atque adeo sensibus inter se divisi quod licet ob eas quas dixi causas, in hoc uno contra Patrem Holtum et Societatem nostram conspirent, quod nos eorum necessitatibus opitulari posse putent, in nullo tamen alio fere conveniunt, id unum aegre ferentes: quod nos qui ex Societate sumus tam unanimes simus in rebus omnibus, cumque Patres Anglos disrumpere aut inter se collidere aliorum hominum more non possint, adeunt patres aliarum nationum, qui rerum hominumque notitiam tantam non habent ac praecipue si quos ob nationis discrimen minori esse affectu suspicantur hosque vel clamoribus ac minis vel argumentis ac querelis falsis aut etiam adulatione inducere conantur, ut vel affectu vel iudicio saltem a nobis discrepent, putant enim (quod etiam verum est) nullum tam efficacem patere eis aditum ad nos fatigandos quam si nostros a nobis separent.

Atque[2] haec quidem Reverentiae Vestrae, occasione hac oblata, dicere volui, non quod omni conatu illud non prosequi velim quod Reverentia Vestra proposuit de mutatione Patris Holti cum Reverendo Patre Nostro Generali, sed ut Reverentia Vestra intelligat quare spem exiguam habeam futurae pacis ex hac mutatione, nisi Dominus rerum et animorum immittat mutationem; quod summis ab eo precibus peto. Nihil omittam Deo volente dum Romae fuero, quod ad pacem hanc procurandam pertinere posse videatur, neque hactenus omisi. Et si quid Reverentiae Vestrae, vel etiam Reverendo Patri Provinciali (cum quo hanc epistolam eo secreto quo convenit communicari desidero) occurrat, quod a me fieri debere iudicant huius pacis conciliandae vel firmandae gratia, libere me admoneant, ero enim obsequentissimus, tantum enim a Reverentias Vestras humiliter peto ut pro sua prudentia videant ne hae voces hominum inquietorum contra patres Societatis apud nostros facilius admittantur, quam ratio et aequitas ferat, inaudita aliorum causa; inde enim magnum damnum et scandalum quoque tandem sequeretur.

2. *Tierney resumes here*

Quod ad Patris vero Holti modum agendi (quousque negotium de mutatione cum Reverendo Patre nostro transigatur) pertinet, si asperior est quam Reverentiae Vestrae videatur expedire, aut nimium invidiae aut emulationi pateat, ut Reverentia Vestra significat, non dubito quin una vestra admonitione Pater Holtus pro ea quam erga Vestram Reverentiam observantia habet in alteram partem facillime se flectet. Ego etiam eadem ipsa de re ad eum scribo, nimirum ut quacunque poterit ratione omnes consoletur, omnes lucretur, invidiam ex modo agendi vitet. A Reverentia autem Vestra peto, ut non gravetur iterum iudicium suum mihi Romae significare de universo hoc negotio, ut maturius statuatur quod ad maiorem Dei gloriam pertineat. Sanctis vestrae reverentiae sacrificiis humiliter me commendo. Barchenoni, 10 Januarii, 1597.

    Servus in Christo
        Robertus Personius.

[*Endorsed*]: Exemplar literarum 10 Jan. 1597 ad P. Oliverium de mutatione P. Holti.
[*Endorsed by Persons*:] 10 Januar. 1597

Translation

Very Reverend Father in Christ
The peace of Christ.

I received a short letter from Your Reverence written from Brussels on October 3,[3] and I have seen a longer one which you wrote to Fr Creswell. Both deal with the same subject, that is, of the dissension among our countrymen who are living there; and it is Your Reverence's opinion that it would go some way to remedying this if Fr Holt were moved from there for a time, thus making a concession to circumstances and men's importunity. Now, I have such regard for Your Reverence's judgement and for your affection for us, which is so well-known, that, even if there were no other reason to persuade me to this very course, the fact of this being Your Reverence's judgement would be enough in itself to incline me to it. But there are other reasons besides, which for two years and more now have moved me to this same conclusion and impelled me to discuss this change in earnest with our father general, namely: first, that in this way Fr Holt's own peace of mind may be considered, and indeed satisfaction be given to his desire, for he has often and urgently begged to be taken away from there; second, because we really need his help very much here in Spain, and it is the wish of each of the seminaries and their rectors to have him. Also, there is the third reason that, since Fr Creswell has now become somewhat versed in Spanish affairs, and is fluent in the language, and is not without that tactfulness which Your Reverence finds lacking in Fr Holt, he would seem likely perhaps, as Your Reverence says, to be for a certain length of time more pleasing and acceptable to some of them. All the same I would not entertain any hope at all that it would bring about that fruit of peace, as Your Reverence supposes, given who they are who seek Fr Holt's removal: from many years' experience and for most compelling reasons I am convinced that they are attacking not this father or that, but the Society. More about that later.

3. B345.

In Rome the dissatisfied students demanded that the Englishman Fr Edmund Harewood, confessor of the college,[4] should be removed, claiming that then everything would be settled. But once he was gone, there was more disturbance than ever, because it was against the whole Society that the disturbers of the peace had openly revolted. Now all I have to say is that, moved by these reasons, I have been mooting Fr Holt's transfer with our father general for a long time already, and with Fr Holt himself, and I am going to broach the matter again as soon as I get to Rome; for I am writing this while already on my way there; and I remember that I explained the reasons for my journey to Your Reverence in previous letters: namely, our reverend father general's wish, and some urgent business of these Spanish seminaries; for if this is not duly transacted with His Holiness and father general, the seminaries will suffer. I hope, with God's good help, that I shall quickly complete it all and return to Spain, for it is on this understanding that I am leaving – unless my superiors decree otherwise. So much for that.

And although this is how matters stand and it is my serious intention to raise the matter, as I have said, with our reverend father general, yet I cannot deny that there are great difficulties standing in the way of my carrying it out, especially at this moment, and these I will put before Your Reverence also.

The first difficulty is that the duke of Feria and Esteban de Ibarra, the ministers of the king who have lately come from you in Belgium,[5] have informed me that in the instructions or memoranda on conditions in Belgium which they left for His Serene Highness the cardinal archduke by order of the king,[6] they laid special stress on this, among other things mentioned: that the Society was of great value to the king's affairs, and that therefore it was advisable to promote its interests in every way; and they went on to say that in the affairs of England, which it is extremely important to the king to have properly dealt with just at the moment, Fr Holt ought to be listened to in preference to all others, on account of his experience and trustworthiness and his prudence in dealing with them; and that no satisfaction was to be given to those who opposed him, by having him removed from Belgium. And this too was the report they made both by letter and by word of mouth to the king. And therefore, how much this has added to the difficulty of making the change, Your Reverence can easily see.

A second difficulty has lately arisen, too: from a conversation which Dr Barret, rector of the seminary at Douai, had with the Supreme Pontiff, it has recently been learnt that those very people who, under the plea of peace, are calling for Fr Holt's removal with Your Reverence and with the rest of our fathers have written to His Holiness attacking not only Fr Holt but all the fathers of the Society besides who are occupied in England. They declare that they are lording it over the rest of the clergy, that indeed they are issuing tyrannical commands on all sides (and they make this assertion expressly too

4. Harewood was in fact the minister rather than the confessor at the college.
5. Esteban de Ibarra (or Yvarra) Emparán (ca. 1538–1610), secretary to the council of the Spanish Netherlands.
6. Archduke Albert was elevated to the status of a cardinal in 1577 without ever taking holy orders. He was appointed cardinal archbishop of Toledo in 1594, but resigned in 1598 when he became sovereign of the Spanish Netherlands (having been governor-general from 1596). He married Isabella Clara Eugenia, the infanta of Spain, in 1599.

about Fr Holt), and they say that for this reason they ought all to be withdrawn; and some of the scholars in Rome, following their example and persuasion, stirred up to rebellion by them and their accomplices, have sought the same object by means of memorials, and have affirmed it by an enormous and most flagrant lie. For those fathers are only serving the interests of all, even of the most ungrateful among them, putting them first; this I can truly vouch for in the case of Fr Holt in particular, who by his letters has often strongly urged in the court of Spain the cause of those who are the foremost to attack him. But this should not surprise Your Reverence: for, in an issue of such importance as the conversion of the kingdom of England, and where there is such poverty and want, such freedom of action and leisure among men in exile and distress, and with the heretics so cunning to nurse these quarrels by means of their spies, it is not to be wondered at that such things occur. With men of other nations too who live outside their native land, if many of them are in want, are laws unto themselves and owe obedience to no one, jealousies, quarrels, and dissensions daily spring up, for beggars fight over a copper, and an embittered mind is easily inclined to quarrels and complaints. But such things ought not to repel or deceive anyone of piety and discretion; it is sufficient for them to examine which party is guided by reason and which by passion; and, in our case, this is very evident: for on the one hand we have – by the grace of God – the closely united band of English fathers of the Society – Cardinal Allen too so long as he lived – along with all the priests from the seminaries, apart from a few malcontents whom these others have corrupted. They are the worthiest Catholics at home and abroad; their works too are in evidence: the erection and maintenance of the seminaries, more than six hundred new priests, more than a hundred and thirty martyrs, more than two hundred confessors, countless heretics converted, numerous books written. On the other hand are a handful of men of restless spirit, without initiative; and although it may seem to Your Reverence that these represent the greater part of those who are living there in Brussels, yet, in comparison with the others who are scattered throughout the whole of Belgium or dwelling elsewhere, they make up a meagre number and are so divided in opinion among themselves that, in spite of being united in this one matter of conspiring against Fr Holt and the Society for the reasons I have mentioned, that is to say, because they imagine that it is in our power to relieve their needs, they agree in scarcely any other matter. This one thing they resent: that we of the Society are in such full agreement on all matters;[7] and, since like other men they are unable to break up or set at variance the English fathers like other men, they approach the fathers of other nations who have not so great a knowledge of men and affairs – especially if they suspect them, on account of difference of nationality, to be less in sympathy with us – and these fathers they try to induce either by clamours and threats or by argument and unfounded complaints, or even by flattery, to be parted from us either in sympathy or at least in opinion; for they think – and this is true – that there is no more efficacious way of wearing us down available to them than by alienating us from Ours.

7. This was meant to be a hallmark of the Society: see *The Constitutions of the Society of Jesus*, ed. George E. Ganss (St Louis, 1970), 285 (no. 655) and 337 (no. 825), cited by McCoog, *And Touching Our Society*, 262.

And indeed it is not because I would not make every effort to obtain from our reverend father general what Your Reverence has proposed with regard to Fr Holt's removal that I wished to take advantage of the opportunity which has arisen, to tell Your Reverence this, but in order that you may know why it is that I have slender hopes of peace from this change, unless God should cause a change of conditions and dispositions – something I am begging Him to do with most earnest prayer. I will leave nothing undone, God willing, while I am in Rome, that looks as if it may help to procure this peace; nor have I left anything undone up to now. And if anything occurs to Your Reverence or even to father provincial[8] – and I wish you to show him this letter with due secrecy – which you consider I ought to do for the sake of bringing about peace or making it more secure, please do not hesitate to advise me; for I shall be most eager to comply. But this one thing I humbly beg of Your Reverences, that you would in your prudence see to it that this clamour of disaffected men against the fathers of the Society is not admitted among Ours more readily than reason and justice demand, and without hearing the other side. For if this is done, great harm, and scandal as well, will eventually follow.

And now about Fr Holt's behaviour (until such time as the negotiation with father general goes through for his removal): if it is more abrasive than Your Reverence deems fitting, or if it exposes him too much to dislike and bad feeling, as Your Reverence suggests, I have no doubt that a single admonition from you will be enough, in view of the respect he has for Your Reverence, to ensure that he will readily turn himself in another direction. I too am writing him to the very same effect, that is, that in every possible reasonable way he ought to conciliate everybody, win everybody over, and avoid provoking enmity by his way of proceeding. And finally, I ask of Your Reverence that you not hold back from telling me your views about all this matter when I am in Rome, so that it may the sooner be determined what tends to the greater glory of God. I commend myself humbly to Your Reverence's holy Sacrifices. Barcelona, 10 January 1597.

Your servant in Christ
Robert Persons.

B353 From Thomas Worthington, Brussels, 10 January 1597

SOURCE: AAW, VI, no. 5, 17–20, holograph.

NOTE: Thomas Worthington (1549–1626) trained at Douai and was closely associated with Allen. In 1589 he became vice president at Douai but clashed with Richard Barret, the president. He then moved to Brussels and Louvain to work on the text of the Douai Old Testament. See Albert J. Loomie, "Worthington, Thomas" (*ODNB*). In 1595 he and William Percy wrote a memorandum to Enrico Caetani, the cardinal protector, supporting the Jesuit authorities at the English College, Rome (Kenny, "Glorious Revolution," 77–78 [part 3]). In his memorandum of 30 August 1596 (B340) regarding the projected enterprise of England, Persons recommended him for a bishopric.

It appears from this letter that Worthington spent several years trying to decide on his vocation, under the guidance of Allen. He now turns to Persons for advice. Unusually, the letter is addressed to "Roberto Parsonio."

8. George Duras.

Most deare and reverend father

Some foure or five yeares agoe, I did impert unto Your Reverence that I had long before that time bound my selfe by expresse vowe, to folowe, and to indevoure (by the assistance of Gods grace) to fulfill the direction of our late Cardinall (of blessed memory) howe, and wheresoever it should seme good to him to appoint me, or to imploy my poore labours, not doubting but the same should be to Gods honour, and better assurance of myn owne salvation. Which vowe and promise made to God, I trust I never notoriously nor wittingly violated, so long as he lived, for so long it did binde me. And truly I found therby (I thank God for it) not only a singular great ease in anie consultation pertaining to my selfe, but also a verie good warrant, as me thought, in all my actions of greatter importance, and no small consolation, quietnes of mind, and peace of conscience, and the like frutes. The consideration wherof caused me even in his liffe time, to purpose to renewe and continue this vowe towardes some other discrete, wise, and Godlike man, if God should take my present superior out of this world before me. And much more I thought to performe this, when in deede God had taken him from me, and from manie, to whom he was a loving father and patron. And[9] so upon the feast of S. Thomas the Martyr, next folowing, (as I trust) to Gods honour, and of our Blessed Ladie, etc., I appointed my selfe two yeares for probation (to the invitation of your Societie) meaning and purposing in the end of the same two yeares to bind my selfe by like vowe, unto Your Reverence, as before I had donne to the good Cardinall, which vowe this last feast of the same St Thomas I have confirmed (I thank God for it) by vowe and promise to God, *in manu confessarii*, who was the rector of your college in Lovain.[10] Who only knoweth this my vowe as yet and no other mortall creature. He asked me, if you knewe of it. I answered, that no, but that I do absolutly bind my selfe, so long as we both shall live in this world, with this one exception, that I am frie to enter, or not to enter into Religion, as I shall be effectually called or not called of God therunto. For as this simple vowe can not hinder me, so my will is not to be bound therto by vertue herof, if you should so direct me. And as for your accepting of this charge over me, I told my strict ghostlie father that I would nowe signifie it unto you, and desire you so to accept me, and that I trust, that of your charitie, you so will. If not, I will notwithstanding for lack of your direction endevoure to folowe your inclination so farre as I can lerne it, in all myn actions of importance. He advised me to write my vowe and kepe it, with my selfe. Which I have donne and here declared to you the summe, and substance therof.

Nowe in all dutifull humilitie, I beseech you for Gods sake thus to accept me into your particular charge, to direct, command and governe me as your subject, in God. It shalbe I trust no newe burden unto you, for you have had still a particular care of me, since I first found you in Rome *anno 79* but especially since you received me with others at Rohan, when we were caried oute of prison in England into a newe banishment *anno 85*.[11]

9. And] *this ed.*; An W

10. Possibly referring to Thomas Stapleton, whose lectures, *Orationes academica* (Antwerp, 1600), Worthington would later edit for publication.

11. Worthington visited Rome with Allen in October 1579; later, he was captured in England, kept in the Tower of London, and banished along with Jasper Heywood and other priests in January 1585 (Anstruther, 387–388). The priests were subsequently succoured by Persons in Rouen (see vol. 1: 557).

It is to me no newe yoke, for I was at your comandment ever since the former of these times mentioned, so farre as could stand with my former vowe, as in deede it stood alwayes right well, for that my Lord Cardinall and your selfe concurred right in imploying me, at least so farre as was intimated unto me, by either of you. So that with confidence to obtaine and with present consolation of future fruit I make this above-mentioned petition, for Gods sake and for our Blessed Ladies, my particular Angel, and particular Patron S. Thomas the Martyr, and for all Santes sake. Thus doing I trust God will adde it to the heape of all your other merites. And then I request agreably herunto that you will assigne me some, by whom I shall be directed here, or in anie other place distant from you, and in your absence. In the meane time, I suppose you will have me to take and folowe Fr Holts direction as your owne, who knoweth, as farre as I can make him knowe or as a mortall man can morally knowe, myn estate, myn inclinations, my small talents, and imperfections. One only thing I am further bold to signifie at this time, that I have an inclination to returne into[12] England, which I have often manifested to Fr Holt and so partly to some others, yet my motives therunto are not so perfect as I would they were, for they are especially these two: want of competent meanes to live here, and litle fruit of my labours in this place, which together with my weakness of bodie and mind (as Fr Holt seeth and knoweth) make me mervelous drearie of this place, and to thinck often, yea dayly and nightly, of the consolations and fruit which I found in England, when I conversed there, and used my function as that place and time permitted. This and all other my desires, griefes, inclinations and whatsoever I referre simply to your judgement and decision. Finally (yet most especially) I crave your prayers, for Gods grace. In myn (such as they be) especially in the Holie Sacrifice, I commend you everie day. And so will continue, God willing. For my nephewes, God will also reward you I doubt not, God make us alwayes gratefull, to whom I commend you, and all your laboures. Bruxels, the 20 of Januarii 97.

    Your Reverences all and for ever
        Thomas Worthington.

[PS] Though I endorse this to you only, yet after your selfe shall have read it, it is in your powre, to communicate the contents, all, or part, at your good discretion, where you suppose it may do good, and no hurt. But before I understand your mind herein, I meane not to communicat it to anie, no not to F. Holt.

[*Addressed:*] Admodum Reverendo in Christo Patri: Patri Roberto Parsonio, Societatis Jesu a ipsi soli.

[*Endorsed:*] D. Worth. 10 Jan 1597. About the vowe that he made to F. Persons.

B354 From Henry Garnet, London, 18 February 1597

    SOURCE: ABSI, Coll P II 548, Grene's excerpts.
    HICKS: Garnet, 418.
    NOTE: Garnet reports on the satisfaction at court about the conflicts between Jesuits and seminarians in Rome and complains that two priests have arrived in England to spread anti-Jesuit sentiment. These would seem to be Sylvester Norris (d. 1630) and Richard But-

---

12. into] *W, obscure*

ton (ca. 1570–post 1643), who were despatched from Rome by the vice-protector Cardinal Toledo on 17 May 1596, and proceeded from Flanders to England in October of that year (see Persons's *Relación* on the disturbances in the English college, 22 May 1597, B378; Kenny, "Inglorious Revolution," 80–81 [part 3]; Anstruther, 60, 255–257; Edwards, 201). Grene identifies two others instead: "The two priests names seem to be *fisher* and *Dudley* as appeares by other letters"; Robert Fisher came to England after visiting Paget, Gifford, and others in Flanders, arriving before Norris (Barret to Persons, 10 August 1597, B338; Renold, *Wisbech Stirs*, 252), and Richard Dudley had been in England since 1591. He tried to arbitrate at Wisbech in 1595 (John Cecil to Persons, 1 November 1591, B126; Renold, *Wisbech Stirs*, 118 and *passim*).

Great speeches and joy there are in the court of dissension between English seminarists at Rome and the Jesuits, &c. (bad reports against the Jesuits by two priests that went to England in September 1596, &c.)[13]

B355 From Henry Garnet, London, 23 February 1597

SOURCE: ABSI, Coll P II 548, Grene's summary.
HICKS: Garnet, 419.
NOTE: Garnet refers to the attempt by John Mush, Christopher Bagshaw, and others, in alliance with Button and Norris, to set up two clerical associations with the aim of instituting order and hierarchy among the secular priests: see Lake and Questier, *All Hail to the Archpriest*, 54–57. Garnet gives further details in his letter of 28 May (B379).

De sodalitatibus duabus quas praetendebant instituere sacerdotes saeculares.

Translation

About the two sodalities which the secular priests were proposing to institute.

B356 To Roger Baynes, Villefranche-sur-Mer, 4 March 1597

SOURCE: ARSI, Angl. 38/II, fol. 197v.
HICKS: 534–35, with English translation.
NOTE: From Barcelona, Persons travelled to Cervera (now Cerbère, on the French side of the border with Spain) and crossed the gulf of Lion to Villefranche-sur-Mer, in the duchy of Savoy. Here he describes his illness on the journey from Spain and asks for Agazzari to meet him at Civitavecchia.

Quatuor menses insumpsimus in hoc itinere a discessu ex oppido Madritensi – omnes, Deo favente, bene valemus, licet bis ipse aegrotaverim in hoc itinere, et bis sanguinem

13. It is unclear whether the previous material in brackets is part of Garnet's letter, or Grene's summary or addition.

emiserim ex visceribus et semel medicinam sumpserim Barcinone et rursus emiserim sanguinem in Colibre ultimo Hispaniae portu, ubi febre continua laboravi et ausus sum in hoc statu mari me committere, et Deus (cui gratias debeo) febri me liberavit in sinu maris (nel golfo) ubi alii ceperunt aegrotari.

[Cupit ut P. Alphonsus obviam illi eat versus Centumcellos Civita Vecchia, ut colloqui simul possent[14] antequam Romam veniat, &c.]

Translation

We have been four months on this journey, since we left the city of Madrid. By the favour of God, all of us are in good health, though I have been ill myself twice during this journey, and twice have passed blood (from my bowels) and on one occasion took medicine at Barcelona and again passed blood at Cervera, our last port in Spain. I suffered from continuous fever there, and even dared to entrust myself to the sea in that state; and the Lord – to whom my thanks are due – freed me from the fever while on the bosom of the sea (in the gulf), where the others began to be ill.

[He desires that Fr Alfonso should come and meet him towards Centumcelli, at Civitavecchia, so that they can confer together before he comes to Rome.]

B357 To William Holt, Genoa, 15 March 1597

SOURCES:

London, Inner Temple, Petyt Collection, MS 538, vol. 38, no. 123, fols. 358 and 359, contemporary fair copies, in English (= *T1, T2*);

AAW, VI, nos. 17, 20–21, Persons's holograph translation from English into Italian, with annotations (= *W*);

ABSI, Anglia A II, item 24, a contemporary fair copy of the Italian translation (= *A*);

ABSI, Coll P I 294–297, Grene's transcription of the Italian translation, "copiata dalla propria scrittura del P. Personio" (= *G*).

HICKS: 536–541, the Italian version, with Hicks's English translation.

EDITION: Partly printed in Tierney, 3: lvii–lix, "MS in the handwriting of Persons, in my possession."

NOTE: Persons gives his reasons for visiting Rome – to deal with the troubles of the English college and persuade Clement VIII to come to an agreement with Philip II over the English succession – and invites Holt to give his opinion on the succession. He is planning to return to Spain before long.

Later, Persons introduced parts of the letter in *A Manifestation of the Great Folly and Bad Spirit of Certayne in England Calling Themselves Secular Priestes* (Antwerp, 1602), fols. 48v–49v, to expose his opponents' "calumniations" in the Archpriest Controversy of 1598–1602. He claimed that a copy was "stolne afterward (as it seemeth) from *F. Holt* and given to

---

14. possent] *R*; possint *Hicks*

his adversayes, which in some places they have shewed, and is like to be that which heere they brag of, saying; *that his owne books & handwrytings wilbe brought out as witnesses against him.* But hitherto they are not brought or alleadged, and it semeth that this in particular wherof we have the copie serveth not their turnes so much, as they dare to alleadge it, finding more sincerity, wisdome and gravity conteyned therin (though wrytten in secret and confidence where he might utter himself boldly) than their malignant envy will suffer them to be glad to see, which yet we be inforced in this place through their malignity, not to thinke amisse to acquaint somwhat the Reader therwith" (see fol. 48v). As Tierney notes (p. lxvii n1), he omitted the passage in which he expresses his personal preference for the infanta. This may have been because the preference is qualified in the letter below, whereas in 1602 there was no longer any hope of James VI's conversion and Persons would no longer need to restrain his commendation of the infanta.

Persons's Italian translation (*W*), made presumably to defend himself to the papal curia, appends hostile annotations (item 20), made (according to the heading) by Dr William Percy. Percy and Henry Constable composed a memorial in favour of the claims of James VI to the succession, which was distributed in Rome in 1601: see McCoog, *Lest Our Lamp be Entirely Extinguished*, 331–332, and Anstruther, 272. Percy's annotations must have been written after the death of Philip II (referred to as "il Re defunto" [*Anot. 10*]) and before the resignation of Patriarch Camillo Caetani as nuncio to Spain, on 24 March 1600 (*Anot. 7*).

The annotations and responses represent in miniature the vehement public debate between Persons and his opponents in the Archpriest Controversy. They also illustrate the interpenetration of scribal and printed texts, as noted in Lake and Questier, *All Hail to the Archpriest*, 137–145.

The text exists in several versions. The scribal copies in the Petyt collection of the Inner Temple (*T1* and *T2*) were hastily copied, probably for Richard Bancroft, bishop of London. Bancroft was compiling a large dossier of materials related to the English Jesuits and various priests, some of whom were to ally themselves with the appellants' party: see Patrick Collinson, "Bishop Richard Bancroft and the Succession," in *Doubtful and Dangerous: The Question of Succession in Late Elizabethan England*, ed. Susan Doran and Paulina Kewes (Manchester, 2014), 92–111, esp. 99–104 and 109–110 n37; Renold, *Wisbech Stirs*, xviii–xxii; and Law, *Archpriest Controversy*, 1: xxvi–xxvii.

The Inner Temple copies contain many errors, including the date, and use the spelling "Parsons," associated with Persons's opponents, such as William Bishop (see the endorsement). The copy at the Westminster archives (*W*), in Persons's hand, is an Italian translation, presumably his own; there is a contemporary scribal copy in the Anglia manuscripts at the Jesuit archives in London (*A*), as well as Grene's transcription (*G*). Persons's version in *Manifestation* contains several minor variations, the more significant of which are recorded here.

G, which often modernizes the spelling, also includes the annotations, with many omissions and variations. In *W*'s Italian text, underlining indicates the *lemmata* for Percy's annotations. In our edition, the annotation number has been inserted in square brackets, both in the English original and in the Italian. It will be noted that Persons began listing the annotations as letters (A–C) and then changed to numbers (4–11) from p. 64.

A not for fa: Holt & such confident freendes as he shall thinke good
to communicat the same

The principall causes of this my jorny are to settle with his holines and fa. Generall all such poyntes as shall seeme necessarie for the upholdinge of the Seminaryes of Spayne, Flanderes, and Italie, and of the missiones[15] of the Societie to Ingland [Annot. A.] And therefore what so ever shall offer it selfe unto yow about any of these poyntes (to witte) for faculties, government, privileges, mayntenances or the like, I praye yow and other frindes to advertise[16] me with the best speed that may be, for I meane to procure that my abode in Italie be as lytel as may be, and so I have promised in Spayne and for dyvers reasons it will be necessarie.

If I cane doe any good also in compounding or accordinge[17] the troubles of the Inglishe Romayne Semynary and of our contraverses betwen those of our nation els wher, I shall do my best, at least I hope I shall make his holines & other principall parties understand the true causes and grounds therof [Annot. B].[18]

About the affayres of Ingland I meane to show to the Pope how things doe stand, and what necessite ther is, that his hollines thinke seriously of the matter with speed, lest after the Queene of Ingland it come into worse handes, the perilles & inevitable daungers, & domages[19] that will ensew if any hereticall prince what[20] so ever prevail,[21] that Inglishe Catholikes do desire onlie a sincer Catholike kinge [Annot. C] without respect of Inglishe, Scottishe or Spanishe, and that in this they depend principally of his holiness.[22] That Fr Parsones[23] is not an enimie to the king of Scotland, nor[24] agent for the King of

15. missiones] MSS; mission Manifestation
16. advertise] MSS; advise Manifestation
17. accordinge] MSS; ending Manifestation
18. Manifestation breaks off here, commenting: "By these two first points we may see that F. Persons jorney to Rome was neyther in post (as these men say, being 5 or 6 monethes in coming) nor to cause the book of English titles to be read in the Refectory (as fondly heere is devised) about which whole matter of succession, he speaketh in his letter so temperately and indifferently, as may shame his adversaryes to alleadge it, for he saith in substance. That he meaneth to proceed therin very softly and coldly, letting his Hol. only to know how matters do stand ... ." Persons refers here to a claim made by William Watson that "he came in post to Rome and would needs have the book of Tytles read in the Refectory of the Colledge if it had not byn resysted" (fol. 47v, paraphrasing Watson's "Epistle Generall" to Thomas Bluet, Important considerations, which ought to move all true and sound-Catholikes ... that the proceedings of Her Majesty ... have bene both mild and mercifull, London, 1601, sig. ***1r).
19. Harms or inconveniences.
20. what] om. T2
21. Manifestation resumes here, introduced as follows: "& that English Catholikes do onlie desire (after her Majestie) some sincere Catholike Prince ..."
22. and that in this they depend principally of his holiness] or other nation in respect of religion Manifestation
23. Parsones] Persons Manifestation (and passim)
24. nor] or T2

Spaine [*Annot. 4*] as some have informed, showinge in the first what offices Fr Parsones[25] hath don for the King of Scotland for many yeares whiles there was hope that he would be Catholike, and in the second, showinge by testemonie[26] of the nuncio of Madrid[27] (who hath wryten effectually in[28] that behalfe) that Fr Parsones hath alwayes perswaded the kinge & his ministers[29] that it will not stand well for his Majestie to pretend England for him selfe [*Annot. 5*], and that Fr Parsones hath obtayned of the kinge of Spayne full promise thereof [*Annot. 6*], about which poynt the nuncio hath seene the papers [*Annot. 7*],[30] & hath ben privie to the speeches which Fr Parsones from tyme to tyme hath had unto[31] that effect.[32] And finally the conclusion must be that the only way were, that his hollines should agree with the kinge of Spaine [*Annot. 8*] upon some reasonable composition for some person that would be fit, & stand well both for his hollines, his Majestie Catholike, English Catholikes, Scotishe, kinge of Navarre, kinge of Denmarke,[33] and all the rest. But who that persone, or persones be, Fr Parsones meaneth to suffer his Hollines to thinke[34] & breake his head for a tyme [*Annot. 9*], but in my opinion there were no such composition more profitable, probabel, and factible,[35] then the Infanta [*Annot. 10*], with Prince Cardinall,[36] yet if yow[37] our good freendes be of an other opinion, & may propose the meanes, I pray yow wryte them, for I shall be glad to hear and conforme my selfe to yow also, for in this other I meane to procede very softly & slowly, until I heare from yow. And remember that we may not respect in this only our owne wishes, desires, or appetites, but the 3. conditions before specified, of profit, probabilite, and factabilite [*Annot. 11*] as well to prevalle and get, as to defend, settell, and continewe after wardes. And this is all that in this poynte[38] I cane say, and so with my most hartie com-

 25. offices Fr Parsones] good offices he *Manifestation*
 26. testemonie] the testimonye *T2*
 27. *Manifestation adds* Patriarke Caëtan
 28. in] *T2 Manifestation*; on *T1*
 29. ministers] *T2*; minsters *T1*; counsel *Manifestation*
 30. Camillo Caetani (1552–1602), titular patriarch of Alexandria, was apostolic nuncio to Spain from 1592 to 24 March 1600.
 31. unto] to *T2*
 32. *Manifestation breaks off here, commenting*: "These are the words of this secret letter, and finally he concludeth; that the best of all would be, yf to avoyd contention, opposition and garboyles after her Majestie ..." *and resuming* "such a person might be thought of as would be fit ..."
 33. kinge of Navarre, kinge of Denmarke] the kings of Fraunce, Denmarke *Manifestation*. Christian IV (1577–1648) reigned as king of Denmark from 1588.
 34. *Manifestation concludes here*
 35. Feasible; see also "factabilite" (feasibility) below. *OED* cites Persons's *Christian Directorie* (1585), 164.
 36. Albert of Austria, cardinal archbishop of Toledo, ruled as governor-general of the Spanish Netherlands from February 1596. It had not yet been decided that he should marry the infanta, Isabella Clara Eugenia. See Luc Duerloo, *Dynasty and Piety: Archduke Albert (1598–1621) and Habsburg Political Culture in an Age of Religious Wars* (London, 2016), 52.
 37. yow] ye *T2*
 38. poynte] *T2*; poyntes *T1*

mendations to all, I byd yow farewell, desieringe in thes[39] matters all possibell secresie, as yow see is nessecarie. Our Lord Jesus be with yow ever, from Genua this 15 of Maye 1597.[40]

  Yours ever whose hande yow know
  [*Endorsed:*] [*T1*] For Mr Dr Bishop &c.
  [*T2*] Persons to Holte.

Italian translation

Copia d'una lettera intercetta[41] del padre Personio, scritta in cifra alli 15 di Marzo del anno 1597 da Genua, al padre Gulielmo Holto residente per alhora in Brussella, intorno le cause vere della sua venuta a Roma.

  La letera in lingua Inglesa[42] comincia cosi:

    Un ricordo per il padre Holto et per altri amici confidenti alli quali
    lui giudicarà conveniente di comunicarlo.

  1. Le cause principali di questo mio viaggio a Roma sono: primo per stabilire con Sua Santità et con il Padre Generale della Compagnia tutti quelli punti che parerano necessarii per sustentar li seminarii nostri in Spagna, Fiandra et Italia, et la Missione Anglicana delli Padri della Compagnia [*Anot. A*], et così tutte quelle cose che vi si offerirano costi, a proposito per questi fini, siano di facultà, governo, privilegii, sustento temporale o altre cose simili, prego la Reverentia Vostra et l'altri amici che me ne voglino advertire, con tutta la prestezza possibile, perché penso di procurare che la mia restata in Italia sia brevissima, et così ancho n'ho promesso partendome da Spagna, et per molte raggioni è necessario.

  2°. Se più di questo potrò far anche alguni[43] buon officio nel comporre o finire li tumulti del Collegio Inglese in[44] Roma et l'altre controversie della nostra natione in altri luoghi, farò lo meglio che potrò, et spero che questo almanco s'effettuarà che si darà a intendere a Sua Santità [*Anot. B*] et all'altri personaggii principali quali sono le vere cause et fundamentali di queste discordie.

  3°. Intorn'al negotio della corona d'Inglaterra, il proposito mio è proporre a Sua Santità il vero stato della cosa in se, et di quanta necessità sia che sua Beatitudine ne pensi seriamente et presto, accioché, doppo la morte della Regina non venga il governo in mani peggiori; li danni grandissimi et pericoli evidenti che seguitarano si qualsivoglia principe heretico vi s'intrasse, et che li Catolici Inglesi solamente desiderano un Re [*Anot. C*] che sia sinceramente Catolico, senza rispetto di che sia o Inglese, Scozzese,

---

39. thes] *T2*; this *T1*
40. The date is correctly given as 15 March in Persons's translation. The mistake here may be accounted for by the fact that Persons's next letter to Holt was dated 15 May (B375).
41. Intercetta] *W A*; om. *G*
42. Inglesa] *W A*; Inglese *G*
43. alguni] *W*; alcun *A G*
44. in] *W A*; di *G*

Spagnolo o d'altra natione, et che in questo punto anche loro dependono principalmente da Sua Santità.

4°. Di più, che il Padre Personio non è contrario al Re di Scotia ni procuratore per il Re di Spagna [*Anot. 4*], come alcuni (per farlo odioso) n'han dato informatione, mostrando per prova del primo (toccante al Re di Scotia) li molti buoni officii che il Padre Personio per molt'anni fece per il detto Re di Scotia, mentre che v'era speranza che si faria Catolico; et nel secondo (toccante al[45] Re di Spagna) se mostrarà per testimonio del Nontio Apostolico che sta in Madrid (il quale anco n' ha scritto effettualmente a Sua Santità) che il Padre Personio ha persuaso sempre al Re di Spagna et alli suoi ministri che non li starà bene pretender il Regno d'Inglaterra per se [*Anot. 5*] et che già ha ottenuto promessa ferma [*Anot. 6*] di Sua Maestà, che non lo farà, et il Noncio n' ha visto le scritture [*Anot. 7*] et è stato consapevole di tutto quello che il Padre Personio ha parlato o trattato in questa materia da tempo in tempo.

5°. Ultimamente, la conclusione con Sua Santità ha d'essere che la sola strada per accordar le cose sarà, che Sua Santità convenga con Sua Maestà Catolica [*Anot. 8*] per via d'alcuna buona compositione in qualche persona idonea, la quale staria bene tanto per Sua Santità quanto per Sua Maestà Catolica, et per li Catolici Inglesi et Scozzesi, et per il Re di Francia et il Re di Denamarca, et per tutti l'altri, ma chi[46] sia quella persona o persone il Padre Personio ha intentione di lasciarlo pensare molto seriamente da Sua Santità per un pezzo [*Anot. 9*], benché, a parer mio, nissun accordo sarebbe più utile, probabile o fattibile, che nella persona della Signora Infanta [*Anot. 10*] maritata al Principe Cardinale. Nientedimeno se voi et l'altri buoni amici che stano costì fussero d'altro parere, et havessero pensato altra cosa con il modo d'effetuarlo, li prego che lo scrivino, poiché io molto volentieri me conformarò ancho alli altri. Et in questa materia penso di proceder molto lentamente spettando quello che scriverano da costì.

6°. Solamente me pare che s'habbia d'advertire, che in questo negotio non habbiamo di risguardar tanto li nostri desiderii, voluntà et appetiti proprii, quanto le tre conditioni specificate di sopra d'utilità, probabilità, et possibilità nella persona che si disegna [*Anot. 11*], et questo non solo per guadagnar la possessione della corona, ma ancho per defenderla dipoi, et per stabilir et mantener le cose. Et quest'è tutto quello che se m'offerisce intorn'a[47] questa materia, et così con raccomandarme cordialmente a tutti fo fine raccomandando il secreto in queste cose, come vederete esser necessario. Nostro Signore Giesù Christo sia con loro sempre. Da Genua a 15 di Marzo 1597.

    Vostro sempre

        215[48]

[*Endorsed:*] [*W, in Persons's hand*] La letera intercetta del pe personio dì 15 Marzo 1597.

[*A*] La copia d'un lettera del Padre Personio di 15 di Marzo 1597. intercetta.

45. al] *W A*; il *G*
46. chi] *W A G*; che *Hicks, Tierney*
47. se m'offerisce intorn'a] *A Tierney*; mi si offerisce in *G*
48. Cipher for Persons.

Annotations[49]

Cert' annotationi maligne[50] del Dottor Perseo sopra la detta lettera
del Padre Personio di 15 di Marzo 1597 con le riposte

Anot. A. La mission anglicana delli padri della Compania.) Già si sa che la maggior parte delli Giesuiti che sono stato mandati a Inghilterra fanno più presto l'officio di spie per il Re di Spagna che non di ministri Catholici, et così dicendo qui Personio che lui tratta queste missioni con il Padre Generale,[51] è cosa manifesta che il Generale ancho sia compagno di quest' inventioni Spagnole. *Risp.* La malignità di quest'annotatione è troppo evidente et non manco la falsità per la quale[52] si può far giudicio dell'altre.

Anot. B. Et spero che si darà a intender a Sua Santità.) Egli ha dato intender al Papa quello che lui ha voluto tanto di falso come di vero,[53] et in queste sue informationi ha dannificato l'honore di molti nobili et honesti Catholici della sua patria, i quali non gl' han voluto adulare, ne[54] dar obedienza. *Risp.* Sua Beatudine potrà giudicare di questo meglio che nissuno, poiché ha inteso li ragionamenti del Padre Personio et ben se ricordarà si sono stato[55] in pregiudicio d'alcuni si non d'heretici o per emendatione d'alcuni inquieti che vanno turbando la pace dell'altri, fra li quali costui se fa capo, massimamente nelle taverne, come quelli turbatori del Collegio Inglese.[56]

Anot. C. Et che li Catolici Inglesi solamente desiderano) Lui essebisce qui il consentimento[57] universali delli Catholici benché non sarà la cinquantessima parte d'essi con lui. *Risp.* La lettera parla assai modestamente dicendo *i Catholici*[58] ma costui volendo calumniarlo fa grande torto all maggior parte di tutti li Catholici d'Inghilterra[59] con dir che la cinquantessima parte d'essi[60] non desideri un re Catholico senza rispetto di natione, o che non voglia depender principalmente dal giudicio di Sua Santità in questa materia.[61]

Anot. 4. Di più che il Padre Personio non è contrario al Re di Scotia ni procuratore per il Re di Spagna) È contrario a se medesimo, poiché mostrando di non far cosa alcuna

 49. *Only in W and G*
 50. Maligne] *W;* calonniose *G*
 51. *G gives the first part of the annotation in Latin*: Notum est Jesuitas pene omnes qui in Angliam mittuntur potius officio fungi exploratorum pro rege Hispaniae quam operariorum pro fide Catholica et dicit Personius agere se de huiusmodi missionibus cum P. Generalem. Dunque [é cosa manifesta, etc.]
 52. per la quale] *W;* onde *G*
 53. tanto di falso come di vero] *W;* falso e vero *G*
 54. ne] *W;* e *G*
 55. stato] *W;* stati *G*
 56. come quelli turbatori del Collegio Inglese] *W;* come quelli turbatori passati del Collegio Inglese di Roma solevano fare *G*
 57. consentimento] *W;* consenso *G*
 58. *G inserts* e non dice tutti
 59. tutti li Catholici d'Inghilterra] *W;* essi *G*
 60. d'essi] *W;* di loro *G*
 61. *G inserts* come diceva il padre

in favore del Re di Spagna mette inanzi nientedimeno la pretensione della figliuola ch'è una cosa medesima, et questo dimostra chiaramente il libro suo della Successione[62] impresso l'anno 94 a sposa del Spagnolo, et perché in questa medesima letera dipoi se resolve nella persona della Infanta. *Risp.* Qui se vede manifesta malitia, poiché il Padre non se risolve in cosa alcuna[63] se non propone la persona della Signora Infanta da considerarsi[64] si sarà buon mezzo per accordarsi il Papa et il Re[65] con altri principi, et nell libro della Successione si fa il medesimo proponendo solamente le ragioni per la Signora Infanta insieme con quelle dell'altri Principi pretendenti per dar più materia a Sua Santità di farne buona elettione[66] ma senza determinar niente in particolare.

Anot. 5. Che non li starà bene pretender il Regno per se) Notese la fraude. *Risp.* Qui non si vide[67] fraude alcuna, si non molta[68] sincerità, se l'huomo lo mira con occhi indifferenti; poiché è verissimo quello ch'il Padre persuadeva a Sua Maestà et l'haverlo[69] scritto questo il Padre in secreto a[70] suo confidente, quando non pensava che sarebbe visto ne letto d'altri,[71] bastarebbe a liberarlo da tutto le calunnie di quelli che malitiosamente interpretano le sue attioni con il Re di Spagna.[72]

Anot. 6. Et che già n'ha ottenuta promessa ferma)[73] Si sappia da chi lui habbi havuto commissione per essiger questa promessa dal Re, à che facultà n' ha havuto di riceverla, et che sicurta di che gli sarà guardata la promessa. *Risp.* Qui se scopre[74] la passione di quest'huomo, poiché ogni Catholico della Nation[75] Inglese, in questi tempi[76] quando non hanno Embasciatori ne Principi che trattino loro cose, può dimandar cose in beneficio publico della patria, et della natione et particularmente il Padre Personio il quale già haveva fondato tre o quatro Seminarii con l'Eleemosine del detto Re, et ottenuto molt' altri beneficii in favore delli Catholici, et per questo poteva esser buon mezzo per trattar fra loro, et dimandar cose in beneficio della patria.

62. G *omits the rest of the annotation*

63. poiché il Padre non se risolve in cosa alcuna] *W*; perché il Padre non risolve cosa alcuna *G*

64. se non propone la persona della Signora Infanta da considerarsi] *W*; ma propone solamente la persona della Infanta per considerarsi *G*

65. si sarà buon mezzo per accordarsi il Papa et il Re] *W*; si sarà buon mezzo per accordarsi il Papa con il Re *G*

66. proponendo] *G omits the rest of this paragrah.*

67. vide] *W*; v'è *G*

68. si non molta] *W*; ma gran *G*

69. se l'huomo lo mira con occhi indifferenti; poiché è verissimo quello ch' il Padre persuadeva a Sua Maestà] *om. G, continuing* e l'haver

70. a] *W*; ad un *G*

71. d'altri] *om. G*

72. di quelli che malitiosamente interpretano le sue attioni con il Re di Spagna] *om. G*

73. G *continues* da chi ebbe lui commissione per essiger questa promessa, e che sicurta che gli sarà osservata la promessa

74. G *inserts* grandemente

75. della Nation'] *om. G*

76. G *concludes the response*; può dimandar cose in beneficio publico della patria, et della natione et particularmente e molto più il Padre Personio

Anot. 7. Et il Noncio n' ha visto le scritture) Può ben[77] esser che lui habbia abusato il Nontio, et il successo dimostra che sia stato vero. *Risp.* Il Nontio sta adesso in Roma Monsignor Patriarca Caëtano, egli potrà esser buon testimonio contra questa calunnia.

Anot. 8. Che Sua Santità convenga con Sua Maestà Catolica) Perché con il Re di Spagna solamente, come se nissun'altro Principe n'havesse interesse. *Risp.* Non dice la lettera solamente, et le parolle seguenti che dicono espressamente che la persona ch'ha di succeder sia a grado del Re di Francia et di Dennamarca, et di tutti li Catholici Inglesi, Scozzesi mostrano, che questa dimanda sia impertinente et per metter seditione solamente.[78]

Anot. 9. Lasciarlo pensare molto seriamente da Sua Santità per un pezzo) Bella arrogantia d'un Giesuita. *Risp.* Qui non si vede[79] arrogantia alcuna, si non[80] multa humiltà, et la phrase Inglese è ordinaria et[81] non vuol dir altro che pensar seriamente,[82] et sbatter le ragioni da tutte le parti.

Anot. 10. Che nella persona della Signora Infanta) Absolutamente se dechiara qui per Spagnolo, dicendo sua opinione,[83] et è cosa d'advertire che mentre visse il Re defunto, credendo Personio, che la figliuola Infanta[84] sarrà in credito et governo, essalto' il dritto di lei sopra quello del Principe suo fratello, ma non potette provarlo, perché la maggior, et[85] la più giusta pretensione del Re di Spagna si funda nella casa di Portugallo, et per quella via s'ha de preferire il maschio alla femina, et così anchora lui l'ha posto nell' arbore della genealogia agionta al libro della successione della corona d'Inghilterra. *Risp.* Si vede che costui *nodos quaerit in sirpo*, come si dice,[86] poiché non s'ha[87] proposto mai la Signora Infanta per la successione d'Inghilterra si non per via di compositione transferendo[88] in lei il padre et il fratello tutt'il dritto che loro hanno per la casa et descendenza delli Re di Portugallo, benché per agionta, lei n'ha anchora un altra pretentione particolar, per la descendenza dalli Duchi di Bretania la quale non hanno ne il Padre ne il fratello ch'adesso regna.

Anot. 11. D'utilità, probabilità et possibilità.) Quant'al profitto o utilità, lui già n'ha ricevuto, et sta assicurato, quant'alla probabilità, gli han mancate le raggioni, et quanto alla

77. ben] *om.* G
78. G *reads* La lettera non dice solamente, et nelle parole seguenti si dice espressamente che la persona che ha da succedere sia a grado del Re di Francia et di Danimarca, et di tutti li Catolici Inglesi, Scozzesi onde si vede l'impertinenza di questa dimanda
79. si vede] W; v'è G
80. si non] W; ma G
81. è ordinaria et] W; (to beate the head) G
82. G *inserts* in una cosa
83. dicendo sua opinione] *om.* G
84. la figliuola Infanta] W; la Infanta figliola del Re G
85. la maggior, et] *om.* G
86. come si dice] *om.* G
87. s'ha] s'è G
88. G *concludes* transferendo il Re il padre et il fratello tutto il loro dritto per la casa e descendenza de' Re di Portugallo, benché per aggionta, lei ne ha ancora un'altra pretensione particolare per la discendenza dalli Duchi di Bretagna

possibilità, o fattibilità,[89] egli n'ha prodotto già per le sue negotiationi (come è cosa notoria) assai tragedie lamentevoli delli più nobili Catholici della sua Patria. *Risp.* Quest' annotation' è troppo maligna et[90] calunniosa, perché quanto al primo d'emolumento temporale tutti sanno che il Padre Personio mai h' havuto cosa particolare da Sua Maestà Catholica, si non[91] tutto in beneficio publico per li seminarii, et per altri Catholici necessitati[92] della sua natione et fra quelli procurò ancho per questo Perseo le lettere del Re di Spagna al Governatore di Fiandra che gli dessero[93] 30 scudi di pensione il mese,[94] la quale godette diversi anni, et venendo a Roma con grandissima necessità, il detto Padre[95] gli procurò una pensione di 100 scudi sopra un beneficio in Spagna et cinquecento scudi dipoi d'un gentilhuomo Spagnuolo per l'esentione di quella pensione, il che s'ottenne[96] solamente per amor del Padre et delli suoi amici,[97] protestando il gentilhuomo, che per via di lite poteva evacuar la detta pensione di che[98] si vede la somma ingratitudine di quest'huomo. Quant'al secondo delle ragioni per la probabilità di poter stabilir la religione Catholica et pace in Inghilterra per via della Signora[99] Infanta, tocca a Sua Santità et alli Principi a considerarle.[100] Ma quant'al terzo della fattibilità o possibilità,[101] benché questo appertenga anchora alli medesimi Principi, a pondezarle,[102] tuttavia è intollerabile questa calumnia di Perseo, dicendo che le negotiationi del Padre[103] Personio fin qui habbino prodotte lamentevoli tragedie delli Catholici, si non intende forze li martirii[104]

    89. *G concludes* egli ne ha prodotte già colle sue negotiationi (com'è notorio) molte tragedie de' più nobili Inglesi

    90. maligna et] *W; om. G*

    91. si non] *W;* ma *G*

    92. necessitati] *W;* poveri *G*

    93. le lettere del Re di Spagna al Governatore di Fiandra che gli dessero] *W; om. G*

    94. *G continues*: dal Re di Spagna, che gli furono pagati parecchi anni: e venendo da poi a Roma in gran necessità

    95. *G inserts* gli soccorse e

    96. solamente] *W; om. G*

    97. et delli suoi amici] *W; om. G*

    98. di che] *W;* onde *G*

    99. Signora] *W; om. G*

    100. alli Principi a considerarle] *W;* alli Principi di considerarle *G, continuing* sono buone o no, e non a costui

    101. o possibilità] *W; om. G*

    102. alli medesimi Principi, a pondezarle] *W;* Principi, di' pondezarle *G*

    103. Padre] *W; om. G*

    104. li martirii] *W;* de martirii *G, concluding*: essendo la maggior parte di questi altrevi del P. Personio o mandati in Inghilterra da lui, ma fuori di questi, non si troverà pur una persona sola nel spatio di più di vinti'anni, che il Padre Personio ha negotiato in questa causa e che per sua culpa habbia patito cosa alcuna, e molto manco sono stati rovinati per le secrete machinationi de' seditiosi contro il Cardinale Alano e li Padri come consta per l'essempio della regina di Scotia e altri. Dunque si dimanda che questa calonnia (essendo gravisssima) s'essamini et insieme che si considerino li effetti seguiti di bene o di male dalle fatiche del Padre Personio, e dalle negotiationi di questi seditiosi nella causa Anglicana, e Sua Santità si degni dar rimedio conforme alla verità e bisogno della causa.

che sono stati per la confesssione della nostra santa fede, poiché fuora di questi, non si trovarà pur una persona nel spacio di più di vinti anni ch'il Padre Personio ha negotiato in questa causa per li Catholici che per sua culpa habbia patito cosa alcuna, ma molti sono stati ruinati per le secrete machinationi di quest' et altri simili seditiosi contr'il Cardinale Alano, et li Padri della Compagnia, et li buoni Sacerdoti delli Seminarii como consta per l'essempio della regina di Scotia et d'altri; et al contrario, quanti beni siano avenuti alli Catholici d'Inghilterra per li fatighe del Padre Personio, l'effetti delli Seminarii da lui fundati, et delli libri scritti et altre cose dimostrano, et tutti li buoni Catholici Inglesi qui et in altri parti lo testificarono unanimi consensu, et così si spera che Sua Santità non permetterà ch'un huomo di lingua sfrennata lo vada infamando senza verità alcuna in questa maniera.

Translation

Certain malicious annotations to the said letter by Fr Persons, 15 March 1597, together with the responses

Annot. A. Of the missiones of the Societie to Ingland) It is now known that the majority of the Jesuits who have been sent to England act as spies for the king of Spain more readily than they perform Catholic ministry, and so when Persons says here that he is carrying out these missions along with father general, it is obvious that the general is also party to these Spanish designs. *Resp.* The malice of this annotation is very evident and is not without the falsehood with which all the others may be judged.

Annot. B. I hope I shall make his holines ... understand) He has made the pope believe whatever he wishes, whether false or true, and in these briefings of his he has impugned the honour of many noble and honest Catholics of his country, whom he does not want to flatter or obey. *Resp.* His Holiness is able to judge this better than anyone, because he understood Fr Persons's reasoning and could well remember if it were to the detriment of anyone except heretics or to correct some discontented people who were disturbing the peace of others, amongst whom he is the leader, especially in the taverns, like those dissidents in the English college.

Annot. C. That Inglishe Catholikes do desire onlie a sincer Catholike kinge) He speaks as if with the universal consent of the Catholics although not even one small fifth of them are with him. *Resp.* The letter speaks very modestly, saying "The Catholics," but this one, wanting to slander him, does a great injustice to the greater part of all the Catholics of England by saying that only the smallest fifth part of them wants a Catholic king, whatever his nationality, or does not want to rely chiefly on the guidance of His Holiness in this matter.

Annot. 4. That Fr Parsones is not an enimie to the king of Scotland, nor agent for the King of Spaine) He contradicts himself, since, while claiming not to be acting at all in favour of the king of Spain he nevertheless puts forward the claim of his daughter, which is one and the same thing, and this clearly indicates that his *Book of the Succession*, printed in 1594, is wedded to the Spanish cause, and because in this very same letter he later decides on the person of the infanta. *Resp.* Here you can see his evident malice, since the father says nothing definitively on anything except to put forward the person of the Lady Infanta for consideration as a possible good means of reconciling the pope and the king with other princes, and in the *Book of Succession* he does the same, merely putting forward the arguments in favour of the Lady Infanta together with the other princely claimants, to provide His Holiness with more information to make a good choice, without predetermining anything in particular.

Annot. 5. That it will not stand well for his Majestie to pretend England for him selfe) Notice the deceit. *Resp.* Here there is no deceit to be seen, but rather much sincerity, if one looks at it with an indifferent eye. For it is absolutely true, that the father persuaded His Majesty, and this is what the father wrote discreetly to his confidant, when he did not think that it would be seen or read by others, and this should be enough to free him from all slander.

Annot. 6. And that Fr Parsones hath obtayned of the kinge of Spayne full promise thereof) Who knows from whom he had a commission to exact this promise from the king, and what faculty he had to receive it, and what certainty he had that the promise would be kept? *Resp.* Here you can see the passion of this man, because every Catholic of the English nation, in these days when they have no ambassadors or princes to deal with their affairs, may ask things to the advantage of their nation – and of that nation, Fr Persons in particular, who has founded three or four seminaries with the alms of the said king, and has obtained many other benefits in favour of the Catholics; and for this reason he is the right intermediary to negotiate on their behalf, and ask things to the benefit of his country.

Annot. 7. About which poynt the nuncio hath seene the papers) It may well be that he has abused the nuncio, and the outcome shows that that is indeed the case. *Resp.* The nuncio is still in Rome at present: the monsignor patriarch Caetani, and he can act as a good witness against this slander.

Annot. 8. That his hollines should agree with the kinge of Spaine) Because he has an interest only in the king of Spain and not in any other prince. *Resp.* The letter does not say "only," and the following words say expressly that the person who should succeed could just as well be the king of France or of Denmark, and all English and Scottish Catholics show that this question is irrelevant and is simply there to sow division.

Annot. 9. To suffer his Hollines to thinke & breake his head for a tyme) Typical Jesuit arrogance. *Resp.* Here there is no arrogance to be seen, but rather humility – and the English phrase ["beat your head"] is commonplace and is not meant to signify anything except to think seriously and toss about the arguments of each on every side.

Annot. 10. Then the Infanta) Here a declaration is made for the Spaniard, giving his own opinion, and it is something worth noting that while the late king was alive, Persons believed that his daughter the infanta would be placed in government, raising her right above that of the prince her brother, but he could not prove that, because the greater and more legitimate claim of the king of Spain is founded on the house of Portugal, and in that case the masculine takes precedence over the feminine – which he himself, again, has indicated on the family tree appended to the *Book of the Succession* to the crown of England. *Resp.* You can see that he is getting tied up in knots, as they say, because the Lady Infanta would not be proposed for the succession of England except by her father and her brother's agreement to transfer to her all the rights that they have through the house and by descent from the king of Portugal – although, in addition, she also has another particular claim through descent from the dukes of Brittany, which is not the case with her father or her brother now regnant.

Annot. 11. Of profit, probabilite, and factabilite) As far as profit and benefit goes, has he not already received it and rests assured of it? As for probability, his reasons are empty; and as for possibility, or feasibility, he has produced nothing through his negotiations (as is a matter of notoriety) except the lamentable ruin of so many noble Catholics of his country. *Resp.* This annotation is very pernicious and slanderous, because on the first point, of temporal emoluments, Fr Persons has never received anything in particular from His Catholic Majesty except what is entirely to the benefit of the seminaries, and for other Catholic necessities of his nation – and amongst them I have obtained, for this very Percy, letters from the king of Spain to the governor of Flanders which gave him a pension of thirty crowns per month, which he has enjoyed for many years; and when he came to Rome in great necessity, the same father obtained a pension for him of one hundred crowns based on a benefice in Spain, and five hundred crowns thereafter from a Spanish gentleman for the reversion of that pension. This was obtained purely through the love of the father and his friends, the gentleman protesting that he might lose the entire pension if he went to law about it – from which you can see the height of ingratitude in this man. As to the second point, of the probability of being able to establish the Catholic religion peacefully in England through the Lady Infanta, it is the business of His Holiness and the princes to consider that. But as for the third point, of feasibility or possibility, although this also is for the same princes, to ponder, nevertheless it is an insufferable slander for Pearce to say that Fr Persons's dealings have produced lamentable ruin for Catholics up to now, unless he means those who have become martyrs for the confession of their holy faith, because apart from these, you will not find a single person, in the space of more than twenty years that Fr Persons has dealt for the Catholics in this cause, who has lost anything at all through his fault, but many have been ruined by the secret machinations of him and others like him who opposed Cardinal Allen and the fathers of the Society and the good priests from the seminaries. The Queen of Scots, and others, can stand as an example of this. And on the other side, how many benefits have accrued to the Catholics of England through the labours of Fr Persons, the effects of the seminaries founded by him, and of the books he has written, and other matters, show, and all the good English Catholics here and elsewhere bear witness with one voice, and so it is to be hoped that His Holiness will not allow one man of unbridled tongue to defame him without any truth in this manner.

B358 To Thomas Stapleton, Genoa, 15 March 1597

SOURCE: Stapleton to Persons, 16 April (B366).

NOTE: Persons wrote to Stapleton by the same post as his letter to Holt, expressing his friendship and enquiring about Stapleton's likely visit to Rome. According to Stapleton's letter of 6 July (B385), he did not receive this letter.

B359 From William Gifford, Brussels, 20 March 1597

SOURCE: AAW, VI, no. 22.
EDITION: Knox, *Douay Diaries*, 395–396.
NOTE: William Gifford, dean of Lille and prominent in the party opposed to Persons, learning that Persons is on his way to Rome, seeks reconciliation. Persons's endorsement suggests that he is not convinced by Gifford's denial that he took the part of the discontented students at the English college in Rome, claiming that he was simply reserving judgement.

Righte Reverende and Lovinge father

I receyved of late youres dated from Madrid the seconde of November which I differred to answer untill this presente for thatt I coulde nott assure my selfe wheare my answer should finde yow, a rumor beinge spred of a journaye yow had in hande to Rome. Butt now perceyvinge by the ordinarie of Spayne[105] thatt yow beganne the saied journaye in the ende of November I hope this my letter will finde yow safe arrived in Rome, whearein I will endeavour playnelie and sincearelie to answer youres, referringe the reste untill oure meetinge which I hope maye be before itt be longe: and truelie as in my laste to you 2 yeares since, soe in this I doe lamente with all my harte the Division and dissention which is betwixte those of oure nation, and as I woulde endeavour by all meanes to bringe them to union and concorde, knowinge the woofull and lamentable effectes which this scisme and discorde hathe bred bothe heare and in other partes, soe my conscience dothe nott accuse me thatt I have given anye occasion theareof, whatt ever the good knighte of blessed memorie by wronge information had conceyved of me, which I doubte nott butt yf ever we had mett I coulde easilie have taken oute of his minde.[106] Truethe itt is I never was of the humor to rayle eyther againste some noble men and gentelmen in thease partes, or to chardge the scollars of Rome with horrible and enormious crimes of heresie, hoardom, sodomye, enmitie to His Catholicke Maiestie, and suche like, and in all places and Companyes to crie oute and exclame againste them, as men woorthie expulsion, gallyes, prisons, degradation, and the like, beinge nott able to prove anye suche thinge againste them; and thearefore I judged itt more secure in conscience to suspende my judgemente and bridle my tonge untill I sawe his holinesse censure and sentence than with the vulgar and unbridled tunges to lavishe rashelie againste them whatt ever was suggested by everie private man; and this perhappes maye be some motive whie some men have conceyved of me as an abetter and favourer of those Romayne broyles, butt I truste a man of youre vertue and wisdome will nott make thatt an argumente of anye my inordinate affection in those troubles.

I endeavored always to continewe and encrease the good knightes uprighte opinion of me, neyther to my knoledge did ever I give him occasion to the contrarie, and yf he lived and died in a wronge conceyte of me I will take itt as a punishemente of my sinnes and exspecte in rewarde of itt (yf I beare itt patientelie) a more favorable sentence of

105. The post from Spain.
106. Sir Francis Englefield died on 13 September 1596. William Gifford was the grandson of Sir George Throckmorton, brother of Englefield's mother, Elizabeth Throckmorton.

almightie God. I am glad thatt att his deathe he bestowed his goodes soe well, butt itt woulde have bene some comforte to me yf he had lefte me some littell memorie consideringe how neare I was to him in bloude and nott soe farre from him in affection as some woulde have made him believe.

For joyninge with yow in one and the same course to serve and helpe oure countrie I am as desirous as he thatt is moste; and yf thatt course consiste in prestelie functions of teachinge, preachinge, sacrificinge and the like I am as yow know nott now to beginne that course, havinge to Gods honor and the profitt of manye spente all my younger yeares thearein. Butt yf itt consiste in anye thinge els, whan I shall knowe youre autoritie of pope or prince to commence and pursue anye suche course I will to the uttermoste of my power joyne with yow, yea yf itt shoulde proceede from youre private judgemente and zeale of sowles; whan yow shall vouchesafe to make me partaker of itt I will assiste yow with all I can, nothinge doubtinge butt thatt youre course will be founded in reason and religion, and yf in the meane season in woorde or affection I differ perhappes from youre course blame me nott, butt youre selfe thatt never vouchesafed to make me privie to itt neyther more nor lesse. Whatt ever you have or maye hereafter promise me I nothinge doubte butt yow will performe and as I will nott require D. Barrett to be youre suertie,[107] soe I will nott admitt him or anye man to be a mediator betwixte us butt assure my selfe thatt whan we meete we shall accorde and yow be·able to comforte me and I to serve yow as well as those whome yow have hithertoe trusted more; and with this I comitt you to Christe Jesus whome I desier longe to conserve yow for the singular good of oure afflicted countrie. Bruxelles this 20^{tie} of Marche 1597.

   Youres moste desirous to serve yow
     in anye thinge he maye
       Wyllyam Gifforde.

[*Addressed:*] To the righte Reverende father [Rob]erte Persons, of the Societie of [Jes]us att Rome.

[*Endorsed:*] D. Giff., 20 March, 1597

[*Endorsed in Persons's hand:*]: his excuse from the roman broyles

[*Another endorsement:*] thease be [a symbol consisting of two identical letters, possibly "d" or "t", joined by a cross stroke]

B360 Minutes of a Meeting with Francisco de Peña, 2 April 1597

  SOURCE: BAV, MS Vat. Lat. 6227, fols. 161–164, with headnote "Padre Personio con Peña cerca de la succession de Inglaterra."

  NOTE: Monsignor Francisco de Peña was a confidant of the Spanish ambassador (the duke of Sessa) and an official of the Apostolic Tribunal of the Roman Rota (the highest ecclesiastical court in the Roman Catholic Church). He acted as an intermediary between Persons, the Spanish embassy, and the papal curia. Persons consulted Peña about his imminent audience with the pope, and was warned about the risks attached to entering too nearly into the question of the English succession.

107. Richard Barret, president of the college at Douai, whom Persons had evidently proposed as someone who could vouch for his integrity.

The codex Vat. Lat. 6227 (summarized by Hicks in a separately paginated list after page 1177 of his transcripts) is packed with materials showing the role of Persons and Roger Baynes, formerly Allen's secretary, in funnelling information and documents to the embassy. It contains copies of letters between Peña, Persons, and Sessa, records of meetings, and memorials written by Persons and others on English affairs. It also contains a collection of despatches from Antwerp which Baynes and Persons delivered to the embassy, gathered by Persons under the title "De Rebus Angliae" (see Persons to Caetani, 1 July, B384).

The symbol § is used here to separate the individual points of the minutes, which are marked by the symbol ⌈ in the MS.

Roma a 2 di Abril 1597.

§ 2 di Abril del año 1597 el Padre Personio vino a casa de Peña y dando cuenta de su venida de Spaña descubrio que avia de tratar con Su Santidad de dos puntos, el primero tocante al estado delos colegios, o, seminarios delos Ingleses, y buena direction dellos; el segundo tocante a la sucesion del reino de Ingleterra: porque hallandose aquella reina vieja, y pudiendo cada momento venir el caso dela sucesion, era necesario discurrir mucho sobre cosa tan importante. En esto se detuvo grande rato el dicho padre; y finalmente deseando entender lo que Peña sentia de cada punto, y del orden con que en ellos se avia de proceder.

§ Respondio quanto al primero, que era necesario con mucha energia representar a Su Santidad el estado delos dichos colegios, o, seminarios y el provecho grande que dellos se avia sacado, y todavia se sacava, pues por medio dellos se avia conservado la fe Catholica en Inglaterra, de manera que les proprios hereges confesavan, que no podia ya faltar, ni ellos prevalecer contra ella: y que por tanto era necesario que Su Santidad pusiese mucho cuidado en procurar que esta obra no faltase, que los colegios se sustentasen y en[108] ellos se conservase aquel modo santo de bivir que hasta oi se avia tenido, del qual avia procedido ofrecerse al martirio tantos sacerdotes y estudiantes criados en dichos colegios, cuia sangre derramada por Christo avia en Inglaterra el efeto que Su Santidad y todo el mundo sabian, pues con aquel medio como queda decho la religion Catholica quedava plantata y establecida en el dicho reino.

§ Quanto al segundo punto Peña representó al Padre Personio quién era él: de donde venía: y la calidad de la causa de que se avia de tratar.

§ Que siendo él, el Padre Personio grande confidente de Su Magestad Catholica y viniendo de España, por consiguiente todos potentados de Italia, y sus embaxadores y agentes en esta corte de Roma, le mirarian a las manos, y contarian los pasos, y esaminarian no solamente las palabras, pero aun los pensamientos, creiendo que su venida non será de balde, sino traia consigo algun misterio, y nuevo secreto en favor del Rei de España, y de sus deseos: y que por tanto me parecia, que en estos principios no devia su paternidad affirmar a Su Santidad y muchos menos a sus sobrinos cosa que tocase a este segundo punto de la sucesion, y que convenia dexar pasar algun tiempo hasta que todos los arriba dichos quedasen enterados que no venia para tratar del Artículo de la sucesion: y que despues con mejor ocasion lo podria hazer.

---

108. en] *interlined with caret B*

§ Al Padre Personio agradó esto parecer: y luego Peña dio avisó de todo al duque de Sessa que tambien aprovo esto mesmo por las razones dichas.

Translation

Rome, 2 April 1597.

§ On 2 April of the year 1597 Fr Persons came to the house of Peña and, explaining why he had come from Spain, revealed that he had two points to discuss with His Holiness: the first touching the condition of the English colleges or seminaries, and the good progress they are making; the second concerning the succession of the realm of England; because, finding that the queen is old, and that the question of the succession could arise at any moment, it was necessary to deliberate seriously about such an important matter. The said father dwelt on this for a long time and finally asked what Peña thought about each point and in what order they should proceed.

§ He [Peña] replied to the first matter, that it was necessary to represent the state of the said colleges or seminaries to His Holiness with much energy: the great profit that had accrued from them, and was still accruing, as it was by their help that the Catholic faith had been conserved in England, to the extent that the heretics themselves admitted that there was no weakness by which they might prevail against them. And that consequently it was necessary that His Holiness should take great care that this work should not fail, that the colleges should be sustained and that the saintly way of living that they had had till now should be preserved. This [saintly way of living] was at the root of the desire for martyrdom of so many priests and students trained in these colleges, whose blood shed for Christ had had the effect in England which His Holiness and all the world recognized. It was in that way that the Catholic faith was planted and established in the said realm, as has been mentioned.

§ With regard to the second point, Peña advised Fr Persons to be mindful who he was, where he came from, and what was the nature of the matter he had come to discuss.[109]

§ That as he, Fr Persons, was a confidant of His Catholic Majesty, and was coming from Spain, all the potentates of Italy, and his ambassadors and agents in this court of Rome, would watch closely what he did and where he went, scrutinizing not only his words, but even his intentions, believing that his coming would not be in vain, but would have behind it some undisclosed purpose and something that would secretly favour the king of Spain and his wishes. And that as far as I could see, at the beginning His Paternity should not recount to His Holiness and even less to his nephews anything touching this second point of the succession, and that it would be fitting to allow some time to pass so that the abovementioned would come to think that he did not come to deal with the succession, and then he could tackle it afterwards on a later occasion.

§ Fr Persons liked his opinion, and then Peña advised the duke of Sessa about everything, who also approved of it for the reasons given.

---

109. Peña is being as cautious as possible in the face of such a sensitive matter as the succession.

B361 Speech to the Scholars at the English College, 5 April 1597

SOURCES:
>ABSI, A IV 1 (*olim* Coll N II), 125–159 (= *A1*);
>ABSI, A IV 1, 161–176, a partial copy, equivalent to 139–155 in *A1* (= *A2*);
>ABSI, Coll P I 260–267, Grene's Latin summary (= *G*).
>There is a note by Grene on *A1*: "A better copy is in the Engl. College," but this has not been located.

HICKS: 542–577.

NOTE: The date given for the speech in *A1* and *G* is "Vigilia Paschalis," 5 April 1597 (with Easter falling on the 6th): Hicks gives the date as 3 April, but the figure resembles the 5 in 1597, in both manuscript copies. It is not certain whether Persons was already residing in the college (see the introduction, "The English College, Rome"), but a welcome party was held for him at the college vineyard on 10 April (Kenny, "Inglorious Revolution," 90 n41 [part 3]).

This speech is one of the very few witnesses to Persons's skill as an orator. It is carefully structured, as the marginal headings indicate. He begins by explaining his reasons for coming to Rome at some length, leading up to the question how to interpret the dissensions in the college. He then states his proposition, "yt hath bene a playne tentation of the enimye, rather then malice or evyll meaninge of sych as have part therin." To confirm that it is Satan's work, he applies the parable of the second sowing from Matthew 13:24–30, extending it to enumerate the fruits or effects by which, as the gospel says, false prophets are to be judged: "We shall know them by the fruites and eventes, what the meaninge ys." He goes on to explain how all good causes are hedged about with difficulties and dissensions, illustrating this theme from the Bible, Christian history, and the experience of English Catholics since the Reformation. In these dissensions he can detect the two hands at work, of God and Satan. Finally, he exhorts the students to see their differences in proportion and put them aside for the common good, to which he commits himself wholeheartedly. He was later to develop the theme at greater length in an unpublished treatise written in 1600, "A Storie of Domesticall Difficulties" (Pollen, *Miscellanea II*, 48–185).

Several scribal errors in *A1* suggest that the copyist was not English-speaking (e.g., "mincaryes" for "seminaryes," n115), but it remains the main source, as *A2* is defective and only partly legible and we have not traced the copy said to be held in the English College, Rome. The Latin summary is of some use in establishing the text, but several doubtful readings remain: for example, it is difficult to distinguish between "these" and "those" in *A1*, and the reader should be cautious accordingly. In two cases the reading is clarified by Grene's marginal note, as indicated. Marginal headings have been incorporated into the main text, marked by square brackets and italics. Marginal Biblical references have been incorporated into the footnotes, using square brackets.

>The speache that Fr Persons had to the Inglishe scolars at Rome some dayes after hys arrivall from Spayne, 1597.

I have beene desyrous ever synce my coming to thys cittye (good contrimen) to relate unto yow with some leyseure the causes of my coming hither after so longe absence: which albeyt I suppose yow have in part alredye understoode by relation of sych as came with me;¹¹⁰ or may safelye gather the same by yowr owne discourse: yett have I bene willinge that yow showld heare what they are from my self.

First then, not to speake of the devotion of thys place, and the comforth I myght receyve by the sighte of thys howse and companye, wherin I have the part and interest which al men know, twoo principall reasons amonge other dyd move my superiors to calle me hether and my self not to reply much against the same: albeyt ther wanted not difficultyes at thys present for my departure out of Spayne.

[*The first cause of coming to Rome.*] The one reason was concerning our new seminaryes and residences that God hath gyven us these later yeares in Spayne, Portugal and Flanders for a supplye, to the helpe and advansment of the Catholike cause, with howses and companyes. Though God be thangked they remayne in reasonable good state, for there temporall maintenance, and in excedinge good for the rest: yet for there better establishment, continuance and perpetuitye, divers poyntes of moment are to be treated with Hys Holynes and with Father General of the Societye and other superiors, as well concerning there government and direction, as also for there facultyes, priveliges, maner of missions, and other lyke necessarye circumstances. All which I hope by the helpe of Almightye God, and by the assistance of your good prayers (which I hartely desire) wylbe well dispached at thys my beinge heare. And when nothinge els were done but onely to gyve accoumpt to our superiors, of that which alredy ys on foote, yt were a necessarye office for my part, lest as S. Paule sayde in a lyke case, *in vacuum currerem aut cucurrissem.*¹¹¹

[*The seminaryes of Spayne.*] But I hope all wyll fal owt well and that our labours in those partes have not bene in vane, but rather to Gods glorye, and to the benefyt of our countrye. And I do not dowbt, but he that should see the numbers of yowthes that are browght up in these new colonyes, and with what alacritye, comforth and other benedictions of God they go forward both in vertew and learninge; he wold say the same. And he that shall consider further, at what tyme and by what occasion and meanes the holye providence of Almightye God provided these new storehowses for us: to wyt, presently upon the losse and fall of the Spanishe armyes that went to assiste our cause, and at the very tyme when our enimyes in Ingland triumphed over our seminarye preistes, and put them to death everye where in greate numbers: and when by the warres and garboyels¹¹² of France they hoped also to extinguish that of Rhemes, whosoever, I say, shall consider these and other lyke circumstances must needes acknowledge the mercifull hand of our Saviour towardes us, and say with the profet, *non fecit taliter omni nationi,* no nation in Christendom infected with heresye hathe receyved lyke favours,¹¹³ for there helpe and reduction, as we have done and doe dalye. Nay, manye Catholyke kingdoms and countryes have not sych helpes for education of there yowth at home as ours hathe fownde in banishment. And we see daly, manye a good wytt to go up and downe poore and full of neede, not finding that sucker in hys owne countrye, which we finde amongst strangers.

110. One of these was John Bennet, brother of Edward Bennet, leader of the dissident students (Anstruther, 31).
111. [Gal. 2]:2, "Lest perhaps I should run or had run in vain".
112. garboyles] *interlined above* broyles (*deleted*) *A1*
113. [Psal. 148] *vere* Ps. 147:20, "He hath not done in like manner to every nation."

What shall we say then to thys but with the profet, *Misericordias Domini in eternum cantabo.*[114]

And to say now a woorde or twoo more of these new seminaryes[115] in other countryes, before I passe any further. [*St Omers.*] The colleige of St Omers serveth to the purpose that all men do see, to receyve the first frye that cometh owt of Ingland, which before must eather have stayed there and bene in deanger of infection, or els lose there tyme and lack mantenance on thys syde the seas, for that there was no fyt place for to receyve them here.

[*Valladolid and Sevill.*] The colleiges of Valladolid and Sevill go forwarde lyke twoo good brotheren helping the one the other in all occasions. As for example yf the health or studyes of anye one man be more to be holpen in one place then in the other, he ys changed and receyved with all love and charitye. And thys ys as often as any neede requireth, withowt respect of cost, labour or other difficultyes. So that albeyt there distance be wel neere 300 myles, the one colleige from the other, yet are there few that stay any number of yeares, that prove not the benefyt of bothe colleiges upon some occasion or other.

[*S. Lucar and Lisbone.*] The twoo residences of St Lucar and Lisbon do serve as well for interteyning of some anciant preestes as also for the receyvinge of scholers that come from Ingland, Irland and other places. And especially for the hospitalitye of sych preistes of the seminaryes as are to imbark towardes Ingland, who lye there without charges and say masse everye day, and have there shyps provided for them to there hands; as also necessarye apparell for there jeorney. And finally, there viaticum of fyftye crownes for ech man delivered wholye in to there owne handes at there departure. And thus much for these poynts.

[*The effectes of the new seminaryes.*] But now if we wyll consider what effectes these howses and companyes have wrought where they are, we shall see also hearby, the wonderfull mercyes of Almightye God unto us. For first they edefy the whole world rounde abowte them, and do gayne excedinge good opinion and love towardes them; and towardes our countrye and whole nation: in so muche as those which before dyd scarsly know what Ingland or Inglish men were, or dyd contemne them, and others that dyd hate them for the infamye of heresy, robrye, pirasye and other wickednes which was publyk:[116] of them do now reverence, respect and honour them, and bistowe benifytes upon them, and both in bookes, pulpites, tribunals and other publyk places, do not cease to speak good of them. Wherby yt cometh to passe that besydes the temporall benefytes which we reape at there handes, we ar prayd for also comonly in all churches and monasteryes; and our cause most zelously commended to Almightye God. Which thinge how much yt may import us, for the obteyninge of Godes favour for the reliefe of our afflicted countrye, all Catholyk men do understand.

Secondly the kinge and hys counsell, the nobilitye and prelates of the realme, captaynes, soldiars and governers of those kingdomes have conceyved a far different opin-

114. [Ps. 88]:1, "The mercies of the Lord I will sing for ever."
115. seminaryes] Hicks; mincaryes A1
116. Although the punctuation in A1 is unreliable, the colon suggests that the following phrase – "of them" – is to be taken to mean "some of them," i.e., of those who previously regarded the English with suspicion.

ion and affection towardes our countrye and countrimen by the notyce they have had and experience of these seminaryes, from that they had before. Which point, what sequel yt doth and may bring forth hearafter in matters that may fal owt betwixt our nation and Spain, ys easye to forsee. And many of our nation do feel yt alredye; sych I meane as are taken prisoners in these warres, and dyvers that are interteyned by hys majestye in hys service upon the galyes, armada, and other partes of Spayne and Portugall, and are well used by hys officers, which before was otherwise.

[*The Inquisition.*] But amonge all other sortes of men, none have founde more benifyte by these seminaryes and by there credytt in Spayne then sych of our countrimen as have fallen in to the handes of the Inquisition, who have bene delt withall, with all favoure, synce the plantinge of our seminaryes in Spayne, and Inglish preestes permitted to treate with them: wherby they have come commonly to be converted as yow have hard I am sure of above nyntye gayned at one tyme at the port of St Maries in Andaluzia some yeares agone, and manye others in sundrye portes and partes synce.[117] And for the most part there ys no man of what estate so ever taken these late yeares, but he hath bene converted. And at thys present there are diverse captaynes and other gentilmen of importance in Sevill of whome they wryte the same from thence, and as for yowthes which have not had sufficient instruction, be they never so much infected with heresye by education, they are all remitted withowt further punishment, imprisonment or restraynt by the governers of that holy tribunall unto the Inglish seminaryes to be delt withall as shalbe thowght most conveniente. And hetherto I do not know anye one that was not perfectly mayde a Catholike.

[*Preestes sent from Spayne and schollers receyved.*] So as these howses serve not onlye for the good of Ingland within Ingland, but without also, yet have there bene sent in to Ingland, Irland and Scotland above 40 preestes from Spayne within these 6 or 7 yeares. And owt of Ingland they have receyved and manteyned welnye twoo hundred persons. And the sayde colledges and residences within Spayne onlye doe manteane yearly litle lesse then a hundred, besydes those of St Omers that are half so manye more. There credyt also and example hathe bene a greate meane to hold the kinges favoure towardes us, as before hath bene towched, and in particular to continew hys yearly almes of 2000 crownes to the colleige of Rhemes that now ys in Doway which otherwyse perhaps in these tymes of so greate and universall want of monye which hys majestye hathe passed, bye reason of so manye warres: and for that he hath had no imbassador lydger in France to pay the same as yt was accustomed,[118] myght chance have fayled wholy, yf the presence and good satisfaction of these other seminaryes of Spayne, together with the deligence of them that do labour for them, had not hetherto drawne owt the same.[119] And albeyt the thing be gotten slowly and with greate toyle and difficultye, yet hetherto yt hathe bene payde, and so I hope yt wylbe heareafter.

117. Persons to Idiáquez, 4 April 1591 (B99).
118. There had been no permanent Spanish ambassador in France since Lorenzo Suárez de Figueroa y Córdoba (1559–1607), second duke of Feria, left Paris with his entire entourage the day after Henry IV's triumphal entry on 22 March 1594.
119. drawne owt the same] drawne *interlined above* borne [*deleted*] A1

[*Other effectes of the seminaries.*] And finallye what helpe and comforth these seminaryes and there procurers have bene and are to all sych of our nation as have passed throwghe Spayne these later yeares; or have come thether for busines or seutes; and what the same have holpen also to hold up and staye in some sort the state and condition of our Inglish in Flanders, that yt showld not utterly break and fall or be cast of by hys majestye and his officers, by reason of the longe and continuall division and contradiction among them selves;[120] how many supplications and petitions have bene geven up in Spayne to thys ende; and how manye letters of hys majestye have bene obteyned to hys officers in Flanders to wynke at these disorders and to have care of the Inglish notwithstanding there owne infirmitye of disagreement: all these poyntes I say God knoweth; and the kinge and hys counsell do also know and have byn edified therby: and our nation in Flanders (thowgh some of them do nether know nor acknowledge yt) have tasted of the benefytt, in that matters have not gone worse, albeyt throwgh the difficultye of the tyme, as I have sayde, and the litle contentment which the kinges officers in those countryes have receyved of some of these procedinges: there necessityes have not bene remedyed so much as all of us have desyred and labored for, and them selves needed.[121] And thys ys so much as I have to say at thys tyme of thys first poynte towchinge matters in Spayne.

[*The 2 cause of cominge &c.*] The seconde cause that moved both my superiors and me to thys my cominge hether was to see wether by my beinge heare I myght doe any good office for the comfort and benefyt of thys howse and companye in particuler after so longe tyme of trowble and discomforth which hath growne to them selves and to there frendes, by that which hath passed in thys place. And albeyt for my part I do verely thyngke that the matter hath bene much lesse in yt self, then the rumor that hathe flyne abrode, nether do I greatly marvell of anye syche successe in syche a communitye as thys ys, consideringe the cause we have in hand, the tyme and state of thinges wherin we are: and some sych other lyke circumstances, and finallye that the remedye of all thys affayre ys far more easye then manye do apprehende yt: yet can not I denye but that the thinge hath geven me much care and griefe, for the opinion that other men have conceyved of yt, and for the longe delaye that hath bene made of the trew meane to heale yt with sweetnes, wherby the sore ys come to be more festred, and both the breach and offence made greater on all sydes.

That which I can judge of the matter by longe thinkinge and beatinge my heade therin, ys that yt hath bene a playne tentation of the enimye, rather then malice or evyll meaninge of sych as have part therin. And for thys I have twoo principall and especiall reasons, besydes the asseveration of the Apòstle St Paul, who holdeth (as ye know) that all these effectes and contentions and disagreementes are of the subtilitye of Satan.[122]

[*The first reason why thys disagerment ys of Satan.*] The first reason ys that which our Saviour hym self alleidged in the Gospell of the husband man which sowed his field at the

---

120. among them selves] amonge *interlined above* against [*deleted*] *A1*

121. The unreliability of payment of Spanish royal pensions was a frequent source of discontent.

122. [Gal. 5]:20, where "enmities, contentions, emulations, wraths, quarrels, dissensions, sects" are listed among the "works of the flesh."

beginninge with very good seed, and afterwarde came hys enimye *et superseminavit zizania*, that ys, he sowed cocle and darnell over and upon that which had bene sowed before, which yett was never discovered, but when the fruites, blossoms and buddes came forthe: for then the good olde father fell into the accowmpte of the matter and sayde: *inimicus homo hoc fecit*, the enimye hath done thys.[123] Which self same reason leadeth me also to mayke the selfsame jugment of the successe of thyse affayres heare. For when I do call to mynde the first seed that was sowed by God in thys gardin, where yt was planted (for I was present and had my parte in the plantinge as some heare wyll beare me wytnes);[124] when I do remember (I say) what sweete, pure, and holy seede God dyd cast in to thys grownde at the beginninge, of jeoe, peace, patience, longanimitye, humilitye, obedience, love, zeale, alacritye, and other sych seed, which St Paule testefieth to be trew seed of good spiritte;[125] and what notable fruytes thys seed browght forth presently in the first plantes and trees of thys gardyn, wherof many have bene martyrs, other confessors, and the rest greate labourers in the vinyearde of our afflicted countrye, to the highe glorye of God, renoune of our nation and edification of the whole worlde abrode: when I thyngk (I say) of thys, and consider withall what lothesome and pernicious cocle hathe appeared synce, at divers tymes, of discontentmentes, greefes, unquietnes, and open breaches, I have nothinge els to say, but that which Christ hym self sayde in the lyke case, *inimicus homo hoc fecit*: Godes enimye hath done thys, hys hande goeth in thys matter, yt ys of hys plantinge, of hys sowinge, hys malice, hys crafte, hys diligence hathe done yt: *non enim fuit sic ab initio*, yt was not soe from the beginninge,[126] yt ys of a later date, of a seconde sowinge, yt ys *superseminatum*, that ys, oversprinkled and oversowen upon that which was well sowen before, even as heresye ys upon the Catholyke religion, and therefore of the same hande and finger, and of the self same malice, thowghe in differente objectes. And thys ys my first reason whye I doe judge all thys matter to be of the enimye.

[*Effectes intended by Satan in thys dissention.*] My seconde reason to the same purpose ys grownded also on the woordes of our Saviour, in an other place of the Ghospell, where he gevethe us a reule, how to frame our judgmentes in lyke cases, sayinge: *ex fructibus cognoscetis*, that ys, that we shall know them by the fruites and eventes, what the meaninge ys.[127] If then we wold looke a litle in to the effectes, which Satan hathe intended and dothe intende whatsoever otherwayes he may pretende, by the disagreementes of thys howse, we shall easelye tayke a scantlinge of hys meaninge. Wherefore some of these effectes I shall discover unto yow.

[*1. Unquietnes of mynde.*] The first and immediate effecte intended no doubt by all thys action ys to depryve the yeowth of thys howse, of that peace of mynde, which pas-

---

123. [Math. 13]:25, 28.
124. Vol. 1: 40–75.
125. [Gal. 5]:22–23, "the fruit of the Spirit."
126. [Math. 19]:8, "ab initio autem non sic fuit" (He saith to them: Because Moses by reason of the hardness of your heart permitted you to put away your wives: but from the beginning it was not so).
127. [Math. 7]:16, "a fructibus eorum cognoscetis eos," referring to "false prophets, who come to you in the clothing of sheep, but inwardly they are ravening wolves" (7:15).

seth all understandinge,[128] as the Apostle sayeth, that heavenly benediction, which our Saviour in all hys meetinges gave unto hys Apostles when he sayde and repeated so often *pax vobis.*[129] And agayne when he wold departe, the greatest gyft and legasye that he left them, was *pacem meam relinquo vobis, pacem meam do vobis, non quomodo mundus dat ego do vobis,*[130] wherby he gave them to understande, that of all the gyftes that can be geven to a servante of God upon earthe, thys ys the greatest, the sweetest, the most pretious and most importante, to have the peace of God within a man hys mynde (which can not be withowte the companye of hys grace), to have thys holye virtew which maketh smooth and easye the yoak of Gods service: and consequently ys the fountaine of all jeoe, comforth, alacritye and mirthe; and on the other syde, the want therof ys the welspringe of all desolation,[131] unquietnesse of mynde, inconstancye and other lyke effectes, wherby a mans hart ys filled with thornes and thystles, hys devotion dryed up, hys alacritye of studye taken away, hys fervour quenched: as I dar affirme that everye one in hym self wyll feell and testefye; if with indifferencye he enter into hym self and do confess what he findeth. And thys ys the first and cheifest effect which Satan hath pretended in turninge upsidown thys gardyne, for that he knoweth that of thys principle all the rest wyll follow to hys purpose; a discontented and unquiet mynde beinge disposed for any temptacion whatsoever.

[2. *Losse of good name.*] The seconde effecte which Satan hath pretended in thys work hath been to deprive us and thys colleige in particuler of that good name and reputation (which the Holy Ghost sayth ys better then anye riches)[132] and of that rare and singular opinion of modestye, humilitye, religion, and sanctitye, which the schollers and preistes of our nation above all other sortes of men have gayned with all good men over the worlde. And well dyd the enimye see what a losse thys wold be unto us, and that procuring these styrres heare in Rome in the eye of the world, whence they would be written in to all other partes, by embassadores, agentes, negotiantes, novellantes,[133] and other sych people, yt wold turne to the disgrace and infamie of our whole nation now in banishmente: and consequentlye diminish princes opinions and good affections not onlye towardes us in particuler, but also to our whole cause, confirminge greatlye by these eventes heare and other lyke in Flanders the sclanderous accusations which the heretiks our enimies of Ingland have spredd abrode in so manye books: to wytt, that the Catholike parte which cometh owt of Ingland ys but a stubborne and headye people that cannot be quiet within there countrye, where they say they myght lyve in peace, yf they wolde; that all thys resistance of our preistes and martyrs at home, cometh but of the same grownd of wylfull obstinacy; and that wheresoever in the world they shall fynde difficultyes, or be checked or restrayned, they wyll showe the same effectes.

128. [Phili. 4]:7.
129. [Luc. 20 & 24]; 20:19, 20:26, and 24:36.
130. [Joan. 14]:27.
131. desolution] *interlined above* dissension [*deleted*] *A1*
132. [Prov. 22]:1.
133. Newsmongers; *OED*'s first citation is from "A Second Narrative" in Law, *Archpriest Controversy*, 2: 37, where Persons is accused of "deliver[ing false rumours] unto the novellantes of Rome to be spreaded among them."

Now how grevous and infamous thys accusation is (deare contrimen) and how false also in the cheefe pointe, which heretiks wold have yt to be beleved, I meane of all Catholiks, we know and God knoweth, and he wyll do us justice at the day of judgment. But yet in the meane how dangerous a temptation thys ys of the dyvell to mayke the matter probable and to deceave streangers in our whole affayre, everye man seyth and must confesse, that yt ys a stratagem worthye of Satan: and whosoever helpeth hym therin, hath hys parte with hym, and geveth a blowe to the very hart of our cause.

[3. *Disablinge of the best wyttes.*] A thyrd effect I do discover also to be intended by the same craftesmaster, which thowgh yt be somewhat more particuler, yet doth yt tende also to the publyke hurte of our cause, which in deede ys the finall ende and butt in all hys indevours. And thys ys, that wheras from the beginninge of thys colleidge of Rome he hath observed, that commonly the best wyttes of our nation were sent hether, who by thys more exquisite institution and by other priviledges of thys place, were lyke to prove greate instrumentes of Gods glory and more eminent then the rest in setting forward the cause of our countrye, Satans devise hath bene from tyme to tyme to crosse the same, partly by the meanes which before I have mentioned of disquietinge there myndes, breakinge there studyes, dryinge up there devotion (in those I meane that by hys art have fallen into discontentment and dissention),[134] and partly also by a particuler maner of disabling them by the same way, to wytt by losse of there opinion and good reputation with those that showld most comfort, helpe and set them forward in thys action, and wold so have done, yf thys diffidence and mislyke browght in by disagreementes, had not been the lett. Wherby to the greate sorow of all good men, and to the greate hurte of our common cause, we have sene divers yowng men of greate expectation so pinioned or rather mixt in the head (even at the begyning) with the prejudice conceyved against them of unquiet spirites, as they might say, with hym in the scripture, *dum adhuc ordirer, succidit me*;[135] a very pitifull case, but yet verefied in manye, which myght have done much and came to nothinge. And perhaps in no one thinge ys the malice and subtiltye of our enimye more to be sene then in thys, wherin *allidit parvulos nostros ad petram*,[136] he cutteth downe our harvest before yt be rype; and casteth sych an aversion and prejudice both in Ingland and other places against some, that otherwyse myght have done infinite good, as when they come to work they fynde the doors shutte against them: that ys they fynde men to flye them, mistruste them, feare them; yea every man redye to shyft them of and to be rydde of them, which otherwise wold have bene most gladd of them. And what great inconveniences do and may follow hereby in sych a worke as ours ys, ys rather to be considered.

[4. *Breache with our nation and the Societye.*] A fourth endevoure of our enimye in thys affayre ys to mayke an open breache betwixte our nacion and the Societye, and consequently to deprive us of all the comforthe, helpe and assistance, which hetherto we have had by them in all places throwghe owt the world at all tymes and in all necessityes and upon all occasions in thys our banishment. And thys I may say unto yow (good con-

134. A2 begins here, with the words "and dissention."
135. [Isa. 58] *vere* Isa. 38:12 ("Whilst I was yet but beginning, he cut me off"), traditionally applied to premature death.
136. [Psal. 136]:9, "beatus qui tenebit et adlidet parvulos tuos ad pertram" (Blessed be he that shall take and dash thy little ones against the rock).

trimen) and so trewly I do with all sinceritye – not as of them but as an Inglishman that hath part and interest in all the good or hurte, credyte or discredyte, honour or infamye that may fall unto our nation in generall, or to any of yow in particuler: I may avouch that in thys place, without offence I hope of anye, that all the world knoweth to be trew, which ys, that of any one sorte of poore frendes which our cause and nation hath hadde in thys longe affliction, these men have bene the most redieste and willinge in all contryes to helpe us. There howses have bene our howses, there frindes our frendes, there credyt our credyt: there woorde alwayes redye to commend us, there handes to helpe us, there labours to assiste us, in all kinde of businesses or necessityes, that have fallen upon us. They have bene our masters, our directors, our confessors, our frendes and fathers; every where they have published the worthynes of our cause, recommended the persons, exalted the work, procured us patrons and benefactors where they have been able. And more then thys, they have jeoned within the very action yt self, laboured with us in Ingland, passed chaynes and imprisonmente with us,[137] shedde there blood with us. All thys ys trew and the whole world seeth yt, and greate shayme yt were to deny yt, and much more ingratitude and evyll nature not to recognise yt, notwithstandinge what disgust soever anye one, twoo or three particuler men may have geven to any, if any have ben geven. And therefore now to loose and overturne all thys union at once and to seperate our selves and break from sych a bodye as hath holpen us, and may helpe us so muche as they have, and may; we standing yet in the tearmes we doe, and needinge dalye more helpe then other, ys sych a pushe of Satan; as he ys very passionate that doth not consider and discover the same. And yf any upon discontentment wolde yeald unto yt, the whole world would crye shayme of us for yt, and the feindes of hell wold laugh us to scorne.

[5. *Breach or jelousye with Spayne.*] Another effect intended by Satan is not much unlyke to thys, which is to breake or put our selves in jelousye with that prince and people, unto whom above all other hetherto for our temporall relief and mantenance in thys our banishment, we have bene and are beholden. Yow know whome I meane and what the matter may importe us, bothe for the present and for the tyme to come. And albeyt yt may be sayde (and perhaps trewly) that no substanciall occasion hath bene geven in these trowbles heare, wherupon that opinion or conceyte may justlye be grownded; yet considering how nyce matters be that belonge to mistruste and jelousye, and how deepelye synke when once they enter, and how hardly they are removed agayne owt of princes myndes when once they are conceyved, and furthermore I havinge seene and redde so manye thinges written and reported in thys behalf of men of authoritye as I have done, I meane bothe of woordes, factes and other signes geven heare and written abroade of aversion or little good wyll borne to that princes procedinges and affayres, I can not but greatlye feare the sequell therof, and so doe other men also that love us. And perhaps we have begonne alredye to feele some parte of the damage. And I pray God we feele not more heareafter, which our enimye wold wyshe and dothe procure by all these meanes. And let thys be sufficient at thys present, of thys matter.

[6. *Falling owt of Seminaryes amonge themselves.*[138]] But yet further of these twoo last effectes dothe insew an other muche rewled also by our enimye, which ys the disagree-

    137. passed = suffered (*OED*, s.v. pass, *v.* 4.18)
    138. *Number 6 supplied in this ed.*

ment and falling owt of thys howse with all thother howses, seminaryes and residences of our nation besydes, which dependinge principally as hathe bene sayde for there temporall mantenance, of the prince and people last mentioned, and receyving dalye benefytts, helpes and assistance from the Societye in the countryes where they resyde, can not but tayke yt grevouslye, that withowt there falt or consent, they beinge farre the greater number, so greate a breache showld be begonne heare againste them and thother of the twoo benefactors, not onely to the infinite shame and greefe of all the other howses and companies, but also to there losse and prejudice; or reather to the utter peryll of all there whole estate, yf the matter goe forwarde, for that they are not able to lyve, or stande withowt them; wherupon diverse cogitations have bene amonge them whether yt were expedient that all the rest of the colleiges and companyes showld jeone together, and jeontly oppose them selves to thys attempte of Rome, which they tayke to be so notorious an injurye offred to them all and to the whole nation. And diverse particuler men have bene of the same opinion and desyre to have yt done. And yf others that have some hande amonge them also to withholde them, had not detayned the matter for avoidinge of publike scandall, no small fyer had bene raysed in thys behalf also before thys day. And what a spectacle thys had bene or may be to the world, and specially to our enimyes, to see the seminaryes at dissention amonge them selves, and then to resiste and impugne thother, every man of judgment can easelye decerne. [*7. & 8. effectes: jeoe of heretikes and greife of Catholykes in Inglande.*] Onelye I wyll saye that twoo other effectes wolde follow hearof, which may be 7th and 8th desyred by our enimye. And are no lesse prejudiciall to our publike cause then thother sixe before observed. And these are, the jeoe and comforthe of our common adversaryes the heretikes in Inglande, and the greife and desolation of our frendes the Catholikes.

And as for the former sort, yt ys evident what an incoragement yt hathe bene and ys unto them to heare what ys alredye done in thys behalf by disunion amonge us, wherby they gather new hopes that albeyt they have not bene able to let the settinge up of seminaryes, nor yet there continuance, nor have bene able to hynder the cominge in of preistes, with all the lawes they have made or can mayke to the contrarye; yet hope they to frustrate and evacuate at length all fruites of these seminaryes, or the greatest parte therof, by thys fier of dissention, which they wyll not fayle to feede and noryshe by all meanes possible: as in reason of estate they are bownde to do, and by former examples we have proved.

[*Catholikes in Inglande.*] The second sorte also which are our frendes and Gods servantes, and suffre for thys cause in Ingland, bothe preistes and others, are infinitelye afflicted by thys accidente, being browght to that estate as they know not what to beleeve, or whom to trust, there lives and Gods cause standinge upon yt, as yt dothe. For wheras hetherto they have treated with men of one spirite, of one mynde, of one harte, so united together in Christian love and faythe and our cause, as no tribulation, tormente, or deathe could separate them in judgment or affection, now to see the same so changed, as in nether of these they do agree: the good people ar at there wyttes ende, and crye owt upon the authors of thys division: and do bothe wryte and sende over dalye, desyringe that in no case anye that are towched with thys disease may come to them or lyve amongst them, persuadinge them selves (as they wryte) that preistes living at dissention, and that do not love one an other, can not possiblye be trustye or secrete one to thother in occasions of tryall that dalye fal owt in Ingland, and consequentlye not to be fytlye disposed to dye for God, who love not there brethren.

And thys ys the estate of thinges in Inglande now, which everye day wold be worse, yf thys dissention showld contenew amonge us heare on thys syde the sees, which I hope in Jesus yt wyl not.

[*Greate causes have ever greate difficultyes.*] By all these effectes then and others which I do omitte to prosequute for brevityes sayke, we may easelye see and discerne how dangerouse a temptation thys hathe bene and ys of our common enimye, for the overthrowgh of our common cause: wherat notwithstandinge I do nothinge at all marvell or am astonished: consideringe the greatnes and weght of our sayde cause and usuall custome of Almightye God to inviron with myghtye difficultyes and batter with strownge temptations all sych causes as ours ys, wherof dependeth not onely the reduction and remedye of our countrye alone, as yow well know, but of all Christian kingdomes infected with heresye that lye rownde abowte yt.

And yf yt be trew, as yt ys, that no one sowle can be gayned withowt greate difficultye, nor any one sainte made withowt contradiction and persecution,[139] as St Paule affirmyth, and yf yt were a good reason of the Angell to Tobias, *quia acceptus eras Deo, necesse fuit ut tentatio probaret te*, because thow was acceptable in the syght of God, yt was necessarye thou showldest be proved by temptation,[140] and yf it were a good consequent as needes yt must be, that Christ made to Ananias in the Actes of the Apostles, when he talked of the greate designmentes he had of St Paules laboures, gyving thys reason of hys election, *ego enim ostendam illi quanta oporteat eum pro nomine meo pati etc.*, which ys, he ys my chosen vessell for that I wyll shewe hym how greate thinges he must suffer for me:[141] if all thys, I say, be so, what marvayle if in so greate and important a cause as ours ys, there be muche to be suffred, manye temptations, manye contradictions, manye difficultyes to be borne and passed throgh, not onelye at the handes of the comon enimye and persecutor (which perhaps ys the leaste), but even amonge our selves that are of the howshowld and domesticall frendes.

I fynde twoo or three greate causes in holye scripture that do muche resemble ours. The one was the reduction of the people of Israell owt of Aegipte into the land of promisse after 400 yeares they had stayde there. The seconde was the restoring of the same people owte of Babilon after 70 yeares banishment into that place. And bothe of these causes have diverse poyntes for our instruction and comforth in the estate wherin we stande.

[*Difficultyes in the retorne from Egypte.*] For in the first we beholde as in a glasse, the difficultyes that fell owt amonge that people of God in there jeorney homewardes not onlye by the persecution and resistance of Pharao, Amelec, Moab, Edom, Madian, and other open enimyes, but also by there owne infirmityes and faltes amongst them selves, by there dissention, contention, murmuringe and emulation upon everye lyght occasion.[142] *Ortum est murmur populi* (sayth the history in one place) *quasi dolentium*

139. [I Tim. 3]:12.
140. [Tob. 12]:13.
141. [Act. 9]:15.
142. [Exod. 14, 16, 17]

pro labore contra Dominum, iratusque est furor Domini. Sed et Moysi res intoleranda visa est: there arose a murmuration of the people against God, for that they were pressed with so muche laboures, and God being exceeding angrye therwith, Moyses also (who at other tymes was wonte to diminishe the offence of the people and to treate for them) thowght now thys fall to be intollerable.[143]

At an other tyme the same people mayde factions amonge them selves and murmured againste there chiefe leaders and directors and those that laboured most for them, to wytt, Moyses and Aaron. And in thys faction the cheife heades were Core, Dathan, Abyron and Hon, who drew after them twoo hundreth and fiftye of the principall men of the Synagoge and complayninge of Moyses and Aaron sayde unto them, as the scripture relateth, *Cur elevamini super populum Domini*:[144] why are yow above the rest, or why do yow tayke upon yow to governe others, seing other men are as good as yow, and presently folowed there lamentable ende by fyer from heaven.

But the matter stayde not heare, for God suffred also emulation to fall owte betwixte Moyses and Aaron them selves, and betweene hys owne sister Marye, in so muche that Aaron and Marye with sych as took there partes came and opposed them selves to Moyses hys owne face and sayd, *Num per solum Moysen loquutus est Dominus, nonne et nobis similiter est loquutus*:[145] hathe God spoken onely by Moyses, and not also to us, why then showld yow be better then we, or more respected then us? Finally the trowbles were so greate, the emulations and murmurations so manye, and the contradictions so strownge which thys good man for 40 yeare together suffred amonge thys people in the daserte (notwithstanding all the myracles he had wrowght and benefytts he had done to them) as he came to say at last to Almightye God, *Obsecro ut interficias me et inveniam gratiam in oculis tuis, ne tantis afficiar malis*: I beseeche the o lord that thow wylt kyll me and that I may fynde thys grace at thy hande, that I may be no longer afflicted with so greate miseryes.[146] And thus muche for the first example.

[*The banishment in Babilon and returne from the same.*] In the seconde returne from Babilon which was 80 yeares and more after the first, there were no lesse difficultyes then the former. The prophettes Ezechiell and Daniell lived in all that banishment with them and laboured muche for them, bothe with God and man. Yet was the former of the twoo so contradicted by hys owne people as God was forced to say for hys comforth unto hym, *fili hominis in medio domus exasperantis tu habitas*, sonne of man, I know thow dwellest amoungste a trowblesome and seditious people, but have a good hart, I shall helpe the owt.[147] But notwithstandinge all thys, he was slayne at lengthe by the same people, as St Epiphanius writeth the storye in hys book of the lyfe and death of prophetes, and thys by the instigation of a certayne emulator of hys, that was a governour in the trybe of Dan.[148]

143. [Num. 12] *vere* Num. 11:1, 11:10.
144. [Num. 16]:3.
145. Num. 12:1–2.
146. [Num. 11]:15.
147. [Ezechie. 12]:2.
148. While he was in Babylon, Ezekiel was said to have pronounced divine judgement on the tribes of Dan and Gad and to have been killed in retribution: *The Lives of the Prophets*, ed. and trans. Charles Cutler Torrey (Philadelphia, 1946), 38; for Epiphanius's recension of the text, see Torrey's introduction, p. 13.

But Daniell thowghe he were not slayne by the sayde people yet had he manye trowbles amonge them, as may appeare by that which happened in the storye of Susanna when he condemned to death for there lewdnesse the twoo wicked judges, that were of power and bare rule amoungst the people, whose kinred and frendes are thowght to have holpen for revenge sayke to gett Daniell into the denne of lyons, and to have jeoned with the Gentils in that persecution agaynst hym, as in the chapter folowinge of the same prophet appearethe.[149]

But above all other in thys action of the returne from Babilon, were Esdras and Nehemias, they that laboured most and had most contradiction and emulation against them, for they were accused that they wold mayke them selves kinges over the rest. And that for thys cause, they had sett a work the 2 prophetes Aggaus and Zacharias to preache in there favoure, and thys was sayde to one of there faces: *levare te vis in regem propter quam causam et prophetas posuisti qui predicent te in Hierusalem*: thow meanest to exalte thy self to be a kinge, and for thys cause hath sett the prophetes to preache the in Hierusalem.[150] But the good man bare all with patience. And wheras they had thowght as he saythe to have terrefied hym and weryed hym owte and have mayde hym cease from the buildinge of those walles, he sayth of hym self: *propter hanc causam magis confortavi manus meas*: even for thys cause I have strengthened my handes the more, and have taken more cowrage to go forward.[151] And finally Tobias and Sanaballat that were hys emulators styrred up one Noadia a prophet to be against hym and corrupted with monye, as he sayth, Simmaia hys frende to betray hym and yet he went forward with hys worke and staggered not. The lyk I myght note of the contradiction of Simon and Jason that were the emulators of holye Onias the high preist in tyme of the Machabees and contradicted hym in all hys actions, thowgh Jason was hys owne brother.[152]

[*The difficultys by domesticall enimyes of the first planting of Christian Religion.*] But in no cause ys thys poynt seene more clearly then in the cause of Christian religion when yt beganne first, which beinge for the restoringe of mankinde from a greater banishment then was ether that of the Jewes from Egypte or from Babilon, and indeed the greatest cause that ever was, shalbe or may be in the worlde, yt was besett with the greatest difficultyes and contradictions that ever cause had or can have, for that besydes the power of the Roman emperours and of all paganisme that was against yt, the Jewes also that were the people of God dyd conspyre to afflicte and persequute the same with all there strengthe. But more then thys amonge the very howshold frendes that mayde profession to follow Christ and to be Christians, there sprownge up a thyrde kynde of enimyes named heritikes; and these in greate numbers and of diverse sortes and sectes that impugned the Apostles no lesse then the forayne enimyes. Nether remayned the rest that were Catholikes all quiet and united, for some of them were factious, as those that made division betweene Paule, Caephas, and Apollo in Corinthe. Some were envious and sedi-

149. [Dan. 13, 14] These chapters, not being in the Hebrew, are omitted from later Protestant bibles. According to the Vulgate, Daniel was twice put in the lions' den, once by Darius the Mede (chapter 6) and once by the Babylonians (chapter 14).
150. [1 Esd. 5; 2 Esd. 4, 5, 6]; the Latin is adapted from 2 Esd. 6:6.
151. 2 Esd. 6:9.
152. [2 Machab. 3, 4] esp. 4:1–10.

tious, as Alexander Aerarius and others of whom S. Paule complaynethe;[153] others were duble and tratours, whome the same Apostle namethe false brethren.[154] Some fell to follow the world, as Demas that left St Paule upon that occasion.[155] And St Jhon the Evangelist compleynethe of a certayne prowde and ambitious felow in the churche of Asia named Diotrephes that alwayes was quarelinge and barkinge against hym: *verbis malignis garriens in nos*, he barkthe against us malitiouslye with spitefull and malignante woordes and nether receyveth those that are united with me, hymself; nor permittethe others to do the same.[156] So that a man may easelye see, that yt was playne spyte and envye.

Thys passed that good man then, and the same hathe passed ever synce in lyke actions belonging to God; and the same wyll passe heareafter to the worldes end; for that alwayes there are some unquiet and wranglinge spirites amonge those that professe the selfsame faythe, which do serve for exercise and humiliation, and for more meryt of the good; and as St Paule addeth: *Ut et qui probati manifesti fiant in vobis*: that those be mayde knowne amonge yow that be of proufe, that be still solide and constante.[157]

[*The domesticall contradiction that hathe bene in the Inglishe cause from the beginge.*] And for that thys poynt may gyve some lyght perhaps to some thynges belonging to thys our present affayre, and discover some growndes that some heare have not thowght upon or well understoode, *Nolo vos ignorare fratres*,[158] to use the Apostles owne woordes, I wold not have yow ignorante (good countrimen) of one poynte, which thowgh for modestyes sayke and for the honour of our countrye, syche as have travelled most in thys action, have ever dissembled, covered, and kept from the syght of the worlde as muche as in them hathe layne, yet now seinge yt ys so broken forth as all princes and people that deale with us do see, that[159] yt ys convenient that yow also be somwhat informed therof. And the pointe ys, that as in all other lyke causes, so in thys of our countrye there hath gone a certen secrett contradiction even from the beginninge.

I can tell yow onlye of my owne knowledge for these 15 or 16 yeares, but our late good Cardinal who was in deede our Moyses,[160] our Esdras, our Nehemias, and as I may say in a certayne sort our first and cheefe Apostle in thys affayre, wold recounte unto me many examples of former tymes. But synce my self have had any parte in thys work, I have seen yt evidently that twoo different handes have gone in the same, the one opposite to the other, and that (as yt seameth) by Gods perticuler order, for that we cowld never remedye the same hetherto by anye meanes possible: thowgh we have not ceased to prove manye: I meane bothe the good Cardinal whyle he lyved, and my self and others with us that have desyred unitye no lesse then we, but yt hathe bene impossible to thys

---

153. [1 Cor. 4]:6; see also 3:22. Alexander Aerarius is Alexander the coppersmith, mentioned in 2 Tim. 4:14.
154. [2 Cor. 11]:26.
155. 2 Tim. 4:9.
156. [3 Joan.]:10.
157. [1 Cor. 11]:19; still *interlined A1; om. A2*
158. 1 Cor. 10:1.
159. that] *A2; om. A1*
160. William Allen.

day, partlye and cheefelye, as I perswade my self, for the reason before alleidged of Gods holye providence in syche affayres. And seinge all those that have laboured zealouslye hetherto in thys cause have passed[161] these difficultyes, what can we say, but that which Elias sayde, *non sumus meliores patribus nostris*, we are no better then our forffathers.[162] If they have passed these difficultyes and had patience, let us do the lyke and follow there example.

[*Causes of discontentment and variance amonge our nation.*] A second reason also for the same ys, the estate and condition of our nation in banishment, where manye miseryes offer them selves to be suffred:[163] muche neede, muche wante, muche sorow to be borne, which yet are the fountaynes of discontentmentes. And a discontented mynde ys easelye browght as ye know to complayne and to tayke aversion and to jeone with anye opposite hande that offreth shew of consolation, be yt trew or be yt false. We reede that when Davyd first fledde owt of kinge Saules cowrte into the fieldes, *Convenerunt ad eum omnes qui erant in angustia constituti et amaro animo*: all ranne after hym that were in necessitye and discontented in mynde,[164] not so muche for that they loved hym or favoured hys cause, as for that by thys meanes they thowght they mygt ease them selves somewhat.

There ys besydes in thys our cause and action some difference of nations as ye know, and some naturall inclination therin to emulation and contention speciallye yf any do incitye and stur upp the same, as betwene Inglishe and Welshe, Scotishe and Inglishe, Irishe and Britishe. There are also different estates and conditions of men, that are capable of the same competence and emulation,[165] when yt ys moved, as betwene seminaryes and souldiours, preistes and laymen, seculer churchmen and religious orders, and of one order against another. All which jeontes and junctures have bene searched and shaken in thys secrett competence and combate, betwene these twoo opposite handes in our Inglishe cause.

And no marvell thowgh owt of sych variety of fountaynes muche water hathe bene derived, and diverted by the left hand from the ryght, and that the force also of thys left hand hathe reached hether to thys Cyttye and wrowght not a litle in some that perhaps never mayde reflexion upon the originall cause, nor from whome the secrete motion came of there disagrementes.

[*Twoo opposite handes in our cause and there differences.*] I meane to towche in thys matter no man at all by name, nor yet to condemne the intentions of anye, but onelye to tell yow that these twoo handes are now manifestlye knowne to the world, and there operations seen and marked notoriouslye, so that nothinge can be dissembled heareafter, but that yt wylbe apparent to what hand yt leaneth. If any man showld desyre to know the differences of these twoo handes, yt seamethe easye to lay them forthe, for they are apparent.

161. As in the instance noted above (n137), "passed" may mean "suffered."
162. [3 Reg. 19], i.e., 1 Kings 19:4.
163. suffred] *in A1, preceded by two indecipherable words and followed by* amonge our nation [deleted] *A1*. This suggests that the copyist was having difficulty reading the copy.
164. [1 Reg. 22], i.e., 1 Sam. 22:2.
165. competence = rivalry (*OED*, s.v. competence, n. 1.1).

1. For first yt ys evident that th'on was before th'other which ys the difference noted before by our Saviour in the Gospell betweene the twoo seedes, good and badde: and betwene the twoo sowers, hym self and hys enimye: to wytt, that th'one sowed first and th'other came after and oversprincled the same.

2. Secondly, yt ys as evidente that th'one of these twoo handes browght forthe good fruytes at the beginninge, for that yt beganne with the good of our countrye, and God was with yt, and the other beganne after to contradicte the former.

3. Thirdly, the one hathe wrowght in publique, in the lyght and syght of all the world: *opera sua in luce fecit*;[166] th'other in secrete, so as in manye yeares yt skearce hathe bene discovered untyll now that the darnell and cockle ys manifestlye growne upp.

4. Fourthlye, yf we consider the persons that have followed the first hande, they are manye and of moment, for they ar our late good Cardinal, Doctor Sanders, Sir Franncys Inglefyld and the rest of that rank now deade,[167] and there frindes and comparteners yet alive of the learnedest and gravest of our nation. And with them have jeoned ever all the fathers of the Societye, all the seminaryes, all the preistes within and withowt Ingland, all the Catholiks in prison and others abrode withowt exception.

And on the other syde, albeyt there may be some[168] numbre united in some poyntes at some tymes (for allwayes and in all poyntes they are never I thyngk at one), yett are they very few in respecte of the other syde; I meane of favourers of th'other hande that in my opinion ys the ryght: and thys other ys left.[169]

5. [*Woorkes of the ryght hand.*] Fyfly yf we respecte woorks and wyll follow the rule which our Saviour gave us to discerne in lyke cases, when he sayde, *operibus credite*, yt seameth that the matter wylbe verye easey to judge, for that the works of the ryght hande may be accowmpted all the fyve seminaryes with the residences:[170] above six or seven hundred preistes that have bene mayde, browght upp, and taken holly orders in seminaryes: above a hundred martyrs: twyse or thryse as many Confessors: infinite numbers of Catholikes converted and mayde by them: infinite yewthes saved that otherwyse might have bene lost: manye books written in defence of Godes cause and of our countrye: manye heretiques converted or confownded: muche love and reputation gotten to our nacion, and union mayde everye where: and finallye, the estate of our countrye browght to that pointe as beinge once more lost and of lesse hope then anye countrye Christian infected with heresye, now the expectation and probabilitye of Inglandes reduction ys greater then of anye other kingdom besydes.

[*Woorks of the left hande.*] But now on th'other syde I do not see what the left hande hathe holpen anye thinge at all to these effectes, but rather hindred (thowgh the intention perhappes was not to hynder), nor that yt hathe browght forthe anye syche woorkes

---

166. He has done his works in the light.

167. William Allen (d. 1594), Nicholas Sander (d. 1581), and Sir Francis Englefield (d. 1596).

168. A2 ends here.

169. other *interlined above* sy[de] [*deleted*] A1

170. fyve] *obscure, blotted or deleted A1, possibly* fayre; foreyne *Hicks.* The five would be Rome, Douai, Valladolid, Seville, and St Omers.

of thys qualitye worthye to be related for the publick good, but rather[171] to be passed over and forgotten, yf any have bene: as for example the overthrow of the poore quene of Scotes, that otherwyse myght yett have lyved manye a fayre yeare, with the ruyne of those fourtene Inglishe Gentilmen that dyed with hyr and for hyr, intrapped bye the rashe and undiscrete treatie of Ballarde,[172] wherin I can assure yow, the ryght hand had nether part nor knowledge. The fall in lyke maner of Gylbert Gifford and hys treatye with the enimye were by thys hand; as also the twoo bookes wrytten by hym and hys compagnion: the one againste our Cardinals epistle for the deliverye of Deventrye, and the other against the fathers of the Societye, which were so fondlye and malitiouslye written as Walsingham hym selfe was asshaymed to lett them be printed:[173] the division and emulation agreed upon at that tyme to be prosequuted betwene preistes and Jesuites: the opposition set upp by name againste our late cardinall hys course in hys lyfe tyme: and an alter indevered to be mainteyned againste an alter, in thys towne, which all the world saw and talked of:[174] the dissention mayde and contenewed to thys day betwene our gentilmen in Flanders, to all our shame and generall prejudice, and the same attempted to be browght in to the colligies also yf yt were possible. These I say are works of the left hande, which I have no desyre to presente any further, nor wold have spoken so muche therof in thys place and at thys tyme, but that diverse men are of opinion, as before I have towched, that some finger of thys left hand hath hadd some secrette force in thys commotion heare; ether to styrr them upp, or to contenew them, or in bothe: thowgh litle marked perhappes by the partyes in whome they had there force and operation.

[*The conclusion.*] With thys then I wyll end, for I have bene longer then at the beginninge I had purposed. Onely I wyll add for a conclusion, that supposinge the lyght that now we have of thys whole matter, the inconveniences that are to follow, the hurtes and damages that are intended, me thinketh that there showld wante no wyll in anye of us all towardes the redresse ether heare, or in anye other place. And so muche the more heare, for that in my opinion the remedye ys most easye and facill, for the contention ys not heare as yt was betwene the howses of Lancaster and Yorke in Ingland for a crowne: nor yet as betwixte twoo Antepapes for a popedom, nor as in Tindall and Ridisdall for dead-

171. Hicks reads "neather"; A1 is obscure, but the Latin summary reads, "Quae silentio magis involvenda quam in lucem proferenda videantur" (Which should rather, it seems, be wrapped up in silence than brought out into the light: Coll P I 267a).

172. The seminary priest John Ballard (d. 20 September 1586) was put to death for treason as one of the fourteen condemned for the Babington Plot (Anstruther, 19–20). Persons may be referring to his imprudent friendship with the apostate priest Anthony Tyrrell (on whom, see p. 276 n149 above), who had incriminated him falsely. In his own account, edited by Persons, Tyrrell wrote: "I looked Mr Ballard full in the face, and he earnestly beheld me, but, good Lord! how I was confounded to behold the man, knowing the abominable slanders I had given out of him, and not knowing what torment he had sustained by reason of my horrible accusations." See Morris, 2: 410.

173. A217.

174. The topos of raising an altar against an altar was common in Catholic polemic of the Reformation era; here it is applied to the rivalry between some seculars and the Jesuites: cf. Persons to Barret, 26/28 September 1596 (B344); Persons's memorandum of 30 August 1596 (B341); etc.

lye foode,[175] for that no man heare hathe shedd the blowde of our parentes or kinsfolkes; and yet yf these causes were, myght ther be some meane of atonemente. But the thinges which we fall owt abowt are mere apprehensions and imaginations *de futuris contingentibusque* and sckearslye hytherto *in rerum natura*.[176] And yf any litle thinge hathe passed or be present that hathe offended us, yt ys scant worthe twoo woordes of stryf, yf yt were weyghed by juste weyght and meseure.

I know well (deere countrimen) by longe experience what yt ys to lyve in a colleige or multitude where once anye motion or blast of contention ys raysed: yt occupyed me and diverse others in our Oxforde colleidges for manye yeares persuadinge our selves that yt imported us muche to go throwghe with our pretensions: but I was no sooner forthe of that ayer and had looked back upon those colleiges agayne, but that I repented my self full hevely of that losse of tyme and marveyled at our follye, that we hadd so trowbled our selves and our frendes abowte syche trifles, and stryved with the ayer.[177] And yet was I farr of then from the feelinge that God hathe gyven me synce of syche losses, and of the greate deangers that are incidente and consequente to those affayres, and the lyke I darr assure yow that any man heare that shall departe thys howse, wyll have the same feelinge and remorce within a few dayes of hys departure hence, and wyll beshrew the day that ever he tooke so depelye to hart and strugled so muche for things of so litle momente which he wold gladlye forget agayne and have to be forgotten.

Wherefore lettinge passe and bringinge under foote all that ys gone, let us for Godes sayke and for our countrye sayke, and for our owne saykes, utterlye mayke an ende of thys tumulte and returne to our olde comforthe and quietnes agayne, wherin I offer my self to laboure most willinglye with all the vaynes of my harte; and perhappes I may be no evyll meane therin beinge on th'on syde an Inglishman, and therby bownde to yow to seeke your good everye way, and on th'other syde of the Societye,[178] and therby not unfytt to deale with them yf any difficultye showld be of that parte, as I hope there wylbe none, for I know they love bothe yow and our countrye intierlye and for God which ys the surest foundation of love in the worlde. They honour also your profession with all there hartes, whatsoever the enimye maye have suggested to the contrarye. Wherof one argumente amongst other may be, that they have imployed bothe me and others in your service, and in the service of the seminaryes so manye yeares and not in there owne affayres as the world seethe. And as for my self yow see that albeyt they have mantayned me some twoo or three and twentye yeares amonge them, yet have I served them litle or

---

175. I.e., feud: Tynedale and Redesdale form part of the English Middle March of the Scottish border, renowned for clan rivalry and cross-border raids. In 1523 the earl of Surrey wrote to King Henry VIII, "Mooste humble besechinge your Grace too loke upon this poure contre which by the contynnell murders and theftes comytted and doon by Tyndale and Ridsdale men and others of Northumbreland and other centres under my Lord Dacre's rewle was nere brought too uttir confusion" (Edward Charlton, *Memorials of North Tyndale and Its Four Surnames* [Newcastle-upon-Tyne, 1871], 39). The area fell under the jurisdiction of the Catholic family Dacre.

176. Things that might be and things that could happen, not in actuality.

177. Persons was expelled from Balliol College, Oxford, in 1574, after a period of conflict with fellow students and fellows; see Edwards, 3–10.

178. I.e., he has the twin advantages of being an Englishman and a Jesuit.

nothinge at all:[179] but my labours syche as they be have bene imployed to the use of Ingland and Inglishmen and of preistes and schollers in particular, so as in thys behalf I darr say with Nehemias to Almightye God at the day of Judgment: *memento mei Domine in bono secundum omnia quae feci huic populo*: I desyre nothinge els at Gods handes but that he wyll vowtsafe to remember me to do me good and perdon my synnes, as I have alwayes bene desyrous and indevored what hathe lane in me to do good to thys kinde of people,[180] to men of your vocation; and the lyke I must and wyll do ever by hys divine grace, let yt be taken or constreued how yt wyll.

In fine I am wholye yours, use me to your best comoditye. Gods holye grace and benediction be upon us all, and upon the cause of our countrye. And thys ys all I have now to saye.

B362 From Henry Garnet, 7 April 1597

SOURCES:
ABSI, Coll P II 548, Grene's excerpt;
ARSI, Angl. 38/II, fol. 177v (Bartoli's Italian translation).
HICKS: Garnet, 421.
NOTE: Garnet relays news of the martyrdom of Christopher Robinson, on whom see Anstruther, 293, who refers us to J.E. Bamber, "The Venerable Christopher Robinson, Martyred at Carlisle in 1597: The Evidence Concerning his Place of Birth and the Place and Date of his Execution," *Recusant History* 4 (1957): 18–35 (Garnet's letter is quoted in full at 29–30). Bamber argues that Robinson must have been put to death before the Lenten Assizes were finished, by Easter, 27 March.

One Robinson a seminary Priest was lately in a purchased gaole-delivery hanged att Carlisle:[181] the rope broke twice and the third time he rebuked the sherif of cruelty, saying that although he meant no way to yield, but was glad of his combat, yet flesh and bloud was weake, and therefore he shewed little humanity to torment a man so long. And when they took order to putt 2 ropes, than sayeth he, "By this meanes I shal be longer a-dying: but it is no matter; I am very willing to suffer all."[182] This is all the particulars I have yet heard.

179. Persons passes over the service he did for Acquaviva in negotiations with the Spanish Jesuits and Philip II.

180. [2 Esd. 5]:19: "Memento mei Deus meus in bonum secundum omnia quae feci populo huic" (Remember me, O my God, for good according to all that I have done for this people).

181. A jail delivery was an occasion when the authorities sought to deal with all outstanding cases and thus clear the prison. Jail sentences were not handed down as a form of punishment; prisoners were either awaiting trial or execution.

182. Bartoli translates: "Un certo Robinsono sacerdote seminarista fu ultimamente fatto morire a Carlisle. Il capestro si ruppe due volte, e la terza volta, accusò il sherifo (officiale di giustitia) di crudeltà, dicendo che concio fusse che non voleva mai lasciarsi vincere nondimeno che la carne e sangue erano in deboli, e pero che gli mostrava poca d'un huomo di tormentarlo così e quando si diede ordine di mettere due capestri insieme, donque disse staro più tempo morendo, ma non importa, patiro il tutto volontieri &c."

B363 From Henry Garnet, London, April 1597

SOURCE: ABSI, Coll P II 595, Grene's excerpt.
HICKS: Garnet, 420.
NOTE: Garnet acknowledges Persons's decision that he should remain in England (cf. Persons to Acquaviva, 10 July 1595, B283). See McCoog, *Building the Faith of St Peter*, 312–313, who suggests that William Baldwin's presence in Rome meant that it was not necessary for Garnet to come to report on the actions of Jesuits in England.

I perceive your will is that I should stay here till further order, which now I acquiett myself in, and soe indeed do all here think best: and I could not otherwise leave things here to my own contentment and others, here being none in all respects fitt to be left in my roome.

B364 To Olivier Mannaerts, Rome, 12 April 1597

SOURCES:
AAW, VI, item 24, 83–86, a copy in Persons's hand (= W);
ABSI, Coll P II 361, Grene's notes (= G).
HICKS: 578–588, with English translation.
EDITION: Tierney, 3: lxxxvi–lxxxix, "Persons's own copy, in my possession."
NOTE: Persons cautions Mannaerts against throwing in his lot with those who were critical of Holt and Owen in Flanders: these included Crichton and other Jesuits. Divisions might develop within the Society there. Persons's concern with Jesuit unity echoes what he wrote to Mannaerts on 10 January (B352). He warns that the rebellious students at the English college in Rome might be encouraged by the example of the faction in Flanders, but is hopeful about the prospects of peace in the English College, Rome. His letter accords with letters written by Acquaviva to Mannaerts and Holt on the same day. In the event, Mannaerts continued to press for Holt's removal. See McCoog, *Building the Faith of St Peter*, 350–353.

Persons claims to be conciliatory towards Holt's opponents, but Tierney, citing Persons's report to Idiáquez, 30 June 1597 (B383), treats this as duplicitous. Cf. Persons's letter to Paget, 20 December 1597 (B429).

Admodum reverende in Christo Pater
Pax Christi.

Hoc ipso fere momento temporis litteras Reverentiae Vestrae, 22° Martii scriptas, accepi, quo fit per tabellarii festinationem non liceat mihi pluribus ad easdem respondere. Laetor valde Reverentiam Vestram viribus adhuc et valitudine frui; et cum minus hinc quam ex Hispaniis impedita sit litterarum transmissio, facilior fiet et frequentior per eas communicatio. Spero autem Reverentiam Vestram adhuc victuram et visuram illud Collegium Londinense, quod aliquando istic una designavimus. Reverentia enim Vestra semper nobis extitit pater amantissimus, ac causae nostrae Anglicanae patronus, ex qua etiam re magis moveor, ut impense cupiam ne tandem, post tot annorum tam singularem unionem, iudiciorum inducatur arte daemonis dissidium, ac ex eo etiam affectuum, quod

Sanctissimus Pater Noster Ignatius prudentissime simul ac piissime precavendum nobis solicite admonet. Video enim Reverentiam Vestram valde serio suscepisse defensionem eorum hominum qui ex gente nostra P. Holtum impugnant: qua in re nonnulla scribit Reverentia Vestra, quibus ego libenter assentior, scilicet, homines istos nullo modo abalienandos esse, aut iniuriis, aut opprobriis, aut contemptu, aut partialitate, ut Vestra Reverentia dicit, exasperandos. Addo etiam, si Hugo Oenus quicquam in eos fecit, iustum est, non solum ut desistat, sed etiam ut satisfaciat: idem etiam dico de P. Holto, vel de meipso, vel alio quolibet nostrorum, qui contra hanc mansuetudinem aut charitatem religiosam vel minimum offenderit. Ex alia tamen parte, aeque iustum est, causam Hugonis Oeni, utpote viri secularis, si qua in re illos laesit, a nostrorum causa seperandam, et non omnia imputanda nostris, id est viris Societatis, quae Hugo gesserit vel dixerit, quanquam nostrorum amicus sit, nobisque bene cupiat: neque aequum esse[183] postulare ut P. Holtus ab eius amicitia discedat, ob aliorum in eum iracundiam, quae multis ab annis manifesta aemulatione duravit; cum nihil Societati nostrae fecerit mali, sed potius e contrario, et gubernatores omnes Belgii fidenter eo usi sint, neque ulla res contra eius fidelitatem hactenus probari potuerit quod ego sciam.

Quod vero Reverentia Vestra toties et ubique in suis literis illos "nobiles" appellat qui P. Holto infensi sunt, aliam vero partem appellat[184] semper "Oen et eius sectatores", tanquam si illi solum nobiles, isti vero ignobiles essent, valde invidiosum est ac male acceptum a pluribus nostratibus, qui Societati nostrae amicissimi hactenus extiterunt et idem se istic observasse ex sermone Reverentiae Vestrae quotidiano affirmant. Putant enim hinc Reverentiam Vestram velle eos ignobiles haberi, cum tamen isti, excepto uno Comitis Vestmerlandiae nomine (qui tamen contra P. Holtum nihil se quaerelae habere apud amicos multos professus est, sed solum contra Oen), longe se aliis nobiliores, vel saltem pares, esse contendunt. Cuiusmodi sunt D. Gulielmus Stanlaeus cum fratribus, cuius maerita in rempublicam aliorum omnium maerita iudicio omnium excedunt. Et plusquam viginti etiam alii qui litteris publicis in P. Holti iustificationem nuper subscripserunt, cum decem et sex sacerdotibus, quorum multi sunt doctores ac viri Ecclesiastici primarii. Sunt deinde in Hispaniis D. Franciscus Inglefildus, nuper mortuus, eques auratus et Senator Regius antiquissimus, D. Thomas Fitzherbertus, D. Jacobus Hillus, et alii, qui D. Caroli Pagetti factioni, aliorumque paucorum variis modis variisque de causis in hac contentione illi coniunctorum, semper se opposuerunt. Numero et dignitate non parum[185] superiores putant, qui ut semper se causae publicae fideles, et Societati nostrae amicissimos, rebus ipsis probaverunt, quod tamen de aliis (quoad Societatem saltem nostram) dici non potest. Nam etsi Reverentia Vestra literis suis ad P. Alfonsum Agazzarium affirmet se credere non posse istos nobiles Societatem nostram petere (neque ego de omnibus nominatim illud affirmaverim, cum non ignorem diversis de causis diversos D. Pagetto hac in causa coniunctos esse, alios nimirum ob inopiam, animique exulcerationem, quae inde sequi solet, alios ob aemulationem Oeni, alios ob nationum differentiam, aliosque similes ob causas, et non ob odium Societatis), praecipuam tamen factionis istius, per Pagettum et Morganum ante quindecim annos coep-

183. esse] W; est Tierney
184. appellat] Tierney; appellet W
185. Tierney inserts se

tae, intentionem contra Societatem fuisse semper ac esse notissimum est iis, qui toto hoc tempore negotia Anglicana tractarunt; quorum e numero P. Alfonsus est, et Dr Barrettus, et Dr Worthingtonus, et alii testes externi, et Cardinalis Alanus sepissime mihi affirmavit; et ego, et P. Creswellus, P. Holtus, et P. Garnettus clarissime probavimus. Dux etiam Feriensis, eodem sensu quo Vestra Reverentia per quosdam istius factionis imbutus, ac multo tempore confirmatus, tandem, perspectis rebus omnibus ac paenitus penetratis, sententiam penitus mutavit, ut nuper Barcanonae mihi significavit.

Et quanquam Reverentia Vestra ad hoc argumentum respondeat, de Anglorum e Societate conspiratione, his litteris suis, quod multorum conspiratio potest aliquid minus provide aliquando agere vel sentire, tamen ad Reverentiae Vestrae prudentiam et aequitatem appello, si probabilius non sit Vestram Reverentiam hac in re posse falli, quae solum 4. mensium commercium cum illis habuisse fatetur, ac verbis eorum tantum credidit, quam nobis omnibus diversarum nationum, statuum, ac locorum hominibus, qui quindecim annorum facta perspeximus ac trutinavimus. Quod si haec ratio adhuc Vestrae Reverentiae non satisfaciat, me admoneat, et demonstrationes aliquot evidentissimas afferam, quibus constabit eos de Societate nostra indigna saepe loquutos, viros nonnullos principes a Societatis nostrae affectu avertisse, libros curasse in Societatem nostram universam scribi, memorialibus contra Societatem subscripsisse et alia istiusmodi. Haec omnia firmis ac indubitatis testibus:[186] quae omnia Dominus scit non me ideo scribere ad Vestram Reverentiam, ut eam ab ullo humanitatis aut benignitatis officio erga eos avertam, in quos ego meipsum libenter impenderem, ut eis serio inservirem, si istic essem (eamque ob causam peto ut haec caute ac prudenter et sine offensione tractentur); sed ideo haec scribenda duxi, ne Vestrae Reverentiae benignitatis huius affectu rapta ac desiderio pacis (quae difficile cum istis sic affectis constituetur) impingat in contrarium incommodum quod aliquousque iam fecisse video; nimirum ut incurrat in offensionem antiquorum amicorum, et istorum novorum amicitiam (Societati saltem) non consequatur firmam. Illud etiam erit valde indignum, ut nostri iudiciis et affectibus hac in causa inter se dimicent, et ut hii alumni rebelles qui istinc animati universam Societatem conviciis indies praescindunt, glorientur (quod modo facere coeperunt) non deesse ex nostris praecipuis in Belgio qui eis faveant, et schisma suum, schisma etiam Jesuitarum commovisse: quo fiet ut difficilius hic remedia tanto morbo adhibeantur; sed mala malis sine fine cumulentur. Atque haec ex nova Reverentiae Vestrae aliorumque patrum cum antiquis nostris aemulis facta amicitia spargi coeperunt, quae licet longissime ab intentione vestra quam sanctissimam esse non dubito, remota sint, tamen haec initio aperienda esse Reverentiae Vestrae duxi, ne longius serpant, si fieri potest.

De P. Holto statuerat Reverendus Pater Noster Generalis, antequam ego huc apellerem, multa esse propter quae in praesentia mutandus esse non videatur; postea commodius fieri posse iudicat. Ego nondum coepi cum summo agere pontifice de rebus nostris: cum Illustrissimis Cardinalibus[187] nepotibus egi; et crastina fortasses die Sua Sanctitas me audiet. Omnia videntur spem bonam facere, fore res Collegii Anglicani pacatiores. Egerunt iam mecum nonnulli ex praecipuis turbatoribus. Ego autem sequar eam

---

186. *Tierney inserts* probabo
187. Illustrissimis Cardinalibus] *W*; Illustrissimi Cardinali *Tierney Hicks*

humanitatis rationem in componendo,[188] quam Vestra Reverentia probat, in quantum virtutis et disciplinae ratio feret, ac Reverentiam Vestram frequentius faciam certiorem de successu, cuius sanctis precibus ac sacrificiis plurimum me commendo. Romae 12 Aprilis, 1597.

[*Endorsed:*] Exemplar P. Pers. literarum ad P. Oliveriu^m 12 Aprilis 1597.

[*At a different time, but in the same hand, probably Persons's*] De mutatione P. Holti.

Translation

Very reverend father in Christ
The peace of Christ.

I have only just this moment received Your Reverence's letter, written on 22 March, with the result that the urgency of the courier prevents my making a longer reply. I am very glad that Your Reverence continues to enjoy good health and strength. As there are fewer impediments to the interchange of letters from here than there are from Spain, our communication will become easier and more frequent. I hope indeed that Your Reverence will yet live to see that college in London which we once planned together there; for Your Reverence has always been conspicuous as a most loving father to us and a patron of our cause in England. And that is also what has increased my earnest desire not to let our understandings be forced apart by the devil's art, after so many years of unparalleled union, nor, as a result, the ties of affection severed, something which our most holy father Ignatius so anxiously, prudently, and piously warns us to be on our guard against. For I observe that Your Reverence has undertaken in all seriousness the defence of those men of our nation who are attacking Fr Holt. On this matter Your Reverence has some things to say which I readily approve: for instance, that those men should by no means be alienated either by injuries, abuse, contempt or prejudice; they must not – as Your Reverence says – be exasperated; I will add also that, if Hugh Owen has acted against them in any way, it is just that he should not only cease to do so but he should give them satisfaction as well. The same applies also to Fr Holt, or to me myself, or to any other of Ours who has offended even in the slightest degree in this way against fair dealing or religious charity. On the other hand it is equally just that the case of Hugh Owen, as a layman, if he has injured them in any way, should be differentiated from Ours. Whatever Hugh may have done or said should not all be laid to the charge of Ours, that is of members of the Society, even though he is a friend of Ours and wishes us well, nor is it fair to ask Fr Holt to break off his friendship with him just because others are angry with him – something that has continued from many years ago, and clearly arises from envy: for he has done no injury to our Society but rather the reverse. All the rulers of Belgium treat him with confidence, and nothing has been brought to light up to now to question his honesty, so far as I know.

The very fact that in your letter Your Reverence so often and in every case speaks of the men who are hostile to Fr Holt as "nobles" but of the other party as "Owen and his following," as though the former alone were of noble birth and the latter of mean birth,

188. *Tierney inserts* negotio

is most invidious and a cause of offence to many of our countrymen who have been so conspicuously friendly to our Society until now; and they say that they have noticed the same thing there in Your Reverence's everyday conversation. They take it from this that Your Reverence considers them lowborn, although as a matter of fact these men argue that they are themselves of far better birth than the other party, or at any rate of equally good birth, with just one exception, namely the earl of Westmorland (and he too has declared before his friends that he has no quarrel with Fr Holt, but only with Owen). Sir William Stanley and his brothers are of the same class, whose services to the state, everyone agrees, exceed in merit those of everybody else; so too with more than twenty other men also who have recently signed their names to a public document approving Fr Holt's conduct, and with them sixteen priests, many of whom are doctors and of high ecclesiastical rank. Then in Spain there are Sir Francis Englefield, recently deceased, a knight and a very old member of the royal council; Mr Thomas Fitzherbert; Mr James Hill; and others, who have always opposed the faction of Mr Charles Paget and the handful of other men who in various ways and for various reasons have been associated with him in this quarrel. They consider that there is not a little superiority in number and worth among those who have always proved themselves, by their very deeds, to be loyal to the common cause and most friendly to our Society; which cannot be said of the others, at any rate as regards our Society. For, although in your letter to Fr Alfonso Agazzari Your Reverence declares that you cannot believe that these noblemen are aiming their blows at our Society (nor would I affirm it expressly of all of them, for I am not unaware that various men from a variety of motives have been associated with Mr Paget in this cause, some for instance on account of poverty and the exasperation of spirit that often accompanies it, some out of dislike for Owen, others on account of difference of nationality, and for other similar reasons, and not from hatred of the Society), yet the fact that the primary intention of that faction, which was begun by Paget and Morgan fifteen years ago, always was, and is, to oppose the Society, is perfectly well-known to those who have had to do with English affairs in all this time. Amongst their number are Fr Alfonso, Dr Barret, Dr Worthington, and other outside witnesses; Cardinal Allen very frequently told me it was so, and I, Fr Creswell, Fr Holt, and Fr Garnet have had very clear proof of it. The duke of Feria too,[189] who was instilled by certain members of that faction with the same sentiments as Your Reverence and had been confirmed in them for a long time, has at last changed his opinion entirely, after examining the whole business and getting to the bottom of it, as he informed me in Barcelona the other day.

Your Reverence may counter this argument, adduced from the consensus of opinion of the English fathers of the Society, by saying in your own letter that a combination of many people is apt sometimes to do things or form opinions with a certain lack of foresight. Nevertheless, I appeal to Your Reverence's prudence and fairness to consider whether it is not more probable that Your Reverence may be deceived in this matter. You admit to having had dealings with them for only four months, and yet you have given as much credit to what they say as to all of us, men of various nationalities and

---

189. The duke of Feria was viceroy of Catalonia (see Persons to Mannaerts, 10 January, B352).

positions in life and stationed in various places, who have been watching and weighing their actions for fifteen years. If Your Reverence is still unconvinced by this argument, let me know, and I will produce some utterly plain proofs which will show conclusively that they have frequently spoken disparagingly of our Society, that they have estranged a number of leading men from the Society, that they have had books written against the whole of our Society, that they have signed memorials against the Society and done other things of that kind. All this by firm and indubitable testimony: God knows that I am telling Your Reverence all this not with the object of dissuading you from any office of humanity or kindness towards them – I myself would willingly devote myself to serving them sincerely if I were there,[190] and for that reason I ask that these matters may be dealt with cautiously and prudently and without giving offence – but I thought it proper that these things be written down for this reason: to prevent Your Reverence, carried away by this sentiment of kindliness and desire for peace (which will be difficult to achieve with men disposed as these are), from laying yourself open to the opposite disadvantage (which to a certain extent I see you have already done): namely, of giving offence to old friends and failing to establish a firm friendship with these new ones, at least so far as the Society is concerned. It will be very unseemly too that Ours should be at variance among themselves in their judgements and sympathies regarding this matter, and that the rebellious students here, who, drawing their inspiration from there, are daily denigrating the whole Society with their abuse, should boast (as they have now begun to do) that they do not lack support from our principal men in Belgium, and that their schism has raised a schism in the Jesuits also: the result of which will be that it will be more difficult to apply a remedy here to such a grave disease, and evil will be piled on evil endlessly. These evils too, arising from this newborn friendship of Your Reverence and other fathers with our long-standing rivals, have begun to spread, and, although this is very far from your intention, which I doubt not to be a most holy one, yet I considered that they ought to be made known to Your Reverence now at the start, so that, if possible, they may not creep in further.

About Fr Holt, our reverend father general had already decided, before I reached here, that there are many reasons why it is not desirable that he should be moved at present; he considers it could be done more conveniently later. I have not yet begun to discuss our affairs with the supreme pontiff; I have done so with the cardinal-nephews, and tomorrow possibly His Holiness will give me audience. Everything seems to promise well for more peaceful times in the English college: some of the principal disturbers have already made approaches to me; and for my part I shall pursue that method of kindliness in composing a quarrel which Your Reverence approves, so far as regard for virtue and discipline will allow; and I will let Your Reverence know from time to time how things go on. To your holy prayers and sacrifices I earnestly commend myself. Rome, 12 April 1597.

190. Tierney comments: "Compare this with his advice to Don Juan d'Idiaquez, in the following June, urging the banishment of some of this party," referring to the memorial dated 30 June 1597 below (B383).

B365 From Henry Garnet, London, 15 April 1597

SOURCE: ABSI, Coll P II 537, Grene's excerpt.
HICKS: Garnet, 422.
NOTE: Garnet consults Persons about admitting Ralph Bickley (ca. 1557–1619) to the Society. Bickley, a student at Douai and Rome, returned to England in 1583, and was arrested and imprisoned, first at the Gatehouse (1585) and then at Wisbech (1588). He entered the Society on 15 August 1597, one of the first to be admitted in England once Acquaviva lifted the restrictions (Foley, 1: 476–85; Anstruther, 35; McCoog, *English and Welsh Jesuits*, 120–21).

Rafe Bickly wrot to you to sue for him that he may be admitted. He is a very singular man. I pray you obtaine it; he hath sued these 12 yeares. He is with Father Weston who desireth it greatly.

B366 From Thomas Stapleton, Louvain, 16 April 1597

SOURCE: AAW VI, no. 27, 95–98, holograph, bearing the note "Tho. Stapletono 1597" at the foot of the first page.
EDITIONS: Knox, *Douay Diaries*, 390–391; James Dallaway, *A History of the Western Division of the County of Sussex* (London, 1815–1832), 2.2: 278–279.
NOTE: Stapleton explains why he has accepted the pope's offer of a position in Rome of protonotary apostolic, i.e., membership in the chief order of prelates attached to the papacy: he hopes to be of some help in settling the disputes at the English college, if it is still necessary, and to be able to return to his scholarly work in Louvain before long. He encloses his letter of acceptance, and expects to travel to Rome at the end of the summer.

+

Right Reverend Father
Your loving letter, dated in Genua the xvth of Marche, was to me most welcome; perceaving thereby the fast frendship and good will it liketh you to beare unto me with more respect then I deserve. Trew it is that almost now a yeare past I have bene sollicited to come to Rome, first by a courteous offer of Cardinal Aldobrandino to be receaved into his family,[191] then by offer of a lesson in the Sapientia,[192] and last by offer of His Holynes to a protonotariat, one of the vii participantes nowe vacant: to the which last offer, being the third letter sent, I gave some eare, rather upon other wordes in the letter then upon the offer it selfe: though to the first and second offer I made great and just exceptions (in my judgement) not to take this viage or make an alteration of my course in this age, and honest state, especially my purpose of writing and perfeyting the commenced concepts.

191. Cardinal Pietro Aldobrandini (1571–1621; created cardinal 1593), nephew to Pope Clement VIII (Ippolito Aldobrandini); see Bruno Boute, *Academic Interests and Catholic Confessionalisation: The Louvain Privileges of Nomination to Ecclesiastical Benefices* (Leiden, 2010), 318.

192. The pontifical university of Rome, founded in 1303, commonly known as "La Sapienza" from the 1560s.

But only for hope to be a meane to helpe my countre and countremen being in this new vocation, I did accept of the last offer more than iii monethes sence, addressing my answer by a meanes that succeeded not: for nowe the xith of Marche last I receaved a fourth letter with a duplicat of the later to have my full resolution; which nowe at this time I send agayne even with these to you, that my answer may be more assuredly delivered, and that, if you thinke good, by your owne handes.[193] And as for my coming thither, assure you I should thinke my selfe very happy to finde you there, and to conferre with you aboute all thinges concerning the good of our countre or the appaisement of that unhappy brawle of the youthes against their Fathers and masters there. Howbeit I hope that point will be utterly appeased by your only endevour. If I do come to Rome at all, it will be the ende of this sommer before I arrive there, not only because it will be nere to August before I have the answer to these, and withall such despatch with His Highnes here[194] as I do require (without the which I minde not to remove), but also because I would have the heates past before I see Rome this yeare. The dimission that I require of his Highnes here is to enjoye the place and roome I have here in all pointes for one yeare and a half at lest after my departure, with liberte to enjoye and continew the same if I returne within that time, which I hope to do:[195] the which I have proposed to Cardinal Aldobrandino in my former, and his Grace hath promised in his last, to deale with His Highnes here for that favour and to employ the Nuncio here to that effect.[196] Nowe, good Father, as I desire sincerely to remayne a trew and trusty servant to His Majesty of Spayne, though I hap to live and perhaps to continew in the Court of Rome, and as I meane before my departure hence to insinuat so much to his Highnes here, so I would wish that some of the Counsel aboute His Majesty in Spayne might understand the same; of which point you may consider, and deale as you thinke good. The favour of His Holynes toward me nowe semeth greate: but what it may be hereafter when he shall see me and knowe me better is very uncertayne, and I builde not a jote thereupon. The dignyte and favour which His Holynes hath offered me is a sufficient motive for me to come and trie for a time, and a sufficient place of credit to do some good to the common cause as long as I shall remayne there; desiring nothing more then to returne with that good provision to my studyes agayne: upon which hope I kepe my lesson here, and will leave my house in such very state as nowe it is for the time before writen, which will be a time of sufficient triall bothe for His Holynes of me and for me of Rome. Many here have greate imaginatyons of this my calling, but surely I have none such. Only the good Cardinal Aldobrandino, as he desired much to have Lipsius, famous in his kinde,[197] so he desireth to have me aboute him, somewhat for lerning famous also: and to accomplish his desire hath (I suppose) enduced His Holynes to offer me the abovesayed dignyte being of some good valew able to mayntayne me in Rome very honestly and with some worship. This I take to be the very

193. and that, if you thinke good, by your owne handes] *added in the margin W*
194. Archduke Albert, governor of the Spanish Netherlands.
195. with liberte to enjoye and continew the same if I returne within that time, which I hope to do] *added in the margin W*
196. Ottavio Mirto Frangipani.
197. Justus Lipsius (1547–1607), author of *De constantia*, was reconciled to the Catholic church in 1590, leading to a spate of invitations from universities and courts.

roote and ground of my calling: and to looke farther, as it were a greate foly in me, so it is an ungrounded imagination of others. I have opened unto you plainly and sincerely this my calling to Rome. If it might be our happe bothe to mete there I should take exceding comfort thereby. You would wonder if you knewe howe some here do feare your coming thither as prejudicial to me, and other some my going thither as prejudiciall to you. But I hope we are bothe wiser, and have bothe better endes of this journey then to geve any just occasion of such fond feares and jalousyes. Much more I have to saye; but this letter hath babled enough. I ende therefore and commit you to God and me most hartely to your good prayers. Lovayne the xvith of Aprill, 1597.

    All youres entierly
        Thomas Stapleton.

[*Addressed*:] Admodum R. Patri, P. Roberto Personio, Societatis Jesu praesbytero. Romae.

[*Endorsed*:] D. Stapleton, 16 Aprilis, 1597.

B367 Minutes of a Meeting with Francisco de Peña, 17 April 1597

SOURCE: BAV, MS Vat. Lat. 6227, fols. 162–164.

NOTE: In a second meeting with Peña, Persons reports on his audience with the pope and the cardinal-nephews, explaining that although Peña had cautioned him against discussing the succession, they had had a fruitful discussion. Another account is given in his memorial of 1 May (B371), prepared for Idiáquez. See McCoog, *Building the Faith of St Peter*, 363–364.

§ A 17 de Abril vino otra vez el Padre Personio, y dio cuenta a Peña de cómo avia tenido larga audiencia con Su Santidad y con los señores cardenales nepotes, y que avia guardado puntualmente su advertimiento, eceto que en algunos ocasiones solamente en general avia dicho lo mucho que importava mirar a lo de la sucesion: y que Su Santidad mostrava gran voluntad de acudir a todo conforme a la calidad de[198] causa tan grave, importante como era esta.

§ Dixo tambien aver tratado con Su Santidad del libro de la Sucesion, y dadole cuenta de lo que contenia, y representadole quán lexos de la verdad estavan los que dezian que aquel libro ofendia a muchos pretensores de aquella corona: pues el autor dél no hazia otra cosa más de referir los derechos que cada pretensor podia tener: y que no era verdad, que[199] en los de la Señora Infanta de España se[200] huviese puesto estudio más particular que en los demas: si bien se señalava ser más conviniente la persona de la Señoria Infanta que los de los otros pretensores, para el remedio de aquella corona, y para establicer la religion en ella, y reduzirla enteramente a la devocion de la Sede Apostolica.

§ Añadio el dicho Padre Personio, como Su Santidad avia mostrado holgarse mucho de entender esto: y de que no avia desgustado lo de la Señora Infanta: Aqui Peña replicó, que si bien de la persona de Su Santidad y de su intencion se podia facilmente creer todo esto, no se podia tener la mesma seguridad de sus parientes y ministros, los quales ultra

198. de] *interlined with caret above* de les [*deleted*] B
199. verdad, que] *supplied from margin* B
200. se] *interlined with caret* B

de tener poco devocion a España, embidiavan su grandeza, y con esta emulacion siguiendo solamente la razon de estado temporal, poniendo mucho esfuerço en contrapesar la grandeza de España, antepondrian a la Señora Infanta[201] para aquella corona de Inglaterra todo otro pretensor, aunque no fuese tan provechoso para el estado de la religion, y que descubriendose[202] este peligro tan claro y evidente todavia me parecia, que era necesario en este punto de la sucesion andar con mucho recato.

§ Conformose con esto el Padre Personio, y dixo que pudiendose deste artículo tratar en dos maneras, en general, y en particular: no trataria dél[203] sino en general: que del decender al particular, bien entendia lo mucho que se aventurava.

§ Peña a este proposito le replicó, que lo que[204] se aventurava era tanto, que iva en ello todo el buen suceso del negocio: porque en decender al particular de constituir sucesor, o, Su Santidad que de su condicion es iresoluto, nunca acabaria, o, finalmente forçado de los persuasiones de los emulos de España, por huir la grandeza de España, y darle contrapeso, vendria en la persona que menos conviniese: y que por tanto deste artículo en particular no se podia, ni devia tratar en Roma sino tan solamente con el duque de Sessa, de quien se podian esperar muy acertados consejos por ser tan prudente, y tener tanta experiencia de cosas de estado, por las muchas que en estos tiempos avian pasado por sus manos no muy diferentes de las de Inglaterra.

§ Y que para acertar convenia en todo caso[205] tener secreto este punto en Roma, pero era necesario prevenirlo con mucho cuidado para que quando muerta la reina, viniese el caso de la Sucesion, todo se hallase dispuesto sin aver[206] las dificultades que se avian en la corona de Francia, que por no aver acudido con presteza, y con resoluciones hechas i efetuar lo que convenia, avia sucedido lo que todo el mundo avia visto sin esperanças de remedio.

§ Y que su paternidad se desengañase que si la resolucion no se hazia en España, y Su Magestad no la alentava, todo lo demas era tiempo perdido: porque tratando desto acá, por las razones arriba dichas avia de suceder una de dos cosas, o, que no se concluiria nada, o, que concluyendose no sería cosa que estuviese bien a la religion, por mirarse tanto acá al estado temporal.

§ Respondio Personio, que asi le parecia, y que en esto pondria él mucho cuidado: y discurriendo sobre el negocio, y reduziendolo a prática individuando las personas dixo que convenia huir mucho del Rei de Escotia por ser notoriamente herege, y porque si él sucediese en Inglaterra y por consiguiente juntandose tres coronas en su persona: la de Escotia, Inglaterra, y Irlanda, y hallandose más poderoso, la religion Catholica estaria en maior peligro: y que quanto a lo temporal tan poco esto convenia a Francia, pues él proprio con este poderio que cobraria, intentaria de nuevo

 201. a la S^a Infanta] *interlined with caret* B
 202. descubriendose] *supplied from margin* B
 203. del] *interlined with caret* B
 204. que] *interlined with caret* B
 205. caso] *interlined with caret* B
 206. aver] *interlined with caret, presumably intended to replace* entrar en *which has not been deleted* B

contra el Frances, todas las antiguas pretensiones que tienen a la corona de Francia, los Reies de Inglaterra.

§ Que de los pretensores Ingleses no avia para que tratar pues todos eran hereges, y que aunque no lo fueran avia otro notable peligro y muy calamitoso para el reino, porque el que fuese Rei para asegurarse cortaria las vidas a los otros principes pretensores como lo avian hecho de cien años a esta parte casi[207] todos los Reies de Inglaterra.

§ Que por tanto lo más acertado era darle Rei estrangero pero no del todo estrangero, como lo era el principe cardenal casandolo con la Señora Infanta; dixo no del todo estrangero, como era el principe cardenal; porque en tiempos pasados de aquella nacion, avian ido a Inglaterra.

§ Concurrio el Padre Personio con la opinion de Peña en que el Rei de Inglaterra que avia de ser para asegurar la religion, y reduzir aquella corona a la obediencia de la Sede Apostolica, avia de ser muy potente, o, depender y tener aiuda de Rei muy potente: porque de otra manera ni podria prevalecer contra los hereges de su reino, ni resistir a los enemigos fuera dél. Y que estas convenientias solamente se hallavan en el Rei de España, i con la Señora Infanta su hija.

Translation

§ On 17 April Fr Persons came another time, and reported to Peña how he had had a lengthy audience with His Holiness and with the cardinal-nephews, and that he had punctiliously followed his advice, except that on some occasions, and only in general terms, he had mentioned how much it was necessary to look into the issue of the succession, and that His Holiness had shown himself very willing to attend to everything according to the nature of such a serious matter, given its importance.

§ He also said that he had discussed the *Book of the Succession* with His Holiness,[208] explaining what it contained and representing to him how far from the truth are those who say that that book gave offence to many of the claimants to the crown – for its author did nothing more than delineate the rights that each claimant might have – and that it was not true that he had given more particular favour to the claim of the Lady Infanta of Spain than to the rest, even though the person of the Lady Infanta was presented as more fitting than the other claimants, for the welfare of that crown, and to establish religion in the realm, and to reduce it entirely to the devotion of the apostolic see.

§ The same Fr Persons added that His Holiness took much pleasure in this information, and that mentioning the issue of the Lady Infanta had not displeased him. To which Peña replied that while as far as the person of His Holiness and his intention were concerned he could easily believe all this, he could not be quite so sure about his kindred [nephews] and ministers, who, besides feeling little attachment to Spain, envied her greatness, and with this emulation simply following temporal reason of state, they put great emphasis on countering the greatness of Spain by setting every other claimant to the crown of England above the Lady Infanta, even if it were less profitable to the state of

207. casi] this ed.; cosi B

208. *Conference about the Next Succession*, variously known as the *Book of the Succession*, the Book of Titles, or Doleman, after the pseudonym used.

religion. Thus exposing the danger so clearly and evidently, it seemed to me that it was [even more] necessary in this point of the succession to proceed with much caution.

§ Fr Persons agreed with this, and said that as this issue could be dealt with in two ways, either in general or in particular, he would not deal with it except in general, as he well understood how much of a risk it would entail to descend to particulars.

§ To this proposition Peña replied that the risks were so great that the good success of the business depended on it. And this was because in getting down to the detail of establishing a successor, either His Holiness, who is by nature indecisive, would never reach a decision, or eventually would be compelled by the persuasions of those who envy Spain, trying to avoid her greatness, to make a counterweight, and consequently would settle on a person who was less fitting. Therefore, this issue in particular could not, and should not, be discussed in Rome except only with the duke of Sessa, of whom he could expect more reliable advice, since he is so prudent and so experienced in state matters, and given how many things he has managed recently that were not greatly different from those of England.

§ And that in order to do things correctly it was fitting in this entire matter to keep this point secret in Rome, but it was necessary to prepare very carefully in advance so that as soon as the queen dies and the issue of succession arises, everything would proceed readily without encountering the difficulties which had been the case with the crown of France, where, because prompt action could not be taken, or resolutions adopted to bring about what was requisite, things had turned out as all the world has seen, without hope of remedy.

§ And that His Paternity should make no mistake: if the decision was not made in Spain, and His Majesty did not support it, all the rest would be a waste of time. If this were discussed here, for the reasons already given, one of two things would transpire: either that no decision would be taken at all, or that something would be concluded that would be really of no good for religion, being considered here mainly from the temporal aspect.

§ Persons responded that he agreed and that he would use much care in this matter, both in deliberating about the business and in putting it into execution: turning to the actual persons themselves, he said it was fitting to keep well clear of the king of Scotland, because of his notorious heresy and because if he succeeded in England the result would be the conjunction of three crowns in his person: those of Scotland, England, and Ireland, and, the more powerful he found himself, the Catholic religion would be in greater danger. And as far as the temporal advantage was concerned, it would be of little benefit to France, because, with this power he had gained, the king would urge against France, with renewed vigour, the ancient claims which the kings of England had to the crown of France.

§ That the English claimants should not be on the table, as they were all heretics, and even if they were not, they posed another notable threat even more calamitous to the kingdom, namely that the one who became king would guarantee his own safety by cutting off the lives of the other claimants, as almost all the kings of England for their part had done throughout the last hundred years.

§ That it was all the more reason why it would be safer to give them a foreign king – but not entirely foreign, as in the case of the prince cardinal, if he married the Lady

Infanta – because on previous occasions in that nation's history, foreign princes had gone to England.

§ Fr Persons concurred with Peña's opinion about what the king of England needed to do to ensure religion and to reduce that crown to obedience to the apostolic see. He would either have to be very powerful himself or else depend on and retain the aid of a more powerful king: because in no other way could he prevail against the heretics within his kingdom, nor withstand the enemies from without. And these helps could only be found in the king of Spain, or the Lady Infanta his daughter.

B368 From Henry Garnet, London, 23 April 1597

> SOURCES:
> ABSI, Coll P II 547, Grene's excerpts;
> ARSI, Angl. 38/II, fol. 173, Bartoli's notes.
> HICKS: Garnet, 423.
> NOTE: Richard Banks (ca. 1569–1643) was a student at the English College, Rome, 1587, and ordained in 1592. He entered the Society in 1597/8 (Anstruther, 20; McCoog, *English and Welsh Jesuits*, 110). On Ralph Bickley, see Garnet to Persons, 15 April, B365; Grene's marginal note here, "Rod. Bickly," is presumably a mistake for "Rad[ulphus]" (Foley, 1: 483).

[*Grene's excerpt:*] John Gerard hath bin sore tortured in the tower:[209] it is thought it was for some letters directed to him out of Spaine, &c. —— Bickly's admittance and Banks I pray you procure, &c.[210] The first — is a notable man, the second is of great towardlynesse and extreme good behaviour, &c.

B369 From Claudio Acquaviva, Naples, about 26 April 1597

> SOURCE: Acquaviva to Persons, 2 May (B372).
> NOTE: Acquaviva, on a visit to Naples, relays a request from the viceroy of Naples, Enrique de Guzmán (1540–1607), second count of Olivares, the former Spanish ambassador to Rome, who wished to see Persons.

B370 From Thomas Covert, 29 April 1597

> SOURCE: Persons to Covert, 31 May (B380).
> NOTE: Thomas Covert had been Allen's agent in Paris, responsible for financial affairs; in 1592 he asked Verstegan to remember him to Persons (Verstegan to Persons, 5 March 1592, B138). When he fell out with William Holt in 1595, he complained to Acquaviva, and a failed attempt was made to settle their differences through the vice provincial in Flanders, Jean d'Heur. After much accusation and counteraccusation, Covert appealed to Persons to intervene. See McCoog, *Building the Faith of St Peter*, 341–348.

> 209. Bartoli translates: "Joannes Gerardi crudeliter tortus fuit in Turri Londinensi."
> 210. [*Grene's sidenote:*] Rod. Bickly.

B371 To Don Juan de Idiáquez, 1 May 1597, *Relacion* of English Affairs in Rome in April

SOURCES:
    AAW VI, no. 32, 113–120, holograph = W;
    ABSI, Angl. A II, no. 26 = A;
    ABSI, Coll P II 463, Grene's note, indicating that there is a copy on fol. 677^e (untraced).

HICKS: 589–601, with English translation.

NOTE: This is the first of five memorials composed in Spanish between May and early July for the attention of the Spanish court, via Idiáquez: an account of events relating to English affairs in Rome during the month of April (1 May, B371); an account of the disturbances in the English college (22 May, B378); a memorial on the partisanship of Charles Paget and Thomas Morgan (30 June, B383); a report on developments at the English college (3 July, B385); and a further account of the promotion of the anti-Jesuit party in England itself (12 July, B390). The present account ends with so fulsome a recommendation of the duke of Sessa, the Spanish ambassador in Rome, that it suggests that Idiáquez, the royal secretary in Madrid, may have had reservations about him. Cf. the beginning of Persons's letter to Idiáquez, 3 July (B385).

Here Persons gives his version of the controversy over the publication of *Conference about the Next Succession* and the developments at the English college. Persons's defence of the book recapitulates the arguments in a similar memorial by Sir Francis Englefield (ABSI, Angl. A II, no. 22); see also Persons to Acquaviva, 4 and 16 June 1594 (B233). In his audience with the pope and the two cardinal-nephews, Pietro and Cinzio Aldobrandini, which was held after a briefing with Francisco de Peña on 2 April, Persons sought to correct the impression, most likely deriving from Innocenzo Malvasia, the papal agent (sometimes treated as nuncio) in Brussels, that the book was designed expressly to promote the candidature of the infanta. The pope expressed his satisfaction with the way Persons had handled the dispute at the English college and asked him to move into residence there. A welcome feast was held for him in the vineyard on 10 April (Kenny, "The Inglorious Revolution," 90 n41 [part 3]).

Lo que hallé en Roma acirca de las
cosas de Inglaterra de Abril Primero 1597[211]

Una grande impression se[212] avia hecho en todos los personages de esta corte contra el libro de la succession de Ynglaterra, como si ubiera sido escritto en favor solamente[213] de Su Magestad de España, y espressamente contra el Rey de Escocia, pero presto se llevó esta impression con mostrar el libro medesimo[214] y las raçones por las quales se escrivio.

---

211. + 1º Maii 1597 *at the foot of the first page*
212. se] W; *om.* A
213. en favor solamente] W; solamente en favor A
214. libro medesimo] W; mismo libro A

Porque por el libro se discubrio que no solamente la causa de Su Magestad se propuso,[215] y se trató en él,[216] si no tan bien de otros nueve o diez pretensores, fuera del Rey de Escocia; los quales todos por differentes vias y raçones pretenden la Corona de Ynglaterra, cada uno en primer lugar, sin ceder nadie a[217] otro, y que de todos estos se ponen con toda indiferençia las raçones y allegaciones en pro y in contra, como las de Su Magestad sin determinar la iusticia de nissuno.[218]

Las raçones eran evidentes de la utilidad y necessidad deste libro: Primero, para obviar a la ley de los hereges de Ynglaterra por lo qual mandavan soto pena de lesa magestad que ninguno scriviesse cosa di questa[219] materia, y esto a fin que offereciendoseles la occasione, hechassen sobre los Catolicos la persona che ellos quesiessen, pues nadie sabia nada de los derechos[220] que avia.

2º Era necessario este libro para resolver las dudas[221] de los Catolicos que avian concebido o podian concebir de la falsa doctrina de las dos[222] appollogias de un cierto Bellay françes el qual ha escrito en nuestros dias que para la admission de un Rey o principe no ay[223] menester mirar otra cosa[224] que solamente la[225] cercania de sangre, y que ni religione ni virtud, ni otra circunstancia avia de entrar en consideracion para esto.

Lo terçero porque[226] convenia que los Catolicos[227] fuessen algo prevenidos en este caso, antes que les sea forçoso determinarse en él, lo qual segun toda probabilidad ha de ser presto, y no sin guerra y rebueltas, pues ay tantos y tales pretensores, y la Reyna es vieja.

Lo quarto para que los demas principes Christianos tan bien y principalmente el Papa, vean juntamente el estado deste negocio, y tengan tiempo y luz[228] para pensar y mirar las pretensiones, possibilidades, conveniencias y disconveniencias de cada uno, y qual estara mejor, no solamente para Ynglaterra, si no tan bien para toda la Christianidad.

Estas raçones con el pareçer de todas las personas más graves casi de la nacionYnglesa que estan en distierro y que vieron el libro antes que se imprimio, y con la[229] approbacion despues de los otros Catolicos de Ynglaterra, que han escrito sobre ello,[230]

215. propuso] *W*; discubrio *A*
216. el] *W*; ello *A*
217. a] *W*; de *A*
218. nessuno] *W*; ninguno *A*
219. di questa] *W*; desta *A*
220. los derechos] *W*; las razones *A*
221. las dudas] *W*; la duda *A*
222. dos] *W*; om. *A*
223. ay] *W*; era *A*
224. cosa] *interlined with caret W*
225. solamente la] *interlined with caret W*
226. porque] *interlined with caret W*
227. Catolicos] *A inserts* de ynglat^a
228. y luz] *W*; om. *A*
229. la] *W*; las *A*
230. que han escrito sobre ello] *interlined with caret W*

y con el successo próspero[231] de la cosa en sí (pues no ha causado este libro persecucion en Ynglaterra, sino más presto calma hasta aora) y[232] porque muchissimos se han reducido a grande temple y moderacion, y se les an abierto los ojos con la licion deste libro, como de alla se avisa; con estas raçones[233] se ha hecho grande mudança tan bien aqui en Roma, y se ha quitado o moderado mucho la suspecha y impression que estava hecha y pegada de[234] los clamores continuos y informaciones falsos que algunos Yngleses en Flandres parciales del Rey de Escocia avian dado en este Corte, para haçer odioso aquel libro.

Se entiende que el medio principal para haçer este impression en este corte, ha sido Monsignor Malvasia que fue Nuncio por un tiempo en Flandres, y enformado de Pagetto, Tressamo, Ligons,[235] y otros yngleses de aquella parcialidad por medio de un cierto[236] Doctor Giffordio hecho Dean novamente de Lila, persona harto appassionada en aquellas cosas (y residia por entonçes[237] en la casa[238] del dicho Malvasia). Vino a Roma con las informaciones que le avian dado en Flandes, y con las que despues le an ydo embiando, ha continuado este mismo camino y hallando disposicion conveniente por las cosas que se tratavan por entonçes en favor de Francia, no es de maravigliar si tales informaciones hallaron entrada.

Tan bien vino a proposito al mismo tiempo la turbacion que se avia començado en este Collegio Ynglés, parte por la passion de algunos pocos estudiantes, que querian más libertad, pero principalmente llevantados por algunos yngleses di fuera del Collegio de la parcialidad del obispo de Cassano y de sus seguaces de Flandes.[239] La qual turbacion pareçio a algunos que no sería mal medio para ygualar, o contrapeçar cosas, como una persona principal y prudente y bien affecta[240] me dixo aqui, porque aviendose dado enformacion que todos los demas seminarios yngleses (cuyo poder se entendia ser muy grande en Ynglaterra) avian caminado hasta aora arrimados al Rey de España, parecia raçon de estado que éste de Roma commençasse con esta[241] occasion a tomar otro camino, bolviendose[242] a la aficion de Francia y Escocia, y aunque esto parecia al principio[243] muy difficultoso para effetuar, por causa del amor antico y arraygado que todos los Catolicos Yngleses tienen ya tanto tiempo a Su Magestad Catolica, toda via la passion destos moços disviados una vez llevantada y fomentada por personas principales, crecio tanto, que yo nunca creyra si no la veyra y la toccara con la mano, porque llegó a tanto, que no

231. prospero] *W*; propero *A*
232. y] *W*; om. *A*
233. raçones] *interlined above* cosas [*deleted*] *W*
234. de] *W*; con *A*
235. Pagetto, Tressamo, Ligons] *W*; Pagetto, Ligons, Tressamo *A*
236. cierto] *W*; om. *A*
237. por entonçes] *interlined with caret W*
238. en la casa] *W*; en casa *A*
239. seguaces de Flandes] *W*; seguacos en Flandes *A*
240. affecta] *W*; affecto *A*
241. esta] *W*; este *A*
242. bolviendose] *interlined above* animandose [*deleted*] *W*
243. esto parecia al principio] *W*; este al principio parecia *A*

podian veer ni oyr con paciencia cosa de España, ni suffrir que se les[244] contasse cosa buena della, pero los otros Estudiantes que vinieron conmigo di España los an vencido en esto particular, contando tantas cosas buenas y tantas obligaciones, y esto con tanto modestia, flemma, humildad y paciencia que al fin se hallaron los otros corridos y confusos, y fue sin duda de mucha importancia aver traydo estos estudiantes de España a Roma, por muchos effetos, y su Santidad restó muy contento dello, y de una oracion que le hizieron la primera ves que le hablaron.

Mandóme su Santidad venir y vivir en este Collegio Ynglés[245] por algunos dias, para provar si con mi presencia se pudiessen aquietar[246] estos humores, pues ya[247] su Santidad veýa claramente por las raçones que se le allegavan[248] que era impossibile llevar adelante el camino de contradicion que algunos avian començado, sino con[249] grande escandalo y manifesta perdita y ruyna de la causa[250] de la religion Catolica en Ynglaterra, y assi vini acá y he estado diez dias y con seis o siete conferencias con la parte estragada del collegio que seran[251] la metad dél, pareçe que anda el negocio mucho mejor, y que todo despues se finira bien, y es cosa cierta, que si de fuera no tubiesse esta juventud alas de personas[252] poderosas (que tanbien les començan a faltar) se reduçerian luego.

El capo principal dellos se ha reducido, y él me ha contado muy a menudo todas las traças del buen Cardinal Toledo en esta[253] materia, como le venia a proposito encaminar el collegio en esta manera, en conformidad de las cosas que se avian resuelto de Francia, y de la poca union que él tenía con los padres de la Compañia, a los quales avia pensado de llevar el gobierno deste Collegio, y mudar tanbien el gobierno del Collegio de Rhemis y meter nuevo orden en el manegio[254] de las cosas[255] dentro de Ynglaterra, todo lo qual fue chimera y imaginacion, que no podia salir por obra, sin infinitas ribueltas y inconvenientes, como él avria probado si ubiesse vivido, y Dios nuestro señor le heço[256] mucha merced de llevarle antes que se veerse[257] embaraçado y fatigado en ello.[258]

Los Catolicos de Ynglaterra escriven grandes quexas contra dos destos sacerdotes[259] destos inquietos que entraron en Ynglaterra poco[260] antes que yo me parti de España; fueron embiados de aqui, con entencion de sus parciales (como por sus cartas se vee)

244. se les se] se *om.* A; les *interlined with caret* W
245. Yngles] *interlined with caret* W
246. aquietar] W; quietar A
247. ya] *om.* A
248. allegavan] W; allegaron A
249. con] *interlined with caret* W
250. A *inserts* y
251. seran] W; será A
252. personas] *followed by* de fuera [*deleted*] A
253. esta] W; este A
254. manegio] W; govierno A
255. A *inserts* de *before* dentro
256. heço] A; hiço W
257. veerse] W; viesse A
258. ello] W; él A
259. destos sacerdotes] W; sacerdotes destos A
260. poco] W; *om.* A

para mover sedicion y division en Ynglaterra, y a este effeto an començado a sparger[261] grandes mentiras y cosas odiosas tanto contra los padres de la Compañia como contra la nacion Española. Los Catolicos los huyan como a ponsoña, y les es grandissima afflicion, en medio de otras tantas affliciones y persecuciones, venirles tanbien este otro[262] açote, el Señor Cardinal Archeduque, avisado por el Duque de Sesa de la entencion y mal ánimo destos, mandó prudentemente que no passassen a Ynglaterra por los Puertos que estan soto[263] de la obediencia de Su Magestad en Flandres, pero luego los nuestros yngleses de la parcialidad contraria les procuraron passage por[264] Hollanda, y assi entraron.

Si estos otros dela misma inficion en Roma, no se enmiendan[265] de veras (de lo qual io tengo mucha duda, particularmente de quatro o cinco que an de partirse[266] este autoño y an sido cabeças desta sedicion y aora pareçe que se rinden[267] por fuerça) será muy importante que Su Magestad mande avisar tanto a su Embaxador por acá, quanto al serenissimo Cardinal Archeduque que se les impida el andar a Ynglaterra por[268] aora, hasta que se vea alguna emendacion, pues la yda suya a Ynglaterra aora podria causar grandes males a los Catolicos y disservicio[269] a Su Magestad.

En las demas cosas me remeto a aquello que escrivera, o, avrá escritto el Duque de Sesa, el qual acude a todo con mucha prudencia, autoridad y voluntad, y es un grande ministro de Su Magestad, y da contento a todos y a mí muy en particular, y trato con él con toda confiança, remetiendome a sus cartas en las cosas más secretas y de más importancia, él avrá avisado de la audiencia que tubi de su Santidad y de dos papeles que despues se le dieron[270] sobre las cosas de Ynglaterra y ansi no digo más en ésta.[271] Sea nuestro Señor con Vuestra Señoria siempre. De Roma al primero de Mayo 1597.

[*Endorsed:*] La pª relacion que se embió a España delas cosas deste collegio 1597.[272]

Translation

What I found out in Rome in relation to English affairs
since 1 April 1597

A very unfavourable impression had been gained by all the dignitaries of the curia here in regard to the book on the English succession, as though it had been written solely to

---

261. sparger] *W*; derramar *A*
262. tanbien este otro] tanbien *interlined above* ancora sobre [*deleted*]; otro *interlined with caret* W
263. que estan soto] *interlined with caret;* de la *possibly deleted*
264. por] *W*; en *A*
265. enmiendan] *A*; emendan *W*
266. partirse] *W*; partir *A*
267. rinden] *W*; enmienden *A*
268. por] *om. A*
269. disservicio] *W*; disservicios *A*
270. despues se le dieron] *W*; se le dieron despues *A*
271. esta] *A*; esto *W*
272. *A is endorsed*: Relacion para el Sᵒʳ Don Juⁿ de Ideaques [*in another ink*] 1597.

support the claim of His Majesty of Spain, and expressly to oppose that of the king of Scotland; but this impression was quickly removed when the book itself was produced[273] and the reasons for which it had been written were made clear.

For on reading the book it was discovered that it was not only the claim of His Majesty that was proposed and discussed in it, but also those of nine or ten other claimants, besides the king of Scotland. All of these in different ways and by various arguments lay claim to the English throne, each preferring his own claim and none of them giving way to any of the rest. It was seen too that in the case of all of these, as well as of His Majesty, the arguments and statements for and against are put with complete impartiality and without pronouncing on the validity of any of them.

The arguments for the usefulness and need of this book were clear: firstly, to counteract the law which the English heretics had passed making it high treason for anyone to write a word on this subject; the intention was that, when the time came, they might impose on the Catholics the person they themselves wanted, since no one had any knowledge what rights were involved.

Second, this book was required in order to resolve the doubts which the Catholics had conceived or were liable to conceive from the false doctrine contained in the treatises of a certain Frenchman, Belloy by name,[274] who, writing in our time, has declared that, in admitting the claim of a king or prince, it is not necessary to take anything else into account except nearness of blood-relationship, and that neither religion nor virtue nor any other circumstance should be taken into consideration for this purpose.

Third, because it was fitting that the [English] Catholics should be to some extent forewarned about this issue, before they were forced to take a decision; and this they will in all probability have to do soon, and not without war and revolts, since there are so many and diverse claimants and the queen is old.

Fourth, in order that the other Christian princes also, and especially the pope, may jointly examine the state of this business, and have time and information to think it over and consider the claims, possibilities, advantages, and disadvantages of each of the claimants, and decide who will be the best choice, not only for England but also for the whole of Christendom.

273. Probably the Latin translation, *De regiae successionis apud Anglos iure libri duo* (*Two Books on the Law of Royal Succession in England*), AAV, Fondo Borghese, IV, 103: Persons to Martín de Idiáquez, 30 August (B340) and to Juan de Idiáquez, 2 September 1596 (B342). An additional chapter (12), argued for papal right to settle the English succession. See Peter Holmes, "The Authorship and Early Reception of *A Conference about the Next Succession to the Crown of England*," *Historical Journal* 23 (1980): 415–429, esp. 423; Stefania Tutino, "The Political Thought of Robert Persons's *Conference* in Historical Context," *Historical Journal* 52 (2009): 43–62; and Dominguez, *Radicals in Exile*, 173–176.

274. Pierre de Belloy (1540–1611/13) was a prominent French jurist and political writer who defended the right of Henry of Navarre against the Catholic League. His *Apologia Catholica ad famosos et seditiosos libellos coniuratorum* (Paris, 1584), published in English translation as *A Catholicke apologie against the libels, declarations, advices, and consultations made, written, and published by those of the League, perturbers of the quiet estate of the realme of France* (London, 1585/6), is frequently challenged in *Conference about the Next Succession*.

These arguments accord with the views of nearly all the most influential people of the English nation who are in exile and saw the book before it was printed; they were endorsed afterwards by the other Catholics in England who have written about it; and they were corroborated by the actual success of the book itself (for it has not caused any persecution in England but a lull rather up to now). Moreover, many people have been brought back to great concord and moderation and their eyes have been opened by reading this book, as we are told from there. And so these arguments have produced a great change here too in Rome and have removed or greatly moderated the suspicions and the impression that had been created and had taken root, thanks to the continual complaints and false reports which some Englishmen in Flanders, adherents of the king of Scotland, had sent to the curia here to make the book odious.

It is understood that the chief instrument in creating this impression in the curia here has been Monsignor Malvasia, who was nuncio for a time in Flanders and received reports from Paget, Tresham, Ligons, and certain other Englishmen of that faction through a Doctor Gifford, recently created dean of Lisle, a man who was choleric in these matters, and was living at that time in Monsignor Malvasia's house.[275] The monsignor came to Rome primed with the reports which had been made to him in Flanders and, making use of those which they proceeded to send afterwards, he has continued the same course of action and, as he found the atmosphere conducive to what was then being attempted on behalf of France, it is no wonder that reports of this kind found acceptance.

At the same time, it so happened that there arose the disturbance which had begun in the English college here, partly from the passionate desire of some few students for a greater liberty, but mainly by the instigation of some Englishmen outside the college belonging to the faction of the bishop of Cassano[276] and his followers in Flanders. It occurred to some people that this disturbance would not be a bad means of balancing affairs or creating a counterpoise – so I was informed here by a person of high position who is a prudent man and well-disposed – because, being informed that all the other English seminaries (whose influence was understood to be very great in England) had hitherto carried on in sympathy with the king of Spain, it seemed politic to them that the one here in Rome should take this opportunity of starting on a different path and giving its allegiance instead to France and Scotland. Although at first this seemed a very difficult thing to bring to pass, owing to the long-existing and deep-rooted love that all English Catholics have borne for so long to His Catholic Majesty, yet the passions of these disaffected youths, once they had been aroused and egged on by men of influence, flared up to such a pitch as I would never have believed if I had not witnessed it and had personal contact with it. For things came to such a pass that they could not bear to see or hear anything having to do with Spain or to allow anything to be said about her that was good.

275. Innocenzo Malvasia, papal agent in Brussels, took a particular interest in the condition of Catholics in Scotland, hoping for the conversion of James VI. Dr William Gifford, Charles Paget, William Tresham, and Ralph Liggons are treated here as opponents of the Society, or at least of Persons and Holt: William Crichton claimed that they were well-disposed to the Jesuits generally; see McCoog, *Building the Faith of St Peter*, 345–347, 368–372. On Liggons, see vol. 1: 523 n456.

276. Owen Lewis.

The other students however, who came with me from Spain,[277] have won them over in this respect by telling them of so many acts of kindness and favours done to them – and they have done so with such modesty, calmness, humility and forbearance – that in the end the others found themselves put to shame and confusion. It was certainly a very useful thing for many purposes to have brought these students from Spain to Rome; His Holiness too was very pleased by it, and by an address they made him the first time they spoke to him.

His Holiness told me to go and live in the English college for a few days, to see if my presence would have the effect of calming these passions; for His Holiness now saw clearly that, for the reasons that had been put forward, it was impossible to allow this path of opposition, on which some of them had started, to be pursued any further without great scandal and evident loss and ruin to the cause of the Catholic religion in England. And so I came here and have remained for ten days, and after six or seven conferences with the infected group in the College – which may amount to the half of it – matters seem to be going much better, and it seems likely that there will eventually be a happy end to the whole affair. It is quite certain too that, if these young men did not find allies in powerful personages outside – and these too are beginning to fail them – they would be brought to order at once.

Their ringleader has made his submission, and he has spoken to me very often of all the good Cardinal Toledo's schemes in connection with this affair: how it suited his purposes to lead the college on in this way, in conformity with the policy that had been decided on in France, and his lack of sympathy with the fathers of the Society.[278] He had formed a plan to deprive them of the government of this college, and also to change the government of the college at Rheims, and to set up a new dispensation in the government of affairs in England; all of which was wishful thinking, which could not come to pass in fact without a multitude of revolts and inconveniences, as he would have found out if he had lived. God our Lord was very merciful to take him away before he became embarrassed and wearied by the affair.

The English Catholics in their letters complain greatly of two priests, belonging to the dissenting party here, who crossed into England shortly before I left Spain;[279] they were sent from here by their confederates with the intention – as is seen from their letters – of raising sedition and discord in England; and with this object they have begun to spread monstrous lies and falsehoods designed to inspire hatred equally to the fathers of the Society and the Spanish nation. The Catholics stay away from them like poison, because it is very distressing for them, in the midst of their other great afflictions and persecutions, that this further calamity should happen to them. The cardinal archduke was

277. Including John Bennet, Edward Bennet's brother.

278. The ringleader was Edward Bennet. Francisco de Toledo Herrera, SJ, had been the cardinal vice-protector of England, with special charge of the English college in Rome, until his death on 14 September 1596. See Agazzari to Persons, 25 September 1596 (B343), and Barret to Persons, 26/28 September 1596 (B344).

279. Richard Button and Sylvester Norris went to England in October 1596 and later joined the appellant party in England; see Garnet to Persons, 18 February 1597 (B354), and Persons's *Relacion* of 22 May 1597 (B378).

informed by the duke of Sessa of their intentions and evil disposition, and so he very prudently gave orders forbidding their passage to England through the ports of Flanders which are subject to His Majesty's obedience; but later our English members of the faction procured them a passage through Holland, and in that way they entered the country.

If these others in Rome who are infected with the same spirit do not sincerely change their attitude – and I have much doubt of their doing so, particularly four or five of them, due to leave this autumn, who have been leaders of this revolt and now look as though they changed their behaviour only under duress – it will be very important for His Majesty to give instructions not only here through his ambassador here but also to His Serene Highness the cardinal archduke to prevent their going to England at present, until some change of heart can be seen: for if they went to England now it might cause great injury to the Catholics and be a disservice to His Majesty.

For the rest I refer you to what the duke of Sessa is going to write or has written; he is helping in every way with great prudence and goodwill, lending the weight of his authority. He is a splendid servant of His Majesty and gives satisfaction to everybody and to me in particular. I deal with him with complete confidence and rely on his letters in matters of greater secrecy and importance. He will have informed you of the audience I had with His Holiness and the two documents which were handed to him afterwards relating to English affairs. And so I will say no more on this subject. May Our Lord be with you always. From Rome on the first of May 1597.

B372 From Claudio Acquaviva, Naples, 2 May 1597

SOURCE: AAW VI, no. 33, 121–122.

NOTE: Acquaviva rehearses Olivares' request for a meeting and expresses hope about the situation at the English College, Rome.

Persons included a free translation of this letter in his *A Briefe Apologie or Defence of the Catholike Ecclesiastical Hierarchie* (Antwerp, 1601), fols. 57v–58r: "If God of his mercy and for the good of your countrey do assist yow in this worke as he hath done in others hertofore, so as yow make an end of those discords in the Colledge, I shall esteeme it for no lesse a benefit to your nation, then the first erection and foundation of the same. This L. Viceroy desyreth much to see yow here shortly, & I have comitted the matter to your owne consideration for the tyme what wilbe most comodious." The MS bears a note, possibly by T.G. Law, referring to the expansion of the text: "Printed, with a strange addition of Parsons's vanity and disregard of truth, in his Briefe apology p. 58."

Molto Reverendo en Christo Padre
Pax Christi.

Despues de haver escrito a Vuestra Reverencia la semana pasada cómo el Señor Virrey desea que venga por acá, reçevi su carta con relacion de la buena audiençia que su Santidad le dio, que segun lo que en ella passó espero que será de mucha utilidad para acomodar ese seminario, que si Dios en eso le da tan buena mano, como en otras cosas se la ha dado, no estimaré io en menos su reparo y reformaçion, que su primera erection, no tengo qué decir en este particular sino esperar que Vuestra Reverencia con su Religion y prudençia yrá viendo todos los particulares, y aplicando los remedios quales, quando, y como converna. En sus oraçiones &c. De Napoles 2 de Mayo 97.

  De Vuestra Reverencia
    siervo en Christo
      Claudio Aquaviva.

[*Addressed:*] Al P^{re} Roberto Personio della Comp^e de Giesu a Roma.
[*Endorsed:*] P. Gen. 2 Maij 1597 de concordia Collegii Anglicani.

Translation

Most Reverend Father in Christ
The peace of Christ.

After I had written to Your Reverence last week, as my lord viceroy wished you to come here, I received your letter with the account of the good audience His Holiness gave you: according to what happened there I hope that it will be of much use in settling that seminary. If God lends a helping hand to you there, as He has done in other matters, I will not esteem its repair and reformation any less than its first foundation. I have no more to say in this matter except that I hope Your Reverence, with your religion and prudence, will see to all the particulars and apply the remedies as and when it is convenient. To your prayers, etc. From Naples, 2 May 1597.

  Your Reverence's
    servant in Christ
      Claudio Acquaviva.

B373 To Pietro Cardinal Aldobrandini, 2 May 1597

  SOURCE: AAV, Fondo Borghese III, 124 g.2, fols. 5 and 12.
  HICKS: 602–605, handwritten transcript, typescript, and English translation.
  NOTE: Persons was still hoping to return to Spain shortly, if the pope and the papal-nephew secretary of state could help to bring the present crisis to a speedy end.

Illustrissimo et Reverendissimo Signor

Questa serà per bacciar le mani di Vostra Signoria Illustrissima, et darla l'hora buona della desideratissima tornata di Sua Santità, et di Vostra Signoria Illustrissima. Et perché ben so le molte et grand'occupationi che n'havera per questi primi giorni Vostra Signoria Illustrissima, non gli vengo a far questo officio in persona, adesso, si lei non me comanda altra cosa, dipoi verro quando Vostra Signoria Illustrissima stara più disoccupata, et in questo mezo mando a Vostra Signoria Illustrissima per il Signor Rogero Secretario del Cardinal Alano certi avisi d'Ingleterra che lui ha cavato di certe letere scritte a me, et andarò facendo lo medessimo da qui inanzi quando verran letere di la, si Vostra Signoria Illustrissima ne sarà servito, mentre io resto qui in Roma, lo qual, con il favor di Nostro Signor, et di Vostra Signoria Illustrissima, spero che sarà poco tempo, per la brevità del buon dispacho che me comandaranno dar nelli nigotiii. Iddio ci conservi et prosperi l'illustrissima persona di Vostra Segnoria Illustrissima come gli supplico. Dal Collegio Inglesi alli 2 di Maggio 1597.

    Di Vostra Signoria Illustrissima ac Reverendissima
       humiissimo servitore
         Roberto Personio.

[*Endorsed:*] Roma al Collegio Inglese 2 di Maggio 1597 il R. P^re Roberto Personio.

Translation

Your Right Reverend Eminence

This letter will serve the purpose of kissing Your Eminence's hands and greeting you on the very welcome return of His Holiness and Your Eminence. And as I well know the immense amount of business which Your Eminence will have during these first days, I am not presenting myself in person, unless you command me otherwise, but will come later on when Your Eminence will be more at leisure. In the meantime I am sending Your Eminence, by Mr Roger,[280] Cardinal Allen's secretary, certain reports on English affairs which he has extracted from some letters written to me, and I shall go on doing the same from now onwards, when letters come from there, if Your Eminence approves, as long as I remain here in Rome. By the favour of His Holiness and of Your Eminence I hope that will be for only a short time, thanks to the speedy and favourable issue which my affairs will enjoy by their command. May God preserve for us and prosper Your Eminence's most illustrious person, as is my prayer to Him. From the English college, 2nd May 1597.

    Your most reverend Eminence's
      most humble servant
        Robert Persons

B374 From Henry Garnet, London, 7 and 14 May 1597

  SOURCE: ABSI, Coll P II 548.
  NOTE: Robert Fisher had come to England from Flanders to canvass support for the anti-Jesuit faction; see Garnet's letter of 18 February 1597.

... de tumultuaribus in Carcere Wisbici: et de Fisheri calumniis contra Societatem, &c. Alia 14 eiusdem, eadem fere narrat, &c.

Translation

About the disturbances in the prison at Wisbech; and Fisher's calumnies against the Society, etc. Another on the 14th of the same month, he writes more or less the same, etc.

  280. Roger Baynes.

B375 To William Holt, Rome, 15 May 1597

SOURCES:
    AAW, MS Anglia VI, no. 106, fol. 491 = *W*;
    Inner Temple, London, Petyt MS 538, vol. 38, nos. 127 and 128, fols. 365–367 = *P1 P2*;
    ABSI, Coll P II 488, Grene's note: "To one of ours, an account of the peace made in the College and of the manner he had used &c. (egregie)" = *G*.

HICKS: 606–609.

EDITION: Tierney, 3: lxxviii–lxxx (modernised), "MS. in my possession."

NOTE: The disaffected students were formally reconciled at a ceremony on Ascension Day, 15 May, in the presence of the vice-protector, Cardinal Camillo Borghese, who approved a memorandum of agreement consisting of nine articles. Borghese instructed Persons to write to Holt about what had happened (Kenny, "Inglorious Revolution," 92–93 [part 3]). Presumably in an attempt to export the spirit of reconciliation to Flanders, the student leader Edward Bennet wrote the next day to Hugh Griffin in Cambrai, effusively expressing his appreciation for what Persons had done: "Father Persons, at his first coming to Rome, lay at the Casa Professa, where many of the scholars visited him; and myself among the rest did the like. You must think that the most of our discourse was, how to end these stirs, and to put an end to that, which was an occasion of so great scandal. He offered us conference to hear our griefs, to give us remedy where we had reason, and desired of us likewise to hear reason, not to be carried away with passion, because it was God's cause; promising us that we should find all charity and indifferency in him, that we could piously desire or expect. This passed on for a sevennight. In the mean time, he visited our protector and the pope's holiness; with whom after a long discourse, the pope did ask him where he lay. He answered him, at the Casa. Then the pope asked him whether he had been at the college:—but, to be brief, the pope desired him to come and lie in the college, to see whether he might do any good. So he came to the college, the next day, and lieth there still: so that then we had better opportunity, with less trouble, to go forward with that whereof we had had some speech. He called us all together, told us we had God's cause in hand, laid before us the detriments that our countrymen suffered abroad because of our troubles, the inconveniences within the college that we found, and, in fine, the harm that the cause of England was like to suffer, if that these factions and dissentions did continue. Such and the like discourses being had, we all agreed to deal with father Persons, and see whether he was able to give that satisfaction, which as yet we had not found. Whereupon we had certain conferences with him, debated and disputed all our whole matter from the beginning, proposed our difficulties and our reasons, which he heard with patience,—he, of the other side, the occasions which he thought to have been always the hinderance of peace, the mediums to get peace again, and gotten to conserve it." See Tierney, 3: lxxx–lxxxii; quotation from lxxxi, transcribed from a copy endorsed by Persons.

Tierney, unusually, has high praise for Persons's letter to Holt: "Here is a letter, penned immediately after the accomplishment of a great work, and flowing from the fulness and sincerity of the writer's heart. How different from the passionate invectives, the defamatory statements, and the distorted narratives, contained in the Briefe Apologie, the Story of Domestic

Difficulties,[281] and the various letters and memorials, which he afterwards composed on the same subject! But there, the spirit of party was at work, justifying its own acts, reviling its opponents, and 'condemning,' as Dr Barret expresses it, 'all but itself.' Here the veil is withdrawn, and we behold the man as he is. We have him acknowledging the errors of both sides, seeking to heal the divisions of the past, and inculcating, with a holy and a beautiful solicitude, the duty of protecting every name of a former adversary from reproach. As an historical testimony, effectually subversive of all the other statements of Persons on the subject to which it refers, this letter is highly important: but as evidence of what nature really is, when unwarped by the prejudices and passions of party, it assumes even an additional degree of interest." See Tierney, 3: lxxx n1.

All three copies, W, P1, and P2, appear to have been made by Persons's opponents, as they use the unusual spelling "Parsons," and the papers in the Petyt collection, probably copied for Bancroft (Law, *Archpriest Controversy*, 1: xxvi), are generally hostile to Persons. The readings in W are generally superior (except for the date), and so it has been adopted as copy text. P1 adds a note in another hand: "Within 4 or 5 monethes after 2 more breeches happned (as Parsons confesseth in a letter to Walley or Blackwell)."

My Reverend Good Father

This lettre shalbe to you (I hope in God) of great comforte, to understand thereby of the happie end which his devine goodnes hath geeven at length to thes troubles and disagreementes here in Rome, which in truth as[282] I found to be greater and more deepelie rooted than ever I could imagine (though I had hard much), so are we more bound to Allmightie God for the remedie, which I beleeve verelie to be sound and from the roote, as yow would also thinke, yf yow saw that which I doe see, and so do manie more besides me,[283] that hadd farre lesse hope of the redresse then ever I hadd.

The meanes have bene, next to Gods holie grace, certaine large conferences that we have had alone (I meane all the aggreved part with me together[284]) wherein we have passed over the whole storie of these troubles and the causes of grief, discontentment, contention, suspition, emulation or exasperation,[285] that have beene geeven or taken on both sides. And as on the one side I have bene content to heare the schollers and to[286] yealde them reason where I thought they hadd yt on ther side,[287] so on the other have thei[288] also beene content to heare me, when I thought my reason was better then theirs, as also to distinguish where I presumed that with some reason there might goe accompanied also some passion, suspicion, exaggeration, or sinister interpretation: and so final-

281. Persons, *A Briefe Apologie or Defence of the Catholike Ecclesiastical Hierarchie* (Antwerp, 1601), "A Storie of Domesticall Difficulties" (Pollen, *Miscellanea II*, 48–185).
282. as] W; om. P1 P2
283. besides me] W; besyde me P1 P2
284. with me together] W; did mete to geather P1 P2
285. grief, discontentment, contention, suspition, emulation or exasperation] W; greifes discontentments contentions suspitions emulations or exasperations P1 P2
286. to] W; om. P1 P2
287. side] W; sides P1 P2
288. have thei] W; they have P1 P2

lie, God be thanked, we are comed[289] to a full end and conclusion, and all inconveniences, that before hadd either happened, or were so presumed, be[290] fullie remedied on both parties. The schollers on their sydes have fullie satisfied me and I have procured to remove all impediments on the behalf of the societie and so shall doe for the tyme to come, so as I greatlie[291] hope that never the like shall happen againe, and that Allmightie God will perfourme in this thing[292] allso, for the good of our countrie, that mercifull pointe which in all other like temptation he is[293] wounte to doe, as the apostle saith, *Faciet etiam cum tentatione proventum*,[294] and that the union of this collegd wilbe better and greater and more solled hereafter than ever it hath bene hitherto from the beginning. And assure your self (my good father) that in untwisting of[295] this clew and unfoulding matters past, I have found errors on both sides, *saltem in modo agendi*,[296] which, you knowe, may stand with the best intentions in the world. And who will marvaile at this? seeing the one were strangers to the other; and the other had to deale with strangers; ech parte did so much as they knew, and could doe noe more; suspicions, aversions, and exasperations were daylie multiplied *et arbiter pacis*[297] was not amongst them. And to conclude, me thinketh that I doe see that yf manie of the thinges that have passed here should have happened in the quietest colledges[298] that we have either in Spaine or Flanders, thei might have putt the peace out of joynt, supposing our English disposition,[299] and the suspicions that such thinges might bring with them, perhaps more then the thinges themselves.

Well, I can saie noe more in this than St Peter, in the Acts of the Apostles, saithe, of the sufferinges of Christ: God had appointed that soe yt should be, *implevit autem sic*.[300] Even soe God had determined that we should passe this crosse: and so he fulfilled yt by diverse men's errors, and as by his infinite providence[301] brought out soe much good to all the world of the former case, so hope I that he will draw noe small good also to our countrie in tyme of this.

Wherefore there remayneth nothing now but to geve thankes to Allmightie God for this[302] singular mercie of his, and that yow signifie the same there to all those of our

289. comed] *W*; comde *P1 corr*; come *P2 Tierney*
290. be] *W*; are *P1 P2*
291. greatlie] *W P1 P2*; heartily *Tierney*
292. this thing] *W*; these thinges *P1 P2*
293. temptation he is] *W*; tentations he was *P1 P2*
294. 1 Cor. 10:13, "God ... will make also with temptation issue, [that you may be able to bear it]." The Vulgate reads "faciet," supporting *W*; *P1* and *P2* read "facit."
295. of] *W*; om. *P1 P2*
296. "At least, in their way of going about things."
297. "A mediator of the peace."
298. colledges] *W P2*; colledge *P1 Tierney*
299. disposition] *W*; dispositions *P1 P2*
300. Acts 3:18, "But [those things which God before had shewed by the mouth of all the prophets, that his Christ should suffer,] he hath so fulfilled."
301. *Tierney inserts* he *before* brought
302. this] *W*; the *P1 P2*

nation, as also to anie others that have hard of thes[303] troubles, for that this[304] union here is not made onelie within the house, but with all in like manner abroade, both of our nation and others and namelie with the Fathers of our Societie everiewhere. And the successe hath so contented His Holinesse and all the Cardinalles of the towne as you would wonder, and this daie (being the Assension of our Saviour)[305] the Cardinal Vice-Protector Borgesio has[306] beene here at the Colledg himself and signified his exceeding great contentment[307] of this event. And the same joye, I doubt not but that Cardenall Caietano the Protector (who is expected verie shortlie) will receave allso at his coming;[308] so as now we must assist,[309] all of us, to appease all rumours that have growen abroade of thes sturs, in everie place, as also to heale such griefes and[310] aversions as thereof have insued: and, in particular, to restore and conserve the good name (as much as in us lieth) of anie that may have bene touched by[311] former reportes, and so doing I trust in Allmightie God that everie daie we shall take much[312] comfort one of an other, and that you shall still have confirmation from me whyle I stay here of the progresse of this good union, and that I shall leave the colledge also[313] att my departure as yt may indure. And this is all[314] I have to saie at thys tyme. The[315] Lord Jhesus be with yow ever, to whom do yow commend me, as also to all frends and countrimen with yow, to whom I pray yow communicate the effect of this lettre. From Rome, this xvth[316] of May, 1597.

    Yours ever, in Christ our Saviour
        Robert Parsons.[317]

B376 To Thomas Stapleton, Rome, about 15 May 1597

SOURCE: Stapleton to Persons, 6 July 1597 (B386).

NOTE: Persons sent a response to Stapleton's letter of 16 April (B366), but Stapleton noted on 6 July that he had not received it.

303. thes] *W*; the *P1 P2*
304. this] *W; om. P1; P2 has* s union
305. The feast of the Ascension was celebrated on 15 May 1597.
306. has] *W*; hath *P1 P2*
307. contentment] *W*; joy *P1 P2*
308. allso at his coming] *W*; also of the same at his coming whom *P1 P2*. The cardinals mentioned are Enrico Caetani and Camillo Borghese (later Pope Paul V).
309. assist] *W*; attende *P1 P2*
310. and] *W*; or *P1 P2*
311. by] *W*; with *P1 P2*
312. much] *W*; more *P1 P2*
313. also] *W; om. P1 P2*
314. all] *P1 P2 insert* that
315. The] *W*; Our *P1 P2*
316. xvth *P1*] 5th *W*; 25 *P2*
317. Parsons] *sic all MSS*

B377 To Pedro Jiménez de Murillo, Rome, 16 and 18 May 1597

SOURCES:
    AAW VI, no. 35, 127–130 (olim X. 851), a contemporary copy endorsed in Persons's hand (= W);
    ABSI, Coll P II 463, Grene's note (= G).
HICKS: 611–612, with English translation.
EDITION: Knox, *Douay Diaries*, 1: 393.
NOTE: On 16 May Jiménez, secretary to the Spanish ambassador, the duke of Sessa, sent Persons a memorial from the ambassador about the proposed visits to Rome of William Gifford and Thomas Stapleton, as well as the advisability of appointing a new English cardinal. Now Persons requests him to facilitate an appointment with the ambassador so that they can discuss these matters. He continues to insist that he would not be available himself for the cardinalate, explaining that he has discussed the matter with leading Spanish courtiers and clerics.

Este memorial que Vuestra Merced me embió ante[a]yer de parte de su Excelencia yo no avía visto ni savia que se avía dado, ni pudiera yo aver consentido que se diera, si lo ubiera savido: porque aunque en el primero que propone acirca de la venida a Roma de los dos Doctores Stapelton y Giffordio he hablado ya con el Señor Duque particularmente del segundo, diciendo mi pareçer qui[318] si commodamente su venida a Roma se pudiera divertir (lo qual me pareçe muy dificultoso, si él lo aprietta) sería bien, por ser el moço de la condicion que en el memorial se diçe, y grande instrumento de la rebuelta deste Collegio juntamente con Ugo, sobrino del Obispo de Cassano. Toda via en lo 2º que propone el Memorial, que es pretar que se haga un Cardenal de la nacion Ynglesa, para el remedio universal de todos estos inconvenientes, yo no soy del mismo pareçer, estando las cosas como estan; no porque, no piense yo que si la Nacion tubiera un Cardenal qual se pudiera pintar, remediaria facilmente a la mayor parte de todas estas quexas y differencias, y tendria los Catolicos unidos con su autoridad, querriendo usar della; mas porque pareçe que al presente no tiene la Nacion Ynglesa, hombre bastante para esta dignidad a Juicio y gusto de todos, y ansi pareçe menos falta y inconveniente no tenerle, que tenerle insufficiente.

En aquello que diçe el memorial que por este fin se ha de romper con los obstaculos de las reglas de religiosos[319] etc., si esto se entendiera en alguna manera de mí, supplico a sua Excelencia que no se mueva con ello, hasta a entender mis raçones en contrario. Las quales dire a su Excelencia quando será servido hablarme en ello, aunque yo me corro de començar esta plática, y de puro corrido he dejado de[320] hablar a su Excelencia en ella hasta agora, aunque con algunos amigos y señores mios más intimos; y que podian haçer me más merced in divertir la Plática, o Impedir la cosa en sí, si se tratara, como son Señor Don Juan de Idiaquez, Garcia Loaysa, el Duque de Feria, y el Señor Cardenal de Guivara, he hablado largamente y dado mis raçones de que no sería ni servicio

    318. qui] W; que *Knox*
    319. religiosos] *this ed.*; religiosas W
    320. de] *supplied in margin* W

a Dios, ni por ventura de Su Magestad pensar en tal cosa, para mi persona, y aunque de todos estos Personages que he nombrado, ninguno a mi pareçer podra ayudarme y haçerme más merced en lo que yo y mi Religion pretendemos que el Señor Embaxador, y que por esto convenia sobre todos que estubiesse bien informada[321] de la verdad y de mi deseo en esta parte, todavía por el respeto arriba dicho, no he podido hasta agora acavar con migo de hablar a su Excelencia en ello, y ansi supplico a Vuestra Merced con esta ocasion que me abra la puerta, y dispongame su Excelencia en esto[322] particular de tal manera que se sirva oyr mis raçones, con la indifferencia que de su piedad y Christiandad se ha de esperar, pues todo va endereçado al servicio y al mayor servicio de nuestro Señor, del qual su Excelencia y Vuestra Merced son tan grandes siervos come se save. Él les guarde siempre como puede. Del Collegio Ynglés en Roma, a 18 de Mayo, 1597.

[*Endorsed in Persons's hand:*] Respuesta al mem^al remisso por el Embaxador sobre el Cardenalato 18 de Mayo, 1597. Esta rispuesta yva al secretario Pedro Xemenes de Murillo para satisficiesse al Duque de Sesa.

Translation

I had not seen the memorial which Your Honour sent me the day before yesterday from His Excellency, nor did I know it had been sent, nor would I have allowed it to be produced if I had known, because in the first place what he proposes about Dr Stapleton and Dr Gifford I had already spoken about to the duke; especially about the latter, saying that it seemed to me that it would be good if his visit could conveniently be delayed (something that seems more difficult to me, if he insists on it), for he is the child of the state of affairs that is dealt with in the memorial, and a major agent in the revolt of this college, along with Hugh, nephew of the bishop of Cassano.[323] In any case, with regard to the second matter proposed in the memorial, which is that he should appoint a cardinal for the English nation, as a general remedy for all these troubles, I do not agree with that, things being as they are; not because I do not think that if the nation had a cardinal who could be appointed, it would easily remedy most of these complaints and differences, and would unite the Catholics under his authority, if he were willing to use it, but rather because at present the English nation does not seem to have anyone suitable to this dignity who would be to everyone's taste and judgement, and it would be less of a deficiency and hindrance not to have one than to have an unsuitable one.

As for what the memorial says to the effect that for this purpose it is necessary to put aside the restrictions imposed on religious, if I understand quite what is meant, I would beg His Excellency not to take it any further, until he has heard my reasons to the contrary. These I will explain to His Excellency when he is pleased to discuss it with me, although I'm embarrassed to start this conversation, and because of this embarrassment I have been unable to talk to His Excellency so far. But I have, with some friends and noblemen of my nearer acquaintance, who are able either to entertain my discussion more readily or to impede the thing in itself, as it were – such as Lord Don Juan de

321. informada] *W*; informado *Knox*
322. esto] *W*; este *Knox*
323. Hugh Griffin, nephew of Owen Lewis.

Idiáquez, García Loaysa, the duke of Feria, and the Lord Cardinal de Guevara[324] – spoken at large and given my reasons why it would not be to the service of God, nor, perhaps, for His Majesty, to think of such a thing for me personally. And although, amongst all those personages whom I have named, none seems to me to be able to help me, and do more for me in what I seek, given my religious profession, than the lord ambassador (and that is the reason why it was appropriate for him, above all, to be well-informed of the truth and what I desire in this respect), nevertheless, for the reason mentioned above, I have not yet been able to get to talk to His Excellency on this matter. Therefore, I beg Your Worship on this occasion that you would open the door for me and dispose His Excellency favourably towards me in this particular in such a way that he would be pleased to hear my reasons with the impartiality that is to be hoped for from his piety and Christian feeling, for everything is directed to the service and greater service of Our Lord, of which His Excellency and Your Honour are such great servants, as is well known. May He protect you always, as He is able. From the English College, Rome, 18 May 1597.

B378 To Don Juan de Idiáquez, 22 May 1597, *Relación* of the Disturbances in the English College

SOURCES:

ACSA, Series II, Legajo 1, item 27, a contemporary copy (= *Vd*);
AAW VI, no. 36, 131–138, a single folded sheet of Roman *carta colomba* (Hicks, 628) (= *W*);
ABSI, Coll P II 463, Grene's excerpts (= *G*).
HICKS: 613–644, with English translation.

NOTE: This memorial is the second prepared for Idiáquez and intended for the Spanish court (see Persons to Idiáquez, 1 May, B371). Persons's version may be compared with the standard account of the disturbances by Kenny, "Inglorious Revolution"; Michael E. Williams, *The Venerable English College* (London, 1979), 16–21; McCoog, *Building the Faith of St Peter*, 259–272 and 356–365; and Lake and Questier, *All Hail to the Archpriest*, 58–72.

Eccentric spelling markers in *Vd* have been silently removed in the text that follows.

---

324. Cardinal García de Loaysa, later archbishop of Toledo, sounded Creswell out on Persons's attitude to the cardinalate (Loomie, *Spanish Elizabethans*, 118–19). He is mentioned in Persons's letter to Juan Ruiz de Velasco, 5 August 1589 (B27), and was in Philip II's retinue during the king's visit to St Alban's college, Valladolid, in 1592 (Persons, *A relation of the King of Spaines receiving in Valliodolid* [Antwerp, 1592], p. 12); Persons consulted the duke of Feria at Barcelona en route to Rome (Persons to Mannaerts, 10 January and 12 April 1597, B352 and B364); Cardinal Fernando Niño de Guevara (1541–1609) was elevated to cardinal on 5 June 1596; he later became archbishop of Seville.

Relacion del principio progresso y fin de la turbacion del Collegio
Ynglés en Roma, que duró más que dos años y medio, y redondó en
prejuicio y peligro de la causa universal de todos[325] los Catolicos
de Ynglaterra.

Lo que se ha savido de todo este negocio por la examinacion de la causa, y de las quexas, memoriales y cartas de ambas partes, y por la confession de los mismos discontentos, despues de reconciliados y apaceguados, es[326] lo siguiente.

La immediata[327] occasion de la discordia entre los estudiantes yngleses fue por causa de algunas facultades que su Santidad avia concedido al Cardinal Alano en su vida para repartir a los Sacerdotes que se embiarian a predicar la nuestra Santa fee en Ynglaterra conforme al talento y merito de cada uno dellos. Las quales facultades despues de la muerte del dicho Cardinal (la qual succedio en el año 94) pretendio que se concediessen a él, el Obispo Cassano como a la persona Ecclesiastica más principal de la naçion Ynglesa, y procuró por medio del rector del dicho Collegio que era Italiano (y no savia mucho de las cosas ni de las personas Ynglesas) que la mayor parte de los estudiantes de su Collegio las pediessen por memorial a Su Santidad allegando por razon que era más justo que un hombre de la misma nacion repartiesse las dichas facultades que no el Cardinal Gaetano que era Protector. Pero Su Santidad no queso darlas al Obispo Cassano, si no al Protector. Con lo qual offendidos los estudiantes y encendidos por algunos Yngleses amigos del dicho Obispo que vivean fuera del Collegio, tomaron aversion no solamente del Cardinal Protector, si no tan bien del Padre General de la Compañia de Jesus, y de todos los demas Padres, que les dissuadian este modo de proceder.

Rompidos una vez los estudiantes con el Cardinal Protector y con los padres que les governavan, se ayudavan de dos suertes de hombres, o por mejor dezir por dos passiones en los mismos. Los unos eran los emulos y los contrarios a la Compañia que hallavan en Roma, como en Flandes Yngleses: y otros, a persuacion tan bien destos de los contrarios o[328] mal affectos a las cosas de España, professando que como no querian ser governados ni dirigidos más por los padres de la Compañia ansi tan poco querian depender de España. Con lo qual dizean que los padres estavan confederados ni querian que este Collegio de Roma anduviesse arrimado al amparo de España como los demas Seminarios: si no que tomasse differente dirotta y camino, y por esta via segun los tiempos que corrian hallaron amparo y ayuda, adonde otramente no hallaron, y reduxeron su discordia a negocio de estado.

Passaron en esta contienda cosas muy disordinadas y escandalosas, por que de una parte las cabeças de los amutinados, perdido el miedo por las alas que avian, no tenian respeto a nady. Y de la otra parte Su Santidad aunque le discontentava mucho el modo de proceder destos,[329] toda via no se resolvia de castigarles por respeto de las interce-

325. todos] W; om. Vd
326. es] W; el Vd
327. Vd inserts causa y after immediata
328. o] W; a Vd
329. le discontentava mucho el modo de proceder destos] supplied in margin W

ssiones de tantos patronos que los amparavan: en tanto, que aviendo Su Santidad mandado una vez, que se echassen del Collegio quatro de los principales inquietos, buelvio les a mandar tornar despues a instancia de los intercessores, con que se animaron más, no solamente ellos, si no tan bien otros muchos que les seguian.

Mandó despues Su Santidad que el Cardinal Sega visitasse al Collegio, y le relatasse la verdad de las cosas, lo qual hizo con mucho cuydado por espacio de seis meses, oyendo a todos con grande paciencia, y dexó escrita la su visita con mucho orden y concierto mostrando en cada cosa donde avia passion o error en los inquietos. Pero veniendo él a morir, el Cardinal Toledo que se succedio en la viceprotecion del Collegio en ausencia del Cardinal Gaetano que era Protector, en otra manera mostrava entender las cosas, y prometio a los inquietos que les daria contento en todo, y que mudaria el modo del govierno, tanto en este Collegio como en aquel de Rheims, y lo mismo haria en las cosas dentro de Ynglaterra, y que apartaria los padres de la Compañia y para comenzar este su pensamiento ordonó por Confessor de los dichos estudiantes inquietos un compañero dellos mismos que avia sido cabeça deste amutinamiento, y más ordenó que este Confessor como un Tribuno de la plebe tuviesse audiencia ordinaria cada Jueves del Protector, para proponer los aggravios o quexas de los estudiantes discontentos, y otras muchas cosas semijantes que tiravan a acrecentar más la discordia, que no a quitarla.

Con estos medios llegó el negocio tan adelante que era cosa de espanto y de lástima, porque el Collegio estava dividido en dos partes casi yguales en el número, aunque los amutinados hazian algo la mayor parte, por ser ellos 28, y los otros 26. Pero el aborecemiento de los unos contra los otros era tal, que ni querian tratar ni conversar el uno con el otro, ni comer en la misma mesa, ni oyer missa en la misma yglesia, y vivian como enemigos, ni obedecian al superior en cosa alguna sin resistencia o murmuracion.

Despues estavan tan aversos de los padres de la Compañia que los governavan y de todos los demas del[330] orden, particularmente de los padres Yngleses que en todas las partes travajavan para ellos, que hablavan mal no solamente de todas sus obras tanto en Ynglaterra como en otras partes, si no tan bien del instituto de la religion diziendo que no compadecia con la vocacion de sacerdotes siglares. Y finalmente no les podian veer más que a herejes, y dizean que más caridad esperavan de los mismos hereges de Ynglaterra que no dellos. Estas fueron las mismas palabras dellos.

En terçero lugar estavan tan aversos de las cosas de España que no podian oyr contar cosa buena della, ni aun de los Seminarios, y otros beneficios y rrecebidas mercedes. De la pérdita de Cadiz mostraron huelgarse, y entrestecerse de la ganancia de Cales. Quando un estudiante que vino con el Padre Personio de España veendo el mal affetto que tenian, dizia, que a lo menos se ha de pensar que el Rey de España haria restituir la Religion Catolica en Ynglaterra, si tuviesse mano por alla. Respondeo otro, esto no savemos. A los maestros Españoles que leen Theologia en Roma, aunque sean hombres muy doctos y eminentes, nunca podian suffrir que se alavassen sus talentos en doctrina, por ser Españoles. Quando topparon al Duque de Sesa Embaxador de Su Magestad en la calle andando todos juntos a las escuelas, aunque le conocian y dizean entresi, a qué viene el Embaxador Español, toda via ninguno de los tentados queria discruverirle la cabeza.

---

330. del] *W*; de la *Vd*

Pero los buenos tanto más le haçian la reverencia. Y en fin avian por esta sola discordia con sus superiores cobrado tanta aversion y mal affetto a las cosas de España, como si por muchos años uviessen recebido muchos[331] grandes daños della.

Del libro de la succession abominavan y dizean mil males dél, no lo aviendo aún visto ni leydo, sino solamente por la mala enformacion que por sus parciales de Flandes avian recebido, diziendo que favorecia mucho a las pretenciones del Rey de España y de la Señora Infanta contra el Rey de Escoçia, y era preambulo de una conquista de Ynglaterra, y que el Padre Personio avia procurado firmes y juramentos de algunas personas principales de la nacionYnglesa en España en favor de la Señora Infanta.

Avian hecho proposito de romper con todos los demas sacerdotes Yngleses que dentro o fuera de Ynglaterra estavan unidos con los padres de la Compañia o con España, y de llevantar otra parcialidad contraria, y por esta causa avian embiado a Ynglaterra en el mes de Otubre passado dos sacerdotes de su banda llamados Button y Nores con comission de pegar este espirito a otros, y de haçer muchos de su parte. Y esto consta claramente por la confession de los mismos amutinados en Roma, los quales dizean al principio quando llegó el Padre Personio que no querian haçer paçes con él hasta a entender el successo destos comissarios en Ynglaterra, y lo mismo consta por una carta de los inquietos encaminada a Carlos Pagetto en Flandes, y por su medio a estos commissarios en Ynglaterra, y esta carta yva postillada de una postilla muy sediciosa del Doctor Giffordo Ynglés Dean en Lyla complice principal del dicho Pagetto, y fue despues intercepta la dicha carta por los Catolicos de Ynglaterra y mandada a Flandes, y de alla a Roma.

Más an confessado algunos de los principales cabeças desta parcialidad en Roma que avian entencion de concurrir con los hereges de Ynglaterra en todo lo que no era professar su religion dellos, como sería en ser contrarios a Jesuitas y a Españoles, y en sustentar y defender el estado presente temporal de la Reyna y opponerse a todos los demas sacerdotes que impugnavan esto, o se le mettian en cosas de estado: y con esto persuadian a sus partiales y compañeros que no serian perseguidos ni martyrizados por los hereges (como es cosa muy cierta que no serian, si no más presto muy favorecidos y regalados dellos) pero los Catolicos no les admitterian ni se fiarian dellos más que de hereges o espiones, quales en effeto en muy poco tiempo avrian sido. Y con todo esto ellos estavan tan porfiados en esto, que dixeron algunos dellos al Padre Personio y a otros, que ninguna potencia humana bastava a mudarles deste parecer, y que moririan de buena gana en esta demanda. Y otros añiadian que lo tenian por señal de su predestinacion ser imobiles en esta discordia.

Veendo esto les hizo una plática el Padre Personio mostrandoles los grandes daños y peligros que seguian desta porfia, tanto a la causa pública de todos los Catolicos de Ynglaterra como a cada uno dellos en particular. Y aunque confessavan ser assi, toda via dizean que los padres de la Compañia eran la causa de todos estos males por los aggravios que les haçian y por no conceder las cosas justas que pedian.

Por esto pareceo necessario abrir más a dentro esta llaga y venir al examen de las cosas en particular, lo qual se hizo por medio de siete o ocho Juntas y conferencias largas que se heçieron commençando del principio de toda esta turbacion y examinando de

331. muchos] *W*; grandes *Vd*

cabo en cabo todas las causas perticulares de disgustos o rompimientos, y los fundamientos que avian estos inquietos de toda su porfia, oyendo el Padre Personio a todas sus quexas con toda paciencia, y dandoles razon donde parecia que en alguna manera la podian tener, y donde no mostrandoles la verdad, y donde[332] podia aver un poquito de razon mesclada con mucha passion, suspicion, mala interpretacion, o exageracion, distinguiendo lo uno de lo otro, y en esta manera venieron a moldarse talmente dentro de pocos dias, que miravan las cosas con otros ochos que antes. Y finalmente venieron a reducirse todos tan de veras que es cosa de maravillar, y particularmente en esto, que quando vinieron a tratar los puntos de accordo con el Padre Personio, que eran las cosas en que differenciavan, y por las quales avian peliado por todo el tiempo passado, hallavan que la differencia era casi question de nombre solamente, por que mirada bien la cosa en si, entre ambas partes venian a querer lo mismo, si no que se entendian, y los estudiantes estavan enagañados y encendidos por otros de fuera, que avian differentes fines y interesses, o estavan movidos de differentes passiones. Segun que ellos mismos an confessado despues, y se ha tocado con la mano. En este examen passó el negocio en la manera siguiente.

El primero fundamento desta turbacion fue el Obispo de Cassano, como se ha dicho, por causa de las facultades, y comenzo el negocio por medio de un Sacerdote de su tierra que estava en el Collegio (que el uno y el otro son de nacion Wallesa, que es una gente en Ynglaterra de differente linguagio y costumbres de los Yngleses, y son reliquias de los antiguos Britannos echados y opprimidos por los Yngleses quando entraron la isla; y por tener ciertas prophetias que an de[333] tornar otra vez a mandar, mantienen siempre en ciertas occasiones, emulacion y competencia contra los Yngleses) aunque dentro de Ynglaterra por ser ellos pocos en respeto de los Yngleses viven pacificamente, y ay muchos hombres principales y prudentes de la nacion que aborecen desta competencia: toda via los demas por lo ordinario la seguen, y con ellos causan nuevas discordias, y ansi en esta occasion por hallarse entonces en este Collegio de Roma algun número destos Wallos, les juntó lluego el dicho sacerdote (el qual se llama Beneto y fue despues cabo del bando y Confessor de todos los amutinados) con el Obispo de Cassano,[334] y pretendiendo que era para el bien público de la nacion Ynglesa traxo al mismo bando al rector del Collegio que era Italiano, y con él muchos de la Juventud Ynglesa engañados con este pretencion, particularmente con dizirles, que los padres Yngleses de la Compañia en España tratavan de poner todas las cosas de Ynglaterra en las manos del Rey y de estrangeros, y de sujetar la patria a ellos. Por lo qual les venia muy a proposito la nueva del libro de la Succession de Ynglaterra que por aquellas dias avia salido, y era cosa muy odiosa a los parciales destos que resedian en Flandes.

Aiudó grandamente a encender este fuego la venida a Roma de un Cavallero Yngles llamado Thomas Throgmorton, el qual siendo de muy buenas partes, avia sido de la parcialidad de Pagetto y Morgano en Flandes por muchos años, y agora se tratava de casarle con la sobrina del Cardinal Alano, el qual siendo muerto antes que llegava Throgmorton

   332. donde] *W*; adonde *Vd*
   333. de] *interlined Vd*
   334. de Cassano] *W* Casano *Vd*

a Roma, se juntó con todas sus fuerças con Cassano, vivio en su casa, y confirmó notabilmente grande parte de los estudiantes en esta su porfia.

Fuera destos dos, en Roma avia de la nacion Italiana Monsignor Mora Visitador Apostolico que les favoreceo mucho, siendo por essos otros informado, y algo encontrado con la Compañia y Monsignor Malvasia poco affeccionado a las cosas de España, como lo mostró estando nuncio en Flandes, donde siendo enformado por Carlos Pagetto que le tratava familiarmente, y por el Doctor Giffordo que era su Capellan y vivia en su casa, hizo despues officios efficaces aqui en Roma en favor de aquella parcialidad y destos inquietos conjuntos con ella. —

De los Yngleses en Roma avia muchos que encendian tan bien este fuego, pero más que otros[335] Ugo Grifinio, sobrino del Obispo de Casano hombre inquietissimo. Nicolas Fizherberto Cuppiero que avia sido del Cardinal Alano, el qual era la persona que embiava y recebia las cartas que sobre este negocio se escrivian a Flandes, Ynglaterra y a otras partes, Fray Gulielmo Secheverello Ynglés de la orden de San Domingo, pero indigno de su hábito como al postre se vio, el qual corria y cansava a Su Santidad y a los Cardinales Sobrinos, y a otros, con memoriales, clamores grandes, y lagrimas en favor de los amutinados.

El prior tan bien que se llama de Ynglaterra Cavallero Yrlandes llegó a Roma y tuvo su parte en favorecer[336] a los inquietos, aunque por ventura no entendia tanto la mala causa que avian. Pero Carlos[337] Pagetto y el Doctor Giffordo con toda aquella parcialidad Escocesa residente en Flandes escrivian continuamente cartas a Su Santidad y a los Sobrinos, y al Cardinal Toledo, y a los dichos Monsignores Mora y Malvasia en favor destos, y a los mismos estudiantes esortandoles que passassen adelante en su porfia. Lo qual ultimamente más que todos tomó a favorecer el Cardinal Toledo, y pensava llevarla muy adelante, y de mudar todo el camino de las cosas Ynglesas, como se ha dicho. Pero Dios que tiene a pecho las cosas de los Catolicos de Ynglaterra que an padecido tanto por su causa no les quiso permiter aruinar por esta via tan violenta. Y asi puso la mano estraniamente y hizo una disposicion maravillosa a la paz que se[338] ha tratada y concluyda aora en esta manera.

Murieron casi de repente y juntamente dentro de dos o tres dias el uno despues del otro, el Obispo de Cassano y Thomas Throgmorton que eran los principales fundamentos de todo. Murio despues el Cardinal Toledo que era el ánimo principalissimo. Murio el Padre Tirio Escoces Assistente de la Compañia de Jesus, el qual aunque era buen Religioso y contrario a la sedicion de los inquietos, toda via simbolizava con ellos y con sus fautores en lo que era favorecer al Rey de Escocia y quitar la dependencia de España.

Partio de Roma el Prior de Ynglaterra sin hacer más daño esta segunda vez que vino de España, porque el Padre Personio le avia hablado en España,[339] y el Duque de Sesa le avia bien amaestrado en Roma. Succedio al frayle que era el principal solicitador un caso adverso que le echó de Roma, y fue que siendo el preso por la justicia en casa de una mala

---

335. otros] *W*; otro *Vd*
336. favorecer] *W*; favocerer *Vd*
337. Carlos] *W*; om. *Vd*
338. se] *interlined with caret Vd*
339. porque el Padre Personio le avia hablado en España] *W*; om. *Vd*

muger de noche fue puesto primero en la carcel pública, y despues azotado por sus frayles en el Capítulo, y recluso en un monasterio fuera de Roma, donde quebrando la carcel huyó despues a Flandes, y aora por cartas de 12 de Abril de Londres se escrive que ha llegado por alla, y que quedó en casa del Tesorero.

Al sobrino del Obispo de Cassano Ugo Grifinio succedio otro caso no muy differente, y fue que aviendo él procurado que se achasse[340] en la carcel un Abad llamado Tiburtio que avia sido mayor domo del Cardinal Farnes el viejo, por causa de una muger casada, de la qual avia suspecha que queria más al Abad que no a Ugo, el qual por muchos años avia[341] sido familiar en su casa, como se dice publicamente en Roma; y le fue necessario retirarse de Roma a sus beneficios de Cambray, para que los amigos del dicho Abad y de la muyer y de su marido (los[342] quales todos estavan presos, y supieron por los examines que Ugo avia sido la causa de las prisiones) no le hiciessen alguna venganza. Pero a la partida de Roma conjuró al sacerdote Beneto su paezano y Confessor de los amutinados (como él despues a confessado) que nunca heciesse paz con los Jesuitas ni desamparasse esta discordia, so pena de serle nimigo mortal. Y aunque el Duque de Sessa le avia dado una buena reprehencion y enstrucion quando se yva a Flandes, toda via no se entiende que dexa el mismo camino hasta aora por alla.

Con estas muertes y partidas de la gente contraria halló el Padre Personio poca resistencia en los de fuera del Collegio en Roma, y los parciales de Flandes tan bien avian abaxado mucho de su porfia, con veer que el Serenissimo Cardinal Archiduque començava a mirar en estas discordias. Y ansi la difficultad de hacer capaces a los mismos estudiantes en Roma era mucho menor, principalmente aviendo ganado primo en cierta manera al sacerdote Wallo ya dicho, que era Confessor y cabeza de todos; y esto por medio de un hermano suyo sacerdote creado en los Seminarios Yngleses de España; el qual vino a Roma con el Padre Personio, y cooperó mucho en ganar a su hermano, y por él[343] se intendieron los fundamentos que tenian los amutinados para perseverar en su porfia, los quales dicia que eran principalmente los dos seguientes.

El primero que los parciales de Flandes les avian persuadido, que hallarian una parcialidad muy grande en la nacion Ynglesa (digo de Catolicos) que se unirian con ellos contra los Jesuitas y contra los Españoles, y en las demas cosas que pretendian, y que sería cosa muy facil, llevar adelante esta parcialidad y acrecentarla con las espaldas que hallavan en Roma.

El otro fundamento era que les prometian, que sin duda sería Cardinal muy presto el Doctor Stapletono, pues Su Santidad le avia mandado ya llamar a Roma quatro veces con muy buenos offrecimientos de hacerle protonotario participante lluego, y que los Monsignores Mora y Malvasia lo negociavan, y lo tenian en buen punto, y que éste siendo Cardinal les favoreceria como hombre que avia salido de la Compañia, y pues él avia ya acceptada la condicion y prometido de estar en Roma para Settembre (para el qual tiempo tan bien estarian por acá los avisos del successo de los Comissarios embiados a Ynglaterra) sería bien no oyr al Padre Personio ni tratar de paces con él hasta entonces.

340. achasse] *W*; echasse *Vd*
341. avia] W; ha *Vd*
342. los] *W*; lo *Vd*
343. él] *interlined with caret Vd*

A estos dos[344] fundamentos deribó el Padre Personio en esta manera: Contra el primero avia procurado (escriviendo a differentes desde España) que veniessen testimonios muy autorizados tanto de Ynglaterra como de Flandes, los quales halló ya[345] en Roma de Catolicos y de sacerdotes de los más principales que testificavan que dentro de Ynglaterra no avia memoria de tal discordia entre los Catolicos, ni de tal emulacion contra Jesuitas ni contra Españoles; si no que al contrario avia summa union entre todos los Catolicos con los padres de la Compañia y grande amor a la nacion Española, y sobre todas, a la persona del Rey por los beneficios recebidos en este distierro, y que los que otro espiritu mostrava en Ynglaterra eran tenidos o por hereges o por espias, y que de los estudiantes deste Collegio Ynglés en Roma avia muy mala opinion y fama entre los Catolicos de alla, par aver mostrado este espiritu, y que si algun dellos llegava a Ynglaterra no le admitterian los Catolicos en sus casas. Y este punto fue testificado en Roma tanto por algunas personas graves que avian venido por esta causa de Ynglaterra como tan bien por cartas muy efficaces de algunos sacerdotes de los principales, y más estimados que travajavan en Ynglaterra.

De Flandes tan bien y de otras partes venian cartas universales y testimonios confirmados por mano de diversos escrivanos publicos testificando lo mismo de la union de todos los Catolicos Yngleses que estavan en distierro entre si y con los padres de la Compañia abominando desta discordia y parcialidad. Y porque esta testificacion contenia el número casi de ochocientos Catolicos parte en los Seminarios, y parte fuera dellos, que avian firmado estas escrituras: conviene a saver, Sacerdotes, Religiosos y Religiosas, estudiantes, Doctores, Capitanes, Cavalleros, y Soldados, y que los que rehusavan de firmar a esta testificacion en Flandes, no eran más de quinze personas en todo, los quales tan bien lo rehusavan por differentes fines y passiones particulares.

Vieron claramente los inquietos (y Su Santidad y los Cardinales tan bien despues quando todo se les mostró) que esta parcialidad dellos no era cosa de momento, como primo avian pensado por el grande ruydo y clamores que avian hecho. Y ansi quedó derivado este primero fundamento por tierra, y tanto más que en el mismo tiempo quando se tratava la paz, llegaron cartas de un de sus Commissarios en Ynglaterra diziendo que por alla no se podia hacer nada en aquel negocio contra los Jesuitas, y que los padres de la Compañia les avia mostrado todo género de caridad.

Al segundo fundamento del Cardinalado del Doctor Stapletono se les respondeo, que aunque esto no era aún cosa muy cierta que Su Santidad hazia venir a Roma al Doctor Stapletono por esta causa, toda vía quando esto ansi succediesse conforme a los meritos del Doctor que eran muchos, ninguna esperanza probable podrian tener los inquietos, de que el Doctor Stapletono hecho ya Cardinal, sería de su parte — lo primero porque siendo el hombre de buen discurso y de mucha virtud, echaria de veer luego el sin razon que tenian los estudiantes, y el mal camino de todos sus parciales de Flandes. Y aunque él uviesse tenido hasta aora alguna amistad con algunos dellos, toda via no bastaria esto (ni tan poco el aver salido de la Compañia pues salio por enfirmidad corporal

344. dos] W; om. Vd
345. ya] W; om. Vd

y con buena gracia de la religion) para hacerle[346] dexar el camino ordinario y comun de todo el cuerpo de la causa Catolica de Ynglaterra y seguir a unos[347] pocos inquietos desviados. Y quando lo quesiesse haçer no lo podria llevar adelante, pues de la otra parte estaria no solamente la union de todos los Catolicos dentro[348] y fuera de Ynglaterra juntamente con los Seminarios, Sacerdotes y Padres de la Compañia, sino tan bien el amparo y favor de su Magistad de España y del Cardinal Archiduque en Flandes. Contra todo[349] lo qual, aunque un Cardinal Ynglés que quesiesse inclinar a estos inquietos y factiosos, podria llevar por ventura[350] alguna parcialidad con sigo y haçer mucho ruydo y daño en la nacion, toda via le sería impossibile prevalecer, o haçer cosa alguna de momento, como lo avia esperimentado el Cardinal Toledo si uviesse vivido, hallandose embarcado de tal manera en el designo que tenía de mudar el camino de las cosas ynglesas, a suggestion destos inquietos, que no avria podido ni passar adelante ni tornar atraz, si no con mucha afflicion y dishonra, pues toda la nacion Ynglesa de los Catolicos se le avrian oppuesto.

    Todas estas razones obravan mucho con los estudiantes rebueltos, y esta postrera, de que el Cardinal Toledo estava engañado, y que no le sería sido possibile passar adelante si viviera. Dio mucha luz a Su Santidad tan bien y a los Cardinales Sobrinos, y al Viceprotector Burghes, y el Cardinal Boronio y a otros, que an echado a veer que sea impossibile apartar la causa Catolica de Ynglaterra del arrimo de España. Y ansi al último vinieron los estudiantes a dexar su porfia, y a remitterse a todo lo que queria el Padre Personio y lo an hecho tan de veras que[351] parece cosa milagrosa y increible a los que conocieron antes su obstinacion.

    Vino el Cardinal Burghese al Collegio, hechas ya las paces para confirmarlas, y le hecieron una oracion los inquietos muy efficaz agradeciendole[352] grandamente lo que avia cooperado a ellas, y mostrando[353] quán de corazon las avian hecho. An escrito tan bien cartas muy humildes al Padre General de la Compañia de Jesus que está[354] al presente en Napoles pidiendole perdon de lo passado, y offreciendole de hacer todo lo que su Paternidad o el Padre Personio les ordenara, y del mismo argumento an escritto muchas cartas tan bien a sus parciales en Flandes, particularmente al Doctor Giffordo y Ugo Grifinio amonestandoles a dexar tan bien ellos esta discordia y porfia. Y en fin aqui en Roma no solamente estos estudiantes, si no tan bien todos los demas Yngleses de fuera del Collegio mostran con las obras de estar muy trocados, y se piensa que nunca podra llevantarse otra tempestad como ésta, pues los mismos autores y fautores principales[355] aqui en Roma (y particularmente los dos Monsignores Mora y Malvasia que estavan engañados) an visto ya por esperiencia que esta porfia no tenía fundamento ni substan-

346. hacerle] *W*; hacerlo *Vd*
347. unos] *W*; uno *Vd*
348. dentro] *Vd*; dentra *W*
349. todo] *interlined with caret Vd*
350. llevar por ventura] *W*; por ventura llevar *Vd*
351. que] *interlined with caret W*
352. agradeciendole] *W, possibly* agradeciendolo
353. mostrando] *W*; mostrado *Vd*
354. está] *W*; sta *Vd*
355. principales] *suppl. in margin W*

cia alguna de verdad, si no passion y emulacion, y asi servira por aviso para otra vez que el Demonio quesiesse attentar otra cosa semijante. Su Santidad ha mostrado grandissimo gusto del fin desta discordia y de la[356] luz que el Padre Personio le a dado en las cosas de Ynglaterra y lo mismo los Sobrinos y otros Cardinales, con que se espera que esta paz será cosa firma placiendo a nuestro Señor el qual guýa todo a su mayor gloria y bien de Ynglaterra. En Roma[357] 22 de mayo, 1597.

[*Endorsed:*] Relacion del principio progresso y fin de la turbacion del Collegio Ynglés en Roma 1597. [*Added in another hand, possibly that of Persons:*] La 2ª que se scrivio.

Translation

An account of the origin, progress, and end of the disturbance in
the English College, Rome, which lasted more than two and a half
years and was the occasion of injury and danger to the common
cause of all the Catholics of England.

What has been discovered about all this affair by examination of the cause and of the complaints, from memorials and letters on both sides, and from the confessions of the malcontents themselves after they had been reconciled and appeased, is as follows:

The immediate occasion of the discord among the English students was the fact that His Holiness granted to Cardinal Allen during his lifetime the allocation of certain faculties to the priests who were to be sent to preach our holy faith in England, according to each one's talents and deserts. After Cardinal Allen's death, which took place in the year 1594, the bishop of Cassano[358] claimed that these powers should be granted to him as the principal ecclesiastic of English nationality. Through the rector of the college,[359] who was an Italian and knew little about English affairs or English people, he induced the majority of the students of his college to petition for them by a memorial to His Holiness, arguing that it was fairer that a man of the same nationality as themselves should allot the faculties, rather than the protector, Cardinal Caetani. His Holiness, however, would not give them to the bishop of Cassano, but only to the protector. The students took offence at this and, incited to anger by some English friends of the bishop who were living outside the college, they adopted a hostile attitude not only to the cardinal protector but also to the father general of the Society of Jesus and to all the other fathers besides who were trying to dissuade them from this sort of conduct.

Once the students had broken with the cardinal protector and the fathers who were governing them, they found support from two kinds of men or, to speak more accurately, from two kinds of passion in them. On the one hand were the rivals and opponents of the Society, whom they found in Rome just as in Flanders; on the other hand, under the influence also of the former, were those averse or ill-disposed to the cause of Spain. They

356. la] *interlined with caret Vd*
357. *Vd inserts* a *after Roma*
358. Owen Lewis.
359. Girolamo Fioravanti.

proclaimed that just as they had no wish to be governed or directed any more by fathers of the Society, so they had no desire either to be dependent on Spain, with whom they said that the fathers were in league. They did not wish this college in Rome to go on leaning on Spain like the other seminaries, but to take a different direction and path; and in this way, following the spirit of that time, they found support and assistance where they had not found it otherwise, and transformed their dispute into a political issue.

Some very unruly and scandalous conduct took place during this dispute, for one reason because the leaders of those in revolt, feeling reckless because of those who protected them, showed no respect for anybody. On the other hand, His Holiness, though much displeased by their manner of behaving, forbore to take the resolution of punishing them, giving in to the intercessions of so many patrons who supported them; so much so that on one occasion, when His Holiness had given orders for four of the principal disturbers of the peace to be expelled from the college, he afterwards gave fresh orders for them to return, under pressure from those who pleaded on their behalf. This encouraged them all the more, and not only them but many others as well who were following their example.

Presently his Holiness gave orders that Cardinal Sega[360] should make a visitation of the College and report to him the true state of affairs. This he did very conscientiously during the space of six months, giving a hearing to everybody with great patience, and he left a written report of his visit, very orderly and well arranged, pointing out in every incident where there had been passion or fault on the part of the rebels. But it so happened that he died, and Cardinal Toledo, who succeeded him as vice-protector of the college in the absence of Cardinal Caetani,[361] the protector, showed that he took a different view of matters. He promised the rebels to give them complete satisfaction in everything and to change the method of government here in this college as well as Rheims; he would deal similarly with matters within England and remove the fathers of the Society. By way of making a beginning of this design of his he appointed one of their comrades who had been the leader of this revolt as confessor of the dissident students. Moreover, he ordered that this confessor, like a tribune of the people, was to have a regular audience of the protector every Thursday, in order to lay before him the grievances and complaints of the discontented students; and he did many other similar things which tended to increase the discord rather than get rid of it.

These measures brought the affair to such a head that it became a source of consternation and grief. For the college was divided into two parties, almost equal in number, although the dissidents had somewhat the larger part, being 28 where the others were 26. But the loathing of the one for the other was such that they did not want to deal with or converse, the one with the other, nor eat at the same table, nor hear Mass in the same church; and they lived as enemies, nor would they obey the superior in any thing at all without resistance and murmuring.

---

360. Mgr Bernardino Morra, notary of the Congregation for Bishops and Religious, conducted a visitation of the college in August 1595; Filippo Sega was appointed cardinal vice-protector at the end of November, and conducted a second visitation with Morra, producing a final report on 14 March 1596. He died on 29 May 1596, to be succeeded by Francisco de Toledo, SJ.

361. Enrico Caetani left Rome for Poland in April 1596, as papal legate (McCoog, *Building the Faith of St Peter*, 270, 357).

Afterwards, they were so averse to the fathers of the Society who governed them and to all the rest of that order, especially the English fathers who were labouring for them in all those parts, that they spoke evil not only of all their works in England, as well as in other parts, but also of their institute of religion,[362] saying that the fathers had no sympathy with the vocation of the secular priests. And finally, they saw them as no better than heretics, and said that they hoped for more charity from the same heretics in England than from them. Such were their very words.

In the third place, they were so averse to all the interests of Spain that they could not listen to any good account of them, not even of the seminaries and other benefits and favours received. They broke out in demonstrations of pleasure at the defeat at Cádiz, and they poured out their grief over the winning of Calais.[363] When a student who came from Spain with Fr Persons, seeing their negative attitude, said that at least it should be considered that the king of Spain would restore the Catholic religion in England if his hand could stretch that far, another replied, "We're not so sure about that!" As for the Spanish masters who teach theology in Rome, they could not bear that their gifts in doctrine should be praised, because they were Spanish, even though they are very learned and eminent men. When they encountered the duke of Sessa, His Majesty's ambassador, in the street as they went all together to the schools, not one of the disaffected ones would uncover his head, although they recognized him and said to one another, "Here comes the Spanish Ambassador." The sound ones, however, made him all the deeper obeisance. In fine, simply on account of this disagreement with their superiors, they had acquired a dislike and aversion for Spanish interests as deep as though they had for many years received many injuries from her.

They loathed the *Book of the Succession* and said a thousand evil things about it, although they had never seen nor read it, based merely on ill-natured reports received from their partisans in Flanders, saying that it was greatly in favour of the claims of the king of Spain and the Lady Infanta as against the king of Scotland; that it was the prelude to a conquest of England; and that Fr Persons had obtained signatures and oaths from some of the foremost men of the English nation in Spain in favour of the Infanta.

They were determined to break with all the other English priests who either within or without England were in sympathy with the fathers of the Society or with Spain, and to set up another party in opposition to them. And with this object they had sent two priests of their body, named Button and Norris, to England in the month of October last, charged with implanting this spirit in others and winning many adherents. This is perfectly evident from the confession of the dissidents in Rome themselves, who used to say, when Fr Persons first arrived, that they would not make peace with him until they had news of the success of these emissaries in England; and the same is proved also by a letter which the disaffected students directed to Charles Paget in Flanders and through him to these emissaries in England. This letter was then forwarded with seditious annotations by Dr Gifford, the English dean of Lisle, who is the chief accomplice of the above-

362. Commonly known in the Society as "our manner of proceeding."
363. Essex raided Cádiz in June–July 1596; Spanish troops seized the citadel of Calais on 24 April 1596.

mentioned Paget. Later it was intercepted by the Catholics in England and sent to Flanders and from there to Rome.

Some of the principal men at the head of this faction in Rome have confessed further that they intended to collaborate with the English heretics in everything except for professing their religion: such as in opposing the Jesuits and Spaniards, upholding and defending the existing temporal status of the queen, and countering all the other priests who were opposed to this or were meddling in affairs of state. In addition, they gave their sympathizers and comrades to understand that by so doing they would escape persecution and martyrdom at the hands of the heretics (as indeed they quite certainly would do and would be more likely to receive favours and presents from them). The Catholics, however, would not receive them or trust them any more than they would have received heretics or spies, which as a matter of fact they would have become in a very short time. And yet in spite of all this they were so stubborn in the matter that some of them told Fr Persons and other persons that no human power was great enough to move them from this attitude and that they would willingly die in this cause. And others went on to say that they took it to be a sign of their predestination to be unyielding in this quarrel.

Perceiving this, Fr Persons made them an address, pointing out to them the great evils and dangers attendant on this obstinacy, to the common cause of all the English Catholics just as much as to each of themselves individually. And though they admitted that this was so, still they continued to say that the fathers of the Society were the cause of all these evils, on account of the injuries they inflicted on them and because they would not grant them their just requests. Upon this it seemed necessary to probe further into this wound and proceed to an examination of the matter in detail. This was done by holding seven or eight long meetings and conferences where, starting from the beginning of all this disturbance, a detailed examination was made into all the particular reasons for annoyances or ruptures of relations and the grounds these rebels had for all their stubborn conduct.[364] Fr Persons listened to all their complaints with great patience, admitting their case where it seemed at all possible that they had one, and where they had none showing them the truth; and where it was possible that there was a small degree of reason mingled with a great deal of passion, suspicion, misunderstanding, or exaggeration, distinguishing the one from the other. In this way it came to pass that they were entirely brought to reason in the course of a few days and so began to look at all things in a different light. And in the end, they were all so genuinely converted that it is cause for astonishment, and especially in this regard: that when they came to the point of negotiating with Fr Persons, that is to say in the matters in which they were at variance and for which they had fought during all the previous period, they found that the difference between them was almost solely a question of terms. For when the matter was examined attentively in its essence, on both sides they came to have the same wish, just to reach an understanding. The students were being deceived and inflamed by other men from outside, who had different objects and interests or were moved by different passions. This is what they themselves have since confessed and it touches to the quick. According to this examination the affair proceeded as follows: —

364. These discussions took place immediately after Persons moved into the college, the day after his audience with the pope.

The original source of this disturbance, as has been mentioned, was the bishop of Cassano in the matter of the faculties, and the affair was started by a priest in the college, a fellow countryman of his.[365] Both of them belong to the Welsh nation, a race of people in England of different language and customs from those of the English.[366] They are the descendants of the ancient Britons, overpowered and driven out by the English when they entered the island. And as there exist certain prophecies that they are to take control again, they always retain, and show on certain occasions, feelings of jealousy and rivalry towards the English, although in England itself, as they are few in number compared with the English, they live peacefully. There are many leading men of that nation who are prudent and detest this rivalry; nevertheless, others habitually pursue it and cause fresh disagreements with the English. And so, as it happened that at that time there were a certain number of Welshmen in this college at Rome, the abovementioned priest (whose name is Bennet and who was later the head of the party and confessor to all the rebels)[367] presently brought them and the bishop of Cassano together, and on the pretence that it was for the common good of the English nation drew into the same party the rector of the College,[368] who was an Italian, and with him many of the young Englishmen, who were taken in by this pretext, especially when told that the fathers of the Society were trying to put all English affairs into the hands of the king and of foreigners and to hand over their country to them. For this purpose, the news of the *Book of the Succession* in England, which had just at that time been published and was an object of much dislike to their partisans who lived in Flanders, came very opportunely. The coming to Rome of an English gentleman named Thomas Throckmorton helped greatly to kindle this fire. He was a man of very good parts and had been one of Paget and Morgan's party in Flanders for many years, and now negotiations were in progress for his marriage to Cardinal Allen's niece. Since the cardinal died before Throckmorton arrived in Rome,[369] he joined Cassano with all his resources, lived in his house, and notably encouraged a large number of the students in this obstinate conduct of theirs.

Besides these two, there were in Rome, of Italian nationality, Monsignor Morra, the Apostolic visitor, who showed them much favour, being primed by the other side, and was somewhat hostile to the Society, and Monsignor Malvasia, who had little sympathy with the interests of Spain, as he made evident when nuncio in Flanders; he got his information there from Charles Paget, who was on familiar terms with him, and from Dr Gifford, who was his chaplain and lived in his house; and he thereupon made effective representations here in Rome in favour of that faction of theirs, and of these turbulent men here who were associated with it.

365. Edward Bennet, from Bryn Canellan, Flint.

366. In this context, "England" refers to the single kingdom of England and Wales; "English" could refer to subjects of this kingdom, or to the Anglo-Saxons who displaced the Britons. Owen Lewis used the term in the former sense when he claimed to be English, as a reason why he should be granted the faculties.

367. Edward Bennet.

368. Girolamo Fioravanti.

369. Cf. Pollen, "Colleges in Spain," 64, suggesting that Throckmorton was received into Allen's household before the cardinal's death.

Among the English in Rome, too, there were many to feed this fire but more than others the following:[370] Hugh Griffin, the bishop of Cassano's nephew, a most turbulent man; Nicholas Fitzherbert, who had been cupbearer to Cardinal Allen (he was the person who sent and received the letters which were written in connection with this affair to Flanders, England, and other places); Friar William Sacheverell, an Englishman of the Order of St Dominic but unworthy of his habit, as was seen later: he kept running to His Holiness and wearying him and the cardinal-nephews and others with memorials and loud outcries and tears in favour of the rebels.

The so-called prior of England, an Irish gentleman, also came to Rome and took his share in showing favour to the rebels, although possibly he was not so well aware what a bad case they had. Charles Paget, moreover, and Dr Gifford, with all that Scottish faction residing in Flanders, were continually writing letters to His Holiness and to the nephews and to Cardinal Toledo and to the Monsignors Morra and Malvasia, mentioned above, in favour of these students, and to the students themselves, exhorting them to persevere in their obstinacy. Finally, it was Cardinal Toledo who more than all the rest undertook to sponsor the affair. He was determined to go to great lengths in the matter and to alter the whole course of English affairs, as I have said. But God, who has care for the interests of the English Catholics who have suffered so greatly in His cause, would not permit them to be brought to ruin by such violent means as these, and so He put forth His hand in a wonderful way and intervened marvellously in the cause of peace which has now been negotiated and concluded in the following way: —

The deaths occurred, rather suddenly and both together in the space of a few days, one after the other, of the bishop of Cassano and Thomas Throckmorton, who were the chief originators of the whole business. Then Cardinal Toledo died, who was the leading spirit in it. Fr Tyrie also, a Scot, died, the assistant of the Society of Jesus, who, though a good religious and opposed to the sedition of the rebels, yet resembled them and their abettors in the matter of favouring the king of Scotland and giving up the dependence on Spain.[371] The prior of England left Rome without doing any further harm on this second occasion of his coming from Spain; for Fr Persons had spoken to him in Spain and the duke of Sessa had briefed him in Rome. The friar who was their chief advocate met with a contretemps which drove him out of Rome; that is, he was arrested by the magistracy at night in the house of a woman of ill fame; he was put first in the public prison and afterwards whipped by his fellow friars in chapter and confined in a monastery outside Rome; from there he broke prison and fled in turn to Flanders. Now, in letters from London dated 12 April they write that he has arrived there and that he stayed in the trea-

---

370. Those mentioned are: Hugh Griffin or Griffith (1555–1600), Lewis's nephew, provost of Cambrai since 1588; Nicholas Fitzherbert, a long-standing English resident in Rome and associate of Owen Lewis (Pollen, *Miscellanea II*, 88); John Sacheverell, a former student of the college, now known as Fr William, OP; and Andrew Wyse (see Persons to Acquaviva, 2 and 9 December 1595, B303).

371. James Tyrie, SJ, the general's assistant for Germany, who acted as agent for the Irish and Scots Jesuits in Rome, died on 20 March 1597. In a later MS work, Persons treats the deaths of Owen Lewis, Thomas Throckmorton, and James Tyrie as "Apparent Judgements" of God (CRS 2: 207–208).

surer's house. The bishop of Cassano's nephew, Hugh Griffin, also met with a not dissimilar embarrassment: he had found means to have an abbot named Tiburtio cast into prison, who had been majordomo to the old man Cardinal Farnese. This was on account of an affair with a married woman whom Hugh suspected of being fonder of the abbot than of himself: Hugh has for many years been on intimate terms in her house, according to common talk in Rome. He was obliged to withdraw from Rome to his benefices at Cambrai, lest the friends of the said abbot and of the woman and her husband should take vengeance on him, for they were all in prison and knew from the examinations that Hugh had been the cause of their imprisonment. At his departure from Rome, however, he conjured the priest Bennet, his fellow countryman and confessor to the rebels (as he has later confessed) never to make peace with the Jesuits or relinquish this quarrel under pain of becoming his mortal enemy.[372] And although the duke of Sessa gave him a stern rebuke and a lecture when he was setting out for Flanders, all the same I do not hear that so far he is refraining from the same conduct there.

In consequence of these deaths and departures of persons of the opposing faction, Fr Persons now encountered little opposition from those outside the college in Rome, and their partisans in Flanders too moderated a good deal of their stubbornness when they saw that His Most Serene Highness the cardinal archduke was beginning to take notice of these quarrels. Consequently, it was much less difficult to bring the students themselves in Rome to reason, chiefly because he had first of all won over to a certain extent the Welsh priest mentioned above, who was their confessor and leader of them all. This he did through a brother of his, a priest, who had been brought up in the English seminaries in Spain.[373] This man came to Rome with Fr Persons and was of great assistance in winning over his brother; and it was through him that the principal matters came to be known that made the rebels persevere in their obstinate conduct. These, he said, were mainly the two points which follow: —

First, that their partisans in Flanders had given them to believe that they would find a very large party in the English nation (I am speaking of the Catholics) who would join with them in opposing the Jesuits and the Spaniards, and in the other aims they had in view; and that it would be a very easy matter to get this party under way and to add to its numbers, considering the protection that they were finding in Rome.

The other ground was the assurance they were given that Dr Stapleton would undoubtedly be a cardinal very soon, for His Holiness four times already had him invited to Rome with very good offers of being made a participating protonotary. Moreover, Monsignors Morra and Malvasia were negotiating the matter and had it well under way; so, when he was cardinal he would favour them, being a man who had left the Society.[374] He had already accepted the appointment and promised to be in Rome for September (at

372. See Patrick M. McGrath, "Apostate and Naughty Priests in England under Elizabeth I," in *Opening the Scrolls: Essays in Catholic History in Honour of Godfrey Anstruther*, ed. Dom A. Bellenger (Bath, 1987), 64–65. Sacheverell subsequently returned to England to join Richard Button and Sylvester Norris.

373. Edward and John Bennet.

374. Stapleton entered the Society in Louvain on 6 August 1584 and was dismissed in February 1587 (McCoog, *English and Welsh Jesuits*, 303).

which time the reports as to the success of the emissaries sent to England would be available), so it would be well not to listen to Fr Persons or negotiate for peace with him until then.[375]

These two grounds were demolished by Fr Persons in the following way: against the first, he had, by writing from Spain to various people,[376] ensured that very well authenticated testimony should come both from England and Flanders – and this he found already waiting in Rome – from the most important Catholics and priests, who bore witness that inside England there was no recollection of any disagreement of this sort among the Catholics, nor of any such jealous dislike of the Jesuits or Spaniards; but on the contrary that there was the greatest harmony between the whole Catholic body and the fathers of the Society, and a great love for the Spanish nation, and above all for the person of the king on account of the benefits received during this their exile. Those in England who showed a different spirit were taken to be either heretics or spies, and the students of the English college here in Rome had a very bad reputation and name with the Catholics there for displaying this spirit; if any one of them came to England the Catholics would not receive him into their houses. This point was vouched for in Rome also, not only by some persons of weight who had come from England in connection with this case, but also by letters which were very much to the point from some of the principal priests and most esteemed of those who were working in England. From Flanders also and other places came joint letters and evidence vouched for by the signatures of various notaries public, bearing witness in the same way to the harmony of all the English Catholic exiles among themselves and with the fathers of the Society, and showing detestation of these quarrels and factions. Since this attestation contained the names of nearly eight hundred signatories in the seminaries and some outside them, let it be known that among them were priests, religious men and women, students, doctors, captains, gentlemen, and soldiers, and that those who refused to sign this evidence in Flanders were not more than fifteen persons in all, and they too refused because of their different aims and individual passions.

The rebels saw clearly (and His Holiness and the cardinals as well afterwards, when it was all shown to them) that this faction of theirs was not so momentous as at first they had believed owing to the great noise and clamour it had made. And thus this first ground was destroyed and levelled to the earth, all the more completely because, just at this time when peace was being negotiated, letters arrived from one of their emissaries in England saying that nothing could be done there in this affair against the Jesuits, and that the fathers of the Society had shown them every sort of kindness.

To the second point, namely, the cardinalate of Dr Stapleton, the answer was made to them that, though it was not as yet very certain that His Holiness was summoning Dr Stapleton to Rome for this purpose, still, even if this should come about, as his many merits deserved, the malcontents could have no reasonable hope that Dr Stapleton, once he was made cardinal, would be on their side. In the first place, being a man of good sense and great virtue, he would be quick to perceive how mistaken the students were, and how destructive the tendencies of all their partisans in Flanders. Even though till now he had

375. See Stapleton to Persons, Louvain, 16 April (B366).
376. Little trace of this correspondence remains.

had some sort of amity with some of them, still this would not be enough (and still less the fact of his having left the Society, because he left it for reasons of his bodily health and with the approval of the order) to make him abandon the ordinary policy commonly followed by the whole body devoted to the Catholic cause in England, and follow instead the lead of a few deluded malcontents. And even if he wanted to do so, he would not be able to make any progress, for on the side of the others there would be not only the united strength of all the Catholics within and without England, including the seminaries, the priests, and the fathers of the Society, but also the support and favour of His Majesty of Spain and of the cardinal archduke in Flanders. Against all this, even though an English cardinal who wished to side with this rebellious and factious party would possibly be able to attract a certain following and cause considerable uproar and damage to the nation, yet it would be impossible for him to prevail or make any appreciable impression. This would have been the experience of Cardinal Toledo, if he had lived, for he would have found himself committed in such a way to the project he had formed of changing the course of English affairs in the way suggested by these malcontents that he would have been able neither to go forward nor to withdraw, except with much distress and loss of prestige, for the whole body of English Catholics would have opposed him.

All these arguments had great effect on the dissident students; and this last one, that Cardinal Toledo had been taken in and that it would not have been possible for him to pursue his course if he were still alive, gave a good deal of light to His Holiness also and to the cardinal-nephews and to the vice-protector Borghese and to Cardinal Baronio and others;[377] they have realized that it is impossible to sever the Catholic cause in England from the protection of Spain. And so, the students finally came to abandon their obstinacy and submit entirely to what Fr Persons desired, and they have done this so genuinely that it seems miraculous and unbelievable to those who knew their stubbornness previously.

Cardinal Borghese came to the college, now that peace was made, to confirm it, and the malcontents addressed him in very appropriate terms, thanking him greatly for his share in bringing it about and making it clear how wholeheartedly they had made peace. They have also written very humble letters to the father general of the Society of Jesus, who is at present in Naples, asking his pardon for what has happened in the past and indicating their willingness to do all that his paternity or Fr Persons may enjoin them. In the same strain they have written many letters also to their partisans in Flanders, in particular to Dr Gifford and Hugh Griffin, admonishing them also to abandon this quarrel and give up their stubborn behaviour. And in short, here in Rome not only these students but all the rest of the Catholics outside the college as well are showing by their deeds a great change of heart, and it is thought that it will never again be possible to raise a storm such as this, for its very authors and principal abettors here in Rome, and the two Monsignors Morra and Malvasia in particular, who were deceived, have now seen from experience that this obstinate dispute had no foundation or substance in truth, but in passion and rivalry; and thus it will serve as a warning on any other occasion when the devil may want to make another attempt of the kind. His Holiness has shown the greatest satisfaction with the ending of this quarrel, and the insight which Fr Persons has given him on

377. Cesare Baronio: see the notes of meetings between Persons and Peña, 2 and 17 April (B360, B367).

English affairs, and so too the nephews and other cardinals. And so, there is hope that this peace will be enduring, if it please Our Lord. May He direct all to His greater glory and the good of England. Rome, 22 May 1597.

B379 From Henry Garnet, London, 28 May 1597

>SOURCES:
>ABSI Coll P II 548, Grene's excerpts;
>ARSI, Angl. 38/II, fol. 173r, Bartoli's Latin translation.
>HICKS: Garnet, 435.
>NOTE: Garnet gives further details of the clerical associations mooted by secular priests in opposition to the Jesuits.

In my last I promised you the rules of the 2 sodalities, the one about London, the other in Lankashire — (all) now see it was nothing but to make a head at the first with pretence of good and afterward to breake out into dissention, especially against Jesuits — when you reade the rules you may ghesse att the intention: it is a very strange case that those which are most forward therein, were those which were most against the rules of Wisbich, as though men that live scattered abroad ought more to live in rule, then those which are continually in tumults in one house.

There is speech that Gerard shal be executed this terme &c.[378] My sute for Bickly I pray you remember.[379]

B380 To Thomas Covert, Rome, 31 May 1597

>SOURCE: AAW VI, no. 37, 139–142, Persons's autograph copy (= W).
>HICKS: 645–652, a handwritten transcript.
>NOTE: Persons responds to Covert's appeal to assist him in his conflict with William Holt, by urging understanding, self-examination, and reconciliation. He has also corresponded with Holt about Covert (no record of that correspondence has been traced).
>This letter is one of very few testimonies to Persons's manner of directly confronting and rebuking someone he believes to be in error. It resonates with his account, in the *Relacion* of 22 May (B378), of how he dealt with the students in Rome, and with his letter to Charles Paget, 20 December 1597 (B429).

Lovinge friende

I have yours of the 29 of April, as I remember for nowe I have not the lettre by me, and full sorrye I ame to see therby the discontented estate wherin you remayne, not

---

378. Bartoli translates: "Fama ... fert Joannem Gerardi brevi morte esse multandum," adding, "ita enim Regina omnino decrevit" (for the Queen has altogether decided it should be so). Gerard was tortured repeatedly in the Tower of London in April and May 1597, and found consolation in a letter from Garnet telling him to "prepare [him]self for execution" (Gerard, *Autobiography*, 123). See also Garnet's letter to Persons, 10/11 June (B381).

379. On Ralph Bickley, see Garnet's letter of 15 April (B365).

perceavinge howe it maye lye in my hande to deliver you therof excepte I sawe better disposition in your self, for often I thinke of those paradoxes of the aunciente philosophers which in deede are some Christian axiomes and propositions in there senses, to witte: *unusquisque sibi fugit fortunam et nemo laeditur nisi a seipso*,[380] for albeit we attribute comonlye ever yvel fortune and hurte unto others and that by natural as Eve did uppon Adam and he uppon the serpente; yet the principal causes therof are we oure selves ether *antecedenter*[381] in procuringe or givinge occasion therof or ells *consequenter* in cooperating therunto or not making oure benefit therof but rather drawinge it on or encreasinge it by oure owne maner of proceding.

I have written to Fr Houlte in your behalf requestinge him to yelde you satisfaction in what he canne and is reasonable and he hathe ever answered me that he desirethe soe to doe but that you are so passionate and soe farre oute of reason as noe reason will contente you, the same doe other men write, also of good accompte and whom I have knowen you to accompte your deere freindes, addinge further also that Fr Houlte hathe borne muche at your handes: what can I doe in this case beinge absente? You saye that if Fr Houlte denye these thinges you accuse him for, you will prove them authenticallye, but can I beinge absente examine these proofes? And do not I prove by experience every daye and especiallye have donne soe heere of late in endinge those scandalouse broyles of Rome that betwene partyes opposite and offended great injuryes are pretended on bothe sydes which when they come to examinasion prove nothing in real substance or at leaste muche lesse and fewer then they were apprehended and blazed?

If reason did rulle amonge you there and not passion you would rather imagyne piouslye and Christianlye that Fr Houlte is a man that desireth to save his soule alsoe amonge others and that by all probabilitye he knowethe what daunger it is to offer injurye or to persequute eny Catholique manne that suffreth for his conscience as you doe, and that you have bene soe trusted and employed in the comon by those that are his frendes as you have, if you should fynde him or others of accompte there shewe themselves otherwise towardes you then heretofore.[382] It were reason for a man somwhat to entre into himself alsoe and see whether his owne maner of proceedinge and desertes be chaunged and not onlye to condemne others (specially being manye and grate and in opinion of good men) and not to call them confederates so easylye as you do in your lettre, and stande uppon innocencye and defence as if yourself onlye were an angel impeccable and others withoute conscience or judgment and consequently to crye for satisfaction at other mens handes (as you doe) and offer none of your owne.

This is not the ryghte waye, my loving freinde, before God or man, and the further you will runne in it the further you will[383] wearye bothe your self and your freindes and the

---

380. "Everyone seeks fortune for himself and no one injures him except himself." The latter part is the title of a treatise by St John Chrysostom, partly based on book 10 of Plato's *Republic*: see *A Select Library of the Nicene and Post-Nicene Fathers of the Christian Church*, ed. Philip Schaff (New York, 1886–1890), 9: 267–284. For *laeditur*, W reads *leditur*.

381. antecedenter] *this ed.*; anteceadenter W

382. It is unclear whether the clause "if you should fynde him ... then heretofore" should be attached to the previous sentence or the following one.

383. will] *duplicated over page break* W

more you will fynde your self entangled in the ende and the lesse meanes lefte you to returne to quietnesse. I see your hande to runne in matters nowe agaynste which I have harde your tonge runne muche at other tymes and your hande and harte alsoe if you dissemble not muche *et Jordanis conversus est retrorsum*.[384] If reason and conscience have leade you to reforme your judgment in your former course it is well, but if passion onlye or offence why this or that man as a storme or tempeste hathe driven you soe much asyde, when this wynde easethe you will fyende your self oute of the waye and wyshe that you had held one when you founde the course firste beganne if it were good. And this I speake not so muche in respecte of eny newe frendes you have as of breache with your oulde, my desyre beinge that all maye be one if it be possible; but the waye is not, assure yourself, for eche syde and for every man to justifye himself at the spears ende and to ask satisfaction of thother, for this is not the waye to make peace or union but to further breaches, and seinge the sperite of God sayethe that *Justus in principio accusator est sui*, that the very wyse man is contente to yelde to accuse himself, those that are not soe wise maye be contente alsoe to yelde alsoe some faulte to have bene on there parte; and this is the waye to union if eny be: to meete half waye together the partyes aggreevid and eche one to acknowledge rather his owne frayeltye and imperfection then still to accuse others malice. And this is all I can saye or doe in this matter, Mr Covarte, wyshinge you to deale with F. Houlte to whom for this purpose I have sente your lettre alsoe requesting him to see and consider your greefe and give you satisfaction wherin it maye be possible and soe I truste he will and that he shall fynde you reasonable on thother syde to be content with reason as Christian Catholique men shuld be; and thoughe you threaten to breake with me alsoe excepte I procure you remedye, yet I hope you will considere that this is all that I can doe in this affayre; nor would I wishe that you should moleste anye more the Fathers or superiors of our Societye in this matter, for in equitye can they do noe more in this matter then I have donne. And so to the Holye Spirite of our Saveoure I committe you. From Rome this 31 of Maye 1597.

[PS] You knowe the writer by the hande and it hathe bene no smal laboure, being in my bedde as I ame these dayes of indisposicion.

[PPS] All matters of descord here in Rome, God be thankd, are well ended, bothe within and withoute the colledge, and as greate comforte and confidence and alacrytye as ever I knewe in this place. I would to God the like were with you.

[*Endorsed by Persons*:] The copie of my lre to Mr Covart 31 May 1597 about the faction.

B381 From Henry Garnet, London, 10/11 June 1597

>SOURCE: ABSI Coll P II 548, Grene's excerpts, incorrectly dated "10. Jan. 1597."
>HICKS: Garnet, 408.
>NOTE: Gerard was moved from the Clink to the Tower of London on 12 April 1597; see Gerard, *Autobiography*, 104 n1; in a note on p. 238, Philip Caraman translates Garnet's letter to Persons [*vere* Acquaviva], 11 June: "We have also lately heard for certain that the Earl of

384. Ps. 113:3: "Mare vidit, et fugit; Jordanis conversus est retrorsum" (The sea saw and fled: Jordan was turned back); verse 5 is even more apposite: "What ailed thee, O thou sea, that thou didst flee: and thou, O Jordan, that thou wast turned back?"

Essex praised his constancy, declaring that he could not help honouring and admiring the man. A secretary of the Royal Council denies that the Queen wished to have him executed. To John this will be a great trouble." See ABSI, Anglia A II 29.

[*Grene's extract:*] I wrott unto you heretofore of the remove of Mr Gerard to the tower: he hath bin thrice hanged up by the hand, every time until he was almost ded and that in one day twice. The cause was (as now I understand pirfectly) for to tell, where his superior was, and by whome he had sent him letters which were delivered him from Father Persons and it was discovered by one of his fellow prisoners: they charged him, &c.

The Earl of Essex sayth he must needs honour him for his constancy.

B382 To Thomas Stapleton, Rome, 15 June 1597

SOURCE: Stapleton to Persons, 6 July (B386).

NOTE: Persons encouraged Stapleton to come to Rome as requested by the pope and cautioned him about the dissidents at the English college. He mentioned writing to Stapleton earlier, most likely in reply to the latter's letter of 16 April (B366), and was disappointed not to have received a reply.

B383 To Don Juan de Idiáquez, Memorial on the Faction of Charles Paget and Thomas Morgan, 30 June 1597

SOURCES:
AAW VI, no. 41, 153–156, a copy endorsed by Persons = *W*;
ABSI, Coll P II 464, Grene's notes = *G*.
HICKS: 653–673, with English translation.
EDITIONS: Knox, *Allen* 386–391; Tierney, 3: lix–lxvii (partial).
NOTE: The memorandum, the third prepared for Idiáquez (see Persons's letter to him, 1 May 1597, B371), is dated 30 June 1597 but enclosed in the letter of 3 July (B385). Its purpose is to alert the Spanish royal council to the threat to their interests posed by Paget, Morgan, and their associates. Persons's account here should be compared with his review of his dealings with Paget and Morgan in his letter to Paget, 20 December 1597 (B429).

Que la parcialidad de Carlos Pagetto y de Tomas Morgano aya sido y sea muy prejudicial al servicio de Su Magestad para las cosas de Ynglaterra.

No ha sido poco daño a la causa pública de todos los Catolicos Yngleses y a las cosas de Su Magestad tocantes aquel Reyno, que algunos ministros suyos no ayan entendido bien o no tenido la cuenta que convenia con la parcialidad y faction de los dichos dos hombres; y muchos mayores daños seguirse han, si de aqui adelante no se mira con más atencion en ella, como, por lo que aora se dira cada uno entendera.

La primera origen desta disunion fue en el año de 82, quando en una junta que se hizo en Paris del Nuncio Apostolico y del ambaxador de España, Juan Baptista de Taxis, y del Duque de Guysa, y del Arzobispo de Glasco, Embaxador de la Reyna de Escocia, y de otros se concluyó, que en la reducion de los Reynos de Ynglaterra y de Escocia se avia de tomar el arrimo del Rey de España y no otro camino. Por confirmacion de lo qual fueron embiados a Lisboa y a Roma el padre Personio y el padre Critonio, para pedir cierto soccorro para Escocia. Y porque avian sido excluydos desta junta los dos dichos Pagetto y Morgano, que se llamavan criados de la dicha Reyna de Escocia, y tenian corespondencia con dos secretarios suyos, Nau Frances, y Curle Escoçes, que residian con ella en Ynglaterra y tenian las cifras y podian mucho con ella, hizieron tanto con ellos estos dos discontentos que resedian en Francia, y todos quatro juntos con la disdechada Reyna, que la divertieron de todo affetto y confianza deste camino comenzado por via de España.

De todo esto es testigo hasta oy el Padre Henrico Samerio, Frances, de la Compañia de Jesus, el qual vive en Flandes, y en esta sazon se halló con la dicha reyna en Ynglaterra con nombre de medico y veýa las cosas que passavan.

Tan bien el Duque de Guysa era testigo desto mientras que vivia, el qual dixo con mucho sentimiento a muchas personas y particularmente al padre Claudio Mateo Loranes de la Compañia de Jesus su Confessor y al Padre Personio y más que los dos dichos Pagetto y Morgano avian puesto en disconfianza con la Reyna a él mismo en cierta cosa[385] por demasado confidente de España y de los padres de la Compañia.

Tras esto se sabe que los dichos dos tratavan algunas veçes con el dicho Duque de Guysa para que tomasse en sí de librar a la Reyna de Escocia y de metterla en el Reyno de Ynglaterra y Escocia con las fuerças de Francia y de sus amigos Franceses, sin admitter a Españoles, y quando el Duque no queria consentir a esto, si no que se resolvio de nuevo en el año de 83 de pedir otra vez soccorro de Su Magestad de España, Carlos Pagetto no podiendo impedir esta resolucion, offreciose de andar a Ynglaterra, para juntar tan bien el Conde de Nortumberland con el Duque. Pero él llegando por alla, hizo officio contrario, divertiendole para que no se juntasse, como el mismo Duque de Guysa lo dixo despues a muchos. Y el mismo Pagetto lo avia dicho en secreto a Guilelmo Wattis, Sacerdote Ynglés, quando estava para embarcarse para yr a Ynglaterra, que tenía esta intencion. Y más se sabe por el testimonio del sobre dicho Padre Samerio y de otros, que Pagetto y Morgano avian por cartas divertido a la misma Reyna de Escocia, y hecho que escreviesse al dicho Conde que en ninguna manera se juntasse con el Duque de Guysa ni con los Españoles en esta empresa. Y esto hizieron Pagetto y Morgano en Paris despues de reconciliados con el Duque de Guysa, y con el Doctor Alano, y con el Padre Personio; los quales por el deseo que tenian de paz y union, y para que estos dos no esturbassen más las cosas, les avian admittido a la participacion de todos los secretos. Pero estos nunca despues les fueron fieles, como parecera por las cosas seguientes.

Passada esta primera traycion de la diversion del Conde de Nortumberland, la qual fue causa tan bien de la perdicion del Conde, andavan cada dia los dos opponendose en secreto por todas vias possibiles (pero principalmente por via de la Reyna de Escocia, la qual ya tenian muy ganada) a todo quanto la otra parte yva haciendo en beneficio de la dicha Reyna y de la causa pública por via de España, quexandose y dando por causa (como oy dia tam bien lo hacen) que los dichos Alano y Personio y Inglefildo, y otros sus

---

385. cosa] *obscure in margin* W

parciales no comunicavan con ellos las cosas de la Reyna de Escocia que les toccavan para ser criados della. Por lo qual los dichos Alano y Personio el año 84 venieron otra vez a Paris a renovar amistad con los dos y communicarles de nuevo los negocios con la occasion que el Baron Pagetto, hermano de Carlos, avia venido de Ynglaterra y avia speranza que por su medio se podia ganar a los dos, aunque succedio al reves, pues los dos ganaron a el Baron a su bando: y heçieron otra traycion que fue que mientras que estavan tratando con el Duque de Guysa, y con Alano y Personio de procurar y aguardar algunas fuerças de España (de las quales ya avia mucha probabilidad que vendrian presto) los dos embiaron secretamente a Ynglaterra un cierto espia que avia sido muchos años de la Reyna de Ynglaterra en Italia y otras partes, llamado Guilemo Parry; el qual descubrio lluego a la Reyna todo lo que passava, como se save por sus confessiones que estan impresas, y más la dixo, como tenía commission para matar tam bien a ella, a su tiempo, para llevantar a la Reyna de Escocia, y para prevenir la invasion Española, la que los Jesuitas pretendian. Y aunque por entonces la Reyna le agradecio y le regaló, todavia despues le hizo ahurcar; y este fue el fin del Doctor Parry.

Despues desto los dos attendian por mucho tiempo a hazer odioso para con todo género de hombres el nombre de invasion Española, y a los que a su parecer, la procuravan o la favorecian; dando nombre de invasion Española a todo género de ayuda o soccoro que se pretendia por via de España. Tam bien llamavan a Alano, Personio, y Ynglefildo y a los demas que seguian este camino de España, o favorecian a este pensamiento, confederados de los Españoles y desyosos de la conquesta y de la perdicion de su patria. Con lo qual les hazen odiosos, y de la otra parte acrecentavan su parcialidad. Pero más que por otra via ninguna tiravan muchos a su bando, con dezir que la misma Reyna de Escocia aborrecia tan bien de esta invasion, y de los que la tratavan, y que queria, más presto qualquier otro género de remedio que no por las fuerças de España, como los Jesuitas pretendian. Y a este effecto escrivia la dicha Reyna una carta al Duque de Guysa en el año 85, diziendo que mirasse bien a los andamentos de los dichos Jesuitas en su causa en quanto que tratavan por via de España, reprehendiendo juntamente al dicho Duque y al Arzobispo de Glasco por que no avian acudido a entregar una cierta summa de deneros, a peticion de Morgano y Pagetto, a un cierto Cavallero mozo en Ynglaterra, el qual avia prometido a los dichos dos de matar a la Reyna de Ynglaterra para la dicha summa de deneros, como ellos hacian creer a la Reyna. Pero por entender el Duque y el Arzobispo que el dicho Cavallero era un perdido y que no haria nada, como en effetto seguio (ni se pone aqui su nombre por ser aún vivo[386]) no quesieron entregar el denero, por lo qual los dichos dos les procuravan una reprehencion como se ha dicho.

Seguio el año de 86 en el qual los dos, viendo que se yva aparejando una armada de España, para el remedio de Ynglaterra, trataron con un cierto Clerigo disviado, llamado Barlardo, persuadiendole que (para devertir este enconveniente de la invasion) andasse a Ynglaterra y tratasse con algunos Cavalleros mozos Catolicos de mattar a la Reyna; y por otra parte que él mismo tratasse con Walsingamo, Secretario de la Reyna, como lo hizo; y no se save las cosas que tratasse, pero el fin fue, que los Cavalleros Catolicos fueron presos y hechos quartos, quatorze dellos, y tam bien la Reyna de Escocia fue muerta y

---

386. [*marginal note:*] I. G.

escaparon solamente los dos Secretarios, el Frances y Escoces, que eran los corespondentes de Pagetto y Morgano, y avian tratado todas las cosas por cifras.

Al mismo tiempo trató Morgano con otro Clerigo Ynglés llamado Gilberto Giffordio, en Paris, y le persuadeo que andasse a Ynglaterra y tratasse con Walsingamo, y se offreciesse a su servicio contra Jesuitas y Españoles; y al mismo Giffordio persuadeo despues y a otro Clerigo de su humor Grateleo, que, en confirmacion deste offrecimiento hecho al Secretario, escreviessen dos libros contra los dichos padres de la Compañia y contra los Españoles; y asi lo hecieron, y los libros quedan hasta oy, y estan llenos de mil mentiras y calumnias contra la nacion Española y contra las intenciones de Su Magestad en particular: y dieron los dichos libros escrittos de mano a Walsingamo, como por las confessiones del dicho Giffordio se hezo despues manifestamente en el año 88°.

Muchas cosas an succedido despues por las quales se ha ydo descubriendo de tiempo en tiempo el mal affetto que estos dos y los de su parcialidad an mostrado a las cosas de Su Magestad, tirando a todos discontentos y tentados a su bando. Pero en ninguna cosa se ha visto más esto, que en lo que an dicho y escritto y travajado contra el libro de la Succession de Ynglaterra, el qual aunque se a escritto con toda la moderacion y indifferencia que se puedo usar en tal materia, prejudicando a nadie, toda via porque allega el dicho libro muchas razones en favor de las pretenciones que Su Magestad y sus hijos por differentes vias pueden tener a la dicha corona entre los demas pretensores, los desta parcialidad no lo han podido tragar; sino con Su Santidad y con otros principes, y con los que han podido de la nacion Ynglesa, tanto en Ynglaterra como fuera, an procurado disacreditar y calumniar al dicho libro, como todos saven, y de llevantar faction en favor del Rey de Escocia para contradicir más por esta via a las cosas de Su Magestad.

Y ultimamente para abrevir las cosas, los desta faction se han conjunta[387] manifestamente con los estudiantes Yngleses llevantados y rebeldes en Roma, los quales han mostrado pública aversion y malissimo affetto a las cosas de Su Magestad tanto por palabras y escritto a Su Santidad y a otros personajes, como tam bien por hechos, abominando del dicho libro de la Succession, y de lo que lo favorecian, y parlando siempre mal de las cosas de España, y mostrando mucho pesadumbre de qualquier buen successo dellas, y gusto y allegria de lo contrario.

En una carta de 7 de noviembre del año 96, la qual estos inquietos de Roma escrivieron al Doctor Guilelmo Giffordio Ynglés, Dean de Lila en Flandes de la faction de Pagetto y su íntimo secretario y consejero en todas estas cosas, va escritto en esta manera, y son las primas palabras de la carta:

> Nos otros vemos y sentimos tanto de sus preparaciones para la monarchia (de la qual vos aveis dicho mucho y muy a proposito), que tenemos ya por comun proverbio entre nos, *qui habet tunicam vendat et emat gladium et certet pro justitia usque ad mortem,* y tenemos esperanza que todos los demas de nuestra patria que no han degenerado, no solamente diran, pero tam bien haran lo mismo.

387. conjunta] W, *possibly corrupt*

Esta carta se escrivio para encender y animar a los clerigos y a algunos otros que los sediciosos de Roma con el apoyo de la autoridad del Cardinal Toledo avian embiado a Ynglaterra para hacer parcialidad de su humor, y divertir la gente de la devocion del Rey de España y de la union con los padres de la Compañia, y se pensava que los dichos agentes quedavan aún en Flandes, pues se avian entendido que el Serenissimo Cardinal Archeduque, avisado por el Duque de Sessa de la mala entencion desta negociacion, les avia negado el passeporte para andar a Ynglaterra por los puertos de Flandes. Pero Pagetto y este Giffordio y algunos otros desta parcialidad, aviendoles regalado mucho y animado a que perseguiessen sus intentos, les avian procurado entrada por otras partes de Germania; y ansi Giffordio les embío lluego esta carta añadiendo la postilla que sigue de su letra.

> Mirad bien lo que haceis. La vuestra esperanza consiste en el secreto, en la brevidad y en la perseverenza. Haçed y acavad presto. Los enimigos vuestros embian y reembian, van a Roma, dan preesa, enforman, travajan, escriven, transladan. Consolad vuestros hermanos; haced lo que aguardan de vosotros; no les dexeis uerphanos y desamparados; os sean por exemplo y encitamiento los vuestros inimigos.

Este mismo Giffordio, en una carta que escrivio a 19 de septiembre de 1596 a los sediciosos de Roma para que la mostrassen a Su Santidad y a los Cardinales contra los padres de la Compañia, les pone estas dos accusaciones entre otras muchas calumnias: *Discordiarum inter summos principes per libellos famosos sine nomine authoris seminatio, et antiquissimi et quondam florentissimi regni Angliae in provinciam reducendi conatus.* Estas son las palabras en Latin, y lo mismo se ha de presumir que él y sus complices an scritto al papa, pues se save que han escritto muchas cartas y muy largas desta materia, usando del medio del Monsignor Malvasia para tratar lo mismo. Y queren dezir en el primero de los cargos que el libro de la Succession es un libello enfamatorio, y que tira a discordia contra el Rey de Escocia: lo qual manifestamente es falso, pues no habla contra la persona de algun principe, y tiene el nombre de su autor. En lo segundo dan a entender que los padres Yngleses de la Compañia tratan de hacer al Rey de España Rey de Ynglaterra, y por esta via reducirla a provincia; la qual cosa aunque sea tan bien muy falsa, toda via los desta faction lo andan publicando por todo, para hacer a los dichos padres y a los demas Catolicos que estan unidos en la dependencia de España odiosos: y con todo esto los dichos parciales y factiosos andan quexandose, diziendo que se les hace aggravio en pensar que no favorecen a las cosas de Su Magestad.

Y aunque estas differencias con la nacion Ynglesa parecen por ventura a algunos de poco momento, por ser de pocos respeto de todo el cuerpo de los Catolicos, toda via se halla por experiencia que los effetos son muy dañosos y de grande importancia y consequencia, porque tienen dividida y inquietada grande parte de la nacion; y mucha gente moza, saliendo de Ynglaterra con buenos intentos y caiendo en manos destos sediciosos, embeven tales impressiones que nunca despues se les pueden quitar hasta a ruynarles, y no tanto a sí mismos si no tan bien a otros; y muchos se hacen finalmente enimigos, espias, apostatas, hereges por esta via, como se a visto, y cada dia se vee, cayendo de un mal o otro. De manera che conviene sumamente que Su Magestad y sus ministros miren con attencion en esta liga de inquietos y contrarios, antes que cresca y se confirme más, porque otramente se veran tantos inconvenientes que no se podran facilmente remediar despues. Y a la reducion de Ynglaterra se hara mucho más difficultosa por la disunion de los Catolicos que estos procuran. Y no a sido poco daño a la causa pública de Ynglaterra y al servicio de Su Magestad el no aver hecho caso hasta agora desta parcialidad; y quanto más se delatara, tanto más daño seguira.

Con apartar uno o dos de las caveças de Flandes, o quitarles los entretenimientos publicamente por inquietos, estubieren ya los demas escarmentados y otros avisados de no unirse con ellos; y se esto no se hace, o alguna otra demostracion de la parte de Su Magestad y de sus ministros, no veo fin que se puede esperar del negocio. Haga nuestro Señor lo que más convenga. A 30 de Junio, 1597.

[*Endorsed by Persons*:] De la parcialidad de Pageto y Morgano en la nacion Ynglesa. 1597.

Translation

That the faction of Charles Paget and Thomas Morgan has been and is very harmful to the interests of His Majesty in English affairs.

It has done no little damage to the common cause of all the Catholics in England, and to the interests of His Majesty touching that realm, that certain of his ministers have not quite understood, or have not taken due account of, the party and faction of the two men above mentioned. And far greater harm is likely to follow if, from now on, they do not pay more attention to it. This will be realized by everybody from what I am about to say.

This disagreement first started in the year '82, when a meeting took place, in Paris, of the apostolic nuncio, the Spanish ambassador Juan Bautista de Tassis; the duke of Guise; the archbishop of Glasgow, ambassador of the queen of Scotland;[388] and others, and it was decided that to deal with the conversion of the kingdoms of England and Scotland they had to obtain the support of the king of Spain and there was no other way. In pursuance of this decision Fr Persons and Fr Crichton were sent to Lisbon and Rome to ask for definite aid for Scotland. The abovementioned Paget and Morgan, who called themselves servants of the said queen of Scotland and kept up a correspondence with her two secretaries, Nau a Frenchman and Curle a Scotsman,[389] who lived with her in England and kept the ciphers and had great influence with her, had been excluded from this meeting and that is why these two disgruntled men, who were living in France, so worked upon the two secretaries, and the four of them together upon the unhappy queen, that they took away from her all liking for and confidence in this plan of action initiated through Spain.

---

388. Juan Bautista de Tassis (1530–1610), Spanish ambassador to France 1581–1584; Henry, duke of Guise (1550–1588); James Beaton (1517–1603), archbishop of Glasgow. See vol. 1: 302.

389. Claude Nau (d. 1605) and Gilbert Curle (1545–1609).

Of all this, Fr Henri Samier,[390] a French father of the Society of Jesus, living in Flanders, remains as a witness to this day. At that period, he was attached to the queen in England, nominally as her physician, and saw what was going on.

The duke of Guise, too, was a witness of it while he lived, and spoke with strong feeling about it to many people, and in particular his confessor Fr Claude Matthieu of the Society of Jesus,[391] a native of Lorraine; Fr Persons; and others, that the abovementioned Paget and Morgan had given rise to distrust between the queen and himself in a certain matter, on the score of his being too intimate with Spain and the fathers of the Society.

Besides this it is known that these two men at various times tried to persuade the duke of Guise to take it upon himself to set the Queen of Scots free and place her on the throne of England and Scotland by using the power of France and her French friends and excluding the Spaniards. When the duke declined this proposal and instead determined once more in the year '83 to ask again for help from His Majesty of Spain, Charles Paget, not being able to prevent this decision, volunteered to go to England and procure the earl of Northumberland's collaboration with the duke. But when he got there, he did the opposite, and prevented him from becoming an ally, as the duke of Guise himself afterwards recounted to many. Paget too, when he was on the point of embarking for England, had himself told William Watts, an English priest, in confidence, that this was his intention. Moreover, it is now known, on the testimony of the abovementioned Fr Samier and others, that Paget and Morgan had written letters which alienated the Queen of Scots herself and caused her to write to the earl of Northumberland, telling him to be sure not to associate himself with the duke of Guise or the Spaniards in this project. And this was done by Paget and Morgan in Paris after they had been reconciled to the duke of Guise and Dr Allen and Fr Persons, who, out of their desire for peace and unity and to prevent these two men from obstructing their policy further, had admitted them to a share in all their secrets. But these two were never loyal to them afterwards, as subsequent events will show.[392]

After this first act of treachery had caused the estrangement of the earl of Northumberland – which was the cause also of the earl's ruin – the two men continued their secret opposition from day to day, in every way they could (but principally through the Queen of Scots, whom they had now largely won over), to all that the opposing party was doing to help the said queen and the common cause by cultivating the Spanish interest. They complained that Allen and Persons and Englefield and others of their party were not keeping them informed of matters connected with the Queen of Scots which were their business as her servants, and gave this as their justification, just as they do today. For this reason, Allen and Persons came again to Paris in the year '84 to renew concord with the two men and put them in touch with affairs again, taking advantage of the fact that Lord Paget, Charles's brother, had come over from England and that there was hope of win-

---

390. Henry Samier or Samerie, SJ (1540–1610); see vol. 1: 293 n408.

391. Claude Matthieu, SJ (1537–1587).

392. A very similar account is given in Persons's autobiography, in Pollen, *Miscellanea II*, 31–36.

ning the two men by his means. Instead, the reverse took place, for the two men won the baron over to their party. They also performed another act of treachery: just when they were negotiating with the duke of Guise and Allen and Persons to obtain the help of some forces from Spain and await their arrival – which there was every probability would soon take place – the two men secretly sent a certain spy to England, named William Parry, who had acted as such for the queen of England for many years in Italy and other countries. This man immediately revealed to the queen all that was going on – as is known from his confessions, which are in print[393] – and told her besides that he had been commissioned also to kill her at the proper moment in order to elevate the Queen of Scots in anticipation of the Spanish invasion which the Jesuits had in mind. The queen thanked and rewarded him at the time, but afterwards she had him hanged. And that was the end of Dr Parry.[394]

After this, the two men made it their business for a long time to render the name of a Spanish invasion, and also of those who, in their opinion, were promoting and favouring it, hateful to every class of person; giving the appellation "Spanish invasion" to every sort of aid or succour that was being attempted with Spanish help. They also called Allen, Persons, and Englefield and the rest who followed the plan of working with Spain or were in favour of this idea the "allies of Spain" and said that they were eager for the conquest and ruin of their own country. In this way they made them unpopular and on the other hand increased their own faction. But, more than by any other means, they attracted a large following by saying that the Queen of Scots herself detested this idea of an invasion and the men who were attempting it, and that she preferred any kind of relief other than the one by means of Spanish forces, for which the Jesuits were working. And the queen wrote a letter to this effect to the duke of Guise in the year '85, telling him to beware of the intrigues of the Jesuits in her cause insofar as they were working with Spain, and finding fault equally with the duke and the archbishop of Glasgow because they had not, at Morgan and Paget's request, hastened to hand over a certain sum of money to a young gentleman in England who had promised the two men to kill the queen of England in return for the said sum of money, as they induced the queen to believe. However, as the duke and the archbishop knew that the said gentleman was a worthless fellow and would do nothing, as in fact happened – I do not give his name, as he is still alive – they would not hand over the money; and for this reason the two men procured them a rebuke, as I have said.[395]

Then came the year '86, in which the two men, seeing that an armada was being got ready to come from Spain for the relief of England, treated with a certain wayward cleric, named Ballard, and persuaded him, in order to avert the misfortune of this invasion, to go to England and negotiate with some young Catholic gentlemen to kill the queen: on

---

393. *A true and plaine declaration of the horrible treasons, practised by William Parry the traitor, against the Queenes Maiestie* (London, 1585).

394. See Alford, 139–151, 179–192.

395. A fuller version of this proposed assassination attempt is given in a letter from Castelli, the nuncio in Paris, to the papal secretary Cardinal Como, 2 May 1583, showing that Mary refused to have anything to do with the scheme (Knox, *Allen*, 412–413). The marginal clue "I. G." may have been added later.

the other hand, he himself was to treat with Walsingham, the queen's secretary, as indeed he did. It is not known what those dealings were, but the final result was that the Catholic gentlemen were arrested and cut in quarters, fourteen of them,[396] and the Queen of Scots also put to death, and the only ones to escape were the two secretaries, the Frenchman and the Scot, with whom Paget and Morgan had corresponded and who had conducted the whole business in cipher.

At the same time Morgan had dealings with another English cleric, named Gilbert Gifford, in Paris, and persuaded him to go to England and treat with Walsingham and volunteer for service with him against Jesuits and Spaniards; and later he persuaded this same Gifford, and another cleric of his humour named Grately, to back up this offer by writing two books against the said fathers of the Society and against the Spaniards. This they did: the books are in existence today and are full of a thousand lies and calumnies against the Spanish nation and the intentions of His Majesty in particular. They gave these books in manuscript to Walsingham, as, according to Gifford's confessions, was done afterwards openly in the year '88.[397]

Many things have happened since then which have continued to reveal from time to time how ill-disposed these two men and their party have shown themselves to His Majesty's interests, drawing to their side all who are discontented and open to temptation. But nowhere has this been more noticeable than in what they have said and written and done in opposition to the *Book of the English Succession*. And, although this book has been written with all the moderation and impartiality which could be exercised when dealing with such a subject, prejudicing nobody, yet, because the book sets forth many arguments to support the claims that His Majesty and his children, among other claimants, can make to the said crown in various ways, the men of this party have been unable to swallow it; and so they have done what they can to discredit and calumniate the said book (as everyone knows) in the eyes of His Holiness and other princes and whoever they could of the English nation, both in England and abroad, and to raise a faction in favour of the king of Scotland, seeking in this way to oppose more surely the interests of His Majesty.

And in fine – to cut the story short – this faction has been associated openly with the English students in Rome who rose in rebellion; and the latter have publicly shown their aversion for and extreme dislike of His Majesty's interests, both by what they have said and written to His Holiness and other personages as well as by their conduct in abusing the *Book of the Succession* and those who approved of it and in forever speaking ill of Spanish policy and showing much melancholy at any success it might have and delight and joy at the opposite.

In a letter of 7 November of the year '96 which these disgruntled men in Rome wrote to Dr William Gifford,[398] the English dean of Lisle in Flanders, who is of Paget's faction

---

396. Anthony Babington and his fellow conspirators were executed on 20 and 21 September 1586, seven on each day.

397. For the involvement of Morgan, Paget, Gilbert Gifford, and Edward Grately in the Babington Plot, see vol. 1: 684–701 and John Hungerford Pollen, ed., *Mary Queen of Scots and the Babington Plot* (Edinburgh, 1922), lxxxvii–civ. Grately's books circulated in manuscript only.

398. On William Gifford's relations with Persons in 1596–1597, see his letter from Brussels, 20 March 1597 (B359).

and his intimate confidant and adviser on all these matters, this is how it is written, forming the opening words of the letter:

> We see and hear so much of the steps he is taking about the kingship – about which you have spoken much and to the point – that this saying is now commonly in our mouths: *He that hath a coat, let him sell it, and buy a sword and strive for justice even unto death;*[399] and we are in hopes that all the rest of our countrymen who are not degenerate will not only say but do the same.

This letter was written with the object of inflaming and rousing the clerics[400] and some others whom the party of sedition in Rome, supported by the authority of Cardinal Toledo, had sent to England to create a faction sympathetic to them and to draw the people away from their devotion to the king of Spain and from union with the fathers of the Society; and it was thought that these agents were still stopping in Flanders, because they had heard that His Serene Highness the cardinal archduke, being informed by the duke of Sessa of the evil intentions latent in these negotiations, had refused them a passport to enable them to go to England through the ports of Flanders. But Paget and this Gifford and others of this same party, after giving them a hearty welcome and encouraging them to carry out their intentions, had procured them entry through other parts of Germany; and so, Gifford presently sent them this letter, adding the following postscript to what they had written:

> Take good care what you do. Your hopes depend on secrecy, speed, and perseverance. Act and get it done quickly. Your enemies are sending to and fro, are going to Rome, are making haste, are sending reports, are working, writing, copying. Console your brethren, do what they expect of you, do not leave them orphans and abandoned, but let your enemies be an example and an incitement to you.

This same Gifford, in a letter which he wrote to the seditious party in Rome on the 19th of September 1596, for them to show to His Holiness and the cardinals, by way of attacking the fathers of the Society, lays against them, among many other calumnies, these two charges: *the sowing of discord among the most powerful princes by means of notorious libels, published anonymously; and attempting to reduce the ancient and once flourishing kingdom of England to the status of a province.* These are the words, written in Latin, and it is to be presumed that he and his accomplices have written the same to the pope, for it is known that they have written many lengthy letters on this subject, using Monsignor Malvasia as their intermediary to deal with the matter. In the first charge they mean to say that the *Book of the Succession* is a defamatory libel and that it conduces to discord and opposition to the king of Scotland. This is manifestly untrue, because it says nothing against the character of any prince and it bears the name of its author.[401] In the second

---

399. Adapted from Lk 22:36 and Ecclus. 4:33. The Roman branch of the group aligned against Persons were warning about his intervention in the succession or about Philip II's aspirations to the succession.

400. Richard Button and Sylvester Norris; see Persons's *Relacion*, 22 May 1597 (B378).

401. The book was in fact published pseudonymously, under the name "R. Doleman."

charge they give it to be understood that the English fathers of the Society are trying to make the king of Spain king of England and in this way reduce England to a province. And, though this also is quite untrue, yet the members of this faction go on publishing it wholesale, in order to heap odium upon the said fathers and the rest of the Catholics who are united in their reliance on Spain. And in spite of all this, this same party and faction carry on complaining, saying that it is an injustice to them to think that they are not supporting His Majesty's interests.

And although these differences within the English nation may perhaps seem insignificant to some, because they relate to a small number compared with the main body of Catholics, yet it is found by experience that the results are very harmful and of great importance and consequence, because they keep a large part of the nation divided and perturbed. Many of the young men too who leave England with good intentions fall into the hands of these seditious men and imbibe such impressions as they are never afterwards able to be rid of, until at length they are ruined, and not themselves only but others as well. Many of them in this way eventually become enemies, spies, apostates, and heretics, as we have seen and are seeing every day, falling away through one evil cause or another. And so it is of the utmost necessity for His Majesty and his ministers to look carefully to this league of unquiet and subversive spirits before it grows and becomes more established, because otherwise such inconveniences will appear as cannot easily be remedied afterwards; and the conversion of England will be rendered much more difficult owing to the discord which these men are causing in the Catholic body. It has been no little hurt to the common cause of England and to His Majesty's service that so far no notice has been taken of this faction; and the longer this continues, the greater the harm that will ensue.

If one or two of the ringleaders were removed from Flanders or deprived publicly of their allowances, as disturbers of the peace, it would be a lesson to the rest, and others would be warned not to join them.[402] If this is not done or some other gesture is made by His Majesty and his ministers, I see no hope of an end to the business. May Our Lord do whatever is best. On the 30th of June 1597.

B384 To Cardinal Enrico Caetani, Rome, 1 July 1597

> SOURCE: AAV, Fondo Borghese II, 448A–B, fol. 426 (olim 331).
>
> HICKS: 677–78, with English translation.
>
> NOTE: Persons sends his apologies for not visiting the cardinal protector in person on his return from Poland, and forwards some advices from England by hand of Roger Baynes, formerly secretary to William Allen. Copies of numerous despatches of this kind, translated into Italian, are collected in BAV, Vat. Lat. 6227, beginning at fol. 53 with a cover page, inscribed by Persons, "De Rebus Angliae" 1597. This is followed by the first despatch, dated January. Most of them would have come first to Baynes and Persons, then to Caetani and the papal curia. Many bear the legend "dedit Rogerius" or "dedit Personius", indicating who it was that made the delivery.

---

402. Tierney argues that this advice contradicts Persons's earlier claim to be entirely well-disposed towards them (Persons to Mannaerts, 12 April 1597, B364).

Illustrissimo et Reverendissimo Signor Protettore Osservandissimo

La causa perché non ho potuto venir questi giorni a visitar Vostra Signoria Illustrissima e stato l'impedimento d'un ginochio che m'ha doluto molto questo mese, et anchora non sta sano benché un poco meglio, et così penso poter presto venir a bacciar le mani di Vostra Signoria Illustrissima et negotiar alcune cose delle molte che n'ho per trattar con lei, alla quale in questo mentre mando con questa per il Signore Rogero, l'avisi ch'ho havuto da Inglaterra, et si v'e qualche cosa che a Vostra Signoria Illustrissima parera degna di comunicar con la Santità di nostro Signor, la supplico humilmente che lo faccia poiché Sua Santità così m'ha commandato far nell'occorenzze. Nostro Signor Iddio ci guardi Vostra Signoria Illustrissima con ogni prosperità come gli supplichiamo. Dal Collegio Inglese hoggi primo de Luglio 1597.
    Di Vostra Signoria Illustrissima
        humilissimo Servitore
            Roberto Personio

Translation

Your Right Reverend Eminence and most Respected Protector

The reason why I have not been able to go and visit Your Eminence these days past has been the inconvenience caused by one of my knees which has been very painful this month, but though still not cured it is a little better; and so I think I shall be able very soon to come and kiss Your Eminence's hands, and deal with some of the many things I should deal with, with you. In the meantime, I am sending you, along with this letter, courtesy of Mr Roger, the reports which I have received from England. And if there is anything that Your Eminence should deem worthy to be imparted to our lord the pope, I humbly beg Your Eminence to do so, for His Holiness has instructed me to do so in case of need. May God our Lord preserve Your Eminence to us in all prosperity, as is our prayer to Him. From the English college today, the first of July 1597.
    Your Eminence's most humble servant
        Robert Persons

B385 To Don Juan de Idiáquez, Rome, 3 July 1597

SOURCES:
    AAW VI, no. 42, 157–160 = W;
    ABSI, Coll P II 464, Grene's notes = G.
HICKS: 674–676 (text); 679–681 (English translation).
NOTE: This letter, enclosing the memorial of 30 June on Paget and Morgan (B383), is in effect a report on recent developments relating to the English college, for the attention of the Spanish court. The opening paragraph indicates that Persons may not always have been in agreement with the Spanish ambassador in Rome; see Persons to Idiáquez, 1 May (B371), headnote, and the report of a meeting with Peña, 9 July (B387). The letter ends with a reference to a recent, satisfactory audience with the pope.

Con todas las occasiones de escrivir he avisado a Vuestra Señoria lo que passa por acá, remetiendome tan bien en algunas cosas al Duque de Sesa.

Las cosas deste Collegio andan por agora pacificas, la relacion de toda la compocision embié con las postreras galeras que se partieron. La semilla que avian sembrado en los animos desta juventud de no sé qué captiverio de nuestra Patria, pretendido por los Españoles, y por los Padres de la Compañia debajo dellos, no se puede tan facilmente sacar de los pensamientos, maximamente siendo la cosa fomentada por los de Flandres, como yo he visto estos dias, y fue la causa por lo qual me resolvi de apuntar la narracion que va con ésta, del principio, occasion, del progresso y de los intentos da aquella parcialidad, la qual si no se remedió con apartar dos o tres de las caveças (o Pagetto a lo menos) no pareçe que avrá fin. Vuestra Señoria lo mire y lo piense, porque entiendo que es cosa de momento para todas las cosas[403] del toccantes a Ynglaterra.

He visto dos cartas estos dias de Flandres, la una del Doctor Giffordio del qual embié a Vuestra Señoria una carta larga y muy maligna, los dias passados, y la otra de Ugo Grifidio preposito de Cambray, sobrino del obispo de Cassano, y la una y la otra anima a estos mancebos a perseverar en su rebeldia, y que rueguen mucho a Dios, y esten unidos en la porfia, y que entonçes, no ay peligro, que no salgan al fin con la suya, las quales cartas aunque no han sido bastantes para estorvar la paz exterior hecha en esta casa toda via han confirmado a algunos de los cavos, en dos cosas como han confessado a algunos amigos suyos, la primera que an de prevalecer con el tiempo en excluyr a los Españoles de sus pretenciones a Ynglaterra, y la, segunda que al último haran odiosos a los Jesuitas en Ynglaterra, como los que procuraran el conquisto y captividad della, y que en lo demas viberan estos quietamente en este Collegio hasta darles dios otro amparo como fue el obispo de Cassano y el Cardenal Toledo.

Por esto veerá Vuestra Señoria que es[404] menester, *ponere securim ad radicem arboris*, yo escrivo esto mismo al sereníssimo Cardenal Archeduque, para que con su prudencia vea lo que conbiene haçer, es lástima veer los ruynes effectos que siguen por muchas vias desta fuente, y entre otros ay estos, que algunos moços que eran bonissimos, quietos y virtuosos quando llegaron aqui, y despues a poco a poco passan a tantos estremos de sedicion con esta imaginacion de querer defender la libertad de la Patria, que dejan los estudios y bolviendo a Ynglaterra, se juntan con los hereges contra Españoles y Jesuitas, y despues perden la fe y se haçen hereges o espias, y destos nos escriven de Ynglaterra que ay hasta quinçe al presente; otros con porfia y sin espiritu entran en algunos Religiones a las quales pareçe que no an vocacion de Dios, si no un cierto zelo de emulacion, y assi no perseveran, y son muchos estos que an salido, y otros dan travajo a la Religion, y dishonra a la Nacion, y ayer me vino acá el procurador del orden de Santo Domingo, a decir de parte del provincial desta Provincia que un frayle Ynglés llamado Guilelmo despues de ser castigado aqui en Roma por ser hallado con una mala muger por la Justicia, fue embiado a Viterbo desde donde huyó a Alemania, y agora ay diversos avisos de que está en Ynglaterra y que ha negado la fe, y que otro estudiante tan bien de los inquietos deste

---

403. cosas] *Hicks*; cosa *W*
404. es] *Hicks*; en *W*

Collegio, llamado Fishero está conjunto con él en la casa de un consejero hereje de Ynglaterra, y que los Catolicos estan con grandissimos temores de los escandalos que destos dos podran seguir, y entrambos an sido muy grandes alboratadores deste Collegio y de la liga de Flandes.

El otro frayle se llama Henrique Clithero y es sobrino del clerigo Clithero íntimo amigo y consejero de Carlos Pagetto en Flandes, y que se dice (y se escrive tan bien de Ynglaterra) que ha embiado por alla instrucciones para responder y escrivir contra el libro de la succession. Este sobrino suyo era de los inquietos y infeccionados de sedicion, y entró quatro años ay sin vocacion, como se piensa en la dicha Religion, y aora da grandissimo travajo a los dichos Padres, pues por dos años no se ha querrido confessar, y al presente despues de quatro meses de prision tan poco quere oyr missa.

Destos y de otros semejantes effectos y estragos en esta Juventud savemos y veemos muchas veçes, por causa desta division causada en la nacion por los tentandos y discontentos que he dicho; y assi será obra de mucha piedad attender al remedio, de las demas cosas escrivera el Embaxador al qual hablaré esta tarde o por la mañana; y le dare quenta de la postrera audiencia que tuvi con Su Santidad, la qual fue larga, y pareçe que Su Santidad está tan adelante y desseoso en lo de la señora Infanta como se puede desear. Dios lo encamine a su mayor gloria, y nos guarde siempre a su Majestad y a Vuestra Señoria como le supplico. De Roma a 3 de Julio 1597.

[*Endorsed in Persons's hand:*] [p. 157] Copia de mi carta al S^r. Don Juan de Idiaquez a 3 de Julio. [p. 162] para el S^{or}. Don Jn° de Idiaquez a 3 de Julio 1597 de las cosas del Collegio ynglés.

Translation

Whenever I get the chance to write, I have informed Your Worship of what is happening here, also taking account the views of the duke of Sessa in certain matters.

Things are going peacefully for the moment in this college; I sent a full account of the settlement by the last galleys that left.[405] The seed that had been sown in the minds of the young men here, of some sort of subjugation of our country by the Spaniards and the fathers of the Society in their service, cannot be so easily withdrawn from their minds, principally because this notion has been encouraged by those in Flanders, as I have perceived during these past days. This is why I determined to put in writing the account, which accompanies this letter, of the beginning and occasion, the progress and the aims of that faction; unless it is countered by the removal of two or three of its leading spirits (or at least of Paget), it seems likely never to end. I pray Your Worship to look into the matter and give it consideration, for I believe this to be urgently called for in regard to everything relating to England.

I have seen two letters, these last few days, from Flanders; one from Dr Gifford – whose long and very perverse letter I sent your worship a few days ago – and the other from Hugh Griffin, provost of Cambrai, nephew of the bishop of Cassano.[406] Both the one and the other encourage these young men to persevere in their rebellion, telling them

---

405. I.e., the *Relacion* of 22 May (B378).
406. Probably letters addressed to students at the English college.

to pray much to God and to be united in their stand; and that in that case there is no fear of their not getting their own way in the end. Though these letters have not been sufficient to hinder the outward peace established in this house, still they have assured some of the leading spirits of two things, as they have confessed to some of their friends: first, that they are bound to succeed eventually in excluding the Spaniards from their claims to England; and, secondly, that in the end they will make the Jesuits hated in England, as those who would bring about her conquest and enslavement; and that for the rest they will live quietly in this college until God gives them some new supporter, such as was the bishop of Cassano and Cardinal Toledo.

Your Worship will see, then, that it is necessary *to put an axe to the root of the tree*. I am writing to this same effect to His Serene Highness the cardinal archduke, so that he may, in his prudence, consider what is to be done. It is pitiful to see the ruinous results flowing in many directions from this source; amongst which are these: that some of the youths, who were most excellent, contented, and virtuous when they arrived here, afterwards little by little come to such extremes of sedition through this illusion of wishing to defend their country's liberty that they abandon their studies and, returning to England, join the heretics in opposing the Spaniards and Jesuits, and later lose their faith and become heretics or spies. We hear from England that there are as many as fifteen of these at the present moment. Others, from obstinacy and without spiritual inclination, enter one of the religious orders, to which they clearly have no vocation from God, but only a certain fervour bred of jealousy. Consequently, they do not persevere; and there are many such who have left the order, and others who make trouble for the order and disgrace their nation. Yesterday the procurator of the order of St Dominic came to me here to tell me, on behalf of the provincial of this province, of an English friar named William,[407] who, after being punished here in Rome for being found by the police with a woman of ill fame, was sent to Viterbo. From there he fled to Germany, and now there are various reports that he is in England and has denied the faith, and that another of the disaffected students of this college, named Fisher,[408] is associated with him and living in the house of one of the heretical councillors of England. The Catholics are grievously afraid of the scandal these two men may cause; both of them have been very serious disturbers of the peace in this college and in the group in Flanders.

The other friar is called Henry Clitherow and is a nephew of the cleric named Clitherow who is an intimate friend and adviser of Charles Paget in Flanders.[409] It is said (and this comes in letters from England also) that he has sent instructions there for a reply to be written in opposition to the *Book of Succession*. This nephew of his was one of

407. John Sacheverell, known as Fr William, OP; see Persons's *Relacion* of 22 May (B378) and his letter to Idiáquez, 12 July (B390).

408. Robert Fisher; see Barret to Persons, 10 August 1597 (B392).

409. The uncle William Clitherow (b. 1542) was brother-in-law of the martyr Margaret Clitherow (d. 25 March 1586). He was ordained priest in 1582 and joined the order of the Carthusians at Louvain (Anstruther, 81). He was rumoured to be the author of the tract defending conformity now usually attributed to Alban Langdale. See Ginevra Crosignani, Thomas M. McCoog and Michael Questier (eds), *Recusancy and Conformity in Early Modern England* (Toronto, 2010), pp. 116–29.

the disaffected who took to rebellion. He entered the said order four years ago without a vocation, it is thought; and now he is giving immense trouble to the fathers: for two years he has refused to go to confession, and at the present moment, after four months of imprisonment, he refuses to hear Mass either.

We often hear of and see similar destructive effects in these young men, resulting from this division effected in our nation by those who, being dissatisfied, have been led astray, as I have said; and so it would be a work of great piety to attempt their remedy. About the other matters the ambassador will write; I will speak to him this evening or tomorrow and give him an account of the last audience I had of His Holiness. It was a lengthy one; it seems as if His Holiness is as ready and eager in the matter of the Lady Infanta as could be wished. May God direct him for His greater glory, and may He ever keep safe for us His Majesty and Your Worship, as I pray Him. From Rome 3 July 1597.

B386 From Thomas Stapleton, Louvain, 6 July 1597

SOURCES:
AAW VI, no. 43, 161–164 = *W*;
ARSI, *Angl.* 38 II, fol. 173v, Bartoli's Latin summary;
Bartoli, *Inghilterra*, 406, Italian summary.

EDITIONS: Knox, *Douay Diaries* 1: 392; Dallaway, *History of the Western Division*, 2.2: 279–281.

NOTE: Stapleton regrets not having received Persons's reply to his letter of 16 April (B366). He has, however, received the letter of 15 June (B382), which took less than three weeks to reach him from Rome. He assures Persons of his friendship, his indifference to any promotion that might be offered in Rome, his disapproval of the dissident students, and his likely departure for Rome. The tone may strike the reader as guarded.

Right reverend father

Youres of the xvth of June I have receaved the ivth of this present with good spede. Your former mencioned in the same I have not receaved, which I would have bene glad to have sene,[410] and not left so longe unanswered. I never doubted of your fast and loving frendship to me, which that I have not by entercourse of letters acknowledged, I pray you impute it, as the truthe is, to my other studyes and writinges, for continuance of the which I have in dede studiously forbearen answering and writing of letters, where no important cause moved. For the good reportes of me in the place you nowe are, I must and do hartely thanke you. But *vide ne quid nimium*.[411] I have of purpose desired a yeare and a half absence with enjoying of my profession and estate here, for this very ende to returne hither after a yeares proofe and triall there, if perhaps (which I worthely feare) my actions and qualytes answer not to their expectation. And for the point of preferment in that place which hath bene so much wreslled for, as I firmely and sincerely beleve you that you pretend no such matter but rather shunneth and avoydeth it, so I pray you beleve me that I am of the same meaning, desire and purpose. To serve

410. have sene] Knox; sene *W*
411. "Take heed of excess."

His Holynes or rather Cardinal Aldobrandino as a man of learning ether in privat affayres or perhaps in some congregation of Doctours adjoyned to the congregatyons of Cardinals, as I trust I shall not be altogether unmete, so I verely thinke my self to be called, and do[412] expect no other office or estate there: hoping yet in that estate to be able to helpe and assist as well the common cause of our countre, as divers in particular whose extreme necessytes here I do lament, and upon which only consideration (except in dede a litle devotion and desire that I have rather to live and dye in those holy places then in any place els of the whole worlde out of my owne native countre) I have consented to this vocation, being otherwise for my selfe sufficiently provided here and in all points well settled.

I am very glad that the troubles and dissensions in the colledg of our nation there are nowe ended and appaised, no doubte by your prudent and laborious endevour. The opinion that I ever favoured those factions, or should favour them if I came thither, may evidently be convinced by two letters by me writen at the request of Fr Gibbons and others here, one to Cardinal Caietan, Protectour, a yeare sence and more, an other to His Holynes the last winter, subscribed by divers others. Not only I never liked, but have allwaies utterly misseliked and condemned such unquiet heades against their Superiours and namely against the Socyete, to whom all our countre Catholike youthes are so highly beholding. And in that sense, especially for the credit and avancement of the Socyete, to which is conjoyned the wealth and avancement of the Catholike religion[413] as well abrode as especially at home, you shall allwayes finde me.

I have nowe thre wekes past receaved a letter from Monsignor Malvasia agnising the receyte of my letters sent to you, contayning also a promise that by the next post I should receave a letter from Cardinal Aldobrandino to His Highnes here, our Gouvernour, and withall a peece of mony assigned for my viaticum. But yet to this howre no such letters are come to my hands. If they come in any good time, I meane (God willing) to sett forward from hence aboute the middest or ende of August, if at lest I obtayne the licence of His Highnes desired, and that my health permit me; for even within these two dayes an issew falling downe to my leg and broken out kepeth me at home, hoping yet by God his grace it will shortly be healed. If not, *Domini voluntas fiat, cuius est disponere, quicquid homo proponat.*[414] And, I thanke God, I am to this howre indifferent either to staye here or to goe as God his providence shall permit. Only if go I must, I do infinitly desire to finde you there, and to communicat with you of all matters largely, openly and roundly. As soone as any effectuall order cometh from thence, and my licence of His Highnes here[415] despatched, you shall by the first understande of my finall resolution and time of setting forward, if it so fall out. In the meane I commend me very humbly to your good prayers with most harty thankes for all your courteous and charitable endevour on my behalfe, which I will not fayle to acquit with all dutifull service when any occasion shall be offred thereunto, assuring you *coram Deo*[416] that I will allwayes remayne a trusty ser-

412. thinke my self to be called, and do] *interlined with caret W*
413. Bartoli quotes this passage in Italian translation.
414. "May the Lord's will be done, to whom it belongs to dispose, whatever man proposes."
415. *W defective.*
416. "Before God."

vant to His Majestie of Spayne; of which point *plura*,[417] if it please God we may mete together. Lovayne, the vith of July, 1597.

Youres assuredly,
THOMAS STAPLETON.

[*Addressed*:] Admodum R. patri, P. Roberto Personio, Anglo, Societatis Jesu presbytero. Romae.

[*Endorsed*:] D. Stapleton, V. [VI.] July, 1597. His cuming to Rome and ... with the Societie.

B387 Report of a Meeting with Francisco de Peña, Rome, 9 July 1597

SOURCE: BAV, MS Vat. Lat. 6227, fol. 39.

NOTE: This report initiates a series of reports and letters relating to Peña's role, as auditor of the Rota, in facilitating discussions between Persons, the Spanish ambassador, and the papal curia, chiefly about measures to be taken to curtail the divisions within the English Catholic communities at home and abroad, and to advance the claim of the infanta to the succession in England.

In a letter to the duke of Sessa, Peña describes a long, wide-ranging discussion that he held with Persons on English affairs. They have finalized the arrangements for a regular Monday meeting between Persons and the ambassador, to begin on Monday, 14 July. There is an indication of unease about the way Persons wrote to Idiáquez about the ambassador (cf. Persons to Idiáquez, 1 May and 3 July, B371, B385).

El Padre Personio a quedado consoladissimo quando a entendido de mí esta mañana, que Vuestra Excellencia no solo se contentava pero aun deseava que cada lunes su paternidad pudiese tener una hora cierta para tratar de las cosas de Inglaterra.

Despues a discurrido largo sobre muchos puntos tocantes a esta materia, y concluido que en la primera conferencia se tratará del remedio que se a de poner en reprimir la audacia y insolencia delos tentados tanto delos de Roma, quanto delos de Flandes; i esto en dos maneras, primeramente considerando los remedios en general, y segundariamente en particular segun la calidad de las personas tentadas.

En respeto de la persona de Gifordo conforme a su condicion y acciones pasadas y presentes, se a concluido que si se permite que venga a Roma, se causará total impedimento al buen progreso de las cosas de Inglaterra y servicio de Su Magestad y que es necesario que el Cardenal Archiduque avisado provea de remedio, que será entretenerlo alla con alguna buena ocasion.

Tanto en esta conferencia quanto en las otras que se iran haziendo traera el padre notado lo que a él le parece, i Vuestra Excellencia lo verá, y con toda libertad dira lo que convendra añadir, quitar, o, poner de otra manera: y conforme quedara asertado se avisará en España, y Flandes, de donde se an de aguardar los efetos destas resoluciones.

Por aver scrito Gifordo de Flandes que alla entre los Ingleses se discurria mucho que Personio avia de ser cardenal, de lo qual este padre a recebido grandissimo pesar,

417. "More."

tenía casi resuelto de dezir a Su Santidad i a los nepotes, que él nunca avia tenido semejante pretension, y que asi lo protestava i io solo e difundido representandole que el Papa que es de su condicion tan sospechoso, creeria que lo dezia para discubrir de su respuesta, y gesto su intencion, y que de aqui naceria que no lo tendria por hombre limpio de pasion, de donde redundaria mucho perjuicio a las cosas que tratava, y que por tanto era más acertado callar, y hazer y dezir lo que convenia como avia començado, y lo demas encomendarlo a Dios. Pareceme que a quedado convencido; con todo esto, no me parece fuera de propósito que Vuestra Excellencia en buena ocasion le acuerde esto mesmo.

Este padre quedará muy consolado de ver que Vuestra Excellencia acude a todo este negocio, y tiene memoria de lo que io le e dicho que e avisado a Vuestra Excellencia certificandole que Vuestra Excellencia queda muy animoso, y deseoso de acudir a todo con mucho cuidado y puntalidad.

Finalmente le e buelto a acordar que scriviendo al Señor Don Juan de Idiaquez en respeto de la persona de Vuestra Excellencia mire bien que no pueda sospechar que es comunicacion con Vuestra Excellencia. Él a añadido que mirará bien en esto, i en que no pueda pensar, que su scrivir nace de quexas que Vuestra Excellencia le aia dado.

Translation

Fr Persons was much consoled to learn from me this morning that Your Excellency was not merely content but eager that His Paternity should meet with him at a fixed hour every Monday to discuss English affairs.

After reflecting on many points regarding this matter, he concluded that in the first conference it will be a question of the remedy to be put into effect for the audacity and insolence of those led astray, both those in Rome and those in Flanders. And this should be done in two ways, first considering the remedies in general, and secondly in particular, according to the rank of the persons who had been led astray.

In respect of the person of Gifford according to his condition and actions past and present, it has been decided that if he is allowed to come to Rome, this will be nothing but an impediment to the good progress of the things of England and to the service of His Majesty and that it is necessary that the cardinal archduke be advised to provide a remedy, which will be to find some good opportunity to delay him with there [i.e., in Flanders].

Both in this conference as in the others which will take place, the father will bring with him notes of what he thinks advisable, and Your Excellency will consider it, and in all freedom say what should be added, removed, or put in another way: and according to what is agreed, notification will be sent to Spain and Flanders, wherever the effects of these resolutions are to be awaited.

Because of the fact that Gifford wrote from Flanders that there was a lot of speculation among the English that Persons was going to be a cardinal, causing this father much distress, he was resolved to say to His Holiness and the nephews that he never entertained such a claim, and that he gave assurances of this. But I sought to dissuade him from this protestation, pointing out that the pope, who is of so suspicious a disposition, would believe that he was saying it so that he would disclose his answer, and indicate his intention, and that from here it would arise that he would not regard him as a man free from passion. From this, much harm would result to the matters under discussion, and for that reason it was more prudent to remain silent, and to do and say what was appropriate, as he had begun, and to entrust the rest to God. It seems to me that he has been convinced; in all this, it does not seem to me inappropriate that Your Excellency should remind him of this at the right time.

This father will be very consoled to see Your Excellency come to the rescue in all this business, and you recall what I have told and informed Your Excellency, assuring him that Your Excellency remains very optimistic, and wishes to take care of everything with great care and punctiliousness.

Finally, I have reminded him that when he writes to His Lordship Don Juan de Idiáquez about Your Excellency, he should take good care that there is no suspicion about the communication he has had with Your Excellency. He added that he would look well into this, and that he cannot think that he has written anything as a reaction against any opposition that Your Excellency has given him.

B388 Notes on Interviews with Cardinal Pietro Aldobrandini, Monsignor Francisco de Peña, Cardinal Cesare Baronio and the Duke of Sessa, 10–15 July 1597

SOURCE: BAV, MS Lat. Vat. 6227, fols. 168–169.

NOTE: These interviews, covering questions of foreign policy and the anti-Jesuit agitation amongst the English, are referred to in several of the letters of this period.

+

A x de Julio 1597.

El Padre Personio estuvo con el Señor Cardenal Aldobrandino el qual le hizo muchas protestas sinificativas de la paz entre España y Francia.

§ Preguntado el Padre Personio respondio que Su Magestad no desearia de venir en lo que fuese justo, aunque en particular no sabia nada cerca desto, de la intencion de Su Magestad.

§ Aldobrandino quedó contento, y dixo que deseava verse con el Señor duque de Sessa el sabado despues de la audiencia del Papa para ablar desta materia.

§ Hizo el Padre Personio muchos favores y caricias.

§ Desea el Padre Personio que el duque scriva al Señor Don Juan de Idiaquez en la propria conformidad del Padre Personio, y represente a Su Santidad o a Su Magestad lo mucho que conviene poner presto el remedio antes que la facion de los sediciosos cresca.

§ Y que en cifra digo lo que el Padre Personio scrive en general de algunos ministros fautores de las cabeças de sediciosos que son en Flandes Juan Baptista de Tassis como lo fue por lo polado[418] Don Bernardino de Mendoça.

418. polado] B obscure

A xi de Julio.

§ Baronio a dicho al Padre Personio que el Papa avia mostrado gusto de lo que avia tratado con Su Santidad.

§ Pregunto Baronio si sería bien embiar un legado a España.

§ Respondio Personio que Su Santidad veria mejor qué convenia: pero que quando se huviese de embiar le parecia que esto avia de ser quando Su Santidad estuviesse cierto del ánimo del Rei de Francia; y por esta causa Personio replicava que convenia embiar uno a Francia.

El Cardenal Baronio dio grandes quexas contra el rei y los ministros, porque llamavan al Rei de Francia que Su Santidad avia absuelto el principe de Bearne, y no Rei: respondiosele que Su Magestad no repugnava la absolucion, pero que en las pretensiones temporales que tenía su hija la Señora Infanta a la corona de Francia, y Su Magestad a la de Navarra, no entendia prejudicarse llamandolo Rei. Peña añadio que esta verdad se comprovava con las protestas que se avian hecho a Su Santidad antes que le absoluiese, y recibiesse su Obediença como constava por el fervor de los memoriales que sobre esto se avian dado Su Santidad por el duque de Sessa.

Julius 1597.

En este principio del mes de Julio el padre Personio en diversas dias se vio diversas vezes con Peña para tratar del remedio de las cosas de Inglaterra:

§ Tomose apuntamiento que el duque de Sessa cada semana diese audiencia al padre Personio una vez: assi lo hizo, y se començo lunes a 14 de Julio: con orden que se prosiguiesse cada lunes por la mañana.

§ En la primera conferencia que se tuvo, se trató del remedio que se avía de poner en reprimir las cabeças de los sediciosos Ingleses que Su Magestad sustenta en Flandes como Señor Pageto, Morgano, y Giffordo, y sobre ello el duque scrivio al Señor Cardenal Archiduque.

Translation

10 July.

Fr Persons was with the Lord Cardinal Aldobrandini, who made several grave entreaties for peace between Spain and France.

When asked, Fr Persons answered that His Majesty would not want to stand in the way of what was just, although in particular he had no intimate knowledge of the intention of His Majesty in this regard.

§ Aldobrandini remained satisfied with the answer and said that he wished to see the Lord Duke of Sessa on Saturday, after the pope's audience, to discuss this matter.

§ Fr Persons responded with many gracious courtesies.

§ Fr Persons would like the duke to write to Don Juan de Idiáquez along the same lines as Fr Persons, and to represent, both to His Holiness and His Majesty, how advisable it is to apply a remedy soon, before the seditious faction grows any further.

§ And that I should put into cipher what Fr Persons generally says of some ministers who tend to support the leaders of the seditious, namely Juan Bautista de Tassis in Flanders,[419] who did so because Don Bernardino de Mendoza was so weak.

11 July.
Baronio told Fr Persons that the pope had shown approval of what he discussed with His Holiness.

§ Baronio asked if it would be good to send a legate to Spain.

§ Persons replied that His Holiness could better judge what was suitable, but regarding when to send the legate, it seemed to him that this should be done when His Holiness would be certain about the king of France's disposition towards it; and for this reason Persons replied that it would be advisable to send one to France.

Cardinal Baronio complained a lot about the king and his ministers, because they continued to call the king of France "prince of Bearne,"[420] and not the king, even though His Holiness had absolved him.[421] He was told that His Majesty did not repudiate the absolution, but that in the temporary claims that his daughter the Lady Infanta had for the crown of France, and His Majesty for that of Navarre, he did not intend to prejudice himself by calling him king. Peña added that this truth was confirmed by the complaints made to His Holiness before he absolved him and received his obedience, as evidenced by the vehemence of the memorials on this matter sent to His Holiness by the duke of Sessa.

July 1597.
At this beginning of the month of July, Fr Persons met with Peña on various days to discuss various possible remedies for English affairs.

§ It was decided that the duke of Sessa would give an audience to Fr Persons once a week: he did so, beginning on Monday July 14, with an indication that they should continue meeting every Monday morning.

§ In the first conference that was held, it was a question of the remedy that should be applied to suppress the leaders of the seditious Englishmen whom His Majesty main-

419. Juan Bautista de Tassis (1530–1610) was Spanish ambassador to France from 1581 until displaced by Mendoza in 1584; he subsequently moved to Flanders to serve with the Spanish army; he was in Paris again in 1594 when the Spanish embassy was evacuated on the entry of Henry IV, and then returned to Flanders. On his involvement in the Guise invasion plans of 1582–1584, see A70. The reading here is puzzling (see textual note).

420. Henry IV was called prince of Bearne or Béarn in a reference to his birthplace and the title of viscount of Béarn, which kings of Navarre held. It was not until the pope acknowledged that his conversion was truthful that Catholics officially termed him king of France.

421. In a letter to Sessa on 12 July (fol. 35), Peña elaborated: on the question of Spain's recognizing Henry IV as king of France, Persons gave a diplomatic and constitutional explanation to Baronio: "El Rei no contradize la absolucion pero que la entiende *prout de iure* sin perjuizio de los derechos de la Señoria Infanta a la corona de Francia" (The king did not contradict the absolution but that he understood it *prout de iure*, without prejudice to the rights of the Lady Infanta to the crown of France).

tains in Flanders, such as Mr Paget, Morgan, and Gifford, and on this matter the duke wrote to the Lord Cardinal Archduke.

B389 To Francisco de Peña, Rome, 11 July 1597

> SOURCE: BAV, MS Vat. Lat. 6227, fol. 165, holograph (= B).
> HICKS: 682–683, with English translation.
> NOTE: This brief note gives a glimpse of Persons's mode of life in Rome: he would be taken by carriage to Peña's residence, bearing news from the letters that had recently arrived from England, with a view to discussions with the Spanish ambassador. Some of the despatches are mentioned in the headnote to Persons's letter to Caetani, 1 July 1597 (B384).

Si Vuestra Señoría Reverendissima pudiesse passar esta tarde por acá, tengo algunas cosas de momento para tratar con ella, para que el Señor Duque de Sesa las sepa luego por medio de Vuestra Señoría. Ayer ablé largo con el Señor Cardenal Aldebrandino, y oy he recebido cartas de Ynglaterra a la vista diremos todo. Guarde Dios a Vuestra Señoría. Del Collegio Ynglés, oy 11 de Julio 1597.
    Roberto Personio
    [PS] Perdoneme Vuestra Señoría del atrevemiento, si yo tubiesse[422] coche,[423] sería venido por aý y vendre se[424] Vuestra Señoría me lo manda.
    [*Addressed, with seal*:] Al R^{mo} Monsig^r de Peña.

Translation

If Your Most Reverend Worship could come this way this evening, I have some important matters to discuss with you, so that the duke of Sessa may then have knowledge of them through Your Worship. Yesterday I had a long conversation with Cardinal Aldobrandini and today I have had letters from England. We will talk it all over when we meet. May God protect Your Worship. From the English college, today, the 11th of July, 1597.
    Robert Persons
    [PS] Your Worship will please pardon my boldness. If I had a carriage, I would have come to you; and I will do so if you tell me to.

B390 To Don Juan de Idiáquez, Rome, 12 July 1597

> SOURCES:
>   BAV, MS Vat. Lat. 6227, fols. 34 and 36, a contemporary copy = B1;
>   BAV, MS Vat. Lat. 6227, fols. 166–67, another contemporary copy = B2.
> HICKS: 684–689, with English translation.
> NOTE: Reacting to news reports from England, Persons pleads with Idiáquez to advise the king of Spain not to favour but confront the rival group of English priests who are now

---

422. tubiesse] *Hicks*; tubresse B
423. coche] *Hicks corr.*; cocho B
424. se] B; si *Hicks*

building up a party in England in opposition to the Jesuits. On Button, Norris, Sacheverell, and the planned clerical associations, see Persons's *Relacion* of 22 May (B378); Garnet to Persons, 23 February (B355); and Persons to Clement VIII, 13 August 1597 (B395).

Persons indicates in this letter that he still plans to return to Spain. In the text, *BV1*'s occasional "i" has been regularized to "y" from *B2*.

Despues de las postreras cartas que scrivi a Vuestra Señoria de 3 deste, e recebido otras de Inglaterra de 6 de Junio y 28 de Mayo, y entre otras cosas cuentan como el negocio que se començo aqui en tiempo del Cardenal Toledo, de hazer parcialidad en Inglaterra contra las cosas de Su Magestad, no se a acabado con su muerte, antes se va tratando por alla con mucho calor por ciertos hombres que se embiaron deste colegio de Roma a Inglaterra para este efeto, de los quales los dos eran sacerdotes llamados Butono, y Noricio, los quales pasando por Flandes fueron regalados por Pageto, Trecamo, y Giffordo, y otros de la facion escosesa, como el mismo Giffordo a scrito acá. Y haviendoles el serenissimo Cardenal Archiduque negato pasaporte por informacion que tuvo de sus intenciones por el duque de Sessa, los dichos parciales les procuraron entrada en Inglaterra por otra via de Alemaña; y assi se scrive que al presente estan negociando por alla.

Con estos se an juntado otros dos: el uno es fraile Inglés, llamado Gulielmo Saceverelo, que solicitava aqui en Roma las cosas de los sediciosos con su Santidad, y[425] con todos los Cardenales con grandissimo calor; y despues preso por la Justicia, por la mala vida que hazia, fue castigado publicamente por sus frailes, y despues embiado a Viterbo: pero de alli huió, y agora anda publicamente en Inglaterra; y otro studiante desvergonçado con él, que tambien salio desta casa llamado Ficero: y estos todos juntos tratan el negocio diziendo mil mentiras. Entre las demas cosas an dicho a un Secretario de la Reina llamado Wad como él mismo lo a afirmado a un Catholico que tiene preso que XXX sacerdotes studiantes Ingleses querian dexar el colegio de Roma, más presto, que no ser de la facion Española con los Jesuitas.

Tambien se scrive que se a començado a tratar de fundar dos cofradias de Catholicos y sacerdotes en Inglaterra, la una en Londres, y la otra en la provincia de Lancastria, que tiran a sedicion. Y entre otros fines dizen que quieren escluir a los Jesuitas como parciales de la facion Española, al exemplo como ellos dizen de los dotores Sorbonicos de Paris; excluieron tambien a los Jesuitas por esta[426] partialidad en favor de España.

Esto[427] scriben de Inglaterra, y de la otra parte yo hallo en este colegio que no obstante la paz y union hecha, todas las cabeças de la sedicion pasada hallan tanto arrimo y ánimo en sus parciales de Flandes (los quales les andan cevando,[428] y fomentado por cartas) que an dicho a algunos amigos suyos en secreto, que ellos seguiran siempre sus[429] desiños en contradezir siempre a Españoles y Jesuitas en Inglaterra: y andan solicitando otros por acá. Y asi pues que siete o ocho dellos, an de partir este Setiembre de acá para

425. y] *B1, B2*; om. *Hicks*
426. esta] *B1, B2*; estar *Hicks*
427. Esto] *B1*; Estos *Hicks*
428. cevando] *B1 B2*; (cellando) *Hicks*
429. sus] *B1 B2*; los *Hicks*

Inglaterra, y se yuntarán con otros en Flandes. Vuestra Señoria podra pensar el daño y confusion que seguira, sino se pone remedio por tiempo.

Años a que hemos propuesto los inconvenientes grandes que se siguirian a las cosas de Su Magestad por esta parcialidad de Pageto y Morgano, y otros aderentes en Flandes, y en otras partes y agora se a derramado tanto (particularmente aqui en Roma, y de acá en Inglaterra y Escocia) que los buenos y fieles a penas pueden resistir: y más estan cansados y desanimados con verse hasta agora tan poco aiudados de Su Magestad y de sus ministros en esta causa, que es tan suya como Vuestra Señoria vee. Nunca se a pedido más de que se mostrase un poco el rostro a dos, o tres; o, a uno de los principales autores en Flandes, y otras partes: porque con solo esto[430] se encogerian los demas, y se bolverian a la union; pero con ver que las cabeças son favorecidas y regaladas y con dezir solamente que sirven al Rei, son creidos de los ministros, no obstante todo lo que hazen contrario,[431] pierden ánimo y paciencia los buenos, y los inquietos cobran vigor, y muchos les siguen: y es cosa certissima que con el tiempo se hará la llaga incurable.

Sé que al contrario diran algunos, que conviene a Su Magestad ganar a todos en Inglaterra, y asi favorecer a entrambes partes, pero esta razon aunque no aya valido en Francia, y otras partes como se a visto por experiencia, toda via podria valer y ser tenida por buena si la parcialidad de Pageto y Morgano fuese muy grande y poderosa entre los Ingleses: pero no puede nada, ni a podido hasta agora pues tenía solamente unos pocos descontentos:[432] pero agora con acrecentamiento de los de Roma y con los favores nuevos[433] de algunos ministros de Su Magestad Dios sabe lo que crecerá: y importa que Su Magestad y los que quieren bien a sus cosas lo miren: pues esta negociacion de Inglaterra toca al bien, o, al mal de todo Setentrion: yo hare lo que pudiere mientras estuviere aqui para informar bien a las personas que conviene, y a la buelta a España diré a Vuestra Señoria cómo an pasado las cosas; pero sin el aiuda de aí no podre dexarlas en puesto para durar. Guarde Dios a Vuestra Señoria. De Roma a 12 de Julio 1597.

Roberto Personio

[*Endorsed in the same hand of the copyist, B1:*] Copia de la carta del padre personio al Señor Don Juan de Idiaquez sobre las cosas de Inglaterra y como crecen alli los de la facion contraria a Su Magestad y Jesuitas y sobre el remedio que conviene poner presto y cómo.

Translation

Since my last letters to Your Worship, written on the 3rd of this month, I have received further letters from England, dated 6 June and 28 May;[434] and, among other things, they tell how the scheme, which was started here in Cardinal Toledo's time, of setting up a party in England to oppose His Majesty's interests, has not come to an end with his death, but, far from that, is being pursued there with much ardour by certain men who were

430. solo esto] *B1*; esto solo *B2*
431. contrario] *B1*; en contrario *B2*
432. descontentos] *B1*; descontolos *B2*
433. y con los favores nuevos] underlined in *B1*
434. BAV, Vat. Lat. 6227, fols. 73–74, presented by Persons to the duke of Sessa on 18 July.

sent to England from this college in Rome for that purpose. Two of these were priests named Button and Norris. Passing through Flanders, they were entertained by Paget, Tresham and Gifford, and others of the Scottish faction – as Gifford himself has written here. And this same party, refused a passport by His Serene Highness the cardinal archduke, owing to the report of their intentions which he had received through the duke of Sessa, procured their entry into England by another route from Germany; and so we hear that at the moment they are carrying on negotiations there.

To these, two others have attached themselves. One is an English friar named William Sacheverell, who used to promote the interests of the seditious party with great vigour here in Rome with the pope and the college of Cardinals; afterwards he was arrested by the magistracy on account of the evil life he was leading, was publicly chastised by his friar brethren and presently sent to Viterbo; however, he fled from there and now he is going about openly in England, along with another impudent student, named Fisher,[435] who also hails from this house; and all these men are working together on the scheme, accompanied by a thousand lies. Among other things they have told one of the queen's secretaries, called Waad,[436] that thirty English priest-students wanted to leave the college in Rome rather than be associated with the Spanish faction along with the Jesuits, as Waad himself has stated to a Catholic whom he is holding under arrest.

They tell us also that steps have been taken to institute two confraternities of Catholics and priests in England, one in London and the other in the county of Lancashire, which they are drawing into sedition. And they say that among their other aims is that of expelling the Jesuits for favouring the Spanish faction – following the example, they say, of the doctors of the Sorbonne in Paris, who also expelled the Jesuits as a party that supported Spain.

This is what they write from England; and, again, I find in the college here that, in spite of the peace and reconciliation effected, all the ringleaders of the late sedition meet with such support and encouragement from their partisans in Flanders – who keep inciting and egging them on in their letters – that they have told some of their friends in confidence that they will pursue their purpose of opposing the Spaniards and Jesuits in England at all times; and they keep making overtures to others here. And so, as seven or eight of them are due to leave here this September for England, and will join others in Flanders, Your Worship will be able to imagine the harm and confusion that will result, unless measures are taken in time against it.

Years ago we suggested what grave inconveniences would result to His Majesty's interests from this faction of Paget and Morgan and their other adherents in Flanders and elsewhere; and now everything has come to a head – especially here in Rome and

435. Robert Fisher arrived in England in October 1596, primed by the anti-Jesuit party in Flanders, and encountering Sacheverell in a tavern, was impressed by his defence of the Catholic faith and concluded that reports of the friar's apostasy were the result of Jesuit propaganda. Later he discovered that Sacheverell was in touch with William Cecil (Kenny, "Inglorious Revolution," 82 n17 [part 3]; Barret to Persons, 10 August 1597, B392).

436. William Waad (1546–1623), who held various responsible posts under Elizabeth and James I, had been involved in negotiations in France and the Netherlands, in the gathering of evidence to incriminate Mary Queen of Scots.

from here passing on to England and Scotland – so that good and loyal people can hardly stand up against it; and they are all the more weary and discouraged, because they see that up to now they have had so little help from His Majesty and his ministers in this cause which is so much his own, as Your Worship can see. They have never asked anything more than that he would act a little more boldly towards two or three of them; or one or two ringleaders in Flanders and elsewhere; because, if only this were done, the rest would be dismayed and would resume their loyalty. But when they see that the leaders receive favour and bounty and that their mere word that they are serving the king is believed by the ministers, in spite of all they do against him, the good lose courage and patience and the unruly gain strength and many follow in their footsteps. And it is perfectly certain that as time passes the wound will become incurable.

I know that some will say in reply that it behoves the king to win the support of everybody in England, and therefore to give his favour to both parties. And although this kind of thinking has not been vindicated in France and other places – as experience has shown – it could still be valid and be adopted by good men, if the faction of Paget and Morgan were a very large and powerful one in England. But it has no power at all and has never yet had, because it has consisted merely of a few disgruntled men. Now, however, with the reinforcement of the men from Rome and with the favour recently shown by certain of His Majesty's ministers, God knows to what it will grow. It would be well for His Majesty and those who have his interests at heart to look to it; for this policy in regard to English affairs affects the whole of the North for good or evil. I will do what I can, while I am here, to enlighten the right people fully; and on my return to Spain, I will let Your Worship know what has been the result; but without help from you there, I shall not be able to leave things in a state to endure. May God protect your worship. From Rome, 12 July 1597.

Robert Persons

B391 To Cardinal Pietro Aldobrandini, Rome, 12 July 1597

SOURCE: AAV, Fondo Borghese III, 124 g.2, fols. 13–14, holograph, with address, seal, and endorsement.

HICKS: 690–695, with English translation.

NOTE: Persons asks the cardinal-nephew to urge the pope, whom Aldobrandini was due to meet on the same day (Saturday), to send an envoy to the nuncio in Paris, Francesco Gonzaga, OFM (d. 1620), to accelerate negotiations about the succession in England. He encloses a synopsis of the discussions they held the previous day. See the summary of meetings held with Peña, Baronio and Aldobrandini, 10–15 July (B388).

Illustrissimo et Reverendissimo Signor

Con questa mando a Vostra Signoria Illustrissima li quatro punti, ch' hieri tratassimo, piaccia a Nuestro Signor che sea per sua magior gloria; Vostra Signoria Illustrissima ha per le mani il magior negotio che sea trattato nella republica Christiana per molti secoli, et vedendo io la prudenza et zelo che sua divina Maestà ha dato a Vostra Signoria Illustrissima (del qual confesso esserne restato edificatissimo et consolatissimo), ho conceputo grandissima speranza di buon successo, però bisogna adoperar li mezzi efficaci per tempo, et così quanto più penso in quello che dissi hieri a Vostra Signoria Illustrissima di mandar algun huomo efficace et prudente a informar il legato di Francia a bocca, tanto più me pare che sarebbe di molta importanza, poiché tutto no se può scrivere, ni se può rispondere all' obgiettioni et difficoltà per letere et così supplico a Vostra Signoria Illustrissima, se degni trattarlo con Sua Santità, et si paresse dipoi bene ch' io parlasse et informasse anchora l'huomo che havesse d'essere mandato, lo faria ampliamente; et io fo instanza per questa diligenza in Francia, perché penso probabilmente che la magior difficultà s'habbia da temer da quella Majestà, benché li profitti saranno a mio giudicio eguali, o più presto magiori da sua banda, tuttavia da parte di Spagna anchora non lasciarà Sua Santità d'usar la diligenza che ne sarà necessaria o convenevole. Et con questo baccio humilissimamente le mani di Vostra Signoria Illustrissima. Dal Collegio Inglese a 12 di Lulio 1597.

    Di Vostra Signoria Illustrissima e Reverendissima
        Humilissimo Servitore
            Roberto Personio.

[PS] Adesso m'han dato un grande presente di vino da parte de V.S.I. Nostro Signor sea la paga di tutto.

[*Addressed in Persons's hand:*] Illmo R^{mo} Sig^{or} il Sor Card^{al} Aldobrandino.

[*Endorsed:*] Lettera del padre Personio al Cardinal Aldobrandino.

Translation

Your Right Reverend Eminence

I am enclosing a note for Your Eminence of the four points we dealt with yesterday; may it please Our Lord that it be for His greater glory. Your Eminence has in hand the most important business that has been undertaken in the Christian commonwealth for many centuries. And when I consider the prudence and zeal with which His Divine Majesty has endowed Your Eminence (and I confess that I have been highly edified and consoled by it), I conceive the highest hopes of good results. But there is need to employ the means that are efficacious in good time, and so, the more I think of what I said yesterday to Your Eminence about sending a capable and discreet man to broach the matter by word of mouth to the legate in France, the more it seems to me that this would be a very important step, because not everything can be put in writing, nor can objections and difficulties be answered by letter. And so, I beg Your Eminence to be so good as to arrange it with His Holiness, and if afterwards it seems advisable for me to speak with the man who is to be sent and give him further information, I would do so in full. I am pressing for this careful approach in France because I think it probable that the greatest difficulties to be feared are from His Majesty there; yet the advantages to be gained from his party will be no less great, in my opinion, or perhaps even greater. Nevertheless, with the Spanish party, too, His Holiness will not, I hope, neglect to take the steps that are necessary or convenient in these matters. And with this, very humbly I kiss Your Eminence's hands. From the English college, 12 July 1597.

> Your Most Reverend Eminence's
> most humble servant
> Robert Persons.

[PS] At this very moment they have given me a magnificent present of wine from Your Eminence. May Our Lord reward you for everything.

B392 From Richard Barret, Liège, 10 August 1597

> SOURCES:
> Persons, *A Briefe Apologie or Defence of the Catholike Ecclesiastical Hierarchie* (Antwerp, 1601), fols. 93v–94, an extract in English;
> AAW, VI, no. 49, Spanish version = *W*;
> BAV, Bib. Vat. Lat. 6227, fol. 29, Spanish version = *B*.
> EDITION: Renold, *Letters of Allen and Barret*, 271–272.
> NOTE: Barret reports to Persons on the movements of Robert Fisher, who, representing the disaffected students at the English college in Rome, was suspected of negotiating with the English authorities for tolerance for Catholics in return for the expulsion of the Jesuits from England. On Fisher's return to Rome in 1598, he was subjected to a papal examination, and sought to conciliate his questioners in a document known as "Fisher's Confessions," 8–14 March (Renold, *Wisbech Stirs*, 230–263, esp. 241–242, 259).

Very loving and reverend Father

This I wryte at Liège, where I am in my way homeward. There passed by this towne one Fisher, that was sent by the seditious schollers into England. From hence he went to Bruxelles, thence to Lille, and so to Doway, and thence to Cambray. He hath bin, as I am informed, in every shire in England to styrre up men against Jesuits and Spaniards, which he uttered to a good man in this towne. I marvaile he escaped at Bruxels, seing they are advertised out of England of his secret conference with a cheefe man of the councel of England and with Sacheverel the Apostata in the said councelors house.[437] Heere he tould one in great secret, that he was to go to Mr Charles Paget and Dr Gifford, and to Mr Morgan about matters of importance;[438] he said also that they were in good hope to

---

437. John Sacheverell, a former soldier, studied at Rheims and the English college in Rome, but left to join the Dominican order. He encouraged the disturbances in Rome and in 1596 fled to England, where he became an informer; for details, see Renold, *Wisbech Stirs*, 216 n4; Persons's *Relacion* of 22 May (B378); and his letter to Idiáquez, 12 July (B390).

438. The Spanish version omits Morgan's name but adds that of Hugh Griffin. Morgan was by this time already in Savoy (Loomie, *Spanish Elizabethans*, 115) or Spain (Alison Plowden, "Morgan, Thomas," *ODNB*). Fisher confessed that he was carrying letters from the anti-Jesuit party at Wisbech Castle to Gifford and others, urging them to redouble their efforts against the Jesuits (Renold, *Wisbech Stirs*, 259).

have liberty of conscience in England in case they might get the Jesuits thence: no doubt this is one part of his busynes. He left his bag at Liège, and I have seene it, yet nothing of importance therin, saving *a litle compendious note* of all their Articles against the Jesuits at Rome which he carried with him to delate to the faction in England, as appeareth, for it is very old and almost worne out.[439] I am to go to Bruxels and to make meanes to have the man examined, in case he may be found, before he returne[440] to this towne, for he is to come backe hither, and to one in this place, he was at his going into England earnestly commended by Dr Gifford, etc.[441]

B393 To Francisco de Peña, Rome, 12 August 1597

> SOURCE: BAV, MS Vat. Lat. 6227, fol. 183a–b, holograph, with seal, address and endorsement.
>
> HICKS: 696–697, with English translation.
>
> NOTE: Persons asks to meet Peña privately at the English vineyard (see "A Brief Account of the Stirs," 18–20 October, in appendix A, item BA 6), so that they can discuss putting together some memorials on the subjects discussed in Persons's regular Monday conference with the duke of Sessa on 11 August. Persons then wrote the "Memorandum on the State of English Affairs" (see appendix A, item BA 1), which Peña mentioned in a note to Sessa on 16 August (fol. 22).
>
> In the next few days, Persons energetically pursued a scheme for the appointment of two bishops, one in Flanders and one in England, which he hoped would contain the opposition to the Jesuits that was being fostered by Paget, Morgan, and William Gifford. This was

439. [*marginal note:*] This note was rather brought out of England. As after wil appeare.
440. returne] returns *Renold*
441. The Spanish version reads: "Capitolo de una carta del Doctor Richardo Barretto Rector del Collegio Yngles de Douay escritta a 10 de agusto en Leige. 1597. Esta carta escrivo en Liege en el camino para bolver a Douay. Aqui ha estado un cierto Fishero embiado a Ynglaterra el año passado por los sediciosos de Roma, entiendo que ha estado en todas las provincias de Ynglaterra incitando a todos contra los padres de la Compañia y contra el Rey de España en favor de la facion de Pagetto, lo qual él mismo confessó aqui a una persona de bien. De aqui passó a Bruxelas, y de alla a Douay, Lila, y Cambray, para conferir con los confiderados. Me aspanto como no le heçieron prender en Bruxelas, pues estan avisados de Ynglaterra que tubo plática secreto con un de los principales Consejeros de la Reyna y con el frayle Sacheverello aposta, todo en la casa del mismo Consejero. Aqui descubrio a una persona en grande secreto que avia de ablar con Pagetto en Bruxelles y con Giffordo en Lila, y con Ugo Griffoni en Cambray de negocios muy importantes. Dixo tan bien a la misma persona que tenian grande esperança de alcançar libertad de consciencia por los Catolicos de Ynglaterra con que se echassen de alli los Jesuitas. Sin duda entiendo que este es un punto principal de sus negociaciones. Él dexó una cierta valisia suya en Liege, y tubimos modo de veerla, pero no hallamos cosa de momento, si no un papel de articulos que proponian contra los padres Jesuitas para hacerles más odiosos. Él ha de bolver por acá a cierta persona, a la qual fue muy encomendado por Giffordo quando passó a Ynglaterra. Estas cosas se an de mirar con mucha attencion y particularmente de Su Alteza, porque altremente llegarán a grandes inconvenientes etc. Esto escribe el Doctor Barretto, diçendo de mas que en llegando a Bruxellas ablará a Su Alteza del Cardenal sobre este negocio."

the subject of his regular Monday meeting with Sessa on the 11th; meetings with Aldobrandini, Peña, and possibly Sessa again on Wednesday 13th; and consultations with Cardinals Allessandrino and Paravicini on Friday 15th or Saturday 16th. Persons wrote to the pope on the 13th (B395), suggesting Cardinals Madruzzo and Tarugi as likely allies. Aldobrandini expected to discuss the matter with the pope on the Monday following, the 18th, and Persons rescheduled his meeting with Sessa to Tuesday 19th.

In support of his scheme, Persons prepared several documents for despatch to the courts in Madrid and Brussels, as well as the papal curia (see appendix A, item BA 3, on the appointment of two bishops; see also the memorandum for Martín de Idiáquez, August 1596 (B341), on creating a council for English affairs in Brussels).

Reverendissimo Monsignor

Yo no escribi anoche a Vuestra Señoria por bolver tarde y cansado y tener mucho que despachar con los correos de España y de Flandres. El Señor Duque y yo discurrimos largo y la conclusion fue que Vuestra Señoria e yo nos viessemos, y pusiessemos en papel todo el negocio, y más puntos aún, de que no ablamos los dos, y esto ha de ser quanto prima y parecieron a Su Excelencia cosas de mucha emportancia, y necessario de[442] assentarlas bien, como verdaderamente son, y el Duque diçe que quando las avremos apuntado, se hallará con nosotros en casa de Vuestra Señoria o donde parecera mejor, y que sería bien commençar luego para que en toda esta semana que entra se pueda despachar el correo.

Conforme a esto vea Vuestra Señoria lo que manda, porque *ego ad oram paratus sum, licet alia negotia satis multa et gravia me premant, sed nihil cum his conferendum.* Si Vuestra Señoria manda que yo venga por aý mañana de mañana y que estemos solos todo el dia, yo vendre; si Vuestra Señoria gusta andar a la nuestra vinea de los Yngleses que está a San Gregorio, mandeme avisar Vuestra Señoria esta tarde con silencio y venga Vuestra Señoria la mañana a buena hora y entraré en el coche y yremos alla y ninguno lo[443] sabra y estaremos solos. De todo y de la hora y del modo[444], aguardo luego rispuesta de Vuestra Señoria para obedecer como hijo amantissimo de Vuestra Señoria a quien nuestro Señor guarde.

Roberto Personio.

[PS] Yo dixi al Señor Rogero que passasse oy por Vuestra Señoria y traxesse la respuesta aora la aguardo luego en papel para disponerme a obedecer si Rogero no ha llegado.

[*Addressed in Persons's hand:*] Al R^{do} Mons^{or} Peña Auditor del Rota.

[*Endorsed by Peña:*] billetes del Padre Personio Roma mes de Aug^{ti} et seq. 1597.

Translation

Most Reverend Monsignor

I did not write to Your Worship last night because I came home late and tired out and had much to get off by the post to Spain and Flanders. The duke and I had a long conference, and we came to a decision that Your Worship and I should get together and put the whole business on paper, and other points also which we two did not discuss; and this

---

442. y necessario de] *interlined B*
443. lo] *interlined with caret B*
444. de la hora y del modo] *this ed.;* de de la hora y del modo *B, with* del *intelined with caret*

is to be done as soon as possible. His Excellency thought that they were matters of great importance and that they should be well settled – as is truly the case – and the duke says that when we have made our notes, he will arrange to meet us at your house, or wherever you think best, and he says that it would be well to make a start immediately so as to be able to dispatch the courier any time during the coming week.

Accordingly, would Your Worship please consider what you would like done, because I am ready at any time, even though quite a lot of other business of considerable importance calls for my attention – nothing, however, to be compared with this in gravity. If Your Worship should tell me to come to you tomorrow morning and that we are to be alone all day, I will come; or if Your Worship would prefer to go to our English vineyard, which is at St Gregory's, please send me word quietly this evening. Come early tomorrow yourself; I will get into the carriage and we will go there, and nobody will know of it and we shall be alone. About all this, and the when and how, I await your reply, in order to obey, as Your Worship's very loving son. And may our Lord protect you.

Robert Persons.

[PS] I have told Mr Roger[445] to call at Your Lordship's today and bring an answer. Now I await a note presently from you, if Roger has not arrived, so that I can make arrangements to do what you ask.

B394 To Francisco de Peña, Rome, 12 August 1597

> SOURCE: BAV, Vat. Lat. 6227, fol. 184, holograph, with remains of a seal.
> HICKS: 698–699, with English translation.
> NOTE: The three Latin papers referred to here were probably
> (a) Persons's memorial on the English succession (see appendix A, item BA 2);
> (b) Persons's own memorial on the appointment of bishops, as an alternative (see appendix A, item BA 3); and
> (c) a copy of the proposed rules for the confraternities proposed by the anti-Jesuit party in Flanders and Rome, prepared for the duke of Sessa to warn against the likely evil consequences, headed "Nonnullae regulae atque ordinationes duarum in Anglia congregationum, quarum una in provincia Londinensi alia vero in Lancastrensi caepta est. Anno Domini 1597" (Some rules and ordinances for the two congregations in England, one of which has been initiated in the province of London, and the other indeed in the province of Lancaster) and endorsed "donde se notan los grandes inconvenientes que nacen dellas. A la Excelencia del Duque de Sessa" (BAV, Vat. Lat. 6227, fols. 23–25).
> Persons was hoping to have these translated into Spanish for Sessa but had to ask Peña to arrange for translation instead: see his letter to him of 14 August (B396).

Vaya Vuestra Señoria muy en buena ora y mandeme avisar lo que se resolviere con Su Excelencia. A mí no se offerece otra cosa fuera dello dicho – los tres papeles en latino yo tendre cuydado de ponerlos en orden para España y despues otros para Flandes, mando avisar Vuestra Señoria quando yran. Yo yre oy a ablar con el Cardenal Aldobrandino si

---

445. Roger Baynes.

será possible para apretar el dispacho de lo de los dos obispos pues es el unico remedio que tenemos para impedir la entrada destos sediciosos a Ynglaterra, si a tiempo se puede despachar. Me consuelo que su Santidad esté ya tan bueno. El vino del Illustrissimo Camerino era bueno, y hará merced Vuestra Señoria a él y no desservicio a Dios nuestro Señor en pedir otros flasquilios. Él guarde a Vuestra Señoria y dé Vuestra Vuecencia[446] mis humildes al Señor Duque.

Roberto Personio.

[*Addressed in Persons's hand:*] Al R^{mo} Mons^{or} Peña

[*Endorsed with a reply from Sessa's secretary:*]

El Duque dize, que a las 20 oras puede Vuestra Señoria venir manaña solo o con el padre Personio, i no antes porque tiene que hazer. De casa 12 d'Agosto 1597. Murillo.

[*Re-addressed:*] A Monseñor Peña.

Translation

Please act as Your Worship thinks best, and let me know what decision is come to with His Excellency. As for me, nothing occurs to me to say beyond what I have already said. I will take care to have the three papers in Latin got ready for Spain, and others afterwards for Flanders. I am giving instructions for Your Worship to be informed when they will go. I am going to speak with Cardinal Aldobrandini today to see if it will be possible to press for a decision on the matter of the two bishops, for it is the only means we have to prevent the entrance of those seditious men into England; if it can be put through in time. I am consoled by His Holiness being now so well. His Eminence's Camerino wine was good,[447] and Your Worship will be paying a compliment to him, and doing no disservice to God our Lord, by asking for some more little flasks. May He protect Your Worship; and give, I pray you, my humble respects to the duke.

Robert Persons.

[*Endorsed with a reply from Sessa's secretary:*]

To Monsignor Peña. The duke says that Your Worship may come tomorrow at 20 hours, alone or with Fr Persons, and not earlier, because he is occupied. From the palace, 12 August 1597. Murillo.

B395 To Pope Clement VIII, 13 August 1597

SOURCE: ABSI, Coll P II 355.

HICKS: 706–708, with English translation.

NOTE: Persons sends the pope some documents recently received from England, which have prompted him to devise the scheme for the appointment of bishops which is contained in the Latin memorials sent first to Sessa and the Spanish court (appendix A, item BA 3). He advises the pope that he would like to consult widely among the cardinals about this, mentioning Ludovico Madruzzo (1532–1600), protector of the German college, and François-

---

446. Vuestra Vuecencia] *this ed.*; V.V. B

447. Presumably Cardinal Aldobrandini's donation (Persons to Aldobrandini, 12 July, B391); less likely, "Cardinal Camerino's wine": Gentile Dolfino, bishop of Camerino, 1596 to 1601.

Marie Tarugi (1525–1608), formerly archbishop of Avignon and about to be appointed (15 September) archbishop of Siena, because of their experience in Protestant-affected regions. On Madruzzo, prince-bishop of Trent, crown cardinal of the Holy Roman Empire, and about to be appointed (18 August) cardinal bishop of Sabina college, see the account of the stirs, 18–20 October, below (BA 6), and Kenny, "Inglorious Revolution," 140 [part 3].

The documents in question may include the rules for the two associations of secular priests proposed by the party opposed to Persons, of which a copy was prepared for the duke of Sessa (see Persons to Peña, 12 August, B394).

Beatissime Pater

Cum ea quae his annexa Beatitudo Vestra videbit, nonnullis abhinc diebus ex Anglia accepissem, volui statim prout debui ea Beatitudinis Vestrae communicare: sed dum nescio quid de adversa Beatitudo Vestra valetudine cum bonorum omnium dolore spargeretur, emittendum iudicavi, ac precibus tantum incumbendum pro sanitate Beatitudinis Vestrae restituenda, qua in re cum misericors Dominus suorum vota iam exaudiverit, animum iterum sumpsi ut ea Beatitudinis Vestrae repraesentarem, quibus ni fallor Beatitudo Vestra debit, quantum intersit ad causam Anglicanam sustentandam ut subordinatio aliqua inter sacerdotes quam primum a Sanctitate Vestra instituatur ad ea incommoda vitanda quae iam ex parte Sanctitati Vestrae aperui, et multa plura timentur nisi maturum adhibeatur remedium. Si Beatitudo Vestra iudicaverit (id quod Illustrissimus Cardinalis Aldobrandinus mihi insinuavit) rem ulterius consultandum esse et cum aliquibus Cardinalibus communicandam, peto humiliter a Beatitudine Vestra ut quanto fieri potest secreto id fiat, atque etiam brevitate, ne si res divulgetur, haeretici Anglicani consilia nostra impediant. Cardinales Madrucius ac Tarugius pro experientia quam de externarum provinciarum rebus ubi haeretici vigent habere videntur, vel eorum alter cum Illustrissimo Cardinale Aldobrandino ac Caetano Protectore facile rem expedirent ac secreto si Vestrae Beatitudini ita videretur; et si qua in re difficultas se offerret, ego facile me eam dissolvere posse confiderem, si me dignati fuerint Beatitudinis Vestrae iussu audire, quam Dominus nobis diutissime ac universae Ecclesiae incolumem tueatur. 13 Augusti 1597. Ad humillima pedum oscula, &c.

Robertus Personius.

Translation

Most Holy Father

When, only a few days ago, I received from England those documents which Your Holiness will see annexed to this letter, I wished to communicate them to Your Holiness immediately, as was my duty. But when, to the grief of all good people, some rumour was doing the rounds of a threat to Your Holiness's health, I judged it best to wait a while, and rather devote myself to prayers for Your Holiness to recover his health. But now that our merciful Lord has heard the prayers of His people in this regard, I have renewed my intention of presenting them to Your Holiness. Unless I am mistaken, Your Holiness will see in them how important it is, if we want to keep the English cause alive, that some form of subordination amongst the priests be established by Your Holiness as soon as possible, to avoid those troubles which I have already in part revealed to Your Holiness. Many more are to be feared unless timely remedy is applied. If Your Holiness has come to the view (as His Eminence Cardinal Aldobrandini has intimated to me) that there should be wider consultation on the matter, and that it should be communicated to a number of cardinals, I humbly beseech Your Holiness that this should take place as secretly as can possibly be done, and also with despatch, lest the thing be divulged and the English heretics obstruct our plans. Cardinals Madruzzo and Tarugi, on account of the experience they apparently have of the affairs of the provinces abroad where the heretics flourish, or one or the other of them, together with His Eminence Cardinal Aldobrandini and the Cardinal Protector Caetani, would get the thing done easily and secretly, if Your Holiness sees fit; and if any difficulty should present itself in this matter, I am confident that I would be able to deal with it easily, if by Your Holiness's command they would deign to hear me. May our Lord grant you great length of days, preserving you for our sake and the sake of all the church. 13 August 1597. Kissing your feet most humbly, etc.

Robert Persons.

B396 To Francisco de Peña, 14 August 1597

SOURCE: BAV, MS Vat. Lat. 6227, fols. 185–186, holograph, with the remains of a seal.
HICKS: 709–710, 700–701 (postscript), with English translation.
NOTE: Persons encloses the first of the three documents mentioned in his letter of 12 August (B394): his memorial on the pretenders for the English succession, for the attention of the duke of Sessa. He refers to this memorial as "papers" because it contains two separate writings, "Scriptum primum" and "Scriptum secundum" (see appendix A, item BA 2). He apologizes that these documents have not yet been translated into Spanish.

Monsignor Reverendissimo

En el enstante que dexé a Vuestra Señoria la otra tarde me tomó una grande ventosidad en el estomago, no sé si era con aver bevido frio, pero me ha travajado siempre despues, y aunque estoy mejor, no quedo aún libre, pero lo que me más preme[448] es, que dos personas que solian con confiança ayudarme a escrivir, estan malas de manera que no pueden trasladar los papeles de la pretension de la Señora Enfanta que van con ésta, y ansi, si es forçoso que vayan, supplico a Vuestra Señoria mande buscar persona de confiança que los traslade o uno a lo menos[449] dellos qual parecera a Vuestra Señoria sea más necessario que se embíe; los otros dos de las reglas de las congregaciones, y de las raçones por los obispos io procuraré en todo caso que Vuestra Señoria los tenga oy o mañana sin falta placiendo a Nuestro Señor, pero para[450] essos otros que embío[451] no es possibile hallar aqui quien lo haga de buena letera y con secreto.

Mucho me huelgo de que Su Excelencia approbasse lo hecho, aunque saliendo de las manos de Vuestra Señoria no podra succeder otra cosa. Dios Nuestro Señor encamine

448. preme] *B, possibly* da pieme ("makes me sad")
449. a lo menos] *interlined with caret B*
450. para] *interlined with caret B*
451. que embío] *interlined with caret B*

todo a su mayor gloria, que es lo que se pretende y nos guarde muchos años a Vuestra Señoria para servirle mucho como lo haçe y ser grande santo, como es su viçino el que embio el flasquilio. Oy 14 de Augusto.

   De Vuestra Señoria Reverendissima[452] siervo
    Roberto Personio.

[PS] Olvideme decir que el Cardenal Aldobrandino me trattó muy cortesemente ayer y me prometio de ablar al papa lunes con muchas veras sobre lo de los dos obispos, lo qual solo si pudiessemos alcançar sería grande reparo contra los sedisiosos, sin a tanto que Dios nos ayudasse más adelante. R.

Translation

Most Reverend Monsignor

  At the moment when I left Your Lordship the other evening, I was seized with a bad attack of flatulence; I do not know whether it came from a chill, but it has troubled me ever since; and, although I have improved, I am not free of it. But what bothers me more is that two trusted persons who usually help me with my correspondence are ill; so badly, that they are unable to copy the papers to be enclosed here, about the claims of the Lady Infanta. So, if it is necessary for them to be included, I beg Your Lordship to have some trustworthy person found to copy them, or one of them at any rate – whichever it seems to Your Lordship most necessary to send. The other two, about the rules of the congregations and the reasons for having two bishops, I will see that Your Lordship gets, in any case, today or tomorrow without fail, God willing; but as for these others which I am sending, it is impossible to find anyone here to do it in a good hand and in secrecy.

  I am very pleased that His Excellency has approved of what has been done, although, since Your Lordship was responsible for it, there could be no other outcome. May God Our Lord direct everything for His greater glory, which is what we seek; and may He preserve Your Lordship to us for many years to give Him great service as you are doing, and to be a great saint – just like your neighbour who sent the little flask. Today, 14 August.

   Your most reverend Lordship's servant
    Robert Persons.

[PS] I forgot to say that Cardinal Aldobrandini treated me very courteously yesterday, and promised me he would speak to the pope on Monday very earnestly about the two bishops, and if only we could obtain that, it would be a great help against the seditious party, until such time as God assists us to make further progress.

B397 To Francisco de Peña, Rome, 15 August 1597

  SOURCE: BAV, MS Vat. Lat. 6227, fol. 188, holograph.
  HICKS: 711–712, with English translation.
  NOTE: As promised, Persons now sends, via Roger Baynes, the two further documents mentioned in his letter of 12 August (B394), on the rules for congregations and the necessity

---

452. Reverendissima] *this ed.*; R^{mo} B

for two bishops, for forwarding to Spain: "Rationes quare Catholici Anglicani subordinationem aliquam petunt inter sacerdotes Anglicanae gentis, tum in Anglia, quam in Belgio degentes" (fols. 26–27 of the same codex; appendix A, item BA 3) and "Nonnullae regulae atque ordinationes duarum in Anglia congregationum, quarum una in provincia Londiniensi alia vero in Lancastrensi caepta est. Anno Domini 1597" (fols. 23–25).

Monsignor Reverendissimo

El Señor Rogero lleva los dos papeles duplicados para España y Flandres. Yo estoy mejor de salud gracias a Dios[453] y deseo mucho que Vuestra Señoria la tenga complida, pues la emplea tanto bien. He tornado a tomar algunos remedios para la rodilla, veeremos qué effetos hacen. Vuestra Señoria me haga merced de avisarme para quando le parece que seran en orden los despachos para embiarse si lo sabe, para que yo tanbien escriba alguna cosa; tanbien Vuestra Señoria ha de hacerme caridad de un translado deste despacho o a lo menos del original para que yo saque la summa para mí. Lo demas dira el Señor Rogero, y digale Vuestra Señoria si se accordo de ablar al Señor Duque, para alguna parte de su entretenimiento y del suo compañero. *Vale Domine mi Reverendissime.* Oy 15 de Augusto 1597.

Roberto Personio.

[*Addressed, in Persons's hand*:] Al Mons^or Peña.

Translation

Most Reverend Monsignor

Mr Roger is taking you the two papers, in duplicate, for Spain and Flanders. My health is improved, thank God; and I do hope that Your Reverence is entirely well, since you make such good use of your good health. I have taken some medicine again for my knees; we shall see what effect it has. I beg Your Reverence to let me know when the despatches are likely to be ready to be sent off, if you know, so that I also may write something. Would Your Reverence have the kindness to let me have a copy of this despatch, or at any rate the original, so that I can make a summary of it for myself. Mr Roger will tell you anything else, and please tell him if you remembered to speak to His Grace the duke about paying a share of his maintenance and that of his companion. *Farewell, my Right Reverend Lord.* This day, 15 August 1597.

Robert Persons.

B398 To Francisco de Peña, Rome, 16 August 1597

SOURCE: BAV, MS Vat. Lat. 6227, fol. 187; holograph, with the remains of a seal.

HICKS: 713–714, with English translation.

NOTE: In pursuit of his aim of creating a new hierarchy for the English Catholic priests, Persons visited the cardinals Alessandrino (Michele Bonelli, OP, 1541–1598), cardinal-bishop of Albano, and Ottavio Paravicini (1552–1611), bishop of Alessandria. Alessandrino

---

453. a Dios] *underlined with caret B*

approved, since Peña had already shown him the memorials on the subject (appendix A, item BA 3). Once Persons showed Paravicini evidence of the factions, the cardinal agreed to have Nicholas Fitzherbert, one of the chief lay supporters of the dissident students, removed from Rome.

Monseñor Reverendissimo

Emos visto al buen Señor Cardenal Alexandrino y admittio con grande amor en su servicio al Cavallier Inglés que Vuestra Señoria le encomendo a su Señoria Illustrissima y despues, si saliere para ello, yrá a estudiar en el collegio. Vuestra Señoria haga merced de agradecerle al Señor Cardenal con la prima occasion, me dixo mucho bien de los dos papeles que Vuestra Señoria le comunicó y está muy persuadido que por esta via se puede hacer la paz.

Passé despues por la casa del Cardenal Paravicino, y ablamos entre otras cosas de su Nicolo ynglés con toda confiança y le mostre algunos papeles en aquela materia de los factiosos y quedó muy capaz de todo y tratamos del modo de sacar a Nicolo suavemente de Roma, a que su Señoria Illustrissima offerecio un mezzo harto a proposito que es embiar le con pretexto de algunos negocios a España, si assi parecera al Señor Duque, de que ablaré con Su Excellencia y con Vuestra Señoria despues; aora *omnia sint in secreto*. Oy escrivere mis cartas y las embiare al Señor Duque o al Secretario parimente. Guarde Dios a Vuestra Señoria. Oy 16 de Augusto.

Roberto Personio.

[*Addressed, in Persons's hand:*] Al Monseñor Reverendissimo Peña Auditor de Rota.

Translation

Most Reverend Monsignor

I have seen the good Lord Cardinal Alessandrino, and he has very charitably received into his service the English gentleman whom Your Worship commended to His Eminence; later on, if he turns out to be suitable for it, he will go and study in the college. Would Your Worship be so good as to thank the lord cardinal on the first possible occasion. He greatly approved of the two documents Your Worship showed him, and he is quite persuaded that that is the way to bring about peace.

I called afterwards at the house of Cardinal Paravicini. We talked, among other things, of his English friend, Nicholas – very confidentially – and I showed him some documents on this matter of the factious group, and he understood everything very well. We discussed ways of getting Nicholas quietly out of Rome, and for this His Eminence suggested a very suitable plan, which is to send him to Spain on the pretext of some kind of business, if this meets with His Grace the duke's approval. I will discuss it with His Excellency and Your Worship later; for the time being, *let everything be kept secret*. Today I shall write my letters and send them to His Grace the duke or to his secretary, one or the other. May God protect Your Reverence. Today, 16th of August.

Robert Persons.

B399 To Francisco de Peña, Rome, 16 August 1597

SOURCE: BAV, MS Vat. Lat. 6227, fol. 189; holograph, with the remains of a seal.
HICKS: 715–716, with English translation.
NOTE: On 16 August (fol. 22 of the same codex), Peña informed Sessa that he had prepared the Spanish memorials for despatch to Spain which Persons had sent him on 14 August, but was unsure whether the despatch to Spain should be delayed so as to accommodate a further document, "el último punto tocante al declar la presension de la Señora Infanta" (probably "Si conviene hazer publicacion de que la Señoria Infanta pretende el Reino de Inglaterra" [Whether it is advisable to publish the Lady Infanta's claims to the kingdom of England]; fols. 31–33; appendix A, item BA 4). Persons now sends a further document on the subject, a response by some Catholics in England on the same topic (fols. 40–42, "La respuesta venida de Inglaterra por diversas cartas de Maio, y Junio deste año 1597 sobre la proposicion de la Serenissima Señora Infanta").

Mirando en los papeles hallé éste que es de la respuesta de algunos Catolicos sobre el negocio de la Señora Enfanta y aunque la de los dias passados al Señor Duque para embiar a España toda via porque Vuestra Señoria es amigo de que los despachos vayan complidos le embío este papel[454] para añadirlo tan bien si le parecera pero con condicion que se me buelva el original como los demas que Vuestra Señoria tiene. Si ha de entrar mencion deste en la narracion parece que entraria bien en el primero capítulo donde se dice de la buena disposicion que ay en los Catolicos de ynglaterra, para el negocio de la Señora Enfanta, al parecer de Vuestra Señoria me remito en todo y por todo. Oy 16 de Augusto 1597.

    Roberto Personio.

[PS] Vuestra Señoria mandeme avisar del recibo del papel con una palabra del Señor Juan Baptista.

[*Addressed, in Persons's hand*:] Al Monseñor Peña.

Translation

While looking over my papers I found this: the reply made by a number of Catholics on the question of the Lady Infanta; and, although I gave it some days ago to the duke for forwarding to Spain, yet, because Your Worship likes the despatches to be complete when they go, I am sending you this paper to add to them as well, if you agree; but on condition that the original is returned to me, along with the others in Your Worship's keeping. If any mention of this paper has to be made in the statement, I think it could well be made in the first paragraph where it is said how well-disposed the Catholics of England are to the project concerning the Lady Infanta. I leave it altogether to Your Reverence's discretion. Today, 16 August 1597.

    Robert Persons.

[PS] Please could Your Worship acknowledge receipt of the document with a word from Señor Juan Bautista.

    454. papel] *this ed.*; paper B

B400 To Francisco de Peña, Rome, 17 August 1597

SOURCE: BAV, MS Vat. Lat. 6227, fol. 190; holograph, with the remains of a seal.
HICKS: 717–718, with English translation.
NOTE: Persons asks for his regular Monday morning audience with the duke of Sessa to be postponed to later in the day or to Tuesday. He would like the imminent post to Spain to be delayed until he has had a chance to talk to the ambassador and Peña about it.

Monseñor Reverendissimo

Por ser mañana lunes disputas de un padre desta casa en el Collegio Romano de la Compañia, a las quales yo no puedo faltar bien ni[455] mattina ni sera, y por ser mi dia de Audiencia ordinaria con el Señor Duque con quien deseo ablar antes que parta este nuestro despacho, por tener tanbien otro papellico nuevo de cosas que an caydo despues de ayer, vea Vuestra Señoria si esto se podra hacer oy a la tarde, y me mande avisar su parecer. Y si Vuestra Señoria ha de andar oy a la Casa del Señor Duque, y quisiera avisarme la hora y passar por acá (que no es muy fuera de camino) accompanaré a Vuestra Señoria. Y si no yrá Vuestra Señoria me haga merced saber de Su Excellencia[456] si yo pudiere andar esta tarde y a qué hora; y si Vuestra Señoria me mandará el coche para llegar alla luego bolvera, porque alli me daran con que bolverme yo, y si Vuestra Señoria ubiesse de servirse de su coche luego despues de comer, mande Vuestra Señoria pedir al Señor Cavallerico que me embíe un coche a la hora que al Señor Duque pareciere conveniente, y si el despacho no ubiesse de partir antes de Martes, y Su Excellencia no tubiesse comodidad de ablarme oy, bastara que vada martes. Vuestra Señoria determine lo que más conbiene, y por tener Vuestra Señoria criados para embiar al Señor Duque e yo no me attrevo a todo esto con Vuestra Señoria a quien Dios guarde. 17 Augusti.

Roberto Personio.

[Addressed, in Persons's hand:] A Mons^{or} R^{mo} Peña.

Translation

Most Reverend Monsignor

Since a father of this house is to defend a thesis at the Roman College of the Society tomorrow, Monday, and I cannot well be absent, either in the morning or the evening, and as it is the day on which I have my usual audience with the duke, and I am anxious to speak with him before this despatch of ours goes, because I have yet another new note containing incidents that have taken place since yesterday, could Your Worship please see if it could be done later today, and let me know what you think. If Your Worship has to go to the duke's today and would inform me of the hour and pass this way – it is not very much out of your way – I will go with you; if you are not going, would you be good

---

455. bien ni] *interlined with caret*
456. de Su Excellencia] *interlined with caret*

enough to find out from His Excellency whether I may go this afternoon and at what time; and if Your Worship will send me your carriage to take me there, it will return at once, for they will provide me there with means to get back; and if Your Worship needs to use your carriage immediately after lunch, please would you send word to the head groom to send me a carriage at the hour that the duke finds convenient? If, however, the despatch does not have to go before Tuesday, and it is not convenient for His Excellency to speak to me today, it will do if I go on Tuesday. Please would Your Worship arrange what suits best? It is because you have servants to send to the duke and I do not that I make bold to ask all this of Your Worship. May God protect you. 17 August.

Robert Persons.

B401 To Cardinal Pietro Aldobrandini, 17 or 18 August 1597

SOURCE: AAV, Fondo Borghese III, 124 g.2, fol. 25, olim fols. 13–14, addressed in Persons's hand, with the remains of a seal, but the letter itself in a scribal hand.

HICKS: 703–705, a handwritten transcript.

NOTE: The date of this letter is unknown, but it anticipates Aldobrandini's meeting with the pope on Monday 18 August (Persons to Peña, 14 August, B396, postscript). Here Persons asks the cardinal-nephew to discuss with the pope the implications of his memorials on the English bishops.

Illustrissimo et Reverendissimo Signor

Roberto Personio supplica humilmente la Signoria Vostra Illustrissima se degne parlar a Nostro Signor per l'espeditione delli tre punti del memoriale delli Catolici d'Ingleterra.

Il primo e un breve apostolico essortandoli et principalmente li sacerdoti a pacientia, longanimità et unione fra loro medessimi.

Il secondo e alcuna subordinatione delli sacerdoti fra di loro con ordinar due vescovi, l'uno in Ingleterra con sei o sette Archipresbyteri per suo conseiglio delli più gravi et antichi. L'altro residente in Fiandra con altro conseiglio simile per il governo delli sacerdoti di fuora et aiuto ancho di quelli di dentro d'Inghilterra come ne memoriale per raggioni evidenti se dimostra la necessità.

Il terzo punto è che per evitar grand'inconvenienti se prohibisca che durante questa heresia di Ingleterra nissuno[457] si faccia dottore senza licenza di suoi superiori et approvatione del vescovo che residera in Fiandra et di suo conseiglio e senza haver passato quatr'anni nelli studii dopo haver finito il corso, si non fusse in caso di alcuna occasione estraordinaria.

Importa multo la brevità et il secreto in questa speditione accioché l'heretici non lo venghino a saper prima che se esseguisca. Li sacerdoti anchora che vennero mandati de la per questo negotio fanno grand istanza per partire.

Li nomi particolari delli più gravi et più antichi sacerdoti che vengono raccommandati per più atti et meritevoli in questa materia se sono dati al Cardinale Protettore per conferir con Vostra Signoria Illustrissima.

Roberto Personio.

[*Addressed, in Persons's hand:*] All'Illmo el R^{mo} Sor Card^{le} Aldobrandino.

457. nissuno] *this ed.*; nissune V

Translation

Your Eminence

Robert Persons humbly begs Your Eminence to vouchsafe to speak to the Holy Father to expedite the three points made in the memorial about the Catholics of England.

The first is an apostolic brief to exhort them, and chiefly the priests, to patience, forbearance and unity among themselves.

The second is to establish a form of subordination of priests among themselves, by ordaining two bishops: one in England, with six or seven archpriests to advise him, chosen from the more respected and older priests; the other resident in Flanders, with a similar set of advisors, to govern the priests in exile and also to help those within England. The necessity of this is shown in the memorial of manifest reasons.

The third point is that to avoid great inconveniences, it should be prohibited that anyone, during this time of heresy in England, should obtain a doctorate without the licence of his superiors and the approval of the bishop who resides in Flanders, along with his advisors, and without spending four years in study after the completion of his course, except in case of some extraordinary circumstance.

Despatch and discretion are of great importance in expediting this business, lest the heretics come to know of it before it is put in execution. The priests, too, who are mandated to carry it out, should make haste to leave.

The particular names of the more respected and older priests who are recommended as more suited and more worthy in this matter have been given to the cardinal protector[458] to discuss with Your Eminence.

Robert Persons.

B402 From Henry Garnet, London, 20 August 1597

> SOURCE: ABSI, Coll P II 548, Garnet's excerpts.
> HICKS: Garnet, 442.
> NOTE: Garnet reports on the death of John Norden (ca. 1565?–1597), a controversial figure at Wisbech, allied with Christopher Bagshaw; see Renold, *Wisbech Stirs*, 323 n26 and *passim*.

Dr Norden is strangely dead being in the beginning of a new tragedy at Wisbich (wherein he only was the speaker with impudent immodesty molesting every where his quiet neighbours so that the Keeper himself was ashamed thereat), suddenly as many men terme it, toung-tyed, a dead lethargy surprizing him, and taking from him almost his memory also, whereof after many daies he dyed.

B403 From Christina Persons, White Webbs, September 1597

> SOURCE: Garnet to Persons, 10 September 1597.

458. Enrico Caetani.

B404 From Henry Garnet, London, 10 September 1597

SOURCE: ABSI, Coll P II 596, Garnet's excerpts, with a transcription of Persons's endorsement, "On the backside be written in f. Persons hand these words."
HICKS: Garnet, 443.

The sodality — is cleane dashed in the North — The old woman is well, and hath endyted a letter unto you &c. —
[*Endorsed by Persons*:] F. Garnet 10 7^{bris} 1597. of Charnock's coming towards Rome and his calling Spanish Papists.

B405 From Thomas Stapleton, Louvain, 15 September 1597

SOURCES:
BAV, MS. Vat. Lat. 6227, fols. 192–193, a contemporary copy;
ABSI, Coll P I 316, Coll P II 488, Grene's notes.
NOTE: Stapleton explains that his health now prevents him from coming to Rome. He leaves it to the pope to choose someone else to take up a high office, possibly as cardinal, in the English interest, but thinks Persons himself is the man for the job. He encloses a letter to Innocenzo Malvasia, the former papal agent in Brussels, now in Rome, who had been a prime mover in the campaign to bring Stapleton to Rome, probably to be elevated to cardinal, as leader of the English Catholics: see Persons to Fitzherbert, 26 September (B411).

The copyist has appended a letter from an English gentleman in Antwerp, registering the dismay of the English exiles over Stapleton's change of plan and their hope that Persons can be persuaded to accept elevation to the cardinalate, now that Stapleton's decision and the death of Owen Lewis have removed the remaining obstacles. It is unclear whether the enclosed letter was addressed to Persons himself.459

459. [Clausula d'un'altra lettera d'Anversa in questa materia. Scritta a un Gentilhouomo Inglese a Roma delli 26 Settembre 1597:] "Per l'ultime mie vi diedi aviso della subita mutatione del intento del Dottore Stapletono per venire a Roma, contraria assai all'aspettatione et desiderio di quelli che per mezzo suo speravano de vedere effetuate grand cose, ma così in questo come nella morte del vescovo di Cassano, si vede chiaramente come Domino Dio rimove l'impedimenti, et riserve il luogo per il P. Personio, il quale sopra ogni altro tutti li Catolici prigioneri et altri in Inghilterra desiderano con grand constanza d'animo, et non dubito che Dio particolarmente dispone l'animi di quelli che lo servino così fidelmente. Et di questo io posso assicure Vostra Signoria che poco fa quando in Inghilterra correva voce che il detto Padre era già fatto Cardinale, li Catolici in tutte le prigioni facevono tanta allegrezza, che più non potevano fare, si la nuova fusse portatogli della lor libertà et ricuperatione del regno alla fede Catolica." = [An enclosure of another letter from Antwerp on this subject, written by an English gentleman to Rome on 26 September:] "In my most recent letter I gave a report of Dr Stapleton's sudden change of his plan to go to Rome, much against the expectation and desire of those who hoped through his efforts to see great things achieved; but in this, just as in the death of the bishop of Casssano, can be seen how God Our Lord is removing the obstacles, and reserving the place for Fr Persons, something which all the Catholic prisoners and others in England desire above anything else, with great constancy of mind, and I

Reverendo Padre

L'ultima mia (come me ricordo) fu del mese di Luglio passato et tra altre cose la diedi d'intendere, d'un male comminciato nella mia gamba, giongendo, che si quello con il suo non guerire impedisse il mio dissegnato viagio a Roma, io con ciò sarei ben contento. Adesso così è accaduto, per providenza divina com'io penso, che essendo quella gamba guerita, l'altra è diventata più gravamente male, non d'esterna accidente ma d'una natural influxione la quale, in un così longo viagio, non lasciandomi comportare il moto del cavallo quantumque portantissimo, et non potendo io trovaremi in luoco del cavallo nissuna carolla tudesca per la quale ho cercato, io facilmente mi son risoluto di non volere fare il viagio né de cambiare il mio presente stato, nondimeno ch'io haveva fatto diverse spese per quel effetto, et ricevuto il viatico di Sua Santità, ma rendutolo poi intieramente a Monsignore Nuntio da chi lo ricevetti, et nelo plico suo ho scritto al Cardinale Aldobrandino amplamente la causa del mio non venire, la quale spero ch'egli accettarà in bona parte, poi che procede dalla providenza di Dio, et non della mia levità o mutabillità, si come a Sua Signoria Illustrissima io lo ho dichiarato per un longo discorso: et in effetto io ho scritto il medesimo a Monsignore Malvasia, et mando con questa la lettera a Vostra Paternità, pregandola di darlila. Et adesso mio bon Padre tutta questa longa aspettatione del mio venire a Roma essendo venuta a questo periodo di nessun effetto, *Providebit sibi Dominus de victima, et alium suscitabit virum secundum cor suum.* Il quale Sua Santità potrà nelle facende della nostra natione, alle quale per dire vero io venendo fuora dell'umbra di questo mio privato studio non fui atto, et per dir vero, né hebbi poco desiderio, altramente si la mia volontà o ambitione m'havesse secondato, potrei havere differito il viagio per 14 giorni più, et allhora sarei stato habile de comportare il cavallo, ma havevo caro et tuttavia ho caro questa occasione data de non venire. Et qalunque piacerà alla Santità Sua da promovere al luoco mio, io heverò così caro viderlo accettato come de vedere me stesso escluso. Io non voglio augurare niente, né usare alcuna sorta d'adulatione (cosa che ho semper abhorita), ma l'elettione è così scarsa, di quelli che hanno età et esperienza, che quasi non vi resta più ch'uno della nostra natione atto per quel posso, et quello è la propria Paternita Vostra, si la vostra ordine lo permette, la quale havendo già una volta comportata quella permitione, non vego per che non la potrà comportare un altra volta in un negotio di tanto grand peso. Ma come già dissi *Deus providebit*, et in questo mezzo, si come io sinceramente vi amo et honoro, così vi prego, *Sit amor noster mutuus, imo quia mutuus est, perseveret mutuus, quicquid casus afferat, aut Deus magis disponat.* Et si per sorte in quel luoco dove siete sentirete alcuno a chi dispicera questa mia ritirata dopo una così certa aspettatione, reputandomi però huomo da poco o forse peggio, prestatemi la vostra bona parolla et scusatemi. *De presenti morbo, ingruente hyeme, senectute ipsa (non tam annis quam laboribus literariis fracta) quae morbus est.* Et veramenta potrete dire, ch'io non potevo partirmi senza il dolore et lamento de tutta l'uni-

---

have no doubts that God specially prepares the hearts of those who so faithfully serve him. And of this I can assure Your Worship, that a little while ago, when rumours were spread in England that the said father was already made cardinal, Catholics in all the prisons made such great cheer that it could not be greater even if news was brought to them of their liberty and the recovery of the kingdom to the Catholic faith."

verstità, anzi della stessa corte di quà, la qual in verità ha lavorata di retenermi, quantunque questa non sia saputa nè a Sua Santità, nè a nessun altro acanto de lui. *Servabo me patriae meae si sic Deus voluerit, docendo, scribendo ecclesiae Dei serviam, mea mediocritate contentus vixero, in plaustro potius quam in honore moriar, de sepulchro magis quam de novis honoribus cogitandum mihi esse haec aetas postulat, crebra mea infirmitas monet.*

Bene vale admodum Reverende Pater, mihi ex animo delectissime, sit mihi mereos qui suorum est mereos magna nimis. Lovanii 15 Septembris 1597.

    Admodum R[everendo] Pat[ernitati] V[estr]ae
        servus in Christo
            Thomas Stapletonus.

[*Endorsed*:] Copia d'un lettera del Dottore Stapletono al P. Personio de 15 di sitiembre 1597 la qual el padre Personio recibio por el mes de octubre del dicho año.

Translation

Reverend Father

My most recent letter (as I recall) was in the middle of July past.[460] Amongst other things I gave it to understand that I had developed such a pain in my leg, upon my arrival, that if it did not improve but prevented me from making my journey to Rome as planned, I would not mind. Now it has so turned out, by divine providence as I think, that while that leg was recovering, the other took a turn for the worse, not from an external accident but by a natural influx, which in such a long journey will not allow me to bear the movement of the horse, however much it is able to carry, and I do not think I can find some German carriage that would meet my need, instead of a horse – and so I have readily persuaded myself that I do not wish to make the journey, nor to change my present condition. Even though I have had various expenses in that regard, and have received my viaticum from His Holiness, I have nevertheless returned it in its entirety to Monsignor Nuncio, from whom I received it,[461] and in the same packet I have also written extensively to Cardinal Aldobrandini of the reasons for my not coming, which I hope that he will accept for the most part, then, since it proceeds from the providence of God, and not from my carelessness or weakness, just as I have explained to His Eminence at some length. In fact, I have written the same to Monsignor Malvasia, and I am sending the letter to Your Paternity with this, praying you to give it to him. And now, my good father, since this long expectation of mine to come to Rome has come at this time to be of none effect: *The Lord will provide a victim for himself, and will raise up another man according to His own heart.*[462] His Holiness will be able to do this on behalf of our nation. To tell the truth, I was not really suitable, emerging from the shadow of this private study of mine, neither did I have much desire. If my will or ambition had supported me, on the other

    460. Stapleton to Persons, 6 July (B386).
    461. Ottavio Frangipani.
    462. A combination of two Biblical passages: [Abraham said to Isaac,] "God will provide himself a victim for an holocaust" (providebit sibi victimam holocausti; Gen. 22:8) and "The Lord hath sought him a man according to his own heart" (quaesivit sibi Dominus virum iuxta cor suum; 1 Kgs 13:14).

hand, I would have deferred the journey for fourteen days more, and then I would have been able to ride the horse, but I have welcomed and still do welcome this occasion for not going. And whoever His Holiness would like to promote in my place, I will be content to see this person approved, just as much as seeing myself left out. I have no need to wish for anything, neither do I want to receive any kind of adulation (something which I have always abhorred), but there is so little choice among those who have age and experience, that hardly more than one remains of our nation suitable for this position and that is precisely Your Paternity, if your order would permit it. However, since you have already obtained it once, I do not see why you could not obtain it again in a business of such great weight.[463] But as I have already said, *God will provide*, and in this even more; by virtue of my sincere love and honour, I beg, *may our mutual love, precisely because it is mutual, continue mutual, whatever chance might bring us, or God ordain*. And if, where you are now, you by any chance hear that anyone, given the level of expectation, is displeased by this withdrawal of mine, regarding me as a man of little value or perhaps worse, please put in a good word for me and make these excuses for me: *my present illness – winter setting in, old age (broken not so much by years as by literary labours) which is itself a sickness*.[464] And you may truly say that I could not leave without causing grief and lamentation to the entire university, even to the very same court here that in truth has tried hard to keep me, however little this is known either to His Holiness or to anyone else close to him. *I shall serve my native land if God desires it; let me serve the church of God by teaching and writing; I shall have lived content with my middle state; let me die rather in a cart than in honour; my age requires me to think of the grave rather than new honours; my frequent infirmity cautions me.*

Farewell, most reverend father, in whom my soul most delights; if only I had the merits which you possess in such great abundance. Louvain, 15 September 1597.

  Your Most Reverend Paternity's
    servant in Christ
      Thomas Stapleton.

B406 To Francisco de Peña, Rome, 17 September 1597

  SOURCE: BAV, MS Vat. Lat. 6227, fol. 30; holograph, with the remains of a seal.
  HICKS: 719–720, with English translation.
  NOTE: With Acquaviva convening a discussion on the situation in Flanders, Persons urgently sends Sessa a document on the subject. This may be the "Memorandum on the State of English Affairs" (appendix A, BA 1), which ends with a proposal for a council to be set up in Brussels. In a postscript, he expresses his confusion about Stapleton's proposed journey to Rome: he has received information confirming Stapleton's imminent departure, while the

---

463. Stapleton may be referring to the fact that, despite the restrictions, Jesuits had been appointed cardinals: for instance, Cardinal Toledo himself, recently deceased cardinal vice-protector of England. Alternatively, he may be referring to the role Persons played in Allen's advancement in 1587.

464. The Latin is grammatically incomplete but presented as a separate sentence. In the translation, it is taken to complete the previous sentence by providing material for an apology.

pope, whom he had seen on Tuesday 15 September, believed that he was no longer coming. Clearly the pope was better informed.

Monseñor Reverendissimo

En esta enstante me llama el Padre General para una Consulta de cosas toccantes a los Yngleses de Flandres, y ansi querriendo que el Señor Duque veesse el papel que va con ésta, y Vuestra Señoria tanbien, y no teniendo tiempo para hacer dos traslados, me resolvi de embiarlo primero a Vuestra Señoria y por su medio al Señor Embaxador con mis humildes encomiendas. Ni puedo más por aora. Guarde Dios a Vuestra Señoria. Del Collegio Ynglés oy Jueves 17 de Septembre 1597.

  De Vuestra Señoria
    siervo in Christo
      Roberto Personio.

[PS] Sigun lo que escriven del Doctor Stapleton y de su venida, me ha hecho pensar *quo tenderet*, aquello que Su Santidad me dixo Martis, que ya pensava que no venia, por no hacer falta a la Universidad de Lovayno.

[*Addressed:*] Para Monseñor Peña.

Translation

Most Reverend Monsignor

At this very moment father general is summoning me to a consultation on matters affecting the English in Flanders, and so, wishing the duke to see the enclosed document, and Your Worship too, and having no time to make two copies, I have decided to send it to Your Worship in the first place, and through you to His Lordship the ambassador with my humble respects. I can write no more, for now. May God preserve Your Worship. From the English college, today, Thursday 17 September 1597.

  Your Reverence's
    servant in Christ
      Robert Persons.

[PS] According to what they write about Dr Stapleton and his coming [to Rome],[465] I have been led to wonder, *Where is this leading?* in response to what His Holiness said to me on Tuesday, i.e., that he now thought that he was not coming, so as not to cause any inconvenience to the University of Louvain.

---

465. Probably referring to a letter from Brussels, 30 August, summarized by Persons on the verso of the extract from Barret's letter of 10 August (B392): "Lunes que viene, se partira de acá el Señor Doctor Stapleton para andar a Roma, la yda suya ha sido muy sollicitada de aý. Aqui se presumen grandes cosas. No le tenemos por muy confidente, por causa de los que trata sus cosas toda via vosotros sabreis las cosas mejor por aý" (On Monday next [1 September], Mr Doctor Stapleton will leave here to set off to Rome: his departure has been much urged from there. Here important matters are presumed. We do not place much confidence in him, on account of those who are dealing with his affairs, although you will understand these matters better over there).

B407 To Francisco de Peña, Rome, 19 and 20 September 1597

SOURCE: BAV, MS Lat. Vat. 6227, fol. 195, holograph.
HICKS: 721–722, with English translation.
NOTE: Persons makes and reschedules arrangements for Peña's carriage to transport him to the cardinal protector. He refers to a note that he received the night before, which raises an important matter for the ambassador's attention. This is very likely the extract he copied from a letter from a "reliable Englishman" in Antwerp, 29 August, probably addressed to Roger Baynes ("Your Honour") and referring to the appearance of the notorious English government agent Thomas Barnes (Gilbert Gifford's cousin), who threatens to deceive the court in Brussels and incline the ministers there to favour the Paget party (see Alford, 258–260). Persons's copy immediately precedes this letter to Peña in the codex (fol. 194).[466]

466. "Por acá ha llegado de Inglaterra un cierto Barnes Ynglés espia conocido por lo passado, y por esto desterrado destos estados antes de algunos años, muy íntimo de Pagetto, el qual Pagetto parece que por medio del Padre Oliverio flamenco de la Compañia y Viceprovincial de Flandes (al qual los de la facion an engañado) ha tornado a ganar tanto credito que aya podirlo procurar passaporto para el dicho Barnes, que veniesse acá, a tratar materia de estados otra vez como solia, para entretener a los ministros del Rey y aun dijar a Pagetto y para espiar cómo las cosas andan por acá y particularmente las de la facion Escoçesa. Ha ablado Barnes con Su Alteza, y aunque no se sabe la respuesta, se sabe que ninguna blanca llevó de denero, porque quando se partio de aqui para embarcarse no tenía más que quarenta reales, y aunque no se saben puntualmente las cosas que traxo de Ynglaterra para proponer a Su Alteza, toda via se sabe que preguntando un amigo en mucho secreto a Gulielmo Clithero (que es íntimo de Pagetto) qué negocios traýa Barnes, suspirando dixo, que traýa cosas que no eramos dinnos dellas, anadiendo que Personio y Holto y sus seguaçes no querrian, si no fuego y sangre a la patria, podiendola remediar por otra via, de las quales palabras entendemos que esta negociacion de Barnes y de Pagetto será alguna proposicion de toleracion o de libertad de Consciencia para engañar, y ganar tiempo como otras veçes, pero con esto vendra Su Alteza a poco a poco a discubrir las negociaciones de Pagetto y de los demas faciosos con el Consejo de Ynglaterra, y como concorren con los desiños de Malvasia y de otros politicos contrarios al Rey en Italia que dan estas traças de toleraciones solamente para haçer odiosas las fuerças de España y a las personas de rectitud y zelo que las favorecen. Por esta ciudad an passado dos hombres, y se an embarcado el uno para Denamarca y el otro por otra via por industria mia el uno no save nada del otro y entrambos van endereçados a los lugares y a las personas y por los negocios que entiendo Vuestra Merced estara advertido ya. Dios les prospere y guarde a Vuestra Merced. De Anvers a 29 de Aug. 1597." (Over here a certain Barnes, an English spy, has arrived, known because he left, and was banished for this from these states some years before, very close with Paget. It appears that the same Paget, who by means of Fr Olivier [Mannaerts], a Fleming of the Society and vice provincial of Flanders (whom those of the faction have deceived) has begun to win so much credit that he has been able to obtain a passport for the said Barnes. He has come here to deal with matters of state again as he used to, to beguile the ministers of the king and tell Paget otherwise and to spy out how things are going over here and particularly what is happening with the Scottish faction. Barnes has spoken with His Highness, and although it is not known what response he received, it is known that he has taken no money, because when he left here to take ship, he had no more than forty reals, and although it is not known in detail what plans he had about England to propose to His Highness, nevertheless it is known that, a friend very secretly asking William

Monseñor mio

Si Vuestra Señoria no va fuera hasta a las 22, mande venir por acá su coche para los 19 para andar al Cardenal Gaetano y bolvera a tiempo el coche.

El aviso que va con esto llegó anoche, si parecera cosa para monstrar al Duque, lo embíe Vuestra Monseñoridad y me se buelva despues el original pues no tengo traslado. Vale. 19.

       Siervo in Christo
          Roberto Personio.

[PS] No mande Vuestra Señoria el coche hasta a las 20 pues en este instante me embia el secretario este villete y hasta a las 20 no puedo despachar mis cartas.

[PPS] Esto escribi ayer, pero no halló la persona a Vuestra Señoria en casa y assi hice trasladar el aviso y lo embié al secretario Ximenes todavia lo he querido que Vuestra Señoria lo vea tanbien, y me lo mande despues bolver. Tengo grandissima priessa en lo que escribi, el mancebo mande Vuestra Señoria al Señor Juan Baptista que le dé priessa. Guarde Dios a Vuestra Señoria. 20 de Septiembre.

[*Addressed:*] a Mons^{or} R^{mo} Peña.

Translation

My dear Monsignor

If you are not going out until 10 o'clock tonight, will you please send your carriage here at 7 o'clock to take me to Cardinal Caetani; it will return in good time.

The enclosed report arrived last night; if you think it should be shown to the duke, would you please send it to him; and let the original be returned to me later, because I have no copy. Farewell, the 19th.

       Your servant in Christ
          Robert Persons.

[PS] Do not send the carriage until 8 o'clock, because the secretary has this moment sent me this note, and I cannot get through my letters before 8 o'clock.

Clitherow (who is close with Paget) what business Barnes was treating, he said in a whisper that he was dealing with matters that we should not be made privy to, adding that Persons and Holt and their followers did not want any other way of bringing remedy to their homeland except by fire and blood, even when there could be other remedies. From these words we understand that this business of Barnes and Paget was some proposal for toleration or liberty of conscience in order to deceive, and gain time, as it has happened at other times, but all the same His Highness will gradually come to discover the machinations of Paget and the rest of the dissidents with the council of England, and how they consort with the designs of Malvasia and other political players opposed to the King and Italy, who make these plans of toleration purely to render hateful the forces of Spain and the just and zealous people who support them. With this brief two men have left, and have taken ship, the one through Denmark and the other by another route. Through my efforts the one does not know anything about the other and both are going straight to the places and the people and for the business which I understand Your Honour already knows about. May God prosper and protect Your Honour. From Antwerp, 29 August 1597.)

[PPS] I wrote the above yesterday, but Your Worship was not to be found at home, and so I had a copy made of the report and sent it to Secretary Jiménez. However I wished Your Worship also to see it; please could you have it sent back to me afterwards. The matter I wrote about is very urgent; please would you send your servant to Señor Juan Bautista to hurry him up. May God protect Your Reverence. 20 September.

B408 To John Bennet in Loreto, Rome, 20 September 1597

SOURCE: Georgetown University, Milton House Collection, box 1, folder 3, fol. 1, holograph, with the remains of a seal, and a modern draft transcript (= *MH*).

HICKS: 723–724.

NOTE: John Bennet (ca. 1570?–1623), who had accompanied Persons from Spain, left for England with his brother Edward and Robert Shepperd on 16 August (Persons to Fitzherbert, 26 September, B411; Kenny, "Inglorious Revolution," 141 n16 [part 4], gives the date as 16 September); although he had received his viaticum from the pope's chamberlain, he was still awaiting faculties from the cardinal protector, Caetani: the uneven granting of faculties was becoming a vexed question among priests in England (see Persons to Garnet, 12 July 1598, cited in Edwards, 214). Persons sends information about several sick priests at the English college, as well as the former minister, Edmund Harewood, who died at Sant'Andrea the following day on 21 September ("A brief account of the stirs," 18–20 October [appendix A, BA 6]).

The Bennet brothers, entrusted with a letter from Persons to Charles Paget in Paris, first went to Loreto, near Macerata, and travelled on to Bologna and Milan, writing to Persons from both cities (Persons to Bennet, 18 October, B423). The famous Marian shrine of Loreto was served by Jesuit confessors and was a common place of retreat for students completing their studies in Rome and proceeding to the English mission or to Spain. Before Henry Piers's departure for Spain in October 1597, Persons took him to pay his respects to the pope. His *Discourse of HP his Travells* (composed about 1604) contains a description of his brief stay in Loreto, together with an extended account of the legendary history of the shrine, based largely on the Jesuit Orazio Torsellino's *Lauretanae historia libri quinque*, published in Rome early in 1598. Continuing to Genoa via Milan, he joined other scholars Persons had despatched for Spain: see *Henry Piers's Continental Travels, 1595–1598*, ed. Brian Mac Cuarta (Cambridge, 2018), 27, 172–197.

The right-hand margin of the verso is decayed; the missing or incomplete words have been supplied in square brackets from the Hicks transcript.

Good father

I hope this shall fynde yow well arrived at Loreto and yowr devotions being ended redy to depart forward in your journy in which I beseech our Saveour Jesus well to prosper yow; heer are fallen syck synce your departure Fr Lassels, Fr Troloppe, Gervase Poole and Fr Siclemor,[467] all of agues but not very vehement nor dangerous I hope. Good Father Edmande Harvode is more syck in S. Andrews and going to God as the phisitians

467. Christopher Lassells; Cuthbert Trollop (b. 1573); Gervase Pole (b. ca. 1572), who entered the Society of Jesus in 1607; and Humphrey Sicklemore (b. 1570). See Anstruther, 206, 280, 315–316; McCoog, *English and Welsh Jesuits*, 268.

do think for that his ague is maligne and his strength almost wholy gone. Our Lord comfort hym.

I dealt with the Cardinal about the faculties yow all requyred me and for the first *de restituendo iure petendi debiti matrimonialis*,[468] he granted it willingly; the other I founde hym much more hard and alleaging many reasons to the contrarie for granting it *promiscue*,[469] yet in the ende he saide (when I urged hym much) that he would wryte to yow hym self and advise yow how much for the present he meant to grant therin, as also to advise yow of two[470] *Breves* that heer are come forth yesterdaye about Inglish affayrs wherof I have not now the tyme to sende you the copies, but the Cardinal saide that he would wryte the substanse of them both and so to his[471] letters I remitte me.[472] He told me that he desyred to have yowr answer and to know how yow all passe in your journy and so in any case you must answer hym and let us also heare in this house how[473] yow for we desyer it much. And with this being very [late] I ende with my hartie commendations to you all, *hoc est omnibus et singulis*.[474] Yesterday was buried Monsignor Diego of the popes chamber; yowr *viaticum* was the last good work he dyd before [his] falling sycke. I pray yow commende his sowle [to] Almighty God for he was a pious yonge [man] and his death is felt and morned[475] by many. Fr Chambers with Mr Standish and that company are to set forth about 2 or 3 dayes hence.[476] His Holines is syck agayne of his gowt [and] so his going forth delayed. And this is all I remember now. And so to our Saveour I commende you. From Rome this 20 of September 1597.

    Yours ever in Christ
        Robert Persons.

[*Addressed*:] Al Molto R^{do} in X^{to} P^{re}, il P^{re} Giovanne Benetto.
[*Endorsed*:] Father Parsons.

B409 To Charles Paget, 20 September 1597

    SOURCE: Persons to Paget, 20 December 1597 (B429).
    NOTE: This letter contained an appeal for unity, in the light of the pacification of the

---

468. The faculty of restoring the right to demand the matrimonial debt, i.e., to allow a couple to live together as man and wife. The confessional divide led to many marital irregularities among English Catholic marriages and became the subject of much casuistry. See Peter Holmes, *Elizabethan Casuistry* (London, 1981).

469. I.e., without discrimination. The faculty involved is not specified.

470. two] *Hicks*; our *Georgetown ts*; *MH* obscure

471. to his] *Hicks*; *MH* obscure

472. Further information about these breves is given in the account of the troubles, 18–20 October (Appendix A, item BA 6), below.

473. how] *Georgetown ts*; from *Hicks*; *MH* obscure

474. That is, to one and all.

475. morned] *MH (obscure)*; moned *Hicks*; moved *Georgetown ts*

476. Robert Chambers (b. 1571) entered the English college, Rome, in 1593 and set off for England in October 1597; James Standish, a graduate of Corpus Christi College, Oxford, studied at Rheims and was sent to England in 1590, returning to Rome via Flanders late in 1596; he appears to have remained in Rome at this time (Anstruther, 70, 331–332).

English College, Rome. It was entrusted to Edward Bennet, who was travelling to England with his brother John. Paget replied on 15 November (B425).

In a note on Persons's letter to Paget of 8 March 1598 (ABSI, Coll P I 306), Grene describes a lively correspondence between them in 1597, showing (he believes) Persons's conciliatory manner: "both these letters [of 20 December 1597 and 8 March 1598] make mention of others written to and fro, all be as it were Apologies for the Society and exhort to union and concord and shew great prudence & patience especiall in F. Persons."

B410 From Henry Garnet, London, 24 September 1597

SOURCE: ARSI, Angl. 38/II, fol. 177v, a brief reference.

HICKS: Garnet, 444.

NOTE: It appears that Gerard consulted Garnet about his planned escape, which took place on 4 October. Bartoli comments: "Videtur P. Garnetus certus esse de exitu rei tam incertae, etc." (It seems that Fr Garnet was sure of the outcome of a somewhat uncertain matter).

Gerardo fra tre o quattro giorni con mio consenso usciva dalla Fortezza, &c.

Translation

Three or four days ago Gerard escaped from the fortress with my permission.

B411 To Thomas Fitzherbert and Joseph Creswell, Rome, 26 September 1597

SOURCE: ABSI, Coll P I 315–316, "Epistola Personii transcripta ex autographo data Roma 26 Sept. 1597."

HICKS: 725–727.

NOTE: Grene describes this letter as "an excellent relation of the stirres in the Engl. College of Rome in great part pacifyed" (Coll P I 304). Persons sent it to Thomas Fitzherbert (1552–1640), Philip II's English secretary in Madrid, in case Creswell was out of town. In it, he warns that Malvasia, the former papal agent in Brussels, has sent Aldobrandini a misleading report about the divisions in Flanders, and is attempting to recruit Stapleton to the anti-Jesuit faction. He also mentions John Bennet's departure and Stapleton's remaining in Flanders.

Right worshipful

For that I doubt Father Creswel at the arryval of this may be forth of Madrid ——— I thought good to direct this packet to you, praying you to impart it with Father Creswel. And first ——— you wil see ——— the necessity that was of somebody's coming to this place to breake the impressions which our politiques and factions had heer made ——— secondly assure yourself this house heer had come before this day to extreame breach and to a most scandalous dissolution; for that the seditious were farre the bigger part and obstinatly or rather desperatly sett to ruin themselves and all with them rather then ever to yield to any composition with the fathers whome they saw most weary and disanimated and so overborn by the clamors and impudent accusations —— of these shamelesse compagnions that cared not what they affirmed of them, as they durst not almost look out or appeer in this matter before any great personages, in respect of the sinister impressions they understood that not only His Holiness but many principal Cardinals had conceaved about this matter as you may perceave by this discourse made by a Monsignor heer, and delyvered up to the Pope himself and to his nephews, in which you shal see that he would have the discontented of this and other colleges maintayned and borne-out, and our fathers for more gayning of the Queen of England recalled from thence – and this is the[477] man that sheweth so extraordinary desire to have Doctor Stapleton come hither quickly —— seeing matters in this state I thought good to follow the course which Physicians are wont to doe in curing a long-festered & greevous wound, which is first to appease the present paine —— secondly to divert the influence and concourse of evil humours to the wound and thirdly to putt locall medecins for the curing and healing the wound it self. The first of these three points I pretended to doe with the peace making, whereby I have had tyme ever since both to appease such schollers themselves with yielding them reasons as would heare reason —— and alsoe to informe His Holiness and other Cardinals without contradiction or outcryes of the factions how matters in truth do passe; and finally to informe myself how matters stood in the house —— The second point of diverting humours I have endeavored to performe, and do think in great part to have attayned, in that I perswade myself that both His Holiness, the Spanish Embassador, our Vice-Protector that was Cardinal Borghese, Cardinal Aldobrandino, &c. —— are better informed then before; and those alsoe of our nation here out of the College that did feede or foster the tumults within are either — satisfyed, or els so putt to silence with the evidence of the truth, as they dare attempt no further stirres for the present. The third point then remaines, which is the[478] application of medicines for the perfect cure which is also begunn, for by letting bloud of late to witt by gentle sending away of 6 or 7 of the most troublesome priests by way of mission, (for that their time was ended) we have much eased the house, and now there is likely to follow a purgation of some more evil humours remayning, which wil not be don perchance with such sweetnesse as the former ——— and after this we shall attend to apply lenitives againe as also defensives for the time to come which wil be good lawes for remedies of disorders past, which have bin more and farr greater then you or I could well have imagined.

Among those that depassed hence upon the 16 August was Father John Benet, whome you knew in Spaine; and he hath behaved himself very well heer and don good to diverse and especially to his brother that was the ring-leader of all the troublesome &c. ———

Doctor Stapleton is sayd to be upon the way,[479] and much expected by Monsignor Malvasia that made the discourse which I abovementioned and do send you heer. It is

 477. is the] *interlined with caret G*
 478. the] *folllowed by blank space G*
 479. [*marginal note:*] Dr Stapleton Being iust to begin his iourny resolued the contrary, as appeereth by his lre to f. Persons from Louain 15 Sept. 1597.

strange to see an Italian so labour for an English man as this good prelate doth, without interest as it seemeth, except he hope that the good Doctor wil concurre with him in his discourse to gaine England to the Catholic religion by dryving Jesuits from thence, &c.
——— Rome 26 September 1597. Yours ever, R[obert] P[ersons].

B412 From Nicholas Bonaert, Brussels, 27 September 1597

SOURCE: AAW, VI, no. 59.

NOTE: Nicholas Bonaert, SJ (1564–1610), superior of a Jesuit house in Brussels, reports that the nuncio Ottavio Frangipani has forwarded a letter from Gifford and Paget to the cardinal-nephew Pietro Aldobrandini: in fact, a memorial by the dissident student Robert Fisher, despatched on 19 September (Renold, *Wisbech Stirs*, 279 n74; Law, *Archpriest Controversy*, 1: 7–15). Frangipani claimed to be providing unbiased information to the papal curia about the divisions among the English Catholics in Flanders, and asked Bonaert to discuss the contents of the letter with Paget.

Bonaert reports his conversation with Paget, who claimed that there was tension between Garnet and Weston over the situation at Wisbech (see Renold, *Wisbech Stirs*, 302–303; McCoog, *Building the Faith of St Peter*, 323 n161) and argued that a superior was needed, to whom both Jesuits and seculars would be accountable.

Marginal comments, in another contemporary hand, questioning Paget's statements, have been supplied in the footnotes.

Admodum Reverendo in Christo Patri
Pax Christi.

Illustrissimus Dominus Nuncius Apostolicus narravit nobis se rogatum esse a D. Giffordo Decano Insulensi et D. Pagetto, ut literas, quas scripserant, ad Illustrissimum Cardinalem Aldobrandinum cum suis, adiuncta commendatione, mitteret; ut Suae Sanctitati relatio fieret de iis quae literis continebantur. Ea autem erant querelae contra Patres Societatis nostrae in Anglia: quot autem querelae fuerint, ignoro: duas retulit nobis Illustrissimus Dominus Nuncius,[480] scilicet, Patres nostros unumquemque in sua Provincia et loco sibi captare et vendicare superioritatem et Jurisdictionem supra caeteros sacerdotes; et sibi tribuere vel arripere dispensationem et distributationem Eleemosynarum, quae contribuuntur a Catholicis ad sustentationem sacerdotum et aliorum.

Illustrissimus Dominus Nuncius literas illas ad Cardinalem misit, quamvis ut nobis dixit, non cum ea commendatione, qua petierant D. Giffordus et Pagettus: sed suggerens ut se informaret de veritate &c. Nobis etiam dixit, se haec ideo communicare, ut Patres Nostri perscriberentur, uti tempestive Illustrissimum Cardinalem Aldobrandinum informaret; petiitque ut loqueremur D. Pagetto, ab eoque intellegeremus, quid esset. Feci: Pagettus multa narravit de dissidiis Catholicorum in Anglia,[481] tam in carceribus quam extra: quae dissidia dicebat etiam inter nostros esse. Narrabat P. Edmundum Vestonum

---

480. [*marginal note:*] utraque falsissima ut postea patebit
481. [*marginal note:*] non sunt tot disidia quot isti dicunt, et non nisi quae ipsi et pauci quidam alii inquieti sustineabat [*obscure*], vel fovebat

in carcere Viscibensi cum multis Catholicis detineri: Catholicos illos omnes tam laicos quam sacerdotes in illo carcere communi mensa uti solitos; iam divisos esse, divisas mensas habere etc.[482] P. Garnetum superiorem Missionis Anglicanae P. Edmundo scrivisse et mandasse ut hoc dissidium componeret pacemque et concordiam conciliaret: P. Edmundum respondisse se hoc non facturum, sed seniorem esse, P. Garneto: P. Garnetum nihil habere, quod sibi prescriberet. Cumque premerem, ut in particulari diceret in quibus dissiderent: respondit facile sciri esse enim 16 articulos, et cepit ab articulo quodam aequivocationis, ut eum nominabat, quo alter alteri non respondet ad mentem: cumque non veniret ad rem petii ab articulo de praetensione Jurisdictionis aut superioritatis: ubi ille, scribi quidem sibi nostros velle aliis imperare, vocare, allegare de loco in locum et similla.[483] Concludebat denique necessarium esse, ut auctoritate Sancti Pontificis, utrique tam nostri quam externi sacerdotes habeant cui pareant, v.g. Episcopum vel vicarium aliquem generalem: alioquin fore perpetua dissidia: se amicum esse Societatis, scripsisse pro bono et pace publica Ecclesiae Anglicanae etc. Neque urgere potui, cur literis suis maxime taxasset Societatem: nam Illustrissimus Dominus Nuncius nolebat illi omnia dici, quae ipse retulerat, sed tantum agi cum eo tanquam pro informatione aliqua capienda super articulis supradictis, ut istuc perscriberet.

Haec absente P. Gulielmo Holto putavi a me ad Reverentiam Vestram scribenda fuisse: addoque quod aliunde intellexerit eundem D. Giffordum cum Pagetto et aliis literas vel scripsisse vel scripturos fuisse ad Suam Sanctitatem ut D. Stapletonum crearet Cardinalem, ad hoc enim huc convenerant: fecerint autem necne, cum iter illud D. Stapletoni sit suspensum, non satis scio. Sanctis Reverentiae Vestrae sacrificiis amice atque humilime me commendo. Bruxellae 27 Septemb. 1597.

 Vestrae Reverentiae
  Servus indignus in Christo
   [N. Bonardus.]

[*Addressed:*] Ex Belgio R^{do} in Chro Patri P. Roberto Personio Soc^{tis} Jesu sacerdoti, Romam.

[*Endorsement by Persons:*] P. Bonardi 27 7^{bris} 1597. De novis memo^{bus} Pagetti et Giffordi.

Translation

Most Reverend Father in Christ
The peace of Christ.

 His Excellency the Apostolic nuncio has told us that he was asked by Dr Gifford, dean of Lille, and Mr Paget, to send the letter which they had written, along with his own, to His Eminence Cardinal Aldobrandini, and to add his support; so that an account could be given to His Holiness of those things contained in the letter. These consisted, however,

---

482. [*marginal note:*] huius separationis nullo fuit causa P. Edmundus sed peccata quaedam scandalosa paucorum dissolutorum ut ex ipsorum literis patet

483. [*marginal note:*] totum hoc colloquium confectum est, nunquam enim auditum est verbum de horum presumptione vel minime dissidio

of complaints against the fathers of our Society in England: how many complaints there were, I cannot tell. His Excellency the nuncio recounted two to us:[484] namely that our fathers, each one in his own province and place, seize for themselves and demand superiority and jurisdiction over the other priests; and [second] they appropriate and lay hold of the dispensation and distribution of alms which are donated by the Catholics for the support of priests and others.

His Excellency the nuncio sent that letter to the cardinal, albeit (as he told us) without endorsing it as Dr Gifford and Paget had desired, but suggesting that he should inform himself of the truth, etc. He even told us that he was communicating these things thus, so that our fathers could explain it fully in writing, in order to inform His Eminence Cardinal Aldobrandini in good time; and he wanted us to speak with Mr Paget so that we could find out from him what was going on. I did so: Paget spoke at length of the divisions among Catholics in England,[485] both in and out of prison: these divisions, he said, even existed among Ours.[486] He told us that Fr Edmund Weston was being held in Wisbech prison with many Catholics: that those Catholics, whether lay or priests, used all to eat at a common table in that prison; now they were divided – they had separate tables, etc.[487] He said that Fr Garnet, superior of the English mission, had written to Fr Edmund and instructed him to settle this division and to bring about peace and concord. Fr Edmund had responded that he would not do this but that he was senior to Fr Garnet and so Fr Garnet had no authority to tell him what to do. And when I urged him to spell out in particular what were the issues in contention, Paget said that there was no difficulty in finding out, for there were sixteen articles; and he began with a certain article concerning equivocation, as he called it, by which one did not reply to the other according to his real meaning. And when he did not get to the point, I asked him about the article on their presumption of jurisdiction or superiority: where he had written indeed that Ours wished to rule others, summon them, and push them from pillar to post, and such like. Finally he drew the conclusion that it was necessary that with the authority of the supreme pontiff, both Ours and the secular priests should have someone to obey, that is to say a bishop or some vicar general: otherwise there would be perpetual discord: he claimed to be a friend of the Society, and that he had written for the good and public peace of the church in England, etc.[488] Nor was I able to press the point, why in his letter he chiefly taxed the Society: for His Excellency the nuncio did not want everything to be said to Paget, which he himself [the nuncio] had reported, but only to deal with what was needed to gain any information about the abovementioned articles, so that he could put it all in writing.

484. [*marginal note:*] Both of these are false, as will be made plain later.

485. [*marginal note:*] There are not so many divisions as those people say, and only those that they themselves and certain few other malcontents have sustained or fostered.

486. Paget appears to mean that there are divisions even among the Jesuits. Alternatively, he means that the divisions in England are also present in Flanders.

487. [*marginal note:*] Fr Edmund was not at all the cause of this separation but certain scandalous misdemeanours of a few dissolute men as is evident from their own letters.

488. [*marginal note:*] This whole conversation is made up, for never was a word heard about their presumption, least of all their divisions.

In the absence of Fr William Holt I thought it advisable that these things should be written by me to Your Reverence; and I add what you may have learnt from another source: that the same Dr Gifford, with Paget and others, had written or were about to write a letter to His Holiness to make Dr Stapleton a cardinal, for they had come together there for this purpose;[489] but whether they did so or not, since Dr Stapleton's journey there has been suspended, I do not know for sure. To Your Reverence's holy sacrifices I commend myself amicably and most humbly. Brussels, 27 September 1597.

    Your Reverence's
        Unworthy servant in Christ
           [Nicholas Bonnaert.]

B413 To Pope Clement VIII, Rome, 28 September 1597

SOURCE: ABSI, Coll P II 358, "Ad Pontificem 28 Sept. 1597."
HICKS: 728–730, with English translation.
NOTE: Persons sends the pope two documents about the troubles at the English college, described as "yours" because it was established under papal auspices: one describing the origins and progress of the conflict, the other an update of developments since the apparent resolution in April. These documents were probably early Italian versions of the narratives copied out by Persons, 18–20 October, "A brief raguaglio of the stirrs" and "A brief relation of such things as have fallen out in the English college in Rome since Fr Persons coming hither" (appendix A, BA 6–7). He points out that he has explained to the cardinal protector, Caetani, and the vice-protector, Borghese, about the management of the college. This would have prompted the letters (B414, B419–421 below) which Persons drafted for the two cardinals to write to the rector of the college, Vitelleschi, and to Frangipani and Barret in Flanders.

Beatissime Pater

Ut Sanctitas Vestra melius intelligat statum huius collegii sui Anglicani, alia dua scripta, praeterea quae iam dignata est legere, cum his transmitto, quorum primum aperiet statum et conditionem rerum durante tumultuatione, et nonnullam quoque causam praecipuam eorundem tumultuum; aliud continet additionem quandam ad ea quae Vestra Sanctitas legit de observatione secundi mensis; ex quibus utrisque Sanctitas Vestra pro summa sua prudentia ac pietate animadvertet in quam infelicem statum devenerit hoc insigne Collegium nisi Sanctitatis Vestrae iussu ad radicem arboris spinas ac vepres atque aconita producentis, hac iustissima data occasione securis adhibeatur. Hodie mihi fassus est rector, se iamdiu animum deposuisse exhortationis faciendae ad scholares quia derridentur omnia quae ad spiritum ac virtutem pertinent: decem vel ii discolorum dimissione ac ad Collegium Duacense transmissione conservabuntur 40 boni, et hi ipsi discoli alibi transplantati ad bonam forte frugem pervenient, quod nullo modo hic Romae sperari poterit. Hanc rem pluribus demonstravi duobus Dominis Cardinalibus

---

489. Either they had held a meeting to draft the letter, or they had come to an agreement about it.

Caietano et Burghesio quibus Sanctitas Vestra Collegii nostri rationes commisit examinandas, atque ii referent Sanctitati Vestrae quid invenerint quidve sentiant: quanquam non dubito quin plura multa iam revelabuntur per examen eorum qui hodie capti fuerunt, aliorum capti fuerunt, aliorumque complicum, ex quibus Sanctitas Vestra statuet quid pro sanando hoc Collegio periculosissime laboranti faciendum erit. Dominus Jesus Sanctitatem Vestram diutissime Ecclesiae Suae incolumem servat. Ex Collegio Anglicano, 28 Septembris 1597.

Translation

Most Holy Father

To give Your Holiness a fuller understanding of the condition of this English college of yours, I am enclosing two further documents, besides those you have vouchsafed to read already. The first of these will show the condition and state of matters during the time of turmoil, and also to some extent the principal cause of the disturbances. The other contains some additional material related to what Your Holiness has read, arising from my observation of the situation during the second month. From these two Your Holiness in your prudence and piety will recognize what an unhappy state this eminent college will fall into, unless by Your Holiness's command it can be saved, as soon as opportunity arises, by putting axe to the root of this tree that is producing thorns and brambles and poisons. Today the rector complained to me that he gave up hope long ago of achieving anything by admonishing the scholars, because they make fun of everything relating to the spirit and virtue. By expelling ten or eleven of the dissidents and transferring them to the college at Douai, forty good students will be kept and even those dissidents who are transplanted elsewhere may perhaps bring forth good fruit, which can by no means be hoped for here in Rome. I have explained this more fully to the two lord cardinals Caetani and Borghese, whom Your Holiness has commissioned to look into the management of our college, and they will report their findings and views to Your Holiness: although I do not doubt that many other things will be discovered in the course of their investigation of those who have been arrested today, both the ones who have been arrested, and others involved. From them Your Holiness may decide what should be done to remedy the condition of this college, which is sinking under such very great dangers. May the Lord Jesus keep Your Holiness in safety for a very long time to come, for the sake of His Church. From the English college, 28 September 1597.

B414 To Muzio Vitelleschi, as from Cardinals Enrico Caetani and Camillo Borghese, Rome, 28 September 1597

SOURCE: ABSI, Coll P I 311–312, Grene's transcription ("Exemplar literarum Illustrissimorum Cardinalium Caetani & Burghesii ad P. Mutium Vitelleschi rectorem Collegii Anglicani [transcriptum ex autographo sive minuta Personii] pro incarcerandis captis in taberna, 28 Sept. 1597"); see also Grene's note, Coll P I 304 ("Minuta della l[etter]a delli Card[ina]li Caetano e Burghesio al P. Mutio Vitelleschi Rett[or]e del Coll[egi]o Ingl[ese] intorno all scolari trovati in una Osteria &c. La minuta è scritta di pegno del P. Personio").

NOTE: Persons drafted several letters in late September and October to Vitelleschi, Frangipani, and Barret, carrying the authority of the cardinal protector and vice-protector, to ensure that a firm line was taken with dissolute students, to transfer difficult students to Douai and revoke the faculties of three unreliable seminary priests en route to England. Grene notes in the margin, "Ep[isto]la Card. Caetani &c. composita a P. Personio 28. Sept. 1597."

Reverende Pater

Sua Sanctitas auditis iis quae pro scholares istius vestri Collegii gesta sunt in tabernis, et quod accidit deinde ut a lictoribus pro Germanis caperentur, valde male ut par est rem accepit, non solum ob delictum ipsum, quod pro se grave erat et Collegio vestro indignum, verum etiam quod Germanorum nomine tabernas frequentates criminis infamia aliam nationem immerito onerare praesumpserint. Itaque initio propendebat Sua Sanctitas ut qui capti sunt ad carcerem publicum deducerentur, sed intercessione facta ut Collegii vestri honori parceret, rem nobis duobus Cardinalibus commisit examinandam ac terminandam: vult tamen Sua Sanctitas ut qui deprehensi in taberna hodie fuerunt, carceris loco in cubicula privata Collegii concludantur sub certa ac secura custodia, quoad de universo negotio examen ac decretum nostrum fiat: quam Sanctitatis Suae voluntatem nostramque significandam Reverentiae Vestrae his literis nostris communibus duximus, quibus etiam facultatem facimus alumnos qui in Taberna a lictoribus detinentur domum avocandi ac sub custodia detinendi, ea lege, ut neque invicem neque cum aliis Alumnis sub publici carceris paena delinquenti statuta colloquantur, nisi nostra habita prius licentia aut eius quem huic rei examinandae praeficiemus: quod eo secreto fieri volumus quantum liceat, ut Collegii ac nationis honori consulatur, eamque ob causam praecipimus omnibus domesticis silentium hac in re, quod Reverentia Vestra diligenter ac severe nostro nomine universis ac singulis denunciet, neque hae nostrae literae cuique extra Collegium ostendantur, sed postquam lectae fuerint, eidem reddantur qui eas vobis nostro nomine detulit. Interea vero temporis dum alia statuantur ad Collegii istius bonum regimen spectantia, ad Reverentiae Vestrae curam pertinebit pacem et quietem inter omnes fovere, et eos notare qui ullo modo illum turbant, ut amoveantur vel gravius etiam si opus fuerit castigentur: nullis alia licentia exeundi detur nisi aut integra cubicula una proficiscantur vel saltem sex aut minimum quattuor simul eant, idque perspecta Reverentiae Vestrae causa, et iis sociis, non quos quisque elegerit, sed qui Reverentiae Vestrae aut P. Sin.^{ro}490 maxime videbuntur idonei. Vale ac nos Deo commenda, Reverende Pater. Romae, ex aedibus nostris, 28 Septembris 1597.

Translation

Reverend Father

When His Holiness heard about what was done by scholars of that college of yours in the taverns, and what happened afterwards, that they were mistaken by the lictors for Germans and arrested, he regarded the matter in a very bad light, as is fitting, not only because of the offence itself, which was serious in itself and unworthy of your college, but also because they presumed to lay the blame of their disgraceful conduct on another

490. P. Sin.^{ro}] *obscure: possibly* P. Fin.^{ro} G

nation undeservedly by frequenting taverns as Germans. And so His Holiness was inclined at first to allow those who were arrested to be led to the public prison, but when he was entreated to spare the reputation of your college, he entrusted the matter to us two cardinals to examine it and come to a decision. Still, His Holiness desires that those who have been taken today in the tavern should be held in separate rooms of the college, in lieu of prison, under strict and secure guard, until we are able to reach a decision about the whole business: we have sent this common letter to Your Reverence to convey His Holiness's will in the matter, and our own. By means of the letter we are also giving you the authority to summon home those students who are being detained by the lictors and to hold them in custody, with this proviso, that they should not discuss the punishment in the public jail ordained for a delinquent, either with each one or with the other students, without prior permission from us or whoever we put in charge of investigating this matter. We would like this to take place as discreetly as possible, for the sake of the reputation of the college and the nation, and for the same reason we instruct that all the servants keep silence about this matter, which we would like Your Reverence to announce strictly in our name to all and sundry. Nor should this letter be shown to anyone outside the college, but as soon as you have read it, please could it be given back to the one who brings it to you in our name. Meanwhile, indeed, during the time while decisions are being made about other things relating to the good government of this college, it will be Your Reverence's responsibility to foster peace and quiet among them all, and to keep a note of those who disturb it in any way, so that they may be admonished or even, if need be, chastised. No one should be given any other leave to go out, unless the whole room goes out together or at least six or, at the very least, four go at the same time, and only if they have explained their reason to Your Reverence, and to their fellows – not just anyone they choose, but those who seem most suitable either to Your Reverence or to Fr Sicklemore.[491] Farewell, and commend us to God, reverend father. From our palaces in Rome, 28 September 1597.

B415 From Edward and John Bennet, Loreto, Bologna, and Milan, September/October 1597

SOURCE: Persons to John Bennet, 18 October (B423).

NOTE: The Bennet brothers responded to Persons's letter of 20 September (B408) by writing regularly as they continued on their journey towards Flanders and England.

---

491. Since Grene's Latin transcript is obscure, the identification of Humphrey Sicklemore is speculative. Sicklemore left Rome in April or May 1598 and in August wrote a letter to Christopher Bagshaw defending Persons as one "whose shoues I wish my selfe worthie to kisse" (Law, *Archpriest Controversy*, 1: 49; see Anstruther, 315, who describes this as "the most glowing tribute to Robert Persons ... ever paid by a secular priest"). Since he was earlier listed by Sega as one of the mutineers, his apparent change of heart under Persons's influence suggests that perhaps he was one whom Persons could now trust.

B416 From Edward Tempest, Milan, September/October 1597

SOURCE: Persons to Bennet, 18 October (B423).
NOTE: Tempest was one of the dissident priests from the English college whom Frangipani was asked to prevent from proceeding to England, in the cardinal protector's letter of 12 October (B419). Along with his fellow seminary priests Hill and Benson, he may have been travelling in company with the Bennets.

B417 To Thomas Fitzherbert, Rome, 4 October 1597

SOURCE: ABSI, Coll P I 304, Grene's note.
HICKS: 731.
NOTE: Persons has fallen ill.

... this is all I can wryte now being in bedd of the [blank] but without ague &c.

B418 From Henry Garnet, Rome, 8 October 1597

SOURCES:
ABSI, Coll P II 548–49, Grene's partial transcription;
ARSI, Angl. 38/II, fols. 172v and 177v, Bartoli's Latin extracts.
HICKS: Garnet, 445–447.
NOTE: This letter is an important witness to attitudes amongst the clergy in England to the question of ecclesiastical hierarchy. It accompanied Garnet's response to a letter from the cardinal protector, Enrico Caetani, on the subject. Here Garnet relays the ambivalence of three of his correspondents – William Weston, SJ; John Bavant, DD (see Renold, *Wisbech Stirs*, 31); and Nicolas Tyrwhit (Anstruther, 365) – as well as the suggestion that George Blackwell or Tyrwhit would be the most suitable candidate for headship. See McCoog, *Building the Faith of St Peter*, 320–321.

The escape of John Gerard and John Arden (a Northamptonshire gentleman implicated in the Babington Plot) from the Tower of London is graphically described in Gerard, *Autobiography*, 128–137.

Thomas Wright, whose difficulties as a Jesuit priest had much exercised Persons during his period as prefect of studies at Valladolid in 1594, returned to England in 1595 under the protection of the earl of Essex but, losing favour, was placed in the custody of Gabriel Goodman, dean of Westminster, where he conferred with the poet William Alabaster (1568–1640). See Peter Milward, "Wright, Thomas" and Francis J. Bremer, "Alabaster, William" (*ODNB*) and the MSS entitled "Alabaster's Conversion" at the Venerable English College, Rome.

Upon St Francis day at night broke out of the tower one Arden — and Mr Gerard the Jesuit.[492] There is yet no great inquiry after him.

492. Bartoli translates: "Il giorno di San Francesco, la notte scappò fuor di prigione un certo Ardeno già condennato, et Signore Gerardo Giesuita, &c." (fol. 177v).

I send you a letter to the Protector, also Mr Blackwells lettre to me and the most think him or Mr Tirwit the fittest for our purpose. Yet Father Weston and D. Bavant and Mr Tirwit think there wil be great difficulty to have hear a head. But they wil submit their judgments to whatsoever shalbe appointed, and that is the cause why they write so generally. The principal doubt is because if such a head meddle with matters, his place of abode wil be subject to dangers: besides there is some feare to be conceived of disobedience, and than no hard course can wel be taken hear. Yet I think the first wil be remedyed, if he have no accesse unto him, but of some few, when he is at home, but that he travail once or twice to London in a yeare and as oft into some one or two countries, and so shal he meete all once a yeare, and many matters may be despatched by letters and many by substitutes. The second may be avoyded by mildnesse of government or remedyed by the fervour & zeale of many others abroade, who undoubtedly wil be united to the heade.[493]

Now I would not think it good to go forth of the Realme presently to be consecrated, but that he after his election and confirmation may begin to practise his jurisdiction and have leave to confirme, and than after at leasure go to be consecrated where and when he will.

M Thomas Wright hath converted one Alabaster, a famous man of Cambridge, &c.[494] — Two theeves were executed the last Assizes at Wisbich and were before reconciled by a priest in the same house, and went with great joy through the towne, professing their faith, till they came to Gallowes.[495] Two others in like sort at Shrewsbury were converted by 2 poor lay Catholick prisoners and with great constancy rejected the ministers, affirming that heresy had brought them to that end, which they acknowledged to have bin deserved; yet that they would dye in the unity of Gods church, and so refused to pray with them, but prayed themselves in Latin. In the same prison to the same lay men, there came a famous preacher of the towne, and being let in by the Keeper who hoped for some mutation in the Catholicks by his secret conference: shutting their chamber dore he came unto them, and "Do you (sayth he) professe the Roman faith?" They fearing he meant to intrappe them, answered that they professed the Catholick faith. He urged again and again that they should answer directly, protesting that he meant not to intrappe them. Att last they plainly said that they professed the Catholick Roman faith: then he suddainly fell down on his knees requesting their praiers and protesting he believed the same faith and that Christ was really present in the Blessed Sacrament, and that for the assured persuasion of the Catholick religion he was giving over his benefice and providing for his wife and children that he might goe over and be reconciled; and that the Puritans falsly thought that they had made him weary of the towne, which was

493. Bartoli summarizes: "Varias affert rationes cur existimet convenire ut constituatur aliquis Episcopus in Anglia: et solvit obiectiones quas P. Westonys & alii afferunt cur non videatur convenire" (fol. 172v).

494. Bartoli translates: "Dominus Thomas Writus convertit ad fidem quendam insignem virum nomine Alabastrum, &c." (fol. 172v).

495. Bartoli translates: "Nelle ultime sessioni furono fatti morire a Wisbico due ladroni, convertiti poco prima a la santa fede da un sacerdote di questo luogo, e andorono con grande allegrezza per tutte le strade facendo professione d.ª loro fede sin'alla forca & &c." (fol. 177v).

not soe, for he neither feared their learning and he had the law on his side to hamper them if he would: all this while with many like speeches the good men being amazed att so unexpected a thing were upon their knees with him and weeping for joy and telling him that the Angels in heaven rejoyced att his conversion: and soe with many friendly speeches they parted and the Minister gave them mony and two Catholick books which he had under his gowne, and which had bin taken from them long before by which it seemeth he gott his resolution.

B419 From Enrico Caetani to Ottavio Frangipani, 12 October 1597

SOURCES:
>ABSI, Coll P II 358–359, "Litterae Cardinalis Caietani ad nuncium in Belgio, quibus reuocat facultates trium sacerdotum in Angliam missorum. [*in margin*:] Litterae Protectoris a Personio compositae, transcriptae ex autographo." Persons's draft, transcribed by Grene, with some omissions = G;
>AAW VI, no. 66, 237–238, dated 10 October, a fair copy of the final version of the letter (see McCoog, *Building the Faith of St Peter*, 397 n. 183) = W.

NOTE: The next two letters provide further evidence of Persons's pursuit of reform among the seminary priests. He drafted letters for the cardinal protector and vice-protector to send to the nuncio in Brussels and the president of the college in Douai. Here Caetani asks Frangipani to summon three priests who are on their way to England from the English college in Rome and revoke their faculties: Edward Tempest, Thomas Hill, and Robert Benson (see Agazzari to Persons, 27 August 1596, B336). In the event, Frangipani was only able to contact Tempest, at Douai (Kenny, "Inglorious Revolution," 141 [part 3]). Tempest wrote to Persons from Milan, but Persons held back his reply, pending Frangipani's intervention (Persons to Bennet, 18 October, B423).

The text below follows *G*, as a record of Persons's draft, with omissions supplied from *W*, as indicated.

Perillustrissime et Reverende Domine

Cum praeter eam curam ac[496] sollicitudinem quam ex Protectionis meae obligatione de rebus Collegii huius Anglicani de urbe ac totius quoque nationis incumbere mihi intelligebam, Sanctissimus Dominus noster aliam quoque his diebus praeteritis[497] speciali[498] mandato iniunxerit, ut de quibusdam excessibus in hoc ipso Collegio per alumnos factis cognoscerem, eaque statuerem quae ad idoneum remedium pertinere posse existimarem,[499] praeficiendum curavi rerum examini (Sanctitate etiam sua annuente) Reverendum ac discretum virum D. Acaritium Apostolicae visitationis fiscalem, ex quo aliisque cognovi tres sacerdotes huius Collegii qui paulo ante (acceptis a me facultatibus pro missione Anglicana) discesserant, diversorum testium depositione de iisdem quoque excessibus aliisque (praesertim vero de frequentandis cum scandalo tabernis dum hic

496. ac] *G*; et *W*
497. his diebus praeteritis] *interlined with caret G*
498. speciali] *G*; speciali quodam *W*
499. eaque statuerem quae ad idoneum remedium pertinere posse existimarem] *W*; *om. G*

adessent) accusari. Cum vero nondum eo usque productus sit processus ut eius copia ad Vestram Dominationem Reverendissimam (quantum ad tres illos sacerdotes pertineat[500]) transmitti nunc possit, ex alia vero parte incommodum omnino ac incongruum tum Suae Sanctitati tum mihi quoque videatur ut hi sacerdotes, priusquam se purgaverint, vel de excessibus commissis aliqua ratione satisfecerint ad Anglicanam messem admittantur, ne simili conversatione scandalum in Anglia Catholicis afferant: scribendum statim hac ipsa de re ad Dominationem Vestram Reverendissimam duxi, eamque rogandum[501] ut pro sua charitate ac auctoritate hos tres sacerdotes Anglos si in Belgio fuerint (quorum nomina sunt Eduardus Tempestius, Thomas Hillus ac Robertus Bensonus) ad se vocandos curet, eisque significet, me ob ea quae hic post eorum discessum, de excessibus per ipsos commissis denunciata sunt, omnino statuisse facultates quas discedentibus pro Anglicana missione eis impertiveram revocandas esse ac per praesentes literas me eas revocare quoad per Reverendissimam Dominationem Vestram aut alia via certa mihi constiterit eos se vel purgasse vel alioquin de obiectis satisfecisse, atque hoc etiam ipsis significandum cupio, quocunque in loco fuerint sive in Belgio sive extra Belgium.[502] Cum vero processus copia, qui ad istos pertinebit, ad Dominationis Vestrae Reverendissimae manus pervenerit, poterit pro sua prudentia ac aucthoritate, eosdem vel reprehendere vel etiam castigare prout expedire causae Anglicanae, et res ipsae quae obiicuntur mereri vel exigere, perpensis loci, temporis ac personarum circumstantiis, Dominatio Vestra Reverendissima indicabit. Neque aliud est, quod modo scribam, nisi ut Reverendissimae Dominationis Vestrae precibus me ex anime commendem. Romae ex aedibus nostris. Die [blank] Octobris 1597.

   Dominationis Vestrae Reverendissimae
    uti frater
      Henricus Cardinalis Caëtanus.

 [*Endorsed:*] Literae Ill^mi Card^lis Caëtani ad Nuncium Apostolicum in Belgio pro tribus sacerdotibus, 1597.

Translation

Your Most Honourable Excellency

 When, besides the responsibility and solicitude for the affairs of this English college in Rome and the entire English nation which I understood to be incumbent on me as a result of my obligation as protector, Our Most Holy Lord added another as well in these days past, by a special instruction: namely, that I should investigate certain excesses committed by students in this same college and decide on such measures as I judged might contribute to a suitable remedy, I arranged (with His Holiness's consent besides) to have put in charge of the examination of the matters the reverend and discreet man Mr Acarizio, fiscal of the apostolic visitation.[503] From him and others I learned that three

---

  500. pertineat] *G*; pertinet *W*
  501. duxi, eamque rogandum] *G*; eamque rogandum duxi *W*
  502. *G omits from here to the end*
  503. Don Acarizio Squarcione (Kenny, "Inglorious Revolution," Part 3, p. 140). He was later responsible for the restraint of William Bishop and Robert Charnock (McCoog, *Lest Our Lamp be Entirely Extinguished*, 186).

priests of this college, who had left a little earlier (after receiving faculties from me for the English mission), were accused, by the deposition of various witnesses, of those very excesses and also others (but especially of scandalously frequenting taverns while they were here). But although the process has not yet reached the point where it would be possible for a copy of the proceedings (as far as it concerns those three priests) to be sent now to Your Excellency – yet it would seem, both to His Holiness and to me too, altogether inconvenient and inappropriate that these priests be admitted to the English mission before they have purged themselves or have made satisfaction for these excesses they have committed by some other means, in case they bring scandal on the Catholics in England by similar behaviour – I have instructed that they write immediately to Your Excellency concerning this very matter, so that you of your charity and authority can arrange for these three priests (whose names are Edward Tempest, Thomas Hill, and Robert Benson) to be summoned to you, if they are in Flanders, and can indicate to them that on account of those things which have been delated to me here, after their departure, of the excesses they have committed, I have absolutely decided that the faculties which I presented to them on their departure for the English mission should be revoked. So, I am revoking them by the present letter until I have been assured, either by Your Excellency or by some other means, that they have purged themselves or in some other way made satisfaction for what has been objected against them. Nor do I wish this to be indicated even to themselves, wherever they may be, either inside or outside Flanders. When indeed the full report of the process relating to those men comes to the hands of Your Excellency, please would you, out of your prudence and authority, either rebuke them or even chide them, so far as is expedient for the English cause, and would Your Most Reverend Lordship please indicate those particular matters which, taking the circumstances of place, time, and the people involved into account, will occur to you as meriting or demanding attention. And there is nothing more for me to write at this time except to commend myself heartily to Your Excellency's prayers. Rome, from our palace, on the ... day of October.

  Your Excellency's
    Brother, so to speak,
      Enrico Cardinal Caetani.

B420 To Muzio Vitelleschi, as from Cardinals Enrico Caetani and Camillo Borghese, Rome, probably 14 October 1597

SOURCES:
  ABSI, MS Anglia II, no. 31, fol. 117r–v, draft in Persons's hand, "Forma quaedam dimissionis, nisi aliquid severius videatur de delictis, etc." = *A*;
  AAW, VI no. 64, 229, with original signatures = *W*.
HICKS: 732–733.
NOTE: Persons arranges for Vitelleschi to send six students from the English college to Douai, using a letter of dismissal signed by the cardinal protector and vice-protector.

Reverende Pater

Post examinatas ac perpensas Collegii istius Anglicani rationes, ac cum Sanctissimis etiam Dominis Nostris communicatas, tam eas quae ad pacem ac disciplinam pertinent, quam quae ad oeconomiam ac ad[504] aes alienum a Collegio contractum dissolvendum, visum est omnino Sanctitati Suae, ac nobis[505] ut hi sex Alumni seguentes,[506] ad Collegium Anglorum Duacensem dimittantur; nimirum P. Cuthbertus Trollopus, P. Georgius Wolleus, Joannes Jaksonus, Gaspar Loberius, Franciscus Fosterus et Georgius Aschuus, quibus etiam pro viatico dabit Collegium viginti quinque aureos unicuique, et vestitum praeterea competentem pro itinere usque ad dictum Collegium Duacensem ex arbitrio rectoris atque Consultorum suorum, quod si quis eo adire recusaverit,[507] ad studia sua persequenda pro Collegii instituto, is sine viatico dimittatur. Nos etiam literas patentes una cum his mittimus pro rectore[508] dicti Collegii Duacensis, ut eos adventantes admittat, et omni caritatis ostensione tractet, donec literarum suarum studia absolvant, modo recte atque[509] pacifice se gerant, quod sperandum est eos facturos. Vestra igitur Reverentia infra triduum post harum literarum acceptionem eos cum caritate ex Collegio isto dimittat, neque ullam admittendam esse hac in re excusationem, appellationem, aut delationem. Sua Sanctitas vult (cuius nomine stricte praecipimus) ut quiete, pacate, ac sine tumultu infra tempus limitatum discedant, neque Romae subsistant vel quisquam eorum, neque ante annum saltem[510] Jubilei proxime sequentis[511] ullo modo ad Urbem redeant, sub poena indignationis Sanctissimi Domini Nostri incurrendae, et sub[512] aliis poenis etiam corporalibus Suae Sanctitatis arbitrio reservatis, nisi licentia nostra prius in scriptis[513] habita, quia haec est mens Sanctitatis Suae: quam Reverentiae Vestrae his literis nostris significandam censuimus, cuius nos precibus commendamus. Ex aedibus nostris die 14 Octobris 1597.

  Paternitatis Vestrae Reverendae
   uti fratres
     Henricus Cardinalis Caetanus
     Protector
     Camillus Cardinalis Borghesius.

[*W is addressed:*] R⁰ in X'o uti fratri: P. Mutius Vitellesco Collegii Anglorum de Urbe rectori etc., Romae

[*A is endorsed:*] Dimissit sex alumnorum 1597. Autographo. Character Personii.

[*W is endorsed:*] literae Cardinalium pro dimittione sex alumnorum. 1597 14 8^{bris}.

---

504. ac ad] *A*; et *W*
505. ac nobis] *A*; et nobis, ob utriusque poneris rationes, *W*
506. *W inserts* ex isto nostro Collegio *after* se[g]uentes
507. *W places* recusaverit *after* instituto
508. pro rectore] *A*; ad rectorem *W*
509. atque] *A*; ac *W*
510. saltem] *W*; *om. A*
511. sequentis] *W*; sequentem *A*
512. et sub] *W*; ac *A*
513. licentia nostra prius in scriptis] *W*; licentia prius scripta *A*

Translation

Reverend Father

After investigating and considering the way this English college is run, and communicating to His Holiness both what makes for peace and discipline and for the internal organization, and to eliminate the alien element in the college, it seemed altogether wise, to His Holiness and ourselves, that the following six students should be transferred to the English college at Douai: Fr Cuthbert Trollop, Fr George Wolly, John Jackson, Jasper Lothbury, Francis Foster, and George Askew.[514] The college should give them twenty-five crowns as viaticum, and besides this, suitable clothing for the journey, until [they reach] the said college of Douai, at the discretion of the rector and his consultors. If any should refuse to go there to pursue his studies according to the institute of the college, he should be sent down without viaticum. Along with them we are also sending letters patent to the rector of the said college of Douai, so that he can welcome them when they arrive, and deal with them with all show of charity, until they have completed their studies of letters, always supposing they behave themselves appropriately and peaceably, which it is to be hoped they will do. Would Your Reverence please therefore send them down from this college within three days of the receipt of this letter, with charity, nor allow any accusation, appeal, or delation in this matter. His Holiness (in whose name we expressly issue this instruction) desires that they depart quietly, peaceably, and without disturbance within the time allocated, nor should any of them remain in Rome, nor should they by any means return to the city before the next Jubilee year, on pain of incurring the wrath of Our Most Holy Lord, and other punishments, even corporal, reserved to His Holiness's discretion, without our written leave given in advance, because this is what His Holiness has resolved: this we thought good to convey to Your Reverence in this letter, and we commend ourselves to your prayers. From our palaces, October 1597.

  As Your Reverend Fatherhood's
    brothers
      Enrico Cardinal Caetani,
      Protector,
      Camillo Cardinal Borghese.

B421 From Enrico Caetani and Camillo Borghese to Richard Barret, Rome, 14 October 1597

SOURCES:

  ABSI, Coll P II 361, Persons's draft, transcribed by Grene "ex autographo Personii" = G;

  AAW VI, no. 63, 227–228, a contemporary fair copy = W.

514. All of these are listed in Knox, *Douai Diaries*, 16, as having been sent from Rome in 1597 to pursue their studies in theology: Cuthbert Trollop (see Persons to John Bennet, 20 September, B408) and George Wolly (b. 1567), priests; John Jackson (b. 1573) and Francis Foster (1572–1631), ordained in 1598; and George Askew (b. 1575) and Jasper Lothbury (b. 1564), ordained in 1599 (Anstruther, 12, 122, 186–187, 213–214, 384).

HICKS: 736.

NOTE: Persons drafted this letter patent for signature by the cardinal protector and vice-protector, requesting Barret to accept the six students whom they were asking Vitelleschi to transfer from the English college in Rome. According to his letter to John Bennet, 18 October (B423), he also wrote a personal letter to Barret, for the six students to bear with them along with this.

Reverende in Christo, uti frater

Sanctissimo Domino Nostro nobisque (quibus Collegii huius Anglicani de urbe rationes, tam quae ad pacem ac disciplinam, quam quae ad oeconomiam pertinent, Sanctitas Sua speciali mandato expendendas, atque moderandas commisit) visum omnino est, ob utriusque generis rationes causasque legitimas, ut hi sequentes alumni, nimirum P. Cuthbertus Trollopus, P. Georgius Wollaeus, Joannes Jacksonus, Gaspar Loberius, Franciscus Fosterus et Georgius Askuus, ad Collegium istud vestrum Duacensem, ad studia sua, pro Seminariorum ratione ac instituto prosequenda, mutantur, ea intentione, ut post studiorum suorum curricula absoluta, in Anglicanam quoque messem, per vos, si idonei videbuntur, et bene se interim gesserint (quod facturos speramus), ad lucrandas Christo animas, suo tempore emittantur. Vult igitur Sua Sanctitas ut benigne a vobis in istius Collegii alumnos recipiantur, ac omni charitatis ostensione tractentur, dum istic apud vos morari eos, studiorum causa, contigerit; ut nos praeterea literis vestris de eorum salvo adventu admoneatis, ac de omni ipsorum, tam in literis quam virtute, sub regiminis vestri obedientia, progressu certiores faciatis: quam Sanctissimi Domini[515] nostramque voluntatem his literis nostris Dominationi Vestrae[516] significandam duximus, omnesque qui in isto vestro Collegio degunt, officiose ex nobis salutandos curabitis. Vale Reverende Pater, ac nos Deo commenda. Romae ex aedibus nostris, die 14[517] Octobris 1597.

   Reverendae Vestrae Dominationis uti fratres
     Henricus Cardinalis Caetanus
      Camillus Cardinalis Borghesius.

[*Endorsed in W*] Lrae patentes pro sex alumnis dimmitendis ad D. Barrettum Collegij Duaceni Praesidem 1597.[518]

Translation

Reverend Brother in Christ, so to speak

  It has seemed good to Our Most Holy Lord and to us (to whom His Holiness has by special commission entrusted the task of considering and reforming the government of this English college in the city, both with regard to the peace and discipline and to the internal organisation), that for valid reasons and causes in either respect, the following students, namely Fr Cuthbert Trollop, Fr George Wolly, John Jackson, Jasper Lothbury,

515. Sanctissimi Domini] G; Sanctissimi Domini Nostri W
516. D[omination]i V[estr]ae] G; om. W
517. Persons's draft, represented by G, omits the date, which is supplied in the fair copy W.
518. W has a similar headnote, "Literae patentes Illustrissimorum Cardinalium Caietani et Burghesij ad Rectorem Collegij Duaceni pro sex alumnis dimittendis."

Francis Foster, and George Askew, should be transferred to your college at Douai, to pursue their studies according to the manner of proceeding of the seminarians, with this intention: that after they have completed the course of their studies, they should be sent by you into the English harvest field, if they seem suitable and have behaved themselves well in the interim (which we hope they will do), in their own time, to win souls for Christ. Therefore, His Holiness desires that they be kindly received by you as students of that college, and treated with all show of charity, so long as it is necessary for them to remain with you for the sake of their studies. He also wishes, besides, that you advise us by letter of their safe arrival, and that you keep us informed of their progress both in learning and virtue, under the obedience of your regimen. We bring this desire of Our Most Holy Lord and ours to Your Worship's attention in this our letter, and you are please to convey our greetings faithfully to all who spend time in that college of yours. Farewell, reverend father, and commend us to God. Rome, from our palaces, on the 14th day of October 1597.

  As it were Your Reverend Worship's brothers
    Enrico Cardinal Caetani
    Camillo Cardinal Borghese.

B422 To Francisco de Peña, Rome, 15 October 1597

  SOURCE: BAV, MS Vat. Lat. 6227, fols. 191–192.
  HICKS: 737–740, with English translation.
  NOTE: Stapleton enclosed a letter to Malvasia in his letter to Persons, 15 September (B405). Here he comments on Malvasia's reaction to the news that Stapleton was not coming to Rome after all, despite the monsignor's efforts (see also Persons to Fitzherbert, 26 September, B411).

Monsignor Reverendissimo
  Oy he dado al Monsignor Malvasia la carta del doctor Stapletono de la su restada en Flandes y que no quiere venir a Roma, lo qual me dixo que havia sabido antes por el secretario del Señor Cardenal Aldobrandino, pues al Cardenal me dixo que no abló por estar su Señoria Illustrissima en la cama del Castron, pero ha quedado Monsignor Malvasia tanto descontento desta nueva que no se puede creer, diciendo y repetiendo muchas veçes que el Doctor avia hecho un grandissimo errore, pues si venia fuera Cardenal sin duda, y que con quedarse en Flandes ha hecho grande daño a sí y a toda la nacion Ynglesa que en él tubiera cabeça porque con esta entençion le llamó Su Santidad y el Señor Cardenal Aldobrandino el qual dixo tanbien que quedava sentido, de que el doctor ubiesse tomado esta resolucion, sin dar parte primero por acá, y quando yo le dixi que por ventura vendria el doctor por la primavera, en aviendo allanado las difficultades que al presente se le offerecian, respondio que si él mismo[519] no lo pedia, los patronos no lo trattarian más, particularmente Su Signoria, pues avia empleado esta vez todas sus fuerças para traerle, mostrando a Su Santidad quando tornó de Flandes quánto era conveniente

---

519. mismo] *interlined with caret* B

y necessario hacer capo de la nacion alguna persona de confiança y valor para consuelo de aquela gente, particularmente de los que estan en Flandes, pues los entretenimientos que les prometia el Rey de España andavan en humo, y nunca se les pagavan, y que aora quando el negocio estava hecho y todo accordado, le pesava grandemente que el doctor por no sé qué pusillanimidad[520] lo uviesse estorbado todo, yo le mostre la carta que el Doctor me escrive,[521] a lo menos las palabras Latinas que ay en ella que son muy buenas y religiosas, pero él no approvo mucho aquel espirito, Vuestra Señoria las vea y despues le dare toda la carta trasladada si Vuestra Señoria la quisiere, porque hasta aora no he tenido tiempo ni tendre por dos o tres dias para traducirla. Las cosas deste Collegio se van preveniendo bien, mañana placiendo a Dios, se intimará el orden a los padres seis que an de partirse. Agradesco mucho a Vuestra Señoria la visita de oy del Señor Juan Baptista. No puedo más por aora. Guarde Dios a Vuestra Señoria como se lo supplico. 15 de Octubre 1597.

De Vuestra Señoria Reverendissima siervo en Christo
Roberto Personio.

[PS] Si parece a V.S. que conviene dar parte deste succeso al Señor Duque de Sesa, supplico a V.S. lo haga.

La Carta de Stapleton o V.S. me haga merced de mandar bolver despues.

[*Addressed:*] A monsignor Reverendisimo Peña Auditor de Rota

Translation

Most Reverend Monsignor

Today I gave Monsignor Malvasia Dr Stapleton's letter about his remaining in Flanders and not wishing to come to Rome. He said that he had heard this before from Cardinal Aldobrandini's secretary; he had not spoken with the cardinal himself, he told me, as His Eminence was in bed with a feverish cold. But Monsignor Malvasia was disgruntled with this news beyond belief: he declared and kept repeating over and over again that the doctor had made a very big mistake: if he came, he would be a cardinal without a doubt, and by staying in Flanders he has done great harm to himself and to all the English nation, which would then have had a leader. This was the very reason why His Holiness and Cardinal Aldobrandini had summoned him; and he said that the latter was grieved that the doctor had taken this decision without first consulting them here. And when I said to him that possibly the doctor would come in the spring when he had overcome the difficulties which were in his way at present, he answered that, unless he himself asked them, his sponsors would not broach the matter again, particularly the monsignor himself,[522] for this time he had used all his influence to have him sent for, pointing out to His Holiness, on his return from Flanders, how suitable and necessary it was to put at the head of the nation some trustworthy person of standing, to comfort these people; especially those in Flanders, because the king of Spain's promise of allowances had gone up in smoke, and they were never paid; and now when the matter had been agreed and everything arranged it grieved him very much that the doctor, through some

520. pusillanimidad] *this ed.*; pusillamidad *B*
521. [*Note at the top of the page:*] la carta di Stapletono era de Lovaina de xv de Setiembre 1597
522. I.e., Malvasia.

sort of diffidence, had brought the whole business to a halt. I showed him the letter which the doctor had written to me – the Latin words it contains at least, which are very fair and pious; but he did not approve very much of that spirit. Please would Your Reverence look at them, and later I will give you a copy of the whole letter, if you like; for up to now I have not had time, and will not for another two or three days, to copy it. College affairs are being well taken care of: tomorrow, God willing, notice will be given to the six fathers of the order to leave. I am much obliged to Your Reverence for Mr Juan Bautista's visit today. I cannot write more at present. May God keep Your Reverence, as is my prayer. 15th of October 1597.

    Your Reverence's servant in Christ
        Robert Persons.

[PS] If Your Reverence thinks it well to inform the duke of Sessa of what has happened, I beg you to do so.

Would Your Reverence please have Stapleton's letter returned to me later on.

B423 To John Bennet, Rome, 18 October 1597

> SOURCE: Georgetown, Milton House Collection, box 1, folder 4, holograph, with the remains of a seal (= MH).
>
> HICKS: 750–751.
>
> NOTE: Responding to letters written by the Bennet brothers from Loreto, Bologna, and Milan, on their way to Flanders, Persons updates them on developments at the English college, especially the hard line taken against the more dissolute students, on instructions from the pope (Persons to Clement VIII, 28 September, B413). The measures taken to improve the situation are substantially those embodied in the letters Persons drafted for Cardinals Caetani and Borghese, 28 September to 14 October (B414, B419–421). It seems likely that Edward Bennet showed this letter to Charles Paget when he delivered Persons's letter to Paget of 20 September (B409).
>
> As in the case of the earlier letter to Bennet, 20 September (B408), defective letters have been supplied in square brackets, normally following Hicks.

Good Father Jhon

I have receaved all your letters from Loreto, Bollon and Millan and do thank you for the same as also your brother for his. I trust you are before the arrivall of this come safe to Flanders wher I do salute you hartely. Father Eli also I perceave is in his way after you as one told me that mette hym some 6 dayes hence about Ancona.[523] Heer in this colleg great alteration hath happened synce your departure, for a complaynt coming to the pope of German schollers that used taverns, His Holiness gave order to the Governour and he to the Isbyrris[524] to apprehend all Germans that went to taverns or hoat howses and

---

523. Possibly William Ellis, a student at the English college who was ordained in Rome in October 1596 (Anstruther, 109–110). Ancona is a city on the Adriatic coast of Italy.

524. Rome was governed by the apostolic vice chamberlain, the *vice camerlengo*; the *bargello* was responsible for maintenance of order, with a force of armed *sbirri*: see Miles Pattenden, "Governor and Government in Sixteenth-Century Rome," *Papers of the British School at Rome* 77 (2009): 257–272, at 262.

so upon Sunday the 28 of September in the morning two companyes of our schollers were taken, to witt Father Trolloppe and Henry Pearse and Mr Middleton at a taverne and Father Robinson and Bannister at Mr Middletons chamber that was at a hoat howse and the pope took the matter so yvell as Mr Middleton was sent to Corte Savella and ther hath remaned thes 20 dayes.[525] And the schollers were sent home with Isbyrris and commanded by His Holiness to be kept in prison within the colleg and examination to be made of all the colleg behaviour synce the bigynning of the trobles and sent the fiscall of the visitation apostolicall to take the examination, who fynding many schollers obstinate and refuse to answer dyrectely was greatly offended and informed the pope therof. And he commanded hym to procede *omnibus iuris viis*,[526] to wit by torture, if they would not answer, and so at last the[y] resolved to confesse and more hath byn confessed in the house then I would have wished had byn, wherupon this day six hath byn dismissed by the popes expresse order, to wit Father Troloppe, Father Wolly, Fathers Jackson, Foster, Askeu, Lober, but yet with good letters patentes to Dr Barret to be receaved in Doway.[527] They are departed hence with m[uch] edification of all as you may see by the copye of my letter that I wrote by them to Dr Barret which I sende you heerwith. They do have apparel and good *viaticum* and so depart contented. Some other I f[ear] are lyke to follow, ether to Flanders or to Spayne or to both, yet shall I do what I can to retayne the frends of yours that you commended heer to me, only [I] dout me that Powell will be sent away; the rest I hope be safe for the present if they behave [them] selves well for the tyme to come. And with this [I] bydde you farewell for this tyme with my hartiest [commend]ations. Rome, this 18 of October 1597.

    Yours ever

        Robert Persons.

[PS] Many matters of taverns are confessed agaynst Father Tempest,[528] Father Hill and Father Benson, which is the cause that I am forced to retayne my letters to Father Tempest untill some cloudes be cleared, and so you may tell hym from me, I had his letter from Millan.

    [*Addressed:*] To the Rev[ent] and verie lovinge fathers, father Edward and Jhon Benet.
    [*Endorsed:*] Father Parsons.

---

    525. For John Middleton and Francis Robinson (b. 1569); see Anstruther, 229–230, 293.
    526. With all the force of the law.
    527. See the letters to Vitelleschi and Barret drafted by Persons for the cardinals, on and around 14 October (B420–421).
    528. Tempest] *Hicks*; Test *MH*. On Tempest, Hill, and Benson, seminary priests who were travelling to England, see Caetani's letter to Frangipani, 12 October (B419). It is unknown whether Persons eventually sent his reply to Tempest, who settled with his brother in Douai (Kenny, "Inglorious Revolution," 142 [part 3]).

B424 To Joseph Creswell, Rome, 12 November 1597

SOURCE: ACSA, Series II, Legajo 1, a contemporary copy = *Vd*.
HICKS: 752–755.
NOTE: Persons took office as rector of the English college at the beginning of November. Here he explains the new order of things: the various halls of residence and the appointment of Jesuits to take charge of study and devotion. Creswell, his assistant in Spain, was a former rector of the college in Rome.

The frequency of eccentric spelling errors ("maine" for "manie," "aine" for "anie," and "reaceue" for "receaue") suggests either a very careless scribe or one not familiar with English.

Taken out of a lettre of Father Persons to Father Creswell the 12th of November 1597, concerning the present estate of the Inglish Colledge in Rome.

Heare in the Colledg all things go passing well, and never so well perhaps, since it was first erected (and without perhapes it is soe) for all are exceeding quiet, mery and contented, and there is no memory of styrrs past, but only a generall detestation therof, for now by the contrayrie put in possession all see the inconveniences of the other,[529] as the losse of tyme, disquietnes, discredit and the like effects, and all do thanke God for the change.

Thes 9 or 10 that weare leaft of them, that had followed the waies of the others, are so well satisfied, as they be the most quiet, dillegent, merrie and contentted in the Colledg, and the formost to sett forward all kinde of discipline and good ordor.

The summe of the reformation consisted in few pointes, by order of His Holynes and the 2 Cardinals, butt are substantiall, to witt, cutting of from traffique with Inglish abroad in the Towne, and seperations of chambers at home, but yet both with convenient moderation, for any may take[530] upon just cause, and at home the chambers are so seperated, as 2 and 2 make recreation together, I meane chambers, and have there particuller Haule made readie to them for the same purpose, with a chimnye for the Wintter and preffectes (as also Vice preffectes) of there owne, and so the 2 chambers of our Ladie and the Apostles, have for ther chamber that wherin the minister last dwelt, to witt, nex the quier that adjoyneth to owr Ladies chamber. The Trinnitie chamber and St Michales, have for there recreation the great haule aboave. The chambers of St Edmond and St George have a perticuller Haule made for them verie faire and great, cut out of the highest gallerie or walking place over the great haule, and it is at thend therof next adjoyning to St Georges chamber, into which it hath a doore. The 2 chambers of St Albanes and St Edwards have there haule over the pointed Haule, there where the congregation was of our Ladie, which hath a chimnie and a new suffit[531] made very faire, and all the teste or covering is raysed 3 or 4 foot higher, and a doore opened into St Edwards chamber, so as it falleth out

---

529. other] *this ed.*; oath *Vd Hicks*
530. take] *Vd*; talke *conj. Hicks*
531. Ceiling.

exceeding commodious and faire, and by this meanes the recreationes are so much more plesant then before, for now they are 12 or fiften together only, or fewer, at a fyer, where there is better conversation then when they were so manie,[532] and our fathers have far better comoditie to goe and sitt amongst them and converse (as on or other doth often tymes and most confidentlie now) then before when they weare so manie.

The congregation surcreaseth[533] for a tyme and the schollers increase them selves no lesse in devotion, otherwise without ambition and contention who shall be officers. They attend to there studies with great ferver and have demaunded repetitors[534] of the Societie, and so have two vere well learned, for there Physiques and methaphisiques, and Father Henrie Tichborne (who assure[535] yow will prove a notable subiect) is prefect of the studyes and heareth the repeticions of Divinitie and logique, to save and spare one place the more. Father Thomas Owen is *confessarious*, a verie grave, learned and spirittuall man,[536] and hath brought in the orders of our meditationes of thos our Spanish seminaries, and all the house doe meditate dalie the selfe same point, and each prefect with his little bell calleth them togethers everie night and readeth the pointes for the morning, before they begin prayers, and warneth again with the same bell a little before the ending of the colloquium[537] or other some good[538] actuating of that they have meditated, and herwith yow will scarse beleeve how this house is altred upon a sudain to the better.

Everie man began presentlie to cut his longe beard, without order of any superiour, as also to lay asside all other signes of distinction or singularitie that were brought up. The preffectes and Vice preffectes have much more authoritie then before, and among other things to cheke and remove any eevill speech or language tending to inquietnes that may hapen in remotion[539] or other wise. The quietnes of the house is exceeding great, God be thanked. The modestie in[540] going through the street and there behavoure at the school is noted alredie to be of great edification, and this induring (as I hope it will) there is no doubt but we may recover our creditt again in short space and owr contrie receave[541] the comfort and helpe that shee expected and hath need out of this colledge.

The schollers that were sent away, departed with so good myndes as could not be wished better, and promised to show the same by workes in Flaunders, which yf they do,

532. so manie] *this ed.*; somaine *Vd*
533. To increase greatly (*OED*, s.v. surcrease, *v.* 1).
534. repetitors] *this ed.*; repitors *Vd Hicks*
535. who assure] *Vd*; who I assure *Hicks conj.*
536. Persons relied on Jesuits: Henry Tichborne, SJ (1570–1606; entered the Society 11 October 1587), remained at the college until 6 October, when he was sent to Madrid and then to the English college at Seville (McCoog, *English and Welsh Jesuits*, 314); Thomas Owens, SJ (1556–1618; entered the Society 13 April 1579), was later appointed rector (McCoog, *English and Welsh Jesuits*, 256)
537. colloquium] *Hicks*; colloqium *Vd*
538. good] *Hicks*; god *Vd*
539. remotion] *Vd*; recreation *conj. Hicks*. "Remotion" means the act of departing.
540. in] *Hicks*; in in *Vd*
541. receave] reaceue *Vd*; reaceve *Hicks*

they shall finde no want of good correspondence of us heere and where soever els, and I do little doubt of it, yf they yeeld not to the new batterie of some in Flaunders, worse affected then them selves, or at least not so much lightened with Gods grace, to see the inconveniencies of thes devisiones and[542] stryfe as thes men seemd to be at there departure, and I do hope they will so Continew.

The Pope is exceeding glad of this change and good successe, and is to conferme all presentlie with a new Bull and therin also to ad such furder orders as shalbe thought best (though few and good[543] and well kept like me best). After this of the spirituall is well setled I meane to sett uppon the Temporall, as well for[544] bringing the Colledg out of dept and, yf it may be, as also for putting good order about the expences, yf anie[545] redresse be to be made or any thing saved of that which now is spent, retaining styll that which is competent and convenient for the schollers, and this being donn I hope to be readie to retourne towards yow again, as greatlie I desire, for my hart is styll with yow. And thus much of the Colledge affaires heere.

[*Endorsed:*] Touchinge the English Colledge at Rome.

B425 From Charles Paget, Paris, 15 November 1597

SOURCE: Persons to Paget, 20 December (B409).

NOTE: Paget replied to Persons's letter of 20 September, brought to him by Edward Bennet. From Persons's reply of 20 December (B429), it seems clear that Paget had also learnt from Bennet about the strict measures now being applied to the students who were in sympathy with Paget's party (Persons to John Bennet, 18 October, B423). Paget expressed his disappointment about this, and complained about the hostility now being shown towards his party in Flanders.

B426 From Henry Garnet, London, 25 November 1597

SOURCES:
ARSI, Angl. 38/II, fol. 173r, Bartoli's partial Latin translation ($=A$);
Bartoli, *Inghilterra* (1667), 406, an Italian translation.
HICKS: Garnet, 448–449, Latin text with English translation.

NOTE: Although Bartoli identifies this as a letter to Persons, the Latin text is addressed to someone, presumably (as Hicks suggests) William Baldwin, who had recently returned to Rome from England (McCoog, *Building the Faith of St Peter*, 191–192, 292–293, 321–322). It is also not clear how much of Bartoli's text reflects the text of a letter, but it is likely that Garnet wrote to Persons and Baldwin at the same time, since Baldwin was now minister at the English college in Rome. The letter provides a picture of Jesuit life in England, as well as the hostility English Jesuits were facing from fellow-Catholics.

542. and] *suppl. Hicks; not in Vd*
543. good] *Hicks;* god *Vd*
544. for] *Vd;* as *Hicks*
545. anie] *Hicks;* aine *Vd*

Hic (inquit) nullus est aperte malevolus: quidquid est, in privatos fumos abiit, paucissimarum linguarum maledicarum, quas flocci facimus. Et confido eos iustam minime habituros occasionem querelarum. Audio tamen in Flandria dici dissidia inter nos esse, qua in re tu testis esse potes. Iidem enim omnino sumus quales nos reliquistis: et hoc tam brevi spatio simul omnes convenimus tribus diversis vicibus, viz. in festis Exaltationis Sanctae Crucis, Sancti Lucae et Praesentationis Beatae Virginis. Solus Holtbaeus abfuit ob necessaria quaedam negotia. Blondus receptus fuit ante Octavianum West, et modo tredecim sumus in missione praeter illos duos quos brevi asciscere statuo, &c.

[*Inghilterra*]
In tanto a'nostri Operai d'entro l'Inghilterra multiplicavasi ogni dia gran misura il che fare, e il che patire, e Iddio scambievolmente, per l'uno inviava loro nuovi Compagni a partecipare nelle fatiche, per l'altro invigoriva loro il cuore con nuovi spiriti, convenienti a quel grande animo, e a quella gran virtù, che si richiedeva a un così arduo ministero. Adunaronsi quest'anno tre volte in tre feste solenni, a spendere alquanti giorni in null' altro che rinfocarsi l'anima in Dio con molte hore d'oratione: rivedere i conti delle loro coscienze, e darli al superiore, ch'era il P. Garnetto; e rinnovar tutto insieme i loro spiriti, e i lor voti religiosi, com'è consueto fra noi. Non però tutti insieme ogni volta, per lo dovuto riguardo al possibile ad avvenire, che qualche vil traditore domestico li desse tutti a una rete presi in mano a'persecutori: ma divisamente, come giàcobbe in somigliante pericolo le sue gregge, e i suoi pastori: e così appunto ne scrive il Garnetto appropriando a sè le parole di quel Patriarca, *Si venerit Esau ad vnam turmam, & percusserit eam, alia turma quae reliqua est, saluabitur*. Tredici erano i Sacerdoti, oltre a gl'imprigionati, ma non perciò inutili, come vedremo ... e verso la fin dell'anno si aggiunse loro P. Oswaldo Tessimondo: e due provatissimi Sacerdoti, ch'erano su l'aggregarsi, e seguire il P. Riccardo Biondi, hora novitio di pochi mesi, poscia grand'huomo, primo provinciale, e secondo padre di quella già non più Missione, ma Provincia da se. Ma un che valeva per molti, e lor si aggiunse quest'anno, fu il P. Giovan Gerardi, rihavuto dalla Torre di Londra, e si può dir dalla morte, giuratagli dalla Reina: e qui si vuol raccontarne tutto seguentemente la presa, l'avuenutogli ne'tre anni che fu prigione, e l'arrischiato, ma felice riuscimento della fuga.

Translation

Here, he says, malice does not come out into the open: whatever there is smoulders away in private, from the speech of a very few detractors, whom we regard as of no account. And I trust that they will have no occasion for complaints at all. Nevertheless, I hear tell that in Flanders there are dissensions among us; you yourself can bear witness to this matter. For we ourselves are exactly as you left us, and even in this short space of time we have all met together on three separate occasions, that is, on the feasts of the Exaltation of the Holy Cross, St Luke, and the Presentation of the Blessed Virgin Mary.[546] Only Holtby was absent,

---

546. 14 September, 18 October, 21 November.

on account of some necessary business. Blount was received before Octavian West,[547] and so there are thirteen of us on the mission besides those two whom I have decided to admit shortly.

[from Bartoli's *Inghilterra*]
In the great work that we were doing in England, every day both action and suffering increased in great measure: and God in equal measure sent them, on the one hand, new companions to share their labours, and on the other invigorated them in the heart with new spirits, conducive to the great courage and great virtue which are needed in such an arduous ministry. They have convened three times this year, for the three solemn feasts, to spend some days doing nothing but rekindling their spirits in God with many hours of prayer, drawing up an account of their consciences, and giving it to their superior, that is, Fr Garnet; thus they renew their spirits entirely together, and they renew their religious vows, as is the custom among Ours. But they do not all gather at the same time because of the distinct possibility that some low traitor in the house might betray them into the hands of the pursuivants; instead, they meet in separate groups, as Jacob did in similar circumstances of danger – he divided his flocks and his shepherds; just so, Fr Garnet writes, taking for himself the words of the patriarch: *If Esau comes to one band, and smites it, the remaining group will be saved.* There were thirteen priests, besides those who were in prison (but not therefore redundant, as we shall see).[548] And towards the end of the year they were joined by Fr Oswald Tesimond and two highly experienced priests who were of his party, and there followed Fr Richard Blount, then a novice, afterwards a great man, the first provincial, and second father of what is now no longer a mission but a province. But one who was worth all the rest and joined us this year was Fr John Gerard, escaped from the Tower of London and, if I may say so, from death, certainly desired by the queen: and here we want to tell everything in order: torture, three years passed while he was in prison, and the risky but happy success of his escape.

B427 From Richard Barret, Douai, 1 December 1597

> SOURCE: BAV, MS Vat. Lat. 6227, fol. 88, a contemporary Italian abstract.
> EDITION: Renold, *Letters of Allen and Barret*, 272–273, with English translation.
> NOTE: Barret warns of a scheme, possibly instigated by Paget and William Gifford, to found an English college in Paris. He mentions Henry Constable and the bishop of Evreux as

---

547. In 1596 Blount appears to have been the first Englishman to be received into the Society on the mission itself. "Octavian West" could be a code name for Richard Banks, who entered the Society in England in 1597/1598 (Garnet to Persons, 23 April 1597, B368). Alternatively, this could refer to the departure of William Baldwin, who used the name Octavian. The text may be corrupt. See McCoog, *English and Welsh Jesuits*, 110 (Baldwin), 111 (Banks), and 122, 180 n31 (Blount).

548. McCoog, *Building the Faith of St Peter*, 321 n157, counts eleven out of prison – Garnet, Holtby, Oldcorne, Lister, Gerard, Jones, Bennet, Pullen, Collins, Stanney, Blount, and Tesimond – with Weston, Pounde, and Emerson in prison. Oswald Tesimond (ca. 1563–1636) entered the Society in 1584. He left Valladolid for England in November 1597 (Pollen, *Valladolid Registers*, xix). In what follows, some details are added retrospectively.

promoters of the plan. Both were concerned to conciliate Protestants: Constable was the author of *Examen pacifique de la doctrine des Huguenots* (1589), later translated as *The Catholike Moderator: Or a moderate examination of the doctrine of the Protestants; Proving against the too rigid Catholikes of these times, and against the arguments especially, of that booke called, The Answer to the Catholike Apologie, that we, who are members of the Catholike, Apostolike, and Roman Church, ought not to condemne the Protestants for heretikes, untill further proofe be made* (1623). In 1598 Constable seems to have been involved in a project to establish a seminary for English priests at Mignon College, University of Paris, although this did not eventuate. Persons wrote to him on 31 August 1598 about this and related matters. See George Wickes, "Henry Constable, Poet and Courtier (1562–1613)," *Biographical Studies* 2 (1954), 272–231, and John Bossy, "A Propos of Henry Constable," *Recusant History* 6 (April 1962): 228–237.

Jacques Davy du Perron (1556–1618), a convert who became bishop of Evreux and later a cardinal, debated with the Huguenot Philippe du Plessis-Mornay in front of King Henry IV in 1600. Persons reported on this conference in *A relation of the triall made before the King of France, upon the yeare 1600 betvveene the Bishop of Evreux, and the L. Plessis Mornay*, a work appended to the second volume of *A Treatise of three conversions of England* (Saint-Omer, 1603–1604).

> Capitulo d'una una lettera del Dottore Bareto Presidente del Collegio dell'Inglesi in Douaco de Fiandra scritta dell primo di Decembre 1597.

Ho visto una lettera da Parigi scritta a uno delli nostri sacerdoti di questo collegio, da parte del Senore Harrigo Conestabile Inglese, de chi ho scritto già per il passato, nella quale egli nel nome de Monsignore D'Ereux alias Perone, cerca de fare venire a Parigi, duo o tre delli nostri Dottori Inglesi, parte per agiutarli a fare un libro de controversie, et parte per fondare la, un seminario Inglese, dicendo ch'il Re ha dato per quell'effetti 12,000 scudi l'anno con concenzo del clero sopra le decime di Francia, li quali il Cardinale Legato ha preso l'assunto de farli pagare, et d'agiutare il negotio; Vostra Reverenza me dia il suo parere et conseglio, che cosa s'haverà da fare quà in quel negotio.

A me pare che quello seminario non sarà altro ch'un recettacolo di tutti quelli Inglesi che saranno nimici delli Spagnolli et delli padri della Compagnia di Giesù, et che sarà agiutato del Carlo Pageto, il Dottore Giffordo, et tutta quella fattione, gli quali senza dubio cercaranno de tirare a quelli bande quanti Inglesi essi[549] possono, et da Inghilterra, et forse anco da questi nostri collegii de qua, con speranza de maggiori commodità che non trovano qua, massimamente in questi tempi che la nostra pensione in Roma è cosi mal pagata, et però sarebbe bono far ogni bon officio in Roma per impedire il fondamento d'una tanta discordia et divisione che ne nasciarebbe tra li stessi Catolici Inglesi, del che l'heretici pigliaranno grand' piacere, et forse hanno parte in questo conseglio et trattato che per quel effetto si fà adesso in Francia.

549. essi] *Renold*; esi B

Translation

Summary of a letter from Dr Barret, president of the English
college in Douai, Flanders, written on 1 December 1597.

I have seen a letter from Paris written to one of our priests in this college, from an English gentleman, Henry Constable – of whom I have already written in the past – in which he attempts, in the name of the bishop of Evreux, also known as Perone, to entice two or three English doctors to come to Paris, partly to help him to produce a book of controversies, and partly to found an English college there, saying that the king has given 12,000 crowns a year for this purpose, with the consent of the clergy, to be levied on the tithes of France, which the cardinal legate has taken on himself the responsibility of ensuring that it is paid, for the support of the enterprise. Please would Your Reverence give me your advice and counsel on what to do here in this business.

It seems to me that such a seminary would be no more than a receptacle for all those Englishmen who are enemies of the Spanish and the fathers of the Society of Jesus, and that it would be supported by Charles Paget, Dr Gifford, and all that faction. They would undoubtedly try to tempt as many Englishmen as possible to those regions, both from England and perhaps even from these colleges of ours here, with the hope of greater convenience than they find here, especially in these times when our pension in Rome is as poorly paid as it is. Consequently, it would be well to do every good office in Rome to prevent the establishment of such great discord and division as would develop among those same English Catholics: from which the heretics would derive great satisfaction, and perhaps they have their part in this plan and in the negotiation that is taking place now in France for this purpose.

B428 From Henry Garnet, London, 3 December 1597

    SOURCES:
        ARSI, Angl. 38/II, fol. 172r–v;
        ABSI, Coll P II 549, Grene's note: "F. Garnet. 3 Xmbris 1597. A letter of two sheets of paper about the seditious."
    HICKS: Garnet, 450–451.
    NOTE: Garnet comments on opinion among the Catholic community in England, reporting that there is confusion about the authorship of *Conference about the Next Succession*, which was published under the pseudonym R. Doleman. On the Marian priest Alban Doleman (b. ca. 1530), see Renold, *Wisbech Stirs*, 30.

Quidam sacerdos Dominus Dolmannus ubique exclamat quod P. Personius illum summa iniuria affecerit, cum librum de successione nomine Roberti Dolmanni edidit, cum tamen ipse omnium iudicio praeterquam suo non adeo doctus sit. Et nomen ipsius sit Albanus non Robertus Dolmannus.

Translation

A certain priest, Mr Dolman, is protesting everywhere that Fr Persons has done him a great injury by publishing a book on the succession in the name of Robert Dolman; whereas, on the contrary, in the opinion of everyone but his own, he has not the learning for it. And his own name is Alban, not Robert, Dolman.

B429 To Charles Paget, Rome, 20 December 1597

> SOURCE: ABSI, Coll II P 452–455, an unsigned copy, endorsed on Coll P II 460 = G.
> HICKS: 757–769.
> EDITION: Knox, *Allen*, 391–394 (partial).
> NOTE: Persons responds to Paget's letter of 15 November (B425), explaining the firm line taken against the dissident students at the English college in Rome, on instructions from the pope (see Persons to John Bennet, 18 October, B423) and defending himself against Paget's outrage over the spreading of criticism of him and his party. He argues that it is unreasonable for Paget to demand, as the price of peace, that his critics retract every statement they have made about him, true or false.
> Persons reviews extensively all their dealings since the Paris conference of 1582, claiming that Paget has consistently reneged on the accords negotiated between them.
> For ease of reading, ampersands have been replaced by "and" throughout this letter.

Jesus.

Right worshipfull

I haue receaved your letter of the xvth of November in answere of myne of the xxthe of September sent you by Fa. Edward Benett, wherin you wryte, that you have understood by the relation of the said father, that by my modest and discreet dealinge heare, all those sturs of Rome have beene appeysed and ended. I am glad if any way my labours have beene profitable to peace, and union. Of modestie and discretion I can affirme nothinge, onlie I knowe there wanted no love, or desire to do them all good. And if since F. Bennetts departure hence His Holynesse hathe resolved him selfe to follow some more seveare course with some others for better remedie of this Colledge, and upon urgente occasion offred of certayne dysorders, yet hathe there not wanted in mee the same desire, nor endevour to procure them[550] moderacion that myght bee, the case standing as it did, and so I thinke the parties themselves interessed did easelie see, as also confesse at their departure, and now remaynethe the Colledge in most perfecte quietnesse, and good order, and so I doubt nott but it will continewe, if it may be permitted from abroad.

Touching the remnant of your letter, wherin you answere to the second parte of myne, and to that I remitted to F. Bennetts reports of the earneste desire I had to see you, and the rest of our nation at union also ther in Flanders, and elsewheare, your com-

---

550. them] *this ed.*; the *followed by* parties [*deleted*] *G*; the parties *Hicks*. In *G*, the next line contains the words "the parties."

playnte is verie vehement, sayinge that you fynd by experience daylie sundry discourses, libells, letters, and speaches divulged agaynste you, and other noble and gentlemen in Rome Spayne and there in Flanders, and delivered to His Holinesse, and to the kinge of Spayne and his ministers to dysgrace and defame you throughout the world and this by my complices or dependants, as namelie F. Holt, Sir Francis Inglefeild, Mr Owen, Rowland alias Vestegan and Banes with others,[551] and that in these reckoninges I am not thought free from suspicion to be an actor, howsoever I may seeme to cleare my self with protestations to the contrarie, and that your differences standinge in these tearmes, untill such as have unjustlie laboured to take away your honours and lives make you reparation, and that the uncharitable practises and informations to these endes be defaced, and publiquely pronounced as wronges, and injuries done unto you, ther is no hope of accord or unitie, no furder then charitie commaundethe. These are your wordes, wherby you seeme to make all union verie hard, if not impossible to be restored amongst you, wherby you greatlie afflicte my harte, and I would God you would but performe the laste clause by you mentioned, yealding to so much as charitie commaundeth, which is not to remitt[552] from the teeth outward (as some perhaps deceavinge themselves do practise) but *ex cordibus* (as Christe himselfe vouchsafed to explane for our instruction), and therfore howsoever men comment or paraphrase upon the matter now, the rigorous performance therof wilbe exacted on day at our handes. But to come to the matter ytself: thoughe by this absolute exclusion of peace or at least wayes by so manny hard and generall condicions sett downe for the same you discourage mee greatlie from further intermedlinge therin (neyther can so many generall and particular poynts of complaynte as you touche appertayninge to so many, partlie dead, partlie alive, be discussed within the compasse of a letter), yett to reduce your self if it be possible (of whom much dependeth no doubt in this poynt) to some more temperate apprehension of the matter, mee thinke yt were convenient to distinguishe your case from those other noble and gentlemen, whom alwayes you, and some other more nearer conjoyned unto you (as namelie Mr Morgane and Mr D. Gifford in all their wrytinges[553]) do name as partakers of all your affayres, under the title of the Englishe Catholike nobilitie and gentry; wheras in my opinion, and of moste indifferent men els, ther case standethe farr otherwise then yours for making of this union. For first touchinge that[554] one nobleman, whose name of late you so much use about the world, I meane the right honorable Earle of Westmerland (for as for the other the Lord Dacres,[555] I have hytherto hard little complaynt of him against such men as you accuse, and no great connection of his with you) it is a matter evident that albeit the said Earle, and some other gentlemen of worshippe there have taken some unkyndnesse ther of later yeares agaynste some particular persons, and namlie agaynste the two persons by you named Mr Owen and Fr Holt, and have byne content to joyne with you in certayne memorialls, and letters agaynste them at your instigation especial-

551. William Holt, Sir Francis Englefield (now deceased), Hugh Owen, Richard Rowlands Verstegan, and Roger Baynes.
552. remitt] *Hicks; G obscure*
553. Thomas Morgan and William Gifford.
554. that] *interlined with caret G*
555. Francis Lord Dacre (Acquaviva to Persons, 22 January 1590, B48).

lie, as many wayes doth appeare, yet do I not thinke that these aversions are either so great, so rooted, or yet founded upon the same causes altogeather agaynste the same men as yours are, and much lesse agaynste other men abroad, whom partlie you name, and partlie I could name, that seeme to stand in farr different termes with them and with you concerninge this poynt, and this as they thinke upon no small reason. For first all Englishe men knowe that those aversions, and dysagreementes of yours are no new thinges, but of many years,[556] and both begonne, and continued upon further groundes, then the late disgustes of those noble and gentlemen, whom now you seeke to drawe into the participation of all your actions. For you will remember your selfe that about xiiij[teene] years agoe, when you and I dealt togeather first in the cytie of Roan in Fraunce you shewed your self no lesse disgusted then now, when yet neyther Fr Holt nor Mr Owen were neare you, or gave you any molestation, but that then all your complaynt was agaynst preistes in generall and agaynst Mr Doctour Allen (after Cardinall) in particular and by name, about whom you and I had longe disputes why hee or other preistes or[557] religious men should meddle in publique matters of our countrie and not you gentlemen, meaninge your self and Mr Morgan, for that other gentlemen of worshipp then present in Fraunce, as Mr Charles Arundell, Mr William Tressam, Mr Thomas Fitzherbert, Mr Fulgiam, Mr James Hill, Mr Hopkinges, Mr Tempeste,[558] and others complayned not of that poynt, but tooke rather part agaynste you in that verie quarrell which you endevred to rayse betweene gentlemen and preistes, repeatinge often (as I well remember) why preistes did not meddle with their breviaries onlie, and the like. And I answeringe you, that if preistes besides ther breviaries, or with ther breviaries, or by ther creditt in Catholike princes courtes where breviarie men were esteemed, could holpe, and assiste, and serve you gentlemen also towards the reduction of our countrey, why should not you be content to use ther labours to your and the publique commoditie without emulation? Upon this you can not but remember also how carefull Mr D. Allen and I did endeavour at that tyme to yeald satisfaction both to my Lord Paggett,[559] your brother, then newlie come over, and to your self and to Mr Morgayne, makinge a jorney of purpose for that cause to Paris, and lyinge in your owne house and impartinge all our affares and secretts with you, and how you brake from us agayne by your secrett sendinge of D. Parry into England without our knowledge,

556. Knox begins his edition with this sentence, "For first all Englishe men knowe that those aversions, and dysagreementes of yours are no new thinges, but of many years," and continues, "For you will remember ... " below.

557. or] interlined with caret G

558. Tempeste] this ed.; G obscure; Timstead Hicks. These lay exiles can tentatively be identified as Charles Arundel, William Tresham, Thomas Fitzherbert, Godfrey Foljambe or Fuljambe, James Hill, Richard Hopkins, and Robert Tempest. For Fitzherbert and Hopkins see the headnote to Persons's letter to an unidentified addressee, 7 November 1590, B85; for Foljambe, see A202 and Pollen, ed., *Mary Queen of Scots*, 7–8. Robert Tempest, who handled correspondence for the exiles, is mentioned by Katy Gibbons, *English Catholic Exiles in Late Sixteenth-Century Paris* (Woodbridge, Suffolk, 2011), 70. This may be Edward Tempest's brother, living in Douai (Kenny, "Inglorious Revolution," 141 [part 3]).

559. Thomas, fourth Lord Paget (A17).

though wee were present;[560] which Parry revealed all (as the world knowethe) and more unto the Queene (though, as I presume, not by your wills or commission in this poynt) and yeat how after this wee made a newe composition and attonement agayne with you in the same Citie of Paris, wher it was concluded that you should goe to Ingland and I to Rome, and that this league[561] was broken agayne by you, and not by us, upon the defeat of all the designements, by that your jorney, and especiallie upon the relation and othe of Mr Wattes, the preiste, who bothe affirmed to the Duke of Guise, to F. Claudius Matheus his confessor,[562] D. Allen and to my self that you had told him in secrett at the seas syde, when you weare to embarke, that you ment in England to overthrowe all our endeavours, and so the effect shewed;[563] and yett you knowe that notwithstandinge all this our desires of peace and union were so great that in the yeare 86, a little before our goinge to Rome togeather,[564] Mr D. Allen and I made a third accord with you and Mr Morgan and desired the continuance of that same, as amonge others Mr Ligons,[565] which was the last man which brought us in our way from the Spaw, can partlie testifie with what myndes we departed in this behalfe, whom wee desired to do his best also to the same effecte with you in Flaunders after our departure.[566] But wee beenge in Rome, you can not forgett how you and your freinds continewed your treatys with Salomon Aldred, that came in and out from England to Paris from the counsaile and professed him self oppositt to our proceadinges.[567] The sendinge also into England of Ballard and Savage without our privities or ever wrytinge one sillable therof unto us, thoughe the one were a preiste, therby subjecte to D. Allen.[568] Afterwardes in licke manner your dealinges with Guilbert Gifford and Grattley, other two preists, were kept secrett from us, as also thear treaties in England with the enemie, their wrytinge of two infamous bookes agaynste D. Allen, Jesuits and Spaniardes,[569] wherof insued the generall and particular hurtes that all men knowe, those matters (I say) and others like passed in Paris amonge you and your secrett freindes alone without any knowledge of ours, or rather any participacion (I dare say) of any of those noble and gentlemen that now you name, participant of your affayrs and disagreements agaynste us.

560. On Thomas Morgan's dealings with Parry, see Leo Hicks, *An Elizabethan Problem: Some Aspects of the Careers of Two Exile-Adventurers* (London, 1964), 61–70; Alford, 139–151.

561. league] *Knox*; leauge G

562. Claude Matthieu, SJ (1537–1587).

563. On Paget's secret mission to England in 1583, see Peter Holmes, "Paget, Charles" (*ODNB*). On William Watts (ca. 1550–1583), a secular priest whom Persons had sent to Scotland in 1581, see vol. 1: 201–234. Claude Matthieu, SJ, former French provincial, was Guise's confessor.

564. In fact, Persons met Allen, who was gravely ill, at Spa in August 1585, and they travelled to Rome from there together, arriving in November (Edwards, 119–121).

565. Ralph Liggons, an agent of Mary Stuart; see Gibbons, *English Catholic Exiles*, 155–156.

566. after our departure] *interlined with caret* G

567. Solomon Aldred was a spy in Walsingham's employ in Rome, an associate of Gilbert Gifford and Edward Grately.

568. For John Ballard, priest, and John Savage, see Pollen, ed., *Mary Queen of Scots*, and Anstruther, 19–20.

569. On Gifford and Grately, see vol. 1: 684–701.

And after this agayne the seditious proceadinge of Mr Morgan, as appeareth by his letters to the Bishopp of Dumblayne the yeare 89, and of the prior Arnold in Spayne agaynst our Lord Cardinall,[570] as is evident by the priors owne letters to the said Morgayne in the same yeare, wherof you could not be ignorant, or at leastwise cannot be so presumed in reason, your intrinsecall conjunction with them beeinge such as it was: which dealinge my Lord Cardinall in his letters to your self yett extant in the yeare 91 affirmeth playnlie to be traytorous to the publique cause.[571]

And after all this agayne the last dealinges now for these two, or three years about the broyles of this Colledge, which have brought forth so great scandall, and losse of creditt to our nation, both ther and in other Nations, and the particular hurtes, or ruynes of so many towardlie youthes as otherwise might have lived quitt, and contentedlie, and proved excellent instrumentes for the good of our countrie, in all which breaches, and notorious iniuries offred therin to the fathers of our Societie for all their love and good works done unto us for so many years, it is well knowen that the chief blowinge of these coales came from Flaunders, and from such as are, and were, most intrinsecall with you, and from whose actions no man of iudgment can deame you to be alienate or ignorant, as they may and doe these other noble and gentlemen whom you make partakers of your disgustes at this present.

And last of all, when all matters were ended, and made upp heare in Rome this last somer, and as well your self, and as others your said frendes had signified your content therof hyther by their letters, you and they beganne a new breache agayne in September last by gevinge up a most slaunderous memoriall ther to the Nuncio, and requestinge him to send yt to Rome to the Cardinall Aldobrandino with his particular commendacions,[572] to the end it might fynd creditt with His Holynesse agaynst both our poore fathers in England (who daylie, and howerlie adventure their lives for Godes cause, whylest others live wastelinge[573] and wranglinge heare) and agaynst the rest of the Soci-

---

570. William Chisholm (1525/6–1593), bishop of Dunblane in Scotland and termed administrator of Vaison, near Avignon, resigned his offices in 1584 to enter the Carthusian order; John Arnold was prior of the English Carthusians in Flanders. As associates of Owen Lewis, they collaborated in attempts to turn Philip II against Allen and Persons and to promote the cause of Lewis's advancement to the cardinalate: Arnold travelled to Spain for this purpose in 1589. Chisholm took part in an abortive mission to James VI of Scotland in 1587–1588, arranged by Pope Sixtus V and Lewis, among others, to try to interest the king in collaborating with Spain to oust the queen of England and restore Catholicism. Chisholm subsequently corresponded with Morgan about a plan to persuade the duke of Savoy to approach the duke of Parma about a possible appointment as governor of the Spanish Netherlands, some time before Morgan's arrest in 1590. See Hicks, *Elizabethan Problem*, 13–14 n37, 73 n221, 79, 84 n243, 85 n245, 137; Yellowlees, 112–114; Mark Dilworth, "Chisholm, William" (*ODNB*); Persons, *A Briefe Apologie or Defence of the Catholike Ecclesiastical Hierarchie* (Antwerp, 1601), fols. 32–33; Knox, *Allen*, 322–323 and 394.

571. See Allen to Paget, 4 January 1591, in Knox, *Allen*, 319. Knox's text of Persons's letter ends here, adding only the salutation at the end.

572. See Persons to Fitzherbert, 27 September 1597 (B411).

573. wastelinge] *Hicks; G obscure, possibly* wrastelinge

etie, to whom yett you professe yourself a great frend whyle you impugne them, and the like do those that are joyned with you in this action, who are not those noble and gentlemen, which you name, if I and others be not deceaved, and I beleeve they will disclame the same, each one of them if they shalbe asked.

Wherfore seeinge it appeareth, that you and such few others as are conjoyned with you in these attempts, etc. and have beene for many yeares do make shew to have resolution to followe these devisions still, I do not marvayle yf you make the conditions of peace so hard, and impossible, for havinge given so great occasion, and ample matter of these discourses, libells and speaches as you mention (if any such have beene) by all these your actions of contradictions for so many years, and others that I name not, it is a hard matter, or rather impossible to have all recalld, anulld and condemned for injurious as you now require, excepte you could make that your said past proceedinges should not have beene, as you can not. Wherfore the onlie way of frendshipp and union agayne (if any bee) is to amende those[574] occasions geven of your parte for the tyme to come, and then will easelie cease those discourses letters and the like, and all men will bothe wryte, and speake as they shall fynd your actions, neyther yett do I goe about to defend or allowe any mans wrytinge or speakinge of yow other wise then becometh, howsoever unfrendlie your owne doinges and speaches may[575] have beene, but onlie I would say that so longe as you are apprehended to be so oppositt to the common course of other mens proceedinges as you are, whose works do shewe that they[576] seeke to promote the common good of Godes cause, and our countrey, they can never want discourses, letters, yea storyes agaynste you and all such as do followe that course, which will remayne not onlie for the present, but also for the posteritie. And the onlie means to avoyd this, and remedie that is past were to ioyne agayne[577] with[578] the bodie of all good Catholike Inglishe both at home and abroad, and to runne unitedlie one and the self same course with them for the reduction of our countrey. And to this I offer my self to serve you, and all yours in all hartie, and dewtifull affection, and I doubt not but all the other noble and gentlemen whom you signified to joyne with you they would joyne most willinglie alsoe in this if you will do your endevour; and this were moste honorable and profitable for all. And if all will not see it or yeald therunto, yett I wishe they did, which have a feelinge of Godes feare, and do consider the strayte obligation of charitie mentioned before. And this is all I can say of this matter, and all that I thinke to be factible when it cometh to the exequution. I meane to forgett and forgive all past, and to unite our selves for the tyme to come, and one to beare the infirmities of the other: for to undoe that which is done, or recall that is past, or to qualifye matters, or speaches with new censures now I take it impossible, seeinge everie man lightlie is bent to defend his owne, and therfore (good Mr Pagett) if you may wynne so much of your self, take this sec-

    574. those] these *Hicks; G obscure*
    575. may] *interlined with caret G*
    576. they] *interlined with caret G*
    577. agayne] *interlined with caret G*
    578. with] *followed by* all, *apparently deleted G*

ond way of attonment, and you shall see that all wilbe well agayne, and if not, God seethe my desire hearin, and so do you also for I speake from my hart, and with this consolation I remayne, and committ you and all to Godes holie providence and protection. From Rome this XXth of December 1597.

[*Endorsed:*] the coppie of f. Persons letter to m[r] Ch. Paget 20 10[bris] 1597.

Appendix A: Memorials and Memoranda, 1597

On his return to Rome in 1597, Persons composed several memorials for the attention of the Spanish court and the papal curia. As these are documents rather than letters, and deal with similar topics in similar ways, they are gathered here for ease of reference.

BA 1 Memorandum on the State of English Affairs, Rome, 13 August 1597

SOURCE: BAV, MS Vat. Lat. 6227, fols. 7–21.

HICKS: One section only, "de los remedios," has been transcribed in a separately paginated section following p. 1177 (pp. 7–12).

NOTE: Persons drew up this memorandum in consultation with Peña to elaborate on matters discussed with the Spanish ambassador on 11 August (Persons's first letter to Peña, 12 August 1597, B393). His proposal for a council to be set up in Brussels to manage English affairs may have been partly prompted by Thomas Morgan's scheme to have Jane Dormer transferred to Brussels to lead the English exiles and support his party (Loomie, *Spanish Elizabethans*, 113–118). The proposal is canvassed at greater length in a memorandum for Idiáquez, August 1596.

Para la conservaçion i buen progresso de las cosas de Inglaterra se an de considerar tres puntos, el primero cerca del estado presente en que hallan asi en respeto de la religion como del estado temporal; el segundo cerca de los peligros y dificultades que se offrecen si no acude en tiempo con el remedio; el tercero cerca de los remedios efficaces que se pueden i parece que se deven tomar para assegurar la religion en aquel Reyno, i pretension de la Señora Infanta de España a la succession dél.

Del estado presente

1. En lo tocante al estado presente de la Religion en el dicho reino considerados los medios que se an tomado de los seminarios que se an erigido fuera dél, en diversas partes, y de los sacerdotes principalmente Jesuitas que alla se an embiado, y cada dia se embian pareçe averse puesto de manera que si se acude con la diligençia que se espera, no se puede ya perder, por ser los Catholicos dentro del Reino declarados i ocultos más en número que los hereticos, y esta es comun opinion y pareçer de hombres prudentes, y discretos no solo Catholicos pero tambien hereges, segun se a entendido por cartas que los meses atras se an recebido de diferentes partes.

2. Cerca del estado temporal por las mesmas vias se a tenido aviso que anda turbado, porque los hereges universalmente estan con mucho cuidado i descontento, parte por la hambre contina que los aprieta, parte por los gastos excesivos de la guerra i armadas, por donde muchos del pueblo andan tristes i descontentos, i principalmente por el temor de lo que puede suceder, viendo la Reina tan adelante en sus dias, y sin sucesion que esto los altera mucho, i mucho más crece la turbaçion, viendo i entendiendo el mucho número de los pretensores en la sucesion, y la incertidumbre del que a con efeto de suceder, i esta turbaçion o confusion a ido i va creciendo cada dia más despues que en aquel Reino pareçio el libro escrito i estampado sobre la sucesion: el qual aviendo sido leido con mucho deseo en causa tan ardua, en que cada qual pretiende tener parte, a impreso en los entendimientos de aquella naçion diversas opiniones i concetos, i grandes dificultades a las quales ellos no saben satisfaçer.

3. Y por la causa arriba dicha pareçe que lo tocante a la pretension de la Señora infanta se va encaminando bien, no solamente por lo que trata el dicho libro de la sucesion en el fin de la segunda parte, a donde aunque no se resuelva cosa firme en su favor se traen grandes conviniençias de que esto estaria bien a aquella Corona pero tambien por otros papeles que se an embiado alla de personas prinçipales particulares de la mesma naçion, como del Cardinal Alano, Francisco Indelfildo, i ultimamente del Padre Personio, cuio breve discurso sobre esta pretension que va con este despacho en el papel sinado A,[1] aviendo visto Su Santidad quedó tan satisfecho que dixo ser esto lo que más convenia, i lo proprio afirmaron despues los dos Cardenales sobrinos diziendo, que esto convenia a toda la Christiandad, i particularmente al Rei de Françia, i que las razones son tan claras i evidentes, que ellos se atreverian a persuadirlos al dicho Rei si se hallasen con él.

Lo que no es poco de considerar, viendo la mala impresion que en contrario avia engendrado un sumario falso sacado del dicho libro por Pageto, Giffordo, i otros Ingleses de la facion escoçesa en Flandes, el qual presentó Monsegnor Malvasia quando bolvio de Flandes a Su Santidad i a los sobrinos i a algunos otros prinçipes de Italia, añadiendo muchos discursos suios contra el dicho libro en favor del Rei de Scoçia segun que él mesmo a dicho a muchos confidentes suios, i en particular al agente del Duque de Memoransi, al qual siendo su grande amigo, i procurando por su medio sacar de mano del dicho Malvesia el dicho libro, Malvesia respondio que de ninguna manera podia mostrarlo porque no se viessen dichos discursos que estavan juntamente con aquel sumario.

4. En quanto al Rei de Scoçia, pareçe que Su Santidad i los sobrinos estan desengañados, no solamente por las muchas i eficaces razones que les a representado el Padre Personio, i en particular por averse declarado por cabeça de la iglesia de Scoçia a imitacion de la Reina de Inglaterra, pero tambien por los muchos i continos avisos que vienen de alla de su mal proceder, i en particular por aver obligado los tres principales Condes, que los años passados se declararon Catholicos, a abjurar la Religion so pena de perder sus estados, para dar contento a sus ministros hereges que lo pedian, por lo qual sus mismos confidentes, i partiales asi Ingleses como Escoçeses en Flandes an començado de

---

1. [*marginal note:*] no va porque a dias se a enviado

perder las speranças que tenian de su conversion, i particularmente el Padre Criton Scoces grande defensor i fautor suio, el qual estos dias atras escrivio una carta a 27 de Junio 1597 al Padre Personio confessandole en secreto que no avia más esperanças del dicho Rei, i otros de la misma façion no esperando más en él, escriven que toda la confiança se haze en la conversion del Principe su hijo, o de su muger del Rei, i que con estas esperanças mientras pudieren se iran entreteniendo sus partiales contra la pretension de la Señora Infanta.

5. Cerca de los Ingleses Catholicos que se hallan fuera de Inglaterra en Flandes que seran de quatrozientos a 500 i en España que seran más de 150, i en Roma que seran pocos menos de 100, es cosa çierta que todos estan concordes y se conforman en la pretension de la Señora Infanta, sacados quinze o veinte tentados que son de la façion Escocesa en Flandes, i veinte ocho studiantes amotinados en el Colegio de Roma, los quales estan unidos, i en grande parte dependen de los de Flandes, con los quales tienen ordinaria correspondençia, i hazen profesion de ser contrarios a las cosas de España, i por cartas de los confidentes de España arriba dichos que estan en Flandes, i por las que scriven algunos padres principales i prudentes que estan en Inglaterra, se entiende que todos los Catholicos de aquel Reino tienen el mesmo desseo fuera de algunos que los meses atras, o por negoçiaçion de los contrarios que estan en Flandes, o de otros sacerdotes i legos que con consentimiento del Cardinal Toledo fueron embiados de Roma a Inglaterra para el mesmo efeto, se an apartado de aquel buen proposito, que antes tenian, i avian profesado o, a lo menos se an resfriado mucho, o, hecho neutrales colgando solamente de lo que suçediere: de donde se asoman grandes peligros de alteraçiones i mudanças come se dize en el Capitulo siguiente.

De los peligros i dificultades que se ofrecen

Los peligros que se assoman son muy grandes, i tales que si no se provee de remedio, facilmente se puede temer que o la religion en aquel reino se irá perdiendo i faltando, o se pondra en tal estado de diminucion, que con dificultad se podra restituir en el estado que oi se halla, y particularmente las cosas tocantes al servicio de Su Magestad i a la pretension de la Señora Infanta recebiran grandissimo daño, como se verá por las cosas siguientes.

1. Estos peligros que se diran tomaron su principio de las divisiones que entre los de la nacion Inglesa se començaron en Flandes el año 1582 quando Pageto, Morgano, i sus sequaces se apartaron de los demas, los quales siempre an ido creciendo dividiendose los Ingleses Catholicos en todas partes en dos faciones, que la una sigue a España, la otra el Rei de Scocia, i reina de Inglaterra, a lo menos en las cosas que abaxo se diran.

En el Colegio Romano de los Ingleses vinieron los studiantes que alli estan por esta causa en tanto rompimiento, i tan grande cisma, que quando vino el Padre Personio, por el mes de Março deste año 1597 casi perdio las speranças de poderlos reconciliar, i hechas grandes diligençias para entender en qué se fundavan los que siguen la facion contraria a España, halló la verdadera causa, la qual a cundido i cunde tanto oi en Inglaterra, que se puede recelar mucho que produzira mui malos efetos, si no se acude con el remedio, porque so color de defender la libertad de la patria da mucho lugar a todo lo que es contrario a la conservaçion de la religion, pues de aquella raiz, deriva i saca esta facion tres ramos, o, proposiçiones: la primera es afirmar que se puede i deve obedeçer a la reina en todo lo que no es contra la religion.

La segunda que se pueden i deven opugnar todos los que van contra el estado temporal de aquel reino, como dizen ellos que son los Españoles i Jesuitas sus aderentes, cuio fin es invadirles i quitarles su natural y patria libertad.

La terçera que se puede i deve obedeçer a la reina en todo lo tocante al estado i govierno temporal i politico.

Y por estas causas pretenden estos del colegio Romano (como dellos mesmos se a entendido) unirse con la Reina i con los hereges en todo lo que no es professar heregia, i especialmente en tres cosas:

La primera en oponerse a la grandeza de España, i qualquiera pretension suia en Inglaterra.

La segunda, oponerse a los Jesuitas Ingleses de la Compañia que (segun ellos dizen) estan confederados con los Españoles para sugetar la patria, i hazerlos señores della so pretesto de religion.

La terçera, oponerse a todos los demas Catholicos y sacerdotes que en alguna manera impugnan el estado temporal de aquella Reina, i prometen a sus parciales, que con estas tres cosas biviran en Inglaterra sin persecuçion i peligro ninguno, antes recebiran favores a lo menos secretos de la Reina, i de su Consejo: i con el tiempo tambien alcançarán libertad en su religion para todos los Catholicos que querran seguir este camino, i finalmente despues de la muerte de la Reina se vendra a levantar un Rei o Reina natural o a lo menos que sea de la mesma Isla (por no escluir al Rei de Scocia si les estuviere bien) y por consiguiente sin daño de la religion quedará del todo excluido el Rei de España i la Infanta su hija.

Y por pareçer este lenguaje en lo esterior tan justificado i aplausible, trae tras sí muchos, y se puede temer que con el tiempo irá atraiendo muchos más, si no se ataja como pareçe que se puede atejar con los remedios que abaxo se apuntarán.

2. Y aunque con las pláticas que el Padre Personio les hizo persuadidos de las bivas razones con que les abló, mostraron quedar confundidos i bien reduzidos, todavia despues de algunos meses, se an buelto a declarar i affirman que eceto en lo tocante a la religion, en lo demas en toda ocasion estaran firmes en su primero proposito, i haran quanto les fuere possible contra los Españoles y Gesuitas sus aderentes, para procurar que no entren ni se apoderen de aquel reino ni de alguna parte dél. I pocos dias a que dos o tres dellos hablando con mucha passion contra el libro de la sucession (no obstante que saben que Su Santidad lo a visto i aprovado) dixeron con palabras mui indecentes que mereçia el autor ser castigado asperamente; de donde se colige, que ellos an tomado nuevos brios, parte por lo que an entendido por cartas de sus aderentes de Flandes, y parte por lo que por diversas vias an sabido que pasa en Inglaterra cerca de çiertas congregaciones o cofadrias de sacerdotes que alli se an començado este año presente de 1597.

3. A estas congregaciones o cofadrias se entiende que dieron ocasion, parte algunos sacerdotes descontentos de Inglaterra i parte algunas personas que fueron de Roma al mesmo reino, con consentimiento i inteligencia del Cardinal Toledo despues de començadas las diferençias i turbationes del Colegio Romano, el uno era Cavallero lla-

mado Griffidio Marcamo cuio padre sirve a la reina en su corte, el qual despues de preso y librado de la Inquisision de Perosa en Italia, vino a Roma donde Toledo i el obispo Casano le hizieron muchos favores i despues se fue a Inglaterra dexando un hermano llamado Roberto Marcamo[2] en Roma, el qual antes avia sido principal cabeça de los sediciosos en el colegio, i agora que está fuera dél recibe su sustento de Inglaterra por via de su hermano y pretende ser comendador de Malta y trata continuamente con los dos Sicilios que estan en Florentia, nietos del Thesorero Sicilio de Inglaterra.

I deste que fue a Inglaterra se entiende que a hecho i haze mui malos offiçios en ella, porque se sabe que un Secretario de la Reina llamado Wade dixo los dias passados a un Catholico que está en prision baxo su custodia que avia trenta sacerdotes en Roma los quales estavan determinados de unirse con ellos contra los Españoles i Jesuitas, i se cree que los estudiantes sediçiosos del Colegio Romano reciben los avisos de Inglaterra, parte por esta via destos dos Marcamos, i parte por medio de otro cavallero que reside en Roma llamado Nicolas Fizharberto el qual tiene un hermano muy perverso i enemigo de Catholicos en Londres con el qual tiene continua correspondencia, aviendo este Nicolas seguido siempre en Roma las partes de los sediciosos, i sido grande fautor dellos.

4. Otros quatro se embiaron de Roma a Inglaterra con el mismo intento, dos de los quales llamados Hatono i Fishero aunque legos eran mui perniciosos i atrevidos, como lo an mostrado en las obras, assi en Roma antes de partir como en Inglaterra con las grandes mentiras que an sembrado. Los otros dos llamados Botono i Noricio eran sacerdotes, a los quales aunque el Señor Cardenal Archiduque avisado por el Duque de Sessa de sus malos intentos nego el pasaporte para Inglaterra, todavia despues de aver sido muy regalados i animados por Pagetto i GifFordo, i otros de la façion Escocesa en Flandes, con el favor destos por otro camino entraron en Inglaterra con los quales despues juntandose Guilielmo Saceverelo fraile de Santo Domingo Inglés el qual por sus delitos huió de Italia, an hecho malos ofiçios en Inglaterra acrecentando la division de los faciosos, i dando grande ocasion a las dichas congregaciones o cofadrias començados por los sacerdotes arriba dichos, los quales ellos an traido a su façion, i les dan mucho calor y aliento, por donde estos estudiantes de Roma de nuevo an cobrado grande brio.

5. Y aunque por estas congregaciones en aparencia esterior los autores dellos no muestran pretender otra cosa que piedad i devocion i subordinacion entre sí por tratarse en ellas lo que se vee por las reglas que se embian en el papel sinado B. Todavia si passan adelante se teme que dellas naceran grandes inconvenientes, lo primero porque con ocasion de las Juntas que se harán conforme a sus reglas como pareçe por el tenor dellas, los Catholicos que oi estan ocultos se descubriran a los hereges con gravissimo daño de los dichos Catholicos i cosas suias: i lo segundo porque meteran discordia, i sembrarán Zizania entre los sacerdotes i legos por las gravezas i coletas que se les impone segun las dichas reglas, como se manifiesta en el dicho papel: y finalmente por entenderse por confesion de algunos de los mismos autores que esta invencion de Congregaciones va encaminada a fin de derribar i aniquilar los sacerdotes Gesuitas ocultos que estan en Inglaterra administrando alli los sacramentos, i que su intento es el proprio que tienen los estudiantes del Colegio Inglés de Roma de contradezir i oponerse a los Españoles, i padres de la Com-

---

2. Marcamo] *this ed.*; Mareamo *B*

pañia: por donde verisimilmente se sospecha que todo o gran parte de aquello pasa con alguna sabiduria de la Reina i de su Consejo, pues tambien se sabe que los sobredichos Griffidio, Saceverelo, i algunos otros an tenido plática secreta con el dicho Consejo.

    6. A los peligros arriba dichos se añade el grande inconveniente que nacera de la ida de nueve, o, diez sacerdotes Ingleses, que este año 1597, por el mes de Setiembre partiran deste Colegio de Roma, de los quales los seis o los siete son de ingenios turbulentos, i muy estraordinarios enemigos de las cosas de España, i no poco exercitados en mover rebueltas i cismas por la plática que en Roma en estos tres años de tumultos an tenido en ella, los quales pasando por Flandes donde seran más informados i encendidos por los sediciosos Ingleses que alli se hallan, llegados a Inglaterra sin duda causarán grandes daños i acrecentarán mucho los peligros arriba dichos, poniendo en grande contingencia el buen progresso de la religion i desbaratando todo quanto se a procurado hasta aqui en caminar tambien al servicio de Su Magestad i de la Señora Infanta: i tanto más porque se entiende que por cartas de los de Flandes, sus aderentes que aqui se an visto se les advierte que se hagan dotores para más autorizarse: i ellos tambien van persuadidos que en Roma tienen grande número de fautores personas de los más principales que en secreto los favorecen: con lo qual sin duda harán grande impression en los animos de muchos, añadiendose a esto el libro que estos meses atras se a publicado por toda Inglaterra escrito como se entiende por uno de los Ingleses descontentos que estavan en Flandes llamado Lauchenero, el qual retirandose en Inglaterra con acuerdo del Consejo de la Reina escrivio este libro, cuio titulo es, de las miserias, despreçios i agravios que padeçen los fugitivos de Inglaterra, del Rei de España, i de sus ministros: en el qual se dizen tantas maldades que bastan para causar aborrecimiento de toda la naçion Española i aversion al Serviçio de Su Magestad.

    7. Por todas estas causas, i por lo que se sabe que en Inglaterra i en otras partes se hazen continuas pláticas por parte del Rei de Scocia, i de otros pretensores particularmente despues de aver descubierto la grande pretension que con razon puede tener la Señora Infanta a aquella Corona, y porque la façion y vando de los sediciosos i contrarios va creciendo, i cobrando más fuerças cada dia, la qual es más peligrosa por salir de los que son tenidos i reputados por Catholicos y algunos dellos stipendiados de Su Magestad, conviene grandemente que Su Magestad i sus ministros principales se resuelvan con brevedad a tomar algunos remedios efficaçes que pareçieren a proposito, para impedir tantos daños pues con la dilacion i disimulaçion se hecha de ver con evidençia que van creciendo: y para más facilitar el negoçio a pareçido apuntar aqui algunos que se an juzgado por convenientes, no escluyendo otros que para el mismo fin i efeto se ofreçeran a la mucha prudencia de Su Magestad i del Serenissimo Cardenal Archiduque.

De los remedios que pareçen a proposito.

El remedio universal para todos los inconvenientes arriba dichos que pareçe que está en nuestra mano, fuera de lo que toca a los fuerças de Su Magestad de que aqui no se trata, es conservar en Inglaterra y fuera della en la nacion Inglesa la parcialidad de los buenos i confidentes para serviçio de la religion i de Su Magestad i de la Señora Infanta, hasta que la providencia divina o por muerte de la Reyna o de otra manera, provea de otros medios para efetuar lo que se dessea, lo qual agora pareçe que se puede alçancar por los medios siguientes:

El primero es procurar por cartas i correspondencia con los sacerdotes confidentes que estan en Inglaterra, y principalmente con los padres de la Compañia que tienen entrada alli con los Catholicos principales, i correspondençia ordinaria con los padres Ingleses de su orden en estas partes de Italia, España, i Flandes que atiendan con todo cuidado como hasta agora han hecho a conservar los Catholicos principales en la devoçion de la Señora Infanta i atraer de nuevo otros a la misma, i avisar en los ocasiones por la misma via de lo que alla passa, i este medio pareçe mui más eficaz y seguro, que embiar otras personas a posta para el dicho efeto, o para tratar otros negoçios de estado alla, pues ni los Catholicos principales se atreveran a comunicar i abrir su pecho con éstos por el grave peligro que ay en ello, ni ellos probablemente pueden entrar i salir sin ser descubiertos lo qual causaria luego grande alteraçion en todo el Reino por el rezelo de los hereges de que ay muchos exemplos i ultimamente[3] se a visto por el mal suceso que a tenido la ida de Palacer sacerdote, el qual aviendo sido imbiado a aquel reino[4] desde el puerto del Ferrol por el mes de Otubre de año passado contra el pareçer de algunas personas pláticas en las cosas de Inglaterra, para avisar a los Catholicos que no perdiesen ánimo por la fortuna que sucedio a nuestra armada, fue preso, y por miedo declaró todo lo que passava: sobre cuia confesion la Reina hizo la persecucion contra los Catholicos que despues se a seguido i a fundado las razones i causas que dize averle movido a embiar esta armada contra España en el manifiesto i declaraçion impressa que a mandado publicar, i tambien los Catholicos quedaron mui ofendidos por averse puesto un sacerdote en este negocio temporal que hazia odioso todo el estado sacerdotal, i particularmente los seminarios.

2. El segundo medio para este mismo efeto pareçe que sería mui importante procurar quanto fuere possible, que no entren sacerdotes Ingleses en aquel Reino que no sean seguros confidentes i bien afetos o a lo menos que no sean de los sediciosos i contrarios, pues el daño que estos pueden causar es tan grande como arriba se a mostrado, i aunque pareçe que no está totalmente en nuestra mano poner esto en execuçion todavia se juzga que se podria conseguir a lo menos alguna parte deste mismo efeto por dos caminos: el uno por la subordinaçion a dos obispos Ingleses que se an propuesto a Su Santidad a petiçion de los Catholicos, de los quales el uno a de residir en Inglaterra, i el otro en Flandes como abaxo se dira, i se contiene en el papel sinado C. El otro reformando el seminario de Roma, en donde se fabrican todas estas malas pláticas, i nacen todos los sediciosos, lo qual poco a poco se podria hazer parte por estos mismos medios que se an dicho, i parte por los otros que se diran más abaxo, pues todos (cada qual segun su oficio i exerciçio) an de concurrir al remedio deste colegio que es (como agora está) verdaderamente seminario i fuente de los dichos inconvenientes, i de otros muchos, por donde es necesario acudir al remedio con mucha brevedad y cuidado.

3. El tercer medio efficacissimo i evidentissimo para el remedio de tantos males, sería hallar modo para que los Catholicos Ingleses que dexada su patria acuden a Su

---

3. ay muchos exemplos i ultimamente] *supplied in margin in B, signalled by letter* F
4. a aquel reino] *this ed.*; aquel reino B

Magestad i a su real proteçion i amparo quedasen contentos, consolados y animados, lo que no solamente cerraria la puerta a Divisiones y cismas, pero daria grande ánimo a otros para que siguiesen el mismo partido, i pondria grande temor i confusion a los hereges, y para alcançar este fin no sería necesario agravar Su Magestad con nuevos o maiores gastos de los que agora haze con la naçion Inglesa, sino poner nueva traça en dispensarlo: de donde nacerian tres grandes i importantes efetos: el uno que los dichos Ingleses quedarian contentos, el otro que si algunos se quexasen no sería la quexa como agora contra Su Magestad i sus ministros: el tercero que con el mesmo gasto de entretenimientos que de presente se dan a Ingleses se podrian sustentar mucho más.

4. Para lo qual, la primera cosa que se offreçe es que Su Magestad ordenase en Flandes como Junta de algunos Ingleses principales Catholicos y confidentes, que sirviesen para consultar i acordar de mano en mano todo lo tocante a las cosas i personas de Inglaterra, juntando con ellos algun Español, o otro del consejo de Su Magestad; y la segunda que por manos destos passassen los repartimientos de los entretenimientos y otras merçedes que Su Magestad hiziesse a los Ingleses, de manera que aunque en efeto esta distribuçion se aia de hazer por orden de Su Magestad o de Su Alteza del Serenissimo Cardenal Archeduque, se entendiesse que se haze con el parecer i recuerdo de la dicha junta con que cesarian las quexas contra Su Magestad i sus ministros i todo caeria sobre estos los quales siendo muchos i de autoritad, i que ternian particular noticia de las personas de aquel reino, i de sus partes, calidad, i seguito, decretando las cosas de comun parecer con más facilidad satisfarian todos.

La tercera cosa que en esta traça⁵ se representa es, que reformando por orden de Su Magestad los entretenimientos que agora se dan, se viese la suma a que montan, i se assignassen en algunas rentas ciertas de manera que con efeto se cobrasen, pues an se servir para conservar la parcialidad que se tiene en reino tan importante, y que se hiziesse nuevo repartimiento de entretenimientos con el parecer desta junta conforme a los merecimientos y necesidades de cada uno, de donde se seguirian los siguientes efetos: el primero es que se tendria relacion verdadera de la qualidad i partes de los Catholicos Ingleses: el otro que segun la dicha relaçion se podria Su Magestad servir dellos en las ocasiones conforme a sus talentos en letras o en guerra por mar o por tierra i en otros exerciçios i no estarian tan ociosos como agora lo estan muchos, de donde se siguen malos efetos: el tercero, que entendiendo los Ingleses, que se camina por merecimientos, cada uno procuraria tenerlos, i muchos dexados otras aderençias solamente seguirian la de España, viendo que se anda con distinçion esaminandose en esta junta los merecimientos, calidad, i sufficiencia de cada uno.

5. Y porque en esta junta de Ingleses en Flandes se a de tratar tambien de otros negoçios tocantes a Inglaterra en serviçio de Su Magestad i de Su Alteza, de aqui nacerian notables bienes por lo que alli se abria de atender, lo primero en tener ordinaria correspondencia en Inglaterra, asi en Londres como en los puertos, para entender a menudo, y con mucha certidumbre lo que alli se trata, assi en lo tocante a la religion, como en lo concerniente a la materia de estado i guerra i serviçio de Su Magestad i de la Señora Infanta.

5. traça] *this ed.*; truça B

Lo otro, que se podria mejor tratar con los nobles de Inglaterra por medios convenientes a este mismo fin que los sabrian bien hallar los Ingleses desta junta, con sabiduria de Su Alteza, a quien mui a menudo se avria de dar cuenta de lo que se tratase, i los dichos nobles más confiadamente se atreverian a tratar con los de la dicha junta, por ser de autoridad i reputaçion que agora con personas particulares i desautorizadas: de donde naceria otro efeto de grandissima consideraçion y provecho porque levantandose altar contra altar, que es esta junta en Flandes contra el consejo de Inglaterra, los meteria en mucho cuidado, principalmente si Su Magestad honrrase algunos particulares benemeritos i de calidad con algunos titulos, como sería armarlos cavalleros, i darles algun hábito, o otra cosa semejante: i con esto en que se gastaria poco, estos quederian contentos, i viendo los demas en Inglaterra su naçion honrrada i estimada, se inclinarian i resolverian a seguir el mismo camino, i Su Magestad ahorraria muchos gastos por otra via.

El terçero efeto que los desta junta harian es, que estando solamente atentos a los cosas de aquel reino, podrian con facilidad dar traça a Su Alteza como se pudiesse ofender en muchas maneras aquella reina, y particularmente armando algunos Vaxeles, de los muchos que ay en Flandes, para molestar la costa de Inglaterra, i metiendo dentro algunos Ingleses mesclados con soldados Españoles, i otros subditos de Su Magestad por la notiçia particular que tienen de su tierra y passos della, podrian de noche y de dia con poco aparato i costa a modo de corsarios[6] infestarlos de manera con daños y presas, que divirtiessen aquella Reina y su consejo del pensar en hazer armadas contra España, como en esperiençia se a visto en algunos pocos cavalleros Ingleses, los quales abrá veinte años, que començando a usar deste medio hizieron en poco tiempo grandissimos daños a la Reina y pusieron en temor a todo el Reyno.

6. El quarto medio efficaz para alcançar lo que se pretiende en la naçion Inglesa, i para quitar las discordias pareçe sería, que Su Magestad i sus ministros principales se resolviesen a declararse en esta causa de los faciosos, dandoles llanamente a entender, i particularmente a los de Flandes que son las cabeças i principio de tanto mal, que Su Magestad i sus ministros saben ia en qué se funda la discordia o differençia desta façion, y que conoçen las personas principales de cada partido, y que no se tiene por servido de los que siguen la facion contraria como perniciosa a la causa de la religion, i contraria a su real serviçio: porque desta declaraçion se siguira que muchos se retirarán i se emendarán, i otros que estan obstinados no se atreveran a manifestar su pecho para inficionar a otros, i los buenos i confidentes cobrando brio tendran autoridad para traer muchos a su partido assi en Flandes como en Inglaterra, porque de lo contrario por el aver callado y disimulado Su Magestad i sus ministros tantos años, i averse mostrado dudosos, de quál parte tenga más razon, los faciosos an cobrado grandissimo brio, i atrevidose a hazer grandes daños, a lo menos en secreto, dando a entender a los simples i otros que no entienden la raiz desta division, que ellos tienen más credito con Su Magestad, por donde traen muchos a su partido que de otra manera no les seguirian: i los buenos i confidentes viendo puesta en contingençia su reputaçion despues de tantos años que sirven, trabajan i esperan, se desaniman i afligen notablemente, i otros con su exemplo padeçen lo mismo: i algunos finalmente con esta tentaçion caen i siguen a los contrarios.

6. corsarios] *this ed.*; cosarios B

7. El quinto medio que se offrece al presente para algun remedio de los inconvenientes sobredichos, i para conservar nuestro partido assi en Inglaterra como en Flandes, hasta que se descubra otro más a proposito, sería satisfaçer al desseo de los Catholicos que piden agora se les concedan dos Obispos, uno de los quales a de residir en Inglaterra i el otro en Flandes, con esta subordinaçion, que el de Inglaterra atienda a las cosas de alla, con consejo i ajuda de seis o siete Archipresbyteros repartidos en diversas provincias, sin tener splendor ni fausto alguno en lo esterior más que si fuera un simple sacerdote, por no descubrirse: y que no pueda ordenar sacerdote alguno sin letras dimissorias del obispo que residiere en Flandes, el qual tendra tambien su consejo de otros seis o siete sacerdotes de los principales dotores que residen en Flandes, i jurisdiçion spiritual sobre todos los demas de la naçion Inglesa, y sobre toda Inglaterra por dos o tres effetos, que son llamar fuera del Reino, i castigar quando fuere menester, los que el obispo i su consejo de Inglaterra juzgaren que lo mereçen, pues este obispo no lo podra hazer dentro del Reino, i esaminar todos los sacerdotes Ingleses de los seminarios, que huvieren de entrar en Inglaterra, dando licencia i facultades a quien lo merece, i deteniendo i empleando en otras cosas los que no fueren idoneos, con lo qual podra librar los Catholicos de Inglaterra del peso i peligro de muchos sacerdotes insufficientes para esta mission.

Este obispo tambien podria assistir i aiudar mucho a la iunta de Ingleses de la qual se a dicho arriba, conforme a las razones que se alegan en el dicho papel sinado C.

[*Endorsed*:] Relaçion sobre la conservaçion i buen progresso de las cosas de Inglaterra, Peligros i dificultades que se offreçen, Y de los remedios contra ellos.

Translation

For the preservation and good progress of things in England three points have to be considered: the first one concerns the present state in which they are both in respect of religion and of the temporal state; the second concerns the dangers and difficulties that arise if the remedy is not applied in time; the third one concerns the effective remedies that can and ought to be taken to assure the religion in that kingdom, and the claim of the Lady Infanta of Spain to the succession.

The Present State

1. Regarding the present state of religion in the said kingdom, having considered the means employed by way of the seminaries that have been set up outside the country in different parts, and from the (mainly Jesuit) priests who have been sent there, and are being sent day by day, it seems to be in such a condition that if it is assisted with the diligence that is expected, it will no longer be lost, since the Catholics within the kingdom both open and hidden are more numerous than the heretics, and this is the common opinion and belief of prudent discreet people, not only Catholics but also heretics, as appears from letters that have been received from different parts in recent months.

2. Concerning the temporal state, by the same means we are advised that it is troubled, because the heretics everywhere are very discontented and anxious, partly as a result

of hunger that continues to oppress them, and partly owing to the excessive expenses of the war and armed forces, causing many of the people to be miserable and discontented. This is mainly because of the fear of what may happen, seeing the queen so advanced in years, and without succession; this disturbs them more and more, and the turbulence is increasing a lot, seeing and understanding how many claimants there are to the succession, and the uncertainty of what is going to happen; and this turmoil and confusion has increased and continues to increase more every day after there appeared in that kingdom the book written and printed about the succession, which has been read avidly, given that the situation is so emotional, in which every claimant plays a part. Its publication has prompted various opinions, imaginations, and interpretations in that nation, and great difficulties which they do not know how to satisfy.

3. And for the aforementioned reason, it seems that the state of affairs with the claim of the Lady Infanta is promising, not only because of what is dealt with in the said *Book of the Succession* at the end of the second part – whence, even if something firm in her favour is not resolved, great advantages arise which would be good for that crown – but also from other papers that have been sent there from the chief particular persons of the same nation, such as Cardinal Allen, Francis Englefield, and finally Fr Persons. His short treatise on this claim, which accompanies this despatch in a separate document labelled A;[7] has been seen by His Holiness, who remained so satisfied that he said that this was the most convenient outcome. Afterwards, the two cardinal-nephews affirmed the same, saying that this suited the whole of Christianity, particularly the king of France, and that the reasons are so clear and evident that they would dare to persuade that king if they met him.

This is food for some thought, in view of the bad impression that a false summary derived from the said book by Paget, Gifford, and other Englishmen of the Scottish faction in Flanders generated, which Monsignor Malvasia presented to His Holiness, to the nephews, and to some other princes of Italy when he returned from Flanders, adding many of his own remarks against the said book, in favour of the king of Scotland. After that he made the same remarks to many of his confidants, and in particular the agent of the duke de Montmorency,[8] who was his great friend. When he tried somehow to get hold of the said book out of the said Malvasia, Malvasia replied that in no way could he show it in such a way that the discourses that went together with that summary would not be seen.

4. And as for the king of Scotland, it seems that His Holiness and his nephews are undeceived, not only through the many effective reasons that Fr Persons has represented to them, and in particular because he has declared himself the head of the church of Scotland in imitation of the queen of England, but also through the many and continuous reports sent from there about his bad behaviour: in particular for having forced the three main earls, who declared themselves Catholics in recent years, to abjure their religion on pain of losing their estates, yielding to the demands of his heretic ministers. For this rea-

---

7. [*marginal note:*] It does not, because it was sent a few days ago. [I.e., the document, BA 2 below, is not attached to this memorandum.]

8. Duke Henri de Montmorency (1534–1614).

son, his very confidants and partisans, both English and Scottish in Flanders, have begun to lose the hopes they had of his conversion, and particularly the Scotsman Father Crichton, his great defender and promoter. In these past days he wrote a letter dated 27 June 1597 to Father Persons, secretly confessing that he no longer entertained hopes for the said king; and others of the same faction, no longer pinning their hopes on him, write that confidence must now depend on the conversion of the prince his son, or the king's wife, and as long as they could nurture these hopes, they will encourage their supporters against the claim of the Lady Infanta.

5. As for the English Catholics who are outside England in Flanders, who are between four and five hundred, and in Spain, more than 150, and in Rome, fewer than 100, it is certain that all are in agreement and support the claim of the Lady Infanta, apart from fifteen or twenty estranged ones who belong to the Scottish faction in Flanders, and twenty-eight mutinous students in the college of Rome, who are in union with, and largely depend on, those of Flanders, with whom they have regular correspondence and make a profession of being contrary to the Spanish interest. From letters from those friendly to Spain mentioned above who are in Flanders, and from what some principal and prudent fathers who are in England write, it is understood that all Catholics of that kingdom have the same desire, apart from some who in recent months, either through the influence of the opponents who are in Flanders or of other priests and laymen who, with the consent of Cardinal Toledo, were sent from Rome to England for the same purpose, have departed from that good purpose which they previously had and professed. Or, at least, they have turned cold, or been made neutral only by waiting to see what will happen. From this, great dangers of alterations and changes appear, as explained in the following chapter.

Of the Dangers and Difficulties that Present Themselves

The dangers that arise are very great, and such that if a remedy is not provided, it can easily be feared that either the religion in that kingdom will be lost or lacking, or it will go into such decline that it will only with difficulty be restored to its present state, and particularly things concerning the service of His Majesty and the claim of the Lady Infanta will suffer very great harm, as can be seen by the following things.

1. These dangers of which we are going to speak originated with the divisions that began among those of the English nation in Flanders in the year 1582, when Paget, Morgan, and their followers were separated from the others. This has continued to grow, dividing English Catholics everywhere into two factions, one following Spain, the other the king of Scotland and the queen of England, at least in the matters mentioned below.

Owing to this cause some students in the English college in Rome came to the point of creating such a disruption, and such a great schism, that when Father Persons came, in the month of March in this year 1597, he almost lost all hope of being able to reconcile them, and did everything he could to understand the underlying motive of those who followed the faction contrary to Spain. He found the true cause, which has been so widespread and continues to be dispersed in England that one may very well suspect that it will produce very bad effects if no remedy is found to counter it, because the pretence of defending the freedom of the homeland gives much scope for everything that is contrary to the preservation of religion, since from that root, this faction derives and generates three branches, or, propositions: the first is to affirm that one can and should obey the queen in everything that is not against religion.

The second is that one can and should attack all those who act against the temporal estate of that queen, as (they say) are the Spaniards and their adherents, the Jesuits, whose purpose is to invade and take away their native liberty inherited from their forefathers.

The third, that they can and should obey the queen in everything touching her temporal and political estate and rule.

And for these reasons those of the college in Rome aim (as is understood from what they say) to be at one with the queen and the heretics in whatever does not involve professing heresy, and especially in three matters:

The first is to oppose the sovereignty of Spain, and whatever claim she might have in England.

The second is to oppose the Jesuits of the Society, who (according to what they say) are confederate with the Spaniards in seeking to subjugate their native land and become lords of it, under pretext of religion.

The third, to oppose all the other Catholics and priests who in some way challenge the temporal estate of that queen. And they promise their supporters that on these three conditions they may live in England without persecution and danger, and then receive favours (at least in secret) from the queen, and her council: and in time they will also achieve freedom of religion for all Catholics who are prepared to follow this path, and finally after the death of the queen they will come to promote a native king or queen or at least one that comes from the same island (thus not excluding the king of Scotland if they see fit), and therefore without doing damage to their religion the king of Spain and his daughter the infanta would be completely excluded.

And it appears that this language, so justified and plausible on the surface, carries many with it, and it is to be feared that over time it will attract many more, if it is not prevented, as seems advisable, by using the remedies listed below.

2. And although, with the talks that Father Persons had with them, they were persuaded by the compelling reasons he explained to them, they showed that they were confounded and well overcome, nevertheless, after a few months, they have reverted to declaring and affirming that, except in things touching religion, in all other respects they will keep firmly to their original purpose, acting as far as possible against the Spaniards and Jesuits their associates, to ensure that they do not enter or seize that kingdom or any part of it. And a few days ago, two or three of them speaking very passionately against the *Book of the Succession* (although they know that His Holiness has seen and approved it) stated, using very strong language, that the author deserved to be harshly punished. From this it can be deduced that they have advanced further, partly because of what they have gleaned from letters from their associates in Flanders, and partly because of what they have learned in various ways in England about certain congregations or confraternities of priests that have been initiated there this year of 1597.

3. These congregations or confraternities are understood to have been occasioned partly by some disgruntled priests from England and partly by some people who went from Rome to the same kingdom, with the consent and knowledge of Cardinal Toledo after the differences and turmoil of the college in Rome began: one was a gentleman named Griffin Markham whose father serves the queen in her court,[9] who, after being imprisoned and freed from the Inquisition at Perosa in Italy,[10] came to Rome, where Toledo and the bishop of Cassano did him many favours, and then left for England leaving a brother named Robert Markham in Rome, who previously had been the main head of the dissidents at the college: now that he is outside, he receives his livelihood from England through his brother and pretends to be commander of Malta and continuously deals with the two Cecils who are in Florence, grandsons of Treasurer Cecil from England.[11]

And since he went to England, it is understood that he has done very bad things there, because it is known that a secretary of the queen, named Waad,[12] said in recent days to a Catholic who is in prison under his custody that there were thirty priests in Rome who were determined to unite with them against the Spaniards and Jesuits, and it is believed that the seditious students of the college in Rome receive despatches from England, partly by way of these two Markhams, and partly by another gentleman residing in Rome called Nicholas Fitzherbert, who has a very perverse brother and an enemy of Catholics in London with whom he keeps a constant correspondence. This Nicholas has always taken the part of the dissidents in Rome, and he has been a great supporter of them.

4. Four others were sent from Rome to England with the same purpose, two of whom were called Hatton and Fisher, very pernicious and daring laymen, as they have shown in their works, both in Rome before leaving as well as in England, with the great lies that they spread. The other two, called Button and Norris, were priests,[13] who,

9. Sir Griffin Markham (ca. 1565–ca. 1644) was the son of Thomas Markham, a standard-bearer in the gentleman pensioners, the personal escort to the queen. He offered his services to Cecil in 1595–1596. See Kenny, "Inglorious Revolution," 149 [part 4], quoting from a letter written on 20 November 1595, describing his "good disposition ... whose virtue doth well resemble his brother's in the College." In part 3, pp. 83 and 87, Kenny gives similar details to those presented here about Robert Markham: see also part 4, p. 150.

10. Villar Perosa, near Turin.

11. Possibly Sir Richard Cecil of Wakerly, who went abroad in 1594, and one of his brothers, William, Edward, or Thomas.

12. William Waad (1546–1623).

13. On Button and Norris, who arrived in England in October 1596, see Garnet to Persons, 18 February 1597 (B354). Robert Fisher and Thomas Hatton were amongst the rebellious students at the English college in Rome: Hatton, a junior scholar, was obliged to leave the college on 28 August 1596, during Morra's first visitation; Fisher, whom Kenny describes as "intelligent and insolent," led the student movement to seek alternative confessors. He was expelled and reinstated in November 1595, and finally sent to Flanders by Cardinal Toledo, the vice-protector, in May 1596 (Kenny, "Inglorious Revolution" 255–257 [part 1]; 14–16 [part 2]; 83 [part 3]; quotation at 255 [part 1]). Fisher's later escapades in Flanders are described by Richard Barret in his letter to Persons, 10 August 1597 (B392); see also Garnet's letter cited above (B354).

although the Lord Cardinal Archduke, warned by the Duke of Sessa of their bad intentions, denied them a passport for England, still after being very well supplied and encouraged by Paget and Gifford, and others from the Scottish faction in Flanders, with their favour entered England by another route. They were later joined by William Sacheverell, an English Dominican friar, who fled from Italy because of his crimes. They have performed bad offices in England, increasing the division of the factious, and giving great opportunity to the said congregations or confraternities begun by the priests mentioned above, which they have brought into their faction. They also give them a lot of heat and animation, as a result of which these students from Rome have once again been prompted to great boldness.

5. And although with regard to these congregations in outward appearance the authors do not show anything other than piety and devotion and subordination in dealing with each other according to what can be seen in the rules which are set forth in the document labelled B,[14] nevertheless if they go ahead, it is to be feared that great inconveniences will arise from them: The first because when the associations are brought into being in conformity with their rules (as it seems, going by the tenor of them), the Catholics who are now hidden will be brought into sight of the heretics, with great harm to the said Catholics and their properties. The second is that they will cause discord, and sow disagreement among the priests and laity as a result of the heavy burdens which will be imposed on them if they follow the said rules, as is made plain in the said document. And finally, it is to be understood, by the confession of some of the same authors, that this invention of congregations goes hand in hand with the purpose of destroying and annihilating the hidden Jesuit priests who are in England, administering the sacraments there, and that their intention is just the same as that of the students of the English college in Rome: to contradict and oppose the Spanish and the fathers of the Society. From this it is very likely to be suspected that all, or a large part, of this is taking place with some connivance of the queen and her Council; it is even known, also, that the abovementioned Griffin, Sacheverell, and some others have held secret talks with the said Council.

6. To the dangers mentioned above can be added the great inconvenience that will arise from the departure of nine or ten English priests, who will leave this college in Rome this year, in the month of September. Of them six or seven are of turbulent spirit and very extraordinary enemies of the Spanish interest, and not a little experienced in promoting rebellion and schism, thanks to the experience they have had in it in Rome in these three years of tumult. After passing through Flanders, where they will be even more influenced and inflamed by those seditious Englishmen that are to be found there, when they arrive in England they will without doubt cause much harm and greatly increase the abovementioned dangers, placing the good progress of religion in great jeopardy and also wrecking all that has been achieved up to now in concert with the service of His Majesty and the Lady Infanta: all the more because, it is understood from letters from those in Flanders, their associates who have been seen here have advised that they will be made doctors to give them more authority. And also, they are persuaded that in Rome they have a large number of supporters among the leading personages, who favour them

---

14. Persons to Peña, 12 August 1597 (B393).

secretly. As a result, they will without doubt make a deep impression on the spirits of many. In addition to this there is a book that has been distributed through all of England these past months, written by one of the estranged Englishmen who reside in Flanders, named Lewkenor; when he withdrew to England with the collusion of the Privy Council he wrote this book, whose title is *Of the miseries, contempt and grievances that the English fugitives have suffered from the king of Spain and his ministers*.[15] In it so many evil things are said that they are enough to cause abhorrence towards the whole Spanish nation and aversion from the service of His Majesty.

7. For all these reasons, and because it is known that in England and in other parts continuous discussions are being held on the part of the king of Scotland and of other claimants, especially since they discovered the great claim which with reason the Lady Infanta is able to make to that crown, and because the faction and association of the dissidents and opposition is growing, and gathering greater force every day, something which is even more dangerous as it originates among those who are held and reputed to be Catholics and some of those who are pensioners of His Majesty, it is most fit that His Majesty and his ministers make the decision to apply some effective measures urgently, such as appear appropriate, to prevent such great harms as with delay and dissimulation come to the surface, with evidence that keeps growing: and to facilitate that business it has been deemed advisable to indicate some [remedies] here which are believed to be suitable, not omitting others which will be offered for the same purpose and to the same effect to the great prudence of His Majesty and His Serene Highness the Cardinal Archduke.

The Measures That Seem Appropriate

The overall remedy for all the abovementioned problems that seems to be practicable – apart from that which involves His Majesty's armed forces, which we cannot deal with at present – is to maintain, both in England and outside, a party of good and trustworthy people in the English nation to serve religion and His Majesty and the Lady Infanta, until such time as divine providence, either through the death of the queen or some other way, should find some other means to bring about what is wanted. This aim, it seems, can now be achieved by the following means:

The first is to obtain, through letters and correspondence with the priests we can trust who are in England (and principally with the fathers of the Society who have access there to the leading Catholics, and are in regular correspondence with the English fathers of their order in other parts of Italy, Spain, and Flanders) that they attend with all care, as they have done so far, to conserve the leading Catholics in their attachment to the Lady Infanta and recruit new ones to it. They should also report from time to time on

15. Lewis Lewkenor, *The estate of English fugitives under the king of Spaine and his ministers* (London, 1595). After serving in Parma's army, Sir Lewis Lewkenor (ca. 1560–1627) entered Burghley's service and became MP for Midhurst in 1597. His uncle Edward was tutor to John Gerard. A George Lewkenor (a fellow of New College, Oxford) travelled with Persons to Padua in 1574 to study medicine (Pollen, *Miscellanea II*, 23; Jonathan Woolfson, *Padua and the Tudors: English Students in Italy, 1485–1604* [Cambridge, 1998], 251.)

what is happening there. This method seems much more effective and secure than to send other persons deliberately for the same end, or to deal with other business of state there, for indeed those leading Catholics will not dare to communicate and disclose their secrets with them for the serious danger which there is in it, nor will they be able, probably, to go in and out without being discovered, which would cause great distress later in the kingdom as a result of suspicion on the part of the heretics. There are many examples of this, and most recently it has been seen from the ill luck attaching to the going of the priest Palasor, who, having been sent to the kingdom via the port of Ferrol in the month of October last year, against the advice of various people versed in English affairs, to caution the Catholics not to lose heart because of the fortune that attended our armada, was imprisoned and, being tortured, declared everything that had passed: following his confession the queen intensified the persecution against the Catholics, it [his confession] has been used to establish the reasons and causes which she said, in a printed manifesto and proclamation which she ordered to be published, had moved her to send this armada against Spain.[16] And also the Catholics were offended that they had placed a priest in this temporal business, which made the entire body of priests hateful, and especially the seminarians.

2. The second means towards the same end would seem to be that it will be very important to ensure, as far as possible, that no English priests come into that kingdom who are not reliable, trustworthy, and well-affected, or at least who are not from the dissidents and objectors, for the damage that they can cause is so great, as has been shown above. And although it seems that it is not entirely within our power to put this into execution, nevertheless it is believed that it will be possible to pursue, at least in some part, this same end in two ways: One through subordination to two English bishops that have been proposed to His Holiness as petitioned by the Catholics, of whom one should reside in England, the other in Flanders, as will be explained below and is contained in the document marked C.[17] The other is by reforming the seminary in Rome, whence all this bad talk originates, and where all the dissidents are brought forth. Little by little this can be achieved, partly through the same means which have been discussed, and partly through others which will be set out below; but everyone (each according to his office and training) must concur in the remedy for this college, which is (and has been until now) truly a seminary and wellspring of those same problems, and many others, for which reason it is necessary that the remedy should come into effect very urgently and attentively.

16. Thomas Palasor, admitted at Valladolid on 3 January 1593, was sent to England from the college there in December 1596 (Pollen, *Valladolid Registers*, 22; cf. Anstruther, 267-268). He was imprisoned in the Gatehouse 12 March 1597, and interrogated. In a letter to William Waad, clerk of the Privy Council, endorsed March 1596/7, he gives details of preparations by the Adelantado of Spain, Martín de Padilla, whom Palasor met in the port city of Ferrol in Galicia, for a possible attack on Ireland or England in the following spring (for Persons's dealings with the Adelantado, see his letter to Acquaviva, 2 and 9 December 1595, B303). In July 1597, the earl of Essex set out with a fleet and a militia to attack Ferrol, where the Spanish fleet was based, but was hampered by storms and sailed for the Azores instead: see Paul E.J. Hammer, *Elizabeth's Wars: War, Government, and Society in Tudor England, 1544-1604* (New York, 2003), 199-203.

17. Appendix BA 3, below.

3. The third most effective and obvious means to remedy so many great evils will be to find a way by which those English Catholics who, having left their homeland, come to His Majesty and to his royal protection and guardianship, remain content, comforted, and encouraged. This will not only close the door on divisions and schisms but will give great encouragement to others so that they share the same disposition of contentment, thereby putting the heretics into great fear and confusion. To achieve this end, it will not be necessary to burden His Majesty with new or greater expenses than those which he already bears in relation to the English nation, but to put together a new method of dispensing it. From this will arise three great and important effects: one, that the said Englishmen will remain content; the other that if any should complain, their quarrel will not be, as it has up to now, against His Majesty and his ministers; the third that with the same expense of hospitality which at present is given to the English many more may be sustained.

4. In this regard, the first matter that presents itself is that His Majesty should set up a kind of council in Flanders of some of the leading, trustworthy English Catholics (together with some Spaniard or other from His Majesty's council), which will serve to consult and settle, from time to time, everything that touches the affairs and personages of England. The second is that the pensions and other payments that His Majesty makes to the English should pass through their hands for distribution in such a way that although in effect this distribution always takes place by order of His Majesty or His Highness the Most Serene Cardinal Archduke, it would be understood that it is done with the approval and recollection of the said council. This would bring to an end the complaints against His Majesty and his ministers, and everything would fall under these men, who will be numerous and carry the weight of authority and will be particularly informed about the personages of that kingdom, their parts, quality, and accomplishments. Their settling the matters of common concern would satisfy everyone more easily.

The third thing that comes to the fore in this plan is that, by reforming the allowances which are now given by order of His Majesty,[18] it will be seen how much this amounts to, and they may be commuted to some specified incomes in such a manner that in effect they grow; and indeed, this will serve to consolidate the support which we enjoy in a kingdom of such importance. Moreover, a new form of distribution of allowances will be established with the approval of this council according to the merits and needs of each one. From this will flow these outcomes: the first is that they will keep a true account of the rank and talents of the English Catholics; the second is that accordingly His Majesty will be able to be served by them when occasion demands, depending on their talents either in letters or in war, by land, or sea and in other offices, and they will not be so idle as many of them are now, which causes much damage; the third is that since the English will understand that it all depends on their individual merits, it will keep a hold on them, and many of them, abandoning other allegiances, will follow that of Spain, seeing that things proceed with discretion, each one's merits, enthusiasm, and competence coming under examination of this council.

18. See Loomie, *The Spanish Elizabethans*, 31–36, on the response of Philip II's Council of State to a memorandum on this subject submitted by Sir William Stanley, Hugh Owen, and William Holt.

5. And because in this council of Englishmen in Flanders there will be discussion also of other business relating to England in the service of His Majesty and His Highness, from this will arise notable benefits for what has to be dealt with there. The first is in maintaining regular correspondence with England, both in London and the ports, so as to gather frequently and with much certainty what is happening there, both in what touches religion and also what concerns business of state and war and service for His Majesty and the Lady Infanta.

The other benefit is to have better dealings with the nobles of England through the means appropriate to that very purpose, which is what the Englishmen of this council should be well able to advise,[19] keeping His Highness informed, to whom regular account will be given of what they are dealing with. The said nobles would feel more confident when dealing with those of the said council, because of its evident authority and reputation, than they are at present, with particular unauthorized personages. From this will flow another effect of the greatest consideration and advantage in that, raising altar against altar, i.e. this council against the council of England, it will make them take great care, especially if His Majesty honours some particular meritorious and worthy people with some titles, for instance by knighting the gentlemen and giving them a military distinction, or something similar: and with this, which will cost little, they will rest content, and others in England, seeing their nation honoured and valued, will lean this way and resolve to follow the same route, and His Majesty will save much expense, which can be used elsewhere.

The third effect which this council will have is that paying attention only to the matters of that kingdom, it will more easily give advice to His Highness, how that queen might be harassed in many ways, and especially by arming some ships, of which already there are many in Flanders, to attack the coast of England repeatedly, and introducing into them some Englishmen, mixed with Spanish soldiers and other subjects of His Majesty; the special familiarity they have with the local terrain and routes, will enable them to infest the country like pirates by day and by night, with minimal equipment and expense, in such a way, causing damage and taking prisoners, that they will distract that queen and her council from planning and setting forth armadas against Spain, as is shown by experience with some few English gentlemen, who some twenty years ago started to use this method and caused very great harm to the queen and spread fear throughout the land.

6. The fourth effective means of promoting what is wanted among the English nation and bringing the discords to an end would be, it seems, if His Majesty and his chief ministers would make a decision to publish the names of the factious ones, giving them to understand clearly (and especially those of Flanders who are the origin and leaders of so great an evil) that His Majesty and his ministers already know where the discord and opposition of this faction originates, and that they know the chief persons of each party, and that he does not consider that he is being well served by those who belong to the enemy faction as it is fatal to the cause of religion and opposed to his royal service. Such

---

19. The proposed council will be much more effective in advising the king and the archduke how to deal with the Privy Council and the English court.

a declaration will have the effect that many will be turned back and put on the right path, and others who remain stubborn will not dare to reveal their real feelings so as to infect others, and the good, trustworthy people, gaining in confidence, will have authority to draw many to their party, both in Flanders and England. Since His Majesty and his ministers have, on the contrary, been keeping silence and reserve for so many years, and shown themselves to be uncertain which side has more reason, the dissidents have achieved extraordinary boldness and have dared to cause great harm, at least in secret, giving the simple people and those who do not understand the root cause of this conflict to believe that they are in more credit with His Majesty – and so they draw many to their party who otherwise would not follow them; and the good, trustworthy ones, seeing their reputation put in jeopardy after so many years of service, labour, and hope, are notably discouraged and afflicted, and others, following their example, suffer the same; and some eventually yield to temptation and follow the opposite side.

7. The fifth measure which comes to mind at present as some remedy for the problems mentioned above, and to maintain our party both in England and Flanders, until some other more suitable can be found, would be to satisfy the request of the Catholics who are now asking that two bishops be granted to them, one of whom will reside in England and the other in Flanders, with this division of responsibilities: the one in England will attend to affairs there, with the advice and assistance of six or seven archpriests distributed among the various provinces. To avoid detection, he would not display any more pomp or outward splendour than an ordinary priest. He would not be able to ordain a priest except with letters dimissory[20] from the bishop resident in Flanders. That bishop will also keep a council of another six or seven priests from the leading doctors who are living in Flanders. He will hold spiritual jurisdiction over the whole of the rest of the English nation, and over all of England in two or three respects: namely, to summon out of the kingdom and punish, where necessary, those whom the bishop and his council in England deem worthy, as this bishop will be unable to deal with it internally; and to examine all the English priests from the seminaries who are about to enter England, granting licence and faculties to those who deserve them, and holding back those who are not suitable, to assign them to other duties. In this way he will free the Catholics in England from the burden and danger of many priests who are unsuitable for this mission.

This bishop could also assist and greatly help the English council spoken of above, according to the reasons given in the said document labelled C.[21]

BA 2 Memorial on Pretenders to the Succession to the Throne of England, August 1597

SOURCE: BAV, MS Lat. Vat. 6227, fols. 170–182, Latin copy.

NOTE: This memorial appears to be one of the three Latin documents prepared for the Spanish ambassador, as mentioned in Persons's letters to Peña, 12 and 14 August 1597 (B394,

---

20. Letters from a superior bishop testifying that the ordinand qualifies according to canon law and may be ordained by the inferior bishop.
21. The memorandum on the appointment of two bishops (BA 3 below).

B396). According to the memorandum on the state of English affairs (BA 1, above), the pope had already seen this memorial, and was persuaded by it.

The memorial consists of two parts: with an eye to his English Catholic critics, Persons pays special attention in the second document to the benefits to France if the infanta should succeed to the English crown.

Examen de principibus, qui regni Anglicani successionem praetendunt, quis aliis praeferendus videatur secundum praesentem Reipublicae Christianae statum[22]

Primo sciendum est, secundum librum Dolmani, de iure successionis regiae apud Anglos, quod licet omnes fere controversiae de hac re reduci possint ad duas antiquas familias regias,[23] Lancastrensem nimirum atque Eboracensem, quae trecentis fere ab hinc annis caeperunt inter se de diademate dimicare (et unaquaeque quatuor ex se Reges habuit) tamen hodie ad quinque familias et ad decem vel eo plures ex eisdem familiis praetensores lis extenditur, quorum omnis et singuli (quod inauditum fortassis alioquin est) rationes suas habent, quibus primo loco sibi deberi regni huius successionem puterit.

§ Familiae sunt:[24] Scotica, et ex ea Rex Scotiae, per primas nuptias senioris filiae Regis Angliae Henrici Septimi, et Arbella nata in Anglia ex secundis nuptiis eiusdem Henrici regis filiae.

§ Alia familia est Ducis Suffolciensis qui iuniorem filiam eiusdem regis Henrici duxit in uxorem, et ex ea habuit duas filias, ex quarum priore natus est Comes Harfordiensis et secunda Comes Derbiensis in Anglia.

§ Tertia familia est Ducis Clarentiae, qui frater fuit Regis Angliae Edouardi quarti ex familia Eboracensi, et ex hac familia existunt hodie in Anglia Comes Huntintonius nomine Hastingus, et Polorum Domus.

§ Quarta familia est Lusitanica sive regum Lusitaniae, qui per matrimonium reginae Lusitanicae nomine Philippae, quae Regis Angliae Henrici quarti soror et heres ex domo Lancastrensi fuit, successionem regni Anglicani petunt, et ex hac familia existunt hodie Rex Hispaniae, Dux Parmensis, et Dux Brigantinus, qui diversis nationibus ad eandem quoque successionem actiones habent.

§ Quinta denique familia est Ducum Britaniae, qui variis de causis ut apud Dolmani librum videre est, ius Angliae corone sibi vendicent, et ex hac familia sunt hodie Elizabetha Hispaniarum Infanta, cum sorore Subaudiae Ducesia, quae ex seniore Regis Galliae filia ortu habent.

§ Deinde sciendum est omnes hos decem praetensores, vel maximum saltem eorum partem ita inter se dissidere de primo successionis loco, et unamquamque partem tot impedimentis et exclusionibus adversarios urgere, ut perpensis omnibus valde difficile et incertum sit, utra pars potiorem habeat actionem, etiamsi solam sanguinis successionem respiciamus.

22. A separate title page prefaces the same text with "R. P. Roberti Personii e Societate Jesu."
23. [*marginal note*:] quinque familia competitorum, et decem competitores
24. Editorial punctuation.

§ Sciendum tertio, non solum sanguinis ius, aut propinquitatem hoc in negotio respiciendum esse, sed alia quoque multa,[25] nimirum possibilitatem facilitatem, vel difficultatem consequendi regni, vel etiam retinendi ac defendendi postea quam fuerit acquisitum. Religionem deinde aliosque partes praetensoris, securitatem quoque vel pericula regni Anglicani, commoda vel incommoda regnorum vicinorum, et ex eis principum quoque externorum affectus, atque voluntates, praecipue vero Galliarum atque Hispaniarum regum, qui vicinissimi ac potentissimi sunt, neque facile patientur praeiudicium sibi suisque statibus ac ditionibus fieri, hac regis Anglicani admissione, secundum omnes ergo haec circunstantias examen sequens faciendum videtur.

De Rege Scotia et Arbella

Jacobus sextus Rex Scotiae, si successionem sanguinis, quam a rege Angliae Henrico septimo habet, qui centum abhinc annis sceptrum per arma acquisivit, respiciamus primam[26] praeceteris habet actionem; quanquam si iterum in questionem vocandum esset, ad quem ius successionis legitimae eo tempore pertinebat, quo Henricus regnum per arma ingressus est, magis Alfonso quinto Regi Lusitaniae, qui tunc vivebat, et infirmus viribus opibusque erat, per Dolmani librum competere videtur actio tanquam haeredi proximo familiae Lancastrensis.

Sed admissa prioritate successionis Regis Scotiae, secundum sanguinis lineam, per hos centum annos proximo deductam, adversarii tamen eius, varias obiiciunt[27] contra eum exclusiones, primo Religionem, quae semper hactenus fuit in eo pessima, neque ullum signum emendationis a pueritia dedit, matrimonium contractum in domo heretica, omnes fere consanguineos et familiares hereticos esse, praeterea non constare dispensationem pontificis petitam, aut obtentam fuisse, cum mater eius matrimonium iniret cum Henrico Darleo in secondo grade sibi consangioneo, ex quo matrimonio Rex iste ortus sit. Denique obiiciunt, per expressam Comitiorum ac parlamenti Anglicani legem ante decem annos latam, exclusum esse regem Scotiae ab omni successionis iure ob matris condemnationem deprocurata Elizabetha Regina morte, quae lex cum ante delictum comissum, et omnium ordinum consensu ad regni securitatem ac pacem conservandam, sancita fuerit, iustam esse affirmant, et legitime potuisse sanciri, atque haec afferunt ad enervandam Regis Scotiae actionem ad regnum Angliae ex iure successionis.

Ceterae vero circumstantiae, si considerentur, multa plura ex is allegari solent ad praetensionem Regis Scotiae infirmandam, ac primo quidem vix possibile esse aiunt, ut Rex Scotiae ad Angliae regnum, vel ab haereticis vel a Catholicis admittatur, nam quanque Anglicanae genti exp[ec]tibilis videatur regnorum illorum unio atque coniunctio, multo tamen potentior est animorum alienatio inter Anglos et Scotos ob vicinitatem ac bella fere perpetua, unde Angli qui digniores se putant, nunquam patientur Scotos sibi dominari, praesertim cum e suis quoque principibus domesticis, praetensores multos habeant, ut dictum iam est, unde semper bella, suspitiones, ac motus futuri essent, si Rex Scotiae sceptrum assequeretur, neque multis saeculis pax esset speranda, praesertim cum neque

---

25. [*marginal note:*] varia consideranda in cuiusque competitores actione
26. primam] *interlined with caret B*
27. [*marginal note:*] variae exclusiones contra Regem Scotiae

ipsi Scoti nobiliores unionem hanc regnorum aequo animo ferant, cum ea re Regi potentiori subiectos se fore videant, qui libertates illas, quibus modo fru[u]ntur, imminuat, ac tandem paulatim Anglis, quos oderunt tanquam nationi potentiori adherere se atque subesse oportere, atque a Gallis divelli quos maxime amant.

Externis etiam principibus incommoda esset valde haec regnorum coniunctio,[28] primum pontifici Romano, cum propter religionem Regis, tum etiam quia magis expedit ecclesiae regna Christiana multa esse quam posse, deinde regi Hispaniarum ob easdam causas, et propter amicitiam ac confederationem antiquam Scotorum cum Gallis, ac denique quia tum sua tum filiae etiam suae actio ad Angliae regnum, hac Regis Scotiae admissione omnino excluderetur.

§ Pro Rege quoque Daniae nonnullae ex his ipsis rationibus militant, sed maxime omnium Regi Franciae incommoda futura esse videtur Regis Scotiae ad Angliae regnum praelatio, tum quia potentiorem inde haberet vicinum, tum etiam quia omnis illa antiqua amicitia ac confederatio Scotorum cum Gallis in hostilitatem transiret, ob ius illud quod reges Angliae, ad Galliae coronam, ac ad varias eiusdem provincias a nonnullis iam saeculis praetendunt, neque persequi desinent cum satis se potentes viderint.

§ Denique cum hactenus Gallia Scotiam habuerit sibi obsequentem, quam Angliae[29] semper potentiae obiiceret, non solum illud subsidium hac regnorum utriusque coniunctione omitteret, sed aliud etiam periculum non leve immineret, nimirum quod cum Rex Angliae accessione hac auctus, varias Galliae provincias legitimo successionis iure sibi pertinere existimet, Rex etiam Hispaniae nonnullos filiae suae esse quoque putet, fieri poterit, ut facta confaederatione ac unitis viribus[30] Galliam aliquando dividant, quod vix unquam fieri poterit dum Angliae Scotiaeque regna divisa manserint.

De Arbella eaedem fere difficultates, quae de Rege Scotiae, vel etiam maiores, ius, nimirum successionis minus certum et explicatum quia ex secundis nuptiis Regina Scotiae descendit, eisque multorum opinione magnisque argumentis non satis legitimis, impotentia deinde Regni consequendi, vel etiam defendendi, ignobilitas patris, qui plebeius fere fuit, religio haeretica, et alia huiusmodi.

De Comitibus Hartfordiensi, Darbiensi, Huntintonio, ac de Polis.

Omnes hi comites Anglicani quoad successionis, ius invicem se oppugnant, nam priores duo qui ex secunda Henrici regis septimi filia descendunt, excluso Rege Scotiae per eas rationes quae supra comemoratae sunt, proximum locum sibi deberi putant, et imprimis Comes Hartfordiensis, qui ex priori nep[o]te Regis Henrici ortum habet, sed comes tamen Darbiensis ex iuniori natus duplici vel triplici illegitimatione eum excludit, Comes vero Huntintonius qui antiquiori ambobus iure ex ducis Clarentiae filia familiae Eboracensis profectus, regnum petit, Comitem quoque Darbiensem ob similem illegitimationis notam impugnat: Polos vero tanquam se longe posteriores in eadem praetentione Domus Eboracensis reiicit, qua etiam ratione et ipse Comes Huntintonius a reliquis iam dictis duobus Comitibus reiicitur tanquam inferior in hoc ipso domus Eboracensis iure,

28. [*marginal note:*] incommoda externorum principum
29. Angliae] *this ed.*; Anglia B
30. viribus] *interlined with caret B*

cum ipsi a filia Edoardi regis quarti senioris fratris ac domus Eboracensis principis descendant, Huntintonius autem tantum a filia Ducis Clarentiae, qui frater natu minor regi Edoardo fuerat, atque haec de successionis iure.

Caeteris vero in rebus, eadem cernuntur incommoda, ac difficultates adipiscendi regni aut tuendi, quae ante sunt exposita, cum enim multi sint praetensores, hii ac inter se divisi, neque externorum principum favorem consanguinitatem aut amicitiam habeant, nemo illorum Regi Scotiae caeterisque simul competitoribus obsistere posse videtur, religio etiam illorum omnium comitum haeretica hactenus, aut valde dubia esse noscitur, adeo ut neque securum neque facile videatur quenquam ex istis ad Regnum evehere, omnes etiam matrimonium iam contraxerunt, ita ut externis nuptiis iuvari opibus aut auxiliis nequeant.

De Rege Hispaniae atque de Ducibus Parmensi ac Bragantino

Tres hii principes, cum omnes ex familia regia Lancastrensi, per Philippam filiam Ducis Lancastriae Lusitaniae reginam descendant, eandem fere disceptationem se huius familiae Lancastrensis successione habere possunt, quam aliquando habuerunt de regni Lusitaniae iure, et paulo fortassis implicatiorem, eo quod nonnullorum opinione leges Anglicanae representationem admittant in regni successione, quae tamen apud Lusitanos eum vim non habeat, ea re caeteris praelatus fuisse Rex Hispaniae videtur pro universo autem iure familiae Lancastrensis, prae Eboracensi si centum annorum praescriptio, qui proxime elapsi sunt excludatur, multa afferuntur argumenta apud Dolmanum in libro de Regiae successionis iure quanquam nihil in ullam partem definiatur.

Caetera vero adiuncta si perpendantur, non exiguae difficultates oriuntur undeque; nam de Rege Hispaniae cum omnes non consentiant in iuris illius aequitatem, tum incommodam etiam fore praetensionem eius affirmant idque non solum Pontifici caeterisque externis principibus, ob tantae potentiae augmentum, verum etiam multo magis Anglis ipsis cuiuscunque tandem conditionis sint, nam uniri regnum Angliae alteri regno, externoque principi subesse, ac in provinciam redigi gravatissime ferrent omnes, unde et dissidia, bella, ac seditiones maximae orirentur, neque sine maximis reipublicae Christianae motibus rem transigi posse putant, ut Hispaniae Rex Angliam sibi subiiciat, licet Catholicorum animos, valde sibi coniunctos ob religionis unionem, ac ob diuturna beneficia in eos collata, habeat.

De Ducibus Parmensi ac Bragantino, licet egregii principes suis et Catholicis Anglicanis acceptissimi cum ob nobilitatem, religionis ardorem, caeterasque virtutes; tum etiam ob familiae Lancastrensis gratissimam memoriam, tamen cum longe absint ab Anglia, neque suis viribus regnum illud consequi aut tueri posse videantur, in tanta praetensorum ac inpugnatorum copia (nisi externorum quoque regum viribus iuventur, de quibus nihil certi promitti posse videtur ob eas rationes, quas unusquisque sibi subiicere poterit); exigua admodum spes affulget, quicquam magni momenti posse confici in horum principum commodum, quod si posset, personae eorum futurae essent Catholicis gratissimae.

De Hispaniarum Principe Infanta

Restat igitur quinta ac postrema familia Britanica, cuius haereditas in eis omnibus quae lege Salica non continentur, in Elizabetham Hispaniarum Infantam primo gradu decidit, quae autem et quot sint Domus Britanicae iura actionesque in regnum Angliae, Dolmani libro abunde explicatur. Potest etiam Rex Hispaniae, ius omne suum quod ex domo Lusitanica vel aliunda habet vel habere poterit, in hanc principem filiam suam transfundere, adeo ut si cetera concurrent, successionis actio deesse ei non poterit.

Reliquae autem circunstanciae omnes, quorum [sic] supra ratio habita est, vel examen factum, adeo favent huic principi, ut nihil optari posse magis videatur:[31] nam quamcunque in partem oculos coniiciamus, commoda plurima occurrunt, primum quidem Anglis ipsis, nam huius principis gubernatione haberent regnum suum ab aliis divisum, quod maxime cupiunt. Religionis deinde Catholicae securitatem obtinerent, quod illis in votis est; haberent praeterea paratas Regis Hispaniae vires ad omnia quae erunt necessaria, vel ad pacem stabiliendam, vel ad rempublicam firmandam. Denique hoc ipsis etiam praetensoribus Anglicanae genti securius multo, utilius ac honorificentius futurum esset, si eminentiori cederent, quam si par pari palmam daret, nam et princeps haec melioribus eos conditionibus remunerari poterit, quam si quisque illorum super alios elevaretur. Is enim metu compulsus, id facere cogeretur, quod omnes fere reges Anglicani posterioribus his saeculis facere consueverunt, nimirum, ut securitati suae aliorum praetensorum exterminio consulerent, haec vero princeps patris innixa potentia, securiorem haberet regnandi conditionem neque tantum reliquorum praetensorum timeret vires, aut subiret odia, unde neque tot suspiciones, seditiones, motusque quod maximum esset reipublicae commodum.

Externis etiam principibus non minora inde commoda nascitura videntur si huius principis causa promoveatur. Nam de Sede Apostolica clarum videtur, cum enim huius principis pietas ardorque incolenda religione adeo sit orbi notus, ut ex eius regimine non tantum Anglicani regni reductio, sed aliorum quoque regnorum sibi cohaerentium, ac maximarum totius septentrionis provinciarum restitio ac reformatio ac ad ecclesiam reditus sperari possit, facile cernitur quantum intersit sedis Apostolicae istiusmodi principis ad regnum evectio. Regis vero Hispaniae quid intersit, omnes vident, ut filia scilicet prospectum sit, non autem quod eius ditio aut potentia magnopere inde augeri possit, ut aliqui fortassis suspicabuntur. Nam princeps haec postquam[32] regno potita fuerit, etiam si Regis Hispaniae sit filia, ratione tamen status cogetur, sua defendere ac securitati magis suae quam patris potentiae studere.

§ Regis demum Daniae hoc ipsum quoque interest, quod aliorum principum Germaniae ac Italiae, nimirum ut regna haec Angliae Scotiaeque divisa maneant, et ut suavi hac compositione regnum Angliae in filiam potius Hispaniarum regis transferatur; alicui principi domus Austriaci nuptam, quam ut vel Rex Scotiae tria regna coniungat, vel Rex aliquis Hispaniae successionis iure munitus ac necessitate adactus, armis aliquando Angliam, vel Hiberniam, vel utramque subigat, suisque regnis subiungat.

31. [*marginal note:*] commoda ex praelatione infantae
32. postquam] *this ed.;* postequam *B*

§ Remanet solum Galliae Rex, cui ut potentissimo Angliaeque vicinissimo, suspecta esse poterit prae caeteris hac filiae Regis Hispaniarum potentia, sed contra plane est, meo iuditio, cum nullum Christiani orbis principem maiora inde emolumenta percepturum existimem quam Galliarum regem, non solum ex illorum incommodorum vitatione, quae regno Galliae eventura per Angliae Scotiaeque adunationem supra comemoravi, sed etiam ex plurimorum maximorumque commodorum perceptione, quae ego scripto potius separato explicanda duxi, quam hic nimia brevitate compingenda, haec igitur in praesentiarum habui, quae de regni Anglicani competitorum inter se comparatione dicenda habui.

[Scriptum secundum:]

> Utilitates ac commoda maxima, quae perventura sunt ad Regem Galliarum, praeceteris principibus, ex praelatione Serenissimae Elizabethae Hispaniarum Infantae ad regnum Anglicanum pro pace publica statuenda

Cum ex priori scripto de principum omnium inter se comparatione, qui successionis iure Anglicanum regnum[33] ambire, aut praetendere possunt, constare iam videatur solos duos esse, qui perpensis omnibus, tum incommodis ac difficultatibus, tum etiam commodis ac adiumentis, probabili aliqua ratione caeteris praeferri possint, si pacifice atque consilio (quod valde optandum est) res transigatur; cumque eodem scripto exposita sint incomoda atque pericula quae regno Galliae accedere possint ex praelatione Regis Scotiae, nimirum ex tanta potentia vicini principis, qui necessario quoque successu temporis inimicus esse regibus Galliae debebit, cum ob vicinitatem tum etiam ob aemulationem imperii, ut se Ducibus Burgundiae visum est, qui licet ex ipsorum regum Galliae domo exierint, inimicissimi tamen semper Galliae regni extiterunt.

Cumque praeterea ostensum sit Regem Galliae Regis Scotiae praelationum faventem non tantum aemulos suos Anglos,[34] universam Galliam ad se pertinere affirmantes, trium regnorum adunatione armaturum, sed se Galliamque quoque eo adminiculo efficacissimo spoliaturum, quod unicum habuerunt a multis saeculis ad Anglos domi refrenandos, quod erat amicitia certissima ac confaederatio Scotorum, cumque universo mundo notum sit, quot quantasque provincias Galliae, Reges Angliae liquidissimo successionis iure (ut nihil de corona Galliae dicam) ad se pertinere existiment: Normandiam scilicet, Andegavensem ac Pictaviensem regionem, ac totam denique Aquitaniam, quas provincias sola vi a Gallis deteneri etiamnum hodie queruntur, cumque ex alia parte Rex quoque Hispaniae, Britaniae provinciam filiae suae esse cum aliis nonnullis in regno Galliae detionibus praesumat, fieri facile potest, ut Rex Scotiae tanto imperio auctus, et Anglicanum animum induens et ab Anglis incitatus, ineat aliquando faedus cum Hispaniarum Rege, aut cum Infanta suisve haeredibus de Franciae provinciis dividendis, quos probabiliter avidere non poterit, si ipsa Infanta Angliae Regnum assignatur, ut paulo post declarabitur.

33. regnum] *interlined with caret B*
34. [*marginal note:*] incommoda Galliae ex praelatione regis Scotiae

Cum tot ergo incomoda regno Galliae immineant ex regis Scotiae praelatione videamus e contrario, quanam utilitates et commoda ex praedictae Infantae ad regnum Angliae admissione, regno Galliae accrescant.

Omnium autem primum illud est,[35] ut cum regnum Galliae gravissimis bellorum incommodis a multis annis afflictum sit, et in praesenti non minorum etiam sentiat, hac ratione ab omnibus non tantum respirare, sed penitus etiam liberari ac securum fieri poterit, quod nulla alia humana via possibile videtur, cum caeteri pacificandi modi, pharmaca tantum sint ad tempus, radices vero inimicitiarum non tollant, pax vero firma cum Hispania atque Angliae regnis hac ratione costituta universam Galliam ac reliquum quoque Christianum orbem paratum reddet.

2^a. Hinc etiam sequitur secunda utilitas quod Rex Galliae pacatus, absolute fiet provinciarum omnium Galliae Dominus, quod allioquin difficile futurum cernitur, dum provinciarum gubernatores regem adeo bellis distractum videant, ac Hispaniae Regis vires semper eis praesto futuras.

3^a. Tertia utilitas est, quod hac ratione Rex Galliae liberabitur a necessitate petendi auxilium ab Anglis aliisque haereticis, qui eum nunc postquam Catholicum se exhibuit, non nisi commodorum suorum causa armis iuvant, maxime vero Angli, quibus fidenter uti non poterit, ob eas praetensiones, quas in multas Galliae provincias eos iam habere diximus, ex alia vero parte dum Rex Galliae horum aliorumque haereticorum confederatione, necessitate licet coactus utetur, reliquos principes[36] Catholicos minus confidenter cum eo agere posse manifestum est, et minus consuletur praeclarissimi nominis Regis Christianissimi existimationi.

4^a. Quarta utilitas est, quod Rex Galliae hac pace constituta cum Anglia Hispaniaque non solum a necessitate auxilii haereticorum externorum, sed domi etiam, hoc est, in ipsa Gal[l]ia (cum Anglia[37] ad unionem ecclesiae reducta fuerit) unam quoque per universum regnum religionem Catholicam stabilire poterit, quae omnis pacis diuturnae ac stabilis fundamentum est, ut[38] experientia demonstrat, neque possibile est alium principem quocunque in principatu securam aut stabilem habere conditionem, ubi duae plurime religiones sustentatur, ut exemplo Galliae, Angliaeque cernitur, et ratio ipsa convincit, nam si princeps uni alicui religioni magis quam alteri adhaereat, odium subibit partis contrariae; si vero omni religioni ex aequo faveat, odio ab omnibus tanquam atheus habibitur.

5^a. Quinta utilitas est, quod hac ratione constituta pace successio coronae Galliae stabiliri poterit, omnesque de ea re controversiae tolli, quod durante bello partiumque contrariarum ac religionum dissidentium differentia ac contentione, nullo modo fieri posse videtur, ex qua re ingens universae Galliae incendium imminere necesse est.

6^a. Sexta utilitas est, quod hoc modo securum redditur regnum Galliae de aliquorum periculo maximo, quod est si regnum Angliae aliquando uniretur coronae Hispaniae,

---

35. [*marginal note:*] utilitates regni Galliae ex D. Infantae praelatione
36. principes] *this ed.*; princeps *B*
37. (cum Anglia] *this ed.*; cum (Anglia *B*
38. ut] *interlined with caret B*

quod nulla alia ratione secure evitare potest, nisi hac compositione, primo quia Rex Hispaniae bello fortasse poterit regnum Angli[a]e obtinere vivente vel mortua Regina qu[a]e modo preest, adiutus Catholicorum ope, qui multum illi favent, et qui ut ex praesenti liberentur persecutionis praessura, cuicunque principi Catholico opem ferenti se adiungerent, deinde etiam cum Rex Hispaniae eam quoque habeat successionis actionem ad regnum Angliae per ius familiae Lancastrensis, quae omnibus nota est, et si modo ius hoc suum persequi omitteret, filius tamen eius ac successores, occasionem nacti semper Angliae regno imminerent, neque ulla via poterit evacuari haec regum Hispanorum actio, nisi per hanc per Infantam, ut dixi, compositionem.

7[a]. Septima utilitas est quod Rex Galliae non tantum recuperabit hac ratione ea oppida et arces quae Infantae nomine retinentur in Britaniae vel alibi, sed etiam efficii potest, ut ipsa Infanta renunciet omni iuri quod habeat in hanc provinciam, vel in aliam, vel in ipsam etiam coronam Franciae, quam tamen actionem persequi nunquam desinent tam ipsa quam eius posteri, nisi hac compositione radix ipsa praecidatur.

8[a]. Octava utilitas est, et omnium forte maxima quod omnes actiones atque praetensiones quas a quatrocentis fere annis Anglorum reges in varias Galliae provincias atque in ipsam tandem Franciae quoque coronam habuerunt, atque infinitorum bellorum ac calamitatum causae fuerunt, hac compositione tolli penitus atque extirpari poterunt, per Infantae scilicet ac mariti sui, renunciationem, ac per omnium ordinum Angliae consensum, quem facile obtinere poterit Infanta cum non precario tantum regnum accipiet, sicut Rex Scotiae, si admitteretur, sed viribus satis munita ad eliciendum illum Parlamenti consensum, quem facilius etiam concedent Catholici qui Infantae favebunt, quam haeretici, quibus niti Rex Scotiae necessario debebit, quia Catholici etiam nunc ex conscientiae dictamine non parum moventur ad renunciandum istiusmodi inanibus titulis ac praetensionibus in regnum Galliae, ex quibus nihil aliud boni consecutum inde a multis saeculis viderunt, quam bella continua ac infiniti sanguinis Christiani effusionem, nullam autem unquam fuisse nec futuram tam idoneam occasionem istiusmodi bellorum causas resecandi quam haec est, manifeste omnes vident; Rex enim Scotiae si Angliae regnum consequeretur, titulo Regis Galliae renunciare, armaque atque insignia Francica ab Anglicis iterum separare, neque volet neque facile ab Anglis permittetur, neque quisque alius qui solo iure successionis haereditatem regni adibit, et Anglorum tantum viribus nitetur, id facile praestaret, Infantam vero iustissimis de causis id ipsum praestare posse nulli dubium esse potest.

Haec igitur aliaque commoda, quae brevitatis causa omitto, regno Galliae obvenient, ex Serenissimae Infantae ad regnum Angliae evectione, quae in universae quoque reipublicae Christianae beneficium emanare quoque necesse est.

Obiectiones contra praedicta

Sed contra haec omnia, solent ab aliis obiici duo, primum quod si princeps Hispaniae sive liberis decenderet, ita ut regnum Hispaniarum in ipsam quoque Serenissimam Infantam deveniret, hac ratione uniretur regnum Angliae corona Hispaniae. éSed haec difficultas facile dissolvitur, lege enim lata caveri poterit, ut si tale aliquid acciderit, ad secundum Infantae filium, vel ad proximum sanguine ex ordinum quoque regni consensu atque approbatione coronae Angliae transiret successio, ita ut numquam alteri coronae maiori uniri possit.

Remanet igitur secunda difficultas adhuc maior, de augmento potentiae Regis Hispaniarum per hanc filiae evectionem,[39] quod quidem in damnum reliquorum principum Christianarum fore posse videtur, praecipue vero Regis Galliae praeiuditium, cum unitis Hispaniae atque Angliae viribus, Gallia impugnari, vel etiam dividi possit ut aliquando de Regno Neapolitano visum est.

Ad hanc obiectionem ac difficultatem respondetur primo, quod si liberum esset caeteris principibus et maxime Regi Galliarum pro suo arbitrio a bellis domi vacare, et optionem quoque facere quamnam vellet rerum Anglicanarum conditionem esse, tunc fortassis praesenti Angliae conditione contentus omnem aliam respuere posset, sed alius longe est rerum status; Gallia enim bello gravissimo foris premitur, neque domi bene sibi cohaeret, Hispania continuis damnis urgetur ut Angliam vel Hiberniam invadat, Angliae conditio ita anceps est ut diu consistere non possit, sed probabiliter cadet, idque brevi, in manus vel Regis Scotiae vel Hispaniae, neque id Rex Galliae facile fortasse impedire poterit: horum vero utrumque, quid adferat preiuditii tum Regi Galliae tum etiam reliquis Christianis principibus facile cernitur. Quare ut istiusmodi maiora vitentur incommoda, difficultates aliquae persuperandae sunt.

Secundo respondetur, quod cum tot et tantae utilitates quae antea explicuimus Regi Galliarum sint obventurae ex hac Infantae praelatione, qui tamen Rex nihil ex suo forte praestabit ad rem conficiendam praeter consensum ac voluntatem, Rex vero Hispaniae universos sumptus facturus sit, et ius insuper successionis quod ad Angliam habet resignaturus, aequum sane est, ut aliquod etiam comodum inde ferat Rex Hispaniae, quod nullo modo moderatius excogitari posse videtur, quam re non sibi sed filiae tantum suae regnum Angliae acquiratur.

Quod vero de augmento potentiae Regis Hispaniae ac de periculo opprimendae vel dividendae Galliae obiicitur, nullo firmo fundamento niti videtur, primum quia etiamsi Serenissima Infanta sit Regis Hispaniae filia, potita tamen Angliae regno, ratione status ac commodi proprii obligabitur, ad regnum illud suum tuendum, ac ad cuiuscunque principis vicini (etiamsi pater fraterve sit) potentiam viresque quantum in se est moderandas[40] ac temperandas cuius rei quotidie exempla prae oculis habemus.

Praeterea per multos annos postquam Infanta Angliae regnum adepta fuerit difficultatibus plurimis excercebitur in pacificando regno,[41] ac vestienda religione Catholica, tum ob reliquos praetensores, qui multi sunt tum etiam ac ob religionis contrariae assertores ac sequaces, praecipue vero ob Regis Scotiae actionem, qui Regi etiam Daniae affinitate est coniunctus, adeo ut his omnibus de causis, Angliae multum intererit, pacem ac amicitiam diuturnam cum Gallia colere, cum vero tandem post longa tempora reges Anglicani, omnia sua pacifica ac stabilita habuerint, iam sanguinis affinitas cum Hispaniae regibus non parum minuetur.

39. [*marginal note:*] De augmento Regis Hispaniae
40. moderandas] *this ed.*; moderandus B
41. [*marginal note:*] Amicitia Galliae necessaria esset Infantae Regno Angliae potitae (France's friendship would be necessary for the Infanta once she has taken possession of the kingdom of England).

Accedit praeterea quod etiamsi reges Hispaniae, atque etiam Angliae (dum a Scotia remanet divisa) coniungere se vellent ad regnum Galliae oppugnandum, parum tamen proficerent si Gallia pacifica unita ac sibi ipsa domi consentiens esset: exemplum vidimus aetate nostra cum Carolus Quintus imperator ex una parte, ac Henricus Octavus Angliae Rex ex alia confaederatis viribus Galliam hostiliter ingressi sunt, neque quicquam tamen magni momenti effecerunt, non enim est regnum Galliae ut regnum Neapolitanum, quod facile dividi inter victores possit, est enim regnum maximarum provinciarum ac viribus immitissimarum adeo ut externos hostes non timeat, si domi sibi unita sit, quicquid autem Angli armis aliquando in eo regno acquisierint, id partim factum est illarum provinciarum ope, quas hereditario iure in Gallia possidebant, praecipue vero ipsorum Gallorum inter se dissensione, ob Ducum nimirum Burgundiae ac Aurelianensium discordias.

Porro si Galliae regnum, quod totius reipublicae Christianae pectus habetur, Hispanorum atque Anglorum sociatis viribus premi cerneretur, status ac politiae ratio omnes statim Germaniae atque Italiae principes, Helvetios etiam atque Danos, excitaret ad auxiliares manus maturae ferendas, praecipue vero Regem Scotiae res moveret, qui moderata admodum pecunia adiutus, magnos excercitus (pro ea quam habet hominum copiam) conscribere facile poterit, ac praeceteris omnibus principibus Anglorum animos domi reprimere.

Denique haec res non tantum rationis vi ac discursu nititur, sed multorum quoque animorum experientia probatur, nam ut de aetate tantum nostra loquamur videmus Henricum Angliae Regem eius nominis septimum, atque octavi patrem, virum bellicosum, Ferdinando se Hispaniae Regi Catholico armis quoque insigni sociasse per matrimonium Catherinae Ferdinandi filiae, Arturo primum principi Henrici filio data est[42] ac Henrico deinde secundo genito, priori mortuo, nupta, neque tamen aut viventibus Henrico Septimo ac Ferdinando, aut postea succedentibus Carolo Imperatore ac Henrico Rege Octavo, ac per viginti fere annos continuos inter se confederatis quicque magni momenti contra Galliam vidimus gestum, aut grande aliquod periculum regibus Galliarum inde natum esse; quod postea etiam perspectum est, cum Philippus Hispaniarum princeps, Rex vero Neapolitano, renunciatus vivente patre Imperatore Carolo, Mariae Angliae Reginae, ex matre Hispana oriundae matrimonio iunctus est, ex quo non tantum Hispaniae, Belgii, Neapolis atque Angliae vires sociare sunt, verum etiam imperii totius, quibus tamen omnibus facile restitit Galliae regnum, iis quae supradiximus adminiculis adiutum, nam quamquam in proelio Quintiano iacturam passus est, Caleti tamen oppido recuperatione quod in Anglorum potestate ad trecentos fere annos extiterat, non parum damnum illatum, resarcivit.

Non est igitur quod regnum Galliae, sociationem hanc Serenissimae Infantae cum Hispaniae regibus multum vereatur, aut suspectam habeat, tum quod nocere plurimum non possit, tum etiam quod rationes plurimae sint, quare neque illam durare diu probabile sit, neque quod Anglicani Regis per multos saltem annos pacem institutam cum Gallia violare velle debebunt: praesertim dum Scotiae regnum a se separatum suique ac regni competitorem aemulum tam vicinum habuerint: ex alia vero parte

---

42. data est] *this ed.*; data est) B

emolumenta illa quae Galliae regno accrescunt ac per illud universae quoque reipublicae Christianae ex ea quae proponitur de Serenissima Infanta compositio tot et tanta sunt, ut sperandum sit Deum optimum maximum huic tanto bono gratia sua affuturum, ac viros omnes pios ac pendentes, pacisque publicae studiosos, auxilium quoque suum prompte allaturos.

Translation

A consideration of which of the princes who make claim to the succession to the English realm ought to be preferred before the others, according to the present state of Christendom

First it should be known, according to Doleman's book about the right of royal succession amongst the English, that although it is possible to reduce virtually all controversies in this matter to two ancient royal lines – to be precise, Lancaster and York, who began almost three centuries ago to contest the crown between them (and each one has had four kings from its own number) – today the suit has been extended to five families and to ten or more claimants from the same families, each and every one of whom (something unheard of elsewhere) has his own reasons why he thinks that the right of succession to this kingdom ought to be given to him in the first place.

§ These are the families: the Scottish, and from it the king of Scotland, through the first marriage of the elder daughter of Henry VII, king of England, and Arbella, born in England from the second marriage of the daughter of the same Henry.[43]

§ Another family is that of the duke of Suffolk, who married the younger daughter of the same king Henry, and from her had two daughters, from the first of which was born, in England, the earl of Hertford and from the second the earl of Derby.[44]

§ The third family is of the duke of Clarence, who was the brother of Edward IV king of England, from the house of York, and from this family there exist in England today the earl of Huntington, Hastings by name, and the house of the Poles.[45]

§ The fourth family is Portuguese, or of the kings of Portugal, who claim the succession to the kingdom of England through the marriage of the Portuguese queen, named Philippa, who was the sister and heir of Henry IV from the house of Lancaster, and from

---

43. Margaret Tudor (1489–1541), elder daughter of Henry VII, was the great-grandmother of James VI of Scotland, through her marriage with James IV (1473–1513), and Lady Arbella Stuart (1575–1615), through her marriage to Archibald Douglas, sixth earl of Douglas.

44. Mary Tudor (1496–1533), younger daughter of Henry VII, was the great-grandmother, through her marriage to Charles Brandon (ca. 1484–1545), first duke of Suffolk, of Edward Seymour (1561–1612), Lord Beauchamp (son of Edward Seymour [1539–1621], first earl of Hertford), and Ferdinando Stanley (ca. 1559–1594), fifth earl of Derby, son of Henry Stanley, fourth earl of Derby (1531–1593).

45. Lady Margaret Pole (1473–1541), eighth countess of Salisbury and daughter of George of York (1449–1478), duke of Clarence, was mother of Cardinal Reginald Pole (ca. 1500–1558) and great-grandmother of Henry Hastings (ca. 1535–1595), third earl of Huntingdon.

this family there exist today the king of Spain, the duke of Parma, and the duke of Braganza.[46]

§ Finally, the fifth family is of the dukes of Brittany, who for various reasons, as can be seen in Doleman's book, arrogate the right to the crown of England to themselves, and of this family there are today Isabella the infanta of Spain, with her sister the duchess of Savoy, who were born of the elder daughter of the king of France.[47]

§ Next it should be known that all ten of these claimants, or at least the greatest part of them, dispute the first place of succession so much among themselves, and each part presses its opponents with so many impediments and exclusions, that if you weigh them all, it is extremely difficult and uncertain which part has the better claim, even if we consider only the bloodline.

§ In the third place it should be known that it is not only the right of blood, or nearness in blood, that should be taken into account, but also many other things, at least the possibility, the easiness or difficulty of attaining the kingdom, or even of holding on to it and defending it after acquiring it. It seems appropriate, therefore, to consider all these circumstances in the examen following: the religion and other qualities of the claimant, also the security or dangers of the realm of England, the advantages and disadvantages to the neighbouring kingdoms, and the wishes and preferences of their princes, especially of the kings of France and Spain, who are the closest and most powerful, nor will they easily allow there to be any prejudice to themselves or their states and sovereignty, by this accession of a king of England.

Of the King of Scotland and Arbella

James VI of Scotland has the first claim of all, if we consider the bloodline of succession, which he holds from Henry VII king of England, who gained the sceptre seventy years ago by force of arms; although if it is called into question to whom the right of legitimate succession belonged at that time, when Henry entered the kingdom in arms, it seems, according to Doleman's book, that a case can be made for Alfonso V, king of Portugal, who was then living, and was defective both in might and wealth, because he was the next heir of the house of Lancaster.

But if priority of succession is conceded to the king of Scotland, according to the line of blood, traced most nearly through these one hundred years, his opponents nevertheless raise various objections to exclude him: first, his religion, which up to now has been of the very worst kind, nor has he ever since boyhood given any sign of amendment. He has contracted marriage to a heretical house and virtually all his relatives and associ-

---

46. Margaret of Parma (1522–1586), Philip II of Spain, and Teodósio II (1568–1630), duke of Braganza, were descended from Philippa of Lancaster (1360–1415), eldest child of John of Gaunt (1340–1399), first duke of Lancaster and son of Edward III, through Manuel I (1469–1521), king of Portugal.

47. Elisabeth of Valois (1545–1568), eldest daughter of Henry II of France (1519–1559), married Philip II of Spain in 1559, and gave birth to the infanta Isabella Clara Eugenia (1566–1633) and Catalina Micaela (1567–1597), duchess of Savoy. Henry II descended from the duchess Anne of Brittany (1477–1514). The name Isabella is equivalent to Elizabeth.

ates are heretics. Besides, no application for papal dispensation was made or obtained when his mother entered into marriage with Henry Darnley, related to her by blood in the second degree. This was the marriage from which that king originated. They object, furthermore, that the king of Scots was excluded from any right of succession by express law laid down ten years ago by the Privy Council and parliament, on account of the condemnation of his mother for seeking the death of Queen Elizabeth. Since this law was ratified before the offence was committed, and by the consensus of all orders, for the sake of preserving the security and peace of the realm, they affirm that it is just, and that it was capable of being lawfully ratified. These are the objections which they raise to weaken the king of Scotland's claim to the kingdom of England by right of succession.

But if other circumstances are taken into account, many more arguments can be alleged from these to weaken the king of Scotland's claim, and first, indeed, they are hardly able to say that the king of Scotland should be admitted to the realm of England either by the heretics or the Catholics, for although to the English people it seems that a union and conjunction is to be expected of those kingdoms, nevertheless the estrangement of feeling between the English and the Scots is much stronger, on account of their being neighbours and almost always at war with each other. From this arises the English belief that they are more worthy and will never allow the Scots to rule over them, especially since they also have many claimants from amongst their leading nobles, as has already been said. As a result, wars, suspicions, and disturbances will arise if the king of Scotland assumes the sceptre, nor can peace be expected for many generations, especially since not even the Scottish nobles themselves will accept this union of the kingdoms with equanimity, when they see that by that means they will be subject to a more powerful king, who will threaten those liberties which they enjoy up to a certain point, and at length little by little they will have to submit and adhere to the English, whom they hate as a more powerful nation, and be sundered from the French, whom they love very greatly.

This conjoining of kingdoms would be very disadvantageous to foreign princes, first to the Roman pontiff, both because of the king's religion, and also because it suits the church more for there to be as many Christian kingdoms as possible; and then to the king of the Spaniards for the same reasons, and because of the ancient friendship and confederation of the Scots with the French, and finally because both his own and his own daughter's claim to the realm of England would be altogether quashed by the accession of the king of Scotland.

§ Quite a few of these same considerations would carry weight with the king of Denmark as well, but most of all the advancement of the king of Scotland to the realm of England would seem to be damaging to the king of France, both because as a result he would have a more powerful neighbour, but also because that ancient friendship and confederation of the Scots with the French would change into enmity, on account of that right by which the kings of England have laid claim to the crown of France, and to various provinces of the same country, for many centuries now, nor will they cease to pursue that claim when they see themselves to be powerful enough.

§ Finally, since France has kept Scotland submissive to herself up to now, which she has always set in opposition to the power of England, not only would she lose that support by this conjunction of the two kingdoms, but another danger would pose a threat, not to be taken lightly: that is to say, that when the king of England has been strengthened by this accession, he would think that various provinces of France would belong to him by a lawful right of succession; the king of Spain, too, would consider that some would belong to his daughter also. It could happen that if this confederation were made, and their strengths combined, they could at some time divide France up, which could hardly happen so long as the kingdoms of England and Scotland remain divided.

With respect to Arbella, virtually the same difficulties apply as to the king of Scotland, or even more: namely, her right of succession being less sure and explicit, because she descends from the Queen of Scots by her second marriage. And if these arguments, which many believe to be powerful, are not sufficiently justified, [we can add] her powerlessness to accede to the realm, or defend it; the lack of nobility in her father, who was virtually a commoner; her religion being heretical; and other considerations of this kind.

Concerning the Earls of Hertford, Derby, and Huntington, and of the Poles

All these English earls are in conflict among themselves about the right of succession, for if the king of Scotland is excluded for the reasons which have been adduced above, the first two, who are descended from the second daughter of King Henry VII, regard the nearest place to belong to them – and first of all the earl of Hertford, who owes his birth to the elder nephew of King Henry. But the earl of Derby, born from the younger, excludes him on the count of a double or triple illegitimacy. Again, the earl of Huntington, who by a more ancient right than both proceeds from the daughter of the duke of Clarence of the house of York, impugns the earl of Derby of a similar mark of illegitimacy: indeed, he rejects the Poles as having a much later position in the same claim from the house of York. For this reason, the earl of Huntington, too, is now himself rejected by the said two earls as holding an inferior place in that very right of the house of York, since both of them are descended from the daughter of the elder brother of King Edward IV and head of the house of York, whereas Huntington only descends from the daughter of the duke of Clarence, who was the younger brother of King Edward: and so much for their right of succession.

But in other respects, the same difficulties and disadvantages, of gaining and guarding the crown, which have been set out above, apply. Since there are many claimants, and they are divided against each other, and they lack the favour of any foreign princes, or consanguinity or alliance with them, none of them seems to be able to stand in the way of the king of Scotland or any of the other competitors. The religion of all of these earls has been heretical heretofore, or at least is known to be dubious, such that it would seem neither secure nor easy to elevate any of them to the kingship. Indeed, all of them have contracted marriage, so they are unable to find aid in the wealth or resources of a foreign alliance.

The King of Spain and the Dukes of Parma and Braganza

These three princes, since they are descended from the royal family of Lancaster through Philippa, the daughter of the duke of Lancaster, queen of Portugal, could advance virtually the same argument, based on succession from the house of Lancaster, as once they used to lay claim to the throne of Portugal. It is even more cogent, perhaps, in that in many people's opinion the laws of England allow representation[48] in the succession to the crown, which however has no force in the case of the Portuguese. This appears to give the king of Spain the foremost place among the rest, since the right of the house of Lancaster, moreover, is generally preferred before that of York, if we pass over the exceptional circumstances of the past hundred years. Many arguments are put forward in Doleman's book of the royal succession, although no final decision is made in favour of any party.

But if other things are added and weighed, not a few difficulties arise on all sides. For in the case of the king of Spain, whereas on the one hand not everyone agrees on the justice of his claim, on the other hand they affirm that his claim would be injurious, not only to the pope and to the rest of the foreign princes, because of the increase of such great power, but also much more to the English themselves: whatever state they find themselves in, ultimately they would all take it very ill that the kingdom of England should be united to another kingdom, to become subject to a foreign prince, and be reduced to the status of a province, whence rebellions, wars, and very great seditions would arise. Neither do they think that it can be achieved without the greatest disturbance to Christendom that the king of Spain should subdue England to himself, even if he has the hearts of the Catholics chiefly attached to him because of the union of religion and the longstanding benefits they have received from him.

As for the dukes of Parma and Braganza, although they are outstanding princes and most acceptable to the English Catholics both because of their nobility, their religious ardour, and other virtues as well as because the house of Lancaster is held in most grateful memory, nevertheless since they are far distant from England, nor does it seem that they can obtain that kingdom and hold it fast by their own strength, seeing that there is such a wealth of opponents and claimants (unless they are also aided by the forces of foreign powers, of which nothing can be promised of certainty, it seems, for those reasons which each one of them could proffer for himself), very little hope shines out, therefore, that anything of moment could be done to the advantage of those princes, but if it could, their personages would be most welcome to the Catholics.

Her Highness the Infanta of Spain

There remains, then, the fifth and last Breton family, whose hereditary line, in all those which are not comprised in the Salic law, descends to Isabella, the infanta of Spain, in the first instance; but it is fully explained in Doleman's book what rights the house of Brittany have to the throne of England, and how many there are. What is more, the king of Spain could transfer the entire right which he himself has, or might have, from the

---

48. This refers to the right of an elder son to represent the person of his mother: Ranuzio Farnese, duke of Parma, claimed to represent his mother, Mary, duchess of Parma, deceased wife of Alessandro Farnese and elder daughter of Edward, former infant of Portugal. Although in Portuguese law, which disallowed representation, this did not give him precedence over Philip II, king of Portugal, in right of his descent from Edward's elder sister Isabel, he could claim that in English law he should be preferred above Philip and Catherine, duchess of Braganza, younger daughter of Edward. See *Conference about the Next Succession*, part 2, 180–188.

house of Portugal to this princess, his daughter, so much so that if other matters are in agreement, her claim to the succession could not fail.

But all the other circumstances, which have been considered or brought under examination above, are so much in favour of this princess, that it seems that nothing more could be hoped for: for wherever we cast our eyes, more advantages occur: first, to be sure, to the English themselves, because if this princess governs them, they will retain their kingdom independent of any others, which is what they want most. Then, they will obtain the security of the Catholic religion, which is in their prayers. Besides, they will have the forces of the king of Spain ready for all their needs, whether to establish peace or strengthen the state. Finally, even to the [other] claimants themselves, it will be much safer for the English people, more useful and more honourable, if they grant it to someone more eminent, rather than if an equal should give the palm to an equal. For this princess would even be able to reward them with better conditions than if any one of them should be raised above the others, for such a one would be compelled by fear to do what virtually all English kings have tended to do in these recent times, that is, to see to their own safety by eliminating other pretenders. This princess, on the other hand, supported by her father's power, would enjoy an assured state of rule, nor would she fear the strength of the remaining pretenders so much, or attract hatred, from which arise so many suspicions, seditions, and movements – which would be of the greatest advantage to the kingdom.

The advantages arising from promoting the princess's cause would seem no less even to foreign princes. For with regard to the apostolic see it seems clear – given the piety of this princess, and her passion for planting religion, so noteworthy, worldwide, that her reign could give rise to hope, not only of the restoration of the English realm, but of those kingdoms also which are allied to her: the restitution of most of the provinces of the whole north, their reformation and return to the church – it is easily observed, how much it is in the interest of the apostolic see that a princess of this kind should be raised to royal power. Anyone can see that it is in the interest of the king of Spain, that there should be such a prospect for his daughter, but not because his sway and power might perhaps be augmented thereby. For even though this princess may be the daughter of the king of Spain, once she has been empowered in the kingdom, she would be driven by reason of state to guard herself and her own security, rather than to care about her father's power.

§ In the end it is equally of interest to the king of Denmark also, as to the princes of Germany and Italy, that is to say, that these kingdoms of England and Scotland remain divided, and that by this pleasant outcome the kingdom of England should rather be transferred to the daughter of the king of the Spaniards, to another prince of the house of Austria, than that either the king of Scotland should unite three kingdoms or that any king of Spain, fortified by the right of succession and compelled by necessity, should someday subdue England or Ireland, or both of them, and join them by force of arms to his own realms.

§ There remains only the king of France, to whom above all, as the most powerful and the closest to England, this power of the daughter of the king of Spain might pose a threat. But it is clearly just the opposite, since I believe no prince in Christendom stands to gain greater profit from this than the king of the French, not only by the clearing away of those inconveniences which I have noted above would accrue to the kingdom of France by the coming together of England and Scotland, but also by the gaining of very many and very great advantages, which I feel should rather be set out in a separate writing than comprised all too briefly here. Therefore, in the present document I have put together those things I feel need to be said in comparing those who are competing among themselves over the realm of England.

[The Second Document:]

The very great advantages and benefits which will accrue to the king of the French, before all other princes, by establishing the priority of Her Highness Isabella the Infanta of Spain to the throne of England for the public peace

Since, from the former document which compares amongst themselves all the princes who are able to solicit or make a claim for the English crown by right of succession, it seems that now only two remain, who, when all is weighed up – both the inconveniences and difficulties as well as the advantages and benefits – may by any reason of probability be preferred to the rest, if the matter can be settled peacefully and with consideration (which is greatly to be wished); and since the inconveniences and dangers which may accrue to the king of France by the accession of the king of Scotland have been set out in the same document, that is, from so great a power of a neighbouring prince, who necessarily will in the course of time be obliged to be hostile to the kings of France, both on account of proximity and also envy of the other's power, as he seems to be to the dukes of Burgundy, who, even though they originate from the house of the selfsame kings of France, have nevertheless always turned out to be very hostile to the kingdom of France —

And since, besides, it has been shown that if the king of France were to favour the advancement of the king of Scotland, he would not only arm his own rivals, the English, with the allegiance of three kingdoms, affirming that the whole of France belongs to them, but also, he would deprive France of that most efficacious support which they have alone enjoyed for many years for keeping the English restrained at home, namely the most assured friendship and alliance of the Scots —

It is known throughout the whole world how many provinces of France, and how large, the kings of England regard as belonging to them by their most evident right of succession (to say nothing about the crown of France) – namely, the regions of Normandy, Anjou, and Poitiers, and the entire province of Aquitaine besides – which provinces are kept from them by the French by force alone, and which they complain of today. From another source also the king of Spain claims the province of Brittany for his daughter, as well as quite a few other regions in the kingdom of France. So, it could easily happen that the king of Scotland, augmented by such great royal power, assuming an English spirit and egged on by the English, would at some time enter into an alliance with the king of Spain, or with the infanta or her heirs, to divide up the provinces of France, which he would probably not be able to aspire to if the kingdom of England is assigned to the infanta, or proclaimed soon afterwards.

When, therefore, so many disadvantages threaten the kingdom of France from the elevation of the king of Scotland, we see on the other hand what kind of benefits and advantages will accrue to the kingdom of France from the accession of the said infanta.

But the first of all is that since the kingdom of France has been afflicted by the gravest problems of wars for many years, and experiences no less weighty wars in the present, by this strategy she may not only get a breathing space from them all, but find internal freedom and become secure, which does not seem humanly possible in any other way, when the other means of making peace are only temporary palliatives, without dealing with the roots of enmity: but firm peace with Spain and the kingdoms of England, established on this principle, will restore the whole of France and also the rest of Christendom to wholeness.

2. Hence indeed follows the second benefit, that if the king of France achieves peace, he will become absolute master of all the provinces of France, which is hard to imagine happening otherwise, so long as the governors of the provinces see the king so distracted by wars, and the strength of the king of Spain always ready at hand.

3. The third benefit is, that by this means the king of France will be freed from the necessity of asking for aid from the English and other heretics, who, now that he has shown himself to be Catholic, do not help him with arms except to their own advantage. He cannot turn to the English, especially, with any confidence, given those claims they still make to many provinces of France, as we have indicated; on the other hand, if the king of France turns to alliance with those other heretics, even though he is forced to do so by necessity, it is clear that the other Catholic princes will have less confidence in their dealings with him, and hold the most excellent name of "most Christian king" of less account.

4. The fourth benefit is that when peace has been established with England and Spain, the king of France will be able to settle one Catholic religion through the entire kingdom not only without the necessity of help from heretics abroad, but also at home, that is in France herself (when England has been restored to the unity of the church). This is the foundation of all lasting and stable peace, as experience shows, nor is it possible for any other prince in any principality whatsoever to enjoy security and stability where two more religions are maintained, as can be gathered from the example of England and France, and reason itself argues, for if the prince leans to one religion rather than the other, he will attract the hatred of the contrary part; but if he favours every religion equally, he will be held in contempt by all as if he were an atheist.

5. The fifth benefit is that if peace is established on this principle, the succession to the crown of France will be able to be settled, and all disputes on the matter removed, which cannot possibly happen as long as war lasts, conflict and contention between the opposing parties and religious dissidents, as a result of which the whole of France necessarily threatens to go up in flames.

6. The sixth benefit is that by this means the kingdom of France is made secure again from the greatest danger of all, which is if the kingdom of England should some time be united with the crown of Spain, which can by no other means be assuredly avoided, except by this settlement, first, because the king of Spain might perhaps be able to obtain the kingdom of England by war (whether the present queen is alive or dead), aided by the power of the Catholics – who are very favourable to him, and who would join themselves

to any Catholic prince bringing aid to them, so that they may be freed from the current pressure of persecution – and second, since the king of Spain also has that claim to the succession to the kingdom of England by the right of the family of Lancaster, which is known to all. Even if he neglects to pursue his own right, his son and successors will always threaten the kingdom of England when opportunity presents itself, nor can this claim of the kings of Spain be eliminated except by this settlement through the infanta, as I have said.

7. The seventh benefit is that by this plan the king of France will not only recover those towns and strongholds which are held in the name of the infanta in Brittany and elsewhere, but it will be possible to ensure that the infanta herself will renounce all the rights she has to that province, or any other, or even to the crown of France. Neither she nor her successors will ever leave off pursuing this claim unless the root itself is cut off by this settlement.

8. The eighth benefit, and probably the greatest of all, is that all the claims and pretensions which the kings of England have entertained for virtually four hundred years to various French provinces and even the crown of France itself, and have been the cause of infinite wars and calamities, can be entirely removed and extirpated through this settlement: that is to say, through the renunciation of them by the infanta and her husband, and by the consent of all classes in England, which the infanta may easily be able to obtain, since she will not receive the kingdom as precariously as the king of Scotland, if he were admitted, but fortified with enough force to be able to elicit that consent of parliament. The Catholics, who will prefer the infanta, will concede that even more easily than the heretics, whom the king of Scotland will necessarily have to rely on, because the Catholics even now, by the dictates of conscience, are moved not a little to renounce empty claims and titles of this kind to the kingdom of France, from which they have seen no good outcome for many ages other than continual war and infinite effusion of Christian blood. That there never has been nor is likely to be such a suitable opportunity as this for cutting off the causes of wars of this kind, everyone can clearly see, for if the king of Scotland should succeed to the kingdom of England, he would not want to renounce his title of king of France and to separate once more the arms and insignia of France from those of the English, nor would he easily be permitted to do so by the English, nor would anyone else who inherited the kingdom by right of succession alone, and depended on the power of the English alone, easily be able to guarantee it. There can be no doubt that the infanta would indeed be able to assure it on the most justifiable grounds.

These, then, and other benefits, which I omit for the sake of brevity, will accrue to the kingdom of France from the elevation of Her Most Serene Highness the infanta to the kingdom of England, which will also necessarily have a happy issue for the whole of Christendom.

Objections against the Aforesaid

But against all these, two things are commonly objected by others: the first, that if the prince of Spain or his children should reach a point where the kingdom of the Spaniards should also fall to the same Most Serene Highness the infanta, by this means the kingdom of England would be united with the crown of Spain. éBut this difficulty is easily cleared away, for by legislation it could be ensured that, if anything of this kind should happen, the succession to the crown of England should pass to the second son of the infanta, or to the nearest in blood, by the consensus and approval of the estates of the realm, such that it could never be united to any greater crown.

There remains, then, the second difficulty, somewhat greater, of the increase of the power of the Spanish king through this elevation of his daughter, which indeed might seem to be to the detriment of the rest of the Christian rulers, but especially to the prejudice of the king of France, since by the joining together of the Spanish and English powers, it would seem that France would be under threat, or even divided up, just as happened at one time to the kingdom of Naples.

In response to this objection and difficulty it can be said, first, that if the other princes, and in particular the king of the French, were free, in their own eyes, to be untroubled by domestic war and make whatever choice they wanted to about the state of English affairs, then perhaps, being satisfied with the present state of England, they would be able to reject any change. But the state of affairs is very different, for France is under the gravest threat of war from without, and is not well at peace with herself at home. Spain is being prompted by continual losses to invade either England or Ireland, and the state of England is so critical that it is not sustainable for long, but will probably fall – and soon – into the hands either of the king of Scotland or Spain. The king of France could not easily prevent this, but of the two, it is easily seen which would be more to the prejudice both of the king of France and the rest of the Christian princes. Therefore, to avoid greater disadvantages of this kind, other difficulties have to be overcome.

In the second place, it can be said in response that so many and such great benefits as we have explained earlier may accrue to the king of the French from this advancement of the infanta, which the king [of Scotland] will not be in any position to achieve in his own strength without consensus and agreement, whereas the king of Spain, on the other hand, will be ready to apply all his resources, and moreover to renounce the right of succession to England which he holds. So, it is quite clear that the king of Spain would draw some advantage even from it, which, it seems, could not be devised in any more measured way, except in fact by the kingdom of England being acquired not for himself but for his own daughter.

As for the objection about the increase in the power of the king of Spain and the danger of his attacking or dividing up France, it seems to stand on no firm foundation, first because even though Her Serene Highness the infanta is the daughter of the king of Spain, nevertheless, once she is placed on the throne of England, she will be obliged by reason of state and her own advantage to concern herself about that kingdom of hers, and only about the power and strength of any nearby prince whatsoever (even if he is her father or brother) so far as it can be moderated or kept in check – examples of which we have before our eyes every day.

Besides, for many years after the infanta has attained the throne of England she will be preoccupied with many difficulties in pacifying the realm and restoring the Catholic religion, both because of the other claimants, of whom there are many, and also because of those who promote and follow the contrary religion, especially on account of the claim of the king of Scotland, who is joined by blood with the king of Denmark. For all these reasons, therefore, it is very much in England's interest to cultivate lasting friendship with France, since in fact, at long last after long ages, the English kings will have taken hold of all things in peace and stability, once the blood tie with the Spanish kings has diminished slightly.

It has happened besides that even if the kings of Spain and England, too, so long as she remained divided from Scotland, wished to join together to attack the kingdom of France, nevertheless they would achieve little if France were peaceful, united, and harmonious in itself at home. We have seen an example in our own day when the emperor Charles V on the one hand and King Henry VIII of England on the other invaded France with their combined powers, but nevertheless did not achieve anything of great moment. For the kingdom of France is not like the kingdom of Naples, which could easily be divided up amongst her conquerors; instead, it is a kingdom of very large, militarily implacable provinces, to the point where she would not fear external enemies, if she were internally united. But whatever the English have acquired by arms in that realm at any time has been accomplished partly with the assistance of those provinces which they possessed in France by hereditary right, but more particularly, in fact, as a result of dissension amongst the French themselves, that is to say, on account of conflicts between the dukes of Burgundy and Orleans.

Moreover, if the kingdom of France, which is regarded as the heart of all Christendom, were perceived to be under pressure from the combined forces of the Spanish and the English, reason of state and polity would immediately induce all the rulers of Germany and Italy, the Swiss too and the Danes, to offer their homegrown help, but the business would especially move the king of Scotland, who, being assisted with a moderate subsidy, would be able to get together a large army (because he has a great store of men), and quell the Englishmen's spirits at home better than any other prince.

Finally, this matter is not decided on the basis of the force of reason or discourse alone, but is also proved by the experience of many souls, for, just to speak of our own time, we see that Henry, king of England, seventh of that name, and father of the eighth, a warlike man, associated himself in his coat of arms with Ferdinand, the Catholic king of Spain, through the marriage of Catherine, Ferdinand's daughter: first she was given to Arthur, Henry's firstborn prince, and then married to Henry, the second-born, after the death of the elder son. Nevertheless, neither during the lifetimes of Henry VII and Ferdinand, nor their successors the Emperor Charles and King Henry VIII, and through a mutual alliance that lasted virtually twenty years together, did we see any significant action taken against France, or any great danger to the kings of France arising from it. Moreover, consider what was seen afterwards: when Philip the ruler of the Spaniards, indeed king of Naples (his father Emperor Charles having abdicated), was joined in matrimony with Mary, Queen of England, born of a Spanish mother, with the result that not only were the forces of Spain, Flanders, Naples, and England joined, but also those of the entire empire – even so, the kingdom of

France was able to resist them all easily, aided by the supports we have spoken of above, for although she suffered defeat in the battle of Saint-Quentin, she repaired the damage done in no small measure by the recovery of the city of Calais,[49] which had continued under English rule for virtually three hundred years.

So it is not that the kingdom of France greatly fears this association of Her Serene Highness the infanta with the kings of Spain, or is suspicious about it, both because it cannot do more harm, and also because there are many reasons why it is unlikely to last long, on the one hand, and because the English kings should not wish to violate a peace established with France for so many years at least, especially when they have the kingdom of Scotland separated from themselves and theirs, and a rival competitor to the throne so close by. But on the other hand, those benefits which accrue to the kingdom of France, and through that to the whole of Christendom as well, from this settlement which is proposed of Her Serene Highness the infanta are so many and so great that it is to be hoped that Almighty God will bestow his grace on such a great good, and all pious and grave men, and those who pursue public peace, will promptly bring their own aid also.

BA 3 Memorandum on the Appointment of Two Bishops, Rome, August 1597

SOURCES:
BAV, MS Vat. Lat. 6227, fols. 26–27 = *B*;
AAV, Fondo Borghese III, 124c, fols. 134–ff. = *V*;
AAW VI, no. 80, 286–287 = *W*.

EDITION: Tierney, 3: cxvii–cxix (appendix no. 21), "From a manuscript in [Tierney's] possession."

NOTE: Tierney argues that this proposed arrangement was designed to ensure that Persons could control the Catholic ecclesiastical hierarchy for England, both at home and abroad (p. cxviii n1). He also notes that although here the document is attributed to the Catholics in England, Persons claimed it as his own in his *Briefe Apologie or Defence of the Catholike Ecclesiastical Hierarchie* (Antwerp, 1601), fol. 102r. There, Persons explains that it was written for the pope and the cardinals of the Inquisition, and that he asked the cardinal protector, Enrico Caetani, to present the arguments to the other cardinals. Persons's claim to have sought to create bishoprics in England following the restoration is supported by his suggestion, in a memorandum of 30 August 1596 (B340), that Stapleton be elevated to a senior bishopric, and by his endorsement of the role of bishops in his *Memorial for the Restoration of England*.

---

49. The Spanish army under Duke Emmanuel Philibert of Savoy defeated the French at Saint-Quentin in Picardy, 10 August 1557. The French reclaimed Calais from the English on 7 January 1558.

Rationes quare Catholici Anglicani subordinationem aliquam
petunt inter sacerdotes Anglicanae gentis, tum in Anglia, quam in
Belgio degentes[50]

Cum ecclesia Catholica Anglicana in corpus magnum per Dei gratiam iam excreverit,[51] atque indies excrescat magis, numerus etiam sacerdotum seminariorum[52] multiplicatione factus sit auctior, humiliter petitur a Vestra Sanctitate, ut, ad incomoda vitanda, quae ex corporis regimine, quod nullam membrorum subordinationem hactenus agnovit, oriri necesse est, et[53] praecipue ad schismatum ac divisionum occasiones tollendas, quae iam alicubi pullulare coeperunt, duo saltem episcopi Anglicanae gentis[54] constituantur, qui reliquos moderentur ac gubernent; alter in Anglia, alter vero in Belgio qui in Anglia moranti correspondeat ac cooperetur, idque ob rationes sequentes.

De Episcopo in Anglia

Necessitas unius episcopi in Anglia pro praesenti rerum Catholicarum statu, magna et multiplex esse videtur: —

1°. Ad roborandum Catholicorum animos[55] in ferendis persecutionibus, episcopi enim arietes gregis esse solebant in persecutionibus antiquis.

2°. Ad sacramentum confirmationis conferendum,[56] quo ad quadraginta fere iam annos caruerunt Catholici Anglicani, ob episcopi inopiam; cum tamen ad fortitudinem in pugna spirituali obtinendam, praecipue conferre, hoc sacramentum noscatur.

3°. Ad chrisma oleumque sacrum conficiendum,[57] cuius maxima inopia premuntur hodie sacerdotes Anglicani, cum aliunde importari sine maximis periculis non possit.

4°. Ad sacros ordines quibusdam conferendos, qui, cum alioqui[58] digni sint, exire tamen regno ad eos suscipiendos non possunt; vel quod carceribus teneantur, vel iusta aliqua alia causa impediti. Aliquando etiam e seminariis remittuntur scholares aliquot, sanitatis recuperandae[59] causa, in Angliam, qui sacerdotio digni sunt, nec tamen, ob aetatis defectum, ordinari possunt ante missionem.

5°. Ad consilium dandum in rebus dubiis, arduis, ac gravioribus, quae cum saepe incidant, his difficillimis Angliae temporibus, neque aliquis modo sit in universo clero, qui aliis auctoritate praeeat, non leve inde damnum rebus communibus accedit.

50. Anglicanae] *W*; Anglicanos *B*; *Tierney's heading reads* Rationes pro Episcopis duobus Anglicanis
51. per Dei gratiam iam] *W B*; *om*. *Tierney*
52. sacerdotum seminariorum] *W*; sacerdotum ex seminariorum *B Tierney*
53. et] *W Tierney*; ac *B*
54. gentis] *W B*; nationis *Tierney*
55. *Tierney omits the rest of this paragraph.*
56. *Tierney omits the rest of this paragraph.*
57. *Tierney omits the rest of this paragraph.*
58. alioqui] *W*; alioquin *B Tierney*
59. recuperandae] *W B*; recuperendae *Tierney*

6°. Ad informationes veras et cum auctoritate, tum ad Vestram Sanctitatem ac[60] cardinalem protectorem, tum ad reliquos principes, de rebus Anglicis mittendas; cuius rei defectu unusquisque modo scribit quae affectus vel[61] error suggerit.

7°. Ad tollendas sacerdotum inter se aemulationes, et terminandas lites, qua una re plurimum paci ac concordiae omnium consuletur.

8°. Ad disponendos ac collocandos sacerdotes locis idoneis, iisque movendos cum erit necesse, aut maioris Dei gloriae ratio postulabit; qua etiam una re multum alleviabuntur patres Societatis tum onere tum invidia[62] aliquorum; cum ipsi hactenus sacerdotibus omnibus, quantum potuerint,[63] hac in re prospexerint,[64] non ex officio, sed tantum ex charitate.

Ad iuvandum hunc episcopum petunt Catholici adiungi numerum aliquem praecipuorum sacerdotum, qui per Angliae provincias degunt, hoc est, ad septem vel octo,[65] qui, vel archipresbyterorum, vel archidiaconorum nomine, episcopo assistant, et a conciliis sint; ita ut vices suas per provincias eis, tanquam commissariis, delegare possit. Horum quattuor nominari statim a Vestra Sanctitate petunt,[66] reliqui vero ab episcopo ipso[67] iam constituto, cum, pro regionum varietate hominumque notitia, ipse melius intelliget quinam magis idonei ad hoc munus erunt.

De Episcopo Anglo in Belgio

Huius etiam episcopi constituendi par necessitas ac utilitas se offerre videntur:

1°. Quia cum episcopus in Anglia iurisdictione episcopali uti non possit in foro exteriori, ob metum persecutorum,[68] hic in Belgio degens illam supplere poterit, evocando ex Anglia, et puniendo (si opus fuerit) quemcumque ille, qui in Anglia vivit, castigare non audebit.

2°. Ut informationes ex Anglia acceptas videat, et, pro diversitate eorum hominum qui ad ipsum scribent, varia conferat, et ea quae certa sunt, ex assistentium suorum consensu, ad Vestram Sanctitatem de rebus Anglicis transmittat.

3°. Ut examinet eos sacerdotes vel scholares qui, ex superiorum suorum mandato, Angliam sunt ingressuri, iisque facultates impertiat, vel non impertiat, pro meritis vel demeritis; et iudicium suum de ipsis ad episcopum in Anglia degentem perscribat, ne omnibus liceat pro libitu ingredi, et causae Catholicorum incommodare, quod modo saepe fit.

4°.[69] Hic episcopus plurimum iuvamenti adferet ad causam Anglicanam promovendam, iuvabit etiam ad unionem et concordiam Catholicorum qui in Belgio vivunt,

60. ac] *W Tierney*; et *B*
61. vel] *W Tierney*; et *B*
62. invidia] *W*; invidiae *Tierney*; odio *B*
63. potuerint] *W B*; potuerit *Tierney*
64. *B inserts* licet *before* non
65. ad septem vel octo] *W Tierney*; ad septimum vel octatum *B*
66. petunt] *W Tierney*; poterunt *B*
67. episcopo ipso] *W Tierney*; ipso episcopo *B*
68. persecutorum] *W Tierney*; persecutionum *B*
69. 4°] *om. W*

praesertim si⁷⁰ sex archipresbyteri adiugantur, ex praecipuis nationis Anglicanae sacerdotibus, quemadmodum supra de episcopo diximus, qui in Anglia victurus est.

Si Vestrae Sanctitati visum fuerit Catholicis Anglicanis has gratias concedere, expediet, primo, ut hi duo *episcopi in partibus* nominentur, et quod non habeant titulos Anglicanos, tum ob vitandas aemulationes, tum etiam ne persecutores magis inde exasperentur: secundo, ut uterque habeat iurisdictionem in universam Angliam, et forsan⁷¹ qui in Belgio victurus est, archiepiscopus sit, ob subordinationem: tertio, ut fiant secreto, per brevia apostolica, unius tantum episcopi ordinatione, ubicunque ille reperiatur, sive in Anglia, Francia, Belgio, Scotia, vel Hibernia; hoc enim necessarium est ad secretum servandum: quarto, ut res expediatur, si fieri possit, antequam innotescat, aut heretici Anglicani aliquid de ea suspicentur, ne maiori diligentia observent portus, ad egressum vel ingressum alicuius episcopi.

[*W endorsed:*] "Rationes pro Episcopis duobus Anglicanis 1597"

[*V endorsed:*] "S. D. N. Relacion de la necessidad que ay de poner dos obispos Ingleses uno en Flandes, i otro en Inglaterra i de los buenos effectos que de aqui se seguiran"

Translation

Reasons why the English Catholics desire some subordination among the priests of the English nation operating both in England and in Belgium

Since the English Catholic church has, by the grace of God, now grown into a large body, and daily continues to grow, the number of priests also being augmented by the increase in seminarians, Your Holiness is humbly requested that – in order to avoid the troubles which will necessarily arise in the constitution of a body which up to now has known no subordination of members, and especially to remove occasions of division and schism, which have begun to break out everywhere – at least two bishops be ordained of the English nation, to regulate and govern the rest: one in England, but the other in Belgium, who would correspond and cooperate with the one remaining in England — and this for the reasons given below.

The Bishop in England

It appears that the need for a bishop in England is great, in many respects, given the present state of Catholic affairs.

First, for strengthening the resolve of the Catholics, in bearing the persecutions, for bishops used to be the rams of the flock, in the persecutions of antiquity.

Second, for conferring the rite of confirmation, which the English Catholics have lacked for almost four decades now for want of a bishop, when in fact this sacrament is known specially to confer the grace of obtaining strength in the spiritual battle.

---

70. si] *W*; si ei *B Tierney*
71. forsan] *W*; forsan ut *B Tierney*

Third, for blessing the chrism and the holy oil, for the lack of which the English priests today suffer extremely, since it is not possible to smuggle them in from elsewhere except with the greatest dangers.

Fourth, for conferring holy orders on some who, although worthy in other respects, are not able to leave the kingdom to receive them, either because they are being held in custody or prevented by some other legitimate cause. Sometimes, indeed, a few scholars are sent back from the seminaries who are worthy of the priesthood but are unable, because they are too young, to be ordained before setting out on the mission.

Fifth, to give advice on dubious, hard, and more serious matters. Since these often occur in these very difficult times in England without there being anyone amongst all the clergy who has authority above the others, great harm is done to the common good.

Sixth, to send accurate and authoritative intelligence, both to Your Holiness and the cardinal protector, as well as to the rest of the princes, on English affairs. In the absence of such authority, each person tends to write according to personal inclination and mistaken point of view.

Seventh, to remove rivalry amongst priests, and bring an end to disputes, by this one action contributing most to the peace and concord of all.

Eighth, to post and assign priests to suitable places, and to relocate them if necessary or if the greater glory of God reasonably requires it. By this very action, also, the burden of the fathers of the Society will be reduced, as well as the envy of others, since up to now they themselves [the Jesuits] have provided for all priests, as far as they are able, not from duty, but from charity.

To assist this bishop, the Catholics ask that a certain number of eminent priests be joined with him, to pass through the counties of England: that is, up to seven or eight, called either archpriests or archdeacons, who may be of assistance to the bishop and offer him counsel: thus he will be able to delegate them to act on his behalf as commissioners in the counties. They would like four of these to be nominated directly by Your Holiness, and the rest by the bishop himself, once he has been established, since, in the light of the diversity of regions and his knowledge of persons, he himself would know better who would be more suitable for this task.

The English Bishop in Belgium

Both necessity and utility present themselves as reasons for establishing this bishop as well:

First, since the bishop in England may not be able to exercise his episcopal jurisdiction in the external forum, for fear of the pursuivants, this one operating in Belgium will be able to make up for it, by summoning from England, and, if need be, punishing whoever the bishop living in England does not dare to chastise.

Second, to scrutinize intelligence reports received from England and, in view of the diversity of people writing to him, compare them and forward to Your Holiness those which, by consensus of his assistants, are trustworthy.

Third, to examine those priests or scholars who are about to enter England by command of their superiors, and furnish them with faculties, or not, depending on their merits or deficiencies; and to make a written report of his judgement on them for the bishop operating in England, so that it should not be lawful for everyone to enter at will and do damage to the cause of the Catholics, as often happens nowadays.

Fourth, this bishop will be of the greatest help in the advancement of the English cause, and he will also contribute to the unity and concord of the Catholics living in Belgium, especially if he is joined by six archpriests from among the leading priests of the English nation, in the same way as we said of the bishop who will be living in England.

If it should seem good to Your Holiness to grant these requests to the English Catholics, it would be prudent, in the first place, for these two bishops to be called "bishops in the lands of the unbelievers,"[72] and that they should not have the titles of English bishops, both to avoid rivalry and also so that the persecutors are not more exasperated thereby. In the second place, that each should have jurisdiction over the whole of England, and, perhaps, that the one living in Belgium should be an archbishop, for the sake of the hierarchy. Third, that these things should happen in secret, through apostolic briefs, by the ordination of only one bishop, wherever he may be found, in England, France, Belgium, Scotland, or Ireland; for this is necessary in order to keep secrecy. Fourth, that the thing should be carried out, if possible, before it is known, or the English heretics suspect anything about it, in case the ports are watched with greater diligence, against the arrival or departure of any bishop.

BA 4 Memorial on the Advisability of Publishing the Infanta's Claims to the Kingdom of England, August 1597

SOURCE: BAV, MS Vat. Lat. 6227, fols. 31–33.

NOTE: This appears to be the document intended for Philip II mentioned in Persons's letter to Peña, 16 August 1597 (B398); it may be by Persons.

Si conviene hazer publicacion de que la Señora Infanta pretende el Reino de Inglaterra

Algunos hombres prudentes i confidentes en Inglaterra, i fuera della an propuesto como remedio mui importante, para aniquilar, o disminuir las controversias sobre la sucesion a aquella corona, i par aventajar mucho la pretension de la Señora Infanta, declararla i publicarla de manera que todos entendiessen, que teniendo Su Alteza derecho a aquel reino lo pretende como suyo, i esto en una de dos maneras, o por declaraçion particular de Su Magestad en que dixesse que no pretende aquella corona para sí, ni para unirla con la de España, sino para la Señora Infanta su hija, a quien toca de derecho por muchas causas: o por medio de algun discurso scrito en lengua Inglesa por persona de autoridad mostrando con buenas razones que esto es lo que más conviene al bien de Inglaterra i que todos lo avian de dessear i pedir, para que el reino huiesse de maiores peligros, ordenando el dicho discurso de manera que aunque no se escriva en nombre de Su Magestad se diesse a entender que se haze con su sabiduria, como se entiende que ya Francisco

---

72. I.e., titular bishops, appointed to sees where the Catholic faith has been displaced.

Inglefildo cavallero Ingles residiendo en Madrid trató de hazerlo el año passado 1596 con aprobaçion de Su Magestad por pareçer persona muy a proposito para ello, tanto por la mucha experiencia que tenía de cosas, por ser de grande edad, quanto por su mucha autoridad con los Catholicos de Inglaterra, por aver sido del consejo secreto, en tiempo de la Reina Maria; i aunque por la muerte que le sobrevino no pudo ordenar el dicho discurso, otro lo podria hazer, i publicarlo en nombre del dicho Inglefildo como Su Magestad aprovase la traça.

Por la qual se alegan las razones siguientes

1. Porque con esta declaraçion se quitarian las sospechas que muchos en Inglaterra i fuera della an sembrado que Su Magestad quiere este reino para sí.

2. Tambien porque con este medio muchos dudosos i indiferentes se vendrian a resolver en qué parte an de seguir.

3. Porque los Catholicos de Inglaterra i los de fuera estavan más unidos, i se animarian más, sabiendo que tienen cabeça çierta a quien seguir, i de quien esperar gratificaçion de sus serviçios.

4. Porque los sediçiosos se reprimirian i estarian mucho sobre si no teniendo qué dezir, como agora que no aviendo cosa determinada cada uno queda libre: y sus proprias cabeças en Flandes mudandose para ganar credito i favor, se harian muy fervorosos, como se a visto por una carta de Giffordo de 27 de Junio deste año 1597, el qual aviendo escrito por lo pasado con mucha vehementia contra la pretension de la Señora Infanta ultimamente aviendo entendido en secreto que Su Alteza del cardinal Archiduque[73] favoreçia esta pretension, scrivio a una persona grave ofreciendo poner su vida, industria i trabajo por aquella pretension, i es verisimil que harian otros lo mesmo quando se entendiesse esta declaraçion.

5. Y tambien porque Su Santidad sabe ia esta pretension i a mostrado aprovarla: y quando se publicase con su consentimiento o no contradiziendolo Su Santidad pareçe que sería de mucha autoridad con todos los Catholicos i prinçipes, i en çierta manera quedarian los sucesores obligados a lo menos a no contradezir lo hecho, i estas son las razones principales desta parte.

Por la parte contraria

Algunos prudentes i confidentes de Su Magestad alegan tambien otras razones de duda diziendo que desta declaraçion podrian naçer algunos inconvenientes, como serian mover a los hereges para resolverse en favor del Rey de Scoçia, o de algun otro pretensor, i declararlo por sucesor i despertar otros que agora callan para el mesmo efeto i incitar a algunos Prinçipes etiam Catholicos para procurar de impedir con maiores veras la pretension de la Señora Infanta, i combidar a los hereges a que pidiessen iuramentos a los Catholicos contra Su Alteza i finalmente si esta declaraçion se huviesse de hazer por medio del sobredicho discurso, pareçe que tendria mucha dificultad en proponer las razones de una parte sin ofender a la otra.

73. del Cardinal Archiduque] *supplied in margin B*

Y aunque a esto se responde que ya en grande parte está entendida esta pretension: la resoluçion deste punto se dexa a la mucha prudencia de Su Magestad.

Translation

Whether it is advisable to publish the Lady Infanta's claims to the kingdom of England

Some wise men and advisors, both in England and abroad, have proposed as a very important measure, to eliminate or reduce the controversies about the succession to that crown, and to advance the claims of the Lady Infanta greatly: to declare and pronounce, in a manner that everyone may understand, that Her Highness holds a direct claim to that kingdom as her own. And this can be done in one of two ways: either by a special declaration of His Majesty, in which he says that he does not make any claim to that crown for himself, or to unite it with that of Spain, but for the Lady Infanta his daughter, to whom the right belongs for many reasons; or by means of some treatise written in the English language by a personage of authority, showing what good reasons there are why this would suit the interests of England and why everyone would want and desire it, because the kingdom suffers from many dangers. This treatise should be set out in such a way that it is not written in the name of His Majesty. It should be made clear that it is done with his knowledge, as it is understood that Sir Francis Englefield, an English gentleman resident in Madrid, drafted it last year, 1596, with the approval of His Majesty, because he seemed to be the person most suitable for the task, both on account of the large experience he had on these matters, being of such a ripe age, and also on account of the great authority he commands with the Catholics of England, since he was a member of the privy council in the time of Queen Mary; but because his death intervened it was not possible to complete the said treatise, and so another could do it and publish it in the name of the said Englefield as approved by His Majesty.

The Following Reasons are Alleged in Favour

1. Because with this declaration the suspicions which many in England and abroad have disseminated about His Majesty's seeking this kingdom for himself would be laid to rest.

2. Equally, because this would be a means of bringing many doubtful and indifferent people to make a decision about which side they will follow.

3. Because the Catholics of England and those in exile would be more unified, and more encouraged, if they knew that they have a definite leader to follow, from whom they could expect some reward for their services.

4. Because the dissidents would be held back and put under much more pressure if they do not get what they want than now, when nothing is determined and each one is a free agent. And their leaders in Flanders, casting about to gain credit and favour, comport themselves more passionately, as is evident in a letter of Gifford of 27 June of this year 1597. He wrote with much vehemence in the past against the claim of the Lady Infanta, but now understanding confidentially that His Highness [the archduke] supports the

claim, has written to a person of influence offering to put his life, industry, and effort into that claim, and in just the same way others will do the same when this declaration is understood.

5. And similarly, because His Holiness is aware of this claim and he has shown his approval of it; and if it is published with his agreement, or at least without His Holiness contradicting it, it seems it will carry much weight with all the Catholics and princes, and in a certain manner the successors would remain obliged at least not to resist what is done. And these are the main reasons on this side.

Some Considerations on the Opposing Side

Some wise men and advisors of His Majesty also allege other reasons to question this, saying that this declaration could give rise to some disadvantages, such as to prompt the heretics to make a decision in favour of the king of Scotland, or some other claimant, and declare for a successor and rouse others to the same effect who are now keeping quiet, and to incite other princes, even Catholic ones, to inhibit the claim of the Lady Infanta with more arguments and join forces with the heretics who would demand oaths of the Catholics against Her Highness. And finally, if this declaration had to be made by way of the abovesaid treatise, it seems likely to have much difficulty in proposing the reasons on one side without offending the other.

And also, to this the answer is given that this claim is already well understood in the main. The resolution of this question depends on the great wisdom of His Majesty.

BA 5 Memorial on the Succession of the King of Spain to the Crown of England

SOURCE: BAV, MS Vat. Lat. 6227, fols 1–6, a fair copy.

HICKS: 708a, overstamped 38–52, with English translation.

NOTE: This Italian analysis of Philip II's claim to the English succession may have been prepared for the papal curia at much the same time as the Latin document above (BA 2).

The MS contains many peculiar spellings, and it is difficult to distinguish between "i", "e", and "a", and between "v" and "b": *caveat lector*.

La successione de Su Maestà Catholica a la corona de Incliterra descendendo de la Casa Reala de Lancastria del Re Enrico VI

Su Magestad Catholica Re Philippo descende de la Corona de Ingilterra descendendo del Re Enrico Terzo[74] il quale Re havea per figlio Edmondo primo duca de Lencastria e questo duca havea una sola figlia fu maritata a Jovani deganti figlo del Re Eduardo Terzo[75] yl quale Giovanne fu fato duca da Lancastria per la eredità de sua moglie, il quale ducca di questo sua prima moglie il detto Blanche era erede de la corona haveva un figlio chia-

---

74. [*marginal note:*] Anno 41 del Re Ricardo 2: chro: Poli: cronico 1494.
75. [*marginal note:*] Cronico: Policronicon fol. 128. vita Eduardo 3 Re de Ingil.

mato Enrico il quale fu chiamato il Re Enrico Quarto, et haveva una figlia femina chiamata Philippe, figlia del detto Blanche, il quale Philippe fu maritata a Giovanne Re di Portugal del quale descende di queste regio sangue Sua Maestà Catholica. Et il detto duca Giovanni de sua seconda moglie chiamata Costança erede di Castiglia, di questa seconda moglie haveva un'altra figlia femina chiamata Caterina il quale fu maritata a Enrico Re di Castiglia in Hispaña del quale è discesso similmente il Re Philippe,[76] intanto que Sua Maestà Catholica tene due potentisimi tituli a la Corona di Ingilterra per di questo Regio sangue de la casa di Lencastria non già ninsuna herede de linea diretta ottuerà successione sino il Re Philippo per il Re Enrico IV fratelo da Philippo et de Caterina. Lasciarono successione de la Corona di Ingilterra Enrico Quinto e questo Re lassava in successione dapoi la morte sua il Re Enrico Sexto e questo Re Enrico Sexto fu lo ultimo vero successore o descendente Ingelterra dela Regia casa de Lancastria. Pertanto que fu iniustamente con falso titulo de Eduardo duca de Yorcho scacciato de la Corona di Ingilterra et amazzato insieme con suo figlio il principe di Valia et questa predetta casa de Yorcho con falso titulo posede la Corona de Ingilterra al di de oggi per usurpacione. Per la Corona de Ingelterra apertene diretamente a la casa de Lencastria de la quale casata non c'è[77] altro vero et legitimo herede e successore in linea direta et preso sangue, si non Sua Maestà Catholica del nostro Re Philippo e queli que sono heredi de la corona de Portugalo descendendo de la predetta Regina Philippe et tutti li altri de questa famiglia, descendendo de la Casa Regia de Alencastra cioè de lo descendente de Etmundo primo duca da Lancastra et figlolo dal Re Enrico Terzo sono tuto extinto in[78] Ingelterra e la heredità toca a Sua Maestà Catholica como descendente de la predetta Corona et famiglia de Alencastra.

Una obcessione che fanno li heretici in Incliterra contra la heredità a la Corona del Re Philippe è questo.[79] Solegano un statuto fato in tempo dal Re Euerdo Terzo il quale era ordinato que ningun forastiero nato oltre il mare de Ingilterra poteva hereditare in Ingilterra. Ma il vero è que questo statuto fu fato per respeto solo de li subditi et vassalli et non per queli que erano descendenti de sangue Reale de la Corona de Ingilterra, e cossi chesto statuto non da impedimento nisuno contra la heredità del Re Philippo a la Corona de Ingilterra. Per sperientia de chesto potramo probari come molti Principi nati oltra il mare sono stati dapoi eletti a la Corona de Inciltera come per exempio el Re Stephano et il Re Enrico Secondo tuti dui de parenti forastieri et loro istessi nati oltra il mare et il Re Artencre ducca da Britanna nato in Franzza[80] et per heredita da su madre chiamata Costanzza fu fato Re de Ingelterra in questo videmo que non se è statuto (in) Ingilterra contra la heredità dal Re Philippe a la preditta corona benché nati in paese alieni.

Li descendenti dal Re Enrico Septimo

Benché il Re Henrico Septimo li soi heredi el dia de hoggi pretendendino per esere descendenti de tute doi casate cioè da Lancastria et la casa de Yorchia se nomina benché

---

76. [*marginal note:*] Policronicon: fol. 140 il Re Henrico.
77. c'è] *conj. Hicks;* che B
78. in] *conj. Hicks;* om. B
79. [*marginal note:*] Anno 26 del Re Eduardo 3.
80. [*marginal note:*] Il Re Ricardo 2. nato in França e fato dapoi Re de Ingilterra.

Jiustamente la cassa da Lancastria per fare bono su titulo a la Corona. Lo vero è che il dito Re Enrico non è descenduto de la vera linea nè herede de la predita cassa da Lencastre per che esto Re pretende su subcesione de Giovani duca di Somarset figlio minor di Giovani di Gante duca di Lancastria la quale moglie non era de sangue Reale cossi il patre ne la matre del ditto duca de Somarset non erano heredi a la Corona.

In questo modo il dito Re Enrico septimo non e dicesso da la Regia cassa da Lencastra. Pertanto che la duquesa da Lencastria chiamata Blanche prima moglie de Giovani di Gante era solo herede de la casa da Lencastria e così quelo que restarono e sono heredi da la ditta duquesa Blanche li quali erano li predetti Re Enrico IV et Philippe Regina de Portugalo e che le Princippi che sono heredi de la detta Regina Philippe e così dapoi de la morte del Re Enrico Sexto in Ingelterra fu extinta tuta la sangue Reale da la casa da Lencastra e la vera subccesione a la Corona di Ingilterra dapoi la morte dal Re Enrico Sixto tocava a li heredi da Philippe, Regina da Portugalo. Intanto che è cosa certissima et aprobatissima che al presente hogi di indubitatamente in vera et diretta iustitia, la Corona di Ingilterra tocca a Sua Maestà Catholica del nostro Re Philippe.[81]

Questo preditto Re Enrico sexto da la casa da Lencastria è predecesor da Sua Maestà Catholica di nostro Re Philippo fue coronato Re di França nela Cita de Pariggi en la chiesa[82] da la madona in presentia de un Cardinal Inglese et la più parte de la nobiltà de Ingilterra e de França, et alora al giorno di hoggi li Regi de Ingilterra sonno stato titolato Re de França ma questo titolo non tocca a la Regina heretica de Ingilterra per non ser membra de aquella familia da la casa da Lencastria. Ma chesto titolo toca justamente a Su Maestà Catholica come vero herede ligitimo[83] descendendo del preditto Re Enrico 6 como vedemo en la chronica et historia antiquisima così toca a la Maestà dal Re Philippe persecuire[84] dal titulo del Re de Françia como herede de la Regia casa da Lencastra et Corona de Ingilterra e non solamente toca al Re Catholico il titulo de Re de França ma anco tocca a Sua Maestà Catholica la arme di França e la heredità di diversi Paessi et provincie de França come potriamo chiaramente probare cioè Normandi Picardi Parigi chiampani, Breton, Poyterus et altri stati de França. E il duce di Bedford fue visto[85] Re di França per il Re Enrico 6 da la casa da Lancastria.

La successione et descendenti del Re Enrico VII

De li descendenti del Re Enrico 7 non è gli restato altro successore in vero e legitimo[86] sangue da quela famiglia in Ingilterra ni in Escotia sino solamente la Regina Maria di Scotia et il Principe Jacobo suo figlio. Per tuti li altri pretendenti a dita casa dal Re Enrico 7º sono bastardi como io probaro dapoi et tuto lo sangue dal Re Enrico 7º dapoi la morte de la ditta Regina Maria et Jacobo suo figlio sarà extinta e alora secondo il dito comuni de tuta Ingelterra la eredità a la Corona de Ingilterra tocarà a li heredi de la Regina

81. [*marginal note:*] anno 4. del Re Enrico 6. Il di 6 de 7bre anno domini 1497.
82. chiesa] *Hicks*; chesia *B*
83. ligitimo] *Hicks*; lix^mo *B*
84. persecuire] *B*; per servire *Hicks*
85. visto] *B obscure: possibly* viz.
86. See previous note.

Philippe di Portugalo il quale e Sua Maestà Catholica, ma secondo la verità toca a Sua Maestà Catholica per il giorno presente per diretto da la casa da Lencastria.

Lo impedimento contra quelli che falsamente pretendono la
corona de Ingilterra

Sono quatro casati in Ingilterra que Injustamente pretendono la corona pretendendo su subcessione dal Re Enrico Septimo il quali pretendono per deshereditare al Re nostro Philippe e questi sonno le casate seguenti.

Una de questa pretendente è Margarita Contesa de Darbi figlia de Dianora Contesa de Cambria il quale de Onara fu figlio de Maria sorela dal Re Enrico Octavo. Et una cossi pretendenti sono doi figlie nati de Caterina figlia da Francesca sorela de Dianora et figlie ambe de Maria figlia dil Re Enrico 7 et sorela dal Re Enrico 8°. Il quale Dionora et Francesco non possono[87] hereditare a la corona por tanto che quando la preditta Maria madre loro maritava con il ducca de Sifolche patre de la ditta de Dionora et Francisco, il preditto ducca de Sifolcha haveva altra moglie viva. Così Dianora predecessora a Margarita Contesa di Darvi et Francisco predecessori di questi dui figli del conte a Harford erano bastardi nati impublico adulterio et non ponno hereditare così questi due pretendenti non ponno dare impedimento contra Il Re Philippe.

Lo impedimento contra il 3° pretendente a la corona

Una altra pretendente chiamata Arbella, figlia di Carlo conte de Lenox, il quale conte pretende la corona per diretto da sua matre chiamada Margarita Duglas figlia dal conte d'Anguise, pretendendo la corona per diritto de sua matre Margarita Regina di Scotia; ma questa pretensa e invalida per Margarita Duglas fu bastarda per quanto la preditta Regina Margarita di Scotia fue maritata a Archobal Duglas conde de Anguisse e il preditto Conte quando maritava la Regina Margarita haveva una sua prima moglie, quale moglie viveva molti anni dapoi di quel matrimonio. Cossi Margarita Duglas fu bastarda nata in adulterio et cossi sua nepote Arbella no po hereditare a la corona de Ingilterra ni dare impedimento contra il Re Philippo.

Lo impedimento contra il Conte Huntiton

La quarta pretendenti a la corona e il Conte de Huntiton, il quale piglia sua successione de Edmundo Anglas Primo ducca de Yorcha. Questo Edmundo fu fratelo minore da Giovani ducca da Lencastria l'quinto figlio dal Re Eduardo 3°. In questo modo il Re Philippo è subcesso dal fratelo mayore, et il deto Edmundo non era de la casa de Alencastra et cossi tocca al Re Phelippe la corona di Ingelterra et non al conte Ultinton. Et è un altro impedimento contra il conte predito que trei de sui predecessori per subcessioni deli quale pretende la corona sonno stati tagliati la teste per traditori chioé de Jiorge duca di Clarense et Aduardos Conte Barguit et Margarita Contesa de Sasbiert de tuti questi fu

---

87. non possono] *this ed.*; nompono B

fata justicia come traditori, iniustamente pretendendo la corona, et le descendenti de questi traditori non sono stati jamai per ordine regio restituti a la perdita dignita que habevano loro antecessori et per questa ragioni secondo el estatuti Inglesi non[88] posono hereditari li subcessori loro a ninguna dignità intanto che sono in questo impedimento contra la heredita et corona del dito conte, massime per non essere descenduto da la vera Regia Casata, così questo conte non po dare impedimento contra il Re Philippo.

Le impedimento perque chesta Regina Tirana Elizabeta Regina de
Ingilterra non debeba posedere la corona

Questa Regina Elizzabetta Regina de Ingilterra a questo presente è bastarda et usurpatora iniustamente. Pertanto que quando il Re Enrico maritava con Anna Bolenna el ditto Re Enrrico repudiando sua moglie legitima, il quale era la Regina Caterina de Aragon, figlia dal Re Catholico alora era viva quando fu fatto questo falso e finto matrimonio et la dita moglie legitima Caterina campo molti anni dapoi cossi, questa Elizzabeta Regina de Ingilterra è bastarda nata in adulterio como tuto il mundo sabe. Per quando il Re Enrrico 8º tagliava la testa di Anna Bolona madre di chesta Elizzabeta fu publicato per bando Reggio que Elizzabeta era bastarda che non tocava la eredità a la corona di Ingelterra et chesta fu cossa publicata per tuto il regno cossi chesta tiranna non deba dare impedimento contra la corona hereditaria de Ingilterra al Re Philippo in tanto che vederemo chiaro e potremo probar molto ben che la corona de Ingilterra tocca per le giorno presente a Sua Maestà Catholica, et chesto saggio provare chiarisimamente che nom può esere negato se la giusticia pue havere su diretto.

Translation

The Claim of His Catholic Majesty to Succeed to the Crown of
England by Descent from King Henry VI
of the Royal House of Lancaster

His Catholic Majesty King Philip is in the line of the English crown through descent from King Henry III. This king had a son, Edmund, who was the first duke of Lancaster, and this duke's only daughter was married to John of Gaunt, the son of King Edward III, and this young man became duke of Lancaster by right of his wife; and this duke, by right of his first wife Blanche, mentioned above, was heir to the crown and had a son named Henry, who became Henry IV, and a daughter named Philippa, by the said Blanche. This Philippa was married to the young king of Portugal and from this royal blood His Catholic Majesty is descended. The abovementioned duke John by his second wife Constance, heiress of Castile, had by this second wife another daughter named Catharine, who was married to Henry king of Castile in Spain; and King Philip is like-

---

88. non] *this ed.*; nom B Hicks

wise descended from him, so that His Catholic Majesty has two very strong titles to the English crown,[89] since no heir in the direct line of the royal blood of the house of Lancaster will make good his claim to succeed except King Philip through Henry IV, brother of Philippa and Catharine, who left Henry V to succeed him in the crown of England, and the latter after his death left the succession to Henry VI. This King Henry VI was the last in the true line of succession to the crown of England from the royal house of Lancaster, for the reason that Edward, duke of York, whose claim was fictitious, unjustly deprived him of the English crown and slew him together with his son the Prince of Wales. And the usurpation of the aforesaid house of York, whose claim to the crown of England was a fictitious one, persists to the present day. For the English crown belongs of right to the house of Lancaster, and of this family there is no true and legitimate heir and successor in the direct line and blood relationship except His Catholic Majesty Philip, our king, and the heirs of the crown of Portugal who are descended from Queen Philippa abovementioned. All others of this family who were descended from the royal house of Lancaster, that is from the descendants of Edmund, first duke of Lancaster and son of Henry III,[90] are quite extinct in England; and so the succession belongs to His Catholic Majesty as heir to the aforesaid crown and family of Lancaster.

An objection made by the heretics in England to King Philip's claim to inherit the crown is as follows: they base their claims upon a statute passed in the time of King Edward III which laid down that no foreigner born out of England could inherit in England; but the truth of the matter is that this statute had reference to subjects only and vassals and not to those who were descended from the royal blood of the English crown, and therefore this statute is no bar to King Philip's succession to the English crown. In witness of this we can prove that many princes born overseas have been afterwards chosen for the English crown: as for example King Stephen and King Henry II, both of whom were of foreign parentage and were themselves born overseas; and the king Arthur, duke of Brittany, who was born in France and by right of his mother, whose name was Constance, was made king of England.[91] Thus, we see that the English statute does not bar King Philip from inheriting the crown although he was born in a foreign country.

---

89. Philip II was descended from John of Gaunt (1340–1399), duke of Lancaster, through both his first wife, Blanche of Lancaster (1342–1368) and his second wife Constance of Castile (1354–1394). Blanche was the mother of Henry Bolingbroke (later King Henry IV) and Philippa of Lancaster (1360–1415), who married King John I of Portugal (1357–1433). Philip was their great-grandson on his mother's side. Constance was the mother of Catherine of Lancaster (1372–1418), from whom Philip descended on his father's side.

90. Edmund Crouchback (1245–1296), second surviving son of King Henry III (1207–1272).

91. Arthur, duke of Brittany (1187–ca. 1203), grandson of Henry II (1133–1189, r. 1154–1189), was the son of Geoffrey II and Constance, duchess of Brittany. He was born in Nantes and recognized as heir to the throne after Richard I, but was displaced by King John.

The Descendants of Henry VII

Although King Henry VII and his heirs today claim to be descended from both houses, that is of Lancaster and York, it is the house of Lancaster that is rightly invoked to make good their title to the crown. But the truth is that the said King Henry is not descended from the true line and is not the heir of the said house of Lancaster; for the king claims descent from John, duke of Somerset,[92] younger son of John of Gaunt, duke of Lancaster, whose wife was not of the royal blood. Thus, neither the father nor the mother of the said duke of Somerset had any inheritance in the crown. And so it appears that the said King Henry VII is not descended from the royal house of Lancaster, inasmuch as the duchess of Lancaster named Blanche, John of Gaunt's first wife, was the sole heiress of the house of Lancaster and so too were those who survived as heirs of the said duchess Blanche, namely the aforesaid Henry IV and Philippa, queen of Portugal, and those princes who are heirs of the said Queen Philippa; and thus, after the death of King Henry VI, the blood royal of the house of Lancaster was entirely extinct in England and the true right of succession to the crown of England after the death of Henry VI devolved on the heirs of Philippa, queen of Portugal. And thus it is most certain and well ascertained that at the present day the crown of England in true and strict justice without doubt belongs to His Catholic Majesty Philip, our king.

This aforesaid king, Henry VI, of the house of Lancaster and ancestor of His Catholic Majesty King Philip, was crowned king of France in the city of Paris in the church of Notre Dame in presence of an English cardinal and of the greater part of the nobility of England and France, and from that time till today the kings of England have had the title of king of France. This title however does not belong to the heretical queen of England, since she is not a member of the family of the house of Lancaster; but it belongs of right to His Catholic Majesty as true and legitimate heir having descent from the aforesaid King Henry VI, as we see in the oldest chronicles and histories. Thus, it is within the right of His Majesty King Philip to pursue[93] the title of king of France as heir of the royal house of Lancaster and of the crown of England; and not only does the title of king of France belong to the Catholic king but also the coat of arms of France, and the succession to various counties and provinces of France, as we can prove conclusively, namely Normandy, Picardy, Paris, Champagne, Brittany, Poitiers, and other departments of France. The duke of Bedford was looked on as being king of France by Henry VI of the house of Lancaster.[94]

The Successors and Descendants of King Henry VII

Of the descendants of King Henry VII there remains to succeed in the true and legitimate right by blood no one of his family in England or Scotland, except only Queen Mary

92. John Beaufort (ca. 1371–1410), first earl of Somerset, was the illegitimate son of John of Gaunt's mistress Katherine Swynford.

93. Or: "use" (see textual note).

94. John of Lancaster (1389–1435), first duke of Bedford, was regent of France during the reign of his nephew Henry IV.

of Scotland and Prince James her son. For all the others who claim to be of the aforesaid house of King Henry VII are bastards, as I will prove later, and the blood of King Henry VII after the death of Queen Mary and James her son will be entirely extinct; and then, in accordance with what is commonly said all over England, the succession to the English crown will devolve on the heirs of Queen Philippa of Portugal, that is on His Catholic Majesty, but in reality it belongs to His Catholic Majesty at the present day by right of the house of Lancaster.

The Impediments That Bar Those Who Falsely Claim the Crown of England[95]

There are four families in England which unjustly claim the crown by descent from King Henry VII, and this they do in order to bar the claim of our King Philip; they are the following families: — One of these claimants is Margaret, countess of Derby, daughter of Diana, countess of Cambridge, this Diana being the daughter of Mary, the sister of Henry VIII; and claimants likewise are the sons born to Catharine, who was the daughter of Frances, Diana's sister, both of whom were daughters of Mary, the daughter of Henry VII and sister of Henry VIII. The same Diana and Frances cannot inherit the crown for the reason that, when the aforesaid Mary their mother married the duke of Suffolk, father of the said Diana and Frances, the aforesaid duke of Suffolk had another wife living. Thus Diana, the ancestress of Margaret, countess of Derby, and Frances, the ancestress of those two sons of the earl of Hertford, were bastards born in open adultery and cannot inherit. Consequently, these two claimants cannot present any impediment to the claim of King Philip.

The Impediment to the Third Claimant to the Crown

Another claimant is named Arbella, the daughter of Charles, earl of Lennox. This earl claims the crown by right of his mother, named Margaret Douglas, daughter of the earl of Angus. They claim the crown by right of his mother Margaret, queen of Scotland, but this claim is invalid, for Margaret Douglas was a bastard, seeing that the aforesaid Queen Margaret of Scotland was married to Archibald Douglas, earl of Angus, and this earl, when he married Queen Margaret, had a former wife, and this wife was alive many years after that marriage. Thus, Margaret Douglas was a bastard born in adultery, and so her granddaughter Arbella cannot inherit the English crown or present an impediment to the claim of King Philip.

The Impediment to the Earl of Huntington's Claim

The fourth claimant to the crown is the earl of Huntington, who traces his descent from Edmund of Langley, first duke of York. This Edmund was the younger brother of John, duke of Lancaster and the fifth son of King Edward III. Thus, King Philip traces from the

---

95. On the following claims, see the notes to BA 2, above.

elder brother, and the said Edmund was not of the house of Lancaster; and so the English crown belongs to King Philip and not to the earl of Huntingdon. There is a further impediment to the claim of the aforesaid earl in that three of his ancestors, by succession from whom he claims the crown, were beheaded as traitors, namely, George, duke of Clarence, and Edward, earl of Warwick, and Margaret, countess of Salisbury. On all of these due sentence was carried out as traitors, claiming the crown unjustly; and the descendants of these traitors have never been restored by order of the king to the lost dignities possessed by their ancestors; and for this reason, according to the statutes of England, their descendants cannot inherit any dignity; and so for these reasons there are impediments to the said earl's inheriting the crown, and above all the fact that he is not descended from the true royal house; and thus the earl cannot bar the claim of King Philip.

> The Impediments Which Ought to Bar This Tyrant Queen Elizabeth of England from Possessing the Crown

This Queen Elizabeth, who is queen of England at the present time, is a bastard and an unjust usurper; for when King Henry married Anne Boleyn, repudiating his lawful wife Queen Catherine of Aragon, daughter of the Catholic king, the latter was living at the time when this false pretended marriage was made, and the same lawful Catholic wife lived for many years afterwards. And so Elizabeth, queen of England, is a bastard, born in adultery, as all the world knows: for, when King Henry VIII cut off the head of Anne Boleyn, the mother of this Elizabeth, it was published by royal decree that Elizabeth was a bastard who had no inheritance in the crown of England; and this is a thing that was published all over the kingdom. Thus, this tyrant should offer no impediment to King Philip's inheriting the crown of England. And thus we see clearly and can prove quite easily that the crown of England belongs at the present day to His Catholic Majesty; and this I have tried to prove quite conclusively, so that it cannot be denied if justice has its rights.

BA 6 A Brief Account of the Stirs at the English College, Rome, 18–20 October 1597

SOURCES:
ABSI, Coll P I 307–310, Grene's transcription of a copy made by Persons (= G).
ABSI, Coll P II 352, Grene's extract (= G2)
HICKS: 741–749.
NOTE: Persons was evidently collecting evidence about his dealing with the crisis at the college. It is uncertain whether this is his own composition, and how it relates to the documents he sent to the pope on 28 September (B413). Unfortunately, Grene was unable to decipher more than the first sentence of the first part, which dealt with the origin and progress of the agitation.

The role of Hugh Griffith/Griffin was confirmed by William Allen's nephew, Thomas Hesketh, in a statement, copied in Persons's hand and dated 15 October 1597 (Coll P II 488):

"De D. Hugone Griffidio nepote Episcopi Cassanensis Attestatio D. Thomae Alani alias Heskett nepotis Card. Alani quod d: Hugo fuerit author turbarum in Collegio" (The testimony of Mr Thomas Allen alias Hesketh, nephew of Cardinal Allen, regarding Hugh Griffith, nephew of the bishop of Cassano, that the said Hugo was the instigator of the troubles in the college).

A brief raguaglio of the stirrs[96]

Cardinal Allen dyed 16 October 1594, and presently after that began the stirrs with a memorial first to the Pope himself with most part of hands of the College exhibited by Signor Silvio for Cassano's preferment and expected answer a good while but had none, and then another to the Monsignor de Camera about January or February ...[97]

A brief relation of such things as have fallen out in the English College of Rome since Father Persons coming hither, which was about the 20th of March unto the 20th of October 1597[98]

The stirrs in this college began in October presently upon the death of Cardinal Allen three yeares now past. — Father Persons arryving heer towards the end of March past,[99] he went to His Holiness about the midst of April — and after many other matters treated, the Pope of himself began to talke of the English College and asked Father Persons if he had bin there, and tould him the exceeding great molestation that he had received by their broyles and obstinacy in the same and seemed highly to mislike all such as he presumed to have bin authors or doers therin, especially out of the College. He identified some of them by name and finally willed Father Persons to goe and lye in the said College and to see what he was able to doe with them to acquyet matters and so to relate to his Holiness what passed, for he was resolved effectually to putt remedy.

The next day after, Father Persons went to lye in the College and found matters in very hard termes: for he found the fathers of the Society wholy weary and desirous to leave the government — the schollers he found devided and the discontented part so

---

96. [*Grene's comment in G2:*] (coppyed out of Father Persons own handwryting). "Raguaglio" means "account." The students sent petitions to Silvio Antoniani, the pope's *maestro de camera*, in August 1595. Various petitions for the promotion of Owen Lewis, bishop of Cassano, were presented after Allen's death, including one from the anti-Jesuit party in Flanders, delivered to Cardinal Aldobrandini by Thomas Throckmorton in the spring of 1595: see Kenny, "Inglorious Revolution," 244–252, 256 (part 1).

97. [*Grene's comment in G2:*] omitto reliqua quia scriptura est difficulter legibilis &c. (I leave out the rest because the handwriting is difficult to read). It has been suggested that he wished to gloss over some of the scandalous contents.

98. [*Grene's prefatory comment in G:*] Many letters about the same [the factions] in 1597. There is also among f. Persons letters [A brief relation, etc.]. (t'is a Copy.) I wil note here the chiefe pointes thereof. [*in margin:*] transcribed out of an other Coppy written by f. Persons.

99. [*Grene's marginal comment in G:*] Arrived in Rome 27 March ut dicitur 179. g. [*Coll P I 179 reads:*] 27 March 1597 f. Persons came to Rome with m^r Worthington etc.

resolute never to agree with the fathers againe as they professed it openly, and one etc. — These schollers also were become such enemies unto the other part of them that were quyet and obeyed the fathers, as they accounted enemies of their country — and of the English Clergy, and so had refused somtimes to eate with them at the same table and to enter[100] into the same church to say or heare masse —— And according to this spirit did all other matters proceede among them, the one part speaking well and reverently of the fathers, the other inveighing every where — etc. (*acerbissime*)[101] ——— the one part shewing comfort for the niew English Seminaries in Spaine; the other part coud scarse abide to heare of them. —— the one part rejoycing att the good successe of the king of Spaine — in Flanders etc.; the other on the contrary advancing still the Queen of England in her affaires — saying they would joyne with her — against any who went about to impugne — her state — And this aversion from forrain princes, especially against Spaniards, went so farre[102] —— that they would not salute any father of the Society when they mett him in the street, except he saluted them first: So would they nether salute the Duke of Sessa, Embassador of the Catholike king, when they mett him — They had also for *Confessarius* of the house one of themselves,[103] a principal doer in these stirres — who kept their mony and gave it to them, as they would spend it, and had lycence also by Cardinal Toledo to write and receave letters without shewing them to the rector, and to give the same licence to others also, and finally as head of the faction had every weeke a certain day appointed for his audience with the Protector, at which time he carryed the memorials of the seditious with him and their complaints against the rector etc. — And in this state stood matters then.

Father Persons after his coming took great paines for many daies calling all the discontented persons together and by many long conferences — gave satisfaction by reason and evident arguments that in most points which they conceived there was manifest error, as namely that there was any intention in him or any other Father of the Society to subjugate our countrye to strangers, but only to provide the best they could to have a Catholike Prince, etc. — etc. — etc. — whereupon they were content at last to come to a good end and to lay down their *Confessarius* which was the Tribune among them — And soe finally upon Ascension-day the 7th of May[104] the full peace was made with exceeding contentment of both partes as it seemed by their words actions and teares — etc. — And the Pope himself took great comfort thereat and Father Persons procured that Father General and all other Fathers of the Society should ask no satisfaction for the injuries and infamations don to them, content to forgett and forgive and to imbrace them with fatherly affection — as appeereth by — courteous letters which Father General wrott from Naples where then he was, in answer to a letter supplicatory which six of the principal discontented priests had written unto him — promising all obedience and quyetnesse for the time to come: and soe they seemed to doe for some 20 daies or a month: but after that, some of the chief of them — began aniew, taking occasion that promises were

100. enter] *this ed.*; ented G
101. Very bitterly or harshly.
102. farre] *followed by* by [*deleted*] G
103. Thomas Hill (Kenny, "Inglorious Revolution," 250–251 [part 1]).
104. 15 May according to the Gregorian calendar (Persons to Holt, 15 May 1597, B375).

not kept with them for having an other vineyard etc.¹⁰⁵ — wherefore they began to murmure — and to make niew conventicles as before, etc. — also they refused to goe any more to the vineyard — and went to tavernes, etc. — Namely in August, all the rest being att the vineyard, one priest — at a tavern having over eaten and overdrunk himself came home sick — vomiting, etc. — and this priest was holden for an Elias among the tumultuous, etc. And for that about this time Father Persons was to have gon to Naples to the bathes there for a paine in one of his knees,¹⁰⁶ these fellowes gave out presently that he went away for that he saw himself able to doe nothing, no more then Dr Barret had don etc. ——

Among other things one was wherewith they vexed much their Superiors: for that they craved all customes of the College to be observed making every thing that once or twice they had obtained by importunity to be a custom inviolable, etc. —— They went very frequently to tavernes, etc. — at last — the rumor came to the German College that dyverse of those schollers haunted tavernes, etc. —the rector of that College and Cardinal Madruccio¹⁰⁷ their Protector made diligent search and found — that they were English, etc., wherat the Germans chafed and so much the more for that the Pope had notice of it — and had given general order to the — *sbirri*¹⁰⁸ — to watch any of that habit that should enter into tavernes, etc. — which Cardinal Madruccio understanding wrot a lettere to our Cardinal Protector Caetan upon the 28 September to advertise him of it: but Cardinal Caetan being abroad that morning — Sonday — when he came home, he had no sooner begunn to reade the letter of Cardinal Madruccio but there came in the Captaine of the Isbirrs to tell him that they had stayd two companies of German schollers that sayd they were English men, two att a taverne besides St Marks att the sign of the rose and with them a Secular English Priest named Middleton, and two other at a certaine hott-house of evill fame where they saye that the said Middleton had a chamber.¹⁰⁹

The Cardinal — sent presently one — to advise Father Persons at the College, who being ready to goe to dinner sent word to the Cardinal —— and desired his grace to intreat the Governor that they should not be sent to prison until he came to speake with his grace after dinner. And soe it was don, and Father Persons intreated the Cardinal to goe in person that day to the Pope to obtaine some remission in the case: but before he came thither His Holiness had understood all and laughed at it that Inglish should both drink-up the good wine for the Germans and also be taken and go to prison for them, as in any case he inclined that they should: but in the end the Cardinal obteined that the 4 schollers should be brought within night by Isbirrs to the College and there remaine prisoners in different chambers until His Holiness should send to examin them as soon after he did: but for Mr Middleton there was noe pardon to be had: but that he must goe to Corte Savilli as he did; and all this appeereth by the lettre of Cardinal Caetan and Cardinal Borghese whome His Holiness joyned with Caetan to trye and punish this matter.

105. See Persons to Peña, 12 August 1597 (B393).

106. Acquaviva was expecting Persons to join him in Naples in early May; see his letter of 2 May 1597 (B372).

107. Ludovico Madruzzo; see Persons to Clement VIII, 13 August 1597 (B395).

108. Watchmen.

109. John Middleton (see Persons to John Bennet, 18 October, B423).

And they wrote their letters to the rector which were read openly in the hall of the College that night:[110] how evil His Holiness took this matter and how he would have those imprisoned that were taken: and two daies after, the same Cardinals sent commission with the fiscall of the Popes[111] — to examen the matter. — The tumultuous — would not — answer directly — whereat the Judge was extremely offended and the Cardinals alsoe. — (Att last) the fiscall — informed the Pope and he willed him to proceed to torture if they persevered in their obstinacy. — Soe the Judge returned — and appointed a niew prison in the College: which when Father Persons saw — he perswaded them to obey — and so they resolved to answer directly. And therupon began the examination and hath lasted these 17 or 18 daies and now I think is ended or neer ended, for that 3 daies agon there came a decree from the Cardinals in the Popes name for six to be sent to Doway, which are Father Trolopp, Father Wolly, Jackson, Foster, Lobbey and Askew,[112] and it is sayd that 5 or 6 are restrained besides and scarse like to have so much favour to be sent with so good letters as these, for that these have reasonable – good letters patents of the Cardinals to Dr Barret to be received in Doway and no fault att all is expressed, as you may see by the said letters which heere I do send you the coppies of.

The examination hath bin made for 3 yeares past, to witt during the tyme since the troubles begann, and much frequenting of tavernes hath bin confessed, as I understand, in so much that one hoste and his servants testify that within 8 daies they had bin of late six times at his taverne, 7, 6, 4, 3 and 2 att a tyme. There hath bin dansing also at dyverse tavernes with many imbracings and other scandalous behaveour, and commonly their drink was *vinum graecum* —— wherwith some have bin so merry as they have gon forth singing of Sellengers rounds throughout the streetes.[113] — Above 20 or 30 tavernes have bin frequented by them besides hoat-houses, which are much more infamous — so as the Judge saith he wil tell the Pope that His Holiness hath not bin so diligent in visitting the churches as the English schollers have bin in visiting tavernes — besides banquetting continually in English mens houses, etc. etc. — And it is noted by the Judge that none of the quyet schollers that obeyed the fathers — are accused for any of these disorders, etc.

You have heard much, I doubt not, of their exclamations against Father Edmond Harewood for defaming them,[114] for that in secret he tould one of them to warne the rest that there was disorders in the College about dishonest touchings, which would come abroade if they proceeded to call in the Apostolical visitation which they cryed for. This good father dyed most godly 21 September, St Matthews day last past.[115] ——

His Holiness hath often said of late that he will remedy (the miserable state of this college) and putt such lawes as may provide for the like inconveniences of sedition and

110. [*Grene's sidenote:*] habes has l[ite]ras fol. 311.e.

111. Acarizio Squarcione, papal fiscal; see Caetani to Frangipani, 12 October 1597 (B419).

112. Wolly] *this ed.*; Welly G. On these six priests, see Caetani and Borghese to Barret and Vitelleschi, 14 October 1597 (B420).

113. Sellenger's round was a popular English country dance. *Vinum Graecum* was an Italian sweet wine made in imitation of wines imported from Greece in antiquity.

114. [*Grene's sidenote:*] f. Edmond Harwood.

115. Persons to Bennet, 20 September 1597 (B408).

dissolution for the tyme to come. And of late — he hath sett forth 2 *Breves*,[116] the one prohibiting English men to proceed Doctors without 4 yeares studdy after their courses ended and licence of their Superiors and the Protector, and the other exhortatory to the Catholics in England to hold union and peace, etc. ——

Rome, this 18 of October 1597.

[PS] After the wryting of this the former six schollers departed with great contentment to themselves and edification to the rest. —— Moreover upon the 20th of October there departed 3 schollers of this College towards the Seminaries of Spaine, and 2 daies after 4 more dismissed to goe to Doway and upon Munday next is to departe Mr Middleton, the priest taken in the taverne with the first schollers.[117] And all are gon with great demonstration of change and contentment of minde; and this night are to be published here in this College the Popes niew orders which we hope wil be the full amendment and reformation of this College.

BA 7 A Further Declaration about Developments at the English College, Rome, 16 November 1597

SOURCES:

AAW VI, no. 68, 241–244, an illegible contemporary copy;

AAW HIS/A/48, MS transcript of the "A" series by Thomas Francis Knox, vol. 1: 271–281, made before the MS was sent for repair and further damaged, "for it crumbled to pieces under the touch." Grateful thanks to Judi McGinley for assistance in locating the transcript.

NOTE: This document complements the other accounts given in the various memorials about the troubles in the English College, Rome. It may be by Persons, and reflects his view of events. It is not uncommon in Persons's anonymous works to refer to himself in the third person.

The declaration records the dismissal of dissident priests from the English college and the appointment and intervention of Cardinals Caetani and Borghese, and rebuts the charge of excessive Jesuit control, claiming that the students were consistently treated with mildness and consideration. The declaration ends by lamenting the fate of those who supported the extremists.

The text below omits square brackets used by Knox to indicate words abbreviated or contracted words in *W*.

116. [*in margin*:] Two Breues of Clement VIII 1^m sub dat. 19 Septemb. 1597 impress. Romae 1601. Persons expressed his concern about plans to confer doctorates on dissident priests to give them more authority, in his "Memorandum on the State of English Affairs," assigned to 13 August 1597 (BA 1).

117. Kenny ("Inglorious Revolution," 141 [part 4]) identifies the seven priests as Francis Robinson (1569–post 1632), Hugh Whitolf (1571–post 1610), Walter Hasels (1574–post 1621), Thomas Curtis, SJ (1576–1657), Powell (see below), William Isham (1578–post 1603), and Robert Pett (ca. 1572–post 1610). William Isham, who entered the college at Valladolid in December 1596 (*Valladolid Registers*, 45), can tentatively be identified as the son of Christopher Isham, a member of Allen's household in 1594 (Knox, *Allen*, 376–377). Powell may be Gervase Pole, who entered the college in Rome in 1593, and was one of the dissidents (Anstruther, 280; Foley, 7.1: 611).

A further declaration of the matter fallen out lately at Rome,
and the causes of the dismission of some priests and schollers
from Rome. 16 of November 1597.

Good Sir.

I writ you some dayes past a certaine relation of things happened in this colleg: of Rome since the arrivall of Father Persons heer, which was in the ende of Marche, untill the myddest of October last (yf I remember not amisse) when the six preest and schollers weer sent awaye, after whom followed four more soone after, to go all to Doway, & fower other weer sent, three to Spaine & one to Millayne;[118] the causes also of this dispertion I signified unto you, and with what good myndes and purposes they departed, to the contentment and edification of all heer. And now I had thought to wryte unto you only at this tyme the most peacable and contented estate that this college is in sithence and at this present, with the good new orders that His Holines hath appoynted the tow Cardenals in comission (to witt Caetan and Burghese) to sett downe for the reformation of inconveniences past and preventing the like to come; which orders, though they be but very few, yet are they so substantial that they have put the whole boddye of the college in joynte agayne, as is much to be rejoysed, and every man feeleth the comfort thereof, as I dowt not but you will understand more at large by other mens letters, even of thos that are remayned heer in the colleg of the former sturres and do see now and confesse the difference of this manner of lyffe in order, peace and disceplyne from that other that was accompaned with the contrary effects.

But for that it is understoode notwithstanding that some of our nation heer in Rome, that had thir partes perhapes in the former broyles and disorders, have spoken upp and downe and of likely hoode wrytten the same also into your partes, reprehending this that hathe byn done as rigorous and injurious and donne without just cause, and therby do seeke to bring in hatred, as well in this as in all other actiones, the fathers of the Societie (to whome in my opinion, if in any other thing owr cowntry is behoulding, it is also greatly in this, that by their long patience and dilligence this college is at length redressed which otherwise would have utterly byn lost and our whole cause therby infinitly prejudiced) for this I say I ame forced, in steade of rehearsing unto you the present benefits we receave, to declare somwhat furder the particular causes of this His Holynes resolution carped by thes men that seeme to lyke of nothinge that tendeth to order and desciplyne.

And first of all it weer enoughe for justefying of thes affayres in the sight of any indifferent man, as I would thinke, that thes have passed not only by the handes of the fathers but of a publique ecclesiasticall judge also, who is fiscall of His Holines whole reformation heer in Rome,[119] and hath examined above thirtie schollers uppon ther othes, and

118. On the six priests sent to Douai, see Persons (as from Caetani and Borghese) to Vitelleschi, 14 October 1597 (B420). On the three sent to Spain, see the preceding document, "A Brief Account of the Stirs ... 18–20 October." The priest sent to Milan may be Middleton, also mentioned in that account.

119. [*marginal note in transcript, following* Cardenal Sega] D. Acaritium, Apostolicae Visitationis fiscalem (Don Acarizio Squarcione; see Caetani to Frangipani, 12 October 1597, B419).

hath ther depositiones subscribed with ther owne handes in above fiftie leaves of paper, and hath conferred the same bothe with the tow Cardinales in comission and also with His Holynes before the resolution taken; so as now to reprehend the saide resolution ys to note of partialitie and injustice not only the fathers but all thes other in lyke manner, as every man seeth.

Secondly, to come to some causes more in particular, the first that perhapes hath weighed much with His Hol. and with the rest of the forenamed judges to make this seperation may be the contynuall broyles that have byn in this college for thes three yeares past, continued by all thes that are departed with such open scandall & obtinacies as all the world knoweth and talketh of it heer, ande specially[120] after the visitation ended by Cardenal Sega,[121] who by His Holines order heard & examined with great patience all the complayntes that could be exhibited agaynst the fathers and took ther memorialls subscribed with their owne handes that would saye any thing, and after all condemned both ther cause and maner of proceeding and re-established all that they would have pulled downe; and albeit His Holines seing the obstinate resistance of the tumultuous not to acept and obey that which Cardenal Sega had sett downe, and some what moved one the other side with the threats of such as would needes make hym beleve certayne desperate resolutiones that some of thes schollers might take if they weer inforced to obey against ther willes, dyd wisely and also piously dissemble the matter for a tyme, and willed Cardenall Toledo to attempt another course with them; yet did hee se well enough the great reasons of Cardenal Sega his determination, and was highly offended inwardly with the schollers heddy dealings, as he signified to divers afterward and tould hym selve plainely to the first preestes that departed by the waye of mission at ther taking leave of hym uppon the 3rd of September,[122] and by this he was the sooner brought to take the resolution he dyd of dispercing them when he perceaved what ensewed uppon ther former obstinacie.

Thirdly, F. Persons being come to Rome and having compounded all things sweetly to the contentation of every side & to the great liking of all persons, but especially of His Holines and of the Cardenals, very soone after certayne trublesome spirites begane agayne (for all I perswade my selfe weer not culpable heerin excepte only for knowing and bearinge it) to move as seditious negotiationes as ever before and to seek by occasion of this now mutual intercourse of conversation together the one with the other not only to confirme such as weer before infected with yvel humor (especially against ther superiours and others of the order or of [wors]hip elsewhere) but after to instille the same to others of the younger sorte that had byn quiet heertofore hitherto, telling them most false and slanderous tales against ther superiours, and namely affirming both glotonie, sensualitie, covetousnes, falshood, thefte, cuseninge, ambition, perjurie, injustice, incontinencie and other such like fowle vices to be among the fathers; which manner of proceeding being

120. ande specially] *Knox, possibly in error for* and especially

121. On Sega's visitation in 1596, see the "The English College, Rome" in the introduction, and Acquaviva to Persons, 15 January, 11 February, and 8 April 1596 (B308, B314, B320); Cowling to Persons, 13 February 1596 (B315).

122. [*marginal note in transcript:*] See supra, no. 56 ("Copy of BRIEF of Clement VIII, about the degree of a Doctor. Printed in Tierney's Dodd, III.cii").

discovered by three or fower schollers at the least to have byn used towards them by dyvers of the othe syde, and that thes thinges have byn affirmed to them with such asseveration and impudencie as if they had not byn most trew (they being indeed most false) it made His Holines and the rest to see that theer was nether love nor conscience remayninge in these reporters towards their superiors and consequently no good to be hoped by them under the other government.

Fowerthly, ther fell owt the publique scandall of those that weer taken in taverns under the name of Germans,[123] whome our men had defamed & greatly injured by going into tavernes under ther name, as then was geven abroade and since[124] has byn confessed by dyvers of our schollers that it hath byn practised; though the greatest rumur therof might arise perhapes of the error of the common people that take for Germans all strangers whom they see love good drinke and to frequent osteries; which frequentation was come to be so great among this sorte of schollers as not only one hoste and his tapster confessed them to have byn in his taverne in divers troopes six tymes in eight daies, but one scholler also confessed to have byn hym selfe five and twentye tymes at different tavernes within the space of tow monethes, and another doth name well neare twentie distinct tavernes that he knew. The judge tould the Pope (or said he would) that His Holynes had not byn so diligent in visiting the churches of Rome as the English schollers had byn in visiting tavernes ... how honorable it is for this colleg, for our whole nation, or rather how shamefull at ... to se schollers in troopes and with the colleg attyre to enter in ... so many tavernes (which commonly are sett heer in Italie ether in market places or blynd corners, and are so beggarly and filthie as none but base or deshonest people will frequent them): what a note (I saie) this is and will remaine unto us for a great while I leave to you to consider.[125]

... theer was ... ther stubborne behaveour[126] at the beginning after the apprehension of some in the taverne, when they made a leage amongst them selfes that no one of ther company should answeer directly unto the judge or confesse any poynte; and so they stood tow it for tow or three days, until His Holines commandyd they should be examined by force; and this also gave great discontentment to His Holines and the Cardenals and yealded suspition of ... pe theer was, though badd enough ... ther[127] could have byn imaginied as such as colleg ... now to committ them unto letter,[128] except necessitie of justifying His Holines and the Cardenals proceedinges in this affayre may heerafter require that the same be published, which I trust shall not bee needfull, nor yet for defence of

---

123. [*marginal note in transcript*:] See supra, No. 49, No. 50 (49. "CAPITOLO de una carta de Doctor Richardo Barretto" concerning Fisher; 50. "Copy of an anonymous deposition [by James Standish] against certain priests in England").

124. since] *this ed.*; sinte *Knox*

125. We have adopted Knox's partial reconstruction of the rest of this letter.

126. I.e., there was other stubborn behaviour, or talk of it.

127. ther] *obscure in Knox; possibly* then

128. The general sense seems to be that the findings were so scandalous that the details should not be put in writing unless it becomes necessary to justify the steps taken.

the fathers against ther detraction; for assure your selfe they have not only used great patience and longanimitie in bearing and dissembling thinges past in tyme of the tumultes agaynst them for the better covering of enormous faultes heer committed (as may yet appeare by a certayne declaration of F. Edward Harwood sett down for his defence by his superiors order a littel before his death)[129] but also now when matters broke out by the happe or providence of God, which before you have heard, notwithstanding the fathers had byn so injuriously handled anew by the slaunders and calumniationes above mentioned (and especially F. Persons by name for his peace and other good turnes done unto them) yet did they and he in particular labor what they could to have all matters mollified, as when His Holines was inclined to have them all sent to publique geale that had been taken in tavernes, thes men procured by Cardenal Caetan's meanes that only they should be put in private chambers at home, and after when, upon ther obstinacie not to aunsweer, the judge had order and resolution to make a geale within the house and to call sbyrres[130] to keep them, the fathers letted it, and procured finally that such as weer to be dismissed should be sent away with the greatest curtesie and best provision that was possible; and he that after all this will yet calumniat still the fathers in this matter, yt is evident that he doth it of malice, and so ether he is to be contempned or to be repressed (if hee be interessed in the matter) with the publishing of thes thinges that are heer under depositiones and may be shewed with authoritie when so ever neede shall require or superiors commaund, and they are such as will make you blushe and your ears burne to read them, and they do evidently show how high tym it was for God of His mercy towards our country to remedie this disordered course of young men in this colleg seeing that otherwise it would have become a synke of ... and ... viciousness. I will saye no more.

Yet[131] her yet do I meane to touch all that are departed from hence with ether fact or suspition of thes later causes, nor any that remayne; for that I hope and verely perswade my selfe that they are not culpable of anye more but of the first fower or five poyntes sett down before, except only some few of the more free and dissolut sorte; but ther is one great inconvenience among other that in sheweth[132] to them that sorde ... t multitude,[133] that whatsoever some few doe shalbe attributed to the whole number; as one the contrarie syde he that followeth the companye of Jesus ... shall alwaies be praysed and well thought of, though hymself doe nothing as of hym selfe praise woorthie. I pray God that this may be an example to the rest of our nation that live in other places to returne to ... and unitie with good Catholique men, as it was at the begynning ... anding

---

129. [*marginal note in transcript:*] See above No. 28 ("A copie of F. EDWARD BENNET his letter to D. Hugh Griffin Provost of Cambray [and to D. Gifford]"; printed in Tierney, 3: lxxx, from vol. 10).

130. The *sbirri* were the armed police force in Rome; see Persons to Bennet, 18 October 1597 (B423).

131. Yet] net *conj. Knox*

132. in sheweth] *Knox, i.e.,* ensueth

133. The sense seems to be that all those who joined ("sorted with"?) the crowd of dissidents were tarred with the brush of the few extremists.

and making factiones:[134] heerwith they have hurted them selfes ... undoe[135] our apostolique cause and be heavely punished[136] .... And so to His holy protection I committ .... 16th of November 1597.

---

134. I.e., before the factions developed.
135. undoe] *Knox, possibly in error for* untoe
136. It is unclear whether it was only the ringleaders who had to be heavily punished for the damage done to the Catholic cause.

Appendix B: List of Rectors of the English Colleges

The Venerable English College, Rome

    SOURCE: Michael E. Williams, *The Venerable English College, Rome: A History 1579–1979* (Leominster, 2008), 292.

Morris/Morys Clynnog/Clennock (1578–1579)
Alfonso Agazzari, SJ (1579–1586)
William Holt, SJ (1586–1588)
Robert Persons, SJ (1588)
Joseph Creswell, SJ (1589–1592)
Muzio Vitelleschi, SJ (1592–1594)
Girolamo Fioravanti, SJ (1594–May 1596)
Alfonso Agazzari, SJ (18 May 1596–)
Muzio Vitelleschi, SJ (1597)
Robert Persons, SJ (November 1597–April 1610)

St Alban's College, Valladolid

    SOURCE: Michael E. Williams, *St. Alban's College Valladolid: Four Centuries of English Catholic Presence in Spain* (London, 1986), 261.

Bartolomé de Sicilia 25 October–26 November 1589
Pedro de Guzmán 1589–24 June 1590
Juan López de Manzano 24 June 1590–1 Sept 1591
Rodrigo de Cabredo 1 Sept 1591
Gonzalo del Río 1 January 1594–Sept 1596
Alonso Rodríguez de Toro September 1596

St Gregory's College, Seville

    SOURCE: Martin Murphy, *St Gregory's College, Seville, 1592–1767* (London, 1992).

Francisco de Peralta 1592–1607

Appendix C: Cardinal Protectors of the English College, Rome

Until 1 Dec 1580	Giovanni Morone (protector of England)
31 Dec 1580–9 Jun 1586	Filippo Buoncampagni
30 June 1586–13 Dec 1599	Enrico Caetani
1599/1600–21 Feb 1626	Odoardo Farnese

Vice-Protectors

Oct 1586–Jan 1592	Ippolito Aldobrandini (later Pope Clement VIII)
Nov 1595–May 1596	Filippo Sega (d. 29 May 1596)
June–Sept 1596	Francisco de Toledo, SJ (d. 14 September 1596)
1596–1605	Camillo Borghese (later Pope Paul V)

Appendix D: Provincial Superiors of the Society of Jesus

SOURCE: *Synopsis historiae Societatis Jesu*, ed. Franz Xaver Wernz, Ludwig Schmitt and Johannes Baptist Goetstouwers (Louvain, 1950).

Belgium

1589–1594	Olivier Mannaerts
1594	Jean d'Heur, vice provincial
1594	George Duras

Toledo

Oct 1588–1593	Gonzalo Dávila
Apr 1593–1595	Francisco de Porres
Dec 1595–1599	Luis de Guzmán

Castile

1585–1590	Pedro Villalba (overlapping with Aragon from 1587)
1589	Gil González Dávila, visitor
1590–1591	Alonso de Montoya, vice provincial
1591–1593	Francisco Galarza, vice provincial
1593–1597	Gonzalo Dávila
1597–1599	Cristóbal de Ribera

Andalusia

1585–1588	Gil González Dávila
1588–1589	Luis de Guzmán
1589	José de Acosta, visitor
March 1589–1593	Bartolomé Pérez de Nueros
May 1593	Cristóbal Méndez, vice provincial until 1596, then provincial
April 1597–1600	Francisco de Quesada

Aragon

1587–1593	Pedro Villalba
1593–1594	Francisco Galarza
1594–1597	Pedro de Villar
1597–1600	Pedro Juste

Index of Persons

This index includes names of persons mentioned in the letters and editorial material (introduction, headnotes, footnotes). For letters to and from individual correspondents (other than Acquaviva and Garnet), see "correspondence with Persons" under their entries.

Acosta, José de, SJ (1540–1600) 31, 193, 250; diplomatic mission to Spain 2, 38–41, 60, 62, 87–88; and Persons's *Philopater* 209; role in fifth general congregation 3–4, 191, 213–215, 252–260, 338–339, 354–355, 364; Valladolid 3, 359, 367, 466–472, 479–486; visitor for Andalusia and Aragon 40 n4, 42–44, 49, 58 n64, 60–61, 74 n106, 91, 191–193

Acquaviva, Claudio, SJ (1543–1615), superior general of the Society of Jesus (in office 1581–1615) 31; commissions Persons and Acosta 1–2, 38–41, 42, 44, 51, 76–77, 512; correspondence with Persons 26–29, 51, 52, 59, 65, 70, 96, 101, 185, 213, 419, 523 n285, 595; English college, Rome 13, 156, 160, 187–189, 434, 478, 501, 504, 528, 537, 541, 586, 595, 629, 707; English college, Seville 127, 153, 154, 189, 205, 222, 248, 464, 487, 501, 586; English college, Saint-Omer 8, 261, 280, 286, 314, 370; English college, Valladolid 76, 97, 107, 111, 117, 119, 158, 160, 179, 337, 398, 489, 502, 536, 548, 586; English colleges in Spain 4, 92, 95 n203, 216; English Jesuits 46, 64, 98, 130, 147, 154–155, 177, 212, 248, 305, 346, 381, 398, 534, 535, 586, 692; Flanders 782, 883 n106; general congregation 3–4, 191, 252, 286, 378; Inquisition 70, 86, 92; *memorialistas* 58, 62, 82, 88, 109, 111, 113, 126; in Naples 698, 707–708, 733, 882–883; and the papacy 127–128, 262; and Philip II 52–59, 78–79, 83, 85, 88, 107, 158, 216

Agazzari, Alfonso, SJ (1549–1602) 31, 527; and William Allen 11; correspondence with Persons 28, 590–591, 623–624; English nation in Rome 582, 623–624; greets Persons at Civitavecchia 649; re-appointed rector at the English college, Rome 13, 562, 582, 590

Alabaster, William (1568–1640), English poet 15, 36–37, 797–798

Alarcón, García de, SJ (1534–1597) 95 n199

Albert VII (1559–1621), Archduke of Austria, viceroy of Portugal 20, 289, 572 n575, 579 n594, 610, 644, 653 n36, 693 n194

Aldobrandini, Cinzio (1551–1610), cardinal-nephew 699

Aldobrandini, Pietro (1571–1621), cardinal-nephew 22, 31, 556 n469, 658, 692 n191, 699, 708, 756, 763, 777, 790

Aldred, Solomon (d. 1592), spy 819

Alexander III, pope (r. 1159–1181) 239–240, 246 n78

Allen (Alano), William (1532–16 October 1594), cardinal 31, 42–43, 46, 52, 77, 85, 87, 162, 411, 725; alliance with Persons 1, 10, 17, 22, 121, 624, 627, 645, 662, 682, 690, 782 n463, 818–819; correspondence with Persons 43, 64, 66, 75, 160, 176, 186, 249, 250, 300; death 1, 11, 18, 411, 564, 881; English college at Douai (Rheims) 41, 63, 66, 499, 508, 633 n673, 646; English college at Saint-Omer 280, 301, 314, 321, 342, 347, 360; English college at Valladolid 75, 77 n120, 82, 119, 186; household of

508, 533, 559, 624, 629 n666, 730, 885 n117; and Owen Lewis 12
—, successor: *see* Englefield, Sir Francis; Lewis, Owen; Persons, Robert; Stapleton, Thomas
Angus, William Douglas (1552–1611), earl of 307, 527 n380, 608
Antoniani, Silvio, papal *maestro de camera* 881 n96
Antonio, Francisco, SJ (1535–1610) 338–340
Archer, James, SJ (ca. 1550–1620) 8, 212–213, 220
Arcos, Rodrigo Ponce de León (ca. 1545–1630), duke of 223, 363
Arcot 634 n677
Arden, John 249
Arden, Robert, SJ (b. ca. 1548) 249
Arnold, John (O.Cart.) 820
Arundel, earl of: *see* Howard, Philip
Arundell, Sir Charles (d. 15 December 1587), Catholic exile 24 n125, 335–336, 818
Arundell, Dorothy (1560–1613), Benedictine nun 534
Arundell, Sir John, of Lanherne (1527–1590) 534
Askew, George (b. 1575), seminary priest 803, 805, 884
Avellaneda, Diego de, SJ (ca. 1529–1598) 39, 40 n4, 44 n7, 61, 338–340, 370, 484
Ayamonte, marquis of: *see* Zúñiga, Francisco de
Aylmer, John (1521–1594), bishop of London 334, 337 n262, 441 n128

Babington, Anthony (d. 1586), conspirator 34, 276 n149, 683 n172, 745 nn396–397, 797
Bagshaw, Christopher (1552–ca. 1625), seminary priest 16, 649, 778, 796 n491
Baldwin IV, king of Jerusalem (r. 1174–1185) 239
Baldwin (Balduino), William, SJ (1562–1632) 14, 129, 248–249, 355, 359, 439–440, 455, 458, 463 n173, 480, 486, 686, 811, 813 n547
Ballard (Barlardo), John (d. 1586), seminary priest 683, 744, 819
Bancroft, Richard (1544–1610), bishop of London 30, 276 n150, 651, 711

Banks, Richard, SJ (ca. 1569–1643) 64, 698, 813 n547
Barbarossa, Frederick I, emperor (r. 1155–1190) 239
Barnes, John, JP 210
Barnes, Thomas, spy 784
Baronio, Cesare (1538–1607), cardinal, historian 23, 623, 625, 627–628, 632 n669, 733, 756–758, 763
Barret (Barrett), Richard (1544–1599), president of English college, Douai (Rheims) 5, 9–10, 26, 31, 41–42, 162, 208, 646, 664; correspondence with Persons 41–42, 100, 122, 508, 565, 595, 629, 803, 813; and English college, Rome 13, 560–567, 592, 594–595, 623–633, 644, 793, 795, 803–808, 883–884; opposition party in Flanders 663, 688, 690, 711, 765, 813
Bavant (Bavand), John (fl. 1550–1598), theologian 797–798
Bayes: *see* Shepperd, Robert
Baynes (Banis), Roger (1546–1623), secretary to William Allen 25 n126, 26, 30 n157, 31, 321, 475–477, 508–511, 519–520, 527–528, 564, 628, 632, 665, 709, 747, 768, 772, 784, 817 n551; correspondence with Persons 540, 585, 649
Beaton, James (1517–1603), exiled archbishop of Glasgow 742 n388
Becket, Thomas: *see* Thomas of Canterbury
Bede, the Venerable 35, 275
Bedingfeld (Silisdon), Matthew (d. 1590) student 124–125
Béjar, duke of: *see* Zúñiga y Mendoza, Francisco Diego de
Bellamy, Richard, of Uxendon 209–210, 282 n170
Bellarmine, St Robert, SJ (1542–1621), cardinal, theologian 84, 277 n152
Belloy (Bellay), Pierre de (c. 1540–1613), political philosopher 704
Belson, Thomas (d. 1589), seminary priest, martyr 84, 633, 634 n677
Bennet, Edward (1569–1637), seminary priest 12, 14–15, 526 n376, 544, 546, 591–594, 627, 632, 706 n278, 710, 729, 731, 786, 788, 796, 807, 811, 816, 889 n129

Index of Persons | 897

Bennet, John (d. 1623), seminary priest 14, 124, 668 n110, 706 n277, 786, 788, 796, 807

Benson, Robert (b. 1571), seminary priest 797, 799, 801, 808

Bernal, Pedro, SJ 471 n195, 479, 483

Bernard of Clairvaux, St 240

Bickley, Ralph, SJ (ca. 1557–1619) 692, 698, 734

Bishop, William (1553/5–1624), later Bishop of Chalcedon 164 n444, 651, 800 n503

Blackfan, John, SJ (c. 1561–1641), annalist 4 n15, 5, 41, 64, 66 n86, 67, 80, 127

Blackwell, George (1547–1612), later archpriest 711, 797–798

Blount (Biondi, Blondus), Richard, SJ (1565–1638), later first provincial of the English province 64, 79 n125, 120, 122, 163, 430, 433, 464–465, 813

Blundell (Blondello), William (1568–1596), seminary priest 593

Bodley, Thomas (1545–1613), diplomat, founder of Bodleian library 336

Bodnam (Bodenham), William 307, 308, 312

Bonaert, Nicolas, SJ (1564–1610) 790

Bonelli, Michele, OP (1541–1598), cardinal 773

Borghese (Borgesio), Camillo (1550–1621), cardinal vice-protector of England, later Pope Paul V (r. 1605–1621) 14, 22–23, 623, 628, 632, 710, 713, 733, 789, 793–794, 801–805, 807, 883, 885

Borromeo, St Charles (1538–1584), cardinal archbishop of Milan 12, 22, 143, 145

Bosseville (Bosvile), John (ca. 1567–ca. 1631), seminary priest 5

Boste, John (ca. 1543–1594), seminary priest, martyr 390–392

Bradford, Samuel (d. 1594), student at Valladolid 407 n509

Brandon, Charles (ca. 1484–1545), duke of Suffolk 853 n44

Brown, Thomas, student at Valladolid 124

Broy, Henry, SJ (b. 1550) 257, 267, 270, 295, 298, 324, 329, 332

Buckhurst, Lord: see Sackville, Thomas

Burghley, Lord: see Cecil, William

Button (Botono), Richard (ca. 1575–post 1643), seminary priest 17, 649, 706 n279, 727, 731 n372, 746 n400, 760, 762, 836

Cabredo, Rodrigo de, SJ (ca. 1558–1618) 6, 110, 153–154, 158–161, 174–175, 206, 209, 252, 254–258, 280–281, 293, 321, 330, 337, 376, 381, 386, 387, 397, 398–400, 447–454, 459, 466, 472, 484, 492, 520, 523, 528, 531, 536–537, 542–543, 548–549

Caetani, Camillo (1552–1602), nuncio to Spain 525, 638, 651, 661

Caetani, Enrico (1550–1599), cardinal protector of England 13, 22, 489, 499, 504, 538, 542, 558 n471, 560–563, 565, 646, 713, 725–726, 747, 771, 778, 785, 786, 793–805, 864, 885

Calvin, John (1509–1564), Protestant reformer 276

Campion (Campiano), St Edmund, SJ (1540–1581), martyr 36, 59, 85 n144, 143–145, 165 n451, 241 n72, 326, 341, 361–363

Carrillo, Juan Bautista, SJ, *memorialista* 2, 126

Carvajal y Mendoza, Luisa de (1566–1614), Spanish missionary to England 17, 28, 354

Castelli, Giovanni Battista (d. 1583), bishop of Rimini, papal nuncio in Paris 744 n395

Castro, Melchor de, SJ (1559–1609), author 9, 222 n2, 354, 529, 531 n393

Castro, Miguel de (1536–1625), cardinal archbishop, patriarch of Lisbon 250

Castro Osorio, Rodrigo de (1523–1600), cardinal archbishop of Seville 7, 223, 225, 234 n47, 264, 338, 471

Catherine of Aragon (1485–1536), queen of England 128, 863, 880

Cecil (Cicilio, Cicilius)(Snowden), John (1558–1626), seminary priest 19–20, 32, 75, 97; agent for Burghley 162–172, 176, 413–414; correspondence with Persons 137–138, 162, 390, 540; departure for England 108 n269, 120, 122–123, 126, 129, 131, 137, 138, 146 n392; English College, Rome 508, 511, 527, 544, 547, 562, 564; English college, Valladolid 75, 540; in Spain 306, 307, 312–314, 335 n254, 390–393, 455, 458, 498 n272; treason 165 n451

Index of Persons

Cecil, Sir Robert (1563–1612), secretary of state 18, 164 n443, 177 n485
Cecil, William (1520–1598), Lord Burghley, Lord Treasurer 10, 18, 167 n461, 181 n491, 335 n254, 762 n435, 836
Chambers, Robert (b. 1571), seminary priest 787
Charles Emmanuel I (1562–1630), duke of Savoy 273 n140
Charnock, Robert (b. 1561), seminary priest 779, 800 n503
Chasteau-Martin, Henri: see d'Or, Pierre
Chinchón, Diego Fernández de Cabrera y Bobadilla (1536–1608), count of 3, 191, 193, 252, 260, 266, 270
Chisholm, William (1525/6–1593), bishop of Dunblane 820 n570
Chrysostom, St John 389, 735 n380
Clement VIII (Ippolito Aldobrandini, 1535–1605), pope (r. 1592–1605) 3, 14, 22, 504, 508, 629, 650, 885 n116; correspondence with Persons 223, 262, 638, 769, 793; English College, Rome 511–512, 542, 546, 561, 629–633, 663, 706, 713, 725–748 *passim*, 789, 795–796, 800–805, 807–808, 881–884; health 769
Clitherow, St Margaret (1556–1586), martyr 19
Clitherow, William (b. 1542) 751, 784 n466
Cobos, Cristóbal de los, SJ 386, 398–399, 485–486
Colford, Gabriel (c. 1563–1628), Catholic exile 282
Collins: *see* Cowling, Richard
Collins, John (ca. 1573–1602), Jesuit lay brother 362 n321
Columna, Alonso de, canon of Seville cathedral 225
Comestor, Peter (1100–1178), French author 240
Como, cardinal of: *see* Galli, Tolomeo
Como, Fabrizio, lay brother 38, 43, 67, 69 n95, 90 n159, 106 n262, 160, 162, 178, 187, 189, 190, 269, 269, 305–306, 316–322, 332–333, 460–462
Copley, John (fl. 1590–1613), seminary priest, apostate 440 n125

Cordeses, Antonio, SJ (1518–1601), spiritual writer 384, 400 n447, 466, 471
Cornelius (O'Mahoney), John, SJ (ca. 1557–1594), martyr 400–402, 534–535
Covert, Thomas, William Allen's agent in Paris 183, 698, 734
Cowling (Collins, Coulingo), Richard, SJ (1562–1618) 13, 20, 28, 289, 292 n189, 295–298, 528, 531, 580, 582, 813 n548; correspondence with Persons 28, 333, 477, 544, 561
Cowling, William (1557–1592) 67, 128, 131, 138 n359, 292
Creswell (Cresuel[l]o), Joseph, SJ (ca. 1556/7–1623) 32, 513, 527, 533, 535, 543; and William Allen 411–413; armada proclamation 21, 616, 621; assistant (procurator) in Madrid 346–347, 360–362, 376, 397, 430–433, 464–466, 472–474, 479–484, 487–488, 508–511, 523–524, 573, 587–589, 621, 638, 643; question of cardinal to succeed Allen 422, 716 n324; correspondence with Persons 26, 30, 50, 59, 63–64, 66, 75, 77–78, 79–80, 82–83, 84–85, 88, 91, 95–96 n203, 97, 98, 100, 110, 113, 120, 126, 128, 137, 144–146, 287, 389, 504–507; Douai 567; and English college, Rome 7, 22, 26, 49, 147, 156–157, 158, 160–163, 213–215, 279 n164, 474–477, 501–502, 537–538, 560–564, 583–585, 590, 595–596, 629, 788, 809–811; English college, Seville 224, 264, 267–270, 355–359, 531; English college, Valladolid 7, 194, 407–409; Flanders 291–292, 295–299, 337, 363, 367–368, 586–587, 690; martyrology 165 n450; and Philip II 549, 577–580; royal proclamation (1591) 24; to Spain 172–190 *passim*, 212–213, 221, 223–224, 249; and Henry Walpole 17, 23, 323 n231, 324–325, 534
Crichton (Criton[io], Creighton), William, SJ (ca. 1534/5–1617) 32, 185, 380; correspondence with Persons 540, 567, 590, 635; Guise invasion plans 742; and William Holt 363, 368, 528, 531–532, 543, 686, 705 n275; and Persons's *Philopater* 209; "Spanish blanks" 307

Cromer, Marcin, prince-bishop of Warmia (in office 1579–1589) 240
Curle, Gilbert (1545–1609), retainer of Mary Stuart 742
Curry (Crureio, Correo), John, SJ (ca. 1552–1596) 155, 285
Curtis, Thomas, SJ (1576–1657) 885 n117

Dacre, Francis Lord (d. 1633) 82, 86–87, 500, 684 n175, 817
Dalmer, Christian, SJ 331 n243
Dávila, Gonzalo, SJ 48 n16, 52, 54, 56 n56, 57, 65, 192–193, 206, 271, 331 n242, 381, 385, 398, 430–432, 536
Dávila y Guzmán, Francisco (1548–1606), inquisitor 80–82
Derby, earl of: *see* Stanley, Ferdinando
Desmond, Gerald FitzGerald (ca. 1538–1583), earl of 559
d'Heur (Orano), Jean, SJ 331 n243, 358, 371, 377, 393–394, 698
Doleman, Alban (b. ca. 1530), Marian priest 815
Doleman, R. (pseud.) 23, 491, 614, 696 n208, 746 n401, 815, 853, 854, 857. *See also* Index of Places and Subjects: *Conference about the Next Succession*
Dolfino, Gentile, bishop of Camerino 769 n447
d'Or, Pierre (Henri Chasteau-Martin), double agent 609
Dormer, Jane (1538–1612), duchess of Feria 11, 67, 418 n42, 627 n661, 823
Drake (Draque), Sir Francis (ca. 1540–1596), naval commander 21, 166, 441, 463 n174, 492, 497–498, 507, 576, 580
Drury, Robert (d. 1607), martyr 124, 126
Duarte, Francisco, SJ (1560–1601) 523, 531
Dudley, Richard (b. 1563), dissident student 122, 126, 163, 649
Duras, George, SJ 298, 358 n314, 370–371, 393–394, 646

Elizabeth I (1533–1603), queen of England (r. 1558–1603) 164, 219, 440, 441 n128, 575; accession 638, 878, 880; assassination plots 335–336, 402–404; evil counsellors 180; excommunication 606; France 207 n200, 335; and John Gerard 734 n378, 737, 812–813; head of the church 833; Ireland 311, 559, 608; and James VI of Scotland 855; military considerations 463 n174, 492–493, 497–498, 580, 621, 841; play about 7; Scotland 307, 311–313, 596–609
Ellis, William (b. 1559) 807 n523
Ely, Humphrey (1539–1604), seminary priest, professor of canon law 10
Emerson, Ralph (1553–1604), Jesuit lay brother 16, 252, 271–274, 403, 513, 525 n373, 543 n422, 573 n578, 813 n548
Emmanuel Philibert (1528–1580), duke of Savoy 864 n49
Englefield (Inglefildo, Ynglefildo), Sir Francis (1522–1596), adviser to the Spanish royal court 21, 22, 25, 32, 66 n86, 207, 209, 282, 285, 341, 375, 416, 422, 444–447, 474, 499, 549, 551, 577–580, 604, 615, 619, 622, 663, 682 n167, 690, 699, 743–744, 817 n551, 833, 869–871
Ernest of Austria (1553–1595), archduke, governor-general of the Netherlands 334 n248, 442 n139
Erroll, Francis Hay (1564–1631), earl of 307, 527 n380, 549, 608 n641
Escobar, Marina de (1554–1633), Bridgettine nun 381
Essex, Robert Devereux (1565–1601), earl of 15, 168 n464, 336, 415, 441 n128, 609 n643, 736–737, 839 n16; Normandy expedition 166–167, 218 n662; raid on Cádiz (1596) 18, 21, 521 n357, 583–585, 594, 727

Farnese, Alessandro (1535–1589), cardinal 731
Farnese, Alessandro (1545–1592), duke of Parma 10, 207, 219, 508
Farnese, Odoardo (1573–1626), cardinal 479
Farnese, Ranuzio (1569–1622), duke of Parma 857 n48
Fénelon, Bertrand de Selignac (1523–1589), seigneur de la Mothe, French ambassador to England 500 n278
Ferdinand II, king of Leon (r. 1157–1188), 239

Feria, duchess of: *see* Dormer, Jane
Feria, Lorenzo Suárez de Figueroa y Córdoba (1559–1607), second duke of 20, 277 n156, 418, 499, 558, 640, 644, 670 n118, 690, 716
Fintry, laird of: *see* Graham, Sir David
Fioravanti, Girolamo, SJ (d. 1630) 12–13, 32, 189, 370–371, 396, 397, 412 n5, 443, 474–477, 513, 528, 533, 560–561, 562, 565, 585 n599, 717–734 *passim*
Fisher, Robert, dissident student 11, 17, 649, 709, 751, 762, 765–766, 790, 836, 888 n123
Fitzherbert (Fitzharbert), Nicholas (1550–1612), resident in Rome 533, 547, 582, 595, 614, 628, 730, 774, 836
Fitzherbert, Thomas (1552–1640), adviser to the Spanish royal court 21, 121, 277, 447, 690, 788–790, 797, 818
Fitzherbert, Sir Thomas (1513/4–1591) 166, 210 n617, 415
Fixer, John (1562–post 1613), seminary priest 19, 79, 97, 120–123, 126, 131, 137–138, 148, 163–164, 176, 274, 413–414
Flack (Flac[c]o), William, SJ (1560–1637) 2, 6, 8, 49, 52, 56, 62 n76, 66, 75, 257, 261, 267–270, 297, 304, 314–315, 324, 325, 331–332, 405–406, 524
Floyd, Henry, SJ (1564–1641) 5, 64, 67
Fonseca, Francisco de, lord of Coca 5–6
Fonseca, Pedro de, SJ 43, 58, 61 n71, 85, 113–114
Forster, Seth (d. 1628), confessor general to the Bridgettine nuns 341
Foster, Francis (1572–1628), seminary priest 803, 805, 808, 884
Foucart, Jean, SJ (1550–1608) 323 n232, 405–406, 561 n480
Frangipani, Ottavio Mirto (1544–1612), papal nuncio to Brussels 20, 32, 693 n196, 781 n461, 790, 793, 795, 797, 799–781
Fuentes, Pedro Henríquez de Acevedo (1525–1610), count of, governor-general of the Netherlands 334 n248, 442 n139
Fuljambe (Folgam), Godfrey (1527–1585) 551, 818 n558

Galarza, Francisco, SJ 161 n434, 179, 187, 331 n242

Galli, Tolomeo (ca. 1525–1607), cardinal Como, papal secretary of state 22
Garnet (Garnett), Henry, SJ (1553–1606) 14, 16–17, 32–33; and Richard Blount 430, 433, 465; clerical associations 648–649, 734, 779; correspondence with Persons 27, 28, 30, 639; (Jesuit) English mission 138, 162–163, 208, 277, 303, 360, 363, 400–405, 413–416, 440, 486, 534, 609, 685, 692, 698, 811–813; and John Gerard 639, 736–737, 788; hierarchy 797–798; Paget–Morgan opposition 690, 709; profession as Jesuit 513, 525 n373, 527, 543; Rome 575, 686; and Robert Southwell 209–212, 287–288; Saint-Omer 274, 290–293, 297; Wisbech 709, 778, 790–792
Garnet, Thomas, SJ (1575–1608), martyr 440 n125
Gerard, John, SJ (1564–1637) 33, 138, 139 n369, 154, 440 n125, 504–506, 838 n15; arrest 492; the Clink 413, 415; Counter in the Poultry 130 n343, 403; Tower of London 17, 18, 698, 734, 736–737, 788, 797, 813
Gervase, Edmund, student at Valladolid 124, 126
Gibbons (Gibbon[i]o), Richard, SJ (ca. 1547–1632) 6–7, 33, 50, 52, 66, 75, 107, 130–131, 154, 213, 286–287, 293, 303, 326, 381–385, 389, 394–398, 405–407, 411, 753
Gifford, Gilbert (1560–1590), conspirator 10, 683, 745, 784, 819 n567
Gifford, William, OSB (1557/1558–1629), dean of Lille 10, 13, 15, 33, 124, 440, 629, 750; correspondence with Persons 11, 26, 663–664; English college, Rome 638, 714–715, 719–734 *passim*, 755; Paget–Morgan group 27, 528, 532, 557, 614, 633, 649, 705, 745–746, 759–766, 790–793, 817, 833, 837, 871; seminary in Paris 813–815
Gilpin, George (ca. 1514–1602), deputy to Thomas Bodley 336, n261
Gonzaga, Francesco, OFM (d. 1620), nuncio to Paris 763
González Dávila, Gil, SJ 3, 33, 40 n4, 42–44, 58 n62, 60–61, 74 n106, 87–88; co-operation with Persons 65; and Joseph Creswell 466,

473, 480–484; English college, Valladolid 76–77, 79, 80–81, 84 n141, 85, 91–95
Goodman, Gabriel (1528–1601), dean of Westminster 797
Gordon, Sir Patrick, of Auchindoun (1538–1594) 307
Graham, Sir David (d. 1592), laird of Fintry 637
Grately (Grateleo), Edward (b. 1555), seminary priest 10, 745, 819 n567 and n569
Green, Thomas (d. 1591), student 124, 126
Gregory XIII (Ugo Buoncampagni, 1502–1585), pope (r. 1572–1585) 13 n70, 22, 573, 607
Gregory XIV (Niccolò Sfondrati, 1535–1591), pope (r. 1590–1591) 22, 119, 127–128, 143
Griffin (Griffith, Grifidio), Hugh (1555–1600), provost of Cambrai 13, 15, 510, 533, 582, 614, 623, 628–629, 710, 715, 721–722, 730–731, 733, 750, 765 n438, 766 n441, 828, 837, 880–881
Griffith, Richard, SJ (ca. 1576–1607) 580–582
Guise, Henry duke of (1550–1588) 16, 819; assassination 41–42, 110; invasion plans 10, 12 n64, 607 n638, 742–744
Guzmán, Luis de, SJ 521 n359
Guzmán, Pedro de, SJ (ca. 1560–1590) 6, 80, 92, 95, 100, 105, 110

Harewood (Harodo, Harvode), Edmund, SJ (1554–1597) 12–13, 27, 365, 367, 437 n96, 501–502, 527, 533, 585, 628, 644, 786, 884; correspondence with Persons 443, 474–477, 503–504, 513, 525
Harpsfield, Nicholas (1519–1575), controversialist and historian 275
Hart, Elizabeth (d. 1609), Bridgettine abbess 341
Hasels, Walter (1574–post 1621), seminary priest 885 n117
Hastings, Henry (1536–1595), third earl of Huntingdon 167, 390, 853, 880
Hatton, Sir Christopher (1540–1591), Lord Chancellor 18, 167 n461, 168, 176 n481, 177 n485, 180, 182 n500
Hatton, Thomas, dissident student 836

Hawkins (Hauquins), Sir John (1532–1595), naval commander 21, 463 n174, 492–493, 497, 507, 576, 577
Haydock (Haddock, Haddoco, Hadoque), Richard (ca. 1551–1605), seminary priest 14, 508, 511, 607, 628–629
Heneage, Sir Thomas (1532–1595), privy councillor 249
Henry II (1133–1189), king of England (r. 1154–1189) 227–248, 877
Henry II (1519–1559), king of France (r. 1547–1559) 854 n47
Henry III (1207–1272), king of England (r. 1216–1272) 876–877
Henry III (1551–1589), king of France (r. 1574–1589) 5, 41, 378 n372
Henry IV (1367–1413), king of England (r. 1399–1413) 497, 534–535 n404, 853, 876–878
Henry IV (Henry of Navarre, 1553–1610), king of France (r. 1589–1610) 13, 22, 126 n327, 166 n453, 207, 272, 273 n140, 377 n369, 512, 577, 670 n118, 758 nn419–421, 814
Henry VI (1421–1471), king of England (r. 1422–1461, 1470–1471) 876–878
Henry VII (1457–1509), king of England (r. 1485–1509) 479, 497–498, 853–854, 856, 863, 878–879
Henry VIII (1491–1547), king of England (r. 1509–1547) 128, 167 n460, 225, 604, 684 n175, 863, 879–880
Hernández, Sebastián, SJ 86–88, 109, 193, 305, 522, 633–634
Hesketh, Richard, conspirator 334–335
Hesketh (Hesquet)(Allen), Thomas, relative of William Allen 13, 335 n254, 413 n8, 533, 557, 582, 595, 614, 624, 628–629, 880–881
Heywood, Jasper, SJ (1535–1598) 647 n11
Hill, James 690, 818
Hill, Thomas (1564–1644), seminary priest 591–594, 797, 799–801, 808, 882 n103
Hoare, Gregory (ca. 1573–1639), Jesuit lay brother 360, 362 n321
Holt (Holto, Olto), William, SJ (1545–1599) 10, 15, 20, 33, 219–220, 325, 402 n473, 793; and Thomas Covert 698, 734–736;

and William Crichton 532, 543; correspondence with Persons 26, 28, 131, 650–662, 710–713; English college, Rome 147, 156–157, 501–502; English college, Saint-Omer 251, 257, 275, 331, 524; opposition in Flanders 628–629, 632, 686–691, 705 n275, 784 n466, 817–818; Scotland 573; Spanish interest 551, 558, 564; proposed transfer 131, 154–156, 160–162, 177, 295–299, 337, 346, 363, 368, 378–380, 560–561, 583, 586–589, 633, 640, 641–646; and Thomas Worthington 648

Holtby, Richard, SJ (1552–1640) 17, 50, 176, 274, 812, 813 n248

Hopkins (Hopquines), Richard (ca. 1546–ca. 1596), translator 121, 551, 818 n558

Howard, Anne (1557–1630), countess of Arundel 7 n64, 35

Howard, Charles (1536–1624), baron Howard of Effingham, Lord Admiral 164 n441, 167 n461

Howard, Jane (d. 1593), countess of Westmorland 337 n262

Howard, Philip (1557–1595), earl of Arundel 17

Hunt (Huncto), Thomas, SJ (1552–1626) 216–217

Huntingdon, earl of: *see* Hastings, Henry

Huntly, George Gordon (ca. 1562–1636), earl of 307, 390, 527 n380, 549, 608 n641

Ibarra Emparán, Esteban de, secretary of the council of the Netherlands 322, 325 n236, 380, 644

Idiáquez, Juan de (1540–1614), secretary to King Philip II 21, 33, 473, 499, 500, 615–623, 737–747; correspondence with Persons 26, 132, 307–314, 354, 367, 508–512, 549, 573, 615, 699, 716, 737, 748, 759; intermediary with Philip II 21, 104, 132–137, 300–301, 522, 549–551, 605 n634, 759–763; relations with Spanish ambassador in Rome 508–512, 748, 757; question of Allen's successor 422, 470, 715–716

Idiáquez, Martin de (1558–1559), royal councillor 596, 597

Ignatius of Loyola, SJ, St (1491–1556) 533, 689; *Spiritual Exercises* 390 n413

Ingram, John (1565–1594), martyr 390–392

Innocent IX (Giovanni Antonio Facchinetti, 1519–1591), pope (r. 29 October–30 December 1591) 22, 176

Isabella Clara Eugenia (1566–1633), infanta of Spain 20, 340 n270; claim to the throne of England 22, 25, 499, 577–579, 582, 604, 614, 620, 651, 653, 660–662, 696–698, 699, 727, 752, 754, 772, 775, 823–864 *passim*, 854 n47, 869–872; claim to the throne of France 758; English college, Valladolid 194; English college, Saint-Omer 257; marriage 20, 378 n372, 644 n6, 653 n36

Isham, William (1578–post 1603), seminary priest 885 n117

Iverson, John, student 440 n125

Jackson, John (b. 1573), seminary priest 803–804, 808, 884

James VI (1566–1625), king of Scotland (r. 1567–1625) 22, 637–638, 820 n570; Catholic lords 390, 544; claim to the throne of England 376, 491, 532, 540, 556, 567–579 *passim*, 620, 651, 835, 838, 843–863 *passim*, 872; heresy 573, 697; Persons regarded as enemy 652–653, 660, 697, 727; potential conversion 574, 577, 579 n593, 651, 705 n275, 834; support of anti-Jesuit party 704–705, 730, 745–746, 833–834

Jiménez, Diego, SJ (ca. 1530–1608), secretary of the Society of Jesus 533

Jiménez de Murillo, Pedro, secretary to the Spanish ambassador, Rome 714, 786

Jones (Jonas), Robert, SJ (ca. 1564–1615) 17, 360–363, 378–380, 411–412, 480, 486, 813 n548

Jonson, Ben (1572–1637), author 15

Kemp, Francis (d. 1598), seminary priest 124

Kenyon, Edward, seminary priest 271, 272 n133

Kerr, George, emissary of Scottish earls 307

Komnenos, Manuel I, Byzantine emperor (r. 1143–1180) 239 n63

Labata, Juan Francisco, SJ (ca. 1549–1631) 386
Langdale, Alban, Marian priest 414, 751 n409
Lassells, Christopher, seminary priest 786
Leslie, John (1527–1596), bishop of Ross 341
Lévêque, Roger de Pont (ca. 1115–1181), archdeacon of Canterbury 241 n73
Lewis, Owen (1533–1595), bishop of Cassano 11, 33–34, 412; Allen's successor 1, 417, 474, 477, 499, 559 n473, 725, 881 n96; anti-Jesuit party 705, 820 n570; death 528, 532 n396, 564, 623, 730 n371, 779; English college, Rome 12–13, 504, 729
Lewkenor (Lauchenero), Sir Lewis (ca. 1560–1627), former Catholic exile 838
Liggons, Ralph, Catholic exile 705, 819
Loaysa, García de (1534–1599), tutor to Prince Philip 69, 194, 716
Lockwood, Francis, seminary priest 67, 123, 126, 131
López, Rodrigo (1517–1594), royal physician 415 n23
López de Manzano, Juan, SJ (d. 1602) 6, 23 n123, 95 n201, 110, 113, 118 n308, 119, 153, 158, 159, 160
Lothbury, Jasper (b. 1564), seminary priest 803, 804
Louis VII (1120–1180), king of France (r. 1137–1180) 239
Loyola: *see* Ignatius of Loyola
Lutte, Jacob (James) 271–274

Madrigal, Pedro (d. 1594), printer 23–24, 84
Madruzzo, Ludovico (1532–1600), cardinal 767, 769–771, 883 n107
Maggio, Lorenzo, SJ (1530/1531–1605) 320
Malcolm IV (1141–1165), king of Scotland (r. 1153–1165) 239
Malvasia, Innocenzo (1552–1612), papal agent in Brussels 10–11, 20, 34, 556, 699, 705, 729–731, 733, 746, 753, 779–781, 784 n466, 788–789, 805–806, 833
Mannaerts (Manaraeo), Olivier, SJ (1523–1605) 8, 10–11, 26, 34, 156 n423, 177, 371, 524; advises Persons on cardinalate 416–419, 423–425, 465; correspondence with Persons 293, 416, 633, 640, 686; opposition party in Flanders 633, 640–646, 686–691, 784 n466; Saint-Omer 257 n104, 261, 280, 286, 289, 293, 355, 358 n314, 370, 393–394
Manrique, Jerónimo (c. 1538–1595), bishop of Cartagena, inquisitor 2, 42, 126
Manríquez, Francisco de, Spanish gentleman 472
Mansfeld, Charles (Karl) (1543–1595), count, military commander 334
Mansfeld, Pierre Ernst (1517–1604), count, governor-general of the Netherlands 278 n160, 282 n178, 322 n225, 334 n248
Marcén, Antonio, SJ 2, 40 n3, 41 n6, 192
Maria of Austria (1528–1603), empress 100, 105 n258, 257, 338
Markham (Marcamo), Sir Griffin (ca. 1565–ca. 1644), soldier and conspirator 544, 546, 836
Markham, Robert 544, 546, 836
Mary I (1516–1558), queen of England (r. 1553–1558) 19, 223, 375, 604, 638, 863, 871
Mary Stuart (1542–1587), queen of Scotland (r. 1542–1567) 10, 441 n128, 491, 573, 638, 662, 738–745, 856, 878–879
Maselli, Luigi, SJ 389
Massi, Cosimo (ca. 1537–1600), secretary to the duke of Parma 220 n675, 299
Matthieu, Claude, SJ (1537–1587) 743, 819
Medina Sidonia, Alonso Pérez de Guzmán (1550–1615), duke of 7, 128, 223, 455–462, 471
Méndez, Cristóbal, SJ 384 n392, 444, 460, 466, 471 n195, 528, 586
Mendoza, Alfonso de, abbot 5, 67
Mendoza, Antonio de, SJ (ca. 1545–1596) 447, 459, 485
Mendoza, Bernardino de (ca. 1540–1604), former Spanish ambassador to England 277 n156, 312 n214, 340, 342 n274, 607 n638, 758
Mendoza, Luis de, SJ 51, 52, 58, 61, 86–87, 193
Mercurian, Everard, SJ (1514–1580), superior

general of the Society of Jesus (in office 1573–1580) 2, 400 n447
Middleton, John, seminary priest 808, 883, 885, 886 n118
Montmorency, duke Henri de (1534–1614) 833
Montoya, Alonso de, SJ 161 n434
Montpesson, Henry, student 440 n125
More, Henry, SJ (ca. 1587–1661), provincial of England 9, 76
Morgan, Thomas (ca. 1542–1606), fomer agent of Mary Stuart 10–12, 27, 34, 136, 220 n671, 499, 510, 532, 556, 558, 627 n661, 690, 699, 729, 737–747, 748, 759, 762–763, 765, 766, 817 n553, 818–820, 823, 834
Morra, Bernardino (ca. 1549–1605), papal official 13, 504, 526 n376, 594 n616, 726 n360, 729–731, 733, 736 n13
Moura y Távora, Cristóbal de (1538–1613), royal councillor 300–301, 522 n361
Mush, John (1552–1612), seminary priest 12, 19, 649; correspondence with Persons 410, 433

Nadal, Jerónimo, SJ (1507–1580) 533
Nannini, Giovanni, SJ (1551–1605) 533 n401
Nau, Claude (d. 1605), retainer of Mary Stuart 742
Navarre: see Henry IV, king of France
Nelson, Martin (ca. 1550–1625), seminary priest 546
Nevill, Lady Margaret 390
Nichols, George (1550–1589), priest and martyr 84, 633, 634 n677
Niño de Guevara, Fernando (1541–1609), cardinal 716
Norden, John (ca. 1565–1597), seminary priest 778
Norris, Sir John (ca. 1547–1597), military commander 66, 167, 172, 218, 497, 507
Norris (Noricio), Sylvester (ca. 1572–1630), seminary priest 17, 648–649, 706 n279, 727, 731 n372, 746 n400, 760, 762, 836

O'Collun, Patrick, soldier 400, 402 n473

O'Donnell, Hugh Roe (1572–1602), of Tyrconnell 311 n211, 441 n129
Ogilvie, John (Pury Ogilvie, fl. 1587–1601), of Pury, political adventurer 544, 579
Olivares, Enrique de Guzmán (1540–1607), count of, viceroy to Naples 57 n58, 499, 698, 707
O'Rourke, Brian (ca. 1540–1591), Irish lord 166 n455
Owen (Oen), Hugh (1538–1618), intelligence agent 10, 20, 34, 121, 551, 558, 595, 609, 615, 686, 689–690, 817–818, 840 n18
Owen, Walter (d. 1591), student at Valladolid 124
Owens, Thomas, SJ (1556–1618) 99 n211, 810

Padilla, Antonio de, SJ (1554–1611) 212–213, 381, 386, 398–400, 485
Padilla, Martín de (1540–1602), adelantado of Castile 132, 512, 521, 560, 616, 621, 622, 839 n16
Paget, Charles (c. 1546–1612), former agent of Mary Stuart 10–11, 26–27, 34, 136, 176, 278, 499, 510, 532, 556–557, 579, 614, 633, 649, 690, 699, 705, 727–730, 737–747, 750–751, 759, 762–763, 765, 766, 784–786, 790–793, 807, 813–822, 833, 834, 837; correspondence with Persons 787–788, 811, 816
Paget, Thomas Lord (c. 1544–1590), Catholic exile 335–336
Palasor (Palacer, Palaser), Thomas (d. 1600), martyr 21, 839
Paravicini, Ottavio (1552–1611), cardinal 767, 773–774
Parma, Margaret of (1522–1586), governor of the Netherlands 854 n46
Parry, William (d. 1585), conspirator 744, 818–819
Paul, apostle and saint 276, 323, 381, 384–385, 622, 668, 671, 672, 677, 679, 680
Paul V, pope: see Borghese, Camillo
Peña, Francisco de (ca. 1540–1612), papal official 14, 22, 30, 34, 664–666, 694–698, 699, 754–759, 763, 766–769, 771–777, 782–786, 805–807, 823

Peralta, Francisco de, SJ (ca. 1554–1622) 8, 34, 248, 258, 269, 300, 330 n240, 381, 384, 452–453, 455, 459, 460–465, 479, 483, 488, 528–531

Percy, Henry (ca. 1532–1585), eighth earl of Northumberland 336 n261, 743

Percy, Henry (1564–1632), ninth earl of Northumberland 167 n460, 168 n466

Percy (Pierse), William (ca. 1550–post 1603), seminary priest 558 n471, 607 n639, 615, 646, 651, 656–662

Pérez de Nueros, Bartolomé, SJ (1548–1614) 3, 7, 50, 96, 97, 128, 153–155, 174, 216 n653, 271, 299, 381–386, 400 n446, 405–407, 444, 460, 466, 471, 484, 516, 523

Perron, Jaques Davy du (1556–1618), bishop of Evreux 814

Perrot (Parrot), Sir John (1528–1592), formerly lord deputy of Ireland 166

Persons, Christina, mother of Robert Persons 576 n589, 778–779

Persons (Parsons, Personio, Personius), Robert, SJ (1546–1610): amanuensis 49, 66; audiences with Philip II 41–42, 49, 63, 65–66, 67, 72–73, 84, 88, 108, 158–159, 252–260, 266–271, 338, 342, 345, 347–352, 492, 496, 512, 522; audiences with pope 489, 627, 660, 666, 691, 696, 707–708, 752, 783; cardinalate 11–12, 417, 421, 425, 430, 442, 465, 540, 714, 716 n324, 779; *conversos* 364; French Jesuits 20, 512; health 43, 46, 48–49, 50, 107, 108 n268, 153, 158–160, 173–174, 177, 189, 420, 649, 883; library 16; orations 194–205, 225–248, 667–685; pastoral role 6–7, 9, 15, 28, 29, 52, 293, 303, 316, 319, 330, 333, 384–385, 389, 394–397, 405–410, 580, 646; political involvement 4, 316, 364, 378, 704 nn273–274; printing and publishing 15, 23–25, 59, 75, 84–85, 139, 194–205, 209, 218, 276 n149, 279, 316, 321, 535, 565, 606, 651, 705, 707, 833; pseudonyms 209, 401 n461, 416 n33, 696 n208, 815; relations with local Spanish Jesuits 5, 8, 92, 117, 119, 158, 160, 174, 179–180, 187, 190, 261, 444, 460, 466, 487, 513, 538, 586–587; spelling of name "Parsons" 15, 121–122, 124, 157, 300–301, 306, 341, 576, 651, 707, 711, 713, 787, 808; superior of the English mission 16, 41; transport in Rome 23, 759, 768, 777, 784–785

—, biography: diplomatic mission to Spain (1588–1591) 1–4, 26, 38–191 *passim*; establishes English college in Valladolid (1589–1590) 1, 4–8, 63–114; visits Andalusia (1590–1591) 128–147; founds English college in Seville (1592) 223–266; founds English college of St Omers (1592–1593) 250–327 *passim*; visits Lisbon (1593) 250, 289, 340; in Madrid to cover for fifth general congregation (1593–1594) 327–346; based in Seville (1594–1596) 419–577; returns to Rome (1596–1597) 640–664; deals with conflicts in the English College, Rome (1597) 667–808; rector (Nov 1597) 809–816

—, memorials 11, 18, 30, 768–778; on bishoprics 864; on condition of England 577, 823; on council in Flanders 610; on English affairs in Rome 699; on English College, Rome 716; on invasion 597–598; on opposition in Flanders 737; on succession to the throne of England 842, 869, 872

—, writings: biography of Campion 59, 326; *Certamen Ecclesiae Anglicanae* 275, 413; *Christian Directory* 322 n226, 324 n234, 653 n35; *Información que da el Padre Personio ... acerca ... del Seminario ... en Valladolid* 23, 67, 75; *A Manifestation of the Great Folly and Bad Spirit of Certayne in England Calling Themselves Secular Priestes* 650–653; *Memorial for the Reformation of England* 18, 25, 69 n96, 604 n632, 864; "Philopater" (*Elizabethae Angliae Reginae ... saevissimum in Catholicos sui regni edictum ... Cum responsione*) 7, 19, 23–24, 168 n466, 176, 209, 218 n656, 279 n163; *Relacion de algunos martyrios* 23, 48 n16, 75, 84, 634 n676; *Relacion ... de la venida de su Magestad a Valliodolid* 24, 75–76, 122, 194; *A relation of the King of Spaines receiving in Valliodolid* 23, 64, 75, 84, 194, 218 n657, 716 n324. *See also* Index of Places and Sub-

jects: *Conference about the Next Succession; Newes from Spayne and Holland*
Peter Lombard (1090–1160), bishop of Paris, theologian 240
Phelippes, Thomas (1556–1625), cipher master 609 n643
Philip II (1527–1598), king of Spain (r. 1556–1598) 13, 166 n454, 223, 259, 327, 375 n366, 633; Bridgettines 340; council of state 840 n18; death 651; distrust of English 131, 135–136, 605 n634; English exiles 293–294; English mission 5, 21, 122; enterprise of England 21, 492–501, 521 n357, 551, 577–580, 607 n638, 616; intelligence networks 121; Society of Jesus 1–2, 38, 52, 62 n78, 83, 191, 342, 685 n179; Spanish Netherlands 219 n669, 220 n675, 322, 334 n251, 627 n661; sponsor of Persons's *Philopater* 24, 209; successor to Allen 417, 442, 551, 820 n570; support of seminaries 8, 100, 186, 252, 257, 278 n162, 508; visit to English College, Valladolid 6, 69 n96, 147, 194–205, 212, 225, 716 n324
Philip III (1578–1621), prince of Asturias, king of Spain (r. 1598–1621) 6, 69 n96, 194, 257, 307, 313, 499, 522, 583, 661
Philips, Peter (1560/1561–1628), musician 334–335, 336 n261
Pickard, Ralph (d. 1591), seminary priest 147–148
Piers, Henry (1567–1623), Irish traveller 8, 14, 508, 786
Pierse: *see* Percy, William
Pineda, Juan de, SJ (1558–1637) 9
Plessis-Mornay, Philippe du (1549–1623), Protestant author 814
Pole, Gervase, SJ (ca. 1572–1641) 478, 557 n470, 786 n467, 885 n117
Pole, Margaret (1473–1541), countess of Salisbury 853 n45
Porres, Francisco de, SJ (1538–1621) 60–61, 94–96, 101, 106, 117, 126–128, 192–193, 288–289, 432 n72, 484 n243, 521 n359
Poza, Francisco de Rojas y Enríquez (1546–1605), marquis of 597, 621
Priego, Pedro Fernández de Córdoba y Figueroa (1563–1606), marquis of 223, 354–357, 471

Pritchard, Humphrey (d. 1589), martyr 633
Puente, Luis de la, SJ (1554–1624) 381, 386
Pullen (Polinus), Joseph, SJ (ca. 1543–1607) 580, 582, 813 n548

Quiñones, Alfonso de, Spanish gentleman 6

Rainolds (Reynoldes), William (1543–1594), theologian 275
Raya Navarrete, Antonio de la (1536–1606), inquisitor 634 n678
Reinosa Baeza, Alfonso de (1534–1601), bishop of Cordoba 6
Ribadeneira, Pedro de, SJ (1526–1611), author 23, 35, 50–52, 58, 60–62, 94–96, 162, 166 n458, 180, 252, 260, 262, 332, 371, 376, 394, 523
Ricci, Bartholomeo, SJ, 314
Río, Gonzalo del, SJ 6, 28, 213 n644, 381, 430–432, 433, 443–444, 447–454, 455, 459, 464, 479, 485, 492, 502, 512, 520, 536, 538, 548, 583
Robinson, Christopher (d. 1597), martyr 685
Robinson, Francis (1569–post 1632), seminary priest 808, 885 n117
Rodríguez, Francisco, SJ (ca. 1548–1627), secretary to Acquaviva 332, 340, 359, 370, 371, 395, 397, 532, 540
Rodríguez, Manuel, SJ 100
Rodríguez de Toro, Alonso, SJ 6, 512
Rojas, Manuel de, SJ 386, 485 n245
Rook, Henry (fl. 1581–1596), seminary priest 123, 126
Ruiz de Velasco, Juan (d. 1605), Spanish courtier 67–70, 300–301
Rye, Marc de (d. 1598), marquis de Varambon 257

Sacheverell, John (Friar William, OP, 1568–1625) 17, 547, 730, 751 n407, 760, 762, 765 n437, 837
Sackville, Thomas (1536–1608), Lord Buckhurst 18, 167 n461, 172
Salway, Thomas (fl. 1583–1619), missionary priest 123, 126
Samier (Samerie), Henry, SJ (1540–1610) 743

Sánchez, Alonso, SJ (1547–1593) 3, 95, 252, 258, 270
Sánchez, Luis (d. 1627), printer 24
Sancho III (1133–1158), king of Castile (r. 1157–1158) 239
Sander (Sanders), Nicholas (ca. 1530–1581), theologian 682; *De schismate Anglicano* 23, 85, 275
Sarmiento de Mendoza, Francisco (1525–1595), bishop of Jaén 113, 471 n194, 479
Savage, John (d. 1586), conspirator 819
Savoy, duke of: *see* Charles Emmanuel I; Emmanuel Philibert
Sega, Filippo (1537–1596), cardinal vice-protector of England 13, 22, 538, 542, 560–564, 726, 796 n491, 887
Semple (Sempill), William (1546–1633), colonel 363, 368, 590, 636
Sessa, Antonio Fernández de Córdoba y Cardona (1550–1606), duke of, Spanish ambassador to Rome 21, 32, 499, 508, 511, 664, 665, 666, 697, 699, 707, 714, 718, 727, 730–731, 746, 750, 754, 756–776, 782, 807, 837, 882
Seymour, Edward (1561–1612), Lord Beauchamp 853 n44
Sfondrati, Niccolò: *see* Gregory XIV
Sfondrati, Paolo Emilio (1560–1618), papal secretary of state 22, 120, 143–147
Shakespeare, William (1564–1616), author 442 n137
Shepperd, Robert (Bayes), student in Rome 544, 546, 562, 786
Sicilia, Bartolomé de, SJ 6, 48, 79, 80–82, 189–190, 213, 344 n279, 346 n283, 347, 512, 521, 543 n418
Sicklemore, Humphrey (b. 1570), seminary priest 786 n467, 796
Sigüenza, Juan de, SJ, 193 n520, 354, 359, 367, 386, 466
Silisdon: *see* Bedingfeld, Matthew
Sixtus V (Felice Peretti di Montalto, OFM 1520–1590), pope (r. 1585–1590) 1, 22, 42, 113, 117, 820 n570
Smith, Nicholas, SJ (1558–1630) 257, 270, 292, 513, 524, 543
Snowden: *see* Cecil, John

Southampton, Henry Wriothesley (1573–1624), earl of 167 n460, 415
Southwell (Bacon), Nathaniel, SJ (1598–1676) 225
Southwell, St Robert, SJ (ca. 1561–1595), poet and martyr 16–17, 35, 122 n317, 138, 162, 166 n452, 176, 183 n504, 207–209, 287–288, 360–362, 415, 439, 534–535; correspondence with Persons 139–143
Squarcione, Azaricio, papal fiscal 800 n503, 884 n111, 886 n119
Standen, Sir Anthony (ca. 1548–ca. 1615), exile, agent of the earl of Essex 19, 490–492
Standish, James (fl. 1587–1608), seminary priest 787, 888 n123
Stanihurst, Richard (1547–1618), author 375 n366, 414 n10
Stanley, Ferdinando (ca. 1559–1594), Lord Strange, earl of Derby 20, 138, 335 n254, 415 n22, 853 n44
Stanley, Sir William (1548–1630), colonel 20, 35, 121, 137, 162 n435, 166 n454, 220 n670, 300, 335, 402 n473, 500, 558–559, 606, 615, 628, 690, 840 n18
Stapleton, Thomas [SJ] (1535–1598), theologian 35, 559, 597, 606–607, 647 n10, 788, 864; cardinalate 12, 731–732, 793; correspondence with Persons 26–27, 662, 692, 713, 737, 752, 779; proposed transfer to Rome 12, 23, 27, 628–629, 631, 632 n669, 662, 692–694, 714–715, 737, 752, 779–783, 789, 793, 805–807; *Apologia pro Rege Catholico Philippo II* 24; *Tres Thomae* 225
Starkey, William: *see* Wiseman, Thomas
Stephenson, Thomas, SJ (1552–1624) 49–50
Sterrell, William (b. 1561), intelligencer 278 n157, 609
Strange, Lord: *see* Stanley, Ferdinando
Stuart, Lady Arbella (1575–1615) 167, 182, 853–856, 879
Suárez, Francisco, SJ (1548–1617), political theorist 58 n61, 316, 321, 479, 485
Suárez, Juan, SJ (1528–1599) 58 n61, 161 n434, 173, 179–180, 386
Sutcliffe, Matthew (1550–1629), Anglican divine 276 n151, 277 n152

Swinburne (Suinborno), Simon, SJ (1562–1638) 128–130, 314, 489, 501

Tancard, Charles, SJ (1564–1599) 6, 21, 50 n22, 52, 56, 62 n76, 66, 75, 95, 118 n310, 120, 122, 269, 292, 319, 330, 387, 389, 409, 444, 447, 459; armada (1596) 560–561, 615–616, 622–623
Tarifa, Ana Téllez-Girón (1555–1625), marchioness of 223, 471
Tarugi, François-Marie (1525–1608), cardinal archbishop of Siena 767, 770–771
Tassis, Juan Bautista de (1530–1610), Spanish ambassador to France 607, 742, 758
Tempest, Edward (b. 1568), seminary priest 591, 593–594, 797, 799, 801, 808, 818 n558
Tesimond, Oswald, SJ (1563–1636) 314, 315, 330 n239, 346 n284, 360, 367, 411, 444, 447, 459 n165, 561, 813
Thomas Aquinas, St 9, 385 n397, 437 n100
Thomas of Canterbury, St 7, 225–248
Thompson, James, student 440 n125
Thomson, John (d. 1616), seminary priest 124
Throckmorton (Throgmortonus), Thomas (fl. 1580–1595), exile 11, 12, 13, 476, 499, 510, 528, 532–533, 557, 594, 623, 627, 729–730, 881 n96; Throckmorton family 12 n64, 499 n273, 663 n106
Tichborne (Touchbornus), Henry, SJ (1570–1606) 13, 28, 544, 548, 580–582, 591, 810
Toledo, Francisco de, SJ (1532–1596), cardinal vice-protector of England 13, 22, 35, 593 n611, 594 n617, 623, 626, 629, 649, 706, 726 n360, 730–733, 746, 751, 761, 782, 834, 836, 882, 887
Topcliffe (Toply), Richard (1531–1604), government agent 17, 164 n445, 166 n452, 171–172, 181 n495, 182, 210–211, 336, 415, 439, 535
Traherne, Gabriel, Catholic exile 615
Tresham (Tressam), William, Catholic exile 614, 705, 762, 818 n558
Trollop, Cuthbert (b. 1573), student 786 n467, 803, 804

Tudor, Margaret (1489–1541), elder daughter of King Henry VII of England 167 n460, 853 n43
Tudor, Mary (1496–1533), younger daughter of Henry VII of England, 853 n44
Turnbull, George, SJ (1569–1633) 544, 548
Tyrie, James, SJ (1543–1597), assistant for Germany 380, 565, 730
Tyrone, Hugh O'Neill (ca. 1550–1616), earl of 311 n211, 441 n129, 559
Tyrrell (Tirrell), Anthony (d. 1615), seminary priest and apostate 275–276, 683 n172
Tyrwhit (Tirwit), Nicolas (fl. 1573–1598), seminary priest 797–798

Urban VII (Giovanni Battista Castagna, 1521–1590), pope (r. 15–27 September 1590) 22, 27, 113, 117, 127

Vendome: see Henry IV, king of France
Vere, Sir Francis (1560–1609), military commander 66, 167 n462, 172
Vernois, Jean de, OP (1540–1599), bishop of Saint-Omer 345 n282, 350 n292
Verstegan (Rowlands), Richard (ca. 1550–1640), Persons's agent in Antwerp 16, 17, 23–24, 36, 182 nn501–502, 183 n504, 208 n610, 209, 211, 221 n679, 258 n108, 401 n452, 609, 639, 698, 817 n551; correspondence with Persons 26, 30, 163, 176, 180, 193, 207, 215, 217–220, 251, 272 n135, 275–280, 281–285, 293, 334, 439, 533–534; *An advertisement written to a secretarie of my L. Treasurers of Ingland* 279 n163; and Persons's *Philopater* 24, 209
Villalba, Pedro, SJ 105 n259, 193 n520
Villerius, Bartholomé, SJ 222
Vitelleschi, Muzio, SJ (1563–1645), superior general of the Society of Jesus (in office 1615–1645) 4, 14, 162 n436, 187, 188–189, 258, 370, 793, 794–795, 801, 804

Waad (Wad, Wade), William (1546–1623), clerk to the Privy Council 21, 211 n628, 762, 836, 839 n16

Walpole, Christopher, SJ (ca. 1570–1606) 363 n324

Walpole (Valpolo), Henry, SJ (1558–1595), priest and martyr 5, 7, 8, 17, 24, 36, 165, 177, 179, 225–226, 234 n46, 248, 277 n153, 279 n164, 300–303, 306, 361–363; correspondence with Persons 321–325

Walpole, Michael, SJ (ca. 1570–1625) 363 n324

Walpole, Richard, SJ (ca. 1562–1607) 8, 147–148, 271, 363 n324, 639

Walsingham, Sir Francis (ca. 1532–1590), secretary of state I 10, 167 n461, 172, 276, 336 n261, 683, 745, 819 n567

Walton, Roger, informer 334–336

Warford, William, SJ (ca. 1560–1608) 28, 97, 122, 138, 148–153, 164, 528, 531, 546, 580, 582

Watson, William (1558–1603), seminary priest 652 n18

Westmorland, Charles Nevill (1542–1601), earl of 337, 390, 500, 579, 690

Weston, William, SJ (ca. 1550–1615), superior of the English mission 16, 17 n92, 66, 360, 362, 402 n465, 513, 525 n373, 527, 543 n422, 692, 790, 792, 797–798, 813 n548

White, Thomas, SJ (1558–1622) 8, 212

Whitolf, Hugh (1571–post 1610), seminary priest 885 n117

Wiseman (Starkey), Thomas, SJ (1572–1596) 580, 582

Wolly, George (b. 1567), seminary priest 803, 804, 808, 884

Worthington, John, SJ (ca. 1572–1652) 124–125, 194, 225

Worthington, Thomas, SJ (1549–1627), translator, vice president of Douai College 9, 11 n53, 36, 124, 225, 553, 558, 565, 567, 607, 615, 690, 881 n99; correspondence with Persons 9, 646–648

Worthington, William, student 440 n125

Wright (Hurit, Vrit), Thomas [SJ] (ca. 1561–1623), theologian 6, 15, 36–37, 85 n143, 98, 155–156, 177, 179, 294–295, 298, 305–306, 316–321; correspondence with Persons 422, 428–429; in England 7, 15, 797–799; and the earl of Essex 15, 36, 797; in Valladolid 330, 332–333, 337, 381, 384, 387–389, 407–410, 420, 430, 432, 438 n115, 464–465

Wright, William, SJ (1563–1639) 49–50

Wyse, Andrew (d. 1631), grand prior of the knights of Malta 510, 730 n370

Yaxley, Richard (d. 1589), martyr 84, 633

Yepes, Diego de (1529–1613), bishop of Tarazona 23–24, 76, 194, 321–333, 341, 506 n291, 534, 633–634

Younger, James (b. 1563), seminary priest 122, 123, 126, 163–164

Zúñiga, Francisco de (d. 1604), fourth marquis of Ayamonte 223, 471 n194

Zúñiga y Mendoza, Francisco Diego de (ca. 1560–1601), fifth duke of Béjar 223, 471 n194

Index of Places and Subjects

Alcalá de Henares 3, 26, 33, 35, 46, 50–51, 56, 58 n62, 66, 75, 95 n198, 252, 258, 512, 520. *See also* Jesús del Monte
alms-giving 97, 112, 122, 217, 242, 262, 265, 300, 345, 384, 418, 462–464, 500–503, 558, 597, 661, 792; conflict of interests 117–119, 460, 463, 466, 471–474, 483–485, 487–488, 523, 548–549, 561, 586–587
Amsterdam 19, 24, 122, 129, 148–153
Andalusia 46–47, 50, 63, 74 n109, 96, 97, 122, 147, 155, 170, 259, 615 n644
Antwerp 23–24, 26, 29, 36, 121, 151, 195, 209, 322, 345, 350, 353, 556, 576, 665, 779, 784
Aragón 195, 313
archpriest controversy 11 n53, 15, 16, 18, 19, 30, 640, 650–651, 711, 796 n491
armadas 21, 137 n357, 493–500, 507, 629 n666, 670; (of 1588) 1, 116, 135, 164 n442, 744; (of 1596) 25, 560, 583, 597–598, 607, 615–616, 621, 624, 839; (of 1597) 839 n16; English armadas 66, 507, 580, 839, 841
Ayamonte 137

Barcelona 26, 397, 615, 620, 635, 640, 649–650, 690, 716 n324
Béarn (Bearne): *see* Index of Persons: Henry IV, king of France
Belgium 9 n47, 246, 303–304 n203, 374, 632 n669, 637, 644, 645, 689, 867–869. *See also* Flanders
Benedictine order 10, 125, 437 n103, 534
Berwick-upon-Tweed 390
Bilbao 64, 87, 146 n392, 303 n203
bishops, proposed 499–500, 607, 646, 766–769, 772–773, 777–778, 792, 839, 842, 864–869

Boetica: *see* Andalusia
Bologna 62, 786, 807
Bridgettine order 28, 289, 340–341
Bruges 334
Brussels 10, 11, 20, 360, 534, 646, 823; council for English affairs 11, 610–615, 782, 840; courier to 26–27, 29, 95–96 n203; Spanish court 219 nn668–669, 322 n225, 415 n23, 524 n369, 561, 605, 614, 767, 784

Cádiz 5, 153, 493. *See also* Index of Persons: Essex
Calatrava, religious order of 240
Camerino 769
Carthusian order 240, 751 n409, 820 n570
Castile 6, 67, 132, 195, 239 n65, 259, 359, 421, 521, 876, 877
Catalonia 640
Catholic community in England 1, 15, 18, 20, 135–151 *passim*, 163–172 *passim*, 225, 604–639 *passim*, 815, 832–842 *passim*, 855–872 *passim*; accused of sedition 285; conversion(s) 15, 40, 163, 166 n458, 224, 264, 298, 483, 631, 645, 742, 747; fervour 165. *See also* loyalism; persecution; prisons; recusancy; toleration
Catholic League 16, 166 n453, 207, 218 n662, 272, 273 n140 and n143, 334 n251, 341, 704 n274
Cerbère (Cervera) 649
chrism 868
ciphers and codes 26–27, 51, 59–60, 87, 111 n278, 129, 191–192, 207, 220, 321–322, 353 n296, 371, 377, 401 nn455–456 and n461, 413, 416 n30, 439–441, 476, 486,

528, 532, 557, 576, 655, 742, 745, 758, 813 n547, 880
Civitavecchia 649–650
Coeverden 334
Coimbra 131, 154–156, 213 n643, 400 n447
colleges: *see* Cordoba; Douai; Huy; Lisbon; Louvain; Madrid; Pont-à-Mousson; Rheims; Rome; Saint-Omer; Salamanca; Seville; Valladolid
Conference about the Next Succession 15, 19 n101, 23–25, 316, 342, 345, 353, 371, 393, 490, 499 n276, 556, 577, 579 n593, 590, 594 n614, 614, 620, 635, 660–661, 696 n208, 699, 704 nn273–274, 727, 729, 745–746, 751, 815, 833, 835, 857 n48
conscience 45, 71, 72, 94, 116, 334, 375, 376, 415, 470, 536 n407, 574, 632, 647, 663, 735–736, 766, 861, 888; cases of 582; examination of 813; liberty of 19, 784–785 n466
conspiracies: *see* Spanish blanks. *See also* Index of Persons: Babington, Anthony; Cecil, John; López, Rodrigo; Parry, William
controversy 23–25, 320
convents 28 n153, 105 n258, 340–341, 506
Cordoba 26, 347, 352, 357 n313, 362, 363 n324; Spanish college 523 n364
correspondence 11, 13, 14, 15, 16, 19, 26–29, 117, 364, 462, 566–567, 596, 623, 742, 772, 818, 834, 836, 838, 841; confidential 6, 26, 28, 29, 48, 52, 88, 128, 130, 146, 156, 191, 350, 389, 394, 396, 447, 521, 587, 589; cost of carriage 583, 595–596; crossing letters 27; dating 27, 48, 82, 117, 122, 135 n354, 158, 160, 162–163, 191, 211–212, 213, 271, 288, 342 n274, 359 n315, 387, 536–537, 629, 651, 654 n40, 711, 736, 737, 804 n517; delays 525 n373; dictation 125, 591, 624; forwarding 280, 286; interception 30, 120, 122, 129, 163, 271, 289, 298, 400, 728; lost/missing letters 29, 52, 72, 80, 88, 104 n255, 122, 125, 162, 208, 213, 274, 298, 321, 346, 387, 414 n17, 447, 548, 587, 732 n376, 734; multiple copies and duplicates 148, 206, 217, 257, 288, 354, 359, 367, 447, 503, 650, 665, 693, 773; postal system 26; routes 26, 152, 220 n671, 273 n139, 288, 476. *See also* ciphers and codes; couriers; language
couriers 16, 26–27, 44, 51, 56, 57, 65, 71, 91–92, 94, 97–98, 117, 141, 148, 206, 216–217, 271, 305, 307, 324, 357, 379, 400–401 n445, 443, 451, 464, 564, 593, 595, 620, 622, 627, 689, 768
Courtrai 292

Deventer 10, 121
devotion, books of 59 n65, 67
disguise 19, 122
dispensations 4, 206, 369, 380, 792, 855
disputations 386 n398, 479
Dominican order 400, 765 n437
Dorchester 504, 506, 534
Douai 67, 281, 304, 567 n494, 590, 629, 646, 799, 808 n528, 818 n558; English college 8–9, 17, 41–42, 377, 393, 451, 508, 524, 628, 631, 682 n170, 794–795, 801–803, 805, 813; Flemish Jesuit college 524 n370
Durham 151 n411, 390, 607
Dutch language 271–274, 336
Dutch war 10, 19, 20, 66, 121, 167, 282, 333, 334–336, 441, 497, 559, 583, 605, 609, 610

El Escorial, San Lorenzo de 46, 59, 70, 104, 137, 188, 295, 299, 300, 303, 375 n366, 384, 633–634
El Pardo, palace of 512, 522
England: royal court 18, 172, 210, 404, 415, 490, 648–649, 836, 841 n19. *See also* parliament of England; Privy Council
espionage 19, 132, 158, 211 n637, 220 n671, 249, 334, 336 n261, 490, 511 n297, 544, 562, 564, 609, 614, 615, 645, 660, 728, 732, 784
Eu, Normandy 110
Évora 26, 105, 152, 250, 266, 271
excommunication: of Elizabeth I 606; of Henry of Navarre 20, 512
exiles 1, 4–5 n16, 10–11, 20, 135, 151, 184, 203 n585, 225, 245, 247, 261, 645, 673, 681, 705, 842, 871, 889; in France 117, 818

n558; Irish 212; leadership 22, 417, 474, 715, 806; pensions 21, 208, 252, 278, 629, 732, 806; Scottish 500, 549; in Spain 28 n153, 77 n120, 128, 258, 278 n159, 727

fasting 165, 172, 242, 247, 259
Ferrol 21, 125, 146 n392, 839
Flanders 41; English "nation" in Flanders 605, 614, 671, 731–732, 778, 779, 816, 823, 834. *See also* Belgium; Brussels
—, Persons's opponents 10–11, 136, 160, 499, 510, 556, 558, 566, 629, 633, 686–690, 709, 729–730, 737–747, 784 n466, 788, 815, 840; anti-Spanish 835–838; pro-French 705–706, 743, 815; pro-Scottish 9, 532, 705, 730, 745, 762, 833–834, 837
France 15, 20, 22, 23, 121, 207, 311–313, 375, 442, 579, 608, 705, 758, 763–764; alliance with Scotland 497, 556; religious wars 282, 285, 384–385, 393, 668, 757
Frascati 359

galleys 122, 128–136, 375, 397, 521, 620, 750
Genoa 26, 48–49, 62, 85 n143, 98, 117, 178 n488, 187, 189, 650, 662, 786
Gertruydenberg 282
Gouda 271–274
Gravelines 246 n78, 340, 344, 350

Hampton court 219
heresy 182 n501, 275, 351 n293, 556, 622, 668–672, 677, 682, 778, 798, 835; *partes infidelium* (infected areas) 5, 67, 92, 95 n203. *See also* Inquisition
Holland 20, 129–130, 138, 151–152, 218, 334–336, 441 n135, 583, 605, 609, 610, 707
Huguenots: *see* France: religious wars
Huy 441

Inquisition 2, 5, 8, 14, 21, 38, 40–41, 42, 44, 62 n80, 67, 70, 74 nn107–108, 83, 86, 92, 94 n197, 95 n203, 96, 101, 176, 351–352, 670, 836, 864; "Cecilian Inquisition" 181, 219
intelligence networks: *see* espionage
Ireland 166 nn454–455, 219, 473, 521 n357, 556, 580, 614, 622, 697, 858, 869; Nine Years' War 18, 311, 441, 497, 507; suitable for invasion 498, 500, 551, 559, 598, 606–608, 621, 623, 839 n16, 862

Jesuits: *see* Society of Jesus
Jesús del Monte 46, 48, 50, 51, 52, 58 n62, 61 n73, 345, 347, 352, 371, 376, 512, 521, 543

Lancashire 163, 208 n610, 313, 335, 607, 762
Lancaster 768; house of Lancaster 683, 853–854, 856–857, 861, 876–879
language 27, 203, 810, 835; ambiguity 90 n160; multilingualism 24, 28, 77, 123, 194, 299, 312, 397, 451, 478 n215, 591, 606, 643, 729, 871
Leicesters Commonwealth 24
León 26, 158, 177–178, 240 n70
Leuven: *see* Louvain
Liège 765
Lisbon 21, 22, 26, 28, 43, 131, 250, 266, 271, 287, 291–292, 333, 573, 616, 621, 669, 742; English college 97; English residence 289, 303, 638. *See also* Bridgettine order
London 29, 129, 171, 172, 185, 209, 211, 238, 403, 458, 498, 504, 558, 576, 609, 730, 798, 841; plague 219, 325; proposed college 689; riot of apprentices 507; xenophobia 282
—, Fleet Street 130, 168; Inner Temple 30, 651; Tyburn 17, 125, 181 n495, 182 n497, 211 n637; Westminster 164 n443, 210, 439, 797
—, prisons: the Clink 403, 413, 492, 639, 736; Counter at the Poultry 130, 403, 492; Gatehouse 211, 414 n13, 692, 839 n16; Newgate 182, 185, 403. *See also* Tower of London
Loreto 2, 56, 249, 786, 807
Louvain (Leuven) 12, 13 n70, 23, 24, 27, 248, 298, 305, 316, 540, 559, 572, 632 n669, 646, 692, 751 n409, 783
loyalism 15, 18, 415 n19, 728, 789, 826, 831, 835, 837, 882
Lyon 24, 26, 209

Madrid 1, 2, 3, 5, 11, 20, 23, 41, 46–48, 52, 60–61, 80–81, 87, 100, 116, 185, 252, 258,

281, 307, 314–315, 363, 367, 389, 414 n10 and n12, 424, 428, 455, 458, 512, 810 n536; English college 535; Jesuits 95, 193, 305, 427, 432, 465–466, 470, 473, 474; postal network 26–29, 65, 78, 251 n84; Spanish college 193 n521, 258, 347, 354, 474, 484, 521 n359

Marchena 26, 363–369

martyrdom 17, 99 n210, 180–183, 324, 392, 493, 557, 575, 662, 672, 682, 685; attendance at 171, 185; benefits 627; contested 125, 162–168, 172, 673; desire for 151, 225, 235, 245, 362, 486, 506, 666; Jesuit pre-eminence 645; martyrology 23–24, 48 n16, 84–85, 326, 534–535, 634 n677; preparation for 247

Medina del Campo 26, 104, 266, 271

memorialistas 1–4, 21, 46, 51, 61–62, 106 n264, 107 n265, 113, 126; proposed transfer of 58 n63, 74

Milan 12, 26, 143–145, 272 n136, 786, 886 n118

Milford Haven 493

missionaries 3, 17, 211 n635, 622; audiences with Philip II 5, 21, 122; routes 16, 122–124, 129, 148, 152, 177, 220 n671, 273 n139, 458, 486, 506, 621

Montilla 324

Naples 698, 862–863

Netherlands: *see* Dutch war; Holland

Newes from Spayne and Holland 23, 24, 36, 132, 225–226, 234–237

news 16, 26, 29, 30 n157, 139, 162–163, 180, 332, 467, 504, 550–551, 576–577, 623, 673 n133, 759. *See also* Index of Persons: Baynes, Roger; Garnet, Henry; Owen, Hugh; Verstegan, Richard

oaths 20, 125, 491, 512, 606, 727, 809 n529, 872

Oxford 18, 84, 633–634, 684; Oxfordshire 163

Palermo 314, 319

papacy 11, 20, 22, 141 n273, 272, 544, 692; apostolic briefs (*breves*) 188, 264, 270, 597, 607, 778, 787, 869, 885, 887 n122; English seminaries 146–147, 186, 224, 644, 666; papal bulls 40, 65, 500, 811; papal curia 11, 14, 30, 50, 51, 62 n80, 546, 626, 651, 664, 703, 705, 747, 754, 767, 790, 823, 872; papal nuncios 27 n139, 32, 34, 117, 128 n336, 352, 525, 556, 607, 638, 651, 653, 661, 693, 699, 705, 729, 742, 744 n395, 763, 781, 790–792, 799, 820

Paris 10, 20, 29, 121, 335–336, 551 n435, 698, 745, 758 n419, 762, 811, 818–819, 878; conference (1582) 10, 742–744, 816; plans for an English college 813–815; Spanish embassy 21, 670 n118

parliament of England 491, 492, 499–500, 855, 861; of 1593 281, 283–285, 303, 404

persecution 19, 28, 139, 166 n458, 217, 303, 361, 400, 403, 404, 405, 506, 637, 706, 728, 835, 867; anti-Catholic legislation 19, 283, 439 n117; contributing factors 25; easing of 363, 637, 705; intensified 176, 181–185, 203 n585, 285, 291, 294, 361, 400–405, 839, 861, 876–879; as justification for invasion 493; of Portuguese 403; of Protestants 168, 172, 219, 281, 285, 404 n493

Peru 634 n678. *See also* Index of Persons: Acosta, José de

Philippines: *see* Index of Persons: Sánchez, Alonso

pilgrims, pilgrimage 46, 240 n70, 419. *See also* Loreto

Poland 442, 560–563

Pont-à-Mousson 10, 99 n211, 285 n181

Portugal 6, 20, 46–47, 64, 75, 85–86, 137, 152 n414, 167 n459, 313, 457, 668, 670; house of Portugal 661–662, 853–858

Prague 85 n144, 208 n612, 414 n12

printing and publishing 23, 25, 48 n16, 69 n96, 75, 84–85, 168 n463, 195, 209, 285, 342, 353, 381, 490, 534, 590, 636–637, 651, 699, 729, 746–747, 786, 815–816, 833; book-smuggling into England and Scotland 271

prisons: *see* Tower of London; Wisbech; York. *See also under* London

Privy Council 166 n453, 167 n461, 172, 176, 177 n485, 277 n155, 282 n174, 284, 335 n254, 415 n28, 838, 841 n19, 855, 871

proclamations, royal 7, 24, 123, 176–177, 184, 209, 219, 327, 332, 404, 839; Spanish 21, 598, 606, 616, 621
propaganda 24, 279 n164, 442 n138, 762 n435
prophets 172, 219; biblical 195, 203, 678–679, 712 n300; false prophets 667, 672 n127; sectarians 168, 172, 219
Protestantism: see persecution; prophets; Puritans. See also Index of Persons: Calvin, John
providence 108, 113, 123, 175, 205, 241, 352, 471, 585, 668, 681, 712, 753, 781, 822, 838, 889; acts of providence 146, 152, 161, 264, 287, 627
Puerto de Santa María 26, 122, 128–132
Puritans 166 n458, 167–168, 172, 280, 281, 285, 404 n493, 798
pursuivants 171, 185, 276 n149, 401 n455, 744, 747, 751, 765, 813, 868

recusancy 18–19, 166, 181, 211 n628, 277, 281, 284, 499 n273, 751 n409
refugees: see exiles
relics 508–510
Rheims, English college at 5, 8, 41–42, 46, 63, 258, 371, 631, 706, 726; funding 43, 56 n55, 340, 342, 345, 347, 350, 377, 597; insecurity 66, 264; martyrs 23 n123, 185, 631; missionaries 164 n444, 171, 184; relocates to Douai 271, 281; royal favour 360; transfer of students 41–42, 63, 67, 75, 79, 105, 110, 117, 120, 125, 126, 131; Rheims/Douai translation of Bible 275 n147
Rochester 99 n210, 400, 404
Rome: English "nation" in Rome 11, 13, 499 n273, 565, 674, 729, 789, 796, 800, 886; persecution of Protestants 478; Roman college 206, 385, 515 n311, 523 n364, 548, 582, 776; watchmen (*sbirri*) 807 n524, 883, 889
—, English College 12–16, 22, 25, 28, 50, 63, 162 n438, 538 n411, 547; discontent among students 213, 433–439, 474–477, 541, 565–567, 586, 667–685, 686, 707, 716–734, 787–788, 880–890; foundation 22, 508, 526 n375, 707–708; Jesuit management 13, 558 n471, 629, 646, 793–794; music 336 n261; rectors 156, 188, 590; vice-protectors 13, 22, 627, 629, 632 n669, 649, 706 n278, 710, 713, 726, 733, 789, 793, 795, 801; vineyard 766–768, 883
Rouen 32, 34, 117, 120–121, 125, 167 n462, 277 n156, 289, 341, 573, 647 n11

Saint-Omer 6, 29, 246, 319, 350, 359, 580; authorities 340, 342, 344–345, 350–351; bishop 345 n282, 350–351, 368; Jesuits 261, 280, 289–291, 293, 314, 331–332, 342 n276, 354–355, 370; Walloon college 331, 342 n276
—, English college of St Omers 8, 36, 250–407 *passim*, 440, 458, 532, 561, 566, 567, 631, 669–670; funding 251, 300, 301, 324, 327, 340–345, 347, 350–351, 513, 524, 543; location 281, 292, 294–297, 304
Saint-Quentin 864
Salamanca: Irish college 8, 212–213, 239 n65
Sanlúcar de Barrameda 5, 26, 128, 269, 289, 455, 459, 513, 527, 638, 669
Santiago de Compostela 240 n70
Scotland 151, 239, 335, 390, 441 n129, 473, 491, 497, 549, 590, 637–638, 670, 681, 683–684, 763, 819 n563, 864, 869; Catholic earls 20, 185, 307–314, 414, 455, 458, 464, 500, 527 n380, 597, 604–609; French alliance 497, 855, 859; invasion plans 16, 307, 498, 507, 614, 621–623, 742–745; Jesuits 10, 333, 380 n380, 405, 544, 548, 594, 730; Scottish colleges 5 n21, 8, 10, 32, 363, 368–369, 405–407, 540, 544, 549, 558, 567–568, 572, 586–587. See also Index of Persons: Crichton, William
secular priests 17, 19, 87, 146–147 n392, 258, 525, 557, 683 n174, 727, 790, 792, 796 n491, 883; clerical associations (confraternities) 649, 734, 762, 768, 770; faculties 123, 143–147, 527, 565, 725, 729, 786–787, 795, 799–801, 842, 868
seminaries: see colleges
Seville 21, 26, 105, 138 n365, 212, 319; Jesuits 460–463, 466, 479, 483–484, 548, 586; Spanish college of St Hermenegild 4, 9, 484 n242
—, English college of St Gregory 7–9, 179,

262–271, 280, 292, 298, 314, 330, 346, 352, 354–360, 381, 384, 397–398, 400, 409, 453–454, 455, 464, 520, 528, 531, 543, 580, 621, 631, 682 n170; anticipated 174, 189–190, 205–206, 209, 213, 216–217, 222–224; benefactors 363, 367, 376, 459, 471, 502 n280, 634; buildings 7, 359, 432, 455–462, 471; chapel 432, 458, 487, 501–502, 504; foundation 7, 24, 224–249, 252–260; royal support 371, 522

Sicily 50, 63–64, 74, 239, 346, 360, 499

Society of Jesus (Jesuits): admission 64–65, 241, 353, 433, 465, 561, 692, 698; annual letters 179–180, 401 n454 and n456, 508; assistants 34, 35, 215 n650, 320 n223, 380 n380, 389 n412, 414, 447, 459 n166, 485 n246, 510, 565, 730; *Constitutions* 96, 117–118, 645 n7; consultors 9, 175 n479, 206 n597, 258, 451–453, 459, 485, 544, 803; curia in Rome 2, 62 n75; (Jesuit) English mission 1–4, 16–17, 38, 46, 64, 143, 362, 401 n454, 480, 534, 580, 786, 792, 801; faculties and instructions 2 n6, 21, 38–41, 46, 50, 84, 622–623, 652, 668; second general congregation 117; fifth general congregation 1–4, 185, 191, 213, 252–271, 286, 304, 316, 342, 364, 371, 378; Institute ("way of proceeding") 2, 38, 52, 57–58, 62, 260, 265, 345, 727; Jewish descent 4, 364, 369, 520 n355; motto *ad maiorem Dei gloriam* 463, 636, 638, 643, 646; novitiate of Sant'Andrea 13, 56, 65, 363, 504, 580, 582, 786; papal interest 286–287, 628, 644; political involvement 4 n14, 364; procurators 3, 7, 90, 128, 142, 193, 252, 258, 269, 332, 430, 433, 466, 473, 479, 484, 524 n366, 531, 585; *ratio studiorum* 9, 178 n489, 385 n397; restrictions on movement of Spanish Jesuits 2, 40, 88, 92, 95 n202, 512, 715; suppression in France 512, 521–523; unity of spirit 645; visitors 2–3, 28, 40–44, 50, 51, 52, 57–63, 65, 70–96 *passim*, 106–119, 126–127, 185, 191, 252, 512, 520–524, 536, 546–548, 560, 589, 623. See also *memorialistas*

—, professed houses 117, 503, 527 n379; Rome 14, 82, 512; Seville 216, 222, 384, 400, 466, 471, 484, 549; Toledo 371, 376, 393; Valladolid 117–119, 158, 191, 359, 367

—, provinces: Andalusia (Boetica) 3, 7, 29, 40, 43, 44 n7, 128, 153, 178, 362, 412; Aragon 179, 187, 193; Austria 40, 49–50; Belgium 9 n47, 416, 464, 631, 691; Castile 29, 40, 44, 206, 213, 266, 271, 287, 353, 362, 386; England 4; France 99, 131, 155–156, 287, 360, 512, 521–522, 543; Milan 298; Naples 371; Peru 2, 38; Philippines 3, 95 n202, 252; Portugal 43, 51; Sicily 314–315; Toledo 2, 29, 40–41, 43, 44, 51, 61–62, 95 n203, 101, 106–108, 288, 305, 362, 419

Spain 10, 20–21, 46, 50, 121, 151, 167 n461, 177, 202, 211, 239–240, 277 n156, 334, 378, 557, 579, 609, 733; enterprise of England 123, 139, 184, 441, 492–501, 507, 558–559, 615–623, 742–754, 784–785 n466; relations with France 121, 207, 273, 757–758, 860–863; relations with papacy 22; relations with Scotland 307, 544–548, 820; rivalry with Italy 579, 666; royal court 21, 25, 30, 32, 34, 43, 180, 307, 364, 369, 421, 466, 645, 699, 714, 716, 748, 767, 769, 823; treasure ships 21, 205, 455, 457, 463 n174, 466, 471 n193, 488 n254

Spanish blanks 307. *See also* Scotland: Catholic earls

Spanish Netherlands: *see* Belgium; Flanders succession to the throne of England 25, 492, 498–499; Clement VIII 620, 652, 660–662, 666, 696–698, 752, 833, 835, 872; Crichton 25, 567–575, 590, 635–638, 830, 833–834; Derby succession 335 n254; French interest 620, 697, 833, 843, 854–864; Persons's memorials 842–864, 869–872, 872–880; Philip II 378, 650, 746 n399, 854, 857 n48, 869, 872–880. *See also Conference about the Next Succession. See also* Index of Persons: Isabella Clara Eugenia; James VI

Toledo 26, 67, 69 n96, 82, 100, 105, 213, 251–252, 272, 572 n575, 653 n36, 716 n324
toleration 15 n83, 18–19, 121, 177 n485, 507, 557, 728, 765, 784–785 n466, 835

torture 165 n450, 171, 181, 211, 403, 439, 698, 734 n378, 808, 813, 839, 884
Tournai 246, 257 n105, 333, 559
Tower of London 17, 18, 166, 168 n465, 185, 362 n323, 402 n473, 413, 415, 439, 492, 574 n580, 639, 647 n11, 698, 734 n378, 736–737, 797, 813
treason 121, 165 n451, 166 nn454–455, 168 n463, 177, 209, 210–211, 335, 403, 414 n13, 439, 637, 683 n172, 704, 744 n393
Trent, Council of 62 n80, 146–147 n393
Tynedale and Redesdale 683–684

Valladolid 5, 8, 26, 62 n80, 64; Irish students 212; Spanish college of St Ambrose 4, 173, 205
—, English College of St Alban's: buildings 6, 67, 303, 330; clothing 95; conflicts among Jesuits 387; employment of students 146–147, 330–331, 353; epidemic 158–160, 177; foundation 1, 23, 66–128 *passim*, 213 n644; hospitality 454, 459; numbers 83, 157, 631; papal authority 188; patrons 5–6, 67, 185–186, 472, 485–486; rectors 79, 80–81, 92, 97–98, 100, 106, 110, 113–114, 118, 153–154, 159, 174, 252, 258, 337, 347, 432, 459, 465, 479–480, 489–490, 492, 512, 520, 528, 531, 536–543, 560–561, 586; refectory 502–503; royal support 216–217, 250, 265; royal visit 6–7, 9, 24, 69 n96, 147, 194–205, 209, 212; satisfactory state 292, 303, 330, 371, 376, 479, 666, 669; teaching 205, 400, 479, 797; tension with Spanish Jesuits 119–120, 190, 191, 466, 472, 479–480; unity of spirit 358; *Vulnerata* statue 583
Villefranche-sur-Mer 649
Vlye 334 n250

Wales 1, 17; Welsh party 13, 594–595; Welsh students 12, 681, 729, 731. *See also* Index of Persons: Lewis, Owen
Wallachia 562–564
White Webbs 576 n589, 778
Winchester 164, 171
Wisbech 16, 17, 362 n323, 400, 402 n465, 410, 433, 649, 692, 709, 765 n438, 778, 790, 792, 798

xenophobia 282 n174, 512

York 17, 164, 171; house of York 497, 683, 853, 856–857, 877–879